U-BOAT OPERATIONS OF THE SECOND WORLD WAR

U-BOAT OPERATIONS
OF THE SECOND WORLD WAR

VOLUME 2: Career Histories, U511-UIT25

KENNETH WYNN

CHATHAM PUBLISHING

LONDON

For Anah
For her constant encouragement,
unfailing support and her always
invaluable commonsense

Copyright © Ken Wynn 1998

First published in Great Britain in 1998 by
Chatham Publishing,
1 & 2 Faulkner's Alley,
Cowcross Street,
London EC1M 6DD

Chatham Publishing is an imprint of Gerald Duckworth & Co Ltd

British Library Cataloguing in Publication Data
A catalogue record for this book is available from the British Library

ISBN 0 86176 069 8

Typeset and Designed by Ken Wynn
Printed and bound in Great Britain by WBC Book Manufacturers Ltd

Contents

Introduction

With this second volume my account of the operations carried out by individual U-boats in the Second World War is completed. The majority of operations covered in this volume occurred in the period from mid-1942 until the German surrender in May 1945.

After the severe losses of Allied ships during 1941, 1942 and the early months of 1943, the Allies gradually built up their own anti-submarine forces. This, coupled with the introduction of new weapons, led to the climax of the Battle of the Atlantic in May 1943, when forty-one U-boats were destroyed during the month.

From that time the Allied naval and air forces gained an ever-greater ascendancy, with sinkings of merchant ships decreasing dramatically and destruction of U-boats becoming more frequent.

The severe losses inflicted in 1943, 1944 and 1945 do not seem to have seriously affected the morale of U-boat commanders and their crews, many of whom did not survive long enough to gain the experience so vital to carry out operations successfully. However, sinkings of Allied ships continued, albeit on a very small scale, until the very last days of the war.

In early May 1945 many U-boats were scuttled by their crews, contrary to the surrender terms, and most of those that were handed over to the Allies were later sunk by them, using various methods.

As far as I am aware, only four wartime U-boats still exist. They are U 505 at Chicago; U 534, currently at Liverpool and due for restoration; the *Wilhelm Bauer,* a much-modified U 2540 now in the museum at Bremerhaven, and U 995 at Laboe, north of Kiel and not far from the U-boat Memorial at Möltenort. The last is my own personal favourite, in the perfect location, overlooking the waters of the Kieler Förde.

I would like to mention some people, to whom I again wish to offer special thanks.

Dr Axel Niestlé of Berlin, for continuing to share his immense wealth of U-boat knowledge. In my experience, he knows more about the subject than probably anyone else in the world. His ever-immediate response to my lists of queries have been invaluable.

Professor Dr Jürgen Rohwer, not only for his invaluable reference works but also for providing me with much up-dated information. Without Professor Rohwer's meticulous research over a very long period on German naval matters, our knowledge of the U-boat war would be very much less than it is.

Herr Horst Bredow, a former U-boat officer and founding director of the U-Boat Archive at Altenbruch, for allowing me to use information from the Archive on U-boat departures from and returns to port. The Archive is without doubt the most important single repository of U-boat material in the world.

Flight Lieutenant E S Cheek AFC DFM RAF, who took part in the Battle of the Atlantic as an aircrew member of 120 and 224 Squadrons. His crew, in 224 Squadron, destroyed two U-boats and damaged another three. Eddie kindly made all his very extensive research on U-boats freely available to me and both he and his wife, Mary, have always been most hospitable on my visits.

The *Alte Kameraden* from Kiel, who have made me so welcome at some of their monthly gatherings at the magnificent U-boat Memorial at Möltenort and were so generous with their hospitality and information.

Mr Ian Sayer, for kindly supplying me with much valuable information from German sources.

Mr David Payne of Auckland, New Zealand, for his help and great kindness in supplying so much useful information.

Mr Lee Norris of Auckland, for his help with my early computing problems and helping me with my original format.

My friend Sam Cope, for his expertise and help with all the computer problems over the years. He has never failed to leave whatever he is doing to sort me out.

Mrs Elizabeth Walker, my daughter, for her ever-continuing patience, accuracy and sheer dogged stickability in doing the word-processing that has gone into these pages. Somehow she manages to do it as well as running her own life and family.

Finally, my dear Anah, always there to encourage me and put me back on track when it was needed. She is still certainly the main contributor to the end product. Without her generous and continual support there would be no books.

It is inevitable that someone, somewhere will know something about a particular U-boat that is not included in this book. If so, I would be most grateful if they would care to send any such information to the publisher, for onward transmission to me.

KEN WYNN

The Boats
U 511 - UIT 25

I wanted to imbue my crews with enthusiasm and a complete faith in their arm and to instil in them a spirit of selfless readiness to serve in it. Only those possessed of such a spirit could hope to succeed in the grim realities of submarine warfare. Professional skill alone would not suffice.

I believed in the fighting powers of the U-boat. I regarded it, as I have always regarded it, as a first class weapon of offence in naval warfare.

ADMIRAL KARL DÖNITZ

Abbreviations used in the text

ab	U-boat under training (Ausbildungsboot)
a/s	Anti-submarine
BdU	U-boat Commander-in-Chief (Befehlshaber der Unterseeboote)
BEM	British Empire Medal
CAM	Catapult-Armed Merchantman
Capt	Captain (RN and USN)
Cdr	Commander (RN and USN)
CGM	Conspicuous Gallantry Medal
CPO	Chief Petty Officer
DFC	Distinguished Flying Cross
DFM	Distinguished Flying Medal
DSO	Distinguished Service Order
dt	Displacement Tons
eb	U-boat on test duties (Erprobungsboot)
EG	Escort Group
FAA	Fleet Air Arm
fb	Operational U-boat (Frontboot)
fb-m	Minelaying U-boat (Frontboot mit überwiegendem Einsatz zu Minenunternehmungen)
fb-oE	Operational U-boat temporarily non-operational (Frontboot ohne Einsatz)
fb-t	Transport and escort U-boat (Frontboot mit überwiegendem Einsatz für Transportunternehmungen)
fb-v	Supply U-boat (Versuchboot)
FdU	Commander of the U-boat arm (Führer der Unterseeboote)
FK	Fregattenkapitän zur See
F/Lt	Flight Lieutenant
F/O	Flying Officer
F/Sgt	Flight Sergeant
G/Capt	Group Captain
grt	Gross Registered Tons
HMS	His Majesty's Ship
HMAS	His Majesty's Australian Ship
HMCS	His Majesty's Canadian Ship
HMIS	His Majesty's Indian Ship
KK	Korvettekapitän zur See
KL	Kapitänleutnant zur See
KzS	Kapitän zur See
LCI	Landing Craft Infantry
LST	Landing Ship Tank
Lt	Leutnant zur See (U-boats)
Lt	Lieutenant (RN and USN)
Lt-Cdr	Lieutenant-Commander (RN and USN)
MAD	Magnetic Anomaly Detector
MTB	Motor Torpedo Boat
MV	Motor Vessel
NEK	Communications Trials Command (Nachrichtenmittelerprobungskommando)
OL	Oberleutnant zur See
OTU	Operational Training Unit
P/O	Pilot Officer
RAAF	Royal Australian Air Force
RAF	Royal Air Force
RCAF	Royal Canadian Air Force
RMS	Royal Mail Ship
RN	Royal Navy
SAAF	South African Air Force
sb	U-boat on training duties (Schulboot)
SG	Support Group
Sgt	Sergeant
S/Ldr	Squadron Leader
Sub-Lt	Sub-Lieutenant (RN)
SO	Staff Officer (Stabsoffizier)
SS	Steam Ship
str-b	U-boat used as a static power generator (Stromboot)
TAF	Tactical Air Force
(temp)	Denotes an officer temporarily in command of a U-boat
ULD	U-boat Training Division (Unterseebootslehrdivision)
U-Fl	U-boat Command unit (Unterseebootsflottille)
USAF	United States Air Force
USCG	United States Coast Guard
US-Fl	U-boat School Flotilla (Unterseebootsschulflottille)
USN	United States Navy
USS	United States Ship
vb	Experimental U-boat (Versuchboot)
VC	Victoria Cross
W/Cdr	Wing Commander

Abbreviations used in the text for the nationality of ships

am	American	eg	Egyptian	it	Italian	pt	Portuguese
ar	Argentinian	es	Estonian	la	Latvian	ro	Romanian
be	Belgian	fa	Faroese	le	Lebanese	sa	South African
br	British	fi	Finnish	li	Lithuanian	sov	Russian
bz	Brazilian	fr	French	me	Mexican	sp	Spanish
ca	Canadian	gr	Greek	ni	Nicaraguan	sw	Swedish
cl	Chile	gre	Greenland	nl	Netherlands	sy	Syrian
co	Colombian	hg	Hungarian	nw	Norwegian	ur	Uruguayan
cu	Cuban	ho	Honduran	pa	Panamanian	ve	Venezuelan
da	Danish	ice	Icelandic	pl	Palestinian	yg	Yugoslavian
do	Dominican	ir	Ireland	po	Polish		

AUTHOR'S NOTES

1. All sailings by U-boats are separately listed and numbered. However, some sailings were for trial and test purposes only or for movements from one port to another. Therefore in many cases the stated number of operational patrols differs from the number of sailings.

2. The total Gross Registered Tonnage (grt) of ships sunk refers only to merchant vessels and armed merchant cruisers and is shown in the accounts as (t) and as (grt) in the Ships Sunk total.

   It does not include warships and auxiliary naval vessels. Their Displacement Tonnage (dt) is not included in the accounts of their damage or sinkings but appears at the bottom of the box if they were sunk by a particular U-boat.

3. When ships are mentioned as 'Possibly sunk' or if the sinking was of an abandoned wreck of a ship previously torpedoed by another boat their tonnages are not included in the Ships Sunk total at the bottom of the box.

4. All U-boat group names are quoted in German.

5. Times of day quoted are based on Central European time, as observed on U-boats.

6. When U-boats were assigned to a particular U-Boat Flotilla they did not necessarily operate from the Headquarters port of that Flotilla.

7. Place names are generally given in the language of the country concerned.

8. Unless specifically stated all aircraft squadrons referred to belong to the RAF.

9. The information in this book is all that the author has been able to find on the subject. Any further information or amendments should be sent to the publisher and will be gratefully received.

U 511 Type IX C

Built by Deutsche Werft, Hamburg
Keel laid 21.2.41   Launched 22.9.41
Commissioned 8.12.41   Feldpost Nr M 42 792

Scuttled 30.4.46 in the Gulf of Maizuru

Served with
4 U-Flottille, Stettin December 1941 - July 1942 (ab)
10 U-Flottille, Lorient August 1942 - 16.9.43 (fb)

Commanded by
KL Friedrich Steinhoff December 1941 - December 1942
KL Fritz Schneewind December 1942 - November 1943

Patrols: 4   Ships sunk: 5 (41,373 grt) + 1 damaged

From May 31st to June 5th 1942 U 511 was used for the testing of special equipment at the research and experimental station at Peenemünde, firing small artillery rockets whilst submerged. Developement ceased because deck-fitted equipment was found to adversely affect the boat's performance.

1. 16.7.42 Left Kiel for the Caribbean.
Outward-bound, U 511 was directed to westbound convoy ON 115, sighted by U 164 on the 29th 480 miles SE of Cape Farewell. U 511 and other boats made contact on the 30th and 31st but were driven off.

On 1.8.42 U 511, U 164, U 210, U 217 and U 553 formed a patrol line, *Pirat*, E of Cape Race, in the anticipated path of the convoy. When it did not appear, searches were carried out, in which the *Pirat* boats were joined on the 2nd by refuelled ex-*Wolf* group boats. The convoy was found by U 552 and an operation was carried out, during which two ships were sunk and another damaged.

U 511 did not take part in the action but resumed her journey to the Caribbean. On the 16th the boat was sighted on the surface and attacked with depth-charges by a Hudson of 53 Squadron (F/Sgt Henderson). U 511's stern rose out of the sea but she was righted and made her escape before the aircraft could make a second approach.

On the 27th U 511 attacked westbound convoy TAW 15 off the tip of Haiti, sinking the tankers SS *San Fabian* (br 13031t) and the MV *Rotterdam* (nl 8968t) and damaging the SS *Esso Aruba* (am 8773t). Her patrol completed, the boat left the Caribbean and in mid-September she was refuelled by U 460 SW of the Azores.

U 511 put in to her new base at Lorient **29.9.42**

2. 24.10.42 Left for operations in the Central Atlantic.
After the Allied landings in North Africa on 8.11.42, all the south-bound boats between the Bay of Biscay and the Cape Verde Islands, including U 511, were ordered to proceed at high speed to the Moroccan coast, as *Schlagetot* group. They were to interrupt sea-borne supplies destined for the Allied forces which had landed at Fedala and Casablanca.

Although there were some sinkings between November 11th and 16th, most of the boats, including U 511, were unable to break through the protective ring formed by Allied naval forces.

U 511 returned to base when her commander became ill. She reached Lorient **28.11.42**

3. 31.12.42 Left for operations in the Central Atlantic.
On 7.1.43 U 511 joined boats of *Delphin* group, moving to intercept convoy TM 1, which was sighted by U 381 on the 8th, heading northeastwards for Gibraltar. U 511 did not have any success against the convoy but on the 9th she sank an independent W of the Canaries, the MV *William Wilberforce* (br 5004t).

After the TM 1 operation ended on the 11th, U 511 remained with *Delphin* group, which reformed from the 16th S of the Azores after some of the boats had been refuelled by U 463. The group moved westwards to intercept an eastbound UGS convoy but turned eastwards again on the 18th. Between the 21st and 29th *Delphin* group waited SW of the Azores but when nothing materialised the group moved further eastwards. From the 31st the patrol line was NW of the Canaries but it then moved to a new position W of Gibraltar for 6.2.43.

On the 7th the five southern boats of *Delphin* went to attack convoy Gib No 2. U 511 and the other boats of the group moved northwards and took up positions W of Portugal from the 11th. Southbound convoy KMS 9 was reported on the 12th, 200 miles W of Cape Finisterre. The *Delphin* boats were ordered to close but the operation failed when the convoy's air escort kept the boats submerged. The situation worsened the nearer the convoy got to Gibraltar. Attacks became impossible and U 442 and U 620 were sunk, both by aircraft.

In mid-February U 511 was refuelled, possibly by another operational boat, and then joined *Robbe* group in a north-south patrol line NE of the Azores. On the 17th the group moved westwards to search the area N of the Azores. With nothing found, a return movement eastwards began on the 20th and from the 21st the boats headed for the Gibraltar area. From the 28th U 511,

3

U 511 (continued)

U 103, U 107, U 410 and U 445 were stationed at the approach to the Straits.

On 4.3.43 the five boats were directed to southbound KMS 10 but Allied air activity was such that they were ordered further west from the 5th. Only U 410 was able to attack, sinking two ships, but she was located and damaged.

U 511 returned to Lorient **8.3.43**

4. 10.5.43 Left, en route to Japan.

U 511 was carrying passengers, amongst them Dr Ernest Woermann, German ambassador to Japan, Vice-Admiral Nomura, Japanese naval attaché and Kriegsmarine engineers.

On the way south, U 511 was refuelled in late May by U 460 W of Freetown. She rounded the Cape and on 27.6.43, SE of Madagascar, she torpedoed and sank the SS *Sebastiano Cermeno* (am 7194t). On 9.7.43 U 511 sank the SS *Samuel Heintzelmann* (am 7176t) ESE of Chagos Archipelago.

The boat reached Penang on 20.7.43 and was handed over to a Japanese crew, who took her on to Kure, where she arrived **7.8.43**

U 511's complement remained in Penang, as spare crew for U-boats operating from there.

On 16.9.43 U 511 was renumbered RO 500 of the Imperial Japanese Navy. She was surrendered to the Americans at Maizuru in August 1945 and scuttled by the US Navy on 30.4.46 in the Gulf of Maizuru.

U 512   Type IX C

Built by Deutsche Werft, Hamburg
Keel laid 24.2.41   Launched 9.10.41
Commissioned 20.12.41   Feldpost Nr M 47 986

Sunk 3.10.42 N of Cayenne (06°50′N 52°25′W)

Served with
4 U-Flottille, Stettin   December 1941 - August 1942 (ab)
10 U-Flottille, Lorient   September 1942 - 3.10.42 (fb)

Commanded by
KL Wolfgang Schultze   December 1941 - 3.10.42

Patrols: 1   Ships sunk: 2 (14,585 grt) + 1 damaged

On 27.12.41 U 512 left Hamburg to begin trials. She reached Kiel on the 29th and left for the eastern Baltic on 10.1.42.

The boat was damaged in diving tests on the 17th and went in to Stettin for repairs, which were completed within ten days. On the 30th U 512 was ordered to allow herself to be frozen in.

On 10.4.42 she resumed trials and left Stettin for final acceptance trials on 13.5.42. In late May U 512 was rammed on the surface by another boat. She returned to Stettin and repairs were completed by 8.7.42.

U 512 left for Danzig on the 11th for final tactical exercises. After these were completed, she had a mechanical failure which caused the boat to ram a small freighter. Again, the boat put in to Stettin for repair. She eventually reached Kiel on 7.8.42.

1. 11.8.42 Left Kiel and arrived Kristiansand **12.8.42**

2. 15.8.42 Left for the Western Atlantic.

In early September U 512 was refuelled by U 462 W of the Azores. Some days later the boat was spotted on the surface by an aircraft in the Sargasso Sea. She remained surfaced and was strafed by the aircraft, which also dropped two bombs astern of the boat. U 512 had a gun jam early in the action and she sustained some damage in

the attack.

A steamship was sighted on the 8th but both torpedoes fired, missed. On the 12th U 512 attacked the tanker SS *Patrick J Hurley* (am 10865t) NE of Guadeloupe. Two torpedoes missed but the vessel was sunk by gunfire. One week later, on the 19th, the SS *Monte Gorbea* (sp 3720t) was torpedoed and sunk just E of Martinique. This vessel, apart from being neutral, belonged to a country sympathetic to Germany and U 512's commander was certain to be court-martialled on his return.

On the 24th the boat sank the abandoned wreck of the SS *Antinous* (am 6034t) SE of Trinidad. This vessel had been seriously damaged by U 515's last torpedo late on the 23rd.

U 512 was sighted on the surface 50 miles N of Cayenne on 3.10.42 by a B 18 aircraft of 99 Squadron (USAF). Four bombs were dropped, two of which hit the boat. She dived and reached bottom at 23 fathoms.

After a time the crew collapsed as sea water reached the batteries, producing chlorine gas. Only three men escaped from the boat, of whom only one reached a dinghy dropped by the aircraft. He was picked up ten days later by the destroyer USS *Ellis* and landed in Trinidad on **30.10.42**

U 513   Type IX C

Built by Deutsche Werft, Hamburg
Keel laid 26.4.41   Launched 29.10.41
Commissioned 10.1.42   Feldpost Nr M 47 994

Sunk 19.7.43 NE of Florianópolis (27°17′S 47°32′W)

Served with
4 U-Flottille, Stettin   January - August 1942 (ab)
10 U-Flottille, Lorient   September 1942 - 19.7.43 (fb)

Commanded by
KK Rolf Rüggeberg   January 1942 - May 1943
KL Friedrich Guggenberger   May 1943 - 19.7.43

Patrols: 4   Ships sunk: 6 (29,940 grt) + 2 damaged

1. 7.8.42 Left Kiel for the North Atlantic.

From the 20th to the 31st U 513 operated off Belle Isle Strait with U 165 and U 517. When these two boats went off to attack convoys, U 513 moved south to patrol off Newfoundland.

On 5.9.42 the boat entered Conception Bay in darkness and reached Wanaba Anchorage, Bell Island, moving on the surface. Before daylight U 513 submerged and later in the day sank two ships, the SS *Saganaga* (br 5454t) and the SS *Lord Strathcona* (br 7335t). The boat came under fire from shore batteries but she escaped despite the rapid arrival of aircraft, which were hampered by very low cloud.

U 513 continued to patrol off Newfoundland but seventeen days of almost continuous fog restricted her activities. Finally, on the 29th she torpedoed and damaged the SS *Ocean Vagabond* (br 7174t) off St John's. On 10.10.42 U 513 set out for home.

She put in to her new base at Lorient **22.10.42**

2. 21.11.42 Left for operations. No details known of this patrol.
U 513 returned to Lorient **18.12.42**

3. 20.2.43 Left for Atlantic operations.

U 513 went to an assembly area W of the Azores, where she was joined by other boats, all intended for operations off the US east coast. On or about 12.3.43 U 513, U 106, U 130, U 167, U 172 and U 515 were to form a patrol line, *Unverzagt*, to operate against approaching, eastbound UGS 6, heading for Gibraltar.

The convoy, which had left New York on the 5th, was sighted by

U 130 in the evening of the 12th, before the line was in position. She began to shadow but was located and sunk during the night and contact was not regained until the 14th.

Unverzagt and *Wohlgemut* groups formed a patrol line W of the Azores, through which the convoy passed on the 14th. *Tümmler* group, then off the Canaries, was ordered to make the 1500 mile journey to intercept before the convoy was too close to Gibraltar. Although there were generally at least six boats in contact and in spite of there being no aircraft and the conditions good, the operation was a failure, with only four ships sunk. The remote screen kept the boats well away from UGS 6, carrying out depth-charge attacks more than ten miles from the convoy. The operation ended on the 19th W of Spain, in the face of increasing air support from Gibraltar. U 513 had no success against the convoy.

After refuelling from returning boats, some of the boats from the UGS 6 operation, including U 513, moved south and joined a new patrol line, *Seeräuber*, S of the Canaries, formed to meet southbound convoy RS 3, expected on the 26th. It was sighted on the 28th and in a two-day operation three ships were sunk, none by U 513, although she did make attacks.

After the operation ended on the 30th, U 513 patrolled off the Canaries for some days. On 14.4.43, approaching Lorient, the boat picked up two survivors from U 526, sunk after striking a British-laid mine that day. U 513 reached Lorient **14.4.43**

4. 18.5.43 Left for operations in the South Atlantic.

In late May U 513 was refuelled by U 460 W of Freetown. She then moved westwards, to operate off the Brazilian coast. On 21.6.43 the SS *Venezia* (sw 1673t) was sunk ESE of Rio de Janeiro and on the 25th the tanker SS *Eagle* (am 6003t) was torpedoed and damaged E of Rio. A Brazilian aircraft, searching for U 513 on the 25th, located U 199 instead. Both boats escaped.

By 1.7.43 U 513 had moved southwards again and early on that day she sank the SS *Tutóia* (bz 1125t) S of São Vicente and on the 3rd the SS *Elihu B Washburne* (am 7176t) was sunk off the Ilha de São Sebastião.

On the 16th U 513 sank the SS *Richard Caswell* (am 7177t) E of Laguna. A USN Mariner of VP-74 (Lt R S Whitcomb) located the boat on the 19th NE of Florianópolis from a radio transmission.

Approaching through flak, the aircraft made two direct hits on U 513, sending it down bow-first. Some 20 survivors were seen in the water but only 7, including the commander, were picked up by the seaplane tender USS *Barnegat* five hours later and made PoW. Of U 513's crew, 46 men were lost.

U 514   Type IX C

Built by Deutsche Werft, Hamburg
Keel laid 29.4.41   Launched 18.11.41
Commissioned 24.1.42   Feldpost Nr M 27 254

Sunk 8.7.43 W of Cape Ortegal (43°37´N 08°59´W)

Served with
4 U-Flottille, Stettin   January - August 1942 (ab)
10 U-Flottille, Lorient   September 1942 - 8.7.43 (fb)

Commanded by
KL Hans-Jürgen Auffermann   January 1942 - 8.7.43

Patrols: 4   Ships sunk: 7 (32,624 grt) + 1 damaged

On 3.6.42 U 514 had an officer killed in an accident.

1. 12.8.42 Left Kiel and arrived Kristiansand **13.8.42**

2. 15.8.42 Left for operations in the western Atlantic.

Outward-bound, U 514 sank the sailing vessel *Helen Forsey* (br 167t), by gunfire SE of Bermuda. In the late evening of the 11th the SS *Cornwallis* (br 5458t) was torpedoed and damaged just W of Bridgetown, Barbados. In the same attack U 514 may have sunk or damaged a second ship but there is no confirmation of this.

On the 15th the SS *Kioto* (br 3297t) was sunk by torpedo and gunfire E of Tobago. The boat was attacked by a USN Mariner of VP-74 on the 16th and seriously damaged. A destroyer arrived and its depth-charge attacks caused further damage to U 514. She managed to escape and moved eastwards, spending the next four days on repairs.

The boat was patrolling off the Amazon Delta on the 28th, on the Equator. On this day she encountered some ships off the Baia de Marajó, escorted by the destroyer USS *Roe*. U 514 torpedoed and sank the SS *Ozório* (bz 2730t) and the SS *Lages* (bz 5472t) in two separate attacks.

On 11.10.42 U 514 had her final success on this patrol, sinking the SS *Steel Scientist* (am 5688t) off Cayenne. After turning for home, the boat was attacked on the 13th by a B 18 of 99 Squadron (USAF) but she escaped.

U 514 put in to her new base at Lorient **9.11.42**

3. 9.12.42 Left for operations in the Caribbean area.

En route on 3.1.43, U 514 sighted eastbound tanker convoy TM 1 1100 miles NE of Trinidad. She torpedoed and damaged the tanker MV *British Vigilance* (br 8093t), the drifting wreck of which was sunk by U 105 on the 24th ENE of Antigua.

U 514 and U 125, also en route to the Caribbean, were ordered to shadow the convoy. *Delphin* group, 900 miles to the north, was ordered to intercept. In the meantime the two shadowers had lost the convoy and after a two-day search they had failed to find it.

The two boats met up with *Delphin* group on the 7th 600 miles W of the Canaries. TM 1 passed through the centre of the *Delphin* line during the afternoon of the 8th. The pursuit ended on the 11th near Madeira, with seven tankers sunk.

U 514 remained with *Delphin* group, which reformed S of the Azores on the 17th after six of its original members had been refuelled by U 463. In search of convoys, the group moved eastwards to the Canaries, then to an area W of Gibraltar. U 514 left the group and patrolled in the area on the southern side of the Azores. On the 27th she sank a straggler from convoy UGS 4, the SS *Charles C Pinckney* (am 7177t) SW of Pico, Azores.

From late January U 514 patrolled the Ponta Delgada. After being refuelled by U 118 in early February, the boat returned to base, reaching Lorient **12.2.43**

4. 15.4.43 Left for the North Atlantic.

Outward-bound, U 514 was directed towards westbound convoy ONS 4, sighted by U 732 on 23.4.43, but she did not make contact.

The boat joined *Specht* group NE of Newfoundland, which on the 27th was directed to HX 235 but the convoy was re-routed to the south. On the 29th *Amsel* group closed up to *Specht* and they moved south. From 1.5.43 the two groups were drawn up in an arc E of Newfoundland, awaiting northbound convoy SC 128. It passed through the *Specht* line and smoke was sighted by U 628 but contact was lost in a southerly gale and when the convoy had not been sighted again by the 3rd a new patrol line, *Fink*, was formed in the expected path of SC 128 from *Specht* and *Star* groups. *Star* had come south after abandoning its pursuit of convoy ONS 5.

SC 128 had not been found by the 4th and the search was called off but almost immediately a southwest-bound convoy appeared in the centre of the *Fink* line. This proved to be ONS 5, delayed by the storm. During the night of the 4/5th some attacks were made and the convoy dispersed into several separate, escorted groups. Fifteen boats were in contact on the 5th but in the late afternoon fog came down and almost all contact was lost. Many boats were attacked by the escorts and damaged. Pursuit was called off on the morning of the 6th.

U 514 then joined *Elbe* group E of Newfoundland. It moved south-

U 514 (continued)

eastwards on the 8th to get ahead of convoy SC 129. On the 10th *Rhein* and *Elbe* groups combined to form *Elbe 1* and *2*. U 514 was in *Elbe 1*. Forming up on the 11th, they passed the convoy. Only two ships were sunk, both by U 402, before the operation ended on the 14th. U 514 supplied fuel to another boat, possibly U 231, on or about the 17th SE of Greenland.

U 514 returned to Lorient **22.5.43**

5. 1.7.43 Left for operations in the Indian Ocean.

U 514 was one of eight boats of *Monsun* group, heading for the South Atlantic. On the 8th the boat was caught on the surface W of Cape Ortegal by a Liberator of 224 Squadron (S/Ldr T M Bulloch). Eight rockets were fired by the aircraft as it swooped in, forcing U 514 to crash-dive. Bulloch dropped eight depth-charges, followed by a homing torpedo, then still on the secret list. U 514 was destroyed.

There were no survivors, 54 dead.

U 515 Type IX C

Built by Deutsche Werft, Hamburg
Keel laid 7.5.41   Launched 2.12.41
Commissioned 21.2.42   Feldpost Nr M 27 988

Sunk 9.4.44 SE of the Azores (34°35´N 19°19´W)

Served with
4 U-Flottille, Stettin February - August 1942 (ab)
10 U-Flottille, Lorient September 1942 - 9.4.44 (fb)

Commanded by
KL Werner Henke February 1942 - 9.4.44

Patrols: 6   Ships sunk: 24 (144,864 grt)
                           1 sloop (1350 dt)
                           1 depôt ship (10,850 dt)

1. 12.8.42 Left Kiel and arrived Kristiansand **13.8.42**

2. 15.8.42 Left to operate in the western Atlantic.

U 515 patrolled initially E of Trinidad and on 12.9.42 she torpedoed two tankers, sinking the MV *Stanvac Melbourne* (pa 10013t) and damaging the MV *Woensdrecht* (nl 4668t). This vessel was taken into port but was declared a total loss.

Four more ships were sunk in the same area, on the 13th the SS *Ocean Vanguard* (br 7174t) and the SS *Nimba* (pa 1854t), on the 14th the SS *Harborough* (br 5415t) by torpedo and gunfire and on the 15th the MV *Sörholt* (nw 4801t). On this day one of the boat's crewmen was killed when a machine-gun misfired.

U 515 sank the SS *Mae* (am 5607t) on the 16th by torpedo and gunfire N of Georgetown and on the 20th the SS *Reedpool* (br 4838t) was sunk NNW of Georgetown. The boat picked up oil-covered survivors from the *Reedpool*. They were cleaned, fed and re-clothed.

On the 23rd U 515 torpedoed two ships SE of Trinidad, sinking the SS *Lindvangen* (nw 2412t) and damaging the SS *Antinous* (am 6034t). This vessel was hit with U 515's last torpedo and the abandoned wreck was sunk next day by U 512.

U 515 put in to her new base at Lorient **14.10.42**

3. 7.11.42 Left for operations in the Central Atlantic.

On the 11th U 515 was attacked and damaged by aircraft S of Cape St Vincent. In the evening of the 11th she sighted a British cruiser force 150 miles S of the Cape. The boat proceeded at high speed for some hours to get ahead of warships for a good attacking position but she was located by the destroyer escorts and driven off.

In the face of heavy opposition from the escort, Henke persisted in his attacks and in the early hours of the 12th he sank the depôt ship HMS *Hecla* and two hours later torpedoed and damaged the destroyer HMS *Marne*. U 515 was spotted by HMS *Venomous* and attacked with gunfire and depth-charges. The boat dived and escaped but when she resurfaced to finish off the *Marne*, she was again attacked by *Venomous*. U 515 evaded further searches by aircraft and warships and left the area.

She joined *Westwall* group, which was carrying out east-west patrols in the area W of Gibraltar, bounded by Cape St Vincent in the north and Casablanca in the south. On the 26th it was decided that the *Westwall* boats should be moved to an area W of the Azores, to meet eastbound UGS convoys beyond the range of land-based aircraft. They formed a north-south patrol line on the 27th, then began a westward movement to take the boats north of the Azores.

By 6.12.42 the 40° W meridian had been reached. Four ships were sunk during the darkness hours of the 6/7th, one of them the troopship SS *Ceramic* (br 18713t), sunk soon after midnight by U 515. The vessel was carrying 656 passengers and crew, including 400 troops and government servants. There was only one survivor, Sapper Eric Munday, picked up by U 515.

No convoys were seen by the *Westwall* boats and it was believed that they were passing further to the south, too far south for boats with limited fuel. So, on the 12th the *Westwall* line began moving eastwards. On the 16th the group was dissolved N of the Azores and the boats took up positions W of Portugal from the 19th. The search for convoys over the next few days found nothing and on the 23rd the boats began their return to base.

U 515 reached Lorient **6.1.43**

4. 21.2.43 Left for operations in the Central Atlantic.

U 515 went to an assembly area W of the Azores. En route, she torpedoed and sank the MV *California Star* (br 8300t) WNW of the Azores on 4.3.43 and picked up her 2nd Officer as a prisoner.

On or about the 12th U 515 and five other boats in the assembly area were to form a patrol line, *Unverzagt*, to operate against approaching eastbound UGS 6, heading for Gibraltar. The convoy which had left New York on the 5th, was sighted by U 130 in the evening of the 12th, before the line could be formed. She began to shadow but was located and sunk during the night and contact was not regained until the 14th.

Unverzagt and *Wohlgemut* groups formed a patrol line W of the Azores, through which the convoy passed on the 14th. *Tümmler* group, then off the Canaries, was ordered to make the 1500 mile journey to intercept before the convoy was too close to Gibraltar. Although there were generally six boats in contact and in spite of there being no aircraft and conditions good, the operation was a failure, with only four ships sunk. The remote screen kept the boats well away from UGS 6, carrying out depth-charge attacks more than ten miles from the convoy. The operation ended on the 19th W of Spain, in the face of increasing air support from Gibraltar. U 515 had no success against the convoy.

After she received fuel from the returning U 106 on the 24th, U 515 went south with other boats from the UGS 6 operation and they joined a new patrol line, *Seeräuber*, formed S of the Canaries to meet southbound convoy RS 3, expected on the 26th. It was sighted on the 28th and in a two-day operation three ships were sunk, none by U 515 which fired no torpedoes, being repeatedly driven down by aircraft and escorts.

After obtaining more fuel from the returning U 67 the boat proceeded south and early on 9.4.43 U 515 sank the MV *Bamako* (fr 2357t) off Dakar. She moved down to the Freetown area, where, on the 29th, she was attacked by a Catalina of 270 Squadron. Six depth-charges were dropped but the boat dived and escaped. The aircraft was damaged by flak in the action. On the 30th U 515 sighted northbound convoy TS 37 90 miles S of Freetown. Late on this day four ships were torpedoed and sunk, the MV *Corabella* (br 5682t), the SS *Bandar Shahpur* (br 5236t), the MV *Kota*

Tjandi (nl 7295t) and in a second attack the SS *Nagina* (br 6551t). U 515 attacked the convoy again in the early morning of 1.5.43, torpedoing three more ships, sinking the SS *Clan MacPherson* (br 6940t) and the SS *City of Singapore* (br 6555t) and damaging the MV *Mokambo* (be 4996t). This last vessel was towed to Freetown roads but sank on May 2nd.

On the 9th U 515 sank the MV *Corneville* (nw 4544t) off Accra. She was refuelled by U 460 on the 22nd W of Freetown. The boat continued to operate W and SW of Freetown and although two convoys were sighted, U 515 had no further success.

She returned to Lorient **24.6.43**

5. 21.8.43 Left Lorient and returned **22.8.43**

6. 29.8.43 Left for operations in the North Atlantic.

On September 5th U 515 sighted OS 54/KMS 25 W of Spain. Near midnight she approached the convoy but was located, attacked and damaged by the frigate HMS *Tavy*. The boat dived deep and escaped.

She returned to Lorient **12.9.43**

7. 1.11.43 Left to pick up new radar equipment and torpedoes at St Nazaire, arriving there **3.11.43**

8. 9.11.43 Left St Nazaire for Atlantic operations.

U 515 joined *Schill 1* group, which by the 18th was drawn up in a patrol line W of Lisbon in the expected path of MKS 30/SL 139, sighted by aircraft on the 15th W of Gibraltar. In the morning of the 18th the convoy was reported to be southeast of the line, which was ordered northeastwards to intercept. The convoy in fact passed through the patrol line during the early afternoon of the 18th but U 515's sighting report was not received by the other boats until late evening. She had been overrun by the convoy and was then located and attacked by the sloops HMS *Chanticleer* and *Crane* before she could report.

U 515 torpedoed and damaged *Chanticleer*, which was towed in to Horta, Azores, where she later became the depôt ship, *Lusitania II*. The boat was tracked by *Crane* for ten hours before slipping away, damaged. The *Schill 1* boats pursued the convoy during the night of the 18/19th but were constantly harassed by aircraft. Only U 262 made contact just before dawn on the 19th, but she was located and driven off. With no chance of the other boats catching up, the pusuit was abandoned and on the 22nd *Schill 1* group was dissolved.

Between the 22nd and 24th U 515 carried out repairs, firstly off La Palma and then Hierro, the westernmost islands of the Canaries. On completion, U 515 requested and received permission to proceed southwards and from early December she was operating S of Freetown. She sank three ships in the Gulf of Guinea; on the 17th the SS *Kingswood* (br 5080t), on the 19th the SS *Phemius* (br 7406t), both off the coast E of Accra, and on the 24th the MV *Dumana* (br 8427t) off Cape Palmas, Ivory Coast. U 515 took one man from a *Phemius* lifeboat as a PoW, to obtain information.

The repairs effected four weeks earlier had begun to deteriorate. U 515 headed north and further repairs were carried out off Santiago, in the Cape Verde Islands. The homeward journey was continued but the batteries, which had also been damaged, now began to give trouble. Off Spain on 11.1.44, they failed.

Unable to dive, U 515 made her way along the coast of France until two German minesweepers arrived to escort her to Lorient. An attack by two aircraft was beaten off and the boat berthed in the evening of **14.1.44**

9. 30.3.44 Left for operations off West Africa.

Late in the evening of 8.4.44 U 515 was located SE of the Azores by an Avenger from the escort-carrier USS *Guadalcanal*. Two other Avengers were dispatched from the carrier one hour later to make a

search. Soon after midnight a boat, U 515, was spotted on the surface. Two depth-charges were dropped and after firing at the aircraft, the boat dived. Meanwhile, the *Guadalcanal* was heading for the scene.

During the night contact with U 515 was lost. Later in the morning she surfaced and after an hour the carrier force was sighted. Almost immediately an aircraft appeared, dropped two depth-charges, which fell short, and U 515 dived. Other aircraft and the escorts USS *Flaherty* and *Pillsbury* were ordered to close. *Pillsbury* (Lt-Cdr G W Casselman) made a contact and carried out two Hedgehog attacks.

The boat dived deep and after two hours it was thought that the two destroyers had gone. In fact they were searching to the west and had been joined by USS *Chatelain*. The fourth destroyer from *Guadalcanal's* escort, USS *Pope*, moved ahead of the carrier to protect her from a possible attack.

Pope (Lt-Cdr E H Headland) established contact about noon on the 9th and made two Hedgehog attacks, followed by three depth-charge attacks, which seriously damaged U 515. Temporary repairs were effected, leaks were plugged but three further depth-charge attacks re-opened them and U 515 began to flood. She began to rise despite all efforts to keep her down. In mid-afternoon the boat broke surface, very near *Chatelain*. The destroyer opened fire at very short range, as U 515's crew emerged from the conning tower, only to be cut down. Aircraft also attacked with rockets and machine-guns. The boat sank within minutes, still being fired at by *Chatelain* (Lt-Cdr J L Foley).

Of U 515's crew, 44 men, including the commander, were picked up. 16 others were killed in the action, some in the water by strafing aircraft.

Werner Henke and his men were landed in the USA, where they underwent interrogation. On June 15 1944, at Fort Hunt, Virginia, Henke was killed whilst apparently attempting to escape.

U 516   Type IX C

Built by Deutsche Werft, Hamburg
Keel laid 12.5.41   Launched 16.12.41
Commissioned 10.3.42   Feldpost Nr M 41 960

Sunk 2.1.46 NW of Malin Head (56°06′N 09°00′W)

Served with
4 U-Flottille, Stettin   March - August 1942 (ab)
10 U-Flottille, Lorient   September 1942 - September 1944 (fb)
33 U-Flottille, Flensburg   October 1944 - 14.5.45 (fb-t)

Commanded by
KK Gerhard Wiebe   March 1942 - June 1943
KL Herbert Kuppisch   June - July 1943
KL Hans-Rutger Tillessen   July 1943 - December 1944
OL Friedrich Petran   December 1944 - 14.5.45

Patrols: 6   Ships sunk: 15 (78,603 grt) + 1 damaged
                         1 submarine depôt ship (10,972 dt)

1. 12.8.42 Left Kiel and arrived Kristiansand **13.8.42**

2. 15.8.42 Left for operations in the western Atlantic.

En route, U 516 encountered the British ship SS *Port Jackson* in the early hours of the 27th some 900 miles W of the southern tip of Ireland. The four torpedoes fired all missed and although two hits were made on the ship with U 516's 105 mm deck-gun, the boat left the scene. Early on the 31st she attacked the tanker SS *Jack Carnes* (am 10907t) N of the Azores, sinking her with six torpedoes and gunfire. This vessel had been attacked by U 705 some hours

U 516 (continued)

earlier, with no apparent result.

In early September U 516 was refuelled by U 462 W of the Azores. The boat went on to operate E of the Caribbean and on 19.9.42 she torpedoed and sank the MV *Wichita* (am 6174t) 500 miles E of Dominica. On the 28th the SS *Antonico* (bz 1223t) was sunk by gunfire off Pointe Isère, French Guiana and in the early morning of the 30th the SS *Alipore* (br 5273t) was torpedoed and sunk NNE of Paramaribo.

On 16.10.42 U 160 sighted an eastbound convoy off Tobago and she, U 516, U 67 and U 332 shadowed it for some days but only U 160 was able to make a successful attack because a full moon and aircraft attacks prevented the other boats closing the convoy.

On the 24th U 516, en route for home, torpedoed and sank the SS *Holmpark* (br 5780t) some 900 miles E of Barbados. In late October the boat was refuelled by U 462 S of the Azores.

U 516 put in to her new base at Lorient **14.11.42**

3. 23.12.42 Left for the Central Atlantic.

In mid-January U 516 was one of a number of boats which assembled S of the Cape Verde Islands. They formed *Seehund* group for operations in South African waters, to interrupt shipping going round the Cape to the Middle East. From the 29th the boats were refuelled by U 459 600 miles S of St Helena.

By 10.2.43 U 516 had rounded the Cape and on the 11th she sank the SS *Helmspey* (br 4764t) SW of Port Elizabeth. On the 17th the SS *Deer Lodge* (am 6187t) was sunk off Algoa Bay and on the 27th the Dutch naval depôt ship *Colombia* in the same area.

U 516 turned back again. In mid-March she was moving up the west coast of South Africa. On the 20th she torpedoed and sank the SS *Nortun* (pa 3663t) SW of Lüderitz. From early April the boats of *Seehund* group began their return journey through the South Atlantic. On the 12th U 516 rendezvoused with the outward-bound U 181 SW of Monrovia, to take off a badly-injured seaman.

In late April U 516 was refuelled by U 117 S of the Azores. She returned to Lorient **4.5.43**

4. 8.7.43 Left for the South Atlantic.

U 516 was one of nine boats intended for operations in the Indian Ocean, as *Monsun* group. U 462 was to accompany the group and then refuel the boats 300 miles E of St Paul Rocks. However, she failed twice to pass through the Bay of Biscay and a new plan was made for the *Monsun* boats to be refuelled by U 487 S of the Azores from 14.7.43.

Five of the boats searched the area for U 487 from the 14th to the 17th but she could not be found and had in fact been sunk by aircraft on the 13th. Three *Monsun* boats had also been sunk en route, U 506, U 509 and U 514. It was then arranged for the remaining six *Monsun* boats to be refuelled by two outward-bound boats, U 155 and U 160 but the latter failed to arrive, having been sunk by carrier-borne aircraft on the 14th.

U 516 was ordered to share the refuelling duty with U 155 and this was carried out 600 miles WNW of the Cape Verde Islands between July 21st and 27th. U 516 supplied U 532 and U 533 and U 155 supplied U 168, U 183 and U 188, after which the five boats continued southwards.

U 516 returned to Lorient **23.8.43**

5. 30.9.43 Left Lorient and arrived Brest **1.10.43**

6. 4.10.43 Left for operations in the Caribbean.

En route, U 516 operated initially off Horta, in the Azores. She went on westwards and on 5.11.43 entered the Caribbean via the Dominica Passage. On the 8th the boat was attacked by a Ventura of VB-133 W of Curaçao but she escaped undamaged.

During the next two weeks U 516 sank four ships, on the 11th the SS *Pompoon* (pa 1082t) off Puerto Colombia, on the 17th the sailing vessel *Ruby* (co 39t) by gunfire N of Còlon, Panama and on

the 23rd and 24th the tankers SS *Elizabeth Kellogg* (am 5189t) and the SS *Melville E Stone* (am 7176t) were both sunk N of Colón.

On 8.12.43 U 516 sank the MV *Colombia* (pa 1064t) just NE of Nombre de Dios and on the 16th the turbine tanker *McDowell* (am 10195t) N of Aruba. U 516's successes had resulted in her being the object of much attention from aircraft. She requested and received permission to move northeastwards to escape the organised searches being carried out for her.

In the late evening of the 18th a searchlight-equipped USN Mariner (Lt R E Pearce) located U 516 and she was caught on the surface and illuminated. Gunfire was exchanged, four depth-charges were dropped and the boat stopped. However, she dived before the Mariner could make a second attack and continued eastwards. U 516 surfaced at dawn on the 19th and some hours later she was sighted and attacked by a Ventura (Lt P J Townsend) as she dived. In spite of many bubbles being seen breaking the surface, the boat was not seriously damaged and temporary repairs were made.

On the 20th U 516 surfaced again and continued eastwards. She passed out of the Caribbean into the Atlantic between the islands of Saint Barthélemy and Barbuda after more that a week of being hunted. With fuel now running low, U 516 was to rendezvous with U 544 360 miles NW of the Azores at dusk on 16.1.44 to receive sufficient fuel to enable her to reach base. U 129, returning from US waters, was also to be refuelled.

The two boats, making a submerged approach to the rendezvous position at the appointed time, heard bombs exploding and the sound of destroyer propellers. This was later presumed to be U 544 being sunk at the rendezvous position by aircraft from the escort-carrier USS *Guadalcanal*.

U 129 continued eastwards and U 516, now desperately short of fuel, was ordered to meet U 539 150 miles further north on the 19th for fuel to be transferred. Both boats were attacked by carrier-borne aircraft after they met and U 516 was also subjected to depth-charge attacks by two destroyers. The boats made contact again on the 21st and after many attempts in difficult sea conditions, U 516 finally received her fuel on 4.2.44.

She returned to Lorient **26.2.44**

7. 7.5.44 Left for operations in the Caribbean.

On June 11th the six boats operating in remote areas, including U 516 and U 539 in the Caribbean, were warned to conserve enough fuel to get them to Norway, if they were so ordered.

Operations in the Caribbean had become extremely difficult and U 516 had only one success, sinking the tanker SS *Esso Harrisburg* (am 9887t) on 7.7.44 NNW of Punta Gallinas, Colombia. On the 8th U 516 fired torpedoes at the American tanker MV *Point Breeze* but without success, the last attack by a U-boat in the Caribbean.

In late July U 516 and U 539 had left the operational area and by mid-August they were near Cape Ortegal. The blockade of the Bay of Biscay prevented their return to French ports and both were ordered to Norway.

U 516 reached Kristiansand **1.10.44**

8. 3.10.44 Left Kristiansand and arrived Flensburg **4.10.44**

9. 24.3.45 Left Kiel and arrived Horten **27.3.45**

10. 1.4.45 Left Horten and arrived Kristiansand **3.4.45**

11. 5.4.45 Left to transport supplies to St Nazaire.

U 516 was still at sea when the U-boat war ended on 4.5.45. She put in to Loch Eriboll on the 14th and surrendered.

U 516 was one of 116 boats disposed of by the Royal Navy in Operation Deadlight. *In late December 1945 she was towed from the assembly point at Lisahally by the destroyer HMS* Quantock.

U 516 was sunk by gunfire by the Polish destroyer Piorun *on 2.1.46 NW of Malin Head.*

U 517   Type IX C

Built by Deutsche Werft, Hamburg
Keel laid 5.6.41   Launched 30.12.41
Commissioned 21.3.42   Feldpost Nr M 41 996

Sunk 21.11.42 NW of Cape Finisterre (46°16′N 17°09′W)

Served with
4 U-Flottille, Stettin March - August 1942 (ab)
10 U-Flottille, Lorient September 1942 - 21.11.42 (fb)

Commanded by
KL Paul Hartwig March 1942 - 21.11.42

Patrols: 2   Ships sunk: 8 (26,383 grt) + 1 damaged
                         1 corvette (900 dt)

1. 8.8.42 Left Kiel for Canadian waters.

U 517 sank the troopship SS *Chatham* (am 5649t) on the 27th at the northern end of Belle Isle Strait. She was part of eastbound SG 6F but was running ahead of the convoy. The *Chatham* was the first US troopship lost in the war. Of her 562 passengers and crew, only 11 were lost. On the 28th, in the same area, U 517 torpedoed and sank the wreck of the SS *Arlyn* (am 3304t) of SG 6S, abandoned after being hit six hours earlier by U 165.

U 517 moved down Belle Isle Strait into the Gulf of St Lawrence. On 3.9.42 she encountered northbound convoy NL 6 E of Cap Mackinnon and sank the SS *Donald Stewart* (br 1781t) in a surface attack in the dark. The boat was sighted by an escorting corvette, HMCS *Weyburn*, which turned to ram. U 517 made off and when the *Weyburn* opened fire, she dived.

On the 6th U 517 sighted convoy QS 33 and shadowed. E of Cap Gaspé late on the 7th, she sank three ships, the SS *Mount Pindus* (gr 5729t), the SS *Oakton* (br 1727t) and the SS *Mount Taygetus* (gr 3286t). The boat was spotted by a Hudson of 113 (RCAF) Squadron from 4,500 feet. The aircraft dived, machine-gunning U 517, but was unable to drop depth-charges until after she had submerged. The boat was undamaged.

U 517 passed through the Détroit d'Honguedo into the St Lawrence River and on the 11th she sank the corvette HMCS *Charlottetown*, escorting convoy SQ 30 off Cap Chat. The boat turned back to re-enter the Gulf of St Lawrence. In the evening of the 15th she met convoy SQ 36 N of Cap des Rosiers and sank the SS *Saturnus* (nl 2741t) and the SS *Inger Elisabeth* (nw 2166t). The boat dived and came under depth-charge attacks by the escorts but suffered no damage. U 517 called up U 165, which attacked the convoy on the 16th, sinking one ship and damaging two others.

Off Cap Gaspé on the 21st, U 517 was surprised on the surface by the minesweeper USS *Georgian*, escorting SQ 38. Her attempt to ram the boat failed. She also made several depth-charge attacks, which probably caused no damage.

U 517 was hunted continuously by aircraft and between the 25th and 29th she was subjected to three heavy attacks, both by depth-bombs and machine-gun fire. These attacks, coupled with very few ships being seen and shortage of fuel and torpedoes led to U 517 leaving the Gulf of St Lawrence on 2.10.42.

She put in to her new base at Lorient **19.10.42**

2. 17.11.42 Left for Atlantic operations.

Outward bound on the 21st, U 517 was attacked NW of Cape Finisterre and sunk by an Albacore of 817 (FAA) Squadron from the aircraft carrier HMS *Victorious*.

Of U 517's crew, 3 men were lost and 52 others, including her commander, were picked up and made PoW.

U 518   Type IX C

Built by Deutsche Werft, Hamburg
Keel laid 11.6.41   Launched 11.2.42
Commissioned 25.4.42   Feldpost Nr M 44 690

Sunk 22.4.45 NW of the Azores (43°26′N 38°23′W)

Served with
4 U-Flottille, Stettin April - September 1942 (ab)
2 U-Flottille, Lorient October 1942 - October 1944 (fb)
33 U-Flottille, Flensburg November 1944 - 22.4.45 (fb)

Commanded by
FK Hans-Günther Brachmann April - September 1942
KL Friedrich-Wilhelm Wissmann September 1942 - January 1944
OL Hans Offermann January 1944 - 22.4.45

Patrols: 7   Ships sunk: 10 (62,923 grt) + 2 damaged

1. 26.9.42 Left Kiel for Canadian waters.

U 518 patrolled initially off Belle Isle Strait. On 2.11.42, en route to put ashore an agent at New Carlisle, Quebec, she went into Conception Bay and torpedoed and sank two ships that were to load iron ore at Wabana Anchorage, the SS *Rose Castle* (br 7803t) and the SS *P.L.M 27* (br 5633t). The boat left the bay and headed south on the surface to go round the end of the Avalon Peninsula. U 518 was surprised by an aircraft 40 miles E of Cape Race, which dropped four depth-charges as the boat submerged, but she escaped undamaged.

She passed through Cabot Strait into the Gulf of St Lawrence and in the early hours of the 10th landed an agent E of Sawyer's Point in Chaleur Bay. The agent, a man named Janowski, was picked up later the same day after his extremely suspicious behaviour had attracted attention.

The boat remained in the Gulf of St Lawrence until the 17th, when she set out for home. In the early morning of the 21st U 518 encountered westbound convoy ON 145 200 miles S of Placentia Bay, Newfoundland. In her first attack she missed a corvette but damaged two tankers, the MV *British Renown* (br 6997t) and the MV *British Promise* (br 8443t). In her second attack, a few minutes later, U 518 sank the MV *Empire Sailor* (br 6140t).

On the 23rd the tanker SS *Caddo* (br 10172t) was torpedoed and sunk SE of Cape Race. Some officers from this vessel were taken aboard as prisoners. In late November U 518 was refuelled by U 460 NW of the Azores.

She put in to her new base at Lorient **15.12.42**

2. 11.1.43 Left for operations in the Central Atlantic.

U 518 was to patrol off the east coast of Brazil, between Bahia (Salvador) and Pernambuco (Recife). On 18.2.43 she sank the MV *Brasiloide* (bz 6075t) E of Bahia. In the same area on the 28th U 518 sighted eastbound convoy BT 6 and on 1.3.43 she torpedoed and sank the SS *Fitz-John Porter* (am 7176t). During a two-day operation against the convoy, KL Wissmann reported that 8 out of 14 torpedoes fired were duds. An enquiry after U 518's return to base showed that Wissmann had fired at excessive range.

The boat continued to patrol off the Brazilian coast and on the 20th and 25th sank two ships off Bahia, the SS *Mariso* (nl 7659t) and the MV *Industria* (sw 1688t). She took some officers from the *Industria* as prisoners.

In late March U 518 was W of St Paul Rocks and in mid-April she was refuelled by U 117 S of the Azores for return to base.

She reached Lorient **27.4.43**

3. 24.6.43 Left for Atlantic operations.

On the 27th U 518 was damaged in two depth-charge attacks, made in the face of intense flak by a Sunderland of 201 Squadron

U 518 (continued)

(F/O B E H Layne). The boat dived and escaped.

Returning to base, she was attacked again on the 30th, this time by a Sunderland of 10 (RAAF) Squadron (F/Lt H W Skinner). One depth-charge attack and strafing attacks were made in the face of heavy flak, in which the aircraft was damaged and the rear gunner was fatally wounded.

U 518 put in to Bordeaux **3.7.43**

4. 18.8.43 Left for operations in the western Atlantic.

U 518 patrolled off Florida and in the Gulf of Mexico but she had no success. She left her operational area in early November.

The boat returned to Lorient **1.12.43**

5. 23.1.44 Left for operations in the Caribbean.

En route, U 518 unsuccessfully attacked a seaplane tender in the central North Atlantic on 13.2.44. Some days afterwards she rendezvoused with the Japanese submarine *I 29*, to hand over equipment and sailing instructions. U 518 continued on her way westwards and after patrolling for a while to the north, she entered the Caribbean via the Mona Passage.

On 7.3.44 the boat torpedoed and sank the tanker SS *Valera* (pa 3401t) NW of Cartagena. During the night of the 15/16th U 518 was attacked by two USN Mariners but escaped.

She returned to Lorient **7.4.44**

6. 4.7.44 Left Lorient and returned, reason unknown, **10.7.44**

7. 15.7.44 Now schnorkel-equipped, left for US waters.

U 518 operated off the US east coast and in early September she managed to survive some intensive searches for her. On the 12th U 518 torpedoed and damaged the SS *George Ade* (am 7176t) SSE of Cape Lookout. She was driven off by the vessel's naval gunners and the minesweeper USS *Project*. The *George Ade* was taken in tow by a salvage vessel, the *Escape*, but went down in a hurricane on the 13th.

From late September U 518 carried out weather-reporting duties in the North Atlantic.

She put in to Kristiansand **24.10.44**

8. 25.10.44 Left Kristiansand and arrived Flensburg **28.10.44**

9. 5.3.45 Left Kiel and arrived Kristiansand **10.3.45**

10. 12.3.45 Left for operations in the western Atlantic.

U 518, U 546, U 805, U 858, U 880 and U 1235 formed *Seewolf* group on 14.4.45 N of the Azores. The group was to sweep westwards in search of convoys, which it was hoped would be less well protected at this late stage of the war. It was thought that any success that the *Seewolf* boats might achieve would result in hunter-killer groups being withdrawn from British coastal waters, thereby reducing the Allied a/s efforts in those waters.

The plan failed and by the 24th only U 805 and U 858 had not been sunk and they were then in the area S of Nova Scotia.

U 518 was sunk on the 22nd NW of the Azores in a Hedgehog attack by the destroyer-escorts USS *Carter* and *Neal A Scott* of the USS *Croatan* carrier group.

There were no survivors, 57 dead.

U 519 Type IX C

Built by Deutsche Werft, Hamburg
Keel laid 23.6.41   Launched 12.2.42
Commissioned 7.5.42   Feldpost Nr M 44 754

Lost 10.2.43 W of the Bay of Biscay, position unknown

Served with
4 U-Flottille, Stettin   May - October 1942 (ab)
2 U-Flottille, Lorient   November 1942 - 10.2.43 (fb)

Commanded by
KL Günter Eppen   May 1942 - 10.2.43

Patrols: 2   Ships sunk: None

1. 17.10.42 Left Kiel for the North Atlantic.

Following the Allied landings in North Africa on 8.11.42, U 519 and other boats in the North Atlantic were ordered to proceed at high speed to the Gibraltar area, where they were to assemble as *Westwall* group.

The boats began to carry out east-west patrols in an area to the west of Gibraltar and bounded by Cape St Vincent in the north and Casablanca in the south, with a view to blocking supplies to the Mediterranean and to ports on the Moroccan coast. During November the group had little success but was at great risk, particularly from Gibraltar-based aircraft.

On the 26th it was decided that *Westwall* group should be moved from the 27th to an area W of the Azores, to meet eastbound UGS convoys beyond the range of land-based aircraft.

U 519 was refuelled on the 28th by U 118 SE of the Azores. She then rejoined *Westwall*, which was moving westwards. By 6.12.42 the group had reached longitude 40°W. After six days and having sighted no convoys, the *Westwall* boats moved eastwards again towards Spain and Portugal. The group dispersed on the 16th and the boats carried out a search W of Portugal from the 19th to the 23rd but with no convoys found, they went home.

U 519 put in to her new base at Lorient **29.12.42**

2. 30.1.43 Left for Atlantic operations.

U 519 joined *Hartherz* group W of the Bay of Biscay, formed to intercept an HG convoy, reported to have left Gibraltar. The group searched between 14° and 19°W from February 4th to the 7th but nothing was seen. *Hartherz* group was dispersed on the 8th.

Soon afterwards, probably on the 10th, U 519 was lost from unknown causes in an area NE of the Azores, the exact position of her sinking unknown.

There were no survivors, 50 dead.

U 520 Type IX C

Built by Deutsche Werft, Hamburg
Keel laid 1.7.41   Launched 2.3.42
Commissioned 19.5.42   Feldpost Nr M 46 364

Sunk 30.10.42 E of Conception Bay (47°47′N 49°50′W)

Served with
4 U-Flottille, Stettin   May - September 1942 (ab)
2 U-Flottille, Lorient   September 1942 - 30.10.42 (fb)

Commanded by
KL Volkmar Schwartzkopff   May 1942 - 30.10.42

Patrols: 1   Ships sunk: None

1. 3.10.42 Left Kiel for Canadian waters.

U 520 was ordered to an area off Newfoundland and to wait there for eastbound convoys, in company with U 521 and U 522. The three boats were to report shipping along their route, which went south of Iceland and via Cape Farewell to Belle Isle Strait.

Climatic conditions had deteriorated in the Gulf of St Lawrence and on arrival the boats were ordered south towards Halifax. On the 30th U 522 sighted eastbound SC 107 ENE of Cape Race and the boats closed in.

U 520 was attacked in fog the same day by a Digby aircraft of 10 (RCAF) Squadron (F/O D F Raynes) and sunk in a four depth-charge attack E of Conception Bay, in the vicinity of the convoy.

There were no survivors, 53 dead.

U 521   Type IX C

Built by Deutsche Werft, Hamburg
Keel laid 3.7.41   Launched 17.3.42
Commissioned 3.6.42   Feldpost Nr M 46 411

Sunk 2.6.43 SE of Delaware Bay (37°43´N 73°16´W)

Served with
4 U-Flottille, Stettin   June - September 1942 (ab)
2 U-Flottille, Lorient   October 1942 - 2.6.43 (fb)

Commanded by
KL Klaus Bargsten   June 1942 - 2.6.43

Patrols: 3   Ships sunk: 3 (19,551 grt)
                            1 a/s trawler (750 dt)

1. 3.10.42 Left Kiel and arrived Kristiansand **4.10.42**

2. 6.10.42 Left for Candian waters.

U 521 was ordered to an area off Newfoundland and to wait there for eastbound convoys, in company with U 520 and U 522. The three boats were to report shipping along their route, which went south of Iceland and via Cape Farewell to Belle Isle Strait.

Climatic conditions had deteriorated in the Gulf of St Lawrence and on arrival the boats were ordered south towards Halifax. On the 30th U 522 sighted eastbound SC 107 ENE of Cape Race and the boats closed in. U 520 was sunk on the 30th and U 521 was driven off next day by a Hudson of 145 (RCAF) Squadron.

Veilchen group joined in the attack on SC 107, when the convoy passed through its patrol line on 1.11.42 E of White Bay, Newfoundland. In the early morning of the 2nd U 521 had a near miss on the escorting HMCS *Moosejaw*, when her torpedo detonated close to the corvette. An hour later, E of Belle Isle, U 521 sank the SS *Hartington* (br 5496t), previously hit with torpedoes by both U 438 and U 522. In the morning of the 3rd U 521 sank the tanker SS *Hahira* (am 6855t) S of Cape Farewell. The operation against SC 107 ended on the 6th in the central North Atlantic, SE of Cape Farewell

U 521 joined *Kreuzotter* group ESE of Cape Farewell, formed from the 9th with boats having limited fuel. On the 15th U 521 reported westbound ONS 144, as it passed through the patrol line. Over the next five days, in spite of fog, five ships and a corvette were sunk. U 521 made two unsuccessful attacks on the convoy, in the evening of the 15th and the early morning of the 18th.

The boat put in to her new base at Lorient **8.12.42**

3. 7.1.43 Left for operations in the Central Atlantic.

U 521 headed for an assembly area W of the Canaries. From the 22nd she, U 43 and U 218 formed *Rochen* group, which was intended to sweep southwards. However, following agents' reports of shipping in the Cap Blanc area, the group was ordered there on

the 23rd. U 66 joined the group there on or about the 27th.

On the 28th the four boats moved north along the coast in search of convoys. U 521 sighted a small convoy, Gib No 2, on 7.2.43 N of the Canaries, heading for Gibraltar. In the morning of the 8th she sank the a/s trawler HMS *Bredon* just NW of Lanzarote, Canaries. The other *Rochen* boats and the five southern boats of *Delphin* group were directed to the convoy, which was thought to be weakly-escorted. However, this was not the case and the operation was abandoned later on the 8th because of a strong air escort.

After briefly pursuing a supposed convoy on the 11th E of Madeira, which in fact was a hunting group, the boats from the Gib No 2 operation dispersed. Those with sufficient fuel, including U 521, moved westwards and five others, all ex-*Delphin* boats, went for refuelling by U 118 SW of Madeira. The boats were re-united on the 16th S of the Azores and a new *Rochen* north-south patrol line was formed.

A search began for convoy UC 1. The group swept westwards until the 20th, then turned east again when no sighting had been made. *Rochen* was ordered to disperse on the 21st, to refuel from U 461 200 miles S of Sao Miguel Island. However, on the 22nd a southwest-bound convoy, the elusive UC 1, was sighted by U 522 east of the replenishment area and the boats were ordered to close.

The action, over five days, saw only three tankers sunk and two damaged, the escort screen of ten warships proving to be too strong. U 521 made an unsuccessful attack on the convoy on the 25th.

U 461 had followed the convoy and from 1.3.43 she refuelled the *Rochen* boats SW of the Azores. U 521 and five other ex-*Rochen* boats then formed a north-south patrol line, *Tümmler*, from the 3rd. They began an eastwards sweep towards the Canaries on the 5th and by the 11th the boats were between the Canaries and the African coast. A small convoy was sighted on the 11th but proved to be too fast.

On the 12th *Tümmler* group was ordered northwest to intercept eastbound convoy UGS 6, heading for Gibraltar but then 1500 miles away. Contact was made with the convoy on the 16th and the operation ended on the 19th near Gibraltar. Although up to nine boats had been in contact with UGS 6 and the weather conditions were good, only four ships were sunk, thanks to the strong surface escort and the appearance of a strong air escort on the final day. In the morning of the 18th U 521 sank the SS *Molly Pitcher* (am 7200t), a straggler from UGS 6, E of the Azores. This vessel had been damaged by U 167 nine hours earlier.

U 521 returned to Lorient **26.3.43**

4. 5.5.43 Left for US waters.

The boat was sighted on the 31st by a Norfolk-based aircraft 225 miles off Cape Hatteras. U 521 dived and moved off in a northwesterly direction. On 1.6.43 she sighted an NG convoy, en route from New York to Guantanamo.

On the 2nd one of the escort, the USN patrol craft *PC 565* (Lt W T Flynn), obtained a contact on U 521 and closed on the boat, apparently undetected. Five depth-charges were dropped, causing severe damage.

U 521 surfaced and *PC 565* opened fire and moved in to ram. The commander of U 521, who had come up immediately the boat surfaced, was the only survivor. The crew had been ordered to abandon ship but did not have time to do so before U 521 sank, with her destruction rapidly completed by more depth-charges from *PC 565*.

51 of the boat's crew were lost.

U 522   Type IX C

Built by Deutsche Werft, Hamburg
Keel laid 9.7.41   Launched 1.4.42
Commissioned 11.6.42   Feldpost Nr M 06 857

Sunk 23.2.43 S of the Azores (31°27′N 26°22′W)

Served with
4 U-Flottille, Stettin   June - September 1942 (ab)
2 U-Flottille, Lorient   October 1942 - 23.2.43 (fb)

Commanded by
KL Herbert Schneider   June 1942 - 23.2.43

Patrols: 2   Ships sunk: 8 (52,809 grt) + 1 damaged

1. 8.10.42 Left Kiel for Canadian waters.

U 522 was ordered to an area off Newfoundland and to wait there for eastbound convoys, in company with U 520 and U 521. The three boats were to report shipping along their route, which went south of Iceland and via Cape Farewell to Belle Isle Strait.

Climatic conditions had deteriorated in the Gulf of St Lawrence and on arrival the boats were ordered south towards Halifax. On the 30th U 522 sighted convoy SC 107 ENE of Cape Race and the boats closed in. U 520 was sunk that day and U 521 was driven off by aircraft. U 522 made an unsuccessful torpedo attack in the early evening on one of the escorts, the destroyer HMCS *Columbia*. On the 31st U 522 was driven off by a destroyer.

Veilchen group was ordered south to intercept the convoy, which passed through its patrol line on 1.11.42. U 522 was still shadowing SC 107 and in the morning of the 2nd she torpedoed three ships E of Belle Isle, damaging the SS *Hartington* (br 5496t) and sinking the SS *Maritima* (br 5801t) and the SS *Mount Pelion* (gr 5655t). In an evening attack, the boat torpedoed and sank the SS *Parthenon* (gr 3189t) a little further northeast. The *Hartington* was also hit by U 438 but she was finally sunk by U 521. The operation against SC 107 ended on the 6th in the central North Atlantic, SE of Cape Farewell.

U 522 joined *Kreuzotter* group, formed from the 9th ESE of Cape Farewell by boats with limited fuel. On the 15th U 521 sighted westbound ONS 144 as it passed through the *Kreuzotter* patrol line. Over the next five days, in spite of fog, five ships and a corvette were sunk. In the morning of the 18th U 522 sank the SS *Yaka* (am 5432t) SSE of Cape Farewell. She had been torpedoed and damaged two hours earlier by U 624. The operation ended on the 21st E of Newfoundland.

A few boats that still had enough fuel to operate, including U 522, formed *Drachen* group from the 24th NE of Newfoundland. They were ordered to search singly for independents. The group sighted no convoys but several ships were seen and two were sunk, by U 262 and U 663. *Drachen* group was dissolved on the 26th.

U 522 put in to her new base at Lorient **2.12.42**

2. 31.12.42 Left for operations in the Central Atlantic.

On 7.1.43 U 522 and other outward-bound boats were ordered to join *Delphin* group in an attack on tanker convoy TM 1, which was sighted by U 381 on the 8th, heading northeast for Gibraltar. In the morning of the 9th U 522 closed the convoy and torpedoed and damaged two tankers, the MV *Minister Wedel* (nw 6833t) and the MV *Norvik* (pa 10034t). They were abandoned by their crews and an unsuccessful attempt was made by the destroyer HMS *Havelock* to sink them by gunfire. In further attacks during the afternoon of the 10th U 522 sank both ships W of the Canaries.

Soon after midnight on the 10th U 522 torpedoed and damaged the tanker SS *British Dominion* (br 6983t), the abandoned wreck of which was sunk some three hours later by U 620.

U 522 remained with *Delphin* group, which reformed from the

16th S of the Azores after six of its original members had been refuelled by U 463. In search of a UGS convoy, the group moved westwards but turned eastwards again on the 18th. Between the 21st and 29th it waited SW of the Azores but when nothing materialised the group moved further eastwards. From the 31st the patrol line was NW of the Canaries but then it moved to a new position W of Gibraltar for 6.2.43.

On the 7th the five southern boats of *Delphin* went to attack convoy Gib No 2. U 522 and the other boats of the group moved northwards and took up positions W of Portugal from the 11th. Southbound KMS 9 was reported on the 12th, 200 miles W of Cape Finisterre. The *Delphin* boats were ordered to close but the operation failed when the convoy's air escort kept the boats submerged. The situation worsened the nearer the convoy got to Gibraltar. Attacks became impossible and U 442 and U 620 were sunk, both by aircraft.

On or about the 21st U 522 was refuelled by U 461 S of the Azores. Next day U 522 reported southwestbound convoy UC 1 WNW of Madeira and *Rochen* group and two *Robbe* boats were ordered to intercept. In the morning of the 23rd U 522 torpedoed and sank the tanker MV *Athelprincess* (br 8882t) S of the Azores.

The boat was located and sunk in a depth-charge attack by one of the escort, the sloop HMS *Totland* (Lt-Cdr L E Woodhouse).

There were no survivors, 51 dead.

U 523   Type IX C

Built by Deutsche Werft, Hamburg
Keel laid 4.8.41   Launched 15.4.42
Commissioned 25.6.42   Feldpost Nr M 06 935

Sunk 25.8.43 W of Vigo (42°03′N 18°02′W)

Served with
4 U-Flottille, Stettin   June 1942 - January 1943 (ab)
10 U-Flottille, Lorient   February 1943 - 25.8.43 (fb)

Commanded by
KL Werner Pietzsch   June 1942 - 25.8.43

Patrols: 3   Ships sunk: None + 1 damaged

On 16.9.42, whilst training, U 523 was involved in a minor collision with the battleship Scharnhorst *in the eastern Baltic.*

1. 9.2.43 Left Kiel for the North Atlantic.

U 523 joined *Burggraf* group, formed on the 26th N of the Azores. The boats began to sweep westwards and by 4.3.43 they were E of Newfoundland, where they joined up with *Wildfang* group, stationed to the north. The two groups formed a long line from the 14th, with a view to intercepting an expected SC convoy.

During the night of the 4/5th the line moved northeastwards but SC 121 passed to the north, sighted by a boat of *Neptun* group, which was waiting to the north of the *Wildfang/Burggraf* line. Seventeen boats were detached from the three groups, including U 523, and sent in pursuit of SC 121, as *Westmark* group. Eleven boats of *Neuland* group were ordered to form a patrol line ahead of the convoy.

In stormy weather and heavy seas, twelve ships were sunk and another damaged but without the loss of any boats. U 523 had no success. After the operation ended on the 11th near Rockall, she joined a new group, *Stürmer*, formed from the 14th in the central North Atlantic, to operate against SC 122.

The group moved westwards until the 16th, then turning southwestwards to intercept the convoy. Contact was made during the night of the 16/17th and so began the biggest convoy action of the war, with forty boats against convoys SC 122 and HX 229.

In the evening of the 19th U 523 sank the abandoned SS *Mathew Luckenbach* (am 5848t), torpedoed and damaged that morning by U 527. This vessel had chosen to leave HX 229 and had moved ahead of the convoy and was completely alone when torpedoed.

The operation against SC 122/HX 229 ended on the 20th W of Ireland, with twenty-one Allied ships sunk for the loss of U 384.

U 523 joined *Seeteufel* group, formed from the 22nd S of Iceland to operate against a feeder convoy, en route from Iceland to join westbound ONS 1. The patrol line was formed but when the convoy did not materialise, the line moved westwards in the expected direction of the main convoy ONS 1.

On the 24th U 306 sighted some escorts to the north of the *Seeteufel* line but the boats she contacted were unable to close. By the 26th the line was running southeast from Cape Farewell and it joined the more southerly *Seewolf* group to form a line running 800 miles south from the Cape. During the afternoon of the 26th masts and an aircraft carrier were sighted in the centre of the *Seeteufel* line. This was an ON convoy but a strong air and surface escort prevented its direction being discovered by the boats.

On the 27th U 305, at the northern end of the *Seewolf* line, sighted eastbound HX 230. *Seewolf* boats were ordered to close the convoy and later *Seeteufel* group was sent against it. The prevailing storm developed into a hurricane on the 28th and only five boats were able to make brief contact with the convoy and torpedo attacks were impossible in the heavy seas. The pursuit continued for three days in very bad weather, in the hope that stragglers would be found. Only one ship was sunk during the operation, which was called off on the 30th.

U 523 put in to her new base at Lorient **16.4.43**

2. 22.5.43 Left for Atlantic operations.

Outward-bound, U 523 was attacked on the 24th by a Whitley of 10 OTU (Sgt S C Chatton) NNW of Cape Ortegal. The aircraft's six depth-charges and strafing attacks damaged the boat.

U 523 returned to Lorient **26.5.43**

3. 1.8.43 Left Lorient and returned **3.8.43**

4. 16.8.43 Left for the North Atlantic, the first boat to be equipped with *Wanze*, a newly-developed radar search receiver which was intended to minimise the risk of boats being detected from the air.

Outward-bound, U 523 encountered southbound convoy OG 92/KMS 24 on the 25th NE of the Azores. She was located by the escort and sunk in an action lasting more than four hours by the destroyer HMS *Wanderer* (Cdr A F St G Orpen) and the corvette HMS *Wallflower* (Lt-Cdr I J Tyson).

The commander and 37 men were picked up by *Wanderer*. 18 other men were lost and two wounded survivors, who died later, were buried at sea with full naval honours.

U 524 Type IX C

Built by Deutsche Werft, Hamburg
Keel laid 7.8.41   Launched 30.4.42
Commissioned 8.7.42   Feldpost Nr M 19 715

Sunk 22.3.43 SSW of Madeira (30°15´N 18°13´W)

Served with
4 U-Flottille, Stettin   July - November 1942 (ab)
10 U-Flottille, Lorient   December 1942 - 22.3.43 (fb)

Commanded by
KL Walter Freiherr von Steinaecker   July 1942 - 22.3.43

Patrols: 2   Ships sunk: 2 (16,256 grt)

1. 10.11.42   Left Kiel and arrived Marviken **12.11.42**

2. 14.11.42   Left for the North Atlantic.

U 524, fitted with a special VHF receiver and carrying a B-Service team to operate it, joined a new group, *Panzer*, formed from the 29th 800 miles W of the North Channel to await a westbound convoy.

On the 29th evidence from hydrophone and radar indicated a convoy not far way and the group searched to the southwest. When nothing was seen the *Panzer* boats continued southwestwards and on 4.12.42 they halted E of Newfoundland. R/T conversations were picked up by U 524 that evening and in the sure knowledge that a convoy was near, *Panzer* group moved northeastwards at high speed.

Eastbound HX 217 was sighted S of Greenland by U 524 on the 6th but contact was lost in bad visibility. She regained contact early on the 7th and brought up U 135, U 254, U 439 and U 465 but they were driven off by a Liberator of 120 Squadron (S/Ldr T M Bulloch). In the early hours of the 8th she torpedoed and damaged the tanker MV *Empire Spenser* (br 8194t) and had a near miss on the escorting destroyer HMS *Fame*. More than three hours later, in a second attack, U 524 sank the *Empire Spenser* SE of Cape Farewell.

Once within range of Iceland, strong air cover appeared from the 10th and the operation was abandoned next day. Two ships had been sunk and two boats lost.

From the 13th U 524 and four ex-*Draufgänger* boats were joined by new arrivals to form *Ungestüm* group S of Iceland, to operate against convoys leaving the North Channel. On the 13th eastbound HX 218 was sighted E of Newfoundland by U 373, which was then driven down by aircraft, losing contact. The *Ungestüm* boats moved westwards at high speed and on the 16th a patrol line was formed SE of Cape Farewell in the expected path of the convoy. However, HX 218 passed unobserved through the line of waiting boats.

Searching for HX 218, U 373 sighted westbound ONS 152 on the 16th to the southeast of the *Ungestüm* line and the boats moved to intercept. Brief contact was made but very bad weather and poor visibility hampered the pursuit. A search for stragglers resulted in only one sinking and the operation ended on the 22nd.

U 524, now low on fuel, left the group and on or about the 24th she was refuelled by U 463 W of the Azores.

She put in to her new base at Lorient **9.1.43**

3. 3.3.43   Left for Atlantic operations.

U 524 went to an area S of the Azores, where she joined four other boats to form *Wohlgemut* group from the 13th. Eastbound convoy UGS 6 had left New York on the 5th and was sighted by U 130 of *Unverzagt* group on the 12th. This boat was sunk the same night and contact was not regained until the 14th, by which time *Wohlgemut* and *Unverzagt* had formed a new patrol line, through which UGS 6 passed on that day.

In the evening of the 15th U 524 torpedoed and sank the SS *Wyoming* (fr 8062t) some 100 miles NNW of Graciosa, Azores. Although there were generally at least six boats in contact and in spite of there being no aircraft and weather conditions good, the operation was a failure, with only four ships sunk. The remote screen kept the boats well away, carrying out depth-charge attacks more that ten miles from the convoy. The operation ended on the 19th just W of Gibraltar, in the face of ever-increasing air support from there. U 524 maintained contact with the convoy until the last but was unable to make an attack.

On the 22nd U 524 was located and sunk in a depth-charge attack by a Liberator of 1 Squadron (USAF) (Lt W L Sanford) SSW of Madeira.

There were no survivors, 51 dead.

U 525   Type IX C

Built by Deutsche Werft, Hamburg
Keel laid 10.9.41   Launched 20.5.42
Commissioned 30.7.42   Feldpost Nr M 20 725

Sunk 11.8.43 WNW of the Azores (41°29′N 38°55′W)

Served with
4 U-Flottille, Stettin   July - December 1942 (ab)
10 U-Flottille, Lorient   January 1943 - 11.8.43 (fb)

Commanded by
KL Hans-Joachim Drewitz   July 1942 - 11.8.43

Patrols: 3   Ships sunk: 1 (3454 grt)

1. 15.12.42   Left Kiel for the North Atlantic.

U 525 joined *Falke* group 500 miles W of Ireland, where it was awaiting an ON convoy. The group was sent against ONS 158 and ON 159 but both were re-routed and avoided the boats.

On 4.1.43 a new north-south patrol line was formed to intercept an expected convoy, probably ONS 160 but that too was re-routed.

From 7.1.43 *Falke* group swept westwards, searching for convoys. This move continued until the 15th with nothing seen. The group turned north next day. *Habicht* group took up a line south of *Falke* and the two groups searched for convoys but on the 19th, with nothing found, they broke up.

The boats with sufficient fuel, including U 525, formed *Haudegen* group, in a patrol line running 300 miles southeastwards from Cape Farewell. On the 22nd a returning boat sighted a British hunting group, which could have been a remote screen for an expected HX convoy. *Haudegen* was ordered southeastwards at high speed to intercept. No convoy was found and a new, long patrol line reformed S of Cape Farewell on the 26th.

Haudegen group began to move southwestwards on 1.2.43, towards Newfoundland. Parts of the moving group were detached to attack convoys SG 19 and SC 118. U 525 remained with the main group, which on the 6th formed into two lines, positioned in an arc 300 miles NE of Cape Race, where they waited until the 15th for HX 225 and SC 119, neither of which materialised.

By then the boats were short of fuel and were ordered to a refuelling area. On the 17th U 69 sighted westbound ONS 165 and the boats, although heading east, were ordered to attack and refuel later. However, contact with the convoy was lost in a storm and the operation ended on the 20th. Two boats had been lost and two ships sunk, one being the SS *Radhurst* (br 3454t), caught straggling by U 525 in the morning of the 20th and sunk E of Newfoundland.

In the last week in February U 525 and other ex-*Haudegen* boats were refuelled by U 460 some 400 to 600 miles N of the Azores. Homeward-bound, U 525 was attacked and damaged during the night of the 2/3rd by a Leigh Light Wellington of 172 Squadron (F/Sgt J L Tweedle).

U 525 put in to her new base at Lorient **3.3.43**

2. 15.4.43   Left for the North Atlantic.

U 525 joined *Amsel* group, formed on the 26th 1400 miles W of Ireland. The group moved south, searching for a convoy that might have been eastbound HX 235. The *Amsel* line linked up with the left wing of *Specht* group on the 29th and the two groups moved south together.

By 1.5.43 the combined line was drawn up in an arc 200 miles E of St John's. On the 3rd the *Specht* boats moved northwards to join a new patrol line, *Fink*, and the *Amsel* boats, augmented by six new-arrivals, formed four new smaller groups, *Amsel 1,2,3* and *4*, in the same arc E of St John's. U 525 was in *Amsel 3*.

Amsel 1 and *2* went north to intercept convoy ONS 5 and on the 7th *Amsel 3* and *4* combined as *Rhein* group, which was ordered

southeastwards at high speed on the 8th to form a patrol line on the 9th for the interception of HX 237.

U 359 sighted a ship of the convoy on the 9th before the line could be formed but lost it in worsening visibility. The boats carried out independent searches before reforming in the morning of the 10th. At noon U 403 sighted a fast independent ship and then a tug, which led to the convoy being located in the afternoon.

The *Rhein* boats were by then too far east, so they were ordered to combine with *Elbe* group, to form *Elbe 1* and *2* groups to pursue the slower convoy SC 129, which was found by U 504 on the 11th. U 525 was in *Elbe 1*. The convoy had a strong surface and carrier-borne air escort, which kept the boats at a distance. The operation against SC 129 ended on the 14th SW of Ireland, with two ships sunk and two boats lost.

U 525 was refuelled by U 459 in the central North Atlantic, SE of Greenland, for return to base.

She returned to Lorient **26.5.43**

3. 25.7.43   Left Lorient and returned **26.7.43**

4. 27.7.43   Left for Atlantic operations.

U 525 was ordered to serve as a U-tanker and refuel U 333, U 571, U 600 and U 618, two at a position 700 to 800 miles S of the Azores and two at a similar distance SW of the Azores.

The boat did not arrive at either position. On 11.8.43 she had been sighted on the surface by aircraft of VC-1 from the escort-carrier USS *Card*, an Avenger (Lt C C Hewitt) and a Wildcat (Ens J Stewart), WNW of the Azores. The fighter made a strafing attack on the apparently-unaware boat, followed by the Avenger dropping two depth-charges near U 525's port side.

As Stewart made a second attack, the boat began to submerge. Hewitt approached again and dropped an acoustic torpedo, which struck U 525's starboard side, astern of the conning tower. After an explosion, bubbles and oil appeared on the surface of the sea.

There were no survivors, 54 dead.

U 526   Type IX C-40

Built by Deutsche Werft, Hamburg
Keel laid 14.10.41   Launched 3.6.42
Commissioned 12.8.42   Feldpost Nr M 49 572

Sunk 14.4.43 SW of the Ile de Groix (47°30′N 03°45′W)

Served with
4 U-Flottille, Stettin   August 1942 - January 1943 (ab)
10 U-Flottille, Lorient   February 1943 - 14.4.43 (fb)

Commanded by
KL Hans Möglich   August 1942 - 14.4.43

Patrols: 1   Ships sunk: 1 (3921 grt)

1. 23.1.43   Left Kiel and arrived Kristiansand **25.1.43**

2. 27.1.43   Left Kristiansand and arrived Bergen **28.1.43**

3. 11.2.43   Left for the North Atlantic.

U 526 joined *Burggraf* group, formed on the 26th in the central North Atlantic, N of the Azores. The boats began to sweep westwards and by 4.3.43 they were E of Newfoundland, where they joined up with *Wildfang* group, stationed to the north.

The two groups formed a long patrol line from the 4th, with a view to intercepting an expected SC convoy. During the night of the 4/5th the line moved northeastwards but SC 121 passed to the north, sighted by a boat of *Neptun* group, which was waiting to the north of the *Wildfang/Burggraf* line. Seventeen boats were detached from the three groups and sent in pursuit of SC 121, as *Westmark*

14

group. Eleven boats of *Neuland* group, which were W of Ireland, were sent northwestwards to form a patrol line ahead of the convoy, as *Ostmark* group.

In stormy weather and heavy seas, attacks began on the convoy. In the morning of the 8th U 526 probably sank the SS *Guido* (br 3921t) which had become separated from the convoy, ESE of Cape Farewell. When the SC 121 operation ended on the 11th near Rockall, twelve ships had been sunk and one damaged. No boats were lost.

U 526 and other ex-*Burggraf* boats with sufficient fuel joined *Stürmer* group, formed on the 14th in the central North Atlantic, S of Iceland, to operate against SC 122. The group moved westwards until the 16th, when it turned southwestwards to intercept the convoy. Contact was made during the night of the 16/17th and so began the biggest convoy action of the war, with some forty boats against convoys SC 122 and HX 229. The operation ended on the 20th W of Ireland, with twenty-one Allied ships sunk for the loss of only one boat, U 384. U 526 had no success.

She joined *Seeteufel* group, formed from the 21st S of Iceland to operate against a feeder convoy en route from Iceland to join westbound ONS 1. The convoy was expected on the 22nd and when it did not materialise, the line moved westwards in the expected direction of the main convoy ONS 1.

On the 24th U 306 of *Seeteufel* sighted some ONS 1 escorts to the north of the patrol line but the boats she called up were unable to close. By the 26th the *Seeteufel* line was running southeast from Cape Farewell and it joined the more southerly *Seewolf* group to form a line running 800 miles south from the Cape. During the afternoon of the 26th some masts and an aircraft carrier were sighted in the centre of the *Seeteufel* line. This was an ON convoy but a strong air and surface escort prevented its direction being discovered by the boats.

On the 27th U 305, at the northern end of the *Seewolf* line, sighted eastbound convoy HX 230 and 22 boats from the two groups were deployed but only five boats were able to make brief contact after the prevailing storm developed into a hurricane on the 28th. Torpedo attacks were impossible in the heavy seas but pursuit continued for three days in the hope that stragglers would be found. Only one ship was sunk during the operation, which was called off on the 30th.

In early April U 526 was refuelled by U 463 in the central North Atlantic for return to base. Homeward-bound on 14.4.43, U 526 was sunk when she struck a British-laid mine SW of Ile de Groix, probably the only loss to British mines in the Bay of Biscay for the whole of the 1943-44 period.

There were 12 survivors, 9 of whom were injured. Two of the survivors were picked up by the inbound U 513. The commander and 41 other crewmen from U 526 were lost.

U 527 Type IX C-40

Built by Deutsche Werft, Hamburg
Keel laid 28.10.41   Launched 3.6.42
Commissioned 2.9.42   Feldpost Nr M 51 963

Sunk 23.7.43 S of the Azores (35°25´N 27°56´W)

Served with
4 U-Flottille, Stettin   September 1942 - January 1943 (ab)
10 U-Flottille, Lorient   February 1943 - 23.7.43 (fb)

Commanded by
KL Herbert Uhlig   September 1942 - 23.7.43

Patrols: 2   Ships sunk: 2 (11,090 grt)
1 LCT (143 dt)

1. 9.2.43   Left Kiel for the North Atlantic.

U 527 joined *Burggraf* group, formed on the 26th in the central North Atlantic, N of the Azores. The boats began to sweep westwards and by 4.3.43 they were E of Newfoundland, where they joined up with *Wildfang* group, stationed to the north.

The two groups formed a long patrol line from the 4th, with a view to intercepting an expected SC convoy. During the night of the 4/5th the line moved northeastwards but SC 121 passed to the north, sighted by a boat of *Neptun* group, which was waiting to the north of the *Wildfang/Burggraf* line. Seventeen boats were detached from the three groups and sent in pursuit of SC 121, as *Westmark* group. Eleven boats of *Neuland* group, which were W of Ireland, were sent northwestwards to form a patrol line ahead of the convoy, as *Ostmark* group.

In stormy weather and heavy seas, attacks began on the convoy. In the evening of the 8th U 527 torpedoed and sank a straggler from the convoy ESE of Cape Farewell, the SS *Fort Lamy* (br 5242t), which had on board *LCT 2480*. When the SC 121 operation ended on the 11th near Rockall, twelve ships had been sunk and one damaged. No boats were lost.

U 527 and other ex-*Burggraf* boats with sufficient fuel joined *Stürmer* group, formed on the 14th in the central North Atlantic, S of Iceland, to operate against SC 122. The group moved westwards until the 16th, when it turned southwestwards to intercept the convoy. Contact was made during the night of the 16/17th and so began the biggest convoy action of the war, with some forty boats against convoys SC 122 and HX 229.

In the morning of the 19th U 527 torpedoed and damaged the SS *Mathew Luckenbach* (am 5848t), which had chosen to leave HX 229 and moved ahead of the convoy. She was completely alone when torpedoed. The crew abandoned ship and she was sunk that evening by U 523.

The operation against the two convoys ended on the 20th W of Ireland. On this day U 527 was attacked with depth-charges by a Sunderland of 201 Squadron (F/Lt D Hewitt) but dived and escaped, probably without damage. Soon afterwards the aircraft probably attacked U 598, also of *Stürmer* group, without serious damage. In the stormy conditions the aircrew thought they had only attacked one boat, sinking it. Hewitt was awarded the DFC.

U 527 joined *Seewolf* group, formed from the 25th in the central North Atlantic, SSE of Cape Farewell, to await convoys. The patrol line moved north on the 26th to search for eastbound HX 230 but a storm, which later became a hurricane, caused the operation to be abandoned on the 30th.

In early April U 527 was refuelled by U 463 in the central North Atlantic. She put in to her new base at Lorient **12.4.43**

2. 10.5.43   Left to operate in the Greater Antilles area.

Outward-bound on the 12th, WSW of Brest, U 527 met a storm-damaged ship being towed to England. The boat was attacked by an escorting corvette with depth-charges but escaped undamaged.

U 527 continued on to her operational area and subsequently patrolled off Florida and later between the Gulf of Mexico and Florida. During June two northwest-bound convoys were sighted but the boat had no success. She began her return journey on 2.7.43 and was to go to a position S of the Azores for refuelling.

Three days from it, U 527 was sighted by an aircraft and one of the two bombs dropped hit the boat, damaging a fuel tank. U 527 dived and soon afterwards oil was seen on the sea and U 527 was attacked with depth-charges and hunted for 19 hours by destroyers before managing to escape. Outward-bound U 648 was ordered to meet the damaged boat S of the Azores and refuel her.

U 527 again headed for the rendezvous position and temporary repairs were carried out en route. The two boats met and on the 23rd, as refuelling was taking place, they were sighted by an Avenger of VC-9 (Lt R L Stearns) from the escort-carrier USS *Bogue*.

U 527's commander, after deciding to remain surfaced and fight it out, cast off the line and made for a nearby fog bank. U 648 dived

U 527 (continued)

and escaped. One of U 527's guns failed and the Avenger was able to approach and drop six depth-charges from low level. The boat was severely damaged and began to sink.

The scene had been marked with a smoke float and the destroyer USS *Clemson* arrived. She picked up U 527's commander and 12 men. 40 others were lost. The survivors were transferred to the *Bogue* and later landed at Casablanca.

U 528   Type IX C-40

Built by Deutsche Werft, Hamburg
Keel laid 10.11.41   Launched 1.7.42
Commissioned 16.9.42   Feldpost Nr M 50 081

Scuttled 11.5.43 NW of Cape Ortegal (46°55′N 14°44′W)

Served with
4 U-Flottille, Stettin   September 1942 - March 1943 (ab)
10 U-Flottille, Lorient   April 1943 - 11.5.43 (fb)

Commanded by
OL Karl-Heinz Fuchs   September - December 1942
OL Georg von Rabenau   December 1942 - 11.5.43

Patrols: 1   Ships sunk: None

1. 15.4.43 Left Kiel for the North Atlantic.

U 528 joined *Star* group, formed from the 27th E of Cape Farewell to operate against expected convoy ONS 5. On the 28th the convoy passed to the north of the patrol line but bad weather made it difficult for the boats to close and attack. On that day U 528 was attacked and damaged by a USN Catalina of VP-84 (Lt W A Shevlin) SW of Iceland.

On 11.5.43 the returning U 528 was sighted on the surface and attacked and damaged by a Halifax of 58 Squadron (P/O J B Stark) in the vicinity of convoy OS 47 NW of Cape Ortegal. The sloop HMS *Fleetwood* (Cdr W B Piggott) came up and began depth-charge attacks.

Unable to dive, von Rabenau scuttled his boat. He and 10 of the crew were lost and the other 45 men were picked up by *Fleetwood* and the corvette HMS *Mignonette* and made PoW.

U 529   Type IX C-40

Built by Deutsche Werft, Hamburg
Keel laid 26.11.41   Launched 15.7.42
Commissioned 30.9.42   Feldpost Nr M 50 148

Lost 15.2.43 SE of Cape Farewell (55°45′N 31°09′W)

Served with
4 U-Flottille, Stettin   September 1942 - January 1943 (ab)
10 U-Flottille, Lorient   January 1943 - 15.2.43 (fb)

Commanded by
KL Georg-Werner Fraatz   September 1942 - 15.2.43

Patrols: 1   Ships sunk: None

1. 30.1.43 Left Kiel for the North Atlantic.

U 529 joined *Ritter* group, formed from the 14th SE of Cape Farewell to operate against eastbound convoy HX 226.

On the 15th U 529 was lost from an unknown cause. There were no survivors, 48 dead. Members of KL Fraatz's previous crew from U 652 may were amongst those men lost in U 529.

U 530   Type IX C-40

Built by Deutsche Werft, Hamburg
Keel laid 8.12.41   Launched 28.7.42
Commissioned 14.10.42   Feldpost Nr M 49 518

Surrendered 10.7.45 at Mar del Plata, Argentina

Served with
4 U-Flottille, Stettin   October 1942 - February 1943 (ab)
10 U-Flottille, Lorient   March 1943 - September 1944 (fb)
33 U-Flottille, Flensburg   October 1944 - May 1945 (fb)

Commanded by
KL Kurt Lange   October 1942 - January 1945
OL Otto Wermuth   January 1945 - 10.7.45

Patrols: 5   Ships sunk: 2 (12,063 grt) + 1 damaged

1. 20.2.43 Left Kiel for the North Atlantic.

U 530 joined *Neuland* group W of Ireland. On 7.3.43 U 530 and ten other boats in the northern section of the patrol line were sent northwestwards, as *Ostmark* group, to form a line from the 8th ahead of SC 121, sighted by U 405 on the 6th S of Greenland.

Seventeen boats of *Wildfang*, *Burggraf* and *Neptun* groups operated against SC 121, as well as the *Ostmark* boats. In the evening of the 9th U 530 torpedoed and sank a straggler from the convoy, the SS *Milos* (sw 3058t). Twelve ships were sunk and one damaged before the operation ended on the 11th S of Iceland.

The *Ostmark* boats were joined by new-arrivals and three *Burggraf* boats to form *Stürmer* group from the 14th in the central North Atlantic, to operate against SC 122. The group moved westwards until the 16th, when it turned southwestwards to intercept the convoy.

Contact was made during the night of the 16/17th and some successful attacks were made by *Stürmer* boats over the next three days, none by U 530. This was the biggest convoy action of the war, with forty boats operating against convoys SC 122 and HX 229. Twenty-one Allied ships were sunk for the loss of U 384. During the action, on the 17th, U 530 was damaged in depth-charge attacks by the destroyer HMS *Beverley*.

U 530 and other ex-*Stürmer* boats joined new arrivals to form *Seewolf* group from the 25th, SE of Cape Farewell and south of the *Seeteufel* line, to operate against reported eastbound SC 123. From the 26th *Seewolf* and *Seeteufel* groups joined to form a line running 800 miles south from Cape Farewell.

U 305, at the northern end of the *Seewolf* line, sighted HX 230 on the 27th. U 530 was one of twenty-two boats from the two groups ordered to close the convoy. However, in the face of a heavy storm, which developed into a hurricane on the 28th, and kept away by a strong air escort from the 29th, the boats involved sank only one ship. Contact was lost on the 30th and the operation ended.

On 4.4.43 the returning U 530 sighted eastbound HX 231 and she brought up boats of *Löwenherz* group, the only ones available to operate against the convoy. In the evening of the 5th U 530 torpedoed and sank a straggler ESE of Cape Farewell, the tanker MV *Sunoil* (am 9005t), torpedoed and damaged ten hours earlier by U 563. Between the 11th and 13th U 530 joined boats of *Lerche* group to attack HX 232 but they were all driven off by the surface and air escort. The operation ended on the 13th W of Ireland.

U 530 put in to her new base at Lorient **22.4.43**

2. 29.5.43 Left for the Central Atlantic.

On 14.6.43 the outward-bound U 530 was ordered to go to an area SW of the Canaries to act as a U-tanker. Some time after mid-June she refuelled the outward-bound U 172, U 572 and U 759 and the inbound U 180 for return to base.

U 530 put in to Bordeaux **3.7.43**

3. 21.9.43 Left Bordeaux and arrived La Pallice **21.9.43**

4. 27.9.43 Left La Pallice and returned **29.9.43**

5. 3.10.43 Left La Pallice and returned **5.10.43**

6. 17.10.43 Left for Caribbean operations.

In early November U 530 was refuelled by U 488 E of Bermuda. She entered the Caribbean on the 21st through the Martinique Channel. U 530 patrolled off the Gulf of Darien and made an unsuccessful attack on a tanker off San Blas. She torpedoed and damaged the turbine tanker *Chapultepec* (am 10195t) on 26.12.43 NNE of Nombre de Dios, Panama. Three days later U 530 had a narrow escape when she was rammed by the tanker *Esso Buffalo* but succeeded in getting away.

U 530 returned to Lorient **22.2.44**

7. 22.5.44 Left for the Caribbean area.

Late in the evening of 23.6.44 U 530 met Japanese submarine *I 52* W of the Cape Verde Islands, to pass over radar warning equipment and put aboard two German technicians to operate it and a Japanese-speaking pilot to take *I 52* into Lorient and to generally advise the Japanese commander Soon after the two submarines parted, *I 52* was attacked by an Avenger of VC-69 (Lt-Cdr J Taylor) from the escort-carrier USS *Bogue*. The carrier, which had been searching for U 530, had picked up a radio report of the meeting.

I 52 dived and Taylor dropped two depth-bombs, followed by an acoustic torpedo, after which an explosion was heard. Short of fuel, Taylor left the scene. Another Avenger (Lt-Cdr W Gordon) arrived and dropped another acoustic torpedo, causing a second explosion. Searchers found debris and oil at the scene, confirming *I 52*'s destruction. Both Avenger pilots were awarded the DFC.

U 530 went on to patrol the area SE of Trinidad and later off the island itself. She failed to make any attacks, with the convoy routes in and out of the Caribbean being so widely dispersed. This patrol was the last to be carried out by a U-boat in the Caribbean area.

The boat put in to Kristiansand on 1.10.44. She went on to Flensburg, arriving there **4.10.44**

8. 19.2.45 Left Kiel and arrived Horten **23.2.45**

9. 3.3.45 Left for the western Atlantic.

U 530 patrolled off the US east coast and later off New York. In early May she was off Long Island and ignored the order to surrender, made by Dönitz on May 4th.

KL Wermuth took U 530 south, reaching Mar del Plata, Argentina on 10.7.45. Her crew was interned and the boat was handed over to US Navy representatives in Buenos Aires. She was later used as an experimental vessel and sunk by a torpedo from the submarine USS *Toro* during tests on 28.11.47 NE of Cape Cod.

U 531   Type IX C-40

Built by Deutsche Werft, Hamburg
Keel laid 22.12.41   Launched 12.8.42
Commissioned 28.10.42   Feldpost Nr M 49 566

Sunk 6.5.43 NE of St John's (52°48′N 45°18′W)

Served with
4 U-Flottille, Stettin October 1942 - March 1943 (ab)
2 U-Flottille, Lorient April 1943 - 6.5.43 (fb)

Commanded by
KL Herbert Neckel October 1942 - 6.5.43

Patrols: 1   Ships sunk: None

1. 13.4.43 Left Kiel for the North Atlantic.

U 531 joined *Star* group, formed from the 27th E of Cape Farewell to operate against expected convoy ONS 5. On the 28th the convoy passed to the north of the patrol line but bad weather made it difficult for the boats to close and attack. In the morning of the 29th only two boats were able to make attacks, sinking one ship. On 1.5.43 the pursuit was called off near Cape Farewell.

The *Star* boats were ordered south to search for SC 128, which was thought to be heading northeastwards. A southerly gale came up and when contact had not been made with the convoy a new patrol line, *Fink,* was formed on the 3rd from twenty-nine boats of *Specht* and *Star* groups, including U 531. The line was drawn up in the expected path of SC 128. The convoy did not materialise but ONS 5, delayed by the storm, was found again on the 4th.

Conditions for an attack were favourable on the 5th but fog came down in the early evening and most boats lost contact. On the 6th U 531 was located NE of Newfoundland by the corvette HMS *Snowflake* and attacked with depth-charges.

After being forced to the surface in dense fog near ONS 5, U 531 dived again and was probably sunk in a Hedgehog attack by the destroyer HMS *Vidette* (Lt R Hart).

There were no survivors, 54 dead.

U 532   Type IX C-40

Built by Deutsche Werft, Hamburg
Keel laid 7.1.42   Launched 26.8.42
Commissioned 11.11.42   Feldpost Nr M 50 614

Sunk 9.12.45 NW of Tory Island (56°08′N 10°07′W)

Served with
4 U-Flottille, Stettin November 1942 - March 1943 (ab)
2 U-Flottille, Lorient April 1943 - September 1944 (fb)
33 U-Flottille, Flensburg October 1944 - 10.5.45 (fb)

Commanded by
FK Ottoheinrich Junker November 1942 - 10.5.45

Patrols: 4   Ships sunk: 8 (46,895 grt) + 2 damaged

1. 25.3.43 Left Kiel for the North Atlantic.

Outward-bound, U 532 was deployed to operate with *Löwenherz* group on 4.4.43 against eastbound HX 231 ESE of Cape Farewell. Conditions were favourable and pursuit of the convoy continued until the 7th, with six ships sunk and four damaged. The constant presence of carrier-borne aircraft made attacks difficult.

U 532 joined *Löwenherz* boats in a new patrol line, *Lerche,* formed SE of Cape Farewell from the 10th to intercept eastbound HX 232. The convoy passed through the line on the 11th and successful attacks were made in the early hours of the 12th, with two ships sunk and another damaged. Further attacks were prevented by aircraft. The operation ended W of the North Channel on the 13th.

U 532, U 203 and U 706 left *Lerche* group, when its boats went to refuel from U 487 and U 462. The three boats joined *Meise* group in the central North Atlantic, E of Newfoundland from the 17th. The group went northwards, searching for convoys. On the 21st HX 234 and ONS 3 were sighted. The group split, with six boats going for ONS 3 and the rest, including U 532, going for HX 234. Fog and snowstorms made closing difficult and on the 25th the operation against HX 234 was called off after all the boats still in contact were driven off by aircraft and the surface escort. Only two ships had been sunk and another damaged.

Meise group was dissolved. Boats with enough fuel, including U 532, joined newly-arrived boats to form *Star* group, E of Cape Farewell, to await a westbound ONS convoy. On the 28th ONS 5 passed the northern end of the *Star* line and again bad weather

U 532 (continued)

made closing difficult. In the early morning of the 29th U 532 fired a 4-torpedo spread at the corvette HMS *Snowflake* but missed and was attacked with depth-charges. Later in the day, near ONS 5, U 532 was attacked again, this time by the frigate HMS *Tay*. The pursuit of ONS 5 was called off on 1.5.43 near Cape Farewell, with only one ship sunk.

The *Star* boats were ordered south to search for SC 128, which was thought to be heading northeastwards. U 532 left the group at this time and was refuelled in the central North Atlantic by U 461 for return to base.

She reached Lorient **15.5.43**

2. 3.7.43 Left for operations in the Indian Ocean.

U 532 was one of nine boats which sailed as *Monsun* group. U-tanker U 462 was to accompany the boats and then refuel them 300 miles E of St Paul Rocks. However, she failed twice to pass through the Bay of Biscay and a new plan was made for the *Monsun* boats to be refuelled by U 487 S of the Azores from 14.7.43.

Five of the boats searched the area for U 487 from the 14th to the 17th but she could not be found and had in fact been sunk by aircraft on the 13th. U 506, U 509 and U 514 of the group had also been sunk en route. It was then arranged for the remaining six *Monsun* boats to be refuelled by the outward-bound U 155 and U 160 but the latter failed to arrive and had been sunk on the 14th.

Refuelling was finally carried out between the 21st and 27th 600 miles WNW of the Cape Verde Islands, three boats by U 155 and U 532 and U 533 by U 516 of *Monsun* group, after which she returned to base.

The five refuelled *Monsun* boats passed through the South Atlantic, rounded the Cape and entered the Indian Ocean. On 11.9.43 they met the German supply tanker *Brake* S of Mauritius and were refuelled. She had been sent from Penang.

The boats then each headed for their own individual area of operations. On the 19th U 532 sank the SS *Fort Longueuil* (br 7128t) SW of the Chago Archipelago and on the 29th the SS *Banffshire* (nw 6479t) WSW of South Island, Lakshadweep.

On 1.10.43 the boat sank the MV *Tahsinia* (br 7267t) by torpedo and gunfire SW of Quilon, Kerala and on the 11th the SS *Jalabala* (br 3610t) was sunk off Badagara, Kerala. In the same area on the 20th U 532 encountered convoy BM 71 and torpedoed and damaged the tanker MV *British Purpose* (br 5845t).

U 532 put in to Penang **30.10.43**

3. 4.1.44 Left to operate SW of India.

On the 11th U 532 torpedoed and damaged the SS *Triona* (br 7283t) S of Ceylon and on the 26th the SS *Walter Camp* (am 7176t) was sunk W of South Island, Lakshadweep.

U 532 rendezvoused with the German supply tanker *Charlotte Schliemann* on 11.2.44 900 miles E of Mauritius, to be refuelled for return to France. Bad weather prevented the transfer of fuel and U 532 lost sight of the tanker, which was sighted by a Catalina flying boat from Mauritius.

The destroyer HMS *Relentless* was directed to the scene and at her approach the *Charlotte Schliemann* scuttled herself soon after midnight on the 11th. U 532 picked up some of the tanker's crew and forty-one more were picked up by *Relentless*. The boat herself was hunted for three days before managing to escape. On the 27th U 532 received fuel from U 178, which had been refuelled by the *Charlotte Schliemann* in late January.

U 532 afterwards operated SE of Mauritius, without success. On 11.3.44 U 168, U 188 and U 532 rendezvoused with the supply tanker *Brake* 1000 miles SE of Mauritius. The three boats had carried out a reconnaissance within a 200 mile radius but had seen no sign of enemy activity. Early on the 12th, after U 532 and U 188 had been refuelled, the weather deteriorated and the four vessels moved southwestwards. Later in the morning they were sighted by a Swordfish from the escort-carrier HMS *Battler*. The three boats

dived. The *Brake* was subsequently attacked with gunfire by the destroyer HMS *Roebuck*, directed to the scene by aircraft. The tanker was under fire for an hour before sinking. She may have been scuttled. Her crew was later picked up by U 168.

On 19.3.44 U 532 refuelled *UIT 24,* which had been due for replenishment by the *Brake*. Now without sufficient fuel to return to France, U 532 went looking for ships. On the 27th she torpedoed and sank the MV *Tulagi* (br 2281t) ESE of the Chagos Archipelago.

On 10.4.44 U 532 refuelled the torpedo-transport U 1062, en route from Bergen to Penang.

U 532 returned to Penang **19.4.44**

4. 17.5.44 Left Penang and arrived Shonan **18.5.44**

5. --.12.44 Left Shonan and arrived Batavia **--.12.44**

6. 13.1.45 Left for France.

On or about 9.2.45 U 532 was refuelled by U 195, which had developed a mechanical defect en route from Batavia to France. After passing over her surplus fuel, U 195 returned to Batavia.

U 532 rounded the Cape and made her way up through the South Atlantic. On 10.3.45 she torpedoed and sank the SS *Baron Jedburgh* (br 3656t) some 700 miles WSW of Ascension and on the 28th the tanker SS *Oklahoma* (am 9298t) 1000 miles W of the Cape Verde Islands.

U 532 was still at sea on May 4th, the final day of the U-boat war. She surrendered at Liverpool on 10.5.45 and was inspected there by Admiral Sir Max Horton, C-in-C Western Approaches. U 532 was carrying strategic materials, 100 tons of tin, 60 tons of rubber, 8 tons of wolfram and 5 tons of molybdenum.

U 532 later went to the assembly point at Loch Ryan. She was one of 116 boats disposed of by the Royal Navy in Operation Deadlight.

In early December 1945 she was towed from Loch Ryan out through the North Channel by the tug HMS Masterful *and sunk by the submarine HMS* Tantivy *on 9.12.45 NW of Tory Island.*

U 533   Type IX C-40

Built by Deutsche Werft, Hamburg
Keel laid 17.2.42   Launched 11.9.42
Commissioned 25.11.42   Feldpost Nr M 50 650

Sunk 16.10.43 ENE of Al Fujayrah (25°28′N 56°50′E)

Served with
4 U-Flottille, Stettin November 1942 - April 1943 (ab)
10 U-Flottille, Lorient May 1943 - 16.10.43 (fb)

Commanded by
KL Helmut Hennig November 1942 - 16.10.43

Patrols: 2   Ships sunk: None

1. 15.4.43 Left Kiel for the North Atlantic.

U 533 joined *Star* group, formed E of Cape Farewell to await an ONS convoy. On the 28th ONS 5 passed the northern end of the *Star* line but bad weather made closing the convoy difficult. On the 29th some of the boats had a brief glimpse of ONS 5 and one ship was sunk, by U 258. The pursuit of the convoy was called off on 1.5.43 near Cape Farewell.

The *Star* boats were ordered south to search for SC 128, which was thought to be heading northeastwards. A southerly gale came up and when contact had not been made with the convoy a new patrol line, *Fink,* was formed on the 3rd from twenty-nine boats of *Specht* and *Star* groups, including U 533.

The line was drawn up in the expected path of SC 128. The

convoy did not materialise but ONS 5, delayed by the storm, was found again on the 4th. Conditions for an attack were favourable on the 5th but fog came down in the early evening and most boats lost contact. In the morning of the 6th the operation was terminated. On the 5th twelve ships were sunk and six boats were lost in the two-day operation.

During the night of the 5/6th U 533 was located by a corvette of the escort, HMS *Sunflower*, which rammed her, causing severe damage. The boat managed to escape and headed for home.

She put in to her new base at Lorient **24.5.43**

2. 3.7.43 Left Lorient and returned **4.7.43**

3. 5.7.43 Left for operations in the Indian Ocean.

U 533 was one of nine boats which sailed as *Monsun* group. U-tanker U 462 was to accompany the boats and then refuel them 300 miles E of St Paul Rocks. However, she failed twice to pass through the Bay of Biscay and a new plan was made for the *Monsun* boats to be refuelled by U 487 S of the Azores from 14.7.43.

Five of the boats searched the area for U 487 from the 14th to the 17th but she could not be found and had in fact been sunk by aircraft on the 13th. U 506, U 509 and U 514 of the group had also been sunk en route. It was then arranged for the remaining six *Monsun* boats to be refuelled by the outward-bound U 155 and U 160 but the latter failed to arrive and had been sunk on the 14th.

Refuelling was finally carried out between the 21st and 27th 600 miles WNW of the Cape Verde Islands, three boats by U 155 and U 532 and U 533 by U 516 of *Monsun* group, after which she returned to base.

The five refuelled *Monsun* boats passed through the South Atlantic, rounded the Cape and entered the Indian Ocean. On 11.9.43 they met the German supply tanker *Brake* S of Mauritius and were refuelled. She had been sent from Penang.

The boats then each headed for their own individual area of operations. U 533 went north to the Gulf of Oman. On 16.10.43 she was sighted by a British Bisley of 244 Squadron (Sgt L Chapman), travelling on the surface ENE of Al Fujayrah.

The aircraft was sighted from U 533 and she began to submerge. The stern was still visible when Chapman dropped four depth-charges, destroying the boat.

U 533's commander and 51 men were lost and the solitary seaman-survivor was picked up and made PoW after 28 hours in the water.

U 534   Type IX C-40

Built by Deutsche Werft, Hamburg
Keel laid 20.2.42   Launched 23.9.42
Commissioned 23.12.42   Feldpost Nr M 49 357

Sunk 5.5.45 E of Anholt (56°45′N 11°52′E)

Served with
4 U-Flottille, Stettin December 1942 - February 1944 (ab)
3 U-Flottille, La Pallice May - November 1944 (fb)
33 U-Flottille, Flensburg November 1944 - 5.5.45 (fb-oE)

Commanded by
KL Herbert Nollau December 1942 - 5.5.45

Patrols: 3   Ships sunk: None

U 534 served as a training boat until February 1944. She then had a yard overhaul before becoming operational.

1. 27.4.44 Left Kiel and arrived Bergen **6.5.44**

2. 8.5.44 Left for the North Atlantic.

U 534, U 853 and U 857 were assigned to weather-reporting duties at 30°W, from Greenland in the north to the Azores in the south. U 534 remained on this duty until mid-July.

She put in to Bordeaux **13.8.44**

3. 25.8.44 Left for Norway.

U 534 was one of a number of not-completely operational boats which left the Biscay bases. Outward-bound on the 27th, she was attacked by a Wellington of 172 Squadron in the Bay of Biscay. The aircraft was shot down.

U 534 put in to Kristiansand **24.10.44**

4. 25.10.44 Left Kristiansand and arrived Flensburg **28.10.44**

5. 1.5.45 Left Kiel and arrived Copenhagen **2.5.45**

6. 5.5.45 Left Copenhagen.

Later the same day U 534 was sunk in a depth-charge attack by a Liberator of 86 Squadron (WO J D Nicol) E of Anholt Island in the Kattegat.

Of U 534's crew, 3 were lost and the commander and 48 men were picked up.

U 534 was raised on 24.8.93. She was laying in 67 metres of water about 25 km from Anholt.
In 1996 she was taken to Liverpool and will be restored and opened to the public, as a memorial for the Battle of the Atlantic.

U 535   Type IX C-40

Built by Deutsche Werft, Hamburg
Keel laid 6.3.42   Launched 8.10.42
Commissioned 23.12.42   Feldpost Nr M 49 383

Sunk 5.7.43 NW of La Coruña (43°38′N 09°13′W)

Served with
4 U-Flottille, Stettin December 1942 - May 1943 (ab)
10 U-Flottille, Lorient May 1943 - 5.7.43 (fb)

Commanded by
KL Helmut Ellmenreich December 1942 - 5.7.43

Patrols: 1   Ships sunk: None

1. 25.5.43 Left Kiel for the North Atlantic.

Outward-bound on 8.6.43, U 535 was attacked S of Iceland and damaged by a Hudson of 269 Squadron (Sgt R B Couchman), escorting convoy SC 132. The boat was apparently undamaged.

On the 14th she, U 170, U 530 and U 536 were ordered to act as U-tankers. U 535, U 170 and U 536 went south and refuelled boats just W of the Azores in support of U 488. U 535 supplied U 415, U 600 and U 615 in late June just W of the Azores and before heading home she transferred her surplus fuel to U 488.

Inbound, U 535, U 170 and U 536 approached the Bay of Biscay in company, for mutual protection against Allied aircraft. On 5.7.43 the three boats were NW of La Coruña when they were attacked with depth-charges by a Liberator of 53 Squadron (F/Sgt W Anderson). U 170 and U 536 were both damaged but they dived and escaped. U 535 was sunk in the attack and the aircraft was damaged by flak from the boats.

There were no survivors, 55 dead.

U 536　Type IX C-40

Built by Deutsche Werft, Hamburg
Keel laid 13.3.42　Launched 21.10.42
Commissioned 13.1.43　Feldpost Nr M 49 397

Sunk 20.11.43 NE of the Azores (43°50´N 19°39´W)

Served with
4 U-Flottille, Stettin　January - May 1943 (ab)
2 U-Flottille, Lorient　June 1943 - 20.11.43 (fb)

Commanded by
KL Rolf Schauenburg　January 1943 - 20.11.43

Patrols: 2　Ships sunk: None

1. 1.6.43 Left Kiel for the North Atlantic.

On the 14th U 536, U 170, U 530 and U 535 were ordered to act as U-tankers. U 536, U 170 and U 535 went south and refuelled boats just W of the Azores, in support of U 488.

In late June U 536 supplied U 84 and before heading for home she transferred her surplus fuel to U 488.

Inbound, U 536, U 170 and U 535 approached the Bay of Biscay in company, for mutual protection against Allied aircraft. On 5.7.43 the three boats were NW of La Coruña when they were attacked with depth-charges by a Liberator of 53 Squadron (F/Sgt W Anderson). U 536 and U 170 were both damaged but they dived and escaped. U 535 was sunk and the attacking aircraft was damaged by flak from the boats.

U 536 put in to her new base at Lorient **9.7.43**

2. 29.8.43 Left for Canadian waters.

U 536 was to carry out Special Task *Kiebitz*, which was to pick up the Lorient Espionage Unit, planning to escape from PoW Camp 30 at Bowmanville, Ontario at some time in September.

U 536 was scheduled to be refuelled by U 460 but on 7.9.43 this order was changed and the tanker supplied five boats of *Leuthen* group instead, between the 10th and 13th N of the Azores. In the same area on the 15th U 536 and U 170 were refuelled by U 460.

There were several captured U-boat commanders in the Lorient Espionage Unit, which was led by Otto Kretschmer and somehow supplied intelligence back to BdU. The plan was for the escapers to exit the camp by a tunnel which had been dug and then make their way to Pointe de Maissonette, Chaleur Bay by September 27th or 28th.

Canadian Naval Intelligence got wind of a breakout and the arrival of a U-boat in Canadian waters. The tunnel was located secretly and books sent through the Red Cross, with concealed escape documents, maps and U-boat pick-up details, were examined, repacked and then passed intact to their intended recipients.

The escape was to be allowed to proceed, with the escapees being taken as they emerged from the tunnel. Details would be broadcast and subsequent recaptures. However, the men that U 536 was expecting to pick up, would not be included among those reported as recaptured. The authorities reasoned, wrongly, that U 536 would hear all this and arrive at the rendezvous point, where it would be easily captured.

The Admiralty persuaded the Canadians to destroy U 536, with warships quickly called when the boat showed herself. In the meantime, another prisoner at Bowmanville, Wolfgang Heyda, ex-commander of U 434, had made his own escape over the wire and made his way to Pointe de Maissonette. Waiting on the beach, he was captured on the 27th and returned to the camp.

U 536 reached the Gulf of St Lawrence on September 16th. She entered Chaleur Bay on the 24th but the commander's suspicions were aroused by the presence of nine warships in the bay. His fears were confirmed by unexpected radio signals and a signal lamp from the shore sending German plain language.

Schauenburg realised that it was time to leave and chose to exit the bay via the shallows of Miscou Flats, believing that his hunters would not expect such a course. U 536 crept out of the bay during the night of the 27/28th at 20 metres depth and able to hear the engines of the searching vessels. The boat was close enough to the shore to become entangled in fishing nets but she made her way safely into the Gulf of St Lawrence and then through Cabot Strait into the Atlantic.

U 536 patrolled for almost four weeks along the southern coast of Nova Scotia and Newfoundland. On 12.10.43 she reported a Liberty ship sunk somewhere SE of Sable Island but there is no confirmation of this.

The returning U 536 joined the *Schill 2* patrol line, formed on 19.11.43 NE of the Azores in the path of combined convoy MKS 30/SL 139. The convoy escort was joined by the 5th SG and on the 20th U 536 was located by the Group and attacked by the frigate HMS *Nene* (Cdr J D Birch) and the corvettes HMCS *Snowberry* (Lt J B O'Brien) and *Calgary* (Lt-Cdr H K Hill). Their depth-charge attacks seriously damaged U 536, sending her down vertically backwards to 240 metres.

The Chief Engineer stabilised the boat, which then rose to the surface. *Snowberry* opened fire, making a direct hit on the conning tower. The crew were cut down as they tried to man their guns. *Nene* and *Calgary* closed in, firing. U 536 was quickly sunk.

Of her crew, 38 were lost and the commander and 16 men were made PoW.

U 537　Type IX C-40

Built by Deutsche Werft, Hamburg
Keel laid 10.4.42　Launched 7.11.42
Commissioned 27.1.43　Feldpost Nr M 49 804

Sunk 9.11.44 E of Surabaya (07°13´S 115°17´E)

Served with
4 U-Flottille, Stettin　January - July 1943 (ab)
10 U-Flottille, Lorient　August 1943 - September 1944 (fb)
33 U-Flottille, Flensburg　October 1944 - 9.11.44 (fb)

Commanded by
KL Peter Schrewe　January 1943 - 9.11.44

Patrols: 3　Ships sunk: None

A USAF bombing raid on Kiel delayed U 537's departure for sea.

1. 18.9.43 Left Kiel and arrived Bergen **23.9.43**

2. 30.9.43 Left for Canadian waters.

U 537 was ordered to set up automatic weather station WFL 26 in northern Labrador. A scientific adviser and a technical assistant were aboard to supervise the operation.

Outward-bound on 13.10.43, heavy seas in the North Atlantic tore off the twin anti-aircraft gun units, which rendered U 537 very vunerable in view of the aircraft presence in Canadian waters.

On the 22nd the boat anchored in Martin Bay, Labrador and the equipment was taken ashore in two large inflatable rafts. Installation was completed within 24 hours. The weather station operated for about three months until the batteries were exhausted, relaying weather conditions in the North Atlantic. In 1944 a boat sent to re-establish the station was sunk en route.

U 537 patrolled for some weeks off the Newfoundland banks but she had no success.

The boat put in to her new base at Lorient **8.12.43**

3. 25.3.44 Left for operations in the Indian Ocean.

U 537 was refuelled on 17.4.44 by U 488 700 miles W of the Cape Verde Islands. The boat passed through the South Atlantic and in May she was operating S and SE of Cape Province but had no success.

In June U 537 was patrolling in the Indian Ocean. On the 25th she was refuelled by U 183, which was returning to Penang. U 537 then patrolled off the southern tip of India. On 8.7.44 the boat made two unsuccessful attacks just S of Ceylon, the first on a ship and a later one on a destroyer. Only two end-of-run detonations were heard. U 537 was subsequently hunted for some days by the destroyers HMS *Racehorse* and *Raider* but she escaped.

The boat put in to Batavia **2.8.44**

4. --.10.44 Left Batavia and arrived Surabaya **--.10.44**

5. 9.11.44 Left for operations in the Indian Ocean.

On this day, en route to a rendezvous with other US submarines in the South China Sea, the USS *Flounder* (Cdr J E Stevens) encountered and sank U 537 E of Surabaya.

There were no survivors, 58 dead.

U 538   Type IX C-40

Built by Deutsche Werft, Hamburg
Keel laid 18.4.42   Launched 20.11.42
Commissioned 10.2.43   Feldpost Nr M 49 827

Sunk 21.11.43 NE of the Azores (45°00´N 19°35´W)

Served with
4 U-Flottille, Stettin February - October 1943 (ab)
2 U-Flottille, Lorient October 1943 - 21.11.43 (fb)

Commanded by
KL Johann-Egbert Gossler February 1943 - 21.11.43

Patrols: 1   Ships sunk: None

1. 19.10.43 Left Kiel and arrived Bergen **24.10.43**

2. 24.10.43 Left for the North Atlantic.

U 538 joined *Eisenhart* group, made up of seven sub-groups of three boats each and drawn up in two lines from 11.11.43, running southeast from Cape Farewell. The lines crossed an area through which most convoys had passed since August 1943.

Reports indicated that convoys were being routed to the south, so the *Eisenhart* boats were ordered southeastwards on the 12th to search for SC 145 and HX 265. By the 16th no convoys had been found and the majority of the boats were then WSW of Ireland. Fuel was now becoming a problem for many of *Eisenhart* group and it was decided to end the operation and send the boats with sufficient fuel, including U 538, to reinforce *Schill* group W of Spain.

U 538 was on her way south when she was sighted NE of the Azores early on the 21st by HMS *Crane* (Lt B M Skinner), from the escort of combined convoy MKS 30/SL 139. As the sloop closed, U 538 dived. *Crane* made several attacks, using most of her depth-charges. She had been joined by the frigate HMS *Foley* (Cdr I J Tyson) and their attacks produced no apparent result. *Foley* made a further attack, with eighteen depth-charges, and U 538 was destroyed.

There were no survivors, 55 dead.

U 539   Type IX C-40

Built by Deutsche Werft, Hamburg
Keel laid 18.5.42   Launched 4.12.42
Commissioned 24.2.43   Feldpost Nr M 50 416

Sunk 4.12.45 NW of Malin Head (55°38´N 07°57´W)

Served with
4 U-Flottille, Stettin February - June 1943 (ab)
2 U-Flottille, Lorient July 1943 - September 1944 (fb)
33 U-Flottille, Flensburg October 1944 - 5.5.45 (fb)

Commanded by
KL Hans-Jürgen Lauterbach-Emden February 1943 - 5.5.45

Patrols: 3   Ships sunk: 1 (1517 grt) + 1 damaged

1. 4.9.43 Left Kiel and arrived Bergen **7.9.43**

2. 14.9.43 Left for the North Atlantic.

U 539 joined *Rossbach* group, formed from the 27th SE of Cape Farewell to operate against ON 203. The line moved 100 miles to the northeast, waited there until the 30th but saw no sign of either ON 203 or the following ONS 19. Both had passed to the north.

The group moved northeastwards on 1.10.43 to a position SW of Iceland, to intercept ON 204. On the 4th U 539 drove off an attacking Hudson of 269 Squadron and shot down a Liberator of 120 Squadron (W/Cdr R M Longmore). This aircraft dropped six depth-charges before crashing into the sea W of Iceland. U 539 was not damaged in the attack.

By the 5th it was realised that convoy ON 204 had also avoided the boats and that pursuit was useless. *Rossbach* group moved southwestwards to form a new line to search for eastbound convoys SC 143 and HX 259, which they expected to intercept on the 8th.

In the evening of the 7th two destroyers were sighted and it was assumed, rightly, that a convoy could be near and a search was made during the night. Although destroyers were seen moving northeastwards, the convoys were not found and the search was called off on the 9th and *Rossbach* dissolved.

U 539 put in to her new base at Lorient **23.10.43**

3. 29.12.43 Left Lorient and returned **30.12.43**

4. 2.1.44 Left for the North Atlantic.

U 539 was to rendezvous with and refuel the returning U 516 NW of the Azores on the 19th. Both boats were attacked by aircraft from the escort-carrier USS *Guadalcanal* after they met, preventing refuelling. U 516 was also attacked by two destroyers.

The two boats made contact again on the 21st and after many attempts in difficult sea conditions, U 516 finally received her fuel on 4.2.44. U 539 went on her way, to operate independently E of Newfoundland but she had no success.

She put in to St Nazaire **21.3.44**

5. 1.5.44 Left for operations in the Caribbean.

On 2.6.44 U 539 was surfaced N of Puerto Rico when she was sighted and attacked by a USN Mariner of VP-204 (Lt J G Tomkins). She escaped undamaged. On the 5th U 539 torpedoed and sank the SS *Pillory* (pa 1517t) off Isabela, after which she was attacked by both aircraft and surface vessels but not badly damaged. The boat probably then entered the Caribbean through the Mona Passage.

In the evening of the 10th U 539 claimed a tanker torpedoed and damaged S of Curaçao but there is no confirmation of this. On the 11th the tanker SS *Casandra* (nl 2701t) was unsuccessfully attacked with torpedo and gunfire a little further south. The tanker returned the fire with machine-guns, damaging the boat, which was driven off by a Mariner of VP-204.

U 539 (continued)

U 539 claimed to have torpedoed four tankers on 4.7.44 N of Nombre de Dios, Panama, damaging the turbine tanker *Kittanning* (am 10195t) and possibly damaging the SS *Hollywood* (am 5498t). The *Kittanning* reached port safely, assisted by a USCG cutter.

U 516 was also operating in the Caribbean and in late July the two boats left the operational area, with instructions to go on to Norway if so ordered. By mid-August they were near Cape Ortegal. The blockade of the Bay of Biscay prevented their return to French ports and both were ordered to Norway.

U 539, by then very short of fuel, was refuelled by U 858, then on weather-reporting duties, in early September some 400 miles SW of Iceland. She put in to Bergen on 17.9.44 and went on to Flensburg, arriving there **22.9.44**

6. 13.4.45 Left Kiel and arrived Horten **20.4.45**

7. 26.4.45 Left Horten for Bergen, where she surrendered **5.5.45**

On 30.5.45 U 539 left Bergen for the assembly area at Loch Ryan. She was one of 116 boats disposed of by the Royal Navy in Operation Deadlight. In early December she was towed out through the North Channel by the tug HMS Saucy.
On 4.12.45 U 539 foundered under tow NW of Malin Head.

U 540   Type IX C-40

Built by Deutsche Werft, Hamburg
Keel laid 12.5.42   Launched 18.12.42
Commissioned 10.3.43   Feldpost Nr M 50 445

Sunk 17.10.43 ESE of Cape Farewell (58°38´N 31°56´W)

Served with
4 U-Flottille, Stettin March - September 1943 (ab)
10 U-Flottille, Lorient September 1943 - 17.10.43 (fb)

Commanded by
KL Lorenz Kasch March 1943 - 17.10.43

Patrols: 1   Ships sunk: None

1. 11.9.43 Left Kiel and arrived Bergen **14.9.43**

2. 4.10.43 Left for the North Atlantic.
Outward-bound, U 540 was ordered to join *Schlieffen* group ESE of Cape Farewell. On the 15th, whilst the patrol line was forming, outward-bound U 844 sighted a westbound convoy W of Rockall, which was presumed to be ONS 20 but was in fact ON 206. She was ordered to shadow and home the *Schlieffen* boats in. She was located and driven off and the boats, kept submerged by Iceland-based aircraft, did not find the convoy.

Early on the 16th U 964 sighted and reported ONS 20, which altered course to the northwest later in the day. Meanwhile, Dönitz had ordered boats to stay on the surface and fight their way to the convoy. During daylight on the 16th reports began arriving of boats being attacked and damaged and the first to be sunk was U 964.

The *Schlieffen* boats moved further eastwards to form a new line for the 17th. ONS 20 passed just north of the line early in the morning of the 17th and an attack was ordered. There was a strong air escort and U 540 was attacked almost simultaneously by two Liberators, one from 59 Squadron (F/Lt E Knowles) and the other from 120 Squadron (WO B W Turnbull).

Each aircraft made two depth-charge attacks and Turnbull also fired his front cannons. His second depth-charge attack sank U 540. He was awarded the DFC for the action.

Survivors were seen in the sea but none was picked up, 55 dead.

U 541   Type IX C-40

Built by Deutsche Werft, Hamburg
Keel laid 5.6.42   Launched 5.1.43
Commissioned 24.3.43   Feldpost Nr M 51 083

Sunk 5.1.46 NNW of Malin Head (55°38´N 07°35´W)

Served with
4 U-Flottille, Stettin March - October 1943 (ab)
10 U-Flottille, Lorient November 1943 - October 1944 (fb)
33 U-Flottille, Flensburg November 1944 - 12.5.45 (fb)

Commanded by
KL Kurt Petersen March 1943 - 12.5.45

Patrols: 4   Ships sunk: 1 (2140 grt)

1. 4.11.43 Left Kiel for the North Atlantic.
U 541 was one of a number of boats which took up submerged, waiting positions W of the British Isles.

In early December they assembled W of the North Channel as *Coronel* group, which searched for westbound ONS 24 but was unsuccessful because aerial reconnaissance failed to find it. The convoy passed to the north of the group.

In mid-December *Coronel* group was enlarged and split into two sub-groups, *Coronel 1* and *3*, to search for westbound ON 214. U 541 was in *Coronel 3*. Again, aircraft failed to find the convoy, which passed to the south. Boats of the group, including U 541, searched far to the south for ONS 25 but it was not found.

From the 20th the *Coronel 3* boats joined with new-arrivals to form a new patrol line, *Borkum*, 400 miles NW of Cape Ortegal, to intercept combined convoy MKS 33/SL 142. When the convoy was not found, the *Borkum* boats were ordered to operate against the carrier-groups of USS *Card* and *Core*, in an effort to cover the returning blockade runner *Osorno*, which was spotted on the 23rd by an aircraft from *Card*.

On the 22nd and 23rd an escorted carrier was sighted by German aircraft. Attacks were made on the escort by some *Borkum* boats after the carrier was sighted by U 305 during the night of the 23/24th. The destroyer USS *Leary* was sunk.

In the evening of the 24th the *Borkum* boats encountered southbound OS 62/KMS 36 and U 415 sank HMS *Hurricane* of the escort, the only success against the convoy. The group continued to operate in the area NE of the Azores between 20° and 25°W, moving from one position to another in the operational area.

Late on the 29th U 541 made several unsuccessful attacks on a hunting group and late on the 31st she reported a destroyer torpedoed and sunk but there is no confirmation of this. During this period U 541 was on the lookout for survivors from the German destroyer and the two torpedo-boats which were sunk by British cruisers on the 27th.

From the 28th *Borkum* group was searching for convoy MKS 34/SL 143, which was finally sighted by aircraft on the 30th and 31st. The convoy passed the patrol line during the night of January 1/2nd 1944. On the 4th *Borkum* was split into three small sub-groups but U 541 left the group at this time and headed home.

She put in to her new base at Lorient **9.1.44**

2. 29.2.44 Left for operations in US waters.
In April U 541 was patrolling between Cape Hatteras and the Bahamas, missing two convoys. On 14.5.44 she unsuccessfully attacked an unescorted tanker SE of Hatteras, expending six torpedoes and hearing only two end-of-run detonations.

On 26.5.44, S of Bermuda, U 541 stopped two neutral steamers, the Portugese SS *Serpa Pinto* and the Greek SS *Thetis*, which was chartered to the Swiss. Among *Serpa Pinto*'s 200 passengers were Jewish refugees. Two US civilian passengers were taken aboard

U 541 as prisoners. After consultation with BdU, both vessels were allowed to proceed.

U 541 returned to Lorient **22.6.44**

3. 6.8.44 Left for operations in Canadian waters.

Outward-bound, U 541 was ordered on the 24th to go into the Gulf of St Lawrence. On 3.9.44 she torpedoed and sank the SS *Livingston* (br 2140t) at the southern end of Cabot Strait, from westbound convoy ONS 251.

In the Gulf, during the night of the 7/8th, U 541's commander sighted what he thought to be an escort-carrier. Unaware that the corvette HMCS *Norsyd* was fast approaching, Petersen surfaced to make a torpedo attack on the 'carrier'.

Norsyd opened fire and U 541 fired her torpedo, which detonated harmlessly after a long run. She then dived. A minesweeper and four frigates were called up and the RCAF alerted. The hunt continued until the 10th but Petersen evaded the searchers and entered the St Lawrence River on the 13th.

After laying on the bottom for two nights, U 541 moved up the river, reaching a position 7 miles NNE of the Matane lighthouse. Petersen made his way back down the river into the Gulf without sighting any targets. On the 21st U 541 was heading through Cabot Strait for the Atlantic.

Knowing that Allied naval vessels would be in strength in the Iceland/Faroes passage, Petersen went north of Iceland through the Denmark Strait. When the surface ice became too much of a problem he submerged and passed beneath it.

With batteries well down, Petersen had to resurface. He went up slowly and had the luck to surface in a hole that was only just bigger than U 541 herself and the only opening to be seen in the icefield. The crew breathed properly again, the boat was aired and put in order and, with batteries recharged, U 541 submerged and moved forward again.

She reached a Norwegian port on 6.11.44 and went on to Flensburg, reaching there **11.11.44**

4. 1.4.45 Left Kiel and arrived Horten **2.4.45**

5. 7.4.45 Left for the Gibraltar area.

When the order to surrender came, U 541 was still at sea. She put in to Gibraltar **12.5.45**

U 541 was one of 116 boats disposed of by the Royal Navy in Operation Deadlight. In early January 1946 she was towed from the assembly point at Lisahally by the frigate HMS Cosby.

U 541 was sunk by gunfire by the destroyer HMS Onslaught *on 5.1.46 NNW of Malin Head.*

U 542   Type IX C

Built by Deutsche Werft, Hamburg
Keel laid 12.6.42   Launched 19.1.43
Commissioned 7.4.43   Feldpost Nr M 51 111

Sunk 28.11.43 W of Lisbon (39°03′N 16°25′W)

Served with
4 U-Flottille, Stettin April - September 1943 (ab)
10 U-Flottille, Lorient October 1943 - 28.11.43 (fb)

Commanded by
OL Christian-Brandt Coester April 1943 - 28.11.43

Patrols: 1   Ships sunk: None

1. 21.10.43 Left Kiel for the North Atlantic.

U 542 joined *Eisenhart* group, made up of seven sub-groups of three boats each and drawn up in two lines from 11.11.43, running southeast from Cape Farewell. The lines crossed an area through which most convoys had passed since August 1943.

Reports indicated that convoys were being routed to the south, so the *Eisenhart* boats were ordered southeastwards on the 12th to search for SC 146 and HX 265. By the 16th no convoys had been found although U 542 sighted destroyers on that day and made an unsuccessful attack on one, hearing only an end-of-run detonation.

By this time the majority of the boats were WSW of Ireland and fuel was becoming a problem for many of *Eisenhart* group. It was then decided to end the operation and send the boats with sufficient fuel, including U 542, to reinforce *Schill* group W of Portugal.

U 542 joined the *Schill 3* patrol line, in the expected path of northbound convoy MKS 30/SL 139 and through which it was expected to pass on the 20th. *Schill 3* surfaced that evening but failed to find the convoy, which was located next morning and attacked by aircraft, resulting in one ship sunk and another damaged, both by glider-bombs.

On the 22nd the remaining fourteen boats of the three *Schill* groups were formed into an east-west patrol line, *Weddigen*, W of Cape Finisterre. On the 23rd the line moved southwestwards but finding nothing, turned southeast on the 25th to intercept northbound MKS 31/SL 140. During the night of the 24/25th U 542 was attacked by Wellingtons of 179 Squadron but not damaged.

Constantly harassed by surface vessels and aircraft and with insufficient information from reconnaissance aircraft, *Weddigen* could not carry out a concentrated attack before the operation was called off on the 28th.

During the early hours of the 28th U 542 was attacked and sunk W of Lisbon by a Leigh Light Wellington of 179 Squadron (F/Sgt D M Cornish). It is possible that U 542 had been previously attacked by another Wellington of 179 Squadron (P/O T B Wilkin). This aircraft did not return to base and may have been shot down by U 542.

There were no survivors from the boat, 56 dead.

U 543   Type IX C-40

Built by Deutsche Werft, Hamburg
Keel laid 3.7.42   Launched 3.2.43
Commissioned 21.4.43   Feldpost Nr M 37 084

Sunk 2.7.44 SW of the Canaries (25°34′N 21°36′W)

Served with
4 U-Flottille, Stettin April - October 1943 (ab)
10 U-Flottille, Lorient November 1943 - 2.7.44 (fb)

Commanded by
KL Hans-Jürgen Hellriegel April 1943 - 2.7.44

Patrols: 2   Ships sunk: None

1. 9.11.43 Left Kiel for the North Atlantic.

U 543 was one of a number of boats which took up submerged waiting positions W of the British Isles.

In early December they assembled W of the North Channel as *Coronel* group, which searched for westbound ONS 24 but was unsuccessful because aerial reconnaissance failed to find it. The convoy passed to the north of the group.

In mid-December *Coronel* group was enlarged and split into two sub-groups, *Coronel 1* and *3*, awaiting westbound ON 214. U 543 was in *Coronel 3*. Again, aircraft failed to find the convoy and it passed to the south.

When the southern boats of the group moved southwards to search for ONS 25, U 543 left to proceed to the area E of Newfoundland, where she operated independently. Early on 3.1.44 she made an

U 543 (continued)

unsuccessful attack on a destroyer E of Cape Race, hearing only an end-of-run detonation.

U 543 put in to her new base at Lorient **24.1.44**

2. 28.3.44 Left for the Central Atlantic.

Outward-bound, U 543 was refuelled on or about 18.4.44 by U 488 some 700 miles W of the Cape Verde Islands. On the 19th U 543 managed to escape the attentions of the escort-carrier USS *Tripoli* and her escorts.

From mid-May U 543 operated W of Freetown and in the Gulf of Guinea but without success. Homeward-bound, she was located SW of the Canaries on 2.7.44 by an Avenger of VC-58 (Ens F L Moore) from the escort-carrier USS *Wake Island*.

In the face of heavy flak, Moore made two depth-bomb attacks, sinking U 543. Nothing was seen afterwards to confirm the sinking and the carrier-group continued to hunt for the boat for another two weeks, supported by Fortresses of RAF Coastal Command from the Azores.

There were no survivors from U 543, 58 dead.

U 544   Type IX C-40

Built by Deutsche Werft, Hamburg
Keel laid 8.7.42   Launched 17.2.43
Commissioned 5.5.43   Feldpost Nr M 37 886

Sunk 16.1.44 WNW of the Azores (40°30′N 37°20′W)

Served with
4 U-Flottille, Stettin   May - October 1943 (ab)
10 U-Flottille, Lorient   November 1943 - 16.1.44 (fb)

Commanded by
KL Willy Mattke   May 1943 - 16.1.44

Patrols: 1   Ships sunk: None

1. 9.11.43 Left Kiel for the North Atlantic.

U 544 was one of a number of boats which took up submerged, waiting positions W of the British Isles.

In early December they assembled W of the North Channel as *Coronel* group, which searched for westbound ONS 24 but was unsuccessful because aerial reconnaissance failed to find it. The convoy passed to the north of the group.

In mid-December *Coronel* group was enlarged and split into two sub-groups, *Coronel 1* and *3*, awaiting westbound ON 214. U 544 was in *Coronel 1*. Again, aircraft failed to find the convoy and it passed to the south.

On the 19th the group was reduced to six boats, U 92, U 421, U 544, U 625, U 653 and U 672, to continue searching for convoys W of the British Isles, as *Föhr* group. Eastbound HX 270 passed to the south of the group between the 20th and 22nd.

From the beginning of January 1944 U 544 was operating as a weather boat around 35°W. U 544 was ordered to rendezvous with U 129 and U 516 at dusk on the 16th 360 miles NW of the Azores, to refuel them.

The two boats, making a submerged approach to the rendezvous position at the appointed time, heard bombs exploding and the sound of destroyer propellers. This was later presumed to be the sinking of U 544. She had been sighted on the 16th by two Avengers of VC-13 (Ens B J Hudson and W M MacLane) from the escort-carrier USS *Guadalcanal*. The boat was attacked with rockets and depth-bombs. U 544's bow rose out of the sea and she then sank stern first and was seen no more.

There were no survivors, 57 dead.

U 545   Type IX C-40

Built by Deutsche Werft, Hamburg
Keel laid 1.8.42   Launched 3.3.43
Commissioned 19.5.43   Feldpost Nr M 52 062

Scuttled 11.2.44 N of Rockall (58°17′N 13°22′W)

Served with
4 U-Flottille, Stettin   May - November 1943 (ab)
2 U-Flottille, Lorient   December 1943 - 11.2.44 (fb)

Commanded by
KL Gert Mannesmann   May 1943 - 11.2.44

Patrols: 1   Ships sunk: 1 (3680 grt) (Shared with U 744)

1. 9.12.43 Left Kiel for the North Atlantic.

U 545 joined *Rügen 2* group, one of six small sub-groups that operated W of Ireland. These groups were constantly moving, changing positions and varying formations, with the objective of preventing the Allies determining the area over which they were operating. When three convoys were sighted, UC 8 on the 23rd, TU 5 on the 26th and CU 9 on the 30th, the groups were each too small to mount an attack.

On the 30th U 545 sighted an unescorted group of stragglers from westbound convoy ON 217 SSW of Reykjavik. She torpedoed and damaged the SS *Empire Housman* (br 7359t) and reported the ship as 'sinking'. The vessel was torpedoed again on 3.1.44 by U 744 and sank under tow two days later.

From 7.1.44 the six small groups were dissolved and the boats operated singly between 50° and 61°N and 18° and 24°W. On the 26th U 545 and other boats formed a patrol line, *Stürmer*, NW of the North Channel, to await expected convoy ON 221, which was sighted by German aircraft on the 27th. Technical difficulties prevented the aircraft homing in the boats and in spite of searches made on the 28th, the convoy was not found. On the 27th one of U 545's officers was lost overboard.

The search for ON 221 was terminated in the morning of the 29th, following a report by an aircraft of a suspected invasion of Western France. After apparent confirmation of this report, all boats in the North Atlantic, which included *Stürmer* group, were ordered to proceed at high speed to the Biscay coast. Shortly after this the 'invasion fleet' was correctly identified as a group of Spanish trawlers and the boats were ordered back to their operational areas.

On the 31st *Stürmer* group was again stationed NW of the North Channel. In early February *Stürmer* and *Hinein* group boats began to withdraw westwards and from the 3rd were reformed into *Igel 1* and *2* groups, U 545 was in *Igel 1* group, which from the 4th to the 10th operated SE of Iceland.

On the 10th U 545 was damaged by a Wellington of 612 Squadron (P/O M H Painter) N of Rockall. Damage was such that the crew abandoned the boat and was taken off by U 714. On the 11th U 545 was scuttled.

Two of U 545's crew lost their lives.

U 546   Type IX C-40

Built by Deutsche Werft, Hamburg
Keel laid 6.8.42   Launched 17.3.43
Commissioned 2.6.43   Feldpost Nr M 51 791

Sunk 24.4.45 SSE of Cape Farewell (53°53′N 40°07′W)

Served with
4 U-Flottille, Stettin   June - December 1943 (ab)
10 U-Flottille, Lorient   January - October 1944 (fb)
33 U-Flottille, Flensburg   November 1944 - 24.4.45 (fb)

Commanded by
KL Paul Just   June 1943 - 24.4.45

Patrols: 3   Ships sunk: None
                      1 destroyer-escort (1200 dt)

1. 22.1.44   Left Kiel and arrived Marviken **23.1.44**

2. 26.1.44   Left for the North Atlantic.
    U 546 joined *Igel 1* group, formed from 3.2.44 NW of Scotland. The boats operated singly SE of Iceland until the 10th, when a withdrawal westwards began. In co-operation with aircraft, an attack on an ONS convoy was planned within a few days.
    Aircraft sighted ONS 29, ON 224 and OS 68 on the 14th W of the North Channel. All boats then W of the British Isles, which included *Igel 1* and *2* groups, assembled in an area 600 miles SW of Ireland and formed two parallel patrol lines, *Hai 1* and *2*, ahead of the convoys from the 18th. It was found that the convoys had turned south on the 17th and passed to the south of the lines. The boats were immediately ordered south, submerged in daylight and at high speed on the surface in the hours of darkness. Instead of sighting any convoys at dawn on the 19th, the boats saw only some destroyers. The operation was called off and the boats submerged to avoid aircraft from the escort-carrier HMS *Striker*.
    The *Hai* groups were dissolved and the boats formed a new group, *Preussen*, but U 546 left to patrol independently off Iceland. She had no success.
    U 546 put in to her new base at Lorient **23.4.44**

3. 15.6.44   Left Lorient and returned, reason unknown **22.6.44**

4. 25.6.44   Left for the Central Atlantic.
    U 546 patrolled off the west coast of Africa and N of Dakar from July 24th to August 30th, during which time she had no success. She was the last boat to operate in that area.
    From early October U 546 was on weather-reporting duties in the North Atlantic.
    The boat put in to Flensburg **11.11.44**

5. 11.3.45   Left Kiel for US waters.
    U 546 and five other outward-bound boats joined to form *Seewolf* group from 14.4.45 N of the Azores. The boats were to sweep westwards across the North Atlantic convoy routes in an effort to draw some of the hunting groups from British coastal waters.
    On the 23rd U 546 was sighted as she surfaced SSE of Cape Farewell by an aircraft of VC-19 (Lt-Cdr W W South) from the escort-carrier USS *Bogue*. South's attack on the boat was unsuccessful.
    Searches were carried out throughout the day but found nothing. The following morning the destroyer-escort USS *Frederick C Davis* made a sound contact. Soon afterwards U 546 torpedoed and sank the warship. In the cold, rough sea only 66 men survived from the *Frederick C Davis*'s complement of 192.
    U 546 was detected under the wreckage by the destroyer-escort USS *Flaherty* (Lt-Cdr H C Dufe), starting a hunt which lasted nearly ten hours, using several escort vessels and every form of attack.
    Badly damaged, U 546 surfaced and fired a torpedo at *Flaherty*, which missed. Four warships opened fire on the boat but this ceased after nine minutes when it became obvious that U 546 was sinking.
    The commander and 4 men were picked up by *Flaherty* and 28 others by other ships. They were all landed in Newfoundland. 24 of U 546's crew were lost.
    At Argentia Just, 2 officers and 5 specialist crewmen were placed in solitary confinement and they were subjected to beatings each day. On the 30th Just collapsed whilst being interrogated. He and the other 7 were sent to Washington and the other 25 survivors went to PoW camps in the US.
    In Washington the interrogations and beatings began again, by the same men from Argentia. On May 9th Just agreed to write a history of U 546. The apparent objective of these brutal interrogations was to ascertain whether U 546 and other *Seewolf* boats had been carrying missile launchers, which they had not.
    U 873's commander, KL Steinhoff, committed suicide in Charles Street Prison, Boston some days after surrendering off Providence, Rhode Island on May 16th. It is believed that he was brutally interrogated on the same subject of missiles by the same men who had beaten the U 546 survivors.

U 547   Type IX C-40

Built by Deutsche Werft, Hamburg
Keel laid 30.8.42   Launched 3.4.43
Commissioned 16.6.43   Feldpost Nr M 52 404

Decommissioned 31.12.44 in Stettin

Served with
4 U-Flottille, Stettin   June - December 1943 (ab)
2 U-Flottille, Lorient   January - October 1944 (fb)
33 U-Flottille, Flensburg   October - November 1944 (--)

Commanded by
FK Kurt Sturm   June 1943 - April 1944
OL Heinrich Niemeyer   April 1944 - 31.12.44

Patrols: 3   Ships sunk: 2 (8371 grt)
                      1 armed trawler (750 dt)

1. 25.12.43   Left Kiel for Atlantic operations.
    From early January U 547 operated with *Rügen* group, whose boats were disposed singly between 50° and 61°N and 18° and 24°W. On the 26th she joined with other boats to form a new patrol line, *Stürmer*, NW of the North Channel, to await expected convoy ON 221, which was sighted by German aircraft on the 27th.
    Technical difficulties prevented the aircraft homing in the boats and in spite of searches made on the 28th, the convoy was not found. The search for ON 221 was terminated in the morning of the 29th, following a report by an aircraft of a suspected invasion of Western France, which stated that 200 to 300 landing craft had been sighted 120 miles W of the Gironde estuary.
    After apparent confirmation of this report, all boats in the North Atlantic, which included *Stürmer* group, were ordered to proceed at high speed to the Biscay coast. Shortly after this the 'invasion fleet' was correctly identified as a group of Spanish trawlers and the boats were ordered back to their operational areas.
    On the 31st *Stürmer* group was again stationed NW of the North Channel. In early February *Stürmer* and *Hinein* groups began to withdraw westwards and from the 3rd were reformed into *Igel 1* and *2* groups. U 547 was in *Igel 1*. From the 4th to the 10th the group operated SE of Iceland, after which a further movement westwards began, to be in position for an attack on an ONS convoy

U 547 (continued)

between the 14th and 18th, in co-operation with aircraft.

Three convoys were sighted by aircraft on the 14th W of the North Channel and *Igel 1* and *2* groups were sent to an assembly area SW of Ireland. U 547 left *Igel 1* group about this time.

She put in to her new base at Lorient **23.2.44**

2. 30.4.44 Left for the Central Atlantic.

From late May U 547 operated W of Freetown and then in the Gulf of Guinea. On 30.5.44 she made a two-torpedo attack on a steamer off Freetown. She heard one detonation and later an explosion but the name of the ship and any possible damage to it are both unknown.

Early on 14.6.44 U 547 encountered a convoy off Greenville, Liberia. She torpedoed and sank the armed trawler HMS *Birdlip* and the SS *Saint Basile* (fr 2778t). In the early hours of 2.7.44 U 547 sank the SS *Bodegraven* (nl 5593t) S of Monrovia. Her captain was taken aboard the boat as a prisoner.

U 547 set out for base soon after this and she was the last boat to enter Bordeaux, arriving there **11.8.44**

3. 23.8.44 Left Bordeaux, in transit for Norway.

On her way out, U 547 struck a mine in the Gironde, near Pauillac. She was badly damaged but continued on her way and put in to Marviken **29.9.44**

4. 1.10.44 Left Marviken and arrived Flensburg **4.10.44**

U 547 was checked and considered to be not repairable and she was decommissioned at Stettin 31.12.44.

U 548 Type IX C-40

Built by Deutsche Werft, Hamburg
Keel laid 4.9.42 Launched 14.4.43
Commissioned 30.6.43 Feldpost Nr M 52 470

Sunk 19.4.45 SW of Sable Island (42°19´N 61°45´W)

Served with
4 U-Flottille, Stettin June 1943 - March 1944 (ab)
2 U-Flottille, Lorient April - September 1944 (fb)
33 U-Flottille, Flensburg October 1944 - 19.4.45 (fb)

Commanded by
KL Eberhard Zimmermann June 1943 - December 1944
KL Günther Pfeffer (temp) August - November 1944
OL Erich Krempl December 1944 - 19.4.45

Patrols: 3   Ships sunk: None
                          1 frigate (1445 dt)

1. 21.3.44 Left Kiel for the North Atlantic.

U 548 called briefly at Kristiansand before heading to the area S of Iceland, where she was to carry out weather-reporting duties. In mid-April the boat set out for Canadian waters, where she patrolled close inshore along the coasts of Newfoundland and Nova Scotia from the 25th onwards.

On 3.5.44 U 548 unsuccessfully attacked a steamer, which may have been the SS *Baltrover*. The boat was spotted by a Liberator, with which it exchanged machine-gun fire. U 548 was afterwards the object of an intensive search, which she avoided by laying on the bottom off Cape Broyle, Newfoundland.

The boat moved south towards Cape Race and southeast of there during the night of the 6/7th she encountered Canadian EG C-1, just relieved from escorting convoy ON 234. Running on the surface, U 548 sighted the frigate HMCS *Valleyfield*. She dived and

after closing, fired an acoustic torpedo, then sheered off out of harm's way. The frigate broke in two after being hit amidships and in the icy waters only 38 of *Valleyfield*'s complement survived.

From the 10th, U 548 patrolled S of Halifax and had no success but remained undetected until 4.6.44, after she had set out for home. U 548 may have been damaged by aircraft on the way through the Bay of Biscay.

She put in to her new base at Lorient **24.6.44**

2. 11.8.44 Left Lorient, in transit to Norway.

In addition to her crew, U 548 was carrying passengers, probably key technical personnel, and had 83 men in all on board. On the 30th one man was lost overboard.

The boat put in to Bergen **25.9.44**

3. 27.9.44 Left Bergen and arrived Hølen **28.9.44**

4. 7.10.44 Left Hølen and arrived Flensburg **12.10.44**

5. 24.2.45 Left Kiel and arrived Horten **28.2.45**

6. 7.3.45 Left Kristiansand for the US east coast.

On the 22nd U 548 was S of Iceland and over the next week she sent a number of weather reports, the last being on the 31st in the Central North Atlantic, NW of the Azores.

On 12.4.45 U 548 was ordered to the Gulf of Maine area. On the 14th she may have sunk the SS *Belgian Airman* (be 6959t) W of Albemarle Sound.

No further reports were ever received from her and it is believed that she was located and sunk on the 19th by the destroyer-escorts USS *Buckley* (Cdr E H Headland) and *Reuben James II* (Lt-Cdr H L Edwards) SW of Sable Island. A sound contact was made in the fog by *Buckley* and 24 Hedgehogs were fired.

There were no survivors, 59 dead.

U 549 Type IX C-40

Built by Deutsche Werft, Hamburg
Keel laid 28.9.42 Launched 28.4.43
Commissioned 14.7.43 Feldpost Nr M 53 434

Sunk 29.5.44 NW of the Canaries (31°13´N 23°03´W)

Served with
4 U-Flottille, Stettin July - December 1943 (ab)
10 U-Flottille, Lorient January 1944 - 29.5.44 (fb)

Commanded by
KL Detlef Krankenhagen July 1943 - 29.5.44

Patrols: 2   Ships sunk: None + 1 damaged
                          1 escort-carrier (8600 dt)

1. 11.1.44 Left Kiel for the North Atlantic.

U 549 was initially on weather-reporting duty but in early February she joined *Igel 1* group NW of Scotland. The *Igel 1* boats operated SE of Iceland from the 4th to the 10th, when a withdrawal westwards began. In co-operation with aircraft, an attack on an ONS convoy was planned within a few days.

Aircraft sighted ONS 29, ON 224 and OS 68 on the 14th W of the North Channel. All boats then W of the British Isles, which included *Igel 1* and *2* groups, assembled in an area 600 miles SW of Ireland and formed two parallel patrol lines, *Hai 1* and *2*, ahead of the convoys from the 18th. It was found that the convoys had turned south on the 17th and passed to the south of the lines.

The boats were immediately ordered south, submerged in daylight and at high speed on the surface in the hours of darkness.

Instead of sighting any convoys at dawn on the 19th, the boats saw only destroyers. The operation was called off and the boats submerged to avoid aircraft from the escort-carrier HMS *Striker*.

The *Hai* groups were dissolved. U 549 moved westwards with the other boats and *Preussen* group was formed from the 22nd 400 to 500 miles N of the Azores. Before the group moved to intercept westbound convoy ON 225, U 549 was detached for weather-reporting duties.

She put in to her new base at Lorient **26.3.44**

2. 14.5.44 Left for operations in Brazilian waters.

Outward-bound, U 549 was sighted and attacked by an aircraft from the escort-carrier USS *Block Island* on the 28th NW of the Canaries. She was found and attacked again next day by another aircraft from the carrier.

Late on the 29th U 549 hit *Block Island* with three torpedoes and she began to sink by the stern. A destroyer-escort, USS *Eugene E Elmore*, sighted the boat's periscope and made an unsuccessful attack. U 549 then fired an acoustic torpedo, which damaged the destroyer-escort USS *Barr*. She was towed into Casablanca and repaired.

Captain Hughes, commanding *Block Island*, gave the order to abandon ship and while this was happening U 549 launched a torpedo at the *Eugene E Elmore* but missed. The USS *Ahrens* and *Eugene E Elmore* both made attacks and U 549 was destroyed.

There were 951 survivors picked up from *Block Island* but there were no survivors from U 549, 58 dead.

U 550   Type IX C-40

Built by Deutsche Werft, Hamburg
Keel laid 2.10.42   Launched 12.5.43
Commissioned 28.7.43   Feldpost Nr M 53 473

Sunk 16.4.44 S of Nantucket Island (40°09′N 69°44′W)

Served with
4 U-Flottille, Stettin   July 1943 - January 1944 (ab)
10 U-Flottille, Lorient   February 1944 - 16.4.44 (fb)

Commanded by
KL Klaus Hänert   July 1943 - 16.4.44

Patrols: 1   Ships sunk: 1 (11,017 grt)

1. 6.2.44 Left Kiel for the North Atlantic.

U 550 initially carried out weather-reporting duties. In the latter part of March she went to the Newfoundland area and later moved south and in mid-April was off the US east coast.

On the 16th U 550 was S of Nantucket Island, when she sighted eastbound convoy CU 21. She torpedoed and sank the tanker SS *Pan Pennsylvania* (am 11017t). Whilst destroyer-escorts were picking up survivors, U 550 was located by USS *Joyce* and depth-charges were dropped.

The boat surfaced close by and USS *Gandy* opened fire and prepared to ram. U 550 tried to manoeuvre clear but was struck near the stern. *Gandy* moved away and began firing again. She was joined by *Joyce* and USS *Peterson*. A muffled explosion was heard from within the boat and some time later she began to sink.

Of U 550's crew, 44 men were lost and the commander and 11 others were picked up and made PoW.

U 551   Type VII C

Built by Blohm & Voss, Hamburg
Keel laid 21.11.39   Launched 14.9.40
Commissioned 7.11.40   Feldpost Nr M 26 026

Sunk 23.3.41 ESE of Vik, Iceland (62°37′N 16°47′W)

Served with
7 U-Flottille, Kiel   November 1940 - 23.3.41 (ab/fb)

Commanded by
KL Karl Schrott   November 1940 - 23.3.41

Patrols: 1   Ships sunk: None

1. 9.3.41 Left Kiel and arrived Bergen **13.3.41**

2. 18.3.41 Left for the North Atlantic.

Outward-bound on the 23rd, U 551 was sunk in a depth-charge attack by the a/s trawler HMS *Visenda* ESE of Vik, Iceland.

There were no survivors, 45 dead.

U 552   Type VII C

Built by Blohm & Voss, Hamburg
Keel laid 1.12.39   Launched 14.9.40
Commissioned 4.12.40   Feldpost Nr M 20 052

Scuttled 2.5.45 at Wilhelmshaven

Served with
7 U-Flottille, Kiel/St Nazaire   December 1940 - April 1944 (ab/fb)
22 U-Flottille, Gotenhafen/Wilhelmshaven   April 1944 - 2.5.45 (sb)

Commanded by
KK Erich Topp   December 1940 - August 1942
KL Klaus Popp   September 1942 - July 1944
OL Günther Lube   July 1944 - 2.5.45

Patrols: 14   Ships sunk: 29 (158,503 grt) + 3 damaged
                          1 destroyer (1190 dt)
                          2 a/s trawlers (747 dt)

1. 13.2.41 Left Kiel and arrived Heligoland **15.2.41**

2. 18.2.41 Left for the North Atlantic.

Outward-bound, U 552 sighted westbound OB 289 NW of the Hebrides on the 23rd. With U 97 and U 108, she pursued the convoy for three days. After first sighting the convoy, U 552 fired seven torpedoes at varying ranges but all failed to detonate. This was fairly common at this time and was attributable to torpedo failure or incorrect settings. Three ships were sunk and another damaged from the convoy, all by U 97 on the 24th. U 552 went on to patrol S of Iceland. Just before midnight on 1.3.41 she torpedoed and sank the tanker SS *Cadillac* (br 12062t) NE of Rockall, from eastbound convoy HX 109.

On the 2nd an aircraft sighted OB 292 leaving the North Channel. U 552 and six other boats formed a patrol line but were unable to find the convoy and were ordered northwards to search. Although OB 292 was sighted again by an aircraft on the 4th, the boats which had then moved eastwards to search were still having no success and the operation ended on the 5th.

On the 10th U 552 sank the fishing vessel *Reykjaborg* (ice 687t) SE of Iceland by gunfire.

U 552 put in to her new base at St Nazaire **16.3.41**

U 552 (continued)

3. 7.4.41 Left for the North Atlantic.

U 552, U 65, U 95, U 96 and U 123 formed a patrol line from the 18th S of Iceland. Nothing was seen until early on the 27th, when U 552 torpedoed and sank the a/s trawler HMS *Commander Horton* S of Iceland. In the afternoon U 552 sank the MV *Beacon Grange* (br 10160t) in the same area.

On the 28th U 123 sighted eastbound convoy HX 121. Before being driven off, she reported to U 65, U 96 and U 552 and they closed in. In the afternoon of the 28th U 552 torpedoed the tanker MV *Capulet* (br 8190t) and she was left burning and abandoned. The wreck was sunk by U 201 in the evening of 2.5.41.

U 552 sank an independent, the SS *Nerissa* (br 5583t), early on 1.5.41 NE of Rockall. The boat returned to St Nazaire **6.5.41**

4. 25.5.41 Left for the North Atlantic.

U 552 patrolled an area NW of Ireland. In the morning of 10.6.41 she sank the SS *Ainderby* (br 4860t) NW of Erris Head, early on the 12th the MV *Chinese Prince* (br 8593t) was sunk S of Rockall and on the 18th the SS *Norfolk* (br 10948t) was sunk ESE of Rockall.

On the 23rd U 203 sighted eastbound convoy HX 133 450 miles S of Cape Farewell. U 552 was one of ten boats which operated against the convoy from the 24th to the 27th. They were hampered by thick fog and a strong escort. Early on the 27th U 552 sank an unidentified ship (c 3000t) by torpedo and gunfire in the central North Atlantic. From HX 133, a total of six ships was sunk.

U 552 returned to St Nazaire **2.7.41**

5. 18.8.41 Left for Atlantic operations.

On the 17th southbound OG 71, heading for Gibraltar, was sighted SW of Ireland by a Kondor. Outward-bound, U 552 was directed to the convoy. In the early morning of the 23rd she sank the SS *Spind* (nw 2129t) by torpedo and gunfire some 160 miles W of Oporto. This vessel had been torpedoed and damaged three hours earlier by U 564. The convoy lost two escorts and eight ships sunk.

U 552 returned to St Nazaire **26.8.41**

6. 4.9.41 Left for the North Atlantic.

U 552 was directed to convoy SC 42, which had been intercepted on the 9th near Cape Farewell. Attacks were carried out but by the 11th air cover from Iceland and a strengthened escort had prevented any further sinkings. During the night of the 12/13th fog came down and U 552 and the other four boats that were still operating against SC 42 lost it in bad visibility. On the 14th U 552 had brief contact with some destroyers but the operation was called off on that day. During the action sixteen ships had been sunk and two boats lost.

From the 16th U 552, U 74, U 373, U 572 and U 575 formed a patrol line S of Greenland. This was later augmented by six more boats and designated *Brandenburg* group. On the 18th U 74 sighted eastbound SC 44 but because of radio interference any form of organised attack could not be carried out and only four boats, U 552, U 94, U 373 and U 562, responded to U 74's report.

During the night of the 19/20th U 552 sank three ships in separate attacks ENE of Cape Farewell, the tanker, SS *T J Williams* (br 8212t), the SS *Pink Star* (pa 4150t) and the tanker MV *Barbro* (nw 6325t). This vessel was already sinking when U 69 hit it with a torpedo that failed to detonate. The convoy also lost another ship and a corvette of the escort, both sunk by U 74.

The *Brandenburg* boats formed a new patrol line SE of Cape Farewell from the 23rd. After some boats left to return to base, the group dispersed on the 26th.

U 552 returned to St Nazaire **5.10.41**

7. 25.10.41 Left for the North Atlantic.

Outward-bound, U 552 was ordered on the 30th to join *Stosstrupp* group E of Newfoundland. En route, she sighted eastbound HX 156 on the 31st in the central North Atlantic. U 552 torpedoed

and sank the destroyer USS *Reuben James* of the escort. She was the first US naval vessel lost in the war, at a time when the US was still neutral. Of the destroyer's complement of 160 men, only 45 survived.

U 552 was driven off but U 567 came up to maintain contact and between them the two boats shadowed the convoy until 3.11.43. U 552 and U 567 made unsuccessful attacks on the 1st.

U 552 and U 567 joined *Störtebecker* group in the central North Atlantic, probably on or about the 12th. From the 15th the group was directed to southbound OS 11 but the convoy changed course to avoid the boats. Searches found nothing and on the 17th a patrol line, 500 miles long, was formed between Ireland and the Azores. This too proved to be unsuccessful. On the 19th all available boats were ordered to form three lines, *Störtebecker*, *Gödecke* and *Benecke*. Again, the convoy was re-routed to miss the groups.

U 552 returned to St Nazaire **26.11.41**

8. 25.12.41 Left for the Gibraltar area.

U 552 was one of six boats en route for the Mediterrranean, which were ordered instead to assemble near the Azores as *Seydlitz* group. On 2.1.42 a decision was made. U 552, U 84 and U 203 were ordered to the Newfoundland Bank and U 71, U 93 and U 571 were ordered to patrol between Gibraltar and the Azores.

In the early hours of the 15th U 552 sank the SS *Dayrose* (br 4113t) S of Cape Race, on the 16th a destroyer was unsuccesfully attacked as it left St John's and on the 18th the SS *Frances Salman* (am 2609t) was sunk off Newfoundland.

U 552 returned to St Nazaire **27.1.42**

9. 7.3.42 Left for operations in US waters.

U 552 was one of eleven boats in the fourth wave of *Operation Paukenschlag*. En route on the 25th, U 552 torpedoed the tanker MV *Ocana* (nl 6256t) S of Cape Sable. The vessel attempted to ram U 552, which set her on fire soon afterwards. The burned-out wreck drifted until 15.4.42, when it was sunk by the minesweeper HMCS *Burlington*.

U 552 reached her operational area in late March and began a run of successes. On 3.4.42 she sank the SS *David H Atwater* by gunfire E of Chincoteague Island. Although the ship was sinking, U 552 continued firing, killing many men as they attempted to launch the lifeboats. Of the vessel's crew of 26, only three men survived.

On the 5th the tanker SS *Byron T Benson* (am 7953t) was torpedoed and sunk E of Albemarle Sound and on the 7th two ships were sunk E of Hatteras, the tanker MV *British Splendour* (br 7138t) and the whaling factory ship SS *Lancing* (nw 7866t).

U 552 sank two tankers E of Cape Lookout, on the 9th the SS *Atlas* (am 7137t) and on the 10th the SS *Tamaulipas* (am 6943t). The boat returned to St Nazaire **27.4.42**

10. 9.6.42 Left for Atlantic operations.

On the 11th a Kondor of 1/KG 40 reported northbound convoy HG 84, which had left Gibraltar on the 9th. U 552 and seven other outward-bound boats were ordered to form a patrol line, *Endrass*, W of Portugal for the 14th, in the expected path of the convoy.

HG 84 was sighted again by a Kondor during the afternoon of the 14th and U 552 was the first *Endrass* boat to be homed in. In the early hours of the 15th she sank five ships NE of the Azores, the SS *Etrib* (br 1943t), the MV *Pelayo* (br 1346t), the tanker MV *Slemdal* (nw 7374t), the SS *City of Oxford* (br 2759t) and the SS *Thurso* (br 2436t). These were the only successes against the convoy. Further attempted attacks by *Endrass* boats were frustrated by the strong air and surface escort.

With no torpedoes left, U 552 returned to St Nazaire **19.6.42**

11. 4.7.42 Left for the North Atlantic.

U 552 joined *Wolf* group, formed from the 12th 600 miles W of the North Channel. The group was to make a circular sweep towards the Newfoundland Bank and then go south.

A convoy was sighted at the northern end of the line on the 13th. Some of the more southerly boats moved northeastwards for some hours but when the convoy was found to be westbound it was not pursued any further, being then too far ahead. When nothing further was seen by the 19th it was decided to move *Wolf* group south. Three days later, as the boats were about to go to a refuelling area, another westbound convoy was reported and a line was formed.

The convoy was sighted on the 23rd and proved to be ON 113, the one originally sighted on the 13th. In the ensuing action, with bad visibility and a strong escort, the convoy lost only two ships and U 90 was sunk. U 552 torpedoed two ships in two attacks in the central North Atlantic in the morning of the 25th, damaging the tanker MV *British Merit* (br 8093t) and sinking the SS *Broompark* (br 5136t). Contact with ON 113 was lost on the 26th and after a fruitless search on the 27th, the operation was terminated.

The *Wolf* boats moved south to a refuelling area W of the Azores, where eight boats of the group were supplied on the 29th and 30th by U 461. The group did not reform but seven of the refuelled boats moved north to close convoy ON 115, reported by U 210 on the 29th. A patrol line, *Pirat*, was formed ahead of the convoy on 1.8.42 and the ex-*Wolf* boats joined this line.

The convoy was sighted by U 552 on the 2nd E of Cape Race and in the early hours of the 3rd she torpedoed and damaged two ships, the tanker MV *G S Walden* (br 10627t) and the SS *Belgian Soldier* (be 7167t). The latter vessel was sunk by U 607 early on the 4th.

U 552 had used her last torpedo. On the 3rd, still near the convoy on the surface, the boat was located by the corvette HMS *Sackville*. She closed with guns firing, as U 552 prepared to dive. A direct hit on the conning tower damaged a shaft, which supplied air to the diesels. After diving, U 552 was attacked with depth-charges. When oil and pieces of debris appeared on the surface of the water, *Sackville* assumed U 552 had been destroyed and news reached Germany to this effect, causing grief and woe to relatives.

U 552 returned to St Nazaire **13.8.42**

12. 10.9.42 Left for the Central Atlantic, KL Popp in command.

U 552 torpedoed and sank the a/s trawler HMS *Alouette* in the early hours of the 19th 75 miles W of Sesimbra, Portugal.

In early October U 552 was operating SW of Freetown and on or about the 11th she was refuelled there by U 459. From early November she was patrolling S of the Cape Verde Islands but not having any success. In mid-November she was refuelled near the Islands by U 462. The returning U 552 sank the SS *Wallsend* (br 3157t) soon after midnight on 2.12.42 NNW of the Islands and picked up her captain as a prisoner.

U 552 returned to St Nazaire **15.12.42**

13. 4.4.43 Left for the North Atlantic.

U 552 joined *Meise* group E of Newfoundland. A patrol line was formed on the 14th to intercept eastbound SC 126 but the convoy was re-routed and in spite of sweeping searches it was not found. From the 21st a new patrol line was formed S of Greenland to intercept HX 234. The convoy was sighted on that day by U 306. Fog and snowstorms made closing difficult and on the 25th the operation was called off after all the boats still in contact were driven off by aircraft and the surface escort. Only two ships had been sunk and another damaged. U 552 had no success.

Meise group was dissolved. The boats joined the newly-formed *Star* group E of Cape Farewell, to await a westbound ONS convoy. On the 28th ONS 5 passed the group's northern wing and again bad weather made closing difficult. In the morning of the 29th only two boats were able to make attacks, sinking one ship. On 1.5.43 the pursuit of ONS 5 was called off near Cape Farewell.

The *Star* boats were ordered south to join *Specht* and *Amsel* groups in an operation against northbound SC 128. The convoy had not been found by the 3rd and a new patrol line, *Fink*, was formed S of Cape Farewell by combining *Star* and *Specht* groups. The twenty-nine *Fink* boats continued to search for SC 128 but by the 4th it was realised that the convoy had been re-routed.

Fink had received orders to take up a new position when a southwest-bound convoy was sighted in the centre of the line. It proved to be ONS 5, which had been delayed by the storm. In daylight on the 5th fifteen boats were in contact with the convoy but before nightfall fog came down and most lost contact.

In the morning of the 6th ONS 5 was again sighted but deteriorating weather conditions caused the operation to be abandoned. In the second action against ONS 5 twelve ships were sunk. U 552 does not seem to have made any attacks on the convoy.

On or about the 10th U 552 was refuelled in the central North Atlantic by U 461. From the 19th she was with *Mosel* group 400 miles S of Cape Farewell, formed to operate against HX 239.

On the 21st it was thought that the convoy might pass south of the patrol line, following a route taken by the convoy's stragglers. *Mosel* group was split into two parts, the southern boats to intercept the stragglers and the other, including U 552, to move east and attack the main convoy. Carrier-borne aircraft kept the boats submerged and HX 239 was never found. With several boats damaged and U 752 sunk, the operation was ended on the 23rd.

From the 24th Dönitz temporarily halted operations against convoys in the North Atlantic. Boats from *Mosel* and *Donau* groups with ample fuel were sent to an area SW of the Azores to operate against US-Gibraltar convoys. Those boats with less fuel, including U 552, ranged over the North Atlantic between 25° and 45°W. Their radio signals were aimed to give the impression that a large U-boat presence was still present across the convoy routes.

On the 29th U 552 was attacked and damaged by a Liberator of 59 Squadron (F/O H A L Moran) SW of Ireland. The aircraft made two attacks, in each of which four depth-charges were dropped, and there was an exchange of fire before the boat dived.

U 552 returned to St Nazaire **13.6.43**

14. 3.10.43 Left for the North Atlantic.

U 552 joined *Siegfried* group, formed for the 24th 500 miles E of Newfoundland to await HX 262 and SC 145. The boats were ordered to remain submerged in daylight, ready for an attack after dark. On the 25th it was thought that a convoy would pass south of the group. The boats moved southwards but nothing was found.

To cover a wider area, *Siegfried* split into three small sub-groups, *Siegfried 1,2* and *3*. U 552 was in *Siegfried 3*. In the constant search for convoys over a wider area of the North Atlantic the boats were split into smaller and smaller groups. After a few days with *Jahn* group, U 552 joined one of the *Tirpitz 1* to *5* sub-groups. In spite of searches being carried out, still no convoys were found.

U 552 next joined *Eisenhart* group, made up of seven sub-groups of three boats each and drawn up in two lines from 11.11.43, running southeast from Cape Farewell.

Reports indicated that convoys were being routed to the south so the *Eisenhart* boats were ordered southeastwards on the 12th to search for SC 146 and HX 265. By the 16th no convoys had been found and the majority of the boats were by then WSW of Ireland. Fuel was now becoming a problem for many of *Eisenhart* group and it was decided to end the operation. Boats with sufficient fuel went to reinforce *Schill* group W of Spain and the others, including U 552, headed for base.

She reached St Nazaire **30.11.43**

15. 8.2.44 Left and returned to rectify a mechanical fault **14.2.44**

16. 16.2.44 Left again for the North Atlantic.

U 552 carried out weather-reporting duties, on what was to be her last Atlantic patrol. The boat put in to Bergen 22.4.44 and then went on, arriving at Danzig **28.4.44**

U 552 joined 22 U-Flottille at Gotenhafen, as a school boat. Late in the war the boat was moved to Wilhelmshaven, where she was scuttled on 2.5.45.

29

U 553   Type VII C

Built by Blohm & Voss, Hamburg
Keel laid 21.11.39   Launched 7.11.40
Commissioned 23.12.40   Feldpost Nr M 23 789

Lost 22.1.43 in the North Atlantic (53°00´N 33°00´W)

Served with
7 U-Flottille, Kiel/St Nazaire December 1940 - November 1942 (ab/fb)
3 U-Flottille, La Pallice November 1942 - 22.1.43 (fb)

Commanded by
KK Karl Thurmann December 1940 - 22.1.43

Patrols: 10   Ships sunk: 15 (85,510 grt)

1. 13.4.41 Left Kiel, in transit for Western France.
U 553 put in to St Nazaire **2.5.41**

2. 7.6.41 Left for the North Atlantic.
In the early hours of the 12th U 553 torpedoed and sank the SS *Susan Maersk* (br 2355t) N of the Azores and in the afternoon the tanker SS *Ranella* (nw 5590t) from southbound convoy OG 64.

U 553 joined *West* group SE of the Newfoundland Bank. On the 20th the group began a movement northeastwards, to operate in a widely-spaced formation in the central North Atlantic. No convoys were seen but some independents were sunk by *West* boats.

On the 24th U 203 sighted westbound OB 336 S of Greenland and sank two ships. U 553, U 77, U 101, U 108 and U 558 closed and shadowed the convoy but fog in the area of the Newfoundland Bank prevented any attacks. The only other success against OB 336 was a straggler sunk by U 108 on the 25th.

U 553, with other ex-*West* boats, continued to operate with some independent boats but in late June a general movement eastwards began. On the 29th they were directed to a convoy sighted by an aircraft 300 miles W of Ireland, probably OG 66. Although sighted again by aircraft on the 30th and July 1st, the boats were unable to close because of bad visibility and fog. Another convoy was briefly sighted on the 2nd but this came to nothing. The boats remained in the area between Greenland and the Azores but saw nothing.

U 553 returned to St Nazaire **19.7.41**

3. 7.8.41 Left for the North Atlantic.
U 553 joined a large group of boats which were operating in a loose formation SW of Iceland. They had no success in locating convoys during August because of skilful re-routing.

From 1.9.41 U 553 and six other boats formed *Kurfürst* group W of the North Channel. The group was directed to convoy OG 73, sighted by a Kondor on the 1st. U 83 and U 557 of *Bosemüller* group, whilst searching for SL 84, encountered OG 73 on the 2nd.

Kurfürst and *Bosemüller* groups were combined into one and directed to attack OG 73 but it was not found, nor was another sighted by U 98 on the 3rd.

U 553 returned to St Nazaire **16.9.41**

4. 7.10.41 Left for the North Atlantic.
U 553 went to an area SE of Cape Farewell, where a new group was to be formed. As the group was forming, convoys ONS 23, ON 24, SC 48 and TC 14 were re-routed to the south. During the night of the 14/15th U 553, at the southern end of the line, sighted SC 48 in the central North Atlantic. She sank two ships on the 15th, the MV *Silvercedar* (br 4354t) and the SS *Ila* (nw 1583t), and early on the 17th she sank the SS *Bold Venture* (pa 6595t).

Outward-bound boats responded to U 553's report and closed the convoy. Successive shadowers were driven off and the escort was strengthened. However, in spite of this the boats persisted in their attacks until the operation ended in the morning of the 18th, with

nine ships and two escorts sunk.
U 553 returned to St Nazaire **22.10.41**

5. 1.1.42 Left for the North Atlantic.
U 553 was to operate in Canadian waters. In the evening of the 15th she torpedoed and sank the tanker MV *Diala* (br 8106t) ESE of St John's, dispersed from convoy ON 52.

On the 22nd U 553 sank an independent S of Sable Island, the tanker MV *Inneröy* (nw 8260t). A few days later the boat headed for home and reached St Nazaire **3.2.43**

6. 24.2.42 Left for the area W of the Faroes and the Hebrides.
In early 1942 Hitler feared an Allied landing in Norway and from January 25th eight boats were stationed W of the Faroes and the Hebrides for the protection of Norway.

In February boats from Germany were unavailable and six were sent from France, U 553, U 87, U 135, U 569, U 701 and U 753.

From 11.3.42 U 553, U 135, U 569 and U 701 were put under the control of Naval Group Command North and, as *York* group, they waited between the Shetlands and Faroes for the return of British naval vessels sighted NE of the Faroes on the 10th. After waiting in vain for two weeks, the boats returned to base.

U 553 reached St Nazaire **1.4.42**

7. 19.4.42 Left for Canadian waters.
U 553 arrived in the Newfoundland Bank area on 3.5.42. On the 6th she sighted a steamer with a corvette escort. A torpedo attack on the steamer failed but alerted the corvette, which dropped a single depth-charge, damaging U 553's periscope. After a second attack caused further minor damage to U 553, the action ceased.

The boat was later attacked by an aircraft and the three depth-charges dropped caused more damage. U 553's commander decided to make for the Gulf of St Lawrence, the first incursion there by a U-boat. On the 10th U 553 was spotted on the surface by a USAF aircraft, which dropped five depth-charges, giving the boat some technical problems. The aircraft reported bubbles and debris but a search by the minesweeper HMCS *Medicine Hat* did not find anything. The boat was further damaged but still operational.

U 553 moved into the St Lawrence River and in the morning of the 12th she sank two ships 10 miles N of Rivière-la-Madeleine, the SS *Nicoya* (br 5364t) and the SS *Leto* (nl 4712t). A third attack that morning saw a third ship hit aft with a torpedo and possibly damaged but not sunk.

On the 21st U 553 left the Gulf of St Lawrence via Cabot Strait. She went south, passed Halifax and then entered the Bay of Fundy. On the 27th U 553 was off the harbour of St John, New Brunswick, where she observed the comings and goings for several days before deciding that St John was not a terminal for convoys.

With nine torpedoes left and enough provisions for 25 days, U 553 moved back into the Atlantic on 1.6.42. In the morning of the 2nd she torpedoed and sank the MV *Mattawin* (br 6919t) S of Cape Sable. Next day an empty, unmarked lifeboat was found, in which were some very welcome provisions.

U 553 began the homeward journey on the 5th and on the 10th, although short of provisions, she turned back to search for a reported UK-Halifax convoy. In the evening of the 11th the boat was caught on the surface by a flying boat, which dropped depth-charges after U 553 dived. The aircraft circled, frustrating any attempt by the boat to approach the convoy. With damage greater than at first thought, the boat turned for home.

U 553 returned to St Nazaire **24.6.42**

8. 19.7.42 Left for the Antilles.
Outward-bound, U 553 was directed to westbound convoy ON 115, sighted by U 164 on the 29th 480 miles SE of Cape Farewell. U 553 and other boats made contact but were driven off. On 1.8.42 U 553, U 164, U 210, U 217 and U 511 formed a patrol line, *Pirat*, ahead of the convoy. It did not arrive by the evening and the boats searched to north and south. The *Pirat* line had by then

been joined by some ex-*Wolf* boats.

The convoy was found by U 552 on the 2nd. In the early morning of the 3rd U 553 torpedoed and sank the MV *Lochkatrine* (br 9419t) ESE of St John's. Three ships in all were sunk before contact was lost in the fog of the Newfoundland Bank, ending the operation.

U 553 resumed her journey southwards to the Caribbean, which she entered on or about the 10th. U 553 encountered Key West-bound convoy TAW 13 on the 18th N of Jamaica. In three morning attacks, she torpedoed three ships, sinking the MV *Blankaholm* (sw 2845t) and the SS *John Hancock* (am 7176t) and damaging the MV *Empire Bede* (br 6959t). After the third attack, U 553 was attacked herself by the corvette HMS *Pimpernel* and kept down. The *Empire Bede* was abandoned and she was sunk by *Pimpernel*.

U 553 left her operational area on or about 1.9.42 and she reached St Nazaire **17.9.42**

9. 23.11.42 Left for the North Atlantic.

U 553 joined *Draufgänger* group, formed on the 30th W of Ireland to operate against an ONS convoy but it did not materialise. On 7.12.42 the group was ordered northwestwards to close convoy HX 217, sighted by U 524 of *Panzer* group on the 6th.

On the 8th the *Draufgänger* boats approached the convoy. U 553 attempted an attack on a destroyer but was forced to submerge by a Liberator of 120 Squadron. Aircraft from this squadron prevented attacks on the convoy by boats of *Panzer* and *Draufgänger* groups.

In the morning of the 9th U 553 torpedoed and sank a straggler from the convoy E of Cape Farewell, the MV *Charles L D* (br 5273t). One other ship was sunk in the operation, which ended on the 11th after strong Iceland-based air cover appeared from the 10th.

U 553 put in to La Pallice **18.12.42**

10. 16.1.43 Left for the North Atlantic.

U 553 joined *Landsknecht* group W of Ireland. The boat was not heard from after the 20th, when she reported that her periscope was unserviceable. Her loss it attributed to an unknown cause, possibly on the 22nd. She was officially declared 'lost' on the 28th.

There were no survivors, 47 dead.

U 554   Type VII C

Built by Blohm & Voss, Hamburg
Keel laid 1.12.39   Launched 7.11.40
Commissioned 15.1.41   Feldpost Nr M 31 379

Scuttled 2.5.45 at Wilhelmshaven

Served with
24 U-Flottille, Danzig/Trondheim/Memel
　　　　　　　　　　　　　　January 1941 - June 1944 (ab)
22 U-Flottille, Gotenhafen July 1944 - February 1945 (sb)
31 U-Flottille, Wilhelmshaven February 1945 - 2.5.45 (ab)

Commanded by
KL Dietrich Lohmann January - June 1941
OL Heinz Stein June 1941 - March 1942
OL Claus von Trotha March - September 1942
KL Karl Hartwig Siebold November 1942 - September 1944
OL Curt Hartmann (temp) June 1944
KL Ernst-Wolfgang Rave October 1944 - March 1945
OL Werner Remus March 1945 - 2.5.45

Patrols: None   Ships sunk: None

U 554 had no operational service. She was at 24, 22 and 31 U-Flottillen, serving always as a training boat.

U 544 was attacked by British aircraft in the Kattegat and damaged by bombs. She was scuttled at Wilhelmshaven on 2.5.45.

U 555   Type VII C

Built by Blohm & Voss, Hamburg
Keel laid 2.1.40   Launched 7.12.40
Commissioned 30.1.41   Feldpost Nr M 34 971

Decommissioned March 1945 at Hamburg

Served with
24 U-Flottille, Danzig/Trondheim/Memel
　　　　　　　　　　　January 1941 - November 1942 (ab)
21 U-Flottille, Pillau December 1942 - March 1945 (sb)

Commanded by
KL Hans-Joachim Horrer January - August 1941
KL Götz von Hartmann August 1941 - February 1942
OL Horst Rendtel February - August 1942
Lt Franz Saar August - October 1942
OL Dieter Erdmann December 1942 - November 1943
OL Detlef Fritz December 1943 - March 1945

Patrols: None   Ships sunk: None

U 555 had no operational service. She was on training duties at 24 and 21 U-Flottillen.

She was taken out of service at Hamburg in 1945 and after the surrender U 555 became a British prize. She was later scrapped.

U 556   Type VII C

Built by Blohm & Voss, Hamburg
Keel laid 2.1.40   Launched 7.12.40
Commissioned 6.2.41   Feldpost Nr M 36 839

Sunk 27.6.41 SW of Reykjavik (60°24′N 29°00′W)

Served with
1 U-Flottille, Kiel/Brest February 1941 - 27.6.41 (ab/fb)

Commanded by
KL Herbert Wohlfarth February 1941 - 27.6.41

Patrols: 2   Ships sunk: 5 (23,557 grt) + 2 damaged

1. 1.5.41 Left Kiel for the North Atlantic.

U 556 was to patrol W of the British Isles and as far as 25°W. On the 6th she sank the fishing vessel *Emanuel* (fa 166t) just W of the Faroes. U 94 sighted westbound OB 318 on the 7th S of Iceland and U 556 was one of the boats directed to it. She closed the convoy E of Cape Farewell in the early morning of the 10th and torpedoed and damaged the SS *Aelybryn* (br 4986t) and missed the British steamer SS *Chaucer*. The *Aelybryn* reached Reykjavik on the 17th. In two further attacks on OB 318 on the 10th U 556 sank the SS *Empire Caribou* (br 4861t) and the SS *Gand* (be 5086t).

U 556 joined up with U 93, U 94 and U 98 on the 11th to form a patrol group SE of Greenland. From the 13th these boats were augmented by U 74, U 97, U 109 and U 111. The group moved to the southwest on the 15th and formed a new patrol line SSE of Cape Farewell.

On the 19th U 94 sighted northbound convoy HX 126 and the other boats closed the convoy one by one over the next two days. U 556 was the first to arrive and make attacks. In the afternoon of the 20th she torpedoed three ships, damaging the tanker MV *San Felix* (br 13037t) and sinking the tanker MV *British Security* (br 8470t) and the MV *Darlington Court* (br 4974t).

U 556 began her return to base on the 24th, the day the *Bismarck*

U 556 (continued)

and *Prinz Eugen* attempted to enter the Atlantic via the Denmark Strait. The plan was that a group of U-boats would form a patrol line running northwest-southeast S of Cape Farewell. After the two battleships had passed through the line the boats would then deal with any shadowing, British naval vessels.

However, the plan was changed. *Bismarck* would make for St Nazaire and *Prinz Eugen* would head southwestwards. During the night of the 24/25th *Bismarck* was damaged in a torpedo attack by carrier-borne aircraft. To assist her into the comparative shelter of the Bay of Biscay the homeward-bound U 556, U 74, U 97, U 98 and U 109 and the outward-bound U 48, U 73 and U 108 were ordered on the 25th to assemble 450 miles W of St Nazaire. They were then directed to form a patrol line running northwest from Cape Ortegal. This was delayed by a heavy storm and the boats were not in position until the 26th. In the evening of that day *Bismarck* was at the northwest end of the line, running parallel to it and just to the east. Boats that still had torpedoes were ordered to go to her assistance but heavy seas prevented their finding her. On the 26th U 556 sighted HMS *Renown* and *Ark Royal*, on their way from Gibraltar to intercept the *Bismarck*, but she had no torpedoes. *Bismarck* was sunk in the morning of the 27th.

U 556 put in to Lorient **30.5.41**

2. 19.6.41 Left for the North Atlantic.

U 556 was one of a number of boats which were to operate in a loose formation in the central North Atlantic. On the 23rd U 203 sighted eastbound HX 133 S of Greenland but after sinking one ship she lost contact.

On the 26th U 556, U 201 and U 564 came up with the convoy. U 556 was located on the 27th SW of Iceland and sunk in depth-charge attacks by the escorting corvettes HMS *Celandine* (Lt-Cdr A Stannard), *Gladiolus* (Lt-Cdr H M C Sanders) and *Nasturtium* (Lt-Cdr R C Freaker).

Of U 556's crew, 5 men were lost and the commander and 40 other men were made PoW.

U 557   Type VII C

Built by Blohm & Voss, Hamburg
Keel laid 6.1.40   Launched 22.12.40
Commissioned 13.2.41   Feldpost Nr M 37 961

Sunk 16.12.41 W of Phalasarna, Crete (35°33´N 23°14´E)

Served with
1 U-Flottille, Kiel/Brest   February - November 1941 (ab/fb)
29 U-Flottille, La Spezia   December 1941 (fb)

Commanded by
KL Ottokar Paulshen   February 1941 - 16.12.41

Patrols: 4   Ships sunk: 6 (31,729 grt)
                         1 cruiser (5220 dt)

1. 13.5.41 Left Kiel for the North Atlantic.

On the 19th U 94 sighted northbound HX 126 SSE of Cape Farewell. Outward-bound, U 557 was directed to the convoy with which she made contact on the 22nd. In a three-day operation nine ships were sunk and another damaged but U 557 had no success.

On the 24th U 557, U 43, U 46, U 66, U 93, U 94 and U 111 were ordered to form a patrol line S of Cape Farewell, ahead of the fleeing *Bismarck*, in the hope of sinking some of her pursuers after she had passed through the line. This plan was cancelled in the evening of the 24th when it was decided that *Bismarck* would head for St Nazaire.

U 557, U 43, U 46, U 66 and U 111 were then ordered to form a

new, broader patrol line SE of Cape Farewell. In the evening of the 29th U 557 sank a straggler from convoy HX 128 SSE of Cape Farewell, the SS *Empire Storm* (br 7290t).

From 1.6.41 U 557 and the other four boats formed a nucleus of *West* group in the western North Atlantic. U 557 was refuelled during the night of the 1/2nd by the German supply ship *Belchen* 120 miles SW of Cape Farewell, after which she rejoined the group. On the 15th U 557 had an engagement with a British submarine.

It was eventually realised that, although independents were being sunk, convoys were being re-routed to avoid *West* group. To counteract this, the *West* boats went into the central North Atlantic from the 20th and operated in a loose formation over a wide area.

On the 29th U 557 and other *West* boats were directed to a convoy, sighted by a Kondor of 1/KG 40 300 miles SW of Ireland. The convoy, probably OG 66, was sighted again by aircraft on the 30th and July 1st. Fog and poor visibility frustrated the boats' attempts to close the convoy. Another convoy, sighted briefly on the 2nd, could not be found either. *West* group broke up and the boats headed for home.

U 557 put in to Lorient **10.7.41**

2. 13.8.41 Left Lorient and returned **15.8.41**

3. 20.8.41 Left to operate W of Ireland.

On the 26th U 141 sighted southbound convoy OS 4 W of Ireland but she was driven down by aircraft. U 557 came up and attacked the convoy during the night of the 26/27th. She sank four ships, the MV *Segundo* (nw 4414t), the SS *Saugor* (br 6303t), the SS *Tremoda* (br 4736t) and the SS *Embassage* (br 4954t).

On 1.9.41 U 557 and other boats formed *Bosemüller* group W to SW of Ireland. The group was directed to convoy SL 84 but could not find it in bad visibility. Whilst searching, U 83 and U 557 sighted ships of OG 73 on the 2nd. *Kurfürst* group was already searching for this convoy and when it appeared that it had been found, *Bosemüller* combined with *Kurfürst* to form one group, which was then directed to attack OG 73. However, the combined group failed to find the convoy and also another one sighted by U 98 on the 3rd.

From the 11th U 557, U 95, U 98, U 558, U 561 and U 565 moved to an area NW of the Hebrides. Three convoys were located by air reconnaissance on the 14th, 15th and 18th but the boats were unable to find them, except for U 98 which sank one ship from SC 42 on the 16th.

U 557 returned to Lorient **19.9.41**

4. 19.11.41 Left for the Mediterranean.

U 557 probably passed through the Straits of Gibraltar during the night of the 26/27th. She remained in the Western Mediterranean and in the evening of 2.12.41 she torpedoed and sank the SS *Fjord* (nw 4032t) off Estepona, Spain.

U 557 put in to Messina **7.12.41**

5. 9.12.41 Left for operations in the Eastern Mediterranean.

U 557 patrolled in the area between Alexandria and Tobruk. On the 15th she sank the cruiser HMS *Galatea* W of Alexandria, which was part of Force B, returning from a foray against Italian convoys going to Benghazi.

The returning U 557 sank on the 16th W of Phalasarna, Crete after being accidentally rammed by the Italian MTB *Orione*.

There were no survivors, 43 dead.

U 558 Type VII C

Built by Blohm & Voss, Hamburg
Keel laid 6.1.40 Launched 23.12.40
Commissioned 20.2.41 Feldpost Nr M 36 167

Sunk 20.7.43 NNW of Cape Ortegal (45°10´N 09°24´W)

Served with
1 U-Flottille, Kiel/Brest February 1941 - 20.7.43 (ab/fb)

Commanded by
KL Günther Krech February 1941 - 20.7.43

Patrols: 10   Ships sunk: 21 (121,783 grt) + 1 damaged
                1 corvette (925 dt)
                1 a/s trawler (913 dt)

1. 1.6.41 Left Kiel for the North Atlantic.

U 558 joined *West* group SE of the Newfoundland Bank. On the 20th the group moved northeastwards, to operate in a widely-spaced formation in the central North Atlantic. No convoys were seen, only independents, some of which were sunk by *West* boats.

On the 24th U 203 sighted westbound OB 336 S of Greenland and sank two ships. U 558, U 77, U 101, U 108 and U 553 closed and shadowed the convoy but fog in the area of the Newfoundland Bank prevented any attacks. The only success against the convoy was a straggler sunk by U 108 on the 25th.

U 558 put in to her new base at Brest **9.7.41**

2. 28.7.41 Left for Atlantic operations.

U 558 went to the area W of the North Channel. On 2.8.41 U 204 made contact with convoy SL 81 SW of Ireland. U 558 was one of the boats which closed the convoy on the 3rd. The strength of the escort prevented any attacks until early on the 5th, when five ships were sunk by three boats. U 558 had no success. The operation ended on the 5th when all boats in contact were driven off by aircraft and the surface escort.

U 558 returned to Brest **7.8.41**

3. 25.8.41 Left for Atlantic operations.

On the 26th U 141 sighted southbound OS 4 W of Ireland. She brought up U 557, which brought up U 751 on the 27th and U 71 and U 558 on the 28th. In the afternoon of that day U 558 sank the MV *Otaio* (br 10298t).

On 1.9.41 U 558 and other boats formed *Bosemüller* group W to SW of Ireland. The group was directed to convoy SL 84, sighted by the returning U 73, but could not find it in bad visibility. Whilst searching, U 83 and U 557 sighted ships of OG 73 on the 2nd.

Kurfürst group was already searching for this convoy and when it appeared that it had been found, *Bosemüller* combined with *Kurfürst* to form one group, which was then directed to attack OG 73. However, the combined group failed to find the convoy and also another sighted by U 98 on the 3rd.

From the 11th U 558, U 95, U 98, U 557, U 561 and U 565 moved to an area NW of the Hebrides. Convoys were sighted by reconnaissance aircraft from the 14th. On that day U 558 and U 557 searched for northbound HG 72 but failed to find it.

U 558 returned to Brest **16.9.41**

4. 11.10.41 Left for Atlantic operations.

Outward-bound, U 558 sank the independent SS *Vancouver Island* (br 9472t) in the late evening of the 15th in the central North Atlantic, W of Ireland. During the night of the 14/15th U 553 had sighted eastbound SC 48 in the central North Atlantic, in an area U 558 was about to enter. U 558 attacked the convoy in the early hours of the 17th some 600 miles W of Rockall, sinking the tankers SS *W C Teagle* (br 9552t) and MV *Erviken* (nw 6595t) and the

SS *Rym* (nw 1369t). She also probably sank a corvette of the escort, HMS *Gladiolus*.

With all torpedoes gone, U 558 returned to Brest **25.10.41**

5. 24.11.41 Left for the Mediterranean.

On 1.12.41 U 558 was attacked and damaged by a Swordfish of 812 (FAA) Squadron, formerly from HMS *Ark Royal* but then operating from the airfield at Gibraltar. She was attacked again by aircraft on the 2nd.

U 558 returned to Brest **7.12.41**

6. 10.2.42 Left for the North Atlantic.

Outward-bound, U 558 was directed to westbound ONS 67, sighted by U 155 on the 21st 600 miles NE of Cape Race. U 558 attacked the convoy in the morning of the 24th WNW of the Azores. In three attacks she torpedoed five ships, sinking the three tankers, SS *Inverarder* (br 5578t), the MV *Anadara* (br 8009t) and the MV *Finnanger* (nw 9551t) and the SS *White Crest* (br 4365t) and damaging the tanker MV *Eidanger* (nw 9432t). In a further attack in the afternoon, U 558 sank the *Eidanger*.

She returned to Brest **11.3.42**

7. 12.4.42 Left for operations in US waters.

U 558 was refuelled by U 459 on the 29th 500 miles NE of Bermuda. On 12.5.42 she sank the a/s trawler HMS *Bedfordshire* off Cape Lookout, North Carolina. The trawler was on loan to the US Navy. There were no survivors but four bodies were washed up on Ocracoke Island. They were buried on the island and the site is now a Commonwealth War Cemetery, the lease being handed over to the Commonwealth War Graves Commission in 1977 at a ceremony attended by the entire population of the island. Two other men from *Bedfordshire*'s crew are buried in the Baptist Cemetery at Creeds, Virginia.

U 558 went southwards and on the 18th she sank the SS *Fauna* (nl 1254t) just NE of Mayaguana Island, Bahamas. The boat entered the Caribbean via the Windward Passage and on the 21st sank the SS *Troisdoc* (br 1925t) W of Jamaica. U 558 torpedoed and damaged the tanker SS *William Boyce Thompson* on the 23rd S of Jamaica, sank the SS *Beatrice* by gunfire on the 25th SE of Kingston and on the 27th the SS *Jack* (am 2622t) S of Haiti.

U 558 left the Caribbean, probably via the Windward Passage. On 1.6.42 she sank the SS *Triton* (nl 2078t) SE of Bermuda. She was refuelled by U 459 in mid-June W of the Azores. U 558 reached Brest **21.6.42**

8. 29.7.42 Left for the Caribbean.

Outward-bound, U 558 was refuelled around mid-August by U 462 W of the Azores. She entered the Caribbean and on the 25th torpedoed and sank a straggler from convoy TAW 15, the SS *Amakura* (br 1987t), E of Port Morant, Jamaica. The boat was afterwards driven off by aircraft.

In September U 558 was in the Eastern Caribbean and on the 13th she encountered convoy TAG 5 W of Grenada, sinking the SS *Suriname* (nl 7915t), the MV *Empire Lugard* (br 7241t) and the tanker MV *Vilja* (nw 6672t).

After leaving the Caribbean U 558 sank the SS *Commercial Trader* (am 2606t) on the 16th E of Trinidad. She was refuelled by U 461 in late September NW of the Azores.

U 558 returned to Brest **16.10.42**

9. 9.1.43 Left for the Central Atlantic for operations against convoys bound for the Mediterranean.

On or about the 23rd U 558 joined *Delphin* group S of the Azores. Towards the end of January the group went eastwards to an area NW of the Canaries, then east again to an area W of Gibraltar.

On 7.2.43 U 521 sighted a small coastal convoy, Gib No 2, N of the Canaries. The five southern *Delphin* boats, U 558, U 87, U 202, U 258 and U 264, were ordered to close the apparently weakly-escorted convoy. However, before the surface escort was

U 558 (continued)

strengthened on the 9th, the operation had already been abandoned on the 8th because of a strong air escort.

After briefly pursuing a reported convoy E of Madeira on the 11th, which in fact was a hunting group, the five boats were refuelled by U 118 SW of Madeira between the 12th and 14th. They then joined *Rochen* group S of the Azores on the 16th, again to search for US-Gibraltar convoys.

The group swept westwards for four days, turning back eastwards on the 20th. Two days later the boats were directed to westbound convoy UC 1, sighted by U 522 WNW of Madeira. In the late evening of the 23rd U 558 torpedoed and sank the tanker SS *Empire Norseman* (br 9811t) 500 miles S of the Azores. This vessel had been hit previously by U 202.

On or about 1.3.43 U 558 and four other *Rochen* boats were refuelled by U 461 SW of the Azores. The boats afterwards formed a north-south patrol line, *Tümmler*, which began an eastwards movement towards the Canaries on the 5th. This move continued until by the 12th the boats were between the Canaries and the Moroccan coast.

A small southbound convoy had been sighted on the 11th but when it proved to be much too fast and its air escort too strong, the *Tümmler* boats were directed northeast to intercept Gibraltar-bound convoy UGS 6, some 1500 miles away.

The group made no real contact with the convoy. On the 17th U 558 fired a 4-torpedo spread against UGS 6 ships E of the Azores but missed. From the 18th strong air cover was provided from Gibraltar and the operation was terminated on the 19th, with only four ships sunk during an eight-day pursuit. On the 24th U 558, U 43 and U 202 received fuel from U 109 for their return to base.

U 558 reached Brest **29.3.43**

10. 8.5.43 Left for Atlantic operations.

From the 18th U 558 was with *Oder* group, formed in the central North Atlantic to operate against eastbound HX 238. However, after the convoy passed well to the north the *Oder* boats became part of a new patrol line, *Mosel*, formed from the 21st 400 miles S of Cape Farewell to intercept HX 239, reported moving eastwards from Newfoundland.

The convoy was sighted on the 22nd by U 305 but she was unable to maintain contact because of aircraft attacks. All attempts to locate the convoy during daylight hours were frustrated by aircraft and several boats were badly damaged and U 569 and U 752 were sunk. With HX 239 still not found, the operation was terminated on the 23rd.

The *Mosel* boats moved to an area SW of the Azores. Convoy operations in the North Atlantic had been suspended whilst the situation was being assessed by BdU. It was decided to try and intercept convoys between the US and the Mediterranean out in the Atlantic, beyond the range of land-based aircraft.

From the boats which assembled SW of the Azores a new patrol line, *Trutz*, was formed during the night of the 30/31st, to await expected convoys UGS 9 and GUS 7A. The line was drawn up on the 43°W meridian and ran between 32° and 38°N. On 4.6.43 the three most southerly boats were attacked by carrier-borne aircraft, which were thought to be part of a convoy's protective cover. The boats closed up to prevent any ships passing through gaps in the line but when nothing had been sighted by the evening of the 5th the convoy was thought to have passed either to north or south.

The group broke up and moved 600 miles to the north to be refuelled by U 488. The UGS convoy was sighted by an outward-bound boat on the 8th 100 miles south of the *Trutz* patrol area of the 5th. The move to refuel had been too premature and the opportunity lost. Refuelling was completed by the 15th and the group reformed in three north-south lines, *Trutz 1,2* and *3*, 1000 miles E of Bermuda. U 558 was in *Trutz 1*.

The boats waited for two other convoys from the 16th until the 22nd and having seen nothing in that time the line began an

eastwards movement which continued until the 27th, when they halted 200 miles SW of the Azores. By the 29th it was realised that the elusive convoys, GUS 8, UGS 10 and GUS 8A had by-passed the lines.

From 2.7.43 three new lines were formed, *Geier 1,2* and *3*. U 558 and U 221 did not become part of any of these but made their way towards the coast of Portugal, where they were to patrol.

On the 15th U 558 was attacked by a Wellington of 179 Squadron off Cape Roca. The aircraft was driven off and the boat dived and escaped. She was attacked again on the 17th and damaged, by a Liberator of 224 Squadron (W/Cdr A E Clouston).

On the 20th the returning U 558 was sunk NNW of Cape Ortegal after depth-charge attacks by a Liberator of 19 Squadron (USAF) (Lt C F Gallimeier) and a Halifax of 58 Squadron (F/Lt G A Sawtell). The Halifax also strafed the boat.

Of U 558's crew, 45 men were lost and the commander, the Chief Engineer and two ratings survived. The four men were sighted in a dinghy on the 24th by a Liberator of 224 Squadron (S/Ldr T M Bulloch) and emergency packs were dropped to them. They were picked up next day by the destroyer HMCS *Athabascan*.

U 559 Type VII C

Built by Blohm & Voss, Hamburg
Keel laid 1.2.40 Launched 8.1.41
Commissioned 27.2.41 Feldpost Nr M 38 782

Sunk 30.10.42 NNE of Port Said (32°30′N 33°00′E)

Served with
1 U-Flottille, Kiel/Brest February - October 1941 (ab/fb)
23 U-Flottille, Salamis November 1941 - April 1942 (fb)
29 U-Flottille, La Spezia April 1942 - 30.10.42 (fb)

Commanded by
KL Hans Heidtmann February 1941 - 30.10.42

Patrols: 10 Ships sunk: 4 (11,811 grt) + 1 damaged
1 sloop (1060 dt)

1. 4.6.41 Left to operate in the central North Atlantic.

U 559 was ordered to the Denmark Strait, with U 79, to support the cruiser *Lützow*, if a planned breakout by the latter took place. The two boats were taken off this duty after the breakout attempt failed during the night of the 12/13th.

From 1.6.41 *West* group had been stationed in the western Atlantic but sinkings were only of independents, with convoys being re-routed to avoid the group. From the 20th the *West* boats moved into the central North Atlantic to operate in a loose formation. To cover a wider area, U 559 and a number of other boats were also ordered to operate in loose formation in the central North Atlantic. The operation was not a success and by the end of June the boats were moving eastwards.

U 559 put in to St Nazaire **5.7.41**

2. 26.7.41 Left for Atlantic operations.

U 559 was one of a number of boats which were to form a new, more compact concentration in the central North Atlantic. On 2.8.41 U 204 made contact with northbound SL 81 and the first boat to close the convoy was U 559. On the 3rd several other boats came up but on that day and the 4th the escort prevented any attacks. In the early hours of the 5th three boats sank five ships. The operation ended on the 5th when all boats still in contact were driven off by aircraft and the surface escort.

Between the 6th and the 10th U 559 and other boats took part in two unsuccessful operations, having no success against HG 68 and then failing to find a reported southbound convoy. After this U 559,

U 559 (continued)

U 75, U 83, U 106 and U 204 assembled W of the North Channel.

On the 17th they were directed to southbound OG 71, reported by a Kondor of 1/KG 40. Outward-bound U 201 made contact in the evening and U 559, U 204 and outward-bound U 552 and U 564 also came up. U 559 torpedoed and sank the SS *Alva* (br 1584t) in the early hours of the 19th SW of Ireland. She claimed another ship sunk and one damaged. Between them the five boats sank eight ships and two escorts before the operation ended on the 23rd.

U 559 returned to St Nazaire **22.8.41**

3. 20.9.41 Left for the Mediterranean.

U 559 was one of the six Type VII boats of *Goeben* group, the first to be sent there. She passed through the Straits of Gibraltar during the night of the 25/26th.

The boat went to the Eastern Mediterranean to operate against shipping on the British supply routes between Alexandria and Tobruk. U 559 made unsuccesful attacks against steamers on October 4th and 10th and on the 18th she claimed a hit on a destroyer that was escorting three barges.

She put in to her new base at Salamis **20.10.41**

4. 24.11.41 Left for the Eastern Mediterranean.

U 559 sank the sloop HMAS *Parramatta* off Bardia on the 27th. The boat returned to Salamis **4.12.41**

5. 8.12.41 Left for operations.

U 559 had no success until the evening of the 23rd, when she torpedoed and sank the SS *Shuntien* (br 3059t) near Tobruk. In the same area on the 26th U 559 torpedoed the SS *Warszawa* (po 2487t). She did not sink and was finished off by U 559 in another attack five hours later. An attack on a convoy made by U 559 on the 28th was unsuccessful.

The boat returned to Salamis **31.12.41**

6. 16.2.42 Left for operations.

U 559 observed two hits on a previously-damaged ship near Bardia on the 21st. It was last seen listing at 45°. There is no confirmation of this.

The boat returned to Salamis **26.2.42**

7. 4.3.42 Left for operations. No details known.

U 559 returned to Salamis **21.3.42**

8. 24.3.42 Left Salamis and arrived Pola **27.3.42**

9. 10.5.42 Left Pola and returned **12.5.42**

10. 18.5.42 Left for operations.

U 559 operated against supply shipping in the Eastern Mediterranean. On 10.6.42 she encountered convoy AT 49 W of Alexandria and torpedoed two ships, sinking the tanker MV *Athene* (nw 4681t) and damaging the fleet oiler SS *Brambleleaf* (br 5917t) W of Alexandria.

The boat returned to Pola **22.6.42**

11. 15.8.42 Left Pola and arrived Salamis **21.8.42**

12. 29.8.42 Left for operations. No details known.

U 559 put in to Messina **21.9.42**

13. 29.9.42 Left for operations.

U 559 operated in the Eastern Mediterranean. On 30.10.42 the boat was located NNE of Port Said. She came under attack by the destroyers HMS *Dulverton* (Cdr W N Petch), *Hero* (Lt-Cdr W Scott), *Hurworth* (Lt D A Shaw), *Pakenham* (Capt E K B Stevens) and *Petard* (Lt-Cdr P C Egan) and a Wellesley of 47 Squadron. 288

depth-charges were dropped and the boat was forced to surface.

The crew abandoned ship and a specially-trained party from *Petard* went aboard. Codebooks and secret code material was taken off. The leader of the party, Lt F A B Fasson, and AB C Grazier, who were trying to recover the M4 cypher machine, went down with the boat when she sank.

Of U 559's crew, 8 men were lost and the commander and 37 men were made PoW.

U 560 Type VII C

Built by Blohm & Voss, Hamburg
Keel laid 1.2.40   Launched 10.1.41
Commissioned 6.3.41   Feldpost Nr M 35 195

Scuttled 3.5.45 at Kiel

Served with
24 U-Flottille, Danzig/Trondheim/Memel
                          March 1941 - November 1943 (ab)
22 U-Flottille, Gotenhafen November 1943 - February 1945 (sb)
31 U-Flottille, Hamburg/Kiel   March 1945 - 3.5.45 (ab)

Commanded by
OL Hansjürgen Zetzsche March - August 1941
OL Ernst Cordes August 1941 - July 1942
KL Konstantin von Rappard July 1942 - August 1943
OL Helmut Wicke August - December 1943
OL Paul Jacobs December 1943 - 3.5.45

Patrols: None   Ships sunk: None

In November 1941 U 560 sank after a collision off Memel. She was raised, put back into service and used as a training boat from 1942.

U 560 saw no operational service, being on training duties at 24, 22 and 31 U-Flottillen. She was scuttled at Kiel on 3.5.45 and broken up in 1946.

U 561 Type VII C

Built by Blohm & Voss, Hamburg
Keel laid 28.2.40   Launched 23.1.41
Commissioned 13.3.41   Feldpost Nr M 40 727

Sunk 12.7.43 in the Straits of Messina (38°16′N 15°39′E)

Served with
1 U-Flottille, Kiel/Brest March 1941 - January 1942 (ab/fb)
23 U-Flottille, Salamis January - September 1942 (fb)
29 U-Flottille, La Spezia October 1942 - 12.7.43 (fb)

Commanded by
KL Robert Bartels March 1941 - August 1942
KL Heinz Schomburg September 1942 - July 1943
OL Fritz Henning July 1943

Patrols: 15   Ships sunk: 6 (22,208 grt) + 1 damaged

1. 25.6.41 Left Kiel for the North Atlantic.

U 561 was one of fifteen boats operating singly over a large area in the central North Atlantic. From 15.7.41 they came together to form a much closer-knit group and moved to the northeast.

On the 17th a Kondor of 1/KG 40 sighted westbound OB 346 W of the North Channel. Although aircraft sighted it again on the 18th, the convoy did not come into contact with a patrol line of five boats formed on the 19th to intercept it. Another line of thirteen boats,

U 561 (continued)

including U 561, was also avoided on the 20th.

On the 24th U 561 was one of a number of boats directed to southbound convoy OG 69 W of Ireland. In the morning of the 28th she attacked the convoy, by then W of Cape Finisterre, sinking the SS *Wrotham* (br 1884t) and claiming a hit on a tanker, for which there is no confirmation. The pursuit of the convoy ended on the 29th, with seven ships sunk.

U 561 put in to her new base at Brest **1.8.41**

2. 20.8.41 Left for Atlantic operations.

U 561 went to the area W of the North Channel. On the 26th U 141 sighted southbound OS 4 W of Ireland but she was driven down by aircraft. U 557 and U 558 had some success against the convoy but U 561 did not make contact.

On 1.9.41 U 561 and other boats formed *Bosemüller* group W to SW of Ireland. The group was directed to convoy SL 84 but did not find it in bad visibility. Whilst searching, U 83 and U 557 sighted ships of OG 73 on the 2nd. *Kurfürst* group was already searching for this convoy and when it appeared that it had been found, *Bosemüller* combined with *Kurfürst* to form one group, which was then directed to attack OG 73. However, the group failed to find the convoy and also another one sighted by U 98 on the 3rd.

From the 11th U 561, U 95, U 98, U 558 and U 565 moved to an area NW of the Hebrides. Convoys were located by aircraft on the 14th, 15th and 18th but the boats did not find them, except for U 98 which sank one ship from SC 42 on the 16th.

U 561 put in to Lorient **20.9.41**

3. 1.11.41 Left for the North Atlantic.

Outward-bound, U 561 sank two stragglers from eastbound convoy SC 53 in the central North Atlantic, the SS *Meridian* (pa 5592t) on the 11th and the SS *Crusader* (pa 2939t) on the 14th.

U 561 met up with U 652 NW of the Azores and from the 17th to the 23rd they escorted the returning *Schiff 45/Komet* as far as the Bay of Biscay. U 652 was ordered to the Mediterranean and U 561 returned to Brest **26.11.41**

4. 3.1.42 Left for the Mediterranean.

U 561, U 73 and U 572 were ordered to wait off the coast of Spain for a new moon before attempting the Straits of Gibraltar. U 73 passed through during the night of the 13/14th, U 561 during the night of the 14/15th but U 572 failed in two attempts.

U 561 put in to Messina **22.1.42**

5. 26.1.42 Left for operations.

U 561 went to the Eastern Mediterranean. On 4.2.42 she unsuccessfully attacked a steamer near Tobruk.

She put in to Pola **20.2.42**

6. 4.4.42 Left for operations.

U 561 laid mines off Port Said on the 15th, which resulted in the sinking of the SS *Mount Olympos* (gr 6692t) and the SS *Hav* (nw 5062t) on 14.5.42. The SS *Fred* (gr 4063t) was damaged by a mine the same day.

U 561 returned to Pola **5.5.42**

7. 11.6.42 Left for operations.

U 561 laid mines off Port Said on the 20th. There are no known sinkings or damage to ships attributed to these mines.

The boat put in to Messina **25.6.42**

8. 2.7.42 Left for operations.

U 561 laid more mines off Port Said on the 9th. Again, there are no known sinkings or damage attributed to these mines.

The boat put in to La Spezia **24.7.42**

9. 9.9.42 Left La Spezia and arrived Messina **11.9.42**

10. 12.9.42 Left for the Eastern Mediterranean.

U 561 claimed a schooner sunk by gunfire off the coast of Syria on the 20th but details are not known. The sailing vessel *Sphinx* (eg 39t) was sunk by gunfire near Haifa on the 24th.

U 561 returned to La Spezia **4.10.42**

11. 7.11.42 Left for the Western Mediterranean.

Whilst U 561 was en route to join other boats waiting west of a line from the Balearics to Algiers, the Allies landed in North Africa.

In the morning of the 10th U 561 unsuccessfully attacked an escort-carrier near Algiers, possibly HMS *Argus*.

U 561 returned to La Spezia **14.11.42**

12. 25.11.42 Left for operations. No details known.

U 561 returned to Messina **18.12.42**

13. 23.12.42 Left for the Eastern Mediterranean.

U 561 attacked a destroyer off Cyprus on the 31st, hearing two detonations but apparently without result.

She returned to Pola **15.1.43**

14. 11.3.43 Left for operations.

U 561 patrolled off the coast of Algeria but had no success. She put in to Toulon **28.3.43**

15. 22.4.43 Left for operations.

U 561 patrolled off Algiers, without success. She returned to Toulon **3.6.43**

16. 10.7.43 Left for operations, with a new commander.

U 561 was on her way to operate against Allied shipping taking part in the invasion of Sicily when she was sunk on the 12th in the Straits of Messina, torpedoed by the British MTB 81.

Of U 561's crew, 42 men were lost and the commander and 4 men were picked up by German forces.

U 562   Type VII C

Built by Blohm & Voss, Hamburg
Keel laid 27.2.40   Launched 24.1.41
Commissioned 20.3.41   Feldpost Nr M 40 608

Sunk 19.2.43 NNE of Benghazi (32°57′N 20°54′E)

Served with
1 U-Flottille, Kiel/Brest March - November 1941 (ab/fb)
29 U-Flottille, La Spezia January 1942 - 19.2.43 (fb)

Commanded by
OL Herwig Collman March - September 1941
KL Horst Hamm September 1941 - 19.2.43

Patrols: 10   Ships sunk: 6 (37,287 grt) + 1 damaged

1. 19.6.41 Left Kiel for the North Atlantic.

U 562 was one of a number of boats sent to operate in a loose formation over a wide area of the central North Atlantic. It was hoped that they would find convoys, re-routed to miss *West* group.

On the 23rd U 203 sighted eastbound HX 133 S of Greenland. After sinking one ship, she lost contact. On the 26th U 201, U 556 and U 564 found the convoy. U 562 was one of the boats which later came up with HX 133 but she made no attacks on the convoy before the boats in contact were driven off on the 28th. Although a Kondor of 1/KG 40 sighted the convoy again on the 29th, there was no further U-boat action against it. Six ships were sunk and another damaged in the operation. U 556 and U 651 were lost.

The boats continued to patrol in the central North Atlantic but from 15.7.41 they came together to form a much closer-knit group and moved to the northeast.

On the 17th a Kondor of 1/KG 40 sighted westbound OB 346 W of the North Channel. Although aircraft sighted the convoy again on the 18th, it did not come into contact with a patrol line of five boats formed on the 19th to intercept it. Another line of thirteen boats, including U 562, was also avoided on the 20th.

On the 24th U 562 was one of a number of boats directed to southbound OG 69. The convoy was sighted by aircraft on the 26th and early on the 27th U 79 and U 203 made successful attacks. U 562, U 68 and U 126 came up on the 27th and the operation continued until the 29th, when the last of the boats in contact were driven off. Seven ships had been sunk, none by U 562.

She put in to Lorient **30.7.41**

2. 25.8.41   Left for Atlantic operations.

U 562 joined other boats to form *Bosemüller* group on 1.9.41 WSW of Ireland. The boat developed mechanical trouble and she put in to Brest **3.9.41**

3. 11.9.41   Left for the North Atlantic, with a new commander.

U 562 joined *Brandenburg* group SE of Greenland, formed from the 18th. On this day U 74 sighted eastbound SC 44 but because of radio interference any form of organised attack could not be carried out and only four boats responded to the sighting report, U 562, U 94, U 373 and U 552. Between them, U 74 and U 552 sank four ships and a corvette. U 562, U 94 and U 373 had no success.

In the early hours of the 22nd U 562 torpedoed and sank an independent, the SS *Erna III* (br 1590t) ENE of Cape Farewell. The *Brandenburg* boats were ordered to form a new patrol line SE of Cape Farewell. After some of them began returning to base, the group was dissolved on the 26th.

On 2.10.41 U 562 sank the CAM ship SS *Empire Wave* (br 7463t) of westbound convoy ON 19, E of Cape Farewell.

She returned to Brest **15.10.41**

4. 17.11.41   Left for the Mediterranean.

U 562 passed through the Straits of Gibraltar during the night of the 27/28th. She took up a position off the coast of Morocco and in the early hours of 2.12.41 she sank the SS *Grelhead* (br 4274t) just off Punta Negri.

The boat put in to Messina **6.12.41**

5. 6.12.41   Left for the Eastern Mediterranean.

U 562 patrolled off the coasts of Egypt and Cyrenaica. On the 23rd she attacked a convoy near Tobruk, missing an escort, and on the 24th she unsuccessfully attacked a steamer.

The boat put in to Pola **29.12.41**

6. 4.4.42   Left for operations.

U 562 laid mines off Famagusta on the 13th, resulting in two sinkings on the 29th, the sailing vessel *Terpsithea* (br 157t) and the steam tug *Alliance* (br 81t), which was towing her.

U 562 returned to Pola **11.5.42**

7. 22.6.42   Left for operations.

U 562 went to the Eastern Mediterranean. On 14.7.42 she torpedoed and damaged the tanker MV *Adinda* (nl 3359t) off Sidon.

The boat put in to La Spezia **25.7.42**

8. 5.9.42   Left for operations.

U 562 operated in the Eastern Mediterranean, without success. She returned to La Spezia **18.10.42**

9. 22.11.42   Left for the Western Mediterranean.

U 562 made an unsuccessful attack on a destroyer on 9.12.42. She encountered convoy KMF 5 on the 21st and torpedoed the troop transport SS *Strathallan* (br 23722t) N of Cap Ferrat, Algeria. The

vessel, which was carrying 4656 troops and nurses and 466 crew, sank next day whilst under tow. 6 of her crew were lost and 2 army officers. The *Strathallan* may also have been hit by a torpedo from an aircraft.

On the 23rd the returning U 562 unwittingly entered a prohibited area, east of the Spanish and south of the French coasts, which was allocated to anti-submarine activities by the Luftwaffe. In the morning of the 23rd U 562 was attacked by German aircraft with depth-charges and machine-gun fire. Damage is unknown.

U 562 reached La Spezia **24.12.42**

10. 7.2.43   Left for the Eastern Mediterranean.

U 562 was sighted and attacked on the 19th NNE of Benghazi by a Wellington of 38 Squadron (F/O I B Butler) in the vicinity of convoy XT 3. The boat was sunk in depth-charge attacks by the destroyers HMS *Hursley* (Lt W J C Church) and *Isis* (Cdr B Jones). There were no survivors, 49 dead.

U 563   Type VII C

Built by Blohm & Voss, Hamburg
Keel laid 30.3.40   Launched 5.2.41
Commissioned 27.3.41   Feldpost Nr M 40 564

Sunk 31.5.43 NNW of Cape Ortegal (46°35´N 10°40´W)

Served with
1 U-Flottille, Kiel/Brest March 1941 - 31.5.43 (ab/fb)

Commanded by
OL Klaus Bargsten March 1941 - March 1942
KL Götz von Hartmann March 1942 - April 1943
OL Gustav Borchardt April 1943 - 31.5.43

Patrols: 8   Ships sunk: 3 (14,689 grt) + 2 damaged
                            1 destroyer (1960 dt)

1. 10.7.41   Left Kiel and arrived Helsingör **10.7.41**

2. 27.7.41   Left Helsingör and arrived Bergen **28.7.41**

3. 31.7.41   Left for the North Atlantic.

U 563 became one of a number of boats which were operating in a loose formation SW of Iceland. On 12.8.41 U 129 sighted a westbound convoy and U 563, U 206 and U 567 were directed to it but failed to find it.

The boats continued to patrol S and SW of Iceland but did not find any convoys. From 1.9.41 U 563 was with *Kurfürst* group W of the North Channel. The group was directed to southbound OG 73, which was sighted on the 1st by a Kondor of 1/KG 40. The convoy was found by U 83 and U 557 of *Bosemüller* group on the 2nd, whilst they were searching for convoy SL 84.

As OG 73 had apparently been found, *Kurfürst* and *Bosemüller* groups combined to attack the convoy but it was not found again, nor was another sighted by U 98 on the 3rd.

U 563 put in to her new base at Brest **10.9.41**

4. 4.10.41   Left for Atlantic operations.

Outward-bound, U 563 and other boats were directed to southbound OG 75. The convoy had been sighted by Kondors on the 2nd W of the North Channel and again daily until the 7th, by which time it was near Cape Finisterre. The boats directed to the convoy failed to close.

OG 75 was sighted again on the 8th but contact was lost next day. U 563 finally came up with the convoy on the 12th but was driven down by an aircraft. A corvette of the escort was sunk early on the 14th by U 206, OG 75's only loss.

U 563 (continued)

U 563 patrolled W of Gibraltar from the 17th, as part of *Breslau* group. The awaited departure of convoy HG 75 took place on the 22nd and contact was made by U 71 soon after midnight on the 23rd. U 563 came up soon afterwards and made an attack SW of Cape St Vincent, torpedoing the destroyer HMS *Cossack*, which sank under tow on the 27th. Operations against the convoy continued until the 28th and four merchant ships were sunk and another damaged. U 563 made further attacks on the convoy and escorts but had no success. With all torpedoes gone, she headed for home.

The boat returned to Brest **1.11.41**

5. 29.11.41 Left for Atlantic operations.

U 563 was attacked and damaged on 1.12.41 W of Brest by a Whitley of 502 Squadron (F/O W W Cave).

She put in to Lorient **3.12.41**

6. 21.1.42 Left Lorient, in transit to Norway.

U 563 put in to Bergen **3.2.42**

7. 7.2.42 Left Bergen and arrived Hamburg **11.2.42**

8. 19.4.42 Left Hamburg and arrived Kiel **20.4.42**

9. 1.10.42 Left Kiel to resume operations in the North Atlantic.

U 563 joined *Panther* group, formed from the 8th 700 to 800 miles W of the North Channel. In the evening of the 11th U 620 sighted ONS 136 and eight boats in the centre of the long *Panther* patrol line were detached to attack the convoy, as *Leopard* group.

On the 16th U 704 sighted ON 137 passing through the southern section of the *Panther* line and eleven boats of the group were ordered to attack. From the remaining *Panther* boats, *Puma* group was formed on the 16th from U 563 and seven others and ordered southwards to seek ONS 138.

By the 22nd the boats were nearly 400 miles south of their original *Puma* line position. On that day the southernmost boat in the line, U 443, sighted ON 139 in the central North Atlantic. The group was ordered to close and attack but the boats were unable to catch the convoy, which was averaging 10 to 12 knots. Only U 443 was able to attack and she sank two ships.

Puma group moved westwards until the 24th, when U 606 reported two destroyers which could have been part of an escort for a westbound ONS convoy. The boats moved northwestwards at high speed to intercept. On the 26th U 436 sighted eastbound HX 212 in the centre of the patrol line. She shadowed and brought up other boats but all were driven off by the escort. On the 28th boats in contact were driven off by Iceland-based aircraft of 120 Squadron. When the same happened on the 29th the operation was abandoned. Despite the difficulty in making attacks, six ships were sunk and another damaged, none by U 563, although she did make attacks.

She returned to Brest **6.11.42**

10. 9.12.42 Left for the eastern Atlantic.

Outward-bound, U 563 torpedoed and sank the SS *Bretwalda* (br 4906t) on the 18th W of Cape Ortegal. From the 19th until the 23rd U 563 operated with boats of *Westwall* group, searching for Mediterranean-bound convoys 200 to 300 miles W of Spain.

U 563 was ordered to join *Falke* group W of Ireland, where it was awaiting an ON convoy. The group was sent against ONS 158 and ON 159 but both were re-routed and avoided the boats.

From 7.1.43 *Falke* group swept westwards, searching for convoys. U 563 left the group soon after this.

She returned to Brest **14.1.43**

11. 20.3.43 Left for the north Atlantic.

U 563 joined *Löwenherz* group, formed from 3.4.43 SE of Greenland. On the 4th eastbound HX 231 was sighted to the west of the patrol line. Conditions were favourable and the pursuit of the

convoy continued until the 7th, with six ships sunk and four damaged. In the morning of the 5th U 563 torpedoed and damaged a straggler ESE of Cape Farewell, the tanker MV *Sunoil* (am 9005t), which was sunk the same evening by U 530. The constant presence of carrier-borne aircraft had made attacks very difficult and on the 7th two of U 563's crew had been lost overboard during an aircraft attack on the boat.

Most of the *Löwenherz* boats, including U 563, formed a new patrol line, *Lerche*, SE of Cape Farewell from the 10th, to intercept eastbound HX 232. The convoy passed through the line on the 11th and in the early morning of the 12th U 563 torpedoed three ships, sinking the MV *Pacific Grove* (br 7117t) and the SS *Ulysses* (nl 2666t) and damaging the MV *Fresno City* (br 7261t), which was sunk by U 706 in the afternoon. Further attacks on the convoy were prevented by aircraft. The operation ended W of the North Channel on the 13th, after which five *Lerche* boats were refuelled by U 487 in the central North Atlantic. Of the other *Lerche* boats, U 203, U 532 and U 706 joined *Meise* group and U 191 and U 563 were refuelled by U 462 N of the Azores.

U 563 returned to Brest **18.4.43**

12. 29.5.43 Left for Atlantic operations.

Outward-bound, U 563 was attacked and damaged by a Halifax of 58 Squadron (W/Cdr W E Oulton) on the 31st NNW of Cape Ortegal. The boat's destruction was completed by two Sunderlands, one from 10 (RAAF) Squadron (F/Lt M S Mainprize) and the other from 228 Squadron (F/O W M French).

There were no survivors, 53 dead.

U 564   Type VII C

Built by Blohm & Voss, Hamburg
Keel laid 30.3.40   Launched 7.2.41
Commissioned 3.4.41   Feldpost Nr M 40 175

Sunk 14.6.43 NW of Cape Finisterre (44°17′N 10°25′W)

Served with
1 U-Flottille, Kiel/Brest   April 1941 - 14.6.43 (ab/fb)

Commanded by
KK Reinhard Suhren   April 1941 - September 1942
OL Hans Fiedler   September 1942 - 14.6.43

Patrols: 9   Ships sunk: 18 (95,544 grt) + 5 damaged
1 corvette (925 dt)

On 22.5.41 U 564 rescued the crew of a German aircraft that had ditched in the Baltic.

1. 17.6.41 Left Kiel for the North Atlantic.

U 564 was one of a number of boats which were to operate in a loose formation in the central North Atlantic. On the 23rd U 203 sighted eastbound HX 133 S of Greenland but after sinking one ship she lost contact.

On the 26th U 564, U 201 and U 556 came up with the convoy. In the early hours of the 27th U 564 torpedoed three ships from the convoy E of Cape Farewell, sinking the SS *Maasdam* (nl 8812t) and the MV *Malaya II* (br 8651t) and damaging the tanker MV *Kongsgaard* (nw 9467t).

On the 28th all boats in contact were driven off, with the exception of U 651. After sinking a ship soon after midnight, she was herself sunk by the escort. Although a Kondor of 1/KG 40 sighted the convoy again on the 29th, there was no further U-boat action against it. Six ships were sunk and another two damaged.

The boats continued to patrol in the central North Atlantic. In the evening of the 29th U 564 torpedoed and sank the independent

SS *Hekla* (ice 1215t) S of Cape Farewell. In mid-July very few ships were seen and the boats were ordered to move northeastwards and to operate in a much closer-knit formation.

On the 17th, before the boats were in position, a Kondor sighted westbound OB 346 W of the North Channel. The convoy was sighted again on the 18th and a line, made up of the five nearest boats, was formed ahead of it for the 19th. This line was avoided, as was one of thirteen boats, which included U 564, formed on the 20th.

Before she headed home, U 564 was briefly with boats directed to convoy OG 69 but she made no contact.

The boat put in to her new base at Brest **27.7.41**

2. 16.8.41 Left for Atlantic operations.

Outward-bound, U 564 was directed to southbound OG 71, sighted by a Kondor W of Spain on the 17th. U 564 was one of several directed boats which did not find the convoy. She did not come up with it until the afternoon of the 22nd, when she reported to U 201, which closed.

In the late evening U 564 sank two ships W of Oporto, the steam tug *Empire Oak* (br 484t) and the SS *Clonlara* (br 1203t). Early on the 23rd U 564 torpedoed and damaged the SS *Spind* (nw 2129t), which was sunk three hours later by U 552.

In an early morning attack on the 23rd, U 564 sank the corvette HMS *Zinnia* of the escort. In the same attack U 564 claimed two ships of the convoy sunk but there is no confirmation of this.

Probably out of torpedoes, U 564 returned to Brest **27.8.41**

3. 16.9.41 Left for Atlantic operations.

U 564 joined *Brandenburg* group, in a patrol line SE of Cape Farewell. After some of the boats began returning to base, the group was dissolved on the 26th.

On 4.10.41 U 564 and other boats were directed to southbound OG 75 but it was not found. The convoy was found again by reconnaissance aircraft on the 8th but contact was lost again next day. A further sighting was made on the 10th but by then the convoy was too far ahead to be caught.

U 564 was refuelled by the German supply ship *Thalia* in Cadiz harbour during the night of the 14/15th. She then joined other boats W of Gibraltar to await the departure of northbound HG 75. From the 17th U 564 was waiting W of Gibraltar, as part of *Breslau* group. The northbound convoy sailed on the 22nd and was sighted by U 71 late on the 23rd. In the early morning of the 24th U 564 torpedoed and sank three ships, the SS *Carsbreck* (br 3670t), the SS *Ariosto* (br 2176t) and the SS *Alhama* (br 1352t).

U 564 and U 71 kept contact but U 563 and U 564 made unsuccessful attacks during the night of the 26/27th. The returning U 432 came up and sank one ship. With all torpedoes gone, the three boats headed home.

U 564 put in to Lorient **1.11.41**

4. 11.1.42 Left Lorient and arrived La Pallice **12.1.42**

5. 18.1.42 Left for the Western Atlantic.

U 564 went to the Newfoundland area and then went southwards. On 11.2.42 she sank the tanker MV *Victolite* (br 11410t) NNW of Bermuda by torpedo and gunfire and on the 16th, 200 miles to the northeast, the tanker MV *Opalia* was attacked and slightly damaged by gunfire.

On the 16th U 564 received fuel from U 107 for return to base. The boat reached Brest **6.3.42**

6. 4.4.42 Left for the US east coast.

Outward-bound, U 564 was refuelled by U 459 on or about the 27th 500 miles NE of Bermuda. In early May U 564 began a run of success. On the 3rd she sank the SS *Ocean Venus* (br 7147t) E of Cape Canaveral, on the 4th the tanker SS *Eclipse* (br 9767t) was torpedoed and damaged E of Delray Beach, Florida and on the 5th the SS *Delisle* (am 3478t) was damaged off Juno Beach, Florida.

Both these vessels were towed in and repaired.

On the 8th the SS *Ohioan* (am 6078t) was sunk and on the 9th the tanker MV *Lubrafol* (pa 7138t), both off Delray Beach. The last sinking on this patrol was the tanker SS *Potrero del Llano* (me 4000t), torpedoed and sunk on the 14th off Sands Key, Florida. As a neutral ship, she was fully lit up, with spotlights illuminating the Mexican flag. 13 of her crew were lost.

U 564 returned to Brest **6.6.42**

7. 9.7.42 Left for the Caribbean area.

In the morning of the 18th the returning U 126 sighted northbound OS 34 N of the Azores. With all torpedoes gone, she called up U 108, U 564 and U 654, all outward-bound. U 564 attacked the convoy early on the 19th, sinking the SS *Empire Hawksbill* (br 5724t) and the MV *Lavington Court* (br 5372t). These were the only losses suffered by the convoy. The four boats were driven off later on the 19th and resumed their journeys.

U 564 and U 654 were refuelled in late July by U 463 W of the Azores. U 564 had no further success until 19.8.42, when she encountered convoy TAW (S) just W of Grenada, sinking the tanker SS *British Consul* (br 6940t) and the SS *Empire Cloud* (br 5969t). On the 30th, just N of Tobago, she sank the tanker MV *Vardaas* (nw 8176t) by torpedo and gunfire.

U 564 returned to Brest **18.9.42**

8. 27.10.42 Left for Atlantic operations.

U 564 and other outward-bound boats joined *Natter* group, formed on 1.11.42 W of Ireland. The boats moved southwards to form a line for the 5th. U 92 sighted westbound convoy ON 143 on the 4th but with none of the other *Natter* boats in position to give support she lost contact. A search was made when the other boats came up but when the convoy had not been found by the 6th the operation was called off. The only successes were two stragglers sunk by U 566 and U 613 during the afternoon of the 7th, after U-tanker U 117, en route to a replenishment area, sighted ON 143 further to the west and reported, enabling four boats to close.

On the 8th all *Natter* boats with sufficient fuel, which included U 564, were ordered to proceed at high speed towards Gibraltar because of the Allied landings in North Africa.

U 564 operated W of Gibraltar with *Westwall* group, which during November had little success but was at great risk, particularly from Gibraltar-based aircraft. On the 26th it was decided that the *Westwall* boats should be moved from the 27th to an area W of the Azores, to meet eastbound UGS convoys beyond the range of land-based aircraft.

On the 28th U 564 was refuelled by U 118 SE of the Azores. The group moved west as far as longitude 40°W, reached on 6.12.42. After six days, with no convoys sighted, the *Westwall* boats moved eastwards again, towards Spain and Portugal. The group dispersed on the 16th and carried out a search W of Portugal from the 19th to the 23rd but with no convoys found, the boats headed home.

U 564 reached Brest **30.12.42**

9. 11.3.43 Left for the North Atlantic.

U 564 joined *Seeteufel* group, formed from the 21st S of Iceland to operate against westbound convoy ONS 1. On the 22nd the group moved westwards and on the 26th was in the path of approaching, eastbound HX 230. In the afternoon of that day U 564 sighted masts and an aircraft carrier in the centre of the patrol line but aircraft and surface vessels prevented the convoy's direction being determined. It was thought to be an ON convoy and was not pursued.

Instead, it was decided that *Seeteufel* should continue to concentrate its efforts on HX 230, which was sighted by U 305 of *Seewolf* group on the 27th. However, the prevailing storm developed into a hurricane on the 28th and only five boats from the two groups were able to make brief contact with the convoy. Although torpedo attacks were vitually impossible in the heavy seas, the boats continued to pursue, in the hope that stragglers would be found.

U 564 (continued)

found. Only one ship was sunk during the operation, which ended on the 30th.

U 564 and other *Seeteufel* boats joined some new-arrivals to form *Löwenherz* group SE of Greenland from 3.4.43. On the 4th eastbound HX 231 was sighted to the west of the patrol line. The operation against the convoy lasted three days, with six ships sunk and others possibly damaged. U 564 had no success.

She put in to Bordeaux **15.4.43**

10. 15.5.43 Left Bordeaux and returned **17.5.43**

11. 31.5.43 Left Bordeaux and returned **3.6.43**

12. 9.6.43 Left for operations.

U 564 was one of five outward-bound boats, with U 159, U 185, U 415 and U 634, travelling in company across the Bay of Biscay.

In the evening of the 13th they were sighted by a Sunderland of 228 Squadron (F/O L B Lee) 250 miles W of Cape Finisterre. Lee carried out a depth-charge attack, straddling U 564, in the face of heavy flak and was shot down into the sea, with the entire crew being lost. U 564 was possibly assisted in shooting down the aircraft by the outward-bound U 358.

The damaged U 564 headed back, escorted by U 185. In the afternoon of the 14th the two boats were sighted by a Whitley of 10 OTU (Sgt A Benson). After waiting two hours for another 10 OTU Whitley to arrive, Benson was given permission to attack on his own. He severely damaged U 564 but his aircraft was badly damaged by flak and was later ditched in the sea after one engine failed. The crew was picked up by the French fishing boat *Jazz Band* and landed at a village south of Brest and made PoW.

U 185 attempted to take U 564 in tow but this was unsuccessful and she sank. U 185 picked up U 564's commander and 17 other survivors and put them aboard German destroyers *Z 24* and *Z 25* in the evening of the 14th, before resuming her journey westwards.

Of U 564's crew, 29 men were lost.

U 565   Type VII C

Built by Blohm & Voss, Hamburg
Keel laid 30.3.40   Launched 20.2.41
Commissioned 10.4.41   Feldpost Nr M 41 992

Scuttled 29.9.44 at Piraeus, Greece

Served with
1 U-Flottille, Kiel/Brest April - November 1941 (ab/fb)
29 U-Flottille, La Spezia December 1941 - 29.9.44 (fb)

Commanded by
OL Johann Jebsen April 1941 - March 1942
KL Wilhelm Franken March 1942 - October 1943
KL Fritz Henning October 1943 - 29.9.44

Patrols: 20   Ships sunk: 4 (11,347 grt) + 3 damaged
                                1 cruiser (5750 dt)
                                1 destroyer (1540 dt)
                                1 submarine (715 dt)

1. 19.6.41 Left Kiel and arrived Trondheim **23.6.41**

2. 8.7.41 Left for Atlantic operations.

U 565 went to the central North Atlantic to join boats which were operating there in a loose formation over a wide area. In mid-July very few ships were seen and so the boats were ordered to move northeastwards and to operate in a much closer-knit group.

On the 17th, before the boats were in position, a Kondor of

1/KG 40 sighted westbound OB 346 W of the North Channel. Although aircraft saw it on the 18th, the convoy did not come into contact with a patrol line of five boats formed on the 19th to intercept it. Another line of thirteen boats, including U 565, was also avoided on the 20th.

Between the 24th and 26th U 565 took part in a failed operation against convoy SL 80 SW of Ireland. On 2.8.41 U 204 sighted northbound SL 81 and she was able to bring up U 565 and other boats to the convoy on the 3rd. The escort was strong and prevented any attacks being made before the early hours of the 5th, when five ships were sunk. All boats still in contact were driven off in daylight on the 5th and the operation ended.

U 565 put in to her new base at Brest **6.8.41**

3. 1.9.41 Left for Atlantic operations.

From the 11th U 565 was with five other boats, U 95, U 98, U 557, U 558 and U 561, in an area NW of the Hebrides. Convoys were located by air reconnaissance on the 14th, 15th and 18th but the boats did not find them.

Searches for convoys or independent ships were carried out as far as 15°W but U 565 had no success. She was the last of the six boats to return to base.

She put in to Lorient **7.10.41**

4. 3.11.41 Left for the Mediterranean.

U 565 was part of *Arnauld* group, with U 81, U 205 and U 433. She passed through the Straits of Gibraltar during the night of the 15/16th. She remained E of Gibraltar until beginning a move eastwards on the 18th.

The boat operated against shipping between Alexandria and Tobruk but had no success.

U 565 put in to La Spezia **25.12.41**

5. 21.1.42 Left for the Eastern Mediterranean.

U 565 again operated against supply shipping, without success. On 9.3.42 British Force B sailed from Alexandria to intercept a damaged Italian cruiser, reported as torpedoed, and to meet warships coming from Malta. The returning Force B was sighted by U 565 on the 11th NNE of Sidi Barrani. In an evening attack, she torpedoed and sank the cruiser HMS *Naiad*, the flagship of the Force, with the loss of 82 of her crew.

U 565 returned to La Spezia **17.3.42**

6. 11.4.42 Left for the Eastern Mediterranean.

On the 23rd U 565 was operating against supply traffic to Tobruk when she torpedoed and sank the SS *Kirkland* (br 1361t) in convoy TA 36 returning to Alexandria. She was sunk between Sollum and Matruh.

U 565 put in to Salamis **30.4.42**

7. 7.5.42 Left for operations.

On 2.6.42 U 565 was attacked by a Blenheim of 203 Squadron but escaped undamaged. U 565 had no success against supply shipping to and from Tobruk. She returned to La Spezia **10.6.42**

8. 9.7.42 Left for the Eastern Mediterranean.

U 565 patrolled off the coast of Palestine. On 3.8.42 she sank a sailing vessel by gunfire.

The boat returned to Salamis **4.8.42**

9. 16.8.42 Left for operations. No details known.

U 565 returned to La Spezia **25.8.42**

10. 31.8.42 Left for operations. No details known.

U 565 returned to La Spezia **4.9.42**

11. 25.10.42 Left for the Western Mediterranean.

On the 29th U 565 made an unsuccessful torpedo attack on the aircraft carrier HMS *Furious*, reporting four hits, with no result.

From 5.11.42 U 565 was one of a large number of boats stationed to the west of a line running from the Balearics to Algiers. They were awaiting developments expected to follow the large concentration of shipping at Gibraltar.

After the landings in North Africa on the 8th, U-boat activity against Allied shipping intensified but U 565 was not involved.

She returned to La Spezia **13.11.42**

12. 23.11.42 Left for the Western Mediterranean.

U 565 patrolled off the Algerian coast. On 18.12.42 she torpedoed and sank the destroyer HMS *Partridge* off Oran and on the 22nd she encountered convoy KMF 5 just N of the Golfe de Bejaïa and torpedoed and damaged the SS *Cameronia* (br 16297t).

The boat returned to La Spezia **1.1.43**

13. 14.2.43 Left for operations.

U 565 again patrolled off the Algerian coast. On the 24th she torpedoed and damaged the SS *Nathanael Green* (am 7176t) 40 miles NE of Oran. This vessel was later hit by an aircraft torpedo. She was towed into harbour but declared to be a total loss.

On the 27th U 565 torpedoed and damaged the tanker MV *Seminole* (br 10389t) from convoy TE 16, ESE of Malaga.

The boat returned to La Spezia **5.3.43**

14. 8.4.43 Left for the Western Mediterranean.

On the 20th U 565 attacked convoy UGS 7 ENE of Oran, sinking the SS *Sidi-Bel-Abbès* (fr 4392t) and the SS *Michigan* (am 5594t). She reported a probable hit on a tanker on 1.5.43 WNW of Alboran.

U 565 returned to La Spezia **12.5.43**

15. 17.6.43 Left for operations. No details known.

U 565 put in to Toulon **23.7.43**

16. 7.9.43 Left for operations.

U 565 operated against Allied shipping at the Salerno bridgehead. On the 12th she reported hits on an LCT S of Salerno and on the 24th she claimed three hits on a southbound convoy 65 miles S of Salerno.

The boat returned to Toulon **1.10.43**

17. 23.10.43 Left for operations.

On the 27th U 565 claimed a hit on a destroyer off western Sicily but there is no report of any warship damaged.

She returned to Salamis **4.11.43**

18. 6.11.43 Left for operations.

On or about the 19th the British submarine HMS *Simoom* was lost in the Karpathos Strait, W of Rhodes from an unknown cause. She may possibly have been sunk by U 565, which reported firing torpedoes soon after midnight on the 19th and hearing detonations.

The boat returned to Salamis **23.11.43**

19. 12.12.43 Left for operations. No details known.

U 565 returned to Salamis **27.12.43**

20. 15.2.44 Left for the Eastern Mediterranean.

U 565 was patrolling off the Libyan coast on 3.3.44. In an early attack she missed a corvette near Benghazi and in a morning attack on the same day she unsuccessfully attacked a cruiser, hearing only two end of run detonations.

The boat returned to Salamis **7.3.44**

21. 1.4.44 Left for operations. No details known.

U 565 returned to Salamis **2.5.44**

U 565 remained in dock at Salamis for the next three months and was probably being fitted with a schnorkel.

22. 26.8.44 Left for operations.

U 565 patrolled N of Crete until 10.9.44, when she was relieved by U 407. After September 1944 there were no further U-boat operations in the Mediterranean.

U 565 returned to Salamis **13.9.44**

On 24.9.44 U 565 was damaged in a USAF bombing raid on Piræus and five of her crew were killed. The damage was such that she was scuttled on the 29th, with three depth-charges.

U 566   Type VII C

Built by Blohm & Voss, Hamburg
Keel laid 30.3.40   Launched 20.2.41
Commissioned 17.4.41   Feldpost Nr M 42 015

Scuttled 24.10.43 W of Oporto (41°12´N 09°31´W)

Served with
1 U-Flottille, Kiel/Brest   April 1941 - 24.10.43 (ab/fb)

Commanded by
KL Dietrich Borchert   April 1941 - June 1942
OL Gerhard Remus   July 1942 - January 1943
KL Hans Hornkohl   January 1943 - 24.10.43

Patrols: 11   Ships sunk: 6 (38,092 grt)
                              1 gunboat (2265 dt)

1. 26.7.41 Left Trondheim and arrived Kirkenes **29.7.41**

2. 30.7.41 Left Kirkenes for Northern Waters.

From August 1st U 566 was patrolling off the Kola coast. She and U 451 were the first U-boats to operate in an area, which from January 1942 was to be the scene of many actions involving the Arctic convoys.

U 566 returned to Kirkenes **19.8.41**

3. 30.8.41 Left for Northern Waters.

U 566 again operated off the Kola coast. On 3.9.41 she made an unsuccessful attack on the British submarine HMS *Trident*, which was returning to Polyarnoe.

U 566 returned to Kirkenes **20.9.41**

4. 22.9.41 Left Kirkenes and arrived Bergen **27.9.41**

5. 29.9.41 Left Bergen and arrived Kiel **2.10.41**

6. 3.12.41 Left Kiel and arrived Kristiansand **4.12.41**

7. 9.12.41 Left, en route to Western France.

U 566 put in to Lorient **23.12.41**

8. 15.1.42 Left for the North Atlantic.

U 566 headed for the Newfoundland area. On the 31st U 82 sighted eastbound convoy NA 2 SSE of Sable Island. U 566, U 86 and U 575 were in the area but were unable to close because the convoy was too fast.

Early on 15.2.42 U 566 torpedoed and sank the SS *Meropi* (gr 4181t) off Halifax, a straggler from westbound convoy ON 60.

The boat put in to her new base at Brest **9.3.42**

9. 8.4.42 Left for operations in US waters.

Outward-bound, U 566 was reprovisioned in late April by U 459 500 miles NE of Bermuda. She went on to operate off New York and later in the Gulf of Maine but had no success.

U 566 joined seven other boats to form *Pfadfinder* group on

U 566 (continued)

21.5.42, 400 miles E of New York. Very few ships had been seen near the coast and the group's objective was to investigate passage of shipping between US east coast ports and Central and South America and find out how far its routes were from the coast. The group dispersed after a few days and most of the boats moved closer to the coast. U 566 moved southwards.

On 1.6.42 she sank the SS *Westmoreland* (br 8967t) by torpedo and gunfire NNE of Bermuda. In mid-June the returning boat was refuelled by U 459 W of the Azores.

U 566 returned to Brest **30.6.42**

10. 6.8.42 Left for operations in the Freetown area, as part of *Blücher* group.

U 566, U 214, U 594 and U 653 arrived in the assembly area SE of the Azores from the 13th. Before the other three boats arrived, U 653 sighted northbound SL 118 entering the assembly area. The boats began to shadow the convoy but the escort prevented any attacks until the evening of the 17th, when U 566 torpedoed and sank the MV *Triton* (nw 6607t) E of the Azores. She also claimed a hit on a second ship. An attack was made on SL 118 the next evening by U 214 but increased air cover made further attacks more difficult and the operation ended on the 20th, after contact was lost. Four ships had been sunk and one damaged.

U 566 took surplus fuel from U 653, which was returning to base. U 566, U 214 and U 406 then moved to an area NE of the Azores, where they were joined by U 107 and became *Iltis* group from the 23rd. The four boats moved southwards and on the 25th U 214 sighted northbound SL 119 W of Lisbon. The other *Iltis* boats and those of *Eisbär* group were directed to the convoy. In the evening of the 28th U 566 torpedoed two ships, the SS *Zuiderkerk* (nl 8424t) and the SS *City of Cardiff* (br 5661t) WNW of Lisbon. The *Zuiderkerk* was sunk by one of the escorts and the *City of Cardiff* sank next day.

During the attack on SL 119, U 566 was rammed whilst submerged. She was badly damaged and after temporary repairs had been made, she set out for home.

U 566 reached Brest **5.9.42**

11. 28.10.42 Left for the North Atlantic.

U 566 and other outward-bound boats joined *Natter* group W of Ireland on 3.11.42. The boats moved southwards to form a line for the 5th. U 92 sighted westbound ON 143 on the 4th but with none of the other boats in position to give support she lost contact.

A search was made when the other boats came up but when the convoy had not been found by the 6th the operation was called off. U 566 had one of the only two successes, when she torpedoed and sank a straggler, the SS *Glenlea* (br 4252t) in the central North Atlantic during the afternoon of the 7th. U 117 had sighted ON 143 further to the west and her report enabled four boats to close. The captain of the *Glenlea* was taken aboard U 566 as a prisoner.

On the 8th all *Natter* boats with sufficient fuel were ordered to proceed at high speed towards Gibraltar because of the Allied landings in North Africa.

U 566 operated W of Gibraltar with *Westwall* group, which in November had little success but was at great risk, particularly from Gibraltar-based aircraft. On the 17th U 566 was attacked and damaged by a Hudson of 233 Squadron (Sgt E H Smith).

The boat returned to Brest **1.12.42**

12. 6.2.43 Left for the North Atlantic.

U 566 joined *Neptun* group, formed from the 18th SW of Iceland, to operate against expected HX 226. The convoy was not found. It had been re-routed to pass north of the *Neptun* line.

On the 20th the group moved southwestwards. It was avoided by the re-routed SC 120 but U 759, at the northern end of the line, sighted HX 227 in the morning of the 27th and the *Neptun* boats pursued. Only U 405 was able to attack the convoy, with bad weather

preventing the other boats closing.

Whilst searching for HX 227, U 608 sighted approaching, westbound convoy ON 168 on 1.3.43 but after she was driven off and the convoy had not been found again by the 3rd the operation was abandoned.

From the 5th the *Neptun* boats took up waiting positions S of Cape Farewell and north of *Wildfang* and *Burggraf* groups. U 405 sighted eastbound SC 121 on the 6th and seventeen boats drawn from *Neptun, Wildfang* and *Burggraf* groups, were detached to pursue the convoy, as *Westmark* group. Another patrol line of eleven *Neuland* boats was formed from the 8th SE of Greenland ahead of the convoy and designated *Ostmark* group.

U 566 made contact during the night of the 6/7th. She shadowed but was driven off on the 9th by Liberators of 120 Squadron. The operation was carried out in stormy weather and despite heavy seas twelve ships were sunk and one damaged, without the loss of any boats. The action against SC 121 ended on the 11th near Rockall.

U 566 was briefly deployed against eastbound HX 228, sighted by U 336 of *Neuland* group on the 10th, but had no success. U 566 was refuelled N of the Azores by U 119 in mid-March.

She returned to Brest **25.3.43**

13. 24.4.43 Left for Atlantic operations.

Outward-bound, U 566 was attacked and damaged on the 26th by a Wellington of 172 Squadron (Sgt A Coumbis).

U 566 returned to Brest **28.4.43**

14. 5.7.43 Left for operations in US waters.

On the 29/30th U 566 is believed to have laid 12 MTB mines off Norfolk, Virginia but no trace of them has ever been recorded. On 2.8.43 the boat was sighted by a USN Mariner 250 miles E of Cape Henry but the aircraft's attack was unsuccessful.

U 566 was now the objective of an extensive but futile search by aircraft and surface vessels. On the 5th she was located by the gunboat USS *Plymouth*, which was escorting a convoy that had been sighted by U 566. The gunboat was torpedoed and sunk NE of Cape Hatteras, which started another search by aircraft and a blimp.

On the 7th U 566 was sighted on the surface and attacked by a USN Ventura of VB-128 (Lt F C Cross) E of Cape Charles. The aircraft was driven off, damaged, and crashed into the sea near its base. The pilot was drowned. A second Ventura attacked the boat but the bombs dropped did not detonate. This aircraft was shot down and its crew killed.

A Mariner appeared, U 566 dived but was forced to resurface by bombs. The aircraft carried out two more attacks and again the boat, was forced to resurface after diving. The boat's gunners held off the Mariner, two other aircraft and two blimps until darkness came and it submerged.

U 566 was later sighted, surfacing in the moonlight, by another Mariner but again she escaped. In the early hours of the 8th the boat was spotted by a Halifax-based Catalina SE of the Nantucket Shoals lightship. Three USN destroyer-escorts from Norfolk came up but U 566 escaped, with the aid of Aphrodite radar decoys.

U 566 returned to Brest **1.9.43**

15. 18.10.43 Left for the Mediterranean.

Outward-bound, U 566 was sighted in the early hours of the 24th by a Leigh Light Wellington of 179 Squadron (Sgt D M Cornish) W of Oporto. In the face of flak, the aircraft dropped six depth-charges and after two hours it returned to base, low on fuel and with a damaged tailplane.

After the attack, the boat had stopped and ceased firing. When Cornish returned to the scene later, no radar contact could be made. It was later discovered that U 566 was seriously damaged and unable to dive and was scuttled by her commander. The entire crew took to dinghies, was picked up by the Spanish trawler *Fina* and landed at Vigo. The men were eventually repatriated to France.

Sgt Cornish was awarded the DFM.

U 567   Type VII C

Built by Blohm & Voss, Hamburg
Keel laid 27.4.40   Launched 6.3.41
Commissioned 24.4.41   Feldpost Nr M 42 135

Sunk 21.12.41 NE of the Azores (44°02′N 20°10′W)

Served with
3 U-Flottille, Kiel/La Pallice   April - October 1941 (ab/fb)
7 U-Flottille, St Nazaire   October 1941 - 21.12.41 (fb)

Commanded by
KL Theodor Fahr   April - September 1941
KL Engelbert Endrass   September 1941 - 21.12.41

Patrols: 3   Ships sunk: 2 (6809 grt)

1. 5.8.41   Left Trondheim for the North Atlantic.

U 567 became one of a number of boats which were operating in a loose formation SW of Iceland. On the 12th U 129 sighted a westbound convoy and U 567, U 206 and U 563 were directed to it but failed to find it. The boats continued to patrol S and SW of Iceland but did not find any convoys. On the 28th U 567 and other boats were directed to an area S of Iceland to intercept eastbound HX 145 but they had no success.

From 1.9.41 U 567 was with *Kurfürst* group W of the North Channel. The group was directed to southbound OG 73, which was sighted on the 1st by a Kondor of 1/KG 40. The convoy was found by U 83 and U 557 of *Bosemüller* group on the 2nd, whilst they were searching for convoy SL 84.

As OG 73 had apparently been found, *Kurfürst* and *Bosemüller* groups combined to attack the convoy but it was not found again, nor was another sighted by U 98 on the 3rd.

U 567 sank an independent in the evening of the 3rd 750 miles W of Ireland, the MV *Fort Richepanse* (br 3485t). On the same day the boat had an engagement with a British submarine.

U 567 put in to St Nazaire **12.9.41**

2. 25.10.41   Left for the North Atlantic.

Outward-bound, U 567 was ordered on the 30th to join *Stosstrupp* group E of the Newfoundland Bank. On the 31st U 552 sighted eastbound HX 156 in the central North Atlantic. After sinking a destroyer of the escort, U 552 was driven off but U 567 came up and took over shadowing. Between them, the two boats maintained contact until 3.11.41. Both made unsuccessful attacks on the 1st.

U 567 and U 552 joined *Störtebecker* group in the central North Atlantic, probably on or about the 12th. From the 15th the group was directed to southbound OS 11 but the convoy changed course to avoid the boats. Searches found nothing and on the 17th a patrol line, 500 miles long, was formed between Ireland and the Azores. This too proved to be unsuccessful.

U 567 left *Störtebecker* group about this time and returned to St Nazaire **26.11.41**

3. 18.12.41   Left for Atlantic operations.

On the 14th northbound convoy HG 76 set out from Gibraltar and *Seeräuber* group was directed to it. U 107, U 108 and U 131 sighted it on the 17th.

U 131 was sunk but the other two boats maintained contact. The outward-bound U 567 was directed to the convoy and after coming up with it in the evening of the 21st, she torpedoed and sank the SS *Annavore* (nw 3324t) NE of the Azores.

The boat was quickly located and sunk in depth-charge attacks by the sloop HMS *Deptford* (Lt-Cdr H C White) and the corvette HMS *Samphire* (Lt-Cdr F T Renny) of the convoy's escort.

There were no survivors, 47 dead.

U 568   Type VII C

Built by Blohm & Voss, Hamburg
Keel laid 27.4.40   Launched 6.3.41
Commissioned 1.5.41   Feldpost Nr M 42 161

Sunk 29.5.42 NE of Tobruk (32°42′N 24°53′E)

Served with
3 U-Flottille, Kiel/La Pallice   May - December 1941 (ab/fb)
29 U-Flottille, La Spezia   January 1942 - 29.5.42 (fb)

Commanded by
KL Joachim Preuss   May 1941 -29.5.42

Patrols: 5   Ships sunk: 1 (6,023 grt) + 1 damaged
2 corvettes (1855 dt)

1. 3.8.41   Left Trondheim for the North Atlantic

U 568 became one of a number of boats which were operating in a loose formation SW of Iceland. On the 11th U 501 sighted westbound ON 5 S of Iceland. U 568 came up with the convoy and in the early hours of the 12th she torpedoed and sank a corvette of the escort, HMS *Picotee*. She also claimed a hit on a tanker but there is no confirmation of this. The boats continued to patrol S and SW of Iceland during the remainder of August but saw no convoys because of skilful re-routing.

From 1.9.41 U 568 was with *Kurfürst* group W of the North Channel. The group was directed to convoy OG 73, sighted by a Kondor of 1/KG 40 on the 1st. U 83 and U 557 of *Bosemüller* group sighted ships of OG 73 on the 2nd. This being so, the two groups were combined into one and directed to OG 73. The convoy was not found, nor was another sighted by U 98 on the 3rd.

U 568 put in to St Nazaire **10.9.41**

2. 9.10.41   Left for the North Atlantic.

U 568 went to the area SE of Cape Farewell, to join other boats assembling there to form a group. Convoys ONS 23, ON 24, SC 48 and TC 14 were re-routed to pass to the south of the boats. As U 568 and other boats arrived to extend the patrol line, the four convoys and ONS 25 were sent even further south.

During the night of the 14/15th SC 48 was sighted by U 553 600 miles W of the North Channel and eight boats, including U 568, were ordered to close and attack the convoy. U 553 was driven off at noon on the 15th and U 568 became the shadower. In the early hours of the 16th she torpedoed and sank the SS *Empire Heron* (br 6023t) in the central North Atlantic, S of Iceland.

Later on the 16th the convoy's escort was strengthened by destroyers of the US escort group TU 4.1.4, coming from dispersed convoy ON 24. In the early morning of the 17th the boats again attacked the convoy. Believing her to be British, U 568 torpedoed and damaged the USS *Kearny*. The destroyer reached Hvalfjordhur, Iceland under her own steam, with 11 men dead and 24 wounded, the first US casualties in the Battle of the Atlantic.

The boats still in contact with SC 48 were driven off by aircraft on the 17th and the operation ended. U 568 and other boats formed *Reissewolf* group 450 miles SE of Greenland from the 22nd. The presence of the group was known and several convoys were re-routed to avoid it. On the 27th the group was directed to westbound ON 28, sighted by U 74 500 miles W of Ireland. Contact was made and U 568 shadowed from the 28th but was driven off by the escorting US destroyers. U 568, U 77, U 502 and U 751 had to break off on the 30th because of fuel shortage.

The returning U 568 was directed to southbound OS 10, sighted by U 96 late on the 31st NNE of the Azores. When she lost contact on 2.11.41 and when aerial reconnaissance failed to find the convoy on the 4th, the search for OS 10 was abandoned.

U 568 returned to St Nazaire **7.11.41**

U 568 (continued)

3. 4.12.41 Left for the Mediterranean.

U 568 passed through the Straits of Gibraltar during the night of the 10/11th. She was ordered to the Eastern Mediterranean to operate off the coasts of Egypt and Cyrenaica.

On the 24th U 568 torpedoed and sank the corvette HMS *Salvia*, escorting a convoy WNW of Alexandria, but escaped detection.

The boat was attacked by a Sunderland of 230 Squadron on 9.1.42 but damage was confined to broken glass.

She put in to La Spezia **17.1.42**

4. 2.3.42 Left for the Eastern Mediterranean.

U 568 called at Messina on the 4th and then went on to operate off Tobruk but had no success.

She returned to La Spezia **30.3.42**

5. 21.5.42 Left for operations.

U 568 was located NE of Tobruk on the 29th and after a hunt lasting 15 hours, she was sunk in depth-charge attacks by the destroyers HMS *Eridge* (Lt-Cdr W F N Gregory-Smith), *Hero* (Lt-Cdr W S Scott) and *Hurworth* (Lt D A Shaw).

U 568's entire crew of 47 was made PoW.

U 569 Type VII C

Built by Blohm & Voss, Hamburg
Keel laid 21.5.40   Launched 20.3.41
Commissioned 8.5.41   Feldpost Nr M 42 293

Sunk 22.5.43 in the central North Atlantic (50°40´N 35°21´W)

Served with
3 U-Flottille, Kiel/La Pallice May 1941 - 22.5.43

Commanded by
KL Hans-Peter Hinsch May 1941 - January 1943
OL Hans Johannsen January 1943 - 22.5.43

Patrols: 9   Ship sunk: 2 (5442 grt)

1. 11.8.41 Left Trondheim for the North Atlantic.

U 569 joined a group of boats which were assembled in a loose formation SW of Iceland. On the 27th eastbound convoy HX 145 was reported S of Iceland and U 569 and ten other boats of the group were directed to close but did not find it.

The boats reformed on the 28th as *Markgraf* group SW of Iceland. On 4.9.41 the group was ordered to form a new patrol line further west. Over the next few days several convoys were re-routed to avoid the line. However, eastbound SC 42 could not be because of bad weather.

The convoy was sighted by U 85 near Cape Farewell on the 9th. The operation continued until the 14th, when poor visibility caused the boats still in contact to lose the convoy. Sixteen ships had been sunk, another was damaged and two boats were lost. U 569 does not appear to have made any attacks.

She put in to St Nazaire **21.9.41**

2. 12.10.41 Left for the North Atlantic.

U 569 joined *Schlagetot* group formed on the 28th 300 to 400 miles S of Greenland. On 1.11.41 U 374 sighted eastbound SC 52. The *Schlagetot* boats combined with several newly-arrived boats to form *Raubritter* group, which was deployed against the convoy.

The shadowing U 374 brought several boats up to the convoy, including U 569. Attacks were made and four ships were sunk, by U 202 and U 203. Contact was lost during the night of the 4/5th and not regained despite a search. The operation, hampered by radio difficulties and misty conditons, was called off after the convoy

was ordered to shelter in the Belle Isle Strait.

U 569 returned to St Nazaire **12.11.41**

3. 10.12.41 Left for the Mediterranean.

During the night of the 16/17th U 569 attempted to pass through the Straits of Gibraltar. After being located and damaged in an attack by a Swordfish of 812 (FAA) Squadron, she turned back.

U 569 returned to St Nazaire **23.12.41**

4. 26.2.42 Left for Atlantic operations.

U 569 patrolled an area W of the Faroes and the Hebrides. From late January a U-boat presence had been maintained there, ostensibly on Hitler's orders, to repel any invasion of Norway. On 8.3.42 U 569 sank the SS *Hengist* (br 984t) in an evening attack SW of the Faroes.

From the 11th U 569, U 135, U 553 and U 701 were put under the control of Naval Group Command North. As *York* group, they waited between the Shetlands and Faroes, for the return of British naval vessels, sighted NE of the Faroes on the 10th. After waiting in vain for two weeks, the boats were ordered home.

U 569 put in to La Pallice **2.4.42**

5. 4.5.42 Left for the North Atlantic.

U 569, U 94, U 96, U 124, U 406 and U 590 were to take part in a planned group-operation, *Hecht*, in the Newfoundland Bank area.

The boats were outward-bound when U 569 sighted westbound ONS 92 on the 11th in the central North Atlantic. Attacks were made during the night of the 11/12th and five ships were sunk. In the early hours of the 12th U 569 claimed a hit on a ship, which was then seen to be sinking. There is no confirmation of this. Contact was lost on the 13th in bad weather and heavy seas.

The *Hecht* patrol line was formed early on the 14th ahead of the lost convoy but contact was not regained. In the evening the group began a northeasterly movement in scouting formation, halting on the 16th. After two days the group moved southwestwards.

On the 20th U 406 sighted southbound ONS 94 but after shadowing for some hours she was driven off. The other boats did not close because of fog and the convoy was not found in spite of a search. The *Hecht* boats went to a refuelling position 600 miles S of Cape Race, where they were refuelled from the 25th by U 116.

The group reformed and on the 30th began a sweep across the known convoy routes. The boats patrolled intially S of the Newfoundland Bank before beginning to move to an area SE of Cape Farewell. En route on the 31st, U 590 sighted westbound ONS 96 but as the weather began to worsen and the convoy neared Newfoundland, the operation was called off on 2.6.42 and the boats continued eastwards.

During the evening of the 8th U 124 sighted westbound ONS 100 in the central North Atlantic and sank a French corvette. On the 9th all *Hecht* boats made contact but U 406, U 96 and U 590 dropped back because of diesel trouble. Contact with the convoy was lost but regained on the 10th by U 94. In the afternoon of the 11th U 569 scored two torpedo hits on the straggling SS *Pontypridd* (br 4458t), badly damaging her. Three hours later U 94 hit her with a torpedo and the ship was finally sunk in a coup de grâce attack by U 569. The operation ended on the 12th, with four ships sunk.

The *Hecht* boats searched northeastwards and on the 16th U 94 sighted westbound ONS 102. Ordered to attack, the boats found the escort to be very strong and U 94 and U 590 were attacked and damaged. The operation ended on the 17th and the boats headed for home.

U 569 returned to La Pallice **28.6.42**

6. 4.8.42 Left for the North Atlantic.

U 569 was one of a number of newly-arrived boats which joined others coming from the operation against SC 94 to form a new patrol line, *Lohs*, 600 miles W of the North Channel. An ON convoy was expected on the 13th. En route to their new positions, some of the boats from SC 94 sighted SC 95 going north. Only three boats closed, sinking one ship before contact was lost.

The *Lohs* patrol line was formed on the 17th W of Scotland. On the 21st the group moved northwards, searching for convoys, and on the 22nd ONS 122 passed to the south and was sighted by *Lohs'* southernmost boat, U 135. She shadowed but contact was lost in bad visibility and not regained until the 24th. By the early hours of the 25th nine boats were in contact, including U 569, and attacks were made. However, fog came down and the operation was called off, with four ships sunk and two boats damaged.

The *Lohs* boats went south, to be refuelled by U 462 W of the Azores from the 29th. They then reformed and from 6.9.42 a new patrol line, 400 miles NE of Cape Race, awaited eastbound convoys. SC 100 was expected to be 150 miles SE of the Cape on the 18th and *Lohs* moved south to intercept but bad weather prevented more than three boats making attacks. When the weather worsened further, the operation was abandoned on the 22nd, with only one ship sunk. However, the convoy was sighted again on the 23rd and U 432 of *Lohs* and U 617 of *Pfeil* group sank one ship and three stragglers between them before the operation was finally called off on the 25th W of Rockall.

U 569 returned to La Pallice **8.10.42**

7. 25.11.42 Left for the North Atlantic.

U 569 joined a new group, *Draufgänger*, W of Ireland, awaiting an ONS convoy but this did not materialise. The patrol line moved north and on 7.12.42 was ordered to close northeastbound convoy HX 217. Once within range of Iceland, the convoy had good air cover from the 10th, causing the operation to be called off next day, with only two ships sunk.

From the 13th U 569 and three other *Draufgänger* boats joined new-arrivals and U 524 to form *Ungestüm* group, to operate against convoys leaving the North Channel. On the 13th eastbound HX 218 was sighted E of Newfoundland by U 373. The *Ungestüm* boats moved westwards at high speed and on the 16th a patrol line was formed SE of Cape Farewell in the expected path of the convoy. However, HX 218 passed unobserved through the waiting boats.

Searching for HX 218, U 373 sighted westbound ONS 152 on the 16th to the southeast of the *Ungestüm* line and the boats were moved towards it. Brief contact was made but bad weather and poorvisibility hampered the pursuit. A search for stragglers continued and one was sunk by U 591. The operation ended on the 22nd.

U 569 returned to La Pallice **28.12.42**

8. 7.2.43 Left for the Gibraltar area.

U 569 was one of six boats which assembled W of Portugal on the 11th. The German Naval Staff feared an Allied invasion and the boats were sent there as a precaution.

However, on the 12th a southbound convoy was sighted by U 382 200 miles W of Cape Finisterre and the waiting boats were directed to it. The air cover, which increased as the convoy approached Gibraltar, forced the boats to remain submerged and no attacks were made.

From the 16th, with the invasion scare forgotten, the boats formed *Robbe* group, in a north-south patrol line NE of the Azores. On the 17th the group moved westwards to search an area N of the Azores. With nothing found, a return movement eastwards began on the 20th and from the 21st the boats headed for the Gibraltar area, except for U 569 and U 382, which went south to join *Rochen* group in an attack on convoy UC 1 W of Madeira. In the evening of the 23rd U 569 fired a 3-torpedo spread against a ship, possibly the British tanker SS *Empire Marvel*, but heard only end-of-run detonations, which at the time were reported as hits. The convoy was pursued until the 27th. By then three tankers had been sunk and two damaged. U 569 was refuelled by U 461 on or about 1.3.43.

The boat returned to La Pallice **13.3.43**

9. 19.4.43 Left for the North Atlantic.

U 569 joined *Amsel 3* group E of St John's, Newfoundland. On 7.5.43 *Amsel 3* combined with *Amsel 4* group to form *Rhein* group, which was ordered southeastwards at high speed on the 8th to form a patrol line for the 9th for the interception of HX 237.

U 359 sighted a ship of the convoy on the 9th, before the line could be formed, but lost it in worsening visibility. The boats carried out independent searches before reforming in the morning of the 10th. At noon U 403 sighted a fast independent ship and then a tug, which led to the convoy being found in the afternoon.

The *Rhein* boats were by then too far east, so they were ordered to combine with *Elbe* group, to form *Elbe 1* and *2* groups and to pursue the slower convoy SC 129, which the boats passed on the 11th as they formed up. U 569 was in *Elbe 1*. Contact with the convoy was made on the 12th but there was a strong surface and carrier-borne air escort, which kept the boats at a distance. The operation against SC 129 ended on the 14th SW of Ireland, with two ships sunk and two boats lost.

U 569 was refuelled by U 459 in the central North Atlantic, after which she joined *Mosel* group, formed on the 19th 400 miles S of Cape Farewell to operate against HX 239. In the evening of the 21st U 569 sighted a convoy, presumably westbound ON 184. Two boats in the *Mosel* line were driven down by destroyers and carrier-borne aircraft and the convoy went through the gap created.

In the afternoon of the 22nd U 569, chasing the convoy, was sighted by an Avenger of VC-9 (Lt W F Chamberlain) from the escort-carrier USS *Bogue*, which was only 20 miles away. The aircraft dropped four depth-bombs close to U 569's conning tower and the boat dived. When she resurfaced later, another Avenger (Lt H Roberts) had arrived and another depth-bomb attack was made.

This time the boat rose out of the sea at an angle and then plunged to 350 feet. U 569 came up again, on her side, sank again and then resurfaced on an even keel. The crew began to abandon ship in very heavy seas and the newly-arrived destroyer HMCS *St Laurent* prepared to send a party aboard.

However, the Chief Engineer opened the valves and U 569 was scuttled before she could be boarded. She was the first U-boat to be sunk by aircraft from an escort-carrier.

21 of the crew were lost and the commander and 24 others were picked up and made PoW.

U 570   Type VII C

Built by Blohm & Voss, Hamburg
Keel laid 21.5.40   Launched 20.3.41
Commissioned 15.5.41   Feldpost Nr M 42 381

Captured 27.8.41 S of Vik, Iceland (62°15′N 18°35′W)

Served with
3 U-Flottille, Kiel   May 1941 - 27.8.41 (ab/fb)

Commanded by
KL Hans-Joachim Rahmlow   May 1941 - 27.8.41

Patrols: 1   Ships sunk: None

1. 23.8.41 Left Trondheim for the North Atlantic.

U 570 went to an area S of Iceland and with other boats was unsuccessfully directed to eastbound convoy HX 145. In the morning of the 27th KL Rahmlow took his boat down because the heavy seas were upsetting his inexperienced crew. Soon after resurfacing two hours later, U 570 was sighted by a Hudson of 269 Squadron (S/Ldr J H Thompson). The aircraft dropped four depth-charges before the boat could dive and then saw the crew coming out of the conning tower and a white flag being shown. The Hudson circled the stationary U 570, continuing to do so until relieved by a Catalina of 209 Squadron (F/O E A Jewiss). Thompson

U 570 (continued)

and his navigator were both awarded the DFC.

The a/s trawler HMS *Northern Chief* arrived early in the evening. U 570 was sent a signal to the effect that if the boat was scuttled, survivors would not be picked up, which was most unlikely. The threat worked and U 570 signalled its agreement. In the morning of the 28th two destroyers and three more trawlers arrived. An aircraft with a Norwegian crew also arrived and not knowing the situation, dropped two depth-charges but caused no damage.

The heavy seas prevented the boat being taken in tow. A line was shot to U 570 and Lt H B Campbell and two ratings from the trawler HMS *Kingston Agate* hauled themselves across to the boat on a liferaft. They also hauled across a tow rope which, at great risk to themselves, they crawled along the casing and secured to the boat's stern. Campbell remained aboard for five hours, leaving only after U 570's crew had all been transferred to the *Kingston Agate*.

In spite of the crew destroying as much of the internal equipment and instruments as they could before the boarding party arrived, U 570 provided a lot of valuable information.

Towing began and the line parted several times. When *Kingston Agate* returned to Iceland with the prisoners, comprising the entire crew less one man killed, the towing was taken over by the *Northern Chief*. The boat was beached at Thorlakshafn late on the 29th and was found to have very little damage.

On 5.9.41 U 570 was towed to Hvalfjord and by the 19th she was again seaworthy. Rechristened HMS Graph, *she sailed for Britain on the 29th and reached Barrow-in-Furness on 3.10.41.* Graph *underwent a refit, after which she carried out extensive sea-trials from the Clyde, which provided more valuable information.*

In late September 1942 Graph *became operational and on 21.10.42 she made an unsuccessful attack on U 333 in the Eastern Atlantic. In the latter part of 1943* Graph *had a major refit at Chatham but with developing defects she went on to the reserve at Aberdeen. In March 1944 she was towed out, en route to the Clyde to be scrapped. On the 20th* Graph *was wrecked on the Island of Islay after the towline parted. She was raised and scrapped in 1947.*

In September 1941 the 1WO, 2WO and Chief Engineer of U 570 arrived at Grizedale Hall PoW Camp in northern England. Otto Kretschmer was the senior German officer and as such convened a Council of Honour, to investigate whether any or all of the three had been guilty of cowardice.

The 2WO and Chief Engineer were found to be not guilty, and were deemed to have been obeying orders. However, the 1WO, Lt Bernhard Berndt, was found guilty and he would face a court-martial after Germany had won the war.

When it was learned that the former U 570 was at Barrow-in-Furness, a plan was made for Berndt to escape, make his way to the shipyard and scuttle the boat, whereby honour would be vindicated. Provided with civilian clothes and assuming the identity of a Dutch seaman, Berndt duly escaped but was caught next day, hiding in a sheep shelter. Although his cover story apparently satisfied his Home Guard captors, they decided to take him to Grizedale Hall for possible indentification. As he was being marched there, he made a run for it and was shot after failing to stop when ordered to do so. Berndt died in a farm house before a doctor arrived and was buried at Grizedale Hall with full military honours.

KL Rahmlow, U 570's former commander, arrived at the camp soon afterwards and he was informed that he would soon face the same Council of Honour. The authorities heard of this, Rahmlow was locked away and next day sent to camp near Carlisle, which contained mostly Luftwaffe officers.

Some time later Rahmlow arrived at Kretschmer's camp at Bowmanville in Canada. He faced a Council of Honour and it seems that during the rest of his captivity Rahmlow was largely ostracised by his fellow-prisoners.

U 571   Type VII C

Built by Blohm & Voss, Hamburg
Keel laid 3.6.40   Launched 4.4.41
Commissioned 22.5.41   Feldpost Nr M 42 483

Sunk 28.1.44 W of Ireland (52°41´N 14°27´W)

Served with
3 U-Flottille, Kiel/La Pallice   May 1941 - 28.1.44 (ab/fb)

Commanded by
KL Helmut Möhlmann   May 1941 - May 1943
OL Gustav Lüssow   May 1943 - 28.1.44

Patrols: 10   Ships sunk: 7 (47,169 grt) + 1 damaged

1. 18.8.41   Left Trondheim for Northern Waters.
U 571, U 451, U 566 and U 752 patrolled off the Kola coast from the 23rd. On the 26th U 571 torpedoed and damaged the MV *Marija Uljanova* (sov 3870t) N of Cape Teriberka. The vessel was beached but declared to be a total loss.
U 571 put in to Kirkenes **27.8.41**

2. 28.8.41   Left Kirkenes and arrived Kiel **5.9.41**

3. 18.10.41   Left Kiel and arrived Arendal **19.10.41**

4. 22.10.41   Left for the North Atlantic.
Outward-bound, U 571 and other boats received orders on the 30th to form *Stosstrupp* group E of the Newfoundland Bank. Late on the 31st U 571 was directed to southbound convoy OS 10, sighted by U 96 NNE of the Azores. The shadower lost contact on 2.11.41 and when aerial reconnaissance failed to find the convoy on the 4th, the search was abandoned.
U 571 joined *Raubritter* group, in a new patrol line formed SE of Cape Farewell from the 8th. When westbound ONS 33 was reported on the 12th, U 571, U 85, U 106, U 133 and U 577 were deployed but did not find the convoy. These boats began their return journey on the 15th. They operated unsuccessfully against westbound ONS 11 on the 16th.
U 571, U 85, U 133 and U 577 formed a patrol line, *Störtebecker,* on the 19th, to await southbound OG 77 but the convoy did not materialise before the group was ordered back to base.
U 571 put in to her new base at La Pallice **26.11.41**

5. 21.12.41   Left for the Gibraltar area.
U 571 was one of six boats en route to the Mediterranean. They were ordered instead to assemble near the Azores, as *Seydlitz* group. On 2.1.42 a decision was made. U 84, U 203 and U 552 were ordered westwards to the Newfoundland Bank and U 571, U 71 and U 93 were ordered to move towards Gibraltar and then patrol between there and the Azores.
On the 11th the three boats were directed against convoy HG 78. They were too few in number to succeed and their attempts to attack the convoy were foiled by the escort and they were driven off. The convoy was shadowed for four days without success and when U 93 was sunk on the 15th the operation was called off.
U 571 returned to La Pallice **27.1.42**

6. 10.3.42   Left for the North Atlantic.
U 571 went to the Newfoundland area and then turned southwards for the US east coast. From the 26th she was operating 300 miles E of Hatteras. On the 29th U 571 torpedoed and sank the SS *Hertford* (br 10932t) E of New York, on 6.4.42 the tanker MV *Koll* (nw 10044t) NE of Bermuda and on the 14th the SS *Margaret* (am 3352t) off Cape Hatteras.
On the 21st U 571 was refuelled by U 459 500 miles NE of

Bermuda for return to base.

She reached La Pallice **7.5.42**

7. 11.6.42 Left to operate in US waters.

With other outward-bound boats, U 571 was directed to northbound HG 84, reported by a Kondor on the 11th W of Portugal. They were to form a patrol line, *Endrass*, for the 14th in the expected path of the convoy. HG 84 was sighted again by a Kondor during the afternoon of the 14th and the *Endrass* boats were homed in. The first boat to close, U 552, sank five ships during the night but these were the only successes. All other boats which approached HG 84 were driven off by the escort or aircraft. The operation ended on the 16th because the good, calm weather and good visibility were unfavourable for U-boat attacks.

In late June five *Endrass* boats, including U 571, were refuelled by U 459 W of the Azores. U 571 continued her journey to US waters, where she operated initially SE of Hatteras, later moving south to the coast of Florida. On 7.7.42 U 571 torpedoed and sank the SS *Umtata* (br 8141t) off Miami, on the 8th the tanker SS *J A Moffet Jr* (am 9788t) was damaged by torpedo and gunfire E of Key West and on the 9th the SS *Nicholas Cuneo* (ho 1051t) was sunk by gunfire SW of Key West. The *J A Moffet Jr* was towed into harbour but was a total loss.

U 571 moved into the Gulf of Mexico and on the 15th she torpedoed and damaged the tanker MV *Pennsylvania Sun* (am 11394t) SE of the Dry Tortugas. This was U 571's final success on this patrol and she re-entered the Atlantic for the homeward journey on or about the 24th.

The boat returned to La Pallice **7.8.42**

8. 3.10.42 Left for the North Atlantic.

U 571 was to join *Panther* group W of Ireland. In the evening of the 16th U 571 approached convoy SC 104. She was located by the Norwegian corvette *Potentilla* and suffered some damage from gunfire and depth-charge attacks before being driven off.

On the 16th the southern boats from *Panther* group and ten from *Wotan* were ordered to attack westbound ON 137, sighted by U 704 that day in the central North Atlantic. U 571 joined this operation, as part of *Panther* group.

The weather worsened and U 704 lost contact after being damaged and driven down. The boats searched but the convoy was not found. A gale developed on the 17th, the *Wotan* boats left for home on the 18th and the operation was terminated on the 19th. U 571 and the other *Panther* boats moved westwards and formed a new line, *Veilchen*, on the 24th 400 miles E of Newfoundland, to await eastbound convoys.

On the 30th SC 107 was sighted by U 522 just S of Cape Race. *Veilchen* group was ordered to attack. The shadower was driven off on the 31st but the convoy was sighted by U 381 of *Veilchen* on 1.11.42. She and two other boats approached but were driven off. Attacks were carried out over three days and when the operation was called off on the 6th, fifteen ships had been sunk and two boats lost. U 571 had no success but she maintained contact with SC 107 until the morning of the 5th, when she was one of the last boats to be driven off by Liberators of 120 Squadron.

U 571 returned to La Pallice **14.11.42**

9. 22.12.42 Left for the Central Atlantic.

U 571 joined *Delphin* group W of Gibraltar, to operate against US-Mediterranean convoys carrying supplies for the Allied armies in North Africa. On the 29th the group was ordered to sweep westwards, searching for convoy GUS 2. Nothing was seen for four days and the boats were then ordered towards Brazil.

However, on 3.1.43 U 514 reported tanker convoy TM 1 900 miles to the south of *Delphin* and probably heading for Gibraltar. The *Delphin* boats turned south to form a patrol line ahead of the convoy for the 7th and on the 8th TM 1 was sighted by U 381. Four homeward- or outward-bound boats had joined the group,

making twelve boats available for an attack. On the night of the 8/9th U 571 approached and was driven off by HMS *Pimpernel*.

The boat made unsuccessful attacks against two Norwegian tankers, on the 10th on the MV *Vanja* and early on the 11th on MV *Cliona*, both W of the Canaries. Seven tankers were sunk in the operation, which ended near Madeira on the 11th.

Delphin group reformed S of the Azores on the 16th after six of its boats, including U 571, had been refuelled by U 463 W of the Azores. The group moved westwards to meet an eastbound UGS convoy but turned east again on the 18th. From the 21st to the 29th the *Delphin* boats waited SW of the Azores but when nothing materialised the group moved further eastwards. From the 31st the line was NW of the Canaries but then moved to a new position W of Gibraltar for 6.2.43.

From the 11th the *Delphin* boats moved north to take up positions W of Portugal. A southbound convoy was reported on the 12th 200 miles W of Cape Finisterre. *Delphin* was ordered to close but the operation failed when the convoy's air escort kept the boats submerged. The situation worsened the nearer the convoy got to Gibraltar. Attacks became impossible and two boats were lost.

U 571 returned to La Pallice **19.2.43**

10. 22.3.43 Left La Pallice and returned **23.3.43**

11. 25.3.43 Left for the North Atlantic.

After German aircraft found convoy SL 126 on the 27th W of the Bay of Biscay, outward-bound U 571, U 181, U 267, U 404 and U 662 were directed to it. Only U 404 and U 662 made contact, sinking four ships and damaging another. When contact was lost U 571 continued westwards.

She joined *Adler* group, formed for 7.4.43 S of Cape Farewell to operate against eastbound SC 125. The convoy passed 200 miles south of the *Adler* line on the 7th and was by then impossible to catch. The group was moved to the southeast to intercept HX 232, thought to be on the same route as SC 125. On the way to the new position, U 404 sighted ON 176 in the afternoon of the 10th.

U571 and U 84, shadowing ON 176, encountered convoy ONS 2 ENE of St John's early on the 11th. Both boats made unsuccessful attacks against the convoy in the morning of the 11th. They afterwards joined the other *Adler* boats in the attack on ON 176. The operation ended on the 13th when the convoy's air cover was increased. One ship and a destroyer of the escort had been sunk.

The *Adler* boats were incorporated into *Meise* group. After a line was formed on the 14th NE of Newfoundland, the group remained in the area until the 19th, when the boats moved northwards to form a new line S of Greenland for the 21st, to intercept eastbound HX 234. U 571 left the group about this time.

She returned to La Pallice **1.5.43**

12. 8.6.43 Left for the Central Atlantic.

U 571 was to operate in the Freetown area. In late June she was refuelled by U 488 W of the Azores, after which she proceeded southwards.

On or about 10.7.43 U 571 may have been damaged but details are not known. On the 22nd she was attacked and damaged by an aircraft of 26 (SAAF) Squadron.

U 571 rendezvoused with U 333 on 5.8.43 to pass over a replacement compressor, which fully restored U 333's operational capability. On or around the 18th U 571 was refuelled by U 129 700 to 800 miles S to SW of the Azores for return to base.

U 571 reached La Pallice **1.9.43**

13. 26.12.43 Left La Pallice and returned **28.12.43**

14. 8.1.44 Left for Atlantic operations.

U 571 joined *Rügen* group W of the British Isles, with boats disposed singly over a large area. On the 18th U 571 unsuccessfully attacked a destroyer W of Fastnet.

U 571 (continued)

On the 26th a KMS convoy was sighted W of the North Channel. The six most southerly *Rügen* boats, including U 571, were formed into a patrol line, *Hinein*, W of Ireland to intercept the southbound convoy on the 27th.

The convoy was further west than reported and by the time the *Hinein* boats had been appraised of this, it was too late to move the patrol line westwards. Boats with 3.7cm anti-aircraft guns were ordered to proceed at high speed on the surface to intercept. Again, communication difficulties between aircraft and boats meant the convoy's position at midnight on the 27th was not passed on and an all-night search by the boats found nothing.

U 571 was attacked on the 28th by a Sunderland of 461 (RAAF) Squadron (F/Lt R D Lucas) W of Fastnet. After the second depth-charge attack the boat blew up. Men were seen in the water but a dinghy dropped by the aircraft failed to inflate.

There were no survivors, 52 dead.

U 572   Type VII C

Built by Blohm & Voss, Hamburg
Keel laid 15.6.40   Launched 5.4.41
Commissioned 29.5.41   Feldpost Nr M 42 493

Sunk 3.8.43 NNE of Paramaribo (11°35´N 54°05´W)

Served with
3 U-Flottille, Kiel/La Pallice   May 1941 - 3.8.43 (ab/fb)

Commanded by
KL Heinz Hirsacker   May 1941 - December 1942
OL Heinz Kummetat   December 1942 - 3.8.43

Patrols: 9   Ships sunk: 6 (19,343 grt) + 1 damaged

1. 2.9.41   Left Trondheim for the North Atlantic.

U 572 joined a number of ex-*Markgraf* boats, which from the 6th were spread over a large area SE of Greenland, across possible convoy routes. Some convoys were routed clear but the course of eastbound SC 42 could not be changed because of very bad weather.

The convoy was sighted by U 85 on the 9th close to Cape Farewell. U 572 had no success in the operation, which lasted until the 14th, by which time sixteen ships had been sunk.

U 572 joined *Brandenburg* group SE of Greenland, formed from the 18th. On this day U 74 sighted eastbound SC 44 but because of radio interference any form of organised attack could not be carried out and only four boats responded to the sighting report. U 74 and U 552 sank four ships and a corvette between them. U 572 and the other *Brandenburg* group boats had no success.

The group was ordered to form a new patrol line SE of Cape Farewell for the 24th but after some boats set out for home, the *Brandenburg* group was dissolved.

U 572 put in to Lorient **2.10.41**

2. 30.10.41   Left for the North Atlantic.

Outward-bound, U 572 was directed to southbound convoy OS 10, sighted by U 96 on the 31st 500 miles W of Ireland. The shadower sank one ship but only U 98 came up but had no success.

On 5.11.41 U 572 joined *Störtebecker* group W of Spain to await convoy HG 76, which had been expected to leave Gibraltar on the 1st. When it was not found by the 7th, the group was directed to convoy SL 91 but by the 11th a sea and air search had not found it.

Störtebecker group now moved westwards to a new position in the central North Atlantic. On the 15th it was directed to southbound OS 11 but no contact was made. The convoy had been re-routed. The *Störtebecker* line was now strung out over 500 miles long, between Ireland and the Azores.

On the 19th all available boats were ordered to form three short lines, *Störtebecker, Gödecke* and *Benecke*, to intercept expected convoy OG 77. U 572 was to be in *Gödecke*.

On the 22nd, before the groups could be formed, all boats with sufficient fuel were ordered to make their way to the Gibraltar area. Boats with less fuel were ordered back to their bases, to be made ready for the Mediterreanean. U 572 was one of these.

She put in to Brest **29.11.41**

3. 7.1.42   Left for the Mediterreanean.

Between the 19th and the 21st U 572 failed in two attempts to pass through the Straits of Gibraltar. She joined U 402 and U 581, carrying out east-west patrols between Gibraltar and the Azores.

On 2.2.42 the MV *Llangibby Castle* sailed from Horta after undergoing repairs to damage incurred in an attack on the vessel by U 402 on January 6th. U 572, U 402 and U 581 were ordered to intercept. Their efforts against her between the 2nd and 4th were unsuccessful and U 581 was sunk by one of her escort.

U 572 returned to Brest **10.2.42**

4. 14.3.42   Left for the US east coast.

U 572 headed for the Newfoundland area and then turned south. On 4.4.42 she attacked the tanker MV *Ensis* (br 6207t) with gun-fire 300 miles NW of Bermuda. The vessel was slightly damaged by 20mm shells.

On the 16th U 572 torpedoed and sank the SS *Desert Light* (pa 2368t) E of Roanoke Island and on the 20th the SS *Empire Dryden* (br 7164t) NNW of Bermuda. On or about the 23rd U 572 was reprovisioned by U 459 500 miles NE of Bermuda.

The boat put in to La Pallice **14.5.42**

5. 30.6.42   Left for the Central Atlantic.

U 572 was one of six boats which were intended for a group operation. They assembled SE of the Azores, as *Hai* group, and on 10.7.42 began to sweep south as far as Dakar between meridians 20° and 25°W. On the 11th southbound convoy OS 33 passed through the patrol line S of Santa Maria, Azores.

After dark a group of ships bound for South America split from the convoy, which continued south. Four *Hai* boats pursued these ships whilst U 572 and U 752 continued southwards after the main part of OS 33. Neither boat had any success and the operation ended on the 13th.

The five surviving *Hai* boats reformed NNE of the Cape Verde Islands on the 15th. U 136 had been sunk on the 11th. The line continued southwards until it passed Dakar. On the 21st the group dispersed and the boats went on to operate independently off Freetown. On 4.8.42 U 572 was refuelled by U 116 W of Freetown. On the 7th U 572 torpedoed and sank the SS *Delfshaven* (nl 5281t) in the same area.

She continued to operate off Freetown for a further ten days before returning northwards.

U 572 returned to La Pallice **3.9.42**

6. 12.10.42   Left for operations in the Freetown area.

U 572 was one of eight boats which assembled E of the Azores. They set off in line abreast for Freetown on the 23rd, as *Streitaxt* group. Off the Canaries on the 25th U 510 sighted a tanker escorted by two destroyers. The group pursued, unsuccessfully.

On the 27th U 409 sighted northbound convoy SL 125 W of the Canaries as it passed through the *Streitaxt* line. U 572 and U 134 were the only *Streitaxt* boats which did not make attacks. When the operation ended on 1.11.42, twelve ships had been sunk.

U 572 then operated off Lisbon for some days but on the 8th, after the Allied landings in North Africa, she moved south at high speed for the Moroccan coast to join *Schlagetot* group. She arrived off Morocco on the 9th but her commander failed to penetrate the anti-submarine defences, as he had failed to pass through the Straits of Gibraltar in January 1942.

Some sinkings were made by other boats on the 11th. However, as the Allied defences strengthened, both at sea and in the air, very few sinkings were made in the areas of the landings at Fedala and Casablanca, in spite of many attempted attacks. U 572 made attacks but had no success.

The boat returned to La Pallice **22.11.42**

After this patrol KL Hirsacker was relieved of his command. He was the only U-boat commander to be tried for cowardice during the war. After being found guilty, Hirsacker was shot 24.4.43.

7. 23.12.42 Left for the North Atlantic.

U 572 joined *Falke* group 500 miles W of Ireland, where it was awaiting an ON convoy. The group was directed to ONS 158, ON 159 and ONS 160 but all were re-routed to avoid the boats.

From 7.1.43 *Falke* group swept westwards, searching for convoys. This move continued until the 15th, with nothing seen. The group turned north next day but again found nothing.

On the 19th *Falke* and *Habicht* groups were formed into two new patrol lines, *Haudegen* and *Landsknecht*, the latter made up of those boats with less fuel, which included U 572. For a week the *Landsknecht* boats waited W of Ireland for an ON convoy but it did not eventuate. The group was dispersed on the 28th.

U 572, U 71 and U 584 joined with outward-bound boats on 4.2.43 to form a new patrol line, *Hartherz*, W of Gibraltar. An HG convoy that was expected did not materialise and the group dispersed on the 8th.

U 572 returned to La Pallice **11.2.43**

8. 10.3.43 Left for the North Atlantic.

U 572 joined *Seeteufel* group S of Iceland, to operate against a feeder convoy en route from Iceland to join westbound ONS 1. A patrol line was formed for the 21st and the convoy was expected on the 22nd but when it did not materialise the line moved westwards in the expected direction of the main convoy ONS 1.

On the 24th U 306 sighted some ONS 1 escorts north of the *Seeteufel* line but the boats contacted were unable to close. By the 26th the *Seeteufel* line ran southeast from Cape Farewell and it joined the more southerly *Seewolf* group to form a line running 800 miles south from the Cape. In the afternoon of the 26th masts and an aircraft carrier were sighted in the centre of the *Seeteufel* line. This was thought to be an ON convoy but a strong air and surface escort prevented its direction being discovered by the boats.

On the 27th U 305, at the northern end of the *Seewolf* line, sighted eastbound convoy HX 230. *Seewolf* and *Seeteufel* boats, including U 572, were ordered to pursue. The prevailing storm developed into a hurricane on the 28th and only five boats were able to make brief contact with the convoy but torpedo attacks were impossible in the heavy seas. The boats continued to pursue in the hope that stragglers would be found but only one ship was sunk during the operation, which ended on the 30th when the last boat lost contact.

U 572 and other *Seeteufel* boats joined some new-arrivals to form *Löwenherz* group SE of Greenland from 3.4.43. On the 4th U 530 sighted eastbound HX 231 to the west of the patrol line. The operation against the convoy lasted three days, with six ships sunk and others possibly damaged. U 572 had no success.

She returned to La Pallice **18.4.43**

9. 2.6.43 Left for the Central Atlantic.

On or about the 16th U 572 was refuelled by U 530 SW of the Canaries. En route to her operational area off Guiana, U 572 encountered convoy UGS 10 on the 22nd in the central North Atlantic. She torpedoed and sank the tanker SS *Lot* (fr 4220t). The boat was hunted for five hours by the escort but escaped.

U 572 patrolled between Barbados and the Guiana coast. On July 14th and 15th she sank two schooners by gunfire NE of Boca Grande, the *Harvard* (br 114t) and the *Gilbert B Walters* (br 176t).

On 3.8.43 the returning U 572 was sighted NNE of Paramaribo

by a USN Mariner of VP-205 (Lt C C Cox). The aircraft reported that an attack was about to made on a U-boat. Neither U 572 or the aircraft were heard from again and a search failed to find any survivors or items of wreckage.

From U 572, 46 men were lost.

U 573   Type VII C

Built by Blohm & Voss, Hamburg
Keel laid 8.6.40   Launched 17.4.41
Commissioned 5.6.41   Feldpost Nr M 42 508

Sold 9.8.42 to Spain

Served with
3 U-Flottille, Kiel/La Pallice   June - December 1941 (ab/fb)
29 U-Flottille, La Spezia   January 1942 - 2.5.42 (fb)

Commanded by
KL Heinrich Heinsohn   June 1941 - 2.5.42

Patrols: 4   Ships sunk: 1 (5289 grt)

1. 27.9.41 Left Kiel for the North Atlantic.

U 573 and other boats assembled SE of Cape Farewell and then formed a patrol line from 7.10.41. Convoys ONS 23, ON 24, SC 48 and TC 14 were re-routed further south to avoid this line. When more boats arrived and the line was extended, the convoys were sent even further south. During the night of the 14/15th U 553 sighted SC 48 and most of the group were deployed against it.

However, U 573, U 109, U 208 and U 374 took no part in the action. They were designated *Mordbrenner* group from the 16th and sent to reconnoitre off Belle Isle.

The boats arrived in the area on the 20th, found no shipping and soon realised that convoys were avoiding them by passing further to the south. On the 28th the four *Mordbrenner* boats went to the area SE of Newfoundland, around Cape Race. On the 31st the group was directed to westbound ON 28 but made no contact. The boats began their homeward journey on the 3rd.

U 573 put in to St Nazaire **15.11.41**

2. 7.12.41 Left St Nazaire and returned **9.12.41**

3. 11.12.41 Left for the Mediterranean.

After several attempts, U 573 passed through the Straits of Gibraltar during the night of the 20/21st. Later on the 21st she torpedoed and sank the SS *Hellen* (nw 5289t) near Cape Negro, Morocco.

U 573 put in to Messina on the 27th and then went on, reaching Pola **30.12.41**

4. 2.2.42 Left to operate in the Eastern Mediterranean.

U 573 returned to Pola **6.3.42**

5. 19.4.42 Left for the Western Mediterranean.

U 573 was attacked and seriously damaged by a Hudson of 233 Squadron (Sgt Brent) on 1.5.42 NW of Ténès, Algeria, with one crewman killed. The boat managed to reach Cartagena, where it was interned by the Spanish authorities.

The crew was temporarily held before being repatriated to Germany. U 573 was sold to Spain on 9.8.42 and renumbered G 7. It was in service until 1970.

U 574 Type VII C

Built by Blohm & Voss, Hamburg
Keel laid 15.6.40   Launched 18.4.41
Commissioned 12.6.41   Feldpost Nr M 43 973

Sunk 19.12.41 N of Madeira (38°12′N 17°23′W)

Served with
1 U-Flottille, Kiel/Brest June 1941 - 19.12.41 (ab/fb)

Commanded by
OL Dietrich Gengelbach June 1941 - 19.12.41

Patrols: 1   Ships sunk: None
                        1 destroyer (1190 dt)

1. 8.11.41 Left Kiel for the North Atlantic.
    U 574 went to an area S of Iceland to join U 105, U 402 and U 434. The boats were to reconnoitre areas S of Iceland and remain there to support a proposed sortie by the pocket-battleship *Admiral Scheer*.
    The *Scheer* operation did not take place and from the 13th the four boats moved southwestwards towards Cape Race. U 574, U 105 and U 434 moved to an area off Newfoundland, where they joined U 43, U 372 and U 575 as *Steuben* group.
    However, on the 23rd all boats with enough fuel, either in or on their way to the Newfoundland area, were ordered eastwards to an area W of Gibraltar. En route, U 574 was directed to southbound convoy OS 12, sighted by U 43 just N of the Azores on the 28th. U 43 also encountered convoy WS 13 on the 30th.
    U 574 and other eastbound boats came up with the convoys but were unable to make any attacks. The boats continued on their way to Gibraltar in scouting formation. No ships were seen and when the boats arrived in the operational area they found strong anti-submarine patrols at the entrance to the Straits, forcing them to remain submerged and preventing any attacks on convoys entering the Mediterranean.
    After the boats had waited in vain for some time BdU decided that searching for convoys should cease and an attack should be made on convoy HG 76, soon to leave Gibraltar. U 574 put in to Vigo and during the night of December 11/12th she was refuelled by the German supply ship *Bessel*.
    Convoy HG 76 left Gibraltar on the 14th and moved south along the coast of Morocco before turning north. It was not found by aircraft until the 16th. *Seeräuber* group was directed to the convoy, as were other boats, including U 574.
    She shadowed HG 76 from the night of the 16/17th. In the evening of the 18th she missed the escorting corvette *Convolvulus* with two torpedoes. As she dived, she was seen and then hunted for two hours by the corvettes HMS *Pentstemon* and *Convolvulus* and the destroyer HMS *Stanley*.
    After they rejoined the convoy, U 574 resurfaced and followed. In the early hours of the 19th the sloop HMS *Stork* (Cdr F J Walker) made contact E of the Azores. *Stanley* sighted the boat but was almost immediately torpedoed and sunk by U 574. *Stork* turned towards the boat, which had dived, and made two depth-charge attacks.
    U 574 resurfaced and *Stork* approached to ram. After both had circled three times, *Stork* rammed U 574, tipping her over. As the sloop moved away, she dropped depth-charges, which destroyed the boat.
    The commander and 27 men of U 574's crew were lost and another 18 were made PoW.

U 575 Type VII C

Built by Blohm & Voss, Hamburg
Keel laid 1.8.40   Launched 30.4.41
Commissioned 19.6.41   Feldpost Nr M 44 068

Sunk 13.3.44 N of the Azores (46°18′N 27°34′W)

Served with
7 U-Flottille, Kiel/St Nazaire June 1941 - 13.3.44 (ab/fb)

Commanded by
KL Günther Heydemann June 1941 - June 1943
OL Wolfgang Boehmer June 1943 - 13.3.44

Patrols: 10   Ships sunk: 8 (36,106 grt) + 1 damaged
                            1 corvette (1015 dt)

1. 2.9.41 Left Kiel and arrived Trondheim **5.9.41**

2. 8.9.41 Left Trondheim for the North Atlantic.
    Outward-bound, U 575 was directed to eastbound SC 42, which was under attack E of Cape Farewell. She was in contact with the convoy from the 13th but contact was lost in poor visibility and the operation ended on the 14th, with sixteen ships sunk.
    U 575 joined *Brandenburg* group SE of Greenland, formed from the 18th. On this day U 74 sighted eastbound SC 44 but because of radio interference any form of organised attack could not be carried out and only four boats responded to the sighting report. U 74 and U 552 sank four ships and a corvette between them. U 575 and other *Brandenburg* boats had no success.
    The group was ordered to form a new patrol line SE of Cape Farewell for the 24th but after some boats set out for home the *Brandenburg* group was dispersed. U 575 continued to patrol S of Greenland and on 2.10.41 attacked a group of four ships in the central North Atlantic with three torpedoes, sinking the MV *Tuva* (nl 4652t) and possibly hitting a second ship.
    U 575 put in to her new base at St Nazaire **9.10.41**

3. 9.11.41 Left for the North Atlantic.
    U 575 went to an area off Newfoundland, joining U 43, U 105, U 372, U 434 and U 574 to form *Steuben* group.
    However, on the 23rd all boats with sufficient fuel, either in or on their way to the Newfoundland area, were ordered eastwards to an area W of Gibraltar. En route, U 575 was directed to southbound convoy OS 12, sighted by U 43 just N of the Azores on the 28th. U 43 also encountered convoy WS 13 on the 30th.
    U 575 and other eastbound boats came up with the convoys but were unable to make any attacks. The boats continued on their way to Gibraltar in scouting formation. No ships were seen and when the boats arrived in the operational area they found strong anti-submarine patrols at the entrance to the Straits, forcing them to remain submerged and preventing any attack on convoys entering the Mediterranean.
    After the boats had waited in vain for some time BdU decided that searching for convoys should cease and an attack should be made on convoy HG 76, soon to leave Gibraltar. U 575 put in to Vigo and during the night of the 12/13th she was refuelled by the German supply ship *Bessel*.
    The boat returned to St Nazaire **17.12.41**

4. 14.1.42 Left for the North Atlantic.
    U 575 was intended to escort the returning blockade-runner *Spreewald* but this vessel did not appear at the rendezvous point on the 31st, having been sunk in error by U 333 on that day, after being in the wrong position.
    U 575 was ordered to make her way to the Newfoundland Bank. On the 31st U 82 sighted eastbound convoy NA 2 SSE of Sable

Island. U 86, U 566 and U 575 were called up but could not close the convoy on 3.2.42 because of its speed. U 575 operated off the Newfoundland Bank until mid-February but had no success.

The boat returned to St Nazaire **26.2.42**

5. 24.3.42 Left for US waters.

U 575 sank the SS *Robin Hood* (am 6887t) by torpedo and gunfire on 16.4.42 SE of Cape Cod. She patrolled as far as 300 miles south of Hatteras but had no further success.

The boat returned to St Nazaire **14.5.42**

6. 10.6.42 Left for the Caribbean area.

With other outward-bound boats, U 575 was directed to northbound HG 84, reported by a Kondor on the 11th W of Portugal. They were to form a patrol line, *Endrass*, for the 14th in the expected path of the convoy.

HG 84 was sighted again by a Kondor during the afternoon of the 14th and the *Endrass* boats were homed in. The first boat to close, U 552, sank five ships during the night but these were the only successes. All other boats which approached HG 84 were driven off by the escort or aircraft. The operation ended on the 16th because the good, calm weather and good visibility were very unfavourable for U-boat attacks. U 575 had made contact with the convoy by day on the 15th. She attacked a ship that night but without result from five torpedoes fired at long range.

U 575 and four other *Endrass* boats were refuelled by U 459 in the latter half of June W of the Azores. She then continued on to the Caribbean. On 4.7.42 U 575 torpedoed and sank the SS *Norlandia* (am 2689t) NE of Cabo Samaná, Dominica.

The boat left the Caribbean and early on the 9th she sank the SS *Empire Explorer* (br 5345t) by torpedo and gunfire N of Tobago. U 575 patrolled an area E of Trinidad and Tobago. On the 18th she attacked three ships, sinking the sailing vessels *Glacier* (br 130t) and *Comrade* (br 110t) by gunfire and torpedoing and damaging the tanker SS *San Gaspar* (br 12910t).

U 575 returned to St Nazaire **7.8.42**

7. 16.9.42 Left for the North Atlantic.

U 575 joined *Luchs* group W of Ireland, awaiting an ON convoy. On the 29th outward-bound U 118 sighted a westbound convoy 250 miles S of Iceland and the *Luchs* boats were ordered northwest to intercept. When nothing was located by the evening of 2.10.42, the group swept slowly southwestwards. On the 3rd U 260 sighted eastbound HX 209 at the northern end of the *Luchs* patrol line.

Bad weather delayed the concentration of the boats for an attack and a strong air escort kept them at a distance. On the 5th two boats were sunk and another damaged. The operation against HX 209 was terminated next day.

From the 8th the boats coming from HX 209 were formed into *Panther* group 700 to 800 miles W of the North Channel. The group was augmented by outward-bound boats. In the evening of the 11th U 620 sighted westbound ONS 136 and eight boats in the centre of the long *Panther* patrol line were detached and directed to the convoy, as *Leopard* group.

On the 16th ONS 137 was sighted by U 704 as it passed through the southern section of the line and eleven boats were ordered to attack. From the remaining *Panther* boats, *Puma* group was formed on the 16th from U 575 and seven others and ordered southwards to seek ONS 138.

By the 22nd the boats were nearly 400 miles south of their original *Puma* line position. On that day the southernmost boat in the line, U 443, sighted ON 139 in the central North Atlantic. The group was ordered to close and attack but the boats were unable to catch the convoy, which was averaging 10 to 12 knots. Only U 443 was able to attack and she sank two ships.

Puma group moved westwards until the 24th, when U 606 reported two destroyers which could have been part of an escort for a westbound ONS convoy. The boats moved northwestwards at

high speed to intercept. On the 26th U 436 sighted eastbound HX 212 in the centre of the patrol line. She shadowed and brought up other boats but all were driven off by the escort. On the 28th the boats which made contact were driven off by Iceland-based aircraft of 120 Squadron. When the same happened again on the 29th the operation was abandoned. Despite the difficulty in making attacks, six ships were sunk and another damaged. U 575 had no success, apparently making no attacks. On the 29th she torpedoed and sank the MV *Abosso* (br 11330t) in the central North Atlantic.

U 575 put in to Lorient **8.11.42**

8. 17.12.42 Left for the Gibraltar area.

U 575 joined *Delphin* group W of Gibraltar, to operate against US-Mediterranean convoys carrying supplies for the Allied armies in North Africa. On the 29th the group was ordered to sweep westwards, to search for convoy GUS 2. Nothing was seen for four days and the boats were then ordered towards Brazil.

However, on 3.1.43 U 514 reported tanker convoy TM 1 900 miles to the south of *Delphin* and probably heading for Gibraltar. The *Delphin* boats turned south to form a patrol line ahead of the convoy for the 7th.

TM 1 was sighted by U 381 on the 8th. Four homeward- or outward-bound boats had joined the group, making twelve boats available for an attack. In the morning of the 9th U 575 fired five torpedoes, claiming one tanker sunk and two others damaged, possibly the MV *Minister Wedel* (nw 6833t) and the MV *Norvik* (pa 10034t), already damaged by U 522. There is no confirmation of this and it is probable that the explosions heard were of depth-charges dropped by HMS *Pimpernel*. When the operation ended near Madeira on the 11th, seven tankers had been sunk.

Delphin group reformed S of the Azores on the 16th after six of its boats, including U 575, had been refuelled by U 463 W of the Azores. The group moved westwards to meet an eastbound UGS convoy but turned east again on the 18th. From the 21st the *Delphin* boats waited SW of the Azores. In the evening of the 25th U 575 torpedoed and sank the SS *City of Flint* (am 4963t), a straggler from convoy UGS 4. The captain of this vessel was picked up as a prisoner.

When nothing further had materialised by the 29th the group moved further eastwards. From the 31st the line was NW of the Canaries but then moved to a position W of Gibraltar for 6.2.43.

From the 11th the *Delphin* boats moved north to take up positions W of Portugal. A southbound convoy was reported on the 12th 200 miles W of Cape Finisterre. *Delphin* was ordered to close but the operation failed when the convoy's air cover kept the boats submerged. The situation worsened the nearer the convoy got to Gibraltar. Attacks became impossible and two boats were lost.

U 575 returned to St Nazaire **18.2.43**

9. 22.4.43 Left for the North Atlantic.

U 575 joined *Amsel 1* group E of Newfoundland on or about 4.5.43 in a patrol line ahead of southwest-bound convoy ONS 5. During the night of the 4/5th the first boats of *Amsel 1* and *2* and *Fink* groups located the convoy. Attacks were made and the convoy was split into several smaller, escorted groups. In the late afternoon of the 5th fog came down and almost all contact was lost. After it was regained briefly in the early morning of the 6th, the operation was abandoned. Twelve ships had been sunk and six boats lost. U 575 had no success and she had been slightly damaged by gunfire by the sloop HMS *Sennen* in the morning of the 6th.

From the 8th *Amsel 1* and *2* groups reformed as *Elbe* group E of Newfoundland. The group was ordered southeastwards to intercept HX 237 but the convoy was too far ahead, so the *Elbe* boats headed southeastwards again to cut off the slower SC 129.

On the 10th *Rhein* and *Elbe* groups were combined to form *Elbe 1* and *2* groups. U 575 was in *Elbe 1*. Whilst the boats were forming their line on the 11th, they passed SC 129, which was sighted by U 504 but she was driven off.

U 575 (continued)

However, contact was made on the 12th but the eleven boats shadowing were driven off. Some were damaged and U 186 was sunk. After the escort-carrier HMS *Biter* arrived, the operation was called off on the 14th. Two ships were sunk and two boats lost.

On or about the 17th U 575 was refuelled for further operations, possibly by another boat. She then joined *Mosel* group 400 miles S of Cape Farewell, to operate against convoy HX 239. It passed south of the patrol line and although some *Mosel* boats moved southeastwards to intercept, they did not find the convoy.

From the 24th Dönitz temporarily halted operations against convoys in the North Atlantic. U 575 and other *Mosel* and *Donau* boats with limited fuel ranged over a large area, their continuing radio signals planned to give the impression that a large U-boat presence was being maintained across the convoy routes.

U 575 returned to St Nazaire **11.6.43**

10. 20.9.43 Left St Nazaire and returned **22.9.43**

11. 25.9.43 Left St Nazaire and returned **27.9.43**

12. 28.9.43 Left St Nazaire and returned **30.9.43**

13. 6.10.43 Left for the North Atlantic.

U 575 joined *Siegfried* group, formed for the 24th 500 miles E of Newfoundland to await HX 262 and SC 145. The boats were ordered to remain submerged in daylight, ready for an attack after dark. On the 25th it was thought that a convoy would pass south of the group. The boats moved southwards but nothing was found.

To cover a wider area, *Siegfried* was split into three small sub-groups, *Siegfried 1,2* and *3*. U 575 was in *Siegfried 3*. The groups continued southwards, searching for SC 145 but it passed by on the 29th. Two days later the boats again reformed, this time into groups *Jahn* and *Körner*. U 575 was in *Jahn*.

On 3.11.43 the boats were redeployed in five small sub-groups, *Tirpitz 1* to *5*, to search for convoy HX 264. It passed the groups late on the 6th and next day the operation was abandoned, it being impossible to surface in daylight because of carrier-borne aircraft.

U 575 next joined *Eisenhart* group, made up of seven sub-groups of three boats each and drawn up in two lines from 11.11.43, running southeast from Cape Farewell.

Reports indicated that convoys were being routed to the south so the *Eisenhart* boats were ordered southeastwards on the 12th to search for SC 146 and HX 265. By the 16th no convoys had been found and the majority of the boats were then WSW of Ireland. Fuel was now becoming a problem for many of *Eisenhart* group and it was decided to end the operation.

Boats of the group with sufficient fuel went to reinforce *Schill* group W of Spain. U 575 set out with the other boats and may have operated briefly against combined convoy MKS 30/SL 139 on the way but without success. She then headed home.

The boat returned to St Nazaire **28.11.43**

14. 29.2.44 Left for the Eastern Atlantic.

U 575 was the second operational boat to be equipped with the schnorkel. The first one, U 264, had been sunk on 19.2.44.

On or about 7.3.44 U 575 joined *Preussen* group. Its boats were operating singly over a wide area in the Western Approaches. Early on the 10th U 575 torpedoed and sank the corvette HMS *Asphodel* WNW of Cape Finisterre, which was escorting northbound convoy MKS 41/SL 150. Later on the 10th U 575 unsuccessfully attacked convoy SC 154, which was sighted and reported by U 845.

U 575 was located on the 13th near convoy ON 227. She was attacked and damaged by three aircraft from Lagens, Azores, a Wellington of 172 Squadron (F/O J P Finnessey), and Fortresses of 206 Squadron (F/O A D Beaty) and 220 Squadron (F/O W R Travell). She came under depth-charge attacks by the frigate HMCS *Prince Rupert* (Lt-Cdr R W Draney), the destroyer-escort USS *Haverfield*

(Lt-Cdr R W Dudley) and the destroyer-minesweeper USS *Hobson*.

The boat was finally sunk N of the Azores, possibly after an attack by an Avenger of VC-95 (Lt-Cdr Adams) from the escort-carrier USS *Bogue*. Before being sunk, U 575 may have shot down a carrier-borne aircraft.

Of U 575's crew, 18 men were lost and the commander and possibly 34 other men were made PoW.

U 576 Type VII C

Built by Blohm & Voss, Hamburg
Keel laid 1.8.40   Launched 30.4.41
Commissioned 26.6.41   Feldpost Nr M 44 117

Sunk 15.7.42 S of Cape Hatteras (34°51′N 75°22′W)

Served with
7 U-Flottille, Kiel/St Nazaire   June 1941 - 15.7.42 (ab/fb)

Commanded by
KL Hans-Dieter Heinicke   June 1941 - 15.7.42

Patrols: 5   Ships sunk: 5 (23,706 grt) + 1 damaged

1. 27.9.41 Left Kiel and arrived Bergen **29.9.41**

2. 30.9.41 Left Bergen and arrived Kirkenes **5.10.41**

3. 6.10.41 Left for Northern Waters.

U 576 operated off the Kola coast and in the entrance to the White Sea. She had no success.

The boat returned to Kirkenes **5.11.41**

4. 8.11.41 Left Kirkenes and arrived Bergen **12.11.41**

5. 11.12.41 Left, in transit to Western France.

U 576 put in to her new base at St Nazaire **23.12.41**

6. 20.1.42 Left for Canadian waters.

U 576 patrolled S of Nova Scotia. Early on 14.2.42 she torpedoed and sank the MV *Empire Spring* (br 6946t) SE of Sable Island.

The boat returned to St Nazaire **28.2.42**

7. 29.3.42 Left for the US east coast.

U 576 was one of twelve boats which made up the fifth wave of *Operation Paukenschlag*. Nearing the US coast, she sank the SS *Pipestone County* (am 5102t) on 21.4.42 N of Bermuda.

The boat turned northwards and on the 24th she hit the SS *Tropic Star* with a dud torpedo E of Nantucket Island. This vessel had aboard survivors from the *Pipestone County*, picked up from lifeboats. The *Tropic Star* was undamaged and reached Boston safely.

On the 30th U 576 torpedoed and sank the SS *Taborfjell* (nw 1339t) E of Cape Cod. From 1.5.42 she attempted to shadow a troop convoy, sighted 80 miles SW of Cape Sable. After being driven off by aircraft, she resumed her return journey.

U 576 reached St Nazaire **16.5.42**

8. 16.6.42 Left for US waters.

In late June U 576 was refuelled by U 460 N of the Azores. She went on to patrol off Hatteras. On 14.7.42 the boat was caught on the surface by two USN OS2U-3 aircraft. The first (Ens W R Jemison), straddled U 576 with depth-charges as she submerged. The boat resurfaced and as the second aircraft (Ens G L Schein) approached, U 576 appeared to be sinking. Schein dropped two depth-sharges as the boat sank beneath the surface, leaving a large oil slick. The two aircraft circled for an hour until relieved by an Army aircraft, whose pilot confirmed the boat's probable sinking.

U 576's commander righted his boat that night and reported that one of the main ballast tanks was damaged beyond repair and that he had lost much fuel.

U 576 set out for home but on the 15th, she sighted an approaching convoy S of Cape Hatteras. Three ships were torpedoed, the tanker MV *J A Mowinckel* (pa 11147t) and the SS *Chilore* (am 8310t) were damaged and the SS *Bluefields* (ni 2063t) was sunk. The two damaged ships left the convoy. The *Chilore* sank later under tow and the *J A Mowinckel* was repaired and went back into service.

Immediately after making her attack, U 576 was herself attacked by two USN Kingfisher aircraft of VS-9 (Ens F C Lewis and C D Webb), escorting the convoy. Their depth-bombs forced the now-seriously damaged U 576 to the surface, where she was fired on by naval guard gunners and also possibly rammed by the SS *Unicoi*. The boat sank quickly.

There were no survivors, 45 dead.

U 577   Type VII C

Built by Blohm & Voss, Hamburg
Keel laid 1.8.40   Launched 15.5.41
Commissioned 3.7.41   Feldpost Nr M 44 228

Sunk 15.1.42 NE of Tobruk (32°40′N 25°08′E)

Served with
7 U-Flottille, Kiel/St Nazaire   July - December 1941 (ab/fb)
29 U-Flottille, La Spezia   December 1941 - 15.1.42 (fb)

Commanded by
KL Herbert Schauenburg   July 1941 - 15.1.42

Patrols: 3   Ships sunk: None

1. 20.10.41   Left Kiel for the North Atlantic.
On the 30th U 577 was ordered to the Newfoundland Bank, to join other boats in the formation of *Stosstrupp* group. En route on the 31st, U 552 sighted eastbound HX 156 in the central North Atlantic but only she and U 567 closed the convoy.

U 577 joined *Raubritter* group, which had just finished operating against convoy SC 52. The group formed a new patrol line on the 8th SE of Cape Farewell. When westbound ONS 33 was reported on the 12th, U 577, U 85, U 106, U 133 and U 571 were deployed but did not find the convoy. These boats began their return journey on the 15th. They operated successfully against westbound ONS 11 on the 16th.

U 577, U 85, U 133 and U 571 formed a patrol line, *Störtebecker*, on the 19th, one of three lines of boats formed to meet expected convoy OG 77. The convoy did not materialise before the boats were ordered to return.

U 577 put in to her new base at St Nazaire **26.11.41**.

2. 16.12.41   Left for the Mediterranean.
During the night of the 22/23rd U 577 passed through the Straits of Gibraltar. She moved on to the Eastern Mediterranean to operate off the coasts of Egypt and Cyrenaica.

U 577 put in to Messina **27.12.41**.

3. 7.1.42   Left for the Eastern Mediterranean.
On the 15th U 577 was located and sunk in a depth-charge attack by a Swordfish of 815 (FAA) Squadron NE of Tobruk.

There were no survivors, 43 dead.

U 578   Type VII C

Built by Blohm & Voss, Hamburg
Keel laid 1.8.40   Launched 15.5.41
Commissioned 10.7.41   Feldpost Nr M 46 136

Sunk 10.8.42 N of Cape Ortegal (45°59′N 07°44′W)

Served with
5 U-Flottille, Kiel   July - August 1941 (ab)
7 U-Flottille, Kiel/St Nazaire   September 1941 - 10.8.42 (ab/fb)

Commanded by
KK Ernst-August Rehwinkel   July 1941 - 10.8.42

Patrols: 5   Ships sunk: 4 (23,635 grt)
                            1 destroyer (1090 dt)

1. 28.10.41   Left Kiel and arrived Trondheim **2.11.41**

2. 5.11.41   Left Trondheim and arrived Kirkenes **8.11.41**

3. 19.11.41   Left for Northern Waters.
U 578 patrolled off the Kola coast, near the entrance to the White Sea. On the 26th the boat was slightly damaged when she was rammed by the Soviet patrol ship *SKR-25/Briz* near Kanin Nos.

The boat returned to Kirkenes **27.11.41**

4. 29.11.41   Left Kirkenes and arrived Bergen **4.12.41**

5. 6.12.41   Left Bergen and arrived Kiel **10.12.41**

6. 15.1.42   Left for the North Atlantic.
U 578 was one of twelve boats from Germany which assembled W of Rockall, as *Schlei* group, to carry out a southwesterly sweep across the convoy routes. The planned operation was called off and U 578 and six other boats went to bases in France to be prepared for service in US waters. The other five *Schlei* boats went to the Iceland/Faroes/Scotland area for the protection of Norway.

U 578 put in to her new base at St Nazaire **28.1.42**

7. 3.2.42   Left for the Western Atlantic.
U 578 went to the area off Nova Scotia and then moved southwards to patrol along the US east coast. On the 27th she torpedoed and sank the tanker SS *R P Resor* (am 7451t) SE of New York and on the 28th the destroyer USS *Jacob Jones* S of Atlantic City. The warship was moving south alone when she was struck by two torpedoes just before dawn, sinking within the hour. Only 11 men survived from the *Jacob Jones'* crew of almost 200. She was the first US warship sunk by enemy action in US coastal waters.

On 12.3.42 U 578 probably sank the SS *Ingerto* (nw 3089t) SSW of Bermuda. She was the only boat known to be in the area and reporting a sinking.

The boat returned to St Nazaire **25.3.42**

8. 7.5.42   Left for operations in US waters.
On the 21st U 578 joined seven other boats to form *Pfadfinder* group 400 miles E of New York. Very few ships had been seen near the coast and the group's objective was to investigate passage of shipping between the US east coast ports and Central and South America and how far its routes were from the coast. The group dispersed after a few days and most of the boats moved closer to the coast.

U 578 stayed out and on the 27th she torpedoed and sank the MV *Polyphemus* (nl 6269t) some 500 miles ESE of New York. On 2.6.42 U 578 sank the MV *Berganger* (nw 6826t) S of Nantucket Island. This vessel had been missed earlier in the day by five torpedoes from U 213 in several attacks.

U 578 (continued)

U 578 went south again and finished her patrol E of Cape Hatteras, setting out for home in mid-June.

She returned to St Nazaire **3.7.42**

9. 6.8.42 Left for Atlantic operations.

Outward-bound, U 578 was sunk on the 10th by a Wellington of 311 (Czech) Squadron (F/O J Nývlt) N of Cape Ortegal.

There were no survivors, 49 dead.

U 579   Type VII C

Built by Blohm & Voss, Hamburg
Keel laid 31.8.40   Launched 28.5.41
Commissioned 17.7.41   Feldpost Nr M 46 268

Sunk 5.5.45 off Fredericia, Denmark

Served with
5 U-Flottille, Kiel   July 1941 - 29.9.41 (ab)
24 U-Flottille, Memel   May 1942 - August 1943 (ab)
23 U-Flottille, Danzig   August 1943 - February 1945 (ab)
4 U-Flottille, Stettin   March 1945 - 5.5.45 (ab)

Commanded by
KL Dietrich Lohmann   July 1941 - 29.9.41
OL Günther Ruppelt   May - October 1942
OL Gerhard Linder   October 1942 - September 1944
OL Hans-Dietrich Schwarzenberg   September 1944 - 5.5.45

Patrols: None   Ships sunk: None

On 29.9.41 U 579 was badly damaged by a fire in the bow torpedo-room, which claimed the lives of two men. The boat was taken out of service and after being successfully repaired, she went back into service again in May 1942.

U 579 saw no operational service but served as a training boat at 24, 23 and 4 U-Flottillen.

On 3.5.45 the boat left Kiel on transfer to Norway. She had passed through the Little Belt, when she was attacked and sunk by a Liberator of 547 Squadron (F/O A A Bruneau) on the 5th off Fredericia. The boat was seen to break in half.

24 men were lost, including U 579's commander.

U 580   Type VII C

Built by Blohm & Voss, Hamburg
Keel laid 31.8.40   Launched 28.5.41
Commissioned 24.7.41   Feldpost Nr M 46 323

Lost 11.11.41 off Memel

Served with
5 U-Flottille, Kiel   July 1941 - 11.11.41 (ab)

Commanded by
OL Hans-Günther Kuhlmann   July 1941 - 11.11.41

Patrols: None   Ships sunk: None

On 11.11.41 U 580 was lost during training exercises off Memel, after colliding with the SS Angelburg. *12 men lost.*

U 581   Type VII C

Built by Blohm & Voss, Hamburg
Keel laid 25.9.40   Launched 12.6.41
Commissioned 31.7.41   Feldpost Nr M 46 386

Sunk 2.2.42 N of Horta, Azores (38°24′N 28°30′W)

Served with
5 U-Flottille, Kiel   July - December 1941 (ab)
7 U-Flottille, St Nazaire   December 1941 - 2.2.42 (fb)

Commanded by
KL Werner Pfeifer   July 1941 - 2.2.42

Patrols: 2   Ships sunk: None

1. 13.12.41 Left Kiel, in transit to Western France.

U 581 put in to her new base at St Nazaire **24.12.41**

2. 11.1.42 Left for the Gibraltar area.

U 581 left in company with U 402. On the 16th they encountered a troop-transport convoy NE of the Azores. U 581 had no success but U 402 torpedoed and damaged the MV *Llangibby Castle* (br 12053t).

The ship was taken in to Horta and after some repairs she sailed again on 2.2.42, with three escorts. U 581, U 402 and U 572 were waiting for her. Their efforts to attack the transport failed and on the 2nd U 581 was driven off and sunk in a depth-charge attack by a destroyer of the escort, HMS *Westcott* (Cdr I H Brockett-Hugh), just NW of Horta.

Of U 581's crew, 4 men were lost and the commander and the rest of the crew were made PoW. However, one source says that one of U 581's officers managed to swim ashore and later got back to Germany. Details he gave of damage caused by depth-charges resulted in gland modifications in the Type VII C's pressure hull.

U 582   Type VII C

Built by Blohm & Voss, Hamburg
Keel laid 25.9.40   Launched 12.6.41
Commissioned 7.8.41   Feldpost Nr M 46 477

Sunk 5.10.42 WNW of Rockall (58°52′N 21°42′W)

Served with
5 U-Flottille, Kiel   August - December 1941 (ab)
1 U-Flottille, Brest   December 1941 - 5.10.42 (fb)

Commanded by
KL Werner Schulte   August 1941 - 5.10.42

Patrols: 4   Ships sunk: 6 (38,826 grt)

1. 20.12.41 Left Kiel and arrived Trondheim **29.12.41**

2. 3.1.42 Left for the North Atlantic.

U 582 went to the Newfoundland Bank area. Extreme cold, snow-storms, fog and heavy seas made operating very difficult. Later in January U-boat commanders were allowed to move further south.

On the 26th U 582 torpedoed and sank the SS *Refast* (br 5189t) of convoy ON 56, S of Cape Race. The boat set out for home and between February 1st and 3rd she took part in the search for survivors of the German blockade-runner *Spreewald*, sunk in error on January 31st by U 333.

U 582 put in to her new base at Brest **7.2.42**

3. 19.3.42 Left for Atlantic operations.

U 582 was intended to escort the returning German blockade-runner *Rio Grande*, coming from Japan. The boat was ordered to meet the ship on 3.4.42 but when *Rio Grande* had not appeared by the 7th, U 582 moved westwards.

From mid-April she was operating NE of Bermuda and late in April U 582 was refuelled by U 459 500 miles NE of Bermuda. She continued to patrol in the area for another two weeks before setting out for base. The boat had no success on this patrol.

She returned to Brest **24.5.42**

4. 22.6.42 Left Brest and returned **26.6.42**

5. 27.6.42 Left for the Central Atlantic.

U 582 was one of six boats intended for operations in the Freetown area. They assembled SE of the Azores, as *Hai* group, and on 10.7.42 began to sweep southwards between meridians 20° and 25°W. On the 11th southbound convoy OS 33 passed through the patrol line S of Santa Maria, Azores.

After dark a group of ships bound for South America split from the convoy, which continued southwards. U 582 shadowed these ships and early on the 12th torpedoed and sank the SS *Port Hunter* (br 8826t) SSE of the Azores. Early on the 15th she sank the SS *Empire Attendant* (br 7524t) SW of the Canaries.

The *Hai* boats reformed and continued southwards and after passing Dakar they dispersed. On the 22nd U 582 sank the SS *Honolulan* (am 7493t) SW of Dakar and on the 23rd the boat was refuelled by U 116 W of Freetown. U 582 attacked the SS *Stella Lykes* (am 6801t) on the 27th WSW of Freetown. This vessel was damaged by torpedoes and gunfire but did not sink until dispatched six and a half hours later, with demolition charges. U 582 took two survivors aboard as prisoners.

The boat returned to Brest **11.8.42**

6. 14.9.42 Left for the North Atlantic.

U 582 headed for the Newfoundland area. On the 23rd she sank the MV *Vibran* (nw 2993t) WNW of the Azores. U 582 joined *Luchs* group formed from the 29th W of Ireland. Immediately, it moved 250 miles northwestwards to search for a westbound convoy, sighted by U 118.

When the convoy had not been found by the evening of the 2nd, the *Luchs* line went southwestwards and on the 3rd U 260 sighted eastbound HX 209. Bad weather and high winds prevented the pursuing boats gathering for a concentrated attack on the 5th. On this day U 582 was located and sunk by a USN Catalina of VP-73 (Lt G F Swanson) WNW of Rockall.

There were no survivors, 46 dead.

U 583 Type VII C

Built by Blohm & Voss, Hamburg
Keel laid 1.10.40   Launched 26.6.41
Commissioned 14.8.41   Feldpost Nr M 04 507

Sunk 15.11.41 off Danzig

Served with
5 U-Flottille, Kiel   August 1941 - 15.11.41 (ab)

Commanded by
KL Heinrich Ratsch   August 1941 - 15.11.41

Patrols: None   Ships sunk: None

On 15.11.41 U 583 was carrying out training exercises in the Baltic off Danzig, when she collided with U 153.
U 583 sank with all hands, 45 dead.

U 584 Type VII C

Built by Blohm & Voss, Hamburg
Keel laid 1.10.40   Launched 26.6.41
Commissioned 21.8.41   Feldpost Nr M 05 347

Sunk 31.10.43 NNE of the Azores (49°14′N 31°55′W)

Served with
5 U-Flottille, Kiel   August - November 1941 (ab)
1 U-Flottille, Brest   November 1941 - 31.10.43 (fb)

Commanded by
KL Joachim Deecke   August 1941 - 31.10.43
KL Kurt Nölke (temp)   20.12.42 - 11.2.43

Patrols: 10   Ships sunk: 3 (18,478 grt)
                              1 submarine (206 dt)

1. 27.11.41 Left Kiel for Northern Waters. No details are known of this first patrol.

U 584 put in to Neidenfjord **20.12.41**

2. 25.12.41 Left for operations.

U 584 joined with U 134 and U 454, as *Ulan* group, the first to operate in Northern Waters. The boats were deployed in the passage S of Bear Island to operate against British convoys going to and from Murmansk.

Ulan group operated against eastbound PQ 7A and PQ 8. U 134 and U 454 had their successes against the convoys but U 584 had none. However, on 10.1.42 U 584 torpedoed and sank the Soviet submarine *M-175* off the Russian coast N of Poluostrov.

U 584 put in to Kirkenes **11.1.42**

3. 23.1.42 Left for operations. No details known of this patrol.

U 584 returned to Kirkenes **20.2.42**

4. 28.2.42 Left for operations.

On 5.3.42 eastbound PQ 12 was found by aerial reconnaissance 70 miles S of Jan Mayen. U 584, U 134, U 377 and U 403 formed a patrol line to intercept. The convoy was not found and the boats also missed westbound QP 8.

U 584 put in to Hamburg **14.3.42**

5. 29.4.42 Left Hamburg and arrived Kiel **30.4.42**

6. 5.5.42 Left, in transit to Western France.

U 584 put in to her new base at Brest **16.5.42**

7. 25.5.42 Left for US waters.

Soon after midnight on 16.6.42 U 584 arrived off Ponte Vedra, S of Jacksonville, Florida. Four agents were put ashore in a rubber dinghy, with four wooden boxes, as part of *Operation Pastorius*. The boxes were buried on the beach and the men, Werner Thiel, Hermann Neubauer, Herbert Haupt and Edward Kerling, went into Jacksonville.

Their mission was to carry out sabotage activities against industrial installations and railways. On the 19th Haupt and Neubauer went to Chicago and Kerling and Thiel to New York. Haupt's parents lived in Chicago and he went to them.

Four other agents had been landed on Long Island by U 202 on the 16th and, rather unaccountably, two of them, George Dasch and Ernst Burger, decided to betray *Operation Pastorius*. After Dasch had revealed all to the FBI in Washington, Burger and the other two men landed by U 202 were arrested in New York, as were Kerling and Thiel on the 23rd. Haupt and Neubauer were arrested in Chicago on the 27th.

Dasch and Burger were tried and imprisoned and in April 1948

U 584 (continued)

they were deported back to Germany. The other six agents were all executed and the German-Americans who had helped the group were sentenced to varying terms of imprisonment.

After landing the agents, U 584 operated off New York and later off Hatteras. She had no success. In early July the boat was refuelled by U 460 W of the Azores.

She returned to Brest **22.7.42**

8. 24.8.42 Left for the North Atlantic.

From the 31st U 584 and five other outward-bound boats formed *Stier* group W of Ireland. It was involved in a failed operation against an ONS convoy on September 1st and 2nd. On the 4th *Stier* combined with *Vorwärts* group to form a long patrol line W of Ireland, to await a westbound convoy.

In the evening of the 9th U 584 sighted ON 127 in the central North Atlantic as it passed through the southern end of the patrol line. Contact was lost during the night but regained on the 10th. In the early hours of the 11th U 584 torpedoed and sank the tanker SS *Empire Oil* (br 8029t), which had stopped after being hit by U 659 four and a half hours earlier.

In the evening of the 11th U 584 torpedoed and damaged the MV *Hindanger* (nw 4884t), sunk some hours later by the corvette HMCS *Amherst* with gunfire and depth-charges. The operation against the convoy ended on the 14th because of bad visibility and the arrival of Newfoundland-based aircraft from the 13th. Seven ships were sunk and it was one of the few times in the war that all participating U-boats fired at least one torpedo each.

U 584 went to an area NW of the Azores, where she was refuelled by U 461 on or about the 20th. From the 22nd a new *Vorwärts* patrol line was formed E of Newfoundland. Next day eastbound RB 1 passed through the centre of the line, sighted by U 404. The convoy was made up of several steamers from the Great Lakes, going to England. The boats reported them to be liners carrying troops. *Vorwärts* group was joined in the attack on the convoy by some boats of *Pfeil* group.

U 584 had no success but the convoy lost three steamers and one escorting destroyer. On the 29th U 584, U 216, U 404 and U 410 formed *Letzte Ritter* group in the central North Atlantic. On 1.10.42 U 216 and U 410 went to refuel and U 404 and U 584 went home.

U 584 reached Brest **10.10.42**

9. 30.12.42 Left for the North Atlantic.

U 584 joined *Falke* group 500 miles W of Ireland, where it was awaiting an ON convoy. The group was directed to ONS 158, ON 159 and ONS 160 but all were re-routed to avoid the boats.

From 7.1.43 *Falke* group swept westwards, searching for convoys. This move continued until the 15th, with nothing seen. The group turned north next day but again found nothing.

On the 19th *Falke* and *Habicht* groups were formed into two new patrol lines, *Haudegen* and *Landsknecht*, the latter made up of those boats with less fuel, which included U 584. For a week the *Landsknecht* boats waited W of Ireland for an ON convoy but it did not eventuate. The group was dispersed on the 28th.

U 584, U 71 and U 572 joined with outward-bound boats on 4.2.43 to form a new patrol line, *Hartherz*, W of Gibraltar. An HG convoy that was expected did not materialise. The group dispersed on the 8th.

U 584 returned to Brest **11.2.43**

10. 23.3.43 Left for the North Atlantic.

U 584 joined *Löwenherz* group, formed from 3.4.43 SE of Greenland. On the 4th the returning U 530 sighted eastbound HX 231 and she brought up some *Löwenherz* boats, the only ones available to operate against the convoy. Conditions were favourable and pursuit of HX 231 continued until the 7th, with six ships sunk and four damaged. The constant presence of carrier-borne aircraft made attacks difficult. U 584 did not make any.

The majority of the *Löwenherz* boats, including U 584, formed a new patrol line, *Lerche*, SE of Cape Farewell from the 10th, to intercept eastbound HX 232. On the 11th U 584 sighted the convoy as it passed through the line. Successful attacks were made early on the 12th by U 563, in which two ships were sunk and another damaged, which was finished off later in the day by U 706. Further attacks on the convoy were prevented by aircraft and the operation against HX 232 ended on the 13th W of the North Channel.

Between the 17th and 20th U 584 and four other *Lerche* boats were refuelled by U 487 in the central North Atlantic, after which they joined a new patrol line, *Specht*, formed from the 20th N of the Azores. From the 22nd the group awaited eastbound SC 127 but when it did not materialise the boats moved northwestwards at high speed and formed a new line from the 25th, ahead of convoy ONS 4. Again, the convoy was re-routed to miss the line.

From the 27th *Specht* was deployed NE of Newfoundland against HX 235 but the convoy was re-routed to the south. On the 29th *Specht* and *Amsel* groups formed a line NE of Newfoundland to intercept eastbound SC 128. Both groups moved south to search but when the convoy had not been found by 1.5.43 the *Specht* boats went north again and a new, long patrol line, *Fink*, was formed on the 3rd from the boats of *Specht* and *Star* groups, S of Cape Farewell.

SC 128 did not appear but in the afternoon of the 4th ONS 5 passed through the centre of the *Fink* line. During the night of the 4/5th attacks were made. The convoy dispersed into a number of small escorted groups. In daylight on the 5th further attacks were made before fog came down. In the afternoon U 584 attacked stragglers escorted by the corvette HMS *Pink*. The SS *West Madaket* (am 5565t) was torpedoed and sunk and U 584 claimed a second ship sunk but this is most unlikely.

In the fog nearly all contact was lost with the convoy and the escorts located and attacked fifteen boats. The convoy was sighted again early on the 6th but by then the weather was deteriorating and the operation was terminated. U 584 then joined *Elbe* group E of Newfoundland. It moved southeastwards on the 8th to get ahead of convoy SC 129. On the 10th *Rhein* and *Elbe* groups combined to form *Elbe 1* and *2*. U 584 was in *Elbe 1*.

Forming up on the 11th, the boats passed the convoy. Only two ships were sunk, both by U 402, before the operation ended on the 14th. U 584 was refuelled by U 119 N of the Azores on or about the 16th for return to base.

U 584 returned to Brest **24.5.43**

11. 2.9.43 Left for the North Atlantic.

U 584 was one of fourteen boats which set out to form a patrol line, *Leuthen*, SSW of Iceland from the 20th, to intercept an ONS convoy. They were joined by six other boats which had assembled N of the Azores and then after refuelling had moved north to take their place in the patrol line. Secrecy had been maintained as far as possible to prevent the presence of the boats becoming known to the Allies. However, on the 19th westbound U 341, which should have been proceeding submerged, was sighted, attacked and sunk by a Canadian aircraft near the planned patrol line position.

Early on the 20th, before the *Leuthen* boats were in position, convoy ON 202 was sighted. Four boats closed but only one was able to make a submerged attack. In the morning contact was lost because of a strong surface and air escort. During the day ON 202 joined up with convoy ONS 18. Contact was regained by the boats in the early evening.

Only five boats closed the convoy, the other *Leuthen* boats being intent on attacking the escorts, in the belief that if the escorts were depleted the convoys could be dealt with during the night of the 21/22nd. In the early morning of the 21st U 584 unsuccessfully attacked HMCS *Chambly* of the escort, her torpedo exploding harmlessly in the corvette's wake.

Fog came down early on the 21st and remained throughout the day and the next night. When it thinned during daylight on the

22nd Allied aircraft re-appeared and boats remained on the surface to fight it out. Further attacks were made on the convoy early on the 23rd and more ships were sunk before the operation ended later in the morning. Six ships had been sunk and another damaged, three escorts had also been sunk and another damaged beyond repair. Two boats were lost.

Some *Leuthen* boats returned home. U 584 and others were joined by new-arrivals and a new patrol line, *Rossbach*, was formed on the 27th in the central North Atlantic to operate against ON 203. The convoy passed north of the patrol line and the group also missed ONS 19, which also passed to the north, in spite of a move in that direction on 1.10.43 by the boats.

From the 3rd the group went eastwards to meet ON 204 but when it was not found the boats, then SW of Iceland, began a sweep southwestwards to search for SC 143 or HX 259, which they expected to intercept on the 8th. The convoys were not found and the search was called off on the 9th.

Now short of fuel, U 584, U 378, U 402, U 603, U 641 and U 731 headed south to refuel. From the 11th the boats made several attempts to rendezvous at different positions with U-tanker U 488 in an area 300 to 600 miles N to NW of the Azores. Each attempt was frustrated by bad weather conditions or the unwelcome attention of carrier-borne aircraft.

U 584 waited for more than fourteen days, until on the 31st she met U 91 SE of Cape Farewell. U 91 was in the process of passing over fuel when the two boats were sighted by an Avenger of VC-9 (Lt W S Fowler) from the escort-carrier USS *Card*. The aircraft circled, waiting for help to arrive. U 91 dived and as two other Avengers (Lts Balliett and McAuslan) came up, U 584 also dived.

Fowler approached and dropped a mine ahead of U 584 and Balliett dropped another further ahead and slightly to port. Explosions were observed and patches of oil and debris were seen. U 584 was destroyed.

There were no survivors, 53 dead, including a team of B-Dienst specialists who had monitored Allied convoy radio signals.

U 585   Type VII C

Built by Blohm & Voss, Hamburg
Keel laid 1.10.40   Launched 9.7.41
Commissioned 28.8.41   Feldpost Nr M 05 506

Sunk 30.3.42 N of Kola Inlet (70°10′N 34°00′E)

Served with
6 U-Flottille, Danzig   August 1941 - 30.3.42 (ab/fb)

Commanded by
KL Bernhard Lohse   August 1941 - 30.3.42

Patrols: 5   Ships sunk: None

1. **20.12.41** Left Kiel for Northern Waters. No details known.
U 585 put in to Neidenfjord **9.1.42**

2. **15.1.42** Left for operations. No details known.
U 585 put in to Kirkenes **21.1.42**

3. **25.1.42** Left for operations. No details known except that on 4.2.42 a crewman was lost overboard.
U 585 returned to Kirkenes **21.2.42**

4. **15.3.42** Left for operations. No details known.
U 585 returned to Kirkenes **25.3.42**

5. **28.3.42** Left for operations.
In the morning of the 27th a German aircraft sighted eastbound

PQ 13, which had been scattered in a storm. U 585, U 435, U 454, U 456 and U 589 were directed to the convoy, as were also German destroyers and aircraft.

On the 30th, whilst operating against the convoy N of Kola Inlet, U 585 sank after striking a mine..

There were no survivors, 45 dead.

U 586   Type VII C

Built by Blohm & Voss, Hamburg
Keel laid 1.10.40   Launched 10.7.41
Commissioned 4.9.41   Feldpost Nr M 05 723

Decommissioned 12.7.44 at Toulon

Served with
6 U-Flottille, Danzig/St Nazaire   September 1941 - June 1942 (ab/fb)
11 U-Flottille, Bergen   July 1942 - May 1943 (fb)
13 U-Flottille, Trondheim   June - September 1943 (fb)
6 U-Flottille, St Nazaire   October 1943 - February 1944 (fb)
29 U-Flottille, Toulon   March 1944 - 12.7.44 (fb)

Commanded by
KL Dietrich von der Esch   September 1941 - August 1943
OL Hans Götze   August 1943 - 12.7.44

Patrols: 13   Ships sunk: 2 (12,716 grt) + 1 damaged

1. **12.1.42** Left Kiel for the North Atlantic.
U 586, U 587 and U 588, all from Germany, and U 94 assembled W of the Hebrides from the 15th. Briefly, on the 18th, the four boats formed a patrol line 40 miles E of the Outer Bailey Bank to intercept ten transports, reported on the 16th to be heading towards England from Reykjavik, but this came to nothing.

More boats arrived from Germany and from the 21st twelve boats, including U 586, assembled W of Rockall as *Schlei* group, for a southwesterly sweep across the convoy routes. However, with favourable reports of operations off the US coast, the *Schlei* boats were ordered to bases in western France to prepare for operations in the Western Atlantic.

Further orders were then received that eight boats were to go to the Iceland/Faroes/Scotland area for the protection of Norway. Five *Schlei* boats, U 586, U 352, U 435, U 455 and U 591, had their previous orders cancelled and went northwards. U 586 patrolled W of the Faroes and from early February she was on weather-reporting duties. In the early morning of the 9th U 586 torpedoed and damaged the tanker MV *Anna Knudsen* (nw 9057t) NW of the Butt of Lewis.

The boat put in to Bergen **12.2.42**

2. **16.2.42** Left Bergen and arrived Trondheim **19.2.42**

3. **14.3.42** Left for operations. No details known.
U 586 returned to Trondheim **22.3.42**

4. **10.5.42** Left for operations in Northern Waters.
U 586 operated against eastbound convoy PQ 16, which set out from Reykjavik on the 21st.
In the early hours of the 29th she made an unsuccessful attack on a tanker in the Barents Sea, N of Kola Inlet. Four torpedoes were fired and four detonations heard.
The boat put in to Skjomenfjord **1.6.42**

5. **4.6.42** Left Skjomenfjord and arrived Trondheim **6.6.42**

6. **25.7.42** Left for operations. No details known.
U 586 put in to Narvik **16.8.42**

U 586 (continued)

7. 27.8.42 Left Narvik and arrived Bergen **31.8.42**

8. 3.10.42 Left Bergen and arrived Skjomenfjord **5.10.42**

9. 11.10.42 Left for operations in the Norwegian Sea.

From the 13th U 586 and U 212 carried out a reconnaissance of Allied installations on the coast of Jan Mayen Island, to gather information for a planned minelaying operation by a German destroyer group. Early on 2.11.42 U 586 torpedoed and sank the SS *Empire Gilbert* (br 6640t) W of Vannøy. She picked up three survivors as prisoners.

The boat returned to Skjomenfjord **5.11.42**

10. 18.11.42 Left for operations. No details known.
U 586 returned to Bergen **1.12.42**

11. 6.12.42 Left Bergen and arrived Hamburg **11.12.42**

12. 7.2.43 Left Hamburg and arrived Kiel **8.2.43**

13. 25.2.43 Left Kiel for Northern Waters.

Westbound RA 53 left Kola Inlet on March 1st. Some days out, the convoy ran into a gale and became scattered. The weather began to be more settled from the 8th and on the 9th U 586 sank the straggling SS *Puerto Rican* (am 6076t) in the Greenland Sea, NE of Iceland.

The boat returned to Narvik **13.3.43**

14. 15.3.43 Left Narvik and arrived Trondheim **16.3.43**

15. 29.3.43 Left for operations. No details known.
U 586 returned to Bergen **2.5.43**

16. 27.5.43 Left Bergen and arrived Hammerfest **31.5.43**

17. 5.6.43 Left for operations. No details known except that on July 4th U 586 had an engagement with a British submarine.
She returned to Narvik **10.7.43**

18. 18.7.43 Left Narvik and arrived Tromsø **19.7.43**

19. 21.7.43 Left for operations.

On the 27th U 586 laid mines E of Pechora Bay, Northern Russia. She returned to Narvik **31.7.43**

20. 3.8.43 Left Narvik and arrived Bergen **7.8.43**

21. 19.10.43 Left for the North Atlantic.

U 586 joined *Jahn* group, formed on the 31st E of Newfoundland. When it was realised that convoys were being re-routed to miss *Jahn* and *Körner* groups, the boats were redisposed in five small sub-groups, *Tirpitz 1* to *5*.

The *Tirpitz* groups were to operate against HX 264, expected on the 5th. The convoy passed unobserved and the operation against it was called off on the 7th because the carrier-borne air escort made it impossible for the boats to surface in daylight.

U 586 moved eastwards and joined *Schill 2* group from the 16th, awaiting the northbound, combined convoy MKS 30/SL 139. On the 18th the group moved northwards and formed an east-west patrol line E of the Azores, which the convoy was expected to reach on the 19th. The convoy passed through the centre of the line late on the 19th but the well-handled surface escort and constant attacks by aircraft prevented any night attacks by the boats, keeping them down most of the time. At dawn on the 20th, with increased air activity expected, the group was ordered to dive, abandoning any hope of attacking the convoy.

With the other remaining boats of *Schill 1,2* and *3* groups, U 586

became part of a new patrol line, *Weddigen*, from the 23rd NE of the Azores, between 18° and 22°W. The group was waiting for convoy information from reconnaissance aircraft. On or about the 25th U 586 was damaged, probably by aircraft, and set off for home.
She reached St Nazaire **3.12.43**

22. 29.1.44 Left for the Mediterranean.

U 586 passed through the Straits of Gibraltar during the night of the 12/13th. She operated initially off the coast of Algeria but had no success.
She put in to her new base at Toulon **22.2.44**

23. 9.5.44 Left for operations. No details known.
U 586 returned to Toulon **21.6.44**

On 5.7.44 U 586 was badly damaged in a USAF bombing raid on Toulon harbour. She was decommissioned on 12.7.44.

U 587 Type VII C

Built by Blohm & Voss, Hamburg
Keel laid 31.10.40   Launched 23.7.41
Commissioned 11.9.41   Feldpost Nr M 19 451

Sunk 27.3.42 NNE of the Azores (47°21´N 21°39´W)

Served with
6 U-Flottille, Danzig/St Nazaire   September 1941 - 27.3.42 (ab/fb)

Commanded by
KL Ulrich Borcherdt   September 1941 - 27.3.42

Patrols: 2   Ships sunk: 2 (6619 grt) + 1 damaged

1. 8.1.42 Left Kiel for the North Atlantic.

U 587, U 586 and U 588, all from Germany, and U 94 assembled W of the Hebrides from the 15th.

Briefly, on the 18th, the four boats formed a patrol line E of the Outer Bailey Bank to intercept ten transports, reported on the 16th to be heading for England from Reykjavik, but this came to nothing.

More boats arrived from Germany and from the 21st twelve boats, including U 587, assembled W of Rockall as *Schlei* group, for a southwesterly sweep across the convoy routes. However, with favourable reports of operations off the US coast, the *Schlei* boats were ordered to bases in western France to prepare for operations in the Western Atlantic.

Further orders were received that eight boats were to go to the Iceland/Faroes/Scotland area for the protection of Norway. In fact only five *Schlei* boats went northwards and U 587 and six others headed for France.
U 587 reached St Nazaire **31.1.42**

2. 12.2.42 Left for Canadian waters.

Outward-bound, U 587 picked up five downed German aircrew on the 18th. Later that day she rendezvoused with the returning U 130 W of the Bay of Biscay and transferred the five men.

U 587 and other boats were ordered to close westbound convoy ONS 67, sighted on the 21st by U 155 60 miles E of Cape Race. En route to the convoy, U 587 reported that a vessel with a cable-laying bow had been torpedoed by her on the 23rd E of Newfoundland but there is no confirmation of this.

On the 24th U 587 reported a tanker from ONS 67 torpedoed but this vessel has not been identified. During a three-day pursuit, eight ships were sunk and one damaged.

By 2.3.42 U 587 was NE of Sable Island when she claimed to have sunk an a/s vessel. Again, there is no confirmation. On the

58

3rd U 587 fired two torpedoes into the harbour at St John's but made no hits. She was searched for by the warships HMCS *Minas*, *The Pas* and *Lunenburg* but she escaped. The boat torpedoed and sank the SS *Hans Egede* (gre 900t) on the 6th E of Cape Breton Island and the SS *Lily* (gr 5719t) from the convoy ONS 68 on the 9th S of Cape Race.

On the 25th the returning U 587 reported a large ship torpedoed on the 25th in the central North Atlantic, which was probably the abandoned wreck of the SS *Empire Celt*, torpedoed and damaged by U 158 on 24.2.42.

U 587 sighted the fast troop-transport convoy WS 17 on the 27th NNE of the Azores. Her radioed position report was picked up by HF/DF and she was sunk in depth-charge attacks by the destroyer HMS *Aldenham* (Lt H A Stuart-Monteith), *Grove* (Lt-Cdr J W Rylands), *Leamington* (Lt-Cdr H G Bowerman) and *Volunteer* (Lt R A Sly). This was the first U-boat to be sunk, using HF/DF.

There were no survivors, 42 dead.

U 588   Type VII C

Built by Blohm & Voss, Hamburg
Keel laid 31.10.40   Launched 23.7.41
Commissioned 18.9.41   Feldpost Nr M 19 687

Sunk 31.7.42 in the central North Atlantic (49°59′N 36°36′W)

Served with
6 U-Flottille, Danzig/St Nazaire   September 1941 - 31.7.42 (ab/fb)

Commanded by
KL Viktor Vogel   September 1941 - 31.7.42

Patrols: 4   Ships sunk: 6 (25,541 grt) + 2 damaged

1. 8.1.42   Left Kiel for the North Atlantic.
U 588, U 586 and U 587, all from Germany, and U 94 assembled W of the Hebrides from the 15th.

Briefly, on the 18th, the four boats formed a patrol line E of the Outer Bailey Bank to intercept ten transports, reported on the 16th to be heading for England from Reykjavik, but it came to nothing.

More boats arrived from Germany and from the 21st twelve boats, including U 588, assembled W of Rockall as *Schlei* group, for a southwesterly sweep acros the convoy routes. En route early on the 22nd, U 588 claimed to have sunk a ship W of the Butt of Lewis.

However, with favourable reports of operations off the US coast, the *Schlei* boats were ordered on the 24th to bases in western France to prepare for operations in the Western Atlantic.

Further orders were received that eight boats were to go to the Iceland/Faroes/ Scotland area for the protection of Norway. In fact only five *Schlei* boats went northwards and U 588 and six others headed for France.

U 588 reached Lorient **30.1.42**

2. 12.2.42   Left for Canadian waters.
U 588 and other boats were ordered to close westbound convoy ONS 67, sighted on the 21st by U 155 600 miles E of Cape Race. During a three-day pursuit eight ships were sunk and another one damaged. U 588 had no success.

On 1.3.42 U 588 torpedoed and sank an independent SE of Sable Island, the SS *Carperby* (br 4890t). The boat continued westwards towards the US east coast and on the 2nd she claimed to have torpedoed an empty tanker and then sunk it after four hours of shelling, ESE of New York. The ship was probably the SS *Consuelo* (br 4847t), which sent out an SOS on the 1st but reached New York on the 3rd, apparently without serious damage.

U 588 moved closer to the coast and on the 10th she torpedoed

and sank the tanker SS *Gulftrade* (am 6676t) NE of Atlantic City. The boat put in to St Nazaire **27.3.42**

3. 19.4.42   Left for the Western Atlantic.
On May 1st U 576 sighted a northeastbound convoy 80 miles SW of Cape Sable. Outward-bound U 588, U 455, U 553 and U 593 were between 600 to 1000 miles to the east. The shadower was unable to maintain contact and although she regained it on the 2nd, she was driven off by aircraft.

U 588 and the other boats were ordered to form a north-south patrol line for the 3rd, running southwards from Cape Race. When it was known that the convoy was staying close inshore, the line moved northwards towards the coast. The operation was abandoned on the 4th and the four boats stationed themselves S of Halifax.

Early on the 9th U 588 torpedoed and damaged the SS *Greylock* (am 7460t) 10 miles from the Halifax lightship. This vessel was eventually sunk by U 255 on 3.2.43 E of Jan Mayen.

U 588 sank the SS *Kitty's Brook* (br 4031t) SE of Cape Sable on the 10th and the SS *Skottland* (nw 2117t) SW of the Cape on the 17th. Next day U 588 struck the SS *Fort Binger* with two dud torpedoes, 60 miles SW of Yarmouth, Nova Scotia. The boat surfaced and the ship turned and tried unsuccessfully to ram. There followed an exchange of gunfire for an hour before U 588 left the scene. The French crew abandoned ship and was picked up by the RCAF rescue launch *Arresteur*, which had come from Yarmouth in response to *Fort Binger's* distress call. The crew later reboarded the *Fort Binger*. There was a search for U 588 but she escaped.

After moving further south, U 588 sank two ships, the SS *Plow City* (am 3282t) on the 21st SE of Rhode Island and the SS *Margot* (br 4545t) on the 23rd SE of Nantucket Island. The *Plow City* was sunk after she stopped to pick up survivors of the MV *Piesander*, sunk by U 653 on the 17th.

U 588 returned to St Nazaire **7.6.42**

4. 19.7.42   Left for the North Atlantic.
On the 29th the outward-bound U 164 sighted westbound ON 115 480 miles SE of Cape Farewell. U 588, then 400 miles away to the southwest, was one of six outward-bound boats ordered to close the convoy.

U 588 made contact but she was located on the 31st and sunk in depth-charge attacks by the corvette HMCS *Wetaskiwin* (Lt-Cdr G S Windeyer) and the destroyer HMCS *Skeena* (Cdr H Kingsley) of the escort.

There were no survivors, 46 dead.

U 589   Type VII C

Built by Blohm & Voss, Hamburg
Keel laid 31.10.40   Launched 6.8.41
Commissioned 25.9.41   Feldpost Nr M 21 775

Sunk 14.9.42 S of Spitzbergen (75°40′N 20°32′E)

Served with
6 U-Flottille, Danzig/St Nazaire   September 1941 - June 1942 (ab/fb)
11 U-Flottille, Bergen   June 1942 - 14.9.42 (fb/fb-m)

Commanded by
KL Hans-Joachim Horrer   September 1941 - 14.9.42

Patrols: 8   Ships sunk: 1 + 2 shared (8222 grt)
                           1 a/s trawler (163 dt)

1. 23.2.42   Left Kiel and arrived Heligoland **26.2.42**

2. 28.2.42   Left for operations. No details known.
U 589 put in to Kirkenes **21.3.42**

U 589 (continued)

3. 24.3.42 Left for operations.

On the morning of the 27th eastbound PQ 13 was located by aerial reconnaissance. U 589, U 435, U 454, U 456 and U 585 were directed to the convoy, as were also German destroyers and aircraft. U 589 unsuccessfully attacked a destroyer of the escort on 1.4.42 N of Kola Inlet.

The boat returned to Kirkenes **2.4.42**

4. 8.4.42 Left for operations. No details known.

U 589 returned to Kirkenes **20.4.42**

5. 29.4.42 Left for operations.

Westbound convoy QP 11 left Murmansk on the 28th and U 589 and six other boats assembled to intercept. The convoy was sighted by aircraft on the 29th and attacks began next day. On May 1st U 589 torpedoed and sank the SS *Ciolkovskij* (sov 2847t) E of Bear Island.

U 589 returned to Kirkenes **6.5.42**

6. 8.5.42 Left Kirkenes and arrived Skjomenfjord **12.5.42**

7. 16.5.42 Left for operations. No details known.

U 589 put in to Narvik **23.5.42**

8. 26.5.42 Left Narvik and arrived Bergen **28.5.42**

9. 17.7.42 Left for operations. No details known.

U 589 returned to Skjomenfjord **12.8.42**

10. 23.8.42 Left for a minelaying operation.

On the 28th U 589 laid mines off the Matochkin Strait. In October the Soviet a/s trawler *SKR-23* sank after striking a mine. However, three different sinking dates appear in records, the 11th, the 13th and the 23rd, and it is not certain whether the trawler struck a mine laid by U 589 or one laid by the German cruiser *Admiral Hipper*.

The boat returned to Narvik **1.9.42**

11. 9.9.42 Left for operations.

On the 12th German aircraft sighted eastbound PQ 18. U 589, outward-bound to lay mines, made contact with the convoy in the morning of the 13th S of Spitzbergen. She fired two torpedoes at the escort-carrier HMS *Avenger*, which missed but possibly ran on to hit the SS *Stalingrad* (sov 3559t) and the SS *Oliver Ellsworth* (am 7191t). Both ships were sunk but one or both were probably also struck by torpedoes from U 408. Sometime on the 13th U 589 picked up four downed German aircrew.

On the 14th U 589 was sighted by a Swordfish of 825 (FAA) Squadron from HMS *Avenger*. The boat dived, the aircraft dropped a smoke float and circled to await the arrival of the destroyer HMS *Onslow*. However, the Swordfish was driven off by a Ju 88. U 589 resurfaced but the *Onslow* was then only six miles away and approaching fast. The boat dived but she had been spotted. A hunt over a three-hour period ended after a depth-charge attack by *Onslow* brought oil and debris to the surface, confirming the destruction of the boat.

There were no survivors, 44 dead.

U 590   Type VII C

Built by Blohm & Voss, Hamburg
Keel laid 31.10.40   Launched 6.8.41
Commissioned 2.10.41   Feldpost Nr M 23 773

Sunk 9.7.43 NE of Ilha de Maracá (03°22′N 48°38′W)

Served with
6 U-Flottille, Danzig/St Nazaire   October 1941 - 9.7.43 (ab/fb)

Commanded by
KL Heinrich Müller-Edzards   October 1941 - June 1943
OL Werner Krüer   June 1943 - 9.7.43

Patrols: 6   Ships sunk: 1 (5228 grt)

1. 4.4.42 Left Kiel, in transit for western France.

On the 14th U 590 was attacked and damaged in the Bay of Biscay area by a Whitley of 502 Squadron (F/O E Cotton).

The boat put in to her new base at St Nazaire **17.4.42**

2. 3.5.42 Left for the North Atlantic.

U 590 together with U 94, U 96, U 124, U 406 and U 569, was to take part in a planned group-operation, *Hecht*, in the area of the Newfoundland Bank. The boats were outward-bound when U 569 sighted westbound ONS 92 on the 11th in the central North Atlantic. Attacks were made during the night of the 11/12th and five ships were sunk, none by U 590. Contact was lost on the 13th.

The *Hecht* patrol line was formed early on the 14th ahead of the lost convoy but contact was not regained. In the evening the group began a northeasterly movement in scouting formation, halting on the 16th. After two days it moved southwestwards. On the 20th U 406 sighted southbound ONS 94, which she shadowed for some hours before being driven off. Contact was lost in the fog close to the Newfoundland Bank. U 590 and the other boats were unable to close and the convoy was not found in spite of a search.

On the 25th U 116 reached a refuelling position 600 miles S of Cape Race and she supplied the *Hecht* boats as they arrived. The group reformed and on the 30th began a sweep across the convoy routes. It patrolled initially S of the Newfoundland Bank before beginning to move to an area 600 miles SE of Cape Farewell.

En route on the 31st, U 590 sighted westbound ONS 96 but as the weather began to worsen and the convoy neared Newfoundland the operation was called off on 2.6.42 and the boats continued eastwards. During the evening of the 8th U 124 sighted westbound ONS 100 in the central North Atlantic and sank a French corvette. On the 9th all *Hecht* boats made contact but U 590, U 96 and U 406 dropped back because of diesel trouble. Contact with the convoy was lost but regained on the 10th by U 94 and before the operation ended on the 12th four ships had been sunk. U 590 had no success.

The *Hecht* boats resumed their search northeastwards. On the 16th U 94 sighted westbound ONS 102. Ordered to attack, the boats found the escort to be very strong and they were driven off. U 590 was damaged in a depth-charge attack.

She returned to St Nazaire **25.6.42**

3. 11.8.42 Left for the Central Atlantic.

U 590 was to be part of *Blücher* group, which was to be formed SE of the Azores from the 13th, intended for operations in the Freetown area. On the 14th, before the seven boats of the group could assemble, northbound SL 118 entered the waiting area. Contact was made with the convoy on the 17th and by the afternoon of the 19th four ships had been sunk and another damaged. The boats in contact had been driven off by aircraft and U 333, U 590 and U 653 had been damaged during the action and afterwards headed back to their bases.

U 590 returned to St Nazaire **23.8.42**

4. 27.8.42 Left for the Central Atlantic.

U 590 again set out for the Freetown area. She joined other boats W of Lisbon and became part of *Iltis* group from 4.9.42. On the 9th the boats moved southwards in line abreast towards the Cape Verde Islands. From the 12th they patrolled an area SW of the Canaries but saw no ships.

On the 24th *Iltis* group dispersed. U 590, U 87, U 107 and U 333 were refuelled from the 25th by U 460 N of the Cape Verde Islands. The four boats continued southwards, to operate independently in the Freetown area. Results were disappointing and U 590 had no success. In late October the returning boat was refuelled by U 462 W of the Cape Verde Islands.

She returned to St Nazaire **24.11.42**

5. 22.2.43 Left for the North Atlantic.

U 590 joined *Neuland* group, formed on 6.3.43 W of Ireland. On the 7th the southern part of the patrol line, including U 590, moved westwards to intercept eastbound HX 228. The convoy was known to have been 300 miles west of the *Neuland* line on the 8th. Anticipating a change of course by the convoy, the *Neuland* line moved north on the 9th to intercept. It was sighted on the 10th by the group's southernmost boat, U 336.

Some of the *Neuland* boats closed the convoy during the night of the 10/11th and in a three-day operation four ships and an escorting destroyer were sunk and two other ships were damaged. In the early hours of the 12th U 590 claimed to have sunk a straggler from the convoy but there is no confirmation of this.

U 590 and eight other *Neuland* boats reformed from the 15th as *Dränger* group in the central North Atlantic, to operate against HX 229. The group took part in the biggest convoy action of the war, against both HX 229 and SC 122 from the 16th to the 19th, during which time twenty-one ships were sunk. U 590 did not carry out any attacks during the operation. The pursuit ended on the 20th because of increasing air attacks on the boats.

After the action ended *Dränger* group moved westwards and from the 25th its seven remaining boats became part of a new patrol line, *Seewolf*, SSE of Cape Farewell. The boats moved north on the 26th to search for eastbound convoy HX 230 but a storm, which later became a hurricane, caused the operation to be abandoned on the 30th.

The *Seewolf* boats then moved to a replenishment area in the central North Atlantic, N of the Azores to meet U 463. On or about April 1st U 590 was refuelled for return to base.

She reached St Nazaire **12.4.43**

6. 8.6.43 Left for the Central Atlantic.

In the latter part of June U 590 was refuelled by U 488 W of the Azores, after which she headed for the northern coast of Brazil. On July 4th U 590 torpedoed and sank the SS *Pelotaslóide* (bz 5228t) off the Baia de Marajó.

U 590 was sighted on the 9th by a USN Catalina of VP-94 (Lt F F Hare) in the vicinity of southbound convoy TJ 1, NE of Ilha de Maracá. The aircraft attacked in the face of heavy flak and the pilot was killed and the radio operator wounded. The second pilot took over, attempted another attack in the damaged aircraft and then flew 350 miles back to base at Belem, where he landed safely.

Two hours after the attack U 590 was located by another Catalina of VP-94 (Lt S E Auslander). An attack was carried out, in which six depth-bombs were dropped, and U 590 was destroyed.

There were no survivors, 45 dead.

U 591   Type VII C

Built by Blohm & Voss, Hamburg
Keel laid 30.11.40   Launched 20.8.41
Commissioned 9.10.41   Feldpost Nr M 37 230

Sunk 30.7.43 SE of Recife (08°36′S 34°34′W)

Served with
6 U-Flottille, Danzig/St Nazaire   October 1941 - June 1942 (ab/fb)
11 U-Flottille, Bergen   July 1942 - May 1943 (fb)
9 U-Flottille, Brest   June 1943 - 30.7.43 (fb)

Commanded by
KL Hansjürgen Zetzsche   October 1941 - June 1943
OL Reimar Ziesmer   June 1943 - 30.7.43

Patrols: 9   Ships sunk: 5 (23,960 grt) + 1 damaged

1. 15.1.42 Left Kiel for Atlantic operations.

U 591 was one of twelve boats which assembled W of Rockall, as *Schlei* group, for a southwesterly sweep across the convoy routes. However, with favourable reports of operations off the US east coast, the *Schlei* boats were ordered on the 24th to go to bases in western France to prepare for operations in the Western Atlantic.

Further orders were received that eight boats were to go to the Iceland/Faroes/Scotland area. In fact U 352, U 435, U 455 and U 586 were sent northwards and U 591 went to an area W of the Hebrides.

On 4.2.42 U 591, U 136 and U 213 located westbound ONS 63 300 miles W of the North Channel. In the late evening of the 5th U 136 sank the corvette HMS *Arbutus* SW of Rockall, the convoy's only casualty in the three-day operation.

U 591 was on weather-reporting duty when she sighted SC 67 on the 10th 500 miles W of the North Channel. She torpedoed and sank the MV *Heina* (nw 4208t) early on the 11th WSW of Rockall. She also reported hits on two other ships in the convoy but there is no confirmation of this. U 136 came up in response to U 591's report and sank the corvette HMCS *Spikenard* early on the 11th.

U 591 put in to Bergen **20.2.42**

2. 1.4.42 Left for operations. No details known.
U 591 put in to Trondheim **11.4.42**

3. 10.5.42 Left for Northern Waters.

On the 25th German aerial reconnaissance found eastbound convoy PQ 16 and aircraft carried out torpedo and bombing attacks. U 591 and other boats operated against the convoy.

U 591 made an unsuccessful attack on the escorting destroyer HMS *Ashanti* on the 26th. The operation ended on June 1st, with six ships sunk by aircraft and one by U 703.

U 591 put in to Narvik **2.6.42**

4. 4.6.42 Left Narvik and arrived Bergen **7.6.42**

5. 27.7.42 Left for operations. No details known.
U 591 returned to Bergen **14.8.42**

6. 8.9.42 Left Bergen and returned **12.9.42**

7. 1.12.42 Left Bergen for the North Atlantic.

U 591 arrived in the area SW of Iceland in the closing stages of *Draufgänger* group's operation against eastbound convoy HX 217. From the 13th U 591 and other new-arrivals joined some of the ex-*Draufgänger* boats to form *Ungestüm* group S of Iceland, to operate against convoys leaving the North Channel.

On the 13th U 373 sighted eastbound HX 218 E of Newfoundland. The *Ungestüm* boats moved westwards at high speed and on

U 591 (continued)

the 16th a patrol line was formed SE of Cape Farewell in the expected path of the convoy. However, HX 218 passed unobserved through the waiting boats.

After U 373 sighted ONS 152 to the southeast of the *Ungestüm* line, the boats were moved towards it. Brief contact was made but bad weather and poor visibility hampered the pursuit. A search for scattered ships was made and U 591 had the only success, when she torpedoed and sank the SS *Montreal City* (br 3066t) early on the 21st in the Central North Atlantic. The operation against ONS 152 ended on the 22nd.

The widely-scattered *Ungestüm* boats formed a new patrol line from the 24th in the central North Atlantic. Next day the line moved northeastwards to meet up with *Spitz* group, moving down towards it from the northwest. Convoy ONS 154 was sighted south of the *Spitz* patrol line.

Both groups moved south to intercept and contact was made on the 27th. In the late evening of the 28th U 591 torpedoed two ships from the convoy, damaging the SS *Norse King* (nw 5701t) and sinking the SS *Zarian* (br 4871t). The *Norse King* was sunk next day by U 435 and the *Zarian* had been previously torpedoed and damaged by U 406. During the ONS 154 operation thirteen ships and one naval special service vessel were sunk and another ship damaged.

Between the 31st and January 5th 1943 U 591 and other *Ungestüm* boats were refuelled by U 117 N of the Azores for return to base.

U 591 reached Brest **12.1.43**

8. 17.2.43 Left for the North Atlantic.

On the 21st outward-bound U 664 sighted convoy ONS 167 WSW of Ireland. She, U 591 and four other outward-bound boats were ordered to form *Sturmbock* group to operate against it. The boats were far apart and only U 664 had any success, sinking two ships of the convoy. From the 24th the *Sturmbock* boats formed a new patrol line, *Wildfang*, E of Newfoundland in the expected path of ONS 167. The convoy was not seen again and the operation ended in bad visibility on the 25th.

From 4.3.43 *Wildfang* linked up with *Burggraf* group S of Greenland. U 405 of *Neptun* group sighted eastbound SC 121 on the 6th and seventeen boats, drawn from the three groups and designated *Westmark* group, were ordered to pursue. U 591 was one of these and in the morning of the 7th she torpedoed and sank the straggling SS *Empire Impala* (br 6116t) SE of Cape Farewell, which had stopped to pick up survivors from the SS *Egyptian*, sunk seven hours earlier by U 230. In the evening of the 8th U 591 sank another straggler ESE of Cape Farewell, the SS *Vojvoda Putnik* (yg 5879t).

After leaving the SC 121 operation, U 591 was refuelled by U 463 in the central North Atlantic. She then joined boats from *Stürmer* and *Dränger* groups to form *Seewolf* group from the 25th SE of Cape Farewell and south of the *Seeteufel* patrol line, to operate against the reported eastbound SC 123. On the 25th U 591 picked up an officer-survivor from the SS *Madoera*, sunk by U 653. From the 26th *Seewolf* and *Seeteufel* groups joined to form a line running 800 miles south from Cape Farewell.

On the 27th U 305, at the northern end of the *Seewolf* line, sighted eastbound HX 230. U 591 was one of twenty-two boats from the two groups which were ordered to close the convoy. She was one of only five boats which closed but gale conditions made attacks impossible. From the 29th a strong air escort kept the boats away and after contact was lost on the 30th the operation ended. One ship had been sunk, by U 610.

U 591 put in to St Naziare **7.4.43**

9. 12.5.43 Left for Atlantic operations.

Outward-bound, U 591 was attacked twice by a Whitley of 10 OTU (F/Sgt G W Brookes) SSW of Ireland. In depth-charge and machine-gun attacks, the boat was damaged and the commander

and one crewman were wounded.

U 591 returned to St Nazaire **17.5.43**

10. 26.6.43 Left for the South Atlantic.

Between July 6th and 12th U 591 was refuelled by U 487 600 miles SW of the Azores. She went on to patrol off the coast of Brazil but had no success.

On the 30th U 591 was sighted by a USN Ventura of VB-126 (Lt W C Young), which was scouting ahead of a convoy off the coast of Brazil near Recife. Young made a rapid attack, straddling the boat with six depth-bombs. U 591 sank in 4 minutes.

19 of her crew were lost and the commander and 27 others were picked up later by the corvette USS *Saucy*.

U 592 Type VII C

Built by Blohm & Voss, Hamburg
Keel laid 30.11.40   Launched 20.8.41
Commissioned 16.10.41   Feldpost Nr M 37 556

Sunk 31.1.44 WSW of Fastnet (50°20´N 17°29´W)

Served with
6 U-Flottille, Danzig/St Nazaire   October 1941 - June 1942 (ab/fb)
11 U-Flottille, Bergen   July 1942 - February 1943 (fb)
6 U-Flottille, St Nazaire   March 1943 - 31.1.44 (fb)

Commanded by
KL Karl Borm   October 1941 - July 1943
OL Heinz Jaschke   September 1943 - 31.1.44

Patrols: 10   Ships sunk: 1 (3770 grt)

1. 19.2.42 Left Hamburg and arrived Heligoland **23.2.42**

2. 3.3.42 Left for operations in Northern Waters.
U 592 put in to Bergen **23.3.42**

3. 1.4.42 Left for operations. No details known.
U 592 returned to Bergen **23.4.42**

4. 20.5.42 Left Bergen and arrived Hamburg **23.5.42**

5. 5.7.42 Left Hamburg and arrived Kiel **5.7.42**

6. 11.7.42 Left Kiel and arrived Bergen **14.7.42**

7. 17.7.42 Left for operations. No details known.
U 592 put in to Skjomenfjord **14.8.42**

8. 10.9.42 Left for operations.
Between the 20th and 22nd U 592 was one of seven boats operating against westbound convoy QP 14 in the Greenland Sea. The convoy, which left Archangel on the 13th, lost six ships to U-boats, including a minesweeper, a destroyer and a navy oiler. U 592 had no success.
She returned to Skjomenfjord **28.9.42**

9. 7.10.42 Left for a minelaying operation.
On the 13th U 592 laid mines off Yugor Strait. On the 14th the SS *Shchors* (sov 3770t) sank after striking one. It was the only sinking attributed to these mines.
U 592 returned to Skjomenfjord **19.10.42**

10. 9.11.42 Left for operations. No details known.
U 592 put in to Narvik **15.12.42**

11. 16.12.42 Left Narvik and arrived Bergen **18.12.42**

12. 9.3.43 Left Bergen for the North Atlantic.

U 592 joined *Seeteufel* group S of Iceland, to operate against a feeder convoy, en route from Iceland to join westbound ONS 1. The patrol line was formed and the convoy was expected on the 22nd but when it did not materialise, the line moved westwards towards Cape Farewell, in the expected direction of the main ONS 1.

On the 24th U 306 sighted some ONS 1 escorts north of the *Seeteufel* line but the boats she contacted were unable to close. By the 26th the line ran southeast from Cape Farewell and it joined the more southerly *Seewolf* group to form a line running 800 miles south from the Cape. In the afternoon of the 26th masts and an aircraft carrier were sighted in the centre of the *Seeteufel* line. This was thought to be an ON convoy but a strong air and surface escort prevented its direction being discovered by the boats.

On the 27th U 305, at the northern end of the *Seewolf* line, sighted eastbound convoy HX 230. *Seewolf* and *Seeteufel*, including U 592 were ordered to pursue. The prevailing storm developed into a hurricane on the 28th and only five boats were able to make brief contact with the convoy and torpedo attacks were impossible in the heavy seas. The pursuit continued for three days in very bad weather, in the hope that stragglers would be found. Only one ship was sunk during the operation, which was called off on the 30th.

U 592 and other *Seeteufel* boats joined some new-arrivals to form *Löwenherz* group SE of Greenland from 3.4.43. On the 4th U 530 sighted eastbound HX 231 to the west of the patrol line. The operation against the convoy lasted three days, with six ships sunk and others possibly damaged. U 592 had no success.

She put in to St Nazaire **18.4.43**

13. 29.5.43 Left for the North Atlantic.

U 592 was one of a number of boats ordered to carry out radio-deception duties, with which it was hoped that the Allies would be deceived into believing that many U-boats were still operating in the North Atlantic.

The boats were positioned in various areas, SW of Ireland and S of Iceland, with others off Greenland and the Azores. The average number of participating boats was generally six and if one was sunk, she was quickly replaced. In early July the scheme was abandoned.

U 592 returned to St Nazaire **14.7.43**

14. 5.10.43 Left for the North Atlantic.

U 592 joined *Siegfried 2* group, which from the 28th formed a patrol line E of Newfoundland, to await eastbound SC 145. The boats were harassed by carrier-borne aircraft from HMS *Fencer* of the 8th SG, which was supporting SC 145's escort. The convoy passed the *Siegfried* line unobserved.

On the 31st *Siegfried 1,2* and *3* groups reformed into two new groups, *Jahn* and *Körner*. U 592 was in *Jahn*. This redisposition was short-lived and on 3.11.43 the boats again reformed, this time into five small groups, *Tirpitz 1* to *5*, to await convoy HX 264, expected on the 5th. Again, the convoy passed by and the operation was called off on the 7th because of the unwelcome attentions of carrier-borne aircraft from HMS *Tracker*, it being impossible to surface in daylight.

The returning U 592 sighted some ships from a convoy, either HX 264 or SC 146, but her attempted attack was unsuccessful.

The boat reached St Nazaire **25.11.43**

15. 10.1.44 Left for Atlantic operations.

U 592 joined *Rügen* group W of the British Isles, with boats disposed singly over a large area. On the 26th a KMS convoy was sighted W of the North Channel. The six most southerly *Rügen* boats, including U 592, were formed into a patrol line, *Hinein*, W of Ireland to intercept the southbound convoy from the 27th.

The convoy was further west than reported and by the time the *Hinein* boats had been appraised of this, it was too late to move the patrol line westwards into the convoy's path. Boats with 3.7cm anti-aircraft guns were ordered to proceed at high speed on the surface to intercept. Communication difficulties between aircraft and boats meant that the convoy's position at midnight on the 27th was not passed on and an all-night search by the boats found nothing. The convoy had passed to the north.

The operation was terminated early on the 29th when an invasion of Western France was reported by an aircraft. After apparent confirmation of this report, all boats in the North Atlantic, which included *Hinein* group, were ordered to proceed at high speed to the Biscay coast. En route on the 29th, U 592 was attacked and damaged by a USN Liberator of VP-110 (Lt H H Budd). The boat set out to return to St Nazaire but she was located WSW of Fastnet in the morning of the 31st by the sloop HMS *Wild Goose* (Lt-Cdr D E G Wemyss) of the 2nd SG, which was escorting the escort-carriers HMS *Activity* and *Nairana*.

Wild Goose dropped depth-charges. Sloops HMS *Starling* (Capt F J Walker) and *Magpie* (Lt-Cdr R S Abram) arrived and they too made depth-charge attacks. U 592 had gone deep. A further depth-charge attack was made by *Starling*, causing a huge underwater explosion, which swamped *Starling* with water. *Wild Goose* made another attack but U 592 had already been destroyed.

There were no survivors, 50 dead.

U 593   Type VII C

Built by Blohm & Voss, Hamburg
Keel laid 17.12.40   Launched 3.9.41
Commissioned 23.10.41   Feldpost Nr M 38 314

Scuttled 13.12.43 NE of Bougie (37°38′N 05°58′E)

Served with
8 U-Flottille, Königsberg   October 1941 - February 1942 (ab)
7 U-Flottille, St Nazaire   March - October 1942 (fb)
29 U-Flottille, La Spezia/Toulon   November 1942 - 13.12.43 (fb)

Commanded by
KL Gerd Kelbing   October 1941 - 13.12.43

Patrols: 15   Ships sunk: 9 (41,384 grt) + 1 damaged
                             2 destroyers (2087 dt)
                             2 LSTs (3250 dt)
                             1 minesweeper (815 dt)

1. 2.3.42 Left Kiel for Atlantic operations.

From late January 1942 a U-boat presence had been maintained in an area W of the Faroes and the Hebrides, ostensibly on Hitler's orders, to repel any invasion of Norway.

U 593 was one of seven boats carrying out this duty in March. Occasionally convoys were seen and attacks made. The scheme was discontinued later in the month and U 593 made her way to France. On the 18th U 507 sighted convoy ONS 76. U 593 was one of three boats directed to the scene but she could not close in time.

In the morning of the 27th, as U 593 surfaced SW of Ushant, she sighted and was seen by destroyers of a British naval force heading to raid St Nazaire. The destroyer HMS *Tynedale* closed and made a depth-charge attack just after U 593 dived. The boat was driven to the surface and *Tynedale* opened fire but the boat dived again and escaped. Several destroyers hunted for two hours before rejoining the main force.

In the early afternoon of the 27th U 593 resurfaced and reported the destroyers. German MTBs were sent out at nightfall to investigate. The raid went ahead and the old ex-US destroyer HMS *Campbeltown* was driven into the lock gates. The explosives

U 593 (continued)

aboard her went up in the afternoon of the 28th, jamming the gates and denying the Germans the use of the only area in France where *Tirpitz* could dock.

U 593 was to meet the *Tynedale* again later in the war, sinking her on 12.12.43 in the Mediterranean.

The boat reached her new base at St Nazaire **28.3.42**

2. 20.4.42 Left for the Western Atlantic.

On May 1st a convoy was reported 80 miles SW of Cape Sable. U 593 and three other outward-bound boats were then between 600 to 1000 miles to the east. They were directed to the convoy and formed a patrol line S of Cape Race for the 3rd.

However, the shadower, the returning U 576, was unable to maintain contact and when it was known that the convoy was hugging the coast, the operation was called off. The four boats split up, to take up positions between Halifax and New York.

On the 14th U 593 torpedoed and damaged the SS *Stavros* (gr 4853t) ENE of Atlantic City. She was under Swiss charter and returned to New York for repairs. U 593 torpedoed and sank the tanker MV *Persephone* (pa 8426t) in the afternoon of the 25th just E of the Barnegat Light, New Jersey. This vessel was part of a convoy and U 593 came under attack several times by the escort before escaping.

The boat returned to St Nazaire **18.6.42**

3. 22.7.42 Left for the North Atlantic.

U 593 was to join *Steinbrinck* group, to be formed E of the Newfoundland Bank for August 7th. On the 5th U 593 sighted eastbound SC 94 and called up other outward-bound boats, some 200 to 300 miles astern and others away to the northeast.

The convoy was pursued by these boats and also some from *Steinbrinck* group that had already joined the patrol line. In spite of the escort carrying out many attacks in the bad visibility and an air escort appearing from the 9th, the boats sank eleven ships for the loss of two boats. U 593 torpedoed and sank the SS *Spar* (nl 3616t) on the 5th E of Newfoundland.

The boat returned to St Nazaire **19.8.42**

4. 3.10.42 Left for the Mediterranean.

U 593 passed through the Straits of Gibraltar during the night of the 10/11th. She put in to her new base at La Spezia **15.10.42**

5. 2.11.42 Left for the Western Mediterranean.

U 593 went to the area W of a line from the Balearic Islands to Algiers, where all available U-boats were stationed to counter any developments arising from the unusually large number of Allied ships at Gibraltar.

On the 8th the landings in North Africa began and the boats operated against invasion and supply shipping. On the 12th U 593 claimed hits on two steamers NE of Oran, with sinking noises heard but there is no confirmation of this.

She returned to La Spezia **16.11.42**

6. 29.11.42 Left for operations. No details known.

U 593 put in to Pola **31.12.42**

7. 6.2.43 Left for the Eastern Mediterranean.

U 593 patrolled off the coasts of Egypt and Cyrenaica but had no success. On 3.3.43 she encountered a convoy W of Alexandria, claiming a torpedo hit on a steamer but again, this is unconfirmed.

She put in to Salamis **8.3.43**

8. 13.3.43 Left for the Eastern Mediterranean.

Patrolling off the Cyrenaican coast, U 593 successfully made attacks on convoys. Off Derna on the 18th, she torpedoed and sank two ships, the SS *Dafila* (br 1940t) and the SS *Kaying* (br 2626t).

U 593 returned to Salamis **21.3.43**

9. 25.3.43 Left for operations.

U 593 returned to her previous operational area and off Derna on the 27th she encountered convoy KMS 10. She sank the SS *City of Guildford* (br 5157t) and claimed a hit on a second ship.

The boat returned to Salamis **4.4.43**

10. 8.4.43 Left for operations.

On the 11th U 593 sank the SS *Runo* (br 1858t) off Tobruk and claimed a hit on a second ship but there is no confirmation.

She returned to Salamis **23.4.43**

11. 24.4.43 Left Salamis and arrived Pola **28.4.43**

12. 13.6.43 Left for operations off the Algerian coast.

U 593 torpedoed and sank two LSTs on the 22nd near Cap Corbelin, the American LST 333 and LST 387.

She had no further success until 5.7.43, when she sank the MV *Devis* (br 6054t) of convoy KMS 18B off the coast, E of Algiers. This vessel is believed to have been carrying troops, among whom there were heavy casualties. She may also have had two LCTs aboard, one of which was sunk and the other damaged.

U 593 put in to her new base at Toulon **11.7.43**

13. 27.7.43 Left for operations. No details known.

U 593 returned to Toulon **8.8.43**

14. 15.9.43 Left for operations in the Salerno bridgehead.

U 593 attacked invasion shipping in the Tyrrhenian Sea, S of Salerno. On the 21st she sank the SS *William W Gerhard* (am 7176t) from convoy NSS 3 and on the 25th the minesweeper USS *Skill*.

The boat returned to Toulon **5.10.43**

15. 26.10.43 Left for operations.

U 593 patrolled off Algeria and on 3.11.43 she attacked convoy KMS 30 just NW of Cherchel, sinking the SS *Mont Viso* (fr 4531t). She returned to Toulon **7.11.43**

16. 25.11.43 Left Toulon and returned **29.11.43**

17. 1.12.43 Left for the Algerian coast.

On the 12th U 593 sighted convoy KMS 34. She attacked the escort, sinking the destroyer HMS *Tynedale* NE of Bougie. A search began for the boat but she was not found.

In the afternoon U 593 torpedoed and sank the searching destroyer HMS *Holcombe*. After a further ten-hour search, the boat was found soon after midnight by a Leigh Light Wellington. The aircraft was damaged by flak and driven off.

The search continued but it was another twelve hours before U 593 was located by the destroyer USS *Wainwright*. She and the destroyer HMS *Calpe* (Lt-Cdr H Kirkwood) made depth-charge attacks. The boat surfaced and came under fire from the two warships.

U 593's crew abandoned ship and her commander scuttled his boat, which went down as an American boarding party came alongside. Thirty-two hours had passed since *Tynedale* had been torpedoed.

The entire crew of U 593 survived, with only one man slightly wounded.

U 594   Type VII C

Built by Blohm & Voss, Hamburg
Keel laid 17.12.40   Launched 3.9.41
Commissioned 30.10.41   Feldpost Nr M 38 516

Sunk 4.6.43 SSW of Cape St Vincent (35°55′N 09°25′W)

Served with
8 U-Flottille, Königsberg   October 1941 - March 1942 (ab)
7 U-Flottille, St Nazaire   March 1942 - 4.6.43 (fb)

Commanded by
KL Dietrich Hoffmann   October 1941 - July 1942
KL Friedrich Mumm   July 1942 - 4.6.43

Patrols: 6   Ships sunk: 1 (6074 grt) + 1 damaged

1. 14.3.42   Left Kiel, in transit to Western France.
U 594 put in to St Nazaire **30.3.42**

2. 11.4.42   Left for the Caribbean.
Outward-bound, U 594 was refuelled in late April by U 459 500 miles NE of Bermuda. She operated NE of the Bahamas and N of Cuba. From 21.5.42 U 594 patrolled between Cuba and Yucatan. On the 25th she had a crewman missing after an engagement with a tanker. U 594 had no success during this patrol.
The returning U 594 was refuelled in mid-June by U 459 W of the Azores.
The boat returned to St Nazaire **25.6.42**

3. 4.8.42   Left for the Central Atlantic.
U 594 was one of seven boats, which were to make up *Blücher* group, intended for operations in the Freetown area. The group was to be formed from the 13th SE of the Azores. However, on the 14th, before all the boats had arrived, northbound convoy SL 118 entered the assembly area.
Contact was made with the convoy on the 17th and by the afternoon of the 19th four ships had been sunk and another one damaged.
The *Blücher* boats split up and U 594 was ordered to the North Atlantic. From the 31st she joined five outward-bound boats to form *Stier* group W of Ireland. The group was involved in a failed operation against an ONS convoy on September 1st and 2nd. On the 4th *Stier* combined with *Vorwärts* group to form a long patrol line W of Ireland, to await a westbound convoy.
In the evening of the 9th U 584 sighted ON 127 in the central North Atlantic as it passed through the southern end of the patrol line. Contact was lost during the night but regained on the 10th. U 594 made unsuccessful attacks during the nights of the 10/11th and 12/13th but torpedoed and sank a straggler, the SS *Stone Street* (pa 6074t), in the afternoon of the 13th in the central North Atlantic, E of Trinity Bay, Newfoundland. Her captain was picked up as a prisoner.
The operation against ON 127 ended on the 14th because of bad visibility and the arrival of Newfoundland-based aircraft from the 13th. Seven ships were sunk and it was one of the few times in the war that all participating U-boats fired at least one torpedo each.
On or about the 16th U 594 was refuelled by U 461 NW of the Azores for return to base.
She reached St Nazaire **28.9.42**

4. 30.12.42   Left for the North Atlantic.
U 594 joined *Jaguar* group, which arrived in its operational area NE of Newfoundland on 12.1.43 and then waited for an HX convoy. However, HX 222 and SC 116 were both re-routed to avoid the boats. HX 223 probably passed the western end of the *Jaguar* line on the 22nd. On this day U 413 sighted eastbound SC 117

SSW of Cape Farewell and sank a straggler but because of radio difficulties she was unable to bring up the other *Jaguar* boats in time to catch the convoy and contact was lost on the 23rd. A search they made for it was unsuccessful.
On the 26th U 594 was involved with a straggler from HX 233, the SS *Kollbjörg* (nw 8259t). This vessel had broken in two during a heavy storm and the stern section sank. However, the fore section remained afloat, even after being hit by two torpedoes from U 607 of *Haudegen* group. It was finally dispatched with a torpedo by U 594 eleven hours later SE of Cape Farewell.
Some ex-*Landsknecht* boats, U 413 and U 594 formed a reconnaissance patrol group, *Pfeil*, from 2.2.43, to intercept an expected eastbound SC convoy.
On the 4th SC 118 was sighted by U 187 as it passed through the centre of the *Pfeil* line. Some *Haudegen* group boats were ordered to close the convoy and some outward-bound boats were also directed to it. In the five days ending the 9th, twenty boats were in contact with the strongly-escorted SC 118. Eleven ships were sunk and two boats lost. U 594 did not make any attacks on the convoy.
After the operation ended, she was refuelled by U 460 in the central North Atlantic for return to base.
U 594 returned to St Nazaire **18.2.43**

5. 23.3.43   Left for the North Atlantic.
U 594 joined *Löwenherz* group, formed SE of Greenland from 3.4.43. On the 4th U 530 sighted eastbound HX 231 to the west of the patrol line. Conditions were favourable and the boats pursued the convoy.
On the 6th U 594 was attacked and damaged by a Liberator of 120 Squadron (F/O J K Moffat) SW of Iceland.
She headed for base, reaching St Nazaire **14.4.43**

6. 23.5.43   Left for the Mediterranean.
On June 4th U 594 was sunk by rocket-fire by a Hudson of 48 Squadron (F/O H C Bailey) SSW of Cape St Vincent. She was the last boat to be sunk by Gibraltar-based Hudsons.
There were no survivors, 50 dead.

U 595   Type VII C

Built by Blohm & Voss, Hamburg
Keel laid 4.1.41   Launched 17.9.41
Commissioned 6.11.41   Feldpost Nr M 38 801

Beached 14.11.42 W of Ténès (36°38′N 00°30′E)

Served with
8 U-Flottille, Königsberg/Danzig   November 1941 - July 1942 (ab)
9 U-Flottille, Brest   July 1942 - 14.11.42 (fb)

Commanded by
KL Jürgen Quaet-Faslem   November 1941 - 14.11.42

Patrols: 3   Ships sunk: 1 (5332 grt)

Whilst on a training exercise in the Baltic on 1.6.42, one crewman was lost overboard.

1. 23.7.42   Left Kiel for the North Atlantic.
U 595 was to join *Steinbrinck* group, to be formed E of the Newfoundland Bank for August 7th. On the 5th U 593 sighted eastbound SC 94 and called up other outward-bound boats, including U 595, some 200 to 300 miles astern.
The convoy was pursued and in spite of the escort carrying out many attacks in the bad visibility and an air escort appearing from the 9th, the attacking boats sank eleven ships for the loss of two boats. In the morning of the 9th U 595 unsuccessfully attacked a

65

U 595 (continued)

destroyer, hearing only what was probably a premature detonation. The boat was afterwards attacked and damaged by gunfire and depth-charges by the corvettes HMCS *Chilliwack* and HMS *Primrose*.

U 595 put in to her new base at Brest **17.8.42**

2. 9.9.42 Left for the North Atlantic.

Outward-bound, U 595 was directed to eastbound convoy SC 100, sighted by U 221 on the 20th S of Greenland. The prevailing westerly gale increased to hurricane force and the pursuit was broken off and then resumed again, finally ending on the 25th. The convoy had a strong air escort and only five ships were sunk, none by U 595.

On the 23rd eastbound convoy RB 1 was sighted by U 404, as it passed through the *Vörwarts* group patrol line. The convoy was made up of several steamers from the Great Lakes, going to England. The boats reported them to be liners carrying troops. *Vörwarts* group was joined in the attack by *Pfeil* group and a few other boats, including U 595, coming from the northeast. U 595 had no success against the convoy.

After the RB 1 operation ended, some of the boats from SC 100 and RB 1, including U 595, were ordered to close westbound ON 131, sighted by U 617 on the 26th. The directed boats were widely-scattered but were ordered to the convoy as *Tiger* group. Contact was lost by the shadower and the boats were unable to mount an efficient search in the worsening weather. The operation was abandoned on the 29th.

U 595 returned to Brest **6.10.42**

3. 31.10.42 Left for the Mediterranean.

U 595 probably passed through the Straits of Gibraltar during the night of the 7/8th. She proceeded to an area west of a line from the Balearics to Algiers, where all available boats were awaiting developments from the heavy concentration of shipping then at Gibraltar.

After the Allied landings in North Africa began on the 8th, the boats began operating against invasion shipping. On the 12th U 595 torpedoed and sank the SS *Browning* (br 5332t) of convoy KMS 2, just NW of Cap de l'Arguille.

U 595 was spotted off Oran on the 14th by two Hudsons of 608 Squadron (F/O G Williams and P/O C A Livingstone). Williams made a four depth-charge attack and U 595 sank. She resurfaced and was strafed by Williams until Livingstone straddled her with four more depth-charges. The boat rose out of the sea and then began to circle, coming under machine gun fire from the aircraft, to which she returned fire.

Six patrolling Hudsons of 500 Squadron appeared and the CO, W/Cdr D Spotswood, made a depth-charge attack but was driven off by flak. Attacks were then made by four of the other Hudsons and, although unable to dive, U 595 was not about to give up.

An hour later another Hudson of 500 Squadron (F/O M A Ensor) appeared and attacked in the face of heavy flak. U 595 was stricken. Secret equipment and documents were destroyed and the boat was beached W of Ténès and later sank.

The entire crew of 45 was taken off by the French and later became prisoners of the Americans.

U 596 Type VII C

Built by Blohm & Voss, Hamburg
Keel laid 4.1.41   Launched 17.9.41
Commissioned 13.11.41   Feldpost Nr M 42 884

Scuttled 24.9.44 at Salamis

Served with
8 U-Flottille, Königsberg/Danzig November 1941 - June 1942 (ab)
3 U-Flottille, La Pallice June - November 1942 (fb)
29 U-Flottille, La Spezia/Pola December 1942 - 24.9.44 (fb)

Commanded by
KL Gunter Jahn November 1941 - June 1943
OL Viktor-Wilhelm Nonn June 1943 - July 1944
OL Hans Kolbus July 1944 - 1.9.44

Patrols: 12   Ships sunk: 11 (41,110 grt) + 2 damaged
                                  1 LCI (380 dt)

1. 25.6.42 Left Kiel and returned **2.7.42**

2. 25.7.42 Left Kiel and arrived Bergen **28.7.42**

3. 8.8.42 Left for the North Atlantic.

U 596 was one of a number of newly-arrived boats which joined others coming from the operation against SC 94 to form a new patrol line, *Lohs*, 600 miles W of the North Channel. An ON convoy was expected on the 13th. En route to their new positions, some of the boats from SC 94 sighted SC 95 going north. Only three boats closed, sinking one ship before contact was lost. During the afternoon of the 16th U 596 torpedoed and sank a straggler from SC 95 in the central North Atlantic, the MV *Suecia* (sw 4966t).

The *Lohs* patrol line was formed on the 17th W of Scotland. On the 21st the group moved northwards, searching for convoys, and on the 22nd ONS 122 passed to the south and was sighted by *Lohs'* southernmost boat, U 135. She shadowed but contact was lost in bad visibility and not regained until the 24th. By the early hours of the 25th nine boats were in contact and attacks were made. However, fog came down and the operation was called off, with four ships sunk and two boats damaged. U 596 had no success.

In late August the *Lohs* boats moved to a position W of the Azores for refuelling. U 596 was probably supplied by U 461. The group reformed and from 6.9.42 a new patrol line, 400 miles NE of Cape Race, awaited eastbound convoys. SC 100 was expected to be 150 miles SE of the Cape on the 18th and *Lohs* moved south to intercept but bad weather prevented more than three boats making attacks. U 596 was one of these and in an attack on the 20th she sank the SS *Empire Hartebeeste* (br 5676t) and may also have hit a second ship.

When the weather worsened further, the operation was abandoned on the 22nd, with only the *Empire Hartebeeste* sunk. However, the convoy was sighted again on the 23rd and U 432 of *Lohs* and U 617 of *Pfeil* group sank one ship and three stragglers between them. The operation against SC 100 finally ended on the 25th W of Rockall.

U 596 put in to St Nazaire **3.10.42**

4. 4.11.42 Left for the Mediterranean.

U 596 possibly passed through the Straits of Gibraltar during the night of the 8/9th and joined other boats operating against Allied shipping taking part in the landings in North Africa.

She put in to her new base at La Spezia **15.11.42**

5. 27.1.43 Left for operations.

U 596 and U 407 made unsuccessful attacks on convoy MKS 7 on 6.2.43 E of Oran, with U 596 reporting detonations on three ships. On the 7th she torpedoed and sank LCI 162 in the same area and on the 8th she claimed an explosion observed after a torpedo hit on a sloop N of Cape Ivi. There is no confirmation of this.

The boat returned to La Spezia **16.2.43**

6. 28.2.43 Left for operations.

U 596 operated off the Algerian coast. On 9.3.43 she torpedoed and damaged two ships NNW of Ténès, the SS *Fort Norman* (br 7133t) and the SS *Empire Standard* (br 7047t), both from convoy KMS 10.

She returned to La Spezia **12.3.43**

7. 23.3.43 Left for operations.

From the 25th U 596 and other boats made unsuccessful attacks on convoys off the Algerian coast. However, on the 30th U 596 attacked convoy ET 16 NW of Ténès, sinking two ships, the tanker MV *Hallanger* (nw 9551t) and the SS *Fort à la Corne* (br 7133t).

On 10.4.43 U 596 unsuccessfully attacked British naval forces near Alboran.

She returned to La Spezia **15.4.43**

8. 26.4.43 Left La Spezia and arrived Pola **30.4.43**

9. 17.6.43 Left for operations. No details are known except that it was KL Jahn's last patrol as commander.

U 596 returned to Pola **26.6.43**

10. 10.8.43 Left for the Eastern Mediterranean.

On the 20th U 596 sank a sailing vessel by gunfire E of Cape Greco, Cyprus, the *Namaz* (br 50t).

She reported a steamer sunk on the 29th 30 miles N of Beirut, which is unconfirmed, and later the same day U 596 sank four sailing vessels by gunfire 20 miles NNW of Beirut. One of them was the *Nagwa* (eg 183t) and another could have been the *Hamdiah*, which was not reported lost until 7.9.43.

U 596 put in to Salamis **10.9.43**

11. 28.9.43 Left for operations.

U 596 patrolled off the coast of Cyrenaica. On 4.10.43 she attacked convoy XT 4 off El Haniyah, sinking the tanker SS *Marit* (nw 5542t).

During the next few days U 596 made unsuccessful attacks on other ships but details are uncertain.

The boat returned to Pola **10.10.43**

12. 30.11.43 Left for operations.

U 596 operated in the Ionian Sea and on 9.12.43 she attacked convoy HA 11 NE of Capo Colonna, torpedoing and sinking the SS *Cap Padaran* (br 8009t). On the 13th U 596 claimed a destroyer and a steamer sunk E of the toe of Italy by a 4-torpedo spread but there is no confirmation of this.

The boat returned to Pola **28.12.43**

In January 1943 U 596 was possibly damaged in an air raid on the harbour at Pola.

13. 12.2.44 Left for operations.

On the 23rd U 596 unsuccessfully attacked an Italian corvette just E of the toe of Italy. On 2.3.44 she attacked an unidentified submarine and on the 7th the boat missed the Italian battleship *Giulio Cesare* S of the Gulf of Taranto.

U 596 returned to Pola **11.3.44**

14. 9.4.44 Left for operations.

U 596, on her first patrol fitted with schnorkel, missed an Italian corvette in the Strait of Otranto on the 13th. She then went on to operate without success in the Gulf of Taranto.

The boat returned to Pola **29.4.44**

15. 29.7.44 Left for operations.

U 596 carried out one of the last U-boat patrols in the Mediterranean. She operated in the Ionian Sea, off Malta and off the coast of Cyrenaica but she had no success.

She put in to Salamis **1.9.44**

On 15.9.44 U 596 was severely damaged in port in a USAF attack on Piraeus/Skaramanga, with the loss of the lives of two crewmen.

The boat was scuttled on the 24th and the wreck was blown up on the 30th.

U 597   Type VII C

Built by Blohm & Voss, Hamburg
Keel laid 13.1.41   Launched 11.10.41
Commissioned 20.11.41   Feldpost Nr M 42 993

Sunk 12.10.42 WSW of Rockall (56°50′N 28°05′W)

Served with
8 U-Flottille, Königsberg/Danzig   November 1941 - June 1942 (ab)
1 U-Flottille, Brest   June 1942 - 12.10.42 (fb)

Commanded by
KL Eberhard Bopst   November 1941 - 12.10.42

Patrols: 2   Ships sunk: None

1. 27.6.42 Left Kiel for the North Atlantic.

U 597 joined *Wolf* group, which was formed from 12.7.42 600 miles W of the North Channel. The group was to make a circular sweep towards the Newfoundland Bank and then go south.

A convoy was sighted at the northern end of the line on the 13th. Some of the more southerly boats moved northeastwards for some hours but when the convoy was found to be westbound it was not pursued further, being then too far ahead. When nothing further was seen by the 19th, it was decided to move *Wolf* group south.

Three days later, as the boats were about to move to a refuelling area, another westbound convoy was reported and a line was formed. The convoy was sighted on the 23rd and proved to be ON 113, the one originally sighted on the 13th. In the ensuing action, with bad visibility and a strong escort, the convoy lost only two ships and U 90 was sunk. U 597 carried out an unsuccessful attack during the night of the 25/26th. Contact was lost on the 26th and after a fruitless search on the 27th, the operation was ended.

The *Wolf* boats moved south to a refuelling area W of the Azores. Eight boats, including U 597, were refuelled on the 29th and 30th by U 461. U 379 was supplied on the 30th. The group did not re-form but after refuelling, seven of the boats, including U 597, moved north to close convoy ON 115, reported by U 210 on the 29th. A new patrol line, *Pirat*, was formed ahead of the convoy on 1.8.42 E of Newfoundland and the ex-*Wolf* boats joined this line on the 2nd.

ON 115 was sighted by U 552 on the 2nd E of Cape Race. The boats were ordered to close and the convoy was pursued as far as the Newfoundland Bank, where fog caused contact to be lost on the 3rd, ending the operation. Attacks had been made on the convoy late on the 2nd and early on the 3rd, sinking two ships and damaging a third. U 597 was unsuccessful against a straggler.

Leaving U 43 and U 552, which had been damaged in the action, U 597 and four other ex-*Wolf* boats headed for a new position 400 miles NE of Newfoundland, to form a patrol line, *Steinbrinck*, for the 7th. Two days before reaching this position, the outward-bound U 593 reported eastbound SC 94 at the northern end of the planned *Steinbrinck* line. The boats closed the convoy and a number of outward-bound boats joined the pursuit.

In the morning of the 10th U 597 made an attack on the convoy and what may have been detonations were heard but there were no

U 597 (continued)

results. The operation against SC 94 ended S of Iceland on the 11th, with eleven ships sunk and two boats lost.

U 597 put in to her new base at Brest **16.8.42**

2. 16.9.42 Left for the North Atlantic.

Outward-bound, U 597 was directed to westbound convoy ON 131, sighted by U 617 S of Iceland on the 26th. The shadower lost contact and bad weather caused the search to be abandoned.

U 597 joined *Luchs* group W of Ireland, to await an ON convoy. On the 29th outward-bound U 118 sighted a westbound convoy 250 miles S of Iceland and the *Luchs* boats were ordered northwestwards to intercept. When nothing had been located by the evening of October 2nd, the group swept southwestwards. On the 3rd U 260 sighted eastbound HX 209 at the northern end of the *Luchs* patrol line. Bad weather delayed the concentration of the boats for an attack and that, coupled with an air escort from the 4th, caused the pursuit to be abandoned on the 6th, with only one ship sunk, that by U 254.

U 437 had sighted a southwestbound ON convoy during the night of the 3/4th 120 miles southeast of HX 209 but her radioed report was delayed by bad conditions. This convoy was nearer to many of the *Luchs* boats and would have been a better attack proposition.

From the 8th the boats coming from HX 209 were formed into *Panther* group W of Ireland, which was augmented by outward-bound boats. During the evening of the 11th U 620 sighted westbound ONS 136 and eight *Panther* boats, including U 597, were directed to it, as *Leopard* group. U 597 made an unsuccessful torpedo attack on a ship of the convoy late on the 11th in the central North Atlantic in atrocious weather conditions.

On the 12th U 597 was sighted on the surface WSW of Rockall by a Liberator of 120 Squadron (S/Ldr T M Bulloch) near convoy ONS 136. Eight depth-charges were selected but only six were released and, perfectly-positioned as they were, they destroyed U 597, which broke up and sank.

It was both Bulloch's and 120 Squadron's first success. He was the pilot with the highest number of attacks on U-boats in the war.

There were no survivors from U 597, 49 dead.

U 598   Type VII C

Built by Blohm & Voss, Hamburg
Keel laid 11.1.41   Launched 2.10.41
Commissioned 27.11.41   Feldpost Nr M 43 201

Sunk 23.7.43 off Atol das Rocas, Brazil (04°04´S 33°23´W)

Served with
8 U-Flottille, Königsberg/Danzig   November 1941 - July 1942 (ab)
6 U-Flottille, St Nazaire   July 1942 - 23.7.43 (fb)

Commanded by
KL Gottfried Holtorf   November 1941 - 23.7.43

Patrols: 4   Ships sunk: 2 (9295 grt) + 1 damaged

1. 7.7.42 Left Kiel for the Western Atlantic.

En route to her operational area, U 598 was refuelled by U 463 W of the Azores in early August. During the transfer of fuel, U 598 had a crewman drowned on August 5th.

During the night of the 12/13th U 658 sighted convoy WAT 13, assembling in the Windward Passage. She called up U 598 and U 600. When the two boats came in to the area they encountered convoy TAW 12. In the morning of the 14th U 598 torpedoed three ships, sinking the SS *Michael Jebsen* (br 2323t) and the tanker SS *Empire Corporal* (br 6972t) and damaging the tanker MV *Standella* (br 6197t), off Gibara, Cuba. The *Standella* was towed into Key

West, later going back into service, only to be attacked again and damaged by U 126 S of Freetown on 2.6.43.

U 598 had no further success on this patrol. In late August she was refuelled for return to base, possibly by U 462 W of the Azores.

The boat put in to St Nazaire **13.9.42**

2. 26.12.42 Left for the North Atlantic.

U 598 joined *Jaguar* group, which was in its operational area NE of Newfoundland from 12.1.43, waiting for an eastbound convoy. HX 223 probably passed the western end of the *Jaguar* patrol line on the 22nd. The *Jaguar* boats pursued eastbound SC 117, sighted by U 413 on the 22nd SSW of Cape Farewell but bad weather and radio conditions that made it difficult to circulate reports did not allow any organised search or attack to be made and contact was lost with the convoy on the 23rd.

U 598 returned to St Nazaire **8.2.43**

3. 6.3.43 Left for the North Atlantic.

U 598 joined *Stürmer* group on the 14th WNW of Ireland. The group took part in the biggest convoy operation of the war, against eastbound convoys HX 229 and SC 122 from March 16th to the 19th. U 598 does not appear to have taken any part in the action.

On the 20th U 598 was probably attacked with depth-charges and strafed by a Sunderland of 201 Squadron (F/Lt D Hewitt). Just prior to this the aircraft had attacked U 527, which had also dived and escaped without serious damage or casualties. The stormy conditions prevented accurate observations and the aircrew reported the attacks to be on only one boat, which had been sunk. Hewitt was awarded the DFC.

On the 21st a new patrol line, *Seeteufel*, was formed S of Iceland to intercept westbound ONS 1. U 598 joined the line soon after its formation. The convoy was expected to cross the line on the 22nd. Masts and an aircraft carrier were seen on the 26th and were thought to be part of an ON convoy, which was not pursued.

It was decided that the *Seeteufel* boats should concentrate their efforts against eastbound HX 230. Only two of the group's boats, U 415 and U 610, were able to approach the convoy. A storm that was blowing developed into a hurricane, making an organised search impossible. The pursuit of HX 230 continued but only one ship was sunk, by U 610. The continuous bad weather and the rough seas made the use of torpedoes virtually impossible and the operation ended on the 30th and *Seeteufel* group broke up.

In mid-April U 598 was refuelled by U 462 N of the Azores. She then joined *Meise* group NE of Newfoundland. On the 20th it was learned that expected convoy HX 234 would pass to the west of the patrol line. The *Meise* boats moved northwestwards at high speed and the convoy was sighted on the 21st by U 306. On her way to close the convoy, U 706 sighted westbound ONS 3. The *Meise* boats divided, some going for each convoy.

U 598 went after HX 234 S of Cape Farewell and on the 22nd the boats were driven off by Catalinas of VP-84. Contact was lost with both convoys because of fog and snowstorms. HX 234 had only two ships sunk and one damaged. The operation was ended in the morning of the 25th S of Iceland because of increasing air cover.

U 598 returned to St Nazaire **13.5.43**

4. 26.6.43 Left for the Central Atlantic.

En route to her operational area off Brazil, U 598 was refuelled between July 6th and 12th by U 487 600 miles SW of the Azores.

On the 22nd U 598 was sighted and attacked near the Rocas Reef by a Natal-based USN Liberator of VB-107 (Lt-Cdr R Turner). Other aircraft came and kept the boat pinned down. In the morning of the 23rd further strafing attacks made U 598 incapable of diving.

One Liberator (Lt G E Waugh) came in too low and the explosion of its depth-bombs caused the aircraft to crash into the sea, killing all twelve members of the crew. A second Liberator (Lt W R Ford) made an attack immediately afterwards, sinking the boat.

Of U 598's crew, 44 were lost and the only 2 survivors were picked up by the tug USS *Seneca* and made PoW.

U 599　Type VII C

Built by Blohm & Voss, Hamburg
Keel laid 27.1.41　　Launched 15.10.41
Commissioned 4.12.41　　Feldpost Nr M 43 202

Sunk 24.10.42 NE of the Azores (46°07′N　17°40′W)

Served with
8 U-Flottille, Königsberg/Danzig　December 1941 - August 1942 (ab)
1 U-Flottille, Brest　August 1942 - 24.10.42 (fb)

Commanded by
KL Wolfgang Breithaupt　December 1941 - 24.10.42

Patrols: 1　　Ships sunk: None

1. 27.8.42　Left Kiel for the North Atlantic.

U 599 joined the reformed *Lohs* patrol line on 13.9.42, 400 miles NE of Cape Race, awaiting an eastbound convoy. SC 100 was expected to be 150 miles SE of the Cape on the 18th and *Lohs* moved south to intercept but bad weather prevented more that three boats making attacks.

When the weather worsened further, the operation was abandoned on the 22nd, with only one ship sunk. However, the convoy was sighted again on the 23rd and U 432 of *Lohs* and U 617 of *Pfeil* group sank one ship and three stragglers between them before the operation was finally called off on the 25th W of Rockall.

U 617 sighted westbound ON 131 on the 26th in the central North Atlantic, SE of Cape Farewell. U 599 was one of the boats coming from the operations against SC 100 and RB 1, which were ordered to close the convoy as *Tiger* group. However, U 617 lost contact and because the weather was bad and the boats so widely scattered, a search for the convoy was impractical and the operation against ON 131 was abandoned. On the 29th eight of the boats were ordered south to an area NW of the Azores to refuel from U 116 and U 118. U 599 was supplied by U 118.

U 599 joined *Wotan* group, formed from 8.10.42, E of Newfoundland, to await eastbound SC 104, expected on the 11th. On this day U 258 sighted a corvette at the northern end of the *Wotan* patrol line but her report did not reach the other boats until the early hours of the 12th, when the *Wotan* boats were ordered northeast at high speed to intercept.

SC 104 was sighted during the night of the 12/13th in the central North Atlantic, S of Greenland. The first attacks were carried out on the convoy in the early morning of the 13th by U 221 and within the next 19 hours she had sunk five ships. U 607, U 618 and U 661 sank another three before the operation was called off in the evening of the 15th as more and more aircraft appeared.

The *Wotan* boats then moved eastwards to intercept ON 137, sighted on the 16th by U 704. Soon after contact was made, the weather worsened and although a search was made, the contact lost was not regained. The operation ended on the 19th.

U 599 headed for home but on the 24th she was sunk in a depth-charge attack by a Liberator of 224 Squadron (P/O B P Liddington) NE of the Azores, near convoy KX 2.

There were no survivors, 44 dead.

U 600　Type VII C

Built by Blohm & Voss, Hamburg
Keel laid 25.1.41　　Launched 16.10.41
Commissioned 11.12.41　　Feldpost Nr M 47 389

Sunk 25.11.43 NE of São Miguel, Azores (40°31′N　22°07′W)

Served with
5 U-Flottille, Kiel　December 1941 - July 1942 (ab)
3 U-Flottille, La Pallice　July 1942 - 25.11.43 (fb)

Commanded by
KL Bernhard Zurmühlen　December 1941 - 25.11.43

Patrols: 6　　Ships sunk: 7 + 1 shared (45,635 grt)

1. 14.7.42　Left Kiel for the Western Atlantic.

En route to her operational area, U 600 was refuelled by U 463 W of the Azores in early August. On the 10th U 600 sank the sailing vessel *Vivian P Smith* (br 130t) by gunfire E of the Turks and Caicos Islands.

During the night of the 12/13th U 658 sighted convoy WAT 13, assembling in the Windward Passage. She called up U 600 and U 598. When the two boats came in to the area they encountered convoy TAW 12. In the morning of the 13th U 600 torpedoed and sank two ships off the eastern tip of Cuba, the SS *Everelza* (la 4520t) and the SS *Delmundo* (am 5032t).

U 600 continued to patrol in the Greater Antilles area and on the 23rd she was sighted in the Windward Passage by a USN Catalina of VP-92. The boat may have been damaged in a depth-charge attack. On the return journey she was refuelled by U 462 in early September W of the Azores.

U 600 put in to her new base at La Pallice **22.9.42**.

2. 22.11.42　Left for the North Atlantic.

U 600 joined *Draufgänger* group W of Ireland, to await an ONS convoy but this did not materialise. On 7.12.42 the group was ordered to close northeast-bound convoy HX 217. En route early on the 8th, U 600 sank an independent ship SSW of Iceland, the SS *James McKay* (am 6762t).

The *Draufgänger* boats came up with convoy HX 217 on the 8th but only U 524 and U 553 of the group had any success, sinking stragglers on the 8th and 9th. The operation was called off on the 11th after strong air cover appeared from Iceland on the 10th.

Draufgänger and *Panzer* groups joined newly-arrived boats to form two new groups S of Iceland, *Ungestüm* and *Raufbold*, from the 13th. U 600 was in *Raufbold*. The groups were to intercept westbound convoys leaving the North Channel.

On the 15th U 609 sighted westbound ON 153 and called up other boats. Despite bad weather from the 17th, contact was maintained until the 21st, when the pursuit ended in the central North Atlantic. Two ships and a destroyer had been sunk and another ship damaged. U 600 had no success.

She returned to La Pallice **27.12.42**.

3. 11.2.43　Left for the North Atlantic.

On the 19th the outward-bound U 600, U 91, U 92 and U 604 were ordered to form a patrol line, *Knappen*, in the expected path of an ON convoy.

The southwest-bound ON 166 was sighted by U 604 on the 20th. The pursuit of the convoy continued for five days, ending ESE of Newfoundland in bad visibility on the 25th. U 600 and U 628 shared in sinking a ship from the convoy on the 24th ESE of St John's, the MV *Ingria* (nw 4391t). In the morning of the 25th U 600 unsuccessfully attacked another ship in the convoy.

The *Knappen* boats returned eastwards to a refuelling area N of the Azores, where U 600, U 91 and U 604 were supplied by

U 600 (continued)

U 462. U 92 had already set out for base.

From March 4th U 600 and U 91 joined *Burggraf* group S of Greenland. From the 7th *Burggraf* and *Wildfang* group boats that had not gone off in pursuit of eastbound convoy SC 121 set up a new patrol line, *Raubgraf*, ENE of Newfoundland. U 600 was in this group, which was awaiting an HX convoy.

On the 9th the boats moved north to intercept southwest-bound ON 170 and on the 13th and 14th they operated unsuccessfully against the convoy, which was pursued in spite of rain, snow and a strong air escort. The operation ended with the reported approach of convoy SC 122.

During the evening of the 15th U 91, in the southern section of the *Raubgraf* line, sighted a destroyer. A search was made for the convoy but it was not found. Next morning a returning boat, U 653, found a convoy southeast of the *Raubgraf* line, thought to be SC 122. *Raubgraf*, *Dränger* and *Stürmer* groups were ordered to attack. During the morning the *Raubgraf* boats made contact. Late on the 16th a second convoy appeared, sailing on a parallel course and slower. It was only then realised that the first convoy was not SC 122 but HX 229.

The largest convoy action of the war was then fought, with more than forty U-boats taking part and twenty-one Allied ships sunk. On the 17th U 600 torpedoed three ships from HX 229 in the central North Atlantic, sinking the whaling factory ship SS *Southern Princess* (br 12156t) and damaging the SS *Nariva* (br 8714t) and the SS *Irenée du Pont* (am 6125t). The abandoned wrecks of these last two vessels were sunk later by U 91, after an attempt by the Norwegian destroyer *Mansfield* failed to do so. The operation against the two convoys ended on the 20th W of Ireland.

U 600 returned to La Pallice **26.3.43**

4. 25.4.43 Left for Atlantic operations.

U 600 was one of eleven outward-bound boats which in late April formed a patrol line, *Drossel*, NW of Cape Finisterre. On May 3rd aerial reconnaissance reported a southbound convoy but when the group moved eastwards to attack, it proved to be fifteen LCTs and two escorts. Sea conditions made torpedo attacks on these flat-bottomed craft very impractical and the operation was abandoned. During the action on the 5th U 600 accidentally rammed U 406, resulting in their both returning to base with possible damage.

U 600 reached La Pallice **11.5.43**

5. 12.6.43 Left for the Central Atlantic.

U 600 went through the Bay of Biscay in company with U 68, U 155, U 257 and U 615, for mutual protection against attack by Allied aircraft. Early on the 14th U 600, U 257 and U 615 were attacked by a Sunderland of 461 (RAAF) Squadron (F/O S White). Depth-charges were dropped but no damage was caused.

The boats dived but on resurfacing six hours later U 600 was attacked by a Whitley of 10 OTU (P/O Orr), suffering slight damage and having one crewman killed. U 257 and U 615 closed up on U 600 and fire was exchanged before Orr left the scene. Four hours later a Fortress of 220 Squadron (F/O C F Callender) appeared, went down to attack U 600 and was shot down by the boat into the sea, with the loss of the entire crew.

Soon afterwards a Wellington of 547 Squadron (W/O J W Hermiston) arrived and attacked U 615. The aircraft was driven off and after circling for some time it left for home.

U 600 and U 257 continued southwards. In late June U 600 was refuelled by U 535 just W of the Azores. She went on through the Central Atlantic to become one of nine boats operating off the African coast from Dakar to the Niger Estuary. In mid-July U 600 rendezvoused with U 333 to pass over spare parts for U 333's ailing air compressor.

From July 23rd U 600 was one of six boats patrolling initially slowly back and forth in an east-west direction off the Ivory Coast, then searching in scouting formation S of Liberia until August 2nd.

Nothing was seen.

U 600 began her return journey on or about the 8th. She, U 333, U 571, U 618 and U 634 were due to have been refuelled by U 525 at positions 700 to 800 miles S to SW of the Azores but she was sunk on the 11th, en route to the rendezvous.

U 129 was sent as a replacement U-tanker and from the 18th she refuelled U 600 and the other four boats and two others that had turned up.

U 600 put in to Brest **10.9.43**

6. 7.11.43 Left for Atlantic operations.

U 600 joined *Schill 1* group, which by the 18th was drawn up in a patrol line W of Lisbon in the expected path of MKS 30/SL 139, sighted by aircraft on the 15th W of Gibraltar. In the morning of the 18th the convoy was reported to the southeast of the line, which was ordered northeastwards to intercept. The convoy in fact passed through the patrol line during the early afternoon of the 18th but U 515's sighting report was not received until late evening.

The *Schill 1* boats pursued the convoy during the night of the 18/19th but were constantly harassed by aircraft. Only U 262 made contact just before dawn on the 19th but she was located and driven off. With no chance of the other boats catching up, the pursuit was abandoned and on the 22nd *Schill 1* group was dissolved.

U 600 was probably on her way to join *Weddigen* group when she was located NE of São Miguel, Azores on the 25th by the frigates HMS *Bazely* (Lt-Cdr J V Brock) and *Blackwood* (Lt-Cdr L T Sly) of the 4th EG and sunk in depth-charge attacks.

There were no survivors, 54 dead.

U 601   Type VII C

Built by Blohm & Voss, Hamburg
Keel laid 10.2.41   Launched 29.10.41
Commissioned 18.12.41   Feldpost Nr M 47 254

Sunk 25.2.44 NW of Harstad (70°25′N 12°40′E)

Served with
5 U-Flottille, Kiel   December 1941 - June 1942 (ab)
11 U-Flottille, Bergen   July 1942 - May 1943 (fb)
13 U-Flottille, Trondheim   June 1943 - 25.2.44 (fb)

Commanded by
KL Peter-Ottmar Grau   December 1941 - October 1943
OL Otto Hansen   October 1943 - 25.2.44

Patrols: 10   Ships sunk: 3 (8819 grt)

1. 4.7.42 Left Kiel and arrived Narvik **10.7.42**

2. 14.7.42 Left Narvik for Northern Waters.

U 601 was directed to search for surviving ships from scattered, eastbound convoy PQ 17, sighted by German reconnaissance aircraft W of Novaya Zemlya but she found none.

On the 26th she shelled the Soviet polar station at Karmakuly, destroying two aircraft. On August 1st U 601 torpedoed and sank the SS *Krest'janin* (sov 2513t) W of Mesduzarskij Island.

U 601 put in to Kirkenes **3.8.42**

3. 9.8.42 Left for operations.

On the 16th the pocket-battleship *Admiral Scheer* left Narvik for the Barents Sea for *Operation Wunderland*, a foray against the Siberian sea route. U 601 and U 251 preceded her into the Kara Sea, to carry out an ice reconnaissance.

U 601 operated in the Kara Sea and on 24.8.42 she torpedoed and sank the SS *Kujbysev* (sov 2332t) E of Yugor Strait.

The boat put in to Neidenfjord **20.9.42**

4. 22.9.42 Left Neidenfjord and arrived Bergen **24.9.42**

5. 31.10.42 Left Bergen and arrived Narvik **3.11.42**

6. 5.11.42 Left Narvik for operations.
Westbound convoy QP 15 left Kola Inlet on the 17th. It ran into a succession of gales from the 20th, scattering the ships. U 601 and other boats were waiting for the convoy off Bear Island.
In spite of the ships being scattered and mostly defenceless, QP 15 lost only two ships, one torpedoed and sunk by U 601 SW of Spitzbergen, the SS *Kusnec Lesov* (sov 3974t).
U 601 returned to Narvik **8.12.42**

7. 15.12.42 Left Narvik and arrived Kiel **24.12.42**

8. 3.4.43 Left Kiel and arrived Bergen **7.4.43**

9. 15.4.43 Left for operations. No details known of this patrol except that one of the boat's officers was killed on May 4th by an artillery misfire.
U 601 returned to Narvik **15.5.43**

10. 7.7.43 Left Narvik and returned **10.7.43**

11. 14.7.43 Left for a minelaying operation.
U 601 laid mines off Belusha, Novaya Zemlya on or about the 20th. There is no record of any sinkings or damage to ships caused by these mines.
The boat put in to Hammerfest **25.7.43**

12. 26.7.43 Left Hammerfest and arrived Tromsø **27.7.43**

13. 29.7.43 Left Tromsø and returned to Hammerfest **29.7.43**

14. 30.7.43 Left for operations.
During this patrol U 601 took part in the establishment of a weather station on Novaya Zemlya and at some time rescued the crew of a ditched German flying boat.
U 601 returned to Narvik **28.8.43**

15. 13.9.43 Left for a minelaying operation.
U 601, as part of *Dachs* group, laid mines off Dikson in the Kara Sea on the 23rd. There appear to have been no sinkings attributed to these mines.
On the 30th U 601, U 703 and U 960 had relieved boats of *Wiking* group. On this day they encountered Russian convoy VA 18. In the evening of 1.10.43 U 601 unsuccessfully attacked the icebreaker *Murman* with the convoy, NE of Ostrova Island in the Kara Sea. U 601 was shelled in retaliation by the icebreaker.
The boat put in to Skjomenfjord **10.10.43**

16. 12.10.43 Left Skjomenfjord and arrived Bergen **19.10.43**

17. 10.12.43 Left Bergen and arrived Trondheim **12.12.43**

18. 18.12.43 Left Trondheim for operations.
U 601 joined *Eisenbart* group. On the 24th she was directed to eastbound convoy JW 55B by reconnaissance aircraft. She and U 716 made contact with the convoy early on the 25th. The latter made an unsuccessful attack on a destroyer of the escort before both boats were driven off. Later in the day the German battlecruiser *Scharnhorst*, with destroyer escort, was deployed against the convoy.
On the 26th *Scharnhorst* was engaged in a day-long running battle with British warships and, very severely damaged, she sank in the evening.
U 601 returned to Skjomenfjord **7.1.44**

19. 10.1.44 Left for operations.
Eastbound JW 56A left Loch Ewe on 12.1.44 but after running into a storm on the 16th the convoy put in to Akureyri, Iceland. On the 21st it sailed again, less five ships which had been damaged. Convoy JW 56B left Loch Ewe on the 22nd.
U 601 was with *Isegrim* group, awaiting these two convoys in Bear Island Passage. On the 25th contact was made with JW 56A and all boats of the group made attacks on either the convoy or escort. U 601 made four unsuccessful attacks on destroyers.
After JW 56A moved on towards Kola Inlet, *Isegrim* group reformed as *Werwolf*, to await JW 56B in the Passage. Contact was made on the 29th and in the early morning of the 30th U 601 made another unsuccessful attack on an escorting destroyer. The convoys lost three ships sunk and a destroyer damaged from JW 56A and the destroyer HMS *Hardy* sunk from JW 56B.
U 601 returned to Hammerfest **2.2.44**

20. 4.2.44 Left Hammerfest and returned **5.2.44**

21. 17.2.44 Left for operations.
Eastbound JW 57 left Loch Ewe on the 20th and was located by aerial reconnaissance on the 23rd. The *Werwolf* group was deployed. U 601, U 425, U 713, U 739 and U 990 closed the convoy on the 24th in the Norwegian Sea.
U 601 was located on the 25th, trailing the convoy NW of Harstad, by a Catalina of 210 Squadron (S/Ldr F J French). The boat was sunk in a depth-charge attack.
There were no survivors, 52 dead.

U 602   Type VII C

Built by Blohm & Voss, Hamburg
Keel laid 8.2.41   Launched 30.10.41
Commissioned 29.12.41   Feldpost Nr M 47 187

Lost 23.4.43 off Oran

Served with
5 U-Flottille, Kiel   December 1941 - September 1942 (ab)
7 U-Flottille, St Nazaire   October - December 1942 (fb)
29 U-Flottille, La Spezia   January 1943 - 23.4.43 (fb)

Commanded by
KL Philipp Schüler   December 1941 - 23.4.43

Patrols: 4   Ships sunk: None + 1 damaged
                                1 destroyer (1540 dt)

1. 26.9.42 Left Kiel for the North Atlantic.
U 602 joined ex-*Luchs* group boats when *Panther* group was formed from 8.10.42 700 to 800 miles W of the North Channel. In the evening of the 11th U 620 sighted westbound ONS 136 and eight boats in the centre of the long *Panther* line were detached and directed to the convoy, as *Leopard* group.
On the 16th ONS 137 was sighted by U 704 as it passed through the southern section of the line and eleven boats were ordered to attack. From the remaining *Panther* boats, *Puma* group was formed on the 16th from U 602 and seven others and ordered southwards to seek ONS 138.
By the 22nd the boats were nearly 400 miles south of their original *Puma* line position. On that day the southernmost boat in the line, U 443, sighted ON 139 in the central North Atlantic. The group was ordered to close and attack but the boats were unable to catch the convoy, which was averaging 10 to 12 knots. Only U 443 was able to attack and she sank two ships.
Puma group moved westwards until the 24th, when U 606 reported two destroyers which could have been part of an escort

U 602 (continued)

for a westbound ONS convoy. The boats moved northwestwards at high speed to intercept. On the 26th U 436 sighted eastbound HX 212 in the centre of the *Puma* line. She shadowed and brought up other boats, which did not include U 602. Attacks were made but the boats were all driven off by the escort. On the 28th the boats which had made contact were driven off by Iceland-based aircraft of 120 Squadron. When the same happened on the 29th the operation was abandoned. Despite the difficulty in making attacks, six ships were sunk and another damaged. U 602 had no success.

She put in to Lorient **6.11.42**

2. 1.12.42 Left for the Mediterranean.

U 602 passed through the Straits of Gibraltar during the night of the 7/8th. In the late evening of the 9th she torpedoed and damaged the destroyer HMS *Porcupine* NNE of Cap Ferrat. The warship broke in two and the parts were towed in to Arzew. The bow section was later towed to the UK but never repaired.

U 602 put in to her new base at La Spezia **21.12.42**

3. 6.2.43 Left for operations.

U 602 patrolled off the Algerian coast but she had no success in any attacks she made.

The boat put in to Toulon **9.3.43**

4. 6.4.43 Left for operations.

U 602 again patrolled off the Algerian coast. She sent a message on the 19th but was not heard from again. It is believed that she was lost on the 23rd off Oran from unknown causes.

There were no survivors, 48 dead.

U 603 Type VII C

Built by Blohm & Voss, Hamburg
Keel laid 27.2.41   Launched 16.11.41
Commissioned 2.1.42   Feldpost Nr M 47 142

Sunk 1.3.44 N of the Azores (48°55′N 26°10′W)

Served with
5 U-Flottille, Kiel   January - November 1942 (ab)
1 U-Flottille, Brest   December 1942 - 1.3.44 (fb)

Commanded by
KL Kurt Kölzer   January - September 1942
OL Hans-Joachim Bertelsmann   September 1942 - May 1943
OL Rudolf Baltz   May 1943 - January 1944
KL Hans-Joachim Bertelsmann   January 1944 - 1.3.44

Patrols: 5   Ships sunk: 3 + 1 shared (19,424 grt)

1. 5.11.42 Left Kiel and arrived at Kristiansand **7.11.42**

2. 13.11.42 Left Kristiansand, in transit for Western France.
U 603 put in to her new base at Brest **9.12.42**

3. 7.2.43 Left for the North Atlantic.

U 603 joined *Ritter* group in the central North Atlantic, formed from the 14th to operate against expected convoy HX 226. During the night of the 14/15th convoy SC 119 passed to the north of the patrol line and on the 18th HX 226 also passed to the north, after a wide detour.

The group had been moving westwards but when it was learned that convoys ON 166 and ONS 167 were being routed south of the *Ritter* line, the movement westwards was halted and the boats moved southeastwards and formed a north-south patrol line with *Neptun* group on the 30° meridian from the 20th. Four outward-bound boats

formed *Knappen* group to the south of *Ritter*, to operate against the two convoys.

ON 166 was sighted by U 604 in the late morning of the 20th but she was driven off during the night before the closing *Ritter* and *Knappen* boats could arrive. In the afternoon of the 21st U 603 and U 332 shared in torpedoing and sinking the tanker MV *Stigstad* (nw 5964t) in the central North Atlantic. In the morning of the 23rd U 603 sank the tanker MV *Glittre* (nw 6409t), which had been torpedoed by U 628 a short time earlier.

The convoy was pursued for 1100 miles and when the operation ended on the 25th E of Newfoundland, fourteen ships had been sunk and another damaged. U 603 and other *Ritter* boats were refuelled by U 462 N of the Azores. They then joined *Burggraf* group, formed from the 26th in the central North Atlantic.

The *Burggraf* boats began a sweep westwards and by 4.3.43 they were E of Newfoundland, where they joined up with *Wildfang* group, stationed to the north. The two groups formed a long patrol line from the 4th, with a view to intercepting an expected SC convoy.

After part of the line was detached to operate against eastbound SC 121, the remaining *Burggraf* boats, including U 603, formed a new patrol line, *Raubgraf*, from the 7th ENE of Newfoundland. On the 9th the group moved north to intercept southwest-bound convoy ON 170. The group operated against the convoy on the 13th and 14th, in spite of rain, snow and a strong escort. The pursuit was called off after a report that SC 122 was approaching.

In the evening of the 15th U 91 of *Raubgraf* sighted a destroyer but a search was unsuccessful. Next day the returning U 653 found a convoy southeast of the *Raubgraf* line, thought to be SC 122. *Raubgraf*, *Dränger* and *Stürmer* boats were ordered to attack. In the morning of the 16th *Raubgraf* group made contact. U 603 torpedoed and sank the MV *Elin K* (nw 5214t) in the evening and late on the 16th a second convoy appeared, sailing on a parallel course and slower. Only then was it realised that the convoy under attack was not SC 122 but HX 229.

The largest convoy action of the war was then fought, with forty U-boats taking part and with twenty-one Allied ships sunk before the operation ended on the 20th. U 603 had no further success. She was refuelled by U 119 N of the Azores for return to base.

The boat reached Brest **26.3.43**

4. 5.5.43 Left for the North Atlantic.

Outward-bound, U 603 was directed to eastbound HX 237 SW of Ireland. On the 12th she was sighted by a Swordfish from the escort-carrier HMS *Biter*. The pilot called up HMS *Pathfinder* to the scene. The destroyer arrived and a depth-charge attack caused slight damage to the boat. Later on the 12th U 603 sank the MV *Brand* (nw 4819t), a straggler from HX 237, NNE of the Azores. The operation against HX 237 ended on the 13th.

U 603 was refuelled by U 461 and then continued westwards towards Newfoundland and from the 18th she was with *Oder* group in the central North Atlantic, formed to operate against eastbound HX 238. However, after the convoy passed well to the north, the *Oder* boats became part of a new patrol line, *Mosel*, formed from the 20th 400 miles S of Cape Farewell to intercept HX 239, reported moving eastwards from Newfoundland.

The convoy was sighted on the 22nd by U 305 but she was unable to maintain contact because of aircraft attacks. All attempts to locate the convoy during daylight hours were frustrated by aircraft. Several boats were badly damaged. U 569 and U 752 were sunk. With HX 239 still not found, the operation was ended on the 23rd.

The *Mosel* boats moved to an area SW of the Azores. Convoy operations in the North Atlantic had been suspended whilst the situation was being assessed by BdU. It was decided to try and intercept US-Mediterranean convoys out in the Atlantic, beyond the range of land-based aircraft.

From the boats which had assembled SW of the Azores, a new patrol line, *Trutz*, was formed during the night of the 30/31st, to await expected convoys UGS 9 and GUS 7A. The line was drawn up on the 43° meridian and ran between 32° and 38°N. On 4.6.43 the three most southerly boats were attacked by carrier-borne aircraft, which were thought to be part of a convoy's protective cover. U 603 was one of these. She was attacked by an Avenger (Lt S H Kinney) from the escort-carrier USS *Bogue*. The boat was near a convoy of LCIs bound for Africa when she was driven down by three depth-bombs. One struck U 603's jump-wire, bounced off and exploded harmlessly.

The boats closed up to prevent any ships passing through gaps in the line but when nothing had been sighted by the evening of the 5th the convoy was thought to have passed either to the north or south. The group broke up and moved 600 miles to the north to be refuelled by U 488. The UGS convoy was sighted by an outward-bound boat on the 8th, 100 miles south of the *Trutz* patrol area of the 5th. The move to refuel had been too premature and the opportunity lost. Refuelling was completed by the 15th and the group reformed in three north-south lines, *Trutz 1,2* and *3*, 1000 miles E of Bermuda. U 603 was in *Trutz 2*.

The boats waited for two other convoys from the 16th until the 22nd and having seen nothing in that time, the line began an eastwards movement, which continued until the 27th, when they halted 200 miles SW of the Azores. By the 29th it was realised that the elusive convoys, GUS 8, UGS 10 and GUS 8A had by-passed the lines.

From 2.7.43 three new lines were formed, *Geier 1,2* and *3*. U 603 was in *Geier 1*. The lines moved in a scouting formation towards the Portugese coast. At 500 miles from the coast air attacks began and by the 8th were such that boat commanders were allowed to return to base if they wished. U 603 was attacked and severely damaged on the 8th by a Catalina of 202 Squadron (F/Lt G Powell)

She returned to Brest **16.7.43**

5. 9.9.43 Left for the North Atlantic.

Outward-bound, U 603 was refuelled by U 460 on or about the 26th N of the Azores. She then joined a new patrol line, *Rossbach*, formed in the central North Atlantic to operate against ON 203. The convoy passed to the north during the night of the 28/29th.

The line was moved 100 miles to the northwest and waited there until the 30th but saw no sign of either ON 203 or the reported ONS 19, which had also passed to the north. The group moved northeastwards on 1.10.43 to a position SW of Iceland, to intercept ON 204 but this convoy was also re-routed. When pursuit was realised to be useless, *Rossbach* went southwestwards on the 5th to form a new patrol line to intercept convoys HX 259 and SC 143.

On the 7th SC 143 was assumed to be in the area when destroyers of the 3rd SG were sighted by U 448. During the night of the 7/8th they were engaged by some boats and the Polish destroyer *Orkan* was sunk by U 378. Liberators of 86 Squadron arrived in the morning and drove off the boats. The convoy was sighted by a German reconnaissance aircraft but its radio signals were not received. The operation ended on the 9th, with SC 143's only loss a straggler sunk early on that day by U 645.

U 603 did not join another group on this patrol. She was refuelled by U 220 on or about the 23rd NNW of the Azores.

The boat returned to Brest **3.11.43**

6. 6.2.44 Left for the North Atlantic.

U 603 was briefly with *Hai* group, formed in two parallel patrol lines, *Hai 1* and *Hai 2*, from the 18th WSW of Ireland in the path of expected convoys ONS 29, ON 224 and OS 68. Aerial reconnaissance failed to find them and it was learned that the convoys had altered course and would pass to the south of the patrol lines, which they did during the night of the 18/19th.

The boats were immediately ordered south, submerged in daylight and at high speed on the surface after dark. Instead of sighting the convoys at dawn on the 19th, the boats saw only some destroyers. Attacks were made by the boats and HMS *Woodpecker*

was damaged by U 256 and later sank under tow. The operation ended in failure on the 20th, with the boats driven down by carrier-borne aircraft.

The *Hai* groups were dissolved and sixteen boats, including U 603, formed *Preussen* group W of Ireland from the 22nd. The boats were concentrated from the 26th between 22° and 30°W in the expected path of westbound ON 225 but the convoy was re-routed.

Soon after midnight on 1.3.44 U 603 was sighted in the vicinity of the escort-carrier USS *Block Island* by the destroyer USS *Bronstein* (Lt H S Kinney) of the escort. The boat was driven off by the approach of the escort and sunk in a depth-charge attack one hour later by *Bronstein*.

There were no survivors, 51 dead.

U 604 Type VII C

Built by Blohm & Voss, Hamburg
Keel laid 27.2.41 Launched 16.11.41
Commissioned 8.1.42 Feldpost Nr M 27 582

Scuttled 11.8.43 SE of St Paul Rocks (05°00´S 20°00´W)

Served with
5 U-Flottille, Kiel January - July 1942 (ab)
9 U-Flottille, Brest August 1942 - 11.8.43 (fb)

Commanded by
KL Horst Höltring January 1942 - 11.8.43

Patrols: 5 Ships sunk: 6 (39,891 grt)

1. 4.8.42 Left Kiel for Atlantic operations.

U 604 went to a waiting area in the eastern North Atlantic, arriving there on the 15th. In the morning of the 25th she torpedoed and sank the MV *Abbekerk* (nl 7906t) in the central North Atlantic.

On the 31st U 609 of *Vorwärts* group sighted eastbound SC 97 SE of Cape Farewell and sank two ships. Other boats from the group and the independent U 604 made contact with the convoy but were driven off. In the morning of 1.9.42 U 604 and U 609 made unsuccessful attacks and during the day the boats in contact were driven off by a USN Catalina of VP-73 from Iceland. The operation was abandoned in daylight on the 2nd because of the aircraft presence.

U 604 put in to her new base at Brest **8.9.42**

2. 14.10.42 Left for the Freetown area.

U 604 was one of eight boats which assembled E of the Azores. On the 23rd they set out in line abreast for Freetown, as *Streitaxt* group. U 203 sighted the escorted tanker MV *Anglo Maersk* (br 7705t) on the 25th just S of the Canaries. She was a straggler from northbound SL 125 and although she was shadowed by U 134, it was U 604's torpedo which sank her in the evening of the 27th. The evening before the vessel had been hit by a torpedo from U 509 but without apparent result.

In the morning of the 27th the main convoy SL 125 had been sighted by U 409 W of the Canaries as it passed through the *Streitaxt* line. The boats pursued. U 604 came up with the convoy in the evening of the 30th and sank two ships N of Madeira, the MV *President Doumer* (br 11898t) and the SS *Baron Vernon* (br 3642t). In this latter attack, U 604 heard a torpedo hit without detonation.

The boat returned to Brest **5.11.42**

3. 26.11.42 Left for the North Atlantic.

U 604 joined a new group, *Draufgänger*, W of Ireland, awaiting an ONS convoy but this did not materialise. On 2.12.42 U 604 may

U 604 (continued)

have sunk the SS *Coamo* (am 7057t) NNE of the Azores. This vessel was reported missing after the 9th, by which time it was expected to be in the Bermuda area.

The *Draufgänger* group was ordered northwards for the 6th, to operate against expected westbound convoy ONS 150. However, on the 7th the boats were ordered to close northeast-bound HX 217, which had been sighted by U 524 of *Panzer* group on the 6th. Some *Panzer* boats came up but strong air cover arrived from the 10th as the convoy came within range of Iceland. The operation against HX 217 was abandoned on the 11th, with two ships sunk and two boats lost.

U 604 and four ex-*Draufgänger* boats were joined by new-arrivals to form *Ungestüm* group S of Iceland from the 13th, to operate against convoys leaving the North Channel. On the 13th eastbound HX 218 was sighted E of Newfoundland by U 373, which was then driven down by aircraft, losing contact. The *Ungestüm* boats moved westwards at high speed and on the 16th a patrol line was formed SE of Cape Farewell in the expected path of the convoy. However, HX 218 passed unobserved through the line of waiting boats.

Searching for HX 218, U 373 sighted westbound ONS 152 on the 16th to the southeast of the *Ungestüm* line and the boats moved to intercept. Brief contact was made but very bad weather and poor visibility hampered the pursuit. A search for stragglers resulted in only one sinking and the operation ended on the 22nd.

U 604 returned to Brest **31.12.42**

4. 8.2.43 Left for the North Atlantic.

On the 19th the outward-bound U 604, U 91, U 92 and U 600 were ordered to form a patrol line, *Knappen*, in the expected path of an ON convoy. In the late morning of the 20th U 604 sighted westbound ON 166. She was located during the night by the USCG cutter *Spencer* and driven down by depth-charges. The pursuit of the convoy continued for five days, ending ESE of Newfoundland in bad visibility on the 25th. U 604 torpedoed and sank the rescue ship SS *Stockport* (br 1683t) early on the 23rd ESE of St John's. The *Stockport* had dropped behind the convoy, searching for survivors from the *Empire Trader*, sunk by U 92. She was on the way to rejoin ON 166 when she was sunk by U 604.

The convoy had been pursued for 1100 miles by the time the operation ended. Fourteen ships had been sunk and another damaged. The *Knappen* boats returned eastwards to a refuelling area N of the Azores, where U 604 was supplied by U 462 for return to base.

U 604 returned to Brest **9.3.43**

5. 22.4.43 Left Brest and returned **26.4.43**

6. 24.6.43 Left for the Central Atlantic.

Between July 6th and 12th U 604 was refuelled by U 487 600 miles SW of the Azores. She went on to patrol off the Brazilian coast but had no success.

U 604 was sighted on the 30th by a USN Ventura of VB-129 (Lt-Cdr T D Davies) some 100 miles off Maceió, as the aircraft swept ahead of convoy TJ 2. The boat turned beam on and began firing as Davies straddled her with four MK 47 bombs. U 604 submerged and the stern rose out of the sea and then went down. Davies flew off, believing U 604 to be destroyed.

The boat's commander, KL Höltring, brought U 604 back to the surface but convinced that he could not recross the Atlantic, he radioed for assistance and a rendezvous 500 miles E of Permambuco was arranged for August 8th with U 185. On the 3rd U 604 was attacked and damaged by a USN Liberator of VP-107. Air activity was such that a new rendezvous was arranged with U 185 400 miles to the northeast. U 172 was ordered to meet U 604 and U 185 at this new position.

The three boats met on the 11th. Whilst fuel and stores were

being transferred from U 604 to the other two boats, a Liberator of VP-107 (Lt-Cdr B J Prueher) appeared. U 172 dived but the other two remained surfaced and opened fire on the aircraft, which made two unsuccessful bombing attacks. On the third run, the Liberator was shot down by U 185 and the crew was lost.

U 185 embarked the survivors of U 604's crew, of whom 16 had been killed and some wounded, and the boat was scuttled as the destroyer USS *Moffett* approached. U 185 moved away from the scene. During the night of the 14/15th U 172 met U 185 and took aboard 23 of U 604's crew.

On the 24th U 185 was sunk by USN aircraft and among the 36 survivors were some men from U 604. As U 185 was flooding, chlorine gas was released from the battery compartment. U 604's commander, KL Höltring, went to the forward torpedo room where two badly-wounded members of his crew lay, unable to move. They pleaded to be shot and Höltring obliged, afterwards turning the gun on himself.

U 605 Type VII C

Built by Blohm & Voss, Hamburg
Keel laid 12.3.41   Launched 27.11.41
Commissioned 15.1.42   Feldpost Nr M 28 117

Sunk 14.11.42 NW of Cap Ferrat (36°20′N 01°01′W)

Served with
5 U-Flottille, Kiel   January - July 1942 (ab)
9 U-Flottille, Brest   August - October 1942 (fb)
29 U-Flottille, La Spezia   October 1942 - 14.11.42 (fb)

Commanded by
KL Herbert-Viktor Schütze   January 1942 - 14.11.42

Patrols: 3   Ships sunk: 3 (8409 grt)

1. 28.7.42 Left Kiel and arrived Bergen **31.7.42**

2. 2.8.42 Left Bergen for the North Atlantic.

Outward-bound, U 605 probably sank the fishing trawler *Bombay* (br 229t) on the 3rd S of Vik, Iceland. She was reported missing after the 5th and U 605 was in the area at the time.

On the 5th U 593 sighted southbound convoy SC 94 900 miles S of Cape Farewell. U 605 was one of seven outward-bound boats, then 200 to 300 miles away, which were directed to the convoy. U 605 was in contact from mid-day on the 8th but her attempt to attack a straggler was unsuccessful. Eleven ships were sunk in the operation, which ended on the 11th WNW of Ireland.

The boats arriving from the SC 94 operation, including U 605, joined with new-arrivals to form *Lohs* group 600 miles W of the North Channel, to intercept an ON convoy expected on the 13th. During the night of the 12/13th, en route to their new positions, a convoy was sighted, heading north. Only three boats were able to close, U 256, U 438 and U 705. One ship was sunk, by U 705, before contact was lost on the 15th.

The *Lohs* patrol line was formed on the 17th W of the British Isles. It moved slowly southwards for two days and then after two days waiting moved northwards in search of convoys. Westbound ONS 122 passed the southern end of the patrol line, sighted by U 135. She shadowed but contact was lost in bad visibility and not regained until the 24th.

Early on the 25th U 605 was one of nine boats which had made contact and she torpedoed and sank two ships in the central North Atlantic, the SS *Katvaldis* (br 3163t) and the SS *Sheaf Mount* (br 5017t). Soon afterwards the boat was located and attacked by the Norwegian corvette *Eglantine* and damaged with depth-charges.

U 605 put in to her new base at Brest **4.9.42**

3. 1.10.42 Left for the Mediterranean.

U 605, U 458, U 593 and U 660 set out, as *Tümmler* group, and all probably passed through the Straits of Gibraltar during the night of the 10/11th.

U 605 put in to her new base at La Spezia **14.10.42**

4. 21.10.42 Left for the Western Mediterranean.

From early November U 605 joined other boats stationed west of a line from the Balearic Islands to Algiers. The Germans were worried by the large number of ships known to be at Gibraltar. On the 8th the Allied landings in North Africa began and the boats operated against invasion shipping.

U 605 reported an escort vessel torpedoed and sunk on the 9th near Algiers but this is unidentified and unconfirmed.

The boat was sunk on the 14th NW of Cap Ferrat in a depth-charge attack by a Hudson of 233 Squadron (P/O J W Barling).

There were no survivors, 46 dead.

U 606   Type VII C

Built by Blohm & Voss, Hamburg
Keel laid 12.3.41   Launched 27.11.41
Commissioned 22.1.42   Feldpost Nr M 28 390

Sunk 22.2.43 NNW of the Azores (47°44′N 33°43′W)

Served with
5 U-Flottille, Kiel   January - August 1942 (ab)
11 U-Flottille, Bergen   September - October 1942 (fb)
9 U-Flottille, Brest   November 1942 - 22.2.43 (fb)

Commanded by
OL Hans Klatt   January 1942 - 14.9.42
KL Dietrich von der Esch   14.9.42 - 27.9.42
OL Hans Döhler   27.9.42 - 22.2.43

Patrols: 3   Ships sunk: 4 (37,493 grt) + 1 damaged

1. 18.8.42 Left Kiel and arrived Bergen **22.8.42**

2. 14.9.42 Left Bergen for operations in Northern Waters. No details known of this patrol except that U 606 probably shot down a Catalina of 330 (Norwegian) Squadron on the 21st.

U 606 returned to Bergen **26.9.42**

3. 17.10.42 Left for the North Atlantic.

Outward-bound, U 606 joined boats of *Puma* group in attacking eastbound convoy HX 212 in the central North Atlantic. In the early morning of the 28th U 606 torpedoed and set fire to the whaling factory ship SS *Kosmos II* (nw 16966t), the abandoned wreck of which was sunk early on the 29th by U 624.

Later in the morning of the 28th U 606 sank the tanker SS *Gurney E Newlin* (am 8225t), torpedoed and damaged late the previous evening by U 436. During daylight on the 28th U 606 and the other boats in contact were kept down by Iceland-based Liberators of 120 Squadron. The same happened on the 29th and the operation ended, with six ships sunk and another damaged.

From 1.11.42 U 606 and five other boats from HX 212 formed *Natter* group W of Ireland. At this time they were the only boats operating in the eastern North Atlantic. On the 2nd the line moved south and on the 3rd was augmented by six new-arrivals.

The boats moved southwards to form a line for the 5th but on the 4th U 92 sighted westbound ON 143 but with none of the other *Natter* boats in position to give support, she lost contact. A search was made when the other boats came up but when the convoy had not been found again by the 6th, the operation was called off. The only successes against ON 143 were two stragglers sunk by U 566

and U 613 during the afternoon of the 7th, after U-tanker U 117, en route to a replenishment area, sighted ON 143 further to the west and reported, enabling four boats to close.

On the 8th all *Natter* boats with sufficient fuel were ordered to proceed at high speed towards Gibraltar because of the Allied landings in North Africa. This did not include U 606. She and U 624 were refuelled by U 117 N of the Azores, after which they joined *Kreuzotter* group 600 miles W of Ireland.

On the 13th the group moved northwards and two days later westbound ONS 144 passed through the centre of the patrol line. In an operation, which ended E of Newfoundland on the 20th, five ships and a corvette of the escort were sunk. U 606 had no success.

Very low on fuel, six of the *Kreuzotter* boats, including U 606, moved southeastwards on the 21st to an area NW of the Azores, where they were refuelled by U 460 on or about the 27th.

U 606 put in to her new base at Brest **5.12.42**

4. 4.1.43 Left for the North Atlantic.

U 606 joined *Falke* group W of Ireland, where it had been awaiting an ON convoy. From the 7th the group swept westwards, searching for convoys. This move continued until the 15th, with nothing seen. The group turned north next day but found nothing.

On the 19th *Falke* and *Habicht* groups were formed into two new patrol lines, *Haudegen* and *Landsknecht*, the latter for boats with less fuel. U 606 was in *Haudegen*, which ran 300 miles southeastwards from Cape Farewell.

A returning boat sighted a British hunting group on the 22nd and this was thought to be possibly the remote screen for an expected HX convoy. *Haudegen* group was ordered southeast at high speed to intercept. Bad weather prevented the boats reaching the planned position and when a search further east found nothing the group returned to a position S of Cape Farewell. The boats began a move southwestwards towards Newfoundland on 1.2.43.

Some *Haudegen* boats were detached to attack convoys SC 118 and SG 19 but U 606 stayed with the main group, which on the 6th was reformed into two lines in an arc E of Newfoundland. With fuel running low, the *Haudegen* boats were ordered to a refuelling area on the 15th. Two days later U 69 sighted westbound ONS 165. The order was given for the boats to attack the convoy, with refuelling to be carried out later. A storm prevented any organised attack and when the operation ended on the 20th two ships had been sunk and two boats lost.

U 606 and other *Haudegen* boats moved eastwards, to be refuelled by U 460 from the 21st. When westbound ON 166 was reported to be passing south of the refuelling area, some of the refuelled boats, including U 606, pursued it. In the late evening of the 22nd U 606 torpedoed three ships from the convoy in the central North Atlantic, sinking the SS *Chattanooga City* (am 5687t) and damaging the SS *Expositor* (am 4959t) and the SS *Empire Redshank* (br 6615t). The *Empire Redshank* was sunk by the corvette HMCS *Trillium*, which also tried to sink the *Expositor*. After the corvette failed, U 303 dispatched the *Expositor* with a torpedo early on the 23rd.

Immediately after torpedoing the three ships, U 606 was sighted by the corvette HMCS *Chilliwack*, which made depth-charge attacks. The boat dived but was located by the Polish destroyer *Burza*, which closed and made two depth-charge attacks. The boat went down to 130 fathoms and her pressure hull ruptured. All tanks were blown and U 606 surfaced.

Badly damaged, she was sighted by the USCG cutter *Campbell* (Cdr R P Heineman). The cutter attempted to ram and her hull was holed by U 606's hydroplanes as she took evasive action. *Campbell's* gunfire killed U 606's commander and the senior officer aboard decided to abandon ship.

Of U 606's crew of 48, only 12 were picked up by boats from *Burza* and *Campbell*. The damaged cutter was towed in by *Burza*.

U 607   Type VII C

Built by Blohm & Voss, Hamburg
Keel laid 27.3.41   Launched 11.12.41
Commissioned 29.1.42   Feldpost Nr M 28 509

Sunk 13.7.43 NNW of Cape Ortegal (45°02´N 09°14´W)

Served with
5 U-Flottille, Kiel   January - July 1942 (ab)
7 U-Flottille, St Nazaire   August 1942 - 13.7.43 (fb)

Commanded by
KL Ernst Mengersen   January 1942 - March 1943
OL Wolf Jeschonnek   March 1943 - 13.7.43

Patrols: 5   Ships sunk: 5 (35,879 grt)

1. 9.7.42 Left Kiel and arrived Kristiansand **10.7.42**

2. 13.7.42 Left Kristiansand for the North Atlantic.
U 607 joined *Wolf* group in its attack on westbound ON 113. The convoy had been sighted on the 23rd at the northern end of the *Wolf* patrol line, SE of Cape Farewell. In the ensuing action, with bad visibility and a strong escort, the convoy lost only two ships and U 90 was sunk. U 607 torpedoed and sank the MV *Empire Rainbow* (br 6942t) from the convoy E of St John's early on the 26th. It is possible that U 704 also scored a hit on this vessel some ten minutes later, which may have contributed to its sinking.

Contact with ON 113 was lost on the 26th and after a fruitless search on the 27th, the operation was terminated. The *Wolf* boats moved south to a refuelling area W of the Azores, where eight boats of the group were supplied on the 29th and 30th by U 461. The group did not reform but seven of the refuelled boats, including U 607, moved north to close convoy ON 115, reported by U 210 on the 29th. A patrol line, *Pirat*, was formed ahead of the convoy on 1.8.42 and the ex-*Wolf* boats joined this line.

The convoy was sighted by U 552 on the 2nd E of Cape Race. Early on the 4th U 607 sank the SS *Belgian Soldier* (be 7167t), torpedoed and damaged by U 552 the previous night. By this time the convoy was entering the fogs of the Newfoundland Bank and the operation ended.

U 607 and other ex-*Wolf* boats were to form *Steinbrinck* group E of the Newfoundland Bank for the 7th. On the 5th U 593 sighted eastbound SC 94 and called up other outward-bound boats, some 200 to 300 miles astern and others away to the northeast. U 607 and other *Steinbrinck* boats that were already in position also joined in the pursuit of the convoy. U 607 made unsuccessful attacks on some stragglers on the 7th and on the escort during the night of the 8/9th, after which she shadowed the convoy. The operation was abandoned on the 11th S of Iceland.

U 607 put in to her new base at St Nazaire **11.8.42**

3. 8.9.42 Left for the North Atlantic.
Outward-bound, U 607 was directed to join boats of *Pfeil* and *Lohs* groups in their attack on eastbound convoy SC 100, sighted by U 221 on the 20th S of Greenland. The prevailing westerly gale increased to hurricane force and the pursuit was broken off and then resumed again, finally ending on the 25th. The convoy had a strong air escort and only five ships were sunk, none by U 607.

With other boats, U 607 had been ordered southwestwards on the 23rd to operate against eastbound RB 1 but she had no success against the convoy, from which three ships and a destroyer were sunk before the operation ended on the 26th.

After the RB 1 operation ended, some of the boats from SC 100 and RB 1, including U 607, were ordered to close westbound ON 131, sighted by U 617 on the 26th. The directed boats were widely scattered but were ordered to the convoy as *Tiger* group.

Contact was lost by the shadower and the boats were unable to mount an efficient search in the worsening weather. The operation was abandoned on the 29th.

U 607 and three other boats then went south to a position NW of the Azores, where they were refuelled by U 118 on or about October 4th. The boats then joined a new patrol line, *Wotan*, formed from the 8th E of Newfoundland to await an SC convoy. In the early hours of the 12th the group was ordered northeastwards at high speed to intercept eastbound SC 104, which had passed the northern end of the *Wotan* line the previous afternoon. The convoy was sighted during the night of the 12/13th and in attacks in the early hours of the 13th and 14th eight ships were sunk. U 607 torpedoed and sank the SS *Nellie* (gr 4826t) soon after midnight on the 13th S of Cape Farewell. She then came under depth-charge attack by the destroyer HMS *Viscount* and was damaged.

During the night of the 14/15th U 607 was driven down and then damaged further by depth-charges from the Norwegian corvette *Acanthus*, after which she set out for base.

U 607 reached St Nazaire **23.10.42**

4. 2.1.43 Left for Atlantic operations.
U 607 joined *Falke* group, which was drawn up in a north-south patrol line 500 miles W of Ireland. When no convoys had been found by the 19th, the boats of *Falke* and *Habicht* groups with sufficient fuel formed a new group, *Haudegen*, in a patrol line running 300 miles southeastwards from Cape Farewell. U 607 was in this line.

On the 22nd a returning boat sighted a British hunting group and this was thought to be possibly the remote screen for an expected HX convoy. *Haudegen* group was ordered southeast at high speed to intercept. Bad weather prevented the boats reaching the planned position and when a search further east found nothing, the group returned to a position S of Cape Farewell. En route on the 26th, U 607 fired two torpedoes in an attempt to sink the bow section of the tanker MV *Kollbjörg*. This vessel broke in two during a storm. The stern section sank but the bow section was finally dispatched by another torpedo from U 594 eleven hours after U 607's attempt.

The *Haudegen* boats moved southwestwards towards Newfoundland on February 1st. Some boats were detached to attack convoys SC 118 and SG 19 but U 607 remained with the main group. On the 6th these boats reformed into two lines, formed in an arc E of Newfoundland.

With fuel running low, the *Haudegen* boats were ordered to a refuelling area on the 15th. On this day U 607 torpedoed and sank an independent, the tanker MV *Atlantic Sun* (am 11355t). On the 17th U 69 sighted westbound ONS 165. The order was given to attack the convoy, with refuelling to be carried out later. A storm prevented any organised attack and when the operation ended on the 20th, two ships had been sunk and two boats lost.

U 607 and other *Haudegen* boats moved eastwards, to be refuelled by U 460 from the 21st. When westbound convoy ON 166 was reported, passing south of the refuelling area, some of the refuelled *Haudegen* boats pursued it. However, U 607 and U 226 went after ONS 167, which passed north of the refuelling area. They made no contact and resumed their homeward journey.

U 607 returned to St Nazaire **9.3.43**

5. 24.4.43 Left for Atlantic operations.
U 607 was one of eleven outward-bound boats which in late April formed a patrol line, *Drossel*, NW of Cape Finisterre.

On 3.5.43 aircraft sighted a southbound convoy and the group moved eastwards to attack. It proved to be fifteen LCTs and two escorts. Sea conditions made torpedo attacks on these flat-bottomed craft impractical and the operation was abandoned.

Drossel group moved southwards to search for two northbound convoys, expected on the 5th. SL 128 was found by aircraft on the 6th but a wrong position-report prevented the boats from making contact early on the 7th. U 607 made an unsuccessful attack in the morning of the 7th W of Lisbon, hearing only an end-of-run detonation. The operation ended on the 8th after the convoy was given a strong air escort.

The group moved westwards at high speed to intercept eastbound HX 237. It was sighted by a *Rhein* group boat on the 9th but lost again in poor visibility. The convoy was intercepted by the *Drossel* boats on the 11th N of the Azores. A strong surface escort and carrier-borne aircraft kept the boats at a distance. The operation against HX 237 ended on the 13th SW of Ireland, with three ships sunk and three boats lost.

In the afternoon of the 15th U 607 torpedoed and sank an independent NNE of the Azores, the SS *Irish Oak* (br 5589t). She was possibly refuelled by another boat before joining *Oder* group, formed in the central North Atlantic from the 18th to operate against eastbound HX 238. However, after the convoy passed well to the north, the *Oder* boats became part of a new patrol line, *Mosel*, formed from the 21st 400 miles S of Cape Farewell to intercept HX 239, reported moving eastwards from Newfoundland.

The convoy was sighted on the 22nd by U 305 but she was unable to maintain contact because of aircraft attacks. All attempts to locate the convoy during daylight hours were frustrated by aircraft and several boats were badly damaged. U 569 and U 752 were sunk. With HX 239 still not found, the operation was terminated on the 23rd.

U 607 returned to St Nazaire **2.6.43**

6. 10.7.43 Left for the Central Atlantic.

U 607, U 445 and U 613 were outward-bound in company when they were attacked in the Bay of Biscay on the 13th by a Halifax of 58 Squadron (F/O A R D Clutterbuck) and a Sunderland of 228 Squadron (F/O R D Hanbury).

U 445 and U 613 dived but U 607 was sunk in a depth-charge attack by the Sunderland. The aircraft dropped a liferaft and seven survivors, including U 607's commander, were saved. They were picked up by the sloop HMS *Wren*.

Of U 607's crew, 46 men lost their lives.

U 608   Type VII C

Built by Blohm & Voss, Hamburg
Keel laid 27.3.41   Launched 11.12.41
Commissioned 5.2.42   Feldpost Nr M 30 340

Sunk 10.8.44 SSW of St Nazaire (46°30´N 03°28´W)

Served with
5 U-Flottille, Kiel   February - August 1942 (ab)
6 U-Flottille, St Nazaire   September 1942 - 10.8.44 (fb)

Commanded by
KL Erwin Struckmeier   February 1942 - January 1944
OL Wolfgang Reisener   January 1944 - 10.8.44

Patrols: 8   Ships sunk: 4 (35,539 grt) + 2 damaged
1 LCT (143 dt)

On 16.7.42, training in the Baltic, U 608 encountered and was almost rammed by a Russian submarine.

1. 20.8.42 Left Kiel for the North Atlantic.

U 608 was one of six boats which formed *Stier* group from the 31st W of Ireland. The group was involved in a failed operation against an ONS convoy on September 1st and 2nd. On the 4th *Stier* combined with *Vörwarts* group to form a long patrol line W of Ireland, to await a westbound convoy.

In the evening of the 9th U 584 sighted ON 127 in the central North Atlantic as it passed through the southern end of the patrol line. Contact was lost during the night but regained on the 10th.

Early on the 11th U 608 may have hit the tanker MV *Marit II*. This vessel had also been struck a few minutes earlier by U 404 and although damaged, she rejoined the convoy on the 12th and reached New York on the 16th.

In the early hours of the 12th U 608 torpedoed three ships from the convoy, sinking the whaling factory ship SS *Hektoria* (br 13795t) and the SS *Empire Moonbeam* (br 6849t), both previously torpedoed by U 211, and possibly sinking the MV *Hindanger* (nw 4884t), which, after being torpedoed by U 584, may have been finished off by the corvette HMCS *Amherst* but this is not absolutely certain.

The operation against the convoy ended on the 14th because of bad visibility and the arrival of Newfoundland-based aircraft from the 13th. Seven ships were sunk and it was one of the few times in the war that all participating boats fired at least one torpedo each.

U 608 put in to her new base at St Nazaire **24.9.42**

2. 20.10.42 Left for the Western Atlantic.

During the night of November 10/11th U 608 laid 10 TMA mines off New York. There are no recorded sinkings or damage to ships attributed to these mines.

Soon after midnight on the 15th U 608 torpedoed and sank a ship near New York, the SS *Irish Pine* (br 5621t). After leaving US waters, U 608 patrolled in the Nova Scotia and Newfoundland areas but had no further success. The returning boat was refuelled by U 460 in late November NW of the Azores for return to base.

She reached St Nazaire **9.12.42**

3. 20.1.43 Left for the North Atlantic.

Outward-bound, U 608 was directed to join boats of *Pfeil* group in their attack on eastbound SC 118. The convoy had been sighted on February 4th in the centre of the *Pfeil* patrol line, E of Newfoundland. During the night of the 4/5th U 608 was driven off twice by the escort. The boats persisted in their attacks. In the early hours of the 8th U 608 sank the abandoned wreck of the tanker MV *Daghild* (br 9272t). This vessel had been torpedoed on the 7th by U 402. She also had aboard LCT 2335, which was lost. The crew was picked up by a corvette, which then failed to sink the ship, leaving it for U 608.

After the SC 118 operation ended, U 608 was refuelled by U 460 in the central North Atlantic. She then joined *Neptun* group E of Cape Farewell, to operate against expected eastbound HX 226. The convoy was not located, having been re-routed to pass to the north of the *Neptun* line. On the 20th the group moved southwestwards. It was avoided by the re-routed SC 120 but U 759, at the northern end of the line, sighted HX 227 in the morning of the 27th and the *Neptun* boats pursued. U 405 sank one ship and possibly damaged another but bad weather prevented any attacks by other boats.

Whilst searching for the convoy on March 1st, U 608 sighted approaching, westbound convoy ON 168. Contact was lost when the shadower was driven off and the operation ended on the 3rd when the convoy had not been found again.

Some days later U 608 was refuelled by U 119 N of the Azores and then joined *Neuland* group, as it moved westwards in search of HX 228, which passed the southern end of the line on the 10th. Attacks on the convoy began that evening and during the three-day operation four ships and a destroyer were sunk, none by U 608.

Neuland boats with sufficient fuel, including U 608, formed *Dränger* group from the 15th in the central North Atlantic, to operate against eastbound HX 229. The group took part in the biggest convoy action of the war, against both HX 229 and SC 122 from the 16th to the 19th, during which time twenty-one ships were sunk. In the early morning of the 19th U 608 made an unsuccessful attack on the destroyer HMS *Highlander*, hearing two hits but no detonations, followed by an explosion and sinking noises. During the operation U 608 was twice attacked with depth-charges by aircraft. On the 17th she was shaken by a Liberator of 86 Squadron and on the 19th she escaped undamaged from a Sunderland of

U 608 (continued)

228 Squadron.

U 608 put in to Bordeaux **29.3.43**

4. 8.5.43 Left for operations.

With the failure of convoy operations in the North Atlantic it was decided by BdU on the 24th to make an effort to intercept convoys between the USA and the Mediterranean. Accordingly, boats with sufficient fuel, including U 608, were ordered to an area W of the Azores, to await expected convoys UGS 9 and GUS 7A.

A patrol line, *Trutz*, was formed during the night of the 30/31st on the 43° meridian WSW of the Azores, made up of sixteen boats. On 4.6.43 the three most southerly boats were attacked by carrier-borne aircraft, which were thought to be part of a convoy's protective cover. The boats closed up to prevent any ships passing through gaps in the line, but when nothing had been sighted by the evening of the 5th the convoy was thought to have passed either to the north or the south.

The group broke up and then moved 600 miles to the north, to be refuelled by U 488. The UGS convoy was sighted by an outward-bound boat on the 8th 100 miles south of the *Trutz* patrol area of the 5th. The move to refuel had been too premature.

On the 16th *Trutz* group reformed in three parallel north-south lines, *Trutz 1,2* and *3*, 1000 miles E of Bermuda. U 608 was in *Trutz 1*. The boats waited for two convoys until the 22nd and having seen nothing in that time, the line began an eastward movement which continued until the 27th, when they halted some 200 miles SW of the Azores. By the 29th it was realised that the elusive convoys had by-passed the lines.

The boats reformed into three new lines, *Geier 1,2* and *3* and from 2.7.43 they moved eastwards towards the coast of Portugal, spaced at one-day intervals. U 608 was in *Geier 1*. At 500 miles from the coast air attacks began and by the 8th were such that boat commanders were allowed to return to base if they wished.

U 608 returned to St Nazaire **18.7.43**

5. 23.9.43 Left St Nazaire and returned **25.9.43**

6. 2.10.43 Left for the North Atlantic.

U 608 joined *Schlieffen* group SW of Iceland. On the 15th a westbound convoy, presumed to be ONS 20 but in fact ON 206, was sighted by the outward-bound U 844. She was ordered to maintain contact and home *Schlieffen* group on to it. U 844 was located by the escort and driven off. She was sunk next day.

It then became difficult to find the convoy because Iceland-based aircraft were keeping the widely-scattered *Schlieffen* boats submerged. Early on the 16th U 964 reported ONS 20. Dönitz decided, against the advice of some of his senior officers, that the boats should remain on the surface and, if necessary, fight their way to the convoy.

Very soon reports were being made of actions being fought. U 964 was sunk and several other boats were severely damaged but the order was not rescinded. Late on the 16th ONS 20 was briefly sighted, then lost again. *Schlieffen* group moved further east and ONS 20 was sighted early on the 17th by U 309. An attack was ordered but again contact was lost and this time it was not regained. The convoy lost only one ship, a straggler sunk late on the 15th by U 426. As the *Schlieffen* boats continued their search during the day, many came under air attack. In the early evening U 608 was overrun by ONS 20 and depth-charged by one of the escort. The operation was finally called off on the 18th.

U 608 joined *Siegfried* group, formed from the 24th 500 miles E of Newfoundland to await HX 262 and SC 145 in submerged positions during daylight. On the 25th it was believed that HX 262 was passing south of the patrol line and although the group moved south, no contact was made. U 608 was attacked by aircraft around this time.

To cover a wider area, *Siegfried* was split into three small sub-groups, *Siegfried 1,2* and *3*. U 608 was in *Siegfried 1*. The groups continued south, searching for SC 145, but it passed by unobserved on the 29th. On this day U 608 and U 405, near SC 145, were attacked by Swordfish from the escort-carrier HMS *Fencer*, which they drove off. Two days later the boats again reformed, this time into groups *Jahn* and *Körner*. U 608 was in *Körner*.

On 3.11.43 the boats were redeployed in five small sub-groups, *Tirpitz 1,2,3,4* and *5*, to search for convoy HX 264. It passed the groups late on the 6th and next day the operation was abandoned, it being impossible to surface in daylight because of carrier-borne aircraft.

U 608 was briefly with *Eisenhart* group from the 12th before setting out for base. En route, she was ordered to join *Schill 2* group W of Spain, in the path of combined convoy MKS 30/SL 139 for interception on the 19th. When the boats surfaced during the evening of the 19th, they were near the convoy but the surface escorts and aircraft kept the boats away, forcing them to submerge for long periods at a time.

In the knowledge that daylight would bring even greater air activity, it was decided that the *Schill 2* boats should dive at dawn and take no further part in the operation.

U 608 returned to St Nazaire **28.11.43**

7. 29.1.44 Left for Atlantic operations.

U 608 joined *Igel 2* group, which from 4.2.44 was patrolling SW of Ireland. On the 6th the boats were deployed against combined convoy MKS 38/SL 147, reported N of the Azores by German aircraft on the 6th, 7th and 8th. Some of the boats came up to the convoy on the 7th but had no success against the strong escort.

On the 10th *Igel 1* and *2* groups began a slow westward withdrawal, which was taken further than intended because of intense Allied anti-submarine activity, both SW of Ireland and NW of Scotland. It was intended to intercept an ONS convoy between the 14th and the 18th, with the aid of aerial reconnaissance.

ONS 29, ON 224 and OS 68 were sighted by aircraft on the 14th W of the North Channel and *Igel 1* and *2* groups were hurried to an assembly area 600 miles SW of Ireland. On the 18th two parallel patrol lines, *Hai 1* and *2*, were formed ahead of the convoys, which were found to have turned south on the 17th and passed the southern end of the *Hai* lines. The boats were immediately ordered south, submerged in daylight and at high speed on the surface in the hours of darkness. Instead of sighting any convoys at dawn on the 19th, the boats saw only some destroyers. The operation was called off and the boats submerged to avoid aircraft from the escort-carrier HMS *Striker*.

U 608 moved westwards with the other boats and *Preussen* group was formed 400 to 500 miles N of the Azores. Between the 27th and 29th the group was concentrated between 22° and 30°W, in the expected path of convoy ON 225 but on March 2nd it was learned that the convoy had altered course, avoiding *Preussen*.

The boats moved northwards on the 6th to search for convoys and they operated singly W of the British Isles. *Preussen* group was dissolved on the 22nd and boats then operated independently.

U 608 returned to St Nazaire **3.4.44**

8. 6.6.44 U 608 was one of nineteen non-schnorkel boats which sailed into the Bay of Biscay as part of *Landwirt* group.

They were to form a line at the 200 metres depth line between Brest and Bordeaux, keeping out of port in case an Allied invasion force arrived and trapped them there. The boats later moved closer in to the 100 metres depth line, where they could lay on the bottom for long periods.

The waiting boats were under constant attack from the air when they surfaced at night. When no invasion had come by the 12th, the boats were recalled to port and placed on six hours notice.

U 608 put in to Lorient **14.6.44**

9. 22.7.44 Left Lorient and returned **23.7.44**

10. 7.8.44 Left Lorient, on transfer to La Pallice.

On the 10th U 608 was attacked and sunk in a depth-charge attack by a Liberator of 53 Squadron (W/Cdr R T F Gates) SSW of St Nazaire. For this action Gates was awarded an immediate DFC.

The aircraft was supported by the sloop HMS *Wren* (Lt-Cdr S R J Woods). She picked up U 608's entire crew of 51 men.

U 609   Type VII C

Built by Blohm & Voss, Hamburg
Keel laid 7.4.41   Launched 23.12.41
Commissioned 12.2.42   Feldpost Nr M 42 154

Sunk 7.2.43 in the central North Atlantic (55°17′N 26°38′W)

Served with
5 U-Flottille, Kiel   February - July 1942 (ab)
6 U-Flottille, St Nazaire   August 1942 - 7.2.43 (fb)

Commanded by
KL Klaus Rudloff   February 1942 - 7.2.43

Patrols: 4   Ships sunk: 2 (10,288 grt)

1. 16.7.42 Left Kiel for the North Atlantic.

Outward-bound, U 609 sighted a UR convoy on the 22nd and, with U 254, she shadowed it to Reykjavik. Thereafter the two boats remained patrolling in the area off Reykjavik.

From early August U 609 patrolled SW of Iceland but she had no success. From the 27th, she was with *Vörwarts* group W of Ireland. The group made a sweep to the southwest and on the 31st U 609, at the northern end of the patrol line, sighted eastbound convoy SC 97. She torpedoed and sank two ships of the convoy, in a surprise, submerged attack SE of Cape Farewell, the MV *Bronxville* (nw 4663t) and the SS *Capira* (pa 5625t). U 609 was then driven off.

As other boats approached from the south, they were driven off by the escort. In the morning of September 1st the first aircraft appeared and from then on continuous air cover kept the boats down. Some unsuccessful attacks were made on the convoy, including one by U 609 in the early morning of the 1st. The aircraft presence forced the abandoning of the operation on the 2nd.

U 609 put in to her new base at St Nazaire **10.9.42**

2. 6.10.42 Left for Atlantic operations.

U 609 joined *Panther* group W of Ireland. On the 16th U 704 sighted westbound ON 137 in the southern section of the patrol line. The twelve southern *Panther* boats and ten from *Wotan* group were ordered to attack the convoy. However, the weather worsened and the shadower lost contact after being damaged and driven off. The boats searched but the convoy was not found. A gale developed on the 17th, the *Wotan* boats went home on the 18th and the operation was called off on the 19th. In bad visiblity on the 16th as U 609 had been shadowing the convoy and trying to make a surface attack, she found herself near the escorting corvette HMS *Celandine*. The boat submerged but was badly damaged by depth-charges. She managed to escape and headed for base.

U 609 reached St Nazaire **22.10.42**

3. 30.11.42 Left for the North Atlantic.

U 609 joined *Draufgänger* group, which on December 7th was some 700 miles W of the North Channel. On this day the group was ordered northwestwards to intercept northeast-bound convoy HX 217. The boats closed with the convoy on the 8th. However, the surface and air escorts kept the boats away and only U 524 and U 553 had any success, sinking stragglers.

On the 10th U 609 was attacked and slightly damaged in a depth-charge attack by a USN Catalina of VP-84 (Lt L L Davis). The operation against HX 217 was called off on the 11th.

Draufgänger and *Panzer* groups joined newly-arrived boats to form two new groups S of Iceland, *Ungestüm* and *Raufbold*, from the 13th. U 609 was in *Raufbold*. The groups were to intercept westbound convoys leaving the North Channel.

On the 15th U 609 sighted westbound ON 153 as it passed through the centre of the patrol line and called up other boats. The seas were heavy and attacks difficult. On the 17th U 609 made an unsuccessful attempt with torpedoes. She continued to maintain contact until the 19th, alternating with U 621. The operation was terminated on the 21st.

U 609 returned to St Nazaire **23.12.42**

4. 16.1.43 Left for the North Atlantic.

U 609 joined *Landsknecht* group W of Ireland. An ON convoy was expected but when it had not appeared by the 28th the group was broken up. From 2.2.43 U 609 and other ex-*Landsknecht* boats formed a reconnaissance patrol group, *Pfeil*, to intercept an expected, eastbound convoy.

On the 4th SC 118 was sighted by U 187 as it passed through the centre of the *Pfeil* line. Some *Haudegen* group boats were also directed to it.

U 609 maintained contact with the convoy from the 4th, after the original shadower, U 187 was sunk by the escort. Over the next three days U 609 was driven off and attacked several times before being finally sunk in a depth-charge attack in the early hours of the 7th by the French corvette *Lobélia* (Lt-Cdr V de Morsier) in the central North Atlantic.

There were no survivors, 46 dead.

U 610   Type VII C

Built by Blohm & Voss, Hamburg
Keel laid 5.4.41   Launched 24.12.41
Commissioned 19.2.42   Feldpost Nr M 42 489

Sunk 8.10.43 WSW of Rockall (55°45′N 24°33′W)

Served with
5 U-Flottille, Kiel   February - September 1942 (ab)
6 U-Flottille, St Nazaire   October 1942 - 8.10.43 (fb)

Commanded by
KL Walter Freiherr von Freyberg-Eisenberg-Allmendingen
                                    February 1942 - 8.10.43

Patrols: 4   Ships sunk: 4 (21,274 grt) + 1 damaged

1. 12.9.42 Left Kiel for Atlantic operations.

U 610 was temporarily stationed in Denmark Strait with U 253 and U 620 from the 20th. U 610 had moved south into the central North Atlantic before torpedoing and sinking the SS *Lifland* (br 2254t), a straggler from convoy SC 101, on the 29th.

On 1.10.42 U 610 and U 620 joined outward-bound boats to form *Luchs* group S of Iceland. Next day the group moved south-westwards, searching for eastbound convoy HX 209, which was sighted on the 3rd by U 260 at the northern end of the line. Bad weather and high winds prevented the boats from gathering for a concerted attack on the 5th and two boats were sunk by aircraft on that day. The pursuit of HX 209 was abandoned on the 6th, in the face of increasing air cover.

From the 8th U 610 joined a new patrol line, *Panther*, W of Ireland. Parts of *Panther* group took part in operations against convoys ONS 136, and ON 137 but U 610 was not involved.

In mid-October the boat was refuelled by U 463 in the central North Atlantic for return to base. On her way back U 610 sank the

79

U 610 (continued)

SS *Steel Navigator* (am 5719t) on the 19th N of the Azores. She was a straggler from convoy ON 137.

U 610 put in to her new base at St Nazaire **31.10.42**

2. 22.11.42 Left for the North Atlantic.

U 610 joined *Draufgänger* group W of Ireland. On the 30th the patrol line began moving north and by December 6th was some 700 miles W of the North Channel. On the 7th the group was ordered northwestwards to intercept northeast-bound convoy HX 217.

The *Draufgänger* boats came up with the convoy on the 8th but only U 524 and U 553 had any success, sinking stragglers on the 8th and 9th. The operation against the convoy was called off on the 11th after strong air cover appeared from Iceland on the 10th.

Draufgänger and *Panzer* groups joined newly-arrived boats to form two new groups S of Iceland, *Ungestüm* and *Raufbold*, from the 13th. U 610 was in *Raufbold*. The groups were to intercept westbound convoys leaving the North Channel.

On the 15th U 609 sighted westbound ON 153 and called up other boats. In the morning of the 16th U 610 torpedoed two tankers, in the central North Atlantic, N of the Azores, sinking the MV *Bello* (nw 6125t) and damaging the MV *Regent Lion* (br 9551t). Despite bad weather from the 17th, contact was maintained until the 21st, when the pursuit ended, with two ships and a destroyer sunk and another ship damaged.

U 610 returned to St Nazaire **26.12.42**

3. 8.3.43 Left for Atlantic operations.

U 610 joined *Stürmer* group, formed on the 14th WNW of Ireland. The group took part in the biggest convoy operation of the war, against eastbound convoys HX 229 and SC 122 from March 16th to the 19th, when 21 ships were sunk and one boat lost. One sinking was claimed by *Stürmer* boats, a straggler shared by U 523 and U 527 on the 19th. On this day U 610 was undamaged after a depth-charge attack by a Liberator of 120 Squadron.

After the operation ended on the 20th, U 610 and some other *Stürmer* boats were joined by new-arrivals and a new patrol line, *Seeteufel*, was formed S of Iceland on the 21st to intercept westbound ONS 1. The convoy was expected to cross the line on the 22nd. Masts and an aircraft carrier were seen on the 26th and were thought to be part of an ON convoy, which was not pursued.

It was decided that the *Seeteufel* boats should concentrate their efforts against eastbound HX 230. Only U 610 and U 415 were able to approach the convoy. A storm that was blowing developed into a hurricane, making an organised search impossible. The pursuit of HX 230 continued but the only success was gained by U 610, when she sank the SS *William Pierce Frye* (am 7176t) in the late evening of the 29th W of Rockall. The continuous bad weather made the use of torpedoes virtually impossible and the operation ended on the 30th and *Seeteufel* broke up.

In early April U 610 was refuelled by U 463 in the central North Atlantic and then joined *Meise* group NE of Newfoundland. On the 20th it was learned that expected convoy HX 234 would pass to the west of the patrol line. The *Meise* boats moved northwestwards at high speed and the convoy was sighted on the 21st by U 306. On her way to close the convoy, U 706 sighted westbound ONS 3. The *Meise* boats divided, some going for each convoy.

A few boats went for ONS 3 but the majority, including U 610, went for HX 234. Two ships were sunk and one damaged and in the morning of the 24th U 610 made an unsuccessful attack on a ship SE of Cape Farewell. USN Catalinas of VP-84 and Liberators of 120 Squadron were very active over the convoy, driving the boats off. The operation was called off on the 25th S of Iceland. In early May U 610 was refuelled by U 461 in the central North Atlantic for return to base.

The boat returned to St Nazaire **12.5.43**

4. 4.9.43 Left St Nazaire and returned **8.9.43**

5. 12.9.43 Left for the North Atlantic.

Outward-bound, U 610 was refuelled by U 460 N of the Azores on or about the 26th. She then joined a new patrol line, *Rossbach*, formed in the central North Atlantic to operate against ON 3. The convoy passed to the north during the night of the 28/29th.

The line was moved 100 miles to the northwest and waited there until the 30th but saw no sign of either ON 203 or the reported ONS 19, which had also passed to the north on the 30th. The group moved northeastwards on 1.10.43 to a position SW of Iceland, to intercept ON 204 but this convoy was also re-routed. When pursuit was realised to be useless, *Rossbach* went southwestwards on the 5th to form a new patrol line to intercept eastbound convoys HX 259 and SC 143.

On the 7th SC 143 was assumed to be in the area, when destroyers were seen. During the early hours of the 8th U 610 made an unsuccessful attack on a destroyer of the convoy's escort. Later in the day the boat was sighted on the surface WSW of Rockall by a Sunderland of 423 (RCAF) Squadron (F/O A H Russell). Three depth-charges were dropped, which sank U 610.

Although some members of her crew were seen in the water, there were no survivors, 51 dead.

U 611   Type VII C

Built by Blohm & Voss, Hamburg
Keel laid 22.4.41   Launched 8.1.42
Commissioned 26.2.42   Feldpost Nr M 42 501

Sunk 8.12.42 ESE of Cape Farewell (57°25´N 35°19´W)

Served with
5 U-Flottille, Kiel February - September 1942 (ab)
3 U-Flottille, La Pallice October 1942 - 8.12.42 (fb)

Commanded by
KL Nikolaus von Jacobs February 1942 - 8.12.42

Patrols: 1   Ships sunk: None

1. 1.10.42 Left Kiel for Northern Waters.
U 611 put in to Skjomenfjord **8.10.42**

2. 4.11.42 Left Harstad for the North Atlantic.

Outward-bound, U 611 was directed to ONS 144, which passed through the centre of the *Kreuzotter* patrol line on the 15th, 600 miles W of Ireland. Over the next five days U 611 operated with the group against the convoy but had no success. However, in spite of foggy conditions, five ships were sunk.

Boats with sufficient fuel, including U 611, joined newly-arrived boats to form *Drachen* group from the 24th NE of the Newfoundland Bank. The other *Kreuzotter* boats had gone off to refuel on the 19th. In early December U 611 was refuelled by U 460 NW of the Azores.

U 611 then joined *Draufgänger* group, which on the 7th was some 700 miles W of the North Channel. On this day the group was ordered northwestwards to intercept northeast-bound HX 217. In the vicinity of the convoy on the 8th, U 611 was attacked and sunk in a depth-charge attack by a Liberator of 120 Squadron (S/Ldr T M Bulloch), ESE of Cape Farewell. The sinking was witnessed by one of the escort, the Norwegian corvette *Potentilla*.

There were no survivors, 45 dead.

U 612   Type VII C

Built by Blohm & Voss, Hamburg
Keel laid 21.4.41   Launched 9.1.42
Commissioned 5.3.42   Feldpost Nr M 42 940

Scuttled 2.5.45 at Warnemünde

Served with
5 U-Flottille, Kiel   March 1942 - 6.8.42 (ab)
24 U-Flottille, Memel   31.5.43 - February 1945 (ab)
31 U-Flottille, Wilhelmshaven   March 1945 - 2.5.45 (ab)

Commanded by
KL Paul Siegmann   March - August 1942
OL Theodor Petersen   May 1943 - February 1944
OL Hans-Peter Dick   February 1944 - 2.5.45

Patrols: None   Ships sunk: None

On 6.8.42, whilst carrying out a training exercise in the Baltic near Warnemünde, U 612 was running submerged when her stern section was rammed by U 444.

Prompt action in resurfacing by U 612's commander, KL Siegmann, enabled all but two of his crew to escape before the boat sank. She was raised and put back into service on 31.5.43, as a training boat. She saw no operational service.

U 612 was scuttled at Warnemünde on 2.5.45 and the wreck was broken up in 1946.

U 613   Type VII C

Built by Blohm & Voss, Hamburg
Keel laid 6.5.41   Launched 29.1.42
Commissioned 12.3.42   Feldpost Nr M 44 892

Sunk 23.7.43 S of Horta, Azores (35°32′N 28°36′W)

Served with
8 U-Flottille, Danzig   March - October 1942 (ab)
3 U-Flottille, La Pallice   November 1942 - 23.7.43 (fb)

Commanded by
KL Helmut Köppe   March 1942 - 23.7.43

Patrols: 4   Ships sunk: 2 (8,087 grt)

1. 22.10.42 Left Kiel for the North Atlantic.

U 613 and other outward-bound boats joined *Natter* group, formed on 1.11.42 W of Ireland. The boats moved southwards to form a line for the 5th. U 92 sighted westbound ON 143 on the 4th but with no other *Natter* boats in position to give support, she lost contact. When other boats came up, a search was made but when the convoy had not been found by the 6th, the operation was called off.

U 613 sank a straggler from the convoy in the central North Atlantic in the afternoon of the 7th, the SS *Roxby* (br 4252t). U 613 was one of four boats that were able to close the convoy on the 7th after the returning U 117 sighted ON 143 further to the west and reported it. One other straggler was also sunk, by U 566.

On the 8th all *Natter* boats with sufficient fuel were ordered to proceed at high speed towards Gibraltar because of the Allied landings in North Africa. U 613 arrived in the operational area W of Gibraltar on or around the 15th.

She was attacked and damaged by a Hudson of 608 Squadron (F/O J B R Petrie) on the 18th and set out for home.

U 613 put in to her new base at La Pallice **27.11.42**

2. 9.1.43 Left for the North Atlantic.

U 613 joined *Habicht* group, formed on the 12th W of Ireland and south of the larger *Falke* group. On the 17th *Habicht* moved westwards in search of ON convoys. By the 19th nothing had been found and the *Habicht* and *Falke* boats combined to form a new patrol line, *Haudegen*, running for 300 miles SE of Cape Farewell.

On the 22nd the group was ordered to go southeastwards to intercept an eastbound HX convoy. Bad weather prevented the interception and the boats returned to a position S of Cape Farewell. On the way back, on the 26th, U 383 sighted escorts of HX 223, which had been scattered in the storm. The convoy was not found.

From 1.2.43 *Haudegen* group began a southwesterly movement towards Newfoundland. On the 2nd the five northern boats of the group were detached to attack convoy SG 19, as *Nordsturm* group.

On the 4th U 187 of *Pfeil* group sighted eastbound SC 118 E of Newfoundland and the southern *Haudegen* boats, U 613, U 438, U 624, U 704 and U 752 were ordered to leave the patrol line and attack the convoy, which by then was already under attack by *Pfeil* group. After the SC 118 operation ended on the 9th WNW of Ireland, with no success for the five *Haudegen* boats, they returned to base.

U 613 put in to Brest **18.2.43**

3. 23.3.43 Left for the North Atlantic.

U 613 joined *Adler* group, formed for 7.4.43 S of Cape Farewell to operate against eastbound SC 125. The convoy passed 200 miles south of the *Adler* line on the 7th and was by then impossible to catch. The group was moved southeastwards to intercept HX 232 but en route on the 10th, U 404 sighted westbound ON 176 and some *Adler* boats, including U 613, closed it E of Newfoundland on the 11th. The boats were driven off by a strong surface and air escort, with only a destroyer sunk in the morning of the 11th.

In the late evening U 613 torpedoed and sank the SS *Ingerfire* (nw 3835t) ENE of St John's. This vessel was a straggler from westbound convoy ONS 2. The operation against ON 176 by the *Adler* boats was called off on the 13th, with one ship sunk by U 404 in the early hours of the 12th.

The *Adler* boats were incorporated into *Meise* group. After a line was formed on the 14th NE of Newfoundland, the group remained in the area until the 19th. The boats then moved north to form a new line S of Greenland for the 21st, to intercept eastbound HX 234. On the 21st the convoy was sighted by U 306. Fog and snowstorms made closing difficult. As she made her way to the convoy, U 706 sighted westbound ONS 3. U 613, U 191, U 203, U 415, U 438 and U 706 left *Adler* group and went for the convoy. Three ships were sunk, none by U 613.

In the evening of the 21st fog and snowstorms caused contact with ONS 3 to be lost. When it had not been regained by the 23rd, the search was called off.

U 613 returned to La Pallice **6.5.43**

4. 10.7.43 Left for the Western Atlantic.

U 613, U 445 and U 607 were outward-bound in company when they were attacked in the Bay of Biscay on the 13th by a Halifax of 58 Squadron (F/O A R D Clutterbuck) and a Sunderland of 228 Squadron (F/O R D Hanbury). U 613 and U 445 dived but U 607 was sunk by the Sunderland.

U 613 was to carry out a mining operation off Jacksonville, Florida. On the 23rd the boat was located S of the Azores by the destroyer USS *George E Badger* (Lt-Cdr T H Byrd), escorting convoy UGS 12.

After a number of depth-charge attacks, U 613 broke up and a lot of debris rose to the surface.

There were no survivors, 48 dead.

U 614 Type VII C

Built by Blohm & Voss, Hamburg
Keel laid 6.5.41   Launched 29.1.42
Commissioned 19.3.42   Feldpost Nr M 44 965

Sunk 29.7.43 NNW of Cape Ortegal (46°42′N 11°03′W)

Served with
8 U-Flottille, Danzig March 1942 - January 1943 (ab)
6 U-Flottille, St Nazaire February 1943 - 29.7.43 (fb)

Commanded by
KL Wolfgang Sträter March 1942 - 29.7.43

Patrols: 3   Ships sunk: 1 (5730 grt)

1. 9.1.43 Left Kiel for the North Atlantic.
    U 614 joined *Landsknecht* group W of Ireland. After waiting for a week for an ON convoy that did not materialise, the group dispersed on the 28th.
    En route to join a new group, U 456 sighted eastbound HX 224 on 1.2.43 in the central North Atlantic. She maintained contact in bad weather for three days and brought up four other ex-*Landsknecht* boats, U 614, U 257, U 265 and U 632. Between them, U 456 and U 632 sank three ships from the convoy. The operation was terminated on the 3rd W of the North Channel.
    On the 4th eastbound SC 118 passed through the centre of the *Pfeil* group patrol line. The *Pfeil* boats were ordered to close, as were the five eastern boats of *Haudegen* group. U 614 and U 456 were also directed to the convoy. In the early morning of the 7th U 614 torpedoed and sank the SS *Harmala* (br 5730t) in the central North Atlantic, SE of Cape Farewell. Twenty boats took part in the operation and before it ended on the 9th W of the North Channel, eleven ships were sunk and two boats lost.
    On the 9th U 614 was attacked and damaged in a depth-charge attack by a Fortress of 206 Squadron (S/Ldr R C Patrick) WSW of Rockall, as she attempted to attack the destroyer HMS *Vimy*, then towing the disabled corvette, *Lobélia*. Some time after the 15th the boat was refuelled by U 460 in the central North Atlantic for return to base.
    U 614 put in to St Nazaire **26.2.43**

2. 12.4.43 Left for Atlantic operations.
    U 614 was one of a number of outward-bound boats directed to the eastbound convoy HX 233, sighted by U 262 on the 15th. One ship was sunk before the operation was called off on the 18th.
    U 614 went on to join *Specht* group, formed from the 20th 400 to 600 miles N of the Azores. The boats moved westwards until the 22nd, halting then to wait in vain for SC 127 until the 23rd, when they moved northwestwards to intercept convoys ON 179 and ONS 4. However, both these convoys were re-routed.
    From the 27th *Specht* group was deployed NE of Newfoundland against HX 235 but the convoy was re-routed to the south. On the 29th *Specht* and *Amsel* groups formed a line NE of Newfoundland to intercept eastbound SC 128. Both groups moved south to search but when the convoy had not been found by 1.5.43 the *Specht* boats went north again and a new, long patrol line, *Fink*, was formed on the 3rd from boats of *Specht* and *Star* groups, S of Cape Farewell.
    SC 128 did not appear but in the afternoon of the 4th ONS 5 passed through the centre of the *Fink* line. During the night of the 4/5th attacks were made. The convoy dispersed into a number of small escorted groups. In daylight on the 5th further attacks were made before fog came down.
    In the fog nearly all contact was lost with the convoy and the escorts located and attacked fifteen boats. The convoy was sighted again early on the 6th but by then weather conditions were deteriorating and the operation was terminated. U 614 then joined

Elbe group E of Newfoundland. It moved southeastwards on the 8th to get ahead of convoy SC 129. On the 10th *Rhein* and *Elbe* groups combined to form *Elbe 1* and 2. U 614 was in *Elbe 1*.
    Forming up on the 11th, the boats passed the convoy. Only two ships were sunk, both by U 402, before the operation ended on the 14th. In mid-May U 614 was refuelled by U 119 N of the Azores for return to base.
    The boat reached St Nazaire **24.5.43**

3. 25.7.43 Left for Atlantic operations.
    Outward-bound, U 614 was attacked and sunk in a depth-charge attack by a Wellington of 172 Squadron (W/Cdr R G Musson) on the 29th NNW of Cape Ortegal.
    There were no survivors, 49 dead.

U 615 Type VII C

Built by Blohm & Voss, Hamburg
Keel laid 20.5.41   Launched 8.2.42
Commissioned 26.3.42   Feldpost Nr M 45 089

Scuttled 7.8.43 NNE of La Blanquilla (12°38′N 64°15′W)

Served with
8 U-Flottille, Danzig March - August 1942 (ab)
3 U-Flottille, La Pallice September 1942 - 7.8.43 (fb)

Commanded by
KL Ralph Kapitzky March 1942 - 7.8.43

Patrols: 4   Ships sunk: 4 (27,231 grt)

1. 5.9.42 Left Kiel for Atlantic operations.
    With other outward-bound boats, U 615 was directed to eastbound SC 99, sighted by U 216 on the 13th W of Ireland. She lost contact when driven down by the escort. The convoy was found again on the 14th by U 440 but when she too was driven off and damaged, the operation was abandoned.
    U 615 and the other newly-arrived boats formed themselves into the *Pfeil* group from the 15th, in an area of the central North Atlantic, W of Ireland. On the 15th U 221 sighted westbound ON 129 and the boats prepared for a concentrated attack but the shadower lost contact in the fog. Briefly sighted again on the 16th, the convoy altered course and the operation was called off.
    Pfeil group was reformed and moved northeastwards on the 18th and then northwestwards on the 19th to close eastbound convoy SC 100. It was sighted by U 221 and *Pfeil* group joined *Lohs* group to attack it. As the boats neared the convoy, the weather worsened and the gale blowing increased to hurricane force. Many boats were left behind and the operation against SC 100 ended on the 22nd.
    A new patrol line, *Blitz*, was formed and it moved southwestwards towards an unidentified northeast-bound convoy, later found to be RB 1. En route early on the 23rd, U 258 sighted SC 100 again, which had been delayed by the weather. U 615, U 221, U 258 and U 617 pursued it while the rest of *Blitz* group went after RB 1. Strong air cover caused the four boats to abandon the SC 100 operation on the 25th. The convoy lost a total of four ships on the 23rd and 24th.
    The *Blitz* boats were now widely scattered and before they could reform U 617 sighted ON 131. They searched for the convoy, as *Tiger* group, but failed to find it. The bad weather would have prevented any reformation of the group in time to attack the convoy. On the 29th all boats were ordered to a refuelling area NW of the Azores.
    U 615 was refuelled by U 118 NW of the Azores for further operations. Nine of the *Tiger* boats, including U 615, formed a new patrol line, *Wotan,* from 8.10.42 E of Newfoundland, awaiting an

SC convoy.

On the 11th U 615 sank a straggler from ONS 136 in the central North Atlantic, the SS *El Lago* (pa 4221t), and picked up two of her surviving officers as prisoners. On the 11th an escort vessel was sighted, heading northeast. In the early hours of the 12th *Wotan* group was ordered northeastwards at high speed to intercept eastbound SC 104, which had passed the northern end of the *Wotan* patrol line the previous afternoon.

The convoy was sighted by U 221 during the night of the 12/13th in the central North Atlantic, S of Cape Farewell. U 615 was one of the boats called up but she was driven off in the early morning of the 14th by the Norwegian corvette *Montbretia*. As more and more aircraft arrived to protect the convoy, the operation was called off late on the 15th, with eight ships sunk.

The returning U 615 torpedoed and sank the independent passenger/cargo ship MV *Empire Star* (br 12656t) in the evening of the 23rd N of the Azores.

U 615 put in to her new base at La Pallice **30.10.42**

2. **25.11.42** Left for the North Atlantic.

U 615 joined a new group, *Draufgänger*, formed on the 30th W of Ireland, awaiting an ONS convoy but this did not materialise. On 7.12.42 the group was ordered to close northeast-bound convoy HX 217. Once within range of Iceland, strong air cover appeared from the 10th and the operation was called off, with two ships sunk.

From the 13th U 615 and three other *Draufgänger* boats joined new-arrivals and U 524 to form *Ungestüm* group, to operate against convoys leaving the North Channel. On the 13th eastbound HX 218 was sighted E of Newfoundland by U 373. The *Ungestüm* boats moved westwards at high speed and on the 16th a patrol line was formed SE of Cape Farewell in the expected path of the convoy. However, HX 218 passed unobserved through the line of waiting boats.

Searching for HX 218, U 373 sighted westbound ONS 152 on the 16th to the southeast of the *Ungestüm* line and the boats were moved towards it. Brief contact was made but bad weather and poor visibility hampered the pursuit. A search for stragglers continued, resulting in one ship being sunk by U 591. The operation ended on the 22nd.

From the 24th the widely-scattered *Ungestüm* boats formed a new patrol line in the central North Atlantic. Next day the line moved northeast to meet up with *Spitz* group, moving down towards it from the northwest. Convoy ONS 154 was sighted south of the *Spitz* patrol line. Both groups moved south to intercept and contact was made on the 27th. In spite of poor visibility on that day, four ships were sunk and another damaged.

In the evening of the 29th HMS *Fidelity*, a special service vessel with ONS 154, was unsuccessfully attacked by U 225 and then by U 615, which missed with five torpedoes. *Fidelity* was sunk the following evening by U 435. The operation against ONS 154 continued until early on the 31st. It ended NW of the Azores, with 13 merchant ships sunk and one damaged. U 615 was refuelled by U 117 N of the Azores for return to base.

The boat returned to La Pallice **9.1.43**

3. **18.2.43** Left for Atlantic operations.

U 615 joined *Burggraf* group in the central North Atlantic, W of Ireland. From the 26th the group swept westwards and from 4.3.43 joined up with *Wildfang* group to form a long, angled patrol line E of Newfoundland, to await an SC convoy, expected on the 5th.

The convoy, SC 121, slipped by during the night and *Neptun* group, together with some boats from *Burggraf*, *Neuland* and *Wildfang* groups, went in pursuit. The remainder of *Burggraf* and *Wildfang* groups, including U 615, formed *Raubgraf* group on the 7th E of Newfoundland, to await HX 228.

A search over the next few days found nothing, the convoy having passed to the south of the line. On the 13th ON 170 was briefly sighted but the pursuit, in bad weather and hampered

further by strong air cover, was soon called off. Now NE of Newfoundland, the *Raubgraf* boats were ordered to shadow an SC convoy, reported on the 14th. Contact was made on the 16th and the convoy, thought to be SC 122 but in fact HX 229, was attacked later the same day.

The four-day operation was the biggest convoy action of the war, with twenty-one ships sunk from the two convoys. U 615 had no success in the action. On the 19th she escaped damage in depth-charge attacks by the destroyer HMS *Volunteer* and the corvette HMS *Anemone*.

U 615 then joined *Seewolf* group, formed from the 25th SSE of Cape Farewell, to operate against eastbound SC 123. The convoy was sighted by U 564 in the afternoon of the 26th and some *Seeteufel* boats went against it, whilst *Seewolf* waited to the south.

On the 27th U 305 sighted westbound HX 230 and *Seewolf* and *Seeteufel* boats were deployed. However, in the face of a heavy gale and kept away by a strong air escort, the twenty-two boats involved sank only one ship, that by U 610. Contact was lost, the operation ended and *Seewolf* group broke up.

U 615 joined a new group, *Adler*, from 7.4.43 S of Greenland, awaiting eastbound SC 125. The convoy passed 200 miles south of the *Adler* line on the 7th and was by then impossible to catch. The group moved southeastwards to intercept HX 232 but on the 10th westbound ON 176 was reported by U 404 and some *Adler* boats were deployed against it, not U 615. She found a straggler from HX 232 in the afternoon of the 10th in the central North Atlantic, the SS *Edward B Dudley* (am 7177t). U 615's first torpedo was a dud but she sank the vessel in another, successful attack in the early hours of the 11th.

U 615 returned to La Pallice **20.4.43**

4. **12.6.43** Left for the Caribbean.

U 615 crossed the Bay of Biscay in company with U 68, U 155, U 257 and U 600, for mutual protection against aircraft. On the 14th U 257, U 600 and U 615 were attacked by a Sunderland of 461 (RAAF) Squadron (F/O S White). Depth-charges were dropped but no damage caused. The boats dived but on resurfacing six hours later, U 600 was attacked by a Whitley of 10 OTU (P/O Orr) and suffered slight damage. U 257 and U 615 closed up on U 600 and fire was exchanged before Orr left the scene.

Four hours later a Fortress of 220 Squadron (F/O C F Callender) appeared, went down to attack U 600 and was shot down by that boat. There were no survivors. Soon afterwards a Wellington of 547 Squadron (W/O J W Hermiston) arrived and attacked U 615, causing minor damage. The aircraft was driven off by the boats and after circling for some time it left for home.

U 615 made her way westwards. En route, she was refuelled by U 535 in late June just W of the Azores. The boat entered the Caribbean via the Anegada Passage on 13.7.43, with orders to disrupt heavy tanker traffic between Lake Maracaibo and the oil refineries at Aruba and Curaçao.

On the 28th U 615 torpedoed and sank the small lake tanker SS *Rosalia* (nl 3177t) just SW of Willemstad, Curaçao. The transmission reporting this to BdU was picked up and a search began. During the night of the 28/29th the boat was attacked by an Army B 18 of 10th Squadron (USAF) (2/Lt T L Merrill) from Aruba and on 1.8.43 by a B 24 from Curaçao. She also came under depth-charge attack on the 2nd by USN patrol craft PC 1196, escorting convoy GAT 77, with which U 615 had made contact. The boat escaped and damage caused was repaired by the crew.

During the night of the 5/6th U 615 was spotted on the surface near La Blanquilla by a Trinidad-based USN Mariner of VP-205 (Lt J M Erskine). The aircraft attacked three times without further damage being caused. In the afternoon of the 6th another Mariner of VP-205 (Lt A R Matuski) made two attacks, damaging U 615 on the first and being shot down on the second, with the loss of the whole crew.

Then began a series of attacks, firstly by a Mariner of VP-204

U 615 (continued)

(Lt L D Crockett) in the face of heavy flak, which set the aircraft alight. Whilst his crew dealt with the blaze, Crockett approached again, dropping depth-bombs close to the boat. He followed this by five strafing attacks. These were followed by a USN Ventura of VB-130 (Lt T M Holmes) coming in through flak and straddling U 615 with depth-bombs. The boat dived and then resurfaced and recommenced firing at the two circling aircraft.

Two hours later another Mariner of VP-204 (Lt J W Dresbach) came in for an attack but Dresbach was killed by flak as he approached. The bombs fell short but the aircraft was saved by the co-pilot regaining control. Another Mariner of VP-205 (Lt-Cdr R S Hull) arrived and the two attacks it made caused further casualties to the crewmen manning U 615's guns.

The final attack of the day was made by an Army B 18 of 10th Squadron (USAF) aided by the light of flares. U 615 was still afloat in the morning of the 7th. The commander, KL Kapitzky, dying of his wounds, ordered the crew to abandon ship and scuttle the boat, he going down with her.

The destroyer USS *Walker* arrived from Port of Spain and picked up 43 survivors and the body of one man who died in his lifejacket.

U 616   Type VII C

Built by Blohm & Voss, Hamburg
Keel laid 20.5.41   Launched 8.2.42
Commissioned 2.4.42   Feldpost Nr M 45 101

Sunk 17.5.44 SE of Cartagena (36°52′N 00°11′E)

Served with
8 U-Flottille, Danzig   April - December 1942 (ab)
6 U-Flottille, St Nazaire   January - May 1943 (fb)
29 U-Flottille, La Spezia/ Toulon   June 1943 - 17.5.44 (fb)

Commanded by
OL Johann Spindlegger   April - October 1942
OL Siegfried Koitschka   October 1942 - 17.5.44

Patrols: 9   Ships sunk: None + 2 damaged
1 destroyer (1,570 dt)

1. 6.2.43   Left Kiel for Atlantic operations.

U 616 joined *Burggraf* group, formed on the 26th in the central North Atlantic, N of the Azores. The boats began to sweep westwards and by 4.3.43 they were E of Newfoundland, where they joined up with *Wildfang* group, stationed to the north.

The two groups formed a long patrol line from the 4th, with a view to intercepting an expected SC convoy. During the night of the 4/5th the line moved northeastwards but SC 121 passed to the north, sighted by a boat of *Neptun* group, which was waiting to the north of the *Wildfang/Burggraf* line. Seventeen boats, including U 616, were detached from the three groups and sent in pursuit of SC 121, as *Westmark* group. Eleven boats of *Neuland* group, which were W of Ireland, were sent northwestwards to form a patrol line ahead of the convoy, as *Ostmark* group.

In stormy weather and heavy seas, attacks began on the convoy. In the afternoon of the 10th U 616 made an unsuccessful attack on a ship. The sound she took to be a detonation was the explosion of a depth-charge dropped by an escorting corvette HMS *Dianthus*. The operation against SC 121 ended on the 11th near Rockall, with twelve ships sunk and one damaged. No boats were lost.

U 616 was refuelled by U 119 N of the Azores and was then directed to convoy HX 229, sighted by U 653 in the morning of the 16th. U 616 made two unsuccessful attacks on the escort on the 17th, against a destroyer and later in the day a corvette, and then the abandoned SS *Nariva* was missed, to be sunk later by U 91.

U 616 left the operation early on the 18th, probably because her torpedoes had all gone.

She put in to her new base at St Nazaire **26.3.43**

2. 19.4.43   Left for the Mediterranean.

U 616 probably passed through the Straits of Gibraltar during the night of May 4/5th. She operated in the Western Mediterranean and on the 12th she attacked a convoy N of Oran, missing an escort but claiming a hit on a ship, which is unconfirmed.

The boat put in to her new base at La Spezia **17.5.43**

3. 28.7.43   Left for operations.

In August, operating off the Algerian coast, U 616 claimed a torpedo-hit on a British cruiser on the 15th NNW of Bougie. In another attack later the same day she claimed detonations heard on two destroyers but none of these claims is confirmed.

The boat put in to her new base at Toulon **18.8.43**

4. 8.9.43   Left for operations.

Patrolling in the area of the Salerno bridgehead, U 616 may have been the U-boat which reported hits on a tanker and a destroyer on the 15th near Salerno. All the vessels are unidentified and claims unsubstantiated.

U 616 returned to Toulon **18.9.43**

5. 3.10.43   Left again for the Salerno area.

Early on the 9th U 616 torpedoed and sank the destroyer USS *Buck* E of Golfo di Policastro, on the 10th she reported a ship torpedoed and left burning N of Sicily and on the 11th U 616 claimed two LSTs torpedoed SW of Golfo di Salerno. The second was reported to be sinking by the stern and may have been either LCT 553 or LCT 618. All details are unconfirmed.

U 616 returned to Toulon **15.10.43**

6. 20.11.43   Left for operations.

On 8.12.43 U 616 reported an attack on a convoy off Cap Takouch, Algeria, in which two ships were claimed as sunk and a third damaged, all unconfirmed.

U 616 reported an attack on a destroyer on the 9th but only an end-of-run detonation appeared to have been heard.

The boat returned to Toulon **12.12.43**

7. 3.1.44   Left for operations.

On the 9th U 616 reported that she had fired two torpedoes at an unidentified submarine E of Algiers, with no results observed. A torpedo attack by U 616 was reported on the 13th ENE of Algiers, on two ships and an escorting destroyer. Only three end-of-run detonations were heard.

U 616 returned to Toulon **15.1.44**

8. 19.2.44   Left for operations.

U 616 may have torpedoed and sunk LST 362 on 2.3.44, from convoy MKS 40, in the Tyrrhenian Sea, S of Anzio. On the 6th, in the same area, she made an unsuccessful attack on a destroyer.

The boat returned to Toulon **15.3.44**

9. 30.4.44   Left for operations.

On May 9th eastbound convoy UGS 40 came into the Mediterranean. U 616 and U 967 attempted to close but were prevented from doing so. On the 13th the destroyers USS *Gleaves, Nields* and *Macomb* were ordered from Oran to a position 100 miles to the west, where U 616 was being kept under scrutiny by British warships.

Contact was lost before the US vessels could arrive and the British warships rejoined convoy GUS 39. During the night of the 13/14th U 616 torpedoed and damaged two ships from the convoy W of Algiers, the tanker MV *G S Walden* (am 10627t) and the SS *Fort Fidler* (br 7127t).

Gleaves, Nields and *Macomb* were joined at the scene by five other US destroyers, as well as aircraft of 36 Squadron. Early on the 14th USS *Hilary P Jones* damaged U 616 in a depth-charge attack and the destroyers searched all day but found nothing. A Wellington of 36 Squadron (WO Cooke) made a radar contact at nightfall, catching U 616 on the surface. She dived, six depth-charges were dropped but contact was lost.

At dawn a 10 mile oil slick was seen. The hunt continued throughout the 15th but it was not until late on the 16th that a Wellington of 36 Squadron (P/O H R Swain) caught U 616 on the surface. Markers were dropped, the searching ships closed and contact was made by *Macomb* just before midnight. She caught U 616 in a searchlight and fired six rounds before she dived.

Contact was regained soon afterwards and depth-charge attacks were made by four destroyers throughout the night. U 616 eventually surfaced and immediately came under gunfire. The crew abandoned ship and the boat was scuttled, sinking in 5 minutes. 47 survivors were picked up by the USS *Ellyson*. This warship was attacked by U 960 five hours later but her three torpedoes missed. *Ellyson* was then on her way back to Oran.

The three-day hunt for U 616 was the longest one for a single U-boat carried out during the war. The US destroyers which took part were the USS *Gleaves, Nields, Macomb, Ellyson, Hambleton, Hilary P Jones, Emmons* and *Rodman*.

U 617   Type VII C

Built by Blohm & Voss, Hamburg
Keel laid 31.5.41   Launched 19.2.42
Commissioned 9.4.42   Feldpost Nr M 46 554

Damaged 11.9.43 N of Sidi Amar (35°13´N 03°29´W)
and beached 12.9.43

Served with
5 U-Flottille, Kiel   April - August 1942 (ab)
7 U-Flottille, St Nazaire   September - November 1942 (fb)
29 U-Flottille, La Spezia/Toulon   December 1942 - 12.9.43 (fb)

Commanded by
KL Albrecht Brandi   April 1941 - 12.9.43

Patrols: 7   Ships sunk: 8 (25,879 grt)
1 destroyer (1050 dt)
1 minelayer (2650 dt)
1 tug (810 dt)

1. 29.8.42   Left Kiel for Atlantic operations.
Outward-bound, U 617 torpedoed and sank the fishing vessel *Tor II* (fa 292t) S of Vik, Iceland. On the 13th eastbound convoy SC 99 was sighted by U 216 W of Ireland and U 617 was one of a number of outward-bound boats directed to it. The shadower was driven off and lost contact. It was regained on the 14th by U 440 but when she too was driven off, the pursuit was abandoned.

U 617 and the outward-bound boats in the area W of Ireland were formed into *Pfeil* group on the 15th. On this day U 221 sighted westbound ON 129 and the boats prepared for a concentrated attack but the shadower lost contact in the fog. Briefly sighted again on the 16th, the convoy altered course and the operation was terminated.

Pfeil group was reformed and moved northeastwards on the 18th and then northwestwards on the 19th to close eastbound SC 100. U 221 sighted the convoy and *Pfeil* group joined *Lohs* group to attack it. As the boats neared the convoy, the weather worsened and the gale blowing increased to hurricane force on the 21st. With many boats left far behind, the operation against the convoy was called off on the 22nd.

A new patrol line, *Blitz*, was formed some 500 miles SE of Cape Farewell and it moved southwestwards towards an unidentified northeast-bound convoy, later found to be RB 1. En route early on the 23rd, U 258 sighted SC 100, which had been delayed by the weather. U 617, U 221, U 258 and U 615 pursued it while the rest of *Pfeil* group went after RB 1.

U 617 attacked SC 100 early on the 23rd SW of Reykjavik and torpedoed and sank the tanker MV *Athelsultan* (br 8882t) and the straggling SS *Tennessee* (br 2342t). Later in the day she sank another straggler, the SS *Roumanie* (be 3563t). A survivor from this vessel was picked up as a prisoner. Strong air cover caused the boats to abandon the operation on the 25th. A total of four ships had been sunk on the 23rd and 24th.

Blitz group was now widely scattered and before the boats could reform, U 617 sighted westbound ON 131 S of Iceland on the 26th All boats ahead of the convoy were ordered to attack. U 617 made an afternoon attack but was unsuccessful, in spite of a claim that two hits were made and sinking noises heard. A third torpedo hit but was a dud. The other *Blitz* boats searched for the convoy, as *Tiger* group, but failed to find it. The bad weather would have prevented any reformation of the group in time to mount an attack. On the 29th the boats were ordered to a refuelling area NW of the Azores. U 617 headed for home.

She put in to her new base at St Nazaire **7.10.42**

2. 2.11.42   Left for the Mediterranean.
U 617 passed through the Straits of Gibraltar during the night of the 7/8th. She operated with other boats W of a line, drawn from the Balearics to Algiers. On the 19th unsuccessful attacks were made by U 617 on a destroyer and two ships between Oran and Algiers, on the 21st several torpedoes were fired at a battleship and on the 23rd a cruiser, said to be the *Jeanne d'Arc*, was attacked and one detonation and two explosions were heard. None of these claims has been substantiated.

U 617 put in to La Spezia **28.11.42**

3. 21.12.42   Left for the Eastern Mediterranean.
On the 27th U 617 torpedoed and sank a naval tug NE of Benghazi, HMS *St Issey*. She was towing a barge. Two other detonations were heard but results were not observed. U 617 claimed a hit on a destroyer on the 28th and from four torpedoes fired in an afternoon attack on ships off the Cyrenaican coast on the 30th, three detonations were heard, followed by sinking noises. All are unconfirmed.

On 13.1.43 U 617 attacked three ships, escorted by a corvette. Detonations were heard and a large steamer was claimed as sunk. On the 15th U 617 sank two ships from a convoy off the Cyrenaican coast, NW of Derna, the SS *Annitsa* (gr 4324t) and the MV *Harboe Jensen* (nw 1862t).

The boat put in to Salamis **17.1.43**

4. 27.1.43   Left for the Eastern Mediterranean.
On February 1st, E of Tobruk, U 617 sank the minelayer HMS *Welshman*, returning from a minelaying operation. The boat encountered a convoy in the same area on the 5th and sank two ships, the SS *Henrik* (nw 1350t) and the SS *Corona* (nw 3264t).

U 617 put in to Pola **13.2.43**

5. 25.3.43   Left for the Western Mediterranean.
On 10.4.43 U 617 claimed the sinking of a British cruiser and the damaging of a British destroyer. On the 13th a hit was claimed on another destroyer and another three on a large troop transport. All attacks took place in the Alboran Sea, S of Spain and all claims are unsubstantiated.

U 617 put in to her new base at Toulon **17.4.43**

6. 31.5.43   Left Toulon and returned **1.6.43**

7. 19.6.43   Left for operations.

U 617 (continued)

On the 26th U 617 reported sinking a British destroyer in the Alboran Sea but this claim is unconfirmed.

The boat reached Toulon **20.7.43**

8. 28.8.43 Left for operations.

U 617 sank the destroyer HMS *Puckeridge* on 6.9.43 E of Gibraltar and on the 11th, in the same area, she claimed the sinking of two destroyers, both unconfirmed.

The boat was attacked and damaged on the 11th in depth-charge attacks by two Leigh Light Wellingtons of 179 Squadron (S/Ldr D B Hodgkinson and P/O W H Brunini), SW of Isla de Alboran. U 617 was pursued by the corvette HMS *Hyacinth* (Cdr R T White), the sloop HMAS *Woolongong* (Lt T H Smith) and the trawler HMS *Haarlem*.

U 617 was beached on the coast of Spanish Morocco near Sidi Amar on the 12th. Her entire crew was interned by the Spanish authorities and later repatriated to Germany.

The beached boat was destroyed by gunfire by the pursuers.

U 618 Type VII C

Built by Blohm & Voss, Hamburg
Keel laid 29.5.41   Launched 20.2.42
Commissioned 16.4.42   Feldpost Nr M 46 602

Sunk 15.8.44 W of St Nazaire (47°22′N 04°39′W)

Served with
5 U-Flottille, Kiel April - August 1942 (ab)
7 U-Flottille, St Nazaire September 1942 - 15.8.44 (fb)

Commanded by
KL Kurt Baberg April 1942 - May 1944
OL Erich Faust May 1944 - 15.8.44

Patrols: 8   Ships sunk: 3 (15,788 grt)

1. 1.9.42 Left Kiel for the North Atlantic.

U 618 and other outward-bound boats went to an area W of Ireland. When U 216 sighted eastbound SC 99 on the 13th, these boats were directed to it but only U 440 came up and she was driven off, damaged. When U 216 was driven off, losing contact, the operation was abandoned on the 14th.

U 618 moved westwards into the central North Atlantic and joined other boats to form *Pfeil* group SE of Greenland from the 15th. On this day U 221 of *Pfeil* sighted westbound ON 129 and the boats prepared for a concentrated attack but U 221 lost contact in the fog. Briefly sighted again on the 16th, the convoy altered course and the operation was terminated.

Pfeil group reformed and moved northeastwards on the 18th and then northwestwards on the 19th to close eastbound SC 100, which was sighted by U 221 on the 20th. *Pfeil* and *Lohs* groups were directed to attack but as they neared the convoy, the weather worsened and the gale blowing increased to hurricane force on the 21st. With many boats left far behind the convoy, the operation was called off on the 22nd some 500 miles SE of Cape Farewell.

The *Pfeil* boats formed a new patrol line, *Blitz*, and late on the 22nd they were ordered southwestwards at high speed to close a convoy, later found to be RB 1. However, early on the 23rd U 617 sighted SC 100, which had been delayed by the storm. U 221, U 258, U 615 and U 617 pursued it whilst U 618, U 216 and U 356 continued on to RB 1.

Contact with this convoy was made on the 24th and the three boats shadowed until early on the 26th. Of the three *Pfeil* boats, U 216 had the only success, sinking a steamer on the 25th.

After the two separate convoy actions, the *Blitz* group was widely

scattered. U 617 sighted westbound ON 131 on the 26th but after an unsuccessful attack on the convoy, she lost contact. U 618 and the other *Blitz* boats were redesignated *Tiger* group and they went in search of ON 131 but failed to find it. The bad weather would have prevented any reformation of the group in time to attack the convoy, had it been found. On the 29th the *Tiger* boats were ordered to an area NW of the Azores, where U 618, U 221, U 258 and U 356 were refuelled by U 116 on or about 2.10.42.

Tiger group formed a new patrol line, *Wotan*, from the 8th E of Newfoundland, awaiting an SC convoy. In the early hours of the 12th the boats were ordered northeastwards at high speed to intercept eastbound SC 104, which had passed the northern end of the *Wotan* line the previous afternoon, sighted by U 258. The convoy was contacted during the night of the 12/13th and in attacks in the early hours of the 13th and 14th, eight ships were sunk. Early on the 14th U 618 torpedoed and sank the SS *Empire Mersey* (br 5791t) SSE of Cape Farewell.

After the operation was terminated late on the 15th, as more aircraft appeared to protect the convoy, the *Wotan* boats were ordered further east to attack ON 137, sighted W of Ireland on the 16th. The deteriorating weather became a gale on the 17th. Early on the 18th U 618 sank a straggler from the convoy, the SS *Angelina* (am 4772t), in the central North Atlantic, N of the Azores. The operation against ON 137 ended next day.

U 618 put in to her new base at St Nazaire **28.10.42**

2. 25.11.42 Left for the Gibraltar area.

U 618 and U 432 moved down to the area W of Gibraltar, lately vacated by *Westwall* group, which had gone westwards to search for UGS convoys beyond the range of land-based aircraft.

From early December U 618 moved north and patrolled off Lisbon but she had no success.

The boat returned to St Nazaire **18.1.43**

3. 21.2.43 Left for the North Atlantic.

U 618 joined *Neuland* group W of Ireland. On 7.3.43 U 618 and ten other boats in the northern section of the patrol line were sent northwestwards, as *Ostmark* group, to form a line from the 8th ahead of SC 121, sighted by U 405 on the 6th S of Greenland.

Seventeen boats of *Wildfang*, *Burggraf* and *Neptun* groups operated against SC 121, as well as those of *Ostmark* group. In the operation twelve ships were sunk and one damaged before it ended on the 11th S of Iceland.

The *Ostmark* boats were joined by new-arrivals and three *Burggraf* boats to form *Stürmer* group from the 14th in the central North Atlantic, to operate against SC 122. The group moved westwards in search of the convoy until the 16th, when it turned southwestwards to intercept. Contact was made during the night of the 16/17th and some successful attacks were made by *Stürmer* boats over the next three days, none by U 618. This was the biggest convoy action of the war, with forty boats operating against convoys SC 122 and HX 229. Twenty-one Allied ships were sunk for the loss of U 384. U 618 made no attacks.

U 618 and other ex-*Stürmer* boats joined new-arrivals to form *Seewolf* group from the 25th, SE of Cape Farewell and south of the *Seeteufel* line, to operate against reported, eastbound SC 123. From the 26th *Seewolf* and *Seeteufel* groups joined to form a line running 800 miles south from Cape Farewell.

U 305, at the northern end of the *Seewolf* line, sighted eastbound HX 230 on the 27th. U 618 was one of twenty-two boats from the two groups which were ordered to close the convoy. However, in the face of a heavy storm, which developed into a hurricane on the 28th, and kept away by a strong air escort from the 29th, the boats involved sank only one ship, that by U 610. Contact was lost on the 30th and the operation ended.

In early April U 618 was refuelled by U 463 in the central North Atlantic, after which she joined *Meise* group, formed from the 14th S of Greenland to await eastbound SC 126. The convoy was re-routed and passed south of the group. On the 20th *Meise* group moved northwards to intercept HX 234. The convoy was sighted by U 306 on the 21st.

U 618, now short on fuel, did not take part in the pursuit of HX 234 but during the last week in April she was refuelled by U 487 in the central North Atlantic for return to base.

The boat returned to St Nazaire **7.5.43**

4. 8.6.43 Left for the Central Atlantic.

U 618 patrolled an area between the Canaries and Freetown. On 2.7.43 U 618 torpedoed and sank the SS *Empire Kohinoor* (br 5225t) SW of Freetown.

Some time in mid-July U 618 and U 600 met up with U 333 to pass over spare parts for that boat's ailing air compressor.

From July 23rd U 618 was one of six boats patrolling slowly back and forth in an east-west direction off the Ivory Coast, then, later, searching in scouting formation S of Liberia until August 2nd. Nothing was seen.

U 618 began her return journey on or about the 5th. She, U 333, U 571, U 600 and U 634 were due to have been refuelled by U 525 at positions 700 to 800 miles S to SW of the Azores but she was sunk on the 11th, en route to the rendezvous. U 129 was sent as a replacement U-tanker and from the 18th she refuelled U 618 and the other four boats and two others that had turned up.

U 618 returned to St Nazaire **5.9.43**

5. 11.11.43 Left for Atlantic operations.

U 618 joined the *Schill 3* patrol line NE of the Azores, in the expected path of northbound convoy MKS 30/SL 139 and through which it was expected to pass on the 20th. On that day U 618 shot down a Sunderland of 422 (RCAF) Squadron (F/Lt J D Uhlrichson). *Schill 3* surfaced on the evening of the 20th but failed to find the convoy, which was located next morning and attacked by aircraft, resulting in one ship sunk and another damaged, both by glider bombs.

On the 22nd the remaining fourteen boats of the three *Schill* groups, including U 618, were formed into an east-west patrol line, *Weddigen*, W of Spain. On the 23rd the line moved southwestwards but finding nothing, turned southeastwards on the 25th to intercept northbound MKS 31/SL 140. Constantly harassed by surface vessels and aircraft and with insufficient information from reconnaissance aircraft, the *Weddigen* boats could not carry out a concentrated attack before the operation was called off on the 28th. U 618 had been attacked on the surface by a Wellington of 179 Squadron from Gibraltar during the night of the 25/26th W of Lisbon. Tracer in U 618's flak was seen by warships of the 4th EG. The destroyers HMS *Bazely* and *Drury* approached and U 618 dived. Depth-charges and Hedgehog attacks were carried out but the boat escaped.

When *Weddigen* was dissolved on 8.12.43, U 618 was directed to join *Coronel* group, which had been formed on the 5th off the North Channel and then moved westwards. U 618 joined the group on or about the 12th SE of Cape Farewell.

On the 15th *Coronel* group was expanded and then split into three sections, *Coronel 1,2* and *3*. U 618 was in *Coronel 3*, which was sent south to find westbound convoy ONS 25. On the 20th *Coronel 3*, now redesignated *Borkum* group, began a move which would take it to an area W of Cape Ortegal to intercept combined convoy MKS 33/SL 142. When the convoy did not materialise, *Borkum* was ordered to operate against the carrier groups of USS *Card* and *Core,* in an effort to cover the returning blockade-runner *Osorno*. This vessel reached the Gironde Estuary safely on the 26th but, after striking a wreck, she had to be beached to save her valuable cargo.

U 618 left *Borkum* group in late December and on her way in she picked up 21 survivors from the German destroyer *Z 27*, which had been sunk by British cruisers on the 28th.

The boat put in to Lorient **4.1.44**

6. 23.2.44 Left for the Mediterranean.

U 618 made several attempts to pass through the Straits of Gibraltar but the defences proved too strong and she failed every time.

The boat returned to St Nazaire **8.4.44**

7. 25.5.44 Left for Atlantic operations.

Outward-bound, U 618 struck a British-laid mine off St Nazaire and was badly damaged.

The boat put back in to St Nazaire **25.5.44**

8. 26.7.44 Left St Nazaire and arrived Brest **30.7.44**

9. 2.8.44 Left Brest.

U 618 and U 766, as *Wiesel* group, operated against Allied escort groups but had no success.

The boat returned **4.8.44**

10. 11.8.44 Left Brest, in transit to La Pallice.

En route, U 618 was badly damaged in a depth-charge attack by a Leigh Light Liberator of 53 Squadron (F/Lt G G Potier) W of St Nazaire.

The boat was finished off in attacks by the frigates HMS *Duckworth* (Cdr R G Mills) and *Essington* (Lt-Cdr W Lambert).

U 618 had some passengers aboard, possibly technical staff. There were no survivors, 61 dead.

U 619   Type VII C

Built by Blohm & Voss, Hamburg
Keel laid 19.6.41   Launched 9.3.42
Commissioned 23.4.42   Feldpost Nr M 00 375

Sunk 5.10.42 SSW of Vik, Iceland (58° 41´N 22° 58´W)

Served with
5 U-Flottille, Kiel April - September 1942 (ab)
3 U-Flottille, La Pallice September 1942 - 5.10.42 (fb)

Commanded by
KL Kurt Makowski April 1942 - 5.10.42

Patrols: 1   Ships sunk: 2 (8723 grt)

1. 10.9.42 Left Kiel for the North Atlantic.

Outward-bound, U 619 sank a straggler from westbound convoy ON 131, the SS *John Winthrop* (am 7176t), on the 24th SW of Iceland by torpedo and gunfire. On the 26th U 619 torpedoed and sank a straggler from eastbound convoy RB 1, the coastal steamer SS *Yorktown* (br 1547t), SW of Rockall.

On 1.10.42 U 619 joined *Luchs* group S of Iceland, to await an ON convoy. The group began a sweep southwestwards on the 2nd and next day U 260 sighted eastbound HX 209 at the northern end of the *Luchs* patrol line.

Bad weather delayed the concentration of the boats for an attack and a strong air escort kept them at a distance. The operation against HX 209 was called off on the 5th, with one ship sunk and two boats lost, U 619 and U 582.

U 619 was sunk on the 5th SSW of Vik, Iceland in a depth-charge attack by a Hudson of 269 Squadron (F/O J Markham).

There were no survivors, 44 dead.

U 620 Type VII C

Built by Blohm & Voss, Hamburg
Keel laid 19.6.41   Launched 9.3.42
Commissioned 30.4.42   Feldpost Nr M 00 459

Sunk 13.2.43 W of Cabo Carvoeiro (39°18´N 11°17´W)

Served with
8 U-Flottille, Danzig   April - September 1942 (ab)
3 U-Flottille, La Pallice   October 1942 - 13.2.43 (fb)

Commanded by
KL Heinz Stein   April 1942 - 13.2.43

Patrols: 2   Ships sunk: None + 1 damaged

1. 12.9.42 Left Kiel for Atlantic operations.

U 620 was temporarily stationed in Denmark Strait with U 253 and U 610 from the 20th. After U 253 was sunk on or about the 25th, U 620 and U 610 moved southwards. They joined some newly-arrived boats to form *Luchs* group on 1.10.42 S of Iceland, to await an ON convoy.

The group began a sweep southwestwards on the 2nd and next day U 260 sighted eastbound convoy HX 209 at the northern end of the *Luchs* patrol line. Bad weather delayed the concentration of the boats for an attack and a strong air escort kept them at a distance. The operation against HX 209 was called off on the 5th, with one ship sunk and two boats lost, sunk by aircraft.

From the 8th the boats coming from HX 209 were augmented and reformed as *Panther* group 700 to 800 miles W of the North Channel. During the evening of the 11th U 620 sighted westbound convoy ONS 136 in the centre of the *Panther* line. Eight boats, including U 620, were directed to attack it, as *Leopard* group. Bad weather and high winds prevented most of the boats closing the convoy and the operation was called off on the 14th, with only two ships sunk.

Leopard group was next directed to approaching convoy SC 104 but only U 254 and U 442 made contact and they were both driven off by the escort. Late on the 15th the *Leopard* boats moved eastwards to search for westbound ON 137. This convoy was sighted by U 704 of *Panther* group in the late morning of the 16th but the weather deteriorated badly and the operation was abandoned on the 19th.

U 620 and most of the other *Leopard* boats went southwards and were refuelled by U 463 in the central North Atlantic on or about the 20th. On the 22nd U 620 was one of a number of boats ordered to pursue westbound ON 139. The convoy's speed was such that only the shadower, U 443, was able to make an attack, sinking two ships.

In late October U 620 and U 260 were ordered to the area of Ponta Delgada, just S of the Azores, to seek information on Allied shipping movements. One crewman of U 620 was killed on 10.11.42 in an aircraft attack.

The boat put in to her new base at La Pallice **12.11.42**

2. 13.12.42 Left La Pallice and returned **14.12.42**

3. 19.12.42 Left for the Central Atlantic.

U 620 joined *Delphin* group W of Gibraltar, to operate against US-Mediterranean convoys carrying supplies for the Allied armies in North Africa. On the 29th the group was ordered to sweep westwards, searching for convoy GUS 2. Nothing was seen for four days and the boats were then ordered towards Brazil.

However, on 3.1.43 U 514 reported convoy TM 1 900 miles to the south of *Delphin* and probably heading for Gibraltar. The *Delphin* boats turned south to intercept and on the 8th the convoy was sighted by U 381 in the centre of the line. Four homeward- or

outward-bound boats joined the group, making twelve boats available for an attack.

On the 10th U 620 reported hits on two tankers WNW of the Canaries but these are unconfirmed and were probably end-of-run detonations. Early on the 11th U 620 sank the abandoned wreck of the tanker SS *British Dominion* (br 6983t) by torpedo and gunfire. The tanker had been torpedoed three hours earlier by U 522. Seven tankers were sunk in the operation, which ended near Madeira on the 11th.

Delphin group reformed S of the Azores after six of its boats, including U 620, had been refuelled by U 463 W of the Azores. The group moved westwards to meet an eastbound UGS convoy but turned east again on the 18th. From the 21st to the 29th *Delphin* waited SW of the Azores but when nothing materialised, the line moved further eastwards.

From the 31st the patrol line was NW of the Canaries but then moved to a new position W of Gibraltar for 6.2.43. From the 11th the *Delphin* boats moved north to take up positions W of Portugal. A southbound convoy was reported on the 12th, 200 miles W of Cape Finisterre. *Delphin* was ordered to close but the operation failed when the convoy's air escort kept the boats submerged. The situation worsened the nearer the convoy got to Gibraltar.

Very late in the evening of the 13th U 620 was sunk W of Cabo Carvoeiro in a depth-charge attack by a Catalina of 202 Squadron (F/Lt H R Sheardown) from Gibraltar.

There were no survivors, 46 dead.

U 621 Type VII C

Built by Blohm & Voss, Hamburg
Keel laid 1.7.41   Launched 29.3.42
Commissioned 7.5.42   Feldpost Nr M 02 062

Sunk 18.8.44 WSW of La Rochelle (45°52´N 02°36´W)

Served with
8 U-Flottille, Danzig   May - September 1942 (ab)
9 U-Flottille, Brest   October 1942 - 18.8.44 (fb)

Commanded by
KL Horst Schünemann   May - December 1942
OL Max Kruschka   December 1942 - May 1944
OL Hermann Stuckmann   May 1944 - 18.8.44

Patrols: 10   Ships sunk: 4 (20,159 grt) + 1 dama1 LST
                             1 LST (1490 dt)
                             1 LSI (2938 dt)

1. 29.9.42 Left Kiel for the North Atlantic.

U 621 joined *Panther* group, formed from 8.10.42 700 to 800 miles W of the North Channel. In the evening of the 11th U 620 sighted westbound ONS 136 and eight boats in the centre of the long *Panther* patrol line were detached and directed to the convoy, as *Leopard* group.

On the 16th U 704 sighted ON 137 passing through the southern section of the *Panther* line and eleven boats of the group were ordered to attack. From the remaining *Panther* boats, *Puma* group was formed on the 16th from U 621 and seven others and ordered southwards to seek ONS 138.

By the 22nd the boats were nearly 400 miles south of their original *Puma* line position. On that day the southernmost boat in the line, U 443, sighted ON 139 in the central North Atlantic. The group was ordered to close and attack but the boats were unable to catch the convoy, which was averaging 10 to 12 knots. Only U 443 was able to attack and she sank two ships on the 23rd. U 621 sank the SS *Empire Turnstone* (br 6113t), a straggler from ONS 136, in the central North Atlantic.

Puma group moved westwards until the 24th, when U 606 reported two destroyers which could have been part of an escort for a westbound ONS convoy. The boats moved northwestwards at high speed to intercept. On the 26th U 436 sighted eastbound HX 212 in the centre of the patrol line. She shadowed and brought up other boats but all were driven off by the escort. Early on the 28th U 621 made unsuccessful attacks on ships in the convoy, hearing only end-of-run detonations. Later on the 28th the Puma boats in contact with the convoy were driven off by Iceland-based aircraft of 120 Squadron. When the same happened on the 29th, the operation was abandoned. Despite the difficulty in making attacks, six ships were sunk and another damaged.

U 621 put in to her new base at Brest **5.11.42**

2. 5.12.42 Left for the North Atlantic.

U 621 joined *Raufbold* group, formed in mid-December W of Ireland. On the 15th U 609 sighted westbound ON 153 and called up other boats. U 621 came up and on the 16th she claimed two hits on a ship in the convoy W of Ireland but this is unconfirmed.

In the early hours of the 18th U 621 attacked an independent in the central North Atlantic, the SS *Oropos* (gr 4474t). A hit was heard, followed by a later explosion and smoke was seen and the smell of burning was noticed. The *Oropos* never arrived at her destination and was reported missing after the 21st. In the evening of the 20th U 621 torpedoed and sank the independent tanker MV *Otina* (br 6217t) in the central North Atlantic.

Despite bad weather from the 17th, *Raufbold* group maintained contact with ON 153 until the 21st. Two ships and a destroyer had been sunk and another ship damaged. *Raufbold* group was dissolved.

U 621 headed home. She was ordered to search for survivors of the blockade-runner *Rhakotis,* sunk on the 28th, but found none.

The boat returned to Brest **5.1.43**

3. 1.2.43 Left for the North Atlantic.

U 621 joined *Hartherz* group W of the Bay of Biscay to operate against convoys on the UK-Gibraltar route. After a week, during which none was seen, the group dispersed on the 8th.

From the 14th U 621 was with *Ritter* group W of Ireland, formed to operate against expected convoy HX 226. During the night of the 15/16th convoy SC 119 passed to the north of the group and on the 18th HX 226 also passed to the north, after a wide detour.

The group had been moving westwards but when it was reported by aircraft that convoys ON 166 and ONS 167 were being routed south of the *Ritter* line, the movement westwards was halted and the boats moved southeastwards and formed a north-south patrol line with *Neptun* group on the 30° meridian from the 20th.

ON 166 was sighted by U 604 in the late morning of the 20th but she was driven off during the night before the closing *Ritter* and *Knappen* boats could arrive. In the evening of the 24th U 621 attacked the convoy. She reported hits on a steamer. The torpedo-tracks were seen from the USCG cutter *Spencer* and she dropped depth-charges but without damage to U 621.

The convoy was pursued for 1100 miles and when the operation ended in bad visibility on the 25th E of Newfoundland, fourteen ships had been sunk and another damaged. After the action U 621 was refuelled by U 462 400 to 600 miles N of the Azores.

The replenished boats then joined *Burggraf* group, formed from the 26th in the central North Atlantic. They began a sweep westwards and by 4.3.43 they were E of Newfoundland, where they joined up with *Wildfang* group, stationed to the north. The two groups formed a long patrol line from the 4th, with a view to intercepting an expected SC convoy.

After part of the line was detached to operate against eastbound SC 121, the remaining *Burggraf* boats, including U 621, formed a new patrol line, *Raubgraf*, from the 7th ENE of Newfoundland. On the 9th the group moved north to intercept southwest-bound convoy ON 170 but U 621 left at this time to return to base. The returning boat torpedoed and sank the SS *Baron Kinnaird* (br 3355t),

a straggler from ONS 169, on the 11th in the central North Atlantic, E of Newfoundland.

U 621 returned to Brest **23.3.43**

4. 22.4.43 Left for the North Atlantic.

U 621 joined *Amsel 1* group E of Newfoundland on or about 4.5.43, in a patrol line ahead of southwest-bound convoy ONS 5. During the night of the 4/5th the first boats of *Amsel 1* and *2* and *Fink* groups located the convoy. Attacks were made and the convoy was split into several smaller, escorted groups. In the late afternoon of the 5th fog came down and almost all contact was lost. After it was regained briefly in the early morning of the 6th, the operation was abandoned. Twelve ships had been sunk and six boats lost. No *Amsel 1* boats made any attack on the convoy.

From the 8th *Amsel 1* and *2* groups reformed as *Elbe* group E of Newfoundland. The group was ordered southeastwards to intercept HX 237 but the convoy was too far ahead, so the *Elbe* boats headed southeastwards again, to cut off the slower SC 129.

On the 10th *Rhein* and *Elbe* groups were combined to form *Elbe 1* and *2* groups. U 621 was in *Elbe 2*. Whilst the boats were forming their line on the 11th, they passed SC 129, which was sighted by U 504 but she was driven off. However, contact was made on the 12th but the eleven boats shadowing were driven off. Some boats were damaged and U 186 was sunk. After the escort-carrier HMS *Biter* arrived on the 13th, the operation was called off on the 14th SW of Ireland. Two ships were sunk but two boats lost.

On or about the 17th U 621 was refuelled for further operations, possibly by another boat. She then joined *Mosel* group 400 miles S of Cape Farewell, to operate against convoy HX 239. It passed south of the patrol line and although some *Mosel* boats moved southeastwards to intercept, they did not find the convoy.

From the 24th Dönitz temporarily halted operations against convoys in the North Atlantic. U 621 and other *Mosel* and *Donau* boats with limited fuel ranged over a wide area, their ongoing radio signals planned to give the impression that a large U-boat presence was still being maintained across the convoy routes.

On the 31st U 621 was sighted on the surface and attacked with six depth-charges by a Liberator of 224 Squadron (F/O R Sweeney) in the Bay of Biscay.

The damaged U 621 put in to Brest **3.6.43**

U 621 was one of seven boats which were converted to flak-boats between May and November 1943. The other six were U 211, U 256, U 263, U 271, U 441 and U 953.

The increased armament reduced the boats' fuel-carrying capacity and made them unsuitable for long-range operations.

5. 22.8.43 Left for operations.

Now converted to a flak-boat, U 621 operated in the Bay of Biscay, presumably escorting boats in and out of that highly dangerous area.

U 621 returned to Brest **28.9.43**

The flak-boat scheme was not a success and on 1.11.43 it was decided to reconvert the flak-boats back to their original state for normal duty.

6. 6.1.44 Left for the North Atlantic.

Outward-bound, U 621 was located on the 13th by a Liberator of 59 Squadron (F/O W G Loney), which was escorting convoy MKS 35/SL 144. Two depth-charge and three machine-gun strafing attacks were made. The boat dived and escaped but she was damaged and one crewman was killed and another six were wounded.

U 621 returned to Brest **23.1.44**

7. 21.2.44 Left for the Eastern Atlantic.

U 621 patrolled N of the outer Hebrides and The Minch. She

U 621 (continued)

was one of five boats, ordered to attack shipping close to the coast, to tie down Allied anti-submarine forces.

Strong defences meant that the boats were unable to operate on the surface and, submerged, they were too slow to close and carry out a successful attack.

On 20.3.44, N of The Minch, U 621 carried out an unsuccessful attack on a destroyer. She had no success on this patrol.

U 621 returned to Brest **19.4.44**

8. 6.6.44 Left Brest, as part of *Landwirt* group.

U 621 was one of eight schnorkel boats ordered to go to the area N of Cherbourg, enter the English Channel and inflict what losses they could on the invasion forces. This was a very difficult and dangerous task, considering the concentration of air and surface forces they would be facing.

Soon after midnight on the 7th U 621 attacked destroyers of the 12th SG but heard only an end-of-run detonation. On the 15th she penetrated the screen escorting 6 LSTs N of Seine Bay and fired three torpedoes, all of which exploded prematurely. Later in the day U 621 sank a straggler, LST 280, NW of Le Havre.

On the 18th she made an unsuccessful attack on two US battleships, which failed because of premature explosions. The boat was driven off.

U 621 returned to Brest **23.6.44**

9. 15.7.44 Left for the English Channel.

U 621 reached her operational area on the 23rd. In attacks on the 29th, SE of the Isle of Wight, U 621 sank the landing ship *Prince Leopold* and claimed a hit on a steamer, which is unconfirmed.

On the 30th, in the same area, U 621 torpedoed and damaged the troop transport SS *Ascanius* (br 10048t) and on 2.8.44, closer to the French coast, she claimed two ships sunk, again unidentified and unconfirmed.

U 621 returned to Brest **11.8.44**

10. 13.8.44 Left, on transfer to La Pallice.

On the 18th U 621 was located and sunk in depth-charge attacks by destroyers of the Canadian 11th SG WSW of La Rochelle, HMCS *Ottawa* (Cdr H F Pullen), *Kootenay* (Lt-Cdr K L Dyer) and *Chaudière* (Lt-Cdr C P Nixon).

There were no survivors, 56 dead.

U 622   Type VII C

Built by Blohm & Voss, Hamburg
Keel laid 1.7.41   Launched 29.3.42
Commissioned 14.5.42   Feldpost Nr M 04 155

Sunk 24.7.43 at Trondheim

Served with
8 U-Flottille, Danzig   May - September 1942 (ab)
11 U-Flottille, Bergen   October 1942 - May 1943 (fb)
13 U-Flottille, Trondheim   June 1943 - 24.7.43 (fb)

Commanded by
KL Horst-Thilo Queck   May 1942 - 24.7.43

Patrols: 5   Ships sunk: None

1. 6.10.42 Left Kiel and arrived Bergen **9.10.42**

2. 12.10.42 Left for Northern Waters. No details known.
U 622 put in to Skjomenfjord **12.11.42**

3. 14.11.42 Left Skjomenfjord and arrived Bergen **17.11.42**

4. 28.12.42 Left Bergen for Northern Waters.

Eastbound convoy JW 52 left Loch Ewe on 17.1.43 and was first reported by a German aircraft on the 23rd. U 622 was one of the U-boats directed to the convoy and the attack she made on it on the 24th was unsuccessful. JW 52 reached Kola Inlet without loss on the 27th.

U 622 returned to Skjomenfjord **29.1.43**

5. 9.2.43 Left for operations.

Eastbound JW 53 left Loch Ewe on 15.2.43 and was reported by aircraft on the 23rd. The convoy passed by the waiting U-boats in bad weather. On the 24th U 622 made unsuccessful attacks against two destroyers. JW 53 reached Kola Inlet without loss on the 27th.

Return convoy RA 53 left Kola Inlet on 1.3.43 and came under attack by U-boats and aircraft. U 622 does not seem to have taken any part in attacks on the convoy.

She put in to Narvik **15.3.43**

6. 16.3.43 Left Narvik and arrived Trondheim **18.3.43**

7. 17.5.43 Left Trondheim and arrived Hammerfest **21.5.43**

8. 29.5.43 Left for operations. No details known.
U 622 returned to Hammerfest **5.6.43**

9. 14.6.43 Left for operations. No details known.
U 622 put in to Trondheim **10.7.43**

On 24.7.43 U 622 was sunk in a USAF bombing raid on the harbour at Trondheim. She may have been raised later and surrendered in May 1945.

U 623   Type VII C

Built by Blohm & Voss, Hamburg
Keel laid 15.7.41   Launched 31.3.42
Commissioned 21.5.42   Feldpost Nr M 04 237

Lost 21.2.43 N of the Azores (48°08′N 29°37′W)

Served with
8 U-Flottille, Danzig   May - November 1942 (ab)
6 U-Flottille, St Nazaire   December 1942 - 21.2.43 (fb)

Commanded by
OL Hermann Schröder   May 1942 - 21.2.43

Patrols: 2   Ships sunk: None

1. 5.11.42 Left Kiel for the North Atlantic.

U 623 joined *Drachen* group, formed from the 24th NE of Newfoundland. The group's orders were for its boats to search independently for single ships. Several were found and two were sunk, neither by U 623. No convoys were seen.

In early December U 623 was refuelled by U 460 NW of the Azores. She then joined *Draufgänger* group, which on the 7th was some 700 miles W of the North Channel. On this day the group was ordered northwestwards to intercept northeast-bound HX 217, with which it made contact next day.

From the 10th the convoy had strong air cover. U 623 approached but was driven off, with the other boats that were still in contact. The operation was abandoned on the 11th, with two ships sunk and two boats lost.

U 623 put in to her new base at St Nazaire **26.12.42**

2. 2.2.43 Left for the North Atlantic.

U 623 joined *Ritter* group in the central North Atlantic, formed from the 14th in the central North Atlantic to operate against expected convoy HX 226. During the night of the 15/16th convoy SC 119 passed to the north of the patrol line and on the 18th HX 226 also passed to the north, after a wide detour.

The group had been moving westwards but when it was learned that convoys ON 166 and ONS 167 were being routed south of the *Ritter* line, the movement westwards was halted and the boats moved southeastwards and formed a north-south patrol line with *Neptun* group on the 30° meridian from the 20th. ON 166 was sighted by U 604 in the late morning of the 20th but she was driven off before the closing *Ritter* boats could arrive.

U 623's last report was made on 9.2.43 and she was never heard from again. She was probably sunk on the 21st N of the Azores by an Iceland-based Liberator of 120 Squadron (S/Ldr D J Isted).

There were no survivors, 46 dead.

U 624   Type VII C

Built by Blohm & Voss, Hamburg
Keel laid 15.7.41   Launched 31.3.42
Commissioned 28.5.42   Feldpost Nr M 04 328

Sunk 7.2.43 WSW of Rockall (55°42′N 26°17′W)

Served with
8 U-Flottille, Danzig May - October 1942 (ab)
7 U-Flottille, St Nazaire October 1942 - 7.2.43 (fb)

Commanded by
KL Ulrich Graf von Soden-Fraunhofen May 1942 - 7.2.43

Patrols: 2   Ships sunk: 4 (22,889 grt) + 2 damaged

1. 10.10.42 Left Kiel for Atlantic operations.
U 624 joined *Puma* group on or about the 22nd in the central North Atlantic. The group moved westwards until the 24th, when U 606 reported two destroyers which could have been part of an escort for a westbound ONS convoy.

The *Puma* boats moved northwestwards at high speed to intercept. On the 26th U 436 sighted eastbound HX 212 in the centre of the patrol line, SE of Greenland. In the morning of the 29th U 624 torpedoed and sank two ships WSW of Rockall, the tanker SS *Pan New York* (am 7701t) and the whaling factory ship SS *Kosmos II* (nw 16966t), which had been abandoned after being torpedoed and set on fire in the morning of the 28th by U 606. The operation ended on the 29th.

On 1.11.42 U 624, four other boats from the HX 212 operation and the newly-arrived U 98 were ordered to form a new patrol line, *Natter*, W of Ireland. During the next three days the group was augmented by six new-arrivals. The boats moved southwards to form a line for the 5th.

U 92 of *Natter* sighted westbound convoy ON 143 on the 4th but with none of the other boats of the group in position to give support, she lost contact. A search was made when other boats came up but when the convoy had not been found again by the 6th, the operation was called off. The only successes were two stragglers sunk by U 566 and U 613 during the afternoon of the 7th, after a reported sighting of the convoy enabled four boats to close.

On the 8th all *Natter* boats with sufficient fuel were ordered to proceed at high speed towards Gibraltar because of the Allied landings in North Africa. This did not include U 624. She and U 606 were refuelled by U 117 N of the Azores, after which they joined *Kreuzotter* group 600 miles W of Ireland.

On the 13th the group moved northwards and two days later westbound ONS 144 passed through the centre of the patrol line. In an operation, which ended E of Newfoundland on the 20th, five ships and a corvette were sunk. In the morning of the 18th U 624

torpedoed three ships from the convoy SSE of Cape Farewell, sinking the SS *Parismina* (am 4732t) and damaging the tanker SS *President Sergent* (br 5344t) and the SS *Yaka* (am 5432t). The *President Sergent* sank seven hours after the attack, probably dispatched by a corvette, and the *Yaka* was sunk by U 522 two hours later. In the same attack U 624 missed the Norwegian corvette *Montbretia,* sunk three hours later by U 262.

U 624 put in to her new base at St Nazaire **4.12.42**

2. 7.1.43 Left for the North Atlantic.
U 624 joined *Habicht* group W of Ireland. On the 17th the group moved westwards in search of ON convoys. By the 19th nothing had been found and the *Habicht* boats combined with those of *Falke* group to form a new patrol line, *Haudegen*, running for 300 miles SE of Cape Farewell.

On the 22nd the group was ordered to go southeastwards to intercept an eastbound HX convoy. Bad weather prevented the interception and the boats returned to their positions SE of Cape Farewell. On the way back U 624 torpedoed and sank a straggler from convoy SC 117 S of Greenland, the SS *Lackenby* (br 5112t). This vessel was reported missing after the 23rd and was possibly sunk by U 624 on the 25th.

On 1.2.43 *Haudegen* group began a southwesterly movement towards Newfoundland. On the 2nd the five northern boats of the group were detached to attack convoy SG 19, as *Nordsturm* group.

U 187 of *Pfeil* group sighted SC 118 on the 4th E of Newfoundland. The southern *Haudegen* boats, U 624, U 438, U 613, U 704 and U 752, were ordered to leave the patrol line and attack the convoy, which was by then already under attack by *Pfeil* group.

On the 7th U 624 was sunk in a depth-charge attack by an Iceland-based Fortress of 220 Squadron (P/O G Robertson) in the vicinity of convoy SC 118.

There were no survivors, 45 dead.

U 625   Type VII C

Built by Blohm & Voss, Hamburg
Keel laid 28.7.41   Launched 15.4.42
Commissioned 4.6.42   Feldpost Nr M 04 401

Sunk 10.3.44 W of Ireland (52°35′N 20°19′W)

Served with
8 U-Flottille, Danzig June - September 1942 (ab)
3 U-Flottille, La Pallice October 1942 (fb)
11 U-Flottille, Bergen November 1942 - May 1943 (fb/fb-m)
13 U-Flottille, Trondheim June - October 1943 (fb)
1 U-Flottille, Brest November 1943 - 10.3.44 (fb)

Commanded by
KL Hans Benker June 1942 - 2.1.44
OL Kurt Sureth (temp) 2.1.44 - 6.1.44
OL Siegfried Straub January 1944 - 10.3.44

Patrols: 9   Ships sunk: 3 (13,688 grt) + 1 damaged
                                1 minesweeper (1165 dt)

1. 1.10.42 Left Kiel and arrived Skjomenfjord **8.10.42**

2. 4.11.42 Left for operations.
In August 1942 the Russians requested that two of their merchant ships, then laying off Iceland, should be sent to Archangel. Each was to sail independently, unescorted and with a one-day interval between departures. Both arrived safely.

In October it was decided to repeat the experiment, with seven British ships, five American and one Russian, each one

U 625 (continued)

independent, unescorted and at some 200 mile intervals. They left Reykjavik for Murmansk between October 29th and November 2nd 1942. As a precaution, six trawlers were positioned along the general route and British submarines were patrolling N of Bear Island. The experiment ended the belief that single ships could successfully get through to Russia. Of the thirteen ships, four were sunk, three were recalled, five arrived safely and one, the SS *Chulmleigh* (br 5445t), ran aground on a reef off South Cape, Spitzbergen soon after midnight on the 5th. The survival of her master, Captain D M Williams, and some of his men is an epic of human endurance. He and the few surviving crew members were not rescued until January 4th 1943 by Norwegian soldiers. They were eventually landed in Scotland on June 15th. The *Chulmleigh* was later bombed by Ju 88s of II/KG 30 and then torpedoed and destroyed by U 625 on November 16th. U 625 had also sunk one of the original thirteen ships, the SS *Empire Sky* (br 7455t), torpedoed S of Spitzbergen on 6.11.42.

On the 23rd U 625 attacked westbound convoy QP 15 S of Spitzbergen, torpedoing and sinking the SS *Goolistan* (br 5851t).

The boat put in to Narvik **29.11.42**

3. 30.11.42 Left Narvik and arrived Bergen **2.12.42**

4. 23.12.42 Left Bergen and arrived Narvik **25.12.42**

5. 30.12.42 Left for operations.
On 1.2.43 U 625 sighted and reported westbound convoy RA 52 SW of Bear Island. She fired five torpedoes, claiming one hit and hearing three detonations but there is no confirmation.
The boat returned to Narvik **6.2.43**

6. 7.2.43 Left Narvik and arrived Bergen **11.2.43**

7. 17.3.43 Left for operations. No details known.
U 625 put in to Hammerfest **16.4.43**

8. 26.4.43 Left for operations. No details known.
U 625 returned to Narvik **31.5.43**

9. 10.6.43 Left Narvik and arrived Hammerfest **11.6.43**

10. 21.6.43 Left for operations. No details known.
U 625 put in to Trondheim **30.6.43**

11. 12.7.43 Left for operations.
On the 20th U 625 laid mines off the Yugor Strait. Five days later the Russian minesweeper TSC-58/T-904 sank after striking one of these mines.
U 625 returned to Narvik **27.7.43**

12. 4.8.43 Left Narvik and arrived Tromsø **5.8.43**

13. 5.8.43 Left Tromsø and arrived Hammerfest **6.8.43**

14. 7.8.43 Left for operations.
On the 13th U 625 laid mines off Yugor Strait. A Russian steam tug (sov 382t), number unknown but formerly the *Skval*, sank on the 25th after striking one of these mines.
U 625 returned to Narvik **20.8.43**

15. 21.8.43 Left Narvik and arrived Trondheim **23.8.43**

16. 4.11.43 Left Trondheim and returned **8.11.43**

17. 15.11.43 Left Trondheim for Atlantic operations.
U 625 was one of a number of boats which took up submerged, waiting positions W of the British Isles.

In early December they assembled W of the North Channel as *Coronel* group, which searched for westbound ONS 24 but was unsuccessful because aerial reconnaissance failed to find it. The convoy passed to the north of the group.

In mid-December *Coronel* group was enlarged and split into two sub-groups, *Coronel 1* and *3*, awaiting convoy ON 214. U 625 was in *Coronel 1*. Air reconnaissance failed to find the convoy and it passed to the south.

On the 19th the group was reduced to six boats, U 625, U 92, U 421, U 544, U 653 and U 672, to search for convoys W of the British Isles, as *Föhr* group. Eastbound HX 270 passed south of the group between the 20th and the 22nd, MKS 33/SL 144 passed on the 22/23rd and KMS 36/OS 62 on the 23/24th.

Föhr then joined with *Amrum* and *Sylt* groups and, together with U 744 and U 390, they formed six small sub-groups, *Rügen 1* to *6* W of Ireland. U 625 was in *Rügen 6*. These small sub-groups were constantly moving, changing positions and varying formations, with the objective of preventing the Allies determining the area over which they were operating. When three convoys were sighted, UC 8 on the 23rd, TU 5 on the 26th and CU 9 on the 30th, the groups were each too small to mount an attack.

On 2.1.44 U 625 was sighted by a Liberator of 224 Squadron (F/O E Allen). A depth-charge attack killed the boat's commander and a crewman on the bridge. The 1WO, OL Sureth, took the boat down and made his way back.
U 625 put in to Brest **6.1.44**

18. 29.2.44 Left for Atlantic operations.
U 625 joined *Preussen* group, whose boats were disposed singly W of the British Isles. On March 10th U 625 was sighted on the surface W of Ireland by a Sunderland of 422 (RCAF) Squadron (F/Lt S W Butler).

As the aircraft came in, the boat began firing but her shells fell short. As U 625 submerged, the Sunderland dropped six depth-charges. The boat soon resurfaced, moving slowly in a circle to the right. The aircraft circled for more than an hour and the crew were then seen abandoning ship and the boat sank.

Although the crew had been seen in their dinghies, there were no survivors, 54 dead.

U 626   Type VII C

Built by Blohm & Voss, Hamburg
Keel laid 28.7.41   Launched 15.4.42
Commissioned 11.6.42   Feldpost Nr M 07 089

Sunk 15.12.42 WSW of Rockall (56°46′N 27°12′W)

Served with
5 U-Flottille, Kiel   June - October 1942 (ab)
6 U-Flottille, St Nazaire   November 1942 - 15.12.42 (fb)

Commanded by
Lt Hans-Botho Bade   June 1942 - 15.12.42

Patrols: 1   Ships sunk: None

During training exercises off Danzig on 2.9.42, U 626 collided with U 222, which sank with the loss of 42 of her crew.

1. 24.11.42 Left Kiel and arrived Bergen **30.11.42**

2. 8.12.42 Left Bergen for the North Atlantic.
Outward-bound, U 626 was located on the 15th WSW of Rockall by the USCG cutter, *Ingham*, from the escort of convoy ONS 152. The boat was sunk in a depth-charge attack.
There were no survivors, 47 dead.

U 627   Type VII C

Built by Blohm & Voss, Hamburg
Keel laid 7.8.41   Launched 29.4.42
Commissioned 18.6.42   Feldpost Nr M 07 218

Sunk 27.10.42 SSW of Reykjavik (59°14´N 22°49´W)

Served with
5 U-Flottille, Kiel   June - October 1942 (ab)
6 U-Flottille, St Nazaire   October 1942 (fb)

Commanded by
KL Robert Kindelbacher   June 1942 - 27.10.42

Patrols: 1   Ships sunk: None

1. 15.10.42 Left Kiel for the North Atlantic.
U 627 was located SSW of Reykjavik near convoy SC 105 on the 27th by a Fortress of 206 Squadron (P/O R L Cowey) and sunk in a depth-charge attack.
There were no survivors, 44 dead.

U 628   Type VII C

Built by Blohm & Voss, Hamburg
Keel laid 7.8.41   Launched 29.4.42
Commissioned 25.6.42   Feldpost Nr M 07 314

Sunk 3.7.43 NW of Cape Ortegal (44°11´N 08°45´W)

Served with
5 U-Flottille, Kiel   June - November 1942 (ab)
1 U-Flottille, Brest   December 1942 - 3.7.43 (fb)

Commanded by
KL Heinrich Hasenschar   June 1942 - 3.7.43

Patrols: 4   Ships sunk: 3 + 2 shared (23,136 grt) + 3 damaged

1. 28.11.42 Left Kiel for the North Atlantic.
Outward-bound, U 628 was directed to convoy HX 217, then under attack E of Cape Farewell. She closed the convoy on December 10th, maintained contact until the 11th and was then driven off. From the 13th U 628 and other new-arrivals combined with some of the ex-*Draufgänger* boats to form a new group, *Ungestüm*, to operate against convoys leaving the North Channel.
On the 13th HX 218 was sighted E of Newfoundland by U 373. The *Ungestüm* boats moved westwards and on the 16th a patrol line was formed SE of Cape Farewell in the expected path of the convoy. However, HX 218 passed unobserved through the waiting line of boats.
After U 373 sighted ONS 152 on the 16th to the southeast of the *Ungestüm* line, the boats were moved towards it. Brief contact was made but bad weather and poor visibility hampered the pursuit. A search for stragglers continued, resulting in a sinking by U 591, but the operation ended on the 22nd.
From the 24th the widely-scattered *Ungestüm* boats formed a new patrol line in the central North Atlantic. On the 25th the line moved northeast to meet up with *Spitz* group, moving down towards it from the northwest. Convoy ONS 154 was sighted just south of the *Spitz* patrol line.
Both groups moved south to intercept and contact was made on the 27th. In spite of poor visibility on that day, four ships were sunk and another damaged. Early on the 29th U 628 torpedoed and sank the SS *Lynton Grange* (br 5029t) N of the Azores, which had been torpedoed two hours earlier by U 406. U 628 also claimed a hit on a corvette, one of several which were picking up survivors from recently-sunk ships, including *Lynton Grange*. There is no confirmation for U 628's report that the corvette was seen to have a broken back.
The pursuit of ONS 154 continued until the 31st, when it ended NW of the Azores, with thirteen ships and a naval special service vessel sunk and another ship damaged. On or about 1.1.43 U 628 and other *Ungestüm* boats were refuelled by U 117 N of the Azores for return to base.
U 628 put in to her new base at Brest **8.1.43**

2. 1.2.43 Left for Atlantic operations.
U 628 joined *Hartherz* group W of the Bay of Biscay, formed to intercept an HG convoy, reported to have left Gibraltar. The group searched between 14° and 19°W from February 4th to the 7th but nothing was seen.
The group broke up on the 8th and from the 14th U 628 was with *Ritter* group, formed W of Ireland to operate against expected convoy HX 226. During the night of the 15/16th convoy SC 119 passed to the north of the group and on the 18th HX 226 also passed to the north, after a wide detour.
Ritter group had been moving westwards but when it was reported by aircraft that convoys ON 166 and ONS 167 were being routed south of the *Ritter* line, the movement westwards was halted and the boats moved southeastwards and formed a north-south patrol line with *Neptun* group on the 30° meridian from the 20th.
ON 166 was sighted by U 604 in the late morning of the 20th but she was driven off during the night before the closing *Ritter* and *Knappen* boats could arrive. U 628 made contact on the 22nd and in the morning of the 23rd she made her first attack on the convoy, torpedoing and damaging two tankers in the central North Atlantic, the MV *Winkler* (pa 6907t) and the MV *Glittre* (nw 6409t). Both were sunk soon afterwards by U 223 and U 603 respectively. Immediately after torpedoing the two tankers, U 628 was probably attacked with gunfire and depth-charges by the escorting USCG cutter *Spencer*.
On the 24th U 628 and U 600 shared in sinking the MV *Ingria* (nw 4391t) from the convoy, ESE of St John's, and on the 25th U 628 sank the SS *Manchester Merchant* (br 7264t) E of Cape Race. ON 166 was pursued for 1100 miles and before the operation ended on the 25th ESE of Newfoundland in bad visibility, fourteen ships were sunk and one damaged. After the action U 628 was refuelled by U 462 400 to 600 miles N of the Azores.
The boat returned to Brest **9.3.43**

3. 8.4.43 Left for the North Atlantic.
During the night of the 14/15th eastbound HX 233 was sighted by U 262 400 miles N of the Azores. U 628 and other outward-bound boats were ahead of the convoy and they were ordered to find it and carry out attacks.
In the morning of the 16th the shadower lost contact but the convoy was found again by U 175 during the night. In the morning of the 17th U 628 scored a torpedo hit on the SS *Fort Rampart* (br 7134t) 900 miles ENE of the Azores. Four hours later this vessel was sunk by a double coup de grâce from U 628 and U 226. HX 233's escort was increased on the 17th and the boats were driven off. The operation was called off on the 18th.
U 628 and other boats from HX 233 joined boats refuelled after operating against HX 232 to form a new patrol line, *Specht*, from the 20th N of the Azores. The group moved westwards and on the 23rd was in a north-south patrol line E of Newfoundland, awaiting convoy SC 127. When it did not materialise, the boats moved northwestwards at high speed and formed a new patrol line from the 25th S of Greenland in the path of convoy ONS 4, sighted by U 732 on the 23rd. The *Specht* boats failed to find the convoy, which was re-routed to miss the line.
On the 27th the *Specht* boats were NE of Newfoundland,

U 628 (continued)

waiting for HX 235 but the convoy was re-routed to the south. From the 29th *Specht* and *Amsel* groups formed a patrol line NE of Newfoundland to intercept eastbound SC 128, reported to be 200 miles E of Cape Race. Both groups moved south to search but when the convoy had not been found by 1.5.43 the *Specht* boats moved north again and on the 3rd a new, long patrol line, *Fink,* was formed from *Specht* and *Star* groups S of Cape Farewell.

In the afternoon of the 4th southwest-bound ONS 5 passed through the *Fink* line, sighted by U 628. By the early hours of the 5th eleven boats had found the convoy and attacks were made, causing the convoy to disperse. Early on the 5th U 628 torpedoed and damaged the SS *Harbury* (br 5081t) S of Cape Farewell, the abandoned wreck of which was sunk some four hours later by U 264.

Later in the morning of the 5th U 628 reported sinking a corvette but this claim is unsubstantiated. Early in the day U 358 torpedoed and damaged the SS *Wentworth* (br 5212t). One of ONS 5's escort, HMS *Loosestrife*, tried but failed to sink the abandoned vessel and she was finally dispatched by U 628 in the early evening with torpedo and gunfire. Fog came down during the evening and most boats lost contact. The radar-equipped escorts made fifteen depth-charge attacks in the fog. The operation was terminated in the morning of the 6th, with twelve ships sunk but six boats lost.

The returning U 628 encountered convoy HX 237 and shadowed it until the 13th. The convoy was already under attack by *Drossel* group. The operation was abandoned after all boats in contact were driven off by the strong surface and air escort.

U 628 returned to Brest **19.5.43**

4. 1.7.43 Left for Atlantic operations.

Outward-bound, U 628 was sighted on the surface on the 3rd SSW of Reykjavik by a Liberator of 224 Squadron (S/Ldr P J Cundy). The boat was sunk in two attacks by the aircraft, the first with 35 lb a/s bombs and the second with 8 depth-charges. The Liberator was severely damaged by flak in the action and after returning safely to base at St Eval, it was written off.

There were no survivors from U 628, 49 dead.

U 629   Type VII C

Built by Blohm & Voss, Hamburg
Keel laid 22.8.41   Launched 12.5.42
Commissioned 2.7.42   Feldpost Nr M 07 337

Sunk 7.6.44 W of Ushant (48°34′N 05°23′W)

Served with
5 U-Flottille, Kiel July - November 1942 (ab)
11 U-Flottille, Bergen   December 1942 - October 1943 (fb/fb-m)
1 U-Flottille, Brest   November 1943 - 7.6.44 (fb)

Commanded by
OL Hans-Helmuth Bugs   July 1942 - 7.6.44

Patrols: 10   Ships sunk: None

1. 12.12.42 Left Kiel and arrived Bergen **17.12.42**

2. 19.12.42 Left Bergen and arrived Narvik **22.12.42**

3. 23.12.42 Left Narvik for operations. No details known.
U 629 returned to Narvik **29.1.43**

4. 31.1.43 Left Narvik and arrived Bergen **3.2.43**

5. 24.2.43 Left Bergen for operations. No details known.
U 629 put in to Trondheim **15.3.43**

6. 30.3.43 Left Trondheim for operations. No details known.
U 629 returned to Bergen **29.4.43**

7. 3.7.43 Left Bergen for operations. No details known.
U 629 returned to Narvik **17.7.43**

8. 19.7.43 Left Narvik for operations.
U 629 laid mines in the Pechora Sea on the 27th. There are no known sinkings or damage to ships attributed to these mines.
The boat returned to Narvik **31.7.43**

9. 4.8.43 Left Narvik for operations.
U 629 laid mines off Russki Savorot on the 10th. There are no known sinkings or damage to ships attributed to these mines.
The boat returned to Narvik **19.8.43**

10. 24.8.43 Left Narvik for operations.
U 629 laid mines NW of Amderma roads on 5.9.43. There are no known sinkings or damage to ships attributed to these mines.
The boat returned to Skjomenfjord **17.9.43**

11. 18.9.43 Left Skjomenfjord and arrived Bergen **21.9.43**

12. 21.11.43 Left Bergen for Atlantic operations.
U 629 joined *Coronel* group W of the North Channel. The group searched for westbound ONS 24 but was unsuccessful because aerial reconnaissance failed to find it. The convoy passed to the north of the group.

In mid-December *Coronel* group was enlarged and split into two sub-groups, *Coronel 1* and *3*, awaiting convoy ON 214. U 629 was in *Coronel 1*. Air reconnaissance failed to find the convoy and it passed to the south.

On the 18th *Coronel 1* group was broken up. Six boats went to form *Föhr* group, U 629 and U 311 went to *Amrum* group and U 761 returned to base, damaged. *Amrum* group was to search for convoys west of the British Isles.

After U 284 was scuttled on the 21st SE of Cape Farewell, her entire crew was picked up by U 629, which then set out for base. On the 29th she made an unsuccessful attack on a destroyer NE of the Azores.

During the night of 4.1.44 U 629 was sighted on the surface in the Bay of Biscay by a Wellington of 304 (Polish) Squadron (F/O H Czyzun).

The boat was damaged in depth-charge and strafing attacks but managed to escape.

She reached Brest **5.1.44**

13. 5.3.44 Left Brest and returned **7.3.44**

14. 9.3.44 Left for Atlantic operations.
Outward-bound on the 12th, U 629 was attacked and damaged by a Wellington of 612 Squadron (F/Sgt D Bretherton) NNW of Cape Ortegal.
The boat returned to Brest **15.3.44**

15. 6.6.44 Left Brest, as part of *Landwirt* group.
U 629 and seven other non-schnorkel boats were ordered to the area between The Lizard and Hartland Point to operate against Allied invasion supply-shipping heading for the English Channel. For an early arrival in the operational area, the boats sailed late in the evening and were ordered to proceed on the surface at high speed. They all came under aircraft attack almost immediately after dropping their escorts off Brest.

With four boats reporting that they were damaged and returning, it was decided that from the 7th the remaining four boats, which included U 629, should proceed to their operational area, submerged in daylight.

In the early morning of the 7th U 629 was sighted on the surface by a Liberator of 53 Squadron (F/Lt J W Carmichael) W of Ushant.

In the face of heavy flak, six depth-charges were dropped, which straddled the boat and lifted her bow out of the water. U 629 had been destroyed.

There were no survivors, 53 dead.

U 630   Type VII C

Built by Blohm & Voss, Hamburg
Keel laid 21.8.41   Launched 12.5.42
Commissioned 9.7.42   Feldpost Nr M 21 203

Sunk 4.5.43 S of Cape Farewell (52°31´N 44°50´W)

Served with
5 U-Flottille, Kiel   July 1942 - March 1943 (ab)
3 U-Flottille, La Pallice   March 1943 - 4.5.43 (fb)

Commanded by
OL Werner Winkler   July 1942 - 4.5.43

Patrols: 1   Ships sunk: 1 (5529 grt)

1. 18.3.43   Left Kiel for the North Atlantic.

U 630 joined *Löwenherz* group, formed from 3.4.43 SE of Greenland. On the 4th U 530 sighted eastbound HX 231 and she brought up U 630 and other *Löwenherz* boats, the only ones available to operate against the convoy. Early on the 5th U 630 torpedoed and sank the MV *Shillong* (br 5529t) ESE of Cape Farewell.

The pursuit of HX 231 continued until the 7th, with six ships sunk and four damaged. The constant presence of carrier-borne aircraft made attacks difficult. The majority of the *Löwenherz* boats, including U 630, formed a new patrol line, *Lerche*, SE of Cape Farewell from the 10th, to intercept eastbound HX 232.

On the 11th U 584 sighted the convoy as it passed through the line. Three ships were sunk on the 12th, by U 563 and U 706, but further attacks on the convoy were prevented by aircraft and the operation against HX 232 ended on the 13th W of the North Channel.

Between the 17th and 20th U 630 and four other *Lerche* boats were refuelled by U 487 in the central North Atlantic, after which they joined a new patrol line, *Specht*, formed from the 20th N of the Azores. From the 22nd the group awaited eastbound SC 127 but when it did not materialise the boats moved northwestwards at high speed and formed a new line from the 25th ahead of convoy ONS 4. Again, the convoy was re-routed to miss the line.

From the 27th *Specht* was deployed NE of Newfoundland against HX 235 but the convoy was re-routed to the south. On the 29th *Specht* and *Amsel* groups formed a line NE of Newfoundland to intercept eastbound SC 128. Both groups moved southwards to search but when the convoy had not been found by 1.5.43 the *Specht* boats went north again and a new long patrol line, *Fink*, was formed on the 3rd from the boats of *Specht* and *Star* groups, S of Cape Farewell.

SC 128 did not appear but in the afternoon of the 4th ONS 5 passed through the centre of the *Fink* line. On this day U 630 was sunk in depth-charge attacks by a destroyer of the escort, HMS *Vidette* (Lt-Cdr R Hart), S of Cape Farewell.

There were no survivors, 47 dead.

U 631   Type VII C

Built by Blohm & Voss, Hamburg
Keel laid 5.9.41   Launched 27.5.42
Commissioned 16.7.42   Feldpost Nr M 22 458

Sunk 17.10.43 ESE of Cape Farewell (58°13´N 32°29´W)

Served with
5 U-Flottille, Kiel   July - December 1942 (ab)
9 U-Flottille, Brest   January 1943 - 17.10.43 (fb)

Commanded by
OL Jürgen Krüger   July 1942 - 17.10.43

Patrols: 3   Ships sunk: 2 (9145 grt)

1. 19.12.42   Left Kiel for the North Atlantic.

Outward-bound, U 631 torpedoed and sank the SS *Ingerfem* (nw 3987t) in the evening of the 29th, WNW of Rockall, a straggler from westbound convoy ONS 156. The boat joined *Falke* group 500 miles W of Ireland, where it was awaiting an ON convoy. The group was sent against ONS 158 and ON 159 but both were re-routed and avoided the boats.

Between January 7th and 15th 1943 *Falke* group swept westwards, searching for convoys. On the 16th it turned north but saw nothing. Three days later *Falke* and *Habicht* groups were formed into two new patrol lines, *Haudegen* and *Landsknecht,* the latter made up of those boats with less fuel, including U 631.

Landsknecht, augmented by newly-arrived boats, waited W of Ireland but expected convoys were not found. At the end of January the boats began to return to base.

U 631 put in to Brest **4.2.43**

2. 6.3.43   Left for the North Atlantic.

U 631 joined *Stürmer* group in the central North Atlantic, formed from the 14th to operate against SC 122. The group moved westwards in search of the convoy until the 16th, when it turned southwestwards to intercept a convoy sighted by the returning U 653 in the morning of that day.

Stürmer, Dränger and *Raubgraf* groups were ordered to attack the convoy and *Raubgraf* made contact later the same morning, with what was assumed to be SC 122. Later in the day a second convoy appeared, sailing on a parallel course and faster. It was only then realised that the convoy already under attack was HX 229, not SC 122. The full force of the three groups was then deployed against the two convoys.

In the afternoon of the 17th U 631 torpedoed and sank the SS *Terkoelei* (nl 5158t) from HX 229. The SC 122/HX 229 operation was the largest convoy action of the war, with forty boats taking part and twenty-one Allied ships sunk. The operation was terminated in the early hours of the 20th, with one boat lost. On the 20th U 631 was attacked by a Sunderland of 210 Squadron (F/O W G Robertson) but escaped damage.

U 631 and other ex-*Stürmer* boats joined new-arrivals to form *Seewolf* group from the 25th, SE of Cape Farewell and south of the *Seeteufel* line, to operate against reported eastbound SC 123. From the 26th *Seewolf* and *Seeteufel* groups joined to form a line running 800 miles south from Cape Farewell.

On the 27th U 305, at the northern end of the *Seewolf* line, sighted eastbound HX 230. U 631 was one of twenty-two boats from the two groups which were ordered to close the convoy. However, in the face of a heavy storm, which developed into a hurricane on the 28th, and kept away by a strong air escort from the 29th, the boats involved sank only one ship, that by U 610. Contact was lost on the 30th and the operation ended. U 631 was the last boat in contact.

Towards mid-April U 631 was refuelled by U 462 N of the Azores.

U 631 (continued)

She then joined *Meise* group NE of Newfoundland. On the 17th U 71 of the group collided with U 631 and left for home two days later, possibly damaged.

On the 20th it was learned that expected convoy HX 234 would pass to the west of the patrol line. The *Meise* boats moved northwestwards at high speed and the convoy was sighted on the 21st by U 306. On her way to close the convoy, U 706 sighted westbound ONS 3. The *Meise* boats divided, some going for each convoy.

The majority, including U 631, went for HX 234. USN Catalinas of VP-84 and Liberators of 120 Squadron were very active over the convoy, driving the boats off. The operation ended on the 25th S of Iceland, with two ships sunk and one damaged. In early May U 631 was refuelled by U 461 in the central North Atlantic for return to base.

The boat reached Brest **11.5.43**

3. 18.9.43 Left for Atlantic operations.

U 631 joined *Rossbach* group, formed from the 27th SE of Cape Farewell to operate against ON 203. The line was moved 100 miles to the northwest and waited there until the 30th but saw no sign of either ON 203 or ONS 19. Both had passed to the north.

The group moved northeastwards on 1.10.43 to a position SW of Iceland, to intercept ON 204. This convoy also avoided the boats and when it was realised that pursuit was useless, *Rossbach* went southwestwards on the 5th to form a new patrol line to intercept eastbound convoys HX 259 and SC 143.

On the 7th SC 143 was assumed to be in the area when destroyers were seen by U 448 and although a reconnaissance aircraft sighted the convoy, its homing signals failed to reach the boats. The main convoy was not found but some attacks were made and before the operation ended on the 9th, one ship and a destroyer were sunk but three boats were lost.

U 631 joined *Schlieffen* group ESE of Cape Farewell from the 15th. Whilst the patrol line was forming, outward-bound U 844 sighted a westbound convoy W of Rockall, which was assumed to be ONS 20 but was in fact ON 206. She was ordered to shadow and home the *Schlieffen* boats in to the convoy.

After U 844 was located and driven off, finding the convoy was difficult because Iceland-based aircraft kept the searching, widely-scattered boats submerged and only by remaining on the surface could contact be re-established, which it never was.

Early on the 16th U 964 sighted and reported ONS 20, which altered course to the northwest later in the day. Meanwhile, Dönitz had ordered boats to stay on the surface and fight their way to the convoy. During daylight on the 16th reports began arriving of boats being attacked and damaged and the first to be sunk was the shadower, U 964.

The *Schlieffen* boats moved further eastwards to form a new line for the 17th, with smaller distances between boats. ONS 20 passed just north of the line early in the morning of the 17th and an attack was ordered. On this day U 631 was located by radar 35 miles from the convoy. She was sunk ESE of Cape Farewell in a depth-charge attack by the corvette HMS *Sunflower* (Lt-Cdr J Plomer), then on her way with EG B7 to support convoy ONS 20.

There were no survivors from U 631, 53 dead.

U 632 Type VII C

Built by Blohm & Voss, Hamburg
Keel laid 4.9.41   Launched 27.5.42
Commissioned 23.7.42   Feldpost Nr M 22 623

Sunk 6.4.43 W of Rockall (58°02′N 28°42′W)

Served with
5 U-Flottille, Kiel   July - December 1942 (ab)
1 U-Flottille, Brest   January 1943 - 6.4.43 (fb)

Commanded by
KL Hans Karpf   July 1942 - 6.4.43

Patrols: 3   Ships sunk: 3 (22,028 grt)

1. 24.12.42   Left Kiel and arrived Marviken **26.12.42**

2. 29.12.42   Left for the North Atlantic.

U 632 joined *Falke* group 500 miles W of Ireland, formed on the 31st to await an ON convoy. The boats waited until January 4th 1943 but after missing ON 159, which was re-routed, they moved northwestwards and formed a north-south patrol line to await ONS 158. This convoy was also re-routed.

Between the 7th and 15th *Falke* group swept westwards, searching for convoys. On the 16th it turned north but saw nothing. On the 10th U 632 encountered and sank a straggler from convoy UGS 3 W of Rockall, the tanker SS *C J Barkdull* (pa 6773t).

On the 19th *Falke* and *Habicht* groups combined to form two new patrol lines, *Haudegen* and *Landsknecht*, the latter for those boats with less fuel, which included U 632. *Landsknecht* was augmented by newly-arrived boats and the group waited W of Ireland but expected convoys were not found. At the end of January some boats set out for base.

U 632 was one of five ex-*Landsknecht* boats which were ordered to pursue eastbound convoy HX 224, sighted by U 456 on 1.2.43 in the central North Atlantic. In the evening of the 3rd U 632 torpedoed and sank a straggler from the convoy WNW of Rockall, the tanker MV *Cordelia* (br 8190t). The sole survivor from this vessel was picked up by U 632. He gave information about a large, slow convoy due in two days time, SC 118, which was reported to BdU. In the ensuing action against that convoy, eleven ships were sunk and two boats lost.

U 632 did not take part in the operation against SC 118. On or about 10.2.43 she was refuelled by U 460 in the central North Atlantic for return to base.

The boat reached Brest **14.2.43**

3. 15.3.43   Left for Atlantic operations.

U 632 joined *Seeteufel* group SW of Iceland. The group had been searching for convoy ONS 1 but without much success. By the 26th the *Seeteufel* line ran southeastwards from Cape Farewell and it joined the more southerly *Seewolf* group to form a line running 800 miles south from the Cape. In the afternoon of the 26th masts and an aircraft carrier were sighted in the centre of the *Seeteufel* line. This was thought to be an ON convoy but a strong air and surface escort prevented its direction being discovered by the boats and it was not pursued.

It was decided on the 28th that *Seeteufel* group should concentrate its efforts on eastbound convoy HX 230, sighted by U 305 of *Seewolf* on the 27th. However, the weather worsened and a hurricane developed. The boats continued to pursue, hoping to find stragglers but only one was sunk because of difficulties of attack in heavy seas. The operation ended on the 30th NW of Ireland.

On 3.4.43 U 632 joined other boats to form *Löwenherz* group 400 miles SE of Cape Farewell. The group moved westwards and

96

on the 4th made contact with HX 231, sighted by the returning U 530. During the early hours of the 6th U 632 attacked the convoy SSW of Reykjavik, sinking the straggling SS *Blitar* (nl 7065t) and missing the corvette HMS *Alisma*.

Later the same day U 632 was sunk in a depth-charge attack by a Liberator of 86 Squadron (F/Lt C W Burcher) W of Rockall.

There were no survivors, 48 dead.

U 633   Type VII C

Built by Blohm & Voss, Hamburg
Keel laid 23.9.41   Launched 10.6.42
Commissioned 30.7.42   Feldpost Nr M 22 922

Lost 10.3.43 WNW of Rockall (58°51′N 19°55′W)

Served with
5 U-Flottille, Kiel July 1942 - February 1943 (ab)
9 U-Flottille, Brest February 1942 - 10.3.43 (fb)

Commanded by
OL Bernhard Müller July 1942 - 10.3.43

Patrols: 1   Ships sunk: None

1. 20.2.43 Left Kiel for the North Atlantic.
U 633 was to have joined *Neuland* group, formed on 6.3.43 W of Ireland, but it is not clear whether she did this.

The boat sank on the 10th WNW of Rockall, after being rammed by the steamer SS *Scorton* of convoy SC 121.

There were no survivors, 43 dead.

U 634   Type VII C

Built by Blohm & Voss, Hamburg
Keel laid 23.9.41   Launched 10.6.42
Commissioned 6.8.42   Feldpost Nr M 23 270

Sunk 30.8.43 ENE of the Azores (40°13′N 19°24′W)

Served with
5 U-Flottille, Kiel August 1942 - January 1943 (ab)
9 U-Flottille, Brest February 1943 - 30.8.43 (fb)

Commanded by
OL Hans-Günther Brosin August 1942 - January 1943
OL Eberhard Dahlhaus January 1943 - 30.8.43

Patrols: 3   Ships sunk: 1 (7176 grt)

1. 9.2.43 Left Kiel and arrived Bergen **13.2.43**

2. 18.2.43 Left Bergen for the North Atlantic.
Outward-bound, U 634 and U 709 joined *Neptun* group boats from the 28th in their pursuit of HX 227. In the early morning of 2.3.43 U 634 torpedoed and sank a straggler from the convoy SW of Reykjavik, the SS *Meriwether Lewis* (am 7176t), which had been shadowed on the 1st by U 759.

From the 5th U 634, U 709 and some *Neptun* boats took up waiting positions S of Cape Farewell and north of *Wildfang* and *Burggraf* groups. On the 6th U 405 sighted eastbound SC 121 and seventeen boats drawn from *Neptun, Wildfang* and *Burggraf* groups, including U 634 and U 709, were detached to pursue the convoy, as *Westmark* group. Another patrol line of eleven *Neuland* boats was formed from the 8th SE of Greenland, ahead of SC 121, as *Ostmark* group. Contact was made during the night of the 6/7th by U 566

and U 230.

On the 7th, in spite of bad weather, U 634 and five other boats maintained contact but could not make any attacks. The weather improved and from the 8th both *Westmark* and *Ostmark* boats made attacks. Before the operation ended on the 11th near Rockall, twelve ships had been sunk and one damaged, without the loss of any boats. U 634 had no success. On the 10th she lost a crewman overboard.

The boat put in to Lorient **23.3.43**

3. 15.4.43 Left for Atlantic operations.
U 634 joined *Amsel* group, formed on the 26th W of Ireland. The group moved south, searching for a convoy which might have been HX 235. On the 28th U 377 made a hydrophone contact with SC 127 but she and four other *Amsel* boats deployed against it were all driven off. The *Amsel* patrol line continued southwestwards towards Newfoundland.

Amsel joined up with *Specht* group on the 29th and they turned south to search for SC 128 E of Newfoundland. A southerly gale made contact impossible and on 3.5.43 *Amsel* group was dissolved and its boats combined with new arrivals to form four smaller formations, *Amsel 1,2,3* and *4,* positioned in an arc around Cape Race from the 4th. U 634 was in *Amsel 2.*

On the 5th *Amsel 1* and *2* groups moved north to meet the approaching westbound ONS 5. During the night of the 4/5th the convoy had been attacked by *Fink* group and dispersed. On the 5th daylight conditions were perfect but in the late afternoon a fog came down and almost all contact was lost. The pursuit was abandoned on the 6th.

From the 7th *Amsel 1* and *2* groups reformed as *Elbe* group E of Newfoundland, to await two eastbound convoys. On the 8th the boats moved southeastwards to intercept HX 237. The convoy was too far ahead, so they headed southeast at high speed to cut off SC 129. *Rhein* and *Elbe* groups combined on the 10th to form a longer patrol line in two parts, *Elbe 1* and *2.* U 634 was in *Elbe 1.* Whilst the boats were forming up on the 11th, they passed SC 129, which was sighted by U 504 but she was driven off.

However, contact was made on the 12th but the eleven boats shadowing were driven off by the escort. From the 13th air cover by Swordfish from the escort-carrier HMS *Biter* kept the boats down. The operation was called off on the 14th SW of Ireland, with two ships sunk but two boats lost.

U 634 put in to Brest **23.5.43**

4. 12.6.43 Left for the Caribbean.
U 634 was one of five outward-bound boats, with U 159, U 185, U 415 and U 564, travelling in company across the Bay of Biscay.

On the 13th U 564 was attacked and damaged by a Sunderland, which she shot down. U 564 set out to return to Brest, escorted by U 185. Again attacked by aircraft, U 564 later sank and U 185 picked up survivors.

U 634, U 159 and U 415 continued westwards. In late June U 634 was refuelled by U 488 W of the Azores. She went on to patrol in the Caribbean but had no success.

The returning U 634 gave fuel to U 230 on or about the 19th, after U 117 failed to meet that boat. U 634 continued eastwards and on 30.8.43 she encountered the northbound, combined convoy MKS 22/SL 135 ENE of the Azores. The boat was located and sunk in depth-charge attacks by warships of the escort, the sloop HMS *Stork* (Cdr G W E Castens) and the corvette HMS *Stonecrop* (Lt-Cdr J P Smythe).

There were no survivors, 48 dead.

U 635   Type VII C

Built by Blohm & Voss, Hamburg
Keel laid 3.10.41   Launched 24.6.42
Commissioned 13.8.42   Feldpost Nr M 51 783

Sunk 6.4.43 WNW of Rockall (58°25′N 19°22′W)

Served with
5 U-Flottille, Kiel   August 1942 - March 1943 (ab)
3 U-Flottille, La Pallice   March 1943 - 6.4.43 (fb)

Commanded by
OL Heinz Eckelmann   August 1942 - 6.4.43

Patrols: 1   Ships sunk: 1 (9365 grt)

1. 16.3.43 Left Kiel for the North Atlantic.

U 635 joined *Löwenherz* group, formed from 3.4.43 SE of
Greenland. On the 4th U 530 sighted eastbound HX 231 and she
brought up U 635 and other *Löwenherz* boats, the only ones
available to operate against the convoy. Early on the 5th U 635
torpedoed and sank the SS *Waroonga* (br 9365t) ESE of Cape
Farewell.

Still pursuing the convoy, U 635 was sunk by an Iceland-based
Liberator of 120 Squadron (F/O G L Hatherly) in a depth-charge
attack on the 6th WNW of Rockall.

There were no survivors, 48 dead.

U 636   Type VII C

Built by Blohm & Voss, Hamburg
Keel laid 2.10.41   Launched 25.6.42
Commissioned 20.8.42   Feldpost Nr M 51 601

Sunk 21.4.45 WNW of Bloody Foreland (55°50′N 10°31′W)

Served with
5 U-Flottille, Kiel   August 1942 - March 1943 (ab)
11 U-Flottille, Bergen   April - October 1943 (fb)
13 U-Flottille, Trondheim   November 1943 - 21.4.45 (fb/fb-m)

Commanded by
KL Hans Hildebrandt   August 1942 - February 1944
OL Eberhard Schendel   February 1944 - 21.4.45

Patrols: 15   Ships sunk: 1 (7169 grt)
                        1 m/s trawler (unknown dt)

1. 17.4.43 Left Kiel and arrived Bergen **20.4.43**

2. 24.4.43 Left Bergen and arrived Trondheim **28.4.43**

3. 2.5.43 Left Trondheim for the North Atlantic.

U 636 and other outward-bound boats, U 340, U 657, U 731 and
U 760, were deployed as *Iller* group to shadow a convoy, sighted by
U 640 early on the 12th SW of Iceland and presumed to be ONS 7.
Contact was lost by U 640 on the 13th and she was sunk next day.

The *Iller* boats, having failed to find the convoy, were moved on the
15th to a new position just SE of Greenland. They joined up with
Inn, Lech, Isar and *Nahe* groups to form *Donau 1* and *2* groups, to
wait for ONS 7 coming from the east and HX 238 coming from the
west. U 636 was in *Donau 1*.

The *Donau* groups moved westwards and took up a line from the
16th, running southeastwards from Cape Farewell. ONS 7 passed
through the line during the night of the 17/18th and HX 238 passed

the southern end of the *Donau* line at about the same time. In the
belief that eastbound SC 130 would be taking the same route, the
Donau groups moved southwards on the 18th into its path.

The convoy was sighted by U 304 during the night of the 18/19th
and the *Donau* boats were ordered to close. SC 130 had continuous
air cover and aircraft attacks out of low cloud made shadowing
almost impossible. On the 19th U 636, preparing for an underwater
attack, was located and subjected to depth-charge attacks by the
destroyer HMS *Duncan* and the corvette HMS *Snowflake*. She
escaped undamaged. The pursuit was abandoned on the 20th, by
which time no ships had been sunk but three boats had been lost,
U 258, U 381 and U 954.

On the 18th HX 239 had been located 200 miles SE of Cape
Race. The surviving *Donau* boats, including U 636, were ordered
southwestwards to meet the approaching convoy. The escort for
HX 239 was joined by the escort-carrier HMS *Archer* and the
strength of the convoy's air cover caused the operation to be called
off on the 23rd before any attacks had been made on the ships.

From the 24th Dönitz temporarily halted operations against
convoys in the North Atlantic. U 636 and other *Mosel* and *Donau*
boats with limited fuel ranged over a wide area, their continuing
radio signals planned to give the impression that a large U-boat
presence was being maintained across the convoy routes.

U 636 returned to Bergen **8.6.43**

4. 24.7.43 Left Bergen for Northern Waters.

On August 3rd U 636 laid mines NE of Sengeyskij in the Pechora
Sea. There are no known sinkings or damage to ships attributed to
these mines.

U 636 put in to Narvik **7.8.43**

5. 14.8.43 Left Narvik for operations.

U 636 laid mines in the Yenisey Estuary in the Kara Sea on the
28th. The SS *Tbilisi* (sov 7169t) sank on 6.9.43, probably after
striking one of these mines. The minesweeper trawler *SKR 14*, which
sank on 17.10.43, was also a probable victim of the mines.

U 636 returned to Narvik **30.8.43**

6. 5.9.43 Left Narvik and arrived Bergen **9.9.43**

7. 24.10.43 Left Bergen and arrived Trondheim **25.10.43**

8. 27.10.43 Left for operations.

U 636 laid mines off Yugor Strait on 14.11.43. There are no
known sinkings or damage to ships attributed to these mines.

The boat put in to Hammerfest **17.11.43**

9. 18.11.43 Left for operations.

U 636 joined *Eisenbart* group between Spitzbergen and Bear
Island. On the 26th westbound convoy RA 54B left Archangel but
passed the waiting boats, almost unseen.

Only U 307 sighted some escort vessels briefly on the 28th. She
was located and driven off, damaged. The convoy reached Loch
Ewe safely on 9.12.43.

In mid-December U 636, U 277, U 354 and U 387 were waiting
E of Bear Island for eastbound JW 55A. The convoy passed the
boats, with only U 636 briefly sighting escort vessels on the 18th,
which she was unable to approach.

U 636 returned to Hammerfest **27.12.43**

10. 30.12.43 Left for operations. No details known.

U 636 returned to Narvik **8.1.44**

11. 26.1.44 Left for operations. No details known.

U 636 returned to Hammerfest **2.2.44**

12. 4.2.44 Left Hammerfest and arrived Narvik **5.2.44**

14. 31.3.44   Left Trondheim and arrived Narvik **2.4.44**

15. 8.4.44   Left Narvik for operations.
   U 636 joined *Donner* group, which was attempting to operate against westbound convoy RA 58. The convoy had set out from Kola Inlet on the 7th and was located by aircraft on the 9th. Boats from *Donner* and *Keil* groups made some unsuccessful attacks against destroyers on the 10th.
   Contact was lost but the convoy was found again by reconnaissance aircraft early on the 11th. By then any pursuit was impractical, the boats being too far behind.
   In late April U 636, U 277, U 278 and U 307 were deployed against westbound convoy RA 59, as *Donner* group. Late in the evening of the 30th boats from *Donner* and *Keil* groups attacked the convoy and escort. One ship was sunk, by U 711 of *Keil*, but attacks made by other boats were unsuccessful.
   U 636 returned to Narvik **3.5.44**

16. 5.5.44   Left Narvik and arrived Trondheim **7.5.44**

17. 23.6.44   Left Trondheim and arrived Narvik **24.6.44**

18. 27.6.44   Left for operations.
   In July U 636 patrolled in the Norwegian Sea, E of Jan Mayen. On the 20th the boat was sighted on the surface by a Liberator of 86 Squadron (S/Ldr T M Bulloch). The aircraft had been spotted from the boat before it was sighted by the Liberator. U 636's commander decided to fight it out and drove off the aircraft, which was severely damaged and made no attack on the boat.
   U 636 returned to Narvik **24.7.44**

19. 25.8.44   Left for operations.
   U 636 was part of *Dachs* group, formed to carry out minelaying in the Pechora Sea. Mines were laid between September 1st and 5th but details are not known.
   The boat returned to Narvik **12.9.44**

20. 16.9.44   Left Narvik and arrived Tromsø **18.9.44**

21. 25.9.44   Left for operations.
   U 636 was one of *Zorn* group, which sailed to intercept westbound RA 60 SW of Bear Island. The convoy, which left Kola Inlet during the night of the 27/28th, avoided the *Zorn* boats and also those of the waiting *Grimm* group. It arrived at Loch Ewe on 5.10.44, less two ships sunk by U 310.
   U 636 returned to Tromsø **3.10.44**

22. 6.10.44   Left for operations.
   Between October 9th and 14th U 636 established and recovered a weather station on Hopen Island.
   On the 20th westbound JW 61 left Loch Ewe. U 636 was part of *Panther* group, awaiting the convoy E of Bear Island. The heavily-escorted convoy passed through the patrol line. Unsuccessful attacks were made on the escort on the 26th and 27th. JW 61 arrived without loss at Kola Inlet on the 28th.
   Return convoy RA 61 sailed on 2.11.44. The strong escort foiled any attempts by *Panther* group to reach the ships. The convoy reached Loch Ewe safely on the 9th.
   U 636 returned to Tromsø **12.11.44**

23. 14.11.44   Left Tromsø and arrived Bogenbucht **16.11.44**

24. 4.12.44   Left for operations.
   On the 10th U 636 landed supplies for a German weather team on Spitzbergen.
   She put in to Kilbotn **16.12.44**

25. 25.12.44   Left for operations.

Eastbound convoy JW 63 sailed from Loch Ewe on the 30th. U 636, U 293 and U 310 waited for it N of Kola. The convoy arrived in Kola Inlet on 8.1.45, without being seen either by *Stier* group, waiting in Bear Island Passage, or the boats N of Kola.
   From the 15th U 636 was one of six boats operating against Soviet shipping and convoys off the Kola coast. She had no success against convoys that were seen. Between the 21st and 24th four Russian destroyers searched for U-boats between Jokanga and Kola. On the 23rd U 636 made an unsuccessful attack on a search vessel, after which she was hunted by sub-chasers.
   U 636 returned to Narvik **30.1.45**

26. 1.2.45   Left Narvik and arrived Trondheim **3.2.45**

27. 1.4.45   Left Trondheim for Atlantic operations.
   U 636 operated W of the North Channel but had no success. On the 21st she was located WNW of Bloody Foreland by the 4th EG and sunk in depth-charge attacks by the frigates HMS *Bazely* (Lt-Cdr J V Brock), *Bentinck* (Lt-Cdr P R G Worth) and *Drury* (Lt N J Parker).
   There were no survivors, 42 dead.

U 637   Type VII C

Built by Blohm & Voss, Hamburg
Keel laid 17.10.41   Launched 7.7.42
Commissioned 27.8.42   Feldpost Nr M 51 550

Sunk 21.12.45 NW of Malin Head (55°35′N 07°46′W)

Served with
5 U-Flottille, Kiel   August 1942 - May 1944 (ab)
1 U-Flottille, Brest   June - July 1944 (fb-oE)
8 U-Flottille, Danzig   July 1944 - January 1945 (fb)
5 U-Flottille, Kiel   January 1945 - 9.5.45 (fb/fb-m)

Commanded by
KL Max Dieterich   August 1942 - February 1943
KL Günther Zedelius   February 1943 - July 1944
OL Fritz Fabricius   July - September 1944
KL Wolfgang Riekeberg   October 1944 - 26.4.45
OL Klaus Weber (temp)   26.4.45 - 9.5.45

Patrols: 2   Ships sunk: None
                   1 patrol boat (56 dt)

1. 7.6.44   Left Kiel and arrived Valløy **9.6.44**

2. 1.7.44   Left Valløy and arrived Arendal **1.7.44**

3. 19.7.44   Left Arendal and arrived Kiel **20.7.44**

4. 13.10.44   Left Kiel and arrived Danzig **16.10.44**

5. 25.11.44   Left Danzig for operations.
   U 637 patrolled in the Batltic but had no success until 20.12.44, when she torpedoed and sank the Russian patrol boat BMO-594/*Batiek* near Pakoj.
   The boat returned to Danzig **13.1.45**

6. 5.4.45   Left Kiel and arrived Stavanger **13.4.45**

7. 23.4.45   Left Stavanger for a minelaying operation.
   Fire broke out in U 637 when she was 36 hours out from port. With the fire put out, the boat headed back to Norway. On the 26th she was attacked by two Norwegian MTBs, Nos 711 and 723, near Utsira Island, WSW of Haugesund.

U 637 (continued)

The MTBs fired torpedoes, which U 637 avoided. In a running battle, four depth-charges were dropped by No 711, which badly damaged the boat. With shore batteries at Karmøy firing at them, a German trawler approaching and U 637 apparently sinking, the MTBs left at high speed for their base at Lerwick in the Shetlands, with one man killed on No 711.

U 637's commander and 7 men had been killed. Escorted by the trawler, the Chief Engineer, OL Weber, assumed command and took the boat in to Ackrehaven, where temporary repairs were made.

U 637 returned to Stavanger **28.4.45**

U 637 was surrendered at Stavanger on 9.5.45 and left there on 29.6.45 for the assembly area at Loch Ryan.

She was one of 116 boats disposed of by the Royal Navy in Operation Deadlight. *In December she was towed out through the North Channel by the tug HMS* Buster.

On 21.12.45 U 637 foundered under tow in 38 fathoms NNW of Malin Head.

U 638 Type VII C

Built by Blohm & Voss, Hamburg
Keel laid 16.10.41   Launched 8.7.42
Commissioned 3.9.42   Feldpost Nr 51 249

Sunk 5.5.43 S of Cape Farewell (54°12′N 44°05′W)

Served with
5 U-Flottille, Kiel   September 1942 - January 1943 (ab)
9 U-Flottille, Brest   February 1943 - 5.5.43 (fb)

Commanded by
OL Oskar Staudinger   September - December 1942
                                        and April 1943 - 5.5.43
KL Hinrich-Oscar Bernbeck   December 1942 - March 1943

Patrols: 2   Ships sunk: 2 (12,044 grt)

1. 4.2.43   Left Kiel for the North Atlantic.

U 638 joined *Wildfang* group, formed from the 25th E of Newfoundland. The group moved north on the 26th, in the hope of catching convoys using a more northerly route.

From 4.3.43 *Wildfang* joined up with *Burggraf* group, to form a long, angled patrol line in the path of an SC convoy expected on the 5th. During the night of the 4/5th the line moved northeastwards but the convoy, SC 121, passed to the north.

Some boats pursued SC 121 but those that did not, including U 638, formed a new line, *Raubgraf*, on the 7th NE of Newfoundland to operate against HX 228. A search over the next few days found nothing, the convoy having passed south of the line. On the 7th U 638 torpedoed and damaged the tanker SS *Empire Light* (br 6537t) S of Greenland, a straggler from westbound convoy ON 168. The abandoned wreck of this vessel was sunk on the 12th by U 468.

On the 13th convoy ON 170 was briefly sighted by U 603 but she and other boats which came up were effectively kept away by the escort, EG B2. Now NE of Newfoundland, the *Raubgraf* boats were ordered to shadow an SC convoy, reported on the 14th. Contact was made early on the 16th and the convoy, thought to be SC 122 but in fact HX 229, was attacked later in the morning.

Later in the day a second convoy appeared, sailing on a parallel course and slower. It was only then realised that the convoy already under attack was HX 229, not SC 122. U 638 does not appear to have made any attack on either of the two convoys in the operation, which developed into the biggest convoy action of the war, with forty U-boats taking part. The operation ended on the 20th, with twenty-one Allied ships sunk for the loss of one boat, U 384. Soon afterwards U 638 was refuelled by U 119 N of the Azores for return to base.

The boat put in to La Pallice **31.3.43**

2. 20.4.43   Left for the North Atlantic.

U 638 joined *Amsel 1* group in early May E of Newfoundland, in a patrol line ahead of southwest-bound convoy ONS 5. During the night of the 4/5th the first boats of *Amsel 1* and 2 and *Fink* groups located the convoy.

In the afternoon of the 5th U 638 torpedoed and sank the MV *Dolius* (br 5507t) S of Cape Farewell. She, herself, was sunk soon afterwards in a depth-charge attack by an escorting corvette, HMS *Sunflower* (Lt-Cdr J Plomer).

There were no survivors, 44 dead.

U 639 Type VII C

Built by Blohm & Voss, Hamburg
Keel laid 31.10.41   Launched 22.7.42
Commissioned 10.9.42   Feldpost Nr M 50 196

Sunk 30.8.43 in the Kara Sea

Served with
5 U-Flottille, Kiel   September 1942 - March 1943 (ab)
11 U-Flottille, Bergen   April - May 1943 (fb)
13 U-Flottille, Trondheim   June 1943 - 30.8.43 (fb/fb-m)

Commanded by
OL Walter Wichmann   September 1942 - 30.8.43

Patrols: 4   Ships sunk: None

1. 18.3.43   Left Kiel and arrived Bergen **22.3.43**

2. 24.3.43   Left Bergen for operations. No details known.
U 639 put in to Hammerfest **25.4.43**

3. 12.5.43   Left Hammerfest for operations. No details known.
U 639 put in to Narvik **8.6.43**

4. 14.6.43   Left Narvik and arrived Trondheim **15.6.43**

5. 24.7.43   Left Trondheim for operations.
U 639 laid mines in the Pechora Sea on 1.8.43. There are no sinkings or damage to ships attributed to these mines.
The boat returned to Narvik **5.8.43**

6. 11.8.43   Left Narvik for operations.
U 639 laid mines in Ob Bay in the Kara Sea on the 21st. There are no sinkings or damage to ships attributed to these mines.

The returning U 639 was sunk in the Kara Sea on the 30th by the Russian submarine *S 101*. She fired three torpedoes, one of which hit U 639.

There were no survivors, 47 dead.

U 640　Type VII C

Built by Blohm & Voss, Hamburg
Keel laid 30.10.41　Launched 23.7.42
Commissioned 17.9.42　Feldpost Nr M 50 291

Sunk 14.5.43 E of Cape Farewell (60°32′N 31°05′W)

Served with
5 U-Flottille, Kiel　September 1942 - April 1943 (ab)
6 U-Flottille, St Nazaire　May 1943 (fb)

Commanded by
OL Karl-Heinz Nagel　September 1942 - 14.5.43

Patrols: 1　Ships sunk: None

1. 1.5.43　Left Kiel for the North Atlantic.

Outward-bound, U 640 sighted westbound convoy ONS 7 SW of Iceland during the night of the 11/12th. Despite being driven off several times, U 640 maintained contact with the convoy until the 13th, enabling U 340, U 636, U 657, U 731 and U 760 to be deployed against it, as *Iller* group.

In the evening of the 13th U 640 attacked the convoy, reporting two hits followed by sinking noises, but there is no confirmation. On the 14th U 640 was sunk in a depth-charge attack by a USN Catalina of VP-84 (Lt E T Allen) E of Cape Farewell.

There were no survivors, 49 dead.

U 641　Type VII C

Built by Blohm & Voss, Hamburg
Keel laid 19.11.41　Launched 6.8.42
Commissioned 24.9.42　Feldpost Nr M 50 387

Sunk 19.1.44 WSW of Ireland (50°25′N 18°49′W)

Served with
5 U-Flottille, Kiel　September 1942 - February 1943 (ab)
7 U-Flottille, St Nazaire　March 1943 - 19.1.44 (fb)

Commanded by
KL Horst Rendtel　September 1942 - 19.1.44

Patrols: 4　Ships sunk: None

1. 20.2.43　Left Kiel for the North Atlantic.

U 641 joined *Neuland* group W of Ireland. On 7.3.43 U 641 and ten other boats in the northern section of the patrol line were sent northwestwards, as *Ostmark* group, to form a line for the 8th ahead of SC 121, sighted by U 405 on the 6th S of Greenland. Later on the 7th U 641 was attacked by a Fortress of 220 Squadron (F/O W Knowles) but escaped undamaged.

Seventeen boats of *Wildfang, Burggraf* and *Neptun* groups operated against SC 121, as well as those of *Ostmark* group. In the operation twelve ships were sunk and one damaged before it ended on the 11th S of Iceland.

The *Ostmark* boats, some new-arrivals and three *Burggraf* boats formed *Stürmer* group from the 14th in the central North Atlantic, to operate against SC 122. The group moved westwards in search of the convoy until the 16th, when it turned southwestwards to intercept. Contact was made during the night of the 16/17th and some successful attacks were made by *Stürmer* boats over the next three days, none by U 641. This was the biggest convoy action of the war, with forty boats operating against convoys SC 122 and HX 229. Twenty-one Allied ships were sunk for the loss of U 384.

U 641 and other ex-*Stürmer* boats joined new-arrivals to form *Seewolf* group from the 25th, SE of Cape Farewell and south of the *Seeteufel* line, to operate against reported eastbound SC 123. From the 26th *Seewolf* and *Seeteufel* groups joined to form a line running 800 miles south from Cape Farewell.

U 305, at the northern end of the *Seewolf* line, sighted eastbound HX 230 on the 27th. U 641 was one of twenty-two boats from the two groups which were ordered to close the convoy. However, in the face of a heavy storm, which developed into a hurricane on the 28th, and kept away by a strong air escort from the 29th, the boats involved sank only one ship, that by U 610. Contact was lost on the 30th and the operation ended. U 641 was refuelled by U 463 in the central North Atlantic for return to base.

U 641 put in to St Nazaire **12.4.43**

2. 9.5.43　Left for the North Atlantic.

U 641 and U 305 joined the boats of *Oder* group in the central North Atlantic. The group was formed on the 18th and was to operate against SC 130. The convoy was located on the 18th to the north of *Oder* group and the more northerly *Donau* and *Iller* groups were ordered to attack it. They had no success, being constantly driven off by aircraft, which took advantage of a low cloud base. The operation was abandoned on the 20th after three boats had been lost. SC 130 is usually thought to be the last convoy seriously threatened in the Battle of the Atlantic.

U 641, U 305 and the *Oder* boats became part of the new *Mosel* group, formed 400 miles S of Cape Farewell to intercept HX 239, reported on the 18th to be moving eastwards from Newfoundland and expected to pass south of the *Mosel* patrol line. The convoy turned north and then northeast on the 21st. *Mosel* group split into two parts, with the southern boats, including U 641, moving southeastwards to intercept any stragglers, whilst the northern boats went eastwards to join *Donau* group in an attack on the main convoy.

On the 22nd U 305 sighted a destroyer and reported before being driven off. Boats carried out searches to the east and northeast but, constantly harassed by aircraft, they did not find HX 239. The destroyer sighted was part of the escort of westbound ON 184, which had passed through the *Mosel* line the previous evening. With HX 239 still not found on the 23rd, the operation was abandoned.

The *Mosel* boats moved to an area SW of the Azores. Convoy operations in the North Atlantic were suspended from the 24th whilst the situation was assessed by BdU. It was decided to try and intercept US-Mediterranean convoys out in the Atlantic, beyond the range of land-based aircraft.

From the boats which had assembled SW of the Azores, a new patrol line, *Trutz*, was formed during the night of 30/31st, to await expected convoys UGS 9 and GUS 7A. The line was drawn up on the 43° meridian and ran between 32° and 38°N. On 4.6.43 the three most southerly *Trutz* boats, U 641, U 603 and U 228, were attacked by carrier-borne aircraft, which were thought to be part of a convoy's protective cover.

U 641 was sighted by a patrolling Avenger (Lt W Fowler) from the escort-carrier USS *Bogue*, off the Azores and only 25 miles from the carrier. A depth-bomb attack caused the boat to circle slowly. Another Avenger (Lt-Cdr W M Drane) arrived and dropped more depth-bombs. The boat stopped circling, fired at the aircraft before diving and apparently escaped undamaged. Drane's aircraft was so badly damaged by the heavy, accurate flak put up from the boat that he was fortunate to reach *Bogue* again.

The boats closed up to prevent any ships passing through gaps in the line but when nothing had been sighted by the evening of the 5th, the convoy was thought to have passed either to north or south.

Trutz group broke up and moved 600 miles to the north to be refuelled by U 488. The UGS convoy was sighted by an outward-bound boat on the 8th 100 miles south of the *Trutz* patrol area of the 5th. The move to refuel had been too premature and the opportunity lost. Refuelling was completed by the 15th and the

U 641 (continued)

group was reformed in three north-south lines, *Trutz 1,2* and *3,*1000 miles E of Bermuda. U 641 was in *Trutz 2*.

The boats waited for two other convoys from the 16th until the 22nd and having seen nothing in that time, the line began an eastwards movement, which continued until the 27th, when they halted 200 miles SW of the Azores. By the 29th it was realised that the elusive convoys, GUS 8, UGS 10 and GUS 8A had by-passed the lines.

From 2.7.43 three new lines were formed, *Geier 1,2* and *3*. U 641 was in *Geier 1*. The lines moved in a scouting formation towards the Portugese coast. At 500 miles from the coast air attacks began and by the 8th were such that boat commanders were allowed to return to base if circumstances warranted.

U 641 returned to St Nazaire **16.7.43**

3. 31.8.43 Left St Nazaire and returned **1.9.43**

4. 4.9.43 Left for the North Atlantic.

U 641 was one of fourteen boats which set out to form a patrol line, *Leuthen*, SSW of Iceland from 20.9.43, to intercept an ONS convoy. They were joined by six other boats which had assembled N of the Azores and then after refuelling had moved north to take their place in the patrol line. Secrecy had been maintained as far as possible to prevent the presence of the boats becoming known to the Allies. However, on the 19th westbound U 341, which should have been proceeding submerged, was sighted, attacked and sunk by a Canadian aircraft near the planned patrol line position.

Early on the 20th, before the *Leuthen* boats were in position, convoy ON 202 was sighted. Four boats closed but only one was able to make a submerged attack. In the morning contact was lost because of aircraft and a strong surface escort. ON 202 joined up with convoy ONS 18 during the day. Contact with the combined convoy was regained in the early evening of the 20th.

Only five boats closed the convoy, the other *Leuthen* boats being intent on attacking the escort, in the belief that if the escort was depleted the convoy could be dealt with during the night of the 21/22nd. In the early hours of the 21st U 641 unsuccessfully attacked a destroyer in the central North Atlantic.

Fog came down early on the 21st and remained throughout the day and next night. When it thinned during daylight on the 22nd, Allied aircraft re-appeared and the boats stayed on the surface to fight it out. Further attacks were made on the convoy in the early hours of the 23rd. The operation was abandoned later in the morning, with six ships and three escorts sunk, another ship damaged and two boats lost.

On the 27th U 641 joined the newly-formed *Rossbach* group in the central North Atlantic to operate against ON 203. The convoy passed north of the patrol line. The group moved northwards on 1.10.43 to intercept westbound ONS 19 but that convoy also passed to the north.

From the 3rd the *Rossbach* boats turned eastwards to meet ON 204 but the convoy was not found. U 641 was attacked and damaged on the 4th by a Hudson of 269 Squadron. On the 5th the *Rossbach* boats, then SW of Iceland, began a sweep southwestwards to search for SC 143 and HX 259, which were expected to be intercepted on the 8th.

Destroyers of the 3rd SG were sighted by U 448 on the 7th and SC 143 was assumed to be in the area. During the night of the 7/8th the destroyers were engaged by *Rossbach* boats and the Polish destroyer *Orkan* was sunk by U 378. Liberators of 86 Squadron arrived in the morning and drove off the boats.

Neither convoy, SC 143 or HX 259, was found and the search was called off on the 9th. One ship from SC 143 was encountered and sunk by U 645 in the morning of the 9th, the only ship seen from the two convoys.

Now short of fuel, U 641, U 378, U 402, U 584, U 603 and U 731 headed southwards to refuel. From the 11th the boats made several attempts to rendezvous at different positions with U-tanker U 488 in an area 300 to 600 miles N and NW of the Azores. On or about the 16th U 641 was finally refuelled by U 488 NNW of the Azores for return to base.

The boat returned to St Nazaire **28.10.43**

5. 11.12.43 Left for the North Atlantic.

U 641 joined *Borkum* group, formed from the 20th 400 miles NW of Cape Ortegal. During the evening of the 24th the *Borkum* boats encountered southbound convoy KMS 36/OS 62 NE of the Azores. The destroyer-leader of the escort was sunk by U 415 that evening but only some unsuccessful attacks could be made against the escort during the night of the 25/26th before the operation was abandoned.

Borkum group then moved to form a new patrol line for the 30th, to intercept convoy MKS 34/SL 143. En route, the group ran into the 6th SG and two boats were attacked but escaped. The convoy was sighted by German aircraft on the 30th and 31st but it passed the *Borkum* patrol line on 1.1.44. The group took part in a failed operation against a southbound convoy on the 2nd and 3rd.

To make detection of the patrol line and avoidance of it by convoys more difficult, *Borkum* group was split into three small sub-groups, *Borkum 1,2* and *3*. U 641 was in *Borkum 2*. On the 5th, 6th and 7th the boats encountered the 5th SG, which was searching for German blockade-runners. U 305 of *Borkum 1* sank a frigate.

From the 8th German aircraft were searching for combined convoy MKS 35/SL 144. It was sighted on the 9th W of Portugal but lost again next day. A chance sighting of it in the evening of the 10th by U 305 at the end of the *Borkum* patrol line led to an order for the three groups to attack. However, with the boats widely disposed, they were unable to close the convoy.

Borkum group was broken up on the 13th. U 641, U 305, U 377 and U 382 operated W of Ireland but within the space of six days three of them had been attacked and sunk and U 382 had returned to base, damaged.

In the evening of the 17th a reconnaissance aircraft sighted convoy OS 65/KMS 39. Of the boats directed to it, only U 641 was able to close and on the 19th she was located WSW of Ireland, 10 miles ahead of the convoy, and sunk in a Hedgehog attack by the corvette HMS *Violet* (Lt C N Stewart).

There were no survivors, 50 dead.

U 642   Type VII C

Built by Blohm & Voss, Hamburg
Keel laid 19.11.41   Launched 6.8.42
Commissioned 1.10.42   Feldpost Nr M 50 471

Decommissioned 12.7.44 at Toulon

Served with
5 U-Flottille, Kiel October 1942 - February 1943 (ab)
6 U-Flottille, St Nazaire March - November 1943 (fb)
29 U-Flottille, Toulon December 1943 - 12.7.44 (fb)

Commanded by
KL Herbert Brünning October 1942 - 12.7.44

Patrols: 4   Ships sunk: 1 (2125 grt)

1. 20.2.43 Left Kiel for the North Atlantic.
U 642 joined *Neuland* group W of Ireland. On 7.3.43 she and ten other boats in the northern section of the patrol line were sent northwestwards, as *Ostmark* group, to form a line for the 8th ahead of SC 121, sighted by U 405 on the 6th S of Greenland.

Seventeen boats of *Wildfang, Burggraf* and *Neptun* groups operated against SC 121, as well as those of *Ostmark* group. In the evening of the 8th U 642 sank an unescorted ship N of Rockall, which was probably a straggler from SC 121, the SS *Leadgate* (br 2125t). During the operation against the convoy, twelve ships were sunk and another damaged.

The *Ostmark* boats, some new-arrivals and three *Burggraf* boats formed *Stürmer* group from the 14th in the central North Atlantic, to operate against SC 122. The group moved westwards in search of the convoy until the 16th, when it turned southwestwards to intercept. Contact was made during the night of the 16/17th and some successful attacks were made by *Stürmer* boats over the next three days, none by U 642. This was the biggest convoy action of the war, with forty boats operating against convoys SC 122 and HX 229. Twenty-one Allied ships were sunk for the loss of U 384. U 642 was one of the last boats to be driven off, early on the 20th.

U 642 and other ex-*Stürmer* boats joined new-arrivals to form *Seewolf* group from the 25th, SE of Cape Farewell and south of the *Seeteufel* line, to operate against reported, eastbound SC 123. From the 26th *Seewolf* and *Seeteufel* groups joined to form a line running 800 miles south from Cape Farewell.

U 305, at the northern end of the *Seewolf* line, sighted eastbound HX 230 on the 27th. U 642 was one of twenty-two boats from the two groups which were ordered to close the convoy. However, in the face of a heavy storm, which developed into a hurricane on the 28th, and kept away by a strong air escort from the 29th, the boats involved sank only one ship, that by U 610. Contact was lost on the 30th and the operation ended. U 642 was refuelled by U 463 in the central North Atlantic for return to base.

U 642 put in to St Nazaire **8.4.43**

2. 4.5.43 Left for the North Atlantic.

U 642 joined *Oder* group in the central North Atlantic, formed from the 18th to be ready to meet eastbound SC 130, should it turn southwards. In fact the convoy did not move too far south and it was intercepted by *Donau 1* and *2* groups north of the *Oder* line. The operation was unsuccessful because of continuous air cover over the convoy from the 19th. Three boats were lost, with none of SC 130's ships sunk. The operation ended on the 20th.

The *Oder* boats became part of the new *Mosel* group, formed 400 miles S of Cape Farewell to intercept HX 239, reported on the 18th to be moving eastwards from Newfoundland and expected to pass south of the *Mosel* patrol line. The convoy turned north and then northeast on the 21st. *Mosel* split into two parts, with the southern boats, including U 642, moving southeastwards to intercept any stragglers, whilst the northern boats went eastwards to join *Donau* group in an attack on the main convoy.

On the 22nd U 305 sighted a destroyer and reported before being driven off. Boats carried out searches to the east and northeast but, constantly harassed by aircraft, they did not find HX 239. The destroyer sighted was part of the escort of westbound ON 184, which had passed through the *Mosel* line the previous evening. With HX 239 still not found on the 23rd, the operation was abandoned.

With the failure of convoy operations in the North Atlantic, it was decided by BdU on the 24th to make an effort to intercept convoys between the USA and the Mediterranean. Accordingly, boats with sufficient fuel, including U 642, were ordered to an area W of the Azores to await expected convoys UGS 9 and GUS 7A.

A patrol line, *Trutz*, was formed during the night of the 30/31st on the 43° meridian WSW of the Azores, made up of sixteen boats. On 4.6.43 the three most southerly boats were attacked by carrier-borne aircraft, which were thought to be part of a convoy's protective cover. The boats closed up to prevent any ships passing through gaps in the line, but when nothing had been sighted by the evening of the 5th the convoy was thought to have passed either to the north or the south.

Trutz group was broken up and moved 600 miles to the north, to be refuelled by U 488. The UGS convoy was sighted by an outward-bound boat on the 8th 100 miles south of the *Trutz* patrol area of the 5th. The move to refuel had been too premature.

On the 16th *Trutz* group reformed in three parallel north-south lines, *Trutz 1,2* and *3*, 1000 miles E of Bermuda. U 642 was in *Trutz 1*. The boats waited for two convoys until the 22nd and then, having seen nothing in that time, the line began an eastwards movement which continued until the 27th, when it halted some 200 miles SW of the Azores. By the 29th it was realised that the elusive convoys had by-passed the lines.

The boats reformed into three new lines, *Geier 1,2* and *3* and from 2.7.43 they moved eastwards towards the coast of Portugal, spaced at one-day intervals. U 642 was in *Geier 1*. At 500 miles from the coast air attacks began. On the 6th U 642 was attacked by US Army Liberators. She was shaken but not damaged. By the 8th air attacks were such that boat commanders were allowed to return to base if circumstances warranted.

U 642 returned to St Nazaire **17.7.43**

3. 11.9.43 Left St Nazaire and returned **12.9.43**

4. 18.10.43 Left for the Mediterranean.

U 642 was one of four boats which set out for Toulon, with U 340, U 450 and U 732. Outward-bound, U 340 and U 732 were sunk and U 450 was damaged but did reach Toulon.

U 642 probably passed through the Straits of Gibraltar during the night of November 2/3rd.

She put in to her new base at Toulon **13.11.43**

5. 22.12.43 Left Toulon for operations.

In early January U 642 was operating against Allied supply convoys en route from Gibraltar, along the Algerian coast to Naples. On the 3rd she claimed a steamer torpedoed and sunk N of Palermo but this is unsubstantiated.

U 642 returned to Toulon **23.1.44**

On 4.2.44 U 642 was damaged in a USAF raid on Toulon. The boat was badly damaged again in a raid by USAF Liberators on Toulon harbour on 5.7.44. Two crewmen were killed.

U 642 was decommissioned 12.7.44.

U 643   Type VII C

Built by Blohm & Voss, Hamburg
Keel laid 1.12.41   Launched 20.8.42
Commissioned 8.10.42   Feldpost Nr M 49 612

Sunk 8.10.43 in the central North Atlantic (56°14′N 26°55′W)

Served with
5 U-Flottille, Kiel   October 1942 - June 1943 (ab)
1 U-Flottille, Brest   July 1943 - 8.10.43 (fb)

Commanded by
KL Hans Harald Speidel   October 1942 - 8.10.43

Patrols: 1   Ships sunk: None

After commissioning, U 643 was beset with many difficulties and modifications and did not leave Kiel until late August 1943.

1. 26.8.43 Left Kiel and arrived Haugesund **28.8.43**

2. 29.8.43 Left Haugesund and arrived Bergen **1.9.43**

3. 14.9.43 Left Bergen for the North Atlantic.

U 643 joined *Rossbach* group, formed from the 27th SE of Cape Farewell to operate against ON 203. The line moved 100 miles to the northeast, waited there until the 30th but saw no sign of either ON 203 or the following ONS 19. Both convoys passed to the north.

U 643 (continued)

The group moved northeastwards on 1.10.43 to a position SW of Iceland, to intercept ON 204. This convoy also avoided the group and when it was realised that pursuit was useless, the *Rossbach* boats went southwestwards on the 5th to search for SC 143 and HX 259, which were expected to be intercepted on the 8th.

Destroyers of the 3rd SG were sighted by U 448 on the 7th and SC 143 was assumed to be in the area. During the night of the 7/8th the destroyers were engaged by *Rossbach* boats and the Polish destroyer *Orkan* was sunk by U 378. Liberators of 86 Squadron arrived in the morning of the 8th and drove off the boats.

A Liberator of 86 Squadron (P/O J Wright) sank U 419 and then spotted the surfaced U 643, which put up light flak. A second Liberator from 86 Squadron (F/O C W Burcher) arrived and carried out a depth-charge attack just after U 643 dived, which Burcher thought to be unsuccessful.

He returned an hour later and after 20 minutes sighted the boat, which was about to be attacked by a Liberator of 120 Squadron (F/O D C L Webber). This aircraft approached through heavy flak and dropped depth-charges. Burcher went in and dropped two more and Webber followed up with a second attack. The boat was strafed by both aircraft. U 643 stopped, down by the bow and listing to starboard.

A large number of the crew came up and inflated dinghies and put on life jackets. There was an explosion in the forward section and the boat immediately slid forward and down. Many of the men on deck were killed by a spout of water, which rose some 150 feet into the air.

The sea was too rough for nearby destroyers to launch boats and survivors who managed to grasp boarding nets were hauled aboard. Many men lost their hold and fell back into the sea.

In all, U 643's commander, chief engineer, doctor and 20 crewmen were picked up as PoWs. Another 25 men lost their lives.

U 644   Type VII C

Built by Blohm & Voss, Hamburg
Keel laid 1.12.41   Launched 20.8.42
Commissioned 15.10.42   Feldpost Nr M 49 683

Sunk 7.4.43 SSE of Jan Mayen (69°38′N 05°40′W)

Served with
5 U-Flottille, Kiel   October 1942 - March 1943 (ab)
11 U-Flottille, Bergen   March 1943 - 7.4.43 (fb)

Commanded by
OL Kurt Jensen   October 1942 - 7.4.43

Patrols: 1   Ships sunk: None

1. 13.3.43 Left Kiel and arrived Bergen **16.3.43**

2. 18.3.43 Left for operations in Northern Waters.
U 644 was sighted on the surface SSE of Jan Mayen by HMS *Tuna* (Lt D S R Martin) on 7.4.43. She was sunk by a torpedo from the British submarine.
There were no survivors, 45 dead.

U 645   Type VII C

Built by Blohm & Voss, Hamburg
Keel laid 17.12.41   Launched 3.9.42
Commissioned 22.10.42   Feldpost Nr M 49 700

Sunk 24.12.43 NNE of the Azores (45°20′N 21°40′W)

Served with
5 U-Flottille, Kiel   October 1942 - April 1943 (ab)
3 U-Flottille, La Pallice   May 1943 - 24.12.43 (fb)

Commanded by
OL Otto Ferro   October 1942 - 24.12.43

Patrols: 3   Ships sunk: 2 (12,788 grt)

1. 24.4.43 Left for the North Atlantic.
From May 11th U 645 joined U 304, U 418 and U 952 to form *Isar* group SE of Cape Farewell. On the 12th outward-bound U 640 sighted westbound ONS 7. *Isar*, *Lech* and *Inn* groups moved northeastwards to intercept but U 640 lost contact on the 13th.

When the convoy was not found the three small groups joined with newly-arrived boats and *Nahe* and *Iller* groups to form *Donau 1* and *2* groups from the 15th SE of Greenland. U 645 was in *Donau 1*. ONS 7 passed north of the patrol line and by the late evening of the 16th was away to the southwest of *Donau 2*.

The boats moved south to intercept eastbound SC 130 and the convoy was sighted by U 304 during the night of the 18/19th. Only U 645 and U 952 closed before contact was lost on the 19th, when SC 130 changed course. Continuous air cover over the convoy frustrated any approach by the *Donau* boats and after two were lost to the escort and one to aircraft, the operation ended on the 20th.

On the 18th HX 239 had been located 200 miles SE of Cape Race. The surviving *Donau* boats were ordered southwestwards to join *Mosel* group to meet the approaching convoy. The escort for HX 239 was joined by the escort-carrier HMS *Archer* and the strength of the convoy's air cover caused the operation to be called off on the 23rd, before any attacks had been made on the ships.

On the 24th Dönitz temporarily halted operations against convoys in the North Atlantic. U 645 and other ex-*Donau* boats with limited fuel were deployed over a wide area, their continuing radio signals planned to give the impression that a large U-boat presence was still being maintained across the convoy routes.

U 645 was ordered to rendezvous with U 450, badly damaged after an aircraft attack on 6.6.43. The two boats met and U 645's doctor was put aboard U 450, to attend seven wounded men. The boats then set out for Brest.

On the 18th they were sighted by a Liberator of 59 Squadron (F/O G B Lynch). U 645 fired at the aircraft as U 450 dived and then went down herself. The boats were sighted again on the 20th, by Beaufighters of 236 and 248 Squadrons, but dived before they could be attacked.

U 645 and U 450 put in to Brest **22.6.43**

2. 23.8.43 Left for the North Atlantic.
U 645 and five other boats took up positions in a waiting area N of the Azores from 2.9.43. Between the 10th and 13th U 645, U 260, U 305, U 338 and U 386 were refuelled by U 460 and then, together with U 731, which was not refuelled, they went north to join fourteen outward-bound boats to form *Leuthen* group SSW of Iceland for the 21st, to intercept the next westbound convoy.

Secrecy had been maintained as far as possible to prevent the presence of the boats becoming known to the Allies. However, U 341, which should have been proceeding submerged, was sighted, attacked and sunk by a Canadian aircraft just east of the planned patrol line position.

Early on the 20th, before the *Leuthen* boats were in position, westbound convoy ON 202 was sighted by U 270 but she was driven off after damaging a frigate. Aircraft and a strong surface escort prevented most boats making any attacks in daylight. During the day ON 202 joined up with convoy ONS 18. In the late evening of the 20th, ESE of Cape Farewell, U 645 torpedoed and sank the SS *Frederick Douglass* (am 7176t), damaged that morning by U 238. U 645 also made an unsuccessful attack on the escorting destroyer HMCS *Gatineau*.

Fog came down early on the 21st and remained throughout the night and the following day. On the 22nd there were some clear patches and when aircraft appeared, some *Leuthen* boats remained surfaced and fought them. When the operation was called off on the 23rd some boats returned to base.

U 645 joined *Rossbach* group, formed from the 27th SE of Cape Farewell to operate against ON 203. The line moved 100 miles to the northeast, waited there until the 30th but saw no sign of either ON 203 or the following ONS 19. Both had passed to the north.

The group moved northeastwards on 1.10.43 to a position SW of Iceland, to intercept ON 204. This convoy also avoided the group and when it was realised that pursuit was useless the *Rossbach* boats went southwestwards on the 5th to search for eastbound convoys SC 143 and HX 259, which they expected to intercept on the 8th.

In the evening of the 7th two destroyers were sighted and it was assumed, rightly, that a convoy could be near and searches were made during the night. Although destroyers were sighted moving northeastwards, the convoys were not found and the search was called off in the morning of the 9th. At some time during the same morning U 645 encountered some ships from SC 143 in bad visibilty WNW of Rockall. She torpedoed and sank the SS *Yorkmar* (am 5162t). With *Rossbach* group now dissolved, the boat set out for home.

U 645 put in to La Pallice **21.10.43**

3. 2.12.43   Left for Atlantic operations.
U 645 joined *Coronel* group W of the North Channel. In mid-December the group was enlarged and split into two sub-groups, *Coronel 1* and *3*, awaiting westbound ON 214. U 645 was in *Coronel 3*. Aircraft failed to find the convoy, which passed to the south. The boats of *Coronel 3* were sent far southwards to search for ONS 25 but it was not found.

From the 20th the *Coronel 3* boats joined with new-arrivals to form a new patrol line, *Borkum*, 400 miles NW of Cape Ortegal, to intercept combined convoy MKS 33/SL 142. When the convoy was not found, the *Borkum* boats were ordered to operate against the carrier-groups of USS *Card* and *Core*, in an effort to cover the returning blockade-runner *Osorno*, which was spotted on the 23rd by an aircraft from *Card*.

In the early hours of the 24th U 645 was sighted as she dived by the destroyer USS *Schenck* of the *Card* group, NNE of the Azores. The boat missed *Schenck* with a torpedo and the destroyer closed and dropped depth-charges.

U 645 resurfaced after some 30 minutes, about two miles away from *Schenck*. The boat dived again. The destroyer came up, located U 645 and fired another pattern of depth-charges. An explosion was heard soon afterwards and U 645 was destroyed.

There were no survivors, 55 dead.

U 646   Type VII C

Built by Blohm & Voss, Hamburg
Keel laid 23.12.41   Launched 3.9.42
Commissioned 29.10.42   Feldpost Nr M 49 751

Sunk 17.5.43 ESE of Vik, Iceland (62°10′N 14°30′W)

Served with
5 U-Flottille, Kiel   October 1942 - March 1943 (ab)
11 U-Flottille, Bergen   April 1943 - 17.5.43 (fb)

Commanded by
OL Heinrich Wulff   October 1942 - 17.5.43

Patrols: 2   Ships sunk: None

1. 23.3.43   Left Kiel and arrived Bergen **26.3.43**

2. 28.3.43   Left Bergen for operations. No details known.
U 646 put in to Trondheim **30.4.43**

3. 12.5.43   Left for the North Atlantic.
Outward-bound, U 646 was sunk in a depth-charge attack by a Hudson of 269 Squadron (Sgt F H W James) on the 17th ESE of Vik, Iceland. There were no survivors, 46 dead.

U 647   Type VII C

Built by Blohm & Voss, Hamburg
Keel laid 30.12.41   Launched 16.9.42
Commissioned 5.11.42   Feldpost Nr M 49 799

Lost 30.7.43 between Iceland and the Faroes

Served with
5 U-Flottille, Kiel   November 1942 - May 1943 (ab)
7 U-Flottille, St Nazaire   June 1943 - 30.7.43 (fb)

Commanded by
KL Willi Hertin   November 1942 - 30.7.43

Patrols: 1   Ships sunk: None

1. 22.7.43   Left Kiel for the North Atlantic.
Outward-bound, U 647 was lost from an unknown cause between Iceland and the Faroes on or about the 30th. She may have sunk after striking a mine. There were no survivors, 48 dead.

U 648   Type VII C

Built by Blohm & Voss, Hamburg
Keel laid 30.12.41   Launched 16.9.42
Commissioned 5.11.42   Feldpost Nr M 50 693

Sunk 23.11.43 NE of the Azores (42°40′N 20°37′W)

Served with
5 U-Flottille, Kiel   November 1942 - April 1943 (ab)
6 U-Flottille, St Nazaire   May 1943 - 23.11.43 (fb)

Commanded by
OL Peter Stahl   November 1942 - 23.11.43

Patrols: 3   Ships sunk: None

U 648 (continued)

1. 3.4.43 Left Kiel for the North Atlantic.

U 648 joined boats of *Meise* group SE of Greenland, to operate against eastbound convoy HX 234 from the 22nd. After contact was lost on the 24th, U 648 became part of a new group, *Star*, in a patrol line S of Iceland, to await a westbound convoy.

On the 28th ONS 5 passed the northern end of the line. The bad weather conditions made it difficult to close the convoy, which was briefly sighted by five boats on the 29th and had one ship sunk that morning, by U 258. The operation ended in the evening of 1.5.43 near Cape Farewell.

The *Star* boats were immediately ordered to join the boats of *Specht* group in the pursuit of eastbound convoy SC 128, sighted during the evening of the 1st. Contact was lost during the night and when it had not been regained by the 3rd a new patrol line, *Fink*, was formed by combining *Star* and *Specht* groups.

The twenty-nine boats continued to search for SC 128 but by the 4th it was realised that the convoy had been re-routed. *Fink* had received orders to take up a new position when a southwest-bound convoy was sighted in the centre of the line. It proved to be ONS 5, which had been delayed by the storm. In daylight on the 5th fifteen boats were in contact with the convoy but before nightfall fog came down and most lost contact. In the fog the escorts made depth-charge attacks on fifteen boats. In the morning of the 6th ONS 5 was again sighted but bad weather conditions caused the operation to be abandoned, with twelve ships sunk but six boats lost.

U 648 does not appear to have made any attacks on ONS 5. After the operation ended, she was refuelled by U 459 in the central North Atlantic. The returning U 648 was attacked by a Sunderland of 10 (RAAF) Squadron (F/Lt M K McKenzie) on the 17th as she entered the Bay of Biscay. The aircraft was probably shot down by the boat, with the loss of the entire crew.

U 648 put in to Brest **19.5.43**

2. 1.7.43 Left for Atlantic operations.

Outward-bound, U 648 was ordered to rendezvous with the damaged U 527 S of the Azores and refuel her.

The boats met and on the 23rd, as refuelling was taking place, they were sighted by an Avenger of VC-9 (Lt R L Stearns) from the escort-carrier USS *Bogue*. U 527's commander, deciding to remain surfaced and fight it out, cast off the line and made for a nearby fog bank. U 648 dived and escaped. U 527 was sunk soon afterwards.

U 648 put in to St Nazaire **10.8.43**

3. 25.9.43 Left St Nazaire and returned **28.9.43**

4. 9.10.43 Left for the North Atlantic.

U 648 joined *Siegfried 3* group in late October, E of Newfoundland, to operate against eastbound SC 145. The convoy passed the line on the 29th. Two days later *Siegfried 1,2* and *3* groups reformed into *Körner* and *Jahn*. U 648 was in *Jahn*.

On 3.11.43 the boats were redeployed in five small sub-groups, *Tirpitz 1* to *5*, to search for convoy HX 264. It passed the groups late on the 6th and next day the operation was terminated, it being impossible to surface in daylight because of carrier-borne aircraft. In the evening of the 8th U 648, with *Tirpitz 5* group, sighted the escort-carrier HMS *Tracker* in the moonlight as she passed the patrol line, 630 miles SE of Cape Race. The boat fired three torpedoes, one of which exploded 1000 yards on the carrier's port quarter. U 648 also missed a sloop of the screen.

No search was mounted for the boat because of worsening weather. The wind increased to hurricane force and U 648 never regained contact with *Tracker*.

U 648 and other *Tirpitz* boats joined *Eisenhart* group, made up of seven sub-groups of three boats each and drawn up in two lines from the 11th, running southeastwards from Cape Farewell. Reports indicated that convoys were being routed to the south, so the *Eisenhart* boats were ordered southeastwards on the 12th to

search for SC 146 and HX 265. The convoys were expected to be in a position 200 miles W of Ireland after the 15th. By the 16th no convoys had been found and the majority of the boats were then WSW of Ireland. Fuel was becoming a problem for many of *Eisenhart* group and it was decided to end the operation. All boats with sufficient fuel, which included U 648, were sent to an area W of Spain to reinforce *Schill* group.

U 648 joined *Schill 2* group in an east-west patrol line W of Cape Finisterre, through which was expected to pass the northbound, combined convoy MKS 30/SL 139. The convoy passed through the eastern end of the *Schill 1* group line, W of Lisbon, in the afternoon of the 18th. The *Schill 2* boats moved northwards and formed an east-west patrol line E of the Azores, which the convoy was expected to reach on the 19th. It passed through the centre of the *Schill 2* line late on that day but the well-handled surface escort and constant attacks by aircraft prevented any night attacks by the boats, keeping them down most of the time. At dawn on the 20th, with increased air activity expected, the group was ordered to dive, abandoning any hope of attacking the convoy.

During the night of the 20/21st U 648 shot down a Liberator of 53 Squadron. Early on the 23rd U 648 was located NE of the Azores by ships of the 4th SG. She was sunk by the frigates HMS *Bazely* (Lt-Cdr J V Brock), *Blackwood* and *Drury*. Twenty-one depth-charge attacks were made and one Hedgehog attack.

There were no survivors, 50 dead.

U 649   Type VII C

Built by Blohm & Voss, Hamburg
Keel laid 12.1.42   Launched 30.9.42
Commissioned 19.11.42   Feldpost Nr M 50 727

Sunk 24.2.43 in the Bay of Danzig

Served with
5 U-Flottille, Kiel   November 1942 - 24.2.43 (ab)

Commanded by
OL Raimund Tiesler   November 1942 - 24.2.43

Patrols: None   Ships sunk: None

Whilst carrying out training exercises in the Bay of Danzig on 24.2.43, U 649 was lost after she collided with U 232.
U 649's commander and 10 men survived. 36 others were lost.

U 650   Type VII C

Built by Blohm & Voss, Hamburg
Keel laid 9.1.42   Launched 11.10.42
Commissioned 26.11.42   Feldpost Nr M 50 801

Missing from 7.1.45 W of the British Isles

Served with
5 U-Flottille, Kiel   November 1942 - May 1943 (ab/fb)
7 U-Flottille, St Nazaire   May 1943 - September 1944 (fb/fb-t)
11 U-Flottille, Bergen   October 1944 - 7.1.45 (fb)

Commanded by
OL Ernst von Witzendorff   November 1942 - July 1944
KL Otto Tinschert (temp)   August - October 1943
OL Rudolf Zorn   July 1944 - 7.1.45

Patrols: 5   Ships sunk: None

1. 10.4.43 Left Kiel and arrived Bergen **13.4.43**

2. 18.4.43 Left Bergen for the North Atlantic.

U 650 joined *Star* group, which formed a patrol line SW of Iceland from the 27th, awaiting westbound convoy ONS 5. At this time ONS convoys were taking routes more northerly then expected. Although the northern end of the *Star* line was at 62°N, ONS 5 still passed it, sighted by U 650 on the 28th. She was driven off by USN Catalinas of VP-84 but managed to bring up U 378 and U 386. The boats moved northwestwards to intercept but bad weather and navigational errors resulted in the convoy being sighted only briefly by U 258, U 378, U 386, U 528 and U 532. Only one ship was sunk, that by U 258. During the night of the 28/29th U 650 came under depth-charge attack after she missed the corvette HMS *Snowflake* with a torpedo.

When the pursuit was called off on 1.5.43 near Cape Farewell, the *Star* boats were ordered south to join *Specht* and *Amsel* groups in an operation against northbound convoy SC 128, The convoy had not been found by the 3rd and a new patrol line, *Fink*, was formed S of Cape Farewell by combining *Star* and *Specht* groups. The twenty-nine *Fink* boats continued to search for SC 128 but by the 4th it was realised that the convoy had been re-routed.

Fink had received orders to take up a new position when a southwest-bound convoy was sighted in the centre of the line. It proved to be ONS 5, which had been delayed by the storm. In daylight on the 5th fifteen boats were in contact with the convoy but before nightfall fog came down and most lost contact. In the fog the escort made depth-charge attacks on fifteen boats. In the morning of the 6th ONS 5 was again sighted but deteriorating weather conditions caused the operation to be abandoned. In this second action against ONS 5 twelve ships were sunk. U 650 does not appear to have made any attacks on the convoy.

From the 8th U 650 was with *Elbe* group E of Newfoundland, which was formed to intercept two expected, eastbound convoys. The group was ordered southeastwards at high speed to intercept convoy HX 237 but when it was realised that the convoy could not be caught, *Elbe* group combined with *Rhein* group on the 10th to form a new, long patrol line, split into two parts, *Elbe 1* and *2*. U 650 was in *Elbe 1*.

As the boats were forming up on the 11th, eastbound SC 129 passed through the *Elbe 2* line. All the *Elbe* boats moved in to attack the convoy but those that approached on the 12th were driven off by the escort. On the 13th a carrier from the HX 237 escort arrived to protect SC 129 and the operation was called off on the 14th, with two ships sunk but two boats lost and others damaged.

On or about the 18th U 650 was refuelled for further operations, by U 459 SE of Greenland. She joined *Mosel* group 400 miles S of Cape Farewell, to operate against convoy HX 239. It passed south of the patrol line and although some *Mosel* boats moved southeastwards to intercept, they did not find the convoy. The search was called off on the 23rd.

On the 24th Dönitz temporarily halted operations against convoys in the North Atlantic. U 650 and other ex-*Mosel* and ex-*Donau* boats with limited fuel were deployed over a wide area, their continuing radio signals planned to give the impression that a U-boat presence was still being maintained across the convoy routes.

The returning U 650 joined up with U 119 and U 449 NW of Cape Finisterre for the perilous journey across the Bay of Biscay. In the early afternoon of 23.6.43 the three boats were sighted by a Liberator of 86 Squadron (F/Lt J Wright). The aircraft came in and dropped depth-charges. All three boats dived but only U 650 was damaged. Later the same day the Liberator again sighted the boats, approached and dropped one depth-charge. The aircraft was driven off by fire from U 119 and U 449, the badly-damaged U 650 having dived when the Liberator was sighted.

The 2nd SG arrived in the early hours of the 24th, called up by the Liberator. Both U 119 and U 449 were located and sunk.

U 650 put in to her new base at St Nazaire **28.6.43**

The damage to U 650 was severe and she was out of service for six months. She was considered for conversion to flak-boat but never went into service as such.

3. 25.12.43 Left St Nazaire and returned **27.12.43**

4. 29.12.43 Left St Nazaire and returned **31.12.43**

5. 1.1.44 Left for the North Atlantic.

U 650 joined *Rügen* group W of the British Isles, with boats disposed singly over a large area. On the 26th a KMS convoy was sighted W of the North Channel. The eight most southerly *Rügen* boats, including U 650, were formed into a patrol line, *Hinein*, W of Ireland, to intercept the southbound convoy on the 27th.

The convoy was further west than reported and by the time the *Hinein* boats had been appraised of this it was too late to move the patrol line westwards into the convoy's path. Boats with 3.7cm anti-aircraft guns were ordered to proceed at high speed on the surface to intercept. Again, communication difficulties between aircraft and boats meant the convoy's position at midnight on the 27th was not passed on and an all-night search by the boats found nothing.

The operation was called off early on the 29th, when an invasion of Western France was reported by an aircraft. After apparent confirmation of this report, all boats in the North Atlantic, which included *Hinein* group, were ordered to proceed at full speed to the Biscay coast. Shortly after this the 'invasion fleet' was correctly identified as a group of Spanish trawlers and the boats were ordered back to their operational areas.

From 3.2.44 U 650 became part of *Igel 2* group, operating W of Ireland, which from the 4th moved up to the area SE of Iceland. On the 10th *Igel 1* and *2* groups began a slow westward withdrawal, which was taken further than was originally intended because of intense Allied anti-submarine activity, both SW of Ireland and NW of Scotland. It was intended to intercept an ONS convoy between the 14th and the 18th, with the aid of aerial reconnaissance.

ONS 29, ON 224 and OS 68 were sighted by aircraft on the 14th W of the North Channel and *Igel 1* and *2* groups were hurried to an assembly area 600 miles to the southwest of Ireland. On the 18th two parallel patrol lines, *Hai 1* and *2*, were formed ahead of the convoys, which were found to have turned south on the 17th and passed the southern end of the *Hai* lines. The boats were immediately ordered south, submerged in daylight and at high speed on the surface in the hours of darkness. Instead of sighting any convoys at dawn on the 19th, the boats saw only some destroyers. The operation was called off and the boats submerged to avoid aircraft, that were operating from a carrier in the convoy's escort.

U 650 returned to St Nazaire **2.3.44**

6. 6.6.44 U 650 was one of nineteen non-schnorkel boats which sailed into the Bay of Biscay as part of *Landwirt* group.

They were to form a line at the 200 metres depth line between Brest and Bordeaux, keeping out of port in case an Allied invasion force arrived and trapped them there. The boats later moved closer in to 100 metres depth line, where they could lay on the bottom for long periods.

The waiting boats were under constant attack from the air when they surfaced at night. When no invasion had come by the 12th, the boats were recalled to port and placed on six hours notice.

U 650 put in to La Pallice **16.6.44**

7. 12.8.44 Left La Pallice, in transit to Norway.

U 650 put in to Lorient **17.8.44**

8. 22.8.44 Left again for Norway.

En route, U 650 unsuccessfully attacked a corvette in the evening of 15.9.44 W of the Faroes, hearing only an end-of-run detonation. The boat reached Bergen **22.9.44**

U 650 (continued)
9. 26.11.44 Left Bergen, possibly training with newly-fitted schnorkel equipment.
U 650 returned **3.12.44**

10. 9.12.44 Left for British coastal waters.
In late December U 650 set out for the English Channel. She is presumed to have been sunk before reaching there and is listed as 'missing' from 7.1.45.
There were no survivors, 47 dead.

U 651 Type VII C

Built by Howaldtswerke, Hamburg
Keel laid 16.1.40   Launched 21.12.40
Commissioned 12.2.41   Feldpost Nr M 35 647

Sunk 29.6.41 NW of Rockall (59°52´N 18°16´W)

Served with
1 U-Flottille, Kiel February 1941 - 29.6.41 (ab/fb)

Commanded by
KL Peter Lohmeyer February 1941 - 29.6.41

Patrols: 1   Ships sunk: 2 (11,639 grt)

1. 7.6.41 Left Hamburg and arrived Bergen **11.6.41**

2. 12.6.41 Left for the North Atlantic.
U 651 was one of a number of boats sent to operate in a loose formation over a wide area of the central North Atlantic. It was hoped that they would find convoys, re-routed to miss *West* group.
On the 23rd U 203 sighted eastbound convoy HX 133 450 miles S of Cape Farewell. Over the next six days ten boats operated against the convoy, sinking six ships and damaging two others.
In the evening of the 24th U 651 torpedoed and sank the SS *Brockley Hill* (br 5297t) E of Cape Farewell and in the early hours of the 29th she sank the SS *Grayburn* (br 6342t) NW of Rockall.
Soon afterwards U 651 was sunk in depth-charge attacks by warships, the destroyers HMS *Malcolm* (Cdr C D Howard-Johnston) and *Scimitar* (Lt R D Franks), the corvettes HMS *Arabis* (Lt-Cdr P Stewart) and *Violet* (Lt F C Reynolds) and the minesweeper HMS *Speedwell* (Lt-Cdr J J Young).
The entire crew of U 651 was picked up and made PoW.

U 652 Type VII C

Built by Howaldtswerke, Hamburg
Keel laid 31.1.40   Launched 7.2.41
Commissioned 3.4.41   Feldpost Nr M 42 644

Sunk 2.6.42 NE of Bardia (31°55´N 25°13´E)

Served with
3 U-Flottille, Kiel April - December 1941 (ab/fb)
29 U-Flottille, La Spezia January 1942 - 2.6.42 (fb)

Commanded by
OL Georg-Werner Fraatz April 1941 - 2.6.42

Patrols: 9   Ships sunk: 3 (11,562 grt) + 2 damaged
                            2 destroyers (2740 dt)
                            1 patrol vessel (558 dt)

1. 19.6.41 Left Kiel and arrived Horten **20.6.41**

2. 29.6.41 Left Horten and arrived Trondheim **3.7.41**

3. 17.7.41 Left to operate in Northern Waters. No details known.
U 652 put in to Bökfjord **22.7.41**

4. 23.7.41 Left for operations.
On the 24th U 652 missed the Russian patrol vessel SKR-23 off Kildin Island. During this patrol U 652 and U 81 carried out the first U-boat operations off the Kola Coast.
On 6.8.41 U 652 torpedoed and sank the Russian patrol vessel *PS-70* off Cape Teriberka.
The boat put in to Kirkenes **7.8.41**

5. 9.8.41 Left Kirkenes and arrived Trondheim **13.8.41**

6. 23.8.41 Left Trondheim for the North Atlantic.
U 652 became one of a large group of boats that were operating in a loose formation SW of Iceland. In the early hours of the 26th She torpedoed and damaged the armed merchant cruiser SS *Southern Prince* (br 11447t) NW of the Faroes. On the 27th eastbound HX 145 was reported S of Iceland. U 652 and ten other boats of the group were directed to it but did not find the convoy.
On the 28th the boats reformed as *Markgraf* group SW of Iceland. U 652 was located by an aircraft on 4.9.41 and reported to the destroyer USS *Greer*, which was en route to Iceland. The aircraft attacked the boat with depth-charges, which U 652 assumed had been dropped by *Greer*, which had arrived on the scene.
U 652 then missed *Greer* with two torpedoes but this failed attack prompted *Greer* to retaliate by making an unsuccessful depth-charge attack on the boat. The two protagonists then went their separate ways but the 'Greer Incident' caused President Roosevelt to issue a 'shoot-on-sight' order to his naval commanders. Although America was neutral at that time, the US Navy was taking a very active part in convoy protection.
On the 4th *Markgraf* group was ordered to form a new patrol line further west but convoy HX 147 was re-routed to the north to avoid it. From the 6th the *Markgraf* boats were deployed over a wider area SE of Greenland, causing several convoys to be diverted.
However, eastbound SC 42 could not be re-routed because of bad weather. The convoy was sighted by U 85 near Cape Farewell on the 9th. In the early morning of the 10th U 652 torpedoed and damaged two ships ENE of the Cape, the tanker SS *Tahchee* (br 6508t) and the SS *Baron Pentland* (br 3410t). The *Tahchee* was towed to Reykjavik by the corvette HMCS *Orillia*. The abandoned *Baron Pentland* remained afloat because of its cargo of timber and was finally sunk on the 19th by U 372. The operation against SC 42 ended on the 14th, with sixteen ships sunk, another three damaged and two boats lost.
U 652 put in to Lorient **18.9.41**

7. 1.11.41 Left for the North Atlantic.
U 652 went to an area NW of the Azores. From the 17th she and U 561 acted as escorts for the returning *Schiff 45/Komet,* taking her to the Bay of Biscay. U 561 then returned to Brest and U 652 was ordered to the Mediterranean.
On the 27th U 652 was refuelled in the harbour at Cadiz by the German supply ship *Thalia.* She then passed through the Straits of Gibraltar during the night of the 28/29th.
The boat remained just east of Gibraltar until the 7th. In the afternoon of the 9th U 652 torpedoed and sank the SS *St Denis* (fr 1595t) S of Balearen.
U 652 put in to Messina **12.12.41**

8. 14.12.41 Left for operations.
U 652 went into the Aegean Sea and on the 19th she torpedoed and sank the tanker MV *Varlaam Avanesov* (sov 6557t) off

Babakale, Turkey.
The boat put in to La Spezia **1.1.42**

9. 5.2.42 Left for operations.
U 652 went to the Eastern Mediterranean and operated against supply-shipping to Tobruk. On the 10th she made an unsuccessful attack on a ship near Matruh, hearing one end-of-run detonation, and on the 13th she was unsuccessful against a destroyer N of Tobruk, hearing an end-of-run detonation and then ten minutes later, 15 depth-charge explosions.
U 652 put in to Salamis **16.2.42**

10. 21.2.42 Left for operations in the Eastern Mediterranean.
On the 25th U 652 attacked a small patrol vessel N of Tobruk but although a hit was heard, the torpedo was a dud.
The boat returned to Salamis **1.3.42**

11. 12.3.42 Left Salamis and returned **14.3.42**

12. 18.3.42 Left for operations off the Egyptian coast.
On the 20th U 652 sank the destroyer HMS *Heythrop* off Bardia and on the 26th the destroyer HMS *Jaguar* off Sidi Barrani.
The boat put in to Pola **31.3.42**

13. 25.5.42 Left for operations off the Egyptian coast.
On 2.6.42 U 652 was attacked by a Sunderland of 202 Squadron NE of Bardia. The depth-charges dropped landed alongside the boat, causing severe damage and rendering her incapable of diving. A further attack by a Swordfish of 815 (FAA) Squadron caused no further damage, with depth-charges exploding astern of the boat.
U 81 came up and took off U 652's crew. The boat was then sunk with a coup-de-grâce torpedo from U 81, fired, very appropriately, by U 652's commander, OL Fraatz.

U 653   Type VII C

Built by Howaldtswerke, Hamburg
Keel laid 9.4.40   Launched 31.3.41
Commissioned 25.5.41   Feldpost Nr M 44 257

Sunk 15.3.44 SW of Rockall (53°46′N 24°35′W)

Served with
1 U-Flottille, Kiel/Brest   May 1941 - 15.3.44 (ab/fb)

Commanded by
KL Gerhard Feiler   May 1941 - September 1943
OL Hans-Albrecht Kandler   October 1943 - 15.3.44

Patrols: 9   Ships sunk: 3 (14,983 grt) + 1 damaged
                1 aircraft tender (840 dt)

1. 13.12.41 Left Kiel for the North Atlantic.
From mid-November strong emphasis was placed on sending boats to the Gibraltar area and into the Mediterranean. The British quickly realised that many boats had been withdrawn from the Atlantic and they increased their a/s forces in the Gibraltar area, making passage through the Straits a very hazardous procedure.
To help counter this movement of warships from the Atlantic, BdU decided to try radio-deception, a tactic to be repeated on a larger scale in May 1943.
U 653 was ordered to carry out this duty and seems to have been the only boat so employed. She ranged over a wide area of the North Atlantic, transmitting signals to give the impression of many boats operating. On the 22nd an officer and 4 crewmen were lost overboard in heavy seas.
U 653 put in to her new base at Brest **13.1.42**

2. 31.1.42 Left for Atlantic operations.
From mid-January Hitler had ordered that six boats should be stationed in an area W of the Hebrides and the Faroes to counter any invasion of Norway. U 653 was on this duty until mid-February, when she headed for the Western Atlantic.
The boat went to the Nova Scotia area and then moved further south. On the 28th she torpedoed and sank the MV *Leif* (nw 1582t) NW of Bermuda. U 653 later operated off the US east coast but had no further success.
She returned to Brest **30.3.42**

3. 25.4.42 Left for the Western Atlantic.
U 653 operated well out from the US east coast. On 17.5.42 she sank the MV *Peisander* (br 6225t) some 400 miles SE of Nantucket Island.
On the 21st U 653 joined seven other boats to form *Pfadfinder* group 400 miles E of New York. Very few ships had been seen near the coast and the group's objective was to investigate passage of shipping between the US east coast ports and Central and South America and how far its routes were from the coast. The group dispersed after a few days and U 653 moved in to operate off New York but she had no success.
On 7.6.42 U 653 attacked two ships N of Bermuda. She made a second attack on them three hours later. This time she torpedoed and sank the small aircraft tender USS *Gannet* and an unidentified patrol yacht took a torpedo hit on the stern but the latter claim is unconfirmed.
U 653 moved north again to an area 300 miles E of New York. Some time after mid-June she was refuelled by U 459 W of the Azores for return to base.
The boat returned to Brest **6.7.42**

4. 5.8.42 Left for the Central Atlantic.
U 653 was one of seven boats, which were to make up *Blücher* group, intended for operations in the Freetown area. The group was to be formed from the 13th SE of the Azores. However, on the 14th, before all the boats had arrived, northbound SL 118 entered the assembly area. U 653 sighted the convoy on the 16th and directed the other *Blücher* boats to it.
The escort prevented any attacks up to the evening of the 17th, when U 566 made the first sinking. When the operation ended on the 20th, four ships had been sunk and one damaged. On the 18th U 653 was seriously damaged in an attack by a Liberator of 120 Squadron (S/Ldr T M Bulloch) near the convoy. Six depth-charges were dropped and the boat was strafed with the aircraft's cannons. The boat submerged after 10 minutes and escaped. One crewman was missing after the action. Before setting out for home, U 653 transferred her surplus fuel to U 406 and U 566.
U 653 returned to Brest **31.8.42**

5. 27.10.42 Left for Atlantic operations.
U 653 and other outward-bound boats joined *Natter* group, formed on 1.11.42 W of Ireland. The boats moved southwards to form a line for the 5th. U 92 sighted westbound convoy ON 143 on the 4th but with none of the other *Natter* boats in position to give support, she lost contact. A search was made when the other boats came up but when the convoy had not been found by the 6th the operation was called off. The only successes were two stragglers sunk by U 566 and U 613 during the afternoon of the 7th, after U-tanker U 117, en route to a replenishment area, sighted ON 143 further to the west and reported, enabling four boats to close.
On the 8th all *Natter* boats with sufficient fuel, which included U 653, were ordered to proceed at high speed towards Gibraltar because of the Allied landings in North Africa.
U 653 operated W of Gibraltar with *Westwall* group, which during November had little success but was at very great risk, particularly from Gibraltar-based aircraft. On the 26th it was decided that from the 27th the *Westwall* boats should be moved to

U 653 (continued)

an area W of the Azores, to meet eastbound UGS convoys beyond the range of land-based aircraft.

On or about the 28th U 653 was refuelled by U 118 SE of the Azores. The *Westwall* group moved west as far as longitude 40°W, reached on 6.12.42. After six days, with no convoys sighted, the *Westwall* boats moved eastwards again, towards Spain and Portugal. The group dispersed on the 16th and carried out a search W of Portugal from the 19th to the 23rd but with no convoys found, the boats headed home.

U 653 reached Brest **29.12.42**

6. 28.1.43 Left for the North Atlantic.

U 653 joined *Hartherz* group W of the Bay of Biscay, formed to intercept an HG convoy, reported to have left Gibraltar. The group searched between 14° and 19°W from February 4th to the 7th but nothing was seen.

The group broke up on the 8th and from the 14th U 653 was with *Ritter* group, formed W of Ireland to operate against expected convoy HX 226. During the night of the 15/16th convoy SC 119 passed to the north of the patrol line and on the 18th HX 226 also passed to the north, after a wide detour.

The group had been moving westwards but when it was learned that convoys ON 166 and ONS 167 were being routed south of the *Ritter* line, the movement westwards was halted and the boats moved southeastwards and formed a north-south patrol line with *Neptun* group on the 30° meridian from the 20th. Four outward-bound boats formed *Knappen* group to the south of *Ritter*, to operate against the convoys.

ON 166 was sighted by U 604 in the late morning of the 20th but she was driven off during the night before the closing *Ritter* and *Knappen* boats could arrive. The convoy was pursued for 1100 miles. When the operation ended in bad visibility on the 25th E of Newfoundland, fourteen ships had been sunk and one damaged. On the 24th U 653 torpedoed and damaged the MV *Madoera* (nl 9382t) from the convoy in the central North Atlantic. In the same attack, U 653 had a torpedo detonate near the British ship SS *Delilian*. The *Madoera* was taken into St John's on 2.3.43.

From February 25th U 653 and other *Ritter* boats were refuelled by U 462 N of the Azores. The replenished boats then joined *Burggraf* group, formed from the 26th in the central North Atlantic. They began a sweep westwards and by 4.3.43 they were E of Newfoundland, where they joined up with *Wildfang* group, stationed to the north. The two groups formed a long patrol line from the 4th, with a view to intercepting an expected SC convoy.

After part of the line was detached to operate against eastbound SC 121, the remaining *Burggraf* boats, including U 653, formed a new patrol line, *Raubgraf*, from the 7th ENE of Newfoundland. On the 9th the group moved north to intercept southwest-bound convoy ON 170. U 653 sank the abandoned wreck of the SS *Thomas Hooker* (am 7176t) on the 12th in the central North Atlantic. This vessel was originally with westbound convoy ON 169. She broke up in a storm on the 7th and her crew was taken off by the corvette HMS *Pimpernel*.

The *Raubgraf* boats operated against ON 170 on the 13th and 14th, in spite of rain, snow and a strong escort, which foiled all attempts to attack the convoy by U 653 and other boats. The operation ended with the reported approach of SC 122. The *Raubgraf* boats formed a short patrol line for the 15th in the expected path of the convoy.

In the morning of the 16th the returning U 653 sighted and reported an eastbound convoy, which was thought to be SC 122 but was in fact HX 229. U 653 was quickly driven off by the escort. She did not take part in what developed into the biggest convoy action of the war, against the two convoys.

U 653 put in to La Pallice **31.3.43**

7. 10.6.43 Left for the Central Atlantic.

Outward-bound, U 653 was refuelled by U 488 in late June W of the Azores. She went on to patrol off the coast N of Guiana but had no success. Many of U 653's crew contracted tropical fever and she set out for home on 4.8.43.

On her return journey U 653 ran very short of fuel. The refuelling situation W of the Azores became very serious after U-tankers U 117 and U 489 were sunk during the first week of August and U 525 was lost on the 11th. U 129 and U 847, both outward-bound for operations, were ordered to act as tankers to supply eleven waiting boats.

Between August 23rd and 27th U 847 supplied six boats 800 miles SW of the Azores, U 653, U 172, U 230, U 257, U 415 and U 508. U 847 was sunk on the 27th.

U 653 returned to Brest **11.9.43**

8. 15.11.43 Left Brest and returned **16.11.43**

9. 21.11.43 Left for Atlantic operations.

U 653 was one of a number of boats which took up submerged, waiting positions, W of the British Isles.

In early December they assembled W of the North Channel as *Coronel* group, which searched for westbound ONS 24 but was unsuccessful because aerial reconnaissance failed to find it. The convoy passed to the north of the group.

In mid-December *Coronel* group was enlarged and split into two sub-groups, *Coronel 1* and *3*, awaiting convoy ON 214. U 653 was in *Coronel 1*. Air reconnaissance failed to find the convoy and it passed to the south.

On the 19th the group was reduced to six boats, U 653, U 92, U 421, U 544, U 625 and U 672, to search for convoys W of the British Isles, as *Föhr* group. Eastbound HX 270 passed south of the group between the 20th and the 22nd, MKS 33/SL 144 passed on the 22/23rd and KMS 36/OS 62 on the 23/24th.

Föhr then joined *Amrum* and *Sylt* groups, and together with U 744 and U 390, they formed six small sub-groups, *Rügen 1* to *6*, W of Ireland. U 653 was in *Rügen 6*. These small sub-groups were constantly moving, changing postitions and varying formations, with the objective of preventing the Allies determining the area over which they were operating. When three convoys were sighted, UC 8 on the 23rd, TU 5 on the 26th and CU 9 on the 30th, the groups were each too small to mount an attack. U 653 made an unsuccessful attack on a corvette of CU 9's escort.

On 5.1.44 the *Rügen* groups were dispersed and the boats were disposed singly W of the British Isles. U 653 left for base about the time this redisposition took place.

She reached Brest **13.1.44**

10. 2.3.44 Left for Atlantic operations.

U 653 joined *Preussen* group, with its boats disposed singly W of the British Isles, searching for convoys.

On the 15th U 653 was sighted on the surface by a Swordfish of 825 (FAA) Squadron (Sub-Lt P Cumberland) from the escort-carrier HMS *Vindex*. The 2nd SG was with the carrier and after the aircraft's report, the sloops HMS *Starling* (Capt F J Walker) and *Wild Goose* (Cdr D E G Wemyss) raced to the scene.

U 653, 10 miles from the carrier, dived when the aircraft was sighted. She was located by *Wild Goose* but sunk by a pattern of depth-charges from *Starling*.

There were no survivors, 51 dead.

U 654   Type VII C

Built by Howaldtswerke, Hamburg
Keel laid 1.6.40   Launched 3.5.41
Commissioned 5.7.41   Feldpost Nr M 46 564

Sunk 22.8.42 ESE of Isla de San Andrés (12°00´N 79°56´W)

Served with
5 U-Flottille, Kiel   July - October 1941 (ab)
11 U-Flottille, Bergen   November 1941 - 22.8.42 (fb)

Commanded by
KK Hans-Joachim Hesse   July - November 1941
OL Ludwig Forster   December 1941 - 22.8.42

Patrols: 4   Ships sunk: 3 (17,755 grt)
                              1 corvette (900 dt)

1. 16.11.41   Left Kiel and arrived Stavanger **19.11.41**

2. 4.12.41   Left Stavanger and arrived Bergen **4.12.41**

3. 7.12.41   Left Bergen and returned **9.12.41**

4. 15.12.41   Left Bergen, in transit to France.
     U 654 arrived at Brest **25.12.41**

5. 3.1.42   Left for the North Atlantic.
     U 654 went to the Newfoundland Bank area. She later patrolled S of Nova Scotia. In the early hours of 9.2.42 the returning U 654 and U 85 attacked southwest-bound ONS 61 some 700 miles E of Cape Race. With three torpedoes, U 654 hit the French corvette *Alysse* and possibly a large steamer in the convoy. The *Alysse* was taken in tow but foundered on the 10th.
     U 654 returned to Brest **19.2.42**

6. 21.3.42   Left for the Western Atlantic.
     U 654 went to the Newfoundland area and then moved south, to operate off the US east coast. On 10.4.42 the boat torpedoed and sank the SS *Empire Prairie* (br 7010t) NE of Bermuda.
     From mid-April U 654 was patrolling 300 to 400 miles E of Hatteras. On the 20th she torpedoed and sank two ships, the SS *Steelmaker* (am 6176t) and 19 hours later the MV *Agra* (sw 4569t). U 654's commander interrogated *Steelmaker*'s captain in his lifeboat. Before leaving, he assured the captain that he would radio the survivors' position. Forster failed to do this. One lifeboat was picked up after two days but the other was not found for ten, by which time two men had died from exposure.
     U 654 returned to Brest **19.5.42**

7. 9.7.42   Left Brest and arrived Lorient **10.7.42**

8. 11.7.42   Left for the Caribbean area.
     On the 18th the returning U 126 sighted southbound OS 34 NE of the Azores. She brought up U 654, U 108 and U 564 but escorting aircraft made it impossible for the boats to remain on the surface for any length of time. U 564 sank two ships but the other boats were unsuccessful.
     In late July U 654 was refuelled by U 463 W of the Azores. The boat entered the Caribbean and in August she was operating N of Panama but had no success.
     On the 22nd U 654 was sunk in a depth-charge attack by a B 18 of 45 Squadron (USAF) (Lt P A Koenig) ESE of Isla de San Andrés. Bubbles, an oil slick and debris appeared within minutes of four depth-charges being dropped.
     There were no survivors, 44 dead.

U 655   Type VII C

Built by Howaldtswerke, Hamburg
Keel laid 10.8.40   Launched 5.6.41
Commissioned 11.8.41   Feldpost Nr M 06 051

Sunk 24.3.42 SSE of Bear Island (73°00´N 21°00´E)

Served with
6 U-Flottille, Danzig   August 1941 - 24.3.42 (ab/fb)

Commanded by
KL Adolf Dumrese   August 1941 - 24.3.42

Patrols: 1   Ships sunk: None

1. 11.3.42   Left Kiel and arrived Heligoland **12.3.42**

2. 15.3.42   Left Heligoland for Northern Waters.
     Westbound QP 9 left Murmansk on the 21st and passed by the waiting boats, U 655, U 209, U 376 and U 378. However, U 655 was sighted by the escorting minesweeper HMS *Sharpshooter* (Lt-Cdr W L O'Mara). The boat was rammed and sunk by the minesweeper before she could dive, SSE of Bear Island.
     There were no survivors, 45 dead.

U 656   Type VII C

Built by Howaldtswerke, Hamburg
Keel laid 3.9.40   Launched 8.7.41
Commissioned 17.9.41   Feldpost Nr M 24 797

Sunk 1.3.42 SSW of Cape Race (46°15´N 53°15´W)

Served with
5 U-Flottille, Kiel   September - December 1941 (ab)
1 U-Flottille, Brest   January 1942 - 1.3.42 (fb)

Commanded by
KL Ernst Kröning   September 1941 - 1.3.42

Patrols: 2   Ships sunk: None

1. 15.1.42   Left Kiel for the North Atlantic.
     U 656 was one of twelve boats from Germany which assembled W of Rockall, as *Schlei* group, to carry out a southwesterly sweep across the convoy routes. The planned operation was called off and U 656 and six other boats went to bases in France to be prepared for service in US waters. The other five *Schlei* boats went to the Iceland/Faroes/Scotland area for the protection of Norway.
     U 656 put in to her new base at Brest **28.1.42**

2. 4.2.42   Left for the North Atlantic.
     U 656 was intended to meet the German blockade-runner *Osorno* on the 20th and escort her in but this did not happen because the *Osorno* had reached port on the 19th.
     In the latter part of February U 656 was patrolling S and SE of Newfoundland. Her last report was made on the 24th. On 1.3.42 the boat was spotted by an Argentia-based USN Hudson of VP-82 (Ens W Tepuni) 25 miles S of Cape Race. The aircraft dropped depth-bombs as U 656 began to dive, straddling the boat.
     The aircraft circled for an hour, returned to Argentia to refuel and then went back to the scene, accompanied by two other Hudsons. Indications were that U 656 had survived and was moving away. Depth-bombs were dropped ahead of oil and air bubbles observed, resulting in more oil appearing.

U 656 (continued)

The aircraft left and surveillance was continued by two US destroyers. During the next 24 hours the search for U 656 continued and 33 depth-charges were dropped. When more oil was seen, the hunt was called off. U 656 was destroyed.

There were no survivors, 45 dead.

U 657   Type VII C

Built by Howaldtswerke, Hamburg
Keel laid 2.10.40   Launched 12.8.41
Commissioned 8.10.41   Feldpost Nr M 38 963

Sunk 17.5.43 S of Cape Farewell (58°54´N 42°33´W)

Served with
8 U-Flottille, Königsberg   October 1941 - February 1942 (ab)
3 U-Flottille, La Pallice   March - June 1942 (fb)
11 U-Flottille, Bergen   July 1942 - 17.5.43 (fb)

Commanded by
OL Hans-Jürgen Radke   October - December 1941
KL Heinrich Göllnitz   December 1941 - 17.5.43

Patrols: 7   Ships sunk: 1 (5196 grt)

1. **21.3.42** Left Hamburg and arrived Heligoland **22.3.42**

2. **26.3.42** Left Heligoland for Northern Waters. No details known.
U 657 put in to Trondheim **11.4.42**

On 14.4.42 one crewman died in an accident on board the boat.

3. **17.6.42** Left Trondheim for operations.
On 1.7.42 eastbound convoy PQ 17 was located E of Jan Mayen, sighted by U 255 and U 408. U 657 and five other boats were ordered to form a patrol line further to the east, to await the convoy.
Brief contact was made with PQ 17 on the 2nd and 3rd and some unsuccessful attacks were made. U 657, U 225, U 376 and U 457 of *Seeteufel* were driven off. When it was suspected that German surface vessels were preparing to attack the convoy, a decision was made by the Admiralty in the late evening of the 4th that the ships of PQ 17 should scatter and proceed to Russian ports. They dispersed on the 5th and sinkings by U-boats and aircraft began.
In the nine-day operation against PQ 17 twenty-four ships were sunk, eight by aircraft, eight by U-boats and another eight by U-boats finishing off ships already damaged by aircraft. U 657 left the PQ 17 operation before the end, with a leaking fuel tank.
She put in to Skjomenfjord **9.7.42**

4. **23.7.42** Left for operations. No details known.
U 657 returned to Skjomenfjord **16.8.42**

5. **17.8.42** Left Skjomenfjord and arrived Bergen **20.8.42**

6. **22.8.42** Left Bergen and arrived Hamburg **27.8.42**

7. **4.11.42** Left Hamburg and arrived Kiel **4.11.42**

8. **12.11.42** Left Kiel and arrived Bergen **15.11.42**

9. **18.11.42** Left Bergen and arrived Narvik **21.11.42**

10. **22.11.42** Left Narvik for operations.
Between November 30th and December 2nd U 657 established an automatic weather station on Bear Island.
U 657 returned to Narvik **25.12.42**

11. **20.1.43** Left Narvik and arrived Tromsø **21.1.43**

12. **23.1.43** Left for operations. No details known.
U 657 put in to Hammerfest **14.2.43**

13. **15.2.43** Left for operations.
Westbound RA 53 left Kola Inlet on 1.3.43 and was first sighted by U 255 on the 2nd. U 657 made an unsuccessful attack on the convoy on the 9th NE of Iceland.
She returned to Narvik **15.3.43**

14. **16.3.43** Left Narvik and arrived Bergen **19.3.43**

15. **24.4.43** Left Bergen and arrived Trondheim **28.4.43**

16. **4.5.43** Left Trondheim for the North Atlantic.
U 657 and other outward-bound boats, U 340, U 636, U 731 and U 760, were deployed as *Iller* group to shadow convoy ONS 7, sighted by U 640 early on the 12th SW of Iceland. Contact was lost by U 640 on the 13th and she was sunk next day.
On the 14th U 657 was attacked by a USN Catalina of VP-84 E of Cape Farewell but suffered no damage. When ONS 7 was not found by the 15th, the *Iller* boats were ordered to a new position just SE of Greenland. The *Iller* group became part of a new group, *Donau 1*, from the 16th.
U 657 was already with *Donau 1* group when ONS 7 passed the northern end of the patrol line early on the 17th. U 657 sighted the convoy and sank the SS *Aymeric* (br 5196t) just E of Cape Farewell. It was to be another four months before the next ship was sunk from a North Atlantic convoy by a U-boat.
An hour after sinking the *Aymeric*, U 657 was sunk in a depth-charge attack by the frigate HMS *Swale*, from ONS 7's escort.
There were no survivors, 51 dead.

U 658   Type VII C

Built by Howaldtswerke, Hamburg
Keel laid 5.11.40   Launched 11.9.41
Commissioned 5.11.41   Feldpost Nr M 43 405

Sunk 30.10.42 NE of St John's (50°32´N 46°32´W)

Served with
8 U-Flottille, Königsberg/Danzig   November 1941 - July 1942 (ab)
6 U-Flottille, St Nazaire   August 1942 - 30.10.42 (fb)

Commanded by
KL Hans Senkel   November 1941 - 30.10.42

Patrols: 2   Ships sunk: 3 (12,146 grt) + 1 damaged

1. **7.7.42** Left Kiel for the Caribbean.
In late July U 658 was refuelled by U 463 W of the Azores. On her way into the Caribbean, U 658 sighted convoy WAT 13 during the night of August 12/13th, assembling in the Windward Passage. Early on the 13th she sank the SS *Medea* (nl 1311t) off the eastern tip of Cuba. Another attack on the convoy three hours later was unsuccessful. She was driven off by the escort.
U 658 called up U 598 and U 600. These two boats encountered convoy TAW 12 and they sank four ships and damaged another.
On the 17th U 658 sighted convoy PG 6 S of Cuba. Before being driven off, she torpedoed three ships, sinking the SS *Fort la Reine* (br 7133t) and the SS *Samir* (eg 3702t) and damaging the MV *Laguna* (br 6466t), W of Anse d'Hainaut, Haiti.
In late August U 658 was refuelled for return to base, possibly by U 462 W of the Azores.
She put in to her new base at St Nazaire **12.9.42**

2. 6.10.42 Left for the North Atlantic.

U 658 joined *Panther* group W of Ireland. On the 16th U 704 sighted ON 137 passing through the southern section of the patrol line. Twelve southern *Panther* boats, including U 658, and ten from *Wotan* group were ordered to attack the convoy.

The weather worsened and the shadower lost contact after being damaged and driven off. The boats searched but the convoy was not found. A gale developed on the 17th, the *Wotan* boats went home on the 18th and the operation was called off on the 19th.

The southern *Panther* boats moved westwards and formed a new patrol line, *Veilchen*, on the 24th 400 miles E of Newfoundland. On the 30th U 658 was sunk in depth-charge attacks by two Hudsons of 145 (RCAF) Squadron NE of St John's.

There were no survivors, 48 dead.

U 659   Type VII C

Built by Howaldtswerke, Hamburg
Keel laid 12.2.41   Launched 14.10.41
Commissioned 9.12.41   Feldpost Nr M 47 074

Sunk 4.5.43 W of Cape Finisterre (43°32´N 13°20´W)

Served with
5 U-Flottille, Kiel   December 1941 - August 1942 (ab)
9 U-Flottille, Brest   September 1942 - 4.5.43 (fb)

Commanded by
KL Hans Stock   December 1941 - 4.5.43

Patrols: 5   Ships sunk: 1 (7519 grt) + 3 damaged

1. 15.8.42 Left Kiel for the North Atlantic.

U 659 joined *Vörwarts* group, formed W of Ireland on the 27th. The group made a sweep to the southwest and on the 31st U 609, at the northern end of the line, sighted eastbound convoy SC 97. As other boats came from the south, they were driven off by the escort.

Next morning, 1.9.42, the first aircraft appeared and from then on continuous air protection kept the boats submerged. Contact was lost that night because of evasive action taken by the convoy and a lack of moonlight. The operation was called off early on the 2nd.

Two days later *Vörwarts* group combined with *Stier* group to form a new long *Vörwarts* line W of Ireland, to await westbound ON 127. The convoy passed the southern end of the line during the evening of the 9th, sighted by U 584. Contact was lost during the night but regained soon after daylight on the 10th. In the evening of the 10th U 659 torpedoed and damaged the tanker SS *Empire Oil* (br 8029t) in the central North Atlantic. This vessel was sunk four hours later by U 584. U 659, attacked and damaged by the escort on the 11th, left the area and set out for home. The operation against ON 127 ended on the 14th.

The boat put in to her new base at Brest **16.9.42**

2. 14.10.42 Left for the Central Atlantic.

U 659 was one of eight boats which assembled E of the Azores. They set off in line abreast for Freetown on the 23rd, as *Streitaxt* group. Off the Canaries on the 25th, the boats pursued a tanker that was escorted by two destroyers but had no success.

On the 27th U 409 sighted northbound SL 125 W of the Canaries as it passed through the *Streitaxt* line. In the evening U 659, U 203 and U 509 came up with the convoy. Early on the 30th U 659 sank the straggling tanker MV *Bullmouth* (br 7519t), torpedoed and damaged an hour earlier by U 409. U 659 next torpedoed the SS *Corinaldo* (br 7131t), previously torpedoed by U 509 and subsequently sunk two hours after U 659's attack by U 203.

In the evening of the 30th U 659 made her last attack on SL 125, torpedoing and damaging the MV *Tasmania* (br 6405t). This vessel

was sunk soon after midnight by U 103. These three attacks by U 659 were made NW of Madeira. During the night of the 30/31st she was damaged in a depth-charge attack and returned to base.

The boat reached Brest **5.11.42**

3. 12.12.42 Left for Atlantic operations.

U 659 joined *Spitz* group, formed from the 23rd W of Ireland. The boats moved southwestwards and by the 26th the *Spitz* line and the *Ungestüm* patrol line were almost joined.

During the afternoon of the 26th westbound ONS 154 passed the southern end of the *Spitz* line, sighted by U 664. Both groups moved to an area N of the Azores to intercept and three ships were sunk and another damaged early on the 27th, all by U 356.

U 659 left the ONS 154 operation on the 29th and searched in vain for the returning German blockade-runner *Rhakotis* until 2.1.43. She was unaware that *Rhakotis* had been sunk late on the 1st by the British cruiser HMS *Scylla*.

U 659 returned to Brest **5.1.43**

4. 8.2.43 Left for the North Atlantic.

U 659 joined *Neptun* group, formed from the 18th SW of Iceland, to operate against expected, eastbound HX 226. The convoy was not found, having been re-routed to pass north of the *Neptun* patrol line.

On the 20th the group moved southwestwards. It was avoided by the re-routed SC 120 but U 759, at the northern end of the line, sighted HX 227 in the morning of the 27th and the *Neptun* boats pursued. Only U 405 was able to attack the convoy, with bad weather preventing the other boats closing.

Whilst searching for HX 227, U 608 sighted approaching, westbound convoy ON 168 on 1.3.43 but after she was driven off and the convoy had not been found again by the 3rd, the operation was abandoned.

From the 5th the *Neptun* boats took up waiting positions S of Cape Farewell and north of *Wildfang* and *Burggraf* groups. U 405 sighted eastbound SC 121 on the 6th and seventeen boats drawn from *Neptun, Wildfang* and *Burggraf* groups were detached to pursue the convoy, as *Westmark* group. Another patrol line of eleven *Neuland* boats was formed from the 8th SE of Greenland, ahead of the convoy and designated *Ostmark* group.

U 566 and U 230 of *Westmark* made contact with SC 121 during the night of the 6/7th. The operation against the convoy was carried out in stormy weather and despite heavy seas, twelve ships were sunk and one damaged, with no boats lost. The action against SC 121 ended on the 11th near Rockall. On or about the 14th U 659 was refuelled by U 119 N of the Azores for return to base.

The boat returned to Brest **20.3.43**

5. 25.4.43 Left for Atlantic operations.

U 659 joined *Drossel* group, which formed a patrol line NW of Cape Finisterre. On 3.5.43 aerial reconnaissance reported a southbound convoy of eleven cargo ships and six escorts NE of the group. The boats moved eastwards to intercept but when contact was made in the late afternoon, the convoy was found to be fifteen LCTs and two escorts.

Sea conditions were bad, making torpedo attacks on these craft impractical. Early on the 4th U 659 and U 439 were attempting to attack. Both were running on the surface when they collided, possibly caused by their lookouts being distracted by one of the escorts, MGB 657, being on fire after an attack by a third U-boat.

U 659 sank immediately and U 439, severely holed in the forward section, settled as it took in water from the heavy seas. The other escort, slowing to investigate oil traces, picked up twelve survivors, three from U 659 and nine from U 439.

From U 659, the commander and 43 men were lost.

U 660 Type VII C

Built by Howaldtswerke, Hamburg
Keel laid 14.2.41   Launched 17.11.41
Commissioned 8.1.42   Feldpost Nr M 31 170

Scuttled 12.11.42 NW of Oran (36°07′N 01°00′W)

Served with
5 U-Flottille, Kiel   January - July 1942 (ab)
9 U-Flottille, Brest   August - October 1942 (fb)
29 U-Flottille, La Spezia   October 1942 - 12.11.42 (fb)

Commanded by
KL Götz Baur   January 1942 - 12.11.42

Patrols: 3   Ships sunk: 2 + 1 shared (12, 286 grt) + 1 damaged

1. 25.7.42 Left Kiel for the North Atlantic.

On August 5th U 593 sighted eastbound convoy SC 94 900 miles S of Cape Farewell. U 660 was one of seven outward-bound boats directed to the convoy and operating against it from the 7th. In the morning of the 8th U 660 torpedoed a steamer. A hit was heard but no detonation.

On the 10th U 660 torpedoed four ships in the convoy, S of Reykjavik, sinking the SS *Empire Reindeer* (br 6259t), the SS *Cape Race* (br 3807t) and the SS *Condylis* (br 4439t) and damaging the SS *Oregon* (br 6008t). The *Condylis* was shared with U 438 and the *Oregon* was sunk later, also by U 438.

The convoy was pursued and in spite of the escort carrying out many attacks in the bad visibility and an air escort appearing from the 9th, the attacking boats sank a total of eleven ships for the loss of two boats.

Some of the boats from SC 94, including U 660, joined with new-arrivals to form a new patrol line, *Lohs,* 600 miles W of the North Channel, to intercept an ON convoy expected on the 13th. During the night of the 12/13th, en route to their new positions, they sighted SC 95 going north. Only three boats closed, U 256, U 438 and U 705, and one ship was sunk by U 705 on the 15th. After contact was lost, the *Lohs* line formed on the 17th W of Ireland.

From the 21st the group moved northwards, searching for convoys, but on the 22nd ONS 122 passed to the south and was sighted by *Lohs'* southernmost boat, U 135. She shadowed but contact was lost in bad visibility on the 23rd and then regained on the 24th by U 660 but she was driven off. In the early hours of the 25th contact was made again with the convoy. Conditions were favourable until a sudden fog came down and the operation was abandoned on the 26th. Four ships were sunk and two boats returned to base after being damaged. The remaining boats moved to an area W of the Azores to refuel. U 660 was refuelled by U 174 for return to base.

U 660 put in to her new base at Brest **6.9.42**

2. 3.10.42 Left for the Mediterranean.

U 660 probably passed through the Straits of Gibraltar during the night of the 10/11th.

She put in to her new base at La Spezia **15.10.42**

3. 24.10.42 Left for the Western Mediterranean.

U 660 was one of a number of U-boats which were assembled from November 5th to the west of a line drawn from the Balearics to Algiers, to counter any outcome of the heavy concentration of shipping at Gibraltar.

After the landings in North Africa on the 8th, U-boat activity against Allied shipping intensified. On the 12th U 660 was operating against eastbound convoy TE 3 when she was located by the escort. The boat was sunk NW of Oran in depth-charge attacks by the corvettes HMS *Lotus* (Lt H J Hall) and *Starwort* (Lt H Kent).

Lotus dropped depth-charges, seriously damaging U 660, which went down to 500 feet. As the boat began to fill with water, *Starwort* dropped her depth-charges. KL Baur took U 660 to the surface, where she immediately came under fire from the corvettes. The crew abandoned ship and U 660 was scuttled.

Of the crew, 2 men were lost and KL Baur and 44 other men were made PoW.

U 661 Type VII C

Built by Howaldtswerke, Hamburg
Keel laid 11.3.41   Launched 11.12.41
Commissioned 12.2.42   Feldpost Nr M 31 365

Sunk 15.10.42 in the central North Atlantic (53°42′N 35°56′W)

Served with
5 U-Flottille, Kiel   February - September 1942 (ab)
3 U-Flottille, La Pallice   September 1942 - 15.10.42 (fb)

Commanded by
OL Erich von Lilienfeld   February 1942 - 15.10.42

Patrols: 1   Ships sunk: 1 (3672 grt)

1. 5.9.42 Left Kiel for the North Atlantic.

Outward-bound, U 661 was directed to westbound convoy ON 131, sighted by U 617 S of Iceland on the 26th. Contact was lost and bad weather caused the search to be abandoned.

On or about October 10th U 661 was refuelled by U 463 in the central North Atlantic. From the 12th U 661 was with *Wotan* group, formed on the 8th E of Newfoundland to await an SC convoy. The group was ordered northeastwards at high speed to intercept eastbound SC 104. U 258 had sighted an escort vessel passing the northern end of the *Wotan* line on the 11th but her report had been very much delayed.

The convoy was sighted during the night of the 12/13th. By the 14th the pursuit had reached an area where *Leopard* group was searching for ONS 136. The *Leopard* boats were ordered to join the attack on SC 104. The surface escort was strong and the boats were kept under for much of the time.

On the 14th U 661 torpedoed and sank the SS *Nikolina Matkovic* (yg 3672t) in the central North Atlantic, S of Cape Farewell. The boat was sunk on the 15th, rammed by the escorting destroyer HMS *Viscount* (Lt Waterhouse).

There were no survivors, 44 dead.

U 662 Type VII C

Built by Howaldtswerke, Hamburg
Keel laid 7.5.41   Launched 22.1.42
Commissioned 9.4.42   Feldpost Nr M 43 109

Sunk 21.7.43 E of Cabo Cassiporé, Brazil (03°56′N 48°46′W)

Served with
5 U-Flottille, Kiel   April - September 1942 (ab)
7 U-Flottille, St Nazaire   September 1942 - 21.7.43 (fb)

Commanded by
KK Wolfgang Hermann   April 1942 - February 1943
KL Heinz-Eberhard Müller   February 1943 - 21.7.43

Patrols: 4   Ships sunk: 3 (18,094 grt) + 1 damaged

1. 22.9.42 Left Kiel for the North Atlantic.

U 662 joined *Panther* group, formed from 8.10.42 700 to 800 miles W of the North Channel. In the evening of the 11th U 620 sighted westbound ONS 136 in the centre of the *Panther* line. Eight boats, including U 662, were detached and directed to it as *Leopard* group. Bad weather and high winds prevented most of the boats closing the convoy and the operation was called off on the 14th, with only two ships of ONS 136 sunk, neither of them by *Leopard* boats.

From the 14th the *Leopard* boats were directed to approaching, eastbound SC 104. They joined *Wotan* group boats in an attack on the convoy. However, the escort drove off any boats which approached, keeping them submerged for long periods. In the evening of the 15th an air escort appeared, driving the boats away. Contact was re-established in the morning of the 16th but again, aircraft prevented any attacks on the convoy and the operation was terminated, with eight ships sunk, U 661 sunk and U 607 damaged.

Late on the 15th the *Leopard* boats began moving eastwards to find westbound ON 137. This convoy was sighted by U 704 of *Panther* group in the late morning of the 16th but the weather deteriorated badly and the operation was called off on the 19th. The *Leopard* boats were refuelled by U 463 on or about the 22nd in the central North Atlantic.

In the evening of the 22nd U 443 sighted ON 139 but her attempts to direct the refuelled *Leopard* boats to the convoy failed. Searches for the convoy were also unsuccessful. In late October U 662 and U 260 were ordered to head for the Azores and patrol the area off Ponta Delgada, to seek information on Allied shipping.

U 662 put in to Lorient **18.11.42**

2. 19.12.42 Left for the North Atlantic.

U 662 joined *Spitz* group, formed from the 23rd in the central North Atlantic, W of Ireland. The group moved southwards and on the 26th westbound ONS 154 was sighted south of the patrol line by U 664. *Spitz* and *Ungestüm* groups were ordered to close..

U 662 made contact with the convoy in the afternoon of the 26th but attacks on it did not begin until the 27th. Early on the 29th U 662 torpedoed and sank the SS *Ville de Rouen* (br 5083t) N of the Azores. This vessel had been damaged by U 225 on the 28th.

Before the operation was called off on the 31st NW of the Azores, fourteen ships had been sunk and another damaged. U 662 and four other boats were still in contact when the operation ended.

On or about 10.1.43 U 662 was refuelled by U 117 in the central North Atlantic as she was on her way to join *Jaguar* group NE of Newfoundland. An HX convoy was expected but it was SC 117 which passed the western end of the *Jaguar* patrol line on the 22nd, sighted by U 413. Radio conditions were bad and *Jaguar* group's pursuit of the convoy did not become known until the 23rd, at which time *Haudegen* group was ordered to form a patrol line S of Cape Farewell to await the convoy. However, bad weather prevented the *Haudegen* boats forming their line and *Jaguar* group had lost contact on the 23rd. In spite of a search, the convoy was not found again. In late January U 662 was again refuelled by U 117, this time for return to base.

She put in to her new base at St Nazaire **7.2.43**

3. 23.3.43 Left for Atlantic operations.

Searching for a returning blockade-runner, German aircraft found northbound convoy SL 126 on the 27th W of Cape Finisterre and outward-bound U 662, U 181, U 267, U 404 and U 571 were directed to it. U 662 made contact on the 29th and late that evening she torpedoed three ships SW of Ireland, damaging the SS *Ocean Viceroy* (br 7174t) and sinking the SS *Empire Whale* (br 6159t) and the SS *Umaria* (br 6852t). In the early morning of the 30th U 662 claimed a hit on a ship but this is unconfirmed. From the convoy, four ships were sunk and one damaged.

After the SL 126 operation, the boats involved joined *Adler* group, formed on 7.4.43 S of Cape Farewell to operate against eastbound SC 125. The convoy passed 200 miles south of the *Adler* line on the

7th and was by then impossible to catch.

The group was moved to the southeast to intercept HX 232 but on the 10th U 404 sighted westbound ON 176 and U 662 was one of nine boats which were directed to it E of Newfoundland on the 11th. U 662 and other boats made brief contact with the convoy but they were all driven off by the strong surface and air escort. One ship and a destroyer from the escort were sunk before the operation was abandoned on the 13th E of St John's.

The *Adler* boats were incorporated into *Meise* group. After a line was formed on the 14th NE of Newfoundland, the group remained in the area until the 19th, when the boats moved northwards at high speed to form a new line S of Greenland for the 21st, to intercept eastbound HX 234.

U 662 had left the group just previous to this move and gone for refuelling by U 487 in the central North Atlantic. She then joined *Specht* group, formed from the 22nd E of Newfoundland to operate against SC 127. However, after the convoy was re-routed to pass north of the *Specht* line, the group was ordered northwestwards to form a patrol line for the 25th ahead of expected convoy ONS 4. Again, the convoy was re-routed to miss the line. From the 27th *Specht* was deployed against HX 235 but it too went south.

From the 29th *Specht* and *Amsel* groups formed a line NE of Newfoundland to intercept eastbound SC 128. Both groups moved south to search but when the convoy had not been found by 1.5.43 the *Specht* boats went north again and a new, long patrol line, *Fink*, was formed on the 3rd S of Cape Farewell from boats of the *Specht* and *Star* groups. In the afternoon of the 4th southwest-bound convoy ONS 5 passed through the centre of the *Fink* line, which was made up of twenty-nine boats.

During the night of the 4/5th attacks were made and the convoy dispersed into a number of small, escorted groups. Further attacks were made in daylight on the 5th but when fog came down in the afternoon almost all contact was lost. The operation was abandoned in the morning of the 6th. Considering that sometimes fifteen or more boats were in contact with the convoy, the total of twelve ships sunk was disappointing for the Germans, especially as six boats were lost. U 662 made no attacks on the convoy.

On or about the 10th she was refuelled for return to base by U 461 in the central North Atlantic.

The boat returned to St Nazaire **19.5.43**

4. 26.6.43 Left for the Central Atlantic.

Outward-bound, U 662 was refuelled between July 6th and 12th by U 487 600 miles SW of the Azores. U 662 went on to be one of seven boats patrolling an area between Trinidad and the mouth of the Amazon.

On the 19th U 662 encountered southbound convoy TF 2 N of the Amazon estuary. Whilst shadowing, the boat was surprised by a US Army Liberator from Surinam but she escaped. Next day she was sighted on the surface and attacked by an Army B 18 E of Cayenne. U 662 held her own against the aircraft for 20 minutes before she dived.

Amapá-based USN Catalinas of VP-94 were escorting convoy TF 2 on the 21st. U 662 had a lengthy engagement with an aircraft captained by Lt Auslander but she was finally sunk in a depth-charge attack by another Catalina (Lt R H Howland) E of Cabo Cassiporé, Brazil.

U 662's commander and one man were picked up 17 days later by the American patrol craft PC 494. 46 other men from the crew lost their lives.

U 663 Type VII C

Built by Howaldtswerke, Hamburg
Keel laid 31.3.41 Launched 26.3.42
Commissioned 14.5.42 Feldpost Nr M 45 175

Sunk 8.5.43 WSW of Brest (46°50´N 10°00´W)

Served with
5 U-Flottille, Kiel May - September 1942 (ab)
11 U-Flottille, Bergen October 1942 (fb)
9 U-Flottille, Brest November 1942 - 8.5.43 (fb)

Commanded by
KL Heinrich Schmid May 1942 - 8.5.43

Patrols: 3 Ships sunk: 2 (10,924 grt)

1. 8.10.42 Left Kiel and arrived Bergen **13.10.42**

2. 5.11.42 Left Bergen for the North Atlantic.
U 663 joined *Drachen* group, formed from the 24th NE of Newfoundland. The group's orders were for its boats to search independently for single ships. Several were found and sunk, one of them by U 663 in the evening of the 26th NE of St John's, the SS *Barberrys* (br 5170t).
In early December *Drachen* group broke up, some boats going home and the others, including U 663, going to refuel. She was supplied by U 460 NW of the Azores for further operations. U 663 then joined with U 373 and U 445, also refuelled by U 460, to form *Büffel* group in the central North Atlantic in the expected path of eastbound HX 218. The convoy was sighted at noon on the 13th by U 373 but she was driven down by the escort and contact was lost. During the night of the 13/14th U 663 came under depth-charge attacks by a destroyer of the escort and headed for home, damaged.
She put in to her new base at Brest **31.12.42**

3. 4.3.43 Left Brest and returned **6.3.43**

4. 10.3.43 Left for the North Atlantic.
Outward-bound, U 663 reported attacking a ship in the central North Atlantic on the 18th. From a 4-torpedo spread she claimed one hit, sinking the vessel, which could have been the SS *Clarissa Radcliffe* (br 5754t). This vessel was reported missing after a storm on the 9th and could have been straggling after her convoy, SC 122.
U 663 joined *Seeteufel* group S of Iceland to operate against convoy ONS 1. When nothing was seen, the group moved westwards on the 22nd and by the 26th was in the path of the convoy. In the afternoon masts were seen but no contact was made. Instead, it was decided to go for approaching, eastbound HX 230, sighted by U 564 on the 26th. About this time U 663 started on her return journey to base.
She reached Brest **4.4.43**

5. 5.5.43 Left for Atlantic operations.
Outward-bound on the 7th, U 663 was attacked and severely damaged in a depth-charge attack by a Sunderland of 10 (RAAF) Squadron (F/Lt G G Rossiter) 250 miles WSW of Brest. A final radio message was received from the boat on the 8th, so it must be assumed that she was lost on this day. Her loss is attributed to unknown causes resulting from the attack the previous day.
There were no survivors, 49 dead.

U 664 Type VII C

Built by Howaldtswerke, Hamburg
Keel laid 11.7.41 Launched 28.4.42
Commissioned 17.6.42 Feldpost Nr M 05 024

Sunk 9.8.43 WNW of the Azores (40°12´N 37°29´W)

Served with
8 U-Flottille, Danzig June - October 1942 (ab)
9 U-Flottille, Brest November 1942 - 9.8.43 (fb)

Commanded by
OL Adolf Graef June 1942 - 9.8.43

Patrols: 5 Ships sunk: 3 (19,325 grt)

1. 20.10.42 Left Kiel for Atlantic operations.
Outward-bound on November 1st, U 664 was sighted, attacked and damaged by a USN Catalina of VP-84 (Lt R C Millard) N of the British Isles.
U 664 put in to her new base at Brest **10.11.42**

2. 5.12.42 Left for the North Atlantic.
U 664 joined *Raufbold* group, formed from the 15th W of Ireland. On that day westbound ON 153 was sighted by U 609 as it passed through the centre of the *Raufbold* patrol line. Some successful attacks were made on the 15th and 16th. In the evening of the 16th U 664 torpedoed and sank the SS *Emile Francqui* (be 5859t) N of the Azores. After four days of bad weather, the pursuit of ON 153 ended on the 21st in the central North Atlantic, with two ships and a destroyer sunk and another ship damaged.
Raufbold group broke up, with U 664, U 203 and U 356 going to *Spitz* group, formed from the 23rd W of Ireland. The line began a movement southwestwards and on the 26th U 664, at the southern end of the line, sighted southwest-bound ONS 154.
Spitz and *Ungestüm* groups were deployed against the convoy. Contact was made on the 27th and in spite of poor visibility, four ships were sunk and another damaged. Early on the 28th some boats passed through the remote screen and during the night of the 28/29th nine more ships were sunk, none by U 664. She and four other boats were still in contact with the convoy when the operation ended on the 31st NW of the Azores. U 664 was refuelled by U 463 in early January for return to base.
She put in to La Pallice **13.1.43**

3. 14.2.43 Left for the North Atlantic.
Outward-bound on the 21st, U 664 sighted convoy ONS 167 WSW of Ireland. She and five other outward-bound boats were ordered to form *Sturmbock* group to operate against it. In the evening of the 21st U 664 torpedoed and sank two ships N of the Azores, the SS *Rosario* (am 4659t) and the tanker SS *H H Rogers* (pa 8807t). U 664 approached the convoy again early on the 22nd, with U 758, but both boats were driven off.
The other boats were too far apart to close and attack the convoy. From the 24th the six *Sturmbock* boats, now ahead of the convoy, formed a new line, *Wildfang*, E of Newfoundland in the expected path of ONS 167. The convoy was not seen again and the operation ended in bad visibility on the 25th.
In early March U 664, U 84 and U 758, from *Wildfang*, joined *Burggraf* group, which on the 7th reformed as *Raubgraf* group NE of Newfoundland. The group moved north until the 10th, then went northwestwards for two days, searching for westbound convoy ONS 169 but failing to find it. On the 13th ON 170 was sighted briefly and although the weather was bad it was decided to pursue. A strong air escort and a report that eastbound SC 122 was approaching caused the operation against ON 170 to be called off.

During the evening of the 15th one of *Raubgraf's* southern boats sighted a destroyer, which led to an unsuccessful search for a convoy. Late in the morning of the 16th the *Raubgraf* boats made contact with an eastbound convoy and later the same day a second convoy was reported ahead of the one then under attack, sailing on a parallel course and slower.

This second one was realised to be SC 122 and the first one sighted to be HX 229. U 664 was unsuccessful against both convoys. The operation ended on the 20th W of Ireland. It was the biggest convoy action of the war, with twenty-one ships sunk and only one boat lost, U 384. After the action U 664 may have been refuelled by U 463 in the central North Atlantic.

U 664 put in to Lorient **28.3.43**

4. 29.4.43 Left for the North Atlantic.

U 664 joined *Lech* group SE of Cape Farewell. In mid-May *Lech* combined with four other small groups to form *Donau 1* and *2* groups. U 664 was in *Donau 2*.

During the night of the 18/19th eastbound convoy SC 130 was located SE of Greenland by U 304 and both *Donau* groups were ordered to close. The convoy had continuous air cover and aircraft attacks out of low cloud made shadowing almost impossible. The operation was abandoned on the 20th, with no ships sunk and three boats lost, U 258, U 381 and U 954, the last having in her crew Dönitz' second son, Peter. SC 130 arrived in the UK on the 25th and was probably the last convoy to be seriously threatened in the Battle of the Atlantic.

The *Donau* boats moved southwards, to intercept eastbound HX 239. The convoy was reported by U 664 and U 413 on the 23rd but no attacks were made on it. On the 24th Dönitz suspended all operations against convoys in the North Atlantic until BdU could assess the situation. *Donau* and *Mosel* group boats with limited fuel supplies, including U 664, were ordered on to radio-deception duties. They ranged over a wide area, their continuing radio signals planned to give the impression that a large U-boat presence was still being maintained across the convoy routes.

U 664 returned to Brest **9.6.43**

5. 21.7.43 Left for the Central Atlantic.

On August 8th U 664 and U 262 were sighted on the surface W of the Azores by aircraft of VC-1 from the escort-carrier USS *Card*, an Avenger (Lt A H Sallenger) and a Wildcat (Ens J F Sprague). The fighter made a strafing attack on the nearer boat and Sallenger followed it in. The Avenger was badly damaged by flak and the radioman was killed. Sallenger managed to drop his depth-bombs close to the boat before ditching his aircraft a mile further on. The pilot and gunner inflated their dinghy and climbed in. As they were doing so, the Wildcat made another strafing run and was shot down into the sea. The pilot was never found. Sallenger and his crewman were picked up later by the destroyer USS *Barry*.

Later that day, in the gathering dusk, a lookout on U 664 reported a tanker ahead. Three torpedoes were fired at what was in fact the USS *Card*. They all missed. Next day, the 9th, U 664 was spotted on the surface by an Avenger (Lt G G Hogan), charging her batteries 65 miles from *Card*. Hogan was flying in company with another Avenger (Lt R H Forney) and a Wildcat (Lt N D Hodson).

Hogan dropped an instantaneous 500 lb bomb near U 664's bow, the fragments from which hit the men on deck. The Wildcat then made a strafing attack as the boat dived. The second Avenger came in fast and dropped two depth-bombs, which exploded under the boat, blowing her back to the surface.

The Wildcat strafed again, along the length of U 664, and some of the crew abandoned ship. The boat then began to dive again, Hogan dropped his second bomb but U 664 still continued to go down. However, leaks were such that the boat resurfaced. In spite of survivors in the water, newly-arrived aircraft from *Card* made further bomb and machine-gun attacks.

U 664's commander gave orders to abandon ship and soon after the last man had jumped, the boat's bow rose vertically and she then slipped under. Aircraft dropped life-jackets and rafts to the men in the sea. The destroyer USS *Borie* arrived seven hours later and she had picked up U 664's commander and 43 men when U 262 came on the scene and fired five torpedoes at her, all of which missed. Rescue operations were called off and *Borie* took the survivors to the *Card*.

Of U 664's crew, eight men lost their lives.

U 665 Type VII C

Built by Howaldtswerke, Hamburg
Keel laid 10.6.41   Launched 9.6.42
Commissioned 22.7.42   Feldpost Nr M 25 463

Sunk 22.3.43 SW of Bishop Rock (48°04′N 10°26′W)

Served with
5 U-Flottille, Kiel July 1942 - January 1943 (ab)
1 U-Flottille, Brest February 1943 - 22.3.43 (fb)

Commanded by
OL Hans-Jürgen Haupt July 1942 - 22.3.43

Patrols: 1   Ships sunk: 1 (7134 grt)

1. 20.2.43 Left Kiel for the North Atlantic.

U 665 joined *Neuland* group W of Ireland. On 7.3.43 she and ten other boats in the northern section of the patrol line were sent northwestwards as *Ostmark* group, to form a line for the 8th ahead of SC 121, sighted by U 405 on the 6th S of Greenland.

As well as the *Ostmark* boats, seventeen others from *Wildfang*, *Burggraf* and *Neptun* groups operated against SC 121. U 665 was one of the boats which closed the convoy during the night of the 9/10th but she had no success. In the operation twelve ships were sunk and another damaged before it ended on the 11th S of Iceland.

The *Ostmark* boats were joined by new-arrivals and three *Burggraf* boats to form *Stürmer* group from the 14th in the central North Atlantic, to operate against SC 122. The group moved westwards in search of the convoy until the 16th, when it turned southwestwards to intercept. Contact was made during the night of the 16/17th and some successful attacks were made by *Stürmer* boats over the next three days.

In the morning of the 17th U 665 sank a straggler from SC 122 N of the Azores, the SS *Fort Cedar Lake* (br 7134t), which had been previously torpedoed and damaged by U 338.

The operation, which had been carried out against convoys SC 122 and HX 229 by forty boats, was the biggest convoy action of the war, with twenty-one Allied ships sunk for the loss of one boat, U 384. After the operation ended on the 20th, U 665 headed for her new base at Brest.

On the 22nd she was located and sunk in a depth-charge attack SW of Bishop Rock by a Whitley of 10 OTU (Sgt J A Marsden), based at St Eval.

There were no survivors, 46 dead.

U 666   Type VII C

Built by Howaldtswerke, Hamburg
Keel laid 10.9.41   Launched 18.7.42
Commissioned 26.8.42   Feldpost Nr M 51 377

Sunk 11.2.44 W of Achill Head (53°56′N 17°16′W)

Served with
5 U-Flottille, Kiel   August 1942 - February 1943 (ab)
6 U-Flottille, St Nazaire   March 1943 - 11.2.44 (fb)

Commanded by
KL Herbert Engel   August 1942 - December 1943
OL Ernst-August Wilberg   December 1943 - 11.2.44

Patrols: 4   Ships sunk: 1 (5234 grt)
                           1 frigate (1370 dt)

1. 25.2.43   Left Kiel for the North Atlantic.

U 666 joined *Neuland* group W of Ireland. On 7.3.43 she and ten other boats in the northern section of the patrol line were sent northwestwards, as *Ostmark* group, to form a line for the 8th ahead of SC 121, sighted by U 405 on the 6th S of Greenland.

As well as those of *Ostmark* group, seventeen boats of *Wildfang*, *Burggraf* and *Neptun* groups operated against SC 121. U 666 had no success in the operation, which ended on the 11th W of the North Channel, with twelve ships sunk and another damaged.

The *Ostmark* boats, some new arrivals and three *Burggraf* boats formed *Stürmer* group from the 14th in the central North Atlantic, to operate against SC 122. The group moved westwards in search of the convoy until the 16th, when it turned southwestwards to intercept. Contact was made during the night of the 16/17th and some successful attacks were made over the next three days. As the *Stürmer* boats closed the convoy, most were driven off by the escort. On the 17th U 666 came under depth-charge attack by the corvette HMS *Godetia*, the destroyer SS *Upshur* and a Liberator of 86 Squadron.

In the early morning of the 19th U 666 claimed three ships hit, with one sinking quickly. The only hit was on the SS *Carras* (gr 5234t), which did not sink after the attack but was dispatched by a coup-de-grâce by U 333 in the evening. On the 19th U 666 was attacked and damaged by a Fortress of 220 Squadron (F/O W Knowles).

The operation was the biggest convoy action of the war, with forty boats against convoys SC 122 and HX 229. Twenty-one Allied ships were sunk for the loss of one boat, U 384. The last boats were driven off early on the 20th.

U 666 and other ex-*Stürmer* boats joined new-arrivals to form *Seewolf* group from the 25th SE of Cape Farewell and south of the *Seeteufel* line, to operate against reported, eastbound SC 123. From the 26th *Seewolf* and *Seeteufel* groups joined to form a line running 800 miles south from Cape Farewell.

U 305, at the northern end of the *Seewolf* line, sighted eastbound HX 230 on the 27th. U 666 may have been one of twenty-two boats from the two groups which were ordered to close the convoy. However, with a rapid deterioration in the weather, only five boats made contact and only one ship was sunk, that by U 610. The operation ended on the 30th and U 666 and other *Stürmer* boats were refuelled by U 463 in the central North Atlantic.

U 666 put in to her new base at St Nazaire **10.4.43**

2. 6.5.43   Left for Atlantic operations.

Outward-bound, U 666 was attacked in the Bay of Biscay by a Halifax of 58 Squadron (F/Sgt J A Hoather), receiving minor damage. The aircraft was shot down and the crew lost.

U 666 joined *Oder* group in the central North Atlantic, formed from the 18th to be ready to meet eastbound SC 130, should it turn southwards. In fact the convoy did not move too far south and it was intercepted by *Donau 1* and 2 groups north of the *Oder* line. The operation was unsuccessful because of continuous air cover over the convoy from the 19th. Three boats were lost with none of SC 130's ships sunk.

The *Oder* boats became part of a new patrol line, *Mosel*, formed from the 21st 400 miles S of Cape Farewell to intercept HX 239, which was reported moving eastwards from Newfoundland.

U 305 made a sighting on the 22nd but was unable to shadow because of aircraft attacks. The *Mosel* boats were constantly harassed by carrier-borne aircraft and after several boats were damaged and the convoy had still not been found the operation was terminated on the 23rd.

The *Mosel* boats moved to an area SW of the Azores. Convoy operations in the North Atlantic had failed and it was decided to try and intercept US-Mediterranean convoys out in the Atlantic, beyond the range of land-based aircraft.

From the boats which had assembled SW of the Azores a new patrol line, *Trutz*, was formed during the night of 30/31st, to await expected convoys UGS 9 and GUS 7A. The line was drawn up on the 43°W meridian and ran between 32° and 38°N. On 4.6.43 the three most southerly boats were attacked by carrier-borne aircraft, which were thought to be part of a convoy's protective cover. The boats closed up to prevent any ships passing through gaps in the line but when nothing had been sighted by the evening of the 5th the convoy was thought to have passed either to the north or south.

The group broke up and moved 600 miles to the north to be refuelled by U 488. The UGS convoy was sighted by an outward-bound boat on the 8th 100 miles south of the *Trutz* patrol area of the 5th. The move to refuel had been too premature and the opportunity lost. Refuelling was completed by the 15th and the group reformed in three north-south lines, *Trutz 1,2* and *3*, 1000 miles E of Bermuda. U 666 was in *Trutz 2*.

The boat waited until the 22nd and having seen nothing in that time, the lines began an eastwards movement, which continued until the 27th, when they halted some 200 miles SW of the Azores. By the 29th it was realised that the elusive convoys, GUS 8, UGS 10 and GUS 8A, had bypassed the lines.

U 666 returned to St Nazaire **9.7.43**

3. 31.8.43   Left for the North Atlantic.

U 666 was one of fourteen boats which set out to form a patrol line, *Leuthen*, SSW of Iceland from 20.9.43, to intercept an ONS convoy. They were joined by six other boats which had assembled N of the Azores and then after refuelling had moved north to take their place in the patrol line. Secrecy had been maintained as far as possible to prevent the presence of the boats becoming known to the Allies. However, on the 19th westbound U 341, which should have been proceeding submerged, was sighted, attacked and sunk by a Canadian aircraft near the planned patrol line position.

Early on the 20th, before the *Leuthen* boats were in position, convoy ON 202 was sighted. Four boats closed but only one was able to make a submerged attack. In the morning contact was lost because of a strong surface and air escort. During the day ON 202 joined up with convoy ONS 18. Contact was regained by the boats in the early evening.

Only five boats closed the convoy, the other *Leuthen* boats being intent on attacking the escorts, in the belief that if the escorts were depleted the convoys could be dealt with during the night of the 21/22nd. Fog came down early on the 21st and remained throughout the day and the next night. When it thinned during daylight on the 22nd, Allied aircraft re-appeared and boats stayed on the surface to fight it out.

In the early hours of the 23rd further attacks were made on the convoys and escorts. U 666 torpedoed and sank the frigate HMS *Itchen* SSE of Cape Farewell and had a second torpedo explode in the wake of the corvette HMCS *Morden*. The operation ended later in the morning of the 23rd, with six ships sunk and another damaged beyond repair. Two boats were lost.

Some of the *Leuthen* boats went home and they were replaced by new-arrivals and a new patrol line, *Rossbach*, was formed on the 27th in the central North Atlantic to operate against ON 203. The convoy passed to the north of the patrol line and the group also missed westbound ONS 19, which also passed to the north, in spite of a move in that direction on 1.10.43 by the *Rossbach* boats.

From the 3rd the group moved eastwards to meet ON 204. On this day U 666 was damaged in a depth-charge attack by two ships of an escort group, supporting westbound convoy ON 204. The boat moved away to carry out temporary repairs. On the 5th she was still unable to dive properly and permission was given for her to return to base.

U 666 reached St Nazaire **16.10.43**

4. 16.12.43   Left St Nazaire and arrived Lorient **18.12.43**

5. 25.12.43   Left for an area W of the British Isles.

From early January U 666 operated with *Rügen* group, whose boats were disposed singly between 50° and 61°N and 18° and 24°W. On the 26th she joined with other boats to form a new patrol line, *Stürmer*, NW of the North Channel, to await expected convoy ON 221, which was sighted by German aircraft on the 27th. Technical difficulties prevented the aircraft homing in the boats and in spite of searches made on the 28th, the convoy was not found. The search for ON 221 was called off in the morning of the 29th, following a report by an aircraft of a suspected invasion of Western France. It was reported that 200 to 300 landing craft had been sighted 120 miles W of the Gironde estuary.

After apparent confirmation of this report, all boats in the North Atlantic, which included *Stürmer* group, were ordered at high speed to the Biscay coast. Shortly after this the 'invasion fleet' was correctly identified as a group of Spanish trawlers and the boats were ordered back to their operational areas.

On the 31st *Stürmer* group was once again stationed NW of the North Channel. In early February *Stürmer* and *Hinein* groups began to withdraw westwards and from the 3rd they were reformed into *Igel 1* and *2* groups. U 666 was in *Igel 1*. From the 4th to the 10th the group operated in loose formation SE of Iceland but an increase in Allied anti-submarine activity then made a further move westwards necessary.

On the 11th U 666 was sunk in a depth-charge attack W of Achill Head, Ireland by a Swordfish of 842 (FAA) Squadron (Sub-Lt W H Thompson) from the escort-carrier HMS *Fencer*.

There were no survivors, 51 dead.

U 667   Type VII C

Built by Howaldtswerke, Hamburg
Keel laid 16.8.41   Launched 29.8.42
Commissioned 20.10.42   Feldpost Nr M 50 568

Sunk 25.8.44 off La Pallice (46°10′N 01°14′W)

Served with
5 U-Flottille, Kiel   October 1942 - May 1943 (ab)
7 U-Flottille, St Nazaire   June 1943 - 25.8.44 (fb)

Commanded by
KL Heinrich Schroeteler   October 1942 - May 1944
OL Karl-Heinz Lange   July 1944 - 25.8.44

Patrols: 5	Ships sunk:	1 (7176 grt)
		1 corvette (925 dt)
		1 LST (1653 dt)
		1 LCI (246 dt)

1. 20.5.43   Left Kiel for the North Atlantic.

On May 24th Dönitz suspended U-boat operations against North Atlantic convoys until BdU could assess the situation. All boats with sufficient fuel were ordered to the area W of Gibraltar.

To give the Allies the impression that a strong U-boat presence was still being maintained across the convoy routes, a number of boats with limited fuel were assigned to radio-deception duties, to move about, transmitting messages. U 667 was ordered to join these boats on her first patrol.

The boats were positioned in various areas, SW of Ireland and S of Iceland, with others off Greenland and the Azores. The average number of participating boats was six and if one was sunk, she was quickly replaced. The scheme was abandoned in early July.

U 667 put in to her new base at St Nazaire **26.7.43**

2. 14.9.43   Left for the Mediterranean.

Outward-bound, U 667 was attacked and damaged on the 24th W of Gibraltar by two Leigh Light Wellingtons of 179 Squadron (F/O A Chiltern and F/Sgt D J MacMahon). The boat escaped but on the 26th she was again attacked and damaged, this time by another Wellington of 179 Squadron and two Hudsons, one from 233 Squadron (F/O A G Frandson) and the other from 48 Squadron (F/O E L Ashbury). The boat again escaped. Her attempts to pass through the Straits of Gibraltar having failed, she returned to base.

U 667 reached St Nazaire **11.10.43**

3. 18.11.43   Left for Atlantic operations.

U 667 was one of a number of boats which took up submerged, waiting positions W of the British Isles.

In early December they assembled W of the North Channel as *Coronel* group, which searched for westbound ONS 24 but was unsuccessful because aerial reconnaissance failed to find it. The convoy passed to the north of the group.

In mid-December *Coronel* group was enlarged and split into two sub-groups, *Coronel 1* and *3*, to search for westbound ON 214. U 667 was in *Coronel 3*. Again, aircraft failed to find the convoy and it passed to the south. Boats of the group, including U 667, searched far to the south for ONS 25 but it was not found.

From the 20th the *Coronel 3* boats joined with new-arrivals to form a new patrol line, *Borkum*, 400 miles NW of Cape Ortegal, to intercept combined convoy MKS 33/SL 142. When the convoy was not found, the *Borkum* boats were ordered to operate against the carrier-groups of USS *Card* and *Core*, in an effort to cover the returning blockade-runner *Osorno*, which had been spotted on the 23rd by aircraft from *Card*.

On the 22nd and 23rd an escorted carrier was sighted by German aircraft. Attacks were made on the escort by some *Borkum* boats after the carrier was sighted by U 305 during the night of 23/24th. The destroyer USS *Leary* was sunk.

In the evening of the 24th the *Borkum* boats encountered southbound OS 62/KMS 36 and U 415 sank HMS *Hurricane* of the escort, the only success against the convoy. The group continued to operate in the area NE of the Azores between 20° and 25°W, moving from one position to another in the operational area. U 667 left the group in late December.

The boat returned to St Nazaire **6.1.44**

4. 8.3.44   Left for Atlantic operations.

Now schnorkel-equipped, U 667 was briefly with *Preussen* group, whose boats were disposed singly W of the British Isles. The group was dissolved on the 22nd for its boats to operate independently between the British Isles and 40°W.

On 16.4.44 U 667 made an unsuccessful attack on a destroyer N of the Azores. Around this time she may have shot down an aircraft. On his return from this patrol, U 667's commander was enthusiastic about the schnorkel, reporting that he had run submerged for nine days from 15°W on the way home.

U 667 reached St Nazaire **19.5.44**

U 667 (continued)

5. **22.7.44** Left for English coastal waters.

U 667 operated initially in the Irish Sea and St George's Channel. From 7.8.44 she patrolled off the northern coast of Cornwall. In the evening of the 8th U 667 encountered coastal convoy EBC 66 just N of Trevose Head and torpedoed and sank two ships, the SS *Ezra Weston* (am 7176t) and the escorting Canadian corvette HMCS *Regina*. On the 14th U 667 attacked convoy EBC 72 off Hartland Point, sinking the American LST 921 and LCI 99.

The returning U 667 sank after striking a mine as she was about to enter La Pallice on the 25th.

There were no survivors, 45 dead.

U 668 Type VII C

Built by Howaldtswerke, Hamburg
Keel laid 3.11.41   Launched 5.10.42
Commissioned 16.11.42   Feldpost Nr M 49 834

Sunk 31.12.45 NW of Malin Head (56°03′N 09°21′N)

Served with
5 U-Flottille, Kiel November 1942 - January 1943 (ab)
22 U-Flottille, Gotenhafen February - December 1943 (ab)
5 U-Flottille, Kiel January - March 1944 (ab)
6 U-Flottille, St Nazaire April - July 1944 (fb)
13 U-Flottille, Trondheim July 1944 - 9.5.45 (fb)

Commanded by
KL Wolfgang von Eickstedt November 1942 - April 1945
KL Fritz Henning April 1945 - 9.5.45

Patrols: 7   Ships sunk: None

1. **1.4.44** Left Kiel and arrived Marviken **2.4.44**

2. **13.5.44** Left Marviken, en route to Northern Waters.

On the 17th U 668 and another boat were sighted on the surface by a Catalina of 333 (Norwegian) Squadron (S/Lt H E Hartmann). The aircraft attacked and was seriously damaged by flak and one of its blister-gunners was killed. One boat may have been damaged, an explosion having been seen in a conning tower after the attack.

U 668 put in to Skjomenfjord **18.5.44**

3. **22.5.44** Left for operations. No details known.
U 668 put in to Hammerfest **25.6.44**

4. **6.7.44** Left Hammerfest and arrived Narvik **7.7.44**

5. **19.7.44** Left for operations.

On 15.8.44 eastbound convoy JW 59 left Loch Ewe. It was sighted by a Ju 88 on the 20th E of Jan Mayen. Next day the convoy reached the patrol line of *Trutz* group, made up of U 668, U 344, U 363, U 394 and U 997. U 344 sank the sloop HMS *Kite* early on the 22nd. Later in the day U 668 and other boats were driven off by aircraft from the escort-carriers HMS *Vindex* and *Striker*.

Driven off again on the 23rd, U 668 made unsuccessful attacks against the escort early on the 24th in the Barents Sea E of Bear Island. After the attacks on JW 59's escort, the boats were kept down and contact with the convoy was lost. JW 59 reached Kola Inlet on the 25th, with no merchant ships lost.

U 668 returned to Hammerfest **27.8.44**

6. **14.9.44** Left Hammerfest for operations.

During the night of the 27/28th westbound convoy RA 60 left Kola Inlet. The *Grimm* group was lying in wait and *Zorn* group, of which U 668 was part, was at sea and intended to intercept SW of Bear Island. However, the convoy was re-routed and avoided the *Grimm* and *Zorn* boats. The only success against the RA 60 was achieved by U 310 of *Zorn* group, which sank two ships after being overrun by the convoy.

U 668 put in to Bogenbucht **3.10.44**

7. **14.10.44** Left Bogenbucht for operations.

On the 20th eastbound JW 61 left Loch Ewe. *Panther* group, which included U 668, was waiting for it but the heavily-escorted convoy passed through the patrol line. Unsuccessful attacks were made on the escort on the 26th and 27th, none by U 668. The convoy reached Kola Inlet on the 28th, without loss.

U 668 put in to Kilbotn **11.11.44**

8. **22.11.44** Left Kilbotn for operations.

U 668 was with *Grube* group, waiting off the Kola coast for eastbound JW 62. From 2.12.44 some of the *Grube* boats operated against Russian coastal convoys. U 668 made no attacks.

JW 62 reached Kola Inlet without loss on the 7th, having by-passed both *Grube* and *Stock* groups.

Grube group was waiting for return convoy RA 62 to sail. Prior to the convoy's departure, a force of Allied and Russian warships tried to drive off the boats waiting at the entrance to Kola Inlet. U 387 of *Grube* group was sunk. RA 62 sailed on the 10th and reached Loch Ewe without loss.

U 668 returned to Bogenbucht **19.12.44**

9. **1.3.45** Left Narvik for operations.

Westbound convoy RA 65 left Kola Inlet on the 23rd. U 668, U 310, U 313, U 992 and some boats of *Hagen* group attempted to form a patrol line ahead of the convoy on the 25th but this was unsuccessful. When the Luftwaffe failed to find the convoy on the 27th, the operation was abandoned.

U 668 returned to Narvik **17.4.45**

U 668 was one of a number of boats which left Narvik, heading for Trondheim. They were met at sea by the 9th EG and escorted to Loch Eriboll, probably arriving there on 19.5.45.

She was one of 116 boats disposed of by the Royal Navy in Operation Deadlight. In late December 1945 U 668 was towed from the assembly point at Lisahally by the destroyer HMS Blencathra. When the towline parted, U 668 was sunk by gunfire by the destroyer HMS Onslaught on 31.12.45 NW of Malin Head.

U 669 Type VII C

Built by Howaldtswerke, Hamburg
Keel laid 25.11.41   Launched 5.10.42
Commissioned 16.12.42   Feldpost Nr M 49 527

Sunk 7.9.43 NW of Cape Ortegal (45°36′N 10°13′W)

Served with
5 U-Flottille, Kiel December 1942 - May 1943 (ab)
1 U-Flottille, Brest June 1943 - 7.9.43 (fb)

Commanded by
OL Kurt Köhl December 1942 - 7.9.43

Patrols: 1   Ships sunk: None

1. **27.5.43** Left Kiel for the North Atlantic.

On May 24th Dönitz suspended U-boat operations against North Atlantic convoys until BdU could assess the situation. All boats with sufficient fuel were ordered to the area W of Gibraltar.

To give the Allies the impression that a strong U-boat presence was still being maintained across the convoy routes, a number of boats with limited fuel were assigned to radio-deception duties, to move about, transmitting messages. U 669 was ordered to join these boats on her first patrol.

The boats were positioned in various areas, SW of Ireland and S of Iceland, with others off Greenland and the Azores. The average number of participating boats was six and if one was sunk, she was quickly replaced. The scheme was abandoned in early July.

U 669 put in to her new base at St Nazaire **14.7.43**

2. 29.8.43 Left for the North Atlantic.

U 669 was to take part in Special Task *Kiebitz*, the plan to pick up escaped German PoWs from Camp 30 at Bowmanville, Ontario.

On 7.9.43 the boat was located NW of Cape Ortegal by a Leigh Light Wellington of 407 (RCAF) Squadron (P/O E M O'Donnell). A radar contact was made and U 669 was found on the surface and illuminated. In the face of heavy flak, the aircraft dropped five depth-charges. The boat, which had already begun to submerge, sank immediately.

There were no survivors, 53 dead.

U 670   Type VII C

Built by Howaldtswerke, Hamburg
Keel laid 2.12.41   Launched 15.12.42
Commissioned 26.1.43   Feldpost Nr M 49 847

Sunk 20.8.43 in Danzig Bay

Served with
5 U-Flottille, Kiel   January 1943 - 20.8.43 (ab)

Commanded by
OL Guido Hyronimus January 1943 - 20.8.43

Patrols: None   Ships sunk: None

Whilst still under training, U 670 was lost in Danzig Bay on 20.8.43 after a collision with the artillery target ship Bolkoburg.

21 men of the crew were lost and the commander and 21 others were rescued.

U 671   Type VII C

Built by Howaldtswerke, Hamburg
Keel laid 24.12.41   Launched 15.12.42
Commissioned 3.3.43   Feldpost Nr M 50 467

Sunk 5.8.44 SSW of Beachy Head (50°23′N 00°06′E)

Served with
5 U-Flottille, Kiel   March 1943 - April 1944 (ab)
3 U-Flottille, La Pallice   May 1944 - 5.8.44 (fb)

Commanded by
OL August-Wilhelm Hewicker March - May 1943
OL Wolfgang Hegewald May 1943 - 5.8.44

Patrols: 2   Ships sunk: None

1. 13.5.44 Left Kiel and arrived Marviken **15.5.44**

2. 26.5.44 Left Marviken and arrived Bergen **27.5.44**

3. 28.5.44 Left Bergen for the North Atlantic.

After the Allied invasion of Normandy on 6.6.44, seven outward-bound schnorkel boats were ordered to the English Channel. U 671

was one of these. After several attempts to enter the invasion area, she succeeded in the latter part of June.

On the 30th U 671 made an unsuccessful attack on a destroyer of a search group. Following another unsuccessful attack, the boat was located on the bottom SW of Beachy Head on 4.7.44. She was damaged in a depth-charge attack but managed to make her way to Boulogne. There were no technical staff at Boulogne, so thirty were sent from St Nazaire and they carried out the necessary repairs.

U 671 put in to Boulogne **5.7.44**

4. 26.7.44 Left Boulogne for operations.

U 671 operated again in the English Channel. On 5.8.44 she was sunk in depth-charge attacks SSW of Beachy Head by the destroyer HMS *Wensleydale* (Lt-Cdr W P Goodfellow) and the frigate HMS *Stayner* (Lt-Cdr H J Hall).

U 672   Type VII C

Built by Howaldtswerke, Hamburg
Keel laid 30.1.42   Launched 27.2.43
Commissioned 6.4.43   Feldpost Nr M 51 135

Sunk 18.7.44 NW of Alderney (50°03′N 02°30′W)

Served with
5 U-Flottille, Kiel April - September 1943 (ab)
6 U-Flottille, St Nazaire October 1943 - 18.7.44 (fb)

Commanded by
OL Ulf Lawaetz April 1943 - 18.7.44

Patrols: 3   Ships sunk: None

1. 13.11.43 Left Kiel for Atlantic operations.

U 672 was one of a number of boats which took up submerged, waiting positions W of the British Isles.

In early December they assembled W of the North Channel as *Coronel* group, which searched for westbound ONS 24 but was unsuccessful because aerial reconnaissance failed to find it. The convoy passed to the north of the group.

In mid-December *Coronel* group was enlarged and split into two sub-groups, *Coronel 1* and *3*, awaiting convoy ON 214. U 672 was in *Coronel 1*. Aerial reconnaissance failed to find the convoy and it passed to the south.

On the 19th the group was reduced to six boats, U 672, U 92, U 421, U 544, U 625 and U 653, to search for convoys W of the British Isles, as *Föhr* group. Eastbound HX 270 passed south of the group between the 20th and the 22nd, MKS 33/SL 144 passed on the 22/23rd and KMS 36/OS 62 during the night of the 23/24th.

Föhr then joined with *Amrum* and *Sylt* groups and together with U 744 and U 390, they formed six small sub-groups, *Rügen 1* to *6* W of Ireland. U 672 was in *Rügen 5*. These small sub-groups were constantly moving, changing positions and varying formations with the objective of preventing the Allies determining the area over which they were operating. When three convoys were sighted, UC 8 on the 23rd, TU 5 on the 26th and CU 9 on the 30th, the groups were each too small to mount an attack.

On 5.1.44 the *Rügen* groups were disposed singly W of the British Isles. U 672 set out for base before this redisposition took place.

The boat reached St Nazaire **15.1.44**

2. 24.2.44 Left for Atlantic operations.

U 672 joined *Preussen* group, whose boats were operating singly W of the British Isles. The group was dissolved on 22.3.44 and from then the boats operated independently between the British Isles and 40°W.

U 672 (continued)

In the first half of April U 672 carried out weather-reporting duties. During the night of the 24th the boat was located by a Leigh Light Liberator of 120 Squadron. Depth-charges were dropped but with no apparent result.

Later the same day U 672 was sighted by a Sunderland of 423 (RCAF) Squadron (F/Lt F G Fellowes). Six depth-charges were dropped in an attack made in the face of heavy flak. The boat was badly damaged and so was the aircraft, when one of the depth-charges exploded prematurely. The Sunderland was able to reach her base.

U 672 returned to St Nazaire **12.5.44**

3. 28.6.44 Left St Nazaire and returned **1.7.44**

4. 6.7.44 Left for the English Channel.

On the 18th U 672 was located by the frigate HMS *Balfour* (Lt-Cdr C D B Coventry) NW of Alderney. During the night of the 18/19th the boat was forced to the surface by depth-charge attacks.

After the crew abandoned ship, U 672 was scuttled. The commander and 51 men were picked up by air/sea rescue launches and made PoW.

U 673 Type VII C

Built by Howaldtswerke, Hamburg
Keel laid 7.4.42 Launched 27.2.43
Commissioned 18.5.43 Feldpost Nr M 37 961

Sunk 24.10.44 between Haugesund and Stavanger

Served with
5 U-Flottille, Kiel May 1943 - May 1944 (ab/vb)
6 U-Flottille, St Nazaire June 1944 (fb/vb)
13 U-Flottille, Trondheim June - July 1944 (fb/vb)
6 U-Flottille, St Nazaire August 1944 - 24.10.44 (fb)

Commanded by
KL Gerhard Haelbich May - August 1943
OL Heinz Sauer August 1943 - July 1944
OL Ernst-August Gerke August 1944 - 24.10.44

Patrols: 5 Ships sunk: None

1. 15.2.44 Left Kiel and arrived Bergen **18.2.44**

2. 20.2.44 Left Bergen for Northern Waters.

On the 23rd eastbound JW 57 was located by German aircraft and shadowed. The *Werwolf* group was deployed and the newly-formed *Hartmut* group, made up of U 673, U 315, U 366 and U 472, was also directed to intercept.

Some *Werwolf* boats made contact on the 25th E of Jan Mayen but two were sunk and the others driven off. Contact was maintained on the 26th and 27th but attacks made on the escort by the boats of both *Werwolf* and *Hartmut* groups were unsuccessful. U 673 did not take part in these attacks. She had gone to refuel.

U 673 put in to Narvik **27.2.44**

3. 29.2.44 Left Narvik and arrived Trondheim **2.3.44**

4. 24.3.44 Left Trondheim and arrived Narvik **26.3.44**

5. 27.3.44 Left for operations. No details known.
U 673 returned to Narvik **4.4.44**

6. 6.4.44 Left Narvik and arrived Trondheim **9.4.44**

7. 4.6.44 Left Trondheim for Atlantic operations.

U 673 had been converted, with an additional anti-aircraft gun platform at the rear of the conning tower structure, the VI arrangement. It proved to make the boat unstable and was not adopted.

U 673 carried out weather-reporting duties in the North Atlantic from the 21st to 7.7.44.

She put in to St Nazaire **24.7.44**

8. 14.9.44 Left St Nazaire, in transit to Norway.

U 673 was one of the not-completely-operational non-schnorkel boats transferred to Norway because of the advance of the Allied land forces in France.

The boat reached Bergen **19.10.44**

9. 22.10.44 Left Bergen for Germany.

U 673 moved down the Norwegian coast in convoy, en route to Germany. On the 24th she was rammed accidentally by U 382 between Haugesund and Stavanger. U 673 sank after running aground. Her entire crew was picked up.

The boat was raised on 9.11.44 and taken in to Stavanger. She was still there in May 1945 and was later broken up.

U 674 Type VII C

Built by Howaldtswerke, Hamburg
Keel laid 9.4.42 Launched 8.5.43
Commissioned 15.6.43 Feldpost Nr M 52 506

Sunk 2.5.44 WNW of the Lofoten Islands (70°32′N 04°37′E)

Served with
5 U-Flottille, Kiel June 1943 - January 1944 (ab)
11 U-Flottille, Bergen February 1944 - 2.5.44 (fb)

Commanded by
OL Harald Muhs June 1943 - 2.5.44

Patrols: 3 Ships sunk: None

1. 6.2.44 Left Kiel for Northern Waters.

U 674 joined *Werwolf* group. On the 23rd a German aircraft sighted eastbound convoy JW 57, which had left Loch Ewe on the 20th. The *Werwolf* boats were ordered to intercept. Some contact was made on the 25th. The boats were driven off but U 990 sank a destroyer of the escort.

Further attacks were made on the escort on the 26th and 27th but all were unsuccessful. The convoy reached Kola Inlet on the 28th. U 674 did not take part in any attacks on the convoy.

U 674 put in to Hammerfest **29.2.44**

2. 4.3.44 Left for operations.

On the 27th convoy JW 58 sailed from Loch Ewe with a very strong surface escort. It was located by German aircraft on the 30th. Three U-boat groups, *Thor*, *Blitz* and *Hammer*, and five outward-bound boats were deployed. U 674 was in *Thor* group.

In the early morning of 1.4.44 U 674 made an unsuccessful attack on a destroyer of the escort E of Jan Mayen, hearing only an end-of-run detonation. She also made what was probably the final attack on JW 58, again an unsuccessful one against a destroyer NNE of Kola inlet, with only an end-of-run detonation heard.

U 674 returned to Hammerfest **5.4.44**

3. 6.4.44 Left Hammerfest and arrived Narvik **7.4.44**

4. 17.4.44 Left Narvik for operations.

From the 30th U 674 was with *Donner* group, deployed against westbound convoy RA 59. Unsuccessful attacks were made against the escorting destroyers from the evening of the 30th. The only success was a ship sunk by U 711.

On 2.5.44, operating against the convoy, U 674 was sunk WNW of the Lofoten Islands in a depth-charge attack by a Swordfish of 842 (FAA) Squadron from the escort-carrier HMS *Fencer*. The same aircraft sank U 959 on the same day.

There were no survivors from U 674, 49 dead.

U 675   Type VII C

Built by Howaldtswerke, Hamburg
Keel laid 13.6.42   Launched 8.5.43
Commissioned 14.7.43   Feldpost Nr M 53 511

Sunk 24.5.44 W of Alesund (62°27´N 03°04´E)

Served with
5 U-Flottille, Kiel July 1943 - April 1944 (ab)
6 U-Flottille, St Nazaire May 1944 (fb)

Commanded by
OL Karl-Heinz Sammler July 1943 - 24.5.44

Patrols: 1   Ships sunk: None

1. 4.5.44 Left Kiel and arrived Kristiansand **6.5.44**

2. 18.5.44 Left for Atlantic operations.
Outward-bound on the 24th, U 675 was sunk W of Alesund in a depth-charge attack by a Sunderland of 4(C)OTU (F/O T F P Frizell). The attack was carried out in the face of heavy flak. Frizell, who was awarded the DFC, was an instructor and all other crew in the aircraft were under instruction.
There were no survivors from U 675, 51 dead.

U 676   Type VII C

Built by Howaldtswerke, Hamburg
Keel laid 13.6.42   Launched 6.7.43
Commissioned 6.8.43   Feldpost Nr M 54 607

Sunk 19.2.45 in the Gulf of Finland

Served with
5 U-Flottille, Kiel August 1943 - August 1944 (ab)
8 U-Flottille, Danzig September 1944 - 19.2.45 (fb)

Commanded by
KL Werner Sass August 1943 - 19.2.45

Patrols: 2   Ships sunk: None

1. 24.8.44 Left Kiel and arrived Danzig **25.8.44**

2. 1.9.44 Left Danzig and arrived Gotenhafen **1.9.44**

3. 3.9.44 Left for operations.
U 676 carried out convoy-escort duties as a flak boat against Soviet aircraft in the eastern Baltic and the Gulf of Finland. She claimed to have shot down two aircraft during this patrol.
U 676 returned to Danzig **25.10.44**

4. 20.1.45 Left for Baltic operations.
After the surrender of Finland in early September 1944, the loss of the use of Finnish harbours severely restricted U-boat activities

in the Baltic.
By the beginning of February 1945 only four boats were still operating, U 676, U 370, U 475 and U 745. On the 4th U 745 was lost by an unknown cause and U 676 sank after striking a mine in the Gulf of Finland on the 19th. The last two boats returned to Danzig on March 5th and 17th.

There were no survivors from U 676, 57 dead.

U 677   Type VII C

Built by Howaldtswerke, Hamburg
Keel laid 3.9.42   Launched 6.7.43
Commissioned 20.9.43   Feldpost Nr M 52 352

Bombed 9.4.45 at Hamburg

Served with
5 U-Flottille, Kiel September 1943 - May 1944 (ab)
3 U-Flottille, La Pallice June - July 1944 (fb)
23 U-Flottille, Danzig July 1944 - February 1945 (sb)
31 U-Flottille, Hamburg February 1945 - 9.4.45 (ab)

Commanded by
OL Paul Weber September 1943 - July 1944
OL Gerhard Ady July 1944 - 9.4.45

Patrols: 1   Ships sunk: None

1. 27.5.44 Left Kiel and arrived Marviken **29.5.44**

U 677 was to have gone on operations in the North Atlantic with 3 U-Flottille, La Pallice from June 1944. Instead, she was assigned to Mitte *group.*

The group was formed on 16.2.44, to stand by at ports in southern Norway in case of an Allied invasion of Norway or Denmark, with four boats at Bergen, four at Kristiansand and two at Stavanger. In March the group was increased from ten to twenty-two boats.

2. 8.6.44 Left Marviken as part of *Mitte* group.
In the early hours of the 6th, when news of the invasion of Normandy was received, the *Mitte* boats were put on immediate notice. U 677 was one of eleven boats which put to sea between the 8th and 10th, to form a reconnaissance line from Trondheim to Lindesnes.
In late June, when the anticipated threat to Norway had receded, U 677 and seven other *Mitte* boats were recalled.
She put in to Bergen **29.6.44**

3. 1.7.44 Left Bergen and arrived Kiel **6.7.44**

U 677 did not see any further operational service. She was one of nine Mitte *boats which were transferred to training duties in early July. Their crews were drafted to 23 and 24 U-Flottillen to man the new Type XXI boats.*

U 677 went to 23 U-Flottille at Danzig and later to 31 U-Flottille at Hamburg. She was destroyed there in an RAF daylight precision bombing attack by 617 Squadron on 9.4.45.

U 678   Type VII C

Built by Howaldtswerke, Hamburg
Keel laid 3.9.42   Launched 18.9.43
Commissioned 25.10.43   Feldpost Nr M 52 381

Sunk 6.7.44 SSW of Brighton (50°32′N 00°23′W)

Served with
5 U-Flottille, Kiel   October 1943 - May 1944 (ab)
7 U-Flottille, St Nazaire   June 1944 - 6.7.44 (fb)

Commanded by
OL Guido Hyronimus   October 1943 - 6.7.44

Patrols: 1   Ships sunk: None

1. 27.5.44   Left Kiel and arrived Marviken **29.5.44**

2. 8.6.44   Left for operations.
  U 678 was one of four schnorkel boats heading for the English Channel. On the 17th it was considered by BdU whether to divert them to operate instead in an area W of the British Isles because of the uncertain situation in the invasion area. However, it was decided to allow them to proceed as planned.
  U 678 reached the operational area. On 6.7.44 she was located whilst attacking a convoy off Beachy Head and sunk in depth-charge attacks SSW of Brighton by the destroyers HMCS *Kootenay* (Lt-Cdr K L Dyer) and *Ottawa* (Cdr H F Pullen) and the corvette HMS *Statice* (Lt R Wolfendon).
  There were no survivors, 52 dead.

U 679   Type VII C

Built by Howaldtswerke, Hamburg
Keel laid 12.10.42   Launched 18.9.43
Commissioned 29.11.43   Feldpost Nr M 53 677

Sunk 10.1.45 in the Gulf of Finland

Served with
31 U-Flottille, Hamburg   November 1943 - July 1944 (ab)
8 U-Flottille, Danzig   August 1944 - 10.1.45 (fb)

Commanded by
OL Friedrich Breckwoldt   November 1943 - October 1944
OL Eduard Aust   October 1944 - 10.1.45

Patrols: 8 at least   Ships sunk: None confirmed

1. 10.6.44   Left Kiel and arrived Marviken **12.6.44**

It is probable that U 679 remained at Marviken on stand-by, as part of Mitte *group.*

2. 29.6.44   Left Marviken and arrived Kiel **1.7.44**

3. 6.7.44   Left Kiel and arrived Helsinki **10.7.44**

4. 11.7.44   Left Helsinki for operations in the Baltic.
  On the 13th U 679 arrived in the area of Koivisto. Next day she had a surface engagement with two Soviet MTBs, one of which was *TKA-57* and the other may have been *MO-104*. Both vessels were hit by gunfire but they escaped.
  U 679 put in to Reval **16.7.44**

5. 18.7.44   Left for operations.
  Over the next seven weeks U 679 carried out short operational sorties of between three and seven days each. In between, a rest period of one or two days was taken in some secluded inlet. Replenishing was done either in Reval or Helsinki.
  U 679 put in to Danzig **10.9.44**

On 2.9.44 Finland broke off diplomatic relations with Germany and surrendered on the 4th. From the 2nd the Germans evacuated their men and as much material as possible from Finnish harbours.
  Further U-boat operations in the Baltic were carried out from Danzig, Gotenhafen and Memel.

6. 2.11.44   Left Danzig for operations.
  On the 18th U 679 reported a Soviet patrol vessel sunk at the entrance to the Gulf of Finland, possibly *SK-62*. On the 27th she claimed a Soviet minesweeper sunk off Baltijsk.
  U 679 put in to Libau **27.12.44**

7. 30.12.44   Left for operations.
  U 679 was sunk by the Soviet submarine *MO-124* on 10.1.45 in the Gulf of Finland.
  There were no survivors, 53 dead.

U 680   Type VII C

Built by Howaldtswerke, Hamburg
Keel laid 21.10.42   Launched 20.11.43
Commissioned 23.12.43   Feldpost Nr M 54 720

Sunk 28.12.45 N of the Giant's Causeway (55°24′N 06°29′W)

Served with
31 U-Flottille, Hamburg   December 1943 - July 1944 (ab)
6 U-Flottille, St Nazaire   August - September 1944 (fb)
11 U-Flottille, Bergen   October 1944 - 9.5.45 (fb)

Commanded by
OL Max Ulber   December 1943 - 9.5.45

Patrols: 4   Ships sunk: None

1. 6.8.44   Left Kiel and arrived Horten **8.8.44**

U 680 was to have to gone on operations in the North Atlantic with 6 U-Flottille, St Nazaire from August 1944. Instead, she operated from bases in Norway.

2. 14.8.44   Left Horten for operations.
  U 680, schnorkel-equipped, operated in the Moray Firth. She made at least one unsuccessful attack on this patrol. In early September she may have been damaged in an attack by Allied a/s forces.
  U 680 put in to Bergen **8.9.44**

3. 25.10.44   Left Bergen for operations. No details known but the patrol was cut short because of damage.
  U 680 returned to Bergen **8.11.44**

4. 13.11.44   Left Bergen and arrived Trondheim **16.11.44**

5. 18.11.44   Left for operations in the English Channel.
  U 680 arrived in her operational area on or about 7.12.44. She made an unsuccessful attack on a trawler on the 15th.
  The boat returned to Bergen **19.1.45**

6. 22.1.45   Left, possibly for operations. No details known.
  U 680 put in to Kristiansand **30.1.45**

7. 1.2.45 Left Kristiansand and arrived Flensburg **5.2.45**

U 680 was surrendered at Wilhelmshaven in early May 1945. She left there for the assembly point at Loch Ryan on 24.6.45.
She was one of 116 boats disposed of by the Royal Navy in Operation Deadlight. In late December 1945 U 680 was towed out from Loch Ryan through the North Channel by the tug HMS Saucy. When the towline parted, the boat was sunk by gunfire on 28.12.45 N of the Giant's Causeway.

U 681   Type VII C

Built by Howaldtswerke, Hamburg
Keel laid 21.12.42   Launched 20.11.43
Commissioned 3.2.44   Feldpost Nr M 49 036

Scuttled 10.3.45 NW of Bishop Rock (49°53´N 06°31´N)

Served with
31 U-Flottille, Hamburg February - October 1944 (ab)
11 U-Flottille, Bergen November 1944 - 10.3.45 (fb)

Commanded by
OL Helmut Bach February - August 1944
OL Werner Gebauer August 1944 - 10.3.45

Patrols: 1   Ships sunk: None

1. 8.2.45 Left Kiel and arrived Horten **13.2.45**

2. 14.2.45 Left for operations in the English Channel.
Outward-bound on 6.3.45, U 681 made an unsuccessful attack on an a/s patrol vessel W of Galway.
On the 10th the boat struck rocks NW of Bishop Rock, damaging her hull and propellers. Diesel oil went into the boat's interior and she was forced to surface.
U 681 was sighted by a USN Liberator of VPB-103 (Lt R N Field) three miles NW of Bishop Rock. After coming under a depth-charge attack, the boat was abandoned whilst moving at speed on the surface. Demolition charges were set and exploded after U 681 submerged.
The commander and 39 men were picked up by British naval vessels and made PoW. 11 others lost their lives.

U 682   Type VII C

Built by Howaldtswerke, Hamburg
Keel laid 23.12.42   Launched 7.3.44
Commissioned 17.4.44   Feldpost Nr M 50 037

Bombed 11.3.45 at Hamburg

Served with
31 U-Flottille, Hamburg April - November 1944 (ab)
11 U-Flottille, Bergen December 1944 - 11.3.45 (fb)

Commanded by
OL Sven Thienemann April 1944 - 11.3.45

Patrols: None   Ships sunk: None

1. 23.12.44 Left Kiel and arrived Horten **26.12.44**

During the night of December 29/30th 1944 U 682 was badly damaged by aircraft in Oslofjord.

2. 3.1.45 Left Horten and arrived Kiel **4.1.45**

U 682 went to Hamburg for repair and was destroyed in a USAF bombing raid there on 11.3.45. One crewman was killed.

U 683   Type VII C

Built by Howaldtswerke, Hamburg
Keel laid 4.3.43   Launched 7.3.44
Commissioned 30.5.44   Feldpost Nr M 00 375

Sunk 12.3.45 SW of Land's End (49°52´N 05°52´W)

Served with
31 U-Flottille, Hamburg May - December 1944 (ab)
11 U-Flottille, Bergen January 1945 - 12.3.45 (fb)

Commanded by
KL Günter Keller May 1944 - 12.3.45

Patrols: 1   Ships sunk: None

1. 22.1.45 Left Kiel and arrived Horten **25.1.45**

2. 3.2.45 Left Horten for operations in the English Channel.
U 683 reached the western entrance to the Channel at the beginning of March. On the 12th the boat was located by ships of the 2nd SG SW of Land's End.
U 683 was sunk in depth-charge attacks by the sloop HMS *Wild Goose* (Lt-Cdr R W Trethewey) and the frigate HMS *Loch Ruthven* (Lt-Cdr R T Horan).
There were no survivors, 49 dead.

U 684 - U 700 were never in service. U 684 - U 688 had their keels laid but construction was never completed. Orders for U 689 - U 700 were cancelled before construction began.

U 701   Type VII C

Built by Stülcken Sohn, Hamburg
Keel laid 13.5.40   Launched 16.4.41
Commissioned 16.7.41   Feldpost Nr M 44 322

Sunk 7.7.42 SE of Cape Hatteras (34°50´N 74°55´W)

Served with
3 U-Flottille, Kiel/La Pallice July 1941 - 7.7.42 (ab/fb/fb-m)

Commanded by
KL Horst Degen July 1941 - 7.7.42

Patrols: 3   Ships sunk: 4 (25,100 grt) + 4 damaged
4 armed trawlers (1840 dt)
1 armed yacht (tonnage unknown)

1. 27.12.41 Left Kiel for the North Atlantic.
Outward-bound on the 31st, U 701's 2 WO was lost overboard. On 6.1.42 the boat torpedoed and sank an independent NW of Rockall, the SS *Baron Erskine* (br 3657t)
U 701 was one of a number of boats which patrolled the Newfoundland Bank area. She had no success there and set out for home on or about the 27th.
The boat put in to St Nazaire **9.2.42**

2. 26.2.42 Left for Atlantic operations.

U 701 (continued)

U 701 patrolled an area W of the Faroes and the Hebrides. From late January 1942 a U-boat presence had been maintained there, ostensibly on Hitler's orders, to repel any invasion of Norway.

In the evening of 6.3.42 U 701 sank a fishing vessel S of Iceland, the *Nyggjaberg* (fa 272t). Late on the 7th she claimed a ship sunk SE of Iceland but this is unconfirmed.

U 701 torpedoed and sank two armed trawlers SE of Iceland, HMS *Notts Country* soon after midnight on the 7th and HMS *Stella Capella* in the early hours of the 11th.

From the 11th U 701, U 135, U 553 and U 569 were placed under the control of Naval Group Command North. As *York* group, they were disposed between the Shetlands and the Faroes to await the return of British naval vessels, sighted NE of the Faroes on the 10th. After waiting in vain for two weeks, the boats were ordered to return to base.

U 701 reached Brest **1.4.42**

3. 19.5.42 Left Brest and arrived Lorient **20.5.42**

4. 20.5.42 Left for operations in US waters.
On 12.6.42 U 701 laid 15 TMB mines at the entrance to Chesapeake Bay. On the 15th a convoy was about to enter the bay when the tanker SS *Robert C Tuttle* (am 11615t) struck a mine, followed by the tanker MV *Esso Augusta* (am 11237t) striking another. The escort thought the two tankers had been torpedoed and the destroyer USS *Bainbridge* dropped eight depth-charges. Another of the mines was set off by the depth-charges, indicating that the *Bainbridge* was in a minefield.

The ships of the convoy made it safely into Chesapeake Bay. A British armed trawler on loan to the US Navy, HMS *Kingston Ceylonite,* was escorting in a ship from the convoy that was being towed in by a tug. The cutter USS *Calypso* had been sent out to warn *Kingston Ceylonite* of the minefield but had missed her. As *Kingston Ceylonite* entered Chesapeake Bay, she struck a mine. The trawler was destroyed, with the loss of her entire crew. The *Robert C Tuttle* was beached but later salvaged and repaired. The *Esso Augusta* was damaged but reached port with assistance.

On the 17th an outward-bound convoy lost the SS *Santore* (am 7117t), which sank after striking a mine in an area pronounced to be clear of mines.

U 701 moved south to Hatteras and had no success until early on the 19th, when the armed trawler YP 389 was sunk by gunfire 10 miles from Diamond Head. Off Cape Hatteras, U 701 had further success, torpedoing and damaging the MV *Tamesis* (nw 7256t) on the 26th and the tanker MV *British Freedom* (br 6985t) on the 27th. The latter vessel was in a convoy and after she had been hit, the auxiliary armed yacht USS *St Augustine* dropped five depth-charges, which caused no damage but prevented U 701 finishing off the tanker.

U 701's final success came on the 28th, when she torpedoed the tanker SS *William Rockefeller* (am 14054t) off Cape Hatteras. The burning tanker drifted for twelve hours before finally sinking.

On 7.7.42 U 701 was spotted on the surface by a Hudson of 396 Squadron (USAF) (Lt H J Kane). The boat dived and the aircraft dropped three depth-charges into and ahead of the swirling sea. The boat resurfaced and all the crewmen that were able to, abandoned ship. Kane flew over and dropped a life raft and five lifejackets. Eventually, U 701's commander and six men were picked up by a USN amphibian. In a naval hospital on the 11th, Horst Degen congratulated Lt Harry Kane on his successful attack on U 701, the first sinking of a U-boat by the USAF.

Of the boat's crew, 40 men lost their lives.

U 702 Type VII C

Built by Stülcken Sohn, Hamburg
Keel laid 8.7.40   Launched 24.5.41
Commissioned 3.9.41   Feldpost Nr M 06 266

Lost 3.4.42 in the North Sea

Served with
5 U-Flottille, Kiel   September 1941 - February 1942 (ab)
7 U-Flottille, St Nazaire   March 1942 - 3.4.42 (fb)

Commanded by
KL Wolf-Rüdiger von Rabenau   September 1941 - 3.4.42

Patrols: 1   Ships sunk: None

1. 21.3.42 Left Hamburg and arrived Heligoland **22.3.42**

2. 29.3.42 Left for operations.
The last message received from U 702 was sent on the 31st. She was lost from an unknown cause, possibly after striking a mine in the North Sea on or about 3.4.42.

There were no survivors, 45 dead.

U 703 Type VII C

Built by Stülcken Sohn, Hamburg
Keel laid 9.8.40   Launched 16.7.41
Commissioned 16.10.41   Feldpost Nr M 25 617

Missing 22.9.44 E of Iceland

Served with
6 U-Flottille, Danzig/St Nazaire   October 1941 - June 1942 (ab/fb)
11 U-Flottille, Bergen   June 1942 - May 1943 (fb)
13 U-Flottille, Trondheim   June 1943 - 22.9.44 (fb)

Commanded by
KL Heinz Bielfeld   October 1941 - July 1943
OL Joachim Brünner   July 1943 - 22.9.44

Patrols: 13   Ships sunk: 5 (29,523 grt)
                              1 destroyer (1870 dt)
                              1 patrol vessel (1050 dt)

U 703 was to operate in the North Atlantic with 6 U-Flottille, St Nazaire but from April 1942 she was based in Norway.

1. 21.3.42 Left Hamburg and arrived Heligoland **22.3.42**

2. 1.4.42 Left Heligoland and arrived Stavanger **4.4.42**

3. 13.4.42 Left Stavanger and arrived Bergen **13.4.42**

4. 26.4.42 Left Bergen for Northern Waters.
Westbound convoy QP 11 left Murmansk on the 28th and U 703 and six other boats assembled to intercept. German aircraft located the convoy on the 29th and some unsuccessful attacks were made next day, both on ships and escort. Of the seven boats taking part in the action, only U 703 and U 405 did not make any attacks.
U 703 put in to Reinöy **7.5.42**

5. 10.5.42 Left Reinöy and arrived Skjomenfjord **13.5.42**

6. 16.5.42 Left for operations.
On the 21st eastbound convoy PQ 16 left Reykjavik and from the

24th had a strong naval escort. German aircraft located the convoy on the 25th and two air attacks were carried out by bombers and torpedo aircraft, resulting in only one ship being damaged.

During the night of the 25/26th U 703 torpedoed and sank the SS *Syros* (am 6191t) NE of Jan Mayen. Attacks en route resulted in seven ships sunk and one returning to Iceland, damaged. U 703's was the only U-boat success, the other ships being sunk by aircraft.

U 703 returned to Skjomenfjord **30.5.42**

7. 1.6.42 Left Skjomenfjord and arrived Bergen **4.6.42**

8. 29.6.42 Left for operations.

On 1.7.42 U 255 and U 408 sighted eastbound PQ 17 E of Jan Mayen and directed other boats to it. U 703 made brief contact on the 3rd but did not make any attack.

When it was suspected that German surface vessels could be preparing to attack the convoy, a decision was made by the Admiralty in the late evening of the 4th that the ships of PQ 17 should scatter and proceed to Russian ports. They dispersed early on the 5th and sinkings by U-boats and aircraft began. In the morning of the 5th U 703 sank the straggling SS *Empire Byron* (br 6645t) E of Bear Island and in the evening the SS *River Afton* (br 5479t) further east. The boat took aboard a British Army REME captain from the *Empire Byron*. He was going to Russia to instruct on the Churchill tanks the ship was carrying.

U 703 continued operating against dispersed ships until the 10th but had no further success. In the operation against PQ 17, twenty-four ships were sunk, eight by aircraft, eight by U-boats and eight more by U-boats finishing off ships, already damaged by aircraft.

U 703 put in to Narvik **15.7.42**

9. 2.8.42 Left Narvik and arrived Trondheim **4.8.42**

10. 9.8.42 Left for operations. No details known of this patrol. U 703 returned to Skjomenfjord **11.9.42**

11. 14.9.42 Left for operations.

Between the 20th and 22nd U 703 was one of seven boats operating against westbound convoy QP 14 in the Greenland Sea. In the evening of the 20th U 703 torpedoed and badly damaged the destroyer HMS *Somali* NNE of Jan Mayen. She was taken in tow by the destroyer HMS *Ashanti* but was lost in a gale on the 24th.

U 703 returned to Narvik **26.9.42**

12. 28.9.42 Left Narvik and arrived Trondheim **30.9.42**

13. 28.12.42 Left Trondheim and arrived Bergen **31.12.42**

14. 7.3.43 Left for operations. No details known of this patrol. U 703 put in to Hammerfest **5.4.43**

15. 17.4.43 Left for operations. No details known of this patrol. U 703 returned to Hammerfest **15.5.43**

16. 18.5.43 Left Hammerfest and arrived Trondheim **21.5.43**

17. 19.7.43 Left for operations.

During a reconnaissance of Hopen Island, U 703 captured four Soviet prisoners. On the 30th she sank Soviet patrol vessel *TSC-65/T 911*, escorting convoy BA 12, WNW of Cape Costin.

U 703 returned to Narvik **3.8.43**

18. 14.8.43 Left for operations.

On the 30th U 703, U 601 and U 960 relieved boats from *Wiking* group and encountered convoy VA 18. On 1.10.43 U 703 attacked the convoy NNE of Dickson, sinking the SS *Sergej Kirov* (sov 4146t) and unsuccessfully attacking the SS *Mossovet*.

U 703 returned to Narvik **10.10.43**

19. 12.10.43 Left Narvik and arrived Trondheim **14.10.43**

20. 18.10.43 Left Trondheim and arrived Bergen **19.10.43**

21. 13.1.44 Left Bergen and arrived Kiel **17.1.44**

22. 24.2.44 Left Kiel and arrived Trondheim **28.2.44**

23. 29.2.44 Left for operations.

U 703 operated against convoy RA 57, which left Kola Inlet on 2.3.44. She torpedoed and sank the SS *Empire Tourist* (br 7062t) on the 4th NNW of North Cape. In a later attack, U 703 missed the escorting destroyer HMS *Milne*. On the 6th U 703 had three men killed and another three wounded in an air attack.

She put in to Narvik **8.3.44**

24. 8.4.44 Left for operations.

Westbound convoy RA 58 set out on the 7th and after aerial reconnaissance found it on the 9th, *Donner* and *Keil* groups were deployed. U 703, with *Donner*, unsuccessfully attacked a destroyer on the 10th SW of Bear Island. Contact was lost and the operation was abandoned on the 11th, when the boats fell too far behind.

U 703 returned to Trondheim **5.5.44**

25. 29.7.44 Left Trondheim and arrived Narvik **1.8.44**

26. 20.8.44 Left for operations.

On the 22nd U 703, U 354, U 365 and U 711 formed a patrol line to intercept eastbound JW 59. After locating and approaching the convoy, the boats were driven down by aircraft from the escort-carriers HMS *Vindex* and *Striker*. The boats were unable to keep up with the convoy and the operation was abandoned on the 25th.

On 1.9.44 U 703 was escorting the German weather observation ship *Kehdingen*, which was trying to establish a weather station on the east coast of Greenland. The USCG cutter *Northland* arrived but left after U 703 fired torpedoes at her.

U 703 returned to Narvik **12.9.44**

27. 17.9.44 Left for operations.

U 703 went missing on or about the 22nd. She was lost, either setting a weather buoy in heavy seas E of Iceland or after striking a mine. There were no survivors, 56 dead.

U 704 Type VII C

Built by Stülcken Sohn, Hamburg
Keel laid 26.8.40   Launched 29.8.41
Commissioned 18.11.41   Feldpost Nr M 43 929

Scuttled April 1945 at Vegesack

Served with
8 U-Flottille, Königsberg/Danzig   November 1941 - June 1942 (ab)
7 U-Flottille, St Nazaire   July 1942 - April 1943 (fb)
21 U-Flottille, Pillau   April - May 1943 (sb)
24 U-Flottille, Memel   June - August 1943 (ab)
23 U-Flottille, Danzig   September 1943 - July 1944 (sb)
21 U-Flottille, Pillau   August 1944 - March 1945 (sb)

Commanded by
KL Horst Kessler   November 1941 - April 1943
OL Karl-Heinz Hagenau   April 1943 - June 1944
OL Gerhard Ady   June - July 1944
OL Wolfgang Schwarzkopf   August 1944 - February 1945
OL Gerhard Nolte   February - March 1945

Patrols: 3   Ships sunk: None + 1 damaged

U 704 (continued)

1. 30.6.42 Left Kiel for the North Atlantic.

U 704 joined *Wolf* group, which formed from 12.7.42 600 miles W of the North Channel. The group was to make a circular sweep towards the Newfoundland Bank, then go south.

A convoy was sighted at the northern end of the line on the 13th. Some of the more southerly boats moved northeastwards for some hours but when the convoy was found to be westbound, it was not pursued further, being then too far ahead. U 704 made brief contact with the convoy on the 14th but was driven off.

The sweep towards the Newfoundland Bank continued but when nothing had been seen by the 19th, it was decided to send the group south. Three days later, as the boats were moving to a refuelling area, another westbound convoy was reported and a line was formed.

The convoy was sighted on the 23rd and proved to be ON 113. In the ensuing action, with bad visibility and a strong escort, the convoy lost only two ships and U 90 was sunk. In the morning of the 26th U 704 torpedoed the MV *Empire Rainbow* (br 6942t) E of Cape Race. This vessel had been hit twice by torpedoes from U 607 15 minutes earlier and U 704's torpedo may or may not have contributed to its sinking. Contact with the convoy was lost on the 26th and after a fruitless search on the 27th, the operation against ON 113 was terminated.

The *Wolf* boats moved south to a refuelling area W of the Azores. Eight boats, including U 704, were refuelled on the 29th and 30th by U 461. The group did not reform but after being refuelled, seven of the boats moved north to close convoy ON 115, reported by U 210 on the 29th. A patrol line, *Pirat*, was formed ahead of the convoy on 1.8.42 E of Newfoundland and the ex-*Wolf* boats joined this line.

The convoy was sighted by U 552 on the 2nd E of Cape Race. The boats were ordered to close and the convoy was pursued as far as the Newfoundland Bank, where fog caused the operation to be terminated on the 3rd. Two ships had been sunk and another one damaged. U 704 had no success.

With U 43 and U 552 damaged in the action against ON 115, the remaining five ex-*Wolf* boats, including U 704, headed to a new position 400 miles NE of Newfoundland, to form a new patrol line, *Steinbrinck*, for the 7th. Two days before reaching this position, outward-bound U 593 reported eastbound SC 94 at the northern end of the planned *Steinbrinck* line. The boats closed the convoy and a number of other outward-bound boats joined the pursuit. In the early morning of the 8th U 704 missed the British steamer *Duchess of Bedford* and in the evening of the 9th she was again unsuccessful against another steamer, possibly because of premature torpedo-detonation. Before the operation ended on the 11th S of Iceland, eleven ships had been sunk and two boats lost, U 210 and U 379.

U 704 put in to her new base at St Nazaire **16.8.42**

2. 9.9.42 Left for operations.

U 704 returned to St Nazaire with technical problems **15.9.42**

3. 5.10.42 Left for the North Atlantic.

U 704 joined *Panther* group W of Ireland. On the 16th twelve boats of the group and ten from *Wotan* were ordered to attack westbound convoy ON 137, sighted by U 704 in the central North Atlantic. The weather worsened and the shadower lost contact after being damaged and driven off. The boats searched but the convoy was not found. A gale developed on the 17th, the *Wotan* boats left for home on the 18th and the operation was terminated on the 19th.

The *Panther* boats moved westwards and formed a new patrol line, *Veilchen*, on the 24th 400 miles E of Newfoundland. On the 30th eastbound SC 107 was sighted by U 522 just S of Cape Race. *Veilchen* group was ordered to attack. This convoy was sighted by U 381. She, U 704 and U 402 made the first approaches to the convoy on 1.11.42 but were driven off and attacks did not begin

until the early hours of the 2nd. U 704 had no success against the convoy.

On the 5th the last boats were driven off by Liberators of 120 Squadron. Others had broken off because of fuel and torpedo shortages. When the operation was called off on the 6th, fifteen ships had been sunk and two boats lost, U 132 and U 520.

U 704 made an unsuccessful attack on the fast, unescorted RMS *Queen Elizabeth* on the 9th in the central North Atlantic. From a 4-torpedo spread, only one detonation was heard.

The boat put in to La Pallice **23.11.42**

4. 1.1.43 Left La Pallice and returned **2.1.43**

5. 7.1.43 Left for the North Atlantic.

U 704 joined *Habicht* group W of Ireland. On 17.1.43 the group moved westwards in search of ON convoys. By the 19th nothing had been found and the *Habicht* boats combined with those of *Falke* group to form a new patrol line, *Haudegen*, running for 300 miles SE of Cape Farewell.

On the 22nd the group was ordered to move southeastwards to intercept an eastbound HX convoy. Bad weather prevented the interception and the boats returned to their original position S of Cape Farewell. On the way back, on the 26th, U 383 sighted escorts of convoy HX 223, which had been scattered in the storm.

From 1.2.43 *Haudegen* group began a southwesterly move towards Newfoundland. On the 2nd the five northern boats of the group were detached to attack convoy SG 19, as *Nordsturm* group.

On the 4th U 187 of *Pfeil* group sighted SC 118 E of Newfoundland and the southern *Haudegen* boats, U 704, U 438, U 613, U 624 and U 752 were ordered to leave the patrol line and attack the convoy, which was also being attacked by *Pfeil* group. After the SC 118 operation ended on the 9th WNW of Ireland, the five *Haudegen* boats did not rejoin their group but returned to base.

U 704 reached St Nazaire **12.2.43**

6. 14.3.43 Left St Nazaire, in transit to Germany.

U 704 put in to Bergen **5.4.43**

7. 6.4.43 Left Bergen and arrived Königsberg **11.4.43**

U 704 saw no further operational service. She went on to training duties and served with 21, 24 and 23 U-Flottillen until March 1945.

She was decommissioned in March and scuttled at Vegesack in April to prevent her falling into Allied hands.

The wreck was broken up in 1947.

U 705   Type VII C

Built by Stülcken Sohn, Hamburg
Keel laid 11.10.40   Launched 23.10.41
Commissioned 30.12.41   Feldpost Nr M 46 975

Sunk 3.9.42 NNW of Cape Ortegal (46°42′N 11°07′W)

Served with
5 U-Flottille, Kiel   December 1941 - July 1942 (ab)
6 U-Flottille, St Nazaire   August 1942 - 3.9.42 (fb)

Commanded by
KL Karl-Horst Horn   December 1941 - 3.9.42

Patrols: 1   Ships sunk: 1 (3279 grt) + 1 damaged

1. 1.8.42 Left Kiel for the North Atlantic.

U 705 was one of eight boats which left Kiel between 21.7.42 and 1.8.42 to join a new line, *Steinbrinck*, 400 miles NE of Newfoundland from 7.8.42. Two days before the first boats reached their positions, U 593 sighted eastbound convoy SC 94. The still outward-bound boats were directed to operate against it from the 7th, in company with the *Steinbrinck* boats which were already in position.

The convoy was pursued for five days and in spite of poor visibility, many attacks from the surface escort and from the 9th the air escort, ten ships were sunk. U 705, on her first patrol, had no success against SC 94. The operation against the convoy ended on the 11th S of Iceland.

After the action, U 705 joined other boats in a new group, *Lohs*, 600 miles W of the North Channel, to search for eastbound SC 95. The convoy was sighted on the 15th by U 256, going north. U 705, U 256 and U 605 were the only boats to make attacks. U 705 had the only success, when she sank the SS *Balladier* (am 3279t) WSW of Rockall. On the 16th U 596 sank a straggler from the convoy. Contact with SC 95 was lost and the *Lohs* group reformed.

On the 21st the *Lohs* boats moved northwards in search of ON and SC convoys and on the 22nd U 135 sighted westbound ONS 122 in the central North Atlantic. She was driven off and contact was not regained until the 24th. During the night of the 24/25th nine boats came up with the convoy. Attacks were made during the early hours of the 25th. Four ships were sunk but further attacks were prevented by a sudden fog.

U 705 did not go with the other *Lohs* boats, when they headed for a refuelling rendezvous. She set out for base. Late on the 30th U 705 torpedoed the tanker SS *Jack Carnes* (am 10907t). Although a detonation was heard, no result was seen. The vessel was sunk by U 516 a few hours later.

On 3.9.42 U 705 was attacked and sunk in a depth-charge attack NNW of Cape Ortegal by a Whitley of 77 Squadron (F/Sgt A A MacInnes). The squadron was on loan from Bomber Command and it was MacInnes' first a/s patrol.

There were no survivors from U 705, 45 dead.

U 706 Type VII C

Built by Stülcken Sohn, Hamburg
Keel laid 22.11.40 Launched 24.11.41
Commissioned 16.3.42 Feldpost Nr M 43 347

Sunk 3.8.43 NNW of Cape Ortegal (46°15′N 10°25′W)

Served with
5 U-Flottille, Kiel March - September 1942 (ab)
3 U-Flottille, La Pallice October 1942 - 3.8.43 (fb)

Commanded by
KL Alexander von Zitzewitz March 1942 - 3.8.43

Patrols: 4 Ships sunk: 3 (18,650 grt)

1. 22.9.42 Left Kiel for the North Atlantic.

U 706 joined *Luchs* group, formed from 1.10.42 W of Ireland. On the 2nd the line began a movement southwestwards and on the 3rd U 260 sighted northeast-bound HX 209. Bad weather and high winds prevented the boats gathering for a concerted attack on the 5th and U 582 was lost. The pursuit was abandoned on the 6th, in the face of increasing air cover.

From the 8th U 706 joined a new patrol line, *Panther*, 700 to 800 miles W of the North Channel. On the 11th U 620 sighted westbound ONS 136 and some of the *Panther* boats were directed to it, as *Leopard* group. U 705 was not part of this group but early on the 13th she torpedoed and sank a ship from ONS 136 in the central North Atlantic, the SS *Stornest* (br 4265t).

On the 22nd westbound ON 139 was sighted by U 443. On the 23rd U 706 sighted some ships and may have carried out an unsuccessful attack. ON 139's escort prevented attacks on the 23rd

and 24th and contact with the convoy was lost on the 25th. Searches failed to find the convoy and U 706 went off to refuel from U 463 in the central North Atlantic. While this was being carried out on the 27th, two of U 706's crewmen were lost overboard, one of whom was rescued by U 463.

U 706 put in to her new base at La Pallice **7.11.42**

2. 8.12.42 Left for Atlantic operations.

U 706 went south to an area W of Portugal, to join other boats searching for UGS convoys bound for Gibraltar with supplies for the North African invasion forces. This deployment was made to comply with a Naval Staff order that twelve boats from the Atlantic were to be on hand to intercept such convoys.

The order was rescinded on the 23rd and U 706 and other boats were sent into the Atlantic. They formed *Falke* group from the 31st 500 miles W of Ireland, to await an ON convoy. The boats waited in vain until 4.1.43, when they moved northwestwards to form a north-south patrol line, hoping to catch on ONS convoy.

U 706 left the group at this time to refuel. She was supplied by U 117 on or after the 11th. U 706, U 123 and U 662 were on their way to join *Jaguar* group NE of Newfoundland. An HX convoy was expected but it was SC 117 which passed the western end of the *Jaguar* patrol line on the 22nd, sighted by U 413.

Radio conditions were bad and *Jaguar* group's pursuit of the convoy did not become known until the 23rd, at which time *Haudegen* group was ordered to form a patrol line S of Cape Farewell to await the convoy.

However, bad weather prevented the *Haudegen* boats forming their line and *Jaguar* group had lost contact on the 23rd. In spite of a search, the convoy was not found again. The *Jaguar* group did not reform and U 706 was refuelled on 7.2.43 for return to base by the outward-bound U 460.

U 706 returned to La Pallice **13.2.43**

3. 15.3.43 Left for the North Atlantic.

U 706 joined *Seeteufel* group SW of Iceland. The group had been searching for convoy ONS 1 but without much success. By the 26th the *Seeteufel* line ran southeast from Cape Farewell and it joined the more southerly *Seewolf* group to form a line running 800 miles south from the Cape. In the afternoon of the 26th masts and an aircraft-carrier were sighted in the centre of the *Seeteufel* line. This was thought to be an ON convoy but a strong air and surface escort kept the boats down and prevented its direction being discovered and it was not pursued.

It was decided on the 28th that *Seeteufel* should concentrate all of its efforts on eastbound convoy HX 230, sighted by U 305 of *Seewolf* on the 27th. However, the weather worsened and a hurricane developed. The boats continued to pursue, hoping to find stragglers but only one was sunk because of difficulties of attack in the heavy seas. The operation ended on the 30th NW of Ireland.

On 3.4.43 U 706 joined other boats to form *Löwenherz* group 400 miles SE of Cape Farewell. The group moved westwards and on the 4th contacted HX 231. Conditions were favourable but carrier-borne aircraft made attacks difficult. In the afternoon of the 5th U 706 attacked the convoy. With a 2-torpedo spread, she sank the tanker SS *British Ardour* (br 7124t) with one and missed the SS *Tyndareus* with the second, SSE of Cape Farewell.

The convoy was pursued until the 7th and six ships were sunk. After the HX 231 action ended, the *Löwenherz* boats which had not headed home, including U 706, formed *Lerche* group on the 11th SE of Greenland, to operate against eastbound HX 232. The convoy passed through the patrol line on that day and attacks were made during the night of the 11/12th. In the afternoon of the 12th U 706 torpedoed and sank a straggler in the central North Atlantic, the SS *Fresno City* (br 7261t). She had been torpedoed earlier in the day by U 563. HX 232 lost a total of three ships but further attacks were prevented by the almost constant harassment of the boats by escorting aircraft.

U 706 (continued)

When the *Lerche* boats went to refuel, U 706, U 203 and U 532 joined *Meise* group E of Newfoundland from the 17th. The group moved northwards, searching for convoys, and on the 21st HX 234 was sighted by U 306. As she closed the convoy, U 706 sighted westbound ONS 3. U 203, U 415, U 438, U 613 and U 732 were detached to join U 706 in the pursuit of ONS 3. The rest of the *Meise* boats went for HX 234.

Contact with ONS 3 was lost in fog and snowstorms and pursuit was abandoned on the 23rd. In early May U 706 was refuelled in the central North Atlantic for return to base.

She reached La Pallice **11.5.43**

4. 4.7.43 Left La Pallice and returned **8.7.43**

5. 26.7.43 Left La Pallice and returned **27.7.43**

6. 29.7.43 Left for Atlantic operations.

Outward-bound on 3.8.43, U 706 was spotted on the surface NNW of Cape Ortegal by a Hampden of 415 (RCAF) Squadron (S/Ldr C G Ruttan). In the face of heavy fire, the aircraft dropped six depth-charges, damaging the boat. A Liberator of 4 Squadron (USAF) (Capt J L Hamilton) arrived and, although hit by flak, dropped twelve depth-charges, which sank U 706. The Liberator dropped a dinghy to survivors and HMS *Waveney* was later sent to pick them up.

Of U 706's crew, the commander and 42 men were lost and 4 were made PoW.

U 707 Type VII C

Built by Stülcken Sohn, Hamburg
Keel laid 2.1.41   Launched 18.12.41
Commissioned 1.7.42   Feldpost Nr M 45 325

Sunk 9.11.43 ENE of the Azores (40°31′N 20°17′W)

Served with
8 U-Flottille, Danzig   July - November 1942 (ab)
7 U-Flottille, St Nazaire   December 1942 - 9.11.43 (fb)

Commanded by
OL Günter Gretschel   July 1942 - 9.11.43

Patrols: 3   Ships sunk: 2 (11,811 grt)

1. 12.1.43 Left Kiel for the North Atlantic.

With other newly-arrived boats, U 707 joined the *Haudegen* group patrol line, which ran southeastwards from Cape Farewell. On the 22nd a returning boat sighted a British hunting group and this was thought to be part of a remote screen for an expected HX convoy. *Haudegen* group was ordered southeastwards at high speed to intercept. Bad weather prevented the boats reaching the planned position. When a search further east found no convoy, the patrol line was moved back to an area SE of Cape Farewell on the 26th.

Haudegen group began to move southwestwards on 1.2.43, towards Newfoundland. On the 2nd small, northbound convoy SG 19 was sighted at the northern end of the line and U 707, U 186, U 223, U 268 and U 358 were detached as *Nordsturm* group to attack it. U 223 sank one ship before contact was lost. After two days of searching the entrances to fjords along the coast of Greenland, the five boats rejoined *Haudegen* group.

Up to mid-February the group was positioned in an arc 300 miles N of Cape Race. On the 15th it was dissolved to go for refuelling but on the 17th the returning U 69 sighted convoy ONS 165, steering southeastwards. Although most of the *Haudegen* boats were very low on fuel and set to return to base, it was decided that they should try for the convoy and refuel later and that the four boats

with sufficient fuel, U 707, U 186, U 223 and U 358 should also attack the convoy, as *Taifun* group. A storm prevented any concerted attack and only two ships were sunk, by U 403 and U 525, but two boats were lost. The operation ended on the 20th.

The *Taifun* boats and the four surviving ex-*Haudegen* boats which had taken part in the action against ONS 165 went for refuelling by U 460 E of Newfoundland. On the 22nd westbound ON 166 passed to the south of the refuelling area. U 707 and other boats, refuelled or not, took off in pursuit of the convoy and in the early hours of the 24th U 707 torpedoed and sank a straggler, the SS *Jonathan Sturges* (am 7176t), in the central North Atlantic. The operation ended on the 25th in bad visibility SE of Newfoundland, with fourteen ships sunk and another damaged. U 707 was refuelled by U 462 in late February 400 to 600 miles N of the Azores for return to base.

She put in to her new base at St Nazaire **8.3.43**

2. 12.4.43 Left for the North Atlantic.

U 707 joined *Specht* group, formed on the 20th N of the Azores. The group moved westwards and on the 23rd was in a north-south patrol line E of Newfoundland, awaiting SC 127. *Specht* moved northwestwards and from the 27th was drawn up in a line S of Greenland, in the path of convoy ONS 4, but it passed to the north.

On the 29th *Amsel* group closed up to *Specht*, they moved south and on 1.5.43 they were positioned in an arc E of Newfoundland, awaiting northbound convoy SC 128. On this day the convoy passed through the *Specht* line but contact was lost in a southerly gale and when the convoy had not been sighted again by the 3rd, a new patrol line, *Fink*, was formed from *Specht* and *Star* groups. *Star* had come south after abandoning its pursuit of convoy ONS 5 on the 1st.

The twenty-nine boats continued to search for SC 128 but by the 4th it was realised that the convoy had been re-routed. *Fink* had received orders to take up a new position when a southwest-bound convoy was sighted in the centre of the line. It proved to be ONS 5, which had been delayed by the storm. In the early hours of the 5th U 707 torpedoed and sank a straggler S of Cape Farewell, the SS *North Britain* (br 4635t).

During daylight on the 5th fifteen *Fink* boats approached the convoy but before nightfall fog came down and most lost contact. In the fog the escorts made fifteen depth-charge attacks. In the morning of the 6th ONS 5 was again sighted but deteriorating weather conditions caused the operation to be abandoned on that day, E of Newfoundland. Twelve ships had been sunk and six boats lost. After the action U 707 was refuelled by U 461 in the central North Atlantic.

Five small groups were formed on the 12th from ex-*Fink* boats and new-arrivals, *Nahe, Iller, Isar, Lech* and *Inn*. U 707 was in *Nahe* with U 92 and U 264. After a few days the small groups were reformed into two new ones, *Donau 1* and *2*, SE of Cape Farewell. U 707 was in *Donau 2*.

The groups moved southwestwards from the 15th and then southwards on the 17th. Contact was made with eastbound SC 130 during the night of the 18/19th, sighted by U 304 S of Cape Farewell. Continuous air cover kept the boats away from the convoy. On the 19th U 707 was damaged in a depth-charge attack by the destroyer HMS *Duncan* and driven off. The operation was terminated on the 20th, with no ships sunk but three boats lost.

U 707 put in to Bordeaux **31.5.43**

3. 12.10.43 Left Bordeaux and arrived La Pallice **13.10.43**

4. 19.10.43 Left La Pallice, one of eight boats that would make up a mobile force, *Schill* group.

The plan was to make a one-night attack on an MKS or KMS convoy off the northwest coast of Spain. Among *Schill*'s boats were three flak-boats, U 211, U 441 and U 953.

The *Schill* patrol line was formed on the 27th 400 miles W of Cape Ortegal, to await northbound convoy MKS 28/SL 138.

Luftwaffe aircraft sighted it on the 27th and 28th but on the 29th, the day of the planned attack, it was not seen, having steered slightly to the west. On the 30th aircraft found it again, to the northwest of the *Schill* line. The boats were ordered to pursue on the surface in daylight and contact was made on the 31st. In a morning attack U 262 sank a ship but U 306 was lost. A strong air escort caused the operation to be broken off.

The *Schill* boats were ordered to form a new patrol line and a move southwards began on 3.11.43, searching for a KMS convoy. On the 5th the Luftwaffe began a search for northbound MKS 29 and it was sighted on the 7th. The *Schill* line was reformed in the expectation that the convoy would pass through it during the evening of the 8th. Again, air reconnaissance failed to sight the convoy on the vital day, when mechanical defects forced aircraft to return to base. At the expected interception time the *Schill* boats moved southwestwards at high speed but when only destroyers were seen it was realised that the convoy had passed through the line. It was found again by aircraft on the morning of the 9th but despite a search, the *Schill* boats never found the convoy.

On the 9th U 707 was attacked and sunk in a depth-charge attack ENE of the Azores by a Fortress of 220 Squadron (F/Lt R P Drummond). One man was seen in the sea. The aircraft dropped a dinghy and a ration pack but it is not known whether or not the man survived. U 707 was the first U-boat to be sunk by an Azores-based aircraft. Drummond was awarded an immediate DFC.

The commander and 49 other men from U 707's crew were lost with the boat.

U 708   Type VII C

Built by Stülcken Sohn, Hamburg
Keel laid 31.3.41   Launched 24.3.42
Commissioned 24.7.42   Feldpost Nr M 28 568

Scuttled 5.5.45 at Wilhelmshaven

Served with
8 U-Flottille, Danzig   July 1942 - October 1943 (ab)
7 U-Flottille, St Nazaire   October 1943 - February 1944 (fb-oE)
5 U-Flottille, Kiel   February - April 1944 (ab)
21 U-Flottille, Pillau   April 1944 - 5.5.45 (sb)

Commanded by
OL Werner Heintze   July 1942 - June 1943
OL Klaus Andersen   June 1943 - February 1944
OL Herbert Kühn   May 1944 - 5.5.45

Patrols: None   Ships sunk: None

From September 1943 to January 1944 U 708 took part in trials in the Baltic, testing equipment to counter airborne radar.

She then went on to training duties, serving with 5 and 21 U-Flottillen. U 708 was scuttled on 5.5.45 at Wilhelmshaven to prevent her falling into Allied hands.

The wreck was broken up in 1947.

U 709   Type VII C

Built by Stülcken Sohn, Hamburg
Keel laid 5.5.41   Launched 14.4.42
Commissioned 12.8.42   Feldpost Nr M 49 765

Sunk 1.3.44 N of the Azores (49°10′N 26°00′W)

Served with
5 U-Flottille, Kiel   August 1942 - February 1943 (ab)
9 U-Flottille, Brest   March 1943 - 1.3.44 (fb)

Commanded by
OL Karl-Otto Weber   August 1942 - December 1943
OL Rudolf Ites   December 1943 - 1.3.44

Patrols: 5   Ships sunk: None

1. 13.2.43   Left Kiel for the North Atlantic.
Outward-bound, U 709 and U 634 joined *Neptun* group boats from the 28th in their pursuit of eastbound HX 227. In the early morning of 2.3.43 U 634 sank a straggler from the convoy.

From the 5th U 709 and U 634 and some *Neptun* boats took up waiting positions S of Cape Farewell and north of *Wildfang* and *Burggraf* groups. On the 6th U 405 sighted eastbound SC 121 and seventeen boats, drawn from *Neptun, Wildfang* and *Burggraf* groups, including U 709 and U 634, were detached to pursue the convoy, as *Westmark* group.

On the 7th, in spite of bad weather, six boats, not including U 709, maintained contact with the convoy but could not make any attacks. The weather improved and from the 8th both *Westmark* and *Ostmark* group boats made attacks. When the operation ended on the 11th near Rockall, twelve ships had been sunk and one damaged, without loss of any boats. U 709 had no success.

The boat put in to her new base at Brest **18.3.43**

2. 15.4.43   Left for the North Atlantic.
U 709 joined *Amsel* group, formed on the 26th 1400 miles W of Ireland. The group moved south, searching for a convoy that might have been eastbound HX 235. The *Amsel* line linked up with the left wing of *Specht* group on the 29th and the two groups moved south together.

By 1.5.43 the combined line was drawn up in an arc 200 miles E of St John's. On the 3rd the *Specht* boats moved northwards to join a new patrol line, *Fink,* and the *Amsel* boats, augmented by six new arrivals, formed four new smaller groups, *Amsel 1,2,3* and *4,* in the same arc E of St John's. U 709 was in *Amsel 3.*

Amsel 1 and *2* went north to intercept convoy ONS 5 and on the 7th *Amsel 3* and *4* combined as *Rhein* group, which was ordered southeastwards at high speed on the 8th to form a patrol line on the 9th for the interception of HX 237.

U 359 sighted a ship of the convoy on the 9th before the line could be formed but lost it in worsening visibility. The boats carried out independent searches before reforming in the morning of the 10th. At noon U 403 sighted a fast independent ship and then a tug, which led to the convoy being located in the afternoon.

The *Rhein* boats were by then too far east, so they were ordered to combine with *Elbe* group, to form *Elbe 1* and *2* groups to pursue the slower convoy SC 129, which was sighted by U 504 on the 11th. U 709 was in *Elbe 1.* The convoy had a strong surface and carrier-borne air-escort, which kept the boats at a distance. The operation against SC 129 ended on the 14th SW of Ireland, with two ships sunk and two boats lost.

U 709 was refuelled by U 459 in the central North Atlantic, SE of Greenland, for return to base.

She returned to Brest **23.5.43**

3. 5.7.43   Left for Atlantic operations.

U 709 (continued)

Outward-bound, U 709 was damaged by a battery explosion. Two crewmen were killed and another injured.

The boat returned to Brest **20.7.43**

4. 2.10.43 Left Brest and returned **3.10.43**

5. 6.10.43 Left for the North Atlantic.

U 709 joined *Siegfried* group, formed for the 24th 500 miles E of Newfoundland to await HX 262 and SC 145. The boats were ordered to remain submerged in daylight, ready for an attack after dark. On the 25th it was thought that a convoy would pass south of the group. The boats moved southwards but nothing was found.

To cover a wider area, *Siegfried* was split into three small sub-groups, *Siegfried 1,2* and *3*. U 709 was in *Siegfried 3*. The groups continued southwards, searching for SC 145 but it passed by on the 29th. Two days later the boats again reformed, this time into groups *Jahn* and *Körner*. U 709 was in *Jahn*.

On 3.11.43 the boats were redeployed in five small sub-groups, *Tirpitz 1* to *5*, to search for convoy HX 264. It passed the groups late on the 6th and next day the operation was abandoned, it being impossible to surface in daylight because of carrier-borne aircraft.

U 709 next joined *Eisenhart* group, made up of seven sub-groups of three boats each and drawn up in two lines from 11.11.43, running southeastwards from Cape Farewell.

Reports indicated that convoys were being routed to the south so the *Eisenhart* boats were ordered southeastwards on the 12th to search for SC 146 and HX 265. By the 16th no convoys had been found and the majority of boats were then WSW of Ireland. Fuel was now becoming a problem for many of *Eisenhart* group and it was decided to end the operation.

Eisenhart boats with sufficient fuel, which included U 709, were sent to an area W of Spain to reinforce *Schill* group. U 709 joined *Schill 2* group in an east-west patrol line W of Cape Finisterre, through which was expected to pass the northbound, combined convoy MKS 30/SL 139. The convoy passed through the eastern end of the *Schill 1* group line in the afternoon of the 18th, W of Lisbon. The *Schill 2* boats moved northwards and formed an east-west patrol line E of the Azores, which the convoy was expected to reach on the 19th. It passed through the centre of the *Schill 2* line late on that day but the well-handled surface escort and constant attacks by aircraft prevented any night attacks by the boats, keeping them down most of the time. At dawn on the 20th, with increased air activity expected, the group was ordered to dive, abandoning any hope of attacking the convoy.

U 709 put in to Lorient **28.11.43**

6. 25.1.44 Left for Atlantic operations.

U 709 joined *Igel 2* group W of Ireland, searching for westbound convoy ON 223. From 4.2.44 the *Igel 2* boats were patrolling SW of Ireland. On the 6th they were deployed against combined convoy MKS 38/SL 147, reported N of the Azores by German aircraft on the 6th, 7th and 8th. Some of the boats came up to the convoy on the 7th but had no success against the strong escort.

From the 10th *Igel 1* and *2* groups began a slow westward withdrawal, which was taken further than intended because of intense Allied anti-submarine activity, both SW of Ireland and NW of Scotland. It was intended to intercept an ONS convoy between the 14th and the 18th, with the aid of aerial reconnaissance.

ONS 29, ON 224 and OS 68 were sighted by aircraft on the 14th W of the North Channel and *Igel 1* and *2* groups were hurried to an assembly area 600 miles SW of Ireland. On the 18th two parallel patrol lines, *Hai 1* and 2, were formed ahead of the convoys. They were found to have turned south on the 17th and passed the southern end of the *Hai* lines. The boats were immediately ordered south, submerged in daylight and at high speed on the surface in the hours of darkness. Instead of sighting any convoys at dawn on the 19th, the boats saw only some destroyers. The operation was

called off and the boats submerged to avoid aircraft from the escort-carrier HMS *Striker.*

U 709 moved westwards with the other boats and *Preussen* group was formed 400 to 500 miles N of the Azores. Between the 27th and 29th the group was concentrated between 22° and 30°W in the expected path of convoy ON 225.

On the 29th U 709 was located by destroyer-escort USS *Thomas* (Lt-Cdr D M Kellogg) of TG 21, which was with the escort-carrier USS *Block Island* 600 miles N of the Azores. A search began and soon afterwards U 709 was illuminated by a star shell from destroyer-escort USS *Bronstein* (Lt H S Kinney), on the surface five miles from the spot where she was first located.

Bronstein opened fire, scoring hits before U 709 dived. *Thomas* carried out nine depth-charge attacks in the early hours of 1.3.44, destroying U 709. USS *Bostwick* also took part in the action.

There were no survivors, 54 dead.

U 710   Type VII C

Built by Stülcken Sohn, Hamburg
Keel laid 4.6.41   Launched 11.5.42
Commissioned 2.9.42   Feldpost Nr M 49 924

Sunk 24.4.43 S of Vik, Iceland (61°25´N 19°48´W)

Served with
5 U-Flottille, Kiel   September 1942 - April 1943 (ab)
7 U-Flottille, St Nazaire   April 1943 (fb)

Commanded by
OL Dietrich von Carlowitz   September 1942 - 24.4.43

Patrols: 1   Ships sunk: None

1. 15.4.43 Left Kiel for the North Atlantic.

Outward-bound on the 24th, U 710 was attacked and sunk in a depth-charge attack S of Vik, Iceland by a Fortress of 206 Squadron (F/O R L Cowey). The boat was apparently heading for eastbound convoy HX 234.

There were no survivors, 49 dead.

U 711   Type VII C

Built by Stülcken Sohn, Hamburg
Keel laid 31.7.41   Launched 25.6.42
Commissioned 26.9.42   Feldpost Nr M 50 659

Sunk 4.5.45 at Kilbotn, Norway

Served with
5 U-Flottille, Kiel   September 1942 - March 1943 (ab)
11 U-Flottille, Bergen   April - May 1943 (fb)
13 U-Flottille, Trondheim   June 1943 - 4.5.45 (fb)

Commanded by
KL Hans-Günther Lange   September 1942 - 4.5.45

Patrols: 12   Ships sunk: 2 (14,376 grt) + 1 damaged
1 corvette (925 dt)

1. 20.3.43 Left Kiel and arrived Bergen **23.3.43**

2. 25.3.43 Left for operations. No details known of this patrol.
U 711 put in to Hammerfest **30.4.43**

3. 12.5.43 Left Hammerfest and returned **14.5.43**

4. 25.5.43 Left for operations. No details known of this patrol.
U 711 put in to Ankenes **18.6.43**

5. 22.7.43 Left for operations in Northern Waters.

In early August U 711, U 302 and U 354 were patrolling as *Wiking* group, in search of Soviet convoys. None was sighted until the 21st, when U 354 sighted a convoy off Dickson. She and U 302 shadowed it into the Vilkitski Strait, where U 354 damaged a ship on the 27th and U 302 sank another on the 28th. U 711 did not take part in attacks on the convoy.

From September 4th to the 6th *Wiking* group again searched for convoys, supported by U 255, but nothing was seen. On the 9th U 711 made a reconnaissance of Wardroper Island, on the 28th she shelled the W/T station at Pravdy, Nansen Island and on the 24th she shelled the W/T station at Blagopoluchiya, Novaya Zemlya.

U 711 lost a man overboard on the 30th and she put in to Narvik the same day, **30.9.43**

6. 2.10.43 Left Narvik and arrived Trondheim **5.10.43**

7. 15.12.43 Left Trondheim and arrived Narvik **17.12.43**

8. 18.12.43 Left Narvik and returned **19.12.43**

9. 20.12.43 Left Narvik and arrived Trondheim **23.12.43**

10. 19.3.44 Left for operations.

U 711 joined *Blitz* group, which in late March was waiting for eastbound JW 58. The convoy set out from Iceland on the 27th and was located by German aircraft on the 30th. *Blitz, Thor* and *Hammer* groups made contact shortly after midnight on 1.4.44.

In the evenings of the 1st and 2nd U 711 made unsuccessful attacks on JW 58's escort SW of Bear Island. The convoy reached Kola Inlet without loss on the 5th.

U 711 returned to Hammerfest **6.4.44**

11. 11.4.44 Left Hammerfest and arrived Narvik **15.4.44**

12. 24.4.44 Left for operations.

Westbound RA 59 left Kola Inlet on the 28th and was located by German aircraft late that evening. U 711 was with *Keil* group, which with *Donner* group was deployed against the convoy.

In the early evening of the 30th U 711 torpedoed and sank the SS *William S Thayer* (am 7176t) S of Bear Island. Later that evening and again soon after midnight the boat made further attacks but heard only end-of-run detonations. In the afternoon of the 2nd she made an unsuccessful attack on a destroyer, with only end-of-run detonations heard.

U 711 returned to Narvik **5.5.44**

13. 30.5.44 Left for operations. No details known of this patrol.
U 711 put in to Bogenbucht **8.7.44**

14. 29.7.44 Left Bogenbucht and arrived Hammerfest **30.7.44**

15. 2.8.44 Left for operations.

U 711 operated with other boats along the Siberian sea route in the Kara Sea, with *Greif* group. U 711 supplied fuel to the other *Greif* boats and then returned to refuel.

She reached Hammerfest **19.8.44**

16. 22.8.44 Left for operations.

On the 23rd U 711 joined a patrol line. She later made some unsuccessful attacks on a Soviet naval task force, which was escorting eastbound JW 59. She failed against the battleship *Archangel'sk* and the destroyer *Zarkij*, E of Bear Island. Early on the 25th U 711 unsuccessfully attacked the destroyer HMS *Keppel.*

In the early morning of the 26th U 711 may have damaged a

Soviet submarine, possibly the *S-56*, or she may have sunk the *M-108,* which was reported missing after the 26th.

U 711 returned to Hammerfest **26.8.44**

17. 27.8.44 Left Hammerfest and arrived Bogenbucht **28.8.44**

18. 3.9.44 Left Bogenbucht and arrived Hammerfest **5.9.44**

19. 7.9.44 Left for operations.

U 711, U 739 and U 957 operated in the Kara Sea. On the 21st they encountered Soviet convoy VD 1, en route from the Vilkitski Strait to Dickson. On that day U 711 claimed to have made six attacks on escort vessels, all of which failed because of torpedo defects. On the 23rd further attacks against the convoy were unsuccessful for the same reason. The other two boats each sank an escort vessel.

The three boats landed a party on Sterligova Island on the 24th and destroyed a wireless station. Four prisoners were taken.

U 711 returned to Narvik **4.10.44**

20. 6.10.44 Left Narvik and arrived Trondheim **8.10.44**

21. 23.1.45 Left Trondheim and arrived Narvik **26.1.45**

22. 9.2.45 Left for operations.

Eastbound JW 64 left Loch Ewe on the 3rd. U 711 joined *Rasmus* group S of Bear Island, to intercept the convoy. The boats were unable to attack because of the strength of the escort and they were sent to join other boats N of Kola Inlet. On the 14th U 711, U 968 and U 992 attacked Soviet convoy BK 3 off the Inlet.

U 711 torpedoed and sank the SS *Horace Gray* (am 7200t) in the morning of the 14th and claimed a second ship sunk in the same attack but this is unconfirmed. On the 16th a combined British and Soviet naval force attempted to drive the boats from the entrance to Kola Inlet, where they were waiting for RA 64 to sail.

When the convoy left on the 17th, it was attacked by U 711 and U 968. The escorting corvette HMS *Bluebell* was sunk on that day by U 711. She evaded the hunt that followed. There was only one survivor from the *Bluebell.* Contact with the convoy was lost on the 18th and the boats moved westwards to Bear Island Passage in the hope of finding it again but they were unsuccessful. Aircraft found the convoy again on the 20th and an unsuccessful attack was made by Ju 88s, in which six German aircraft were shot down. U-boats which approached the convoy were driven off. In a second attack by Ju 88s, the straggling SS *Henry Bacon* was sunk. She was the last ship to be sunk by German aircraft in the Second World War.

U 711 put in to Harstad **24.2.45**

23. 14.3.45 Left for operations.

On the 11th eastbound JW 65 set out from the Clyde and *Hagen* group took up a waiting position in Bear Island Passage. U 711 later joined this group. When aerial reconnaissance had not found the convoy by the 17th, the *Hagen* boats moved eastwards to join those waiting at the entrance to Kola Inlet and two patrol lines were formed, one of six boats and one of seven.

Early on the 20th JW 65 passed through the first line in a snowstorm and reached the second at noon. Attacks were made and one ship and a sloop were sunk. After the convoy entered the Inlet, the boats attempted to operate against the escort-carriers HMS *Campania* and *Trumpeter* from JW 65's escort, believed to be in the Barents Sea, but this was unsuccessful. On the 22nd U 711 torpedoed the Soviet armed trawler *BPS-5* off Kola Inlet, damaging her stern.

Westbound RA 65 sailed on the 23rd. U 711 and other boats tried to form a patrol line ahead of it on the 25th but the convoy failed to appear as expected. When aerial reconnaissance had not located it by the 27th, the operation was abandoned.

U 711 returned to Harstad **31.3.45**

U 711 (continued)

24. 15.4.45 Left for operations.

U 711 joined *Faust* group W of Bear Island, awaiting JW 66, which sailed from the Clyde on the 16th. When aerial reconnaissance failed to find it, the boats moved to a position off Kola Inlet. En route with other boats, U 711 reported sinking a small steamer from an eastbound convoy on the 19th near the Inlet.

JW 66 avoided the waiting boats and reached Kola safely on the 25th. At noon on this day U 711 unsuccessfully attacked a destroyer of the escort after penetrating further into the Inlet than any of the other boats.

In late April U 711 was one of fourteen boats waiting off Kola Inlet for the departure of return convoy RA 66. On the 29th, prior to the convoy sailing, Allied and Soviet warships attempted to drive off the waiting boats. A British frigate was sunk, two boats were lost and the remainder left the area.

When the convoy set out, the boats did not approach. Contact was lost and could not be regained by aerial reconnaissance. On the 30th U 711 unsuccessfully attacked a destroyer. The operation was abandoned. Thus ended what would have been the last convoy action of the war.

U 711 returned to Harstad **2.5.45**

In the afternoon of 4.5.45 British aircraft from a naval task force attacked the naval installation at Kilbotn, near Harstad. U 711 was moored alongside the depôt ship MV Black Watch, formerly the flagship of the Olsen Line.

20 Wildcats of 882 (FAA) Squadron from HMS Searcher, 8 Avengers and 4 Wildcats of 846 (FAA) Squadron from HMS Trumpeter and 9 Avengers and 4 Wildcats of 853 (FAA) Squadron from HMS Queen took part. U 711 and Black Watch were sunk at their moorings.

Of U 711's crew, 32 men were killed.

U 712   Type VII C

Built by Stülcken Sohn, Hamburg
Keel laid 4.9.41   Launched 10.8.42
Commissioned 5.11.42   Feldpost Nr M 50 836

Surrendered 5.5.45 at Kristiansand-Süd

Served with
8 U-Flottille, Danzig   November 1942 - October 1943 (ab)
3 U-Flottille, La Pallice   November - December 1943 (fb-oE)
23 U-Flottille, Danzig   January 1944 - February 1945 (ab)
31 U-Flottille, Hamburg   March 1945 - 5.5.45 (ab)

Commanded by
OL Walter Pietschmann   November 1942 - December 1943
OL Walter-Ernst Koch   December 1943 - June 1944
OL Eberhard Freiherr von Ketelhodt   July 1944 - 5.5.45

Patrols: None   Ships sunk: None

1. 23.10.43 Left Kiel and arrived Bergen **29.10.43**

2. 4.11.43 Left Bergen, possibly after damage to her hull made her unfit for operational service.
U 712 returned to Kiel **10.11.43**

In January 1944 U 712 went on to training duties, serving at 23 and 31 U-Flottillen.

She was surrendered at Kristiansand-Süd on 5.5.45. She left there on the 29th for Loch Ryan. U 712 served with the Royal Navy from 1946 and was scrapped in 1949.

U 713   Type VII C

Built by Stülcken Sohn, Hamburg
Keel laid 22.10.41   Launched 23.9.42
Commissioned 29.12.42   Feldpost Nr M 49 449

Sunk 24.2.44 SSE of Jan Mayen (69°27´N 04°53´W)

Served with
8 U-Flottille, Danzig   December 1942 - June 1943 (ab)
11 U-Flottille, Bergen   July - October 1943 (fb)
13 U-Flottille, Trondheim   November 1943 - 24.2.44 (fb)

Commanded by
OL Henri Gosejakob   December 1942 - 24.2.44

Patrols: 4   Ships sunk: None

1. 29.6.43 Left Kiel and arrived Bergen **2.7.43**

2. 3.7.43 Left for operations. No details known of this patrol.
U 713 put in to Skjomenfjord **20.8.43**

3. 8.9.43 Left for operations.
In early October U 713 was with *Monsun* group between Spitzbergen and Bear Island. The last Allied convoy, RA 53, had left Kola Inlet on 1.3.43. The convoys were then suspended and the next one would not sail for Russia until mid-November 1943. The U-boats in Northern Waters were somewhat under-employed and the number of Soviet ships sunk, damaged or attacked by U-boats during the eight-month period of suspension did not exceed twenty.
U 713 put in to Narvik **27.10.43**

4. 22.11.43 Left for operations.
Westbound RA 54B left Archangel on the 26th. U 713 was with *Eisenbart* group, awaiting the convoy. Only U 307 sighted some escort vessels of the convoy but she was located and driven off, damaged by depth-charges. RA 54B reached Loch Ewe without loss.
Between November 29th and December 1st 1943 U 713 established a weather station on the north coast of Bear Island.
The boat returned to Narvik **9.12.43**

5. 12.12.43 Left Narvik and arrived Trondheim **14.12.43**

6. 3.2.44 Left Trondheim and arrived Narvik **5.2.44**

7. 5.2.44 Left for operations.
U 713 joined *Werwolf* group in Bear Island Passage. Westbound RA 56 left Kola Inlet on the 3rd. The convoy avoided the waiting boats and when it was located by aircraft on the 6th, the boats were given incorrect information, which sent them searching in the wrong direction.
Eastbound JW 57 left Loch Ewe on the 20th and was found by German aircraft on the 23rd. The *Werwolf* group was deployed. U 713, U 425, U 601, U 739 and U 990 closed the convoy on the 24th in the Norwegian Sea.
Operating against the convoy on the 24th, U 713 was sunk in a depth-charge attack SSE of Jan Mayen by the destroyer HMS *Keppel* (Cdr R J Tyson).
There were no survivors, 50 dead.

U 714   Type VII C

Built by Stülcken Sohn, Hamburg
Keel laid 24.12.41   Launched 12.11.42
Commissioned 10.2.43   Feldpost Nr M 50 495

Sunk 14.3.45 off St Abb's Head (55°57′N 01°57′W)

Served with
5 U-Flottille, Kiel   May - July 1943 (ab)
7 U-Flottille, St Nazaire   August 1943 - October 1944 (fb)
33 U-Flottille, Flensburg   November 1944 - 14.3.45 (fb)

Commanded by
KL Hans-Joachim Schwebcke   February 1943 - 14.3.45

Patrols: 5   Ships sunk: 1 (1226 grt)
                             1 m/s trawler (425 dt)

1. 23.9.43   Left Kiel and arrived Trondheim **29.9.43**

2. 13.10.43   Left for operations in the North Atlantic.
U 714 joined *Körner* group, formed E of Newfoundland from the 31st to search for convoys HX 263 and ONS 21. Both convoys went round the *Körner* patrol line.

The *Körner* and *Jahn* group boats were deployed in five smaller sub-groups, *Tirpitz 1,2,3,4* and *5,* each with four or five boats. They were to search for eastbound HX 264, which was expected in the area on 5.11.43.

Two boats were destroyed by the convoy's escort, aided by the 2nd SG, and the convoy passed the *Tirpitz* boats. The operation against HX 264 ended on the 7th, the convoy's air escort keeping the boats submerged.

The *Tirpitz* groups were dissolved and the boats reformed as *Eisenhart* group, made up of seven sub-groups of three boats each and drawn up in two lines from the 11th, running southeastwards from Cape Farewell. The lines crossed an area through which most convoys had passed since August 1943.

Reports indicated that convoys were now being routed further south, so the *Eisenhart* boats were ordered southeastwards on the 12th to search for SC 146 and HX 265. By the 16th no convoys had been found and the majority of boats were then WSW of Ireland. Fuel was now becoming a problem and it was decided to end the operation and send the boats to join *Schill* group W of Portugal.

U 714 joined the *Schill 3* patrol line, in the expected path of northbound convoy MKS 30/SL 139 and through which it was expected to pass on the 20th. *Schill 3* surfaced that evening but failed to find the convoy, which was located next morning and attacked by aircraft, resulting in one ship sunk and another damaged, both by glider bombs.

On the 22nd the remaining fourteen boats of the the three *Schill* groups were formed into an east-west patrol line, *Weddigen,* positioned between 18° and 22°W. On the 23rd the line moved southwestwards.

During the night of the 23/24th the 4th SG passed the patrol line. U 648 was detected and sunk and U 714 and U 424 were hunted and driven off after being subjected to depth-charge attacks for almost 12 hours. After finding no convoys, the *Weddigen* boats made a turn southeastwards on the 25th to intercept northbound MKS 31/SL 140.

Constantly harassed by surface vessels and aircraft and with insufficient information from reconnaissance aircraft, *Weddigen* could not carry out a concentrated attack before the operation was called off on the 28th.

U 714 put in to Lorient **2.12.43**

3. 11.1.44   Left Lorient and returned **15.1.44**

4. 20.1.44   Left for the North Atlantic.
U 714 joined *Igel 1* group W of Ireland. From February 4th to the 10th the boats operated singly SE of Iceland, after which they began a slow withdrawal westwards. In co-operation with aircraft, an attack on an ONS convoy was planned within a few days.

On the 11th U 714 took aboard the crew of U 545, which was scuttled that day N of Rockall, after being damaged by an aircraft on the 10th.

U 714 put in to St Nazaire **25.2.44**

5. 6.6.44   U 714 was one of nineteen non-schnorkel boats which sailed into the Bay of Biscay as *Landwirt* group.

They were to form a line at the 200 metres depth line between Brest and Bordeaux, keeping out of port in case an Allied invasion force arrived and trapped them there. The boats later moved in to the 100 metres depth line, where they could lay on the bottom.

The waiting boats were under constant attack from the air when they surfaced at night. When no invasion had come by the 12th, the boats were recalled to port and placed on six hours notice.

U 714 put in to La Pallice **15.6.44**

6. 21.8.44   Left La Pallice and returned **25.8.44**

7. 27.8.44   Left for operations.
Now schnorkel-equipped, U 714 headed for British coastal waters and from early September she was patrolling in the mouth of the Bristol Channel. After two weeks without success, she left the operational area.

U 714 put in to Farsund, Norway **20.10.44**

8. 23.10.44   Left Farsund and arrived Flensburg **28.10.44**

9. 17.2.45   Left Kiel and arrived Horten **22.2.45**

10. 3.3.45   Left for operations in British coastal waters.
U 714 patrolled off the east coast of Scotland. On the 10th she torpedoed and sank the Norwegian auxiliary fleet minesweeper *Nordhav II* off Dundee.

On the 14th U 714 sank the SS *Magne* (sw 1226t) off the coast, just N of Berwick. Very soon afterwards the boat was detected and sunk in a depth-charge attack off St Abb's Head by the frigate HMSAS *Natal.*

There were no survivors, 51 dead.

U 715   Type VII C

Built by Stülcken Sohn, Hamburg
Keel laid 28.3.42   Launched 14.12.42
Commissioned 17.3.43   Feldpost Nr M 51 222

Sunk 13.6.44 ENE of the Faroes (62°45′N 02°59′W)

Served with
5 U-Flottille, Kiel   March 1943 - May 1944 (ab)
9 U-Flottille/FdU Mitte, Norway   May 1944 - 13.6.44 (fb)

Commanded by
KL Helmut Röttger   March 1943 - 13.6.44

Patrols: 1   Ships sunk: None

1. 27.5.43   Left Kiel and arrived Stavanger **30.5.43**

2. 8.6.43   Left for Atlantic operations.
Outward-bound on the 13th, U 715 was located by a Canso of 162 (RCAF) Squadron (W/Cdr C St G W Chapman) ENE of the Faroes. After sighting a periscope, the aircraft came in to attack at

U 715 (continued)

50 feet and dropped four depth-charges. The boat half-surfaced and began turning to the right. Her stern rose out of the sea and men were seen jumping overboard.

The aircraft, which had been circling some two miles away, flew over the boat. A man ran to U 715's guns, fired and hit the aircraft's port engine, which began to smoke. The hull had also been holed and when the Canso hit the water, it sank very quickly.

The aircrew got out but one dinghy was unusable and the other was damaged. An ASR Warwick dropped a lifeboat, which was also damaged. Seven of the crew managed to climb in but one man was lost in the sea. The lifeboat was half under water. A dinghy was dropped by another aircraft but this was damaged when the men tried to get in to it. Now back in the lifeboat, the men were unable to reach a second dinghy and the sea carried it way.

They were later picked up by an ASR launch but by then two more men had died. Chapman was awarded the DSO and the four other surviving members of his crew were awarded either the DFC of DFM, according to their rank.

Of U 715's crew, the commander and 35 men were lost.

U 716 Type VII C

Built by Stülcken Sohn, Hamburg
Keel laid 16.4.42   Launched 15.1.43
Commissioned 15.4.43   Feldpost Nr M 40 428

Sunk 11.12.45 NW of Bloody Foreland (55°50´N 10°05´W)

Served with
5 U-Flottille, Kiel   April - December 1943 (ab)
11 U-Flottille, Bergen   January - September 1944 (fb)
13 U-Flottille, Trondheim   October 1944 - 9.5.45 (fb)

Commanded by
OL Hans Dunkelberg   April 1943 - January 1945
OL Jürgen Thimme   January 1945 - 9.5.45

Patrols: 12   Ships sunk: 1 (7200 grt)

1. 11.12.43   Left Kiel and arrived Bergen **14.12.43**

2. 15.12.43   Left Bergen for Northern Waters.
Eastbound JW 55B left Loch Ewe on the 20th and was located by German aircraft on the 22nd. An aerial attack against the convoy failed on the 23rd. Next day U 601 was homed in and she was joined by U 716, which made an unsuccessful torpedo attack on a destroyer early on the 25th before both boats were driven off.

Later in the day the battlecruiser *Scharnhorst*, with destroyer escort, was deployed against the convoy. On the 26th *Scharnhorst* was engaged in a day-long running battle with British warships and, very severely damaged, she sank in the evening.

U 716 put in to Hammerfest **16.1.44**

3. 25.1.44   Left for operations.
Eastbound JW 56A left Loch Ewe on the 12th but after running into a storm on the 16th, the convoy put in to Akureyri, Iceland. On the 21st it sailed again, less five ships which had been damaged. JW 56B left Loch Ewe on the 22nd.

Contact was made with JW 56A on the 25th and soon after midnight U 716 torpedoed and sank the SS *Andrew G Curtin* (am 7200t) N of North Cape. She also claimed a hit on a second ship but this is unconfirmed. U 716 was with *Isegrim* group. Its boats made many attacks on the convoy and escort, resulting in three ships being sunk and a destroyer damaged. The convoy reached Kola Inlet on the 28th.

After JW 56A had passed, *Isegrim* group reformed as *Werwolf*,

to await oncoming convoy JW 56B. Contact was made on the 29th. Attacks were made on the escort but the boats were unable to reach the convoy. Their only success was the destroyer HMS *Hardy*, sunk after being torpedoed by U 278. The convoy reached Kola Inlet on 1.2.44 without further loss. U 716 made no attacks on the convoy.

The boat returned to Hammerfest **18.2.44**

4. 23.2.44   Left for operations. No details known of this patrol.
U 716 may have rejoined *Werwolf* group in its operation against convoy JW 57 but this is not certain.

The boat put in to Narvik **7.3.44**

5. 10.3.44   Left Narvik and arrived Hammerfest **11.3.44**

6. 30.3.44   Left for operations.
On the 27th JW 58 left Loch Ewe. The convoy was located by German aircraft on the 30th. *Thor*, *Blitz* and *Hammer* groups were deployed against the convoy and they were joined by outward-bound boats, including U 716. Attacks were made against the escort but all were unsuccessful and the convoy reached Kola Inlet without loss on 5.4.44. U 716 did not carry out any attacks.

The return convoy, RA 58, sailed on the 7th but was not found by aircraft until the 9th. *Donner* and *Keil* groups were sent against it. U 716 was with one of these groups. Some unsuccessful attacks were made on the escort on the 10th and then contact was lost. Aircraft found the convoy early next morning but the operation was abandoned, the boats being too far behind.

U 716 put in to Bergen **17.4.44**

7. 14.6.44   Left Bergen and arrived Skjomenfjord **17.6.44**

8. 20.6.44   Left for operations. No details known of this patrol.
U 716 returned to Hammerfest **10.7.44**

9. 17.7.44   Left for operations.
U 716 was on her way to join *Trutz* group E of Jan Mayen, when she was sighted on the 19th by a Liberator of 59 Squadron (F/O R C Penning). In the face of heavy flak, the aircraft came in and dropped six depth-charges. Smoke was seen coming from the conning tower area.

The aircraft made a second attack, dropping two more depth-charges. Eventually, the damaged U 716 submerged.

She returned to Hammerfest **21.7.44**

10. 26.7.44   Left Hammerfest and arrived Bergen **31.7.44**

11. 17.9.44   Left Bergen and arrived Kiel **22.9.44**

12. 20.11.44   Left Kiel and arrived Horten **24.11.44**

13. 3.12.44   Left Horten and arrived Harstad **7.12.44**

14. 7.1.45   Left Harstad on a special operation.
U 716, U 295 and U 739 sailed, each with two Biber midget submarines lashed to their casings. They were to go into Kola Inlet, where the Bibers would make attacks on the Soviet battleship *Archangel'sk* and any Allied naval vessels found.

Technical troubles with the Bibers caused the operation to be abandoned. The three boats returned.

U 716 put in to Bogenbucht **12.1.45**

15. 27.1.45   Left Bogenbucht and arrived Kilbotn **27.1.45**

16. 3.2.45   Left Kilbotn and arrived Narvik **4.2.45**

17. 6.2.45   Left for operations.
U 716 joined *Rasmus* group, waiting in Bear Island Passage for eastbound convoy JW 64, which had been sighted by aircraft on the

6th. Aerial attacks made on the convoy on the 7th and 8th failed and twelve Ju 88s were destroyed.

The boats were unable to attack JW 64 because of the strength of the escort, which included the escort-carriers HMS *Campania* and *Nairana*. The *Rasmus* boats were sent to an area off Kola Inlet but U 716 returned to base.

She reached Kilbotn **12.2.45**

18. 18.2.45   Left for operations.
U 716, U 286, U 307, U 711, U 968 and U 992 were ordered to Bear Island Passage to try and make contact with westbound RA 64. It was found by aircraft on the 20th and attacked, with twelve ships claimed as sunk or damaged. U 716, U 286 and U 307 were directed to the convoy to finish off the damaged ships but none was found. The boats were driven off by escorting aircraft.
U 716 returned to Harstad **24.2.45**

19. 25.2.45   Left Harstad and arrived Bogenbucht **26.2.45**

20. 12.3.45   Left for operations.
U 716 joined *Hagen* group, which was stationed in Bear Island Passage, awaiting eastbound JW 65, which had left the Clyde on the 11th.
Aerial reconnaissance failed to find the convoy and the waiting boats moved to the entrance of Kola Inlet to join others and two lines were formed, one of six boats and one of seven. In the morning of the 20th the convoy passed the first line in a snowstorm. One ship was torpedoed and damaged. U 716 claimed to have sunk a Soviet destroyer but it is possible that she fired at and missed a British destroyer of the convoy's escort.
The second patrol line was passed at noon and U 968 sank a ship and a sloop of the escort. After the convoy entered Kola Inlet on the 21st, the boats attempted to operate against the aircraft carriers HMS *Campania* and *Trumpeter* from JW 65's escort, which were believed to be in the Barents Sea, but this was unsuccessful.
On the 23rd return convoy RA 65 sailed from Kola Inlet. U 716 was one of a number of boats which attempted to form a patrol line on the 25th ahead of the convoy but were unsuccessful. Two days later aerial reconnaissance had not found the convoy and the operation was abandoned. The convoy arrived without loss off Kirkwall on the 31st.
U 716 returned to Narvik **9.4.45**

21. 21.4.45   Left for operations.
U 716 was one of a number of boats which were sent to Kola Inlet to join *Faust* group boats, which were waiting there for eastbound JW 66. The strongly-escorted convoy was taken into the Inlet on the 25th, without loss.
U 716 returned to Narvik **28.4.45**

U 716 was surrendered at Narvik on 9.5.45. Later she left for Loch Eriboll. She was one of 116 boats disposed of by the Royal Navy in Operation Deadlight.
In December 1945 U 716 was towed from the assembly point at Loch Ryan and out through the North Channel by the destroyer HMS Rupert.
U 716 was sunk by aircraft on 11.12.45 NW of Bloody Foreland.

U 717   Type VII C

Built by Stülcken Sohn, Hamburg
Keel laid 24.4.42   Launched 19.2.43
Commissioned 19.5.43   Feldpost Nr M 52 559

Scuttled 5.5.45 near Glücksburg

Served with
5 U-Flottille, Kiel   May - July 1943 (ab)
22 U-Flottille, Gotenhafen   August 1943 - June 1944 (sb)
8 U-Flottille, Danzig   August 1944 - February 1945 (fb/ab)
5 U-Flottille, Kiel   February 1945 - 5.5.45 (ab)

Commanded by
OL Siegfried von Rothkirch und Panthen   May 1943 - 5.5.45

Patrols: 4   Ships sunk: None

U 717 had her training halted in August 1943 at 5 U-Flottille and was detached to serve with 22 U-Flottille as a school boat. In June 1944 she returned to 5 U-Flottille, to complete her training before becoming operational.

1. 16.8.44   Left Kiel for operations in the Baltic.
U 717 put in to Helsinki **19.8.44**

2. 21.8.44   Left Helsinki and arrived Grand Hotel **21.8.44**

3. 26.8.44   Left Grand Hotel for operations.
U 717 operated in the area near Koivisto and in Narva Bay.
She returned to Grand Hotel **31.8.44**

On 2.9.44 Finland broke off diplomatic relations with Germany and surrendered on the 4th. From the 2nd the Germans evacuated their men and what material they could from Finnish harbours.

4. 3.9.44   Left Grand Hotel for operations.
U 717 operated off the entrance to the Gulf of Finland.
The boat put in to Windau, Latvia **25.9.44**

5. 30.9.44   Left Windau for operations.
Whilst docked at Libau, Latvia on 14.10.44, U 717 came under air attack. She had two crewmen killed and three others wounded.
She put in to Danzig **17.10.44**

U 717 resumed her training duties at 8 U-Flottille, Danzig. She returned to 5 U-Flottille, Kiel in February 1945.
The boat was scuttled near Glücksburg on 5.5.45, whilst she was there awaiting further orders.

U 718   Type VII C

Built by Stülcken Sohn, Hamburg
Keel laid 18.5.42   Launched 26.3.43
Commissioned 25.6.43   Feldpost Nr M 53 527

Sunk 18.11.43 NE of Bornholm

Served with
5 U-Flottille, Kiel   June 1943 - 18.11.43 (ab)

Commanded by
OL Helmut Wieduwilt   June 1943 - 18.11.43

Patrols: None   Ships sunk: None

U 718 (continued)

On 18.11.43, whilst carrying out training exercises in the Baltic, U 718 collided with U 476 20 miles NE of Bornholm.

Of U 718's crew, the commander and 6 men survived and 43 others lost their lives.

U 719   Type VII C

Built by Stülcken Sohn, Hamburg
Keel laid 3.7.42   Launched 28.4.43
Commissioned 27.7.43   Feldpost Nr M 53 569

Sunk 26.6.44 WNW of Bloody Foreland (55°33′N 11°02′W)

Served with
5 U-Flottille, Kiel   July 1943 - April 1944 (ab)
3 U-Flottille, La Pallice   May 1944 - 26.6.44 (fb)

Commanded by
OL Klaus-Dietrich Steffens   July 1943 - 26.6.44

Patrols: 1   Ships sunk: None

1. 6.5.44   Left Kiel and arrived Arendal **9.5.44**

2. 19.5.44   Left for Atlantic operations.
   U 719, a schnorkel boat, was ordered to operate in the area of the North Channel, to tie down Allied anti-submarine forces.
   Later in June she was patrolling further west and on the 26th U 719 was sunk after a long search by the destroyer HMS *Bulldog* (Cdr A J Baker-Creswell) in a depth-charge attack WNW of Bloody Foreland.
   There were no survivors, 52 dead.

U 720   Type VII C

Built by Stülcken Sohn, Hamburg
Keel laid 17.8.42   Launched 5.6.43
Commissioned 17.9.43   Feldpost Nr M 54 671

Sunk 21.12.45 NW of Bloody Foreland (56°04′N 09°35′W)

Served with
21 U-Flottille, Pillau   September 1943 - February 1945 (sb)
31 U-Flottille, Wilhelmshaven   March 1945 - 9.5.45 (ab)

Commanded by
OL Wolf-Harald Schüler   September 1943 - May 1944
OL Walter Boldt   May - November 1944
OL Erhard Wendelberger   November 1944 - 9.5.45

Patrols: None   Ships sunk: None

U 720 saw no operational service. She was on training duties at 21 and 31 U-Flottillen throughout her service life. The boat was surrendered at Wilhelmshaven in early May 1945.

She left there for Loch Ryan on 24.6.45. U 720 was one of 116 boats disposed of by the Royal Navy in Operation Deadlight. *She was towed out through the North Channel in December 1945 by the destroyer HMS* Quantock.

U 720 was sunk by gunfire on 21.12.45 NW of Bloody Foreland in over 500 fathoms.

U 721   Type VII C

Built by Stülcken Sohn, Hamburg
Keel laid 16.11.42   Launched 22.7.43
Commissioned 8.11.43   Feldpost Nr M 53 697

Scuttled 5.5.45 in Geltinger Bucht

Served with
22 U-Flottille, Gotenhafen   November 1943 - February 1945 (sb)
31 U-Flottille, Hamburg   March 1945 - 5.5.45 (ab)

Commanded by
OL Otto Wollschläger   November 1943 - December 1944
OL Ludwig Fabricius   December 1944 - 5.5.45

Patrols: None   Ships sunk: None

U 721 saw no operational service. She was on training duties at 22 and 31 U-Flottillen throughout her service life.

The boat was awaiting further orders when was scuttled in Geltinger Bucht on 5.5.45, complying with the Regenbogen *order of 30.4.45 but contrary to the surrender terms.*

U 722   Type VII C

Built by Stülcken Sohn, Hamburg
Keel laid 21.11.42   Launched 18.9.43
Commissioned 15.12.43   Feldpost Nr M 54 762

Sunk 27.3.45 E of Eriskay, Hebrides (57°09′N 06°55′W)

Served with
31 U-Flottille, Hamburg   December 1943 - July 1944 (ab)
1 U-Flottille, Brest   August - October 1944 (fb-oE)
11 U-Flottille, Bergen   October 1944 - 27.3.45 (fb-t/fb)

Commanded by
OL Hans Reimers   December 1943 - 27.3.45

Patrols: 3   Ships sunk:1 (2,190 grt)

U 722 was nominally with 1 U-Flottille, Brest from August to October 1944 but she was non-operational for that period, probably at Kiel.

1. 7.10.44   Left Kiel and arrived Horten **9.10.44**

2. 13.10.44   Left Horten and arrived Marviken **14.10.44**

3. 16.10.44   Left Marviken on transport duties.
   U 722 went to St Nazaire, carrying a cargo of anti-tank weapons, ammunition and medical supplies.
   She reached St Nazaire **20.11.44**

4. 7.12.44   Left for Norway.
   U 722 was carrying a cargo of 3.2 tons of non-ferrous metals and four dockyard specialists as passengers. In the morning of the 13th she made an unsuccessful attack on a steamer W of the British Isles, hearing only an end-of-run detonation.
   The boat put in to Bergen **29.12.44**

5. 21.2.45   Left Trondheim for British coastal waters.
   From the second week in March U 722 was operating in the Sea of the Hebrides, between the Inner and Outer Hebrides. In the morning of the 16th U 722 attacked convoy RU 156 at the southern

end of the Little Minch, sinking the SS *Inger Toft* (br 2190t).

The boat was still patrolling in the Sea of the Hebrides when she was located by frigates of the 21st EG on the 27th E of Eriskay. U 722 was sunk in depth-charge attacks by HMS *Byron* (Lt J B Burfield), *Fitzroy* (Cdr A J M Miller) and *Redmill* (Lt G Pitt).

There were no survivors, 44 dead.

U 723 - U 730 never went into service. Construction was halted on 30.9.43. U 723 and U 724 were wrecked in an air raid on Hamburg and the orders for U 725 - U 730 were cancelled on 22.7.44.

U 731 Type VII C

Built by Schichau, Danzig
Keel laid 1.10.41   Launched 25.7.42
Commissioned 3.10.42   Feldpost Nr M 50 791

Sunk 15.5.44 off Tangier (35°54′N 05°45′W)

Served with
8 U-Flottille, Danzig October 1942 - April 1943 (ab)
1 U-Flottille, Brest May 1943 - 15.5.44 (fb)

Commanded by
OL Werner Techand October 1942 - November 1943
OL Alexander Graf von Keller November 1943 - 15.5.44

Patrols: 4   Ships sunk: None

1. 29.4.43 Left Kiel for the North Atlantic.

U 731 and other outward-bound boats, U 340, U 636, U 657 and U 760, were deployed as *Iller* group to shadow a convoy, sighted by U 640 early on the 12th SW of Iceland and presumed to be ONS 7. Contact was lost by U 640 on the 13th and she was sunk next day.

The *Iller* boats, having failed to find the convoy, were sent on the 15th to a new position just SE of Greenland. They joined up with *Inn, Loch, Isar* and *Nahe* groups to form *Donau 1* and *2* groups, to wait for ONS 7 coming from the east and HX 238 coming from the west. U 731 was in *Donau 1*.

The *Donau* groups moved westwards and took up a line from the 16th, running southeastwards from Cape Farewell. ONS 7 passed through the line during the night of the 17/18th and HX 238 passed the southern end of the *Donau* line at about the same time. In anticipation of eastbound SC 130 taking the same route, the *Donau* groups moved southwards on the 18th into its path.

The convoy was sighted by U 304 of *Donau 1* group during the night of the 18/19th and the *Donau* boats were ordered to close. SC 130 had continuous air cover and aircraft attacks out of low cloud made shadowing almost impossible. On the 19th U 731 was attacked by a Liberator of 120 Squadron (F/Sgt W Stoves) but she escaped undamaged. The boats were driven away from the convoy before dusk on the 19th and the pursuit was abandoned on the 20th, by which time the convoy had lost no ships but U 258, U 381 and U 954 had been sunk.

On the 18th HX 239 had been located 200 miles SE of Cape Race. The surviving *Donau* boats, including U 731, were ordered southwestwards to meet the approaching convoy. The escort for HX 239 was joined by the escort-carrier HMS *Archer* and the strength of the convoy's air cover caused the operation to be called off on the 23rd before any attacks had been made on the ships.

From the 24th Dönitz temporarily halted operations against convoys in the North Atlantic. U 731 and other *Donau* and *Mosel* boats with limited fuel ranged over a wide area, their continuing radio signals planned to give the impression that a large U-boat presence was being maintained across the convoy routes.

U 731 put in to her new base at Brest **12.6.43**

2. 29.8.43 Left for the North Atlantic.

U 731 and five other boats took up positions in a waiting area N of the Azores from 2.9.43. Between the 10th and 13th U 260, U 305, U 338, U 386 and U 645 were refuelled by U 460 and then, together with U 731, which was not refuelled, they moved northwards to join fourteen outward-bound boats to form a patrol line, *Leuthen*, SSW of Iceland for the 21st, to intercept the next westbound convoy.

Secrecy had been maintained as far as possible to prevent the presence of the boats becoming known to the Allies. However, U 341, which should have been proceeding submerged, was sighted, attacked and sunk by a Canadian aircraft just east of the planned patrol line position.

Early on the 20th, before the *Leuthen* boats were in position, westbound convoy ON 202 was sighted by U 270 but she was driven off after damaging a frigate. Aircraft and a strong surface escort prevented most boats making any attacks in daylight. During the day ON 202 joined up with convoy ONS 18.

Fog came down early on the 21st and remained throughout the night and the following day. On the 22nd there were some clear patches and when aircraft appeared, some of the *Leuthen* boats remained surfaced and fought them. In the late afternoon the fog cleared and five boats approached but encountered a strong escort.

In the early hours of the 23rd the convoy was close to the Newfoundland Bank, an area noted for its fog. The operation ended later in the morning. Six ships had been sunk and another damaged, three escorts had also been sunk and another damaged beyond repair. Two boats were lost.

Augmented by new arrivals, the *Leuthen* boats formed *Rossbach* group S of Iceland from the 27th. The group moved northwards on 1.10.43 to intercept ONS 19 and then from the 3rd went eastwards to meet ON 204. On the 4th U 731 was attacked three times by a Hudson of 269 Squadron (P/O H M Smith). U 731's commander and five ratings were wounded in the attacks.

Neither convoy was found and from the 5th the *Rossbach* boats began a southwestwards sweep, to search for SC 143 and HX 259. The former was sighted by German aircraft on the 8th but the boats did not receive the aircraft's homing signals and the convoy was not found. The search was called off on the 9th.

Now short of fuel, U 731 and other *Rossbach* boats headed southwards. From the 11th they made several attempts to rendezvous at different positions with U 488 in an area 300 to 600 miles N and NW of the Azores. Each attempt was frustrated by bad weather or the unwelcome attention of carrier-borne aircraft. On or about the 15th U 731 was probably damaged in an aircraft attack. She was finally refuelled by U 488 between the 15th and 17th for return to base.

U 731 reached Brest **1.11.43**

3. 19.12.43 Left for Atlantic operations.

U 731 was to join one of the small *Rügen* sub-groups, which were operating from the 22nd W of Ireland. Their object was to constantly change position, to give the impression of many boats over a wide area. When convoys were found, the groups were too small to mount a successful attack.

The *Rügen* groups were dissolved on 7.1.44 and their boats, including U 731, then operated singly in specified areas.

On the 26th U 731 and other *Rügen* boats formed a patrol line, *Stürmer*, NW of the North Channel, to await expected convoy ON 221, which was sighted by German aircraft on the 27th. Technical difficulties prevented the aircraft homing in the boats, which made searches on the 28th but did not find the convoy.

On the morning of the 29th the operation was terminated, following a report by an aircraft of a suspected invasion of Western France. After apparent confirmation of this report all boats in the North Atlantic, including *Stürmer* group, were ordered to proceed at high speed to the Biscay coast. Shortly after this the 'invasion fleet' was correctly identified as a group of Spanish trawlers and

U 731 (continued)

the boats were ordered back to their operational areas.

On the 31st *Stürmer* group was again stationed NW of the North Channel. From early February Allied a/s defences were increased and the waiting boats began a slow withdrawal westwards.

From 3.2.44 U 731 was with *Igel 2* group W of Ireland, searching for westbound convoy ON 223. From the 4th the boats patrolled SW of Ireland, until the 10th, when they began a slow withdrawal further westwards. During the night of the 10/11th U 731, U 413 and U 437 made unsuccessful attacks against the escort of convoy KMS 41/OS 67. The boats were hunted but shook off their pursuers with anti-radar metal foil.

U 731 put in to Lorient **18.2.44**

4. 18.4.44 Left for the Mediterranean.

U 731 was attempting to enter the Straits of Gibraltar on 15.5.44 when she was located by two MAD-equipped USN Catalinas of VP-63 (Lts M T Vopacek and H L Worrell) off Tangier. Both of the aircraft made retro-bomb attacks, which probably damaged the boat.

The sloop HMS *Kilmarnock* (Lt-Cdr K B Brown) and the a/s trawler HMS *Blackfly* (Lt A P Hughes) arrived at the scene. U 731 was destroyed by a Hedgehog pattern fired by *Kilmarnock* and depth-charges dropped by *Blackfly*.

There were no survivors, 53 dead.

U 732   Type VII C

Built by Schichau, Danzig
Keel laid 6.10.41   Launched 25.8.42
Commissioned 24.10.42   Feldpost Nr M 49 880

Sunk 1.11.43 off Tangier (35°54′N 05°52′W)

Served with
8 U-Flottille, Danzig   October 1942 - April 1943 (ab)
1 U-Flottille, Brest   May 1943 - 1.11.43 (fb)

Commanded by
OL Klaus-Peter Carlsen   October 1942 - 1.11.43

Patrols: 3   Ships sunk: None

1. 8.4.43 Left Kiel for the North Atlantic.

Outward-bound, U 732 reported a ship torpedoed and sunk SSW of Iceland on the 19th but there is no confirmation of this. U 732 joined *Meise* group E of Newfoundland. From the 21st a new patrol line was formed S of Greenland to intercept HX 234. The convoy was sighted on that day by U 306 but fog and snowstorms made closing difficult and USN Catalinas of VP-84 drove the boats away from the convoy.

Searching for HX 234, U 732 encountered southwest-bound ONS 4 SE of Cape Farewell on the 23rd. She began to shadow but was driven down by Swordfish from the escort-carrier HMS *Biter*. U 191 took over as shadower but she was sunk the same afternoon. Although other boats managed to establish contact with the convoy, the operation did not develop and no ships were sunk.

In late April U 732 joined *Specht* group NE of Newfoundland, which on the 27th was directed to HX 235 but the convoy was re-routed to the south. On the 29th *Amsel* group closed up to *Specht* and they moved southwards. From 1.5.43 the two groups were drawn up in an arc E of Newfoundland, awaiting northbound convoy SC 128. It passed through the *Specht* line and smoke was sighted by U 628 but contact was lost in a southerly gale and when the convoy had not been sighted again by the 3rd, a new patrol line, *Fink*, was formed in the expected path of SC 128 from *Specht* and *Star* groups. *Star* had come south after abandoning its pursuit of convoy ONS 5.

SC 128 had not been found by the 4th and the search was called off but almost immediately a southwest-bound convoy appeared in the centre of the *Fink* line, reported by U 628. This proved to be ONS 5, delayed by the storm. During the night of the 4/5th some attacks were made, none by U 732, and the convoy dispersed into several separate, escorted groups. Fifteen boats were in contact on the 5th but in the late afternoon fog came down and almost all contact was lost. Many boats were attacked by the escorts and damaged. Pursuit was called off in the morning of the 6th. Soon afterwards U 732 headed home.

She put in to her new base at Brest **15.5.43**

2. 10.6.43 Left for the Western Atlantic.

U 732 passed through the Bay of Biscay in company with U 84 and U 306, for mutual protection against air attacks.

In late June U 732 was refuelled by U 488 W of the Azores. During the night of July 10/11th the boat entered the Caribbean via the Windward Passage. On the 12th she was sighted by two USN Kingfisher aircraft near Navassa Island. U 732 dived and went northwards back to the Windward Passage.

On the 28th U 732 met three naval repair ships but she was driven off by their escort. Late on 1.8.43 she sighted southbound convoy NG 376 30 miles W of Great Inagua Island. U 732 was located and driven off by the corvette USS *Brisk* with depth-charges. U 732's commander reported that he had torpedoed two ships in the convoy in the early hours of the 2nd, sinking one of them. However, NG 376 reached Guantanamo without loss.

The boat returned to Brest **31.8.43**

3. 17.10.43 Left for the Mediterranean.

U 732 was heading for Toulon. On 31.10.43 she was detected off Tangier by the a/s trawler HMS *Imperialist* (Lt-Cdr B H C Rodgers). Ten depth-charges were dropped, forcing U 732 to resurface.

Imperialist approached and its guns put those on the boat out of action. U 732 dived and the trawler dropped ten more depth-charges, followed by a further eight. When contact was lost by *Imperialist*, the boat was claimed as probably sunk. For this action Rodgers was awarded the DSC.

U 732 lay on the bottom at 585 feet for eight hours. When she surfaced, she could still move forward, although listing badly. The boat was spotted and caught in a searchlight. The destroyer HMS *Douglas* (Lt-Cdr K H J L Phibbs) opened fire, causing severe damage.

U 732's commander ordered his men to abandon ship and scuttled his boat. *Douglas* dropped ten depth-charges to make sure of complete destruction. The commander and 18 men were picked up by *Douglas*. The other 31 members of the crew lost their lives.

U 733   Type VII C

Built by Schichau, Danzig
Keel laid 15.10.41   Launched 5.9.42
Commissioned 14.11.42   Feldpost Nr M 50 883

Scuttled 5.5.45 in Geltinger Bucht

Served with
8 U-Flottille, Danzig   November 1942 - May 1943 (ab)
21 U-Flottille, Pillau   December 1943 - February 1945 (sb)
31 U-Flottille, Hamburg   March 1945 - 5.5.45 (ab)

Commanded by
OL Wilhelm von Trotha   November 1942 - May 1943
OL Hans Hellmann   December 1943 - March 1945
OL Ulrich Hammer   April 1945 - 5.5.45

Patrols: None   Ships sunk: None

On 8.8.43 U 733 sank at Gotenhafen after a collision with an unidentified U-boat. She was raised, repaired and went back into service in December 1943.

U 733 went on to training duties at 21 and 31 U-Flottillen. In early May 1945 she was en route to Norway in company with U 746 when she was attacked and damaged on the 4th by Typhoons of 2nd TAF. Two of the crew were killed.

U 733 was scuttled in Gelting Bay on 5.5.45, complying with the Regenbogen order of 30.4.45 but contrary to the surrender terms.

U 734   Type VII C

Built by Schichau, Danzig
Keel laid 20.10.41   Launched 19.9.42
Commissioned 5.12.42   Feldpost Nr M 50 912

Sunk 9.2.44 WSW of Ireland (49°43′N 16°23′W)

Served with
8 U-Flottille, Danzig   December 1942 - July 1943 (ab)
3 U-Flottille, La Pallice   August 1943 - 9.2.44 (fb)

Commanded by
OL Hans-Jörg Blauert   December 1942 - 9.2.44

Patrols: 2   Ships sunk: None

1. 6.11.43   Left Kiel for Atlantic operations.

U 734 was one of a number of boats which took up submerged, waiting positions W of the British Isles.

In early December they assembled W of the North Channel as *Coronel* group, which searched for convoy ONS 24 but was unsuccessful because aerial reconnaissance failed to find it. From the 5th the group operated between 20° and 35°W but failed to find HX 268, which passed north of the patrol line on the 8th. A few days later ON 215 also avoided the line.

U 734 put in to Lorient **25.12.43**

2. 31.1.44   Left for the North Atlantic.

U 734 joined *Igel 2* group, which from 4.2.44 was patrolling SW of Ireland. On the 6th the boats were deployed against combined convoy MKS 38/SL 147, reported N of the Azores by German aircraft on the 6th, 7th and 8th. Some *Igel 2* boats came up to the convoy on the 7th but had no success against the strong escort.

In the early hours of the 9th U 734 was detected and then sighted by the sloop HMS *Wild Goose* (Cdr D E G Wemyss) of the 2nd SG, which was supporting the convoy escort. As she dived, U 734 fired a torpedo, which exploded astern of the sloop.

Wild Goose dropped depth-charges, sending U 734 deep. The sloop HMS *Starling* (Capt F J Walker) came up and the two sloops carried out depth-charge attacks, which brought some oil to the surface. Soon afterwards a torpedo track was seen heading straight for *Starling*. U 734 had come up, fired and then gone down again. Too late to take avoiding action, Walker gave the command to go hard a'port and ordered shallow-set depth-charges to be fired, the explosions from which detonated the approaching torpedo just before it struck the sloop, swamping her decks with water.

Starling and *Wild Goose* recommenced depth-charge attacks, which were followed by an underwater explosion and the appearance of wreckage over a wide area of sea. U 734 had come so close to destroying the formidable Captain Walker and his ship but had paid the price.

There were no survivors, 50 dead.

U 735   Type VII C

Built by Schichau, Danzig
Keel laid 29.11.41   Launched 10.10.42
Commissioned 28.12.42   Feldpost Nr M 49 502

Sunk 28.12.44 at Horten

Served with
8 U-Flottille, Danzig   December 1942 - July 1944 (ab)
11 U-Flottille, Bergen   August 1944 - 28.12.44 (fb-oE)

Commanded by
OL Hans-Joachim Börner   December 1942 - 28.12.44

Patrols: 1 (?)   Ships sunk: None

1. 7.6.44   Left Kiel and arrived Marviken **9.6.44**

2. 13.7.44   Left Marviken and returned **14.7.44**

3. 16.7.44   Left Marviken and arrived Bergen **16.7.44**

4. 29.7.44   Left Bergen, possibly on an operation. No details known. U 735 put in to Larvik **5.8.44**

5. 7.9.44   Left Larvik and arrived Kiel **11.9.44**

6. 21.12.44   Left Kiel and arrived Horten **23.12.44**

7. 24.12.44   Left Horten and returned **25.12.44**

During the night of December 28/29th 1944 68 aircraft of RAF Bomber Command raided shipping in Oslofjord, in the Horten area. U 735 was sunk at her moorings. There were no survivors, 39 dead.

U 736   Type VII C

Built by Schichau, Danzig
Keel laid 29.11.41   Launched 31.10.42
Commissioned 16.1.43   Feldpost Nr M 49 866

Sunk 6.8.44 SW of Lorient (47°19′N 04°16′W)

Served with
8 U-Flottille, Danzig   January 1943 - March 1944 (ab)
1 U-Flottille, Brest   April 1944 - 6.8.44 (fb)

Commanded by
OL Reinhard Reff   January 1943 - 6.8.44

Patrols: 2   Ships sunk: None

1. 11.3.44   Left Kiel and arrived Stavanger **14.3.44**

2. 31.3.44   Left Stavanger for the North Atlantic.

U 736, schnorkel-equipped, was one of a number of boats, operating independently between Ireland and Newfoundland. For a short period in early May U 736 was on weather-reporting duties.

On the 17th U 736 encountered a convoy SW of Ireland but her attack on it was unsuccessful. The returning boat was attacked in the Bay of Biscay on the 24th by a Wellington of 612 Squadron (F/O K H Davies), which she shot down. Later in the day U 736 was attacked and damaged by a Liberator of 224 Squadron (F/Lt E W Lindsay). She was escorted into Lorient by five minesweepers.

U 736 reached Lorient **26.5.44**

U 736 (continued)

3. **5.8.44** Left for operations.

Outward-bound, U 736 was detected by the frigate HMS *Loch Killin* (Lt-Cdr S Darling) 50 miles SW of Lorient. A pattern of depth-charges was dropped.

U 736 attempted to surface and came up directly under *Loch Killin*'s stern. The commander and seven men emerged from the conning tower hatch and then stepped on to the frigate's quarter-deck. The boat remained locked there for some minutes and then dropped away into the depths.

Of U 736's crew, 28 men were lost and the commander and 18 others were made PoW.

U 737   Type VII C

Built by Schichau, Danzig
Keel laid 10.2.42   Launched 21.11.42
Commissioned 30.1.43   Feldpost Nr M 49 907

Sunk 19.12.44 in Vestfjord, Norway (68°09´ 15°39´)

Served with
8 U-Flottille, Danzig   January - June 1943 (ab)
13 U-Flottille, Trondheim   July 1943 - 19.12.44 (fb)

Commanded by
Lt Wolfgang Poeschel   January - February 1943
KL Paul Brasack   February 1943 - November 1944
OL Friedrich-August Gréus   November 1944 - 19.12.44

Patrols: 11   Ships sunk: None

1. **20.7.43** Left Kiel for Northern Waters. No details known.
U 737 put in to Hammerfest **29.7.43**

2. **8.8.43** Left for operations. No details known of this patrol.
U 737 returned to Hammerfest **20.9.43**

3. **4.10.43** Left for operations. No details known of this patrol.
U 737 put in to Narvik **24.10.43**

4. **27.10.43** Left Narvik and arrived Trondheim **29.10.43**

5. **13.1.44** Left Trondheim and arrived Narvik **15.1.44**

6. **16.1.44** Left for operations.

Eastbound JW 56A left Loch Ewe on 12.1.44 but after running into a storm on the 16th the convoy put in to Akureyri, Iceland. On the 21st it sailed again, less five ships which had been damaged. Convoy JW 56B left Loch Ewe on the 22nd.

U 737 was with *Isegrim* group, which was awaiting these convoys in Bear Island Passage. On the 25th contact was made with JW 56A and during that day and the night of the 25/26th nine of the ten boats of *Isegrim* group made attacks on the convoy and escort. Three ships were sunk and the destroyer HMS *Obdurate* was damaged. U 737 had no success.

After JW 56A moved on towards Kola Inlet, *Isegrim* group reformed as *Werwolf*, to await JW 56B in the Passage. Contact was made on the 29th and early on the 30th U 737 had a near miss on the destroyer HMS *Milne*, with a torpedo exploding in her wake. In the late evening of the 30th U 737 made an unsuccessful attack on a destroyer, hearing only an end-of-run detonation.

U 737 may still have been with *Werwolf* group when it took part in a failed operation against return convoy RA 56 but this is not certain.

The boat put in to Skjomenfjord **12.2.44**

7. **28.2.44** Left Skjomenfjord and arrived Hammerfest **29.2.44**

8. **1.3.44** Left for operations.

On the 6th U 737 was attacked and damaged by a Liberator of 120 Squadron (F/Lt H F Kerrigan). In the face of intense flak, six depth-charges were dropped by the aircraft, which was badly damaged. Soon afterwards Kerrigan sighted another boat and pressed home an attack, again in the face of heavy flak.

Now very seriously damaged and with two of his crew badly wounded, Kerrigan jettisoned his remaining depth-charges and went on to land at Skitten on two engines. For his part in the action, he was awarded the DSO.

U 737 returned, putting in to Skjomenfjord **8.3.44**

9. **9.3.44** Left Skjomenfjord and arrived Trondheim **12.3.44**

10. **2.5.44** Left Trondheim and arrived Narvik **4.5.44**

11. **8.5.44** Left Narvik and arrived Hammerfest **8.5.44**

12. **13.5.44** Left for operations. No details known of this patrol.
U 737 put in to Bogenbucht **7.6.44**

13. **11.6.44** Left Bogenbucht and arrived Hammerfest **12.6.44**

14. **14.6.44** Left for operations. No details known.
U 737 returned to Hammerfest **18.6.44**

15. **24.6.44** Left for operations. No details known.
U 737 returned to Bogenbucht **9.7.44**

16. **15.7.44** Left Bogenbucht and arrived Trondheim **17.7.44**

17. **16.9.44** Left for operations.

Eastbound JW 60 left Loch Ewe on the 15th. U 737 was with *Grimm* group, awaiting the convoy. It passed, unobserved by the searching aircraft and waiting U-boats and arrived safely at Kola Inlet on the 23rd.

Return convoy RA 60 avoided the waiting *Grimm* and *Zorn* groups but lost two ships to U 310, which it overran in the afternoon of the 29th.

U 737 returned to Skjomenfjord **3.10.44**

18. **12.10.44** Left for operations. No details known.
U 737 returned to Hammerfest **24.10.44**

19. **25.10.44** Left for operations.

On the 20th eastbound JW 61 left Loch Ewe. U 737 was with *Panther* group, awaiting the convoy E of Bear Island. The heavily-escorted contvoy passed through the patrol line. Unsuccessful attacks were made against the convoy's escort on the 26th and 27th by the *Panther* boats. JW 61 arrived without loss at Kola Inlet on the 28th.

U 737 returned to Trondheim **31.10.44**

20. **7.12.44** Left for operations. No details known of this patrol.

On the 19th the returning U 737 was in collison with the German minesweeper *MRS 25* in Vestfjord. She sank, with the loss of 31 men of her crew. U 737's commander was among the survivors.

U 738   Type VII C

Built by Schichau, Danzig
Keel laid 25.2.42   Launched 12.12.42
Commissioned 20.2.43   Feldpost Nr M 50 527

Decommissioned 3.3.44 at Danzig

Served with
8 U-Flottille, Danzig February 1943 - 3.3.44 (ab)

Commanded by
OL Erich-Michael Hoffmann February 1943 - 14.2.44

Patrols: None   Ships sunk: None

U 738 was sunk in the Baltic, off Gdynia on 14.2.44 after colliding with the SS Erna *whilst carrying out exercises. The commander and 23 men were lost and 24 others survived.*

The boat was raised and then decommissioned on 3.3.44. U 738 was sent to the training establishment 3 ULD. She was later scrapped.

U 739   Type VII C

Built by Schichau, Danzig
Keel laid 17.4.42   Launched 23.12.42
Commissioned 6.3.43   Feldpost Nr M 50 545

Sunk 16.12.45 NW of Bloody Foreland (55°50´N 10°05´W)

Served with
8 U-Flottille, Danzig March - October 1943 (ab)
9 U-Flottille, Brest November - December 1943 (fb)
13 U-Flottille, Trondheim January 1944 - May 1945 (fb)

Commanded by
OL Ernst Mangold March 1943 - February 1945
OL Johannes Ney (temp) February - March 1945
OL Fritz Kosnick March - May 1945

Patrols: 9   Ships sunk: None
                         1 minesweeper (625 dt)

Although she was nominally with 9 U-Flottille, Brest in November and December 1943, U 739 did not carry out any operations at that time and was probably at Kiel.

1. 1.1.44 Left Kiel and arrived Bergen **6.1.44**

2. 8.1.44 Left for operations.
Eastbound JW 56A left Loch Ewe on the 12.1.44 but after running into a storm on the 16th the convoy put in to Akureyri, Iceland. On the 21st it sailed again, less five ships which had been damaged. Convoy JW 56B left Loch Ewe on the 22nd.
U 739 was with *Isegrim* group, which was awaiting these two convoys in Bear Island Passage. On the 25th contact was made with JW 56A and all boats of the group except U 739 made attacks on either the convoy or escort. U 739 was too far away to the north.
After JW 56A moved on towards Kola Inlet, *Isegrim* group reformed as *Werwolf*, to await JW 56B in the Passage. Contact was made on the 29th and in the early hours of the 30th the attacks began. U 278 torpedoed the escorting destroyer HMS *Hardy*, which was later sunk by another destroyer, HMS *Venus*. This was the only success against JW 56B, which reached Kola Inlet on 1.2.44.
U 739 put in to Narvik **3.2.44**

3. 21.2.44 Left for operations.
Eastbound JW 57 left Loch Ewe on the 20th and was located by aerial reconnaissance on the 23rd. *Werwolf* group was deployed. U 739, U 425, U 601, U 713 and U 990 closed the convoy on the 24th in the Norwegian Sea. The boats were driven off on the 25th but in the evening U 990 sank the destroyer HMS *Mahratta*, the convoy's only loss. JW 57 reached Kola Inlet on the 28th.
U 739, U 307, U 315 and U 472 formed *Boreas* group to await the returning, westbound convoy. The group was joined by other boats. RA 57 sailed on 2.3.44 and during the early hours of the 4th U 739 made the first attack on the convoy, just missing the escorting destroyer HMS *Swift*.
Only U 703 had any success, sinking a ship on the 4th. U 366 and U 973 were sunk during the operation against RA 57, which reached Loch Ewe on the 10th.
U 739 put in to Trondheim **8.3.44**

4. 27.3.44 Left Trondheim and arrived Narvik **29.3.44**

5. 30.3.44 Left for operations.
Eastbound JW 58 left Loch Ewe on the 27th and was located by German aircraft on the 30th. Three U-boats groups, *Thor, Blitz* and *Hammer,* were awaiting the convoy. In addition outward-bound U 739, U 360, U 361, U 716 and U 990 were also deployed. Contact was made soon after midnight on the 30th.
Although many attacks were made on April 1st, 2nd and 3rd by the boats on the convoy's escort, all were unsuccessful. U 739 fired two Gnat torpedoes at the destroyer HMS *Ashanti* in the evening of the 2nd. Two detonations were heard, with the second being reported as an explosion but the *Ashanti* was not hit. The convoy reached Kola Inlet on the 5th.
U 739 put in to Bogenbucht **13.4.44**

6. 16.4.44 Left for operations.
U 739 joined *Keil* group, which was waiting S of Bear Island for the next eastbound convoy. Late on the 28th German aircraft sighted westbound RA 59.
Keil and *Donner* groups were deployed. Many attacks were made, mostly against the escort, from the evening of the 30th to the afternoon of 2.5.44. Only one ship was sunk, by U 711. During the action U 277, U 674 and U 959 were sunk by Swordfish from the escort-carrier HMS *Fencer*. U 739 did not attack the convoy.
The boat returned to Bogenbucht **9.5.44**

7. 11.5.44 Left Bogenbucht and arrived Trondheim **13.5.44**

8. 30.6.44 Left Trondheim and arrived Bogenbucht **1.7.44**

9. 7.7.44 Left for operations. No details known of this patrol.
U 739 returned to Bogenbucht **12.7.44**

10. 2.8.44 Left for operations.
U 739 was ordered to the Kara Sea, to operate with other boats along the Siberian Sea route. The boats, U 739, U 278, U 362, U 365, U 711 and U 957, made up *Greif* group. During August only U 365 and U 711 had any success, on the 12th and 26th.
From early September *Greif* group was down to three boats only, U 739, U 278 and U 362. They had taken on fuel from U 711 and U 957, which had gone to Hammerfest to refuel. On the 5th U 739 and U 362 tried to attack a Soviet convoy near Krakowa Island. U 362 was sunk by an escorting minesweeper on that day and on the 6th U 739 unsuccessfully attacked a Soviet destroyer.
After refuelling, U 711 and U 957 rejoined U 278 and U 739. From the 21st the boats attempted attacks on Soviet convoy VD 1. In the eastern Kara Sea on the 22nd U 739 unsuccessfully attacked a steamer and in the morning of the 24th she torpedoed and sank the Soviet minesweeper *TSC-120.*
Later on the 24th U 739, U 711 and U 957 landed a party on

U 739 (continued)

Sterligova Island to knock out a wireless station.

U 739 put in to Skjomenfjord **3.10.44**

11. 6.10.44 Left Skjomenfjord and arrived Trondheim **8.10.44**

12. 15.12.44 Left Trondheim and arrived Harstad **18.12.44**

13. 7.1.45 Left Harstad on a special operation.

U 739, U 295 and U 716 sailed, each with two Biber midget submarines lashed to their casings. They were to go into Kola Inlet, where the Bibers would make attacks on the Soviet battleship *Archangel'sk* and any Allied naval vessels found.

Technical trouble with the Bibers caused the operation to be abandoned. The three boats returned.

U 739 put in to Kilbotn **10.1.45**

14. 16.1.45 Left for operations.

In early February U 739 was with *Rasmus* group in Bear Island Passage, waiting for the next convoy. Eastbound JW 64 left the Clyde on the 3rd and was reported by a German weather aircraft on the 6th. Aerial attacks on the convoy were made on the 7th and 10th but they failed and twelve aircraft were destroyed.

The *Rasmus* boats were unable to reach the convoy because of the strength of the escort, which included the escort-carriers HMS *Campania* and *Nairana*. After JW 64 had passed, the *Rasmus* boats joined others waiting off Kola Inlet.

On the 16th a combined force of British and Soviet naval vessels attempted to drive the waiting boats away before return convoy RA 64 sailed. It left on the 17th and on that day U 968 sank a ship and torpedoed and damaged a sloop and U 711 sank a corvette. Contact with the convoy was lost on the 18th. Some boats moved to Bear Island Passage but they were unable to regain contact.

RA 64 was found by aircraft on the 20th. Further aerial attacks were made and although the straggling SS *Henry Bacon* was sunk, the Luftwaffe lost another six aircraft. The *Henry Bacon* was the last ship sunk by a German aircraft in the war.

U 739 returned to Harstad **25.2.45**

15. 1.4.45 Left for operations in British coastal waters.

U 739 patrolled in the North Minch and off the north coast of Scotland from the 12th to the 26th but had no success.

The boat put in to Wilhelmshaven **4.5.45**

U 739 was surrendered at Wilhelmshaven and on 30.6.45 she left for Loch Eriboll, Scotland. She was one of 116 boats disposed of by the Royal Navy in Operation Deadlight.

In mid-December 1945 the boat was towed from Loch Ryan out through the North Channel by the tug HMS Freedom. *U 739 was sunk by RAF aircraft on 16.12.45 NW of Bloody Foreland.*

U 740   Type VII C

Built by Schichau, Danzig
Keel laid 26.4.42   Launched 23.12.42
Commissioned 27.3.43   Feldpost Nr M 51 233

Sunk 9.6.44 WSW of the Scillies (49°09′N 08°37′W)

Served with
8 U-Flottille, Danzig   March 1943 - March 1944 (ab)
1 U-Flottille, Brest   April 1944 - 9.6.44 (fb)

Commanded by
KL Günther Stark   March 1943 - 9.6.44

Patrols: 2   Ships sunk: None

1. 11.3.44 Left Kiel and arrived Bergen **14.3.44**

2. 27.3.44 Left Bergen for the North Atlantic.

Outward-bound, U 740 and other boats were ordered to go to bases in Western France to join *Landwirt* group.

U 740 put in to Brest **21.4.44**

3. 6.6.44 Left Brest, as part of *Landwirt* group.

U 740 and seven other non-schnorkel boats were ordered to the area between The Lizard and Hartland Point to operate against Allied invasion supply-shipping heading for the English Channel. For an early arrival the boats sailed late in the evening and were ordered to proceed on the surface at high speed. They all came under aircraft attack almost immediately after dropping their escorts off Brest.

With four boats reporting that they were damaged and returning, it was decided that from the 7th the remaining four boats, U 740, U 413, U 629 and U 821, should proceed to their operational area, submerged in daylight. On the 9th U 740 was sunk in a depth-charge attack by a Liberator of 120 Squadron (F/Lt A K Sherwood) WSW of the Scillies On the 11th the boat was advised to return to base but it was too late.

There were no survivors, 51 dead.

U 741   Type VII C

Built by Schichau, Danzig
Keel laid 30.4.42   Launched 4.2.43
Commissioned 10.4.43   Feldpost Nr M 41 306

Sunk 15.8.44 NW of Le Havre (50°02′N 00°36′W)

Served with
8 U-Flottille, Danzig   April - October 1943 (ab)
1 U-Flottille, Brest   November 1943 - 15.8.44 (fb/fb-t)

Commanded by
OL Gerhard Palmgren   April 1943 - 15.8.44

Patrols: 5   Ships sunk: None

1. 25.11.43 Left Kiel for Atlantic operations.

U 741 joined a number of boats assembled off the North Channel to search for convoys W of the British Isles. On 15.12.43 U 741, U 284, U 364, U 471, U 976 and U 981 formed *Coronel 2* group to continue their search.

On the 19th *Coronel 1* and 2 groups were reformed as *Sylt, Amrum* and *Föhr* groups. U 741 was in *Sylt*. From the 22nd the boats were reformed again W of Ireland, this time into six small sub-groups, *Rügen 1* to *6*. These small groups, mostly of three boats each, were constantly moving, changing positions and varying formations, with the objective of preventing the Allies determining the area over which they were operating.

When three convoys were sighted in late December, the groups were each too small to mount an attack. From 7.1.44 the groups were dissolved and the boats operated singly W of Ireland, as *Rügen* group. They had no success.

U 741 put in to her new base at Brest **27.1.44**

2. 29.2.44 Left for Atlantic operations.

Outward-bound, U 741 was ordered to a position SW of Ireland, where U 625 had been sunk on 10.3.44. She joined U 256 there and they searched for survivors. Although liferafts were seen after the sinking, no survivors were found. Whilst the two boats were searching, they were attacked by a Wellington of 407 (RCAF) Squadron (P/O E M O'Donnell), which they shot down.

U 741 joined *Preussen* group, whose boats were operating singly

W of the British Isles. The group was dissolved on 22.3.44 and the boats then operated independently between the British Isles and 40°W. From early April U 741 was on weather-reporting duties.

She returned to Brest **3.5.44**

3. 19.6.44 Left for a transport operation.

U 741, now schnorkel-equipped, was one of four boats ordered to transport anti-tank and machine gun ammunition to Cherbourg, which was cut off from the land side.They were recalled on the 23rd, when it was learned that the entrance to Cherbourg harbour was blocked.

U 741 returned to Brest **29.6.44**

4. 5.7.44 Left for the English Channel.

On the 12th U 741's port propeller was fouled by sweep wires. On the 13th the boat's schnorkel and periscope were damaged when a vessel passed over her.

U 741 put in to Le Havre **15.7.44**

5. 3.8.44 After repairs, left Le Havre for operations.

On the 15th U 741 attacked a convoy NW of Le Havre, She was located and sunk in a depth-charge attack by an escorting corvette, HMS *Orchis* (Lt B W Harris).

There were no survivors, 48 dead.

U 742   Type VII C

Built by Schichau, Danzig
Keel laid 12.5.42   Launched 4.2.43
Commissioned 1.5.43   Feldpost Nr M 41 587

Sunk 18.7.44 W of Hadselfjord (68°24′N 09°51′E)

Served with
8 U-Flottille, Danzig   May 1943 - March 1944 (ab)
6 U-Flottille, St Nazaire   April - May 1944 (fb)
13 U-Flottille, Trondheim   June 1944 - 18.7.44 (fb)

Commanded by
KL Heinz Schwassmann   May 1943 - 18.7.44

Patrols: 2   Ships sunk: None

Nominally with 6 U-Flottille, St Nazaire in April and May 1944, U 742 was operating from Norwegian bases.

1. 20.4.44 Left Kiel and arrived Marviken **22.4.44**

2. 13.5.44 Left Marviken and arrived Skjomenfjord **18.5.44**

3. 20.5.44 Left for operations. No details known of this patrol.
U 742 returned to Skjomenfjord **8.6.44**

4. 3.7.44 Left for operations.

On the 18th U 742 was en route to join *Trutz* group E of Jan Mayen. The boat was sighted on the surface by a Catalina of 210 Squadron (F/O R W G Vaughan) W of Hadselfjord. The aircraft approached in the face of heavy flak and dropped depth-charges, which sank U 742. Many survivors were seen in dinghies but none was ever found.

The Catalina had been damaged in the action and its port fuel tank was holed. The loss of fuel was such that on the homeward flight, one engine was switched off. With enough fuel left for two hours and suspecting that the hull was damaged, Vaughan decided to fly for as long as possible and then, hopefully, land at Heinkel Bay. He achieved this and ran the aircraft up on to the beach there.

There were no survivors from U 742, 52 dead.

U 743   Type VII C

Built by Schichau, Danzig
Keel laid 30.5.42   Launched 11.3.43
Commissioned 15.5.43   Feldpost Nr M 51 797

Sunk mid/late September 1944 NW of Ireland

Served with
8 U-Flottille, Danzig   May 1943 - June 1944 (ab)
1 U-Flottille, Brest   July - September 1944 (fb)

Commanded by
OL Helmut Kandzior   May 1943 - September 1944

Patrols: 2   Ships sunk: None

In August 1943 U 743 carried out equipment tests in the Baltic.

1. 15.6.44 Left Kiel for Atlantic operations.

On the 20th U 743 was sighted on the surface by a Liberator of 86 Squadron (F/O E D Moffitt) W of Norway. Two depth-charge attacks were made and fire was exchanged between the aircraft and the boat. The Liberator reached base safely.

U 743 put in to Bergen **21.6.44**

2. 18.8.44 Left Bergen and returned **20.8.44**

3. 21.8.44 Left for operations.

U 743, now schnorkel-equipped, was ordered to an area W of the Hebrides. She was lost at some time mid to late September NW of Ireland due to an unknown cause.

There were no survivors, 50 dead.

U 744   Type VII C

Built by Schichau, Danzig
Keel laid 5.6.42   Launched 11.3.43
Commissioned 5.6.43   Feldpost Nr M 51 807

Sunk 6.3.44 W of Dingle Bay (52°01′N 22°37′W)

Served with
8 U-Flottille, Danzig   June - November 1943 (ab)
9 U-Flottille, Brest   December 1943 - 6.3.44 (fb)

Commanded by
OL Heinz Blischke   June 1943 - 6.3.44

Patrols: 2   Ships sunk: 1 (3680 grt) (shared with U 545)
                                 1 LST (2750 dt)

1. 2.12.43 Left Kiel for the North Atlantic.

U 744 went to the area W of Ireland and from the 24th she was with a small group, *Rügen 2*, which was one of six small sub-groups spread over a wide area. They were constantly moving, changing positions and varying formations, with the objective of preventing the Allies determining the area over which they were operating.

On the 30th U 744 probably attacked the MV *Empire Housman* (br 7359t) SSW of Reykjavik, which had been torpedoed and damaged a little earlier by U 545 of *Rügen 2*. The vessel was one of an unescorted group of stragglers from westbound convoy ON 217. She was sighted again by U 744 early on 3.1.44 and torpedoed. The *Empire Housman* was taken in tow but sank on the 5th.

U 744 put in to Brest **15.1.44**

U 744 (continued)

2. 24.2.44 Left for Atlantic operations.

U 744 joined *Preussen* group, whose boats were operating singly W of the British Isles. Early on 2.3.44 U 744 encountered northbound MKS 40/SL 149 SW of Ireland. She attacked the convoy and reported three small tankers sunk. U 744 did sink LST 362 and may also possibly have sunk LST 324.

On the 6th the boat was located some 550 miles W of Dingle Bay by warships of the 6th EG, escorting eastbound convoy HX 280. She became the object of a hunt, which eventually lasted 30 hours. U 744 was depth-charged by the destroyers HMCS *Chaudière* (Lt-Cdr C P Nixon) and *Gatineau* (Lt-Cdr H V W Groos) and HMS *Icarus* (Lt-Cdr R Dyer), the frigates HMCS *St Catherine* (Lt-Cdr H C R Davis), *Chilliwack* (Lt-Cdr G R Coughlin) and *Fennel* (Lt-Cdr W P Moffat) and the corvette HMS *Kenilworth Castle* (Lt J J Allon), which was summoned to the scene to give support.

U 744 was forced to the surface and was boarded by a party from *Chilliwack*, who hoisted the White Ensign and captured books, documents and important equipment. In the heavy seas, all attempts to take the boat in tow failed and she was finally sunk by a torpedo from *Icarus*.

U 744's commander and 12 men were lost.

U 745   Type VII C

Built by Schichau, Danzig
Keel laid 8.7.42   Launched 16.4.43
Commissioned 19.6.43   Feldpost Nr M 52 636

Missing 4.2.45 in the Gulf of Finland

Served with
8 U-Flottille, Danzig   June 1943 - 4.2.45 (ab/fb)

Commanded by
KL Wilhelm von Trotha   June 1943 - 4.2.45

Patrols: 6 at least   Ships sunk: None
                         1 m/s trawler (600 dt)
                         1 patrol vessel (140 dt)

On 20.11.43, in an accident at night in the Baltic, U 745 rammed U 768, which was en route from Pillau to Gotenhafen. U 768 sank but there were no casualties.

1. 24.5.44 Left Kiel and arrived Larvik **26.5.44**

U 745 joined Mitte *group, formed on 16.2.44 and made up of twenty-two non-schnorkel boats on six hours standby, mostly at Bergen, Stavanger and Kristiansand, to counter any invasion of southern Norway and Denmark. On 6.6.44, after news of the Allied landings in Normandy, the boats were brought to immediate action.*

2. 9.6.44 Left Larvik, as one of eleven *Mitte* boats which formed a reconnaissance line running from Trondheim to Lindesnes.

The boats were ordered to remain submerged, unless recharging batteries, to escape the attention of Allied aircraft. Eight *Mitte* boats were recalled in the latter part of June when the invasion threat had lessened. U 745 was not one of these and she remained patrolling between 57° and 61°N with original *Mitte* boats U 1001 and U 1165 and U 771 and U 994, both of which had arrived in mid-June.

U 745 put in to Bergen **7.7.44**

3. 15.7.44 Left Bergen and arrived Marviken **17.7.44**

4. 29.7.44 Left Marviken and arrived Kiel **1.8.44**

5. 3.8.44 Left Kiel for operations in the Baltic.
U 745 operated in the Koivisto and Narva Bay areas.
The boat put in to Helsinki **7.8.44**

6. 8.8.44 Left Helsinki and arrived Gotenhafen **9.8.44**

7. 14.8.44 Left for operations. No details known of this patrol.
U 745 returned to Helsinki **18.8.44**

8. 20.8.44 Left Helsinki and arrived Kalasika **20.8.44**

9. 23.8.44 Left for operations.
On the 26th U 745 torpedoed and sank Soviet patrol vessel *TSC-48* just E of Malyy Island at the eastern end of the Gulf of Finland.
The boat put in to Rüsiö **27.8.44**

10. 29.8.44 Left Rüsiö and arrived Helsinki **29.8.44**

On 2.9.44 Finland broke off diplomatic relations with Germany and surrendered on the 4th. From the 2nd the Germans evacuated their men and as much material as possible from Finnish harbours.

Further U-boat operations in the Baltic were carried out from Danzig, Gotenhafen and Memel.

11. 11.9.44 Left Helsinki for operations.
U 745 patrolled in the entrance to the Gulf of Finland, On 12.10.44 she made an unsuccessful torpedo attack on Soviet vessels.
She put in to Libau on the 17th and returned to Danzig **20.10.44**

12. 23.12.44 Left Danzig for operations.
U 745 took part in the final phase of U-boat operations in the Baltic. On 11.1.45 she reported hearing two torpedo detonations in an attack on two tugs and a floating crane.
Material from Russian sources indicates that U 745 sank m/s trawler *T-76/Korall* on 11.1.45 S of Helsinki.
U 745 went missing in the Gulf of Finland from 4.2.45, possibly sinking after striking a mine.
There were no survivors, 48 dead.

U 746   Type VII C

Built by Schichau, Danzig
Keel laid 15.7.42   Launched 16.4.43
Commissioned 4.7.43   Feldpost Nr M 55 392

Scuttled 5.5.45 in Geltinger Bucht

Served with
21 U-Flottille, Pillau   September 1943 - February 1945 (sb)
31 U-Flottille, Wilhelmshaven   March 1945 - 5.5.45 (ab)

Commanded by
Lt Herbert Kaschke   October 1943 - January 1944
OL Ernst Lottner   January 1944 - 5.5.45

Patrols: None   Ships sunk: None

U 746 was commissioned on 4.7.43 as submarine S 2 for the Italian Navy. After Italy surrendered on 8.9.43, the boat was taken over by the Kriegsmarine. She afterwards served with 21 and 31 U-Flottillen as a training boat.

On 2.5.45 all fully-operational boats were ordered to head for Norway. U 746 was on her way when she was attacked and damaged by an aircraft on the 4th, with one crewman being killed.

U 746 was scuttled in Geltinger Bucht early on the 5th, in compliance with the Regenbogen *order of 30.4.45.*

U 747   Type VII C

Built by Schichau, Danzig
Keel laid 16.8.42   Launched 13.5.43
Commissioned 17.7.43   Feldpost Nr M 55 433

Scuttled 3.5.45 at Hamburg

Served with
24 U-Flottille, Memel   September 1943 - April 1945 (ab)
31 U-Flottille, Hamburg   April 1945 (ab)

Commanded by
OL Erich Jewinski   October 1943 - May 1944
OL Günter Zahnow   May 1944 - 3.5.45

Patrols: None   Ships sunk: None

U 747 was commissioned on 17.7.43 as submarine S3 for the Italian Navy. After Italy surrendered on 8.9.43 the boat was taken over by the Kriegsmarine.

She afterwards served with 24 U-Flottille as a training boat. In early April 1945 U 747 was in the Deutsche Werke yard at Hamburg-Finkenwerder. She was scuttled there on 3.5.45 to prevent her falling into Allied hands.

U 748   Type VII C

Built by Schichau, Danzig
Keel laid 20.8.42   Launched 13.5.43
Commissioned 31.7.43   Feldpost Nr M 55 456

Scuttled 3.5.45 at Rendsburg

Served with
24 U-Flottille, Memel   September 1943 - April 1945 (ab)
31 U-Flottille, Hamburg   April 1945 - 3.5.45 (ab)

Commanded by
OL Götz Roth   September 1943 - September 1944
OL Joachim Knecht   September - November 1944
OL Hans-Friedrich Puschmann   November 1944 - April 1945
OL Gottfried Dingler   April 1945 - 3.5.45

Patrols: Unknown   Ships sunk: None

U 748 was commissioned on 31.7.43 as submarine S5 for the Italian Navy. After Italy surrendered on 8.9.43 the boat was taken over by the Kriegsmarine.

She went on to training duties at 24 U-Flottille. From 26.6.44 U 748 was in the Baltic for operations. The boats there carried out short patrols in the Koivisto and Narva Bay areas, relieving each other every two days. No details known.

1. 5.7.44   Left Reval and arrived Nuokko **7.7.44**

2. 11.7.44   Left Nuokko and arrived Helsinki **12.7.44**

U 748 returned to 24 U-Flottille, and remained there until moving to 31 U-Flottille, in April 1945.

The boat was awaiting further orders when she was scuttled at Rendsburg in the Kiel Canal on 3.5.45.

U 749   Type VII C

Built by Schichau, Danzig
Keel laid 28.9.42   Launched 10.6.43
Commissioned 14.8.43   Feldpost Nr M 55 485

Sunk 4.4.45 at Kiel

Served with
24 U-Flottille, Memel   September 1943 - April 1945 (ab)
5 U-Flottille, Kiel   April 1945 (ab)

Commanded by
OL Rupprecht Fischler Graf von Treuberg
                                        September - December 1943
OL Ernst Fischer   December 1943 - November 1944
OL Friedrich Huisgen   December 1944 - 4.4.45

Patrols: None   Ships sunk: None

U 749 was commissioned on 14.8.43 as submarine S7 for the Italian Navy. After Italy surrendered on 8.9.43 the boat was taken over by the Kriegsmarine.

She went on to training duties at 24 and 5 U-Flottillen. U 749 was sunk on 4.4.45 in a USAF bombing raid on Kiel. Two crewmen were killed.

U 750   Type VII C

Built by Schichau, Danzig
Keel laid 29.9.42   Launched 10.6.43
Commissioned 26.8.43   Feldpost Nr M 55 404

Scuttled 5.5.45 in Flensburger Förde

Served with
24 U-Flottille, Memel   September 1943 - April 1945 (ab)
5 U-Flottille, Kiel   April 1945 - 5.5.45 (ab)

Commanded by
OL Georg von Bitter   September 1943 - August 1944
OL Justus Grawert   August 1944 - 5.5.45

Patrols: None   Ships sunk: None

U 750 was commissioned on 26.8.43 as submarine S9 for the Italian Navy. After Italy surrendered on 8.9.43 the boat was taken over by the Kriegsmarine.

She went on to training duties at 24 and 5 U-Flottillen. U 750 was one of many boats which left their bases in early May and went to the bays of Northern Germany, to await further orders.

She was scuttled in Flensburger Förde on 5.5.45, in compliance with the Regenbogen order but contrary to the surrender terms.

U 751 Type VII C

Built by Kriegsmarine-Werft, Wilhelmshaven
Keel laid 2.1.40   Launched 16.11.40
Commissioned 31.1.41   Feldpost Nr M 30 807

Sunk 17.7.42 NW of Cape Finisterre (45°15′N 12°22′W)

Served with
7 U-Flottille, Kiel/St Nazaire   January 1941 - 17.7.42 (ab/fb)

Commanded by
KL Gerhard Bigalk   January 1941 - 17.7.42

Patrols: 7   Ships sunk: 5 (21,412 grt) + 1 damaged
                        1 aircraft carrier (11,000 dt)

1. 3.6.41   Left Kiel for the North Atlantic.
Outward-bound early on the 14th, U 751 torpedoed a ship in the central North Atlantic, N of the Azores. The vessel, which exploded and sank, was probably the SS *St Lindsay* (br 5370t), which was reported missing after the 13th.
U 751 went on to join *West* group SE of the Newfoundland Bank. On the 20th the group moved northeastwards, to operate in a widely-spaced formation in the central North Atlantic. No convoys were seen, only independents, some of which were sunk by *West* boats. U 751 was not successful.
She put in to her new base at St Nazaire **5.7.41**

2. 2.8.41   Left for Atlantic operations.
On the 4th outward-bound U 751, U 43, U 71, U 77 and U 96 were directed to a convoy sighted by U 565 S of Iceland but they had no success. From the 6th these boats and others operated unsuccessfully against convoy HG 68 and between the 8th and the 10th they failed to find a reported, southbound convoy.
From the 22nd U 751 was stationed with other boats W of the North Channel. Southbound convoy OS 4 was sighted by U 141 on the 26th NW of Bloody Foreland. U 557 came up during the night and sank four ships. She brought up U 751 on the 27th but that boat was unable to carry out an attack.
On 1.9.41 U 751 and other boats formed *Bosemüller* group WSW of Ireland. It was directed to convoy SL 84, sighted by U 73, but failed to find the northbound convoy in poor visibility. Whilst searching, U 83 and U 557 of *Bosemüller* sighted ships of OG 73 on the 2nd. *Kurfürst* group was already searching for this convoy and when it appeared that it had been found, *Bosemüller* combined with *Kurfürst* to form one group, which was then directed to attack OG 73. However, the boats failed to find the convoy and also another one sighted by U 98 on the 3rd.
U 751 returned to St Nazaire **8.9.41**

3. 11.10.41   Left for the North Atlantic.
The outward-bound U 751 was directed to eastbound SC 48, sighted by U 553 in the central North Atlantic, SE of Greenland during the night of the 15/16th. U 751 closed the convoy but had no success. The operation ended in the morning of the 18th, with nine ships, a corvette and destroyer sunk and the destroyer USS *Kearny* damaged.
On the 22nd U 751 joined *Reissewolf* group in the central North Atlantic, which on the 27th was directed to westbound ON 28, sighted by U 74 500 miles W of Ireland. U 751 made contact with the convoy but was driven off by the US destroyer escort. With fuel running low, U 751, U 77, U 502 and U 568 were forced to break off on the 30th.
U 751 returned to St Nazaire **8.11.41**

4. 16.12.41   Left for Atlantic operations.
On the 4th northbound convoy HG 76 set out from Gibraltar and

Seeräuber group was directed to it. U 107, U 108 and U 131 sighted it on the 17th. U 131 was sunk but the other two boats kept contact.
Outward-bound, U 751, U 71 and U 567 were directed to join the attack and they closed the convoy NE of the Azores in the evening of the 21st. U 751 attacked the escort-carrier HMS *Audacity*. Her first spread of torpedoes stopped the carrier and two more fired at short range sank her. U 751 was driven off early on the 23rd.
She returned to St Nazaire **26.12.41**

5. 14.1.42   Left for Canadian waters.
U 751 went to the Nova Scotia area. On 2.2.42 she attacked convoy HX 173 in bad weather E of Halifax. In difficult conditions three torpedoes were fired at the tanker MV *Corilla* (nl 8096t), one of which struck, causing damage. A further attack was prevented by the tanker zig-zagging. The boat was driven off by one of the escort. The *Corilla* reached port and was repaired. U 751 managed to evade searching warships and aircraft.
On the 4th she torpedoed and sank the MV *Silveray* (br 4535t) off Hunt's Point and was driven off by RCAF aircraft as she pursued another vessel. After escaping an intensive search, U 751 sank the SS *Empire Sun* (br 6952t) on the 7th, again off Hunt's Point.
With all torpedoes gone, U 751 made a gunfire attack at night on a ship S of the Sambro Island light. The vessel fired back. She received a hit on her afterdeck before moving away at full speed. With heavy sea conditions making gunnery difficult and restricting speed, U 751 did not pursue.
She returned to St Nazaire **23.2.42**

6. 15.4.42   Left for US waters.
In early May the outward-bound U 751 was refuelled by U 459 500 miles NE of Bermuda. She then patrolled E and SE of Hatteras before moving south and from mid-May patrolled off the Bahamas.
On the 16th U 751 torpedoed and sank the SS *Nicarao* (am 1445t) NE of Cat Island. The boat passed through the Windward Passage into the Caribbean and on the 19th she sank the SS *Isabela* (am 3110t) ENE of Morant Cays. U 751 operated in the Eastern Mediterranean but had no further success.
She returned to St Nazaire **15.6.42**

7. 14.7.42   Left for the North Atlantic.
On the 17th U 751 was sunk NW of Cape Finisterre in depth-charge attacks by two aircraft, a Lancaster of 61 Squadron (F/Lt P R Casement) and a Whitley of 502 Squadron (P/O A R A Hunt). Casement's squadron was on loan from Bomber to Coastal Command and it was his first a/s patrol.
There were no survivors from U 751, 47 dead.

U 752 Type VII C

Built by Kriegsmarine-Werft, Wilhelmshaven
Keel laid 5.1.40   Launched 29.3.41
Commissioned 24.5.41   Feldpost Nr M 44 442

Sunk 23.5.43 in the central North Atlantic (51°40′N 29°49′W)

Served with
3 U-Flottille, Kiel/La Pallice   May 1941 - 23.5.43 (ab/fb)

Commanded by
KL Karl-Ernst Schroeter   May 1941 - 23.5.43

Patrols: 8   Ships sunk: 7 (37,157 grt) + 1 damaged
                        2 m/s trawlers (2150 dt)

1. 23.7.41   Left Kiel and arrived Horten **24.7.41**

2. 31.7.41   Left Horten and arrived Trondheim **2.8.41**

3. 18.8.41 Left Trondheim and arrived Kirkenes **22.8.41**

4. 23.8.41 Left Kirkenes for Northern Waters.

U 752 operated off the Kola Coast and on the 25th she torpedoed and sank the Soviet m/s trawler *TSC-898/T-44* NW of Svyatoy Nos. In the same area two days later U 752 reported sinking a Soviet patrol vessel, possibly the *SKR-11,* but there is no confirmation of this. The boat had no further success on this patrol.

She returned to Kirkenes **17.9.41**

5. 19.9.41 Left Kirkenes and arrived Trondheim **23.9.41**

6. 18.10.41 Left Trondheim and arrived Kirkenes **22.10.41**

7. 7.11.41 Left for operations.

From the 12th U 752 was operating in the entrance to the White Sea. On the 15th she attacked a coastal convoy near Cape Gorodetski, torpedoing the lumber-carrier *ZM-93/Jusar* (sov 2020t), which was hit but did not stop. In a second attack, U 752 missed the listing *ZM-93* and the torpedo went on to sink Soviet m/s trawler *TSC-889/T34.*

The boat returned to Kirkenes **18.11.41**

8. 22.11.41 Left Kirkenes and arrived Kiel **10.12.41**

9. 4.2.42 Left Kiel and arrived Heligoland **5.2.42**

10. 7.2.42 Left Heligoland and arrived Bergen **10.2.42**

11. 12.2 42 Left for Atlantic operations.

From mid-January 1942 Hitler had ordered that six boats should be stationed in an area W of the Hebrides and the Faroes to counter any invasion of Norway. U 752 was on this duty until the 22nd, when she, U 136 and U 213 were directed to eastbound convoy HX 175, sighted by U 154 800 miles W of the North Channel.

On the 24th U 752 attacked the convoy SW of Rockall, afterwards reporting two detonations on a tanker but without any apparent result. The boat returned to the area W of the Hebrides and Faroes.

She put in to her new base at La Pallice **13.3.42**

12. 28.3.42 Left for US waters.

U 752 was one of twelve boats in the fifth wave of *Operation Paukenschlag.* She patrolled off the east coast of America from New York southwards.

On 21.4.42 U 752 sank the SS *West Imboden* (am 5751t) by torpedo and gunfire E of New York, on the 23rd the MV *Reinholt* (am 4799t) was sunk by gunfire E of Delaware Bay and on 1.5.42 the MV *Bidewind* (nw 4956t) was torpedoed and sunk E of Asbury Park, New Jersey.

U 752 put in to St Nazaire **21.5.42**

13. 2.7.42 Left for the Central Atlantic.

U 752 was one of six boats intended for operations in the Freetown area. They assembled SE of the Azores, as *Hai* group, and on the 10th began a sweep southwards between meridians 20° and 25°W. On the 11th southbound convoy OS 33 passed through the patrol line S of Santa Maria, Azores.

After dark a group of ships bound for South America split from the convoy, which continued southwards. Four of the *Hai* boats pursued these ships whilst U 752 and U 572 maintained contact with the convoy. Neither boat had any success and the operation ended on the 13th.

The five surviving *Hai* boats reformed NNE of the Cape Verde Island on the 15th. U 136 had been sunk on the 11th. The line continued southwards until it passed Dakar. On the 21st the group dispersed and the boats then operated independently off Freetown.

U 752 torpedoed and sank the SS *Garmula* (br 5254t) on the

23rd SSW of Freetown. Two days later the boat attacked convoy FN 20 and sank the SS *Leikanger* (nw 4003t) SW of Freetown. On 4.8.42 U 752 was refuelled W of Freetown by U 116.

Patrolling SW of Freetown, U 752 sank two more ships in August, on the 9th the SS *Mendenau* (nl 6047t) and on the 13th the SS *Cripple Creek* (am 6347t). The boat picked up three survivors from the *Mendenau* as prisoners.

U 752 returned to La Pallice **4.9.42**

14. 19.10.42 Left for the Central Atlantic.

U 752 was proceeding southwards when the Allied landings were made in North Africa on 8.11.42. She was one of the boats between the Bay of Biscay and the Cape Verde Islands that were ordered to head at high speed for the Moroccan coast, as *Schlagetot* group. They were to interrupt sea-borne supplies destined for the Allied forces which had landed at Fedala and Casablanca.

Although there were some sinkings between November 11th and 16th, most of the boats, including U 752, were unable to break through the protective ring formed by Allied naval forces. Early on the 18th U 752 made an unsuccessful attack on a steamer NW of Casablanca.

She returned to La Pallice **3.12.42**

15. 9.1.43 Left for the North Atlantic.

U 752 joined *Habicht* group W of Ireland. On the 17th the group moved westwards in search of ON convoys. By the 19th nothing had been found and the *Habicht* boats combined with those of *Falke* group to form a new patrol line, *Haudegen,* running for 300 miles SE of Cape Farewell.

On the 22nd the group was ordered to go southeastwards to intercept an eastbound HX convoy. Bad weather prevented the interception and the boats returned to a position S of Cape Farewell. On the way back, on the 26th, U 383 sighted escorts of HX 223, which had been scattered in the storm.

From 1.2.43 *Haudegen* group began a southwesterly movement towards Newfoundland. On the 2nd the five northern boats of the group were detached to attack convoy SG 19, as *Nordsturm* group.

On the 4th U 187 of *Pfeil* group sighted eastbound SC 118 E of Newfoundland and the southern *Haudegen* boats, U 752, U 438, U 613, U 624 and U 704, were ordered to leave the patrol line and attack the convoy, which was also being attacked by *Pfeil* group. The *Haudegen* boats had no success. After the SC 118 operation ended on the 9th WNW of Ireland, they did not rejoin the group but returned to base.

On the 10th the returning U 752 was attacked by a Liberator of 2 A/S Squadron (USAF) (Lt W L Sandford) NE of the Azores. The boat was only slightly damaged by depth-charges.

She reached La Pallice **15.2.43**

16. 22.4.43 Left for the North Atlantic.

Outward-bound on the 29th, U 752 made an unsuccessful torpedo attack on a large passenger liner SW of Ireland. One detonation was heard but without apparent result.

U 752 joined *Amsel 3* group, which with *Amsel 1,2* and *4* groups, was stationed in an arc E of St John's, Newfoundland. *Amsel 1* and *2* went north to intercept convoy ONS 5 and on the 7th *Amsel 3* and *4* combined as *Rhein* group, which was ordered southeastwards at high speed on the 8th to form a patrol line on the 9th for the interception of HX 237.

U 359 sighted a ship of the convoy on the 9th before the line could be formed but lost it in worsening visibility. The boats carried out independent searches before reforming in the morning of the 10th. At noon U 403 sighted a fast independent ship and then a tug, which led to HX 237 being located in the afternoon.

The *Rhein* boats were by then too far east, so they were ordered to combine with *Elbe* group to form *Elbe 1* and *2* groups to pursue the slower convoy SC 129. U 752 was in *Elbe 1.* As the boats were forming up on the 11th, the convoy passed by, sighted in the evening

U 752 (continued)

by U 504. The *Elbe* boats moved in to attack but those that approached the convoy on the 12th were driven off by the escort. On the 13th a carrier from the HX 237 escort arrived to protect SC 129 and the operation was called off on the 14th, with two ships sunk but two boats lost and others damaged.

U 752 was possibly refuelled by U 459 in the central North Atlantic for further operations. She then joined *Oder* group, formed on the 18th from mainly ex-*Elbe* boats to be ready to meet eastbound SC 130, should it turn southwards. In fact the convoy did not move too far south and it was intercepted by *Donau 1* and *2* groups north of the *Oder* line.

The *Oder* boats became part of the new *Mosel* group, formed 400 miles S of Cape Farewell to intercept HX 239, reported on the 18th to be moving eastwards from Newfoundland and expected to pass south of the *Mosel* patrol line. The convoy took evasive action and whilst the southern part of the line went south to intercept stragglers the other *Mosel* boats, including U 752, moved eastwards on the 21st to attack the convoy itself.

Early on the 23rd, in the vicinity of HX 239, U 752 was sighted by a Swordfish of 819 (FAA) Squadron from the escort-carrier HMS *Archer*. Depth-charges were dropped but the boat dived and escaped.

About one hour later U 752 resurfaced and was sighted by another Swordfish (Sub-Lt H Horrocks), this one armed with rocket-projectiles. Four salvoes of two were fired, the last striking the boat as it dived. U 752 surfaced again and began to circle, losing oil.

Crewmen came up and manned the guns. The Swordfish called for fighter assistance and a Martlet of 892 (FAA) Squadron arrived from *Archer*. A long burst of machine-gun fire into the conning tower killed U 752's commander, KL Schroeter. After briefly firing at the Martlet, the gunners went below again. A short time afterwards men came up and began to abandon ship as U 752 sank, the first boat to be sunk by an aircraft from an escort-carrier, firing rocket projectiles.

Directed by the Martlet, the destroyer HMS *Escapade* came up and picked up 13 survivors. Another 4 were picked up later by U 91. From U 752's crew, 29 men lost their lives.

U 753   Type VII C

Built by Kriegsmarine-Werft, Wilhelmshaven
Keel laid 3.1.40   Launched 26.4.41
Commissioned 18.6.41   Feldpost Nr M 44 578

Sunk 13.5.43 NNE of the Azores (48°37′N 22°39′W)

Served with
3 U-Flottille, Kiel/La Pallice   June 1941 - 13.5.43 (ab/fb)

Commanded by
KK Alfred Manhardt von Mannstein   June 1941 - 13.5.43

Patrols: 6   Ships sunk: 2 (13,769 grt) + 3 damaged

1. 24.12.41 Left Kiel for operations.
U 753 had engine damage on the 27th and returned **30.12.41**

2. 17.1.42 Left for Atlantic operations.
U 753 was one of twelve boats from Germany which assembled W of Rockall, as *Schlei* group, to carry out a southwesterly sweep across the convoy routes. The planned operation was called off and U 753 and six other boats went to bases in France to be prepared for service in US waters. The other five *Schlei* boats went to the Iceland/Faroes/Scotland area for the protection of Norway.
U 753 put in to St Nazaire **1.2.42**

3. 26.2.42 Left for Atlantic operations.
U 753 patrolled an area W of the Faroes and the Hebrides. From late January 1942 a U-boat presence had been maintained there, ostensibly on Hitler's orders, to repel any invasion of Norway.
On 18.3.42 U 507, in transit to Western France, sighted westbound convoy ONS 76 200 miles W of the North Channel. She called up U 753, U 506 and U 593 but they were unable to come up before U 507 lost contact with the convoy. The operation was abandoned on the 20th.
U 753 put in to La Pallice **26.3.42**

4. 22.4.42 Left for US waters.
In early May the outward-bound U 753 was refuelled by U 459 500 miles NE of Bermuda. The boat initially operated off Cape Hatteras and then from mid-May in the Florida area.
On the 19th U 753 sighted a convoy near the southern end of the Florida Strait. She submerged and approached but went too close and the boat was sucked upwards, striking the keel of one of the ships, which apparently heard and felt nothing. U 753 moved away and surfaced for an assessment of the damage. The net-deflector was smashed and the deck-gun badly damaged. Unable to carry out any repairs in daylight, U 753 surfaced after dark and makeshift repairs were made.
In the evening of the 20th she attacked two ships N of the western tip of Cuba, sinking the SS *George Calvert* (am 7191t) by torpedo and damaging the sailing vessel *E P Theriault* (br 326t), which was stopped by gunfire and then not quite sunk with scuttling charges.
U 753 entered the Gulf of Mexico. On the 25th she torpedoed and damaged the tanker MV *Haakon Hauan* (nw 6582t) off Grand Isle, Louisiana and on the 27th she sank the tanker MV *Hamlet* (nw 6578t) S of Atchafalaya Bay, Louisiana.
The returning boat was attacked and damaged by a Whitley of 58 Squadron (F/Sgt W Jones) on 23.6.42 in the Bay of Biscay.
U 753 returned to La Pallice **25.6.42**

5. 1.9.42 Left La Pallice and returned **4.9.42**

6. 20.9.42 Left for the North Atlantic.
U 753 joined *Luchs* group W of Ireland, awaiting an ON convoy. On the 29th outward-bound U 118 sighted a westbound convoy 250 miles S of Iceland and the *Luchs* boats were ordered northwest to intercept. When nothing had been located by the evening of 2.10.42 the group swept slowly southwestwards. On the 3rd U 260 sighted eastbound HX 209 at the northern end of the *Luchs* patrol line.
Bad weather delayed the concentration of the boats for an attack and a strong air escort kept them at a distance. On the 5th two boats were sunk and another damaged. The operation against HX 209 was terminated next day.
From the 8th the boats coming from HX 209 were formed into *Panther* group 700 to 800 miles W of the North Channel. The group was augmented by outward-bound boats. In the evening of the 11th U 620 sighted westbound ONS 136 and eight boats in the centre of the long *Panther* patrol line were detached and directed to the convoy as *Leopard* group.
On the 16th ONS 137 was sighted by U 704 as it passed through the southern section of the line and eleven boats were ordered to attack. From the remaining *Panther* boats, *Puma* group was formed on the 16th from U 753 and seven other boats and ordered southwards to seek ONS 138.
By the 22nd the boats were nearly 400 miles south of their original *Puma* line position. On that day the southernmost boat in the line, U 443, sighted ON 139 in the central North Atlantic. The group was ordered to catch the convoy, which was averaging 10 to 12 knots. Only U 443 was able to attack and she sank two ships.
Puma group moved westwards until the 24th, when U 606 reported two destroyers which could have been part of an escort for a westbound ONS convoy. The boats moved northwestwards at

high speed to intercept. On the 26th U 436 sighted eastbound HX 212 in the centre of the patrol line. She shadowed and brought up other boats but all were driven off by the escort.

Short of fuel, U 753 did not take part in this operation but moved south for replenishment by U 463 in the central North Atlantic. The boat then joined boats of *Natter* group in the search for westbound ON 143 from 4.11.42 but with no convoy found the operation was called off on the 6th.

On the 8th U 753 was refuelled by U 117 N of the Azores. She then joined *Kreuzotter* group 600 miles W of Ireland. The group moved northwards on the 13th and two days later westbound ONS 144 passed through the centre of the patrol line. On the 18th U 753 missed the corvette HMS *Rose* and the rescue ship *Perth*. In the operation, which ended E of Newfoundland on the 20th, five ships and a corvette of the escort were sunk.

Very low on fuel, six of the *Kreuzotter* boats, including U 753, moved southeastwards on the 21st to an area NW of the Azores, where they were refuelled by U 460 on or about the 27th.

U 753 returned to La Pallice **8.12.42**

7. 28.1.43 Left for the North Atlantic.

U 753 joined *Hartherz* group W of the Bay of Biscay, formed to intercept an HG convoy, reported to have left Gibraltar. The group searched between 14° and 19°W from February 4th to the 7th but nothing was seen. The group broke up on the 8th and from the 14th U 753 was with *Ritter* group, formed W of Ireland to operate against expected convoy HX 226. During the night of the 15/16th convoy SC 119 passed to the north of the group and on the 18th HX 226 also passed to the north, after a wide detour.

Ritter group had been moving westwards but when it was reported by aircraft that convoys ON 166 and ONS 167 were being routed south of the *Ritter* line, the movement westwards was halted and the boats moved southeastwards and formed a north-south patrol line with *Neptun* group on the 30° meridian from the 20th.

ON 166 was sighted by U 604 in the late morning of the 20th but she was driven off during the night before the closing *Ritter* and *Knappen* boats could arrive. U 753 made contact NNW of the Azores on the 21st but was driven off. In the morning of the 22nd she made a torpedo hit on the whaling factory ship MV *N T Nielsen Alonso* (nw 9348t), struck three hours earlier by two torpedoes from U 92. The abandoned wreck of this vessel was sunk some hours later by the Polish destroyer *Burza*. Later on the 22nd U 753 was attacked with depth-charges by the corvettes HMCS *Rosthern* and *Trillium*.

The convoy, ON 166, was pursued for 1100 miles and before the operation ended on the 25th ESE of Newfoundland in bad visibility, fourteen ships were sunk and another damaged. On the 27th U 753 picked up six survivors of the MV *Madoera*, sunk by U 653 early on the 24th. On or about March 1st U 753 was refuelled by U 462 N of the Azores for return to base.

The boat reached La Pallice **10.3.43**

8. 5.5.43 Left for Atlantic operations.

Outward-bound, U 753 was directed to northeast-bound convoy HX 237 SW of Ireland. In the evening of the 11th she made an unsuccessful attack against a ship of the convoy. The operation ended on the 13th, with three ships sunk. U 89, U 456 and U 753 were destroyed by the escort.

In the morning of the 13th U 753 was spotted on the surface 10 miles from the convoy by a Sunderland of 423 (RCAF) Squadron (F/Lt J Musgrave), NNE of the Azores. As the aircraft approached, U 753 opened fire and the Sunderland moved out of range and requested assistance.

The frigate HMS *Lagan* (Lt-Cdr A Ayre) and the corvette HMCS *Drumheller* (Lt P Denny) were sent from the escort. As they came up, U 753 dived. The Sunderland came in and dropped two depth-charges. *Lagan* and *Drumheller* made depth-charge and Hedgehog attacks and eventually oil and debris was seen. U 753 was destroyed.

There were no survivors, 47 dead.

U 754   Type VII C

Built by Kriegsmarine-Werft, Wilhelmshaven
Keel laid 8.1.40   Launched 5.7.41
Commissioned 28.8.41   Feldpost Nr M 46 656

Sunk 31.7.42 SE of Cape Sable (43°02´N 64°52´W)

Served with
5 U-Flottille, Kiel August - November 1941 (ab)
1 U-Flottille, Brest December 1941 - 31.7.42 (fb)

Commanded by
KL Johannes Oestermann August 1941 - 31.7.42

Patrols: 3   Ships sunk: 13 (55,659 grt) + 1 damaged

1. 30.12.41 Left Kiel for Canadian waters.

U 754 went to the Newfoundland Bank area. On 21.1.42 she torpedoed and sank two ships E of St John's, the MV *Belize* (nw 2153t) and the SS *William Hansen* (nw 1344t). The *Belize* sailed from New York on the 15th and one of her waterfilled lifeboats was found on the 24th by the corvette HMCS *Spikenard*.

On the 25th U 754 sank the SS *Mount Kitheron* (gr 3876t) off St John's and on the 26th the SS *Icarion* (gr 4013t) was sunk SE of Cape Race.

U 754 put in to her new base at Brest **9.2.42**

2. 7.3.42 Left for the North Atlantic.

U 754 again headed for the Newfoundland area. On the 23rd she torpedoed and sank the tanker MV *British Prudence* (br 8620t) S of St Pierre Island. Towards the end of March U 754 moved south into US waters. On the 31st, E of Cedar Island, Virginia, the boat attacked a tug and three barges by gunfire. She sank the tug *Menominee* (am 441t), the barges *Barnegat* (am 914t) and *Alleghany* (am 914t) and damaged the barge *Ontario* (am 490t).

On 1.4.42 U 754 sank the tanker SS *Tiger* (am 5992t) E of Cape Henry, on the 3rd the SS *Otho* (am 4839t) E of Albermarle Sound and on the 6th the tanker MV *Kollskegg* (nw 9858t) E of Cape Hatteras.

U 754 returned to Brest **25.4.42**

3. 19.6.42 Left for the Western Atlantic.

On the 29th the outward-bound U 754 sank the MV *Waiwera* (br 12,435t) NNW of the Azores. Some time later the boat was refuelled by U 459 W of the Azores.

She operated initially S of Hatteras but at this time unescorted ships were very seldom seen. U 754 was one of the last seven U-boats operating off the US east coast.

On July 19th U 754, U 89, U 132 and U 458 were moved to an area SE of Nova Scotia. On the 28th U 754 sank the trawler *Ebb* (am 260t) by gunfire S of Halifax.

The boat was sighted on the surface on the 31st SE of Cape Sable by a Hudson of 113 (RCAF) Squadron (S/Ldr N E Small), based at Yarmouth, Nova Scotia.

Taken by surprise, U 754 was unable to dive before the aircraft dropped depth-charges. The Hudson then quickly turned and machine-gunned the conning tower before the boat submerged. Almost an hour later a large explosion brought oil and debris to the surface. U 754 was destroyed.

There were no survivors, 43 dead.

U 755   Type VII C

Built by Kriegsmarine-Werft, Wilhelmshaven
Keel laid 11.1.40   Launched 23.8.41
Commissioned 3.11.41   Feldpost Nr unknown

Sunk 28.5.43 WNW of Majorca (39°58′N 01°41′E)

Served with
5 U-Flottille, Kiel November 1941 - July 1942 (ab)
9 U-Flottille, Brest August - November 1942 (ab)
29 U-Flottille, La Spezia December 1942 - 28.5.43 (fb)

Commanded by
KL Walter Göing November 1941 - 28.5.43

Patrols: 5   Ships sunk: 2 (2075 grt)
                        1 patrol yacht (1827 dt)

1. 4.8.42 Left Kiel for the North Atlantic.

U 755 was one of a number of newly-arrived boats which joined others coming from the operation against convoy SC 94 to form a new patrol line, *Lohs*, 600 miles W of the North Channel. An ON convoy was expected on the 13th.

En route to their new positions, some of the boats from SC 94 sighted SC 95 going north. Only three boats closed, sinking one ship before contact was lost.

The *Lohs* patrol line was formed on the 17th W of Scotland. On the 21st the group moved northwards, searching for convoys, and on the 22nd ONS 122 passed to the south and was sighted by *Lohs'* southernmost boat, U 135. She shadowed but contact was lost and not regained until the 24th. By the early hours of the 25th nine boats were in contact and attacks were made. However, fog came down and the operation was called off, with four ships sunk and two boats damaged. U 755 had no success.

In late August the *Lohs* boats moved to a position W of the Azores for refuelling. U 755 was supplied by U 462 on or about the 30th. The group reformed and from 6.9.42 a new patrol line, 400 miles NE of Cape Race, awaited eastbound convoys. On the 9th U 755 torpedoed and sank the US patrol yacht *Muskeget* (AG 48) NE of St John's. She was on weather-reporting duty and was on her way from Norfolk, Virginia to Iceland.

Eastbound SC 100 was expected to be 150 miles SE of Cape Race on the 18th and *Lohs* moved south to intercept but bad weather prevented more than three boats making attacks. When the weather worsened further, the operation was abandoned on the 22nd, with only one ship sunk. The convoy was sighted again on the 23rd and U 432 of *Lohs* and U 617 of *Pfeil* group sank one ship and three stragglers between them. The operation against SC 100 finally ended on the 25th W of Rockall.

When U 617 sighted westbound ON 131 on the 26th, U 755 and other boats from the SC 100 operation were directed to it as *Tiger* group. When contact was lost, the operation against ON 131 was abandoned because of threatening weather and the widely-scattered positions of the boats.

U 755 was briefly with *Luchs* group, formed on 1.10.42 W of Ireland but did not take part in the operation against eastbound convoy HX 209.

The boat put in to her new base at Brest **6.10.42**.

2. 1.11.42 Left for the Mediterranean.

U 755 passed through the Straits of Gibraltar during the night of the 9/10th and joined other boats which were operating against Allied ships taking part in the invasion of North Africa. She had no success.

The boat put in to her new base at La Spezia **22.11.42**.

3. 27.1.43 Left for operations.

U 755 operated off the Algerian coast against Allied supply shipping. She made only unsuccessful attacks.

The boat returned to La Spezia **20.2.43**.

4. 21.3.43 Left for operations.

U 755 operated against convoys along the Moroccan and Algerian coasts. On the 26th she torpedoed and sank the SS *Sergeant Gouarne* (fr 1147t) N of Ceuta, at the eastern exit of the Straits of Gibraltar.

On 2.4.43 U 755 sank a straggler from convoy TE 20, the SS *Simon Duhamel II* (fr 928t), NNE of Cap Des Trois Fourches, Morocco.

U 755 put in to Toulon **12.4.43**.

5. 18.5.43 Left for operations in the Western Mediterranean.

On the 28th U 755 was sighted NNW of Majorca by a Hudson of 608 Squadron (F/O G A K Ogilvie), which was equipped with rocket projectiles. On sighting the aircraft, the boat did not submerge but began to fire at the circling Hudson.

Two rocket attacks were made against the boat, each scoring hits. U 755 began to circle and flames and smoke were seen, after which she began to sink. As the crew leapt into the sea, the aircraft fired at them.

U 755's bow rose up and then slid, stern first, into the depths. Many men were seen in the water but only nine, all wounded, were landed at Valencia after being picked up by Spanish naval vessels.

From U 755's crew, the commander and 39 men were lost.

U 756   Type VII C

Built by Kriegsmarine-Werft, Wilhelmshaven
Keel laid 18.1.40   Launched 18.10.41
Commissioned 30.12.41   Feldpost Nr M 39 246

Sunk 1.9.42 ESE of Cape Farewell (57°41′N 31°30′W)

Served with
6 U-Flottille, Danzig/St Nazaire December 1941 - 1.9.42 (ab/fb)

Commanded by
KL Klaus Harney December 1941 - 1.9.42

Patrols: 1   Ships sunk: None

1. 15.8.42 Left Kiel for the North Atlantic.

U 756 joined *Vörwarts* group, formed on the 27th W of Ireland. The group began a sweep to the southwest and on the 31st U 609, at the northern end of the patrol line, sighted eastbound convoy SC 97 and sank two ships before being driven off.

In the late evening U 756 made an unsuccessful attack on the convoy. On the morning of September 1st she was one of six boats near the convoy, ESE of Cape Farewell. The boat was located and sunk in a depth-charge attack by the corvette HMCS *Morden* (Lt J J Hodgkinson).

There were no survivors, 43 dead.

U 757　Type VII C

Built by Kriegsmarine-Werft, Wilhelmshaven
Keel laid 18.5.40　Launched 14.12.41
Commissioned 28.2.42　Feldpost Nr M 39 567

Sunk 8.1.44 WSW of Bantry Bay (50°33′N 18°03′W)

Served with
6 U-Flottille, Danzig/St Nazaire　February 1942 - 8.1.44 (ab/fb)

Commanded by
KL Friedrich Deetz　February 1942 - 8.1.44

Patrols: 5　　Ships sunk: 2 (9117 grt) + 1 damaged

1. 15.9.42　Left Kiel and arrived Kristiansand **16.9.42**

2. 18.9.42　Left Kristiansand and arrived Bergen **19.9.42**

3. 26.9.42　Left Bergen for the North Atlantic.
　U 757 joined ex-*Luchs* group boats when *Panther* group was formed from 8.10.42 700 to 800 miles W of the North Channel. She remained with the group until about the 16th but took no part in any of its operations.
　The boat put in to her new base at St Nazaire **24.10.42**

4. 12.12.42　Left for Atlantic operations.
　U 757 was damaged by an explosion on board on the 19th. She returned to St Nazaire **25.12.42**

5. 22.2.43　Left for the North Atlantic.
　Outward-bound on the 28th, U 757 reported a possible torpedo hit on a steamer NE of the Azores but this is unconfirmed. From 6.3.43 the boat was with the newly-formed *Neuland* group W of Ireland. On the 7th the patrol line split, with the northern section moving northwestwards, as *Ostmark* group to attack SC 121 and the southern boats, including U 757, moving westwards in search of HX 228. On the 9th this line moved northwards and on the 10th the convoy was sighted by U 336 at the southern end of the *Neuland* line. In the early hours of the 11th U 757 torpedoed two ships of HX 228 in the central North Atlantic, the SS *Brant County* (nw 5001t) and the abandoned wreck of the SS *William C Gorgas* (am 7197t), which had been torpedoed previously by U 444.
　When the *Brant County*'s cargo of munitions exploded, U 757 was damaged by the blast. Although she managed to sink the wreck of the *William C Gorgas*, the boat was sufficiently damaged to warrant her return to base.
　U 757 reached St Nazaire **18.3.43**

6. 7.7.43　Left for the Central Atlantic.
　U 757 operated off Freetown. On 7.8.43 she torpedoed and sank the MV *Fernhill* (nw 4116t) WSW of Freetown and picked up one survivor as a prisoner. U 757 turned for home in mid-August.
　She returned to St Nazaire **4.9.43**

7. 31.10.43　Left St Nazaire and returned **2.11.43**

8. 16.11.43　Left St Nazaire and returned **18.11.43**

9. 20.11.43　Left St Nazaire and returned **22.11.43**

10. 29.11.43　Left St Nazaire and returned **1.12.43**

11. 29.12.43　Left for Atlantic operations.
　U 757 joined other boats which were operating independently W to SW of Ireland. On 8.1.44 the boat was located by the escort of convoy KMS 38/OS 64 WSW of Bantry Bay.

She came under repeated depth-charge attacks by the frigate HMS *Bayntun* (Lt-Cdr L P Bourke) and the corvette HMCS *Camrose* (Lt L R Pavillard) and her destruction was confirmed by the appearance of wreckage.
　There were no survivors, 49 dead.

U 758　Type VII C

Built by Kriegsmarine-Werft, Wilhelmshaven
Keel laid 18.5.40　Launched 1.3.42
Commissioned 5.5.42　Feldpost Nr M 47 033

Decommissioned 24.3.45 at Kiel

Served with
6 U-Flottille, Danzig/St Nazaire　May 1942 - October 1944 (ab/fb)
33 U-Flottille, Flensburg　October 1944 - 24.3.45 (ab)

Commanded by
KL Helmut Manseck　May 1942 - April 1944
OL Hans-Arend Feindt　April 1944 - 24.3.45

Patrols: 7　　Ships sunk: 1 (6813 grt) + 1 damaged

1. 14.11.42　Left Kiel for the North Atlantic.
　U 758 joined other boats to form *Panzer* group, which on the 29th was in a position 800 miles W of the North Channel, awaiting an ONS convoy. Evidence from hydrophone and radar indicated a convoy not far away and the group searched to the southwest. When nothing was seen, the *Panzer* boats continued southwestwards and on 4.12.42 they halted E of Newfoundland.
　That evening U 524 picked up R/T conversations and in the very sure knowledge that a convoy was near, *Panzer* group moved northeastwards at high speed. Eastbound HX 217 was sighted by U 524 on the 6th S of Greenland but contact was lost in bad visibility. It was regained on the 7th and U 135, U 254, U 439 and U 465 came up but were driven off by a Liberator of 120 Squadron (S/Ldr T M Bulloch).
　In the morning of the 8th U 758 claimed a hit on a steamer and in the early hours of the 10th she claimed hits on three ships of the convoy but all are unconfirmed. Once within range of Iceland, strong air cover appeared from the 10th and the operation was abandoned next day. Two ships had been sunk and two boats lost.
　U 758 put in to her new base at St Nazaire **24.12.42**

2. 14.2.43　Left for Atlantic operations.
　Outward-bound on the 21st, U 664 sighted westbound convoy ONS 167 WSW of Ireland. She, U 758 and four other outward-bound boats were ordered to form *Sturmbock* group to operate against it. U 664 sank two ships in the evening of the 21st but when she made a second approach in company with U 758 early on the 22nd both boats were driven off.
　The other *Sturmbock* boats were too far apart to close and attack the convoy. From the 24th the six boats, now ahead of the convoy, formed a new line, *Wildfang*, E of Newfoundland in the expected path of ONS 167. The convoy was not seen again and the operation ended in bad visibility on the 25th.
　In early March U 758, U 664 and U 84 joined *Burggraf* group, which on the 7th was reformed as *Raubgraf* group NE of Newfoundland. The group moved northwards until the 10th, then went northwestwards for two days, searching for westbound convoy ONS 169 but failed to find it. On the 13th ON 170 was sighted briefly and although the weather was bad it was decided to pursue. A strong air escort and a report that eastbound SC 122 was approaching caused the operation against ON 170 to be called off.
　During the evening of the 15th one of *Raubgraf*'s southern boats sighted a destroyer, which led to an unsuccessful search for a

U 758 (continued)

convoy. Late in the morning of the 16th the *Raubgraf* boats made contact with an eastbound convoy and later the same day a second convoy was reported ahead of the one then under attack, sailing on a parallel course and slower.

The second one was realised to be SC 122 and the first one sighted to be HX 229. Early on the 17th U 758 attacked ships in HX 229, sinking the SS *Zaanland* (nl 6813t), damaging the SS *James Oglethorpe* (am 7176t), which was sunk eight hours later by U 91, and claiming a hit on a tanker, possibly the MV *Magdala* (nl), but there is no confirmation of this.

The operation against the two convoys ended on the 20th W of Ireland. It was the biggest convoy action of the war, with twenty-one ships sunk and only one boat lost, U 384. On or about the 19th U 758 was possibly refuelled by U 463 in the central North Atlantic for return to base.

The boat put in to Bordeaux **30.3.43**

U 758's armament was modified by the replacement of her existing light anti-aircraft guns with a quadruple 2cm gun set-up. Trials were carried out in April and May.

3. 15.5.43   Left Bordeaux and returned **16.5.43**

4. 26.5.43   Left for Atlantic operations.

Outward-bound on June 8th, U 758 sighted a destroyer W of the Azores, one of the escort for eastbound convoy UGS 9. The escort-carrier USS *Bogue* was with the convoy and U 758's experimental armament was about to be tested.

In the evening of the 8th the boat was sighted, moving fast on the surface, by an Avenger from *Bogue* (Lt L S Balliett). In the face of heavy flak, the aircraft dropped four depth-bombs which fell wide. The boat moved away southwestwards but was soon after attacked by another Avenger (Lt W S Fowler), again in the face of heavy fire. Four more depth-bombs were dropped and the aircraft was badly damaged and her radioman wounded. Fowler managed to get his aircraft back to *Bogue*.

The boat circled slowly on the surface and several Wildcats made strafing attacks but were driven off. One, flown by Lt P Perabo, put two of the four 2cm guns out of action A third Avenger (Lt F D Fogde) approached and dropped depth-bombs as the boat dived.

Ten minutes later U 758 resurfaced and put up intense flak at the two circling aircraft. Before the boat dived again, Perabo made two more strafing attacks in his Wildcat. The pilots had signalled that no surface assistance was required and three approaching escort vessels were recalled.

The destroyer USS *Clemson* was later sent to the scene but her one depth-charge attack caused no further damage to the boat. In the early hours of the 9th U 758 resurfaced to recharge her batteries and then headed for a rendezvous with U 118 on or about the 10th to pass over some of the eleven crewmen wounded in the action. U 118 was sunk by carrier-borne aircraft on the 12th and some of U 758's men were among the 15 survivors.

U 758's performance against the attacking aircraft was considered sufficient justification for the increased armament and the flak-boat conversions went ahead.

U 758 returned to St Nazaire **25.6.43**

5. 1.9.43   Left for the North Atlantic

U 758 was one of fourteen boats which set out to form a patrol line, *Leuthen*, SSW of Iceland from 20.9.43, to intercept an ONS convoy. They were joined by six other boats which had assembled N of the Azores and then after refuelling had moved north to take their place in the patrol line. Secrecy had been maintained as far as possible to prevent the presence of the boats becoming known to the Allies. However, on the 19th westbound U 341, which should have been proceeding submerged, was sighted, attacked and sunk by a Canadian aircraft near the planned patrol line position.

Early on the 20th, before the *Leuthen* boats were in position, convoy ON 202 was sighted. Four boats closed but only one was able to make a submerged attack. In the morning contact was lost because of aircraft and a strong surface escort. ON 202 joined up with convoy ONS 18 during the day. Contact with the combined convoy was regained in the early evening of the 20th.

Only five boats closed the convoy, the other *Leuthen* boats being intent on attacking the escort, in the belief that if the escort was depleted, the convoy could be dealt with during the night of the 21/22nd.

Fog came down early on the 21st and remained throughout the day and the next night. When it thinned during daylight on the 22nd Allied aircraft re-appeared and the boats stayed on the surface to fight it out. In the morning of the 23rd U 758 made attacks on a ship and a destroyer and although detonations were heard the boat had no success. The operation was abandoned later in the morning, with six ships and three escorts sunk, another ship damaged and two boats lost.

On the 27th U 758 joined the newly-formed *Rossbach* group in the central North Atlantic, SW of Iceland, to operate against ON 203. The group moved 100 miles northwestwards towards Cape Farewell and waited until the 29th but the expected convoy was not seen.

The group moved northwards on 1.10.43 to intercept westbound ONS 19 but the convoy also passed to the north. From the 3rd the *Rossbach* boats turned eastwards to meet ON 204 but the convoy was not found. On the 5th the boats, then SW of Iceland, began a sweep southwestwards to search for SC 143 and HX 259, which were expected to be intercepted on the 8th.

In the evening of the 7th U 448 sighted ships of the 3rd SG, on their way to support SC 143. During the night U 758 was one of eight boats which made contact with the warships. She was located by the destroyer HMS *Musketeer* and then attacked by the Polish destroyer *Orkan*. A defensive torpedo fired by U 758 exploded in *Orkan*'s wake.

Liberators of 86 Squadron arrived in the morning and drove off the boats. Neither convoy, SC 143 or HX 259, was found and the search was called off on the 9th, with SC 143's only loss a straggler sunk early on that day by U 645.

Now short of fuel, U 758 and other *Rossbach* boats headed southwards to refuel. From the 11th they made several attempts to rendezvous with U-tanker U 488 in an area 300 to 600 miles N and NW of the Azores. U 758 was finally refuelled between the 15th and the 17th.

She put in to Lorient **24.10.43**

6. 16.12.43   Left for Atlantic operations.

U 758 joined *Borkum* group, which was searching in an area 400 miles NW of Cape Ortegal for combined convoy MKS 33/SL 142. When the convoy was not found, the *Borkum* boats were ordered to operate against the carrier groups of USS *Card* and *Core*, in an effort to cover the returning blockade-runner *Osorno*, which had been spotted on the 23rd by aircraft from *Card*. The ship reached the Gironde estuary safely on the 26th but after striking a wreck she had to be beached to save her valuable cargo.

On the 22nd and 23rd an escorted carrier was sighted by German aircraft. Attacks were made on the escort by the *Borkum* boats from the late evening of the 23rd. In the early morning of the 24th the destroyer USS *Leary* was sunk by U 275 and U 382.

In the evening of the 24th the *Borkum* boats encountered southbound OS 62/KMS 36 and U 415 sank the destroyer-leader of the escort. There were no other sinkings. The group continued to operate in the area NE of the Azores, between 20° and 25°W, moving from one position to another in the operational area.

On the 28th *Borkum* group was directed to search for convoy MKS 34/SL 143, which was finally sighted by aircraft on the 30th and 31st. En route to a new area, some *Borkum* boats encountered the 6th SG and some unsuccessful attacks were made by both sides.

MKS 34/SL 143 passed the *Borkum* patrol line on 1.1.44 and some unsuccessful attacks were made on the escort. The group took part in a failed operation against a southbound convoy on the 2nd and 3rd To make detection of the patrol line and avoidance of it by convoys more difficult, *Borkum* group was split into three small sub-groups, *Borkum 1,2 and 3*. U 758 was in *Borkum 2*. On the 5th, 6th and 7th the boats were frequently in contact with ships of the 5th SG, out searching for blockade-runners. On the 5th U 578 made an unsuccessful attack on a corvette.

From the 8th aircraft supported *Borkum* group, then searching for MKS 35/SL 144. The convoy was sighted by an aircraft on the 9th W of Portugal but could not be found during daylight on the 10th. A chance sighting of it by U 305 that evening at the end of the *Borkum* patrol line led to an order for the three groups to close. Harassed by carrier-borne aircraft, the boats were unable to make any concentrated attack. On the 11th U 758 was damaged in a rocket attack by aircraft from USS *Block Island*.

The boat returned to St Nazaire **20.1.44**

7. 6.6.44 U 758 was one of nineteen non-schnorkel boats which sailed into the Bay of Biscay as part of *Landwirt* group.

They were to form a line at the 200 metres depth line between Brest and Bordeaux, keeping out of port in case an Allied invasion force arrived and trapped them there. The boats later moved in to the 100 metres depth line, where they could lay on the bottom for long periods.

The waiting boats were under constant attack from the air when they surfaced at night. When no invasion had come by the 12th, the boats were recalled to port and placed on six hours notice.

U 758 returned to St Nazaire **15.6.44**

8. 23.8.44 Left for British coastal waters.

Now schnorkel-equipped, U 758 patrolled in the Bristol Channel for two weeks from the end of August. Very few independent ships were seen and individual boats in inshore waters could do little against convoys. U 758 had no success on this patrol.

The boat put into Bergen **10.10.44**

9. 13.10.44 Left Bergen and arrived Stavanger **14.10.44**

10. 19.10.44 Left Stavanger and arrived Flensburg **25.10.44**

On 24.3.45 U 758 was decommissioned at Kiel after being badly damaged in an air attack. She was handed over to the Allies in May 1945 and broken up in 1946/47.

U 759   Type VII C

Built by Kriegsmarine-Werft, Wilhelmshaven
Keel laid 15.11.40   Launched 30.5.42
Commissioned 15.8.42   Feldpost Nr M 46 926

Sunk 26.7.43 S of Navassa Island (18°06´N 75°00´W)

Served with
5 U-Flottille, Kiel   August 1942 - January 1943 (ab)
9 U-Flottille, Brest   February 1943 - 26.7.43 (fb)

Commanded by
KL Rudolf Friedrich   August 1942 - 26.7.43

Patrols: 2   Ships sunk: 2 (12,764 grt)

1. 2.2.43 Left Kiel for the North Atlantic.

U 759 joined *Neptun* group, formed from the 18th SW of Iceland to operate against expected, eastbound HX 226. The convoy was not found, having been re-routed to pass north of the *Neptun* line.

On the 20th the group moved southwestwards but was avoided by the re-routed SC 120. U 759, at the northern end of the line, sighted HX 227 S of Greenland in the morning of the 27th but she was driven off by the escort. The *Neptun* boats pursued but only U 759 was able to attack the convoy, with bad weather preventing the other boats closing.

On 1.3.43 U 759 sighted and missed the SS *Meriwether Lewis* (am 7176t) but the vessel, a straggler from HX 227, was sunk by U 634 in the early morning of the 2nd. Whilst searching for HX 227, U 608 sighted approaching, westbound ON 168 on the 1st but after she was driven off and the *Neptun* boats had not found the convoy again by the 3rd, the operation was abandoned.

From the 5th the *Neptun* boats took up waiting positions S of Cape Farewell and north of *Wildfang* and *Burggraf* groups. On the 6th U 405 sighted eastbound SC 121 and seventeen boats, drawn from the three groups, were detached to pursue the convoy, as *Westmark* group. U 759 did not take part in this operation.

She put in to Lorient **14.3.43**

2. 7.6.43 Left for the Caribbean.

Outward-bound, U 759 was refuelled some time after mid-June by U 530 SW of the Canaries. The boat entered the Caribbean via the Mona Passage and on the 30th she reported sinking a sailing vessel by gunfire SSE of Santo Domingo, Dominican Republic.

On 5.7.43 U 759 torpedoed and sank the SS *Maltran* (am 3513t) off Navassa Island and escaped attack by an escorting subchaser. Next day the boat encountered a convoy off Morant Point, Jamaica and on the 7th sank the MV *Poelau Roebiah* (nl 9251t) just E of Jamaica. U 759 was undamaged after a depth-charge attack by the destroyer USS *Tatnall*.

On the 10th the boat made an unsuccessful attack on a convoy S of the Windward Passage. She was sighted by a Kingfisher aircraft from Guantanamo, which made a depth-bomb attack and called for surface assistance. U 759 was subjected to depth-charge attacks by ships and aircraft for several hours before she was able to slip away.

On the 26th U 759 was sighted just before dawn by a Mariner of VP-32 (Lt R W Rawson) S of Navassa Island. Rawson dropped a flare and made a depth-charge attack, which destroyed the boat.

There were no survivors, 47 dead.

U 760   Type VII C

Built by Kriegsmarine-Werft, Wilhelmshaven
Keel laid 5.8.40   Launched 21.6.42
Commissioned 15.10.42   Feldpost Nr M 49 952

Sunk 13.12.45 NW of Bloody Foreland (55°50´N 10°05´W)

Served with
8 U-Flottille, Danzig   October 1942 - April 1943 (ab)
3 U-Flottille, La Pallice   May 1943 - 8.9.43 (fb)

Commanded by
OL Otto-Ulrich Blum   October 1942 - 8.9.43

Patrols: 2   Ships sunk: None

1. 29.4.43 Left Kiel for the North Atlantic.

U 760 and other outward-bound boats, U 340, U 636, U 657 and U 731, were deployed as *Iller* group to shadow convoy ONS 7, sighted by U 640 on 12.5.43 SW of Iceland. Contact was lost by U 640 on the 13th and she was sunk next day.

The *Iller* boats, having failed to find the convoy, were sent on the 15th to a new position just SE of Greenland. They joined up with *Inn, Lech, Isar* and *Nahe* groups to form *Donau 1* and 2 groups, to wait for ONS 7 coming from the east and HX 238 coming from the west. U 760 was in *Donau 1*.

U 760 (continued)

The *Donau* groups moved westwards and took up a patrol line from the 16th, running southeastwards from Cape Farewell. ONS 7 passed through the line during the night of the 17/18th and HX 238 passed the southern end of the *Donau* line at more or less the same time. Neither convoy was pursued.

Anticipating eastbound SC 130 taking the same route, the *Donau* groups moved southwards on the 18th into the convoy's path. It was sighted by U 304 during the night of the 18/19th and the boats were ordered to close.

SC 130 had continuous air cover and aircraft attacks out of low cloud made shadowing almost impossible. The pursuit was abandoned on the 20th, by which time no ships had been sunk but three boats had been lost, U 258, U 381 and U 954.

On the 18th eastbound HX 239 had been located 200 miles SE of Cape Race. The surviving *Donau* boats, including U 760, were ordered southwestwards to meet the approaching convoy. HX 239's escort had been joined by the escort-carrier HMS *Archer* and the strength of the convoy's air cover caused the operation to be called off on the 23rd, before any attacks had been made on the ships.

U 760 put in to her new base at La Pallice **31.5.43**

2. 24.7.43 Left for the Central Atlantic.

Outward-bound, U 760 and U 262 were in company when they were detected on the 28th by two MAD-equipped Catalinas 150 miles NW of Cape Finisterre. The aircraft, based at Pembroke Dock, circled, awaiting reinforcements, but the boats dived and escaped.

U 760 probably was on weather-reporting duties W of the Azores and in early August she was refuelled by U 664. On the 11th U 760 was sighted on the surface by the USCG cutter *Menemsha*. She called for assistance from the escort-carrier USS *Croatan* but searching aircraft found no trace of the boat in the squally conditions.

On the 12th U 760 was attacked and damaged by a Wellington of 179 Squadron. The boat was to meet and refuel U 84 at a position 700 miles SW of the Azores. When U 760 arrived there on the 18th, she was attacked and damaged by two destroyers but managed to escape. The refuelling of U 84 never took place and that boat was sunk on the 24th.

The returning U 760 was attacked during the night of September 6/7th by a Leigh Light Wellington of 179 Squadron (F/O D F McRae) W of La Coruña. The boat was badly damaged and was towed into Vigo on the 8th and interned.

U 760 was later moved to El Ferrol, where she remained until the end of the war. In July 1945 she was taken to the assembly area at Loch Ryan.

U 760 was one of 116 boats disposed of by the Royal Navy in Operation Deadlight. In December 1945 she was towed out through the North Channel by the destroyer HMS Mendip. *The boat was sunk by aircraft on 13.12.45 NW of Bloody Foreland.*

U 761   Type VII C

Built by Kriegsmarine-Werft, Wilhelmshaven
Keel laid 16.12.40   Launched 26.9.42
Commissioned 3.12.42   Feldpost Nr M 51 100

Sunk 24.2.44 in the Straits of Gibraltar (35°55′N 05°45′W)

Served with
8 U-Flottille, Danzig   December 1942 - July 1943 (ab)
9 U-Flottille, Brest   August 1943 - 24.2.44 (fb)

Commanded by
OL Horst Geider   December 1942 - 24.2.44

Patrols: 2   Ships sunk: None

1. 9.9.43 Left Kiel and arrived Trondheim **18.9.43**

2. 17.11.43 Left for Atlantic operations.

U 761 was one of a number of boats which took up submerged, waiting positions W of the British Isles.

In early December they assembled W of the North Channel as *Coronel* group, which searched for westbound ONS 24 but was unsuccessful because aerial reconnaissnce failed to find it. The convoy passed to the north of the group.

In mid-December *Coronel* group was enlarged and split into two sub-groups, *Coronel 1* and *3*, awaiting convoy ON 214. U 761 was in *Coronel 1*. Aerial reconnaisance again failed to find the convoy and it passed to the south.

On or about the 16th U 761 was damaged, probably by heavy seas, and returned.

The boat put in to her new base at Brest **26.12.43**

3. 8.2.44 Left for the Mediterranean.

Attempting to enter the Straits of Gibraltar on the 24th, U 761 was located by two MAD-equipped USN Catalinas of VP-63 (Lts T R Woolley and H J Baker). Contact was lost but a smoke-float dropped was seen by the destroyers HMS *Anthony* (Lt-Cdr J H Wallace) and *Wishart* (Lt J A Holdsworth), patrolling the Straits.

When contact was regained, the two Catalinas each made retro-bomb attacks. *Anthony* had arrived and she dropped depth-charges, which brought U 761 to the surface but she then slid back down, stern first.

Wishart made an attack, followed by another from *Anthony* and U 761 again surfaced, to be attacked by a Catalina of 202 Squadron (F/Lt J Finch) and a USN Ventura of VPB-127. There was an explosion and as U 761 sank, her crew abandoned ship.

The boat's commander and 47 men were picked up by the destroyers and 9 others lost their lives.

U 762   Type VII C

Built by Kriegsmarine-Werft, Wilhelmshaven
Keel laid 2.1.41   Launched 21.11.42
Commissioned 30.1.43   Feldpost Nr M 49 943

Sunk 8.2.44 WSW of Bantry Bay (49°02′N 16°58′W)

Served with
8 U-Flottille, Danzig   January - July 1943 (ab)
9 U-Flottille, Brest   August 1943 - 8.2.44 (fb)

Commanded by
KL Wolfgang Hille   January - December 1943
OL Walter Pietschmann   December 1943 - 8.2.44

Patrols: 2   Ships sunk: None

1. 11.9.43 Left Kiel and arrived Bergen **15.9.43**

2. 28.9.43 Left for the North Atlantic.

U 762 joined the boats of *Rossbach* group SW of Iceland, where they were searching for eastbound convoys. Having been avoided by several convoys, the *Rossbach* boats moved southwards on 5.10.43 to look for HX 259 and SC 143 and to form a new patrol line.

On the 7th SC 143 was assumed to be in the area when some destroyers were seen by U 448. During the night of the 7/8th eight boats sighted destroyers moving northeastwards. The search for the convoy continued and in daylight on the 8th SC 143 was sighted by a reconnaissance aircraft but her homing signals were not received by the searching boats. Allied air patrols increased during the day and U 419, U 610 and U 643 were sunk. U 762 was attacked and damaged by a Liberator of 120 Squadron (WO B W Turnbull) SE of Cape Farewell and about 80 miles from SC 143. The operation against the convoy was called off on the 9th.

U 762 then moved to join *Schlieffen* group, in the process of being formed SE of Greenland to search for westbound convoy ONS 20. On the 14th the group moved northwards but in the evening of the 15th outward-bound U 844 sighted a westbound convoy, presumed to be ONS 20 but in fact ON 206. She was ordered to shadow and home the *Schlieffen* boats in to the convoy.

After U 844 was located and driven off, finding the convoy was difficult because Iceland-based aircraft kept the searching, widely-scattered boats submerged and only by remaining on the surface could contact be re-established, which it never was.

Early on the 16th U 964 sighted and reported convoy ONS 20, which altered course to the northwest later in the day. Meanwhile, Dönitz had ordered boats to stay on the surface and fight their way to the convoy. During daylight on the 16th reports began arriving of boats being attacked and damaged and the first to be sunk was the shadower, U 964.

The *Schlieffen* boats moved further eastwards to form a new line for the 17th, with smaller distances between boats. ONS 20 passed just north of the line early in the morning of the 17th and an attack was ordered. However, contact was lost soon afterwards and although U 309 sighted the convoy again during the morning the boats were constantly harassed by aircraft. The search for ONS 20 was given up in the evening of the 17th and the boats moved further westwards to escape the aircraft. The operation ended at noon on the 18th, with only one straggler sunk but six boats lost.

U 762 joined *Siegfried* group, formed from the 24th 500 miles E of Newfoundland to await HX 262 and SC 145 in submerged positions during daylight. On the 25th it was believed that HX 262 was passing south of the *Siegfried* patrol line and although the group moved southwards, no contact was made.

Short of fuel, U 762 went southwards to meet U-tanker U 488. Bad weather and the presence of Allied aircraft and surface vessels made the operation extremely difficult for U 488 to rendezvous with and refuel all the boats that were awaiting her. Eventually U 762 was refuelled by U 343 for return to base.

The boat put in to her new base at Brest **15.11.43**

3. 28.12.43 Left for Atlantic operations.

U 762 was one of a number of boats operating independently W of the British Isles. From mid-January the boats took up positions W of the North Channel. Few ships were seen.

From 27.1.44 U 762 joined with other boats to form a new patrol line, *Stürmer*, NW of the North Channel, to await expected convoy ON 221, which was sighted by German aircraft on the 27th.

Technical difficulties prevented the aircraft homing in the boats and in spite of searches made on the 28th, the convoy was not found. The search for ON 221 was called off in the morning of the 29th, following a report by an aircraft of a suspected invasion of Western France. It was reported that 200 to 300 landing craft had been sighted 120 miles W of the Gironde estuary.

After apparent confirmation of this report, all boats in the North Atlantic, which included *Stürmer* group, were ordered at high speed to the Biscay coast. Soon after this the 'invasion fleet' was correctly identified as a group of Spanish trawlers and the boats were ordered back to their operational areas.

On the 31st *Stürmer* group was once again stationed NW of the North Channel. In early February *Stürmer* and *Hinein* groups began to withdraw westwards and from the 3rd they reformed as *Igel 1* and 2 groups, NW of Scotland and SW of Ireland respectively. U 762 was in *Igel 2*.

From the 6th *Igel 2* was deployed against northbound, combined convoy MKS 38/SL 147 N of the Azores. The convoy was protected by EG B3, which was joined by the 2nd SG. In the evening of the 8th U 762 was sighted on the surface by a look-out on the sloop HMS *Wild Goose* (Cdr D E G Wemyss), ahead of the convoy.

A change of course was ordered for the convoy and *Wild Goose* turned towards the boat, intending to ram. U 762 dived but kept on coming towards the sloop. The same look-out saw her periscope very close by. This was fired at and hit by *Wild Goose*'s light guns.

The sloop HMS *Woodpecker* (Cdr H L Pryse) came up and the two warships made depth-charge attacks and wreckage rising to the surface confirmed the destruction of U 762.

There were no survivors, 51 dead.

U 763   Type VII C

Built by Kriegsmarine-Werft, Wilhelmshaven
Keel laid 21.1.41   Launched 16.1.43
Commissioned 13.3.43   Feldpost Nr M 51 254

Bombed 24.1.45 at Königsberg

Served with
8 U-Flottille, Danzig   March - October 1943 (ab)
3 U-Flottille, La Pallice   November 1943 - September 1944 (fb)
33 U-Flottille, Flensburg   October 1944 (fb)
24 U-Flottille, Memel   November 1944 - 24.1.45 (ab)

Commanded by
KL Ernst Cordes   March 1943 - October 1944
Lt Kurt Braun (temp)   July - October 1944
Ol Karl-Heinz Schröter   November 1944 -24.1.45

Patrols: 4   Ships sunk: 1 (1499 grt)

1. 14.12.43   Left Kiel for the North Atlantic.

U 763 was employed on weather-reporting duties throughout this patrol. The returning boat was attacked in the Bay of Biscay on 5.2.44 by a Halifax of 502 Squadron (F/O Culling-Mannix). The aircraft was shot down.

U 763 put in to her new base at La Pallice **7.2.44**

2. 19.3.44   Left for Atlantic operations.

U 763 returned to base, recalled to join *Landwirt* group.

She reached La Pallice **27.3.44**

3. 10.6.44   Left for the English Channel, now schnorkel-equipped.

During the night of the 22/23rd U 763 made an unsuccessful attack on a search group with two torpedoes.

In the evening of 5.7.44 U 763 attacked feeder convoy ETC 26 NE of Pointe de Barfleur, sinking the SS *Ringen* (nw 1499t). Later the same evening she made unsuccessful attacks on two ships and a destroyer, after which she was hunted for 30 hours. The crew became distressed with the foul air. During the submerged period, 364 depth-charges were counted, of which 252 were in the near vicinity of the boat.

When the attacks ceased, the commander was unable to fix his position, the boat having drifted. He surfaced in the early hours of the 8th and decided, from observations of anchored warships, that he had drifted into the Royal Navy base at Spithead.

U 763 submerged again and lay on the bottom throughout the 8th and into the early hours of the 9th. She moved away in the late afternoon and reached deep water in the evening. On the 11th U 763 made another attack on a destroyer of an escort group SSW of Plymouth but was unsuccessful.

The boat returned to Brest **15.7.44**

4. 9.8.44   Left Brest and arrived La Pallice **14.8.44**

5. 23.8.44   Left La Pallice, in transit for Norway.

U 763 was one of eighteen boats which left the Biscay bases from mid-August onwards.

U 763 (continued)

Nearing Bergen, she was sighted on the surface on 24.9.44 by a Leigh Light Liberator of 224 Squadron (S/Ldr J C T Downey). The light was switched on but U 763 took no evasive action and did not fire at the aircraft. Depth-charges were dropped, U 763's stern rose out of the water and then the boat disappeared from view.

The damaged boat put in to Bergen **25.9.44**

6. 6.10.44 Left Bergen for Germany.

On the 8th U 763 was damaged after striking a mine in the Skagerrak.

The boat put in to Flensburg **11.10.44**

U 763 was sent to Königsberg for repairs. She was destroyed there on 24.1.45 in a raid by Soviet aircraft.

U 764 Type VII C

Built by Kriegsmarine-Werft, Wilhelmshaven
Keel laid 1.2.41   Launched 13.3.43
Commissioned 6.5.43   Feldpost Nr M 51 834

Sunk 2.1.46 NNW of Tory Island (56°06′N 09°00′W)

Served with
8 U-Flottille, Danzig May - October 1943 (ab)
9 U-Flottille, Brest November 1943 - September 1944 (fb)
11 U-Flottille, Bergen October 1944 -14.5.45 (fb)

Commanded by
OL Hanskurt von Bremen May 1943 - 14.5.45

Patrols: 7   Ships sunk: 1 (638 grt) + 1 damaged
                            1 destroyer (1085 dt)

1. 26.10.43 Left Kiel for the North Atlantic.

U 763 joined *Eisenhart* group, made up of seven sub-groups of three boats each and drawn up in two lines from 11.11.43, running southeastwards from Cape Farewell. The lines crossed an area through which most convoys had passed since August 1943.

Reports indicated that convoys were being routed to the south, so the *Eisenhart* boats were ordered southeastwards on the 12th to search for SC 146 and HX 265. By the 16th no convoys had been found, although U 542 sighted destroyers on that day.

By this time the majority of the *Eisenhart* boats were WSW of Ireland and fuel was becoming a problem for many of the group. It was decided to end the search-operation and send the boats with sufficient fuel, including U 764, to reinforce *Schill* group, then W of Portugal.

U 764 joined the *Schill 3* patrol line, in the expected path of northbound MKS 30/SL 139 and through which it was expected the convoy would pass on the 20th. *Schill 3* surfaced that evening but failed to find the convoy, which was located next morning and attacked by aircraft, resulting in one ship being sunk and another damaged, both by glider-bombs.

On the 22nd the remaining fourteen boats of the three *Schill* groups were formed into a patrol line, *Weddigen,* between 18° and 22°W, to operate against southbound KMS 30/OG 95 W of Cape Finisterre On the 23rd the line moved southwestwards but finding nothing, turned southeastwards on the 25th to intercept northbound MKS 31/SL 140. During the night of the 26/27th U 764 made an unsuccessful attack on a destroyer of the 4th SG and came under depth-charge attack.

Constantly harassed by surface vessels and aircraft and lacking information from reconnaissance aircraft, *Weddigen* could not carry out a concentrated attack before the operation was called off on the 28th, after the convoy had passed to the east of the patrol line.

During the night of the 27/28th U 746 attacked a frigate but heard only an end-of-run detonation. She may also have shot down a Fortress of 220 Squadron but this is not certain.

In the morning of the 29th U 764 was attacked by aircraft from the escort-carrier USS *Bogue* but she managed to escape.

The boat put in to her new base at Brest **11.12.43**

2. 17.1.44 Left for Atlantic operations.

U 764 joined *Sturmer* group, formed on the 26th NW of the North Channel to await expected convoy ON 221, which was sighted by German aircraft on the 27th.

Technical difficulties prevented the aircraft homing in the boats and in spite of searches made on the 28th, the convoy was not found. The search for ON 221 was called off in the morning of the 29th, following a report by an aircraft of a suspected invasion of Western France. It was reported that 200 to 300 landing craft had been sighted 120 miles W of the Gironde estuary.

After apparent confirmation of this report, all boats in the North Atlantic, which included *Stürmer* group, were ordered at high speed to the Bay of Biscay coast. Shortly after this the 'invasion fleet' was correctly identified as a group of Spanish trawlers and the boats were ordered back to their operational areas.

On the 31st *Stürmer* group was once again stationed NW of the North Channel. In early February *Stürmer* and *Hinein* groups began to withdraw westwards and from the 3rd they reformed into *Igel 1* and 2 groups. U 764 was in *Igel 1*, which was in an area NW of Scotland. *Igel 2* was SW of Ireland.

From the 10th both groups moved further west, to wait W of the British Isles for an ONS convoy, expected between the 14th and 18th. ONS 29, ON 224 and OS 68 were sighted by aircraft on the 14th W of the North Channel and *Igel 1* and 2 groups were hurried to an assembly area SW of Ireland. On the 18th two parallel patrol lines, *Hai 1* and *2,* were formed ahead of the convoys.

It was found that the convoys had turned south on the 17th and passed the southern end of the *Hai* lines. The boats were immediately ordered south, submerged in daylight and at high speed on the surface in the hours of darkness. Instead of sighting any convoys at dawn on the 19th, the boats saw only destroyers. The operation was called off and the boats submerged to avoid aircraft from the escort-carrier HMS *Striker.*

The *Hai* groups were dissolved and sixteen boats, including U 764, formed *Preussen* group W of Ireland from the 22nd. The group was concentrated from the 26th between 22° and 30°W in the expected path of ON 225 but the convoy was re-routed.

The boats moved northwards on 6.3.44 to search for convoys and they operated singly W of the British Isles.

U 764 returned to Brest **15.3.44**

3. 26.4.44 Left Brest and returned **28.4.44**

4. 18.5.44 Left for the English Channel.

Now schnorkel-equipped, U 764 joined U 269, U 441, U 953 and U 984 to form *Dragoner* group.

The group was to operate in the western part of the English Channel, N of Ushant, in co-operation with shore radar against Allied cruiser and destroyer formations. The objective was to test the effectiveness of the schnorkel and to assess tactics required in areas patrolled by many enemy aircraft. Some experience was gained but in general results were discouraging. When U 764 surfaced on the 23rd, she was attacked three times by aircraft but undamaged.

The boats were recalled and U 764 returned to Brest **28.5.44**

5. 6.6.44 Left Brest, as part of *Landwirt* group.

U 764 was one of eight schnorkel boats ordered to go to the area N of Cherbourg, enter the English Channel and inflict what losses they could on the invasion forces. This was a very difficult and dangerous task, considering the concentration of air and surface forces they would be facing.

On the 9th U 764 was unsuccessful against a destroyer when her four torpedoes all missed. However, on the 15th the boat torpedoed the destroyer-escort HMS *Blackwood* NW of Cap de la Hague, blowing off her bows. *Blackwood* was taken in tow but sank next day. During the action U 764 was attacked and her stern damaged in a Hedgehog attack by the destroyer-escort HMS *Duckworth*.

The boat returned to Brest **23.6.44**

6. 6.8.44 Left for the English Channel.

On the 20th U 764 made three attacks on convoy ETC 72 SE of the Isle of Wight and torpedoed and sank the SS *Coral* (br 638t). The boat was afterwards subjected to eight depth-charge attacks.

ENE of Barfleur on the 25th, U 764 attacked a group of landing craft and damaged LCT 1074. With the worsening situation in Western France and the capture of the Biscay bases by the Allies becoming more than likely, the boats still in the English Channel were ordered to make for Norway.

U 764 reached Bergen **19.9.44**

7. 26.12.44 Left for Atlantic operations.

U 764 went to an area W of the British Isles. On 9.1.45 she set out to return to base after the exhaust conduit on her schnorkel was damaged when the boat went down to 135 metres.

On the 14th U 764 was overrun by the French liner *Ile de France* but the opportunity to attack was missed by the boat's commander.

U 764 returned to Bergen **4.2.45**

8. 15.3.45 Left Bergen and returned **18.3.45**

9. 19.3.45 Left Bergen and returned **23.3.45**

10. 26.4.45 Left for Antlantic operations.

U 764 went to an area W of the British Isles. She was still at sea when the war ended. The boat, acting on instructions given, went into Loch Eriboll on May 14th and surrendered.

She put in to Loch Alsh on the 16th and reached Lisahally **17.5.45**

U 764 was one of 116 boats disposed of by the Royal Navy in Operation Deadlight. *At the end of December 1945 she was towed from Lisahally by the Polish destroyer* Krakowiak.

The boat was sunk by gunfire by the Polish destroyer Piorun *on 2.1.46 NNW of Tory Island.*

U 765   Type VII C

Built by Kriegsmarine-Werft, Wilhelmshaven
Keel laid 15.2.41   Launched 22.4.43
Commissioned 19.6.43   Feldpost Nr M 52 665

Sunk 6.5.44 in the central North Atlantic (52°30′N 28°28′W)

Served with
8 U-Flottille, Danzig   June 1943 - March 1944 (ab)
7 U-Flottille, St Nazaire   April 1944 - 6.5.44 (fb)

Commanded by
OL Werner Wendt   June 1943 - 6.5.44

Patrols: 1   Ships sunk: None

1. 18.3.44 Left Kiel and arrived Bergen **22.3.44**

2. 3.4.44 Left for Atlantic operations.

In early May U 765 was one of only five boats that were still W of the British Isles. She was on weather-reporting duty, necessitating immediate evasive action after transmitting reports.

U 765 followed this procedure but at the beginning of May one

of her reports was picked up. The escort-carrier HMS *Vindex* and the 5th SG were ordered to make a search. In the evening of the 5th the boat made an unsuccessful attack on the frigates HMS *Bickerton* and *Bligh* of the 5th SG. Early on the 6th U 765 was sighted by a Swordfish of 825 (FAA) Squadron. The destroyer-escort HMS *Keats* made a radar contact at the scene but her search was unsuccessful.

The frigates HMS *Aylmer* (Lt A D P Campbell), *Bickerton* (Lt-Cdr E M Thorpe) and *Bligh* (Lt-Cdr R E Blyth) arrived and a Hedgehog attack was carried out after *Bickerton* made a contact some miles from where *Keats* was searching. A creeping attack with depth-charges followed and U 765 surfaced.

The frigates opened fire and another Swordfish (Lt-Cdr F G B Sheffield) dropped two depth-charges, which destroyed U 765.

37 men lost their lives and 8 survivors, including the commander, were picked up by *Bickerton*.

U 766   Type VII C

Built by Kriegsmarine-Werft, Wilhelmshaven
Keel laid 1.3.41   Launched 29.5.43
Commissioned 30.7.43   Feldpost Nr M 53 610

Decommissioned 21.8.44 at La Pallice

Served with
8 U-Flottille, Danzig   July 1943 - February 1944 (ab)
6 U-Flottille, St Nazaire   March 1944 - 21.8.44 (fb)

Commanded by
OL Hans-Dietrich Wilke   July 1943 - 21.8.44

Patrols: 3   Ships sunk: None

1. 9.3.44 Left Kiel and arrived Marviken **11.3.44**

2. 21.3.44 Left Marviken and arrived Bergen **22.3.44**

3. 23.3.44 Left for the North Atlantic.

Outward-bound through the Shetlands-Faroes Passage, U 766 was ordered to go to Western France to join *Landwirt* group.

She put into St Nazaire **16.4.44**

4. 6.6.44 Left St Nazaire, as part of *Landwirt* group.

U 766 was one of nineteen non-schnorkel boats which were ordered to form a line at the 200 metre depth line between Brest and Bordeaux, keeping out of port in case an Allied invasion force arrived and trapped them. The boats later went to the 100 metre depth line, where they could lay on the bottom for long periods.

The waiting boats were under constant attack from the air when they surfaced at night. When no invasion had come by the 12th, the boats were recalled to port and placed on six hours notice.

U 766 returned to St Nazaire **15.6.44**

5. 26.7.44 Left St Nazaire and arrived Brest **30.7.44**

6. 2.8.44 Left Brest for operations.

U 766 and U 618, as *Wiesel* group, operated against Allied escort groups. U 766 returned to Brest **6.8.44**

7. 8.8.44 Left Brest for La Pallice.

U 766 carried 14 additional personnel from Brest. She reached La Pallice **18.8.44**

U 766 was decommissioned on 21.8.44, unable to put to sea.

Handed over in May 1945, she entered the French Navy in 1947 as the Laubie.

She was paid off on 11.3.63 as Q 335 and broken up.

U 767   Type VII C

Built by Kriegsmarine-Werft, Wilhelmshaven
Keel laid 5.4.41   Launched 10.7.43
Commissioned 11.9.43   Feldpost Nr M 52 399

Sunk 18.6.44 NW of Les Sept Îles (49°03′N 03°13′W)

Served with
8 U-Flottille, Danzig   September 1943 - April 1944 (ab)
1 U-Flottille, Brest   May 1944 - 18.6.44 (fb)

Commanded by
OL Walter Dankleff   September 1943 - 18.6.44

Patrols: 1   Ships sunk: None
                               1 frigate (1370 dt)

1. 9.5.44   Left Kiel and arrived Marviken **11.5.44**

2. 22.5.44   Left for the North Atlantic.
   U 767 was one of only eight boats which managed to pass from Norwegian waters into the Atlantic during the latter half of May, escaping the attentions of patrolling aircraft of 18 Group RAF Coastal Command, then conducting an offensive.
   On 9.6.44 she was ordered to go to the English Channel and on the 15th she sank the frigate HMS *Mourne* of the 5th SG, SSE of Wolf Rock.
   In the morning of the 18th U 767 was detected by the 14th EG in the Golfe de St Malo. In the afternoon the destroyer HMS *Fame* (Cdr R A Currie) made a Hedgehog attack NW of Les Sept Iles, followed by depth-charges. HMS *Havelock* (Lt-Cdr R Hart) arrived and dropped more depth-charges.
   At this point a survivor with escape gear burst on to the surface and was picked up by *Fame*. HMS *Inconstant* (Lt-Cdr J H Eaden) made a Hedgehog attack. U 767 was almost certainly destroyed by then but the three ships made sure with more depth-charges.
   German shore batteries opened up but under cover of a smokescreen from HMS *Hotspur* the three destroyers moved off.
   U 767's commander and 47 men were killed. The sole survivor had been ejected from the aft section of the boat in an air bubble.

U 768   Type VII C

Built by Kriegsmarine-Werft, Wilhemshaven
Keel laid 5.4.41   Launched 22.8.43
Commissioned 14.10.43   Feldpost Nr M 53 733

Sunk 20.11.43 in the Baltic

Served with
31 U-Flottille, Hamburg   October 1943 - 20.11.43 (ab)

Commanded by
OL Johann Buttjer   October 1943 - 20.11.43

Patrols: None   Ships sunk: None

On the night of 20.11.43 U 768 was en route to Gotenhafen from Pillau when she was accidentally rammed by U 745.
   U 768 sank but there were no casualties.

U 769 and U 770 were never built, orders cancelled.

U 771   Type VII C

Built by Kriegsmarine-Werft, Wilhelmshaven
Keel laid 21.8.41   Launched 26.9.43
Commissioned 18.11.43   Feldpost Nr M 54 806

Sunk 11.11.44 E of Andenes, Norway (69°17′N 16°28′E)

Served with
31 U-Flottille, Hamburg   November 1943 - May 1944 (ab)
9 U-Flottille, Brest   June - July 1944 (fb)
11 U-Flottille, Bergen   August - September 1944 (fb-oE)
13 U-Flottille, Trondheim   October 1944 - 11.11.44 (fb)

Commanded by
OL Helmut Block   November 1943 - 11.11.44

Patrols: 3   Ships sunk: None

1. 27.5.44   Left Kiel and arrived Hatvik **30.5.44**

2. 2.6.44   Left Hatvik and arrived Bergen **2.6.44**

Although nominally on the strength of 9 U-Flottille at Brest in June/July 1944, U 771 was with Mitte *group, based in Norway.*

3. 19.6.44   Left Bergen and arrived Stavanger **20.6.44**

4. 21.6.44   Left for operations.
   U 771 joined four other boats that were in waiting positions off the Norwegian coast, as part of *Mitte* group.
   The boat returned to Bergen **15.7.44**

5. 26.7.44   Left Bergen and arrived Trondheim **28.7.44**

6. 29.7.44   Left Trondheim and arrived Stavanger **1.8.44**

7. 2.8.44   Left Stavanger
   On the 2nd U 771 was being escorted when it was sighted by two Mosquitos of 333 (Norwegian) Squadron. One of the aircraft made a strafing attack with its 20mm cannons and then dropped two depth-charges, damaging the boat.
   The second aircraft came in too low and struck the escort vessel's mast. It went into the sea and straight under, taking its crew with it.
   U 771 put in to Kristiansand **3.8.44**

8. 5.8.44   Left Kristiansand and went to Bergen for repairs to be carried out. U 771 reached there **6.8.44**

9. 27.9.44   With repairs completed, U 771 went north to carry out operations in Northern Waters.
   The boat put in to Bogenbucht **30.9.44**

10. 2.10.44   Left Bogenbucht and arrived Hammerfest **4.10.44**

11. 14.10.44   Left Hammerfest for operations.
   On the 20th eastbound JW 61 set out from Loch Ewe. U 771 was one of the boats of *Panther* group, through which the convoy passed without loss, arriving off Kola Inlet on the 28th.
   From 5.11.44 U 771, U 956 and U 997 were operating against Soviet escort vessels in the Barents Sea. In the evening of the 8th U 771 made an unsuccessful attack on a destroyer, hearing only an end-of-run detonation.
   The returning boat was sighted by the submarine HMS *Venturer* (Lt J S Launders) on the 11th E of Andenes. Four torpedoes were fired and U 771 was destroyed.
   There were no survivors, 51 dead.

U 772   Type VII C

Built by Kriegsmarine-Werft, Wilhelmshaven
Keel laid 21.9.41   Launched 31.10.43
Commissioned 23.12.43   Feldpost Nr M 14 151

Sunk 30.12.44 S of Portland Bill (50º05′N 02°31′W)

Served with
31 U-Flottille, Hamburg   December 1943 - July 1944 (ab)
9 U-Flottille, Brest   August - October 1944 (fb)
11 U-Flottille, Bergen   October 1944 - 30.12.44 (fb)

Commanded by
KL Ewald Rademacher   December 1943 - 30.12.44

Patrols: 2   Ships sunk: 4 (21,053 grt) + 1 damaged

1. **3.8.44**   Left Kiel and arrived Horten **5.8.44**

2. **7.8.44**   Left Horten and arrived Trondheim **11.8.44**

3. **13.8.44**   Left for the North Atlantic.
    U 772 went initially to an area W of the British Isles and then from the beginning of September she was on weather-reporting duties in the North Atlantic.
    The boat returned to Trondheim **6.10.44**

4. **19.11.44**   Left Trondheim for the English Channel.
    In the morning of 23.12.44 U 772 attacked two convoys, sinking one ship from each, the SS *Slemish* (br 1536t) of WEG 14 N of Cherbourg and the SS *Dumfries* (br 5149t) SW of the Isle of Wight.
    On the 28th U 772 torpedoed and sank the infantry landing ship SS *Empire Javelin* (br 7177t) NE of Cherbourg. A well-disciplined crew and good seamanship shown by the escorts kept the loss of life down to only 7 men.
    U 772 attacked convoy TBC 21 late on the 29th off Portland Bill. She torpedoed and damaged two ships, the SS *Black Hawk* (am 7191t) and the SS *Arthur Sewall* (am 7176t). The *Black Hawk* was beached and later declared a total loss.
    As she was leaving the scene, U 772's periscope and schnorkel were spotted by a Leigh Light Wellington of 407 (RCAF) Squadron (S/Ldr C W Taylor). The area was illuminated and six depth-charges were dropped, which destroyed U 772.
    There were no survivors, 48 dead.

U 773   Type VII C

Built by Kriegsmarine-Werft, Wilhelmshaven
Keel laid 13.10.41   Launched 8.12.43
Commissioned 20.1.44   Feldpost Nr M 49 058

Sunk 8.12.45 NW of Bloody Foreland (56°10′N 10°05′W)

Served with
31 U-Flottille, Hamburg   January - July 1944 (ab)
1 U-Flottille, Brest   August - September 1944 (fb)
11 U-Flottille, Bergen   October 1944 - 9.5.45 (fb-t/fb)

Commanded by
OL Richard Lange   January - April 1944
OL Hugo Baldus   April 1944 - 9.5.45

Patrols: Ships sunk: None

1. **7.10.44**   Left Kiel and arrived Horten **9.10.44**

2. **13.10.44**   Left Horten and arrived Marviken **14.10.44**

3. **15.10.44**   Left for operations.
    U 773 was on transport duty, with a cargo of anti-tank weapons, ammunition and medical supplies for St Nazaire.
    She reached there **18.11.44**

4. **7.12.44**   Left for operations.
    U 773 left St Nazaire on transport duty, carrying four dockyard specialists and a cargo of non-ferrous metals.
    She put into Bergen **10.1.45**

5. **14.1.45**   Left Bergen and arrived Bogenbucht **23.1.45**

6. **19.2.45**   Left for operations.
    U773 operated off Reykjavik and the coast of Iceland but she had no success.
    The boat put in to Trondheim **14.4.45**

U 773 was surrendered at Trondheim on 9.5.45. She left Lo-fjord on the 29th for the assembly point at Loch Ryan.
    She was one of 116 boats disposed of by the Royal Navy in Operation Deadlight. *In early December 1945 U 773 was towed out through the North Channel by the tug HMS* Freedom.
    U 773 was sunk by the submarine HMS Tantivy *on 8.12.45 NW of Bloody Foreland.*

U 774   Type VII C

Built by Kriegsmarine-Werft, Wilhelmshaven
Keel laid 17.12.41   Launched 23.12.43
Commissioned 17.2.44   Feldpost Nr M 50 064

Sunk 8.4.45 SW of Cape Clear (49°58′N 11°51′W)

Served with
31 U-Flottille, Hamburg   February 1944 - January 1945 (ab)
11 U-Flottille, Bergen   February 1945 - 8.4.45 (fb)

Commanded by
OL Johann Buttjer   February - October 1944
KL Werner Sausmikat   October 1944 - 8.4.45

Patrols: 1   Ships sunk: None

1. **1.3.45**   Left Kiel and arrived Bergen **13.3.45**

2. **14.3.45**   Left for operations.
    U 774 was one of seven boats which sailed from Norwegian ports to operate in the English Channel. They were diverted to areas 200 to 300 miles west of the western entrance to the Channel because of the significant increase in losses of boats in the English and North Channels.
    On 8.4.45 U 774 was sunk SW of Cape Clear in depth-charge attacks by the frigates HMS *Bentinck* (Lt-Cdr P R G Worth) and *Calder* (Lt-Cdr E Playne) of the 4th EG.
    There were no survivors, 44 dead.

U 775　Type VII C

Built by Kriegsmarine-Werft, Wilhelmshaven
Keel laid 22.1.42　Launched 11.2.44
Commissioned 23.3.44　Feldpost Nr M 00 412

Sunk 8.12.45 N of Tory Island (55°40´N 08°25´W)

Served with
31 U-Flottille, Hamburg　March - October 1944 (ab)
11 U-Flottille, Bergen　November 1944 - 9.5.45 (fb)

Commanded by
OL Erich Taschenmacher　March 1944 - 9.5.45

Patrols: 2　　Ships sunk:　1 (1926 grt) + 1 damaged
　　　　　　　　　　　　　　　1 frigate (1300 dt)

1. 31.10.44　Left Kiel and arrived Horten **3.11.44**

2. 7.11.44　Left Horten and arrived Bergen **11.11.44**

3. 18.11.44　Left for British coastal waters.
　U 775 operated N of Scotland, from Cape Wrath to the Pentland Firth. On 6.12.44 she torpedoed and sank the frigate HMS *Bullen* off Strathy Point. The boat was hunted for 14 hours afterwards by the frigates HMS *Loch Insh* and *Goodall* but she escaped.
　U 775 returned to Bergen **21.12.44**

On 12.1.45 U 775 was damaged in a raid on the U-boat pens at Bergen by Lancasters of RAF Bomber Command.

4. 7.2.45　Left for operations.
　In late February U 775 was operating in St George's Channel. On the 28th she sank the SS *Soreldoc* (pa 1926t) NW of St David's Head and on 2.3.45 she claimed two ships torpedoed W of Ireland. This seems unlikely because on the 6th U 775 probably attacked and damaged the SS *Empire Geraint* (br 6991t) W of Hartland Point.
　The boat put in to Trondheim **30.3.45**

U 775 was surrendered at Trondheim on 9.5.45. She left for Scapa Flow on the 29th, later going on to the assembly area at Loch Ryan.
　She was one of 116 boats disposed of by the Royal Navy in Operation Deadlight. In early December 1945 she was towed out through the North Channel by the destroyer HMS Obedient.
　U 775 was sunk by gunfire on 8.12.45 N of Tory Island.

U 776　Type VII C

Built by Kriegsmarine-Werft, Wilhelmshaven
Keel laid 4.3.42　Launched 4.3.44
Commissioned 13.4.44　Feldpost Nr M 15 421

Sunk 3.12.45 WNW of Loch Ryan (55°08´N 05°30´W)

Served with
31 U-Flottille, Hamburg　April 1944 - 16.5.45 (ab/fb)

Commanded by
KL Lothar Martin　April 1944 - 16.5.45

Patrols: 1　　Ships sunk: None

1. 12.3.45　Left Kiel and arrived Horten **18.3.45**

2. 22.3.45　Left for operations.

U 776 went to British coastal waters and operated in the western English Channel and off Ushant. She had no success.
　When the war ended, U 776 was still at sea in her operational area. In accordance with instructions given, she put in to Weymouth on 16.5.45 and surrendered.

U 776 went from Weymouth to Lough Foyle and became No N 65 for tests carried out by the Royal Navy.
　She was one of the 116 boats disposed of by the Royal Navy in Operation Deadlight. In early December 1945 she was towed from the assembly area at Loch Ryan into the North Channel by the tug HMS Enforcer.
　U 776 foundered on 3.12.45 in 48 fathoms WNW of Loch Ryan.

U 777　Type VII C

Built by Kriegsmarine-Werft, Wilhelmshaven
Keel laid 5.6.42　Launched 25.3.44
Commissioned 9.5.44　Feldpost Nr M 17 108

Bombed 15/16.10.44 at Wilhelmshaven

Served with
31 U-Flottille, Hamburg　May 1944 - 15.10.44 (ab)

Commanded by
OL Günter Ruperti　May 1944 - 15.10.44

Patrols: None　　Ships sunk: None

During the night of October 15/16th 1944 U 777 was destroyed in a raid by aircraft of RAF Bomber Command on Wilhelmshaven. One crewman was killed.

U 778　Type VII C

Built by Kriegsmarine-Werft, Wilhelmshaven
Keel laid 3.7.42　Launched 6.5.44
Commissioned 7.7.44　Feldpost Nr M 33 584

Sunk 4.12.45 N of Malin Head (55°34´N 07°26´W)

Served with
31 U-Flottille, Hamburg　July 1944 - February 1945 (ab)
11 U-Flottille, Bergen　March 1945 - 9.5.45 (fb)

Commanded by
KL Ralf Jürs　July 1944 - 9.5.45

Patrols: 1　　Ships sunk: None

1. 24.2.45　Left Kiel and arrived Horten **28.2.45**

2. 4.3.45　Left for operations.
　U 778 operated off the Moray Firth and eastwards along the Scottish coast as far as Peterhead. She had no success.
　The boat put in to Bergen **26.3.45**

U 778 was surrendered at Bergen on 9.5.45. On the 31st she left for the assembly point at Loch Ryan.
　She was one off 116 boats disposed of by the Royal Navy in Operation Deadlight. In early December 1945 U 778 was towed from Loch Ryan out through the North Channel by the frigate HMS Cubitt.
　U 778 foundered in 34 fathoms on 4.12.45 N of Malin Head.

U 779   Type VII C

Built by Kriegsmarine-Werft, Wilhelmshaven
Keel laid 21.7.42   Launched 17.6.44
Commissioned 24.8.44   Feldpost Nr M 25 447

Sunk 17.12.45 NW of Bloody Foreland (55°50´N 10°05´W)

Served with
31 U-Flottille, Hamburg/Wilhelmshaven August 1944 - 9.5.45 (ab)

Commanded by
OL Johann Stegmann August 1944 - 9.5.45

Patrols: None   Ships sunk: None

U 779 saw no operational service. She was surrendered at Wilhelmshaven in May 1945. On 24.6.45 the boat left there for the assembly area at Loch Ryan.

She was one of 116 boats disposed of by the Royal Navy in Operation Deadlight. In December 1945 U 779 was towed out through the North Channel by the destroyer HMS Southdown.

The boat was sunk by gunfire on 17.12.45 NW of Bloody Foreland.

U 780 - U791 were never in service. U 780 - 782 had their keels laid but construction was never completed. Orders for U783-U790 were cancelled before construction began.

U 790 was an experimental boat, Type V300. A contract to produce it was given to Germaniawerft, Kiel on 18.2.42 but with very little done, the project was scrapped on 15.7.42.

U 792   Type Wa 201

Built by Blohm & Voss, Hamburg
Keel laid 1.12.42   Launched 28.9.43
Commissioned 16.11.43   Feldpost Nr M 52 546

Scuttled 4.5.45 in Audorfer See, near Rendsburg

Served with
8 U-Flottille, Danzig November 1943 - January 1945 (vb)
5 U-Flottille, Kiel February 1945 - 4.5.45 (vb)

Commanded by
OL Horst Heitz November 1943 - October 1944
OL Hans Diederich Duis October 1944 - 4.5.45

Patrols: None   Ships sunk: None

On 2.8.43 U 792 was damaged in an RAF raid on Hamburg whilst still under construction.

U 792 was an experimental coastal boat, powered by Walter turbine diesels. In June 1944 she achieved a submerged speed of 25 knots in trials. Soon afterwards she was damaged in a collision and was still under repair in early May 1945.

On 4.5.45 the boat was scuttled in Audorfer See, near Rendsburg. It is possible that U 792 was later salved and used by the Royal Navy in 1947.

U 793   Type Wa 201

Built by Blohm & Voss, Hamburg
Keel laid 1.12.42   Launched 4.3.44
Commissioned 24.4.44   Feldpost Nr M 53 805

Scuttled 4.5.45 in Audorfer See, near Rendsburg

Served with
8 U-Flottille, Danzig April 1944 - February 1945 (vb)
5 U-Flottille, Kiel February 1945 - 4.5.45 (vb)

Commanded by
OL Günther Schauenburg April 1944 - January 1945
OL Friedrich Schmidt January 1945 - 4.5.45

Patrols: None   Ships sunk: None

On 2.8.43 U 793 was damaged in an RAF raid on Hamburg whilst still under construction.

U 793 was an experimental coastal boat, powered by Walter turbine diesels. In March 1944 she achieved a submerged speed of 22 knots in trials. The boat was used for sea training of crews destined for service in future Walter boats.

On 4.5.45 U 793 was scuttled in Audorfer See, near Rendsburg. It is possible that the boat was later salved and used by the Royal Navy in 1947.

U 794   Type Wk 202

Built by Germania Werft, Kiel
Keel laid 1.2.43   Launched 7.10.43
Commissioned 14.11.43   Feldpost Nr M 52 496

Scuttled 5.5.45 in Geltinger Bucht

Served with
8 U-Flottille, Danzig November 1943 - January 1945 (vb)
5 U-Flottille, Kiel February 1945 - 5.5.45 (vb)

Commanded by
OL Werner Klug November 1943 - September 1944
OL Philipp Becker September 1944 - 5.5.45

Patrols: None   Ships sunk: None

U 794 was only used experimentally. In late March 1944 Dönitz went to the test establishment at Hela and he and four other admirals took part in a trial in U 794. They were all most enthusiastic.

The boat was scuttled on 5.5.45 in Geltinger Bucht. She was later raised and broken up.

U 795   Type Wk 202

Built by Germania Werft, Kiel
Keel laid 8.2.43   Launched 21.3.44
Commissioned 22.4.44   Feldpost Nr M 53 834

Scuttled 3.5.45 at Kiel

Served with
8 U-Flottille, Danzig   April 1944 - February 1945 (vb)
5 U-Flottille, Kiel   February 1945 - 3.5.45 (vb)

Commanded by
OL Horst Selle   April 1944 - 3.5.45

Patrols: None   Ships sunk: None

U 795 was only used experimentally. She was scuttled on 3.5.45 at Kiel. The boat was possibly salved later and used by the Royal Navy in 1947.

U 796 and U 797 were ordered on 4.1.43 from Deutsche Werke, Kiel. Although U 796's keel was laid on 13.12.43, neither she nor U 797 were completed.
U 798 was ordered on 15.2.44 from Germania Werft, Kiel. Although her keel was laid on 23.4.44, she was never completed.
U 799 and U 800 were never built.

U 801   Type IX C-40

Built by Seebeckwerft, Wesermünde
Keel laid 1.10.41   Launched 31.10.42
Commissioned 24.3.43   Feldpost Nr M 51 307

Sunk 17.3.44 W of the Cape Verde Islands (16°42´N 30°28´W)

Served with
4 U-Flottille, Stettin   March - November 1943 (ab)
2 U-Flottille, Lorient   November 1943 - 17.3.44 (fb)

Commanded by
KL Hans-Joachim Brans   March 1943 - 17.3.44

Patrols: 2   Ships sunk: None

1. 6.11.43 Left Kiel and arrived Bergen **9.11.43**

2. 13.11.43 Left for Atlantic operations.
U 801 was one of a number of boats which took up submerged, waiting positions W of the British Isles. In early December they assembled W of the North Channel as *Coronel* group, which searched for westbound ONS 24 but was unsuccessful because aircraft failed to find it. The convoy passed to the north of the group.
In mid-December *Coronel* group was enlarged and split into two sub-groups, *Coronel 1* and *3*, to search for westbound ON 214. U 801 was in *Coronel 3*. Again, aircraft failed to find the convoy and it passed to the south. Boats of the group, including U 801, searched far to the south for ONS 25 but it was not found.
From the 20th the *Coronel 3* boats joined with new-arrivals to form a new patrol line, *Borkum*, 400 miles NW of Cape Ortegal, to intercept combined convoy MKS 33/SL 142. When the convoy was not found, the *Borkum* boats were ordered to operate against the carrier-groups of USS *Card* and *Core*, in an effort to cover the returning blockade runner *Osorno*, which was spotted on the 23rd by an aircraft from *Card*.

On the 22nd and 23rd an escorted carrier was sighted by German aircraft. Attacks were made on the escort by some *Borkum* boats after the carrier was sighted by U 305 during the night of the 23/24th. The destroyer USS *Leary* was sunk.
In the evening of the 24th the *Borkum* boats encountered southbound OS 62/KMS 36 and U 415 sank HMS *Hurricane* of the escort, the only success against the convoy. The group continued to operate in the area NE of the Azores between 20° and 25°W, moving from one position to another in the operational area. U 801 left the group in early January.
The boat put in to her new base at Lorient **8.1.44**

3. 26.2.44 Left for operations in the Indian Ocean.
Outward-bound, U 801 was located in the morning of the 15th 300 miles W of the Cape Verde Islands by the escort-carrier USS *Block Island*. A search by aircraft failed to find the boat. In the evening of the 16th U 801 was sighted on the surface by an Avenger (Lt C A Woodell) and a Wildcat of VC-6 from *Block Island*.
A strafing attack was carried out and the Avenger dropped an accoutstic torpedo. U 801 dived and escaped but she had sustained casualties in the attack. Early on the 17th the boat radioed, requesting a rendezvous with a U-tanker and reporting her casualties. It was arranged that U 801 would meet U 488 on the 20th. The transmission was heard and a search for U 801 began.
Just before dawn on the 17th the boat was sighted on the surface by another Avenger (Lt N Dowty). A depth-bomb was dropped, causing damage in U 801's engine room. She dived but an oil leak marked her position. The aircraft called for assistance and the destroyers USS *Bronstein* (Lt H S Kinney) and *Corry* arrived.
Eight depth-charge attacks were carried out in two hours, damaging U 801 to such an extent that her commander decided to surface and scuttle her. The boat surfaced and immediately came under fire from the destroyers and the commander and one of the crew were killed as they came out of the conning tower hatch. The crew abandoned ship as best they could and after opening the sea cocks, the Chief Engineer went down with the boat.
10 of U 801's crew were lost. The survivors were picked up by the destroyers.

U 802   Type IX C-40

Built by Seebeckwerft, Wesermünde
Keel laid 1.12.41   Launched 31.10.42
Commissioned 12.6.43   Feldpost Nr M 52 697

Sunk 31.12.45 NNW of Tory Island (55°30´N 08°25´W)

Served with
4 U-Flottille, Stettin   June 1943 - January 1944 (ab)
2 U-Flottille, Lorient   February - November 1944 (fb)
33 U-Flottille, Flensburg   December 1944 - 11.5.45 (fb)

Commanded by
KL Rolf Steinhaus   June - December 1943
KL Helmut Schmoeckel   December 1943 - 11.5.45

Patrols: 4   Ships sunk: 1 (1621 grt)

1. 29.1.44 Left Kiel for the North Atlantic.
U 802 was initially on weather-reporting duty. In late February she was ordered to the Newfoundland area.
On 23.3.44 U 802 torpedoed and sank the SS *Watuka* (br 1621t) of convoy SH 125 E of Halifax and reported three small steamers sunk in the same attack but there is no confirmation of this claim.
On 9.4.44 U 802 attacked convoy HX 286 SW of Sable Island. She heard detonations and claimed one steamer sunk and another damaged but there is no confirmation of this. She patrolled off Nova

Scotia until mid-April.

U 802 put in to her new base at Lorient **2.5.44**

2. 22.6.44 Left for operations.

U 802 returned to base because of technical problems with her schnorkel equipment.

She reached Lorient **9.7.44**

3. 16.7.44 Left for the North Atlantic.

U 802 was one of the last few schnorkel boats to leave from a base in Western France. The boat went initially to an area S of Newfoundland. In the early hours of 15.8.44 an Avenger(Lt W A Dixon) from the escort-carrier USS *Bogue* reported a radar contact, U 802, off Grand Bank, 38 miles north of the carrier. The aircraft was never heard from again.

Late on the 18th another Avenger (Lt C E Lair) made a contact 70 miles S of Grand Bank and 65 miles north of *Bogue*. U 802 was spotted on the surface and three depth-bombs were dropped but the boat was undamaged.

On 2.9.44 U 802 passed through Cabot Strait into the Gulf of St Lawrence. By the 6th she was at the mouth of the St Lawrence River. The boat left the river on the 13th and on the 14th sighted the *Bogue* and her escort in the Détroit d'Honguedo. U 802 fired a torpedo at a destroyer but heard a premature detonation.

The boat patrolled S of Nova Scotia until early October but had no success. She then made her way towards Norway.

U 802 put in to Bergen **12.11.44**

4. 13.11.44 Left Bergen and arrived Horten **20.11.44**

5. 21.11.44 Left Horten and arrived Flensburg **23.11.44**

6. 8.4.45 Left Kiel and arrived Horten **12.4.45**

7. 22.4.45 Left Horten and arrived Kristiansand **12.4.45**

8. 28.4.45 Left for US waters.

Outward-bound, U 802 was still at sea when the war ended. In accordance with instructions given, she put in to Loch Eriboll on 11.5.45 and surrendered.

U 802 was one of 116 boats disposed of by the Royal Navy in Operation Deadlight. *In late December 1945 she was towed from the assembly area at Lisahally by the destroyer HMS* Pytchley.

On 31.12.45 U 802 is believed to have foundered NNW of Tory Island.

U 803 Type IX C-40

Built by Seebeckwerft, Wesermünde
Keel laid 30.6.42   Launched 1.4.43
Commissioned 7.9.43   Feldpost Nr M 52 544

Sunk 27.4.44 in the Wismarer Bucht (53°55′N 14°17′E)

Served with
4 U-Flottille, Stettin September 1943 - 27.4.44 (ab)

Commanded by
KL Karl Schimpf September 1943 - 27.4.44

Patrols: None   Ships sunk: None

On 27.4.44 U 803 was sunk by a mine laid by the RAF in the Wismarer Bucht. Of her crew, 13 men were lost and the commander and 34 others survived.

The boat was raised on 9.8.44 and decommissioned.

U 804 Type IX C-40

Built by Seebeckwerft, Wesermünde
Keel laid 15.3.42   Launched 1.4.43
Commissioned 4.12.43   Feldpost Nr M 55 307

Sunk 9.4.45 W of Skärhamn (57°58′N 11°15′E)

Served with
4 U-Flottille, Stettin December 1943 - June 1944 (ab)
10 U-Flottille, Lorient July - September 1944 (fb)
33 U-Flottille, Flensburg October 1944 - 9.4.45 (fb)

Commanded by
OL Herbert Meyer December 1943 - 9.4.45

Patrols: 3   Ships sunk: None
                 1 destroyer-escort (1300 dt)

1. 12.6.44 Left Kiel, possibly for operations.

On the 16th U 998 was attacked by aircraft NW of Bergen. U 804 was ordered to go to her assistance. A twin-engined aircraft was seen, which sent up the correct colours of the day when the boat began firing at it.

When U 804 ceased fire, the aircraft, a Mosquito of 333 (Norwegian) Squadron (Lt J M Jacobsen), dived and strafed the conning tower with cannon fire, wounding eight crewmen.

U 804 put in to Bergen **17.6.44**

2. 19.6.44 Left for the North Atlantic.

U 804 was one of three Type IX C boats, which from the end of June carried out weather-reporting duties between Greenland and the Azores. From 24.7.44 the escort-carrier USS *Wake Island* and her escort searched for the weather boats.

On 2.8.44 the boat surfaced 8 miles from the destroyer-escort USS *Douglas L Howard* of the carrier's escort, some 500 miles N of Flores, Azores. U 804 was spotted by aircraft and the *Douglas L Howard* and another destroyer-escort, USS *Fiske,* were directed to the scene.

The boat fired three torpedoes, which missed the *Douglas L Howard* but two hit *Fiske* on the starboard side amidships, breaking her in two. The order was given to abandon ship and in spite of danger of more torpedoes, the other escorts picked up survivors. Of the crew of 213, 30 men were killed and another 50 were wounded, all of whom survived. U 804 slipped away northeastwards.

She remained on weather-reporting duties until mid-September. U 804 put in to Kristiansand 7.10.44, then went on to Flensburg, arriving there **12.10.44**

3. 17.10.44 Left Flensburg and arrived Kiel **17.10.44**

4. 4.4.45 Left Kiel, in transit to Norway.

On the 9th U 804 and U 1065 were moving northwards up the Kattegat, close to the Swedish coast. They were sighted on the surface by 34 Mosquitos of the Banff Strike Wing. 22 aircraft from 143 and 235 Squadrons went down and strafed the boats with rocket, cannon and machine-gun fire. 248 Squadron aircraft did not take part.

Both boats sank, one exploding with such force that four Mosquitos were badly damaged, one of them going down into the sea.

There were no survivors from either boat. 56 men lost their lives in U 804, one of whom was KL Ruprecht Fischer, commander of U 244, who was travelling as a passenger.

U 805   Type IX C-40

Built by Seebeckwerft, Wesermünde
Keel laid 24.12.42   Launched --.--.--
Commissioned 12.2.44   Feldpost Nr M 49 091

Surrendered 14.5.45 at Kittery, Maine

Served with
4 U-Flottille, Stettin   February 1944 - February 1945 (ab)
33 U-Flottille, Flensburg   March 1945 - 14.5.45 (fb)

Commanded by
KK Richard Bernardelli   February 1944 - 14.5.45

Patrols: 1   Ships sunk: None

1. 10.2.45   Left Kiel and arrived Horten **14.2.45**

2. 19.2.45   Left Horten and arrived Kristiansand **20.2.45**

3. 3.3.45   Left Kristiansand and arrived Bergen **11.3.45**

4. 17.3.45   Left for the Western Atlantic.
U 805 and five other outward-bound boats joined to form *Seewolf* group from 14.4.45 N of the Azores. The boats were to sweep westwards across the North Atlantic convoy routes in an effort to draw some of the hunting groups from British coastal waters.

During the nights of the 18/19th and 19/20th U 805 was sighted on the surface by USN Leigh Light Liberators of VPB-14 from Teceira, at 420 miles N of Flores, Azores and 50 miles from the escort-carrier USS *Mission Bay*. The boat submerged each time before an attack could be made. During the night of the 20/21st she was located and attacked with depth-charges for two hours by the destroyer-escort USS *Mosely*. Again, she escaped.

The *Seewolf* group plan failed and by the 24th only U 805 and U 858 had not been sunk. U 805 patrolled in the Halifax area.

When the war ended she was still at sea. U 805's commander radioed his position in the morning of 9.5.45 and rendezvoused with the destroyer-escorts USS *Otter* and *Varian* on the 13th, 15 miles S of Cape Race. The warships had come out from Argentia.

The boat went into the Portsmouth Navy Yard at Kittery, Maine, where she surrendered on 14.5.45. The crew was interrogated there about missile-launching equipment being fitted to U-boats.

U 805 was used for 'Victory Visits' to ports on the US east coast. She was later used experimentally by the US Navy. The boat was scuttled on 4.2.46 off the east coast.

U 806   Type IX C-40

Built by Seebeckwerft, Wesermünde
Keel laid 27.4.43   Launched --.--.43
Commissioned 29.4.44   Feldpost Nr M 17 549

Sunk 21.12.45 N of Tory Island (55°44´N 08°18´W)

Served with
4 U-Flottille, Stettin   April - October 1944 (ab)
33 U-Flottille, Flensburg   November 1944 - 5.5.45 (fb)

Commanded by
KL Klaus Hornbostel   April 1944 - 5.5.45

Patrols: 1   Ships sunk: None + 1 damaged
1 minesweeper (672 dt)

1. 20.10.44   Left Kiel and arrived Horten **23.10.44**

2. 27.10.44   Left Horten and arrived Kristiansand **28.10.44**

3. 30.10.44   Left for the North Atlantic.
Outward-bound, U 806 was ordered on 13.11.44 to make for Nova Scotia. At the end of November she was directed to the Halifax area, to be one of four boats operating off the port.

On 21.12.44 U 806 torpedoed and damaged the SS *Samtucky* (br 7219t) off Halifax. She was one of four ships then forming into convoy HX 327. The *Samtucky* was beached next day, later repaired and eventually put back into service. On the 22nd U 806 fired three torpedoes at a merchant vessel and a corvette but missed.

U 806 sighted convoy XB 139 leaving Halifax on the 24th. One of the rendezvousing escorts, the minesweeper HMCS *Clayoquot*, moved at speed to take her assigned place at one side of the convoy. The commander of U 806 assumed that he had been spotted by her and fired an acoustic torpedo, diving immediately afterwards to be safe from his own torpedo. The *Clayoquot* was hit and sank, with the loss of 9 of her crew.

Some minutes later U 806 fired at a steamer but the torpedo exploded in the anti-torpedo gear of another escorting minesweeper, HMCS *Transcona*. A task force was quickly assembled to search for U 806. Late at night the boat left its inshore bottom position, moving southwards, not to the north as the searching ships anticipated. She kept going for 21 hours before the commander felt it safe enough to use the schnorkel. On the 26th U 806 returned to the sea-bottom for a Christmas celebration.

In the later part of January the boat carried out weather-reporting duties.
U 806 returned to Kristiansand **21.2.45**

4. 25.2.45   Left Kristiansand and arrived Flensburg **27.2.45**

At the end of the war U 806 was at Arhus, Denmark. She was surrendered at Wilhelmshaven on 5.5.45. On 21.6.45 she left for the assembly area at Loch Ryan.

U 806 was one of 116 boats disposed of by the Royal Navy in Operation Deadlight. Some time after mid-December 1945 she was towed out through the North Channel by the tug HMS Masterful.
The boat became waterlogged and was sunk by gunfire on 21.12.45 N of Tory Island.

U 807 - U820 were never built.

U 821   Type VII C

Built by Oderwerke, Stettin
Keel laid 2.10.41   Launched 26.6.43
Commissioned 11.10.43   Feldpost Nr M 52 715

Sunk 10.6.44 NW of Ushant (48°31´N 05°11´W)

Served with
4 U-Flottille, Stettin   October - November 1943 (ab)
24 U-Flottille, Memel   November - December 1943 (ab)
4 U-Flottille, Stettin   January - March 1944 (ab)
1 U-Flottille, Brest   March 1944 - 10.6.44 (fb)

Commanded by
Lt Ludwig Fabricius   October - November 1943
OL Ernst Fischer   November - December 1943
OL Ulrich Knackfuss   January 1944 - 10.6.44

Patrols: 2   Ships sunk: None

1. 7.3.44   Left Kiel and arrived Kristiansand **9.3.44**

2. 17.3.44   Left Kristiansand and arrived Bergen **18.3.44**

3. 19.3.44   Left for the North Atlantic.
Outward-bound through the Shetlands-Faroes Passage, U 821 was ordered to make her way to Western France to join *Landwirt* group.
She put in to her new base at Brest **12.4.44**

4. 6.6.44   Left Brest, as part of *Landwirt* group.
U 821 and seven other non-schnorkel boats were ordered to the area between The Lizard and Hartland Point to operate against Allied invasion supply-shipping heading for the English Channel. For an early arrival in the operational area, the boats sailed late in the evening and were ordered to proceed on the surface at high speed. They all came under aircraft attack almost immediately after dropping their escorts off Brest.

With four boats reporting that they were damaged and returning, it was decided that from the 7th the remaining four boats, which included U 821, should proceed to their operational area submerged in daylight.

On the 10th U 821 was sighted surfacing NW of Ushant by four Mosquitos of 248 Squadron, led by F/Lt S G Nunn and flying just above the sea. Unseen by the boat, the aircraft approached and made strafing attacks. The crew was seen to be abandoning ship, which appeared to be sinking. A Liberator of 206 Squadron (F/Lt A D S Dundas) arrived and made two depth-charge attacks, destroying U 821. Considering how near U 821 was to Brest, it seems likely that she was returning to base when sunk.

The survivors were picked up by a German harbour patrol craft, which was attacked and sunk by six Mosquitos of 248 Squadron later in the day as it made its way to Brest. One of the attacking aircraft was shot down by the launch in the action.

Of the combined launch and U 821 crews, there was only one survivor. 50 men from U 821 lost their lives.

U 822   Type VII C

Built by Oderwerke, Stettin
Keel laid 29.10.41   Launched 20.2.44
Commissioned 1.7.44   Feldpost Nr M 17 865

Scuttled 3.5.45 at Wesermünde

Served with
4 U-Flottille, Stettin   July 1944 - 3.5.45 (ab)

Commanded by
OL Josef Elsinghorst   July 1944 - 3.5.45

Patrols: None   Ships sunk: None

U 822 saw no operational service. On 3.5.45 she was scuttled in the Weser Estuary at Wesermünde.
The wreck was broken up in 1948.

U 823 and U 824 were never built.

U 825   Type VII C

Built by Schichau, Danzig
Keel laid 19.7.43   Launched 27.2.44
Commissioned 25.5.44   Feldpost Nr M 19 192

Sunk 3.1.46 N of Malin Head (55°31´N 07°31´W)

Served with
8 U-Flottille, Danzig   May - November 1944 (ab)
11 U-Flottille, Bergen   December 1944 - 10.5.45 (fb)

Commanded by
OL Gerhard Stoelker   May 1944 - 10.5.45

Patrols: 2   Ships sunk: 1 (8262 grt) + 1 damaged

1. 13.12.44   Left Kiel and arrived Horten **16.12.44**

2. 27.12.44   Left Horten and arrived Kristiansand **28.12.44**

3. 29.12.44   Left for British coastal waters.
U 825 operated initially S of Ireland and later in the Bristol and St George's Channels.
On 27.1.45 U 825 attacked convoy HX 332 WSW of Bardsey Island in Cardigan Bay. She torpedoed and damaged two ships, the tanker MV *Solör* (nw 8262t) and the SS *Ruben Dario* (am 7198t). The boat was attacked and damaged by the escort but escaped. The *Solör* was towed in but was declared to be a total loss.
U 825 put in to Bergen **18.2.45**

4. 1.4.45   Left for the Irish Sea.
U 825 had no success on this patrol. At the end of the war the boat was still in the Irish Sea. In accordance with instructions received, U 825 surrendered at Portland on 10.5.45. She was later moved to Lough Foyle.

U 825 was one of 116 boats disposed of by the Royal Navy in Operation Deadlight. At the beginning of January 1946 the boat was towed from the assembly point at Lisahally by the destroyer HMS Mendip. *The towline parted and on 3.1.46 U 825 was sunk by gunfire by the Polish destroyer* Blyskawica *N of Malin Head.*

U 826   Type VII C

Built by Schichau, Danzig
Keel laid 6.8.43   Launched 9.3.44
Commissioned 11.5.44   Feldpost Nr M 35 882

Sunk 1.12.45 NW of Bloody Foreland (56°10´N 10°05´W)

Served with
8 U-Flottille, Danzig   May - December 1944 (ab)
11 U-Flottille, Bergen   January 1945 - 11.5.45

Commanded by
KL Olaf Lübcke   May 1944 - 11.5.45

Patrols: 1   Ships sunk: None

1. 25.2.45   Left Kiel and arrived Horten **28.2.45**

2. 9.3.45   Left Kristiansand for British coastal waters.
On the 30th U 826 and three other boats, U 774, U 1001 and U 1063, were ordered to attack-areas 200 to 300 miles to the west of the western entrance to the English Channel.

U 826 (continued)

U 826 had no success there. When the war ended she was on her return journey to Norway. In accordance with instructions received, the boat made for Loch Eriboll and surrendered there on **11.5.45**

U 826 was one of 116 boats disposed of by the Royal Navy in Operation Deadlight. In late November 1945 she was towed from the assembly point at Loch Ryan out through the North Channel by the destroyer HMS Pytchley.
On 1.12.45 U 826 was sunk by gunfire NW of Bloody Foreland.

U 827   Type VII C

Built by Schichau, Danzig
Keel laid 7.8.43   Launched 9.3.44
Commissioned 25.5.44   Feldpost Nr M 36 350

Scuttled 4.5.45 in Flensburger Förde

Served with
8 U-Flottille, Danzig   May 1944 - February 1945 (ab)
11 U-Flottille, Bergen   March 1945 - 4.5.45 (fb)

Commanded by
KL Wilhelm Hunck   May 1944 - March 1945
KL Kurt Baberg   April 1945 - 4.5.45

Patrols: None   Ships sunk: None

When surrender was announced on 4.5.45 U 827 was one of a large number of boats awaiting further orders in the bays of Northern Germany.
On 30.4.45 instructions for the scuttling of the German fleet, Operation Regenbogen, had gone out to commanders. On the 4th these orders were carried out by some U-boat commanders, in accordance with Regenbogen but contrary to the surrender terms.
U 827 was scuttled on the 4th in the inner Flensburger Förde.

U 828   Type VII C

Built by Schichau, Danzig
Keel laid 16.8.43   Launched 16.3.44
Commissioned 17.6.44   Feldpost Nr M 25 463

Scuttled 3.5.45 at Wesermünde

Served with
8 U-Flottille, Danzig   June 1944 - February 1945 (ab)
5 U-Flottille, Kiel   February 1945 - 3.5.45 (ab)

Commanded by
OL Alfred John   June 1944 - 3.5.45

Patrols: None   Ships sunk: None

U 828 saw no operational service. She was scuttled on 3.5.45 in the Weser Estuary at Wesermünde.
The wreck was broken up in 1948.

U 829 - U 840 were never built.

U 841   Type IX C-40

Built by AG Weser, Bremen
Keel laid 20.3.42   Launched 21.10.42
Commissioned 6.2.43   Feldpost Nr M 49 972

Scuttled 17.10.43 E of Cape Farewell (59°57′N 31°06′W)

Served with
4 U-Flottille, Stettin   February - June 1943 (ab)
2 U-Flottille, Lorient   July 1943 - 17.10.43 (fb)

Commanded by
KL Werner Bender   February 1943 - 17.10.43

Patrols: 1   Ships sunk: None

1. 26.8.43   Left Kiel and arrived Bergen **1.9.43**

2. 9.9.43   Left Bergen and arrived Trondheim **10.9.43**

3. 4.10.43   Left for the North Atlantic.
Outward-bound, U 841 was ordered to join *Schlieffen* group ESE of Cape Farewell. On the 15th, whilst the patrol line was forming, outward-bound U 844 sighted a westbound convoy W of Rockall, which was presumed to be ONS 20 but was in fact ON 206. She was ordered to shadow and home the *Schlieffen* boats in. U 844 was located and driven off and the boats, kept submerged by Iceland-based aircraft, did not find the convoy.
Early on the 16th U 964 sighted and reported ONS 20, which altered course to the northwest later in the day. Meanwhile Dönitz had ordered the boats to stay on the surface and fight their way to the convoy. During daylight on the 16th reports began arriving of boats being attacked and damaged and the first to be sunk was the shadower, U 964.
The *Schlieffen* boats moved further eastwards to form a new line for the 17th. ONS 20 passed just north of the line early in the morning of the 17th and an attack was ordered.
U 841 was located E of Cape Farewell by the destroyer-escort HMS *Byard* on the 17th, following ONS 20 and nine miles astern. A depth-charge attack forced U 841 to the surface. Although *Byard* was in a perfect position to ram, her captain (Cdr Paramor) decided to resort to gunfire, knowing that he was far from home and that the convoy was threatened.
Firing commenced and soon the boat's crew began to come up. U 841's commander was seen firing a pistol but an Austrian crewman was more practical and waved a white handkerchief. The *Byard* moved in as the scuttled boat sank. She picked up 27 survivors. The commander and 25 men were lost.

U 842   Type IX C-40

Built by AG Weser, Bremen
Keel laid 6.4.42   Launched 14.11.42
Commissioned 1.3.43   Feldpost Nr M 50 566

Sunk 6.11.43 WNW of the Azores (43°42′N 42°08′W)

Served with
4 U-Flottille, Stettin   March - July 1943 (ab)
2 U-Flottille, Lorient   August 1943 - 6.11.43 (fb)

Commanded by
KK Wolfgang Heller   March 1943 - 6.11.43

Patrols: 1   Ships sunk: None

1. 14.9.43 Left Bergen and returned **17.9.43**

2. 5.10.43 Left for the North Atlantic.
Outward-bound, U 842 was ordered to join *Schlieffen* group ESE of Cape Farewell. On the 15th, whilst the patrol line was forming, outward-bound U 844 sighted a westbound convoy W of Rockall, which was presumed to be ONS 20 but was in fact ON 206. She was ordered to shadow and home the *Schlieffen* boats in. U 844 was located and driven off and the boats, kept submerged by Iceland-based aircraft, did not find the convoy.

Early on the 16th U 964 sighted and reported ONS 20, which altered course to the northwest later in the day. Meanwhile Dönitz had ordered the boats to stay on the surface and fight their way to the convoy. During daylight on the 16th reports arrived of boats being attacked. The first to be sunk was the shadower, U 964.

The *Schlieffen* boats moved further eastwards to form a new line for the 17th. ONS 20 passed just north of the line early in the morning of the 17th and an attack was ordered. Again, contact was lost and this time it was not regained.

As the *Schlieffen* boats continued their search during the day, many came under air attack and the operation was called off at noon on the 18th. Six boats were lost for only one ship sunk.

The surviving boats were joined by new-arrivals to form *Siegfried* group from the 24th 500 miles E of Newfoundland to await HX 262 and SC 145. The boats were ordered to remain submerged in daylight, ready for an attack after dark. On the 25th it was thought that a convoy would pass south of the group. The boats moved southwards but nothing was found.

To cover a wider area, *Siegfried* was split into three small sub-groups, *Siegfried 1,2* and *3*. U 842 was in *Siegfried 3*. The groups continued southwards, searching for SC 145 but it passed by on the 29th. Two days later the boats again reformed, this time into *Jahn* and *Körner* groups. U 842 in was *Jahn*.

On 3.11.43 the boats were redeployed in five small sub-groups, *Tirpitz 1* to *5*, to search for convoy HX 264, expected on the 5th. The convoy's escort was supported by the 2nd SG and it was sloops HMS *Starling* (Capt F J Walker), *Wild Goose* (Cdr D E G Wemyss) and *Magpie* of the group that were sent to the scene after an aircraft sighted U 842 submerging 20 miles away, WNW of the Azores.

A Liberator of 10 (RCAF) Squadron and a Swordfish from the escort-carrier HMS *Tracker* were already there but had seen nothing. In the early afternoon *Wild Goose* made contact and *Starling* carried out a depth-charge attack, which failed.

Wild Goose was then ordered by Walker to make a creeping attack, with 26 depth-charges set deep. The attack was late and the full quota of depth-charges was not dropped. Walker's fury was cut short when there was an underwater explosion reported and oil, wreckage and human remains began to surface. U 842 was destroyed.

There were no survivors, 56 dead.

U 843   Type IX C-40

Built by AG Weser, Bremen
Keel laid 21.4.42   Launched 15.12.42
Commissioned 24.3.43   Feldpost Nr M 51 370

Sunk 9.4.45 off Skagen (57°48′N 11°26′E)

Served with
4 U-Flottille, Stettin   March - October 1943 (ab)
2 U-Flottille, Lorient   November 1943 - September 1944 (fb)
33 U-Flottille, Flensburg   October 1944 - 9.4.45 (fb)

Commanded by
KL Oskar Herwartz   March 1943 - 9.4.45

Patrols: 4   Ships sunk: 1 (8261 grt)

1. 7.10.43 Left Kiel and arrived Trondheim **12.10.43**

2. 15.10.43 Left for the North Atlantic.
U 843 joined *Körner* group, which was formed from the 31st E of Newfoundland to search for convoys HX 263 and ONS 21. Both convoys went round the *Körner* patrol line.

The *Körner* and *Jahn* group boats were redeployed in five smaller sub-groups, *Tirpitz 1* to *5*, each with four or five boats. They searched for eastbound HX 264, expected in the area on 5.11.43.

Two boats were destroyed by the convoy's escort, aided by the 2nd SG, and the convoy passed the *Tirpitz* boats. The operation against HX 264 ended on the 7th, the convoy's air escort keeping the boats submerged.

The *Tirpitz* groups were dissolved and the boats reformed as *Eisenhart* group, made up of seven sub-groups of three boats each and drawn up in two lines from the 11th, running southeastwards from Cape Farewell. The lines crossed an area through which most convoys had passed since August 1943.

Reports indicated that convoys were now being routed further to the south so the *Eisenhart* boats were ordered southeastwards on the 12th, to search for SC 146 and HX 265. By the 16th no convoys had been found and the majority of the boats were now WSW of Ireland. Fuel was now becoming a problem and it was decided to end the operation and send the boats to join *Schill* group, operating W of Portugal.

U 843 joined the *Schill 3* patrol line, in the expected path of northbound convoy MKS 30/SL 139 and through which it was expected to pass on the 20th. *Schill 3* surfaced that evening but failed to find the convoy, which was located next morning and attacked by aircraft, resulting in one ship sunk and another damaged, both by glider-bombs.

On the 22nd the remaining fourteen boats of the three *Schill* groups were formed into an east-west patrol line, *Weddigen*, between 18° and 22°W to operate against convoy KMS 30/OG 95. On the 23rd the line moved southwestwards.

Finding nothing, the boats turned southeastwards on the 25th to intercept northbound MKS 31/SL 140. Constantly harassed by surface vessels and aircraft and with insufficient information from reconnaissance aircraft, *Weddigen* could not carry out a concentrated attack before the operation was called off on the 28th. U 843 was driven off by the 2nd SG.

Weddigen group moved to operate against KMS 34/OS 60 but it was not found, either by aircraft or U-boats. The group was directed northwestwards to join *Coronel* group in an operation on 6.12.43 against ONS 24 but this was unsuccessful. On the 7th *Weddigen* group was broken up and U 843 set out for home.

She put in to her new base at Lorient **15.12.43**

3. 19.2.44 Left for the Indian Ocean.
U 843 was refuelled in late March by U 488 W of the Azores. In early April she stopped two steamers, one Portugese and the other Spanish, and after examination, released them.

On 8.4.44 U 843 torpedoed and sank the SS *Nebraska* (br 8261t) WSW of Ascension and on or about the 10th she was twice attacked by aircraft S of Ascension and damaged.

In late April U 843 rounded the Cape and entered the Indian Ocean and in mid-May, after being damaged, she headed for Batavia, reaching there **11.6.44**

4. 13.6.44 Left Batavia and arrived Shonan **15.6.44**

5. --.11.44 Left Shonan and returned Batavia **--.11.44**

6. 10.12.44 Left to return to Europe.
U 843, which was carrying 100 tons of zinc, was refuelled on the 20th by U 195, at the end of her voyage from France and heading for Batavia. On the 23/24th U 843 took aboard surplus fuel from U 181, also heading for Batavia.

U 843 (continued)

In mid-January 1945 U 843 entered the South Atlantic and crossed the Equator in early February.

She reached Bergen **3.4.45**

7. 6.4.45 Left Bergen, en route to Kiel.

On the 9th U 843 was heading southwards into the Kattegat as U 804 and U 1065 were heading northwards and about to leave it. The three boats were sighted on the surface by Mosquitos of the Banff Strike Wing.

U 843 was attacked with rockets and cannon fire by a Mosquito of 235 Squadron (F/O A J Randell) and sunk off Skagen, Denmark. U 804 and U 1065 were also sunk.

There were no survivors from U 843, 44 dead.

The wreck of U 843 was raised on 22.8.58 and scrapped.

U 844   Type IX C-40

Built by AG Weser, Bremen
Keel laid 21.5.42   Launched 30.12.42
Commissioned 7.4.43   Feldpost Nr M 51 391

Sunk 16.10.43 SW of Iceland (58°30′N 27°16′W)

Served with
4 U-Flottille, Stettin   April - September 1943 (ab)
10 U-Flottille, Lorient   October 1943 (fb)

Commanded by
OL Günther Möller   April 1943 - 16.10.43

Patrols: 1   Ships sunk: None

1. 14.9.43 Left Kiel and arrived Bergen **19.9.43**

2. 6.10.43 Left for the North Atlantic.

Outward-bound, U 844 was ordered to join *Schlieffen* group ESE of Cape Farewell. However, on the 15th U 844 sighted a westbound convoy W of Rockall, which was presumed to be ONS 20 but was in fact ON 206. She was ordered to shadow and home the *Schlieffen* boats in.

U 844 was located and driven off during the night of the 15/16th by the destroyers HMS *Duncan* and *Vanquisher* of the escort. The *Schlieffen* boats, kept submerged by Iceland-based aircraft, did not find the convoy.

Early on the 16th U 844 was sighted on the surface SW of Iceland, 15 miles south of the convoy, by a Liberator of 86 Squadron (F/Lt E A Bland). In the face of heavy flak, the aircraft came in but its depth-charges failed to release. Badly-damaged, the aircraft circled, unable to make another attack, but Bland homed in other aircraft.

A Liberator of 59 Squadron (P/O W J Thomas) arrived and dropped four depth-charges but was badly damaged by flak. The boat began to submerge and four more depth-charges were dropped by Thomas ahead of the swirl.

HMS *Duncan* came up and fired some depth-charges but probably U 844 was already finished. Bland, in the 86 Squadron Liberator, decided to ditch his aircraft near the convoy. It broke up on impact with the sea. All the crew were picked up by the corvette HMS *Pink* but two died and Bland and his navigator were wounded. For his part in the action, Bland was awarded the DSO.

There were no survivors from U 844, 53 dead.

U 845   Type IX C-40

Built by AG Weser, Bremen
Keel laid 21.6.42   Launched 22.1.43
Commissioned 1.5.43   Feldpost Nr M 41 779

Scuttled 10.3.44 NW of Cape Finisterre (48°20′N 20°33′W)

Served with
4 U-Flottille, Stettin   May - December 1943 (ab)
10 U-Flottille, Lorient   January 1944 - 10.3.44 (fb)

Commanded by
KK Udo Behrens   May - July 1943
KL Rudolf Hoffman   July - October 1943
KK Werner Weber   October 1943 - 10.3.44

Patrols: 1   Ships sunk: None + 1 damaged

1. 1.1.44 Left Kiel and arrived Bergen **6.1.44**

2. 8.1.44 Left for Canadian waters.

U 845 operated E of Newfoundland from the 25th. On 5.2.44 she made an unsuccessful attack on a steamer E of St John's, hearing only an end-of-run detonation. On the 9th the boat torpedoed and damaged the SS *Kelmscott* (br 7039t) off St John's. The explosion was thought to have been caused by a mine and the port was closed and convoy JH 81 diverted. The *Kelmscott* was towed back by the tug *Samsonia*.

On the 14th U 845 was sighted on the surface by a Liberator of 10 (RCAF) Squadron (F/O A P V Cheater) off Flemish Cap, Newfoundland. The boat put up heavy flak with her 3.7cm gun and the aircraft returned the fire, killing one of U 845's crew and wounding another. Six depth-charges were dropped, without damage to the boat.

The aircraft attacked again, the boat's gun jammed and two more depth-charges were dropped, very close the to conning tower. The damaged U 845 crash-dived and went very deep, out of control. Eventually trim was restored. The Liberator circled the area for more than an hour but there was no further contact.

On or about the 16th U 845 made an unsuccessful attack on the SS *Pacesham*, which had sailed alone from St John's.

With icing conditions in the area now severe, U 845 began her return journey. Nearing home, the boat was NW of Cape Finisterre early on 10.3.44 when she sighted eastbound convoy SC 154. U 845 began to shadow, following the convoy at a distance. With constant danger from air attack, the boat sailed submerged and almost exhausted her batteries.

In the afternoon U 845's commander surfaced to recharge but after a short time the boat was sighted by the destroyer HMCS *St Laurent* (Lt-Cdr G H Stephen) and the corvette HMCS *Owensound* (Lt J M Watson) of EG C1, at a distance of eight miles. The two warships closed and U 845 dived deep, batteries uncharged. A series of depth-charge and Hedgehog attacks were carried out, which were added to by the destroyer HMS *Forester* (Lt-Cdr J A Burnett). Having seen no results, the ships waited for developments, now joined by the frigate HMCS *Swansea* (Cdr C A King).

After six hours of manoeuvring, U 845's batteries failed and her commander decided to surface and make a run for it. He fired two torpedoes, which missed. The boat moved off at high speed, firing her guns. The warships took off after her, all firing, but it was *St Laurent* which was able to act quickest. She passed U 845, scored three direct hits on the conning tower, killing every man on it, including the commander, and then fired ten shallow-set depth-charges ahead of the boat.

The crew were already abandoning ship before the depth-charges exploded and the Engineering Officer was below, setting scuttling charges. He escaped through the galley hatch.

For such an action, it was remarkable that there were 45 survivors, picked up by *Forester* and *Swansea*. 10 others, including the commander, lost their lives.

U 846   Type IX C-40

Built by AG Weser, Bremen
Keel laid 21.7.42   Launched 17.2.43
Commissioned 29.5.43   Feldpost Nr M 51 907

Sunk 4.5.44 NNW of Cape Ortegal (46°04′N 09°20′W)

Served with
4 U-Flottille, Stettin May - November 1943 (ab)
10 U-Flottille, Lorient December 1943 - 4.5.44 (fb)

Commanded by
OL Berthold Hashagen May 1943 - 4.5.44

Patrols: 2   Ships sunk: None

1. 4.12.43 Left Kiel for the North Atlantic.

U 846 joined *Rügen* group W of Ireland. From 5.1.44 the boats operated singly W of the British Isles. After mid-January U 846 was detached for weather-reporting duty.

She put in to her new base at Lorient **3.3.44**

2. 29.4.44 Left for Atlantic operations.

Outward-bound on 2.5.44, U 846 was attacked in the Bay of Biscay by a Halifax of 58 Squadron. She was undamaged and she shot the aircraft down.

During darkness on the 4th U 846 was sighted on the surface in bright moonlight by a Wellington of 407 (RCAF) Squadron (F/Lt L J Bateman). The aircraft dropped six depth-charges and the boat was destroyed. For this action Bateman was awarded the DFC.

There were no survivors from U 846, 57 dead.

U 847   Type IX D-2

Built by AG Weser, Bremen
Keel laid 24.11.41   Launched 5.9.42
Commissioned 23.1.43   Feldpost Nr M 49 998

Sunk 27.8.43 SW of the Azores (28°19′N 37°58′W)

Served with
4 U-Flottille, Stettin January - June 1943 (ab)
12 U-Flottille, Bordeaux July 1943 - 27.8.43 (fb)

Commanded by
KL Friedrich Guggenberger January - February 1943
KL Jost Metzler February - July 1943
KL Herbert Kuppisch July 1943 - 27.8.43

Patrols: 2   Ships sunk: None

Whilst U 847's crew were under training, two men were killed and two others injured.

1. 6.7.43 Left Kiel for Atlantic operations.

U 847 was damaged by pack-ice in Denmark Strait. She returned, putting in to Bergen **20.7.43**

2. 29.7.43 Left for the Indian Ocean.

Outward-bound, U 847 was ordered to undertake the duty of a

U-tanker, following the loss of tankers U 117 and U 525. She was ordered to an area 800 miles SW of the Azores.

On 19.8.43 U 847 supplied U 66, returning from US waters. Between the 23rd and 27th U 847 refuelled U 172, U 230, U 257, U 415, U 508 and U 653. The fuel was transferred using fire hoses.

On completion of the operation, U 847 radioed to that effect. The transmission was picked up and three hours later the boat was sighted on the surface by three aircraft of VC-1 from the escort-carrier USS *Card*, an Avenger (Lt R W Long) and two Wildcats.

The boat was forced to submerge by strafing attacks by the Wildcats. The Avenger then dropped a homing torpedo, which destroyed U 847.

There were no survivors, 63 dead.

U 848   Type IX D-2

Built by AG Weser, Bremen
Keel laid 6.1.42   Launched 6.10.42
Commissioned 20.2.43   Feldpost Nr M 50 593

Sunk 5.11.43 SW of Ascension (10°09′S 18°00′W)

Served with
4 U-Flottille, Stettin February - July 1943 (ab)
12 U-Flottille, Bordeaux August 1943 - 5.11.43 (fb)

Commanded by
KK Wilhelm Rollmann February 1943 - 5.11.43

Patrols: 1   Ships sunk: 1 (4573 grt)

1. 18.9.43 Left Kiel for the Indian Ocean

U 848 torpedoed and sank the SS *Baron Semple* (br 4573t) on 2.11.43 NW of Ascension.

In the morning of the 5th U 848 was sighted on the surface SW of Ascension by a USN Liberator (Lt C A Baldwin) of VP-107. The aircraft came in and dropped six depth-bombs, straddling the boat. Another Liberator (Lt W R Ford) arrived 30 minutes later, inflicted further damage but did not silence U 848's guns. A third Liberator (Lt W E Hill) met with heavy flak and returned to base on Ascension with one engine knocked out.

In the afternoon two Army B 25s from the 1st Composite Squadron (USAF) dropped 500 lb bombs from 4000 feet but caused no further damage to the boat. Two Liberators appeared, one captained by Lt S K Taylor and the other by Lt C A Baldwin. The latter aircraft had made the first attack in the morning and then had returned to Ascension to refuel and re-arm. Both aircraft made depth-bomb attacks and U 848 was destroyed.

Liferafts were dropped to the 20 or so survivors seen in the water and a ship was requested to pick them up. However, only one delirious survivor was picked up by the light cruiser USS *Marblehead* one month later. He died within a few days.

There were no other survivors from U 848, 64 dead.

U 849   Type IX D-2

Built by AG Weser, Bremen
Keel laid 20.1.42   Launched 31.10.42
Commissioned 11.3.43   Feldpost Nr M 51 402

Sunk 25.11.43 ENE of Ascension (06°30′S 05°40′W)

Served with
4 U-Flottille, Stettin   March - September 1943 (ab)
12 U-Flottille, Bordeaux   October 1943 - 25.11.43 (fb)

Commanded by
KL Heinz-Otto Schultze   March 1943 - 25.11.43

Patrols: 1   Ships sunk: None

1. 2.10.43 Left Kiel for the Indian Ocean.
Outward-bound, U 849 was first reported off St Paul Rocks on 17.11.43 by the light cruiser USS *Memphis*. A search by Ascension-based Liberators of VP-107 began but the boat was not sighted until the 25th, by a Liberator (Lt M V Dawkins) 600 miles ENE of Ascension.
Taken completely unawares, the boat was straddled by six depth-bombs from 25 feet. One fin and rudder of the aircraft was damaged when one of the bombs bounced. U 849 began to sink and the crew abandoned ship before she exploded. A liferaft was dropped by the aircraft but never found.
There were no survivors, 63 dead.

U 850   Type IX D-2

Built by AG Weser, Bremen
Keel laid 17.3.42   Launched 7.12.42
Commissioned 17.4.43   Feldpost Nr M 41 858

Sunk 20.12.43 SW of the Azores (32°54′N 37°01′W)

Served with
4 U-Flottille, Stettin   April - October 1943 (ab)
12 U-Flottille, Bordeaux   October 1943 - 20.12.43 (fb)

Commanded by
FK Klaus Ewerth   April 1943 - 20.12.43

Patrols: 1   Ships sunk: None

1. 18.11.43 Left Kiel for the Indian Ocean.
U 850 was sighted on the surface by an Avenger of VC-19 (Lt W A La Fleur) from the escort-carrier USS *Bogue* in the afternoon of 20.12.43 SW of the Azores. The aircraft made two attacks but the depth-bombs fell short.
Following La Fleur's report of the sighting, two Wildcats and two more Avengers (Lt H Bradshaw and Ens G Goodwin) were dispatched from *Bogue*. The Wildcats made strafing attacks and a depth-bomb attack by Goodwin damaged the boat, slowing her down. Acoustic torpedoes were then dropped by La Fleur and Bradshaw, both of which struck U 850 aft of the conning tower on the starboard side as she submerged. The boat sank stern first.
The destroyers USS *Dupont* and *George E Badger* arrived later and picked up wreckage and other evidence of U 850's destruction.
There were no survivors, 66 dead.

U 851   Type IX D-2

Built by AG Weser, Bremen
Keel laid 18.3.42   Launched 15.1.43
Commissioned 21.5.43   Feldpost Nr M 51 969

Sunk late March/early April 1944, position unknown

Served with
4 U-Flottille, Stettin   May 1943 - January 1944 (ab)
12 U-Flottille, Bordeaux   February 1944 - c 30.3.44 (fb)

Commanded by
KK Hannes Weingaertner   May 1943 - c 30.3.44

Patrols: 1   Ships sunk: None

1. 26.2.44 Left Kiel for the Indian Ocean.
Outward-bound, U 851 went missing in late March/early April 1944. The last report from the boat was made on 27.3.44.
Although a BdU report of 20.7.44 gives U 851's official 'missing' date as 8.6.44, a British report says it was sunk in March 1944, presumably in the last three days of the month, which seems a much more likely time.
There were no survivors, 70 dead.

U 852   Type IX D-2

Built by AG Weser, Bremen
Keel laid 15.4.42   Launched 28.1.43
Commissioned 15.6.43   Feldpost Nr M 52 771

Scuttled 3.5.44 near Ras Mabber (09°32′N 50°59′E)

Served with
4 U-Flottille, Stettin   June 1943 - January 1944 (ab)
12 U-Flottille, Bordeaux   February 1944 - 3.5.44 (fb)

Commanded by
KL Heinz-Wilhelm Eck   June 1943 - 3.5.44

Patrols: 1   Ships sunk: 2 (9972 grt)

1. 18.1.44 Left Kiel for the Indian Ocean.
U 852 moved out of the Baltic, up the Norwegian coast, north of the British Isles, to the central North Atlantic, and then southwards.
In the evening of 13.3.44 U 852 torpedoed and sank the SS *Peleus* (gr 4695t) S of Liberia. Survivors in the water were machine-gunned and hand grenades used to try and destroy floating wreckage. Eck and those others involved were tried at Hamburg in October 1945.
On 1.4.44 U 852 torpedoed and sank the SS *Dahomian* (br 5277t) off Cape Town. The boat then turned eastwards into the Indian Ocean. As she went northwards up the coast of East Africa her progress was monitored.
U 852 was located on 2.5.44 by an Aden-based Wellington of 621 Squadron (F/O H R Mitchell) 100 miles SE of Cape Guardafui. As the boat submerged, she was straddled by six depth-charges and strafed by machine-gun fire. She resurfaced soon afterwards, damaged and unable to dive again, and came under attack by Wellingtons of 8 and 621 Squadrons throughout the day.
Early on the 3rd the decisive attack was made by a Wellington of 8 Squadron (F/O J R Forrester). The damage caused to U 852 decided her commander, KL Eck, to beach the boat. This was done near Ras Mabber, Somaliland on the 3rd. Scuttling charges were set in U 852's bow and stern, effectively destroying the boat.
Eck and 58 members of his crew were captured by the Somaliland

Camel Corps and a naval landing party. Another 7 men of U 852's crew were killed.

Heinz Eck and four members of his crew were tried at the War Crimes Court in Hamburg on October 17th 1945, charged with 'Committing a war crime in that you in the Atlantic Ocean on the night of 13/14th March 1944, when Captain and members of the crew of Unterseeboot 852 which had sunk the steamship Peleus *in violation of the laws and usages of war were concerned in the killing of members of the crew of the said steamship, Allied nationals, by·firing and throwing grenades at them'.*

In evidence, it transpired that after sinking the Peleus *U 852 remained in the area, in darkness, for five hours, time which could have been used to move away from the scene on the surface before daylight.*

After midnight U 852 moved amongst the survivors in the water and on rafts and two men on her foredeck asked the name of the ship, where she was from and where bound and other questions about convoy routine and warships at Freetown. U 852 then moved off but re-appeared and hailed the rafts to approach. As they did so, they came under machine-gun fire but when the rafts did not sink, hand grenades were thrown. A signalling lamp was used to see if any men had survived and intermittent bursts of machine-gun followed, presumbably finishing off wounded men. Just before dawn U 852 left the scene. However, three men survived and were picked up on April 20th by the Portugese steamer Alexandre Silva *and reached Lobito on the 27th.*

When U 852 was scuttled, her log was not destroyed and it stated that the boat had sunk a ship on 13.3.44 in the approximate position where Peleus *was sunk.*

Eck's defence was that he tried to destroy pieces of wreckage and the rafts so that no trace of the sinking would remain to be seen by patrolling ships or aircraft. Thus U 852's presence would be undiscovered. This defence was not accepted by the prosecution and after a four-day trial, all five defendants were found guilty. KL Heinz Eck, Lt August Hoffman (2WO), Oberstabsarzt Walter Weisspfennig (medical officer) were sentenced to be shot. KL Hans Lenz (chief engineer) sentenced to life imprisonment and Matrosen-Gefreiter Wolfgang Schwender to 15 years' imprisonment. The executions were carried out on Lüneburg Heath on November 30th 1945.

Ten days before he was shot, Eck made a deposition to be used in defence of Dönitz at his trial at Nuremburg. Of 29 questions and answers, three were as follows:-

Q 21 Have you ever been taught or encouraged by Admiral Dönitz to fire at survivors of a shipwreck or anything which might help save them or to destroy by an other means such survivors?

A 21 No.

Q 22 Have you made a report to the Commander-in-Chief of the Submarine Arm concering the sinking of the Peleus *and your action in destroying the survivors and their means of rescue?*

A 22 No, I did not have the opportunity of making a report with all the necessary details.

Q 23 Does this mean that you have not made any report to any higher officer of the Submarine Arm concerning your actions?

A 23 Yes.

U 853 Type IX C-40

Built by AG Weser, Bremen
Keel laid 21.8.42   Launched 11.3.43
Commissioned 25.6.43   Feldpost Nr M 52 793

Sunk 6.5.45 E of Block Island (41°13′N 71°27′W)

Served with
4 U-Flottille, Stettin   June 1943 - March 1944 (ab)
10 U-Flottille, Lorient   April - October 1944 (fb)
33 U-Flottille, Flensburg   October 1944 - 6.5.45 (fb)

Commanded by
KL Helmut Sommer   June 1943 - July 1944
OL Otto Wermuth   July - August 1944
KK Günter Kuhnke   August - October 1944
OL Helmut Frömsdorf   October 1944 - 6.5.45

Patrols: 3   Ships sunk: 1 (5353 grt)
                                1 patrol craft (430 dt)

1. 11.4.44   Left Kiel and returned **14.4.44**

2. 20.4.44   Left Kiel and arrived Marviken **22.4.44**

3. 25.4.44   Left Marviken and arrived Bergen **26.4.44**

4. 29.4.44   Left Bergen for the North Atlantic.
U 853 was on weather-reporting duties at 30°W. On 25.5.44 the boat was attacked with rockets by three Swordfish aircraft from the auxiliary escort-carriers *Ancylus* and *Empire Mackendrick*. U 853 was undamaged and escaped.
On 17.6.44 she was attacked and damaged in strafing attacks by two Wildcats from the escort-carrier USS *Croatan*, after being located following the transmission of a weather report. The boat had 2 men killed and another 12 wounded, including her commander. The 1WO OL Frömsdorf, took command.
U 853, which was then only 30 miles south of the carrier, submerged and escaped before the Avengers arrived with their depth-bombs and torpedoes. The boat then set out for base because of her casualties.
She put in to Lorient **4.7.44**

5. 27.8.44   Left Lorient, in transit to Germany.
The boat was commanded by KK Günter Kuhnke, the commander of 10 U-Flottille at Lorient. In addition to her crew, U 853 was carrying seven technical staff, evacuated from Lorient.
The boat put in to Flensburg **14.10.44**

6. 6.2.45   Left Kiel and arrived Horten **11.2.45**

7. 14.2.45   Left Horten and arrived Stavanger **17.2.45**

8. 23.2.45   Left for US waters.
U 853 possibly sank the patrol vessel USS *Eagle 56* on 23.4.45, which sank off Portland, Maine after an explosion. On 5.5.45 U 853 sank the SS *Black Point* (am 5353t) off Narragansett Bay. She had probably not heard the Dönitz surrender order of May 4th. The boat was briefly sighted by another ship and reported.
Within two hours the frigate USS *Moberly* (Lt-Cdr L B Tollakson) arrived, followed later by two other vessels of a hastily-convened hunter-killer group. A scouting line was formed and the destroyer-escort USS *Atherton* (Lt-Cdr L Iselin) made a sound contact 5 miles E of Grove Point, Block Island.
She carried out depth-charge and Hedgehog attacks before contact with the boat was lost. U 853 was laying on the bottom, hoping to eventually slip away. *Atherton* made contact again after

U 853 (continued)

three hours and carried out a Hedgehog attack which probably destroyed the boat.

However, with no wreckage seen, attacks continued throughout the night and into the morning of the 6th. At noon the boat's chart table and the commander's cap surfaced, confirming U 853's destruction.

There were no survivors, 56 dead.

U 854   Type IX C-40

Built by AG Weser, Bremen
Keel laid 21.9.42   Launched 5.4.43
Commissioned 19.7.43   Feldpost Nr M 53 631

Sunk 4.2.44 off Swinemünde (53°55′N 14°17′E)

Served with
4 U-Flottille, Stettin   July 1943 - 4.2.44 (ab)

Commanded by
KL Horst Weiher   July 1943 - 4.2.44

Patrols: None   Ships sunk: None

U 854 saw no operational service. She was near the end of her training when she sank on 4.2.44 off Swinemünde after striking an Allied air-laid mine.

The commander and 50 members of the crew lost their lives. There were 7 survivors.

U 855   Type IX C-40

Built by AG Weser, Bremen
Keel laid 21.10.42   Launched 17.4.43
Commissioned 2.8.43   Feldpost Nr M 53 689

Missing after mid-September 1944 W of Bergen

Served with
4 U-Flottille, Stettin   August 1943 - March 1944 (ab)
10 U-Flottille, Lorient   April - September 1944 (fb)

Commanded by
KL Albert Sürenhagen   August 1943 - April 1944
OL Prosper Ohlsen   April - September 1944

Patrols: 1   Ships sunk: None

1. **22.6.44**   Left Kiel and arrived Marviken **24.6.44**

2. **25.6.44**   Left Marviken and returned Kiel **27.6.44**

3. **1.7.44**   Left Kiel for the North Atlantic.
U 855 was on weather-reporting duty. The boat did not return to base. She is believed to have been lost in the latter half of September 1944, possibly W of Bergen from some unknown cause or striking a mine in the Iceland-Faroes Passage.

There were no known survivors, 56 dead.

U 856   Type IX C-40

Built by AG Weser, Bremen
Keel laid 31.10.42   Launched 11.5.43
Commissioned 19.8.43   Feldpost Nr M 54 791

Sunk 7.4.44 SE of Cape Sable (40°18′N 62°22′W)

Served with
4 U-Flottille, Stettin   August 1943 - February 1944 (ab)
2 U-Flottille, Lorient   March 1944 - 7.4.44 (fb)

Commanded by
OL Friedrich Wittenberg   August 1943 - 7.4.44

Patrols: 1   Ships sunk: None

1. **24.2.44**   Left Kiel for the North Atlantic.
U 856 operated S of Newfoundland from the end of the third week of March. On 7.4.44 the boat was located SE of Cape Sable and sunk in depth-charge attacks by the destroyer USS *Champlin* and the destroyer-escort USS *Huse* (Lt-Cdr R H Wanless).

The commander and 27 men were picked up. 27 other men of U 856's crew lost their lives.

U 857   Type IX C-40

Built by AG Weser, Bremen
Keel laid 26.11.42   Launched 23.5.43
Commissioned 16.9.43   Feldpost Nr M 52 607

Sunk 7.4.45 NE of Cape Cod (42°22′N 69°46′W)

Served with
4 U-Flottille, Stettin   September 1943 - May 1944 (ab)
10 U-Flottille, Lorient   June 1944 - September 1944 (fb)
33 U-Flottille, Flensburg   October 1944 - 7.4.45 (fb)

Commanded by
KL Rudolf Premauer   September 1943 - 7.4.45

Patrols: 3   Ships sunk: None + 1 damaged

1. **9.5.44**   Left Kiel for the North Atlantic.
U 857, U 534 and U 853 carried out weather-reporting duties at 30°W, from Greenland in the north to the Azores in the south. U 857 remained on this duty until the end of July.
She put in to Bordeaux **13.8.44**

2. **25.8.44**   Left Bordeaux, in transit to Norway.
U 857 reached Kristiansand **7.10.44**

3. **9.10.44**   Left Kristiansand and arrived Flensburg **11.10.44**

4. **17.10.44**   Left Flensburg and arrived Hamburg **19.10.44**

5. **--.12.44**   Left Hamburg and arrived Kiel **--.12.44**

6. **30.1.45**   Left Kiel and arrived Horten **2.2.45**

7. **6.2.45**   Left for US waters.
In late March U 857 was operating in the Gulf of Maine. On 5.4.45 she torpedoed and damaged the turbine tanker *Atlantic States* (am 8537t) just N of Cape Cod. This vessel was taken into port and a hunt began for the boat.

A hunting group was formed, comprising two frigates and two

destroyer-escorts. One of the latter, the USS *Gustafson,* located U 857 on the 7th, lying on the bottom NE of Cape Cod. The boat was destroyed in Hedgehog attacks.

There were no survivors, 59 dead.

U 858   Type IX C-40

Built by AG Weser, Bremen
Keel laid 11.12.42   Launched 17.6.43
Commissioned 30.9.43   Feldpost Nr M 52 646

Surrendered 14.5.45 at Cape May

Served with
4 U-Flottille, Stettin   September 1943 - April 1944 (ab)
2 U-Flottille, Lorient   May - September 1944 (fb)
33 U-Flottille, Flensburg   October 1944 - 14.5.45 (fb)

Commanded by
KL Thilo Bode   September 1943 - 14.5.45

Patrols: 2   Ships sunk: None

1. 12.6.44   Left Kiel for the North Atlantic.
U 858, U 804 and U 855 operated as weather boats. From 24.7.44 the escort-carrier USS *Wake Island* and her escort searched for them. Only U 804 was located and she escaped after sinking one of the destroyer-escorts.
U 858 put in to Farsund **27.9.44**

2. 28.9.44   Left Farsund and arrived Marviken **29.9.44**

3. 1.10.44   Left Marviken and arrived Flensburg **4.10.44**

4. 2.3.45   Left Kiel and arrived Horten **9.3.45**

5. 11.3.45   Left for the Western Atlantic.
On 14.4.45 the outward-bound U 858, U 518, U 546, U 805, U 880 and U 1235 were formed into *Seewolf* group N of the Azores. The boats were to sweep westwards across the North Atlantic convoy routes in an effort to draw some of the hunting groups from British coastal waters.
The USS *Block Island* and *Croatan* escort-carrier groups formed two lines in the expected path of *Seewolf* group. This was to prevent the boats reaching the US east coast to fire V2 rockets from towed launching pads, which was believed by the Americans to be their mission.
By the 24th only U 858 and U 805 had not been sunk and had succeeded in reaching the US coast. When the surrender order was given by Dönitz on 4.5.45 U 858 was still at sea and she was intercepted 300 miles S of Cape Race by the destroyer-escorts USS *Carter* and *Muir.* In accordance with instructions received, she was escorted to Cape May, where she surrendered on the 14th. U 858's crew were later interrogated at Portsmouth Navy Yard on the subject of missile-launching equipment being fitted to U-boats.

U 858 was later used by the US Navy. She was scuttled in 1947 after being used for torpedo trials.

U 859   Type IX D-2

Built by AG Weser, Bremen
Keel laid 15.5.42   Launched 2.3.43
Commissioned 8.7.43   Feldpost Nr M 53 706

Sunk 23.9.44 off Penang (05°46′N 100°04′E)

Served with
4 U-Flottille, Stettin   July 1943 - March 1944 (ab)
12 U-Flottille, Bordeaux   April 1944 - 23.9.44 (fb)

Commanded by
KL Johann Jebsen   July 1943 - 23.9.44

Patrols: 1   Ships sunk: 3 (20,853 grt)

1. 4.4.44   Left Kiel and arrived Marviken **6.4.44**

2. 8.4.44   Left for the Indian Ocean.
On the 26th U 859 torpedoed and sank the MV *Colin* (pa 6255t), a straggler from convoy SC 157, SE of Cape Farewell.
In late June U 859 arrived in the Indian Ocean and in the afternoon of 5.7.44 she was sighted as she surfaced by a St Lucia-based Catalina of 262 Squadron, 270 miles ESE of Durban. The aircraft was damaged by fire from the boat but she dropped five depth-charges, causing damage, including a punctured fuel tank. One crewman was killed and 3 others were wounded. U 198 was in the area at the time and she was also attacked and damaged. Both boats were hunted by aircraft and surface vessels but they managed to escape.
U 859 was hunted on August 22-23rd by aircraft and the sloop HMS *Banff* and the frigate HMS *Tay.* She escaped and made her way into the Gulf of Aden.
On the 27th U 859 reported an escorted tanker sunk but there is no confirmation of this. The SS *John Barry* (am 7176t) was torpedoed and sunk on the 28th S of Mirbat, Oman and on 1.9.44 the SS *Troilus* (br 7422t) was sunk E of Socotra, in the Arabian Sea.
U 859 then headed for Penang. She arrived and was about to go in when she was sighted by a patrolling British submarine, HMS *Trenchant* (Lt-Cdr A R Hezlet). Of the three torpedoes fired, one hit and sank U 859.
Trenchant surfaced and picked up 11 survivors, who were later landed at Trincomalee. 8 other survivors were picked up by the Japanese. U 859's commander and 46 other men lost their lives.

U 860   Type IX D-2

Built by AG Weser, Bremen
Keel laid 15.6.42   Launched 23.3.43
Commissioned 12.8.43   Feldpost Nr M 54 813

Sunk 15.6.44 S of St Helena (25°27′S 05°30′W)

Served with
4 U-Flottille, Stettin   August 1943 - March 1944 (ab)
12 U-Flottille, Bordeaux   April 1944 - 15.6.44 (fb)

Commanded by
FK Paul Büchel   August 1943 - 15.6.44

Patrols: 1   Ships sunk: None

On 24.10.43 Reichsminister Albert Speer was aboard U 860 during test drives.

U 860 (continued)

1. 11.4.44 Left Kiel for the Indian Ocean.

U 860 entered the South Atlantic at the beginning of June. In the morning of the 15th the boat was located some 600 miles S of St Helena by an Avenger of VC-9 (Ens G E Edwards) from the escort-carrier USS *Solomons*. The aircraft was shot down before Edwards could report his position.

A search began and U 860 was found on the surface in the late afternoon by Lt-Cdr H M Avery, the CO of VC-9. He circled until Wildcats and Avengers arrived on the scene from *Solomons*. The Wildcats made strafing attacks. U 860 remained surfaced and fired back against rocket attacks.

One of the Avengers (Lt W F Chamberlain) came in low and his depth-charges exploded as they hit U 860's casing. The aircraft was caught by the explosions and crashed into the sea. Chamberlain and his two crewmen were lost and U 860 sank soon afterwards.

The commander and 19 men were picked up and 44 others were lost.

U 861   Type IX D-2

Built by AG Weser, Bremen
Keel laid 15.7.42   Launched 29.4.43
Commissioned 2.9.43   Feldpost Nr M 54 873

Sunk 8.12.45 NE of Malin Head (55°25′N 07°16′W)

Served with
4 U-Flottille, Stettin   September 1943 - March 1944 (ab)
12 U-Flottille, Bordeaux   April - September 1944 (fb)
33 U-Flottille, Flensburg   October 1944 - 9.5.45 (fb)

Commanded by
KK Jürgen Oesten   September 1943 - 9.5.45

Patrols: 2   Ships sunk: 4 (22,048 grt) + 1 damaged

1. 20.4.44 Left for the South Atlantic.

U 861 operated off the coast of Brazil but failed to spot the US transport *William A Mann*, which left Rio de Janeiro on 2.7.44, carrying the first contingent of the Brazilian Expeditionary Force to Italy.

On the 20th U 861 torpedoed and sank the troop transport *Vital d'Oliveira* (bz 1737t) E of Rio de Janeiro and made an unsuccessful attack on the sub-chaser *Javari*. On the 24th the boat attacked convoy JT 39 SSW of Rio and sank the SS *William Gaston* (am 7177t).

U 861 was ordered to head for the southern tip of Africa, where she was to operate with U 862 in the area of Cape Town. She reached the Cape in early August but was then ordered to move up the east coast of South Africa.

Early on the 20th U 861 torpedoed and sank the SS *Berwickshire* (br 7464t) 400 miles E of Durban and in the evening the boat attacked convoy DN 68 and damaged the tanker MV *Daronia* (br 8139t). This vessel reached Durban on the 24th under her own power.

U 861 went up through the Mozambique Channel and on 5.9.44 sank the SS *Ioannis Fafalios* (gr 5670t) E of Mombasa.

The boat put in to Penang **23.9.44**

2. 1.11.44 Left Penang and arrived Shonan **2.11.44**

3. 3.11.44 Left Shonan and arrived Surabaya **5.11.44**

4. 15.1.45 Left Surabaya for Europe.

U 861 was one of the last Type IX boats to leave with a cargo of strategic material. She was carrying 100 tons of zinc. She moved

up through the South Atlantic and crossed the Equator in mid-March.

The boat put in to Trondheim **19.4.45**

U 861 was surrendered at Trondheim on 9.5.45. She left there on the 29th for a British assembly area.

She was one of 116 boats disposed of by the Royal Navy in Operation Deadlight. In early December 1945 she was towed from Lisahally by the tug HMS Freedom.

U 861 was sunk by gunfire on 8.12.45 by the Polish destroyer Blyskawica NE of Malin Head.

U 862   Type IX D-2

Built by AG Weser, Bremen
Keel laid 15.8.42   Launched 5.6.43
Commissioned 7.10.43   Feldpost Nr M 52 685

Handed over 6.5.45 at Singapore

Served with
4 U-Flottille, Stettin   October 1943 - April 1944 (ab)
12 U-Flottille, Bordeaux   May - September 1944 (fb)
33 U-Flottille, Flensburg   October 1944 - 6.5.45 (fb)

Commanded by
KK Heinrich Timm   October 1943 - 6.5.45

Patrols: 2   Ships sunk: 7 (42,374 grt)

1. 20.5.44 Left Kiel and arrived Bergen **26.5.44**

2. 27.5.44 Left Bergen and arrived Narvik **30.5.44**

3. 3.6.44 Left for the Indian Ocean.

U 862 passed through Denmark Strait into the North Atlantic. By the 24th she was W of the Azores and moving south into the Central Atlantic.

Early on 25.7.44 U 862 torpedoed and sank the SS *Robin Goodfellow* (am 6885t) WSW of St Helena. An order for U 862 to operate with U 861 off Cape Town was changed and both boats were ordered to move up the east coast of South Africa.

On 13.8.44 U 862 torpedoed and sank the SS *Radbury* (br 3614t) at the southern end of the Mozambique Channel. The boat moved up through the Channel and at the northern end she sank three ships, the SS *Empire Lancer* (br 7037t) on the 16th, the SS *Nairung* (br 5414t) and the SS *Wayfarer* (br 5068t) on the 19th.

U 862 was sighted on the surface on the 20th by a Catalina of 265 Squadron (F/Lt J S Lough). The boat stayed surfaced and awaited the aircraft's approach. The Catalina flew in low through heavy flak. When it seemed that Lough would hit U 862, Timm put her hard astarboard and the aircraft just missed the conning tower, crashed into the sea and exploded. Her entire crew was lost.

Knowing that a search for him was inevitable, Timm abandoned any thought of going to the Gulf of Aden and headed for Penang.

U 862 reached there on **9.9.44**

4. 12.9.44 Left Penang and arrived Shonan **13.9.44**

5. 6.11.44 Left Shonan and arrived Batavia **8.11.44**

6. 18.11.44 Left Batavia for operations.

U 862 was to cruise around the coast of Australia. She set out through the Sunda Strait and then due south, passing west of Australia. On the 23rd the boat steered southeastwards and then from the 28th moved eastwards along the southern coast of Australia.

On 9.12.44 the SS *Ilissos* (gr 4724t) was found off the coast S of

Adelaide. U 862's commander attempted to sink the vessel by gunfire, a difficult task in the prevailing rough sea conditions. *Ilissos'* naval gunners returned U 862's fire, forcing the boat to submerge. The vessel escaped in heavy rain.

U 862 evaded a search by ships and aircraft and made her way south of Tasmania. In the early hours of the 25th she torpedoed and sank the SS *Robert J Walker* (am 7180t) off shore S of Sydney. Once again, U 862 evaded the searching ships and aircraft.

The boat moved northeastwards from the 27th until 1.1.45, when she went due east across the Tasman Sea. The northernmost point in New Zealand, Cape Reinga, was rounded on the 7th and U 862 moved down the east coast. No ships large enough to be worthy of attention were sighted during the boat's progress southwards and on the 21st U 862 was once again in the Tasman Sea, heading westwards back towards Australia.

The boat did not go close to land this time but kept well to the south. U 862 was already 1000 miles W of Flinders Bay, Western Australia on 6.2.45, when she torpedoed and sank the SS *Peter Silvester* (am 7176t).

U 862 returned to Batavia **15.2.45**

On U 862's two cruises she carried a Bachstelze (Water Wagtail), a small, folding rotorkite. This machine, the Focke Angelis FA 330 A-1, carried a man and when towed behind a U-boat on 500 feet of cable, could rise to 400 feet, lifted by the unpowered three-blade rotor, which revolved as the Bachstelze was towed into the wind by the U-boat.

At maximum height, the Bachstelze pilot, who had a parachute, could see 25 miles in every direction, as opposed to the view from the conning tower of 5 miles. The Bachstelze could only be used in remote situations, with no fear of disturbance by aircraft or ships, the U-boat being completely unable to submerge while it was being used.

On U 862, the ship's doctor, Jobst Schaefer, was the Bachstelze pilot.

7. 18.2.45 Left Batavia and arrived Shonan **20.2.45**

U 862 was to return to Europe but she had not left Singapore before the German surrender was announced.

On 6.5.45 the Japanese informed the German senior officers in Singapore that all German service personnel were to be interned. U 862 was taken over and became part of the Imperial Japanese Navy as I 502.

When the British took over Singapore in late August the Germans went to Pasir Panjang camp there. On 17.10.45 they were marched to Changi Prison, where they were housed in the barracks.

U 862's men left Singapore on 28.6.46 in the Empress of Australia, *arriving at Liverpool on July 20th. Repatriation for most did not begin until 1947 and some did not get home until the end of the year.*

On 14.2.46 U 862 was towed out of Singapore by the tug HMS Growler. The boat was scuttled in 52 fathoms in the Malacca Strait in the evening of the 15th and finally dispatched by three Squid mortar bombs from the frigate HMS Loch Lomond.

U 863 Type IX D-2

Built by AG Weser, Bremen
Keel laid 15.9.42   Launched 29.6.43
Commissioned 3.11.43   Feldpost Nr M 53 881

Sunk 29.9.44 ESE of Recife (10°45´S 25°30´W)

Served with
4 U-Flottille, Stettin November 1943 - June 1944 (ab)
12 U-Flottille, Bordeaux July 1944 - 29.9.44 (fb)

Commanded by
KL Dietrich von der Esch November 1943 - 29.9.44

Patrols: 2   Ships sunk: None

1. 3.7.44 Left Kiel and arrived Horten **5.7.44**

2. 10.7.44 Left Horten and arrived Bergen **13.7.44**

3. 20.7.44 Left for the Indian Ocean.
Outward-bound, U 863 was attacked on the 21st by a Mosquito of 333 (Norwegian) Squadron (Lt R Leithe). She was damaged in attacks with depth-charges and cannon and machine-gun fire.
The boat returned to Bergen **21.7.44**

4. 26.7.44 Left for the Indian Ocean.
U 863 was moving through the South Atlantic when she was spotted on the surface on 29.9.44 ESE of Recife by a USN Liberator of VP-107 (Lt J T Burton) from Natal, Brazil. The aircraft approached and dropped five depth-bombs which straddled the boat. U 863 lost speed, leaving an oil slick. She did not put up any flak.
The Liberator made a second run. The remaining bombs hung up and a strafing attack was met by return fire. Another Liberator (Lt E A Krug) arrived but as it approached U 863 turned sharply to port. The two aircraft ran in together and their strafing silenced U 863's guns. Burton's depth-bombs again failed to release. Krug dropped six bombs in his second attack but all fell short and the aircraft was damaged by return fire. In his third attack, Krug dropped three depth-bombs, straddling the boat and seriously damaging her. His aircraft also received further damage.
U 863's crew were seen to be abandoning ship, as she sank very rapidly. Burton made another approach and finally dropped his remaining bombs in the oil slick after U 863 sank. A third Liberator arrived (Lt Roewer) and the three aircraft dropped liferafts to about 20 men seen in the oil slick.
No survivors were ever picked up, 68 dead.

U 864 Type IX D-2

Built by AG Weser, Bremen
Keel laid 26.10.42   Launched 12.8.43
Commissioned 9.12.43   Feldpost Nr M 54 842

Sunk 9.2.45 off Fedje (60°46´N 04°35´E)

Served with
4 U-Flottille, Stettin December 1943 - October 1944 (ab)
33 U-Flottille, Flensburg November 1944 - 9.2.45 (fb)

Commanded by
KK Rolf-Reimar Wolfram December 1943 - 9.2.45

Patrols: 1   Ships sunk: None

U 864 (continued)

1. 5.12.44 Left Kiel and arrived Horten **9.12.44**

2. 27.12.44 Left Horten and arrived Farsund **30.12.44**

3. 1.1.45 Left Farsund and arrived Bergen **5.1.45**

On 12.1.45 U 864 was damaged in a raid on the U-boat pens at Bergen by 9 and 617 Squadrons of RAF Bomber Command.

4. 7.2.45 Left Bergen for operations.
Outward-bound, U 864 was detected off Fedje by the patrolling British submarine *Venturer* (Lt J S Launders). Her periscope and radio mast were sighted.
Still submerged, *Venturer* ran on a parallel course with U 864 for an hour before firing four torpedoes. One positive explosion was heard, followed by breaking-up noises. Launders went to investigate and the oil slick and floating wreckage confirmed U 864's destruction. It is possibly the only occasion when one submarine sank another whilst both were submerged.
There were no survivors from U 864, 73 dead.

U 865   Type IX C-40

Built by AG Weser, Bremen
Keel laid 5.1.43   Launched 11.7.43
Commissioned 25.10.43   Feldpost Nr M 53 961

Missing after 8.9.44, position unknown

Served with
4 U-Flottille, Stettin October 1943 - June 1944 (ab)
10 U-Flottille, Lorient July - September 1944 (fb)

Commanded by
OL Dietrich Stellmacher October 1943 - September 1944

Patrols: 5   Ships sunk: None

1. 20.6.44 Left Kiel for operations.
Outward-bound, U 865 developed trouble with her schnorkel and returned, putting into Trondheim **5.7.44**

2. 27.7.44 Left for operations.
Outward-bound the same day, U 865 was attacked by a Liberator of 86 Squadron (F/O G G Gates). In the face of heavy flak, the aircraft dropped six depth-charges which damaged the boat. The Liberator had two engines damaged.
U 865 returned to Trondheim **28.7.44**

3. 1.8.44 Left for operations.
U 865 again developed a schnorkel defect.
She returned to Trondheim **3.8.44**

4. 10.8.44 Left for operations.
For the third time U 865 returned to base with schnorkel trouble.
She reached Trondheim **13.8.44**

5. 8.9.44 Left for operations.
U 865 was not heard from again and her loss is attributed to an unknown cause. However, it would seem likely that she was the victim of a schnorkel accident.
There were no known survivors, 59 dead.

U 866   Type IX C-40

Built by AG Weser, Bremen
Keel laid 23.1.43   Launched 29.7.43
Commissioned 17.11.43   Feldpost Nr M 54 899

Sunk 16.3.45 SW of Sable Island (43°18′N 61°08′W)

Served with
4 U-Flottille, Stettin November 1943 - July 1944 (ab)
10 U-Flottille, Lorient July - October 1944 (fb)
33 U-Flottille, Flensburg October 1944 - 16.3.45 (fb)

Commanded by
KK Walter Pommerehne November 1943 - September 1944
OL Peter Rogowsky September 1944 - 16.3.45

Patrols: 1   Ships sunk: None

On 24.6.44 U 866 was badly damaged in an RAF bombing raid on Bremen. She underwent lengthy repairs.

1. 21.1.45 Left Kiel and arrived Horten **23.1.45**

2. 26.1.45 Left Horten and arrived Kristiansand **27.1.45**

3. 30.1.45 Left Kristiansand and arrived Bergen **2.2.45**

4. 6.2.45 Left for US waters.
U 866 was one of the last boats to operate off the US east coast. On 10.3.45 she unsuccessfully attacked two ships E of Cape Cod. Two Canadian naval groups, EG 16 and EG 27, were already searching for U 866 after transmissions from the boat had been picked up.
Also searching for U 866 was a USCG group, TG 22.14, and it was the destroyer-escort USS *Lowe* from this group which located the boat on the 16th SW of Sable Island. After an unsuccessful Hedgehog attack by *Lowe*, U 866 went to the bottom. Following a second attack, wreckage and oil came to the surface. Many depth-charges were fired in the area later on the 16th and again on the 17th by *Lowe* and the other destroyer-escorts of the group, USS *Menges* (Lt-Cdr F M McCabe), *Pride* (Lt-Cdr H W Buxton) and *Mosely* (Lt-Cdr E P MacBride). When the group commander was sure of U 866's destruction, the attacks ceased. EG 16 and EG 27, which had gone to other duties, did not come up in time.
There were no survivors from U 866, 55 dead.

U 867   Type IX C-40

Built by AG Weser, Bremen
Keel laid 5.2.43   Launched 24.8.43
Commissioned 12.12.43   Feldpost Nr M 54 950

Sunk 19.9.44 W of Stadlandet (62°15′N 01°50′E)

Served with
4 U-Flottille, Stettin December 1943 - August 1944 (ab)
11 U-Flottille, Bergen September 1944 (fb)

Commanded by
KzS Arved von Mühlendahl December 1943 - 19.9.44

Patrols: 1   Ships sunk: None

1. 9.9.44 Left Kiel and arrived Kristiansand **11.9.44**

2. 12.9.44 Left Kristiansand for the North Atlantic.

U 867 was ordered to set up an unmanned weather station in North America. Outward-bound on the 18th, the boat was attacked by a Mosquito of 248 Squadron (WO H A Corbin).

The boat may have been damaged in this attack because she was sighted on the surface next day in the Norwegian Sea, W of Stadlandet by a Liberator of 224 Squadron (F/Lt H J Rayner). It is possible that U 867 was unable to dive because of a diesel defect.

The aircraft approached through heavy flak and the six depth-charges dropped all overshot. U 867 sank soon afterwards, going down on an even keel, which suggests that she was scuttled. Some 50 men were seen in dinghies in the oily sea.

There were no survivors picked up, 60 dead.

U 868   Type IX C-40

Built by AG Weser, Bremen
Keel laid 21.3.43   Launched 18.9.43
Commissioned 23.12.43   Feldpost Nr M 16 800

Sunk 28.11.45 NW of Malin Head (55°48′N 08°33′W)

Served with
4 U-Flottille, Stettin   December 1943 - July 1944 (ab)
2 U-Flottille, Lorient   August - September 1944 (fb)
33 U-Flottille, Flensburg   October 1944 - 9.5.45 (fb-t)

Commanded by
KL Dietrich Rauch   December 1943 - July 1944
OL Eduard Turre   July 1944 - 9.5.45

Patrols: 2   Ships sunk: None
                1 minesweeper (672 dt)

1. **5.1.45**   Left Kiel and arrived Horten **9.1.45**

2. **21.1.45**   Left Horten on transport duty.
U 868 carried essential stores and ammuntion to St Nazaire. Whilst there, she supplied fuel to U 255.
U 868 put in to St Nazaire **18.2.45**

3. **14.3.45**   Left to return to Norway.
Outward-bound, U 868 torpedoed and sank the minesweeper HMCS *Guysborough* in the evening of the 17th SW of Brest.
U 868 put in to Kristiansand **10.4.45**

4. **14.4.45**   Left Kristiansand and arrived Bergen **17.4.45**

U 868 was surrendered at Bergen on 9.9.45. She left there on the 30th for an assembly point in Britain.

She was one of 116 boats disposed of by the Royal Navy in Operation Deadlight. *In late December 1945 U 868 was towed from Loch Ryan out through the North Channel by the tug HMS* Saucy.

The boat sank on 28.11.45, when the towline parted and she went in a steep dive down to 70 fathoms NW of Malin Head.

U 869   Type IX C-40

Built by AG Weser, Bremen
Keel laid 5.4.43   Launched 5.10.43
Commissioned 26.1.44   Feldpost Nr M 49 163

Sunk 28.2.45 ENE of Atlantic City (39°33′N 73°02′W)

Served with
4 U-Flottille, Stettin   January - November 1944 (ab)
33 U-Flottille, Flensburg   December 1944 - 28.2.45 (fb)

Commanded by
KL Hellmut Neuerburg   January 1944 - 28.2.45

Patrols: 1   Ships sunk: None

1. **23.11.44**   Left Kiel and arrived Horten **27.11.44**

2. **3.12.44**   Left Horten and arrived Kristiansand **4.12.44**

3. **8.12.44**   Left for operations.
U 869 was to operate in the Gibraltar area. On 31.1.45 she may have attacked a destroyer W of the Straits.
On 28.2.45 U 869 was off the US east coast, ENE of Atlantic City. She was located and sunk in depth-charge attacks by two destroyer-escorts, the USS *Fowler* (Lt-Cdr S F Morris) and the French *L'Indescret*.
There were no survivors, 57 dead.

U 870   Type IX C-40

Built by AG Weser, Bremen
Keel laid 29.4.43   Launched 29.10.43
Commissioned 3.2.44   Feldpost Nr M 49 432

Bombed 30.3.45 at Bremen

Served with
4 U-Flottille, Stettin   February - September 1944 (ab)
33 U-Flottille, Flensburg   October 1944 - 30.3.45 (fb)

Commanded by
KK Ernst Hechler   February 1944 - 30.3.45

Patrols: 1   Ships sunk: 1 (4637 grt) + 2 damaged
                              1 LST (1490 dt)
                              1 patrol craft (335 dt)

1. **31.10.44**   Left Kiel and arrived Horten **3.11.44**

2. **10.11.44**   Left for the North Atlantic.
U 870 was one of four boats on weather-reporting duties, as part of the information-gathering preparations for the forthcoming offensive in the Ardennes.
With her duty completed, U 870 headed for the Gibraltar area. On 20.12.44 she was overrun by a convoy of 21 ships, including some under tow that had been damaged in the invasion of Normandy. U 870 torpedoed two ships ENE of the Azores, sinking LST 359 and hitting the destroyer-escort USS *Fogg*, which was towed into port with a damaged stern.
U 870 operated W of Gibraltar for three weeks and attacked several convoys. On 3.1.45 she damaged the SS *Henry Miller* (am 7207t) of convoy GUS 63, just W of the Straits. In the same area U 870 claimed two ships torpedoed on the 8th but there is no confirmation of this. On the 9th she sank the French patrol craft

U 870 (continued)

L'Enjoue and on the 10th she torpedoed and sank the SS *Blackheath* (br 4637t).

The boat returned to Norway and put in to Kristiansand **20.2.45**

3. 25.2.45 Left Kristiansand and arrived Flensburg **27.2.45**

U 870 was destroyed on 30.3.45 in a USAF daylight raid by B17s on Bremen.

U 871 Type IX D-2

Built by AG Weser, Bremen
Keel laid 14.11.42   Launched 7.9.43
Commissioned 15.1.44   Feldpost Nr M 19 451

Sunk 26.9.44 NW of the Azores (43°18′N 36°28′W)

Served with
4 U-Flottille, Stettin   January - July 1944 (ab)
12 U-Flottille, Bordeaux   August 1944 - 26.9.44 (fb)

Commanded by
KL Erwin Ganzer   January 1944 - 26.9.44

Patrols: 1   Ships sunk: None

1. 19.8.44 Left Kiel and arrived Kristiansand **21.8.44**

2. 24.8.44 Left Kristiansand and arrived Trondheim **28.8.44**

3. 31.8.44 Left Trondheim for operations.
U 871 was en route to the Indian Ocean. On 26.9.44 she was sunk in a depth-charge attack by a Fortress of 220 Squadron (F/Lt A F Wallace) NW of the Azores.
There were no survivors, 69 dead.

U 872 Type IX D-2

Built by AG Weser, Bremen
Keel laid 23.12.42   Launched 20.10.43
Commissioned 10.2.44   Feldpost Nr M 50 158

Decommissioned 10.8.44 at Bremen

Served with
4 U-Flottille, Stettin   February 1944 - 29.7.44 (ab)

Commanded by
KL Peter-Ottmar Grau   February 1944 - 29.7.44

Patrols: None   Ships sunk: None

U 872 had presumably completed her training at 4 U-Flottille and had gone to Bremen for an overhaul before going on operations.

On 29.7.44 the boat was badly damaged in a USAF bombing raid on Bremen and one crewman was killed and three others wounded.

U 872 was decommissioned on 10.8.44 and later broken up.

U 873 Type IX D-2

Built by AG Weser, Bremen
Keel laid 17.2.43   Launched 16.11.43
Commissioned 1.3.44   Feldpost Nr M 50 271

Surrendered 17.5.45 at Portsmouth, Maine

Served with
4 U-Flottille, Stettin   March 1944 - January 1945 (ab)
33 U-Flottille, Flensburg   February 1945 - 17.5.45 (fb)

Commanded by
KL Friedrich Steinhoff   March 1944 - 17.5.45

Patrols: 1   Ships sunk: None

1. 17.2.45 Left Kiel and arrived Horten **22.2.45**

2. 21.3.45 Left Horten and arrived Kristiansand **22.3.45**

3. 30.3.45 Left for operations.
U 873 was still at sea when the U-boat war ended on May 4th. In accordance with instructions given, the boat made her way to the Portsmouth Navy Yard, New Hampshire, arriving there **17.5.45.**

After surrendering, U 873's commander, KL Steinhoff, was interrogated at the Navy Yard on missile-launching equipment on U-boats. He had taken part in the submerged rocket-launching trials at Peenemünde in June 1942.

A few days after surrendering, Steinhoff committed suicide in Charles Street Prison, Boston. It seems likely that he received the same sort of rough treatment as that meted out to the men from U 546 on the same subject and probably by the same American interrogation team.

U 873 became a US war prize and she was broken up in 1948.

U 874 Type IX D-2

Built by AG Weser, Bremen
Keel laid 27.3.43   Launched 21.12.43
Commissioned 8.4.44   Feldpost Nr M 00 459

Sunk 31.12.45 NW of Bloody Foreland (55°47′N 09°27′W)

Served with
4 U-Flottille, Stettin   April 1944 - February 1945 (ab)
33 U-Flottille, Flensburg   March 1945 - 9.5.45 (fb-oE)

Commanded by
OL Theodor Petersen   April 1944 - 9.5.45

Patrols: None   Ships sunk: None

At the end of the war U 874 may have been scheduled to transport mercury, lead and optical glass to Japan but she never sailed.

The boat was surrendered at Horten on 9.5.45 and on the 29th left for a British assembly area. She was one of 116 boats disposed of by the Royal Navy in Operation Deadlight.

In late December 1945 U 874 was towed from Lisahally by the destroyer HMS Mendip. When the towline parted, the boat was sunk by gunfire by the destroyer HMS Offa on 31.12.45 NW of Bloody Foreland.

U 875   Type IX D-2

Built by AG Weser, Bremen
Keel laid 12.5.43   Launched 16.2.44
Commissioned 21.4.44   Feldpost Nr M 19 456

Sunk 31.12.45 NW of Malin Head (55°41′N 08°28′W)

Served with
4 U-Flottille, Stettin   April 1944 - February 1945 (ab)
33 U-Flottille, Flensburg   March 1945 - 9.5.45 (fb-oE)

Commanded by
KL Georg Preuss   April 1944 - 9.5.45

Patrols: None   Ships sunk: None

*At the end of the war U 875 may have been scheduled to transport
mercury, lead and optical glass to Japan but she never sailed.*

*The boat was surrendered at Bergen on 9.5.45 and on the 30th
she left for a British assembly area. She was one of 116 boats
disposed of by the Royal Navy in* Operation Deadlight.

*In late December 1945 U 875 was towed from Lisahally by the
frigate HMS* Cubitt. *She was sunk by gunfire by the destroyer HMS*
Offa *on 31.12.45 NW of Malin Head.*

U 876   Type IX D-2

Built by AG Weser, Bremen
Keel laid 5.6.43   Launched 29.2.44
Commissioned 24.5.44   Feldpost Nr M 36 700

Scuttled 4.5.45 in Eckernförder Bucht

Served with
4 U-Flottille, Stettin   May 1944 - 4.5.45 (ab)

Commanded by
KL Rolf Bahn   May 1944 - 4.5.45

Patrols: None   Ships sunk: None

*In the final days of the war U-boats that were able to dive were
ordered to proceed to Norway.*

*U 876 may have been on her way there when she was attacked
and damaged by RAF aircraft on 3.5.45. The boat was scuttled off
Aschau in Eckernförder Bucht on the 4th.*

U 877   Type IX C-40

Built by AG Weser, Bremen
Keel laid 22.5.43   Launched 10.12.43
Commissioned 24.3.44   Feldpost Nr M 50 294

Sunk 27.12.44 NW of the Azores (46°25′N 36°38′W)

Served with
4 U-Flottille, Stettin   March - November 1944 (ab)
33 U-Flottille, Flensburg   December 1944 (fb)

Commanded by
KL Eberhard Findeisen   March 1944 - 27.12.44

Patrols: 1   Ships sunk: None

1. 11.11.44   Left Kiel and arrived Horten **18.11.44**

2. 25.11.44   Left for the North Atlantic.
   U 877 was to have carried out weather-reporting but after
difficulties with her radio she was released from this duty.
   On 27.12.44 U 877 was overrun by eastbound convoy HX 327
NW of the Azores. She was located by one of the escorts, the
corvette HMCS *St Thomas* (Lt-Cdr L P Denny) of the 3rd EG. Two
Squid bombs were fired, the second of which seriously damaged
the boat.
   U 877 surfaced and immediately came under fire from *St Thomas*.
The boat's crew began to abandon ship, the firing ceased and U 877
quickly sank.
   There were no casualties, 55 survivors.

U 878   Type IX C-40

Built by AG Weser, Bremen
Keel laid 16.6.43   Launched 6.1.44
Commissioned 14.4.44   Feldpost Nr M 00 518

Sunk 10.4.45 WSW of Brest (47°35′N 10°33′W)

Served with
4 U-Flottille, Stettin   April 1944 - January 1945 (ab)
33 U-Flottille, Flensburg   February 1945 - 10.4.45 (fb-t)

Commanded by
KL Johannes Rodig   April 1944 - 10.4.45

Patrols: 2   Ships sunk: None

1. 30.1.45   Left Kiel and arrived Horten **2.2.45**

2. 9.2.45   Left Horten on transport duty.
   U 878 carried essential stores and ammunition to St Nazaire.
Whilst there, she supplied fuel to U 255.
   U 878 put in to St Nazaire **20.3.45**

3. 6.4.45   Left to return to Norway.
   On the 10th U 878 attempted to attack convoy ON 295 WSW of
Brest. She was located and sunk by the destroyer HMS *Vanquisher*
(Lt-Cdr F M Osbourne) and the corvette HMS *Tintagel Castle*
(Lt R Atkinson).
   There were no survivors, 51 dead.

U 879   Type IX C-40

Built by AG Weser, Bremen
Keel laid 26.6.43   Launched 11.1.44
Commissioned 19.4.44   Feldpost Nr M 00 832

Sunk 30.4.45 E of Norfolk, Virginia (36°34′N 74°00′W)

Served with
4 U-Flottille, Stettin   April 1944 - January 1945 (ab)
33 U-Flottille, Flensburg   February 1945 - 30.4.45 (fb)

Commanded by
KL Erwin Manchen   April 1944 - 30.4.45

Patrols: 1   Ships sunk: 2 (15,259 grt) + 1 damaged

1. 27.1.45   Left Kiel and arrived Horten **31.1.45**

2. 9.2.45   Left Horten and arrived Kristiansand **10.2.45**

U 879 (continued)

3. 11.2.45 Left for US waters.

U 879 transmitted weather reports between March 6th and 15th, after which she was ordered to operate in the Cape Hatteras area.

On 14.4.45 U 879 torpedoed and sank the SS *Belgian Airman* (be 6959t) ESE of Cape Henry. In foggy weather on the 18th she sank the tanker SS *Swiftscout* (am 8300t) E of Cape Charles. On the 23rd U 879 torpedoed and damaged the tanker MV *Katy* (nw 6825t) E of Kitty Hawk. This vessel was taken into Lynnhaven Bay and later repaired.

During the night of the 29/30th U 879 was preparing to attack convoy KN 382 E of Norfolk, Virginia when she was located by the escort. The boat was sunk in the early morning of the 30th in depth-charge attacks by the destroyer-escorts USS *Natchez*, *Coffman*, *Bostwick* (Lt-Cdr H J Church) and *Thomas* (Lt-Cdr D M Kellogg) of TG 02.10.

There were no survivors, 52 dead.

U 880   Type IX C-40

Built by AG Weser, Bremen
Keel laid 17.7.43   Launched 10.2.44
Commissioned 11.5.44   Feldpost Nr M 19 687

Sunk 16.4.45 N of the Azores (47°53′N 30°26′W)

Served with
4 U-Flottille, Stettin May - November 1944 (ab)
33 U-Flottille, Flensburg November 1944 - 16.4.45 (fb)

Commanded by
KL Gerhard Schötzau May 1944 - 16.4.45

Patrols: 1   Ships sunk: None

1. 11.1.45 Left Kiel and arrived Horten **15.1.45**

2. 23.1.45 Left Horten and arrived Bergen **29.1.45**

3. 7.2.45 Left Bergen and returned **9.2.45**

4. 14.3.45 Left Bergen for the Western Atlantic.

The outward-bound U 880, U 518, U 546, U 805, U 858 and U 1235 were formed into *Seewolf* group on 14.4.45 N of the Azores. The boats were to sweep westwards across the North Atlantic convoy routes in an effort to draw some of the hunting groups from British coastal waters.

The USS *Block Island* and *Croatan* escort-carrier groups formed two lines in the expected path of *Seewolf* group. This was to prevent the boats reaching the US east coast to fire V2 rockets from towed launching pads, which was believed by the Americans to be their mission.

Late on the 15th the destroyer-escort USS Stanton had located U 1235 and then sunk her soon after midnight. Forty minutes later USS *Frost* (Lt-Cdr A E Ritchie) made contact with another boat, this one moving on the surface, U 880. *Frost* pursued in the fog and heavy seas, followed by the *Stanton* (Lt-Cdr J C Kiley) and U 880 was finally caught in a searchlight. *Frost* began firing and the boat dived. The two warships carried out Hedgehog attacks in appalling conditions for their crews. Eventually there were underwater explosions and U 880 had been destroyed.

There were no survivors, 49 dead.

U 881   Type IX C-40

Built by AG Weser, Bremen
Keel laid 7.8.43   Launched 4.3.44
Commissioned 27.5.44   Feldpost Nr M 19 715

Sunk 6.5.45 SE of Cape Race (43°18′N 47°44′W)

Served with
4 U-Flottille, Stettin May 1944 - February 1945 (ab)
33 U-Flottille, Flensburg March 1945 - 6.5.45 (fb)

Commanded by
KL Dr Karl-Heinz Frischke May 1944 - 6.5.45

Patrols: 1   Ships sunk: None

1. 11.3.45 Left Kiel and arrived Horten **16.3.45**

2. 19.3.45 Left Horten but turned back with schnorkel failure. U 881 put in to Bergen **30.3.45**

3. 7.4.45 Left for US waters.

U 881 was originally ordered to join *Seewolf* group but did not do so because of having to put in to Bergen. She headed for the US east coast independently and was probably the boat sighted by an Avenger of VC-19 (Lt-Cdr W W South) in the afternoon of the 23rd 70 miles northwest of the escort-carrier USS *Bogue*. The boat dived as two depth-charges straddled her and she escaped.

Early on 6.5.45 U 881 was located SE of Cape Race by the destroyer-escort USS *Farquhar* (Lt-Cdr D E Walter) as she approached the escort-carrier USS *Mission Bay*. The boat was sunk in one depth-charge attack. She possibly had not heard the surrender order of May 4th.

There were no survivors, 52 dead.

U 882 had not been completed when she was destroyed in the AG Weser yard at Bremen on 30.3.45 in a USAF daylight raid.

U 883   Type IX C-42

Built by AG Weser, Bremen
Keel laid 27.7.43   Launched 28.4.44
Commissioned 27.3.45   Feldpost Nr M 32 765

Sunk 31.12.45 NNW of Bloody Foreland (55°44′N 08°46′W)

Served with
4 U-Flottille, Stettin March - May 1945 (ab)

Commanded by
OL Johannes Uebel March - May 1945

Patrols: None   Ships sunk: None

U 883's transfer journey from Bremerhaven to Norway was interrrupted by the surrender on May 4th. She put in to Cuxhaven and was surrendered there to the Allies.

The boat was moved later to Wilhelmshaven and on 21.6.45 she was taken to the assembly area at Lisahally in Lough Foyle.

U 883 was one of 116 boats disposed of by the Royal Navy in Operation Deadlight. *In late December 1945 she was towed from Lisahally by the frigate HMS* Cosby.

The boat was sunk by gunfire on 31.12.45 by the destroyer HMS Offa *NNW of Bloody Foreland.*

U 884 was destroyed on 30.3.45 in a bombing raid on the AG Weser shipyard at Bremen. She was still under construction.

U 885 - U 888 were never completed, orders cancelled.

U 889   Type IX C-40

Built by AG Weser, Bremen
Keel laid 13.9.43   Launched 5.4.44
Commissioned 4.8.44   Feldpost Nr M 37 894

Surrendered 13.5.45 at Shelburne, Nova Scotia

Served with
4 U-Flottille, Stettin   August 1944 - March 1945 (ab)
33 U-Flottille, Flensburg   March 1945 - 13.5.45 (fb)

Commanded by
KL Friedrich Braeucker   August 1944 - 13.5.45

Patrols: 1   Ships sunk: None

1. 26.3.45   Left Kiel and arrived Horten **30.3.45**

2. 2.4.45   Left Horten and arrived Kristiansand **3.4.45**

3. 5.4.45   Left for US waters.
   U 889 was ordered to harass shipping off the Port of New York. She was sighted by an RCAF Liberator on 10.5.45 250 miles SE of Flemish Cap. The aircraft reported the sighting and approached the boat. The black flag of surrender was hoisted and U 889's crew waved their arms. A Canadian escort group intercepted the boat 175 miles SSE of Cape Race and escorted her in to the RCN base at Shelburne, Nova Scotia, where she surrendered on the 13th. U 889 and U 190 were the last two U-boats in Canadian waters.

In June 1945 U 889 was commissioned into the Royal Canadian Navy. In late 1945 she was allocated to the US under the terms of the Tripartite Naval Commission agreement.
   On 11.1.46 the boat was sailed by an RCN crew to Portsmouth Navy Yard and handed over to the US Navy. She was scuttled in 1947 after being used for torpedo trials.

U 890 and U 891 were damaged in a bombing raid on Bremen on 29.7.44, whilst still under construction. They were never rebuilt.

U 892 - U 900 were never built, orders cancelled.

U 901   Type VII C

Built by AG Vulkan, Stettin
Keel laid 10.1.42   Launched 9.10.43
Commissioned 29.4.44   Feldpost Nr M 24 797

Sunk 6.1.46 NW of Malin Head (55°50´N 08°30´W)

Served with
4 U-Flottille, Stettin   April 1944 - March 1945 (ab)
11 U-Flottille, Bergen   March 1945 - 15.5.45 (fb)

Commanded by
KL Hans Schrenk   April 1944 - 15.5.45

Patrols: 1   Ships sunk: None

1. 29.3.45   Left Kiel and arrived Stavanger **6.4.45**

2. 14.4.45   Left for operations.
   U 901 went to an area W of the British Isles. She was still at sea when surrender was announced on May 4th.
   The boat returned to Stavanger and surrendered **15.5.45**

U 901 left Stavanger on 29.5.45 for an assembly area in Britain.
   She was one of 116 boats disposed of by the Royal Navy in Operation Deadlight. In early January 1946 she was towed from Lisahally by the frigate HMS Loch Shin *and sunk by gunfire on 6.1.46 NW of Malin Head.*

U 902 was never built, order cancelled.

U 903   Type VII C

Built by Flender Werft, Lübeck
Keel laid 31.8.42   Launched 17.7.43
Commissioned 4.9.43   Feldpost Nr M 54 904

Scuttled 3.5.45 at Kiel

Served with
23 U-Flottille, Danzig   September 1943 - February 1945 (ab)
31 U-Flottille, Hamburg   February 1945 - 3.5.45 (ab)

Commanded by
OL Otto Fränzel   September 1943 - April 1945
KL Otto Tinschert   April 1945 - 3.5.45

Patrols: None   Ships sunk: None

U 903 was on training duties. She was scuttled at Kiel on 3.5.45 and the wreck was broken up in 1947.

U 904   Type VII C

Built by Flender Werft, Lübeck
Keel laid 10.9.42   Launched 7.8.43
Commissioned 25.9.43   Feldpost Nr M 52 703

Scuttled 5.5.45 at Eckernförde

Served with
23 U-Flottille, Danzig   September 1943 - February 1945 (ab)
5 U-Flottille, Kiel   March 1945 - 5.5.45 (ab)

Commanded by
OL Detlef Fritz   September - November 1943
OL Dieter Erdmann   December 1943 - June 1944
OL Günter Stührmann   June 1944 - 5.5.45

Patrols: None   Ships sunk: None

U 904 was on training duties.On 4.5.45, when the surrender order was made, she was one of many boats awaiting further orders in the bays of Northern Germany. She was in Eckernförder Bucht when she was damaged on that day in a rocket attack by RAF Typhoons.
   On 30.4.45 instructions for the scuttling of the German fleet, Operation Regenbogen, had gone out from Dönitz to commanders. On May 4th these orders were carried ot by some commanders, contrary to the surrender terms.
   The damaged U 904 was scuttled on 5.5.45 in Eckernförder Bucht.

U 905   Type VII C

Built by Stülcken Sohn, Hamburg
Keel laid 26.1.43   Launched 20.11.43
Commissioned 8.3.44   Feldpost Nr M 49 263

Sunk 20.3.45 N of Cape Wrath (59°42′N 04°55′W)

Served with
31 U-Flottille, Hamburg   March - November 1944 (ab)
11 U-Flottille, Bergen   December 1944 - 20.3.45 (fb)

Commanded by
OL Heinz Brüllau   March - June 1944
OL Bernhard Schwarting   June 1944 - 20.3.45

Patrols: 2   Ships sunk: None

1. **1.12.44**   Left Kiel and arrived Horten **4.12.44**

2. **9.12.44**   Left Horten and arrived Kristiansand **10.12.44**

3. **11.12.44**   Left for operations.
   Schnorkel-equipped, U 905 was to operate in the English Channel but she failed to reach her operational area, possibly because of schnorkel-equipment defects.
   The boat put in to Bergen **31.1.45**

4. **1.2.45**   Left Bergen and arrived Trondheim **3.2.45**

5. **13.3.45**   Left for British coastal waters.
   U 905 was almost certainly sunk on 20.3.45 by a Liberator of 86 Squadron (F/Lt N E M Smith) N of Cape Wrath. The aircraft made a radar contact but on investigation nothing could be found. Sonobuoys were placed and a propeller sound was heard.
   Two homing torpedoes were dropped and after six minutes the sonobuoy operator heard a long echoing sound. U 905 was known to have been in the area and she disappeared at about that time.
   There were no known survivors, 45 dead.

U 906   Type VII C

Built by Stülcken Sohn, Hamburg
Keel laid 27.2.43   Launched 28.6.44
Commissioned 15.7.44   Feldpost Nr M 50 824

Bombed 31.12.44 at Hamburg

Served with
4 U-Flottille, Stettin   July - December 1944 (ab)

Commanded by
Unknown

Patrols: None   Ships sunk: None

On 31.12.44 U 906 was sunk in harbour at Hamburg in a USAF bombing raid. The wreck was further damaged in another raid in April 1945 and was presumably scrapped.

U 907   Type VII C

Built by Stülcken Sohn, Hamburg
Keel laid 1.4.43   Launched 1.3.44
Commissioned 12.5.44   Feldpost Nr M 01 308

Sunk 7.12.45 off Fair Head (55°17′N 05°59′W)

Served with
31 U-Flottille, Hamburg   May - November 1944 (ab)
11 U-Flottille, Bergen   December 1944 - 9.5.45 (fb)

Commanded by
OL Servais Cabolet   May 1944 - 9.5.45

Patrols: 2   Ships sunk: None

1. **18.12.44**   Left Kiel and arrived Horten **22.12.44**

2. **28.12.44**   Left Horten and arrived Kristiansand **29.12.44**

3. **31.12.44**   Left Kristiansand and arrived Bergen **3.1.45**

4. **4.1.45**   Left for the North Atlantic.
   U 907 operated off Reykjavik but had no success. In the latter part of January and for most of February she carried out weather-reporting duty.
   The boat returned to Kristiansand **15.3.45**

5. **16.3.45**   Left Kristiansand and arrived Bergen **18.3.45**

6. **29.4.45**   Left for operations.
   Recalled, returned to Bergen **5.5.45**

U 907 was surrendered at Bergen on 9.5.45. She left there on the 29th for an assembly area in Britain.
She was one of 116 boats disposed of by the Royal Navy in Operation Deadlight. In early December 1945 U 907 was towed from Loch Ryan out through the North Channel by the tug HMS Prosperous and sunk on 7.12.45 in 77 fathoms off Fair Head.

U 908 was still in the shipyard, uncompleted, when she was sunk in a USAF bombing raid on Hamburg on 31.12.44.

U 909 - U920 were never built, orders cancelled.

U 921   Type VII C

Built by Neptun Werft, Rostock
Keel laid 15.10.41   Launched 3.4.43
Commissioned 30.5.43   Feldpost Nr M 50 627

Sunk 30.9.44 SW of Bear Island (72°32′N 12°55′E)

Served with
8 U-Flottille, Danzig   May 1943 - May 1944 (ab)
13 U-Flottille, Trondheim   June 1944 - 30.9.44 (fb)

Commanded by
OL Wolfgang Leu   May 1943 - May 1944
Lt Hans Neumann (temp)   May 1944
OL Alfred Werner   June 1944 - 30.9.44

Patrols: 3   Ships sunk: None

1. 18.5.44 Left Kiel for Northern waters.

Outward-bound, U 921 was attacked on the 24th in the Norwegian Sea by a Sunderland of 423 (RCAF) Squadron (F/Lt R H Nesbitt). The aircraft dropped five depth-charges and the boat submerged, damaged, and was not seen again. The boat's commander was missing and three crewmen wounded. The 1 WO, Lt Hans Neumann, took command.

U 921 put in to Trondheim **26.5.44**

2. 30.6.44 Left Trondheim and arrived Narvik **1.7.44**

3. 2.7.44 Left for operations.

In July U 921 was operating in the Norwegian Sea, E of Jan Mayen. On the 20th the boat may have been attacked by an aircraft and damaged.

U 921 put in to Hammerfest **7.8.44**

4. 8.8.44 Left Hammerfest and arrived Narvik **9.8.44**

5. 2.9.44 Left Narvik and returned **3.9.44**

6. 5.9.44 Left for operations.

On the 15th eastbound JW 60 set out from Loch Ewe. U 921 was with *Grimm* group, awaiting it. However, the convoy was not located by the boats or the aircraft searching for it and reached Kola Inlet on the 23rd.

Return convoy RA 60 set out during the night of the 27/28th and again bypassed *Grimm* group. Attempting to close the convoy, U 921 was sighted by a Swordfish of 813 (FAA) Squadron from the escort-carrier HMS *Campania*. The boat was sunk in a depth-charge attack SW of Bear Island.

There were no survivors, 51 dead.

U 922   Type VII C

Built by Neptun Werft, Rostock
Keel laid 15.12.41   Launched 1.6.43
Commissioned 1.8.43   Feldpost Nr M 54 991

Scuttled 3.5.45 at Kiel

Served with
21 U-Flottille, Pillau   August 1943 (ab)
23 U-Flottille, Danzig   September 1943 - February 1945 (ab)
31 U-Flottille, Hamburg   February 1945 - 3.5.45 (ab)

Commanded by
OL Ulrich-Philipp Graf von und zu Arco-Zinneberg
                          August - November 1943
OL Eduard Aust   November 1943 - October 1944
OL Erich Käselau   October 1944 - 3.5.45

Patrols: None   Ships sunk: None

U 992 saw no operational service. She was on training duties at 21, 23 and 31 U-Flottillen.

The boat was scuttled on 3.5.45 at Kiel to prevent her falling into Allied hands.

The wreck was broken up in 1947.

U 923   Type VII C

Built by Neptun Werft, Rostock
Keel laid 21.2.42   Launched 7.8.43
Commissioned 4.10.43   Feldpost Nr M 53 015

Sunk 9.2.45 in Kieler Bucht

Served with
23 U-Flottille, Danzig   October 1943 - 9.2.45 (ab)

Commanded by
OL Heinz Frömmer   October 1943 - 9.2.45

Patrols: None   Ships sunk: None

U 923 sank after striking a mine in Kiel Bucht on 9.2.45, east of the Kiel fire-ship. There were no survivors, 48 dead. The boat was on training duties.

She was raised in January 1953 and scrapped.

U 924   Type VII C

Built by Neptun Werft, Rostock
Keel laid 15.4.42   Launched 25.9.43
Commissioned 20.11.43   Feldpost Nr M 54 999

Scuttled 3.5.45 at Kiel

Served with
22 U-Flottille, Gotenhafen   November 1943 - February 1945 (ab)
31 U-Flottille, Hamburg   March 1945 - 3.5.45 (ab)

Commanded by
OL Hans-Jürg Schild   November 1943 - 3.5.45

Patrols: None   Ships sunk: None

U 924 served on training duties at 22 and 31 U-Flottillen. She was scuttled at Kiel on 3.5.45 to prevent her falling into Allied hands. The wreck was broken up in 1947.

U 925   Type VII C

Built by Neptun Werft, Rostock
Keel laid 15.6.42   Launched 6.11.43
Commissioned 30.12.43   Feldpost Nr M 43 854

Lost about 14.9.44, possibly between Iceland and the Faroes

Served with
4 U-Flottille, Stettin   December 1943 - July 1944 (ab)
1 U-Flottille, Brest   August 1944 - c 14.9.44 (fb)

Commanded by
OL Helmuth Knoke   December 1943 - c 14.9.44

Patrols: 1   Ships sunk: None

1. 15.8.44 Left Kiel and arrived Horten **19.8.44**

2. 21.8.44 Left Horten and arrived Kristiansand **22.8.44**

3. 24.8.44 Left for the North Atlantic.

U 925 was not heard from after early September and is presumed

U 925 (continued)

lost from an unknown cause between Iceland and the Faroes on or about 14.9.44.

There were no known survivors, 51 dead.

U 926 Type VII C

Built by Neptun Werft, Rostock
Keel laid 1.7.42   Launched 28.12.43
Commissioned 29.2.44   Feldpost Nr M 50 939

Surrendered 9.5.45 at Bergen

Served with
4 U-Flottille, Stettin   February 1944 - March 1945 (ab)
11 U-Flottille, Bergen   March 1945 - 9.5.45 (ab)

Commanded by
OL Eberhard von Wenden   February - July 1944
OL Werner Roost   August 1944 - February 1945
OL Hellmut Rehren   February 1945 - 9.5.45

Patrols: None   Ships sunk: None

U 926 was surrendered at Bergen on 9.5.45. She was later taken to the assembly area at Loch Ryan.

Allocated to Norway in October 1948, U 926 was commissioned into the Norwegian Navy as the Kya on 10.1.49.

She was paid off in March 1964 and broken up.

U 927 Type VII C

Built by Neptun Werft, Rostock
Keel laid 1.12.42   Launched 3.5.44
Commissioned 27.6.44   Feldpost Nr M 21 755

Sunk 24.2.45 SE of Falmouth (49°54´N 04°45´W)

Served with
4 U-Flottille, Stettin   June 1944 - January 1945 (ab)
11 U-Flottille, Bergen   February 1945 (fb)

Commanded by
KL Jürgen Ebert   June 1944 - 24.2.45

Patrols: 1   Ships sunk: None

1. **11.1.45**   Left Kiel and arrived Horten **15.1.45**

2. **23.1.45**   Left Horten and arrived Kristiansand **24.1.45**

3. **31.1.45**   Left for operations.
U 927 was to operate in the English Channel. She had reached its western entrance when she was detected in the evening of 24.2.45 SE of Falmouth by a Warwick of 179 Squadron (F/Lt A G Brownhill).

The boat's schnorkel was caught by the aircraft's Leigh Light and six depth-charges were dropped, straddling U 927. Oil and wreckage were subsequently seen on the sea. The boat was destroyed, the only victory by a Warwick aircraft.

There were no survivors, 47 dead.

U 928 Type VII C

Built by Neptun Werft, Rostock
Keel laid 5.1.43   Launched 15.4.44
Commissioned 11.7.44   Feldpost Nr M 38 859

Sunk 16.12.45 NW of Bloody Foreland (55°50´N 10°05´W)

Served with
4 U-Flottille, Stettin   July 1944 - 9.5.45 (ab)

Commanded by
KL Hellmut Stähler   July 1944 - 9.5.45

Patrols: None   Ships sunk: None

U 928 saw no operational service. She was surrendered at Bergen on 5.5.45 and left there on the 30th for an assembly area in Britain.

The boat was one of 116 disposed of by the Royal Navy in Operation Deadlight. In December 1945 she was towed from Loch Ryan out through the North Channel by the frigate HMS Rupert.

U 928 was sunk by aircraft on 16.12.45 NW of Bloody Foreland.

U 929 Type VII C-41

Built by Neptun Werft, Rostock
Keel laid 20.3.43   Launched 23.7.44
Commissioned 6.9.44   Feldpost Nr M 43 666

Scuttled 3.5.45 at Warnemünde

Served with
4 U-Flottille, Stettin   September 1944 - 3.5.45

Commanded by
OL Werner Schulz   September 1944 - 3.5.45

Patrols: None   Ships sunk: None

U 929 saw no operational service. She was scuttled off Warnemünde on 3.5.45 to prevent her falling into Allied hands.

U 930 Type VII C-41

Built by Neptun Werft, Rostock
Keel laid 20.4.43   Launched 5.10.44
Commissioned 6.12.44   Feldpost Nr M 47 074

Sunk 8.12.45 W of Malin Head (55°22´N 07°35´W)

Served with
4 U-Flottille, Stettin   December 1944 - 9.5.45

Commanded by
OL Kurt Mohr   December 1944 - 9.5.45

Patrols: None   Ships sunk: None

U 930 saw no operational service. She was surrendered at Bergen on 9.5.45 and left there on the 30th for an assembly area in Britain.

The boat was one of 116 disposed of by the Royal Navy in Operation Deadlight. In early December 1945 she was towed from Lisahally by the destroyer HMS Zetland.

U 930 was sunk by gunfire on 8.12.45 by the destroyer HMS Onslow *W of Malin Head.*

U 931 - U 942 were never built, orders cancelled.

U 943 - U 950 were projected but never ordered.

U 951   Type VII C

Built by Blohm & Voss, Hamburg
Keel laid 31.1.42   Launched 14.10.42
Commissioned 3.12.42   Feldpost Nr M 50 964

Sunk 7.7.43 WSW of Lisbon (37°40′N 15°30′W)

Served with
5 U-Flottille, Kiel   December 1942 - May 1943 (ab)
9 U-Flottille, Brest   June 1943 - 7.7.43 (fb)

Commanded by
OL Kurt Pressel   December 1942 - 7.7.43

Patrols: 1   Ships sunk: None

1. 13.5.43   Left Kiel for Atlantic operations.
U 951 joined other boats that were waiting W of the Azores for expected convoys UGS 9 and GUS 7A. A patrol line, *Trutz*, was formed during the night of the 30/31st on the 43°W meridian WSW of the Azores, running between 32° and 38°N.

On 4.6.43 the three most southerly boats were attacked by carrier-borne aircraft, which were thought to be part of a convoy's protective cover. The boats closed up to prevent any ships passing through gaps in the line but when nothing had been sighted by the evening of the 5th, the convoy was thought to have passed either to the north or south.

The group broke up and moved 600 miles to the north to be refuelled by U 488. The UGS convoy was sighted by an outward-bound boat on the 8th 100 miles south of the *Trutz* patrol area of the 5th. The move to refuel had been much too premature and the opportunity lost. Refuelling was completed by the 15th and the group reformed in three parallel north-south lines, *Trutz 1,2* and *3*, 1000 miles E of Bermuda. U 951 was in *Trutz 2*.

The boats waited for convoys until the 22nd and having seen nothing in that time, the line began an eastwards movement which continued until the 27th, when they halted some 200 miles SW of the Azores. By the 29th it was realised that the elusive convoys GUS 8, UGS 10 and GUS 8A, had bypassed the lines.

The boats reformed into three new lines, *Geier 1,2* and *3* and from 2.7.43 they moved eastwards towards the coast of Portugal, the lines spaced at one-day intervals. U 951 was in *Geier 2*. At 500 miles from the coast air attacks began.

On the 7th U 951 was sighted on the surface WSW of Lisbon by a Liberator of 1 A/S Squadron (USAF) (Lt W S McDonnell). The boat remained surfaced and manoeuvred to meet the approaching aircraft with flak. Seven depth-bombs were dropped from a low level, straddling the boat and destroying her.

The Liberator was badly damaged and several of her crew had been wounded by flak during the run-in. McDonnell managed to get back to his base at Port Lyautey, Morocco.

There were no survivors from U 951, 46 dead.

U 952   Type VII C

Built by Blohm & Voss, Hamburg
Keel laid 1.2.42   Launched 14.10.42
Commissioned 10.12.42   Feldpost Nr M 49 527

Bombed 6.8.44 at Toulon

Served with
5 U-Flottille, Kiel   December 1942 - April 1943 (ab)
3 U-Flottille, La Pallice   May 1943 - January 1944 (fb)
29 U-Flottille, Toulon   February 1944 - 6.8.44 (fb)

Commanded by
KL Oskar Curio   December 1942 - 6.8.44

Patrols: 6   Ships sunk: 3 (18,111 grt) + 1 damaged
                          1 corvette (925 dt)

1. 22.4.43   Left Kiel and arrived Bergen **26.4.43**

2. 27.4.43   Left for the North Atlantic.
Outward-bound on 4.5.43, U 952 encountered and sank a straggler from convoy ONS 5, the SS *Lorient* (br 4737t), S of Cape Farewell. On the 5th U 952 made an unsuccessful attack on the convoy itself, her torpedo detonated prematurely.

From the 11th U 952 joined U 304, U 418 and U 645 to form *Isar* group SE of Cape Farewell. On the 12th outward-bound U 640 sighted westbound ONS 7. *Isar, Lech* and *Inn* groups moved northeastwards to intercept but U 640 lost contact on the 13th.

When the convoy was not found the three small groups joined up with newly-arrived boats and *Nahe* and *Iller* groups to form *Donau 1* and *2* groups from the 15th SE of Greenland. U 952 was in *Donau 1*. ONS 7 passed north of the patrol line and by the late evening of the 16th was away to the southwest of *Donau 2*.

The boats moved southwards to intercept eastbound SC 130 and the convoy was sighted by U 304 during the night of the 18/19th. Only U 952 and U 645 closed before contact was lost on the 19th, when SC 130 changed course. The boats were driven off by a Liberator of 120 Squadron (F/Sgt W Stoves) and U 952 was damaged in a depth-charge attack by one of the escorts, the frigate HMS *Tay*.

U 952 put in to Bordeaux **31.5.43**

3. 2.8.43   Left Bordeaux and arrived La Pallice **2.8.43**

4. 26.8.43   Left for the North Atlantic.
U 952 returned with technical trouble after a deep-diving test. She reached La Pallice **27.8.43**

5. 31.8.43   Left for operations and again returned with technical trouble, reaching La Pallice **1.9.43**

6. 4.9.43   Left for operations and yet again returned with technical trouble, reaching la Pallice **6.9.43**

7. 6.9.43   Left for the North Atlantic.
U 952 was one of fourteen boats which were to form *Leuthen* group SSW of Iceland from the 20th, to intercept an ON convoy.

Secrecy had been maintained as far as possible to prevent the presence of the boats becoming known to the Allies. However, U 341, which should have been proceeding submerged, was sighted, attacked and sunk by a Canadian aircraft just east of the planned patrol line position.

Early on the 20th, before the *Leuthen* boats were in position, westbound convoy ON 202 was sighted by U 270 but she was driven off after damaging a frigate. Aircraft and a strong surface escort prevented most boats making any attacks in daylight. During the

U 952 (continued)

day ON 202 joined up with convoy ONS 18.

Soon after midnight of the 20th U 952 torpedoed and sank the corvette HMS *Polyanthus* of ON 202's escort, SE of Cape Farewell. The corvette broke up and the sole survivor was picked up by the frigate HMS *Itchen*. She had earlier picked up survivors from the destroyer HMCS *St Croix*, sunk by U 305. When *Itchen* herself was sunk early on the 23rd, only three men survived, the sum total from these three ships.

After U 952 sank *Polyanthus*, fog came down and remained throughout the night and next day. On the 22nd there were some clear patches and when aircraft appeared some *Leuthen* boats remained surfaced and fought them. In the late afternoon the fog cleared and five boats approached the convoy, including U 952, but they encountered a strong escort.

U 952 was sighted near the convoy by the a/s trawler HMS *Northern Waters*. She tried unsuccessfully to ram the boat and then made a depth-charge attack after U 952 dived. The boat resurfaced later and moved away.

In the evening of the 22nd U 952 made an unsuccessful attack on the French corvette *Renoncule*, hearing only an end-of-run detonation. U 952 torpedoed two ships from ON 202 in the morning of the 23rd SSE of Cape Farewell, sinking the SS *Steel Voyager* (am 6198t) and hitting the SS *James Gordon Bennett* (am 7176t) with a dud. Soon afterwards, the operation was terminated. Six ships had been sunk and another damaged, three escorts had also been sunk and another damaged beyond repair. Two boats were lost.

Augmented by new arrivals, the *Leuthen* boats formed *Rossbach* group S of Iceland from the 27th. The group moved northwards on 1.10.43 to intercept ONS 19 and then from the 3rd went eastwards to meet ON 204. Neither convoy was found and from the 5th the *Rossbach* boats began a southwestwards sweep, to search for SC 143 or HX 259. The former was sighted by German aircraft on the 8th but the boats did not receive the aircraft's homing signals and the convoy was not found, although attacks were made on some escorts. The search was called off on the 9th. U 952 left the group soon after this.

The boat returned to La Pallice **23.10.43**

8. 11.12.43 Left La Pallice and returned **15.12.43**

9. 16.12.43 Left for the Mediterranean.

U 952 passed through the Straits of Gibraltar during the night of January 3/4th 1944. The boat then probably patrolled in the Western Mediterranean but had no success.

She put in to her new base at Toulon **15.1.44**

10. 17.2.44 Left for operations.

On the 26th U 952 unsuccessfully attacked a destroyer off Anzio and on 4.3.44 she missed a corvette N of Isola Ustica, hearing only an end-of-run detonation.

On the 10th U 952 torpedoed and sank the SS *William B Woods* (am 7176t) NNE of Palermo.

The boat put in to La Spezia **20.3.44**

11. 3.5.44 Left La Spezia and arrived Toulon **7.5.44**

12. 8.5.44 Left for operations. No details known of this patrol.

U 952 returned to Toulon **21.6.44**

On 5.7.44 U 952 was damaged in a USAF bombing raid on Toulon and decommissioned there on the 12th. She was finally sunk in another USAF raid on Toulon on 6.8.44.

U 953   Type VII C

Built by Blohm & Voss, Hamburg
Keel laid 10.2.42   Launched 28.10.42
Commissioned 17.12.42   Feldpost Nr M 49 558

Surrendered 9.5.45 at Trondheim

Served with
5 U-Flottille, Kiel   December 1942 - May 1943 (ab)
3 U-Flottille, La Pallice   June 1943 - October 1944 (fb)
33 U-Flottille, Flensburg   October 1944 - 9.5.45 (fb)

Commanded by
OL Karl-Heinz Marbach   December 1942 - July 1944
OL Herbert Werner   August 1944 - March 1945
OL Erich Steinbrink   March 1945 - 9.5.45

Patrols: 9   Ships sunk: 1 (1927grt)

1. 13.5.43 Left Kiel for Atlantic operations.

U 953 joined other boats that were waiting W of the Azores for expected convoys UGS 9 and GUS 7A. A patrol line, *Trutz*, was formed during the night of the 30/31st on the 43° meridian WSW of the Azores, running between 32° and 38°N.

On 4.6.43 the three most southerly boats were attacked by carrier-borne aircraft, which were thought to be part of a convoy's protective cover. The boats closed up to prevent any ships passing through gaps in the line but when nothing had been sighted by the evening of the 5th the convoy was thought to have passed either to the north or south.

The group broke up and moved 600 miles to the north to be refuelled by U 488. The UGS convoy was sighted by an outward-bound boat on the 8th 100 miles south of the *Trutz* patrol area of the 5th. The move to refuel had been much too premature and the opportunity lost. Refuelling was completed by the 15th and the group reformed in three parallel north-south lines, *Trutz 1,2* and *3*, 1000 miles E of Bermuda. U 953 was in *Trutz 2*.

The boats waited for convoys until the 22nd and having seen nothing in that time, the line began an eastwards movement which continued until the 27th, when they halted some 200 miles SW of the Azores. By the 29th it was realised that the elusive convoys, GUS 8, UGS 10 and GUS 8A, had bypassed the lines.

The boats reformed into three new lines, *Geier 1,2* and *3* and from 2.7.43 they moved eastwards towards the coast of Portugal, the lines spaced at one-day intervals. U 953 was in *Geier 2*. At 500 miles from the coast air attacks began and by the 8th were such that boat commanders were allowed to return to base if circumstances warranted. On the 9th U 953 was attacked by a USAF Liberator. The boat was badly shaken but undamaged. One crewman was killed and two wounded.

U 953 put in to her new base at La Pallice **22.7.43**

U 953 was one of seven boats which were converted to flak-boats between May and November 1943. The other six were U 211, U 256, U 263, U 271, U 441 and U 621.

The increased armament reduced the boats' fuel-carrying capacity and made them unsuitable for long-range operations.

2. 2.10.43 Left for operations.

U 953 went to an area W of the Bay of Biscay, to give protection against aircraft for outgoing and returning boats. Later in October she joined seven other boats, which included flak-boats U 211 and U 441, to form a mobile force, *Schill* group, to make a one-night attack on an MKS or KMS convoy off the northwest coast of Spain.

The *Schill* patrol line was formed on the 27th 400 miles W of Cape Ortegal, to await northbound convoy MKS 28/SL 138. Luftwaffe aircraft sighted it on the 27th and 28th but on the 29th, the day of the planned attack, it was not seen, having steered slightly to the west.

On the 30th aircraft found the convoy again, to the northwest of the *Schill* line. The boats were ordered to pursue on the surface in daylight and contact was made on the 31st. Only two boats, U 262 and U 333, made attacks. One ship was sunk and U 306 was lost.

On 1.11.43 U 953 sighted an MKF convoy but it was too fast for the *Schill* boats to attack. They were ordered to form a new patrol line and a move southwards began on the 3rd, searching for a KMS convoy. On the 5th the Luftwaffe began a search for northbound MKS 29 and it was sighted on the 7th. The *Schill* line was reformed in the expectation that the convoy would pass through it during the evening of the 8th. Again, air reconnaissance failed to sight the convoy on the vital day, when mechanical defects forced aircraft to return to base.

At the expected interception time the *Schill* boats moved southwestwards at high speed but when only destroyers were seen it was realised that the convoy had passed through the line. It was found again by aircraft in the morning of the 9th but despite a search the *Schill* boats never found the convoy.

U 953 returned to La Pallice **17.11.43**

The flak-boat experiment was not a success and U 953 was restored to her original state and returned to normal duty.

3. 26.12.43 Left for the North Atlantic.

U 953 joined *Borkum* group W of Ireland. In the first few days of January 1944 the group took part in two failed convoy operations. From the 4th the group was split into three small sub-groups, *Borkum 1,2* and *3*. U 953 was in *Borkum 3*.

From the 8th aircraft were searching for combined convoy MKS 35/SL 144 and it was sighted on the 9th W of Portugal. U 305 of *Borkum 1* made contact with the convoy during the evening of the 11th. The *Borkum* groups approached the convoy and although they held their own against carrier-borne aircraft from USS *Block Island* they were unable to make any concerted attacks and no ships were sunk.

In the early evening of the 11th U 953 claimed a hit on the corvette HMCS *Lunenburg*, escorting convoy KMS 38/OS 64 W of Cape Finisterre.

The *Borkum* groups were dissolved on the 13th. U 953 then went owards Casablanca and from the 21st she was operating off the west coast of Morocco. She had no success.

The boat returned to La Pallice **20.2.44**

4. 30.3.44 Left La Pallice and returned **1.4.44**

5. 23.4.44 Left La Pallice and arrived Brest **26.4.44**

6. 22.5.44 Left for the English Channel.

U 953 was one of five schnorkel boats which joined up to form *Dragoner* group. It was to operate in the western part of the English Channel, N of Ushant, in co-operation with shore radar against Allied cruiser and destroyer formations.

The objective was to test the effectiveness of the schnorkel and to assess tactics required in areas patrolled by many enemy aircraft. Some experience was gained but in general results were discouraging.

U 953 returned to Brest **28.5.44**

7. 6.6.44 Left Brest, as part of *Landwirt* group.

U 953 was one of eight schnorkel boats ordered to go to the area N of Cherbourg, enter the English Channel and inflict what losses they could on the invasion forces. This was a very difficult and dangerous task, considering the concentration of air and surface forces they would be facing.

In the morning of the 8th U 953 fired four torpedoes at destroyers of the 12th EG at the western entrance of the Channel, HMCS

Qu'Appelle, Restigouche and *Skeena*. Three torpedoes detonated near the warships but no damage was caused. Some days later U 953 was forced to return to base with an exhausted crew.

She reached Brest **18.6.44**

8. 24.6.44 Left for the English Channel.

In the morning of 5.7.44 U 953 attacked a convoy S of Worthing, sinking the SS *Glendinning* (br 1927t) and claiming a hit on a second ship. On the 11th U 953 attacked a convoy near the Isle of Wight, claiming one ship sunk and a destroyer hit. None of these claims is confirmed.

U 953 returned to Brest **22.7.44**

After returning from this patrol U 953's commander, OL Marbach, went to Berlin to receive his Knight's Cross. He was unable to return to Brest because of the advance of Allied forces. OL Werner took over command of the boat in early August.

9. 10.8.44 Left Brest and returned **11.8.44**

10. 12.8.44 Left on transport duty.

U 953 left Brest for La Pallice, carrying scientific equipment and some 40 technical personnel.

The boat reached La Pallice **19.8.44**

11. 31.8.44 Left for British coastal waters.

U 953 was one of three schnorkel boats operating in the North Channel from mid-September. They remained there for a short time, there being very few ships to be seen.

U 953 put in to Bergen **11.10.44**

12. 16.10.44 Left Bergen and arrived Flensburg **25.10.44**

13. 4.2.45 Left Kiel and arrived Kristiansand **9.2.45**

14. 12.2.45 Left Kristiansand and arrived Bergen **15.2.45**

15. 21.2.45 Left Bergen for the English Channel.

U 953 operated at the western entrance of the Channel from mid-March but had no success.

She returned to Bergen **3.4.45**

16. 6.4.45 Left Bergen and arrived Trondheim **9.4.45**

U 953 was surrendered at Trondheim on 9.5.45. She left there on the 29th for Scapa Flow. After experimental use as an N series submarine by the Royal Navy, the boat was scrapped in June 1949.

U 954   Type VII C

Built by Blohm & Voss, Hamburg
Keel laid 10.2.42   Launched 28.10.42
Commissioned 23.12.42   Feldpost Nr M 49 568

Sunk 19.5.43 in the central North Atlantic (54°54′N 34°19′W)

Served with
5 U-Flottille, Kiel   December 1942 - April 1943 (ab)
9 U-Flottille, Brest   May 1943 (fb)

Commanded by
KL Odo Loewe   December 1942 - 19.5.43

Patrols: 1   Ships sunk: None + 1 damaged

1. 8.4.43 Left Kiel for the North Atlantic.

U 954 joined boats of *Meise* group SE of Greenland, to operate

U 954 (continued)

against eastbound convoy HX 234 from the 22nd. The boat torpedoed and damaged the MV *Silvermaple* (br 5313t) in the afternoon of the 23rd E of Cape Farewell. After contact was lost with the convoy on the 24th, U 954 became part of a new group, *Star*, in a patrol line S of Iceland, to await a westbound convoy.

On the 28th ONS 5 passed the northern end of the line. The bad weather conditions made it difficult to close the convoy, which was briefly sighted by five boats on the 29th and had one ship sunk that morning, by U 258. The operation ended in the evening of 1.5.43 near Cape Farewell.

The *Star* boats were immediately ordered to join the boats of *Specht* group in the pursuit of eastbound convoy SC 128, sighted during the evening of the 1st. Contact was lost during the night and when it had not been regained by the 3rd a new patrol line, *Fink*, was formed by combining *Star* and *Specht* groups.

The twenty-nine boats continued to search for SC 128 but by the 4th it was realised that the convoy had been re-routed. *Fink* had received orders to take up a new position when a southwest-bound convoy was sighted in the centre of the line. It proved to be ONS 5, which had been delayed by the storm. In daylight on the 5th fifteen boats were in contact with the convoy but before nightfall fog came down and most lost contact. In the fog the escorts made depth-charge attacks on fifteen boats. In the morning of the 6th ONS 5 was again sighted but deteriorating weather conditions caused the operation to be abandoned, with twelve ships sunk but six boats lost.

U 954 joined U 258 and U 381 to form *Inn* group SSE of Cape Farewell on the 12th. The three *Inn* boats became part of *Donau 1* group from the 15th. On this day *Donau 1* and *2* and *Iller* groups began a southwesterly movement in search of convoys.

On the 17th SC 130 was reported to be 150 miles SE of Cape Farewell and the groups moved southeastwards to intercept. The convoy was found during the night of the 18/19th by U 304 and the boats pursued.

U 954 was sunk on the 19th in the vicinity of convoy SC 130, in depth-charge attacks by the frigate HMS *Jed* (Lt-Cdr R C Freaker) and the sloop HMS *Sennen*.

There were no survivors, 47 dead. The 2WO on U 954 was Leutnant Peter Dönitz, second son of Admiral Karl Dönitz. It was his first patrol.

U 955   Type VII C

Built by Blohm & Voss, Hamburg
Keel laid 23.2.42   Launched 13.11.42
Commissioned 31.12.42   Feldpost Nr M 49 601

Sunk 7.6.44 N of Cape Ortegal (45°13´N 08°30´W)

Served with
5 U-Flottille, Kiel December 1942 - March 1944 (ab)
9 U-Flottille, Brest April 1944 - 7.6.44 (fb)

Commanded by
OL Hans-Heinrich Baden December 1942 - 7.6.44

Patrols: 1   Ships sunk: None

1. **23.3.44** Left Kiel and arrived Kristiansand **26.3.44**

2. **13.4.44** Left Kristiansand and arrived Bergen **14.4.44**

3. **16.4.44** Left for the North Atlantic.
   U 955 carried out weather-reporting duties until late May. She claimed to have shot down an Allied aircraft on 5.5.44.
   The returning boat was N of Cape Ortegal just before midnight

on 6.6.44 when a radar contact was made by a Sunderland of 201 Squadron (F/Lt L H Baveystock). The aircraft turned on, losing height as it approached the boat's expected position.

Baveystock dropped a flare, which illuminated a swirl where U 955 had submerged. A Sunderland of 461 (RAAF) Squadron had homed in on to Baveystock and they crossed each other's course at 300 mph, the second flying boat passing below Baveystock's.

Knowing that the U-boat was there and estimating when it would surface to recharge batteries, Baveystock flew out for eight miles, later increasing this distance to twelve.

At 03.00 hrs radar contact was made at eleven miles. The Sunderland approached but before a flare could be dropped, two streams of tracer came up at the aircraft. Flares were dropped and in the face of heavy flak, Baveystock dropped six depth-charges. The boat sank immediately. For the action Baveystock was awarded a Bar to the DFC.

There were no survivors from U 955, 50 dead.

U 956   Type VII C

Built by Blohm & Voss, Hamburg
Keel laid 20.2.42   Launched 14.11.22
Commissioned 6.1.43   Feldpost Nr M 49 622

Sunk 17.12.45 NW of Bloody Foreland (55°50´N 10°05´W)

Served with
5 U-Flottille, Kiel January - June 1943 (ab)
1 U-Flottille, Brest July - December 1943 (fb)
11 U-Flottille, Bergen January - September 1944 (fb)
13 U-Flottille, Trondheim October 1944 - 13.5.45 (fb)

Commanded by
OL Hans-Dieter Mohs January 1943 - 13.5.45

Patrols: 13   Ships sunk: None + 1 damaged

1. **3.8.43** Left Kiel and arrived Bergen **6.8.43**

2. **14.8.43** Left Bergen and arrived Narvik **17.8.43**

3. **18.8.43** Left for Northern Waters. No details known.
   U 956 returned to Narvik **13.9.43**

4. **23.9.43** Left for operations.
   In early October U 956 was with *Monsun* group between Spitzbergen and Bear Island. The last Allied convoy, RA 53, had left Kola Inlet on 1.3.43. The convoys were suspended and the next one would not sail for Russia until mid-November 1943. The U-boats in Northern Waters were somewhat under-employed and the number of Soviet ships sunk, damaged or attacked by U-boats during the eight-month period of suspension did not exceed twenty.
   U 956 returned to Narvik **4.11.43**

5. **5.11.43** Left Narvik and arrived Bergen **8.11.43**

6. **28.12.43** Left Bergen for operations. No details known.
   U 956 put in to Narvik **7.1.44**

7. **8.1.44** Left for operations. No details known.
   U 956 put in to Skjomenfjord **18.1.44**

8. **25.1.44** Left for operations.
   U 956 joined *Werwolf* group in the Bear Island Passage, awaiting eastbound convoy JW 56B, which was sighted by U 956 at noon on the 29th. Before midnight the boat had been attacked three times by escorting destroyers. She fired defensive torpedoes but without

success. On January 31st and February 1st U 956 made several unsuccessful attacks against the escort.

The boat put in to Hammerfest **2.2.44**

9. 15.2.44 Left for operations.

Convoy JW 57 left Loch Ewe on the 20th. U 956 was again with *Werwolf* group. Contact was made on the 25th in the Norwegian Sea. U 956 and other boats made unsuccessful attacks on the convoy NW of Tromsø on the 26th.

JW 57 reached Kola Inlet on the 28th, with no ships lost but HMS *Mahratta* of the escort sunk by U 990.

U 956 returned to Narvik **2.3.44**

10. 23.3.44 Left for operations.

U 956 joined *Blitz* group, which in late March was waiting for eastbound JW 58. The convoy set out from Iceland on the 27th and was located by German aircraft on the 30th. *Blitz, Thor* and *Hammer* groups made contact shortly after midnight on the 31st.

Unsuccessful attacks were made by the boats until the evening of 3.4.44. The only ship which failed to reach Kola Inlet on the 5th was one which returned to Iceland with ice damage.

U 956 returned to Narvik **8.4.44**

11. 9.4.44 Left Narvik and arrived Bergen **12.4.44**

12. 3.6.44 Left Bergen and arrived Hammerfest **10.6.44**

13. 23.6.44 Left Hammerfest and returned **23.6.44**

14. 26.6.44 Left for operations. No details known.

U 956 returned to Narvik **24.7.44**

15. 27.8.44 Left for operations.

U 956, U 425, U 636, U 968, U 992 and U 995 formed *Dachs* group to lay mines in the Pechora Sea. U 956 laid her mines off Novaya Zemlya on 3.9.44.

The boat returned to Skjomenfjord **8.9.44**

16. 14.9.44 Left for operations.

On the 15th eastbound JW 60 set out from Loch Ewe. U 956 was with *Grimm* group, awaiting it. However, the convoy was not located either by the boats or the aircraft searching for it and reached Kola Inlet on the 23rd.

Return convoy RA 60 set out during the night of the 27/28th and again bypassed *Grimm* group.

U 956 returned to Narvik **3.10.44**

17. 15.10.44 Left for operations.

On the 20th eastbound JW 61 left Loch Ewe. U 956 was one of the boats of *Panther* group, through which the convoy had passed without loss, arriving off Kola Inlet on the 28th. During the night of the 26/27th U 956 and other *Panther* boats made unsuccessful attacks on the escorts N of Kola Inlet.

Between November 5th and 8th U 956, U 771 and U 997 were operating against Soviet escort vessels in the Barents Sea. Their attacks were unsuccessful.

U 956 returned to Narvik **24.11.44**

18. 11.12.44 Left for operations.

On the 20th U 956 reported one ship and a patrol craft sunk E of Kola Inlet but there is no confirmation of this. On the 30th she torpedoed and damaged the SS *Tbilisi* (sov 7176t) of convoy KP 24 in Skorbeyevskij Bay. The vessel was towed into Kildin and beached.

In early January U 956 was with *Stier* group in Bear Island Passage, awaiting eastbound JW 63. The convoy passed through unobserved, reaching Kola Inlet on the 8th.

U 956 unsuccessfully attacked a Soviet patrol craft on the 12th E of Kola Inlet. From mid-January she was one of six boats operating

against Soviet inshore shipping on the Kola coast.

The boat returned to Narvik **20.1.45**

19. 22.1.45 Left Narvik and arrived Trondheim **25.1.45**

20. 2.4.45 Left for operations in British coastal waters.

In the latter half of April U 956 was operating W of the North Channel but she had no success. At the end of the U-boat war on 4.5.45 U 956 was in the Irish Sea. In accordance with instructions given, she put into Loch Eriboll on 13.5.45 and surrendered.

U 956 was one of 116 boats disposed of by the Royal Navy in Operation Deadlight. *In mid-December 1945 she was towed from Loch Ryan out through the North Channel by the tug HMS Prosperous.*

The boat was sunk by gunfire on 17.12.45 NW of Bloody Foreland.

U 957   Type VII C

Built by Blohm & Voss, Hamburg
Keel laid 11.3.42   Launched 21.11.42
Commissioned 7.1.43   Feldpost Nr M 50 029

Decommissioned 21.10.44 at Narvik

Served with
5 U-Flottille, Kiel   January - July 1943 (ab)
3 U-Flottille, La Pallice   August - December 1943 (fb-oE)
11 U-Flottille, Bergen   January - September 1944 (fb)
13 U-Flottille, Trondheim   October 1944 (fb)

Commanded by
OL Franz Saar   January 1943 - 20.3.43
OL Gerd Schaar   March 1943 - 21.10.44

Patrols: 7   Ships sunk: 1 (7153 grt)
                             1 patrol craft (580 dt)
                             1 survey ship (200 dt)

During training in the Baltic, U 957 collided with the U-boat tender Wilhelm Bauer. *The boat's conning tower was damaged and it may have been in this incident that U 957's commander, OL Saar, lost his life on 20.3.43.*

1. 14.12.43 Left Kiel for Northern Waters.

U 957 joined *Eisenbart* group. On the 24th U 601 of the group was directed to convoy JW 55B by reconnaissance aircraft but only she and U 716 of *Eisenbart* made contact with the convoy and they were quickly driven off.

On the 25th the German battlecruiser *Scharnhorst* with destroyer-escort, was deployed against JW 55B. On the 26th *Scharnhorst* was engaged in a day-long running battle with British warships and, very severely damaged, she sank in the evening.

In the evening of the 28th U 957 made unsuccessful attacks on the escort of JW 55B, hearing two end-of-run detonations. The convoy reached Kola Inlet without loss on the 29th.

U 957 also operated against westbound RA 55B, which left Kola Inlet on the 31st and reached Loch Ewe safely on 8.1.44. U 957 made an unsuccessful attack against the escort.

The boat put in to Narvik **12.1.44**

2. 24.1.44 Left for operations.

U 957 joined *Isegrim* group in Bear Island Passage, waiting for eastbound JW 56A, which sailed from Akureyri, Iceland on the 21st. In the afternoon of the 25th the *Isegrim* boats closed the convoy SE of Bear Island and torpedo attacks began, continuing

U 957 (continued)

throughout the night. On the 25th U 957 missed a destroyer and on the 26th, after claiming a hit on a ship, she torpedoed and sank the SS *Fort Bellingham* (br 7153t), torpedoed and damaged six hours earlier by U 360. Forty of the crew of the *Fort Bellingham* abandoned ship without orders. Only two survived, picked up by U 957. Their interrogation provided valuable information.

On the 30th U 957 made unsuccessful attacks on the escort of JW 56B, including the destroyer HMS *Hardy*, sunk soon afterwards by U 278.

U 957 put in to Hammerfest **2.2.44**

3. **6.2.44** Left for operations.
U 957 joined *Werwolf* group, waiting for westbound RA 56, which sailed on the 3rd and was located by aerial reconniassance on the 5th. Supplied with inaccurate information, the *Werwolf* boats did not find the convoy.
U 957 returned to Narvik **20.2.44**

4. **22.2.44** Left Narvik and arrived Hammerfest **25.2.44**

5. **26.2.44** Left Hammerfest and arrived Bergen **4.3.44**

6. **29.4.44** Left Bergen and arrived Narvik **2.5.44**

7. **11.5.44** Left for operations.
On the 30th, E of Jan Mayen, U 957 made an unsuccessful attack on the escort of the aircraft carriers HMS *Furious* and *Victorious* of a British naval task force sent to attack the *Tirpitz*. The operation against the battleship, scheduled for the 28th, was abandoned because of bad weather.
U 957 returned to Narvik **8.6.44**

8. **14.6.44** Left Narvik and arrived Tromsø **15.6.44**

9. **23.6.44** Left Tromsø and returned **23.6.44**

10. **26.6.44** Left Tromsø and returned **28.6.44**

11. **2.7.44** Left Tromsø and arrived Narvik **3.7.44**

12. **18.7.44** Left Narvik and arrived Hammerfest **20.7.44**

13. **23.7.44** Left for operations.
U 957 was ordered to the Kara Sea, to operate with other boats along the Siberian Sea route. The boats, U 957, U 278, U 362, U365, U 711 and U 739, made up *Greif* group.
On 26.8.44 U 957 sank the Soviet survey ship *Nord* by gunfire off the north coast of Taymyr Peninsula.
After supplying fuel to other *Greif* boats, U 957 returned to refuel. On this patrol U 957 had B-Dienst specialists aboard to monitor Soviet communications.
She put in to Hammerfest **3.9.44**

14. **7.9.44** Left for operations.
U 957 rejoined U 711 and U 739 in the Kara Sea. On the 21st they encountered Soviet convoy VD 1, en route from the Vilkitski Strait to Dickson. Unsuccessful attacks were made on the convoy on the 21st and 22nd. U 957 torpedoed and sank the patrol craft *SKR-29/Brilliant* early on the 23rd N of Krakovka Island.
The three boats landed a party on Sterligova Island on the 24th. A wireless station was destroyed and four prisoners taken.
U 957 returned to Narvik **3.10.44**

15. **6.10.44** Left Narvik and arrived Trondheim **8.10.44**

16. **17.10.44** Left Trondheim.
U 957 was en route for operations when she came into collision

with pack-ice. She made for Narvik, heavily damaged. There were no casualties.
U 957 reached Narvik on **21.10.44** and was decommissioned on the same day.

U 958   Type VII C

Built by Blohm & Voss, Hamburg
Keel laid 10.3.42   Launched 21.11.42
Commissioned 14.1.43   Feldpost Nr M 50 044

Scuttled 3.5.45 at Kiel

Served with
5 U-Flottille, Kiel   January 1943 - July 1944 (ab)
8 U-Flottille, Danzig   August 1944 - February 1945 (fb)
5 U-Flottille, Kiel   February 1945 - 3.5.45 (fb-oE)

Commanded by
KL Gerhard Groth   January 1943 - April 1945
OL Friedrich Stege   April 1945 - 3.5.45

Patrols: 4   Ships sunk: 2 (c 80 dt)

In March 1943 the uncoated U 958 was used in sea trials off Arendal, Norway in comparison to the Alberich-coated U 470.

Whilst on a training exercise in the Baltic between Hela and Gotland during the night of February 9/10th 1944 U 958 collided with U 290. Neither sank but U 290's conning tower was damaged.

1. **6.5.44** Left Kiel and arrived Stavanger **9.5.44**

2. **22.5.44** Left for operations.
On the 26th U 958 was attacked and damaged by the cannon fire of two Mosquitos of 333 (Norwegian) Squadron (Lts J M Jacobsen and H Engebrigsten). The boat put up defensive flak. She had one crewman killed and two wounded.
U 958 put in to Bergen **27.5.44**

3. **3.6.44** Left for operations.
U 958 was one of five boats which set out for the North Atlantic. On the 6th, after news came of the invasion of Normandy, the boats were halted W of Norway, to await further orders. On the 9th they were ordered to specific patrol areas within reach of Norway.
U 958 returned to Bergen **23.6.44**

4. **3.7.44** Left Bergen and arrived Haugesund **3.7.44**

5. **27.7.44** Left Haugesund and arrived Kiel **1.8.44**

6. **3.8.44** Left Kiel for operations in the Baltic.
U 958 put in to Gotenhafen **5.8.44**

On 2.9.44 Finland broke off diplomatic relations with Germany and surrendered on the 4th. From the 2nd the Germans evacuated their men and as much material as possible from Finnish harbours.
Further U-boat operations in the Baltic were carried out from Danzig, Gotenhafen and Memel.

7. **4.9.44** Left Gotenhafen and arrived Reval **5.9.44**

8. **7.9.44** Left for operations.
U 958 was one of several boats operating in the entrances to the Gulfs of Bothnia and Finland. She had no success on this patrol.
She put in to Danzig **11.10.44**

9. 13.10.44 Left for operations.

U 958 operated again in the same area. On the 24th she sank two small Finnish fishing vessels by gunfire off Odensholm, the *Linnea* and *Piikiö*.

The boat continued to operate in the Baltic until mid-December but had no further success.

She returned to Danzig **17.12.44**

10. 23.3.45 Left Danzig and arrived Kiel **26.3.45**

U 958 was scuttled at Kiel on 3.5.45 to prevent her falling into Allied hands.
She was raised in 1947 and broken up.

U 959   Type VII C

Built by Blohm & Voss, Hamburg
Keel laid 21.3.42   Launched 3.12.42
Commissioned 21.1.43   Feldpost Nr M 50 076

Sunk 2.5.44 ESE of Jan Mayen (69°20′N 00°20′W)

Served with
5 U-Flottille, Kiel   January 1943 - February 1944 (ab)
13 U-Flottille, Trondheim   March 1944 - 2.5.44 (fb)

Commanded by
OL Martin Duppel   January - July 1943
OL Friedrich Weitz   July 1943 - 2.5.44

Patrols: 2   Ships sunk: None

1. 22.2.44 Left Kiel and arrived Bergen **24.2.44**

2. 25.2.44 Left for Northern Waters.

Westbound convoy RA 57 left Kola Inlet on 2.3.44 and was engaged by boats of *Boreas* group on the 4th. U 959 and other boats were on their way to join the group.

U 959, U 278 and U 288 closed the convoy NW of Vestfjord but their attacks on the escort on the 5th and 6th were unsuccessful. U 959 heard only an end-of-run detonation. The convoy lost one ship, sunk by U 703, and reached Loch Ewe on the 10th.

U 959 put in to Narvik **16.3.44**

3. 17.3.44 Left Narvik and arrived Trondheim **20.3.44**

4. 19.4.44 Left Trondheim and arrived Narvik **21.4.44**

5. 22.4.44 Left for operations.

U 959 joined *Keil* group. Westbound RA 59 set out from Kola Inlet on the 28th and the *Keil* boats were deployed against it.

Contact was made with the convoy during the evening of the 30th but U 959 did not make any attacks until late on 1.5.44, when she was unsuccessful against destroyers of the escort.

On the 2nd U 959 was sighted ESE of Jan Mayen by a Swordfish of 842 (FAA) Squadron and sunk in a depth-charge attack. The aircraft, from the escort-carrier HMS *Fencer*, also sank U 674 on the same day.

There were no survivors from U 959, 53 dead.

U 960   Type VII C

Built by Blohm & Voss, Hamburg
Keel laid 20.3.42   Launched 3.12.42
Commissioned 28.1.43   Feldpost Nr M 50 098

Sunk 19.5.44 N of Ténès (37°20′N 01°35′E)

Served with
5 U-Flottille, Kiel   January - July 1943 (ab)
3 U-Flottille, La Pallice   August 1943 - 19.5.44 (fb)

Commanded by
OL Günther Heinrich   January 1943 - 19.5.44

Patrols: 5   Ships sunk: 2 (9656 grt) + 1 damaged
                              1 m/s trawler (611 dt)

1. 3.8.43 Left Kiel and arrived Bergen **6.8.43**

2. 12.8.43 Left Bergen and arrived Narvik **15.8.43**

3. 18.8.43 Left for operations.

On the 28th U 960 laid mines E of the Matochkin Strait.

The boat returned to Narvik **1.9.43**

4. 14.9.43 Left for operations.

On the 23rd U 960 laid mines off Dickson. There are no known sinkings attributed to these mines.

In late September U 960, U 601 and U 703 relieved boats of *Wiking* group. On the 30th they encountered westbound Soviet convoy VA 18 NE of Dickson. U 960 torpedoed and sank the SS *Archangel'sk* (sov 2480t) on the 30th, sank the m/s trawler *TSC-42* on 1.10.43 and she may also have damaged the SS *A Andreev* (sov 2487t) in the same attack on the convoy.

U 960 returned to Narvik **10.10.43**

5. 14.10.43 Left Narvik and arrived Trondheim **16.10.43**

6. 4.12.43 Left for operations W of the British Isles.

U 960 joined *Amrum* group, formed on the 18th in the central North Atlantic. From the 23rd *Amrum, Föhr* and *Sylt* groups were redisposed in six small sub-groups, *Rügen 1* to *6*, each with three or four boats. U 960 was in *Rügen 4*. These groups were constantly changing positions and varying formations to prevent the Allies determining the area over which they were operating.

When convoys UC 8, TU 5 and CU 9 were sighted by various *Rügen* groups in late December, the group involved in the sighting was always too small to mount an attack. From 7.1.44 the groups were dissolved and the boats operated singly.

U 960 left *Rügen* group and went on to weather-reporting duty in the central North Atlantic. On the 16th she torpedoed and sank a straggler from westbound convoy ON 219, the SS *Sumner I Kimball* (am 7176t), SE of Cape Farewell.

U 960 put in to La Pallice **3.2.44**

7. 16.3.44 Left La Pallice and returned **18.3.44**

8. 19.3.44 Left for Atlantic operations.

On the 27th U 960, possibly returning after being recalled, was attacked and damaged by two Mosquitos of 618 Squadron (F/O D J Turner and A Hilliard), equipped with 57mm guns. The aircraft sighted a convoy of nine armed trawlers, two U-boats, one minesweeper and a merchant ship. In the face of heavy flak, Hilliard scored hits on U 960. Ten of her crew were wounded, four of them seriously. Hilliard's Mosquito was damaged.

U 960 returned to La Pallice **27.3.44**

U 960 (continued)

9. 27.4.44 Left for the Mediterranean.

U 960 probably passed throught the Straits of Gibraltar during the night of May 14/15th. Early on the 17th the boat attacked the destroyer USS *Ellyson* with a 3-torpedo spread that missed. The destroyer had aboard 47 survivors from the recently-sunk U 616.

Torpedo tracks were sighted by an RAF aircraft near the *Ellyson* N of Ténès. Four destroyers, USS *Ludlow, Niblack, Woolsey* and *Benson*, were ordered to the scene. Searching aircraft from 36 and 500 Squadrons made a contact in the evening. The destroyers paired off, 20 miles apart in U 960's possible track. In the early hours of the 19th an aircraft made a radar contact ahead of *Ludlow* and *Niblack*. The two destroyers raced to the spot and after locating the boat, they dropped depth-charges.

Four hours later U 960 surfaced about a mile away and the two destroyers opened fire. They were joined in the attack by the *Woolsey* and *Benson* and USS *Madison*. Whilst fire was being exchanged between U 960 and the destroyers, a Wellington of 36 Squadron (P/O K H N Bulmer) and a Ventura of 500 Squadron (WO E A K Munday) came in and dropped depth-charges. U 960 dived but depth-charges from *Niblack* forced her back to the surface. The crew abandoned ship and U960 sank. The hunt had lasted more than 40 hours.

U 960's commander and 21 men were picked up and 31 others of the crew lost their lives.

U 961   Type VII C

Built by Blohm & Voss, Hamburg
Keel laid 7.4.42   Launched 17.12.42
Commissioned 4.2.43   Feldpost Nr M 50 655

Sunk 29.3.44 NNE of the Faroes (64°31′ 03°19′W)

Served with
5 U-Flottille, Kiel   February 1943 - 29.3.44 (ab/fb)

Commanded by
OL Klaus Fischer   February 1943 - 29.3.44

Patrols: 1   Ships sunk: None

1. 23.3.44 Left Marviken for Atlantic operations.

U 961 was NNE of the Faroes on the 29th, heading westwards, when she passed close to the eastbound convoy JW 58. The 2nd SG was escorting this convoy and the sloop HMS *Starling* (Capt F J Walker) located U 961. Two hasty depth-charge patterns were fired whilst other 2nd SG ships moved into position. The boat exploded almost immediately, sending wreckage and bodies to the surface.

There were no survivors, 49 dead.

U 962   Type VII C

Built by Blohm & Voss, Hamburg
Keel laid 7.4.42   Launched 17.12.42
Commissioned 11.2.43   Feldpost Nr M 50 679

Sunk 8.4.44 NE of the Azores (45°43′N 19°57′W)

Served with
4 U-Flottille, Stettin   February 1943 - July 1943 (ab)
7 U-Flottille, St Nazaire   August 1943 - 8.4.44 (fb)

Commanded by
OL Ernst Liesberg   February 1943 - 8.4.44

Patrols: 2   Ships sunk: None

1. 23.9.43 Left Kiel and arrived Bergen **27.9.43**

2. 3.11.43 Left Bergen for Atlantic operations.

U 962 was one of a number of boats which took up submerged, waiting positions W of the British Isles.

In early December they assembled W of the North Channel as *Coronel* group, which searched for westbound ONS 24 but was unsuccessful because aerial reconnaissance failed to find it. The convoy passed to the north of the group.

In mid-December *Coronel* group was enlarged and split into two sub-groups, *Coronel 1* and *3*, to search for westbound ON 214. U 962 was in *Coronel 3*. Again, aircraft failed to find the convoy and it passed to the south. Boats of the group, including U 962, searched far to the south for ONS 25 but it was not found.

From the 20th the *Coronel 3* boats joined with new-arrivals to form a new patrol line, *Borkum*, 400 miles NW of Cape Ortegal, to intercept combined convoy MKS 33/SL 142. When the convoy was not found, the *Borkum* boats were ordered to operate against the carrier groups of USS *Card* and *Core*, in an effort to cover the returning blockade-runner *Osorno*, which had been spotted on the 23rd by aircraft from *Card*.

U 962 left *Borkum* group about this time and made her way to St Nazaire, reaching there **28.12.43**

2. 14.2.44 Left for the North Atlantic.

U 962 joined *Preussen* group, formed 400 to 500 miles N of the Azores. Between the 27th and 29th the group was concentrated between 22° and 30°W, in the expected path of convoy ON 225 but on March 2nd it was learned that the convoy had altered course, avoiding *Preussen*.

The boats moved northwards on the 6th to search for convoys and they operated singly W of the British Isles. *Preussen* group was dissolved on the 22nd and boats then operated independently.

From early April U 962 was on weather-reporting duty. On 8.4.44 she was located NE of the Azores and sunk in depth-charge attacks by the sloops HMS *Crane* (Lt B M Skinner) and *Cygnet* (Cdr D M Maclean) of the 7th SG.

There were no survivors, 50 dead.

U 963   Type VII C

Built by Blohm & Voss, Hamburg
Keel laid 20.4.42   Launched 30.12.42
Commissioned 17.2.43   Feldpost Nr M 50 702

Scuttled 20.5.45 near Nazaré, Portugal

Served with
5 U-Flottille, Kiel   February - July 1943 (ab)
1 U-Flottille, Brest   August 1943 - October 1944 (fb)
11 U-Flottille, Bergen   November 1944 - 5.5.45 (fb)

Commanded by
OL Karl Boddenberg   February 1943 - October 1944
OL Werner Müller (temp)   19.7.44 - 21.8.44
OL Rolf-Werner Wentz   December 1944 - 5.5.45

Patrols: 8   Ships sunk: None

1. 17.8.43 Left Kiel and arrived Bergen **20.8.43**

2. 24.8.43 Left Bergen and arrived Trondheim **26.8.43**

3. 4.9.43 Left for the North Atlantic.

Making her way out through the Denmark Strait, U 963 suffered damage from pack-ice.

She returned to Trondheim **18.9.43**

4. 5.10.43   Left for the North Atlantic.

U 963 joined *Siegfried* group, formed for the 24th 500 miles E of Newfoundland to await HX 262 and SC 145. The boats were ordered to remain submerged in daylight, ready for an attack after dark. On the 25th it was thought that a convoy would pass south of the group. The boats moved southwards but nothing was found.

To cover a wider area, *Siegfried* was split into three small sub-groups, *Siegfried 1,2* and *3*. U 963 was in *Siegfried 2*. The groups continued southwards, searching for SC 145 but it passed by on the 29th. Two days later the boats again reformed, this time into groups *Jahn* and *Körner*. U 963 was in *Körner*.

On 3.11.43 the boats were again redisposed, in five small sub-groups, *Tirpitz 1* to *5*, to search for convoy HX 264. It passed by late on the 6th and next day the operation was abandoned, it being impossible to surface in daylight because of carrier-borne aircraft.

U 963 next joined *Eisenhart* group, made up of seven sub-groups of three boats each and drawn up in two lines from 11.11.43, running southeastwards from Cape Farewell. The lines crossed an area through which most convoys had passed since August 1943.

Reports indicated that convoys were being routed to the south so the *Eisenhart* boats were ordered southeastwards on the 12th to search for SC 146 and HX 265. By the 16th no convoys had been found and the majority of the boats were by then WSW of Ireland. Fuel was now becoming a problem for many of *Eisenhart* group and it was decided to end the operation. Boats with sufficient fuel went to reinforce *Schill* group W of Spain and the others, including U 963, headed for base.

She reached Lorient **3.12.43**

5. 23.1.44   Left Lorient and returned **24.1.44**

6. 26.1.44   Left for Atlantic operations.

U 963 joined *Igel 2* group W of Ireland, searching for westbound convoy ON 223. From 4.2.44 the *Igel 2* boats were patrolling SW of Ireland. On the 6th they were deployed against combined convoy MKS 38/SL 147, reported N of the Azores by German aircraft on the 6th, 7th and 8th. Some of the boats came up to the convoy on the 7th but had no success against the strong escort.

From the 10th *Igel 1* and *2* groups began a slow westward withdrawal, which was taken further than intended because of intense Allied anti-submarine activity, both SW of Ireland and NW of Scotland. It was intended to intercept an ONS convoy between the 14th and 18th, with the aid of aerial-reconnaissance.

ONS 29, ON 224 and OS 68 were sighted by aircraft on the 14th W of the North Channel and *Igel 1* and *2* groups were hurried to an assembly area 600 miles SW of Ireland. On the 18th two parallel patrol lines, *Hai 1* and *2*, were formed ahead of the convoys. They were found to have turned south on the 17th and passed the southern end of the *Hai* lines. The boats were immediately ordered southwards, submerged in daylight and at high speed on the surface in the hours of darkness. Instead of sighting any convoys at dawn on the 19th, the boats saw only some destroyers. The operation was called off and the boats submerged to avoid aircraft from the escort-carrier HMS *Striker*.

U 963 moved westwards with the other boats and *Preussen* group was formed 400 to 500 miles N of the Azores. Between the 27th and 29th the group was concentrated between 22° and 30°W in the expected path of convoy ON 225 but on March 2nd it was learned that the convoy had altered course, avoiding *Preussen*.

The boats moved northwards on the 6th to search for convoys and they operated singly W of the British Isles. *Preussen* group was dissolved on the 22nd.

U 963 put in to Brest **27.3.44**

7. 6.6.44   Left Brest, as part of *Landwirt* group.

Outward-bound on the 7th, U 963 was attacked and damaged by a Liberator of 53 Squadron (F/Lt J W Carmichael) NW of Ushant. She returned to Brest **8.6.44**

8. 11.7.44   Left Brest and returned **13.7.44**

9. 17.7.44   Left Brest and returned **19.7.44**

10. 13.8.44   Left Brest, in transit to La Pallice.

U 963 lost one crewman in a crash-dive on the 21st. She put in to La Pallice later the same day **21.8.44**

11. 29.8.44   Left La Pallice for British coastal waters.

U 963 was one of three schnorkel boats which operated in the North Channel from mid-September. Whilst some ships were sunk there in the first weeks of September, the traffic became very much reduced. U 963 stayed in the area for only a few days and had no success.

U 963 put in to Bergen **7.10.44**

12. 16.1.45   Left Bergen for British coastal waters.

In the first week of February U 963 was patrolling in the Irish Sea but she had no success. From the 10th repairs were carried out on her schnorkel.

The boat returned to Trondheim **6.3.45**

13. 23.4.45   Left for the Western Atlantic.

U 963 was to carry out a mining operation off Portland, Maine. She was outward-bound when the U-boat war ended on May 4.

The boat made her way back eastwards and on the 20th, in contravention of the surrender terms, she was beached by her crew and scuttled near Nazaré, W of Oporto, Portugal.

U 964   Type VII C

Built by Blohm & Voss, Hamburg
Keel laid 20.4.42   Launched 30.12.42
Commissioned 18.2.43   Feldpost Nr M 50 718

Sunk 16.10.43 SW of Reykjavik (57°27′N 28°17′W)

Served with
5 U-Flottille, Kiel   February - September 1943 (ab)
6 U-Flottille, St Nazaire   October 1943 (fb)

Commanded by
OL Emmo Hummerjohann   February 1943 - 16.10.43

Patrols: 1   Ships sunk: None

1. 30.9.43   Left Kiel and arrived Bergen **4.10.43**

2. 5.10.43   Left for the North Atlantic.

Outward-bound, U 964 was ordered to join *Schlieffen* group, which on the 15th was searching for westbound ONS 20. The convoy was sighted by U 844 in the evening of the 15th W of Rockall but she was located and driven off during the night.

Early on the 16th ONS 20 was sighted by U 964. In the afternoon the shadowing boat was sighted ahead of the convoy by a Liberator of 86 Squadron (F/O G D Gamble). The aircraft dropped three depth-charges but apparently without causing damage. Further attacks could not be pressed home because of heavy flak.

When Gamble's request for surface assistance was turned down, he went in and dropped three more depth-charges. U 964 moved northwards, still on the surface but gradually sinking. She went down within the hour.

Several boats answered U 964's call for assistance but despite many of her crew being seen in the water, only four men were picked up by U 231, one of whom died soon afterwards.

The commander and 46 other men were lost.

U 965　Type VII C

Built by Blohm & Voss, Hamburg
Keel laid 4.5.42　Launched 14.1.43
Commissioned 25.2.43　Feldpost Nr M 51 414

Sunk 27.3.45 SW of Cape Wrath (58°34´N 05°46´W)

Served with
5 U-Flottille, Kiel　February - December 1943 (ab)
11 U-Flottille, Bergen　January - September 1944 (fb)
13 U-Flottille, Trondheim　October 1944 - 27.3.45 (fb)

Commanded by
KL Klaus Ohling　February 1943 - June 1944
OL Günter Unverzagt　June 1944 - 27.3.45

Patrols: 8　Ships sunk: None

1. 14.12.43　Left Kiel and arrived Arendal **16.12.43**

2. 29.12.43　Left Arendal and arrived Bergen **31.12.43**

3. 1.1.44　Left for Northern Waters.
Eastbound JW 56A left Loch Ewe on the 12th but after running into a storm on the 16th the convoy put in to Akureyri, Iceland. On the 21st it sailed again, less five ships which had been damaged. Convoy JW 56B left Loch Ewe on the 22nd.
U 965 was with *Isegrim* group, which was awaiting these two convoys in Bear Island Passage. On the 25th contact was made with JW 56A and during that day and the night of the 25/26th nine of the ten boats of *Isegrim* group made attacks on the convoy and escort. U 965 made the first attack on the escort, an unsuccessful one with only end-of-run detonations heard. JW 56A had three ships sunk and the destroyer HMS *Obdurate* damaged.
After the convoy moved on towards Kola Inlet, *Isegrim* group reformed as *Werwolf*, to await JW 56B in the Passage. Contact was made on the 29th and next day U 965 made an unsuccessful attack on an escorting destroyer SE of Bear Island.
The boat put in to Narvik **3.2.44**

4. 5.2.44　Left Narvik and arrived Bergen **9.2.44**

5. 14.5.44　Left Bergen and arrived Bogenbucht **18.5.44**

6. 23.6.44　Left for operations.
In July U 965 was with *Trutz* group E of Jan Mayen. On 20.7.44 one crewman was killed and another wounded when an aircraft attacked the boat. Immediately after this the group was dissolved.
U 965 returned to Narvik **23.7.44**

7. 19.8.44　Left Narvik.
On the 22nd U 965 was within 45 minutes of Hammerfest when she was attacked by FAA Seafires. In the attack she had 3 men killed and 8 others wounded.
The boat put in to Hammerfest **22.8.44**

8. 1.9.44　Left Hammerfest and arrived Narvik **3.9.44**

9. 8.9.44　Left Narvik and arrived Tromsø **9.9.44**

10. 16.9.44　Left Tromsø and arrived Altafjord **19.9.44**

11. 21.9.44　Left Altafjord and arrived Tromsø **23.9.44**

12. 26.9.44　Left for operations.
Westbound convoy RA 60 left Kola Inlet during the night of the 27/28th. U 965 was with *Zorn* group, which was at sea and intended to intercept the convoy SW of Bear Island. However, RA 60 was re-routed and avoided both *Zorn* and *Grimm* groups. The only success achieved was by U 310. She sank two ships after being overrun by the convoy.
U 965 returned to Narvik **3.10.44**

13. 15.10.44　Left for operations. No details known.
U 965 returned to Hammerfest **23.10.44**

14. 24.10.44　Left for operations.
On the 20th eastbound JW 61 left Loch Ewe. U 965 was with *Panther* group, through which the convoy passed without loss, arriving off Kola Inlet on the 28th. Unsuccessful attacks were made against the convoy's escort on the 26th and 27th by *Panther* boats.
U 965 probably also operated against eastbound JW 61A. The *Panther* boats were unable to reach the convoy because of the strength of the escort. It was the same situation with westbound RA 61, although the destroyer-escort HMS *Mounsey* was damaged by U 295 and a Soviet destroyer was probably sunk by U 997.
U 965 put in to Kilbotn **11.11.44**

15. 13.11.44　Left Kilbotn and arrived Narvik **14.11.44**

16. 21.11.44　Left for operations.
U 965 was with *Grube* group, waiting off the Kola coast for eastbound JW 62. From 2.12.44 some *Grube* boats operated against Russian coastal convoys. U 965 did not take part in any attacks. JW 62 reached Kola Inlet without loss on the 7th, having bypassed both *Grube* and *Stock* groups.
Grube group was waiting for return convoy RA 62 to sail. Prior to the convoy's departure, a force of Allied and Russian warships tried to drive off the boats waiting at the entrance to Kola Inlet. U 387 of *Grube* group was sunk. RA 62 sailed on the 10th and reached Loch Ewe without loss.
U 965 returned to Kilbotn **14.12.44**

17. 17.12.44　Left Kilbotn and arrived Trondheim **20.12.44**

18. 15.2.45　Left Trondheim for operations. No details known.
U 965 returned **27.2.45**

19. 5.3.45　Left Trondheim for British coastal waters.
U 965 operated in The Minch and around the northwest coast of Scotland. On the 16th she made an unsuccessful attack on a ship.
The 21st EG was searching for U-boats in the area of the Hebrides and The Minch in the latter part of March. On the 27th U 965 was located by the frigate HMS *Conn* (Lt-Cdr C T D Williams) SW of Cape Wrath and sunk in depth-charge attacks.
There were no survivors, 53 dead.

U 966　Type VII C

Built by Blohm & Voss, Hamburg
Keel laid 1.5.42　Launched 14.1.43
Commissioned 4.3.43　Feldpost Nr M 51 418

Scuttled 10.11.43 near De Santafata Bay, Spain

Served with
5 U-Flottille, Kiel　March - July 1943 (ab)
9 U-Flottille, Brest　August 1943 - 10.11.43 (fb)

Commanded by
OL Eckehard Wolf　March 1943 - 10.11.43

Patrols: 1　Ships sunk: None

1. 9.9.43 Left Kiel and arrived Molde **15.9.43**

2. 17.9.43 Left Molde and arrived Trondheim **18.9.43**

3. 5.10.43 Left for the North Atlantic.
U 966 had no success on this patrol. She was making for Western France when she was located in the early morning of 10.11.43 NW of Cape Ortegal by a Wellington of 612 Squadron (WO I D Gunn).
Six depth-charges were dropped and fire was exchanged. The boat was damaged and whilst temporary repairs were being made a Wellington of 407 (RCAF) Squadron arrived, which had been directed to the scene. This aircraft was shot down and the boat then headed for the Spanish coast.
She was unsuccessfully attacked by a USN Liberator of VP-105 and later came under depth-charge attacks by Liberators of VP-103 (Lt K L Wright) and VP-110 (Lt J A Parrish).
U 966 was finally attacked by a Liberator of 311 (Czech) Squadron (F/Sgt Zanta) with rockets. The boat was scuttled offshore of De Santafata Bay, Spain. The crew went ashore in dinghies or were picked up by Spanish fishing trawlers.
8 men were killed or missing. 42 others, including U 966's commander, were interned by the Spanish authorities. 9 were later repatriated to Germany.

U 967 Type VII C

Built by Blohm & Voss, Hamburg
Keel laid 16.5.42   Launched 28.1.43
Commissioned 11.3.43   Feldpost Nr M 51 480

Scuttled 19.8.44 at Toulon

Served with
5 U-Flottille, Kiel   March - September 1943 (ab)
6 U-Flottille, St Nazaire   October 1943 - February 1944 (fb)
29 U-Flottille, Toulon   March 1944 - 19.8.44 (fb)

Commanded by
OL Herbert Loeder   March 1943 - March 1944
FK Albrecht Brandi   March - July 1944
OL Heinz-Eugen Eberbach   July 1944 - 19.8.44

Patrols: 3   Ships sunk: None
                              1 destroyer-escort (1300 dt)

1. 5.10.43 Left Kiel and arrived Bergen **9.10.43**

2. 11.10.43 Left for the North Atlantic. On the 12th one crewman was lost overboard.
U 967 joined *Siegfried* group 500 miles E of Newfoundland, which was in position on the 24th awaiting convoys HX 262 and SC 145. When carrier-borne aircraft were seen next day it was assumed a convoy had passed to the south and the group moved to intercept but nothing was found.
On the 27th, to widen the search, the group was split into three, *Siegfried 1,2* and *3*. U 967 was in *Siegfried 1*. A further redisposition was made on 1.11.43, when the boats reformed as two larger groups, *Körner* and *Jahn*. U 967 was in *Körner* but not for long because on the 3rd yet another redisposition saw the boats split into five small sub-groups, *Tirpitz 1* to *5*.
On the 7th after failing to find convoys HX 264 and SC 146, the *Tirpitz* groups were dissolved and the boats moved eastwards. From the 11th they reformed as *Eisenhart* group, disposed in seven subsections of three boats each, strung out in two lines running southeastwards from Cape Farewell to 48°N. When convoys were found to be passing south of the lines, the *Eisenhart* boats began to

move southeastwards on the 12th. By the 14th they were between 43° and 50°N, awaiting HX 265 and SC 146. When neither convoy appeared, the groups were broken up on the 16th and the boats were sent to reinforce *Schill* group, waiting W of Portugal for northbound convoy MKS 30/SL 139. U 967 joined *Schill 3*.
The convoy was expected to pass through the line on the 20th. *Schill 3* surfaced that evening but failed to find the convoy, which was located next morning and attacked by aircraft, resulting in one ship sunk and another damaged, both by glider-bombs. Thus the operation ended in complete failure for the U-boats. Early on the 21st U 967 was attacked with depth-charges by the destroyer-escort HMS *Essington* but was probably undamaged.
U 967 put in to her new base at St Nazaire **1.12.43**

3. 20.1.44 Left for the Mediterranean.
U 967 passed through the Straits of Gibraltar during the night of 12/13.2.44. She operated initially off the Algerian coast but she had no success.
The boat put in to her new base at Toulon **23.2.44**

4. 11.4.44 Left for operations.
U 967 operated in the Eastern Mediterranean. On the 26th she unsuccessfully attacked a destroyer E of Gibraltar, hearing only an end-of-run detonation.
During the night of May 4/5th U 967 was located by the destroyer-escort USS *Laning* after attempting to attack a ship in convoy GUS 38 E of Gibraltar. Shortly afterwards U 967 torpedoed and sank the destroyer-escort USS *Fechteler*. 188 of *Fechteler's* crew were picked up by the *Laning* and the tug HMS *Hengist*.
On the 8th U 967 missed a destroyer N of the Isla de Alboran. She was also unable to get through to the ships of eastbound convoy UGS 40 on the 10th.
U 967 returned to Toulon **17.5.44**

On 5.7.44 U 967 was slightly damaged in a USAF raid on Toulon harbour. After being further damaged in another USAF raid on 6.8.44, the boat was scuttled on the 19th to prevent her falling into Allied hands. Two of U 967's crew were killed in Toulon.

U 968 Type VII C

Built by Blohm & Voss, Hamburg
Keel laid 14.5.42   Launched 28.1.43
Commissioned 18.3.43   Feldpost Nr M 51 536

Sunk 29.11.45 N of Rathlin Island (55°24´N 06°23´W)

Served with
5 U-Flottille, Kiel   March 1943 - February 1944 (ab)
13 U-Flottille, Trondheim   March 1944 - 16.5.45 (fb)

Commanded by
OL Otto Westphalen   March 1943 - 16.5.45

Patrols: 8   Ships sunk: 2 (14,386 grt) + 1 damaged
                              2 sloops (2700 dt)
                              1 frigate (1150 dt)

From September 1943 U 968 took part in trials in the Baltic, testing equipment to counter airborne radar.

1. 7.3.44 Left Kiel for Northern Waters.
Eastbound convoy JW 58 left Loch Ewe on the 27th and was located by German aircraft on the 30th. Three small U-boat groups, *Hammer, Thor* and *Blitz*, were waiting for the convoy. U 968 was in *Hammer.*
Most of the boats made contact with the convoy early on 1.4.44

U 968 (continued)

ENE of Jan Mayen. U 968 was one of the first to attack but she was unsuccessful against two destroyers of the escort and was probably located and damaged.

She put in to Narvik **2.4.44**

2. 4.4.44 Left Narvik and arrived Trondheim **6.4.44**

3. 11.7.44 Left Trondheim and arrived Narvik **14.7.44**

4. 17.7.44 Left for operations.

On the 18th U 968 was sighted by a Liberator of 86 Squadron (F/Lt W F J Harwood). Two depth-charge attacks were made in the face of heavy flak and the aircraft was shot down. Six of her crew were picked up by a Catalina three days later.

U 968 was further damaged in three attacks by another Liberator in the morning of the 19th. One crewman was killed and six wounded.

The boat put in to Bogenbucht **21.7.44**

5. 20.8.44 Left Bogenbucht and arrived Hammerfest **22.8.44**

6. 29.8.44 Left for operations.

U 968 was with *Dachs* group, which carried out minelaying operations. On 4.9.44 she laid mines off the coast at Mys Kanin Nos, Pechora Sea. As far as is known, there are no known sinkings or damage to ships attributed to these mines.

U 968 returned to Bogenbucht **10.9.44**

7. 24.9.44 Left for operations.

Westbound convoy RA 60 left Kola Inlet during the night of the 27/28th. U 968 was with *Zorn* group, which was awaiting the convoy. However, RA 60 avoided both *Zorn* and *Grimm* groups but two ships were sunk by U 310 of *Zorn*, after she had been overrun by the convoy in the afternoon of the 29th.

U 968 returned to Narvik **3.10.44**

8. 14.10.44 Left for operations.

U 968 was with *Panther* group, awaiting eastbound JW 61, which had left Loch Ewe on the 20th. The convoy passed through the waiting boats. Some attacks were made on the escort but were unsuccessful.

U 968 put in to Ramsund **11.11.44**

9. 13.11.44 Left Ramsund and arrived Rörvik **16.11.44**

10. 23.1.45 Left Rörvik and arrived Narvik **25.1.45**

11. 1.2.45 Left Narvik and arrived Harstad **1.2.45**

12. 7.2.45 Left for operations.

U 968 joined *Rasmus* group in Bear Island Passage. The group was attempting to reach eastbound convoy JW 64 but failed because of the very strong escort. After the convoy had passed, the *Rasmus* boats joined others waiting off Kola Inlet.

On the 14th U 968 torpedoed and damaged the tanker SS *Norfjell* (nw 8129t) of Soviet convoy BK 3 off Kola Inlet. This vessel was towed to Rosta and taken over by the Soviet Navy in June 1945.

On the 16th a combined force of British and Soviet naval vessels attempted to drive the waiting boats away before return convoy RA 64 sailed. It left on the 17th and on that day U 968 attacked the convoy and torpedoed two ships, damaging the escorting sloop HMS *Lark* and the SS *Thomas Scott* (am 7176t). The *Lark* was beached and later handed over to the Russians but was probably never repaired. The *Thomas Scott* was abandoned after being hit and sank under tow. U 968 also claimed a Soviet destroyer hit.

Contact with the convoy was lost on the 18th. Some boats moved to Bear Island Passage but they were unable to find the convoy. It was found by German aircraft and attacked on the 20th and 23rd. One straggler was sunk in the second attack but the Luftwaffe lost six more aircraft.

U 968 put in to Kilbotn **20.2.45**

13. 12.3.45 Left for operations.

U 968 joined *Hagen* group in Bear Island Passage, awaiting eastbound JW 65, which had left the Clyde on the 11th.

Aerial reconnaissance failed to find the convoy and the waiting boats moved to the the entrance of Kola Inlet to join others already there and two lines were formed, one of six boats and one of seven. In the morning of the 20th the convoy passed the first line in a snowstorm. On ship was torpedoed and damaged.

The second line was passed at noon. U 968 sank the sloop HMS *Lapwing* and the SS *Thomas Donaldson* (am 7210t). After the convoy entered Kola Inlet on the 21st, the boats attempted to operate against the aircraft carriers HMS *Campania* and *Trumpeter* from JW 65's escort, which were believed to be in the Barents Sea, but this was unsuccessful.

On the 23rd return convoy RA 65 sailed from Kola Inlet. U 968 sighted the convoy and its carrier escort as it left the Inlet but was unable to attack. Waiting boats tried to form a patrol line ahead of the convoy but were unable to. JW 65 arrived without loss off Kirkwall on the 31st.

U 968 returned to Kilbotn **30.3.45**

14. 21.4.45 Left for operations.

U 968 and other boats left their bases to move to Kola Inlet. En route, some came into contact with a Soviet coastal convoy on the 21st and 22nd. U 968 did not take part in the ensuing action.

On the 29th before return convoy RA 66 sailed, Allied and Russian warships attempted to drive the boats away from the Inlet.

The boats were waiting for the convoy. U 968 had a torpedo explode in the wake of the corvette HMS *Alnwick Castle* and she torpedoed and severely damaged the frigate HMS *Goodall*. The corvette HMS *Honeysuckle* went alongside *Goodall* to take off her crew but almost immediately *Goodall* exploded, damaging the corvette and forcing her away. It is possible that U 286 may have put another torpedo into *Goodall* at some time but this is not certain. The frigate HMS *Anguilla* sank the abandoned *Goodall*.

When Dönitz declared the end of the U-boat war on May 4th, U 968 was still at sea. She put in to Harstad on the 6th, left on the 7th and went to Skjomenfjord. The boat left again, probably to go to Narvik.

U 968 was one of a number of boats which headed for Trondheim. They were met at sea by the 9th EG and escorted to Loch Eriboll, probably reaching there on 19.5.45.

U 968 was one of 116 boats disposed of by the Royal Navy in Operation Deadlight. In late November 1945 she was towed from Loch Ryan out through the North Channel by the tug HMS Prosperous.

U 968 foundered under tow on 29.11.45 N of Rathlin Island.

U 969 Type VII C

Built by Blohm & Voss, Hamburg
Keel laid 29.5.42   Launched 11.2.43
Commissioned 24.3.43   Feldpost Nr M 51 543

Destroyed 19.8.44 at Toulon

Served with
5 U-Flottille, Kiel March - September 1943 (ab)
7 U-Flottille, St Nazaire October 1943 - February 1944 (fb)
29 U-Flottille, Toulon March 1944 - 19.8.44 (fb)

Commanded by
OL Max Dobbert March 1943 - 19.8.44

Patrols: 3   Ships sunk: 2 (14,352 grt)

1. 30.9.43   Left Kiel and arrived Bergen **4.10.43**

2. 5.10.43   Left for the North Atlantic.
U 969 joined *Siegfried* group, formed for the 24th 500 miles E of Newfoundland to await HX 262 and SC 145. The boats were ordered to remain submerged in daylight, ready for an attack after dark. On the 25th it was believed that HX 262 was passing south of the patrol line. The group moved southwards. No contact was made.

To cover a wider area, *Siegfried* was split into three small sub-groups, *Siegfried 1,2* and *3*. U 969 was in *Siegfried 1*. The group continued southwards, searching for SC 145 but it passed by unobserved on the 29th. Two days later the boats again reformed, this time into groups *Körner* and *Jahn* E of Newfoundland. U 969 was in *Körner*.

On 3.11.43 the boats were redeployed in five small sub-groups, *Tirpitz 1* to *5*, to search for convoy HX 264. It passed the groups late on the 6th and next day the operation was abandoned, it being impossible to surface in daylight because of the constant presence of carrier-borne aircraft.

U 969 joined *Eisenhart* group, made up of seven sub-groups of three boats each and drawn up in two lines from the 11th, running southeastwards from Cape Farewell. The lines crossed an area through which most convoys had passed since August 1943.

Reports indicated that convoys were being routed to the south, so the *Eisenhart* boats were ordered southeastwards on the 12th to search for SC 146 and HX 265. By the 16th no convoys had been found although U 969 and U 542 sighted destroyers on that day.

By this time the majority of boats were WSW of Ireland and fuel was becoming a problem for many of *Eisenhart* group. It was then decided to end the operation and send the boats with sufficient fuel, including U 969, to reinforce *Schill* group W of Portugal.

U 969 joined *Schill 2* group on or about the 17th. The group moved northwards on the 18th to take up an east-west patrol line in the expected path of MKS 30/SL 139 and through which the convoy was expected to pass late on the 19th. When the *Schill 2* boats surfaced that evening, the convoy was reported to be 20 miles south of the line.

However, night-flying aircraft constantly harassed the boats, keeping them down, and the convoy's escort kept them at a distance. *Schill 2* took no further part in the operation against MKS 30/SL 139. On the 22nd the boats from *Schill 1,2* and *3* groups, which had not returned to base, formed *Weddigen* group, in an east-west patrol line between 18° and 22°W W of Spain, to await convoys KMS 33/OG 95 and OS 59.

When the convoys were not found by aircraft, the patrol line moved southwestwards at high speed to make a possible interception. When nothing had been found by the evening of the 25th, the *Weddigen* line moved southeastwards, to intercept MKS 31/SL 140.

The combined convoy was sighted on the 26th, moving westwards, but it later headed north and next morning was reported to the east of the patrol line. The boats moved northeastwards, submerged in daylight and at high speed on the surface in darkness. In the face of Allied aircraft and surface vessel activity, the boats made slow progress and the pursuit ended on the 28th.
U 969 put in to Lorient **6.12.43**

3. 18.1.44   Left for the Mediterranean.
U 969 passed through the Straits of Gibraltar during the night of February 4/5th and then operated off the coast of Algeria. On the 22nd the boat attacked a westbound convoy near Philippeville. She torpedoed and damaged two ships, the SS *George Cleeve* (am 7176t) and the SS *Peter Skene Ogden* (am 7176t). Both vessels were beached but both were declared total losses.
U 969 put in to her new base at Toulon **26.2.44**

4. 20.3.44   Left for operations.
On the 31st U 969 and U 421 were deployed against convoy UGS 36, which had just entered the Mediterranean, but the escort prevented both boats from making an attack.

U 969, U 421 and the newly-arrived U 471 were sent against convoy UGS 37, which had passed through the Straits of Gibraltar on 10.4.44, but they had no success.

On the 20th U 969 was unsuccessful against convoy UGS 38, which had entered the Mediterranean the previous day.
The boat returned to Toulon **28.4.44**

On 5.7.44 U 969 was badly damaged in a USAF raid on Toulon harbour. She was further damaged in another USAF raid on 6.8.44.

U 969 was blown up on 19.8.44 to prevent any Allied attempt to salvage the boat.

U 970 Type VII C

Built by Blohm & Voss, Hamburg
Keel laid 29.5.42   Launched 11.2.43
Commissioned 25.3.43   Feldpost Nr M 51 558

Sunk 8.6.44 in the Bay of Biscay (45°15′N 04°10′W)

Served with
5 U-Flottille, Kiel March 1943 - February 1944 (ab)
3 U-Flottille, La Pallice March 1944 - 8.6.44 (fb)

Commanded by
KL Hans-Heinrich Ketels March 1943 - 8.6.44

Patrols: 2   Ships sunk: None

1. 24.2.44   Left Kiel and arrived Bergen **26.2.44**

2. 16.3.44   Left Bergen for the North Atlantic.
In early April U 970 was ordered to proceed to Western France and join *Landwirt* group.
She put in to La Pallice **22.4.44**

3. 6.6.44   U 970 was one of nineteen non-schnorkel boats which sailed into the Bay of Biscay as part of *Landwirt* group.

They were to form a line at the 200 metres depth line between Brest and Bordeaux, keeping out of port in case an Allied invasion force arrived and trapped them there.

U 970 was located early on the 8th by a Sunderland of 228 Squadron (F/Lt C G D Lancaster). A depth-charge attack was carried out after the boat had been illuminated by flares. She was not seen again.

The commander and 13 members of the crew were picked up by the German rescue service. 38 men lost their lives.

U 971   Type VII C

Built by Blohm & Voss, Hamburg
Keel laid 15.6.42   Launched 22.2.43
Commissioned 1.4.43   Feldpost Nr M 41 942

Scuttled 24.6.44 S of Land's End (49°01´N 05°35´W)

Served with
5 U-Flottille, Kiel   April 1943 - May 1944 (ab)
3 U-Flottille/FdU Mitte, Norway   June 1944 (fb)

Commanded by
OL Walter Zeplien   April 1943 - 24.6.44

Patrols: 1   Ships sunk: None

1. **21.5.44**   Left Kiel and arrived Marviken **23.5.44**

2. **8.6.44**   Left for the English Channel.
  Outward-bound, U 971 was located on the 20th by a Wellington of 407 (RCAF) Squadron (F/O F H Foster). The boat was damaged in a depth-charge attack. She was attacked again on the same day by a Halifax of 502 Squadron.
  After receiving further damage, U 971's commander headed for Brest. On the 24th the boat was attacked by a Liberator of 311 (Czech) Squadron (F/O J Vella). The aircraft brought up the destroyers HMCS *Haida* (Cdr H G de Wolf) and HMS *Eskimo* (Lt-Cdr E N Sinclair).
  Depth-charges forced U 971 to the surface. The crew abandoned ship as the two destroyers blazed away. Two men were killed. The commander and 50 others were picked up and made PoW.

U 972   Type VII C

Built by Blohm & Voss, Hamburg
Keel laid 15.6.42   Launched 22.2.43
Commissioned 8.4.43   Feldpost Nr M 42 135

Missing early to mid-January 1944, position unknown

Served with
5 U-Flottille, Kiel   April - November 1943 (ab)
6 U-Flottille, St Nazaire   December 1943 - January 1944 (fb)

Commanded by
OL Klaus-Dietrich König   April 1943 - January 1944

Patrols: 1   Ships sunk: None

1. **30.11.43**   Left Kiel for the North Atlantic.
  U 972 was to have joined *Sylt* group, formed from 19.12.43 W of the British Isles. From the 22nd *Sylt, Amrum* and *Föhr* groups were reformed again W of Ireland, this time into six small sub-groups, *Rügen 1* to *6*. U 972 was to have been in *Rügen 1*.
  These small groups, mostly of three boats each, were constantly moving, changing positions and varying formations, with the objective of preventing the Allies determining the area over which they were operating.
  The last radio message from U 972 was sent on 15.12.43. She is thought to have been lost between January 5th and 15th 1944.
  There were no known survivors, 50 dead.

U 973   Type VII C

Built by Blohm & Voss, Hamburg
Keel laid 26.6.42   Launched 10.3.43
Commissioned 15.4.43   Feldpost Nr M 42 381

Sunk 6.3.44 NW of Bodø (70°04´N 05°48´E)

Served with
5 U-Flottille, Kiel   April 1943 - 6.3.44 (ab)

Commanded by
OL Klaus Paepenmöller   April 1943 - 6.3.44

Patrols: 2   Ships sunk: None

U 973 had the V1 conversion to her conning tower, to include an additional anti-aircraft gun platform.

1. **22.1.44**   Left Kiel and arrived Marviken **23.1.44**

2. **26.1.44**   Left Marviken and arrived Bergen **29.1.44**

3. **2.2.44**   Left for operations.
  U 973 was with *Werwolf* group in Bear Island Passage awaiting westbound RA 56. The boats searched for the convoy in the wrong direction, misled by incorrect information. RA 56 passed by the waiting boats and reached Loch Ewe without loss.
  U 973 put in to Narvik **12.2.44**

4. **19.2.44**   Left Narvik and arrived Trondheim **21.2.44**

5. **1.3.44**   Left for operations.
  On the 2nd westbound RA 57 left Kola Inlet. U 973 was one of a number of boats which operated against it in the Norwegian Sea.
  U 973 was sighted on the 6th and sunk in a rocket attack by a Swordfish of 816 (FAA) Squadron (Sub-Lt L E B Bennett) from the escort-carrier HMS *Chaser*.
  There were no survivors, 51 dead.

U 974   Type VII C

Built by Blohm & Voss, Hamburg
Keel laid 26.6.42   Launched 11.3.43
Commissioned 22.4.43   Feldpost Nr M 43 387

Sunk 19.4.44 just W of Stavanger (59°08´N 05°23´E)

Served with
5 U-Flottille, Kiel   April - October 1943 (ab)
7 U-Flottille, St Nazaire   November 1943 - 19.4.44 (fb)

Commanded by
OL Joachim Zaubitzer   April - November 1943
OL Heinz Wolff   November 1943 - 19.4.44

Patrols: 1   Ships sunk: None

1. **23.3.44**   Left Kiel and arrived Marviken **26.3.44**

2. **18.4.44**   Left Marviken.
  On the 19th U 974 and an escort were sighted by the Norwegian submarine *Ula* (Lt-Cdr R M Sars) just W of Stavanger. A 4-torpedo spread was fired, one of which struck and sank U 974.
  The commander and 7 men were picked up by the German escort and 42 other members of the crew lost their lives.

U 975　Type VII C

Built by Blohm & Voss, Hamburg
Keel laid 10.7.42　Launched 24.3.43
Commissioned 29.4.43　Feldpost Nr M 43 633

Sunk 10.2.46 NW of Bloody Foreland (55°42´N 09°01´W)

Served with
5 U-Flottille, Kiel　April 1943 - January 1944 (ab)
3 U-Flottille, La Pallice　January - July 1944 (fb)
23 U-Flottille, Danzig　July 1944 - February 1945 (ab)
31 U-Flottille, Hamburg　March 1945 - 9.5.45 (ab/fb-m)

Commanded by
OL Hans-Joachim Ebersbach　April - November 1943
OL Paul Frerks　November 1943 - March 1944
OL Hubert Jeschke　March - July 1944
OL Walter-Ernst Koch　July 1944 - April 1945
KL Wilhelm Brauel　April 1945 - 9.5.45

Patrols: 1　　Ships sunk: None

1. 24.5.44　Left Kiel and arrived Stavanger **28.5.44**

2. 8.6.44　Left Stavanger, as part of *Mitte* group.
　Early on the 6th, when news of the invasion of Normandy was received, the *Mitte* boats were put on immediate notice. U 975 was one of eleven boats which put to sea to form a line from Trondheim to Lindesnes. In late June, when the anticipated threat to Norway had receded, U 975 and eight other *Mitte* boats were recalled.
　She returned to Stavanger **26.6.44**

3. 28.6.44　Left Stavanger and arrived Bergen **28.6.44**

4. 30.6.44　Left Bergen and arrived Kristiansand **1.7.44**

5. 2.7.44　Left Kristiansand and returned Kiel **4.7.44**

U 975 did not see any further operational service. She was one of nine Mitte *group boats which were transferred to training duties in early July. Their crews were drafted to 23 and 24 U-Flottillen to man the new Type XXI boats.*

On 9.5.45 U 975 was surrendered at Horten. She left there on the 29th for an assembly area in Britain. She was one of 116 boats disposed of by the Royal Navy in Operation Deadlight.
　In February 1946 U 975 was towed from Lisahally by HMS Loch Arkaig *and sunk by gunfire on 10.2.46 NW of Bloody Foreland.*

U 976　Type VII C

Built by Blohm & Voss, Hamburg
Keel laid 9.7.42　Launched 25.3.43
Commissioned 5.5.43　Feldpost Nr M 51 982

Sunk 25.3.44 just NW of Île d'Yeu (46°48´N 02°43´W)

Served with
5 U-Flottille, Kiel　May - October 1943 (ab)
7 U-Flottille, St Nazaire　November 1943 - 25.3.44 (fb)

Commanded by
OL Raimund Tiesler　May 1943 - 25.3.44

Patrols: 2　　Ships sunk: None

1. 25.11.43　Left Kiel for Atlantic operations.
　U 976 joined a number of boats assembled off the North Channel to search for convoys W of the British Isles. On 15.12.43 U 976, U 284, U 364, U 471, U 741 and U 981 formed *Coronel 2* group to continue their search.
　On the 19th *Coronel 1* and *2* groups were reformed as *Sylt, Amrum* and *Föhr* groups. U 976 was in *Amrum*. From the 22nd the boats were reformed again W of Ireland, this time into six small subgroups, *Rügen 1* to *6*. U 976 was in *Rügen 4*. These small groups, mostly of three boats each, were constantly moving, changing positions and varying formations, with the objective of preventing the Allies determining the area over which they were operating.
　When three convoys were sighted in late December, the groups were each too small to mount an attack. From 7.1.44 the groups were dissolved and the boats operated singly W of Ireland as *Rügen* group. They had no success.
　U 976 put in to her new base at St Nazaire **29.1.44**

2. 20.3.44　Left for operations.
　U 976 was returning to St Nazaire with an escort of two minesweepers and a destroyer on the 25th, probably recalled to become part of *Landwirt* group.
　She was on the surface about 40 miles SW of St Nazaire when she came under attack by two Mosquitos of 618 Squadron (F/Os D J Turner and A Hilliard), equipped with 57mm guns. Hits were scored on U 976's conning tower and forward casing. The batteries were damaged and the resulting chlorine gas forced the crew to abandon ship.
　Four men were killed and the rest of the crew, including the commander, were picked up by German forces.

U 977　Type VII C

Built by Blohm & Voss, Hamburg
Keel laid 24.7.42　Launched 31.3.43
Commissioned 6.5.43　Feldpost Nr M 51 994

Sunk 13.11.46 off US east coast

Served with
5 U-Flottille, Kiel　May - September 1943 (ab)
21 U-Flottille, Pillau　October 1943 - February 1945 (sb)
31 U-Flottille, Hamburg　March - May 1945 (ab/fb)

Commanded by
KL Hans Leilich　May 1943 - March 1945
OL Heinz Schäffer　March 1945 - 17.8.45

Patrols: None　　Ships sunk: None

1. 13.4.45　Left Kiel and arrived Horten **20.4.45**

2. 29.4.45　Left Horten and arrived Kristiansand **30.4.45**

3. 2.5.45　Left for operations in British coastal waters.
　When the U-boat war ended on May 4th, U 977 was off the Norwegian coast. Ignoring the order to surrender, the boat headed westwards across the Atlantic.
　According to Schäffer's book 'U 977', the decision to head for Argentina was made after the surrender order. 30 of the crew agreed, 2 wanted to go to Spain and the other 16, many of whom had families, wished to return to Germany. These men were put ashore next night near Bergen, leaving the boat without most of her older, experienced men.
　After 66 days submerged, the condition of both boat and crew was very bad. On 10.7.45 a radio report told of U 530's arrival at Mar del Plata, a great encouragement to U 977's crew.

U 977 (continued)

The boat completed the voyage on the surface and after 105 days at sea U 977 put in to Mar del Plata on 17.8.45. Boat and crew were interned by the Argentinian authorities and later handed over to the Americans.

On 13.11.46 U 977 was sunk off the US coast by the submarine USS *Atule*.

U 978   Type VII C

Built by Blohm & Voss, Hamburg
Keel laid 24.7.42   Launched 1.4.43
Commissioned 12.5.43   Feldpost Nr M 51 997

Sunk 11.12.45 NW of Bloody Foreland (56°10′N 10°05′W)

Served with
5 U-Flottille, Kiel May 1943 - July 1944 (ab)
11 U-Flottille, Bergen August 1944 - 9.5.45 (fb)

Commanded by
KL Günther Pulst May 1943 - 9.5.45

Patrols: 2   Ships sunk: 1 (7176 grt)

1. 22.8.44 Left Kiel and arrived Horten **24.8.44**

2. 5.9.44 Left Horten and arrived Flekkefjord **13.9.44**

3. 13.9.44 Left Flekkefjord and arrived Egersund **13.9.44**

4. 7.10.44 Left Egersund and arrived Bergen **8.10.44**

5. 9.10.44 Left for operations in British coastal waters.
U 978 entered the English Channel on 2.11.44. On the 19th she claimed a ship sunk just N of Barfleur but this is unconfirmed. In the same area on the 23rd U 978 torpedoed and sank the SS *William D Burnham* (am 7176t).
The boat returned to Bergen **16.12.44**

6. 25.2.45 Left Bergen for British coastal waters.
From early March U 978 operated off the Pentland Firth. On 4.4.45 she reported a ship sunk but this claim is unconfirmed and on the 6th U 978 unsuccessfully attacked an aircraft carrier. From a 3-torpedo spread only end-of-run detonations were heard
The boat put in to Trondheim **20.4.45**

U 978 was surrendered at Trondheim 5.5.45. She left Lofjord on the 29th for an assembly area in Britain.
The boat was one of 116 disposed of by the Royal Navy in Operation Deadlight. *In December 1945 she was towed from Loch Ryan out through the North Channel by the tug HMS* Enchanter.
On 11.12.45 U 978 was sunk by the submarine HMS Tantivy *NW of Bloody Foreland.*

U 979   Type VII C

Built by Blohm & Voss, Hamburg
Keel laid 10.8.42   Launched 15.4.43
Commissioned 20.5.43   Feldpost Nr M 52 107

Scuttled 24.5.45 at Amrum Island

Served with
5 U-Flottille, Kiel May 1943 - July 1944 (ab)
9 U-Flottille, Brest August - October 1944 (fb)
11 U-Flottille, Bergen October 1944 - 24.5.45 (fb)

Commanded by
KL Johannes Meermeier May 1943 - 24.5.45

Patrols: 4   Ships sunk: 1 (348 grt) + 2 damaged

1. 6.8.44 Left Kiel and arrived Horten **8.8.44**

2. 14.8.44 Left Horten for operations.
The patrol was cut short because of schnorkel failure. U 979 put in to Bergen **27.8.44**

3. 29.8.44 Left for Atlantic operations.
U 979 operated S of Iceland and later off Reykjavik. On 22.9.44 she fired a 3-torpedo spread at the SS *Yukon* (am 5747t) SW of Reykjavik, one torpedo of which hit. A coup de grâce shot missed. The vessel was towed in. On the 23rd U 979 attacked a convoy but she was unsuccessful against a steamer.
The boat put in to Trondheim **10.10.44**

4. 9.11.44 Left for Atlantic operations.
From November 23rd to December 1st U 979 operated off Reykjavik, and probably made unsuccessful attacks on a trawler, a frigate and a convoy. Later in the patrol U 979 went into St George's Channel but, again, she had no success.
U 979 put in to Stavanger **16.1.45**

5. 26.3.45 Left Bergen and returned **29.3.45**

6. 29.3.45 Left for Atlantic operations.
On 2.5.45 U 979 torpedoed and sank the fishing trawler *Ebor Wyke* (br 348t) W of Reykjavik. In the same area on the 4th the boat damaged the tanker MV *Empire Unity* (br 6386t).
When the surrender order was given on the 4th, U 979 began her return journey. On 24.5.45 she was scuttled after running aground on the beach at Amrum, one of the North Frisian Islands.
It is believed that there were no casualties.

U 980   Type VII C

Built by Blohm & Voss, Hamburg
Keel laid 10.8.42   Launched 15.4.43
Commissioned 27.5.43   Feldpost Nr M 52 816

Sunk 11.6.44 WNW of Alesund (63°07′N 00°26′E)

Served with
5 U-Flottille, Kiel May 1943 - May 1944 (ab)
7 U-Flottille/FdU Mitte, Norway June 1944 (fb)

Commanded by
KL Hermann Dahms May 1943 - 11.6.44

Patrols: 1   Ships sunk: None

1. **18.5.44** Left Kiel and arrived Kristiansand **19.5.44**

2. **20.5.44** Left Kristiansand and arrived Bergen **21.5.44**

3. **3.6.44** Left for the North Atlantic.

U 980 was one of five outward-bound non-schnorkel boats which were halted W of Norway when news of the Normandy invasion came through early on the 6th. They were to wait for further orders.

On the 11th U 980 was sighted on the surface by a Canso of 162 (RCAF) Squadron (F/O L Sherman) WNW of Alesund. The aircraft ran in through heavy flak and dropped four depth-charges from 50 feet. There was a further exchange of fire and then U 980 was seen to be sinking, with her crew abandoning ship.

There were no survivors, 52 dead.

On his return to base, Sherman was awarded an immediate DFC for this action. Two days later he and his crew took off from Wick and later reported sighting a U-boat. They were not heard from again and it is assumed that the aircraft was shot down.

U 981   Type VII C

Built by Blohm & Voss, Hamburg
Keel laid 24.8.42   Launched 29.4.43
Commissioned 3.6.43   Feldpost Nr M 52 873

Sunk 12.8.44 SW of La Pallice (45°41′N 01°25′W)

Served with
5 U-Flottille, Kiel June - November 1943 (ab)
6 U-Flottille, St Nazaire December 1943 - 12.8.44 (fb)

Commanded by
OL Walter Sitek June 1943 - June 1944
OL Günther Keller June 1944 - 12.8.44

Patrols: 3   Ships sunk: None

1. **27.11.43** Left for the North Atlantic.

U 981 joined a number of boats assembled off the North Channel to search for convoys W of the British Isles. On 15.12.43 U 981, U 284, U 364, U 471, U 741 and U 976 formed *Coronel 2* group to continue their search.

On the 19th *Coronel 1* and *2* groups were reformed as *Sylt, Amrum* and *Föhr* groups. U 981 was in *Sylt*. From the 22nd the boats were reformed again W of Ireland, this time into six small sub-groups, *Rügen 1* to *6*. U 981 was in *Rügen 1*.

These small groups, mostly of three boats each, were constantly moving, changing positions and varying formations, with the objective of preventing the Allies determining the area over which they were operating. When three convoys were sighted, UC 8 on the 23rd, TU 5 on the 26th and CU 9 on the 30th, the groups were each too small to mount an attack.

From 7.1.44 the groups were dissolved and the boats operated singly W of Ireland, as *Rügen* group. They had no success.

U 981 put in to her new base at St Nazaire **30.1.44**

2. **12.4.44** Left St Nazaire and arrived Lorient **15.4.44**

3. **6.6.44** Left Lorient, as part of *Landwirt* group.

U 981 was one of nineteen non-schnorkel boats ordered to form a line at the 200 metre depth line between Brest and Bordeaux, keeping out of port in case an Allied invasion force arrived and trapped them there. The boats later went to the 100 metre depth line, where they could lay on the bottom for long periods.

The waiting boats came under constant attack from the air when they surfaced at night. When no invasion had come by the 12th, the boats were recalled to port and placed on six hours notice.

U 981 returned to Lorient **17.6.44**

4. **7.8.44** Left Lorient for La Pallice.

U 981, in company with U 309, was approaching the escort-rendezvous point SW of La Pallice early on the 12th when she struck a mine. With engines not working and unable to dive, U 981 requested an immediate escort.

U 309 remained with U 981 and two hours after the mine explosion the two stationary boats were sighted by a Halifax of 502 Squadron (F/O J Capey), which dropped flares.

Just then U 981's electric motors were restarted and the two boats moved slowly ahead. The Halifax approached and dropped an a/s bomb. A second mine exploded alongside U 981 and this was followed by another aircraft attack with more bombs. Some 20 minutes later U 981's crew began to abandon ship as the boat sank.

U 309 closed and picked up 40 survivors, including the commander. 12 of U 981's crew lost their lives.

U 982   Type VII C

Built by Blohm & Voss, Hamburg
Keel laid 24.8.42   Launched 29.4.43
Commissioned 10.6.43   Feldpost Nr M 52 885

Bombed 9.4.45 at Hamburg

Served with
5 U-Flottille, Kiel June 1943 - January 1944 (ab)
6 U-Flottille, St Nazaire February - June 1944 (fb)
6 U-Flottille/FdU Mitte, Norway June - July 1944 (fb)
24 U-Flottille, Memel July 1944 - February 1945 (ab)
31 U-Flottille, Hamburg March 1945 - 9.4.45 (ab)

Commanded by
OL Edmund Grochowiak June 1943 - April 1944
OL Ernst-Werner Schwirley April - July 1944
OL Curt Hartmann July 1944 - 9.4.45

Patrols: 1   Ships sunk: None

1. **3.6.44** Left Kiel and arrived Egersund **5.6.44**

2. **10.6.44** Left, as part of *Mitte* group.

In the early hours of the 6th, when news of the invasion of Normandy was received, the *Mitte* boats were put on immediate notice. U 982 was one of eleven boats which put to sea between the 8th and 10th, to form a reconnaissance line from Trondheim to Lindesnes.

In late June, when the anticipated threat to Norway had receded, U 982 and eight other *Mitte* boats were recalled.

She put in to Haugesund **28.6.44**

3. **29.6.44** Left Haugesund and arrived Bergen **1.7.44**

4. **3.7.44** Left Bergen and arrived Marviken **4.7.44**

5. **6.7.44** Left Marviken and arrived Kiel **8.7.44**

U 982 did not see any further operational service. She was one of nine Mitte *group boats which were transferred to training duties in July 1944. Their crews were drafted to 23 and 24 U-Flottillen to man the new Type XXI boats.*

U 982 was destroyed on 9.4.45 in a precision daylight attack by 617 Squadron on the U-boat pens at Hamburg-Finkenwerder.

U 983   Type VII C

Built by Blohm & Voss, Hamburg
Keel laid 7.9.42   Launched 12.5.43
Commissioned 16.6.43   Feldpost Nr M 52 911

Sunk 8.9.43 NW of Leba (54°56´N 17°14´E)

Served with
5 U-Flottille, Kiel   June 1943 - 8.9.43 (ab)

Commanded by
Lt Hans Reimers   June 1943 - 8.9.43

Patrols: None   Ships sunk: None

On 8.9.43, whilst on a training exercise in the Baltic, U 983 sank after a collision with U 988 NW of Leba.
Of U 983's crew, 5 men lost their lives.

U 984   Type VII C

Built by Blohm & Voss, Hamburg
Keel laid 7.9.42   Launched 12.5.43
Commissioned 17.6.43   Feldpost Nr M 53 784

Sunk 20.8.44 SW of Ushant (48°16´N 05°33´W)

Served with
5 U-Flottille, Kiel   June - December 1943 (ab)
9 U-Flottille, Brest   January 1944 - 20.8.44 (fb)

Commanded by
OL Heinz Sieder   June 1943 -20.8.44

Patrols: 5   Ships sunk: 3 (21,550 grt) + 2 damaged

1. 30.12.43   Left Kiel and arrived Egersund **2.1.44**

2. 4.1.44   Left for the North Atlantic.
U 984 operated independently for a while before joining *Stürmer* group, formed from the 26th NW of the North Channel to await an ONS convoy.
German aircraft sighted ON 221 on the 27th. Technical difficulties prevented them homing in the boats and in spite of searches made on the 28th the convoy was not found.
The operation was terminated in the morning of the 29th, following a report by an aircraft of a suspected invasion of Western France. After apparent confirmation of this report, all boats in the North Atlantic, which included *Stürmer* group, were ordered to proceed at high speed to the Biscay coast. Shortly after this the 'invasion fleet' was correctly identified as a group of Spanish trawlers and the boats were ordered back to their operational areas.
On the 31st *Stürmer* group was again stationed NW of the North Channel. From early February Allied anti-submarine defences were being noticeably increased and the waiting boats began a slow withdrawal westwards.
U 984 was with *Igel 1* group NW of Scotland from 3.2.44. The boats operated singly SE of Iceland until the 10th, when a further withdrawal westwards began. In co-operation with aircraft, an attack on an ONS convoy was planned within a few days. Aircraft sighted ONS 29 on the 14th W of the North Channel.
U 984 did not take part in the operation against this convoy. She appears to have left the group about this time. Early on the 15th she made an unsuccessful attack on a destroyer, hearing only an end-of-run detonation During the night of the 16/17th the boat managed

to beat off attacks by aircraft.
U 984 put in to her new base at Brest **24.2.44**

3. 22.5.44   Left for the English Channel.
Now schnorkel-equipped, U 984 joined U 269, U 441, U 764 and U 953 to form *Dragoner* group.
The group was to operate in the western part of the English Channel, N of Ushant, in co-operation with shore radar against Allied cruiser and destroyer formations.
The objective was to test the effectiveness of the schnorkel and to assess tactics required in areas that were patrolled by many enemy aircraft. Some experience was gained but in general results were discouraging.
U 984 returned to Brest **27.5.44**

4. 6.6.44   Left for the English Channel, as part of *Landwirt* group.
In the evening of the 7th U 984 fired three torpedoes at destroyers of the 12th EG, one of which detonated in the wake of HMCS *Saskatchewan*.
The boat returned to recharge her batteries and take on more torpedoes. She reached Brest **10.6.44**

5. 12.6.44   Left again for the English Channel.
On the 14th U 984 was unsuccessful against a search group. She put in to St Peter Port, Guernsey on the 18th, to re-charge batteries. A few hours after her arrival, fighter-bombers arrived and attacked the port area. U 269 and U 275 had put in there some days previously and in both cases, fighter-bombers had attacked within hours of the boats' arrivals. St Peter Port had been previously unmolested. In these attacks the aircraft sank one patrol vessel and damaged two others.
U 984 left St Peter Port on the 21st and on the 25th she torpedoed and damaged the destroyer-escort HMS *Goodson* SSW of Portland Bill. *Goodson* was towed into Portland by HMS *Bligh*.
On the 29th U 984 attacked convoy EMC 17 SSE of the Isle of Wight, torpedoing four ships, the SS *Henry G Blasdel* (am 7176t), the SS *Edward M House* (am 7240t), the SS *John A Treutlen* (am 7198t) and the SS *James A Farrell* (am 7176t).
The *Henry G Blasdel* and *John A Treutlen* were towed into Southampton, the *James A Farrell* was towed into Spithead and the *Edward M House* was taken to the Tyne. Only the *Edward M House* was repaired.
U 984 returned to Brest **5.7.44**

6. 26.7.44   Left for the English Channel.
U 984 had no success on this patrol. She was probably returning to Brest when she was detected in the evening of 20.8.44 SW of Ushant by the destroyer HMCS *Ottawa* (Cdr H F Pullen).
Two other destroyers of the 11th EG, HMCS *Chaudière* (Lt-Cdr C P Nixon) and *Kootenay* (Lt-Cdr K L Dyer), were with *Ottawa*. U 984 was destroyed, probably by a depth-charge attack carried out by *Chaudière* but no tangible evidence of her destruction was seen at the time.
There were no survivors, 45 dead.

U 985   Type VII C

Built by Blohm & Voss, Hamburg
Keel laid 18.9.42   Launched 20.5.43
Commissioned 24.6.43   Feldpost Nr M 53 813

Decommissioned 15.11.44 at Kristiansand

Served with
5 U-Flottille, Kiel   June - December 1943 (ab)
7 U-Flottille, St Nazaire   January 1944 - 15.11.44 (fb)

Commanded by
KL Horst Kessler   June 1943 - April 1944
KL Heinz Wolff   May 1944 - 15.11.44

Patrols: 3   Ships sunk: 1 (1735 grt)

1. 30.12.43   Left Kiel and arrived Bergen **5.1.44**

2. 19.1.44   Left for Atlantic operations.
   U 985 was with *Igel 1* group NW of Scotland from 3.2.44. The boats operated SE of Iceland until the 10th, when a further withdrawal westwards began. U 985, at the northern end of the *Igel 1* patrol line, torpedoed and sank the SS *Margit* (br 1735t) from convoy RA 56, on the 8th WSW of the Faroes.
   In co-operation with aircraft, an attack on an ONS convoy was planned for *Igel 1* and 2 groups within a few days. Aircraft sighted ONS 29, ON 224 and OS 68 on the 14th W of the North Channel. All boats then west of the British Isles assembled in an area 600 miles SW of Ireland and formed two lines, *Hai 1* and 2, ahead of the convoys. However, the convoys turned southwards on the 17th and the *Hai* boats went south to intercept, submerged in daylight and at high speed on the surface in the hours of darkness. Instead of sighting any convoys at dawn on the 19th, the boats saw only destroyers. The operation was called off and the boats submerged to avoid aircraft from the escort-carrier HMS *Striker*.
   U 985 joined *Preussen* group, formed from the 22nd 400 to 500 miles N of the Azores. On the 25th ON 225 was thought to be just W of the North Channel, from a radio report of the 24th. From the 26th *Preussen* group was concentrated between 22° and 30°W, in the expected path of the convoy but it was routed clear.
   U 985 put in to her new base at St Nazaire **12.3.44**

3. 6.6.44   U 985 was one of nineteen non-schnorkel boats which sailed into the Bay of Biscay as part of *Landwirt* group.
   They formed a line at the 200 metres depth line between Brest and Bordeaux, keeping out of port in case an Allied invasion force arrived and trapped them there. The boats later moved in to the 100 metres depth line, where they could lay on the bottom.
   The waiting boats were under constant attack from the air when they surfaced at night. When no invasion had come by the 12th, they were recalled to port, and placed on six hours notice.
   U 985 returned to St Nazaire **15.6.44**

4. 30.8.44   Left St Nazaire for British coastal waters.
   U 985 was one of three schnorkel boats which operated in the North Channel from mid-September. Whilst some ships were sunk there in the first weeks of September, the traffic became very much reduced. U 985 was in the area for ten days but had no success.
   On 23.10.44 the returning boat struck a mine just W of Farsund. She put in to Flekkefjord **23.10.44**

5. 25.10.44   Left Flekkefjord and arrived Kristiansand **26.10.44**

U 985 was surveyed and found to be so severely damaged that she was decommissioned on 15.11.44 at Kristiansand.

U 986   Type VII C

Built by Blohm & Voss, Hamburg
Keel laid 18.9.42   Launched 20.5.43
Commissioned 1.7.43   Feldpost Nr M 53 856

Sunk 17.4.44 SW of Bantry Bay (50°09´N 12°51´W)

Served with
5 U-Flottille, Kiel   July 1943 - February 1944 (ab)
6 U-Flottille, St Nazaire   March 1944 - 17.4.44 (fb)

Commanded by
OL Karl-Ernst Kaiser   July 1943 - 17.4.44

Patrols: 1   Ships sunk: None

1. 8.2.44   Left Kiel for Atlantic operations.
   U 986 joined *Preussen* group, whose boats were operating singly W of the British Isles. The group was dissolved on 22.3.44 and from then the boats operated independently between the British Isles and 40°W.
   On 17.4.44 U 986 attempted to attack a small coastal convoy SW of Bantry Bay. She was sunk in depth-charge attacks by the minesweeper USS *Swift* and the US sub-chaser PC 619.
   There were no survivors, 50 dead.

U 987   Type VII C

Built by Blohm & Voss, Hamburg
Keel laid 2.10.42   Launched 2.6.43
Commissioned 8.7.43   Feldpost Nr M 53 910

Sunk 15.6.44 W of Bodø (68°01´N 05°08´E)

Served with
5 U-Flottille, Kiel   July 1943 - February 1944 (ab)
1 U-Flottille/FdU Mitte, Norway   March - May 1944 (fb)
11 U-Flottille, Bergen   June 1944 (fb)

Commanded by
OL Hilmar Schreyer   July 1943 - 15.6.44

Patrols: 1   Ships sunk: None

On 2.2.44, whilst carrying out training exercises in the Baltic, U 987 collided with German patrol vessel V 1702, which sank.

1. 13.5.44   Left Kiel and arrived Marviken **15.5.44**

2. 21.5.44   Left Marviken and arrived Stavanger **22.5.44**

3. 28.5.44   Left Stavanger for operations.
   U 987 later joined the boats of *Mitte* group, which had left Norwegian ports between June 8th and 10th to form a reconnaissance line off the coast from Trondheim to Lindesnes.
   On 15.6.44 U 987 was sighted on the surface W of Bodø by the submarine HMS *Satyr* (Lt T S Weston). Six torpedoes were fired, two of which hit U 987, breaking her in half.
   There were no survivors, 52 dead.

U 988　Type VII C

Built by Blohm & Voss, Hamburg
Keel laid 2.10.42　Launched 3.6.43
Commissioned 15.7.43　Feldpost Nr M 53 999

Sunk 30.6.44 S of Start Point (49°37´N 03°41´W)

Served with
5 U-Flottille, Kiel　July 1943 - May 1944 (ab)
7 U-Flottille, St Nazaire　June 1944 (fb)

Commanded by
OL Erich Dobberstein　July 1943 - 30.6.44

Patrols: 1　　Ships sunk:　2 (9444 grt)
　　　　　　　　　　　　1 corvette (925 dt)

On 8.9.43 U 988 collided with U 983 whilst both boats were carry-ing out training exercises in the Baltic. U 983 sank and five of her crew were lost.

1. 11.5.44 Left Kiel and arrived Marviken **13.5.44**

2. 22.5.44 Left for the North Atlantic.
　On 6.6.44 U 988 was ordered to proceed to the English Channel, passing south of Ireland. On the 27th she torpedoed and severely damaged the corvette HMS *Pink* in the Baie de la Seine, E of Barfleur. She was towed to Portsmouth but never repaired.
　On the 28th U 988 attacked convoy FXP 18 SSE of the Isle of Wight and sank the SS *Maid of Orleans* (br 2386t). There is a possibility that *Pink* and *Maid of Orleans* may have struck mines but it is more likely that they were sunk by U 988.
　The boat torpedoed and sank the SS *Empire Portia* (br 7058t) on the 29th from convoy FMT 22, SE of Portsmouth. On the 30th U 988 was attacked and damaged by a Liberator of 224 Squadron (F/Lt J W Barling) S of Start Point.
　The aircraft called up the 3rd EG and depth-charge attacks were made by the frigates HMS *Domett* (Lt-Cdr S Gordon), *Duckworth* (Cdr R G Mills) and *Essington* (Lt-Cdr W Lambert). U 988 was destroyed.
　There were no survivors, 50 dead.

U 989　Type VII C

Built by Blohm & Voss, Hamburg
Keel laid 16.10.42　Launched 16.6.43
Commissioned 22.7.43　Feldpost Nr M 54 065

Sunk 14.2.45 N of the Shetlands (61°36´N 01°35´W)

Served with
5 U-Flottille, Kiel　July 1943 - January 1944 (ab)
9 U-Flottille, Brest　February - September 1944 (fb)
33 U-Flottille, Flensburg　October 1944 - 14.2.45 (fb)

Commanded by
KL Hardo Rodler von Roithberg　July 1943 - 14.2.45
OL Wilhelm Brauel (temp)　8.6.44 - 24.6.44

Patrols: 4　　Ships sunk: 1 (1719 grt) + 1 damaged

1. 11.1.44 Left Kiel for the North Atlantic.
　U 989 joined *Stürmer* group, formed from the 26th NW of the North Channel to await an ONS convoy. German aircraft sighted ON 221 on the 27th. Technical difficulties prevented them homing in the boats and in spite of searches made on the 28th the convoy was not found.
　The operation was terminated in the morning of the 29th, following a report by an aircraft of a suspected invasion of Western France and after apparent confirmation of this, all boats in the North Atlantic had been ordered to the scene. Shortly after this the 'invasion fleet' was correctly identified as a group of Spanish trawlers and the boats were ordered back to their operational areas.
　On the 31st *Stürmer* group was again stationed NW of the North Channel. From early February Allied anti-submarine defences were being noticeably increased and the waiting boats began a slow withdrawal westwards.
　U 989 was with *Igel 1* group NW of Scotland from 3.2.44. The boats operated SE of Iceland until the 10th, when an even further withdrawal westwards began. In co-operation with aircraft, an attack on an ONS convoy was planned for *Igel 1* and 2 groups within a few days.
　Aircraft sighted ONS 29, ON 224 and OS 68 on the 14th W of the North Channel. All boats then W of the British Isles assembled in an area 600 miles SW of Ireland and formed two patrol lines, *Hai 1* and 2, ahead of the convoys.
　However, the convoys turned southwards on the 17th and the *Hai* boats went south to intercept, submerged in daylight and at high speed on the surface in the hours of darkness. Instead of sight-ing any convoys at dawn on the 19th, the boats saw only destroyers. The operation was called off and the boats submerged to avoid aircraft from the escort-carrier HMS *Striker.*
　U 989 put in to her new base at Brest **4.3.44**

2. 6.6.44 Left Brest, as part of *Landwirt* group.
　Outward-bound on the 7th, U 989 was attacked and damaged by a Wellington of 407 (RCAF) Squadron (S/Ldr D W Farrell) and also attacked by a Liberator of 224 Squadron (F/O E Allen). U 989 shot down the Wellington.
　The boat returned to Brest **8.6.44**

3. 8.7.44 Left Brest and returned **10.7.44**

4. 9.8.44 Left Brest for the English Channel.
　U 989, now schnorkel-equipped, reached her operational area. In the evening of the 23rd she torpedoed and damaged the SS *Louis Kossuth* (am 7176t) SW of the Isle of Wight and on the 26th, in the same area, she sank the SS *Ashmun J Clough* (br 1791t), which was en route to Normandy.
　The seven boats that were thought to be still operating in the Channel were ordered in late August to head for Norway. U 989 and five others responded to this order.
　U 989 put in to Marviken **26.9.44**

5. 28.9.44 Left Marviken and arrived Flensburg **3.10.44**

6. 3.2.45 Left Kiel and arrived Horten **5.2.45**

7. 7.2.45 Left for British coastal waters.
　Outward-bound, U 989 was located by the 10th EG on the 14th N of the Shetlands. She was sunk in depth-charge attacks by the frigates HMS *Bayntun* (Lt-Cdr L P Bourke), *Braithwaite* (Lt-Cdr E M MacKay), *Loch Dunvegan* (Cdr E Wheeler) and *Loch Eck* (Lt-Cdr N McInnes).
　The commander and one crewman were picked up but both died soon afterwards. 46 other members of U 989's crew were also lost.

U 990   Type VII C

Built by Blohm & Voss, Hamburg
Keel laid 16.10.42   Launched 16.6.43
Commissioned 28.7.43   Feldpost Nr M 54 093

Sunk 25.5.44 NW of Trondheim (65°05´N 07°28´E)

Served with
5 U-Flottille, Kiel   July - December 1943 (ab)
11 U-Flottille, Bergen   January 1944 - 25.5.44 (fb)

Commanded by
KL Hubert Nordheimer   July 1943 - 25.5.44

Patrols: 4   Ships sunk: None
                              1 destroyer (1920 dt)

1. 22.1.44   Left Kiel and arrived Marviken **23.1.44**

2. 26.1.44   Left for Northern Waters.
    U 990 joined *Werwolf* group in Bear Island Passage, awaiting the next convoy. On the 31st the boat made an unsuccessful attack on a destroyer, which was escorting eastbound convoy JW 56B in the Barents Sea, N of Kola.
    The return convoy, RA 56, managed to avoid *Werwolf* group, which had been given wrong information by aerial reconnaissance and was searching in the wrong direction. The convoy reached Loch Ewe on 11.2.44 without loss.
    On 20.2.44 eastbound JW 57 left Loch Ewe and was located by German aircraft on the 23rd. *Werwolf* group boats, including U 990, were deployed against it. In the evening of the 25th U 990 torpedoed and sank an escorting destroyer, HMS *Mahratta,* NNW of Harstad.
    U 990 put in to Hammerfest **28.2.44**

3. 4.3.44   Left for operations. No details known of this patrol.
    U 990 put in to Narvik **27.3.44**

4. 31.3.44   Left for operations.
    On the 27th convoy JW 58 set out from Loch Ewe and was found by aerial reconnaissance on the 30th. Soon after midnight *Thor, Blitz* and *Hammer* groups were in contact. They were later joined by U 990 and several other outward-bound boats. Attacks were made on the convoy over three days but JW 58 reached Kola Inlet without loss on 5.4.44. U 990 made an unsuccessful attack on destroyers of the escort on the 2nd SSE of Bear Island.
    The boat returned to Narvik **5.4.44**

5. 8.4.44   Left Narvik and arrived Bergen **12.4.44**

6. 22.5.44   Left Bergen, bound for Narvik.
    On the 4th U 990 picked up 21 survivors from U 476, sunk by a Catalina NNW of Kristiansand. U 990 also sank the still-afloat U 476 with a coup-de-grâce torpedo.
    Next day U 990 was sighted on the surface NW of Trondheim by a Liberator of 59 Squadron (S/Ldr B A Sisson). The aircraft came in under cover of a rain squall. Six depth-charges were dropped and U 990 began to sink.
    There were 52 survivors, of which 19 were probably from U 476. Both boat-commanders survived. From U 990's crew, 19 men lost their lives.

U 991   Type VII C

Built by Blohm & Voss, Hamburg
Keel laid 30.10.42   Launched 24.6.43
Commissioned 29.7.43   Feldpost Nr M 54 105

Sunk 11.12.45 NW of Bloody Foreland (56°10´N 10°05´W)

Served with
5 U-Flottille, Kiel   July 1943 - August 1944 (ab)
11 U-Flottille, Bergen   September 1944 - 9.5.45 (fb)

Commanded by
KL Diethelm Balke   July 1943 - 9.5.45

Patrols: 1   Ships sunk: None

1. 5.10.44   Left Kiel and arrived Horten **7.10.44**

2. 11.10.44   Left Horten and arrived Kristiansand **12.10.44**

3. 15.10.44   Left for operations in the English Channel.
    U 991 reached her operational area on 12.11.44. On the 27th she made an unsuccessful attack on a large steamer SSW of the Isle of Wight, firing a 3-torpedo spread but hearing only two end-of-run detonations.
    On 15.12.44 U 991 claimed a Liberty ship torpedoed and sunk S of Fastnet but this is unconfirmed.
    She put in to Bergen **26.12.44**

4. 27.12.44   Left Bergen and arrived Marviken **29.12.44**

5. 2.1.45   Left Marviken and arrived Flensburg **4.1.45**

6. 20.4.45   Left Kiel and arrived Horten **27.4.45**

7. 29.4.45   Left Horten and arrived Bergen **4.5.45**

U 991 was surrendered at Bergen on 9.5.45. She set out from there on the 29th for the assembly area at Loch Ryan.
    She was one of 116 boats disposed of by the Royal Navy in Operational Deadlight. *In early December 1945 the boat was towed out through the North Channel by the tug HMS* Freedom.
    U 991 was sunk on 11.12.45 by the submarine HMS Tantivy *NW of Bloody Foreland.*

U 992   Type VII C

Built by Blohm & Voss, Hamburg
Keel laid 30.10.42   Launched 24.6.43
Commissioned 2.8.43   Feldpost Nr M 54 132

Sunk 16.12.45 NW of Bloody Foreland (56°10´N 10°05´W)

Served with
5 U-Flottille, Kiel   August 1943 - February 1944 (ab)
3 U-Flottille, La Pallice   March - May 1944 (fb-oE)
11 U-Flottille, Bergen   June - September 1944 (fb)
13 U-Flottille, Trondheim   October 1944 - 19.5.45 (fb)

Commanded by
OL Hans Falke   August 1943 - 19.5.45

Patrols: 9   Ships sunk: None
                              1 corvette (1060 dt)
                              1 minesweeper (625 dt)

U 992 (continued)

1. **30.3.44** Left Kiel and arrived Stavanger **2.4.44**

2. **13.5.44** Left Stavanger and arrived Bergen **14.5.44**

3. **7.6.44** Left Bergen and arrived Ramsund **12.6.44**

4. **15.6.44** Left Ramsund and arrived Skjomenfjord **15.6.44**

5. **18.6.44** Left for operations.
U 992 may have operated with *Trutz* group E of Jan Mayen. On 17.7.44 she established an automatic weather station on Jan Mayen.
Returning to base, U 992 was approaching Vestfjord on the 23rd, when she was attacked with depth-charges by a Sunderland of 330 (Norwegian) Squadron. The boat dived and escaped without serious damage.
U 992 reached Narvik **24.7.44**

6. **21.8.44** Left Narvik and arrived Hammerfest **24.8.44**

7. **29.8.44** Left for operations.
U 992 took part in minelaying operations with *Dachs* group. During the night of September 2/3rd she laid mines off southwestern Novaya Zemlya. There are no known sinkings or damage to ships attributed to these mines.
The boat returned to Narvik **7.9.44**

8. **12.9.44** Left for operations.
Westbound convoy RA 60 left Kola Inlet during the night of the 27/28th. U 992 was with *Zorn* group, which was awaiting the convoy. However, RA 60 avoided both *Zorn* and *Grimm* groups but two ships were sunk by U 310 of *Zorn*, after she had been overrun by the convoy in the afternoon of the 29th.
U 992 returned to Narvik **4.10.44**

9. **18.10.44** Left for operations.
U 992 joined *Panther* group, which was awaiting eastbound JW 61. The convoy, which had left Loch Ewe on the 20th, passed through the patrol line. Unsuccessful attacks were made against the escort on the 26th and 27th, none by U 992. The convoy reached Kola Inlet without loss on the 28th.
U 992 returned to Narvik **10.11.44**

10. **30.11.44** Left for operations.
U 992 joined *Stock* group, deployed W of Bear Island, waiting for convoy JW 62, which had been located by German aircraft on the 27th.
On 1.12.44 the *Stock* boats moved to the Kola coast, when it was assumed that JW 62 had passed through Bear Island Passage unobserved. U 992 attacked a westbound Soviet coastal convoy NNE of Kola Inlet. She was unsuccessful against two minesweepers and a large steamer.
Between the 5th and 7th U 992 made attacks on Soviet a/s groups and against the eastbound JW 62 but she had no success.
The boat put in to Bogenbucht **8.12.44**

11. **16.1.45** Left for operations.
U 992 was one of four boats operating off Kola Inlet from early February. On the 5th she torpedoed and sank the Soviet minesweeper *TSC-116* and on the 8th she unsuccessfully attacked a destroyer.
Eastbound JW 64 reached Kola Inlet on the 13th. It had been subjected to aircraft attacks but had passed by the waiting *Rasmus* group. After the convoy entered the Inlet, U 992 torpedoed and severely damaged the corvette HMS *Denbigh Castle* of the escort. She was towed into Kola by HMS *Bluebell* but in spite of every effort made she had to be beached and became a total wreck.
On the 14th U 992 may have torpedoed and hit the tanker SS *Norfjell* (nw 8129t) from Soviet convoy BK 3. This vessel had

previously been hit by U 968. She was towed to Rosta and taken over by the Soviet Navy in June 1945.
On the 18th U 992 was one of six boats moved to Bear Island Passage to try and make contact with westbound RA 64. They failed to do so but on the 20th the convoy was found and attacked by torpedo aircraft.
U 992 returned to Narvik **21.2.45**

12. **17.3.45** Left for operations.
U 992 and U 313 went to Kola Inlet to join U 995, waiting there for the arrival of convoy JW 65. *Hagen* group boats, which had been waiting for the convoy in Bear Island Passage, also moved to the Inlet after aerial reconnaissance failed to find JW 65.
Two lines were formed, one of six boats and one of seven. Early on the 20th the convoy passed through the first line in a snowstorm and reached the second at noon. Attacks were made and one ship and a sloop were sunk. After JW 65 entered Kola Inlet, the boats attempted to operate against the escort-carriers HMS *Campania* and *Trumpeter* from JW 65's escort, believed to be in the Barents Sea, but this was unsuccessful.
Return convoy RA 65 left Kola Inlet on the 23rd. U 992 was one of a number of boats which attempted to form a patrol line ahead of the convoy on the 25th but this was unsuccessful. Two days later aerial reconnaissance failed to find the convoy and the operation was abandoned. RA 65 reached Scapa Flow safely on the 31st.
U 992 returned to Narvik **1.4.45**

13. **1.5.45** Left for operations.
U 992 was to operate against westbound convoy RA 66 but the operation against it was abandoned on the 2nd. The boat was still at sea when the surrender order was given on the 4th.
She returned to Narvik **9.5.45**

U 992 was one of a number of boats which left Narvik for Trondheim. They were met at sea by the 9th EG and escorted to Loch Eriboll, probably arriving there on 19.5.45.

U 992 was one of 116 boats disposed of by the Royal Navy in Operation Deadlight. In December 1945 she was towed from Loch Ryan out through the North Channel by the destroyer HMS Fowey.

The boat was sunk by gunfire on 16.12.45 NW of Bloody Foreland.

U 993 Type VII C

Built by Blohm & Voss, Hamburg
Keel laid 16.11.42   Launched 5.7.43
Commissioned 19.8.43   Feldpost Nr M 55 038

Bombed 4.10.44 at Bergen

Served with
5 U-Flottille, Kiel August 1943 - February 1944 (ab)
3 U-Flottille, La Pallice March 1944 - 4.10.44 (fb)

Commanded by
OL Kurt Hilbig August 1943 - July 1944
OL Karl-Heinz Steinmetz July 1944 - 4.10.44

Patrols: 3   Ships sunk: None

1. **9.3.44** Left Kiel and arrived Marviken **11.3.44**

2. **23.3.44** Left for the North Atlantic.
In early April U 993 was ordered to proceed to Western France to join *Landwirt* group. On the 16th she was attacked by a Liberator of 53 Squadron (F/Lt F M Burton), which she shot down.
The boat put in to Lorient **22.4.44**

3. 6.6.44 U 993 was one of nineteen non-schnorkel boats which sailed into the Bay of Biscay as part of *Landwirt* group.

They were to form a line at the 200 metres depth line between Brest and Bordeaux, keeping out of port in case an Allied invasion force arrived and trapped them there. The boats later moved in to the 100 metres depth line, where they could lay on the bottom for long periods.

The waiting boats were under constant attack from the air when they surfaced at night. Early on the 12th U 993 had one crewman killed and another wounded in an aircraft attack.

When no invasion had come by the 12th, the boats were recalled to port and placed on six hours notice.

U 993 put in to Brest **14.6.44**

4. 17.8.44 Left for Norway.

U 993 was one of a number of not-completely operational boats which left the Biscay bases for the safer Norwegian ports. En route, a crewman died of yellow jaundice on the 12th.

She reached Bergen **18.9.44**

On 4.10.44 U 993 was severely damaged in an RAF Bomber Command raid on Bergen. She was in the Laksevag dockyard there. 2 of her crew were killed.

All equipment was removed from U 993 and she was broken up.

U 994   Type VII C

Built by Blohm & Voss, Hamburg
Keel laid 14.12.42   Launched 6.7.43
Commissioned 2.9.43   Feldpost Nr M 55 083

Sunk 5.12.45 N of Tory Island (55°50´N 08°30´W)

Served with
5 U-Flottille, Kiel   September 1943 - May 1944 (ab)
7 U-Flottille, St Nazaire   June - July 1944 (fb)
5 U-Flottille, Kiel   July - September 1944 (ab)
11 U-Flottille, Bergen   September - October 1944 (fb-oE)
13 U-Flottille, Trondheim   November 1944 - 9.5.45 (fb-oE)

Commanded by
OL Wolf Ackermann   September 1943 - March 1944
OL Volker Melzer   April 1944 - 9.5.45

Patrols: 1   Ships sunk: None

1. 22.6.44 Left Kiel for Norwegian waters.

U 994 was one of five boats sent out in June to relieve *Mitte* group boats. They were to stand by off southern Norway, between Trondheim and Lindesnes, to counter any invasion threat.

On 17.7.44 U 994 had five crewmen wounded in an aircraft attack, which also damaged the boat.

She put into Bergen **17.7.44**

2. 27.7.44 Left Bergen and arrived Vallöy **28.7.44**

U 994 returned to Kiel to undergo repairs. She joined 11 U-Flottille at Bergen in September 1944 and later moved to 13 U-Flottille at Trondheim. She was non-operational at both units and was surrendered at Trondheim on 9.5.45. She left there on the 29th for an assembly area in Britain.

U 994 was one of 116 boats disposed of by the Royal Navy in Operation Deadlight. *In early December 1945 she was towed from Loch Ryan out through the North Channel by the tug HMS Prosperous.*

The boat foundered under tow on 5.12.45 N of Tory Island.

U 995   Type VII C-41

Built by Blohm & Voss, Hamburg
Keel laid 25.11.42   Launched 22.7.43
Commissioned 16.9.43   Feldpost Nr M 55 095

Surrendered 9.5.45 at Trondheim

Served with
5 U-Flottille, Kiel   September 1943 - May 1944 (ab)
13 U-Flottille, Trondheim   June 1944 - February 1945 (fb)
14 U-Flottille, Narvik   March 1945 - 9.5.45 (fb)

Commanded by
KL Walter Köhntopp   September 1943 - October 1944
OL Hans-Georg Hess   October 1944 - 9.5.45

Patrols: 9   Ships sunk: 2 (7734 grt)
                            1 patrol craft (1165 dt)
                            1 m/s trawler (500 dt)
                            1 subchaser (105 dt)

1. 25.4.44 Left Kiel and arrived Flekkefjord **28.4.44**

2. 16.5.44 Left Flekkefjord and arrived Bergen **16.5.44**

3. 18.5.44 Left Bergen, possibly for operations.

On the 21st U 995 was sighted as she surfaced by a Sunderland of 4(C)OTU (P/O E T King). The aircraft dropped six depth-charges and the boat appeared to sink. She was only damaged but 5 of her crew had been wounded.

U 995 put in to Trondheim **23.5.44**

4. 30.6.44 Left Trondheim for operations.

U 995 patrolled in the Norwegian Sea, E of Jan Mayen. There were no UK-Russia convoys at this time. JW 59 was to be the next eastbound convoy and she did not leave Loch Ewe until 15.8.44. No Allied ships were sunk in Northern Waters in July 1944.

U 995 put in to Narvik **28.7.44**

5. 30.7.44 Left Narvik and arrived Trondheim **2.8.44**

6. 17.8.44 Left Trondheim and arrived Narvik **19.8.44**

7. 23.8.44 Left Narvik and arrived Tromsø **24.8.44**

8. 26.8.44 Left Tromsø and arrived Hammerfest **26.8.44**

9. 29.8.44 Left for operations.

U 995 was with *Dachs* group, which was to carry out minelaying operations. The boat laid mines on 4.9.44 S of Novaya Zemlya. There are no sinkings or damage to ships attributed to these mines.

U 995 returned to Hammerfest **11.9.44**

10. 12.9.44 Left Hammerfest and arrived Narvik **14.9.44**

11. 25.9.44 Left for operations.

Westbound convoy RA 60 left Kola Inlet during the night of the 27/28th. U 995 was with *Zorn* group, which was awaiting the convoy. However, RA 60 avoided both *Zorn* and *Grimm* groups but two ships were sunk by U 310 of *Zorn*, after she had been overrun by the convoy in the afternoon of the 29th.

U 995 put in to Skjomenfjord **3.10.44**

12. 14.10.44 Left for operations.

U 995 joined *Panther* group. Eastbound JW 61 left Loch Ewe on the 20th. The convoy passed through the *Panther* patrol line in Bear

U 995 (continued)

Island Passage. Unsuccessful attacks were made against the escorting destroyers, two by U 995 N of Kola Inlet on the 27th, with only an end-of-run detonation heard.

The boat put in to Harstad 10.11.44 and then went on to Narvik, reaching there **11.11.44**

13. 30.11.44 Left Narvik for operations.

U 995 joined *Stock* group W of Bear Island Passage. Convoy JW 62, which left Loch Ewe on the 27th, passed the waiting boats unobserved. *Stock* group moved to the Kola coast and U 995 attacked Soviet coastal convoy PK 20 on 2.12.44, without success. On the 4th she was unsuccessful against a Soviet KP convoy off Kola Inlet.

From the 5th to the 7th U 995 and other boats attacked a Soviet PK convoy off Kola. On the 5th U 995 torpedoed and sank the Soviet m/s trawler *TSC-107* and probably sank the SS *Proletarij* (sov 1123t), both off Kola.

U 995 put in to Bogenbucht **9.12.44**

14. 11.12.44 Left for operations.

U 995 patrolled along the Kola coast. On the 21st she picked up a survivor from a Russian fishing vessel that had been sunk and on the 23rd a landing party was put ashore briefly on Litzki Island.

On the 26th U 995 sank the SS *RT-52* (sov 558t) near Uda and on the 29th she attacked Soviet coastal convoy KB 37, sinking the patrol craft *T-883/T-37* and probably damaging a steamer. U 995 probably picked up a survivor from *T-883*.

In early January 1945 U 995 was briefly with *Stier* group in Bear Island Passage. The awaited convoy, JW 63, passed by unobserved.

U 995 put in to Tromsø 5.1.45 and returned to Narvik **7.1.45**

15. 2.2.45 Left Narvik for operations.

En route to Kola Inlet, U 995 entered Kirkenes harbour on the 9th and narrowly missed with a shot at the Norwegian ship SS *Idefjord*, tied up at the wharf there.

U 995, U 293, U 318 and U 992 waited off Kola Inlet for approaching convoy JW 64, sighted by German aircraft on the 6th. U 992 had the only success against the convoy, when she torpedoed the corvette HMS *Denbigh Castle*.

On the 14th U 995 was waiting with other boats for return convoy RA 64. A combined force of British and Soviet naval vessels attempted to drive the waiting boats away from Kola Inlet before RA 64 sailed. It left on the 17th and two boats made attacks but contact was lost on the 18th. Some boats, not U 995, moved to Bear Island Passage but failed to find the convoy.

On 2.3.45 U 995 torpedoed and sank the Soviet sub-chaser *BO-224* NNE of Kola Inlet.

The boat returned to Narvik **6.3.45**

16. 13.3.45 Left for operations.

U 995 again went to a waiting position off Kola Inlet and she was joined there by U 313 and U 992. When aerial reconnaissance failed to find approaching convoy JW 65 on the 17th, *Hagen* group boats moved from Bear Island Passage to join those waiting at Kola Inlet. Two lines were formed, one of six boats and one of seven.

In the morning of the 20th the convoy passed through the first line in a snowstorm. U 995 torpedoed the SS *Horace Bushnell* (am 7176t) and claimed two hits on other ships. The second patrol line was passed at noon and one ship and a sloop were sunk. The *Horace Bushnell* was beached and declared a total loss.

After JW 65 entered Kola Inlet on the 21st, the boats attempted to operate against the escort-carriers HMS *Campania* and *Trumpeter* from JW 65's escort, which were believed to be in the Barents Sea, but this was unsuccessful.

U 995 put in to Harstad **25.3.45**

17. 26.3.45 Left Harstad and arrived Trondheim **28.3.45**

U 995 was surrendered at Trondheim on 8.5.45 and decommissioned there. On 1.12.52 she entered the service of the Royal Norwegian Navy as the Kaura.

The boat was decommissioned again in October 1965. She was offered by the Norwegians to the German Federal Navy with the proviso that she was to be preserved and suitably exhibited at some future time. The offer was accepted and U 995 returned once again to the naval dockyard at Kiel.

After much consideration and with many difficulties surmounted, U 995 was started off on a programme of repair and restoration at Kiel on 25.9.70. This work was completed on 1.10.71 and she was officially handed over as a Museum boat next day.

On 13.3.1972 U 995 was installed on the beach at Laboe, near Kiel in front of the 1914-1918 German Naval War Memorial, to serve as a memorial for all those who lost their lives in the war at sea in the years 1939 to 1945.

U 996 was never completed. Her keel was laid on 25.11.42 and she was launched on 22.7.43.

Whilst fitting out in the Blohm & Voss yard basin at Hamburg, U 996 was destroyed in one of a series of bombing raids carried out on Hamburg by the RAF and USAF between July 24th and August 3rd 1943.

The exact date of U 996's destruction is not known.

U 997 Type VII C-41

Built by Blohm & Voss, Hamburg
Keel laid 5.12.42   Launched 18.8.43
Commissioned 23.9.43   Feldpost Nr M 55 164

Sunk 11.12.45 WNW of Bloody Foreland (55°50´N 10°05´W)

Served with
5 U-Flottille, Kiel   September 1943 - April 1944 (ab)
9 U-Flottille, Brest   May 1944 (fb)
13 U-Flottille, Trondheim   June 1944 - March 1945 (fb)
14 U-Flottille, Narvik   March 1945 - 19.5.45 (fb)

Commanded by
KL Hans Lehmann   September 1943 - 19.5.45

Patrols: 8   Ships sunk: 1 (1603 grt) + 1 damaged
                               3 patrol craft (225 dt)

1. 25.4.44 Left Kiel and arrived Egersund **29.4.44**

2. 16.5.44 Left Egersund and arrived Bergen **16.5.44**

3. 18.5.44 Left Bergen and arrived Bogenbucht **22.5.44**

4. 25.5.44 Left for operations. No details known of this patrol. U 997 put in to Hammerfest **22.6.44**

5. 18.7.44 Left Hammerfest and returned **20.7.44**

6. 6.8.44 Left for operations.

U 997 was with *Trutz* group. Early on the 21st eastbound convoy JW 59 reached the *Trutz* patrol line and U 344 of the group sank the escorting sloop HMS *Kite*. On the 22nd, near the convoy, the boats were attacked by surface vessels and aircraft.

U 997 was attacked by Swordfish and Martlets from the escort-carriers HMS *Vindex* and *Striker* and also a Soviet Catalina from the 118th Reconnaissance Regiment. She was forced to submerge and driven off.

In the early hours of the 24th U 997 attacked two destroyers of the escort N of Vardø but without success. JW 59 reached Kola Inlet on the 25th and *Trutz* group moved to Bear Island Passage to await return convoy RA 59A. It sailed on the 28th but en route neither aircraft or U-boats approached it.

U 997 put in to Narvik **2.9.44**

7. 13.9.44   Left for operations.

U 997 was with *Grimm* group. Convoy JW 60 left Loch Ewe on the 15th and arrived without loss at Kola Inlet on the 23rd, not located either by reconnaissance aircraft or by the searching boats of *Grimm* group.

The return convoy, RA 60, sailed during the night of the 27/28th and also avoided both *Grimm* and *Zorn* groups.

U 997 returned to Bogenbucht **2.10.44**

8. 8.10.44   Left Bogenbucht and arrived Hammerfest **10.10.44**

9. 14.10.44   Left for operations.

U 997 was with *Panther* group, which later in October was waiting for eastbound convoy JW 61, which left Loch Ewe on the 20th. The convoy passed through the *Panther* line and during the night of the 26/27th attacks were made by some boats on the escort but without success.

Between November 5th and 8th U 997, U 771 and U 956 were operating against Soviet escort vessels in the Barents Sea. On the 5th U 997 may have sunk a Soviet destroyer, possibly the *Spokojnyj*, but this is not certain.

U 997 returned to Narvik **9.11.44**

10. 21.11.44   Left for operations.

U 997 was with *Grube* group, deployed off the Kola coast and waiting for eastbound JW 62. The convoy was located by aerial reconnaissance on the 27th. It bypassed the boats whilst the escort attacked them, without success.

On 4.12.44 U 997 torpedoed and sank the Soviet patrol craft *BO-230* E of Kola Inlet. In the same area on the 7th, U 997 sank another patrol craft, *BO-229*. Off Kola on the 9th she unsuccessfully attacked Soviet destroyer *Zhivuchiy*, one of a Soviet/British naval force that was trying to drive U-boats away from the entrance to Kola Inlet.

U 997 sank an auxiliary patrol craft on the 21st in Kola Fjord, the motor boat *Resitel'nyj*, by gunfire.

The boat returned to Narvik **26.12.44**

11. 27.12.44   Left Narvik and arrived Trondheim **29.12.44**

12. 22.2.45   Left Trondheim.

On the 24th U 997 lost a crewman overboard. On this short journey there was some carbon monoxide poisoning amongst the crew because of a defective schnorkel.

U 997 put in to Kilbotn **26.2.45**

13. 7.3.45   Left Kilbotn and returned **8.3.45**

14. 12.3.45   Left for operations.

U 997 was with *Hagen* group in Bear Island Passage. Convoy JW 65 had sailed from the Clyde on the 11th but aerial reconnaissance failed to find it. On the 17th the waiting boats were moved to Kola Inlet and formed into two lines, one of six boats and one of seven.

In the morning of the 20th the convoy passed through the first line in a snowstorm and one ship was torpedoed. The second patrol line was passed at noon and one ship and a sloop were sunk.

After JW 65 entered Kola Inlet on the 21st, the boats attempted to operate against the escort-carriers HMS *Campania* and *Trumpeter* from JW 65's escort, which were believed to be in the Barents Sea, but this was unsuccessful.

U 997 returned to Narvik **24.3.45**

15. 17.4.45   Left for operations.

U 997 and other boats left their bases and made for Kola Inlet, to be joined there by boats of *Faust* group, to await approaching convoy JW 66.

On the 22nd U 997 made several attacks on Soviet coastal convoy PK 9 off Kola Inlet. In the morning the boat missed the Soviet destroyer *Karl Libknecht* and the patrol craft *BO-225* and a little later she torpedoed two ships, damaging the SS *Idefjord* (nw 4287t) and sinking the SS *Onega* (sov 1603t).

In late April U 997 was one of fourteen boats waiting off Kola Inlet for return convoy RA 66. On the 29th the boats were driven off by a combined Allied and Soviet naval force before RA 66 sailed.

The boat returned to Narvik **30.4.45**

U 997 was at Narvik when the war ended and she was one of a number of boats which set out from there for Trondheim. They were met at sea by the 9th EG and escorted to Loch Eriboll, probably arriving there on the 9th.5.45.

U 997 was one of 116 boats disposed of by the Royal Navy in Operation Deadlight. In December 1945 she was towed from Loch Ryan out through the North Channel by the tug HMS Bustler.

The boat was sunk by aircraft on 11.12.45 WNW of Bloody Foreland.

U 998   Type VII C-41

Built by Blohm & Voss, Hamburg
Keel laid 7.12.42   Launched 18.8.43
Commissioned 7.10.43   Feldpost Nr M 52 749

Decommissioned 27.6.44 at Bergen

Served with
5 U-Flottille, Kiel   October 1943 - 27.6.44 (ab/fb)

Commanded by
KL Hans Fiedler   October 1943 - 27.6.44

Patrols: 1   Ships sunk: None

1. 12.6.44   Left Kiel to join *Mitte* group, at that time stationed off Norway.

On the 16th U 998 was attacked with rockets and cannon fire by a Mosquito of 333 (Norwegian) Squadron (Lt E U Johansen) N of the Shetlands. U 804 was sent to help but she was attacked by another Mosquito of 333 Squadron and had to put in to Bergen with casualties.

The badly-damaged U 998 put in to Bergen **17.6.44**

U 998 was decommissioned at Bergen on 27.6.44 and she was surrendered there on 9.5.45.

After the war all equipment was removed from the boat by the Norwegians and she was scrapped.

U 999 Type VII C-41

Built by Blohm & Voss, Hamburg
Keel laid 18.12.42   Launched 17.9.43
Commissioned 21.10.43   Feldpost Nr M 52 784

Scuttled 5.5.45 in Geltinger Bucht

Served with
5 U-Flottille, Kiel October 1943 - May 1944 (ab)
6 U-Flottille, St Nazaire June 1944 (fb)
24 U-Flottille, Memel June 1944 - February 1945 (ab)
31 U-Flottille, Hamburg March 1945 - 5.5.45 (ab)

Commanded by
OL Hermann Hansen October 1943 - July 1944
OL Wilhelm Peters July - November 1944
OL Wolfgang Heibges November 1944 - 5.5.45

Patrols: 1   Ships sunk: None

1. 24.5.44 Left Kiel and arrived Arendal **26.5.44**

In late May U 999 and U 247 were used in sea trials, serving as a comparison with the Alberich-coated U 480.

U 999 was to have gone to operations in the North Atlantic with 6 U-Flottille, St Nazaire. Instead, she was assigned to Mitte group. The group was formed on 16.2.44, to stand by at ports in southern Norway in case of an Allied invasion of Norway or Denmark, with four boats at Bergen, four at Kristiansand and two at Stavanger. In March the group was increased from 10 to 22 boats and in June to 30, with boats such as U 999 being sent from Kiel.

2. 8.6.44 Left Marviken, as part of *Mitte* group.
    In the early hours of the 6th, when news of the invasion of Normandy was received, the *Mitte* boats were put on immediate notice. U 999 was one of eleven boats which put to sea between the 8th and 10th, to form a reconnaissance line from Trondheim to Lindesnes.
    In late June, when the anticipated threat to Norway had receded, U 999 and eight other *Mitte* boats were recalled.
    She put in to Kristiansand **27.6.44**

3. 1.7.44 Left Kristiansand and arrived Bergen **1.7.44**

4. 3.7.44 Left Bergen and arrived Marviken **4.7.44**

5. 6.7.44 Left Marviken and arrived Kiel **8.7.44**

U 999 did not see any further operational service. She was one of nine Mitte boats which were transferred to training duties in July. Their crews were drafted to 23 and 24 U-Flottillen to man the new Type XXI boats.
    U 999 went to 24 U-Flottille at Memel and later to 31 U-Flottille at Hamburg. As the war drew to a close, a large number of boats moved from their bases to the bays of Northern Germany, there to await further orders. U 999 was one of these.
    In accordance with the Operation Regenbogen order issued by Dönitz on April 30th 1945 but contrary to the surrender terms, U 999 was scuttled on 5.5.45 in Geltinger Bucht.

U 1000 Type VII C-41

Built by Blohm & Voss, Hamburg
Keel laid 19.12.42   Launched 17.9.43
Commissioned 4.11.43   Feldpost Nr M 52 805

Decommissioned 29.9.44 at Kiel

Served with
31 U-Flottille, Hamburg November 1943 - July 1944 (ab)
8 U-Flottille, Danzig August 1944 - 29.9.44 (ab)

Commanded by
OL Willi Müller November 1943 - 29.9.44

Patrols: 1   Ships sunk: None

1. 18.5.44 Left Kiel and arrived Egersund **20.5.44**

2. 4.6.44 Left for the North Atlantic.
    U 1000 was one of five outward-bound non-schnorkel boats which were halted W of Norway when news of the Normandy invasion came through early on the 6th. They were to wait for further orders before proceeding. On the 9th the boats were ordered to specific patrol areas within reach of Norway.
    U 1000 put in to Bergen **19.6.44**

3. 25.6.44 Left Bergen and arrived Arnöy **25.6.44**

4. 27.7.44 Left Arnöy and arrived Arendal **29.7.44**

5. 12.8.44 Left Arendal and arrived Kiel **13.8.44**

6. 15.8.44 Left Kiel and arrived Gotenhafen **17.8.44**

7. 26.8.44 Left Gotenhafen and arrived Königsberg **26.8.44**

8. 29.8.44 Left Königsberg and arrived Pillau **29.8.44**

9. 31.8.44 Left Pillau.
    U 1000 struck a mine soon after sailing. She was very badly damaged and returned to Pillau **31.8.44**

U 1000 was surveyed and then decommissioned at Kiel on 29.9.44.
    All equipment was later removed from the boat and she was broken up.

U 1001 Type VII C-41

Built by Blohm & Voss, Hamburg
Keel laid 31.12.42   Launched 6.10.43
Commissioned 8.11.43   Feldpost Nr M 52 852

Sunk 8.4.45 SSW of Fastnet (49°19'N 10°23'W)

Served with
31 U-Flottille, Hamburg November 1943 - July 1944 (ab)
8 U-Flottille, Danzig August 1944 - February 1945 (fb)
5 U-Flottille, Kiel February 1945 - 8.4.45 (fb)

Commanded by
KL Ernst-Ulrich Blaudow November 1943 - 8.4.45

Patrols: 8   Ships sunk: None

1. 21.5.44 Left Kiel and arrived Marviken **23.5.44**

2. 8.6.44 Left Marviken, as one of eleven *Mitte* group boats which formed a reconnaissance line running from Trondheim to Lindesnes.

The boats were ordered to remain submerged, unless recharging batteries, to escape the attention of Allied aircraft. Eight *Mitte* boats were recalled in the latter part of June when the invasion threat had lessened. U 1001 was not one of these and she remained patrolling between 57° and 61°N with original *Mitte* boats U745 and U 1165, and U 771 and U 994, which had arrived in mid-June.

U 1001 put in to Bergen **5.7.44**

3. 9.7.44 Left Bergen and arrived Stavanger **9.7.44**

4. 28.7.44 Left Stavanger and arrived Kiel **1.8.44**

5. 3.8.44 Left Kiel for operations in the Baltic.
U 1001 put in to Reval **6.8.44**

6. 7.8.44 Left Reval and arrived Grand Hotel **9.8.44**

7. 10.8.44 Left Grand Hotel and returned **10.8.44**

8. 11.8.44 Left for operations.
U 1001 patrolled in the Koivisto and Narva Bay areas.
She returned to Grand Hotel **15.8.44**

9. 20.8.44 Left for operations. No details known.
U 1001 returned to Grand Hotel **24.8.44**

10. 26.8.44 Left Grand Hotel and arrived Mira Mare **26.8.44**

On 2.9.44 Finland broke off diplomatic relations with Germany and surrendered on the 4th. From the 2nd the Germans evacuated their men and as much material as possible from Finnish harbours.

Further U-boat operations in the Baltic were mostly carried out from Danzig, Gotenhafen and Memel.

11. 29.8.44 Left Mira Mare for operations. No details known.
U 1001 returned to Reval **9.9.44**

12. 12.9.44 Left Reval and returned **12.9.44**

13. 21.9.44 Left for operations.
On the 21st U 1001 laid mines near Porkkala, off the northern Estonian coast. Next day she rescued 13 German soldiers from a sunken steamer.
The boat put in to Libau **2.10.44**

14. 4.10.44 Left for operations.
On the 25th U 1001 made a gunfire attack on a tug towing barges in the entrance to the Gulf of Finland. Hits were observed.
The boat put in to Danzig **1.11.44**

15. 4.1.45 Left Danzig for operations.
U 1001, U 242 and U 348 carried out reconnaissance patrols into the Gulfs of Bothnia and Finland. U-boat operations in the Baltic were greatly curtailed after the end of January 1945.
U 1001 returned to Kiel **30.1.45**

16. 5.3.45 Left Kiel and arrived Horten **8.3.45**

17. 10.3.45 Left Horten and arrived Kristiansand **11.3.45**

18. 11.3.45 Left for operations in British coastal waters.
Although bound for the English Channel, U 1001 was one of seven boats diverted to an area SW of Ireland.
On 8.4.45 U 1001 was sunk SW of Fastnet by the frigates HMS *Byron* (Lt J R Burfield) and *Fitzroy* (Lt-Cdr A J M Miller). There were no survivors, 46 dead.

U 1002   Type VII C-41

Built by Blohm & Voss, Hamburg
Keel laid 4.1.43   Launched 6.10.43
Commissioned 30.11.43   Feldpost Nr M 52 880

Sunk 11.12.45 NW of Bloody Foreland (56°10′N 10°05′W)

Served with
31 U-Flottille, Hamburg   November 1943 - February 1945 (ab)
11 U-Flottille, Bergen   February 1945 - 9.5.45 (fb)

Commanded by
OL Albrecht Schubart   November 1943 - July 1944
OL Hans-Heinz Boos   July 1944 - 9.5.45

Patrols: 1   Ships sunk: None

1. 9.2.45 Left Kiel and arrived Horten **13.2.45**

2. 20.2.45 Left for operations in British coastal waters.
From mid-March U 1002 operated initially W of the English Channel. She later moved eastwards and patrolled in the mouth of the Channel. The boat had no success.
U 1002 put in to Bergen **9.4.45**

U 1002 was surrendered at Bergen on 9.5.45 and left there on the 30th for an assembly area in Britain.

She was one of 116 boats disposed of by the Royal Navy in Operation Deadlight. In early December 1945 the boat was towed from Loch Ryan out through the North Channel by the tug HMS Prosperous.

U 1002 was sunk on 11.12.45 NW of Bloody Foreland by the submarine HMS Tantivy.

U 1003   Type VII C-41

Built by Blohm & Voss, Hamburg
Keel laid 18.1.43   Launched 27.10.43
Commissioned 9.12.43   Feldpost Nr M 34 077

Scuttled 23.3.45 NW of the Giant's Causeway (55°25′N 06°53′W)

Served with
31 U-Flottille, Hamburg   December 1943 - August 1944 (ab)
11 U-Flottille, Bergen   September 1944 - 23.3.45 (fb)

Commanded by
OL Werner Strübing   December 1943 - 23.3.45

Patrols: 2   Ships sunk: None

On 7.2.44 U 1003 had one crewman killed in an accident whilst the boat was training in the Baltic.

1. 19.9.44 Left Kiel and arrived Horten **22.9.44**

2. 27.9.44 Left Horten and arrived Marviken **28.9.44**

3. 11.10.44 Left for operations in British coastal waters.
U 1003 patrolled in the North Channel throughout November.
The boat put in to Stavanger **16.12.44**

4. 10.1.45 Left Stavanger and arrived Bergen **11.1.45**

5. 19.2.45 Left for British coastal waters.

U 1003 (continued)

From early March U 1003 operated in the North Channel. On the 20th she was attacked by a Liberator of 120 Squadron but escaped undamaged.

In the evening of the 21st U 1003 collided with the frigate HMCS *New Glasgow*. She was moving at periscope depth at the entrance to the North Channel and somehow failed to see the frigate. The seriously-damaged boat went to the bottom and was subjected to depth-charge attacks by other warships which had arrived at the scene.

Early on the 22nd U 1003 went up for the commander to assess the damage to the superstructure, which was severe. The boat dived again at the sound of an approaching ship. U 1003 proceeded northwestwards, leaking badly. She surfaced again after dark to recharge batteries but was quickly forced down by approaching a/s vessels. When the batteries failed and the pumps stopped working in the early hours of the 23rd, the commander surfaced and the crew abandoned ship.

31 men were picked up by the frigate HMCS *Thetford Mines* and another 18 men, including the commander, died. Two survivors died soon after being picked up and were buried at sea.

U 1004   Type VII C-41

Built by Blohm & Voss, Hamburg
Keel laid 15.1.43   Launched 27.10.43
Commissioned 16.12.43   Feldpost Nr M 54 101

Sunk 1.12.45 NW of Bloody Foreland (56°10′N 10°05′W)

Served with
31 U-Flottille, Hamburg December 1943 - July 1944 (ab)
7 U-Flottille, St Nazaire August - October 1944 (fb)
11 U-Flottille, Bergen November 1944 - 9.5.45 (fb)

Commanded by
OL Hartmuth Schimmelpfennig December 1943 - January 1945
OL Rudolf Hinz January 1945 - 9.5.45

Patrols: 2   Ships sunk: 1 (1313 grt)
                            1 corvette (980 dt)

1. **22.8.44** Left Kiel and arrived Horten **24.8.44**

2. **26.8.44** Left Horten and arrived Marviken **27.8.44**

3. **29.8.44** Left for operations in British coastal waters.
From late September U 1004 operated in the North Channel until 10.10.44. The returning boat made an unsuccessful attack on a destroyer on the 17th NW of the Orkneys.
U 1004 put in to Bergen **23.10.44**

4. **26.10.44** Left Bergen and arrived Stavanger **27.10.44**

5. **2.1.45** Left Bergen for operations.
The patrol was cut short because of schnorkel failure.
U 1004 returned to Bergen **11.1.45**

6. **27.1.45** Left for British coastal waters.
From 20.2.45 U 1004 operated at the western entrance to the English Channel. On the 22nd she encountered convoy BTC 76 SE of Falmouth. In two afternoon attacks she torpedoed and sank the SS *Alexander Kennedy* (br 1313t) and the escorting corvette HMCS *Trentonian*. The boat missed a second ship, hearing only an end-of-run detonation. U 110 was hunted afterwards and although many depth-charges were dropped, she suffered only minor damage.
She returned to Bergen **20.3.45**

U 1004 was surrendered at Bergen on 9.5.45. She left there on the 30th for an assembly area in Britain.

The boat was one of 116 disposed of by the Royal Navy in Operation Deadlight. In late November she was towed from Loch Ryan out through the North Channel by the tug HMS Bustler.

U 1004 was sunk by gunfire on 1.12.45 NW of Bloody Foreland.

U 1005   Type VII C-41

Built by Blohm & Voss, Hamburg
Keel laid 29.1.43   Launched 17.11.43
Commissioned 30.12.43   Feldpost Nr M 54 124

Sunk 5.12.45 N of Tory Island (55°33′N 08°27′W)

Served with
31 U-Flottille, Hamburg December 1943 - January 1945 (ab)
11 U-Flottille, Bergen February 1945 - 14.5.45 (fb)

Commanded by
OL Joachim Methner December 1943 - July 1944
Ol Hermann Lauth July 1944 - 14.5.45

Patrols: 1   Ships sunk: None

1. **8.2.45** Left Kiel and arrived Horten **14.2.45**

2. **19.2.45** Left for British coastal waters.
U 1005 operated in the North Minch. On 3.3.45 the boat claimed to have sunk a corvette but there is no confirmation of this. Whilst in the North Minch U 1005 was damaged when she ran aground.
She put in to Bergen **20.3.45**

3. **3.5.45** Left Bergen for operations.
The boat returned after the surrender order of May 4th called for all those still at sea to cease hostilities and return to base.
U 1005 reached Bergen **14.5.45**

U 1005 was surrendered at Bergen on 14.5.45. She left there on the 30th for an assembly area in Britain.

The boat was one of 116 disposed of by the Royal Navy in Operation Deadlight. In early December she was towed from Loch Ryan out through the North Channel by the destroyer HMS Fowey.

U 1005 foundered under tow on 5.12.45 in 48 fathoms N of Tory Island.

U 1006   Type VII C-41

Built by Blohm & Voss, Hamburg
Keel laid 30.1.43   Launched 17.11.43
Commissioned 11.1.44   Feldpost Nr M 54 173

Sunk 16.10.44 SW of the Faroes (60°59′N 04°49′W)

Served with
31 U-Flottille, Hamburg January - August 1944 (ab)
11 U-Flottille, Bergen September 1944 - 16.10.44 (fb)

Commanded by
OL Horst Voigt January 1944 - 16.10.44

Patrols: 1   Ships sunk: None

1. **13.9.44** Left Kiel and arrived Bergen **18.9.44**

2. **9.10.44** Left for operations in the English Channel.

Outward-bound, U 1006 was located on the 16th SW of the Faroes by the frigate HMCS *Annan* (Lt-Cdr C P Balfrey). A depth-charge attack was made and the boat was badly damaged. However, the contact was thought not to be a U-boat and *Annan* went off to rejoin the 6th EG. A contact was made by HMS *Loch Achanalt* and *Annan* was ordered back to the scene. U 1005 fired a torpedo at the approaching frigate, which exploded very near her. *Annan* fired rockets, illuminating the surfaced U 1005. There was an exchange of gunfire but the frigate's superior firepower was decisive. The boat was finished off with two depth-charges.

U 1006's commander and 43 men were picked up and 6 other men lost their lives.

U 1007 Type VII C-41

Built by Blohm & Voss, Hamburg
Keel laid 15.2.43   Launched 8.12.43
Commissioned 18.1.44   Feldpost Nr M 54 196

Scuttled 2.5.45 near Lübeck (53°54′N 10°50′E)

Served with
31 U-Flottille, Hamburg   January - May 1944 (ab)
1 U-Flottille, Brest   June - July 1944 (fb)
24 U-Flottille, Memel   August 1944 - February 1945 (ab)
31 U-Flottille, Hamburg   March 1945 - 2.5.45 (ab)

Commanded by
KL Hans Hornkohl   January - July 1944
OL Leonhard Klingspor (temp)   3.7.44 - 7.7.44
OL Helmut Wicke   July 1944 - March 1945
KL Ernst von Witzendorff   March 1945 - 2.5.45

Patrols: 1   Ships sunk: None

1. 31.5.44   Left Kiel and arrived Flekkefjord 1.6.44

U 1007 was to have gone to operations in the North Atlantic with 1 U-Flottille, Brest. Instead, she was assigned to Mitte *group.*

The group was formed on 16.2.44, to stand by at ports in southern Norway in case of an Allied invasion of Norway or Denmark, with four boats at Bergen, four at Kristiansand and two at Stavanger.

In March the group was increased to 22 boats and in June to 30, when boats such as U 1007 were sent from Kiel.

2. 10.6.44   Left Flekkefjord, as part of *Mitte* group.

In the early hours of the 6th, when news of the Normandy invasion was received, the *Mitte* boats were put on immediate notice. U 1007 was one of eleven boats which put to sea between the 8th and 10th, to form a reconnaissance line from Trondheim to Lindesnes.

In late June, when the anticipated threat to Norway had receded, U 1007 and eight other *Mitte* boats were recalled.

She put in to Marviken 27.6.44

3. 3.7.44   Left Marviken and arrived Bergen 5.7.44

4. 5.7.44   Left Bergen and arrived Stavanger 6.7.44

5. 7.7.44   Left Stavanger and arrived Kristiansand 7.7.44

6. 7.7.44   Left Kristiansand and arrived Kiel 9.7.44

U 1007 did not see any further operational service. She was one of nine Mitte *boats which were transferred to training duties in July. Their crews were drafted to 23 and 24 U-Flottillen to man the new Type XXI boats.*

U 1007 went to 24 U-Flottille at Memel and later to 31 U-Flottille at Hamburg. As the war drew to a close a large number of boats moved from their bases to the bays of Northern Germany, there to await orders. U 1007 was one of these.

She was in Lübecker Bucht when she was sighted by Typhoons of 2nd TAF on 2.5.45. The boat was badly damaged in rocket and cannon attacks.

Her commander beached and scuttled her, with the loss of one crewman. The wreck was raised and broken up in May 1946.

U 1008 Type VII C-41

Built by Blohm & Voss, Hamburg
Keel laid 12.2.43   Launched 8.12.43
Commissioned 1.2.44   Feldpost Nr M 55 064

Scuttled 6.5.45 in the Kattegat (56°22′N 10°51′E)

Served with
31 U-Flottille, Hamburg   February - October 1944 (ab)
24 U-Flottille, Memel   November 1944 - January 1945 (eb)
5 U-Flottille, Kiel   February 1945 - 6.5.45 (fb)

Commanded by
OL Dieter Todenhagen   February - November 1944
OL Hans Gessner   November 1944 - 6.5.45

Patrols: None   Ships sunk: None

U 1008 was on experimental duties at 24 U-Flottille Memel, on underwater detection research.

U 1008 was probably on her way from Kiel to Norway when she was attacked on 5.5.45 in the Kattegat by a Liberator of 224 Squadron (W/Cdr M A Ensor).

The depth-charges dropped only slightly damaged the boat. She was scuttled next day, the 6th. There were 49 survivors, no casualties.

U 1009 Type VII C-41

Built by Blohm & Voss, Hamburg
Keel laid 24.2.43   Launched 5.1.44
Commissioned 10.2.44   Feldpost Nr M 55 087

Sunk 5.1.46 N of Tory Island (55°50′N 08°30′W)

Served with
31 U-Flottille, Hamburg   February - October 1944 (ab)
11 U-Flottille, Bergen   November 1944 - 10.5.45 (fb)

Commanded by
OL Klaus Hilgendorf   February 1944 - 10.5.45
OL Dietrich Zehle (temp)   November 1944 - February 1945

Patrols: 2   Ships sunk: None

1. 12.10.44   Left Kiel and arrived Horten 14.10.44

2. 22.10.44   Left Horten and arrived Kristiansand 23.10.44

3. 27.10.44   Left Kristiansand and arrived Horten 28.10.44

4. 17.11.44   Left Horten and arrived Kristiansand 19.11.44

5. 20.11.44   Left Kristiansand and arrived Egersund 20.11.44

U 1009 (continued)

6. 26.11.44 Left Egersund and arrived Bergen **27.11.44**

7. 28.11.44 Left for operations.
U 1009 had to return to base because of schnorkel trouble. She reached Bergen **3.12.44**

8. 11.12.44 Left for operations.
U 1009 headed for British coastal waters and from mid-January 1945 she was operating in the North Channel. The boat made unsuccessful attacks against a patrol boat and a destroyer.
U 1009 took a turn at weather-reporting duties during the latter part of this patrol.
She put in to Trondheim **8.2.45**

9. 29.3.45 Left for weather-reporting duties.
U 1009 was still at sea in the North Atlantic when the U-boat war ended on 4.5.45. In accordance with instructions given, the boat put in to Loch Eriboll on the 10th and surrendered.

U 1009 was one of 116 boats disposed of by the Royal Navy in Operation Deadlight. *In early January 1946 she was towed from the assembly area at Lisahally by the frigate HMS* Loch Shin.
The boat was sunk by gunfire on 5.1.46 N of Tory Island.

U 1010   Type VII C-41

Built by Blohm & Voss, Hamburg
Keel laid 23.2.43   Launched 5.1.44
Commissioned 22.2.44   Feldpost Nr M 55 109

Sunk 7.1.46 NW of Malin Head (55°37′N 07°49′W)

Served with
31 U-Flottille, Hamburg   February 1944 - April 1945 (ab)
11 U-Flottille, Bergen   April 1945 - 14.5.45 (fb)

Commanded by
OL Otto Bitter   February - July 1944
KL Günter Strauch   July 1944 - 14.5.45

Patrols: 1   Ships sunk: None

1. 19.3.45 Left Kiel and arrived Kristiansand **27.3.45**

2. 31.3.45 Left Kristiansand and arrived Stavanger **2.4.45**

3. 15.4.45 Left for operations in British coastal waters.
When the U-boat war ended on 4.5.45, U 1010 was still at sea W of the British Isles. In accordance with instructions given, the boat put in to Loch Eriboll on the 14th and surrendered.

U 1010 was one of 116 boats disposed of by the Royal Navy in Operation Deadlight. *In early January 1946 she was towed from the assembly point at Lisahally by the frigate HMS* Loch Shin.
The boat was sunk by gunfire by the Polish destroyer Garland *on 7.1.46 NW of Malin Head.*

U 1011 and U 1012 had their keels laid at the Blohm & Voss yard on March 12th and 11th 1943 respectively. Both boats were damaged in a bombing raid on Hamburg in late July 1943. No further work was done on either boat and the orders for them were cancelled.

U 1013   Type VII C-41

Built by Blohm & Voss, Hamburg
Keel laid 26.3.43   Launched 19.1.44
Commissioned 2.3.44   Feldpost Nr M 50 346

Sunk 17.3.44 E of Rügen Island

Served with
31 U-Flottille, Hamburg   March 1944 (ab)

Commanded by
OL Gerhard Linck   March 1944

Patrols: None   Ships sunk: None

U 1013 was in the early stages of her training when she was lost on 17.3.44 after a collision with U 286 E of Rügen Island.
There were 26 survivors from U 1013. The commander and 24 other men were lost.

U 1014   Type VII C-41

Built by Blohm & Voss, Hamburg
Keel laid 25.3.43   Launched 30.1.44
Commissioned 14.3.44   Feldpost Nr M 01 524

Sunk 4.2.45 N of Portrush (55°17′N 06°44′W)

Served with
31 U-Flottille, Hamburg   March - December 1944 (ab)
11 U-Flottille, Bergen   January 1945 - 4.2.45 (fb)

Commanded by
OL Wolfgang Glaser   March 1944 - 4.2.45

Patrols: 1   Ships sunk: None

On 19.5.44 U 1014 collided with U 1015 in the Gulf of Danzig, W of Pillau. U 1015 sank with the loss of 36 men.

On 16.9.44 U 1014 had two crewmen killed and three wounded in a Soviet air attack on Libau harbour.

1. 8.1.45 Left Kiel and arrived Bergen **13.1.45**

2. 18.1.45 Left for operations in British coastal waters.
Soon after arriving in her operational area, U 1014 was detected on 4.2.45, lying on the bottom N of Portrush by the frigate HMS *Loch Scavaig* of the 23rd EG.
She was joined by the frigates HMS *Loch Shin* (Cdr J P de W Kitcat), *Nyasaland* (Lt A E Selby) and *Papua* (Lt-Cdr E H Lynes). U 1014 was destroyed in depth-charge attacks.
There were no survivors, 48 dead.

U 1015   Type VII C-41

Built by Blohm & Voss, Hamburg
Keel laid 25.3.43   Launched 7.2.44
Commissioned 23.3.44   Feldpost Nr unknown

Sunk 19.5.44 W of Pillau

Served with
31 U-Flottille, Hamburg March 1944 - 19.5.44 (ab)

Commanded by
OL Hans-Heinz Boos March 1944 - 19.5.44

Patrols: None   Ships sunk: None

U 1015 sank after colliding with U 1014 on 19.5.44 W of Pillau. 14 men, including the commander, were rescued and another 36 men were lost.

U 1016   Type VII C-41

Built by Blohm & Voss, Hamburg
Keel laid 1.4.43   Launched 8.2.44
Commissioned 4.4.44   Feldpost Nr M 03 110

Scuttled 5.5.45 in Lübecker Bucht

Served with
31 U-Flottille, Hamburg April 1944 - 5.5.45 (ab)

Commanded by
OL Walther Ehrhardt April 1944 - 5.5.45

Patrols: None   Ships sunk: None

As the war neared its end U-boats moved from their bases to prevent them falling into Allied hands. Some went to Norway but many others went to the bays of Northern Germany to await further orders.

In accordance with the Regenbogen *order given to commanders by Dönitz on 30.4.45 but contrary to the surrender terms, U 1016 was scuttled in Lübecker Bucht on 6.5.45.*

U 1017   Type VII C-41

Built by Blohm & Voss, Hamburg
Keel laid 17.5.43   Launched 1.3.44
Commissioned 13.4.44   Feldpost Nr M 03 373

Sunk 29.4.45 WNW of Bloody Foreland (56°04´N 11°06´W)

Served with
31 U-Flottille, Hamburg April - October 1944 (ab)
11 U-Flottille, Bergen October 1944 - 29.4.45 (fb)

Commanded by
KL Graf von Reventlow April - September 1944
OL Werner Riecken September 1944 - 29.4.45

Patrols: 2   Ships sunk: 2 (10,604 grt)

1. 18.12.44 Left Kiel and arrived Horten **23.12.44**

2. 28.12.44 Left for British coastal waters.

From 22.1.45 U 1017 was operating in the English Channel. On the 26th the boat reported one ship sunk off Cherbourg, possibly the SS *Sibert* (am 7176t) but there is no confirmation of this. In the same area in the morning of the 27th U 1017 made an unsuccessful attack on a corvette.

On 6.2.45 the boat encountered convoy TBC 60 SW of the Isle of Wight. She torpedoed and sank the SS *Everleigh* (br 5222t) and claimed a second ship sunk but this is unconfirmed.

U 1017 attacked convoy BTC 65 on the 11th SW of Plymouth and sank the SS *Persier* (be 5382t).

The boat put in to Trondheim **2.3.45**

3. 14.4.45 Left for British coastal waters.

U 1017 was en route to her operational area W of the North Channel when she was located by a Liberator of 120 Squadron (F/O H J Oliver) 125 miles WNW of Bloody Foreland after the wake and smoke from her schnorkel were sighted.

Four depth-charges and a homing torpedo were dropped and U 1017 was destroyed.

The commander and 32 men were lost. There were no survivors.

U 1018   Type VII C-41

Built by Blohm & Voss, Hamburg
Keel laid 19.5.43   Launched 1.3.44
Commissioned 25.4.44   Feldpost Nr M 22 623

Sunk 27.2.45 SW of The Lizard (49°56´N 05°20´W)

Served with
31 U-Flottille, Hamburg April - December 1944 (ab)
11 U-Flottille, Kiel December 1944 - 27.2.45 (fb)

Commanded by
KL Ulrich Faber April - December 1944
KL Walter Burmeister December 1944 - 27.2.45

Patrols: 1   Ships sunk: 1 (1317 grt)

On 27.6.44 U 1018 had one crewman killed and two injured during training exercises in the Baltic.

1. 7.12.44 Left Kiel and arrived Horten **10.12.44**

2. 21.1.45 Left for British coastal waters.

From mid-February U 1018 was operating at the western entrance of the English Channel. On the 27th she encountered convoy BTC 81 SW of The Lizard and torpedoed and sank the SS *Corvus* (nw 1317t).

The boat was immediately searched for by the 2nd EG. She was located by the frigate HMS *Loch Fada* (Lt-Cdr B A Rogers) and sunk in Squid attacks.

Of U 1018's crew, 51, including the commander, died and two survivors were picked up.

U 1019 Type VII C-41

Built by Blohm & Voss, Hamburg
Keel laid 28.4.43   Launched 22.3.44
Commissioned 4.5.44   Feldpost Nr M 22 922

Sunk 7.12.45 WNW of Malin Head (55°27′N 07°56′W)

Served with
31 U-Flottille, Hamburg May - November 1944 (ab)
11 U-Flottille, Bergen December 1944 - 9.5.45 (fb)

Commanded by
OL Hans Rinck May 1944 - 9.5.45

Patrols: 1   Ships sunk: None

1. **22.1.45** Left Kiel and arrived Horten **25.1.45**

2. **3.2.45** Left for British coastal waters.
On the 16th U 1019 was attacked W of the North Channel by a Liberator using sonobuoys and homing torpedoes. The boat managed to escape. During March U 1019 operated in the southern Irish Sea. On the 12th she reported a large steamer sunk S of Ireland but there is no confirmation of this.
She put in to Trondheim **9.4.45**

U 1019 was surrendered at Trondheim on 9.5.45. She left there on the 29th for an assembly area in Britain.
She was one of 116 boats disposed of by the Royal Navy in Operation Deadlight. *In early December 1945 the boat was towed from Loch Ryan out through the North Channel by the destroyer HMS* Pytchley.
U 1019 lost buoyancy and was sunk by gunfire on 7.12.45 WNW of Malin Head.

U 1020 Type VII C-41

Built by Blohm & Voss, Hamburg
Keel laid 30.4.43   Launched 22.3.44
Commissioned 17.5.44   Feldpost Nr M 22 946

Missing from 3.1.45 off Northeast Scotland

Served with
31 U-Flottille, Hamburg May - November 1944 (ab)
11 U-Flottille, Bergen December 1944 - January 1945 (fb)

Commanded by
OL Otto Eberlein May 1944 - January 1945

Patrols: 1   Ships sunk: None + 1 damaged

1. **14.11.44** Left Kiel and arrived Horten **17.11.44**

2. **22.11.44** Left for British coastal waters.
U 1020 operated off the northeast coast of Scotland and around the Orkneys from 7.12.44. On the 31st she torpedoed and damaged the destroyer HMS *Zephyr* W of Mainland, Orkney.
The boat went missing on or about 3.1.45, possibly in the Dornoch Firth area, cause of sinking unknown.

U 1021 Type VII C-41

Built by Blohm & Voss, Hamburg
Keel laid 6.5.43   Launched 13.4.44
Commissioned 25.5.44   Feldpost Nr M 23 789

Missing after 10.3.45 in the English Channel

Served with
31 U-Flottille, Hamburg May - November 1944 (ab)
11 U-Flottille, Bergen December 1944 - March 1945 (fb)

Commanded by
OL William Holpert May 1944 - March 1945

Patrols: 1   Ships sunk: None

1. **4.2.45** Left Kiel and arrived Horten **8.2.45**

2. **10.2.45** Left Horten and arrived Bergen **13.2.45**

3. **16.2.45** Left Bergen and returned **19.2.45**

4. **20.2.45** Left for British coastal waters.
From early March U 1021 was operating S of Ireland and in St George's Channel.
The boat went missing on or about the 10th, cause and position unknown but could have been a mine off Trevose Head.
There were no known survivors, 43 dead.

U 1022 Type VII C-41

Built by Blohm & Voss, Hamburg
Keel laid 6.5.43   Launched 13.4.44
Commissioned 7.6.44   Feldpost Nr M 38 350

Sunk 29.12.45 NW of Malin Head (55°40′N 08°15′W)

Served with
31 U-Flottille, Hamburg June 1944 - January 1945 (ab)
11 U-Flottille, Bergen February 1945 - 9.5.45 (fb)

Commanded by
KL Hans-Joachim Ernst June 1944 - 9.5.45

Patrols: 1   Ships sunk: 2 (1720 grt)

The KTB states that during training exercises in the Baltic U 1022 was attacked several times by Allied aircraft but suffered neither casualties or damage.

1. **16.1.45** Left Kiel and arrived Kalundborg **17.1.45**

2. **22.1.45** Left Kalundborg and arrived Horten **23.1.45**

3. **29.1.45** Left Horten and arrived Bergen **8.2.45**

4. **12.2.45** Left for Atlantic operations.
U 1022 operated off Iceland. On the 28th she attacked convoy UR 155 just W of Reykjavik and sank the SS *Alcedo* (pa 1392t). She also claimed to have hit a second vessel in the same attack.
On 3.3.45 U 1022 torpedoed and sank the fishing trawler *Southern Flower* (br 328t) W of Reykjavik. On or about the 11th U 1022 was attacked and damaged by surface forces after she surfaced to attack a group of trawlers.
The boat returned to Bergen **1.4.45**

U 1022 was surrendered at Bergen 9.5.45. She left there on the 30th for an assembly area in Britain.

She was one of 116 boats disposed of by the Royal Navy in Operation Deadlight. In late December 1945 the boat was towed from Lisahally by the destroyer HMS Quantock.

After the towline parted, U 1022 was sunk by gunfire on 29.12.45 by the Polish destroyer Piorun.

U 1023 Type VII C-41

Built by Blohm & Voss, Hamburg
Keel laid 20.5.43   Launched 3.5.44
Commissioned 15.6.44   Feldpost Nr M 38 963

Sunk 9.1.46 NW of Malin Head (55°49´N 08°24´W)

Served with
31 U-Flottille, Hamburg   June 1944 - February 1945 (ab)
11 U-Flottille, Bergen   March 1945 - 10.5.45 (fb)

Commanded by
OL Wolfgang Strenger   June 1944 - March 1945
KL Heinrich Schroeteler   March 1945 - 10.5.45

Patrols: 1   Ships sunk: None
                          1 minesweeper (335 dt)

1. 20.2.45   Left Kiel and arrived Horten **23.2.45**

2. 2.3.45   Left Horten and arrived Bergen **9.3.45**

3. 25.3.45   Left for British coastal waters.

From mid-April U 1023 operated in the Irish Sea and on the 19th she made an unsuccessful attack on a convoy just S of Ireland.

When the U-boat war ended on 4.5.45, U 1023 was in the Irish Sea. In accordance with instructions received, U 1023 headed for Weymouth. En route, she torpedoed and sank the Norwegian minesweeper NYMS 382 in the evening of the 7th ESE of Torbay.

She put in to Weymouth and surrendered **10.5.45**

U 1023 was one of 116 boats disposed of by the Royal Navy in Operation Deadlight. In January 1946 she was towed from Lisahally by the tug HMS Saucy.

U 1023 foundered under tow on 9.1.46 NW of Malin Head. She had been used by the Royal Navy for tests as submarine N 83.

U 1024 Type VII C-41

Built by Blohm & Voss, Hamburg
Keel laid 20.5.43   Launched 3.5.44
Commissioned 28.6.44   Feldpost Nr M 39 246

Sunk 13.4.45 SSW of the Isle of Man (53°39´N 05°03´W)

Served with
31 U-Flottille, Hamburg   June 1944 - January 1945 (ab)
11 U-Flottille, Bergen   February 1945 - 12.4.45 (fb)

Commanded by
KL Hans-Joachim Gutteck   June 1944 - 12.4.45

Patrols: 1   Ships sunk: 1 (7176 grt) + 1 damaged

1. 30.12.44   Left Kiel and arrived Horten **2.1.45**

2. 28.2.45   Left Horten and arrived Marviken **1.3.45**

3. 3.3.45   Left for British coastal waters.

From late March U 1024 was operating in the Irish Sea. On 5.4.45 she reported a corvette sunk but there is no confirmation of this.

U 1024 attacked convoy HX 346 on the 7th NNW of Holyhead, sinking the SS *James W Nesmith* (am 7176t), and on the 12th, in the same area, the boat torpedoed and damaged the SS *Will Rogers* (am 7200t). She also reported two ships sunk in the same attack but there is no confirmation of this.

In the late evening of the 12th U 1024 was located by the frigate HMS *Loch Glendhu* (Lt-Cdr E G P B Knapton) of the 8th EG. The boat was forced to the surface by a Squid attack. Ships of the 8th EG opened fire and HMS *Loch Achray* fired depth-charges. U 1024's crew was seen to be abandoning ship and the firing ceased. It is believed that U 1024's commander, KL Gutteck, was wounded during the firing and that he then shot himself.

The boat was boarded by a party from HMS *Loch More* and valuable documents were found. U 1024 was taken in tow by *Loch More* but she foundered in the morning of the 13th after the towline parted in thick fog.

9 men, including the commander, were lost and another 37 men were picked up.

U 1025 Type VII C-41

Built by Blohm & Voss, Hamburg
Keel laid 3.6.43   Launched 24.5.44
Commissioned 12.4.45   Feldpost Nr M 40 175

Scuttled 5.5.45 in Flensburger Förde

Served with
33 U-Flottille, Flensburg   April 1945 - 5.5.45 (ab)

Commanded by
OL Ewald Pick   April 1945 - 5.5.45

Patrols: None   Ships sunk: None

U 1025 did not go into service. In accordance with Operation Regenbogen *but contrary to the surrender terms, she was scuttled on 5.5.45 in Flensburger Förde, where she awaited further orders.*

U 1026 - U 1032 were all launched in the Blohm & Voss yard at Hamburg but construction was never completed. They were all either scuttled in early May 1945 or broken up earlier.

U 1033 - U 1050 were never built, orders cancelled.

U 1051 Type VII C

Built by Germania Werft, Kiel
Keel laid 11.2.43   Launched 3.2.44
Commissioned 4.3.44   Feldpost Nr M 50 396

Sunk 26.1.45 SW of the Isle of Man (53°39´N 05°23´W)

Served with
5 U-Flottille, Kiel   March - December 1944 (ab)
11 U-Flottille, Bergen   January 1945 (fb)

Commanded by
OL Heinrich von Holleben   March 1944 - 26.1.45

Patrols: 1   Ships sunk: 1 (1152 grt)
                              1 frigate (1300 dt)

U 1051 (continued)

1. 18.12.44 Left Kiel and arrived Horten **23.12.44**

2. 28.12.44 Left for British coastal waters.

From 20.1.45 U 1051 was operating in the Irish Sea. On the 21st she probably sank the SS *Galatea* (nw 1152t) SW of Bardsey Island and on the 26th she probably torpedoed and damaged the frigate HMS *Manners* W of the Isle of Man. *Manners* was towed to Barrow-in-Furness but never repaired.

The hunt for U 1051 intensified after the frigate HMS *Bentinck* made contact and carried out a depth-charge attack. She was joined by HMS *Aylmer* and *Calder*. After further attacks, U 1051 surfaced and came under fire from the three frigates. The boat sank after being rammed by *Aylmer*.

There were no survivors, 47 dead.

U 1052 Type VII C

Built by Germania Werft, Kiel
Keel laid 10.3.43   Launched 16.12.43
Commissioned 20.1.44   Feldpost Nr M 49 477

Sunk 7.12.45 NW of Bloody Foreland (55°50′N 10°05′W)

Served with
5 U-Flottille, Kiel   January - June 1944 (ab)
U-Abwehrschule, Bergen   July 1944 - 9.5.45 (sb)

Commanded by
OL Friedrich Weidner   January - July 1944
OL Günther Scholz   July 1944 - 9.5.45

Patrols: None   Ships sunk: None

U 1052 was on training duties. She was surrendered at Bergen on 9.5.45. She left there on the 29th for an assembly area in Britain.

She was one of 116 disposed of by the Royal Navy in Operation Deadlight. *In early December 1945 the boat was towed from Loch Ryan out through the North Channel by the frigate HMS* Cubitt.

On 7.12.45 U 1052 was sunk in rocket-projectile attacks by aircraft of 816 (FAA) Squadron.

U 1053 Type VII C

Built by Germania Werft, Kiel
Keel laid 15.3.43   Launched 17.1.44
Commissioned 12.2.44   Feldpost Nr M 49 500

Sunk 15.2.45 off Bergen (60°22′N 05°10′E)

Served with
5 U-Flottille, Kiel   February - October 1944 (ab)
11 U-Flottille, Bergen   November 1944 - 15.2.45 (fb)

Commanded by
OL Helmut Lange   February 1944 - 15.2.45

Patrols: 1   Ships sunk: None

1. 28.10.44 Left Kiel and arrived Horten **31.10.44**

2. 7.11.44 Left for Atlantic operations.

From early December U 1053 was on weather-reporting duties. She sent daily reports from 5.12.44 from a position 150 miles W of Rockall. The information gathered was used in preparation for the forthcoming German offensive in the Ardennes.

U 1053 was relieved from this duty by U 248 in early January 1945 and headed for home.

U 1053 put in to Stavanger **21.1.45**

3. 15.2.45 Left Stavanger.

On this day U 1053 sank off Bergen, the result of a marine accident during deep-diving exercises.

There were no survivors, 54 dead.

U 1054 Type VII C

Built by Germania Werft, Kiel
Keel laid 27.3.43   Launched 24.2.44
Commissioned 25.3.44   Feldpost Nr M 50 425

Decommissioned 16.9.44 at Kiel

Served with
5 U-Flottille, Kiel   March 1944 - 16.9.44 (ab)

Commanded by
KL Wolfgang Riekeberg   March 1944 - 16.9.44

Patrols: None   Ships sunk: None

On 18.8.44 U 1054 was irreparably damaged when she was rammed by the motor ferry Peter Wessel *off Hela.*

The boat was decommissioned at Kiel 16.9.44 and later scrapped.

U 1055 Type VII C

Built by Germania Werft, Kiel
Keel laid 12.3.43   Launched 9.3.44
Commissioned 8.4.44   Feldpost Nr M 04 059

Lost 30.4.45 WSW of Brest (48°00′N 06°30′W)

Served with
5 U-Flottille, Kiel   April - November 1944 (ab)
11 U-Flottille, Bergen   December 1944 - 30.4.45 (fb/fb-m)

Commanded by
OL Rudolf Meyer   April 1944 - 30.4.45

Patrols: 2   Ships sunk: 4 (19,413 grt)

1. 1.12.44 Left Kiel and arrived Horten **4.12.44**

2. 9.12.44 Left Horten and arrived Marviken **10.12.44**

3. 11.12.44 Left for British coastal waters.

From early January U 1055 operated in St George's Channel and the Irish Sea. On the 9th she attacked convoy ON 271 W of St Bride's Bay and sank the SS *Jonas Lie* (am 7198t). The abandoned wreck drifted until finally sinking on the 14th.

U 1055 torpedoed three ships off Holyhead on the 11th, missing the Yugoslav SS *Senga* but sinking the SS *Roanoake* (am 2606t) and the SS *Normandy Coast* (br 1428t). The boat was attacked by a Liberator on the 12th W of Holyhead but she managed to escape without damage.

On the 15th U 1055 sank the tanker MV *Maja* (br 8181t) SW of the Isle of Man and on the 16th she may have unsuccessfully atttacked a steamer but this is not certain.

U 1055 put in to Stavanger **1.2.45**

4. 22.3.45 Left Stavanger and arrived Bergen **23.3.45**

5. 5.4.45 Left for British coastal waters.

U 1055 was to operate at the western entrance to the English Channel. On the 30th the boat was lost WSW of Brest from an unknown cause but possibly after striking a mine.

There were no survivors, 49 dead.

U 1056   Type VII C

Built by Germania Werft, Kiel
Keel laid 2.7.43   Launched 30.3.44
Commissioned 29.4.44   Feldpost Nr M 23 837

Scuttled 5.5.45 in Geltinger Bucht

Served with
5 U-Flottille, Kiel   April 1944 - 5.5.45 (ab)

Commanded by
OL Rudolf Schwarz   April 1944 - January 1945
OL Gustav Schröder   January 1945 - 5.5.45

Patrols: None   Ships sunk: None

U 1056 did not go into service. In accordance with Operation Regenbogen *but contrary to the surrender terms, she was scuttled on 5.5.45 in Geltinger Bucht, where she had been sent to await further orders.*

U 1057   Type VII C

Built by Germania Werft, Kiel
Keel laid 22.6.43   Launched 20.4.44
Commissioned 20.5.44   Feldpost Nr M 25 172

Surrendered 10.5.45 at Bergen

Served with
5 U-Flottille, Kiel   May 1944 - 10.5.45 (ab/fb)

Commanded by
OL Günter Lüth   May 1944 - 10.5.45

Patrols: 1   Ships sunk: None

1. 23.4.45 Left Kiel and arrived Horten **25.4.45**

2. 26.4.45 Left for British coastal waters.

When the U-boat surrender order came on 4.5.45, U 1057 was in her operational area W of the British Isles.

The boat put in to Bergen **9.5.45**

U 1057 surrrendered at Bergen on 10.5.45 and she left there on the 30th for an assembly area in Britain.

In November 1945 U 1057 was given to the Soviet Navy and became submarine S-81.

U 1058   Type VII C

Built by Germania Werft, Kiel
Keel laid 20.8.43   Launched 11.4.44
Commissioned 10.6.44   Feldpost Nr M 40 307

Surrendered 10.5.45 at Lough Foyle

Served with
5 U-Flottille, Kiel   June - December 1944 (ab)
11 U-Flottille, Bergen   January 1945 - 10.5.45 (fb)

Commanded by
OL Hermann Bruder   June 1944 - 10.5.45

Patrols: 2   Ships sunk: None

1. 30.12.44 Left Kiel and arrived Horten **2.1.45**

2. 8.1.45 Left Horten and arrived Stavanger **10.1.45**

3. 15.1.45 Left for British coastal waters.

U 1058 operated in the Irish Sea from 9.2.45. On or about the 18th she claimed a large freighter sunk but this is unconfirmed.

The boat put in to Bergen **26.3.45**

4. 28.4.45 Left Bergen for British coastal waters.

When the U-boat war ended on 4.5.45, U 1058 was still at sea W of the British Isles. In accordance with instructions given, she put in to Lough Foyle on 10.5.45 and surrendered.

In November 1945 U 1058 was handed over to the Soviet Navy and became submarine S-82.

U 1059   Type VII F

Built by Germania Werft, Kiel
Keel laid 4.6.42   Launched 12.3.43
Commissioned 1.5.43   Feldpost Nr M 43 973

Sunk 19.3.44 WSW of the Cape Verde Islands (13°10´N 33°44´W)

Served with
5 U-Flottille, Kiel   May - December 1943 (ab)
12 U-Flottille, Bordeaux   January 1944 - 19.3.44 (fb-v)

Commanded by
OL Herbert Brüninghaus   May - September 1943
OL Günter Leupold   October 1943 - 19.3.44

Patrols: 1   Ships sunk: None

1. 4.2.44 Left Kiel and arrived Bergen **10.2.44**

2. 12.2.44 Left for the Far East.

U 1059 was heading for Penang, carrying a cargo of Monsun torpedoes.

On 19.3.44 she was sighted on the surface WSW of the Cape Verde Islands by an aircraft from the escort-carrier USS *Block Island*. Some of the crew were swimming in the sea but all except one managed to scramble aboard before the conning tower was strafed by a Wildcat of VC-6 (Lt W H Cole).

An Avenger of VC-6 (Lt N T Dowty) came in through heavy flak. The aircraft was hit and the pilot fatally wounded but before crashing into the sea he dropped two depth-charges, one of which exploded U 1059's ammunition, destroying the boat, which rose from

U 1059 (continued)

the sea and then sank by the stern.

The sole survivor of the Avenger's crew, Ensign Fitzgerald, took to his dinghy and found himself among U 1059's survivors in the sea. Fitzgerald pulled aboard a badly-wounded German and after applying a tourniquet he pushed the man back into the sea. Fitzgerald discouraged any would-be boarders with a knife and a .38 pistol.

The destroyer USS *Corry* arrived and picked up Fitzgerald and eight survivors from U 1059, including her commander.

U 1060 Type VII F

Built by Germania Werft, Kiel
Keel laid 7.7.42   Launched 8.4.43
Commissioned 15.5.43   Feldpost Nr M 52 184

Sunk 27.10.44 just W of Velfjord (65°24´N 12°00´E)

Served with
5 U-Flottille, Kiel   May 1943 - 27.10.44 (ab/fb-t)

Commanded by
OL Herbert Brammer   May 1943 - 27.10.44

Patrols: 13 (?)   Ships sunk: None

U 1060 carried out torpedo-transport duties between Kiel and the Norwegian ports.

1. **14.12.43**   Left Kiel and arrived Narvik **23.12.43**

2. **29.12.43**   Left Narvik and returned to Kiel **7.1.44**

3. **18.1.44**   Left Kiel and arrived Ramsund **27.1.44**

4. **1.2.44**   Left Ramsund and returned to Kiel **12.2.44**

5. **28.3.44**   Left Kiel and arrived Ramsund **6.4.44**

6. **10.4.44**   Left Ramsund and returned to Kiel **27.4.44**

7. **13.5.44**   Left Kiel and arrived Ramsund **20.5.44**

8. **23.5.44**   Left Ramsund and returned to Kiel **3.6.44**

9. **20.6.44**   Left Kiel and arrived Trondheim **26.6.44**

10. **30.6.44**   Left Trondheim and arrived Kristiansand **7.7.44**

11. **8.7.44**   Left Kristiansand and arrived Bergen **10.7.44**

12. **11.7.44**   Left Bergen and returned to Kiel **15.7.44**

13. **7.10.44**   Left Kiel and arrived Horten **9.10.44**

14. **12.10.44**   Left Horten and arrived Bergen **17.10.44**

15. **22.10.44**   Left Bergen and arrived Bodø **25.10.44**

16. **26.10.44**   Left Bodø for Bergen.
On the 27th U 1060 was attacked just W of Velfjord by Fireflies of 1771 (FAA) Squadron from the aircraft carrier HMS *Implacable*. The damaged boat ran aground off the island of Fleina.

Later the same day U 1060 was attacked by two Liberators of 311 (Czech) Squadron (S/Ldr A Sedivy and F/O P Pavelka) and two Halifaxes of 502 Squadron (S/Ldr H H C Holderness and

F/Lt W G Powell). During the attacks the boat keeled over and then slid into deeper water.

12 of the crew, including the commander, died and 43 survived.

At the time of her sinking, U 1060 had aboard 28 men from the crew of U 957, which had been badly damaged in a collision on 19.10.44. 4 of the U 957 men were lost in addition to the 12 from U 1060's own crew.

U 1061 Type VII F

Built by Germania Werft, Kiel
Keel laid 21.8.42   Launched 22.4.43
Commissioned 25.8.43   Feldpost Nr M 52 982

Sunk 1.12.45 NW of Bloody Foreland (56°10´N 10°05´W)

Served with
5 U-Flottille, Kiel   August 1943 - 9.5.45 (ab/fb-t)
12 U-Flottille, Bordeaux   January - March & May -October 1944 (fb-t)

Commanded by
OL Otto Hinrichs   August 1943 - March 1945
OL Walter Jäger   March 1945 - 9.5.45

Patrols: 9 (?)   Ships sunk: None

U 1061 carried out torpedo-transport duties between Kiel and the Norwegian ports.

1. **22.2.44**   Left Kiel and arrived Narvik **2.3.44**

2. **5.3.44**   Left Narvik and returned to Kiel **14.3.44**

3. **6.4.44**   Left Kiel and arrived Narvik **13.4.44**

4. **18.4.44**   Left Narvik and returned to Kiel **29.4.44**

5. **18.5.44**   Left Kiel and arrived Gotenhafen **20.5.44**

6. **22.5.44**   Left Gotenhafen and returned to Kiel **24.5.44**

7. **27.5.44**   Left Kiel and arrived Skjomenfjord **5.6.44**

8. **8.6.44**   Left Skjomenfjord and arrived Trondheim **10.6.44**

9. **12.6.44**   Left Trondheim and returned to Kiel **17.6.44**

10. **1.7.44**   Left Kiel and arrived Narvik **12.7.44**

11. **13.7.44**   Left Narvik and returned to Kiel **23.7.44**

12. **17.10.44**   Left Kiel and arrived Horten **19.10.44**

13. **22.10.44**   Left Horten and arrived Kristiansand **23.10.44**

14. **26.10.44**   Left Kristiansand.
On the 27th U 1061 was located by a Leigh Light Wellington of 407 (RCAF) Squadron (F/O J E Neelin). The boat was illuminated and then attacked with six depth-charges. A Liberator of 224 Squadron (F/Lt W S Blackden) appeared and also made a depth-charge attack in the face of heavy flak. The boat was damaged.
U 1061 put in to Trondheim **3.11.44**

15. **20.1.45**   Left Trondheim and arrived Bergen **21.1.45**

16. **7.2.45**   Left Bergen and returned **9.2.45**

17. 24.4.45 Left Bergen and arrived Kristiansand **29.4.45**

18. 1.5.45 Left Kristiansand and returned Bergen **4.5.45**

U 1061 was surrendered at Bergen on 9.5.45. She left there on the 30th for an assembly point in Britain.
The boat was one of 116 boats disposed of by the Royal Navy in Operation Deadlight. *In late November 1945 she was towed from Loch Ryan and out through the North Channel by the tug HMS Enchanter.*
U 1061 was sunk by gunfire on 1.12.45 NW of Bloody Foreland.

U 1062   Type VII F

Built by Germania Werft, Kiel
Keel laid 14.8.42   Launched 8.5.43
Commissioned 19.6.43   Feldpost Nr M 53 002

Sunk 30.9.44 WSW of the Cape Verde Islands (11°36´N 34°44´W)

Served with
5 U-Flottille, Kiel   June - December 1943 (ab)
12 U-Flottille, Bordeaux   January 1944 - 30.9.44 (fb-t)

Commanded by
OL Karl Albrecht   June 1943 - 30.9.44

Patrols: 4   Ships sunk: None

1. 18.12.43 Left Kiel for Bergen.
On the 22nd U 1062 was sighted on the surface by Beaufighters of 144 and 404 (RCAF) Squadrons. The boat was in company with a destroyer and the nine aircraft made their attacks in the face of heavy fire from both vessels and shore installations. Two of 404's aircraft crashed into the sea. U 1062 was slightly damaged in the conning tower area and had some casualties.
She put in to Bergen **24.12.43**

2. 3.1.44 Left Bergen for the Far East.
U 1062 was carrying a cargo of 39 Monsun torpedoes. On 10.4.44 she was refuelled in the Indian Ocean by U 532.
U 1062 put in to Penang **19.4.44**

3. 19.6.44 Left Penang for Europe.
On the 20th U 1062 was unsuccessfully attacked by the British submarine HMS Storm.
The boat returned to Penang **2.7.44**

4. 15.7.44 Left again for Europe.
On the 16th U 1062 was unsuccessfully attacked by the British submarine HMS *Templar*. The boat was carrying a cargo of strategic war material.
She passed through the Indian Ocean and the South Atlantic. In late September U 1062 was ordered to refuel U 219, outward-bound for the Far East. They were to meet 600 miles WSW of Fargo, the most southerly of the Cape Verde Islands.
On the 30th three destroyer-escorts of the escort-carrier USS *Mission Bay's* screen were sent to investigate reports of a U-boat. USS *Fessenden* (Lt-Cdr W A Dobby) made a contact and she fired Hedgehogs, which resulted in four explosions being heard. *Fessenden* then dropped depth-charges and U 1062 was destroyed. There were no survivors, 55 dead.

U 1063   Type VII C-41

Built by Germania Werft, Kiel
Keel laid 7.9.43   Launched 8.6.44
Commissioned 8.7.44   Feldpost Nr M 40 438

Sunk 16.4.45 just NW of Land's End (50°08´N 05°52´W)

Served with
5 U-Flottille, Kiel   July 1944 - February 1945 (ab)
11 U-Flottille, Bergen   March 1945 - 16.4.45 (fb)

Commanded by
KL Karl-Heinz Stephan   July 1944 - 16.4.45

Patrols: 1   Ships sunk: None

1. 4.3.45 Left Kiel and arrived Horten **9.3.45**

2. 11.3.45 Left for British coastal waters.
En route to the English Channel, U 1063 was diverted to an area 200 to 300 miles W of the western entrance to the Channel. In early April she moved eastwards. On the 16th U 1063 was attempting to attack convoy TBC 128 off Land's End when she was located by the escorting frigate HMS *Loch Killin* (Lt-Cdr S Darling) of the 17th EG. The boat was sunk by her in a depth-charge attack.
Of U 1063's crew, the commander and 28 men were lost and 17 others were picked up and made PoW, of whom 6 were wounded.

U 1064   Type VII C-41

Built by Germania Werft, Kiel
Keel laid 23.9.43   Launched 22.6.44
Commissioned 29.7.44 Feldpost Nr M 41 096

Surrendered 9.5.45 at Trondheim

Served with
5 U-Flottille, Kiel   July 1944 - January 1945 (ab)
11 U-Flottille, Bergen   February 1945 - 9.5.45 (fb)

Commanded by
KK Hermann Schneidewind   July 1944 - 9.5.45

Patrols: 1   Ships sunk: 1 (1564 grt)

1. 16.1.45 Left Kiel and arrived Kalundborg **17.1.45**

2. 22.1.45 Left Kalundborg and arrived Horten **23.1.45**

3. 29.1.45 Left Horten and arrived Bergen **2.2.45**

4. 7.2.45 Left for operations in the North Channel.
On the 21st U 1064 encountered and attacked a convoy NE of Larne. She reported three ships sunk but only the SS *Dettifoss* (ice 1564t) was confirmed.
From the 22nd U 1064 operated in the Irish Sea and from 9.3.45 she was on weather-reporting duties for two weeks. During February and March some of U 1064's crew suffered from carbon monoxide poisoning because of a defective schnorkel.
The boat put in to Trondheim **9.4.45**

U 1064 was surrendered at Trondheim on 9.5.45. She left there on the 29th for an assembly area in Britain.
In November 1945 the boat was handed over to the Soviet Navy and became submarine S-83.

U 1065   Type VII C-41

Built by Germania Werft, Kiel
Keel laid 5.10.43   Launched 3.8.44
Commissioned 23.9.44   Feldpost Nr M 43 832

Sunk 9.4.45 W of Skärhamn (57°58´N 11°15´E)

Served with
5 U-Flottille, Kiel   September 1944 - 9.4.45 (ab/fb)

Commanded by
OL Johannes Panitz   September 1944 - 9.5.45

Patrols: None   Ships sunk: None

1. **4.4.45** Left Kiel for Horten.
  On the 9th U 1065 and U 804 were moving northwards up the Kattegat, close to the Swedish coast. They were sighted on the surface by 34 Mosquitos of the Banff Strike Wing. 22 aircraft from 143 and 235 Squadrons went down and strafed the boats with rocket, cannon and machine-gun fire. 248 Squadron did not take part.
  Both boats sank, one exploding with such force that four Mosquitos were badly damaged, one of them going into the sea.
  There were no survivors from either boat. 45 men died in U 1065.

U 1066 - U 1100 were never built, orders cancelled.

U 1101   Type VII C

Built by Nordseewerke, Emden
Keel laid 18.3.43   Launched 13.9.43
Commissioned 10.11.43   Feldpost Nr M 55 209

Scuttled 5.5.45 in Geltinger Bucht

Served with
22 U-Flottille, Gotenhafen November 1943 - February 1945 (sb)
31 U-Flottille, Hamburg March 1945 - 5.5.45 (fb)

Commanded by
OL Rudolf Dübler   November 1943 - 5.5.45

Patrols: None   Ships sunk: None

Awaiting orders, U 1101 was scuttled on 5.5.45 in Geltinger Bucht.

U 1102   Type VII C

Built by Nordseewerke, Emden
Keel laid 16.4.43   Launched 15.1.44
Commissioned 22.2.44   Feldpost Nr M 55 331

Sunk 21.12.45 NW of Bloody Foreland (56°04´N 09°35´W)

Served with
31 U-Flottille, Hamburg February - May 1944 (ab)
U-Abwehrschule, Bergen September 1944 - 9.5.45 (sb)

Commanded by
OL Bernhard Schwarting February - May 1944
OL Erwin Sell   August 1944 - 9.5.45

Patrols: None   Ships sunk: None

U 1102 was taken out of service at Königsberg on 12.5.44 after being badly damaged in a USAF bombing raid. She was towed to Kiel and after repair she went to the U-Abwehrschule in September 1944 as a school boat.
  U 1102 was surrendered at Kiel on 9.5.45. She left Wilhelmshaven on 23.6.45 for an assembly area in Britain. She was one of 116 boats disposed of by the Royal Navy in Operation Deadlight.
  In December 1945 U 1102 was towed from Loch Ryan out through the North Channel by the destroyer HMS Zetland.
  U 1102 was sunk by gunfire on 21.12.45 in 500 fathoms NW of Bloody Foreland.

U 1103   Type VII C

Built by Nordseewerke, Emden
Keel laid 26.5.43   Launched 12.10.43
Commissioned 8.1.44   Feldpost Nr M 31 936

Sunk 30.12.45 NW of Bloody Foreland (56°03´N 10°05´W)

Served with
8 U-Flottille, Danzig January - September 1944 (ab)
22 U-Flottille, Gotenhafen September 1944 - February 1945 (sb)
31 U-Flottille, Hamburg/Wilhelmshaven March 1945 - 9.5.45 (sb)

Commanded by
KL Hans Bungards January - July 1944
OL Werner Sausmikat July - October 1944
OL Karl-Heinz Schmidt October - November 1944
OL Jürgen Iversen November 1944 - February 1945
KL Wilhelm Eisele March 1945 -9.5.45

Patrols: None   Ships sunk: None

U 1103 was on training duties. She surrendered at Wilhelmshaven on 9.5.45 and left there on 23.6.45 for an assembly area in Britain.
  The boat was one of 116 disposed of by the Royal Navy in Operation Deadlight. In late December 1945 U 1103 was towed from Loch Ryan and out through the North Channel by the frigate HMS Cawsand Bay.
  The boat was sunk by gunfire on 30.12.45 NW of Bloody Foreland.

U 1104   Type VII C

Built by Nordseewerke, Emden
Keel laid 26.6.43   Launched 7.12.43
Commissioned 15.3.44   Feldpost Nr unknown

Served with
8 U-Flottille, Danzig March 1944 - January 1945 (ab)
11 U-Flottille, Bergen February 1945 - 9.5.45 (fb)

Commanded by
OL Rüdiger Perleberg March 1944 - 9.5.45

Patrols: 1   Ships sunk: None

1. **22.1.45** Left Kiel and arrived Horten **25.1.45**

2. **1.2.45** Left for British coastal waters.
  From the 9th U 1104 began operating in the area from The Minch to Loch Ewe. During the latter part of February, on or about the 25th, she claimed to have sunk a freighter and a tanker at the northern end of The Minch but there is no confirmation of this.
  U 1104 put in to Bergen **22.3.45**

U 1104 was surrendered at Bergen on 9.5.45 and she left there on the 30th for an assembly area in Britain.

She was one of 116 boats disposed of by the Royal Navy in Operation Deadlight. In December 1945 the boat was towed from Loch Ryan out through the North Channel by the frigate HMS Cawsand Bay.

U 1104 lost buoyancy on 15.12.45 and she was scuttled with demolition charges NW of Malin Head.

U 1105   Type VII C

Built by Nordseewerke, Emden
Keel laid 6.7.43   Launched 20.4.44
Commissioned 3.6.44   Feldpost Nr M 50 444

Surrendered 10.5.45 at Loch Eriboll

Served with
8 U-Flottille, Danzig   June 1944 - February 1945 (ab)
5 U-Flottille, Kiel   February 1945 - 10.5.45 (fb)

Commanded by
OL Hans-Joachim Schwarz   June 1944 - 10.5.45

Patrols: 1   Ships sunk: None
                         1 frigate (1300 dt)

1. 2.4.45   Left Kiel and arrived Horten **6.4.45**

2. 9.4.45   Left Horten and arrived Marviken **11.4.45**

3. 12.4.45   Left for British coastal waters.
U 1105 was schnorkel-equipped and Alberich-coated. The boat operated off the west coast of Ireland. On the 27th the boat torpedoed and damaged the frigate HMS *Redmill* NNW of Black Rock. She was towed to Londonderry but never repaired. The boat avoided detection, probably because of her Alberich-coating.

From the 28th U 1105 operated W of the North Channel. She was in her operational area when the U-boat war ended on 4.5.45. In accordance with instructions given, U 1105 made her way to Loch Eriboll and surrendered there **10.5.45**

U 1105 was taken over by the Royal Navy as submarine N 16. She later went to the US Navy and was sunk on 18.11.48 during explosives trials in Chesapeake Bay.

U 1106   Type VII C

Built by Nordseewerke, Emden
Keel laid 28.7.43   Launched 26.5.44
Commissioned 5.7.44   Feldpost Nr M 04 237

Sunk 29.3.45 NNW of the Shetlands (61°46′N 02°16′W)

Served with
8 U-Flottille, Danzig   July 1944 - February 1945 (ab)
5 U-Flottille, Kiel   February 1945 - 29.3.45 (fb)

Commanded by
OL Erwin Bartke   July 1944 - 29.3.45

Patrols: 1   Ships sunk: None

1. 14.3.45   Left Kiel and arrived Horten **18.3.45**

2. 21.3.45   Left for British coastal waters.

U 1106 was schnorkel-equipped and Alberich-coated. Outward-bound, she was sighted on the 29th NNW of the Shetlands by a Liberator of 224 Squadron (F/Lt M A Graham) and sunk in a depth-charge attack.

There were no survivors, 46 dead.

U 1107   Type VII C-41

Built by Nordseewerke, Emden
Keel laid 20.8.43   Launched 30.6.44
Commissioned 8.8.44   Feldpost Nr unknown

Sunk 30.4.45 WSW of Ushant (48°00′N 06°30′W)

Served with
8 U-Flottille, Danzig   August 1944 - February 1945 (ab)
11 U-Flottille, Bergen   February 1945 - 30.4.45 (fb)

Commanded by
KL Fritz Parduhn   August 1944 - 30.4.45

Patrols: 1   Ships sunk: 2 (15,209 grt)

1. 24.3.45   Left Kiel and arrived Horten **27.3.45**

2. 29.3.45   Left for British coastal waters.
U 1107 was schnorkel-equipped and Alberich-coated. From 16.4.45 she was operating at the western entrance to the English Channel. On the 18th the boat attacked convoy HX 348 WSW of Brest and sank two ships, the SS *Cyrus H McCormick* (am 7181t) and the tanker MV *Empire Gold* (br 8028t). U 1107 was hunted by the escort but she evaded them.

On the 30th the boat was attacked and sunk WSW of Ushant by a MAD-equipped USN Catalina of VP-63 (Lt F G Lake).

Of U 1107's crew, the commander and at least 36 men were lost.

U 1108   Type VII C-41

Built by Nordseewerke, Emden
Keel laid 20.9.43   Launched 5.9.44
Commissioned 18.11.44   Feldpost Nr M 27 527

Surrendered 9.5.45 at Horten

Served with
8 U-Flottille, Danzig   November 1944 - February 1945 (ab)
5 U-Flottille, Kiel   February 1945 - 9.5.45 (ab)

Commanded by
OL Wolf Wigand   November 1944 - 9.5.45

Patrols: None   Ships sunk: None

U 1108 left Kiel in early May and was surrendered at Horten on 9.5.45. She left there on the 29th for an assembly area in Britain.

The boat was taken over by the Royal Navy and after some experimental use, she was scrapped in 1949 at Briton Ferry.

U 1109   Type VII C-41

Built by Nordseewerke, Kiel
Keel laid 22.10.43   Launched 19.6.44
Commissioned 31.8.44   Feldpost Nr M 41 181

Sunk 5.1.46 NNW of Tory Island (59°49′N 08°31′W)

Served with
8 U-Flottille, Danzig   August 1944 - February 1945 (ab)
11 U-Flottille, Bergen   February 1945 - 12.5.45 (fb)

Commanded by
OL Friedrich van Riesen   August 1944 - 12.5.45

Patrols: 2   Ships sunk: None

1. **11.3.45**   Left Kiel and arrived Horten **16.3.45**

2. **19.3.45**   Left Horten and arrived Kristiansand **20.3.45**

3. **22.3.45**   Left for British coastal waters.
   She returned with engine damage, reaching Bergen **6.4.45**

4. **17.4.45**   Left again for British coastal waters.
   U 1109 was still in her operational area on 4.5.45 when the
   U-boat war ended. In accordance with instructions received, she
   made for Loch Eriboll and surrendered there **12.5.45**

U 1109 was one of 116 boats disposed of by the Royal Navy in
Operation Deadlight. *In early January 1946 the boat was towed
from Lisahally by the destroyer HMS* Zetland.
    *U 1109 was sunk on 5.1.46 NNW of Tory Island by gunfire by the
submarine HMS* Templar.

U 1110   Type VII C-41

Built by Nordseewerke, Emden
Keel laid 18.12.43   Launched 21.7.44
Commissioned 24.9.44   Feldpost Nr M 47 389

Sunk 21.12.45 N of Tory Island (55°45′N 08°19′W)

Served with
8 U-Flottille, Danzig   September 1944 - February 1945 (ab)
5 U-Flottille, Kiel   February 1945 - 9.5.45 (fb)

Commanded by
OL Joachim-Werner Bach   September 1944 - 9.5.45

Patrols: None   Ships sunk: None

*U 1110 was surrendered at Wilhelmshaven on 9.5.45. She left there
on 23.6.45 for an assembly area in Britain.*
    The boat was one of 116 disposed of by the Royal Navy in
Operation Deadlight. *In December 1945 she was towed from Loch
Ryan out through the North Channel by the frigate HMS* Rupert.
    *After the towline parted on 21.12.45, U 1110 was sunk by
gunfire N of Tory Island.*

U 1111 - U 1120 were never built, orders cancelled.

U 1121 - U 1130 were projected but never ordered.

U 1131   Type VII C

Built by Howaldtswerke, Kiel
Keel laid 6.2.43   Launched 3.4.44
Commissioned 20.5.44   Feldpost Nr M 04 328

Bombed 31.3.45 at Hamburg

Served with
5 U-Flottille, Kiel   May 1944 - 31.3.45 (ab)

Commanded by
OL Günter Fiebig   May 1944 - 31.3.45

Patrols: None   Ships sunk: None

*On 11.3.45 U 1131 was damaged in a USAF bombing raid on Kiel.
She was transferred to Hamburg for repair and destroyed in the
Deutsche Werke yard at Hamburg-Finkenwerder in an RAF
bombing raid on 31.3.45.*

U 1132   Type VII C

Built by Howaldtswerke, Kiel
Keel laid 15.2.43   Launched 29.4.44
Commissioned 24.6.44   Feldpost Nr M 27 945

Scuttled 4.5.45 at Flensburger Förde

Served with
5 U-Flottille, Kiel   June 1944 - 4.5.45 (ab)

Commanded by
OL Walter Koch   June 1944 - 4.5.45

Patrols: None   Ships sunk: None

U 1132 did not go into service. In accordance with Operation
Regenbogen *but contrary to the surrender terms, she was
scuttled on 4.5.45 in Flensburger Förde, where she was awaiting
further orders.*

U 1133 - U 1152 were never built, orders cancelled.

U 1153 - U 1160 were projected but never built.

U 1161   Type VII C

Built by Danziger Werft
Keel laid 27.10.42   Launched 8.5.43
Commissioned 25.8.43   Feldpost Nr M 55 412

Scuttled 4.5.45 at Flensburger Förde

Served with
24 U-Flottille, Memel   September 1943 - January 1945 (sb)
18 U-Flottille, Gotenhafen   January -February 1945 (ab)
5 U-Flottille, Kiel   March 1945 - 4.5.45 (ab)

Commanded by
OL Karl-Heinz Raabe   September 1943 - January 1945
KL Bruno Schwalbach   January 1945 - 4.5.45

Patrols: None   Ships sunk: None

U 1161 was commissioned on 25.8.43 as Italian submarine S 8. When Italy surrendered on 8.9.43, the boat was taken over by the Kriegsmarine and numbered U 1161.

She went on to training duties at 24,18 and 5 U-Flottillen. Near the war's end the boat left Kiel and went to Flensburger Förde to await further orders.

On 4.5.45 she was scuttled there, in accordance with Operation Regenbogen *but contrary to the surrender terms. The wreck was later broken up.*

U 1162   Type VII C

Built by Danziger Werft
Keel laid 14.11.42   Launched 29.5.43
Commissioned 15.9.43   Feldpost Nr M 52 909

Scuttled 5.5.45 in Geltinger Bucht

Served with
24 U-Flottille, Memel September 1943 - January 1945 (ab)
18 U-Flottille, Gotenhafen January - February 1945 (ab)
5 U-Flottille, Kiel March 1945 - 5.5.45 (ab)

Commanded by
OL Dietrich Sachse September - December 1943
OL Erich Krempl December 1943 - January 1945
KL Klaus Euler January - April 1945
KL Hans-Heinrich Ketels April 1945 - 5.5.45

Patrols: None   Ships sunk: None

U 1162 was to be Italian submarine S 10 but Italy surrendered on 8.9.43 before the boat was commissioned. She was taken over by the Kriegsmarine as U 1162.

She went on to training duties at 24, 18 and 5 U-Flottillen. Near the war's end U 1162 left Kiel and went to Geltinger Bucht to await further orders.

On 5.5.45 she was scuttled there, in accordance with Operation Regenbogen *but contrary to the surrender terms. The wreck was later broken up.*

U 1163   Type VII C-41

Built by Danziger Werft,
Keel laid 5.12.42   Launched 12.6.43
Commissioned 6.10.43   Feldpost Nr M 52 936

Sunk 11.12.45 WNW of Bloody Foreland (55°50´N 10°05´W)

Served with
8 U-Flottille, Danzig October 1943 - July 1944 (ab)
11 U-Flottille, Bergen August - September 1944 (fb)
13 U-Flottille, Trondheim October 1944 - 9.5.45 (fb)

Commanded by
OL Ernst-Ludwig Balduhn October 1943 - 9.5.45

Patrols: 6   Ships sunk: 1 (433 grt)

1. 10.6.44   Left Kiel and arrived Flekkefjord **13.6.44**

2. 13.7.44   Left Flekkefjord and went to a waiting position off the Norwegian coast. U 1163 was recalled on the 16th.
  She put in to Arnöy **19.7.44**

3. 1.8.44   Left Arnöy. On the 2nd U 1163 may have shot down an Allied aircraft.

U 1163 arrived Egersund **2.8.44**

4. 17.8.44   Left Egersund and arrived Bergen **17.8.44**

5. 22.8.44   Left Bergen and arrived Stavanger **23.8.44**

6. 26.8.44   Left Stavanger and arrived Marviken **27.8.44**

7. 21.9.44   Left Marviken and arrived Trondheim **24.9.44**

8. 3.10.44   Left Trondheim and arrived Skjomenfjord **6.10.44**

9. 12.10.44   Left Skjomenfjord and arrived Bogenbucht **13.10.44**

10. 15.10.44   Left for operations.
  U 1163 was with *Panther* group, awaiting eastbound JW 61, which left Loch Ewe on the 20th. The convoy passed through the patrol line. During the night of the 26/27th U 1163 was one of a number of *Panther* boats which unsuccessfully attacked the escorting destroyers. The convoy arrived off Kola Inlet on the 28th.
  U 1163 put in to Hammerfest **31.10.44**

11. 2.11.44   Left Hammerfest and arrived Narvik **4.11.44**

12. 8.11.44   Left Narvik.
  On the 11th U 1163 established a weather station on the Norwegian arctic coast.
  The boat put in to Tromsø **12.11.44**

13. 14.11.44   Left Tromsø.
  From the 16th to the 20th U 1163 was engaged in establishing a weather station on Bear Island.
  She put in to Kilbotn **22.11.44**

14. 25.11.44   Left Kilbotn for operations.
  U 1163 joined *Grube* group, which waited off the Kola coast for approaching, eastbound JW 62. The convoy passed through Bear Island Passage, unobserved by the waiting *Stock* group, which then moved to the Kola coast.
  On 3.12.44 U 1163 attacked Soviet coastal convoy KB 35 N of Cape Cernyj, sinking the trawler *Revoljucioner* (sov 433t). Between the 5th and 7th U 1163 and other boats attacked Soviet a/s groups as well as convoy JW 62. Three small Soviet craft were sunk but JW 62 entered Kola Inlet without loss on the 7th.
  U 1163 may have taken part in the operation against return convoy RA 62 but if she did, she had no success.
  The boat put in to Bogenbucht **16.12.44**

15. 12.1.45   Left Bogenbucht and arrived Trondheim **15.1.45**

16. 28.1.45   Left Trondheim.
  On the 28th U 1163 collided with German motor minesweeper R 57 in Trondheim fjord. R57 sank.
  U 1163 put in to Kristiansand **4.2.45**

17. 15.4.45   Left Kristiansand for operations. No details are known of this final patrol. U 1163 was still at sea when the U-boat war ended on 4.5.45.
  She put in to Marviken and surrendered **9.5.45**

U 1163 left Kristiansand-Süd on 29.5.45 for an assembly area in Britain. She was one of 116 boats disposed of by the Royal Navy in Operation Deadlight. In December 1945 she was towed from Loch Ryan out through the North Channel by the tug HMS Emulous.

U 1163 was sunk by aircraft on 11.12.45 WNW of Bloody Foreland.

U 1164 Type VII C-41

Built by Danziger Werft
Keel laid 11.1.43   Launched 3.7.43
Commissioned 27.10.43   Feldpost Nr M 54 201

Decommissioned 24.7.44 at Kiel

Served with
8 U-Flottille, Danzig   October 1943 - 24.7.44 (ab/fb-oE)

Commanded by
KL Fokko Schlömer   October 1943 - June 1944
KL Hans Wengel   June 1944 - 24.7.44

Patrols: None   Ships sunk: None

During the night of July 23/24th 1944 U 1164 was very seriously damaged in an RAF raid on Kiel. The boat was decommissioned on 24.7.44 and broken up.

U 1165 Type VII C-41

Built by Danziger Werft
Keel laid 31.12.42   Launched 20.7.43
Commissioned 17.11.43   Feldpost Nr M 55 256

Sunk 31.12.45 NW of Fanad Head (55°44′N 08°40′W)

Served with
8 U-Flottille, Danzig   November 1943 - May 1944 (ab)
9 U-Flottille, Brest   June - August 1944 (fb)
11 U-Flottille, Bergen   August 1944 - 9.5.45 (fb)

Commanded by
OL Hans Homann   November 1943 - 9.5.45

Patrols: 4   Ships sunk: None
                    1 minesweeper (tonnage unknown)

1. **18.5.44**   Left Kiel and arrived Larvik **19.5.44**

2. **9.6.44**   Left Larvik, as one of eleven *Mitte* boats which formed a reconnaissance line running from Trondheim to Lindesnes.
   The boats were ordered to remain submerged, unless recharging batteries, to escape the attention of Allied aircraft. Nine *Mitte* boats were recalled in the latter part of June when the invasion threat had lessened. U 1165 was not one of these and she remained patrolling between 57° and 61°N with original *Mitte* boats U 745 and U 1001, and U 771 and U 994, both of which had arrived in mid-June.
   U 1165 put in to Bergen **5.7.44**

3. **9.7.44**   Left Bergen and arrived Stavanger **10.7.44**

4. **28.7.44**   Left Stavanger and arrived Egersund **28.7.44**

5. **11.8.44**   Left Egersund and arrived Kiel **13.8.44**

6. **15.8.44**   Left Kiel and arrived Gotenhafen **17.8.44**

In September, October and November 1944 U 1165 was one of ten boats operating in the Baltic.

7. **7.9.44**   Left Gotenhafen and arrived at a Baltic port **12.9.44**

8. **16.9.44**   Left a Baltic point and arrived Reval **17.9.44**

9. **23.9.44**   Left Reval for operations.
   U 1165 torpedoed and sank the Soviet minesweeper *BMB-512* WNW of Reval on 17.10.44. In the same area on the 19th she attacked a convoy of one submarine, two patrol craft and a tug. U 1165 claimed three hits but there is no confirmation of this.
   The boat put in to Libau **24.10.44**

10. **12.11.44**   Left Libau for operations.
    U 1165 operated in the Gulf of Bothnia and in the entrance to the Gulf of Finland but she had no success.
    She put in to Danzig **25.11.44**

11. **22.1.45**   Left Danzig and arrived Kiel **26.1.45**

12. **7.4.45**   Left Kiel and arrived Horten **11.4.45**

13. **18.4.45**   Left Frederikstad and arrived Kristiansand **20.4.45**

14. **21.4.45**   Left for operations.
    When the U-boat war ended on 4.5.45, U 1165 was still at sea in Northern Waters.
    She put in to Narvik on **5.5.45**

U 1165 was one of a number of boats which set out from Narvik for Trondheim. They were met at sea by the 9th EG and escorted to Loch Eriboll, probably arriving there on 19.5.45.
   U 1165 was one of 116 boats disposed of by the Royal Navy in Operation Deadlight. In late December she was towed from the assembly area at Lisahally by the Polish destroyer Krakowiak.
   The boat was sunk by gunfire on 31.12.45 NW of Fanad Head by the destroyer HMS Offa.

U 1166 Type VII C-41

Built by Danziger Werft
Keel laid 4.2.43   Launched 28.8.43
Commissioned 8.12.43   Feldpost Nr M 32 853

Scuttled 3.5.45 at Kiel

Served with
8 U-Flottille, Danzig   December 1943 - 28.7.44 (ab)

Commanded by
OL Herbert Wagner   December 1943 - April 1944
OL Sarto Ballert   April 1944 - 28.7.44

Patrols: None   Ships sunk: None

On 28.7.44 U 1166 was damaged at Eckernförde after an accidental torpedo explosion on board. The boat rose to the surface by herself. There were no casualties.
   She was taken to Flensburg and, after being made water-tight, was then taken to Kiel, where she was decommissioned on 28.8.44.
   Near the war's end, U 1166 was scuttled on 3.5.45 at Dock 2 in the Deutsche Werke yard at Kiel to prevent her falling into Allied hands.

U 1167   Type VII C-41

Built by Danziger Werft
Keel laid 2.3.43   Launched 28.8.43
Commissioned 29.12.43   Feldpost Nr M 40 885

Bombed 31.3.45 at Hamburg

Served with
8 U-Flottille, Danzig   December 1943 - July 1944 (ab)
22 U-Flottille, Gotenhafen   August 1944 - February 1945 (sb)
31 U-Flottille, Hamburg   March 1945 (ab)

Commanded by
KL Hans Roeder-Pesch   December 1943 - July 1944
OL Karl-Hermann Bortfeldt   August 1944 - 31.3.45

Patrols: None   Ships sunk: None

U 1167 was on training duties. On 31.3.45 the boat was destroyed in an RAF bombing raid on Hamburg. She was in the Deutsche Werke yard at Hamburg-Finkenwerder. One man was killed.

U 1168   Type VII C-41

Built by Danziger Werft
Keel laid 16.3.43   Launched 2.10.43
Commissioned 19.1.44   Feldpost Nr M 49 689

Scuttled 5.5.45 at Flensburger Förde

Served with
8 U-Flottille, Danzig   January 1944 - January 1945 (ab)
5 U-Flottille, Kiel   February 1945 - 5.5.45 (ab)

Commanded by
OL Martin Grasse   January - July 1944
KL Hans Umlauf   July 1944 - 5.5.45

Patrols: None   Ships sunk: None

U 1168 went on to training duties. As the war neared its end she was one of many boats which left their bases and headed for the bays of Northern Germany, there to wait for further orders.
U 1168 ran aground on 5.5.45 near Holnis, Flensburger Förde, after a depth-charge attack by an unidentified aircraft. She was scuttled, in accordance with Operation Regenbogen *but contrary to the surrender terms.*

U 1169   Type VII C-41

Built by Danziger Werft
Keel laid 9.4.43   Launched 2.10.43
Commissioned 9.2.44   Feldpost Nr M 50 520

Lost after 8.3.45, possibly SW of Ireland

Served with
8 U-Flottille, Danzig   February 1944 - January 1945 (sb)
11 U-Flottille, Bergen   February 1945 - 8.3.45 (fb)

Commanded by
OL Heinz Goldbeck   February 1944 - 8.3.45

Patrols: 1   Ships sunk: None

During training in the Baltic, U 1169 had three crewmen killed and another two injured in two accidents.

1. 8.2.45   Left Kiel and arrived Horten **13.2.45**

2. 18.2.45   Left Horten and arrived Kristiansand **19.2.45**

3. 20.2.45   Left for British coastal waters.
    In early March U 1169's engines were damaged. The boat was lost from an unknown cause after the 8th, either SW of Ireland or in her operational area in the English Channel.
    There were no known survivors, 50 dead.

U 1170   Type VII C-41

Built by Danziger Werft
Keel laid 30.4.43   Launched 14.10.43
Commissioned 1.3.44   Feldpost Nr M 50 530

Scuttled 3.5.45 at Travemünde

Served with
8 U-Flottille, Danzig   March - September 1944 (ab)
33 U-Flottille, Flensburg   October 1944 - 3.5.45 (ab)

Commanded by
KL Friedrich Justi   March 1944 - 3.5.45

Patrols: None   Ships sunk: None

U 1170 went on to training duties. As the war neared its end she was one of many boats which went to the bays of Northern Germany, there to wait for further orders.
The boat was scuttled at Travemünde on 3.5.45 in accordance with Operation Regenbogen *but contrary to the surrender terms.*

U 1171   Type VII C-41

Built by Danziger Werft
Keel laid 5.5.43   Launched 23.11.43
Commissioned 22.3.44   Feldpost Nr M 05 459

Surrendered 9.5.45 at Stavanger

Served with
8 U-Flottille, Danzig   March 1944 - February 1945 (ab)
11 U-Flottille, Bergen   March 1945 - 9.5.45 (fb-oE)

Commanded by
OL Richard Nachtigall   March - July 1944
OL Hermann Koopmann   July 1944 - 9.5.45

Patrols: None   Ships sunk: None

U 1171 was originally commissioned 12.1.44 but she was returned to the dockyard and then recommissioned 22.3.44.

1. 8.4.45   Left Kiel and arrived Horten **12.4.45**

2. 19.4.45   Left Horten and arrived Stavanger **23.4.45**

U 1171 was surrendered at Stavanger on 9.5.45. She left there on the 29th for an assembly area in Britain.
The boat was taken over by the Royal Navy and became submarine N 19. She was broken up at Sunderland in April 1949.

U 1172   Type VII C-41

Built by Danziger Werft
Keel laid 7.6.43   Launched 3.12.43
Commissioned 20.4.44   Feldpost Nr M 05 593

Sunk 27.1.45 WNW of Holyhead (53°29´N 05°23´W)

Served with
8 U-Flottille, Danzig April - November 1944 (ab)
11 U-Flottille, Bergen December 1944 - 27.1.45 (fb)

Commanded by
OL Jürgen Kuhlmann April 1944 - 27.1.45

Patrols: 1   Ships sunk: 1 (1599 grt)

1. 7.12.44 Left Kiel and arrived Horten **10.12.44**

2. 22.12.44 Left for British coastal waters.
    From mid-January 1945 U 1172 operated in the Irish Sea. On the 23rd she torpedoed and sank the SS *Vigsnes* (nw 1599t) from convoy MH 1, NNE of Point Lynas, Angelsey.
    U 1172 was sunk in depth-charge attacks on the 27th by the frigates HMS *Bligh* (Lt-Cdr R E Blyth), *Keats* (Lt-Cdr N F Israel) and *Tyler* of the 5th EG, WNW of Holyhead.
    There were no survivors, 52 dead.

U 1173 - U 1179 Work was halted on the construction of these boats on 6.11.43. Orders were cancelled on 22.7.44 and the partly-completed boats were scrapped.

U 1180 - U 1190 were never built, orders cancelled.

U 1191   Type VII C

Built by Schichau, Danzig
Keel laid 14.11.42   Launched 6.7.43
Commissioned 9.9.43   Feldpost Nr M 52 991

Sunk 18.6.44 NNE of Plouguerneau (49°03´N 04°48´W)

Served with
8 U-Flottille, Danzig September 1943 - April 1944 (sb)
7 U-Flottille, St Nazaire May 1944 - 18.6.44 (fb)

Commanded by
OL Peter Grau September 1943 - 18.6.44

Patrols: 1   Ships sunk: None

1. 9.5.44 Left Kiel and arrived Stavanger **15.5.44**

2. 22.5.44 Left for operations.
    U 1191 managed to evade the Coastal Command aircraft that were patrolling off Norway, looking out for boats heading for the North Atlantic.
    On 9.6.44 U 1191 was ordered to make her way to the English Channel. She reported on the 12th, sending a weather report from 54°N, 18°W, being then W of Achill Head, Ireland.
    In the evening of the 18th U 1191 was sighted by a Wellington of 304 (Polish) Squadron NNE of Plouguerneau and six depth-charges were dropped, straddling the boat and bringing oil and wreckage to the surface. U 1191 was destroyed.
    There were no survivors, 50 dead.

U 1192   Type VII C

Built by Schichau, Danzig
Keel laid 14.11.42   Launched 16.7.43
Commissioned 23.9.43   Feldpost Nr M 53 051

Scuttled 3.5.45 at Aussenförde, Kiel

Served with
8 U-Flottille, Danzig September 1943 - April 1944 (ab)
7 U-Flottille, St Nazaire May - July 1944 (fb)
24 U-Flottille, Memel August 1944 - February 1945 (ab)
31 U-Flottille, Hamburg March 1945 - 3.5.45 (ab)

Commanded by
OL Herbert Zeissler September 1943 - July 1944
OL Erich Jewinski July - December 1944
OL Karl-Heinz Meenen December 1944 - 3.5.45

Patrols: 1   Ships sunk: None

1. 13.5.44 Left Kiel and arrived Vallöy **14.5.44**

2. 7.6.44 Left Vallöy and arrived Bergen **9.6.44**

3. 13.6.44 Left Bergen and arrived Hatvik **13.6.44**

4. 19.6.44 Left Hatvik and arrived Bergen **20.6.44**

5. 22.6.44 Left for operations.
    U 1192 relieved a boat of *Mitte* group in a waiting position off Norway. In late June, when the anticipated threat to Norway had receded, U 1192 and eight other *Mitte* boats returned to base.
    She returned to Bergen **27.6.44**

6. 30.6.44 Left Bergen and returned to Kiel **4.7.44**

U 1192 did not see any further operational service. She and the eight other Mitte *boats were transferred to training duties in July. Their crews were drafted to 23 and 24 U-Flottillen to man the new Type XXI boats.*
    U 1192 went to 24 U-Flottille at Memel and later to 31 U-Flottille at Hamburg. As the war drew to a close many boats moved from their bases to the bays of Northern Germany, there to await further orders. U 1192 was one of these.
    In accordance with the Operation Regenbogen *order issued by Dönitz on April 30th 1945, but contrary to the surrender terms, U 1192 was scuttled on 3.5.45 at Aussenförde, Kiel.*

U 1193   Type VII C

Built by Schichau, Danzig
Keel laid 28.12.42   Launched 5.8.43
Commissioned 7.10.43   Feldpost Nr M 53 065

Scuttled 5.5.45 in Geltinger Bucht

Served with
24 U-Flottille, Memel October 1943 - February 1945 (ab)
8 U-Flottille, Danzig June - August 1944 (fb)
31 U-Flottille, Hamburg March 1945 - 5.5.45 (ab/fb)

Commanded by
OL Joachim Guse October 1943 - 5.5.45

Patrols: 4   Ships sunk: None

U 1193 went on to training duties at 24 U-Flottille, Memel. In June 1944 she was detached to operate in the Baltic.

1. 20.6.44   Left Gotenhafen and arrived Reval **21.6.44**

2. 27.6.44   Left Reval for operations.
     U 1193 and other boats operated in the Koivisto and Narva Bay areas, generally in patrols lasting two or three days only. Very little Soviet shipping was seen.
     The boat returned to Reval **30.6.44**

3. 5.7.44   Left for operations.
     U 1193 put in to Nuokko **8.7.44**

4. 11.7.44   Left for operations.
     U 1193 put in to Helsinki **19.7.44**

5. 23.8.44   Left Helsinki for operations.
     U 1193 returned to Gotenhafen **27.8.44**

U 1193 left the Baltic and returned to 24 U-Flottille, Memel.

At the war's end U 1193 was one of many boats waiting in the bays of Northern Germany for further orders.
     On 5.5.45 she was scuttled in Geltinger Bucht, in accordance with Operation Regenbogen but contrary to the surrender terms. The wreck was later broken up.

U 1194   Type VII C

Built by Schichau, Danzig
Keel laid 29.12.42   Launched 5.8.43
Commissioned 21.10.43   Feldpost Nr M 54 219

Sunk 22.12.45 NW of Bloody Foreland (55°59´N 09°55´W)

Served with
22 U-Flottille, Gotenhafen   October 1943 - February 1945 (sb)
31 U-Flottille, Hamburg/Wilhelmshaven   March 1945 - 9.5.45 (ab)

Commanded by
OL Gerhard Nolte   October 1943 - October 1944
OL Karl-Heinz Laudahn (temp)   October - November 1944
OL Herbert Zeissler   November 1944 - 9.5.45

Patrols: None   Ships sunk: None

U 1194 went on to training duties. She was surrendered at Wilhelmshaven on 9.5.45. She left there on 23.6.45 for an assembly area in Britain.
     The boat was one of 116 disposed of by the Royal Navy in Operation Deadlight. In December 1945 she was towed from Loch Ryan out through the North Channel by the destroyer HMS Mendip.
     When the towline parted, U 1194 was sunk by gunfire on 22.12.45 NW of Bloody Foreland.

U 1195   Type VII C

Built by Shichau, Danzig
Keel laid 6.2.43   Launched 2.9.43
Commissioned 4.11.43   Feldpost Nr M 54 254

Sunk 6.4.45 SSW of Selsey Bill (50°33´N 00°55´W)

Served with
21 U-Flottille, Pillau   November - December 1943 (sb)
24 U-Flottille, Memel   January - October 1944 (ab)
5 U-Flottille, Kiel   November - December 1944 (ab)
11 U-Flottille, Bergen   January 1945 - 6.4.45 (fb)

Commanded by
OL Karl-Heinz Schröter   November 1943 - October 1944
KL Ernst Cordes   November 1944 - 6.4.45

Patrols: 1   Ships sunk: 2 (18,604 grt)

1. 4.2.45   Left Kiel and arrived Horten **8.2.45**

2. 13.2.45   Left Horten and arrived Kristiansand **14.2.45**

3. 16.2.45   Left Kristiansand and arrived Bergen **22.2.45**

4. 25.2.45   Left for English coastal waters.
     U 1195 headed for the English Channel. On 21.3.45 she torpedoed and sank the SS *John R Park* (am 7184t) from convoy TBC 102, W of Lizard Point.
     On 6.4.45 U 1195 attacked convoy VWP 16 SSW of Selsey Bill and sank the troop transport SS *Cuba* (br 11420t). The boat was located by an escorting destroyer, HMS *Watchman* (Lt-Cdr J R Clarke) and sunk in depth-charge attacks. Attempts to salvage the boat were abandoned.
     Of U 1195's crew, the commander and 30 men were lost and the 18 survivors were picked up by the French warship *L'Escarmouche*.

U 1196   Type VII C

Built by Shichau, Danzig
Keel laid 8.2.43   Launched 2.9.43
Commissioned 18.11.43   Feldpost Nr M 55 261

Scuttled 3.5.45 at Travemünde

Served with
21 U-Flottille, Pillau   November 1943 - February 1945 (sb)
31 U-Flottille, Hamburg   March 1945 - 3.5.45 (ab)

Commanded by
OL Wilhelm Brand   November 1943 - February 1944
OL René Ballert   February 1944 - 3.5.45

Patrols: None   Ships sunk: None

U 1196 went on to training duties at 21 and then 31 U-Flottille. In August 1944 she was decommissioned after an internal torpedo explosion, which killed two men.
     Near the war's end, U 1196 was one of many boats sent into the bays of Northern Germany to wait for further orders.
     She was scuttled at Travemünde on 3.5.45, in accordance with Operation Regenbogen but contrary to the surrender terms.

U 1197 Type VII C

Built by Schichau, Danzig
Keel laid 13.3.43   Launched 30.9.43
Commissioned 2.12.43   Feldpost Nr M 55 272

Bombed 25.4.45 at Wesermünde

Served with
21 U-Flottille, Pillau   December 1943 - February 1945 (sb)
31 U-Flottille, Hamburg/Wesermünde   March 1945 - 25.4.45 (ab)

Commanded by
OL Heinz Baum   December 1943 - March 1944
OL Kurt Lau   March 1944 - 25.4.45

Patrols: None   Ships sunk: None

U 1197 was damaged in a USAF bombing raid on Wesermünde on 30.4.45. The boat was captured by the Allies and transferred to Wilhelmshaven.

She was sent to Britain on 24.6.45 as a war prize. U 1197 was sunk in February 1946 by the US Navy in the North Sea.

U 1198 Type VII C

Built by Schichau, Danzig
Keel laid 13.3.43   Launched 30.9.43
Commissioned 9.12.43   Feldpost Nr M 40 935

Sunk 17.12.45 NW of Bloody Foreland (56°14´N 10°37´W)

Served with
21 U-Flottille, Pillau   December 1943 - February 1945 (sb)
31 U-Flottille, Hamburg/Wilhelmshaven   March 1945 - 9.5.45 (ab)

Commanded by
OL Gerhard Peters   December 1943 - 9.5.45

Patrols: None   Ships sunk: None

U 1198 was on training duties. She was surrendered at Wilhelmhaven on 9.5.45. She left there on 24.6.45 for an assembly area in Britain.

In mid-December 1945 U 1198 was towed from Loch Ryan out through the North Channel by the destroyer HMS Orwell.

The boat was sunk by gunfire on 17.12.45 NW of Bloody Foreland.

U 1199 Type VII C

Built by Shichau, Danzig
Keel laid 23.3.43   Launched 12.10.43
Commissioned 23.12.43   Feldpost Nr M 42 161

Sunk 21.1.45 S of Land's End (49°57´N 05°42´W)

Served with
8 U-Flottille, Danzig   December 1943 - August 1944 (ab)
1 U-Flottille, Brest   August - October 1944 (fb)
11 U-Flottille, Bergen   November 1944 - 21.1.45 (fb)

Commanded by
KL Rolf Nollmann   December 1943 - 21.1.45

Patrols: 2   Ships sunk: None + 1 damaged

Nominally with 1 U-Flottille, Brest from August to October 1944, U 1199 operated from Bergen during that period.

1. 18.8.44   Left Kiel and arrived Horten **20.8.44**

2. 23.8.44   Left Horten and arrived Bergen **25.8.44**

3. 14.9.44   Left for British coastal waters.
   U 1199 was to operate in the Moray Firth but from early October she patrolled off the northeast coast of Scotland between Peterhead and Aberdeen. On the 21st she reported sinking a freighter E of Aberdeen but there is no confirmation of this. During this patrol the schnorkel-equipped U 1199 remained under water for 50 days.
   The boat returned to Bergen **5.11.44**

4. 1.1.45   Left Bergen for British coastal waters.
   U 1199 patrolled in the western entrance to the English Channel. On the 21st she encountered convoy TBC 43 and torpedoed and damaged the SS *George Hawley* (am 7176t) near Wolf Rock. This vessel was towed in but was probably a total loss.
   The boat was located by an escorting corvette, HMS *Mignonette* (Lt H H Brown), and she was sunk in depth-charge attacks by *Mignonette* and the destroyer HMS *Icarus* (Lt-Cdr R Dyer).
   There were no survivors from U 1199, 47 dead.

U 1200 Type VII C

Built by Schichau, Danzig
Keel laid 17.4.43   Launched 4.11.43
Commissioned 5.1.44   Feldpost Nr M 42 508

Sunk 11.11.44 SSE of Fastnet (50°24´N 09°10´W)

Served with
8 U-Flottille, Danzig   January - August 1944 (ab)
11 U-Flottille, Bergen   September 1944 - 11.11.44 (fb)

Commanded by
OL Hinrich Mangels   January 1944 - 11.11.44

Patrols: 1   Ships sunk: None

1. 9.9.44   Left Kiel and arrived Horten **11.9.44**

2. 29.9.44   Left Horten and arrived Marviken **30.9.44**

3. 1.10.44   Left Marviken and arrived Larvik **1.10.44**

4. 2.10.44   Left Larvik and returned to Marviken **3.10.44**

5. 7.10.44   Left Marviken for operations.
This patrol was cut short because of schnorkel failure.
U 1200 put in to Bergen **17.10.44**

6. 19.10.44   Left for British coastal waters.
U 1200 was to operate S of Ireland. On 11.11.44 the boat was sunk in depth-charge attacks by the corvettes HMS *Kenilworth Castle* (Lt J J Allen), *Launceston Castle* (Lt R M Roberts), *Pevensey Castle* (Lt-Cdr J P G Lewis) and *Portchester Castle* (Lt A G Scott), 75 miles SSE of Fastnet.
There were no survivors, 52 dead.

U 1201 Type VII C

Built by Schichau, Danzig
Keel laid 18.4.43   Launched 4.11.43
Commissioned 13.1.44   Feldpost Nr M 49 693

Scuttled 3.5.45 at Hamburg

Served with
8 U-Flottille, Danzig   January - June 1944 (ab)
21 U-Flottille, Pillau   July 1944 - February 1945 (sb)
31 U-Flottille, Hamburg   March 1945 - 3.5.45 (ab)

Commanded by
OL Eberhard Ebert   January - July 1944
OL Kurt Ahlers   July - October 1944
OL Reinhold Merkle   October 1944 - 3.5.45

Patrols: None   Ships sunk: None

U 1201 was on training duties. To prevent her falling into Allied hands, she was scuttled on 3.5.45 at Hamburg-Finkenwerder and later scrapped.

U 1202 Type VII C

Built by Schichau, Danzig
Keel laid 28.4.43   Launched 11.11.43
Commissioned 27.1.44   Feldpost Nr M 49 757

Surrendered 9.5.45 at Bergen

Served with
8 U-Flottille, Danzig   January - August 1944 (ab)
11 U-Flottille, Bergen   September 1944 - 9.5.45 (fb)

Commanded by
KL Rolf Thomsen   January 1944 - April 1945

Patrols: 2   Ships sunk: 1 (7176 grt)

1. 21.10.44   Left Kiel and arrived Horten **24.10.44**

2. 26.10.44   Left Horten and arrived Kristiansand **28.10.44**

3. 30.10.44   Left for British coastal waters.
U 1202 was to operate in the Irish Sea. On 10.12.44 she reported sinking four ships from a convoy she attacked NW of St David's Head. Only one was confirmed, the SS *Dan Beard* (am 7176t).
The boat put in to Bergen **1.1.45**

4. 4.3.45   Left for Atlantic operations.
U 1202 operated in an area SW of Ireland. On the 21st she claimed one destroyer sunk and an escort-carrier damaged SW of Ireland. Neither was confirmed.
The boat reported two ships sunk on the 31st SW of Ireland but, again, there was no confirmation. On 1.4.45 U 1202 claimed two corvettes sunk and a ship torpedoed and damaged. These claims were also unconfirmed.
The boat returned to Bergen **26.4.45**

U 1202 was surrendered at Bergen on 9.5.45. She was taken over by the Royal Navy in 1947 and transferred to the Royal Norwegian Navy in October 1948.
She was commissioned as submarine Kynn *on 1.7.51 and decommissioned on 1.6.61. The boat was broken up in 1963.*

U 1203 Type VII C

Built by Schichau, Danzig
Keel laid 15.5.43   Launched 9.12.43
Commissioned 10.2.44   Feldpost Nr M 50 595

Sunk 8.12.45 WNW of Bloody Foreland (55°50´N 10°05´W)

Served with
8 U-Flottille, Danzig   February - November 1944 (ab)
11 U-Flottille, Bergen   December 1944 - 9.5.45 (fb)

Commanded by
OL Erich Steinbrink   February - July 1944
OL Sigurd Seeger   July 1944 - 9.5.45

Patrols: 1   Ships sunk: None
                        1 a/s trawler (580 dt)

1. 4.1.45   Left Kiel and arrived Horten **7.1.45**

2. 15.1.45   Left for British coastal waters.
U 1203 operated in the English Channel. On 24.2.45 she torpedoed and sank the a/s trawler HMS *Ellesmere* NNW of Ushant. In late February/early March U 1203 reported one ship torpedoed and a destroyer attacked in the area off Land's End but there are no details.
The boat put in to Trondheim **30.3.45**

U 1203 was surrendered at Trondheim on 9.5.45. She left from Lofjord on the 29th for an assembly area in Britain.
The boat was one of 116 disposed of by the Royal Navy in Operation Deadlight. In early December she was towed from Loch Ryan out through the North Channel by the destroyer HMS Mendip.
U 1203 was sunk by gunfire on 8.12.45 WNW of Bloody Foreland.

U 1204 Type VII C

Built by Schichau, Danzig
Keel laid 15.5.43   Launched 9.12.43
Commissioned 17.2.44   Feldpost Nr M 50 642

Scuttled 5.5.45 in Geltinger Bucht

Served with
8 U-Flottille, Danzig   February - August 1944 (ab)
21 U-Flottille, Pillau   August 1944 - 5.5.45 (sb)

Commanded by
OL Heinrich Mäueler   February - August 1944
OL Erwin Jestel   August 1944 - 5.5.45

Patrols: None   Ships sunk: None

U 1204 was on training duties. She was one of many boats which were moved from their bases in early May to bays in Northern Germany, there to await further orders.
She was scuttled in Geltinger Bucht on 5.5.45 in accordance with Operation Regenbogen but contrary to the surrender terms. The wreck was later broken up.

U 1205   Type VII C

Built by Schichau, Danzig
Keel laid 12.6.43   Launched 30.12.43
Commissioned 2.3.44   Feldpost Nr M 50 693

Scuttled 3.5.45 at Kiel

Served with
8 U-Flottille, Danzig   March - September 1944 (ab)
33 U-Flottille, Flensburg   October 1944 - 3.5.45 (ab)

Commanded by
KL Hermann Zander   March 1944 - 3.5.45

Patrols: None   Ships sunk: None

U 1205 was on training duties. To prevent her falling into Allied hands, the boat was scuttled at Kiel on 3.5.45.

U 1206   Type VII C

Built by Schichau, Danzig
Keel laid 12.6.43   Launched 30.12.43
Commissioned 16.3.44   Feldpost Nr M 50 897

Lost 14.4.45 SSE of Peterhead (57°21′N 01°39′W)

Served with
8 U-Flottille, Danzig   March 1944 - January 1945 (ab)
11 U-Flottille, Bergen   February 1945 - 14.4.45 (fb)

Commanded by
OL Günther Fritze   March - July 1944
KL Karl-Adolf Schlitt   July 1944 - 14.4.45

Patrols: 1   Ships sunk: None

1. 28.3.45   Left Kiel and arrived Horten **30.3.45**

2. 2.4.45   Left Horten and arrived Kristiansand **3.4.45**

3. 6.4.45   U 1206 was to operate off northeast Scotland. On the 14th the submerged boat ran into difficulties, possibly after a toilet malfunction. She surfaced and then ran aground near Buchan Ness, where she was abandoned and scuttled.
   3 men died and the commander and 45 others were made PoW.

U 1207   Type VII C

Built by Schichau, Danzig
Keel laid 26.6.43   Launched 6.1.44
Commissioned 23.3.44   Feldpost Nr M 05 834

Scuttled 5.5.45 in Geltinger Bucht

Served with
8 U-Flottille, Danzig   March - October 1944 (ab)
24 U-Flottille, Memel   November 1944 - February 1945 (eb)
5 U-Flottille, Kiel   March 1945 - 5.5.45 (ab)

Commanded by
OL Kurt Lindemann   March 1944 - 5.5.45

Patrols: None   Ship sunk: None

From late 1944 U 1207 took part in trials in the Baltic, using centimetric radar.

As the war drew to a close, U 1207 was one of many boats moved from their bases to bays in Northern Germany, there to wait for further orders.
   On 5.5.45 she was scuttled in Geltinger Bucht, in accordance with Operation Regenbogen, *the Dönitz order of 30.4.45, but contrary to the surrender terms.*

U 1208   Type VII C

Built by Schichau, Danzig
Keel laid 30.6.43   Launched 13.1.44
Commissioned 6.4.44   Feldpost Nr M 05 973

Sunk 27.2.45 S of Wolf Rock (49°46′N 05°47′W)

Served with
8 U-Flottille, Danzig   April - December 1944 (ab)
11 U-Flottille, Bergen   January 1945 - 27.2.45 (fb)

Commanded by
KK Georg Hagene   April 1944 - 27.2.45

Patrols: 1   Ships sunk: None

1. 30.12.44   Left Kiel and arrived Horten **2.1.45**

2. 13.1.45   Left Horten and arrived Kristiansand **14.1.45**

3. 16.1.45   Left for British coastal waters.
   From early February U 1208 operated S of Ireland. She was sunk in depth-charge attacks by ships of the 2nd EG, on the 27th, S of Wolf Rock in the western English Channel.
   There were no survivors, 49 dead.

U 1209   Type VII C

Built by Schichau, Danzig
Keel laid 14.7.43   Launched 9.2.44
Commissioned 13.4.44   Feldpost Nr M 28 716

Scuttled 18.12.44 just E of Wolf Rock (49°57′N 05°47′W)

Served with
8 U-Flottille, Danzig   April - October 1944 (ab)
11 U-Flottille, Bergen   November 1944 - 18.12.44 (fb)

Commanded by
OL Ewald Hülsenbeck   April 1944 - 18.12.44

Patrols: 1   Ships sunk: None

1. 14.11.44   Left Kiel and arrived Horten **17.11.44**

2. 22.11.44   Left Horten and arrived Kristiansand **23.11.44**

3. 23.11.44   Left Kristiansand and arrived Farsund **25.11.44**

4. 26.11.44   Left for British coastal waters.
   U 1209 was to operate in the English Channel. On 18.12.44 the submerged boat struck a rock. She ran aground near Wolf Rock, the crew abandoned ship and U 1209 was scuttled.
   10 of the crew lost their lives, including the commander.

U 1210 Type VII C

Built by Schichau, Danzig
Keel laid 14.7.43   Launched 9.2.44
Commissioned 22.4.44   Feldpost Nr M 28 986

Sunk 3.5.45 off Eckernförde (54°27´N 09°51´E)

Served with
8 U-Flottille, Danzig   April 1944 - February 1945 (ab)
5 U-Flottille, Kiel   February 1945 - 3.5.45 (ab)

Commanded by
KL Paul Gabert   April 1944 - 3.5.45

Patrols: None   Ships sunk: None

From late 1944 U 1210 took part in trials in the Baltic using centimetric radar.

She was one of many boats which left their bases in early May 1945 to go into the bays of Northern Germany, there to await further orders.
    On 3.5.45 she was attacked and sunk by Typhoons of 2nd TAF off Eckernförde. Casualties unknown.

U 1211 - U 1220 were never built, orders cancelled.

U 1221 Type IX C-40

Built by Deutsche Werft, Hamburg
Keel laid 28.10.42   Launched 2.5.43
Commissioned 11.8.43   Feldpost Nr M 55 188

Bombed 3.4.45 at Kiel

Served with
4 U-Flottille, Stettin   August 1943 - June 1944 (ab)
10 U-Flottille, Lorient   July - November 1944 (fb)
33 U-Flottille, Flensburg   December 1944 - 3.4.45 (fb)

Commanded by
OL Karl Kölzer   August 1943 - January 1944
OL Paul Ackermann   January 1944 - 3.4.45

Patrols: 1   Ships sunk: None

1. **8.8.44**   Left Kiel and arrived Horten **10.8.44**

2. **14.8.44**   Left Horten and arrived Bergen **17.8.44**

3. **20.8.44**   Left for Canadian waters.
    U 1221 operated S of Nova Scotia from mid-September. On the 24th, SSW of Sable Island, a crewman went overboard. A search failed to find him. He had been given extra work as a punishment for falling asleep on look-out. The suggestion that he had committed suicide was later rejected.
    U 1221 operated off Halifax from 30.9.44 until 24.10.44, when she again moved south of Nova Scotia. The boat had no success.
    She put in to Marviken **28.11.44**

4. **1.12.44**   Left Marviken and arrived Flensburg **5.12.44**

U 1221 was sunk at Buoy 7 in Kiel harbour in a USAF bombing raid on 3.4.45. 7 of the crew were killed. The boat was later scrapped.

U 1222 Type IX C-40

Built by Deutsche Werft, Hamburg
Keel laid 2.11.42   Launched 9.6.43
Commissioned 1.9.43   Feldpost Nr M 55 214

Sunk 11.7.44 SW of Lorient (46°31´N 05°29´W)

Served with
4 U-Flottille, Stettin   September 1943 - February 1944 (ab)
10 U-Flottille, Lorient   March 1944 - 11.7.44 (fb)

Commanded by
KL Heinz Bielfeld   September 1943 - 11.7.44

Patrols: 1   Ships sunk: None

1. **13.4.44**   Left Kiel and arrived Marviken **15.4.44**

2. **16.4.44**   Left for Canadian waters.
    From mid-May U 1222 operated S of Nova Scotia and made some unsuccessful attacks on convoys. On 22.5.44 she failed in a torpedo attack on the British tanker SS *Bulkoil* 65 miles S of Halifax. The tanker's radio report led aircraft and the corvettes HMCS *Agassiz* and *Norsyd* to the scene. U 1222 evaded their attacks and escaped.
    On 13.6.44 the boat was ordered to return to France but to conserve enough fuel to reach Bergen, in the event that the Allied land forces had captured the Biscay bases.
    The returning U 1222's schnorkel was sighted SW of Lorient on 11.7.44 by a Sunderland of 201 Squadron (F/Lt I B F Walters). As the aircraft approached to make an attack, the boat dived so steeply that her stern broke the surface.
    Three depth-charges were dropped, straddling U 1222 amidships. Wreckage was strewn over a wide area and the boat was destroyed. Walters was awarded a Bar to the DFC.
    There were no survivors, 56 dead.

U 1223 Type IX C-40

Built by Deutsche Werft, Hamburg
Keel laid 25.11.42   Launched 16.6.43
Commissioned 6.10.43   Feldpost Nr M 53 099

Bombed 28.4.45 off Wesermünde

Served with
4 U-Flottille, Stettin   October 1943 - July 1944 (ab)
2 U-Flottille, Lorient   August - December 1944 (fb)
33 U-Flottille, Flensburg   January 1945 - 28.4.45 (fb)

Commanded by
KL Harald Bosüner   October 1943 - March 1944
OL Albert Kneip   March 1944 - 28.4.45

Patrols: 1   Ships sunk: None + 1 damaged
                          1 frigate (1370 dt)

1. **6.8.44**   Left Kiel and arrived Horten **8.8.44**

2. **14.8.44**   Left Horten and arrived Bergen **17.8.44**

3. **28.8.44**   Left for Canadian waters.
    U 1223 operated S of Nova Scotia and from early October in the Gulf of St Lawrence. On the 4th the boat unsuccessfully attacked the frigate HMCS *Toronto*. On the 14th she attacked the escort of convoy ONS 33 in the Baie aux Outardes, in the St Lawrence River,

U 1223 (continued)

torpedoing and damaging the frigate HMCS *Magog*. The warship was towed into port but never repaired.

U 1223 continued up-river. On the way down, on 2.11.44, she torpedoed and damaged the SS *Fort Thompson* (br 7134t) 6 miles N of Matane. The boat left the Gulf of St Lawrence on the 21st and headed for home.

She put in to Kristiansand **24.12.44**

On 28.4.45 U 1223 was sunk off Wesermünde in an Allied bombing raid. 7 of her crew were killed.

U 1224   Type IX C-40

Built by Deutsche Werft, Hamburg
Keel laid 30.11.42   Launched 7.7.43
Commissioned 20.10.43   Feldpost Nr M 53 122

Sunk 13.5.44 NW of the Cape Verde Islands

Served with
31 U-Flottille, Hamburg October 1943 - 15.2.44

Commanded by
KL Georg Preuss October 1943 - 15.2.44

Patrols: None   Ships sunk: None

U 1224 was given to the Japanese Navy on 15.2.44 and renumbered Ro 501. She was formally handed over on 28.2.44.

The boat was to be crewed by 48 Japanese, who were taken to France in Japanese submarine I 8. They underwent training at 31 U-Flottille, Hamburg until 30.3.44.

The Ro 501 left for Japan on 16.4.44. She was located and sunk NW of the Cape Verde Islands on 13.5.44 by the destroyer USS Francis M Robinson (Lt J E Johansen) in one Hedgehog and two depth-charge attacks.

U 1225   Type IX C-40

Built by Deutsche Werft, Kiel
Keel laid 28.12.42   Launched 21.7.43
Commissioned 10.11.43   Feldpost Nr M 53 196

Sunk 24.6.44 NW of Bergen (63°00´N 00°50´W)

Served with
31 U-Flottille, Hamburg November 1943 - May 1944 (ab)
2 U-Flottille, Lorient June 1944 (fb)

Commanded by
OL Ernst Sauerberg November 1943 - 24.6.44

Patrols: 1   Ships sunk: None

1. 17.6.44 Left Kiel for Kristiansand **19.6.44**

2. 20.6.44 Left for the North Atlantic.
Outward-bound on the 24th, U 1225 was sighted on the surface NW of Bergen by a Canso of 162 (RCAF) Squadron (F/Lt D Hornell). U 1225 stayed on the surface to fight in out and the aircraft's attack was made in the face of heavy and accurate return fire. The four depth-charges, dropped from 50 feet, straddled and sank the boat.

The aircraft was set on fire and vibrating badly. She was ditched in the sea by Hornell and the second pilot, with none of the crew injured. The eight men took turns in one four-man dinghy but later

they all managed to squeeze in together.

Later they were sighted by a Catalina of 333 (Norwegian) Squadron. A Wellington arrived and dropped a dinghy but the ditched crew were unable to reach it.

After 21 hours in the original dinghy in heavy, icy seas, the crew were picked up by a high-speed launch. Two men had died of exposure and Hornell died soon after being rescued. He was awarded a posthumous VC for gallantry during the attack and courage in the dinghy. The five surviving members of the crew were awarded decorations, one DSO, two DFCs and two DFMs.

There were no survivors from U 1225's crew, 56 dead.

U 1226   Type IX C-40

Built by Deutsche Werft, Hamburg
Keel laid 11.1.43   Launched 21.8.43
Commissioned 24.11.43   Feldpost Nr M 54 305

Missing from 28.10.44 in the North Atlantic

Served with
31 U-Flottille, Hamburg November 1943 - July 1944 (ab)
2 U-Flottille, Lorient September 1944 (fb)
33 U-Flottille, Flensburg October 1944 (fb)

Commanded by
OL August-Wilhelm Claussen November 1943 - 28.10.44

Patrols: 1   Ships sunk: None

1. 23.9.44 Left Kiel and arrived Horten **26.9.44**

2. 30.9.44 Left for US coastal waters.
U 1226 is believed to have had a defective schnorkel. She went missing after 28.10.44, position unknown.

There were no known survivors, 56 dead.

In June 1993 a diver claimed to have found the wreck of U 1226 about 4 miles E of Cape Cod.

U 1227   Type IX C-40

Built by Deutsche Werft, Hamburg
Keel laid 1.2.43   Launched 18.9.43
Commissioned 8.12.43   Feldpost Nr M 54 328

Scuttled 3.5.45 at Kiel

Served with
31 U-Flottille, Hamburg December 1943 - July 1944 (ab)
2 U-Flottille, Lorient August - December 1944 (fb)
33 U-Flottille, Flensburg January 1945 - 10.4.45 (fb)

Commanded by
OL Friedrich Altmeier December 1943 - 10.4.45

Patrols: 1   Ships sunk: None
                        1 frigate (1370 dt)

1. 31.8.44 Left Kiel and arrived Horten **2.9.44**

2. 5.9.44 Left Horten and arrived Marviken **6.9.44**

3. 7.9.44 Left Marviken and arrived Bergen **10.9.44**

4. 14.9.44 Left for Atlantic operations.

En route to her operational area off Gibraltar, U 1227 encountered convoy ONS 33 NNE of the Azores. On 4.10.44 the boat torpedoed and damaged the escorting frigate HMCS *Chebogue*. She was towed in to Port Talbot, South Wales but never repaired.

U 1227 moved down to the Gibraltar area and on 8.11.44 she reported sinking a tanker from convoy UGS 58 W of Gibraltar but there is no confirmation of this. U 1227 remained in the area until mid-November, when she began her return journey to Norway, possibly after being badly damaged in a depth-charge attack.

The boat returned to Bergen **26.12.44**

5. 27.12.44 Left Bergen and arrived Marviken **29.12.44**

6. 2.1.45 Left Marviken and arrived Flensburg **4.1.45**

U 1227 was badly damaged in a bombing raid on Kiel by the RAF during the night of 9.4.45. The boat was decommissioned on the 10th.

She was scuttled at Kiel on 3.5.45 and later broken up.

U 1228   Type IX C-40

Built by Deutsche Werft, Hamburg
Keel laid 16.2.43   Launched 2.10.43
Commissioned 22.12.43   Feldpost Nr M 55 286

Surrendered 13.5.45 at Portsmouth, New Hampshire.

Served with
31 U-Flottille, Hamburg   December 1943 - July 1944 (ab)
2 U-Flottille, Lorient   August - October 1944 (fb)
33 U-Flottille, Flensburg   November 1944 - 13.5.45 (fb)

Commanded by
OL Friedrich-Wilhelm Marienfeld   December 1943 - 13.5.45

Patrols: 3   Ships sunk: None
1 corvette (900 dt)

1. 5.9.44 Left Kiel and arrived Horten **9.9.44**

2. 11.9.44 Left Horten and arrived Bergen **15.9.44**

3. 17.9.44 Left for the North Atlantic.
On the 18th U 1228 was detected by radar at night by a Liberator of 224 Squadron (F/O P M Hill). The boat was illuminated on the surface by the aircraft's Leigh Light and came under depth-charge attack. The schnorkel was damaged and cases of carbon monoxide poisoning occurred, killing one crewman.
U 1228 returned to Bergen **20.9.44**

4. 12.10.44 Left for Canadian waters.
U 1228 was S of Newfoundland on 11.11.44. Her commander decided to operate in Cabot Strait. The boat moved along the southern coast of Newfoundland and went into Connoire Bay, for equipment-repairs to be carried out before entering Cabot Strait.
Moving again, U 1228 sighted the corvette HMCS *Shawinigan* early on the 25th off Mouse Island. An acoustic torpedo caused the corvette to explode and sink immediately. The *Shawinigan* was to have escorted the ferry *Burgeo* from Porte aux Basques to Sydney but when she did not appear, the ferry captain, expecting her to arrive at any moment, proceeded to Sydney unescorted. Only on his arriving there did the naval authorities know that the destroyer was missing. A search found only six bodies and an unmarked float.
U 1228, with further technical problems, set out for home, incurring the extreme displeasure of BdU.
She put in to Stavanger **29.12.44**

5. 31.12.44 Left Stavanger and arrived Flensburg **4.1.45**

6. 1.4.45 Left Kiel and arrived Horten **3.4.45**

7. 9.4.45 Left Horten and arrived Kristiansand **11.4.45**

8. 14.4.45 Left for the US east coast.
U 1228 was still at sea when the war ended. On 11.5.45 she was intercepted by the destroyers USS *Scott* and *Sutton* 350 miles E of Cape Race. They escorted her to Casco Bay, Maine and she surrendered at Portsmouth on the 13th.

The boat was taken by the US as a war prize. She was scuttled on 5.2.46 off the US east coast.

U 1229   Type IX C-40

Built by Deutsche Werft, Hamburg
Keel laid 2.3.43   Launched 22.10.43
Commissioned 13.1.44   Feldpost Nr M 55 295

Sunk 20.8.44 SSE of Cape Race (42°20′N 51°39′W)

Served with
31 U-Flottille, Hamburg   January - July 1944 (ab)
10 U-Flottille, Lorient   August 1944 (fb)

Commanded by
KK Armin Zinke   January 1944 - 20.8.44

Patrols: 1   Ships sunk: None

1. 13.7.44 Left Kiel and arrived Kristiansand **15.7.44**

2. 16.7.44 Left Kristiansand and arrived Trondheim **18.7.44**

3. 26.7.44 Left for the US east coast.
U 1229 was carrying an agent, who was to be landed in the Gulf of Maine. En route during the night of August 18/19th, the boat was sighted on the surface by an Avenger from the escort-carrier USS *Bogue* 300 miles S of St John's, Newfoundland. She was attacked with depth-charges but escaped.
On the 20th U 1229 was sighted by an Avenger of VC-42 (Lt A X Brokas), on the surface 300 miles SSE of Cape Race. The Avenger attacked with rockets and bombs, causing casualties amongst U 1229's gunners and flooding the batteries, releasing chlorine gase inside the boat. The commander submerged and went down to schnorkel depth in the hope of venting the gas.
The batteries were unable to provide sufficient power and two hours later he was forced to resurface and order abandon ship. Five Avengers were waiting and the boat came under immediate rocket and bomb attacks. U 1229 sank quickly, as the crew struggled to release liferafts.
There were 42 survivors and 18 men lost their lives, including the commander.

Among the survivors was the agent Oskar Mantel. He had formerly worked as a bar tender in Yorkville, New York State and was to be landed at Winter Harbour, Maine.

Under interrogation Mantel told the FBI that U-boats with missile-launchers were being prepared for attacks against the US east coast. This apparently confirmed rumours that V2 rockets might be directed against US eastern seaboard cities.

This information, further augmented by the interrogation of two agents landed by U 1230 on 29.11.44, led to the unfortunate and brutal interrogations of the commanders and crews of U 546 and U 873 (qv).

U 1230   Type IX C-40

Built by Deutsche Werft, Hamburg
Keel laid 15.3.43   Launched 8.11.43
Commissioned 16.1.44   Feldpost Nr M 42 644

Sunk 17.12.45 WNW of Bloody Foreland (55°50′N 10°05′W)

Served with
31 U-Flottille, Hamburg   January - July 1944 (ab)
10 U-Flottille, Lorient   August - September 1944 (fb)
33 U-Flottille, Flensburg   October 1944 - 9.5.45 (fb)

Commanded by
KL Hans Hilbig   January 1944 - 9.5.45

Patrols: 1   Ships sunk: 1 (5458 grt)

1. 26.9.44   Left Kiel and arrived Horten **30.9.44**

2. 8.10.44   Left for the US east coast.
U 1230 was carrying two agents. She went to Canadian waters, then passed south of Nova Scotia down to the US east coast. Cape Cod was reached on 27.11.44 and the boat then made for Mount Desert Island.
During the night of the 29/30th the two agents, one German and the other American, were landed in a dinghy at Hancock Point in Frenchman Bay. They were spotted, followed and arrested soon afterwards in New York. U 1230 remained in the area for several days, torpedoing and sinking the SS *Cornwallis* (br 5458t) near Swans Island on 3.12.44.
The returning boat carried out weather-reporting duty in the North Atlantic until mid-January 1945.
U 1230 put in to Kristiansand **13.2.45**

3. 20.2.45   Left Kristiansand and arrived Flensburg **23.2.45**

U 1230 was surrendered at Wilhelmshaven on 9.5.45. She left there on 21.6.45 for an assembly area in Britain.
U 1230 was one of 116 boats diposed of by the Royal Navy in Operation Deadlight. *In mid-December 1945 she was towed from Loch Ryan out through the North Channel by the frigate HMS Cubitt. She was sunk by gunfire on 17.12.45 WNW of Bloody Foreland.*

U 1231   Type IX C-40

Built by Deutsche Werft, Hamburg
Keel laid 31.3.43   Launched 18.11.43
Commissioned 9.2.44   Feldpost Nr M 43 319

Surrendered 14.5.45 at Lough Foyle

Served with
31 U-Flottille, Hamburg   February - August 1944 (ab)
11 U-Flottille, Bergen   September 1944 (fb)
33 U-Flottille, Flensburg   October 1944 - 14.5.45 (fb)

Commanded by
KzS Hermann Lessing   February 1944 - March 1945
OL Helmut Wicke   March 1945 - 14.5.45

Patrols: 2   Ships sunk: None

1. 5.10.44   Left Kiel and arrived Horten **7.10.44**

2. 11.10.44   Left Horten and arrived Marviken **12.10.44**

3. 15.10.44   Left Marviken and arrived Bergen **17.10.44**

4. 18.10.44   Left for Canadian waters.
In late November U 1231 entered the Gulf of St Lawrence. On the 30th she made an unsuccessful attack against a destroyer in the Détroit d'Honguedo at the mouth of the St Lawrence River and on 3.12.44 the boat missed the corvette HMCS *Matapedia* W of Matane. These failures were put down to faulty torpedoes.
U 1231 passed out of the Gulf via Cabot Strait and then patrolled off Nova Scotia and later off Halifax. She had no success. The returning boat was on weather-reporting duty for a short time in mid-January.
U 1231 put in to Farsund **31.1.45**

5. 1.2.45   Left Farsund and arrived Flensburg **5.2.45**

6. 13.4.45   Left Kiel and arrived Horten **20.4.45**

7. 22.4.45   Left Horten and arrived Kristiansand **24.4.45**

8. 27.4.45   Left for US coastal waters.
U 1231 was still at sea when the war ended. As instructed, she put in to Lough Foyle and surrendered there **14.5.45**

U 1231 was handed over to the Russians as a war prize in 1947 and became submarine N-25. She was broken up in 1960.

U 1232   Type IX C-40

Built by Deutsche Werft, Hamburg
Keel laid 14.4.43   Launched 20.12.43
Commissioned 8.3.44   Feldpost Nr M 49 759

Surrendered 5.5.45 at Wesermünde

Served with
31 U-Flottille, Hamburg   March - October 1944 (ab)
33 U-Flottille, Flensburg   November 1944 - 5.5.45 (fb)

Commanded by
KzS Kurt Dobratz   March 1944 - March 1945
OL Götz Roth   March 1945 - 5.5.45

Patrols: 1   Ships sunk: 4 (24,531 grt) + 1 damaged

1. 28.10.44   Left Kiel and arrived Horten **31.10.44**

2. 10.11.44   Left for the North Atlantic.
U 1232 was one of four boats on weather-reporting duties, as part of the information-gathering preparations for the forthcoming offensive in the Ardennes. The boat sent reports from 5.12.44 from an area between the Faroes and Greenland.
With this duty completed, U 1232 headed for Canadian waters. En route, the boat was damaged in heavy seas and the patrol was delayed by stops for repairs whenever conditions permitted.
In early January 1945 U 1232 searched for targets off Nova Scotia. On the 2nd a destroyer was reported as sunk but this is unconfirmed and on the 3rd U 1232 missed the troop transport *Nieuw Amsterdam*. On the 4th she sighted convoy SH 194 E of Halifax. The boat torpedoed two ships, sinking the SS *Polarland* (nw 1591t) and damaging the tanker MV *Nipiwan Park* (br 2373t). U 1232 also reported an unsuccessful attack on the 4th on the Canadian harbour defence motor launch HDML 163, which was hit by a torpedo, apparently without result.
U 1232 attacked convoy BX 141 on the 14th off Halifax. She torpedoed three ships, sinking the tankers MV *British Freedom* (br 6985t) and the MV *Athelviking* (br 8779t) and damaging the

SS *Martin van Buren* (am 7176t). This vessel was beached and declared a total loss.

A torpedo was fired at a fourth ship but although an explosion was heard there was no other ship sunk from the convoy. As U 1232 dived, she was struck by the escort vessel HMS *Ettrick*, which she had missed with a torpedo. The boat suffered some structural damage.

U 1232 headed southwards and after midnight on the 15th the boat had reached the open sea beyond the many banks. Between then and the attack on BX 141 U 1232's crew counted 134 depth-charges and depth-bombs dropped by the forces searching for them.

Near the Norwegian coast a German patrol boat appeared to lead U 1232 in. It led the boat on to a reef, from where she was pulled off by a tug and towed in to Marviken, reaching there **14.2.45**

On 5.5.45 U 1232 was surrendered at Wesermünde. She was taken to Britain from Wilhelmshaven in July 1945 and later scrapped.

U 1233   Type IX C-40

Built by Deutsche Werft, Hamburg
Keel laid 29.4.43   Launched 23.12.43
Commissioned 22.3.44   Feldpost Nr M 49 604

Sunk 29.12.45 NW of Tory Island (55°51´N 08°54´W)

Served with
31 U-Flottille, Hamburg   March - October 1944 (ab)
33 U-Flottille, Flensburg   November 1944 - 9.5.45 (fb)

Commanded by
KK Joachim Kuhn   March 1944 - April 1945
OL Heinrich Niemeyer   April 1945 - 9.5.45

Patrols: 1   Ships sunk: None

1. 18.11.44   Left Kiel and arrived Horten **24.11.44**

2. 11.12.44   Left Horten and arrived Bergen **16.12.44**

3. 17.12.44   Left Bergen but cut short the patrol after experiencing schnorkel failure.
U 1233 returned to Bergen **21.12.44**

4. 24.12.44   Left for the Western Atlantic.
U 1233 headed for Bermuda, moved up to the Gulf of Maine and finally patrolled S of Nova Scotia. Some attacks were made on ships but without success.
The boat put in to Kristiansand **28.3.45**

5. 31.3.45   Left Kristiansand and arrived Flensburg **3.4.45**

At the war's end U 1233 was at Fredericia, Denmark, possibly being sent there from Flensburg to prevent the boat falling into Allied hands.
U 1233 surrendered at Wilhelmshaven on 9.5.45. She left there on 21.6.45 for an assembly area in Britain.
The boat was one of 116 diposed of by the Royal Navy in Operation Deadlight. In late December 1945 U 1233 was towed from Loch Ryan and out through the North Channel by the tug HMS Freedom.
When the towline parted, U 1233 was sunk by gunfire on 29.12.45 NW of Tory Island.

U 1234   Type IX C-40

Built by Deutsche Werft, Hamburg
Keel laid 11.5.43   Launched 7.1.44
Commissioned 19.4.44   Feldpost Nr M 50 706

Scuttled 5.5.45 at Höruphaff

Served with
31 U-Flottille, Hamburg   April 1944 - January 1945 (ab)
4 U-Flottille, Stettin   February 1945 - 5.5.45 (ab)

Commanded by
KL Helmut Thurmann   April - May 1944
OL Hans-Christian Wrede   October 1944 - 5.5.45

Patrols: None   Ships sunk: None

On 15.5.44, whilst on exercises in the Baltic, U 1234 sank after colliding with the tugboat Anton *off Gotenhafen in fog. 13 men were lost and 32 were rescued. She went back into service 17.10.44.*
In early May 1945 she was one of many boats which left their bases for the bays of Northern Germany, to await further orders.
On 5.5.45 U 1234 was scuttled at Höruphaff, in accordance with Operation Regenbogen *but contrary to the surrender terms.*

U 1235   Type IX C-40

Built by Deutsche Werft, Hamburg
Keel laid 25.5.43   Launched 25.1.44
Commissioned 17.5.44   Feldpost Nr M 50 796

Sunk 15.4.45 N of the Azores (47°54´N 30°25´W)

Served with
31 U-Flottille, Hamburg   May - November 1944 (ab)
33 U-Flottille, Flensburg   December 1944 - 15.4.45 (fb)

Commanded by
KL Franz Barsch   May 1944 - 15.4.45

Patrols: 1   Ships sunk: None

1. 21.12.44   Left Kiel and arrived Horten **23.12.44**

2. 28.12.44   Left Horten and arrived Kristiansand **29.12.44**

3. 31.12.44   Left Kristiansand and arrived Stavanger **3.1.45**

4. 6.2.45   Left Stavanger. The patrol was cut short because of schnorkel failure. U 1235 put in to Bergen **19.2.45**

5. 14.3.45   Left Bergen and returned **15.3.45**

6. 19.3.45   Left for the Western Atlantic.
The outward-bound U 1235, U 518, U 546, U 805, U 858 and U 880 were formed into *Seewolf* group on 14.4.45 N of the Azores. The boats were to sweep westwards across the North Atlantic convoy routes in an effort to draw some of the hunting groups from British coastal waters.
The USS *Block Island* and *Croatan* escort-carriers formed two lines in the expected path of *Seewolf* group. This was to prevent the boats reaching the US east coast to fire V2 rockets from towed launching pads, which the Americans believed to be their mission.
On 15.4.45 U 1235 was picked up on radar by the destroyer-escort USS *Stanton* (Lt-Cdr J C Kiley), of *Croatan's* screen, 500

U 1235 (continued)

miles N of the Azores. *Stanton* closed in fog and found the boat on the surface, airing and recharging batteries.

The boat dived and *Stanton* fired a Hedgehog pattern. Some minutes later a large underwater explosion was heard. A further attack produced more explosions. More Hedgehogs were fired and 90 minutes after the first sighting an explosion occurred which shook the *Croatan* 12 miles away. U 1235 was destroyed.

There were no survivors, 57 dead.

U 1236 - U 1238 were launched in February 1944 but construction was never completed. They were scrapped in May 1945.

U 1239 - U 1262 were never built, orders cancelled.

U 1263 - 1270 were projected but never built.

U 1271   Type VII C-41

Built by Bremer Vulkan, Vegesack
Keel laid 17.4.43   Launched 8.12.43
Commissioned 12.1.44   Feldpost Nr M 49 790

Sunk 8.12.45 N of Malin Head (55°29´N 07°21´W)

Served with
8 U-Flottille, Danzig January - September 1944 (ab)
33 U-Flottille, Flensburg October 1944 - 9.5.45 (ab)

Commanded by
OL Erwin Knipping January 1944 - April 1945
OL Sven Thienemann April 1945 - 9.5.45

Patrols: None   Ships sunk: None

At the end of the war U 1271 was at the Torpedo School at Bergen and she was surrendered there on 9.5.45, leaving on the 30th for an assembly area in Britain.
U 1271 was one of 116 boats disposed of by the Royal Navy in Operation Deadlight. In early December 1945 she was towed from Loch Ryan out through the North Channel by the destroyer HMS Southdown.
The boat foundered in 30 fathoms on 8.12.45 N of Malin Head.

U 1272   Type VII C-41

Built by Bremer Vulkan, Vegesack
Keel laid 31.5.43   Launched 23.12.43
Commissioned 28.1.44   Feldpost Nr M 49 841

Sunk 8.12.45 WNW of Bloody Foreland (55°50´N 10°05´W)

Served with
8 U-Flottille, Danzig January 1944 - February 1945 (ab)
11 U-Flottille, Bergen March 1945 - 10.5.45 (fb)

Commanded by
OL Bernhard Meentzen January - July 1944
OL Hans Schatteburg July 1944 - 10.5.45

Patrols: None   Ships sunk: None

1. **12.4.45** Left Kiel and arrived Horten **15.4.45**

2. **26.4.45** Left Horten and arrived Kristiansand **28.4.45**

3. **29.4.45** Left for British coastal waters.
U 1272 was at sea W of the British Isles when the war ended. The boat put in to Bergen and surrendered **10.5.45**

U 1272 left Bergen on 30.5.45 for an assembly area in Britain.
The boat was one of 116 disposed of by the Royal Navy in Operation Deadlight. In early December 1945 she was towed from Loch Ryan out through the North Channel by the frigate HMS Rupert.
U 1272 was sunk by aircraft on 8.12.45 WNW of Bloody Foreland.

U 1273   Type VII C-41

Built by Bremer Vulkan, Vegesack
Keel laid 7.6.43   Launched 10.1.44
Commissioned 16.2.44   Feldpost Nr M 50 803

Sunk 17.2.45 in Oslofjord

Served with
8 U-Flottille, Danzig February 1944 - January 1945 (ab)
11 U-Flottille, Bergen February 1945 (fb)

Commanded by
OL Karl-Heinz Voswinkel February - July 1944
KL Helmut Knollmann July 1944 - 17.2.45

Patrols: None   Ships sunk: None

1. **10.2.45** Left Kiel and arrived Horten **14.2.45**

2. **17.2.45** Left Horten.
After leaving harbour, U 1273 was moving down Oslofjord when she struck a mine and quickly sank.
The commander and 56 men were lost. 8 men survived.

U 1274   Type VII C-41

Built by Bremer Vulkan, Vegesack
Keel laid 21.6.43   Launched 25.1.44
Commissioned 1.3.44   Feldpost Nr M 50 816

Sunk 16.4.45 ESE of Holy Island (55°36´N 01°24´W)

Served with
8 U-Flottille, Danzig March 1944 - April 1945 (ab)
5 U-Flottille, Kiel April 1945 (fb)

Commanded by
OL Fedor Kuscher March - July 1944
OL Hans-Hermann Fitting July 1944 - 16.4.45

Patrols: 1   Ships sunk 1 (8966 grt)

1. **24.3.45** Left Kiel and arrived Horten **27.3.45**

2. **1.4.45** Left to operate in the Firth of Forth.
On the 16th U 1274 attacked convoy FS 1784 off the northeast coast of England. She torpedoed and sank the tanker MV *Athelduke* (br 8966t).
Soon afterwards the boat was sunk in a depth-charge attack by the escorting destroyer HMS *Viceroy* (Lt-Cdr J M J Sinclair) ESE of Holy Island.
There were no survivors, 44 dead.

U 1275 Type VII C-41

Built by Bremer Vulkan, Vegesack
Keel laid 7.7.43   Launched 8.2.44
Commissioned 22.3.44   Feldpost Nr M 50 862

Surrendered 9.5.45 at Bergen

Served with
8 U-Flottille, Danzig   March 1944 - February 1945 (ab)
5 U-Flottille, Kiel   February 1945 - 9.5.45 (sb)

Commanded by
OL Hellmut Niss   March - July 1944
OL Günther Frohberg   July 1944 - 9.5.45

Patrols: None   Ships sunk: None

When the war ended, U 1275 was in Bergen. She was surrendered there on 9.5.45. The boat was later scrapped.

U 1276 Type VII C-41

Built by Bremer Vulkan, Vegesack
Keel laid 13.7.43   Launched 25.2.44
Commissioned 6.4.44   Feldpost Nr M 07 089

Sunk 20.2.45 SSW of Waterford Harbour (51°48´N 07°07´W)

Served with
8 U-Flottille, Danzig   April - October 1944 (ab)
11 U-Flottille, Bergen   November 1944 - 20.2.45 (fb)

Commanded by
OL Karl-Heinz Wendt   April 1944 - 20.2.45

Patrols: 1   Ships sunk: None
                    1 corvette (925 dt)

1. 4.11.44   Left Kiel and arrived Horten **11.11.44**

2. 15.11.44   Left Horten, possibly for operations.
    On the 16th the boat was damaged when she struck a mine off the Norwegian coast.
    U 1276 put in to Kristiansand **17.11.44**

3. 19.11.44   Left Kristiansand and arrived Farsund **20.11.44**

4. 16.1.45   Left Farsund and arrived Bergen **17.1.45**

5. 19.1.45   Left Bergen and returned **22.1.45**

6. 28.1.45   Left for British coastal waters.
    U 1276 operated initially in the Irish Sea and later in St George's Channel. On 20.2.45 she torpedoed and sank the corvette HMS *Vervain*, from the escort of convoy HX 337, S of Waterford Harbour.
    Soon afterwards U 1276 was herself sunk in a depth-charge attack by the sloop HMS *Amethyst* (Lt N Scott-Elliott).
    There were no survivors, 49 dead.

U 1277 Type VII C-41

Built by Bremer Vulkan, Vegesack
Keel laid 6.8.43   Launched 18.3.44
Commissioned 3.5.44   Feldpost Nr M 07 218

Scuttled 3.6.45 W of Oporto

Served with
8 U-Flottille, Danzig   May 1944 - January 1945 (ab/vb)
11 U-Flottille, Bergen   February 1945 - 9.5.45 (fb)

Commanded by
KL Ehrenreich Stever   May 1944 - 3.6.45

Patrols: 1   Ships sunk: None

1. 5.4.45   Left Kiel and arrived Stavanger **13.4.45**

2. 21.4.45   Left for Atlantic operations.
    U 1277 remained at sea after the war ended. She was finally scuttled on 3.6.45 W of Oporto, Portugal. It is believed that U 1277's commander was severely punished by a British court-martial.

U 1278 Type VII C-41

Built by Bremer Vulkan, Vegesack
Keel laid 12.8.43   Launched 15.4.44
Commissioned 31.5.44   Feldpost Nr M 30 549

Sunk 17.2.45 N of the Shetlands (61°32´N 01°36´W)

Served with
8 U-Flottille, Danzig   May - November 1944 (ab)
11 U-Flottille, Bergen   December 1944 - 17.2.45 (fb)

Commanded by
KL Erich Müller-Bethke   May 1944 - 17.2.45

Patrols: 1   Ships sunk: None

1. 31.1.45   Left Kiel and arrived Horten **2.2.45**

2. 11.2.45   Left for British coastal waters.
    Outward-bound, U 1278 was sunk in depth-charge attacks on the 17th by the frigates HMS *Bayntun* (Lt-Cdr L P Bourke) and *Loch Eck* (Lt-Cdr N McInnes), N of the Shetlands.
    There were no survivors, 48 dead.

U 1279 Type VII C-41

Built by Bremer Vulkan, Vegesack
Keel laid 26.8.43   Launched --.5.44
Commissioned 5.7.44   Feldpost Nr M 30 807

Sunk 3.2.45 NNW of the Shetlands (61°21´N 02°00´W)

Served with
8 U-Flottille, Danzig   July 1944 - January 1945 (ab)
11 U-Flottille, Bergen   February 1945 (fb)

Commanded by
OL Hans Falke   July 1944 - 3.2.45

Patrols: 1   Ships sunk: None

U 1279 (continued)

1. **20.1.45** Left Kiel and arrived Horten **23.1.45**

2. **29.1.45** Left for British coastal waters.

Outward-bound, U 1279 was sunk in depth-charge attacks by the frigates HMS *Bayntun* (Lt-Cdr L P Bourke), *Braithwaite* (Lt-Cdr E M MacKay) and *Loch Eck* (Lt-Cdr N McInnes), on 3.2.45 NNW of the Shetlands.

There were no survivors, 48 dead.

U 1280 - U 1282 were never completed. Keels were laid but construction was halted on 6.11.43

U 1283 - U 1297 were never built, orders cancelled.

U 1298 - U 1300 were projected but never built.

U 1301   Type VII C-41

Built by Flensburger Schiffbau
Keel laid 20.1.43   Launched 22.12.43
Commissioned 11.2.44   Feldpost Nr M 50 897

Sunk 16.12.45 NW of Bloody Foreland (56°10´N 10°05´W)

Served with
4 U-Flottille, Stettin   February 1944 - 9.5.45 (ab)

Commanded by
OL Karl Feufel   February - July 1944
KL Paul Ehrenfried Lenkeit   July 1944 - 9.5.45

Patrols: None   Ships sunk: None

On 29.3.45 U 1301 collided with U 234, which was carrying out sea tests with the schnorkel off Kristiansand. Both boats sustained damage but that received by U 1301 to her bow and torpedo caps was not repairable.

She was surrendered at Bergen on 9.5.45 and left there on the 30th for an assembly area in Britain. U 1301 was one of 116 boats disposed of by the Royal Navy in Operation Deadlight.

In mid-December 1945 she was towed from Loch Ryan out through the North Channel by the tug HMS Bustler. *U 1301 was sunk by gunfire on 16.12.45 NW of Bloody Foreland.*

U 1302   Type VII C-41

Built by Flensburger Schiffbau
Keel laid 6.3.43   Launched 4.4.44
Commissioned 25.5.44   Feldpost Nr M 38 782

Sunk 7.3.45 NW of Dinas Head (52°19´N 05°23´W)

Served with
4 U-Flottille, Stettin   May - December 1944 (ab)
11 U-Flottille, Bergen   January 1945 - 7.3.45 (fb)

Commanded by
KL Wolfgang Herwartz   May 1944 - 7.3.45

Patrols: 1   Ships sunk: 3 (8386 grt)

U 1302 had one fatal accident during her training period.

1. **22.1.45** Left Kiel and arrived Horten **25.1.45**

2. **3.2.45** Left for British coastal waters.

U 1302 entered the Irish Sea via St George's Channel. On the 28th she sank the MV *Norfolk Coast* (br 646t) NW of St David's Head and in the same area on 2.3.45 U 1302 attacked convoy SC 167, sinking the MV *King Edgar* (br 4536t) and the SS *Novasli* (nw 3204t).

On the 7th the boat was located after a five-day search NW of Dinas Head by warships of the 25th EG. She was sunk in depth-charge attacks by the three Canadian frigates HMCS *La Hulloise* (Lt-Cdr J Brock), *Strathadam* (Lt-Cdr H L Quinn) and *Thetford Mines* (Lt-Cdr J A R Allen).

There were no survivors, 48 dead.

U 1303   Type VII C-41

Built by Flensburger Schiffbau
Keel laid 8.4.43   Launched 10.2.44
Commissioned 5.4.44   Feldpost Nr M 07 970

Scuttled 6.5.45 in Geltinger Bucht

Served with
4 U-Flottille, Stettin   April 1944 - 6.5.45 (ab)

Commanded by
OL Heinz Baum   April 1944 - April 1945
OL Helmut Herglotz   April 1945 - 6.5.45

Patrols: None   Ships sunk: None

U 1303 was en route to Norway when she was scuttled on 6.5.45 in Geltinger Bucht.

The wreck was later broken up.

U 1304   Type VII C-41

Built by Flensburger Schiffbau
Keel laid 17.5.43   Launched 4.8.44
Commissioned 6.9.44   Feldpost Nr M 47 644

Scuttled 5.5.45 in Kupfermühlen Bay

Served with
4 U-Flottille, Stettin   September 1944 - 5.5.45 (ab)

Commanded by
OL Walter Süss   September 1944 - 5.5.45

Patrols: None   Ships sunk: None

U 1304 was coated with the rubber Alberich anti-sonar covering.

U 1304 was one of many boats sent from their bases in early May to the bays of Northern Germany, there to await further orders.

She was scuttled on 5.5.45 in Kupfermühlen Bay, in accordance with Operation Regenbogen *but contrary to the surrender terms.*

The wreck was later broken up.

U 1305   Type VII C-41

Built by Flensburger Schiffbau
Keel laid 30.7.43   Launched 10.7.44
Commissioned 13.9.44   Feldpost Nr M 44 117

Surrendered 10.5.45 at Loch Eriboll

Served with
4 U-Flottille, Stettin   September 1944 - March 1945 (ab)
33 U-Flottille, Flensburg   March 1945 - 10.5.45 (fb)

Commanded by
OL Helmut Christiansen   September 1944 - 10.5.45

Patrols: 1   Ships sunk: 1 (878 grt)

1. **17.3.45**   Left Kiel and arrived Horten **25.3.45**

2. **29.3.45**   Left Horten and arrived Stavanger **2.4.45**

3. **4.4.45**   Left for British coastal waters.
    U 1305 torpedoed and sank a ship in the afternoon of the 24th 80 miles off Sligo, almost certainly the SS *Monmouth Coast* (br 878t).
    At the end of the U-boat war on 4.5.45 U 1305 was W of the North Channel. In accordance with instructions received, the boat headed for Loch Eriboll and surrendered there **10.5.45**

U 1305 was given as a war prize to Russia in November 1945 and became submarine S-84.

U 1306   Type VII C-41

Built by Flensburger Schiffbau
Keel laid 23.9.43   Launched 25.10.44
Commissioned 20.12.44   Feldpost Nr M 49 039

Scuttled 5.5.45 in Flensburger Förde

Served with
4 U-Flottille, Stettin   December 1944 - 5.5.45 (ab)

Commanded by
OL Ulrich Kiessling   December 1944 - 5.5.45

Patrols: None   Ships sunk: None

U 1306 was coated with Alberich, the rubber anti-sonar coating.

U 1306 was one of many boats which left their bases in early May and went to the bays of Northern Germany, there to await further orders.
    She was scuttled on 5.5.45 in Flensburger Förde, in accordance with Operation Regenbogen *but contrary to the surrender terms.*
    The wreck was later broken up.

U 1307   Type VII C-41

Built by Flensburger Schiffbau
Keel laid 2.12.43   Launched 29.9.44
Commissioned 17.11.44   Feldpost Nr M 47 679

Sunk 9.12.45 WNW of Bloody Foreland (55°50′N 10°05′W)

Served with
4 U-Flottille, Stettin   November 1944 - 9.5.45 (ab)

Commanded by
OL Hans Buscher   November 1944 - 9.5.45

Patrols: None   Ships sunk: None

At the end of the war U 1307 was at Bergen. She was surrendered there on 9.5.45 and on the 30th she left for an assembly area in Britain.
    U 1307 was one of 116 boats disposed of by the Royal Navy in Operation Deadlight. *In December 1945 she was towed from Loch Ryan out through the North Channel by the destroyer HMS* Fowey.
    The boat was sunk in rocket attacks on 9.12.45 by aircraft of 816 (FAA) Squadron.

U 1308   Type VII C-41

Built by Flensburger Schiffbau
Keel laid 28.1.44   Launched 22.11.44
Commissioned 17.1.45   Feldpost Nr M 49 103

Scuttled 2.5.45 NW of Warnemünde

Served with
4 U-Flottille, Stettin   January 1945 - 2.5.45 (ab)

Commanded by
OL Heinrich Besold   January 1945 - 2.5.45

Patrols: None   Ships sunk: None

U 1308 was scuttled on 2.5.45 NW of Warnemünde to prevent her falling into Allied hands.
    The wreck was raised in October 1952 and broken up at the Neptun yard at Rostock.

U 1309 - 1404 were never built, orders cancelled or only projected.

U 1405   Type XVII B

Built by Blohm & Voss, Hamburg
Keel laid 15.10.43   Launched 1.12.44
Commissioned 21.12.44   Feldpost Nr M 38 801

Scuttled 4/5.5.45 in Eckernförder Bucht

Served with
8 U-Flottille, Danzig   December 1944 - April 1945 (ab/vb)
5 U-Flottille, Kiel   April 1945 - 4/5.5.45 (ab/vb)

Commanded by
OL Wilhelm Rex   December 1944 - 4/5.5.45

Patrols: None   Ships sunk: None

U 1405 (continued)

U 1405 was an experimental boat. She was one of many which left their bases in early May and went to the bays of Northern Germany, there to await further orders.

She was scuttled in Eckernförder Bucht on 4/5.5.45, in accordance with Operation Regenbogen *but contrary to the surrender terms. She was broken up later.*

U 1406   Type XVII B

Built by Blohm & Voss, Hamburg
Keel laid 30.10.43   Launched 2.1.45
Commissioned 8.2.45   Feldpost Nr M 47 655

Scuttled 5.5.45 at Cuxhaven

Served with
8 U-Flottille, Danzig February - April 1945 (ab/vb)
5 U-Flottille, Kiel April 1945 - 5.5.45 (ab/vb)

Commanded by
OL Werner Klug February 1945 - 5.5.45

Patrols: None   Ships sunk: None

U 1406, an experimental boat, was decommissioned at Cuxhaven on 2.5.45. She was scuttled on 5.5.45 to prevent her falling into Allied hands.

The boat was raised on 15.9.45 and transported to the US on the deck of the transport SS Shoemaker. *After being used in trials, U 1406 was broken up at New York in 1948.*

U 1407   Type XVII B

Built by Blohm & Voss, Hamburg
Keel laid 13.11.43   Launched --.2.45
Commissioned 13.3.45   Feldpost Nr M 47 665

Scuttled 5.5.45 at Cuxhaven

Served with
8 U-Flottille, Danzig March - April 1945 (ab/vb)
5 U-Flottille, Kiel April 1945 - 5.5.45 (ab/vb)

Commanded by
OL Horst Heitz March 1945 - 5.5.45

Patrols: None   Ships sunk: None

U 1407 was an experimental boat. She was decommissioned at Cuxhaven on 2.5.45 and scuttled on 5.5.45 to prevent her falling into Allied hands.

The boat was later raised and taken to England. She served with the Royal Navy as HMS Meteorite *from 1946 to 1950, when she was scrapped at Barrow-in-Furness.*

U 1408 - U 2110 and U 2301 - U 2320 were never built and were either ordered and cancelled or projected only and never ordered.

U 2111 - U 2300 were midget submarines, Type XXVIIA (Hecht). Some were built but were used for training purposes only and were never operational.

U 2321   Type XXIII

Built by Deutsche Werft, Hamburg
Keel laid 10.3.44   Launched 17.4.44
Commissioned 12.6.44   Feldpost Nr M 41 224

Sunk 27.11.45 NW of Bloody Foreland (56°10´N 10°05´W)

Served with
4 U-Flottille, Stettin June - August 1944 (ab)
32 U-Flottille, Königsberg August 1944 - January 1945 (ab)
11 U-Flottille, Bergen February 1945 - 9.5.45 (fb)

Commanded by
OL Hans-Heinrich Barschkis June 1944 - 9.5.45

Patrols: 1   Ships sunk: 1 (1406 grt)

1. 2.3.45 Left Kiel and arrived Horten **5.3.45**

2. 9.3.45 Left for British coastal waters.
   U 2321 was to operate E of the British Isles. On 5.4.45 she torpedoed and sank the SS *Gasray* (br 1406t) off St Abb's Head.
   The boat put in to Marviken **13.4.45**

U 2321 was surrendered at Kristiansand on 9.5.45. She left there on the 29th for an assembly area in Britain. The boat was one of 116 disposed of by the Royal Navy in Operation Deadlight.

In late November she was towed from Loch Ryan out through the North Channel by the frigate HMS Cubitt. *U 2321 was sunk by gunfire on 27.11.45 NW of Bloody Foreland.*

U 2322   Type XXIII

Built by Deutsche Werft, Hamburg
Keel laid 22.3.44   Launched 30.4.44
Commissioned 1.7.44   Feldpost Nr M 41 243

Sunk 27.11.45 NW of Bloody Foreland (56°10´N 10°05´W)

Served with
4 U-Flottille, Stettin July - August 1944 (ab)
32 U-Flottille, Königsberg August 1944 - January 1945 (ab)
11 U-Flottille, Bergen February 1945 - 9.5.45 (fb)

Commanded by
OL Fridtjof Heckel July 1944 - 9.5.45

Patrols: 2   Ships sunk: 1 (1317 grt)

1. 21.1.45 Left Kiel and arrived Horten **25.1.45**

2. 6.2.45 Left for British coastal waters.
   U 2322 operated off the Scottish coast from the Firth of Forth southwards. On the 25th she encountered convoy FS 1739 E of Berwick and sank the SS *Egholm* (br 1317t).
   The boat put in to Stavanger **3.3.45**

3. 4.4.45 Left for British coastal waters.
   U 2322 operated off the east coast of England and the Thames Estuary. On the 29th she reported one ship sunk off the Norfolk/Suffolk coast but there is no confirmation of this claim.
   The boat returned to Stavanger **30.4.45**

U 2322 was surrendered at Stavanger on 9.5.45. She left there on the 31st for an assembly area in Britain.

The boat was one of 116 disposed of by the Royal Navy in Operation Deadlight. In late November 1945 she was towed from Loch Ryan out through the North Channel by the tug HMS Saucy.

U 2322 was sunk by gunfire on 27.11.45 NW of Bloody Foreland.

U 2323   Type XXIII

Built by Deutsche Werft, Hamburg
Keel laid 11.4.44   Launched 31.5.44
Commissioned 18.7.44   Feldpost Nr M 41 284

Sunk 26.7.44 in Kieler Förde (54°23´N 10°11´E)

Served with
4 U-Flottille, Stettin   July 1944 (ab)

Commanded by
Lt Walter Angermann   July 1944

Patrols: None   Ships sunk: None

U 2323 sank on 26.7.44 after striking an Allied air-laid mine in Kieler Förde, off Möltenort. 2 crewmen were killed and 12 others, including the commander, survived.

The boat was raised and decommissioned at Kiel. She was blown up there on 3.5.45 to prevent her falling into Allied hands.

U 2324   Type XXIII

Built by Deutsche Werft, Hamburg
Keel laid 21.4.44   Launched 16.6.44
Commissioned 25.7.44   Feldpost Nr M 41 384

Sunk 27.11.45 NW of Bloody Foreland (56°10´N 10°05´W)

Served with
4 U-Flottille, Stettin   July - August 1944 (ab)
32 U-Flottille, Königsberg   August 1944 - January 1945 (ab)
11 U-Flottille, Bergen   February 1945 - 9.5.45

Commanded by
OL Hans-Heinrich Hass   July 1944 - February 1945
KL Konstantin von Rappard   March 1945 - 9.5.45

Patrols: 2   Ships sunk: None

1. **18.1.45**   Left Kiel and arrived Kalundborg **19.1.45**

2. **22.1.45**   Left Kalundborg and arrived Horten **23.1.45**

3. **29.1.45**   Left for British coastal waters.
   U 2324 encountered a convoy on 18.2.45 in bad visibility 15 miles E of Coquet Light. She fired two torpedoes, both of which missed because of gyro-angling failure.
   The boat put in to Marviken **25.2.45**

4. **30.3.45**   Left Marviken and returned **31.3.45**

5. **2.4.45**   Left for British coastal waters.
   U 2324 again patrolled off the east coast of England. The boat was still at sea when the U-boat ended on 4.5.45.
   She put in to Stavanger **8.5.45**

U 2324 was surrendered at Stavanger on 9.5.45. She left there on

the 31st for an assembly area in Britain.

The boat was one of 116 disposed of by the Royal Navy in Operation Deadlight. In late November she was towed from Loch Ryan out through the North Channel by the destroyer HMS Southdown.

U 2324 was sunk by gunfire on 27.11.45 NW of Bloody Foreland.

U 2325   Type XXIII

Built by Deutsche Werft, Hamburg
Keel laid 29.4.44   Launched 13.7.44
Commissioned 3.8.44   Feldpost Nr M 41 387

Sunk 28.11.45 NW of Bloody Foreland (56°10´N 10°05´W)

Served with
4 U-Flottille, Stettin   August 1944 (ab)
32 U-Flottille, Königsberg   August 1944 - January 1945 (ab)
11 U-Flottille, Bergen   February 1945 - 9.5.45 (fb)

Commanded by
OL Wolf-Harald Schüler   August 1944 - April 1945
OL Kurt Eckel   April 1945 - 9.5.45

Patrols: None   Ships sunk: None

U 2325 was surrendered at Kristiansand on 9.5.45 and left there on the 29th for an assembly area in Britain.

The boat was one of 116 disposed of by the Royal Navy in Operation Deadlight. In November 1945 she was towed from Loch Ryan out through the North Channel by the destroyer HMS Mendip.

U 2325 was sunk by gunfire on 28.11.45 NW of Bloody Foreland.

U 2326   Type XXIII

Built by Deutsche Werft, Hamburg
Keel laid 8.5.44   Launched 17.7.44
Commissioned 10.8.44   Feldpost Nr M 41 468

Surrendered 14.5.45 at Dundee

Served with
4 U-Flottille, Stettin   August 1944 (ab)
32 U-Flottille, Königsberg   August 1944 - January 1945 (ab)
11 U-Flottille, Bergen   February 1945 - 14.5.45 (fb)

Commanded by
OL Karl Jobst   August 1944 - 14.5.45

Patrols: 2   Ships sunk: None

1. **30.3.45**   Left Kiel and arrived Larvik **3.4.45**

2. **5.4.45**   Left Larvik and arrived Kristiansand **6.4.45**

3. **9.4.45**   Left Kristiansand and arrived Stavanger **11.4.45**

4. **19.4.45**   Left for British coastal waters.
   U 2326 operated off the east coast of England but had no success, missing one ship.
   She returned to Stavanger **27.4.45**

5. **4.5.45**   Left for operations.

U 2326 (continued)

U 2326 was outward-bound when the surrender order was made on the 4th. The boat was sighted on the 12th in the North Sea by a Liberator of 206 Squadron (F/O M J Frost), heading southwards.

U 2326 stopped when ordered to do so but the commander either could not or would not understand the instruction to head for Scotland. The aircraft dropped a depth-charge ahead of the boat, after which she was escorted by relays of aircraft to Dundee, where she surrendered on 14.5.45.

U 2326 was used by the Royal Navy as submarine N 35. In 1946 she was handed over to France and was lost in an accident off Toulon on 6.12.46 with the loss of 17 lives.

The boat was later raised and scrapped.

U 2327   Type XXIII

Built by Deutsche Werft, Hamburg
Keel laid 16.5.44   Launched 29.7.44
Commissioned 19.8.44   Feldpost Nr M 41 495

Scuttled 2.5.45 at Hamburg

Served with
32 U-Flottille, Königsberg/Hamburg   August 1944 - 2.5.45 (ab)

Commanded by
OL Heinrich Mürl   August 1944 - February 1945
OL Werner Müller   February - March 1945
OL Hans-Walter Pahl   March - April 1945
OL Herman Schulz   April 1945 - 2.5.45

Patrols: None   Ships sunk: None

U 2327 saw no operational service. She was scuttled on 2.5.45 to prevent her falling into Allied hands.
The wreck was later broken up.

U 2328   Type XXIII

Built by Deutsche Werft, Hamburg
Keel laid 19.5.44   Launched 17.8.44
Commissioned 25.8.44   Feldpost Nr M 41 556

Sunk 27.11.45 NW of Bloody Foreland (56°12´N 09°48´W)

Served with
32 U-Flottille, Königsberg/Hamburg   August 1944 - April 1945 (ab)
11 U-Flottille, Bergen   April 1945 - 9.5.45 (fb)

Commanded by
OL Hans-Ulrich Scholle   August - November 1944
OL Peter Lawrence   December 1944 - 9.5.45

Patrols: None   Ships sunk: None

U 2328 saw no operational service. She was surrendered at Bergen on 9.5.45 and left there on the 30th for an assembly area in Britain.
The boat was one of 116 disposed of by the Royal Navy in Operation Deadlight. In late November 1945 she was towed from Loch Ryan out through the North Channel by the frigate HMS Loch Shin.
After the towline parted, U 2328 was sunk by gunfire on 27.11.45 NW of Bloody Foreland.

U 2329   Type XXIII

Built by Deutsche Werft, Hamburg
Keel laid 2.6.44   Launched 11.8.44
Commissioned 1.9.44   Feldpost Nr M 41 607

Sunk 28.11.45 NW of Bloody Foreland (56°10´N 10°05´W)

Served with
32 U-Flottille, Königsberg   September 1944 - April 1945 (ab)
11 U-Flottille, Bergen   April 1945 - 9.5.45 (fb)

Commanded by
OL Heinrich Schlott   September 1944 - 9.5.45

Patrols: 1   Ships sunk: None + 1 damaged

1. 1.4.45   Left Kiel and arrived Stavanger **6.4.45**

2. 11.4.45   Left for British coastal waters.
U 2329 operated off the east coast of England. On the 23rd she torpedoed and damaged the SS *Sverre Helmersen* (nw 7209t).
The boat returned to Stavanger **26.4.45**

U 2329 was surrendered at Stavanger on 9.5.45. She left there on the 31st for an assembly area in Britain. The boat was one of 116 disposed of by the Royal Navy in Operation Deadlight.
In late November 1945 she was towed out through the North Channel by the tug HMS Masterful.
U 2329 was sunk on 28.11.45 NW of Bloody Foreland.

U 2330   Type XXIII

Built by Deutsche Werft, Hamburg
Keel laid 12.6.44   Launched 19.8.44
Commissioned 7.9.44   Feldpost Nr M 44 194

Scuttled 3.5.45 at Kiel

Served with
32 U-Flottille, Königsberg   September 1944 - February 1945 (ab)
11 U-Flottille, Bergen   March 1945 - 3.5.45 (fb)

Commanded by
OL Hans Beckmann   September 1944 - 3.5.45

Patrols: None   Ships sunk: None

U 2330 was scuttled on 3.5.45 at Kiel.

U 2331   Type XXIII

Built by Deutsche Werft, Hamburg
Keel laid 30.6.44   Launched 22.8.44
Commissioned 12.9.44   Feldpost Nr M 44 322

Lost 10.10.44 off Hela

Served with
32 U-Flottille, Königsberg   September 1944 - 10.10.44 (ab)

Commanded by
OL Hans-Walter Pahl   September 1944 - 10.10.44

Patrols: None   Ships sunk: None

During training exercises in the Baltic on 10.10.44, U 2331 was lost in an accident off Hela. 15 men lost their lives and 4 survivors were rescued, including the commander.

The boat was raised and towed to Gotenhafen, where she was decommissioned.

U 2332   Type XXIII

Built by Deutsche Werft, Hamburg/Germania Werft, Kiel
Keel laid --.9.44   Launched 18.10.44
Commissioned 11.11.44   Feldpost Nr M 44 381

Scuttled 2.5.45 at Hamburg

Served with
5 U-Flottille, Kiel   November 1944 - 2.5.45 (ab)

Commanded by
OL Dieter Bornkessel   November 1944 - April 1945
OL Hanns-Joachim Junker   April 1945 - 2.5.45

Patrols: None   Ships sunk: None

U 2332 was originally ordered from Deutsche Werft, Hamburg on 20.9.43. Some time after July 1944 finished sections of the boat were delivered to Germania Werft, Kiel for assembly to the keel and completion.

U 2332 saw no operational service. She was scuttled at Hamburg on 2.5.45 to prevent her falling into Allied hands.

The wreck was later broken up.

U 2333   Type XXIII

Built by Deutsche Werft, Hamburg/Germania Werft, Kiel
Keel laid --. 10.44   Launched 16.11.44
Commissioned 18.12.44   Feldpost Nr M 44 442

Scuttled 5.5.45 in Flensburger Förde

Served with
5 U-Flottille, Kiel   December 1944 - 5.5.45 (ab)

Commanded by
OL Heinz Baumann   December 1944 - 5.5.45

Patrols: None   Ships sunk: None

U 2333 was originally ordered from Deutsche Werft, Hamburg on 20.9.43. Some time after July 1944 finished sections of the boat were delivered to Germania Werft, Kiel for assembly to the keel and completion.

U 2333 was one of the many boats sent from their bases in early May to the bays of Northern Germany, there to await further orders.

She was scuttled on 5.5.45 in Flensburger Förde, in accordance with Operation Regenbogen *but contrary to the surrender terms.*

The wreck was later broken up.

U 2334   Type XXIII

Built by Deutsche Werft, Hamburg
Keel laid 14.7.44   Launched 26.8.44
Commissioned 21.9.44   Feldpost Nr M 44 455

Sunk 28.11.45 NW of Bloody Foreland (56°10´N 10°05´W)

Served with
32 U-Flottille, Königsberg/Hamburg
                    September 1944 - April 1945 (ab)
11 U-Flottille, Bergen   April 1945 - 9.5.45 (fb)

Commanded by
OL Walter Angermann   September 1944 - 9.5.45

Patrols: None   Ships sunk: None

U 2334 saw no operational service. She was surrendered at Kristiansand on 9.5.45 and left there on the 29th for an assembly area in Britain.

The boat was one of 116 disposed of by the Royal Navy in Operation Deadlight. In late November 1945 she was towed from Loch Ryan out through the North Channel by the frigate HMS Rupert.

U 2334 was sunk by gunfire on 28.11.45 NW of Bloody Foreland.

U 2335   Type XXIII

Built by Deutsche Werft, Hamburg
Keel laid 20.7.44   Launched 31.8.44
Commissioned 27.9.44   Feldpost Nr M 44 578

Sunk 28.11.45 NW of Bloody Foreland (56°10´N 10°05´W)

Served with
32 U-Flottille, Königsberg/Hamburg
                    September 1944 - April 1945 (ab)
11 U-Flottille, Bergen   May 1945 (fb)

Commanded by
OL Karl-Dietrich Benthin   September 1944 - 9.5.45

Patrols: None   Ships sunk: None

On 19.4.45 U 2335 was on her way from Kiel to Kristiansand when she was attacked in the Kattegat by Mosquitos of the Banff Strike Wing, looking for targets of opportunity.

The boat was damaged by rocket and cannon fire by aircraft from the force of 22 Mosquitos, which were drawn from 143, 235, 248 and 333 (Norwegian) Squadrons.

U 2335 surrendered at Kristiansand on 9.5.45. She left there on the 29th for an assembly area in Britain.

The boat was one of 116 disposed of by the Royal Navy in Operation Deadlight. In late November 1945 she was towed from Loch Ryan out through the North Channel by the naval tug HMS Enchanter.

U 2335 was sunk by gunfire on 28.11.45 NW of Bloody Foreland.

U 2336　Type XXIII

Built by Deutsche Werft, Hamburg
Keel laid 27.7.44　Launched 10.9.44
Commissioned 30.9.44　Feldpost Nr M 44 599

Sunk 2.1.46 NW of Fanad Head (56°00´N 09°00´W)

Served with
32 U-Flottille, Königsberg/Hamburg
　　　　　　　September 1944 - February 1945 (ab)
4 U-Flottille, Stettin　February 1945 - 14.5.45 (ab)

Commanded by
OL Jürgen Vockel　September 1944 - March 1945
KL Emil Klusmeier　April 1945 - 14.5.45

Patrols: 1　　Ships sunk: 2 (4669 grt)

On 18.2.45 U 2336 collided with U 2344 off Heiligendamm. U 2344 sank with the loss of 6 lives.

1. 18.4.45　Left Kiel and arrived Larvik **23.4.45**

2. 1.5.45　Left for British coastal waters.
　U 2336 was to operate in the Firth of Forth area. On the 7th she sank two ships off Dunbar, the SS *Sneland I* (nw 1791t) and the SS *Avondale Park* (br 2878t). These were the last two ships sunk by U-boat attack in the Second World War.
　The boat returned to Kiel and surrendered **14.5.45**

On 21.6.45 U 2336 left Wilhelmshaven for an assembly area in Britain. She was one of 116 boats disposed of by the Royal Navy in Operation Deadlight. *In late December 1945 U 2336 was towed from Lisahally by the destroyer HMS* Pytchley.
　The boat was sunk by gunfire on 2.1.46 NW of Fanad Head.

U 2337　Type XXIII

Built by Deutsche Werft, Hamburg
Keel laid 2.8.44　Launched 15.9.44
Commissioned 4.10.44　Feldpost Nr M 44 676

Sunk 28.11.45 NW of Bloody Foreland (56°10´N 10°05´W)

Served with
32 U-Flottille, Königsberg/Hamburg
　　　　　　　October 1944 - February 1945 (ab)
4 U-Flottille, Stettin　February 1945 - 9.5.45 (ab)

Commanded by
OL Günther Behnisch　October 1944 - 9.5.45

Patrols: None　　Ships sunk: None

U 2337 saw no operational service. She was surrendered at Kristiansand on 9.5.45 and left there on the 29th for an assembly area in Britain.
　She was one of 116 boats disposed of by the Royal Navy in Operation Deadlight. *In late November 1945 U 2337 was towed from Loch Ryan out through the North Channel by the Polish destroyer* Krakowiac.
　The boat was sunk by gunfire on 28.11.45 NW of Bloody Foreland.

U 2338　Type XXIII

Built by Deutsche Werft, Hamburg
Keel laid 10.8.44　Launched 18.9.44
Commissioned 9.10.44　Feldpost Nr M 44 754

Sunk 4.5.45 off Fredericia (55°34´N 09°49´E)

Served with
32 U-Flottille, Königsberg/Hamburg　October 1944 - 4.5.45 (ab)

Commanded by
OL Hans-Dietrich Kaiser　October 1944 - 4.5.45

Patrols: None　　Ships sunk: None

U 2338 was moving close in shore along the Danish coast on 4.5.45, en route to Norway. She was sighted on the surface off Fredericia and attacked with rocket and cannon fire by 12 Beaufighters of the North Coates Wing, from 236 and 254 Squadrons. The boat was sunk. Of U 2338's crew, the commander and 11 men were killed and only 2 men survived.

U 2339　Type XXIII

Built by Deutsche Werft, Hamburg
Keel laid 15.8.44　Launched 22.9.44
Commissioned 16.11.44　Feldpost Nr M 44 892

Scuttled 5.5.45 in Geltinger Bucht

Served with
32 U-Flottille, Königsberg　November - December 1944 (ab)
8 U-Flottille, Danzig　December 1944 - 5.5.45 (--)

Commanded by
OL Germanus Woermann　November 1944 - 5.5.45

Patrols: None　　Ships sunk: None

In December 1944 U 2339 was damaged. She was transferred to 8 U-Flottille and attached to the War Ship Training Centre (KLA).
　In early May 1945 U 2339 was one of many boats which left their bases and went to the bays of Northern Germany, there to await further orders. On 5.5.45 she was scuttled in Geltinger Bucht, in accordance with Operation Regenbogen.

U 2340　Type XXIII

Built by Deutsche Werft, Hamburg
Keel laid 18.8.44　Launched 28.9.44
Commissioned 16.10.44　Feldpost Nr M 44 965

Destroyed 31.3.45 at Hamburg

Served with
32 U-Flottille, Königsberg/Hamburg　October 1944 - 31.3.45 (ab)

Commanded by
OL Emil Klusmeier　October 1944 - 31.3.45

Patrols: None　　Ships sunk: None

U 2340 was destroyed in the Deutsche Werke yard at Hamburg-Finkenwerder in an RAF Bomber Command raid on 31.3.45.

U 2341   Type XXIII

Built by Deutsche Werft, Hamburg
Keel laid 23.8.44   Launched 3.10.44
Commissioned 21.10.44   Feldpost Nr M 45 089

Sunk 31.12.45 NNW of Fanad Head (55°44´N 08°19´W)

Served with
32 U-Flottille, Königsberg/Hamburg October 1944 - 9.5.45 (ab)

Commanded by
OL Hermann Böhm October 1944 - 9.5.45

Patrols: None   Ships sunk: None

*U 2341 was surrendered at Wilhelmshaven on 9.5.45. She left there
on 21.6.45 for an assembly area in Britain.*
The boat was one of 116 disposed of by the Royal Navy in
Operation Deadlight. *In late December 1945 U 2341 was towed
from Lisahally by the destroyer HMS* Zetland.
U 2341 was sunk by gunfire on 31.12.45 by the Polish destroyer
Blyskawica *NNW of Fanad Head.*

U 2342   Type XXIII

Built by Deutsche Werft, Hamburg
Keel laid 29.8.44   Launched 13.10.44
Commissioned 1.11.44   Feldpost Nr M 45 175

Sunk 26.12.44 off Swinemünde

Served with
32 U-Flottille, Königsberg November 1944 - 26.12.44 (ab)

Commanded by
OL Berchtold Schad von Mittelbiberach November 1944 - 26.12.44

Patrols: None   Ships sunk: None

*On 26.12.44 U 2342 was proceeding in a convoy of ten U-boats,
escorted by minesweeper M 502, when she struck an RAF-laid mine
and sank off Swinemünde.*
The commander and 7 of the boat's crew lost their lives.

U 2343   Type XXIII

Built by Deutsche Werft, Hamburg
Keel laid 31.8.44   Launched 18.10.44
Commissioned 6.11.44   Feldpost Nr M 45 207

Scuttled 5.5.45 in Geltinger Bucht

Served with
32 U-Flottille, Königsberg/Hamburg
                    November 1944 - February 1945 (ab)
4 U-Flottille, Stettin February 1945 - 5.5.45 (ab)

Commanded by
OL Harald Fuhlendorf November 1944 - April 1945
KL Hans-Ludwig Gaude April 1945 - 5.5.45

Patrols: None   Ships sunk: None

U 2343 was one of many boats which left their bases in early May

and went to the bays of Northern Germany, to await further orders.
*She was scuttled on 5.5.45 in Geltinger Bucht, in accordance
with* Operation Regenbogen *but contrary to the surrender terms.*

U 2344   Type XXIII

Built by Deutsche Werft, Hamburg
Keel laid 4.9.44   Launched 24.10.44
Commissioned 10.11.44   Feldpost Nr M 45 325

Lost 18.2.45 off Heiligendamm

Served with
32 U-Flottille, Königsberg/Hamburg November 1944 - 18.2.45 (ab)

Commanded by
OL Hermann Ellerlage November 1944 - 18.2.45

Patrols: None   Ships sunk: None

*On 18.2.45 U 2344 collided with U 2336 off Heiligendamm in the
Baltic. U 2344 sank with the loss of 6 lives.*
She was raised in June 1956 and scrapped at Rostock in 1958.

U 2345   Type XXIII

Built by Deutsche Werft, Hamburg
Keel laid 7.9.44   Launched 28.10.44
Commissioned 15.11.44   Feldpost Nr M 50 159

Sunk 27.11.45 NW of Bloody Foreland (56°10´N 10°05´W)

Served with
32 U-Flottille, Königsberg/Hamburg November 1944 - 9.5.45 (ab)

Commanded by
OL Karl Steffen November 1944 - 9.5.45

Patrols: None   Ships sunk: None

*U 2345 was surrendered at Stavanger on 9.5.45 and left there on
the 31st for an assembly area in Britain.The boat was one of 116
disposed of by the Royal Navy in* Operation Deadlight.
*In late November 1945 she was towed from Loch Ryan out through
the North Channel by the naval tug HMS* Prosperous.
*U 2345 was sunk by demolition charges on 27.11.45 NW of Bloody
Foreland.*

U 2346   Type XXIII

Built by Deutsche Werft, Hamburg
Keel laid 14.9.44   Launched 31.10.44
Commissioned 20.11.44   Feldpost Nr M 50 188

Scuttled 5.5.45 in Geltinger Bucht

Served with
32 U-Flottille, Königsberg November 1944 - February 1945 (ab)
4 U-Flottille, Stettin February 1945 - 5.5.45 (ab)

Commanded by
OL Hermann von der Höh November 1944 - 5.5.45

Patrols: None   Ships sunk: None

U 2346 (continued)

U 2346 was one of many boats which left their bases in early May for the bays of Northern Germany, there to await further orders.

She was scuttled on 5.5.45 in Geltinger Bucht, in accordance with Operation Regenbogen *but contrary to the surrender terms. The wreck was later broken up.*

U 2347 Type XXIII

Built by Deutsche Werft, Hamburg
Keel laid 19.9.44   Launched 6.11.44
Commissioned 2.12.44   Feldpost Nr M 50 196

Scuttled 5.5.45 in Geltinger Bucht

Served with
32 U-Flottille, Königsberg/Hamburg
              December 1944 - February 1945 (ab)
4 U-Flottille, Stettin   February 1945 - 5.5.45 (ab)

Commanded by
OL Willibald Ulbing   December 1944 - 5.5.45

Patrols: None   Ships sunk: None

U 2347 was one of many boats which left their bases in early May for the bays of Northern Germany, there to await further orders.

She was scuttled on 5.5.45 in Geltinger Bucht, in accordance with Operation Regenbogen *but contrary to the surrender terms. The wreck was later broken up.*

U 2348 Type XXIII

Built by Deutsche Werft, Hamburg
Keel laid 22.9.44   Launched 11.11.44
Commissioned 4.12.44   Feldpost Nr M 50 203

Surrendered 9.5.45 at Stavanger

Served with
32 U-Flottille, Königsberg/Hamburg
              December 1944 - February 1945 (ab)
4 U-Flottille, Stettin   February 1945 - 9.5.45 (ab)

Commanded by
OL Georg Goschzik   December 1944 - 9.5.45

Patrols: None   Ships sunk: None

U 2348 was surrendered at Stavanger on 9.5.45. She left there on the 29th for an assembly area in Britain.

In 1946 U 2348 may have gone to France. The boat was broken up in Belfast in April 1949.

U 2349 Type XXIII

Built by Deutsche Werft, Hamburg
Keel laid 25.9.44   Launched 20.11.44
Commissioned 11.12.44   Feldpost Nr M 50 232

Scuttled 5.5.45 in Geltinger Bucht

Served with
32 U-Flottille, Königsberg   December 1944 - February 1945 (ab)
4 U-Flottille, Stettin   February 1945 - 5.5.45 (ab)

Commanded by
OL Hans-Georg Müller   December 1944 - 5.5.45

Patrols: None   Ships sunk: None

U 2349 was one of many boats which left their bases in early May and went to the bays of Northern Germany, to await further orders.

She was scuttled on 5.5.45 in Geltinger Bucht, in accordance with Operation Regenbogen *but contrary to the surrender terms. The wreck was later broken up.*

U 2350 Type XXIII

Built by Deutsche Werft, Hamburg
Keel laid 28.9.44   Launched 22.11.44
Commissioned 23.12.44   Feldpost Nr M 50 247

Sunk 26.11.45 NW of Bloody Foreland (56°10′N 10°05′W)

Served with
32 U-Flottille, Königsberg   December 1944 - February 1945 (ab)
4 U-Flottille, Stettin   February 1945 - 9.5.45 (ab)

Commanded by
OL Werner Schauer   December 1944 - 9.5.45

Patrols: None   Ships sunk: None

U 2350 was surrendered at Kristiansand on 9.5.45 and on the 29th she left for an assembly area in Britain.

She was one of 116 boats disposed of by the Royal Navy in Operation Deadlight. *In November 1945 she was towed from Loch Ryan out through the North Channel by the destroyer HMS* Pytchley.

U 2350 was sunk by gunfire on 26.11.45 NW of Bloody Foreland.

U 2351 Type XXIII

Built by Deutsche Werft, Hamburg
Keel laid 3.10.44   Launched 25.11.44
Commissioned 30.12.44   Feldpost Nr M 50 291

Sunk 31.12.45 NNW of Fanad Head (55°44′N 08°19′W)

Served with
32 U-Flottille, Königsberg   December 1944 - February 1945 (ab)
4 U-Flottille, Stettin   February 1945 - 9.5.45 (ab)

Commanded by
OL Werner Brückner   December 1944 - 9.5.45

Patrols: None   Ships sunk: None

U 2351 was surrendered at Kiel on 9.5.45. She was moved to Flensburg and later to Wilhelmshaven from where she left on 21.6.45 for an assembly area in Britain.

The boat was one of 116 disposed of by the Royal Navy in Operation Deadlight. In late December 1945 U 2351 was towed from Lisahally by the tug HMS Enchanter.

The boat was sunk by gunfire on 31.12.45 by the Polish destroyer Blyskawica NNW of Fanad Head.

U 2352   Type XXIII

Built by Deutsche Werft, Hamburg
Keel laid 9.10.44   Launched 5.12.44
Commissioned 11.1.45   Feldpost Nr M 50 300

Scuttled 4.5.45 at Höruphaff

Served with
32 U-Flottille, Königsberg/Hamburg   January - February 1945 (ab)
4 U-Flottille, Stettin   February 1945 - 4.5.45 (ab)

Commanded by
OL Sigmund Budzyn   January 1945 - 4.5.45

Patrols: None   Ships sunk: None

U 2352 was one of many boats which left their bases in early May and went to the bays of Northern Germany, there to wait for further orders.

She was scuttled on 4.5.45 at Höruphaff, in accordance with Operation Regenbogen but contrary to the surrender terms.

U 2353   Type XXIII

Built by Deutsche Werft, Hamburg
Keel laid 10.10.44   Launched 6.12.44
Commissioned 9.1.45   Feldpost Nr M 50 310

Surrendered 9.5.45 at Kristiansand

Served with
32 U-Flottille, Hamburg   January - February 1945 (ab)
4 U-Flottille, Stettin   February 1945 - 9.5.45 (ab)

Commanded by
OL Jürgen Hillmann   January 1945 - 9.5.45

Patrols: None   Ships sunk: None

U 2353 was surrendered at Kristiansand on 9.5.45. She left there on the 29th for an assembly area in Britain.

The boat became British submarine N 37. She was handed over to Russia in 1947 and broken up in 1963.

U 2354   Type XXIII

Built by Deutsche Werft, Hamburg
Keel laid 14.10.44   Launched 10.12.44
Commissioned 11.1.45   Feldpost Nr M 50 312

Sunk 22.12.45 NW of Bloody Foreland (56°00´N 10°05´W)

Served with
32 U-Flottille, Hamburg   January - February 1945 (ab)
4 U-Flottille, Stettin   February 1945 - 9.5.45 (ab)

Commanded by
OL Dieter Wex   January 1945 - 9.5.45

Patrols: None   Ships sunk: None

U 2354 was surrendered at Kristiansand on 9.5.45 and left there on the 29th for an assembly area in Britain.

She was one of 116 boats disposed of by the Royal Navy in Operation Deadlight. In December 1945 she was towed from Loch Ryan out through the North Channel by the frigate HMS Cosby.

U 2354 was sunk by gunfire on 22.12.45 NW of Bloody Foreland.

U 2355   Type XXIII

Built by Deutsche Werft, Hamburg
Keel laid 18.10.44   Launched 13.12.44
Commissioned 12.1.45   Feldpost Nr M 50 330

Scuttled 3.5.45 in Kieler Förde

Served with
32 U-Flottille, Hamburg   January - February 1945 (ab)
4 U-Flottille, Stettin   February 1945 - 3.5.45 (ab)

Commanded by
OL Hans-Heino Franke   January 1945 - 3.5.45

Patrols: None   Ships sunk: None

U 2355 saw no operational service. She was scuttled on 3.5.45 in Kieler Förde, off Laboe, to prevent her falling into Allied hands.

U 2356   Type XXIII

Built by Deutsche Werft, Hamburg
Keel laid 21.10.44   Launched 19.12.44
Commissioned 12.1.45   Feldpost Nr M 50 346

Sunk 5.1.46 NW of Malin Head (55°50´N 08°20´W)

Served with
32 U-Flottille, Hamburg   January - February 1945 (ab)
4 U-Flottille, Stettin   February 1945 - 9.5.45 (ab)

Commanded by
OL Friedrich Hartel   January 1945 - 9.5.45

Patrols: None   Ships sunk: None

U 2356 saw no operational service. She was surrendered at Wilhelmshaven on 9.5.45 and left there on 21.6.45 for an assembly area in Britain.

U 2356 (continued)

U 2356 was one of 116 boats disposed of by the Royal Navy in Operation Deadlight. *In early January 1946 she was towed from Lisahally by the destroyer HMS* Blencathra.

The boat was sunk by gunfire on 5.1.46 NW of Malin Head.

U 2357   Type XXIII

Built by Deutsche Werft, Hamburg
Keel laid 21.10.44   Launched 19.12.44
Commissioned 13.1.45   Feldpost Nr M 50 387

Scuttled 5.5.45 in Geltinger Bucht

Served with
32 U-Flottille, Hamburg   January - February 1945 (ab)
4 U-Flottille, Stettin   February 1945 - 5.5.45 (ab)

Commanded by
OL Erwin Heinrich   January 1945 - 5.5.45

Patrols: None   Ships sunk: None

U 2357 was one of many boats which left their bases in early May and went to the bays of Northern Germany, there to wait for further orders.

On 5.5.45 she was scuttled in Geltinger Bucht, in accordance with Operation Regenbogen *but contrary to the surrender terms. The wreck was later broken up.*

U 2358   Type XXIII

Built by Deutsche Werft, Hamburg
Keel laid 1.11.44   Launched 20.12.44
Commissioned 16.1.45   Feldpost Nr M 50 390

Scuttled 5.5.45 in Geltinger Bucht

Served with
32 U-Flottille, Hamburg   January - February 1945 (ab)
4 U-Flottille, Stettin   February 1945 - 5.5.45 (ab)

Commanded by
OL Gerhard Breun   January 1945 - 5.5.45

Patrols: None   Ships sunk: None

U 2358 was one of many boats which left their bases in early May and went to the bays of Northern Germany, there to wait for further orders.

On 5.5.45 she was scuttled in Geltinger Bucht, in accordance with Operation Regenbogen *but contrary to the surrender terms. The wreck was later broken up.*

U 2359   Type XXIII

Built by Deutsche Werft, Hamburg
Keel laid 3.11.44   Launched 23.12.44
Commissioned 16.1.45   Feldpost Nr M 50 445

Sunk 2.5.45 E of Frederikshavn (57°29´N 11°24´E)

Served with
32 U-Flottille, Hamburg   January - February 1945 (ab)
4 U-Flottille, Stettin   February 1945 - 2.5.45 (ab)

Commanded by
OL Gustav Bischoff   January 1945 - 2.5.45

Patrols: None   Ships sunk: None

U 2359 was moving from Kiel to Horten when she was attacked in the Kattegat and sunk by Mosquitos of 143 and 235 Squadrons. The 33 aircraft were part of the Banff Strike Wing.

Of U 2359's crew, 12 men were lost, including her commander.

U 2360   Type XXIII

Built by Deutsche Werft, Hamburg
Keel laid 7.11.44   Launched 29.12.44
Commissioned 23.1.45   Feldpost Nr M 50 527

Scuttled 5.5.45 in Geltinger Bucht

Served with
32 U-Flottille, Hamburg   January - February 1945 (ab)
4 U-Flottille, Stettin   February 1945 - 5.5.45 (ab)

Commanded by
OL Kurt Schrobach   January 1945 - 5.5.45

Patrols: None   Ships sunk: None

U 2360 was one of many boats which left their bases in early May for the bays of Northern Germany, there to await further orders.

On 5.5.45 the boat was scuttled in Geltinger Bucht, in accordance with Operation Regenbogen *but contrary to the surrender terms. The wreck was later broken up.*

U 2361   Type XXIII

Built by Deutsche Werft, Hamburg
Keel laid 12.11.44   Launched 3.1.45
Commissioned 3.2.45   Feldpost Nr M 51 111

Sunk 27.11.45 NW of Bloody Foreland (56°10´N 10°05´W)

Served with
32 U-Flottille, Hamburg   February 1945 (ab)
4 U-Flottille, Stettin   February 1945 - 9.5.45 (ab)

Commanded by
OL Heinz von Hennig   February 1945 - 9.5.45

Patrols: None   Ships sunk: None

U 2361 was surrendered at Kristiansand on 9.5.45 and left there on the 29th for an assembly area in Britain.

She was one of 116 boats which were disposed of by the Royal

Navy in Operation Deadlight. *In late November 1945 U 2361 was towed from Loch Ryan out through the North Channel by the frigate HMS* Cubitt.

The boat was sunk by gunfire on 27.11.45 NW of Bloody Foreland.

U 2362   Type XXIII

Built by Deutsche Werft, Hamburg
Keel laid 22.11.44   Launched 11.1.45
Commissioned 5.2.45   Feldpost Nr M 51 115

Scuttled 5.5.45 in Geltinger Bucht

Served with
32 U-Flottille, Hamburg February 1945 (ab)
4 U-Flottille, Stettin February 1945 - 5.5.45 (ab)

Commanded by
OL Martin Czekowski February 1945 - 5.5.45

Patrols: None   Ships sunk: None

U 2362 was one of many boats which left their bases in early May and went to the bays of Northern Germany, there to wait for further orders.

On 5.5.45 she was scuttled in Geltinger Bucht, in accordance with Operation Regenbogen *but contrary to the surrender terms. The wreck was later broken up.*

U 2363   Type XXIII

Built by Deutsche Werft, Hamburg
Keel laid 22.11.44   Launched 18.1.45
Commissioned 5.2.45   Feldpost Nr M 51 249

Sunk 27.11.45 NW of Bloody Foreland (56°10´N 10°05´W)

Served with
32 U-Flottille, Hamburg February 1945 (ab)
4 U-Flottille, Stettin February 1945 - 9.5.45 (ab)

Commanded by
OL Karl Frahm February 1945 - 9.5.45

Patrols: None   Ships sunk: None

U 2363 was surrendered at Kristiansand on 9.5.45 and left there on the 29th for an assembly area in Britain.

She was one of 116 boats disposed of by the Royal Navy in Operation Deadlight. *In late November 1945 U 2363 was towed from Loch Ryan out through the North Channel by the naval tug HMS* Saucy.

The boat was sunk by gunfire on 27.11.45 NW of Bloody Foreland.

U 2364   Type XXIII

Built by Deutsche Werft, Hamburg
Keel laid 27.11.44   Launched 23.1.45
Commissioned 14.2.45   Feldpost Nr M 51 307

Scuttled 5.5.45 in Geltinger Bucht

Served with
32 U-Flottille, Hamburg February 1945 (ab)
4 U-Flottille, Stettin February 1945 - 5.5.45 (ab)

Commanded by
OL Dieter Hengen February - April 1945
KL Gerhard Remus April 1945 - 5.5.45

Patrols: None   Ships sunk: None

U 2364 was one of many boats which left their bases in early May and went to the bays of Northern Germany, to await further orders.

On 5.5.45 she was scuttled in Geltinger Bucht, in accordance with Operation Regenbogen *but contrary to the surrender terms.*

U 2365   Type XXIII

Built by Deutsche Werft, Hamburg
Keel laid 6.12.44   Launched 26.1.45
Commissioned 2.3.45   Feldpost Nr M 51 377

Scuttled 8.5.45 SW of Varberg (56°51´N 11°49´E)

Served with
4 U-Flottille, Stettin March 1945 - 8.5.45 (ab)

Commanded by
OL Fritz-Otto Korfmann March - May 1945
OL Uwe Christiansen May 1945

Patrols: None   Ships sunk: None

U 2365 may have been en route to Norway when she was scuttled in the Kattegat on 8.5.45, possibly as ordered in Operation Regenbogen *but contrary to the surrender terms.*

Raised in June 1956 and commissioned in the Bundesmarine on 15.8.57 as U-Hai, Germany's first post-war U-boat. On 14.9.66 she was exercising in the North Sea when a welded seam in the hull split and the boat flooded. 19 men died and there was one survivor.

The boat was raised on 24.9.66 and broken up.

U 2366   Type XXIII

Built by Deutsche Werft, Hamburg
Keel laid 6.12.44   Launched 17.2.45
Commissioned 10.3.45   Feldpost Nr M 51 391

Scuttled 5.5.45 in Geltinger Bucht

Served with
4 U-Flottille, Stettin March 1945 - 5.5.45 (ab)

Commanded by
OL Kurt Jäckel March 1945 - 5.5.45

Patrols: None   Ships sunk: None

U 2366 (continued)

U 2366 was one of many boats which left their bases in early May and went to the bays of Northern Germany, there to wait for further orders.

On 5.5.45 she was scuttled in Geltinger Bucht, in accordance with Operation Regenbogen *but contrary to the surrender terms. The wreck was later broken up.*

U 2367   Type XXIII

Built by Deutsche Werft, Hamburg
Keel laid 11.12.44   Launched 23.2.45
Commissioned 9.3.45   Feldpost Nr M 51 402

Scuttled 5.5.45 at Schleimünde

Served with
4 U-Flottille, Stettin   March 1945 - 5.5.45 (ab)

Commanded by
OL Heinrich Schröder   March 1945 - 5.5.45

Patrols: None   Ships sunk: None

U 2367 was scuttled at Schleimünde on 5.5.45 after she was badly damaged in a collision with an unidentified U-boat.

The boat was raised in August 1956. She was commissioned into the Bundesmarine on 1.10.57 as U-Hecht.
She was broken up at Kiel in 1969.

U 2368   Type XXIII

Built by Deutsche Werft, Hamburg
Keel laid 15.12.44   Launched 19.3.45
Commissioned 11.4.45   Feldpost Nr M 51 418

Scuttled 5.5.45 in Geltinger Bucht

Served with
4 U-Flottille, Stettin   April 1945 - 5.5.45 (ab)

Commanded by
OL Fritz Ufermann   April 1945 - 5.5.45

Patrols: None   Ships sunk: None

U 2368 was one of many boats which left their bases in early May and went to the bays of Northern Germany, there to wait for further orders.

On 5.5.45 she was scuttled in Geltinger Bucht, in accordance with Operation Regenbogen *but contrary to the surrender terms. The wreck was later broken up.*

U 2369   Type XXIII

Built by Deutsche Werft, Hamburg
Keel laid 20.12.44   Launched 24.3.45
Commissioned 18.4.45   Feldpost Nr M 51 783

Scuttled 5.5.45 in Geltinger Bucht

Served with
4 U-Flottille, Stettin   April 1945 - 5.5.45 (ab)

Commanded by
OL Hermann Schulz   April 1945
OL Hans-Walter Pahl   April 1945 - 5.5.45

Patrols: None   Ships sunk: None

U 2369 was one of many boats which left their bases in early May and went to the bays of Northern Germany, there to wait for further orders.

On 5.5.45 she was scuttled in Geltinger Bucht, in accordance with Operation Regenbogen *but contrary to the surrender terms. The wreck was later broken up.*

U 2370   Type XXIII

Built by Deutsche Werft, Hamburg
Keel laid 20.12.44   Launched --.3.45
Commissioned 15.4.45   Feldpost Nr M 51 813

Scuttled 3.5.45 at Hamburg

Served with
4 U-Flottille, Stettin   April 1945 - 3.5.45 (ab)

Commanded by
OL Dieter Bornkessel   April 1945 - 3.5.45

Patrols: None   Ships sunk: None

U 2370 was scuttled at Hamburg-Finkenwerder on 3.5.45 to prevent her falling into Allied hands.
The wreck was later broken up.

U 2371   Type XXIII

Built by Deutsche Werft, Hamburg
Keel laid 19.1.45   Launched 18.4.45
Commissioned 20.4.45   Feldpost Nr M 45 477

Scuttled 3.5.45 at Hamburg

Served with
4 U-Flottille, Stettin   April 1945 - 3.5.45 (ab)

Commanded by
OL Johannes Kühne   April 1945 - 3.5.45

Patrols: None   Ships sunk: None

U 2371 was originally scheduled to be built by Deutsche Werft at Toulon but she was built at the Hamburg yard.

The boat was scuttled at Hamburg-Finkenwerder on 3.5.45 to prevent her falling into Allied hands. The wreck was later broken up.

U 2372 - U2377 were under construction but were scrapped before completion.

U 23798 - U 2460 were never built, orders cancelled.

U 2461 - U 2500 were projected but never built.

U 2501   Type XXI

Built by Blohm & Voss, Hamburg
Keel laid 3.4.44   Launched 12.5.44
Commissioned 28.6.44   Feldpost Nr M 43 526

Scuttled 3.5.45 at Hamburg

Served with
31 U-Flottille, Hamburg   June - November 1944 (ab)
8 U-Flottille, Danzig   November 1944 - 3.5.45 (ab)

Commanded by
OL Otto Hübschen   June - November 1944

Patrols: None   Ships sunk: None

When U 2501 was with 8 U-Flottille, she was attached to the War Ship Training Centre (KLA) and did not have a commander as such.
The boat was scuttled at Hamburg on 3.5.45 to prevent her falling into Allied hands.
The wreck was later broken up.

U 2502   Type XXI

Built by Blohm & Voss, Hamburg
Keel laid 25.4.44   Launched 15.6.44
Commissioned 19.7.44   Feldpost Nr M 41 658

Sunk 28.11.45 NW of Bloody Foreland (56°10´N 10°05´W)

Served with
31 U-Flottille, Hamburg   July 1944 - March 1945 (ab)
11 U-Flottille, Bergen   March 1945 - 9.5.45 (fb-oE)

Commanded by
KL Gert Mannesmann   July 1944 - 8.4.45 (killed in air raid)
KL Hans Hornkohl   April 1945
KL Heinz Franke   April 1945 - 9.5.45

Patrols: None   Ships sunk: None

On 19.4.45 U 2502 was in the Kattegat en route from Kiel to Horten when she was attacked and damaged by Mosquitos of the Banff Strike Wing. She reached Horten and was surrendered there on 9.5.45 and left on the 29th for an assembly area in Britain.
U 2502 was one of 116 boats disposed of by the Royal Navy in Operation Deadlight. *In late November 1945 she was towed from Loch Ryan and out through the North Channel by the destroyer HMS* Mendip.
The boat was sunk by gunfire on 28.11.45 NW of Bloody Foreland.

U 2503   Type XXI

Built by Blohm & Voss, Hamburg
Keel laid 2.5.44   Launched 29.6.44
Commissioned 1.8.44   Feldpost Nr M 41 704

Scuttled 4.5.45 S of Korsør (55°09´N 11°07´E)

Served with
31 U-Flottille, Hamburg   August 1944 - April 1945 (ab)
11 U-Flottille, Bergen   April 1945 - 4.5.45 (fb)

Commanded by
OL Raimund Tiesler   August - October 1944
KL Richard Becker   October - November 1944
KL Karl-Jürg Wächter   November 1944 - 3.5.45

Patrols: None   Ships sunk: None

U 2503 was en route from Kiel to Norway on 3.5.45 when she was attacked S of Korsør by Mosquitos of 236 and 254 Squadrons of the North Coates Strike Wing.
The boat was severely damaged by rocket and cannon fire and 14 men, including her commander, were killed. U 2503 was beached next day on the Danish coast and scuttled.

U 2504   Type XXI

Built by Blohm & Voss, Hamburg
Keel laid 20.5.44   Launched 18.7.44
Commissioned 12.8.44   Feldpost Nr M 41 815

Scuttled 3.5.45 at Hamburg

Served with
31 U-Flottille, Hamburg   August - November 1944 (ab)
8 U-Flottille, Danzig   November 1944 - 3.5.45 (ab)

Commanded by
OL Horst Günther   August - November 1944

Patrols: None   Ships sunk: None

When U 2504 was with 8 U-Flottille, she was attached to the War Ship Training Centre (KLA) and did not have a commander as such.
The boat was scuttled at Hamburg on 3.5.45.

U 2505   Type XXI

Built by Blohm & Voss, Hamburg
Keel laid 23.5.44   Launched 27.7.44
Commissioned 7.11.44   Feldpost Nr M 41 903

Scuttled 3.5.45 at Hamburg

Served with
31 U-Flottille, Hamburg   November 1944 - 3.5.45 (ab)

Commanded by
OL Joachim Düppe   November 1944 - 3.5.45

Patrols: None   Ships sunk: None

The boat was scuttled at Hamburg on 3.5.45 to prevent her falling into Allied hands. The wreck was later broken up.

U 2506   Type XXI

Built by Blohm & Voss, Hamburg
Keel laid 29.5.44   Launched 5.8.44
Commissioned 21.8.44   Feldpost Nr M 41 996

Sunk 5.1.46 N of Malin Head (55°37´N 07°30´W)

Served with
31 U-Flottille, Hamburg August 1944 - April 1945 (ab)
11 U-Flottille, Bergen April 1945 - 9.5.45 (fb-oE)

Commanded by
KL Horst von Schroeter August 1944 - 9.5.45

Patrols: None   Ships sunk: None

*U 2506 was surrendered at Bergen on 9.5.45 and left there on the
30th for an assembly area in Britain.*
  She was one of 116 boats disposed of by the Royal Navy in
Operation Deadlight. *In early January 1946 U 2506 was towed
from Lisahally by the naval tug HMS* Saucy.
  The boat was sunk on 5.1.46 N of Malin Head.

U 2507   Type XXI

Built by Blohm & Voss, Hamburg
Keel laid 4.6.44   Launched 14.8.44
Commissioned 8.9.44   Feldpost Nr M 42 090

Scuttled 5.5.45 in Geltinger Bucht

Served with
31 U-Flottille, Hamburg September 1944 - 5.5.45 (ab)

Commanded by
KL Paul Siegmann September 1944 - 5.5.45

Patrols: None   Ships sunk: None

*U 2507 was one of many boats which left their bases in early May
and went to the bays of Northern Germany, to await further orders.*
  *The boat was scuttled on 5.5.45 in Geltinger Bucht, in accord-
ance with* Operation Regenbogen.

U 2508   Type XXI

Built by Blohm & Voss, Hamburg
Keel laid 13.6.44   Launched 19.8.44
Commissioned 26.9.44   Feldpost Nr M 42 154

Scuttled 3.5.45 at Kiel

Served with
31 U-Flottille, Hamburg September 1944 - 3.5.45 (ab)

Commanded by
OL Uwe Christiansen September 1944 - 3.5.45

Patrols: None   Ships sunk: None

*On 14.11.44 U 2508 sank in the Kattegat after submerging with the
diesel air intake open. She was raised and put back into service.*
  *U 2508 was scuttled at Kiel on 3.5.45 to prevent her falling into
Allied hands. The wreck was later broken up.*

U 2509   Type XXI

Built by Blohm & Voss, Hamburg
Keel laid 17.6.44   Launched 27.8.44
Commissioned 21.9.44   Feldpost Nr M 45 671

Destroyed 8.4.45 at Hamburg

Served with
31 U-Flottille, Hamburg September 1944 - 8.4.45 (ab)

Commanded by
KK Rudolf Schendel September 1944 - 8.4.45

Patrols: None   Ships sunk: None

*U 2509 was destroyed in an RAF bombing raid on Hamburg on
8.4.45. Two of the crew were killed.*

U 2510   Type XXI

Built by Blohm & Voss, Hamburg
Keel laid 5.7.44   Launched 29.8.44
Commissioned 27.9.44   Feldpost Nr M 45 783

Scuttled 3.5.45 at Travemünde

Served with
31 U-Flottille, Hamburg September 1944 - 3.5.45 (ab)

Commanded by
OL Werner Hermann September 1944 - 3.5.45

Patrols: None   Ships sunk: None

*U 2510 was scuttled on 3.5.45 off Travemünde to prevent her fall-
ing into Allied hands. The wreck was later broken up.*

U 2511   Type XXI

Built by Blohm & Voss, Hamburg
Keel laid 7.7.44   Launched 2.9.44
Commissioned 29.9.44   Feldpost Nr M 45 912

Sunk 7.1.46 NNW of Malin Head (55°33´N 07°38´W)

Served with
31 U-Flottille, Hamburg September 1944 - March 1945 (ab)
11 U-Flottille, Bergen March 1945 - 9.5.45 (fb)

Commanded by
KK Adalbert Schnee September 1944 - 9.5.45

Patrols: 1   Ships sunk: None

1. 17.3.45 Left Kiel and arrived Horten **23.3.45**

2. 3.4.45 Left Horten and arrived Bergen **8.4.45**

3. 17.4.45 Left Bergen and returned **20.4.45**

4. 3.5.45 Left on the first operational patrol by a Type XXI boat.
On the 4th, after a return-to-base order had been received, U 2511
encountered a hunting group N of the Faroes.
  The boat's schnorkel was retracted. She increased speed to 16

knots and escaped.
U 2511 returned to Bergen **6.5.45**

She was surrendered on 9.5.45 at Bergen and left there on the 30th for an assembly area in Britain.
U 2511 was one of 116 boats disposed of by the Royal Navy in Operation Deadlight. *In early January 1946 the boat was towed from Lisahally by the tug HMS* Enchanter.
U 2511 was sunk by gunfire by the frigate HMS Sole Bay *on 7.1.46 NNW of Malin Head.*

U 2512   Type XXI

Built by Blohm & Voss, Hamburg
Keel laid 13.7.44   Launched 7.9.44
Commissioned 10.10.44   Feldpost Nr M 45 926

Scuttled 3.5.45 at Eckernförde

Served with
31 U-Flottille, Hamburg   October 1944 - 3.5.45 (ab)

Commanded by
KL Hubert Nordheimer   October 1944 - 3.5.45

Patrols: None   Ships sunk: None

U 2512 was scuttled on 3.5.45 at Eckernförde to prevent her falling into Allied hands.
The wreck was later broken up.

U 2513   Type XXI

Built by Blohm & Voss, Hamburg
Keel laid 19.7.44   Launched 14.9.44
Commissioned 12.10.44   Feldpost Nr M 46 136

Surrendered 9.5.45 at Horten

Served with
31 U-Flottille, Hamburg   October 1944 - April 1945 (ab)
11 U-Flottille, Bergen   April 1945 - 9.5.45 (fb)

Commanded by
KL Hans Bungards   October 1944 - April 1945
FK Erich Topp   April 1945 - 9.5.45

Patrols: None   Ships sunk: None

1. 1.5.45   Left Kiel for Horten.
    As U 2513 entered Oslofjord she had to dive to avoid an aircraft attack.
    The boat put in to Horten **3.5.45**

U 2513 was surrendered at Horten on 9.5.45 and left there on the 29th for an assembly area in Britain.
In August 1945 the boat went to the US Navy and was used experimentally. She was sunk off Key West on 7.10.51 in rocket attacks.

U 2514   Type XXI

Built by Blohm & Voss, Hamburg
Keel laid 24.7.44   Launched 17.9.44
Commissioned 17.10.44   Feldpost Nr M 46 179

Destroyed 8.4.45 at Hamburg

Served with
31 U-Flottille, Hamburg   October 1944 - 8.4.45 (ab)

Commanded by
KL Rolf-Birger Wahlen   October 1944 - 8.4.45

Patrols: None   Ships sunk: None

U2514 was destroyed on 8.4.45 in an RAF Bomber Command raid on Hamburg.
The wreck was later broken up.

U 2515   Type XXI

Built by Blohm & Voss, Hamburg
Keel laid 29.7.44   Launched 22.9.44
Commissioned 19.10.44   Feldpost Nr M 47 884

Destroyed 11.3.45 at Hamburg

Served with
31 U-Flottille, Hamburg   October 1944 - 11.3.45 (ab)

Commanded by
OL Gerhard Linder   October 1944 - 11.3.45

Patrols: None   Ships sunk: None

On 31.12.44 U 2515 was severely damaged in a USAF bombing raid on Hamburg. One section was wrecked.
The boat was placed in Dock III, where she was cut to allow replacement of the section wrecked in the air raid of 31.12.44. On 17.1.45 Dock III was sunk in a USAF raid on Hamburg and U 2515 was further damaged.
She was finally destroyed in a third USAF raid on 11.3.45.

U 2516   Type XXI

Built by Blohm & Voss, Hamburg
Keel laid 3.8.44   Launched 27.9.44
Commissioned 24.10.44   Feldpost Nr M 47 956

Destroyed 8.4.45 at Hamburg

Served with
31 U-Flottille, Hamburg   October 1944 - 8.4.45 (ab)

Commanded by
OL Fritz Kallipke   October 1944 - 8.4.45

Patrols: None   Ships sunk: None

On 3.4.45 U 2516 was damaged in a USAF bombing raid on the Deutsche Werke yard at Hamburg. In the next raid by RAF Bomber Command on the 8th, the boat was destroyed.
The wreck was later broken up.

U 2517   Type XXI

Built by Blohm & Voss, Hamburg
Keel laid 8.8.44   Launched 4.10.44
Commissioned 31.10.44   Feldpost Nr M 47 966

Scuttled 5.5.45 in Geltinger Bucht

Served with
31 U-Flottille, Hamburg   October 1944 - 5.5.45 (ab)

Commanded by
OL Hermann Hansen   October 1944 - 5.5.45

Patrols: None   Ships sunk: None

*U 2517 was one of many boats which left their bases in early May
for the bays of Northern Germany, there to await further orders.*
*   The boat was scuttled on 5.5.45 in Geltinger Bucht, in accordance with* Operation Regenbogen *but contrary to the surrender
terms.*

U 2518   Type XXI

Built by Blohm & Voss, Hamburg
Keel laid 16.8.44   Launched 4.10.44
Commissioned 4.11.44   Feldpost Nr M 49 105

Surrendered 9.5.45 at Horten

Served with
31 U-Flottille, Hamburg   November 1944 - April 1945 (ab)
11 U-Flottille, Bergen   April 1945 - 9.5.45 (fb-oE)

Commanded by
KL Friedrich Wiedner   November 1944 - 9.5.45

Patrols: None   Ships sunk: None

*U 2518 was surrendered at Horten on 9.5.45 and left there on the
29th for an assembly area in Britain.*
*   The boat went to the French Navy in 1947 and became the
submarine* Roland Morillot. *She was decommissioned on 17.10.67
and broken up in 1968.*

U 2519   Type XXI

Built by Blohm & Voss, Hamburg
Keel laid 24.8.44   Launched 18.10.44
Commissioned 15.11.44   Feldpost Nr M 49 106

Scuttled 3.5.45 at Kiel

Served with
31 U-Flottille, Hamburg   November 1944 - 3.5.45 (ab)

Commanded by
KK Peter Erich Cremer   November 1944 - 3.5.45

Patrols: None   Ships sunk: None

On 8.4.45 U 2519 was damaged in an RAF raid on Hamburg.
*   She was scuttled at Kiel on 3.5.45 to prevent her falling into
Allied hands. The wreck was later broken up.*

U 2520   Type XXI

Built by Blohm & Voss, Hamburg
Keel laid 24.8.44   Launched 16.10.44
Commissioned 14.11.44   Feldpost Nr M 49 177

Scuttled 3.5.45 at Kiel

Served with
31 U-Flottille, Hamburg   November 1944 - 3.5.45 (ab)

Commanded by
OL Albrecht Schubart   November 1944 - 3.5.45

Patrols: None   Ships sunk: None

*U 2520 was scuttled at Kiel on 3.5.45 to prevent her falling into
Allied hands.*
*   The wreck was later broken up.*

U 2521   Type XXI

Built by Blohm & Voss, Hamburg
Keel laid 31.8.44   Launched 18.10.44
Commissioned 31.10.44   Feldpost Nr M 49 231

Sunk 4.5.45 just N of Geltinger Bucht (54°49´N 09°50´E)

Served with
31 U-Flottille, Hamburg   October 1944 - 4.5.45 (ab)

Commanded by
OL Joachim Methner   October 1944 - 4.5.45

Patrols: None   Ships sunk: None

*U 2521 was one of many boats which left their bases in early May
for the bays of Northern Germany, there to await further orders.*
*   The boat was ordered to proceed to Norway and on 4.5.45 she
had just moved out of Geltinger Bucht when she was attacked and
sunk by Typhoons of 184 Squadron, 2nd TAF.*
*   The commander and 40 men lost their lives.*

U 2522   Type XXI

Built by Blohm & Voss, Hamburg
Keel laid 26.8.44   Launched 22.10.44
Commissioned 22.11.44   Feldpost Nr M 49 267

Scuttled 5.5.45 in Geltinger Bucht

Served with
31 U-Flottille, Hamburg   November 1944 - 5.5.45 (ab)

Commanded by
KL Horst-Thilo Queck   November 1944 - 5.5.45

Patrols: None   Ships sunk: None

*U 2522 was one of many boats which left their bases in early May
and went to the bays of Northern Germany, to await further orders.*
*   She was scuttled on 5.5.45 in Geltinger Bucht, in accordance
with* Operation Regenbogen *but contrary to the surrender terms.*
*   The wreck was later broken up.*

U 2523   Type XXI

Built by Blohm & Voss, Hamburg
Keel laid 6.9.44   Launched 25.10.44
Commissioned 26.12.44   Feldpost Nr M 49 281

Destroyed 17.1.45 at Hamburg

Served with
31 U-Flottille, Hamburg   December 1944 - 17.1.45 (ab)

Commanded by
KL Hans-Heinrich Ketels   December 1944 - 17.1.45

Patrols: None   Ships sunk: None

*U 2523 was sunk on 17.1.45 in a USAF bombing raid on Hamburg.
The wreck was later scrapped.*

U 2524   Type XXI

Built by Blohm & Voss, Hamburg
Keel laid 6.9.44   Launched 30.10.44
Commissioned 16.1.45   Feldpost Nr M 49 299

Scuttled 3.5.45 in the Fehmarn Belt

Served with
31 U-Flottille, Hamburg   January 1945 - 3.5.45 (ab)

Commanded by
KL Ernst von Witzendorff   January 1945 - 3.5.45

Patrols: None   Ships sunk: None

*Soon after being commissioned, U 2524 was sunk in a USAF
bombing raid on Hamburg on 17.1.45. She was later raised and
recommissioned.
    The boat was scuttled on 3.5.45 in the Fehmarn Belt after air-
craft made cannon and rocket attacks. 2 crewmen were killed.*

U 2525   Type XXI

Built by Blohm & Voss, Hamburg
Keel laid 13.9.44   Launched 30.10.44
Commissioned 12.12.44   Feldpost Nr M 49 365

Scuttled 5.5.45 in Geltinger Bucht

Served with
31 U-Flottille, Hamburg   December 1944 - 5.5.45 (ab)

Commanded by
KL Paul-Friedrich Otto   December 1944 - 5.5.45

Patrols: None   Ships sunk: None

*U 2525 was one of many boats which left their bases in early May
for the bays of Northern Germany, there to await further orders.
    She was scuttled on 5.5.45 in Geltinger Bucht, in accordance
with* Operation Regenbogen *but contrary to the surrender terms.*

U 2526   Type XXI

Built by Blohm & Voss, Hamburg
Keel laid 16.9.44   Launched 30.11.44
Commissioned 15.12.44   Feldpost Nr M 49 312

Scuttled 2.5.45 at Travemünde

Served with
31 U-Flottille, Hamburg   December 1944 - 2.5.45 (ab)

Commanded by
OL Otto Hohmann   December 1944 - 2.5.45

Patrols: None   Ships sunk: None

*A daylight raid by the USAF on Hamburg, probably on 4.11.44,
blocked U 2526 on its slip in the Blohm & Voss yard.
    U 2526 was scuttled on 2.5.45 at Travemünde to prevent her
falling into Allied hands.
    The wreck was later broken up.*

U 2527   Type XXI

Built by Blohm & Voss, Hamburg
Keel laid 20.9.44   Launched 30.11.44
Commissioned 23.12.44   Feldpost Nr M 49 344

Scuttled 2.5.45 at Travemünde

Served with
31 U-Flottille, Hamburg   December 1944 - 2.5.45 (ab)

Commanded by
OL Hans Götze   December 1944 - 2.5.45

Patrols: None   Ships sunk: None

*U 2527 was damaged in a daylight bombing raid by the USAF on
Hamburg, probably on 4.11.44, whilst under construction in the
Blohm & Voss yard.
    She was scuttled on 2.5.45 at Travemünde to prevent her falling
into Allied hands.
    The wreck was later broken up.*

U 2528   Type XXI

Built by Blohm & Voss, Hamburg
Keel laid 25.9.44   Launched 18.11.44
Commissioned 9.12.44   Feldpost Nr M 49 352

Scuttled 2.5.45 at Travemünde

Served with
31 U-Flottille, Hamburg   December 1944 - 2.5.45 (ab)

Commanded by
KL Oskar Curio   December 1944 - 2.5.45

Patrols: None   Ships sunk: None

*She was scuttled on 2.5.45 at Travemünde to prevent her falling
into Allied hands.
    The wreck was later broken up.*

U 2529 Type XXI

Built by Blohm & Voss, Hamburg
Keel laid 29.9.44   Launched 18.11.44
Commissioned 22.2.45   Feldpost Nr M 49 368

Surrendered 9.5.45 at Kristiansand

Served with
31 U-Flottille, Hamburg February 1945 - 9.5.45 (ab)

Commanded by
OL Karl Feufel February - April 1945
KL Fritz Kallipke April 1945 - 9.5.45

Patrols: None   Ships sunk: None

*U 2529 was surrendered at Kristiansand on 9.5.45 and left there
on the 29th for an assembly area in Britain.*
   *The boat became British submarine N 27. She was handed over
to the Russians in 1947 and broken up in 1963.*

U 2530 Type XXI

Built by Blohm & Voss, Hamburg
Keel laid 30.9.44   Launched 23.11.44
Commissioned 30.12.44   Feldpost Nr M 49 383

Destroyed 11.3.45 at Hamburg

Served with
31 U-Flottille, Hamburg December 1944 - 11.3.45 (ab)

Commanded by
KL Max Bokelberg December 1944 - 11.3.45

Patrols: None   Ships sunk: None

*On 31.12.44, the day after commissioning, U 2530 was sunk in a
bombing raid on Hamburg docks. The boat was raised in January
1945 and put into dry dock.*
   *U 2530 received further damage in a USAF raid on the docks on
17.1.45 and was finally destroyed in a third bombing raid on 11.3.45.*
   The wreck was broken up.

U 2531 Type XXI

Built by Blohm & Voss, Hamburg
Keel laid 3.10.44   Launched 5.12.44
Commissioned 10.1.45   Feldpost Nr M 49 394

Scuttled 2.5.45 at Travemünde

Served with
31 U-Flottille, Hamburg January 1945 - 2.5.45 (ab)

Commanded by
KL Helmut Niss January 1945 - 2.5.45

Patrols: None   Ships sunk: None

*U 2531 was scuttled on 2.5.45 at Travemünde to prevent her
falling into Allied hands.*
   The wreck was later broken up.

*U 2532 was never commissioned. She was sunk in a bombing raid
on the Blohm & Voss yard at Hamburg on 31.12.44 and later
scrapped.*

U 2533 Type XXI

Built by Blohm & Voss, Hamburg
Keel laid 13.10.44   Launched 7.12.44
Commissioned 18.1.45   Feldpost Nr M 49 401

Scuttled 3.5.45 at Travemünde

Served with
31 U-Flottille, Hamburg January 1945 - 3.5.45 (ab)

Commanded by
OL Horst Günther January 1945 - 3.5.45

Patrols: None   Ships sunk: None

*U 2533 was scuttled on 3.5.45 at Travemünde to prevent her fall-
ing into Allied hands. The wreck was later broken up.*

U 2534 Type XXI

Built by Blohm & Voss, Hamburg
Keel laid 17.10.44   Launched 11.12.44
Commissioned 17.1.45   Feldpost Nr M 49 427

Scuttled 3.5.45 in the Kattegat

Served with
31 U-Flottille, Hamburg January 1945 - 3.5.45

Commanded by
KL Ulrich Drews January 1945 - 3.5.45

Patrols: None   Ships sunk: None

*On her commissioning day, U 2534 was damaged in a USAF
bombing raid on the Blohm & Voss yard at Hamburg. She was
repaired and recommissioned in March 1945.*
   The boat was scuttled on 3.5.45 in the Kattegat.

U 2535 Type XXI

Built by Blohm & Voss, Hamburg
Keel laid 18.10.44   Launched 16.12.44
Commissioned 28.1.45   Feldpost Nr M 49 435

Scuttled 2.5.45 at Travemünde

Served with
31 U-Flottille, Hamburg January 1945 - 2.5.45 (ab)

Commanded by
KL Otto Bitter January 1945 - 2.5.45

Patrols: None   Ships sunk: None

*U 2535 was scuttled on 2.5.45 at Travemünde to prevent her fall-
ing into Allied hands.*
   The wreck was later broken up.

U 2536　Type XXI

Built by Blohm & Voss, Hamburg
Keel laid 21.10.44　Launched 16.12.44
Commissioned 6.2.45　Feldpost Nr M 49 449

Scuttled 3.5.45 at Travemünde

Served with
31 U-Flottille, Hamburg　February 1945 - 3.5.45 (ab)

Commanded by
OL Ulrich Vöge　February 1945 - 3.5.45

Patrols: None　　Ships sunk: None

*She was scuttled on 3.5.45 at Travemünde to prevent her falling
into Allied hands.*
　　The wreck was later broken up.

U 2537　Type XXI

Built by Blohm & Voss, Hamburg
Keel laid 22.10.44　Launched 22.12.44
Commissioned 21.3.45　Feldpost Nr M 52 015

Destroyed 8.4.45 at Hamburg

Served with
31 U-Flottille, Hamburg　March 1945 - 8.4.45 (ab)

Commanded by
OL Max Dobbert　March 1945 - 8.4.45

Patrols: None　　Ships sunk: None

*On 31.12.44 U 2537 was sunk in a USAF bombing raid on
Hamburg docks. The boat was raised in January but she was
slightly damaged in a USAF raid on 17.1.45.*
　　*U 2537 was commissioned on 21.3.45 but then destroyed in an
RAF bombing raid on Hamburg on 8.4.45.*

U 2538　Type XXI

Built by Blohm & Voss, Hamburg
Keel laid 24.10.44　Launched 6.1.45
Commissioned 16.2.45　Feldpost Nr M 52 021

Scuttled 9.5.45 off Marstal

Served with
31 U-Flottille, Hamburg　February 1945 - 9.5.45 (ab)

Commanded by
OL Heinrich Klapdor　February 1945 - 9.5.45

Patrols: None　　Ships sunk: None

*U 2538 was at sea from 3.5.45 in the western Baltic, as were other
boats, transferring from Swinemünde to Neustadt. The Baltic coast
was occupied by British troops and the boats stayed at sea whilst
deciding where to scuttle.*
　　*U 2538 was finally scuttled on 9.5.45 off Marstal, Aeröe Island,
Denmark.*
　　The wreck was raised and scrapped in 1948.

U 2539　Type XXI

Built by Blohm & Voss, Hamburg
Keel laid 27.10.44　Launched 6.1.45
Commissioned 21.2.45　Feldpost Nr M 52 044

Scuttled 3.5.45 at Kiel

Served with
31 U-Flottille, Hamburg　February 1945 - 3.5.45 (ab)

Commanded by
OL Erich Jewinski　February - April 1945
OL Johann Johann (temp)　April 1945 - 3.5.45

Patrols: None　　Ships sunk: None

U 2539 was scuttled on 3.5.45 at Kiel, to prevent capture.
　　The wreck was later broken up.

U 2540　Type XXI

Built by Blohm & Voss, Hamburg
Keel laid 29.10.44　Launched 13.1.45
Commissioned 24.2.45　Feldpost Nr M 52 062

Scuttled 4.5.45 off the Flensburg Fireship

Served with
31 U-Flottille, Hamburg　February 1945 - 4.5.45 (ab)

Commanded by
OL Rudolf Schultze　February 1945 - 4.5.45

Patrols: None　　Ships sunk: None

*U 2540 one of the many boats which left their bases in early May
for the bays of Northern Germany, there to await further orders.*
　　*En route, on the 3rd, she was attacked by aircraft of 2nd TAF.
U 2540 was scuttled on the 4th off the Flensburg Fireship.*

*The boat was raised in 1957 and rebuilt at the Howaldtswerke yard
at Kiel. On 31.8.60 she was commissioned into the Bundesmarine
as the experimental boat* Wilhelm Bauer.
　　She was handed over to the Museum in Bremerhaven in 1983.

U 2541　Type XXI

Built by Blohm & Voss, Hamburg
Keel laid 31.10.44　Launched 13.1.45
Commissioned 1.3.45　Feldpost Nr M 52 146

Scuttled 5.5.45 in Geltinger Bucht

Served with
31 U-Flottille, Hamburg　March 1945 - 5.5.45 (ab)

Commanded by
OL Ernst-August Stellmann　March - April 1945
KL Rolf-Birger Wahlen　April 1945 - 5.5.45

Patrols: None　　Ships sunk: None

*Whilst still under construction, U 2541 was damaged on 17.1.45,
in a USAF bombing raid on Kiel.*

U 2541 (continued)

U 2541 was one of many boats which left their bases in early May and went to the bays of Northern Germany, to await further orders.
She was scuttled on 5.5.45 in Geltinger Bucht, in accordance with Operation Regenbogen *but contrary to the surrender terms.*

U 2542 Type XXI

Built by Blohm & Voss, Hamburg
Keel laid 10.11.44   Launched 22.1.45
Commissioned 5.3.45   Feldpost Nr M 52 386

Destroyed 3.4.45 at Kiel

Served with
31 U-Flottille, Hamburg   March 1945 - 3.4.45 (ab)

Commanded by
OL Otto Hübschen   March 1945 - 3.4.45

Patrols: None   Ships sunk: None

Whilst still under construction, U 2542 was slightly damaged in a USAF bombing raid on Hamburg on 17.1.45.
She was destroyed in a USAF raid on Kiel on 3.4.45.

U 2543 Type XXI

Built by Blohm & Voss, Hamburg
Keel laid 13.11.44   Launched 9.2.45
Commissioned 7.3.45   Feldpost Nr M 52 395

Scuttled 3.5.45 at Kiel

Served with
31 U-Flottille, Hamburg   March 1945 - 3.5.45 (ab)

Commanded by
OL Gottfried Stolzenburg   March 1945 - 3.5.45

Patrols: None   Ships sunk: None

U 2543 was scuttled on 3.5.45 at Kiel. The wreck was broken up.

U 2544 Type XXI

Built by Blohm & Voss, Hamburg
Keel laid 10.11.44   Launched 9.2.45
Commissioned 10.3.45   Feldpost Nr M 52 436

Scuttled 5.5.45 off Aarhus, Denmark

Served with
31 U-Flottille, Hamburg   March 1945 - 5.5.45 (ab)

Commanded by
OL Rudolf Meinlschmidt   March 1945 - 5.5.45

Patrols None   Ships sunk: None

U 2544 was slightly damaged in a USAF raid on Hamburg on 17.1.45, whilst still under construction.
She was scuttled on 5.5.45 off Aarhus, Denmark. The boat was raised in 1952 and scrapped.

U 2545 Type XXI

Built by Blohm & Voss, Hamburg
Keel laid 20.11.44   Launched 12.2.45
Commissioned 9.3.45   Feldpost Nr M 52 467

Scuttled 3.5.45 at Kiel

Served with
31 U-Flottille, Hamburg   March 1945 - 3.5.45 (ab)

Commanded by
OL Hans-Bruno Freiherr von Müffling   March 1945 - 3.5.45

Patrols: None   Ships sunk: None

Whilst still under construction, U 2545 was slightly damaged in a USAF bombing raid on Hamburg on 17.1.45.
She was scuttled on 3.5.45 at Kiel.

U 2546 Type XXI

Built by Blohm & Voss, Hamburg
Keel laid 22.11.44   Launched 19.2.45
Commissioned --.4.45   Feldpost Nr unknown

Scuttled 3.5.45 at Kiel

Served with
31 U-Flottille, Hamburg   March 1945 - 3.5.45 (ab)

Commanded by
OL Max Dobbert   April 1945 - 3.5.45

Patrols: None   Ships sunk: None

Whilst still under construction, U 2546 was slightly damaged in a USAF bombing raid on Hamburg on 17.1.45.
She was scuttled on 3.5.45 at Kiel.

U 2547 was bombed in the Blohm & Voss yard in Hamburg on 11.3.45, whilst fitting out. She was never commissioned.
The wreck was later broken up.

U 2548 Type XXI

Built by Blohm & Voss, Hamburg
Keel laid 30.11.44   Launched 9.3.45
Commissioned 31.3.45   Feldpost Nr M 53 122

Scuttled 3.5.45 at Kiel

Served with
31 U-Flottille, Hamburg   March 1945 - 3.5.45 (ab)

Commanded by
OL Karl-Erich Utischill   March 1945 - 3.5.45

Patrols: None   Ships sunk: None

Whilst still under construction, U 2548 was slightly damaged in a USAF bombing raid on Hamburg on 17.1.45.
The boat was scuttled on 3.5.45 at Kiel to prevent her falling into Allied hands. The wreck was later broken up.

U 2549 and U 2550 were never commissioned. Both boats were badly damaged in a USAF raid on Hamburg on 11.3.45, whilst still under construction.

U 2549 was scuttled at Hamburg on 2.5.45 to prevent her falling into Allied hands and U 2250 was destroyed in attacks by RAF Bomber Command on April 8th and 9th 1945.

U 2551   Type XXI

Built by Blohm & Voss, Hamburg
Keel laid 8.12.44   Launched 31.3.45
Commissioned --.4.45   Feldpost Nr M 53 631

Scuttled 5.5.45 at Flensburg

Served with
31 U-Flottille, Hamburg   April 1945 - 5.5.45 (ab)

Commanded by
KL Gerd Schaar   April 1945 - 5.5.45

Patrols: None   Ships sunk: None

Whilst still under construction, U 2551 was slightly damaged in a USAF raid on Hamburg on 17.1.45.
The boat was scuttled at Flensburg-Solitude on 5.5.45. The wreck was later broken up.

U 2552   Type XXI

Built by Blohm & Voss, Hamburg
Keel laid 10.12.44   Launched 31.3.45
Commissioned 20.4.45   Feldpost Nr M 53 733

Scuttled 3.5.45 at Kiel

Served with
31 U-Flottille, Hamburg   April 1945 - 3.5.45 (ab)

Commanded by
KL Johannes Rudolph   April 1945 - 3.5.45

Patrols: None   Ships sunk: None

U 2552 was scuttled at Kiel-Wik on 3.5.45, to prevent her falling into Allied hands.
The wreck was later broken up.

U 2553 - U 2564 had their keels laid but construction was never completed and they were broken up.

U 2565 - U 2761 were never built, orders cancelled.

U 2762 - U 3000 were projected but never built.

U 3001   Type XXI

Built by AG Weser, Bremen
Keel laid 15.4.44   Launched 30.5.44
Commissioned 20.7.44   Feldpost Nr M 54 524

Scuttled 3.5.45 at Wesermünde

Served with
32 U-Flottille, Königsberg   July - August 1944 (ab)
4 U-Flottille, Stettin   August - November 1944 (ab)
6 KLA, Wesermünde   November 1944 - 3.5.45 (ab)

Commanded by
OL Hans Vogel   July - November 1944
KL Wilhelm Peters   April 1945 - 3.5.45

Patrols: None   Ships sunk: None

U 3001 was scuttled on 3.5.45 in the Weser Estuary at Wesermünde to prevent her falling into Allied hands.
The wreck was later broken up.

U 3002   Type XXI

Built by AG Weser, Bremen
Keel laid 23.5.44   Launched 9.7.44
Commissioned 6.8.44   Feldpost Nr M 42 293

Scuttled 2.5.45 at Travemünde

Served with
32 U-Flottille, Königsberg   August - September 1944 (ab)
4 U-Flottille, Stettin   September 1944 - 2.5.45 (ab)

Commanded by
KL Helmut Manseck   August - September 1944
FK Hermann Kaiser   October 1944 - 2.5.45

Patrols: None   Ships sunk: None

U 3002 was scuttled on 2.5.45 at Travemünde to prevent her falling into Allied hands.
The wreck was later broken up.

U 3003   Type XXI

Built by Blohm & Voss, Hamburg
Keel laid 27.5.44   Launched 18.7.44
Commissioned 22.8.44   Feldpost Nr M 42 302

Destroyed 4.4.45 at Kiel

Served with
4 U-Flottille, Stettin   August 1944 - 4.4.45 (vb)

Commanded by
OL Ludo Kregelin   August 1944 - 4.4.45

Patrols: None   Ships sunk: None

U 3003 was destroyed in a USAF bombing raid on Kiel on 4.4.45.
The wreck was later broken up.

U 3004   Type XXI

Built by AG Weser, Bremen
Keel laid 4.6.44   Launched 26.7.44
Commissioned 30.8.44   Feldpost Nr M 42 501

Scuttled 2.5.45 at Hamburg

Served with
4 U-Flottille, Stettin   August 1944 - 2.5.45 (vb)

Commanded by
KL Helmut Thurmann   August 1944 - February 1945
KL Otto Peschel   March 1945 - 2.5.45

Patrols: None   Ships sunk: None

U 3004 was scuttled on 2.5.45 at Hamburg to prevent her falling into Allied hands.
    The wreck was later broken up.

U 3005   Type XXI

Built by AG Weser, Bremen
Keel laid 2.6.44   Launched 18.8.44
Commissioned 20.9.44   Feldpost Nr M 42 792

Scuttled 3.5.45 at Kiel

Served with
4 U-Flottille, Stettin   September 1944 - 3.5.45 (ab)

Commanded by
KL Johannes Hinrichs   January 1945 - 3.5.45

Patrols: None   Ships sunk: None

U 3005 was scuttled on 3.5.45 at Kiel to prevent her falling into Allied hands.
    The wreck was later broken up.

U 3006   Type XXI

Built by AG Weser, Bremen
Keel laid 12.6.44   Launched 25.8.44
Commissioned 5.10.44   Feldpost Nr M 42 993

Scuttled 1.5.45 at Wilhelmshaven

Served with
4 U-Flottille, Stettin   October 1944 - 1.5.45 (ab)

Commanded by
OL Hans-Ferdinand Geisler   October - December 1944
OL Gerhard Linder   December 1944 - January 1945
OL Ernst Fischer   January 1945 - 1.5.45

Patrols: None   Ships sunk: None

U 3006 was scuttled at Wilhelmshaven on 1.5.45.
    The wreck was later broken up.

U 3007   Type XXI

Built by AG Weser, Bremen
Keel laid 9.7.44   Launched 4.9.44
Commissioned 22.10.44   Feldpost Nr M 46 289

Destroyed 24.2.45 at Bremen

Served with
4 U-Flottille, Stettin   October 1944 - 24.2.45 (ab)

Commanded by
KL Helmut Manseck   October 1944 - 24.2.45

Patrols: None   Ships sunk: None

U 3007 was destroyed in a USAF bombing raid on Bremen on 24.2.45. She had been cleared for final fitting out and was sunk at the quay.
    The wreck was later broken up.

U 3008   Type XXI

Built by AG Weser, Bremen
Keel laid 2.7.44   Launched 15.9.44
Commissioned 19.10.44   Feldpost Nr M 46 364

Surrendered 9.5.45 at Wilhelmshaven

Served with
4 U-Flottille, Stettin   October 1944 - April 1945 (ab)
11 U-Flottille, Bergen   April 1945 - 9.5.45 (fb)

Commanded by
KL Fokko Schlömer   October 1944 - February 1945
KL Helmut Manseck   March 1945 - 9.5.45

Patrols: None   Ships sunk: None

On 9.5.45 U 3008 was surrendered at Wilhelmshaven and left there on 21.6.45 for an assembly area in Britain.
    The boat was handed over to the US Navy and used experimentally in trials until expended as a target in 1954.
    She was broken up in Puerto Rico.

U 3009   Type XXI

Built by AG Weser, Bremen
Keel laid 21.7.44   Launched 30.9.44
Commissioned 10.11.44   Feldpost Nr M 46 411

Scuttled 1.5.45 at Wesermünde

Served with
4 U-Flottille, Stettin   November 1944 - 1.5.45 (ab)

Commanded by
KL Karl Schimpf   November 1944 - 1.5.45

Patrols: None   Ships sunk: None

U 3009 was scuttled on 1.5.45 at Wesermünde to prevent her falling into Allied hands.
    The wreck was later broken up.

U 3010 Type XXI

Built by AG Weser, Bremen
Keel laid 13.7.44   Launched 20.10.44
Commissioned 11.11.44   Feldpost Nr M 46 477

Scuttled 3.5.45 at Kiel

Served with
4 U-Flottille, Stettin   November 1944 - 3.5.45 (ab)

Commanded by
OL Eberhard Ebert   November 1944 - March 1945
FK Erich Topp   March - April 1945
KL Hans Bungards   April 1945 - 3.5.45

Patrols: None   Ships sunk: None

U 3010 was scuttled on 3.5.45 at Kiel to prevent her falling into Allied hands.
   The wreck was later broken up.

U 3011 Type XXI

Built by AG Weser, Bremen
Keel laid 14.8.44   Launched 20.10.44
Commissioned 21.12.44   Feldpost Nr M 46 554

Scuttled 3.5.45 at Travemünde

Served with
4 U-Flottille, Stettin   December 1944 - 3.5.45 (ab)

Commanded by
KL Otto Tinschert   December 1944 - April 1945
OL Otto Fränzel   April 1945 - 3.5.45

Patrols: None   Ships sunk: None

U 3011 was scuttled on 3.5.45 at Kiel to prevent her falling into Allied hands.
   The wreck was later broken up.

U 3012 Type XXI

Built by AG Weser, Bremen
Keel laid 26.8.44   Launched 20.10.44
Commissioned 21.12.44   Feldpost Nr M 46 564

Scuttled 3.5.45 at Travemünde

Served with
4 U-Flottille, Stettin   December 1944 - 3.5.45 (ab)

Commanded by
KL Friedrich Kloevekorn   December 1944 - 3.5.45

Patrols: None   Ships sunk: None

U 3012 was scuttled on 3.5.45 at Travemünde to prevent her falling into Allied hands.
   The wreck was later broken up.

U 3013 Type XXI

Built by AG Weser, Bremen
Keel laid 18.8.44   Launched 19.10.44
Commissioned 22.11.44   Feldpost Nr M 49 799

Scuttled 3.5.45 at Travemünde

Served with
4 U-Flottille, Stettin   November 1944 - 3.5.45 (ab)

Commanded by
KL Volker Simmermacher   November 1944 - 3.5.45

Patrols: None   Ships sunk: None

U 3013 was scuttled on 3.5.45 at Travemünde to prevent her falling into Allied hands.
   The wreck was later broken up.

U 3014 Type XXI

Built by AG Weser, Bremen
Keel laid 28.8.44   Launched 25.10.44
Commissioned 17.12.44   Feldpost Nr M 48 818

Scuttled 3.5.45 at Neustadt

Served with
4 U-Flottille, Stettin   December 1944 - 3.5.45 (ab)

Commanded by
KL Karl-Heinz Marbach   December 1944 - 3.5.45

Patrols: None   Ships sunk: None

U 3014 was scuttled on 3.5.45 at Neustadt to prevent her falling into Allied hands.
   The wreck was later broken up.

U 3015 Type XXI

Built by AG Weser, Bremen
Keel laid 28.8.44   Launched 27.10.44
Commissioned 17.12.44   Feldpost Nr M 49 827

Scuttled 5.5.45 in Geltinger Bucht

Served with
4 U-Flottille, Stettin   December 1944 - 5.5.45 (ab)

Commanded by
KL Peter-Ottmar Grau   December 1944 - 5.5.45

Patrols: None   Ships sunk: None

U 3015 was one of many boats which left their bases in early May for the bays of Northern Germany, there to await further orders.
   She was scuttled on 5.5.45 in Geltinger Bucht, in accordance with Operation Regenbogen *but contrary to the surrender terms.*

U 3016 Type XXI

Built by AG Weser, Bremen
Keel laid 7.9.44   Launched 2.11.44
Commissioned 5.1.45   Feldpost Nr M 49 847

Scuttled 2.5.45 at Travemünde

Served with
4 U-Flottille, Stettin   January 1945 - 2.5.45 (ab)

Commanded by
OL Bernhard Meentzen   January 1945 - 2.5.45

Patrols: None   Ships sunk: None

U 3016 was scuttled on 2.5.45 at Travemünde to prevent her falling into Allied hands.
   The wreck was later broken up.

U 3017 Type XXI

Built by AG Weser, Bremen
Keel laid 2.9.44   Launched 5.11.44
Commissioned 5.1.45   Feldpost Nr M 49 880

Surrendered 9.5.45 at Horten

Served with
4 U-Flottille, Stettin   January 1945 - 9.5.45 (ab/fb)

Commanded by
OL Rudolf Lindschau   January 1945 - 9.5.45

Patrols: None   Ships sunk: None

U 3017 was surrendered at Horten on 9.5.45 and left there on the 29th for an assembly area in Britain.
   She was taken over by the Royal Navy and became submarine N 41. The boat was scrapped in November 1949.

U 3018 Type XXI

Built by AG Weser, Bremen
Keel laid 18.9.44   Launched 29.11.44
Commissioned 6.1.45   Feldpost Nr M 49 924

Scuttled 2.5.45 at Travemünde

Served with
4 U-Flottille, Stettin   January 1945 - 2.5.45 (ab)

Commanded by
OL Siegfried Breinlinger   January 1945 - 2.5.45

Patrols: None   Ships sunk: None

U 3018 was scuttled on 2.5.45 at Travemünde to prevent her falling into Allied hands.
   The wreck was later broken up.

U 3019 Type XXI

Built by AG Weser, Bremen
Keel laid 20.9.44   Launched 15.11.44
Commissioned 23.12.44   Feldpost Nr M 49 943

Scuttled 2.5.45 at Travemünde

Served with
4 U-Flottille, Stettin   December 1944 - 2.5.45 (ab)

Commanded by
OL Ernst-August Racky   December 1944 - 2.5.45

Patrols: None   Ships sunk: None

U 3019 was scuttled on 2.5.45 at Travemünde to prevent her falling into Allied hands.
   The wreck was later broken up.

U 3020 Type XXI

Built by AG Weser, Bremen
Keel laid 1.10.44   Launched 16.11.44
Commissioned 23.12.44   Feldpost Nr M 49 952

Scuttled 2.5.45 at Travemünde

Served with
4 U-Flottille, Stettin   December 1944 - 2.5.45 (ab)

Commanded by
OL Heinrich Mäueler   December 1944 - 2.5.45

Patrols: None   Ships sunk: None

U 3020 was scuttled on 2.5.45 at Travemünde to prevent her falling into Allied hands.
   The wreck was later broken up.

U 3021 Type XXI

Built by AG Weser, Bremen
Keel laid 26.9.44   Launched 27.11.44
Commissioned 12.1.45   Feldpost Nr M 49 972

Scuttled 2.5.45 at Travemünde

Served with
4 U-Flottille, Stettin   January 1945 - 2.5.45 (ab)

Commanded by
OL Kurt van Meeteren   January 1945 - 2.5.45

Patrols: None   Ships sunk: None

U 3021 was scuttled on 2.5.45 at Travemünde to prevent her falling into Allied hands.
   The wreck was later broken up.

U 3022 Type XXI

Built by AG Weser, Bremen
Keel laid 6.10.44   Launched 30.11.44
Commissioned 25.1.45   Feldpost Nr M 49 979

Scuttled 5.5.45 in Geltinger Bucht

Served with
4 U-Flottille, Stettin   January 1945 - 5.5.45 (ab)

Commanded by
KL Paul Weber   January 1945 - 5.5.45

Patrols: None   Ships sunk: None

U 3022 was one of many boat which left their bases in early May for the bays of Northern Germany, there to await further orders.
She was scuttled on 5.5.45 in Geltinger Bucht, in accordance with Operation Regenbogen *but contrary to the surrender terms.*

U 3023 Type XXI

Built by AG Weser, Bremen
Keel laid 3.10.44   Launched 2.12.44
Commissioned 22.1.45   Feldpost Nr M 49 998

Scuttled 3.5.45 at Travemünde

Served with
4 U-Flottille, Stettin   January 1945 - 3.5.45 (ab)

Commanded by
OL Erich Harms   January 1945 - 3.5.45

Patrols: None   Ships sunk: None

U 3023 was scuttled on 3.5.45 at Travemünde to prevent her falling into Allied hands.
The wreck was later broken up.

U 3024 Type XXI

Built by AG Weser, Bremen
Keel laid 15.10.44   Launched 6.12.44
Commissioned 13.1.45   Feldpost Nr M 50 010

Scuttled 3.5.45 at Neustadt

Served with
4 U-Flottille, Stettin   January 1945 - 3.5.45 (ab)

Commanded by
OL Ferdinand Blaich   January 1945 - 3.5.45

Patrols: None   Ships sunk: None

U 3024 was scuttled on 3.5.45 at Neustadt to prevent her falling into Allied hands.
The wreck was later broken up.

U 3025 Type XXI

Built by AG Weser, Bremen
Keel laid 22.10.44   Launched 9.12.44
Commissioned 20.1.45   Feldpost Nr M 50 034

Scuttled 3.5.45 at Travemünde

Served with
4 U-Flottille, Stettin   January 1945 - 3.5.45 (ab)

Commanded by
KL Hans Vogel   January 1945 - 3.5.45

Patrols: None   Ships sunk: None

U 3025 was scuttled on 3.5.45 at Travemünde to prevent her falling into Allied hands.
The wreck was later broken up.

U 3026 Type XXI

Built by AG Weser, Bremen
Keel laid 20.10.44   Launched 14.12.44
Commissioned 22.1.45   Feldpost Nr M 50 081

Scuttled 3.5.45 in Lübecker Bucht

Served with
4 U-Flottille, Stettin   January 1945 - 3.5.45 (ab)

Commanded by
OL Günther Drescher   January 1945 - 3.5.45

Patrols: None   Ships sunk: None

U 3026 was scuttled on 3.5.45 in Lübecker Bucht to prevent her falling into Allied hands.
The wreck was later broken up.

U 3027 Type XXI

Built by AG Weser, Bremen
Keel laid 18.10.44   Launched 18.12.44
Commissioned 25.1.45   Feldpost Nr M 50 115

Scuttled 3.5.45 at Travemünde

Served with
4 U-Flottille, Stettin   January 1945 - 3.5.45 (ab)

Commanded by
KL Karl Mehne   January 1945 - 3.5.45

Patrols: None   Ships sunk: None

U 3027 was scuttled on 3.5.45 at Travemünde to prevent her falling into Allied hands.
The wreck was later broken up.

U 3028   Type XXI

Built by AG Weser, Bremen
Keel laid 26.10.44   Launched 22.12.44
Commissioned 27.1.45   Feldpost Nr M 50 141

Scuttled 3.5.45 at Kiel

Served with
4 U-Flottille, Stettin   January 1945 - 3.5.45 (ab)

Commanded by
KL Erwin Christophersen   January 1945 - 3.5.45

Patrols: None   Ships sunk: None

The boat was scuttled on 3.5.45 at Kiel to prevent her falling into Allied hands.
   Casualties are unknown.

U 3029   Type XXI

Built by AG Weser, Bremen
Keel laid 24.10.44   Launched 28.12.44
Commissioned 5.2.45   Feldpost Nr M 50 148

Scuttled 3.5.45 at Kiel

Served with
4 U-Flottille, Stettin   February 1945 - 3.5.45 (ab)

Commanded by
KL Hermann Lamby   February 1945 - 3.5.45

Patrols: None   Ships sunk: None

U 3029 was scuttled on 3.5.45 in Kieler Aussenförde to prevent her falling into Allied hands.

U 3030   Type XXI

Built by AG Weser, Bremen
Keel laid 2.11.44   Launched 31.12.44
Commissioned 14.2.45   Feldpost Nr M 52

Scuttled 8.5.45 in Eckernförder Bucht

Served with
4 U-Flottille, Stettin   February 1945 - 3.5.45 (ab)

Commanded by
OL Bernhard Luttmann   February 1945 - 3.5.45

Patrols: None   Ships sunk: None

U 3030 was at sea from 3.5.45 in the western Baltic, as were other boats, transferring from Swinemünde to Neustadt. The Baltic coast was occupied by British troops and the boats stayed at sea, whilst deciding where to scuttle.
   U 3030 was finally scuttled on 8.5.45 in Eckernförde Bucht.

U 3031   Type XXI

Built by AG Weser, Bremen
Keel laid 30.10.44   Launched 6.1.45
Commissioned 18.2.45   Feldpost Nr M 52 101

Scuttled 3.5.45 at Kiel

Served with
4 U-Flottille, Stettin   February 1945 - 3.5.45 (ab)

Commanded by
OL Heinrich Sach   February 1945 - 3.5.45

Patrols: None   Ships sunk: None

U 3031 was scuttled on 3.5.45 at Kiel to prevent her falling into Allied hands.
   The wreck was later broken up.

U 3032   Type XXI

Built by AG Weser, Bremen
Keel laid 9.11.44   Launched 10.1.45
Commissioned 12.2.45   Feldpost Nr M 52 110

Sunk 3.5.45 E of Fredericia

Served with
4 U-Flottille, Stettin   February 1945 - 3.5.45 (ab)

Commanded by
OL Horst Slevogt   February 1945 - 3.5.45

Patrols: None   Ships sunk: None

U 3032 was attacked and sunk by Typhoons of 184 Squadron on 3.5.45 E of Fredericia.
   Of U 3032's crew, 28 men lost their lives. The boat's commander was among the survivors.

U 3033   Type XXI

Built by AG Weser, Bremen
Keel laid 6.11.44   Launched 20.1.45
Commissioned 27.2.45   Feldpost Nr M 52 191

Scuttled 4.5.45 in Flensburger Förde

Served with
4 U-Flottille, Stettin   February 1945 - 4.5.45 (ab)

Commanded by
OL Peter Callsen   February 1945 - 4.5.45

Patrols: None   Ships sunk: None

U 3033 was scuttled on 4.5.45 in Wasserslebener Bucht, in Flensburger Förde, in accordance with Operation Regenbogen *but contrary to the surrender terms.*
   The wreck was later broken up.

U 3034   Type XXI

Built by AG Weser, Bremen
Keel laid 14.11.44   Launched 21.1.45
Commissioned 31.3.45   Feldpost Nr M 52 197'

Scuttled 5.5.45 in Flensburger Förde

Served with
4 U-Flottille, Stettin   March 1945 - 5.5.45 (ab)

Commanded by
OL Wilhelm Prehn   March 1945 - 5.5.45

Patrols: None   Ships sunk: None

U 3034 was scuttled on 5.5.45 in Wasserslebener Bucht, where she was awaiting further orders. The scuttling was in accordance with Operation Regenbogen *but contrary to the surrender terms.*
The wreck was later broken up.

U 3035   Type XXI

Built by AG Weser, Bremen
Keel 11.11.44   Launched 24.1.45
Commissioned 1.3.45   Feldpost Nr M 52 251

Surrendered 9.5.45 at Stavanger

Served with
4 U-Flottille, Stettin   March 1945 - 9.5.45 (ab)

Commanded by
OL Ernst-August Gerke   March 1945 - 9.5.45

Patrols: None   Ships sunk: None

U 3035 was surrendered at Stavanger on 9.5.45 and left there on the 31st for an assembly area in Britain.
She was taken over by the Royal Navy and became submarine N 28. The boat was handed over to Russia in 1947.

U 3036 was delivered by the yard on 6.2.45 but shortly before commissioning she was badly damaged in an air raid.
In another bombing raid on Bremen on 30.3.45, the boat was destroyed.

U 3037   Type XXI

Built by AG Weser, Bremen
Keel laid 18.11.44   Launched 31.1.45
Commissioned 3.3.45   Feldpost Nr M 52 552

Scuttled 3.5.45 at Travemünde

Served with
4 U-Flottille, Stettin   March 1945 - 3.5.45 (ab)

Commanded by
KK Carl Emmermann   March - April 1945
KL Gustav-Adolf Janssen   April 1945 - 3.5.45

Patrols: None   Ships sunk: None

U 3037 was scuttled at Travemünde on 3.5.45 to prevent her falling into Allied hands.
The wreck was later broken up.

U 3038   Type XXI

Built by AG Weser, Bremen
Keel laid 1.12.44   Launched 7.2.45
Commissioned 4.3.45   Feldpost Nr M 52 580

Scuttled 3.5.45 at Kiel

Served with
4 U-Flottille, Stettin   March 1945 - 3.5.45 (ab)

Commanded by
OL Matthias Brünig   March - April 1945

Patrols: None   Ships sunk: None

U 3038 was scuttled on 3.5.45 at Kiel to prevent her falling into Allied hands.
The wreck was later broken up.

U 3039   Type XXI

Built by AG Weser, Bremen
Keel laid 29.11.44   Launched 14.2.45
Commissioned 8.3.45   Feldpost Nr M 52 652

Scuttled 3.5.45 at Kiel

Served with
4 U-Flottille, Stettin   March 1945 - 3.5.45 (ab)

Commanded by
KL Günter Ruperti   March 1945 - 3.5.45

Patrols: None   Ships sunk: None

U 3039 was scuttled on 3.5.45 at Kiel to prevent her falling into Allied hands.
The wreck was later broken up.

U 3040   Type XXI

Built by AG Weser, Bremen
Keel laid 9.12.44   Launched 10.2.45
Commissioned 8.3.45   Feldpost Nr M 52 673

Scuttled 3.5.45 at Kiel

Served with
4 U-Flottille, Stettin   March 1945 - 3.5.45 (ab)

Commanded by
OL Heinz Robbert   March 1945 - 3.5.45

Patrols: None   Ships sunk: None

U 3040 was scuttled on 3.5.45 at Kiel to prevent her falling into Allied hands.
The wreck was later broken up.

U 3041   Type XXI

Built by AG Weser, Bremen
Keel laid 7.12.44   Launched 23.2.45
Commissioned 12.3.45   Feldpost Nr M 52 673

Surrendered 9.5.45 at Horten

Served with
4 U-Flottille, Stettin   March 1945 - 9.5.45 (ab)

Commanded by
OL Joachim Vieth   March - April 1945
KL Hans Hornkohl   April 1945 - 9.5.45

Patrols: None   Ships sunk: None

U 3041 was surrendered at Horten on 9.5.45 and she left there on the 29th for an assembly area in Britain.
    She was taken over by the Royal Navy and became submarine N 29. The boat was handed over to Russia in 1947.

U 3042 and U 3043 were both destroyed in a bombing raid whilst under construction.

U 3044   Type XXI

Built by AG Weser, Bremen
Keel laid 21.12.44   Launched 1.3.45
Commissioned 27.3.45   Feldpost Nr M 55 611

Scuttled 5.5.45 in Geltinger Bucht

Served with
4 U-Flottille, Stettin   March 1945 - 5.5.45 (ab)

Commanded by
KL Bernhard Jaek   March - April 1945
KL Detlef von Lehsten   April 1945 - 5.5.45

Patrols: None   Ships sunk: None

U 3044 was one of many boats which left their bases in early May for the bays of Northern Germany, there to await further orders.
    She was scuttled on 5.5.45 in Geltinger Bucht, in accordance with Operation Regenbogen *but contrary to the surrender terms.*

U 3045 and U 3046 were destroyed in a daylight bombing raid on Bremen on 30.3.45, just before the boats were due to be commissioned.

U 3047, U 3050 and U 3051 were scuttled at Wesermünde on 5.5.45 before commissioning. The wrecks were broken up.

U 3048 and U 3049 were broken up after being bombed whilst still under construction.

U 3052 - U 3063 were broken up before completion.

U 3064 - U 3500 were projected but never built.

U 3501   Type XXI

Built by Schichau, Danzig
Keel laid 20.3.44   Launched 19.4.44
Commissioned 29.7.44   Feldpost Nr M 40 608

Scuttled 5.5.45 at Wesermünde

Served with
8 U-Flottille, Danzig   July - November 1944 (ab)
7 KLA, Danzig   November 1944 - 5.5.45 (ab)

Commanded by
OL Helmut Münster   July - October 1944

Patrols: None   Ships sunk: None

When at 7 KLA, U 3501 did not have a commander as such.

U 3501 was scuttled at Wesermünde on 5.5.45.
    The wreck was later broken up.

U 3502   Type XXI

Built by Schichau, Danzig
Keel laid 16.4.44   Launched 6.7.44
Commissioned 19.8.44   Feldpost Nr M 43 288

Scuttled 3.5.45 at Hamburg

Served with
8 U-Flottille, Danzig   August 1944 - January 1945 (vb)
5 U-Flottille, Kiel   January 1945 - 3.5.45 (vb)

Commanded by
OL Hermann Schultz   August 1944 - 3.5.45

Patrols: None   Ships sunk: None

U 3502 received severe damage to her stern and electricity plant in an RAF bombing raid on Hamburg on 8.4.45.
    The boat was taken out of service and scuttled at Hamburg on 3.5.45 to prevent her falling into Allied hands.
    The wreck was later broken up.

U 3503   Type XXI

Built by Schichau, Danzig
Keel laid 12.5.44   Launched 27.7.44
Commissioned 9.9.44   Feldpost Nr M 43 302

Scuttled 8.5.45 off Göteborg, Sweden

Served with
8 U-Flottille, Danzig   September 1944 - January 1945 (sb/vb)
5 U-Flottille, Kiel   January 1945 - 8.5.45 (sb/vb)

Commanded by
OL Hugo Deiring   September 1944 - 8.5.45

Patrols: None   Ships sunk: None

U 3503 was scuttled off Göteborg, Sweden on 8.5.45 and her crew was interned.
    The wreck was raised by Sweden in 1948 and scrapped.

U 3504 Type XXI

Built by Schichau, Danzig
Keel laid 30.6.44   Launched 19.8.44
Commissioned 23.9.44   Feldpost Nr M 43 405

Scuttled 2.5.45 at Wesermünde

Served with
8 U-Flottille, Danzig September 1944 - January 1945 (ab)
5 U-Flottille, Kiel January 1945 - 2.5.45 (ab)

Commanded by
KL Karl Hartwig Siebold September 1944 - 2.5.45

Patrols: None   Ships sunk: None

U 3504 was scuttled on 2.5.45 at Wesermünde to prevent her falling into Allied hands.
The wreck was later broken up.

U 3505 Type XXI

Built by Schichau, Danzig
Keel laid 9.7.44   Launched 25.8.44
Commissioned 7.10.44   Feldpost Nr M 46 656

Sunk 3.4.45 at Kiel

Served with
8 U-Flottille, Danzig October 1944 - January 1945 (ab)
5 U-Flottille, Kiel   January 1945 - 3.4.45 (ab)

Commanded by
OL Horst Willner October 1944 - 3.4.45

Patrols: None   Ships sunk: None

U 3505 was sunk in a USAF bombing raid on Kiel on 3.4.45. One crewman was killed.
The wreck was later broken up.

U 3506 Type XXI

Built by Schichau, Danzig
Keel laid 9.7.44   Launched 25.8.44
Commissioned 7.10.44   Feldpost Nr M 46 726

Scuttled 2.5.45 at Hamburg

Served with
8 U-Flottille, Danzig October 1944 - January 1945 (ab)
5 U-Flottille, Kiel January 1945 - 2.5.45 (ab)

Commanded by
KL Gerhard Thäter October 1944 - 2.5.45

Patrols: None   Ships sunk: None

U 3506 was scuttled on 2.5.45 at Hamburg to prevent her falling into Allied hands.
The wreck was later broken up.

U 3507 Type XXI

Built by Schichau, Danzig
Keel laid 19.7.44   Launched 16.9.44
Commissioned 19.10.44   Feldpost Nr M 46 894

Scuttled 3.5.45 at Travemünde

Served with
8 U-Flottille, Danzig October 1944 - March 1945 (ab)
5 U-Flottille, Kiel January 1945 - 3.5.45 (ab)

Commanded by
OL Otto Niethmann October 1944 - January 1945
OL Hans-Jürgen Schley March 1945 - 3.5.45

Patrols: None   Ships sunk: None

U 3507 was scuttled on 3.5.45 at Travemünde to prevent her falling into Allied hands.
The wreck was later broken up.

U 3508 Type XXI

Built by Schichau, Danzig
Keel laid 25.7.44   Launched 22.9.44
Commissioned 2.11.44   Feldpost Nr M 46 926

Sunk 30.3.45 at Wilhelmshaven

Served with
8 U-Flottille, Danzig November 1944 - January 1945 (ab)
5 U-Flottille, Kiel January 1945 - 30.3.45 (ab)

Commanded by
KL Detlef von Lehsten November 1944 - 30.3.45

Patrols: None   Ships sunk: None

U 3508 was sunk in a USAF bombing raid on Wilhelmshaven in daylight on 30.3.45.

U 3509 Type XXI

Built by Schichau, Danzig
Keel laid 29.7.44   Launched 27.9.44
Commissioned 29.1.45   Feldpost Nr M 47 968

Scuttled 3.5.45 in the Weser estuary

Served with
5 U-Flottille, Kiel January 1945 - 3.5.45 (ab)

Commanded by
KL Karl-Heinz Voswinkel January - March 1945
KL Heinz Franke March - April 1945
OL Wilhelm Neitzch April 1945 - 3.5.45

Patrols: None   Ships sunk: None

U 3509 was damaged in a bombing raid in September 1944, whilst still under construction. She was repaired and completed.
The boat was scuttled on 3.5.45 in the Weser estuary to prevent her falling into Allied hands.

U 3510   Type XXI

Built by Schichau, Danzig
Keel laid 6.8.44   Launched 4.10.44
Commissioned 11.11.44   Feldpost Nr M 47 968

Scuttled 5.5.45 in Geltinger Bucht

Served with
8 U-Flottille, Danzig   November 1944 - January 1945 (ab)
5 U-Flottille, Kiel   January 1945 - 5.5.45 (--)

Commanded by
OL Ernst-Werner Schwirley   November 1944 - 5.5.45

Patrols: None   Ships sunk: None

U 3510 was one of many boats which left their bases in early May and went to the bays of Northern Germany, to await further orders.
She was scuttled on 5.5.45 in Geltinger Bucht, in accordance with Operation Regenbogen *but contrary to the surrender terms.*
The wreck was later broken up.

U 3511   Type XXI

Built by Schichau, Danzig
Keel laid 14.8.44   Launched 11.10.44
Commissioned 18.11.44   Feldpost Nr M 49 533

Scuttled 3.5.45 at Travemünde

Served with
8 U-Flottille, Danzig   November 1944 - January 1945 (ab)
5 U-Flottille, Kiel   January 1945 - 3.5.45 (--)

Commanded by
OL Martin Grasse   November 1944 - January 1945
KL Hans-Heinrich Ketels   January - March 1945
KL Hermann Schrenk   April 1945 - 3.5.45

Patrols: None   Ships sunk: None

U 3511 was scuttled on 3.5.45 at Travemünde to prevent her falling into Allied hands.
The wreck was later broken up.

U 3512   Type XXI

Built by Schichau, Danzig
Keel laid 15.8.44   Launched 11.10.44
Commissioned 27.11.44   Feldpost Nr M 49 566

Destroyed 9.4.45 at Kiel

Served with
8 U-Flottille, Danzig   November 1944 - January 1945 (ab)
5 U-Flottille, Kiel   January 1945 - 9.4.45 (ab)

Commanded by
KL Hans Hornkohl   November 1944 - 9.4.45

Patrols: None   Ships sunk: None

U 3512 was destroyed in an RAF bombing raid on Kiel during the night of 9.4.45. The wreck was later broken up.

U 3513   Type XXI

Built by Schichau, Danzig
Keel laid 20.8.44   Launched 21.10.44
Commissioned 2.12.44   Feldpost Nr M 49 568

Scuttled 3.5.45 at Travemünde

Served with
8 U-Flottille, Danzig   December 1944 - January 1945 (ab)
5 U-Flottille, Kiel   January 1945 - 3.5.45 (ab)

Commanded by
OL Richard Nachtigall   December 1944 - 3.5.45

Patrols: None   Ships sunk: None

U 3513 was scuttled on 3.5.45 at Travemünde to prevent her falling into Allied hands. The wreck was later broken up.

U 3514   Type XXI

Built by Schichau, Danzig
Keel laid 21.8.44   Launched 21.10.44
Commissioned 9.12.44   Feldpost Nr M 49 572

Sunk 11.2.46 NW of Bloody Foreland (56°00′N 10°05′W)

Served with
8 U-Flottille, Danzig   December 1944 - January 1945 (ab)
5 U-Flottille, Kiel   January 1945 - 9.5.45 (ab)

Commanded by
OL Günther Fritze   December 1944 - 9.5.45

Patrols: None   Ships sunk: None

U 3514 was surrendered at Bergen on 9.5.45 and left there on the 30th for an assembly area in Britain.
She was the last of 116 boats to be disposed of by the Royal Navy in Operation Deadlight. *In February 1946 she was towed from Lisahally by the frigate HMS* Loch Arkaig.
U 3514 was sunk by gunfire on 11.2.46 NW of Bloody Foreland.

U 3515   Type XXI

Built by Schichau, Danzig
Keel laid 27.8.44   Launched 4.11.44
Commissioned 14.12.44   Feldpost Nr M 49 612

Surrendered 9.5.45 at Horten

Served with
8 U-Flottille, Danzig   December 1944 - January 1945 (ab)
5 U-Flottille, Kiel   January 1945 - 9.5.45 (ab)

Commanded by
OL Fedor Kuscher   December 1944 - 9.5.45

Patrols: None   Ships sunk: None

U 3515 was surrendered at Horten on 9.5.45 and left there on the 29th for an assembly area in Britain.
She was taken over by the Royal Navy and became submarine N 30. The boat was handed over to Russia in 1946.

U 3516   Type XXI

Built by Schichau, Danzig
Keel laid 28.8.44   Launched 4.11.44
Commissioned 18.12.44   Feldpost Nr M 49 638

Scuttled 2.5.45 at Travemünde

Served with
8 U-Flottille, Danzig December 1944 - January 1945 (ab)
5 U-Flottille, Kiel January 1945 - 2.5.45 (ab)

Commanded by
KL Hans Wengel December 1944 - March 1945
OL Heinrich Grote March 1945 - 2.5.45

Patrols: None   Ships sunk: None

U 3516 was scuttled at Travemünde on 2.5.45 to prevent her falling into Allied hands.
   The wreck was later broken up.

U 3517   Type XXI

Built by Schichau, Danzig
Keel laid 12.9.44   Launched 6.12.44
Commissioned 22.12.44   Feldpost Nr M 49 683

Scuttled 2.5.45 at Travemünde

Served with
8 U-Flottille, Danzig December 1944 - January 1945 (ab)
5 U-Flottille, Kiel January 1945 - 2.5.45 (ab)

Commanded by
KL Helmut Münster December 1944 - April 1945

Patrols: None   Ships sunk: None

U 3517 was scuttled on 2.5.45 at Travemünde to prevent her falling into Allied hands.
   The wreck was later broken up.

U 3518   Type XXI

Built by Schichau, Danzig
Keel laid 12.9.44   Launched 11.12.44
Commissioned 29.12.44   Feldpost Nr M 49 695

Scuttled 3.5.45 at Kiel

Served with
8 U-Flottille, Danzig December 1944 - January 1945 (ab)
5 U-Flottille, Kiel January 1945 - 3.5.45 (ab)

Commanded by
KL Herbert Brünning December 1944 - March 1945

Patrols: None   Ships sunk: None

The boat was scuttled on 3.5.45 at Kiel to prevent her falling into Allied hands.
   The wreck was later broken up.

U 3519   Type XXI

Built by Schichau, Danzig
Keel laid 19.9.44   Launched 23.11.44
Commissioned 7.1.45   Feldpost Nr M 49 699

Sunk 2.3.45 off Warnemünde

Served with
8 U-Flottille, Danzig January 1945 (ab)
5 U-Flottille, Kiel January 1945 - 2.3.45 (--)

Commanded by
KL Richard von Harpe January 1945 - 2.3.45

Patrols: None   Ships sunk: None

U 3519 was sunk by an RAF-laid mine off Warnemünde on 2.3.45. The commander and 64 men lost their lives.

U 3520   Type XXI

Built by Schichau, Danzig
Keel laid 20.9.44   Launched 23.11.44
Commissioned 12.1.45   Feldpost Nr M 49 700

Sunk 31.1.45 off Bülk (54°27´N 09°26´E)

Served with
8 U-Flottille, Danzig January 1945 (ab)

Commanded by
KL Sarto Ballert January 1945

Patrols: None   Ships sunk: None

U 3520 sank after striking a mine off Bülk, in Eckernförde Bucht. The commander and 58 men were lost. The wreck was later raised and broken up.

U 3521   Type XXI

Built by Schichau, Danzig
Keel laid --.10.44   Launched 3.12.44
Commissioned 14.1.45   Feldpost Nr M 49 708

Scuttled 3.5.45 at Travemünde

Served with
8 U-Flottille, Danzig January 1945 (ab)
5 U-Flottille, Kiel January 1945 - 3.5.45 (ab)

Commanded by
OL Günther Keller January 1945 - 3.5.45

Patrols: None   Ships sunk: None

U 3521 was scuttled on 3.5.45 at Travemünde to prevent her falling into Allied hands.
   The wreck was later broken up.

U 3522   Type XXI

Built by Schichau, Danzig
Keel laid --.10.44   Launched 3.12.44
Commissioned 14.1.45   Feldpost Nr M 49 751

Scuttled 2.5.45 at Travemünde

Served with
5 U-Flottille, Kiel   January 1945 - 2.5.45 (ab)

Commanded by
OL Dieter Lenzmann   January 1945 - 2.5.45

Patrols: None   Ships sunk: None

U 3522 was scuttled on 2.5.45 off Travemünde to prevent her falling into Allied hands.
   The wreck was later broken up.

U 3523   Type XXI

Built by Schichau, Danzig
Keel laid --.10.44   Launched 14.12.44
Commissioned 29.1.45   Feldpost Nr M 49 765

Sunk 6.5.45 NNE of Skagen (57°52´N 10°49´E)

Served with
5 U-Flottille, Kiel   January 1945 - 6.5.45 (ab)

Commanded by
OL Willi Müller   January 1945 - 6.5.45

Patrols: None   Ships sunk: None

U 3523 was outward-bound from Kiel when she was attacked and sunk on 6.5.45 NNE of Skagen by a Liberator of 86 Squadron (F/Lt T H E Goldie).
   The commander and 56 men were lost.

U 3524   Type XXI

Built by Schichau, Danzig
Keel laid --. 10.44   Launched 14.12.44
Commissioned 26.1.45   Feldpost Nr M 52 272

Scuttled 5.5.45 in Geltinger Bucht

Served with
5 U-Flottille, Kiel   January 1945 - 5.5.45 (ab)

Commanded by
KK Hans-Ludwig Witt   January 1945 - 5.5.45

Patrols: None   Ships sunk: None

U 3524 was one of many boats which left their bases in early May and went to the bays of Northern Germany, to await further orders.
   She was scuttled on 5.5.45 in Geltinger Bucht, in accordance with Operation Regenbogen *but contrary to the surrender terms.*

U 3525   Type XXI

Built by Schichau, Danzig
Keel laid 17.10.44   Launched 23.12.44
Commissioned 31.1.45   Feldpost Nr M 52 280

Scuttled 3.5.45 at Kiel

Served with
5 U-Flottille, Kiel   January 1945 - 3.5.45 (ab)

Commanded by
KL Hans-Ludwig Gaude   January - April 1945
KL Franz Kranich   April 1945 - 3.5.45

Patrols: None   Ships sunk: None

After being bombed in the western Baltic on 30.4.45, U 3525 was taken to Kiel. She was scuttled there on 3.5.45 to prevent her falling into Allied hands.
   The wreck was later broken up.

U 3526   Type XXI

Built by Schichau, Danzig
Keel laid 15.10.44   Launched 23.12.44
Commissioned 22.3.45   Feldpost Nr M 52 300

Scuttled 5.5.45 in Flensburger Förde

Served with
5 U-Flottille, Kiel   March 1945 - 5.5.45 (ab)

Commanded by
OL Kurt Hilbig   March 1945 - 5.5.45

Patrols: None   Ships sunk: None

When Danzig was threatened by the advance of the Red Army, U 3526 was moved to the Bremer Vulkan yard to be completed.
   The boat was one of many which left their bases in early May and went to the bays of Northern Germany, to await further orders.
   She was scuttled on 5.5.45 in Flensburger Förde, in accordance with Operation Regenbogen *but contrary to the surrender terms.*

U 3527   Type XXI

Built by Shichau, Danzig
Keel laid 25.10.44   Launched 10.1.45
Commissioned 10.3.45   Feldpost Nr M 52 331

Scuttled 5.5.45 at Wesermünde

Served with
5 U-Flottille, Kiel   March 1945 - 5.5.45 (ab)

Commanded by
KL Willy Kronenbitter   March 1945 - 5.5.45

Patrols: None   Ships sunk: None

When Danzig was threatened by the advance of the Red Army, U 3527 was moved to the Bremer Vulkan yard to be completed.
   She was scuttled on 5.5.45 at Wesermünde, in accordance with Operation Regenbogen *but contrary to the surrender terms.*

U 3528 Type XXI

Built by Schichau, Danzig
Keel laid 26.10.44   Launched 10.1.45
Commissioned 18.3.45   Feldpost Nr M 52 347

Scuttled 5.5.45 at Wesermünde

Served with
5 U-Flottille, Kiel March 1945 - 5.5.45 (ab)

Commanded by
KL Heinz Zwarg March 1945 - 5.5.45

Patrols: None   Ships sunk: None

When Danzig was threatened by the advance of the Red Army, U 3528 was moved to the Bremer Vulkan yard to be completed.
    She was scuttled on 5.5.45 at Wesermünde, in accordance with Operation Regenbogen *but contrary to the surrender terms.*
    The wreck was later broken up.

U 3529 Type XXI

Built by Schichau, Danzig
Keel laid 2.11.44   Launched 26.1.45
Commissioned 22.3.45   Feldpost Nr M 52 359

Scuttled 5.5.45 in Flensburger Förde

Served with
5 U-Flottille, Kiel March 1945 - 5.5.45 (ab)

Commanded by
OL Karl-Heinz Schmidt March 1945 - 5.5.45

Patrols: None   Ships sunk: None

When Danzig was threatened by the advance of the Red Army, U 3529 was moved to the Bremer Vulkan yard to be completed.
    She was scuttled on 5.5.45 in Flensburger Förde, in accordance with Operation Regenbogen *but contrary to the surrender terms.*
    The wreck was later broken up.

U 3530 Type XXI

Built by Schichau, Danzig
Keel laid 3.11.44   Launched 26.1.45
Commissioned 23.3.45   Feldpost Nr M 52 375

Scuttled 3.5.45 at Kiel

Served with
5 U-Flottille, Kiel March 1945 - 3.5.45 (ab)

Commanded by
KL Wilhelm Brauel March - April 1945

Patrols: None   Ships sunk: None

When Danzig was threatened by the advance of the Red Army, U 3530 was moved to the Bremer Vulkan yard to be completed.
    She was scuttled on 3.5.45 at Kiel to prevent her falling into Allied hands.
    The wreck was later broken up.

U 3531 - U 3695 were never completed during the war. Some boats may have been finished off by the Russians.

U 3696 - U 4000 were projected but never built.

U 4001 - U 4120 were never completed.

U 4121 - U 4500 were projected but never built.

U 4501 - U 4600 were never completed.

U 4601 - U 4700 were never built, orders cancelled.

U 4701 Type XXIII

Built by Germania Werft, Kiel
Keel laid 13.10.44   Launched 14.12.44
Commissioned 10.1.45   Feldpost Nr M 50 536

Scuttled 5.5.45 at Höruphaff

Served with
5 U-Flottille, Kiel January 1945 - 5.5.45 (ab)

Commanded by
OL Arnold Wiechmann January 1945 - 5.5.45

Patrols: None   Ships sunk: None

U 4701 was one of many boats which left their bases in early May and went to the bays of Northern Germany, to await further orders.
    She was scuttled at Höruphaff on 5.5.45, in accordance with Operation Regenbogen *but contrary to the surrender terms.*

U 4702 Type XXIII

Built by Germania Werft, Kiel
Keel laid 15.10.44   Launched 20.12.44
Commissioned 22.1.45   Feldpost Nr M 50 558

Scuttled 5.5.45 at Höruphaff

Served with
5 U-Flottille, Kiel January 1945 - 5.5.45 (ab)

Commanded by
OL Edgar Seeliger January 1945 - 5.5.45

Patrols: None   Ships sunk: None

U 4702 was one of many boats which left their bases in early May and went to the bays of Northern Germany, to await further orders.
    She was scuttled on 5.5.45 at Höruphaff, in accordance with Operation Regenbogen *but contrary to the surrender terms.*

U 4703   Type XXIII

Built by Germania Werft, Kiel
Keel laid 27.10.44   Launched 3.1.45
Commissioned 21.1.45   Feldpost Nr M 50 566

Scuttled 5.5.45 at Höruphaff

Served with
5 U-Flottille, Kiel   January 1945 - 5.5.45 (ab)

Commanded by
OL Hans-Ulrich Scholz   January 1945 - 5.5.45

Patrols: None   Ships sunk: None

*U 4703 was one of many boats which left their bases in early May
and went to the bays of Northern Germany, to await further orders.*
  She was scuttled on 5.5.45 at Höruphaff, in accordance with
Operation Regenbogen *but contrary to the surrender terms.*

U 4704   Type XXIII

Built by Germania Werft, Kiel
Keel laid --.11.44   Launched 13.2.45
Commissioned 14.3.45   Feldpost Nr M 50 593

Scuttled 5.5.45 at Höruphaff

Served with
5 U-Flottille, Kiel   March 1945 - 5.5.45

Commanded by
OL Gerhard Franceschi   March 1945 - 5.5.45

Patrols: None   Ships sunk: None

U 4704 was covered in Alberich, the rubber anti-sonar coating.

*She was one of many boats which left their bases in early May and
went to the bays of Northern Germany, to await further orders.*
  U 4704 was scuttled on 5.5.45 at Höruphaff, in accordance with
Operation Regenbogen *but contrary to the surrender terms.*

U 4705   Type XXIII

Built by Germania Werft, Kiel
Keel laid 11.11.44   Launched 11.1.45
Commissioned 2.2.45   Feldpost Nr M 50 646

Scuttled 3.5.45 at Kiel

Served with
5 U-Flottille, Kiel   February 1945 - 3.5.45 (ab)

Commanded by
OL Martin Landt-Hayen   February 1945 - 3.5.45

Patrols: None   Ships sunk: None

*U 4705 was scuttled on 3.5.45 at Kiel to prevent her falling into
Allied hands.*

U 4706   Type XXIII

Built by Germania Werft, Kiel
Keel laid 14.11.44   Launched 19.1.45
Commissioned 7.2.45   Feldpost Nr M 50 650

Surrendered 9.5.45 at Kristiansand

Served with
5 U-Flottille, Kiel   February 1945 - 9.5.45 (ab)

Commanded by
OL Manfred Schneider   February 1945 - 9.5.45

Patrols: None   Ships sunk: None

*U 4706 was surrendered at Kristiansand on 9.5.45. In July 1945
the boat was handed over to the Royal Norwegian Navy and later
became submarine* Knerter.
  She was taken out of service in 1953 and scrapped.

U 4707   Type XXIII

Built by Germania Werft, Kiel
Keel laid 23.11.44   Launched 25.1.45
Commissioned 20.2.45   Feldpost Nr M 50 698

Scuttled 5.5.45 in Geltinger Bucht

Served with
5 U-Flottille, Kiel   February 1945 - 5.5.45 (ab)

Commanded by
OL Joachim Leder   February 1945 - 5.5.45

Patrols: None   Ships sunk: None

*U 4707 was one of many boats which left their bases in early May
and went ot the bays of Northern Germany, to await further orders.*
  *She was scuttled on 5.5.45 in Geltinger Bucht, in accordance
with* Operation Regenbogen *but contrary to the surrender terms.*

*U 4708 was destroyed in a bombing raid on the Germania Werft
yard at Kiel on 9.4.45, three days before commissioning.*

U 4709   Type XXIII

Built by Germania Werft, Kiel
Keel laid --.12.44   Launched 8.2.45
Commissioned 3.3.45   Feldpost Nr M 50 727

Scuttled 4.5.45 at Kiel

Served with
5 U-Flottille, Kiel   March 1945 - 4.5.45 (ab)

Commanded by
OL Paul Berkemann   March 1945 - 4.5.45

Patrols: None   Ships sunk: None

*U 4709 was scuttled on 4.5.45 at Kiel to prevent her falling into
Allied hands.*

U 4710 Type XXIII

Built by Germania Werft, Kiel
Keel laid --.12.44 Launched 14.4.45
Commissioned 1.5.45 Feldpost Nr M 52 881

Scuttled 5.5.45 in Geltinger Bucht

Served with
5 U-Flottille, Kiel May 1945 (ab)

Commanded by
OL Ludwig-Ferdinand von Friedeburg May 1945

Patrols: None Ships sunk: None

*U 4710 was one of many boats which left their bases in early May
and went to the bays of Northern Germany, to await further orders.*
*She was scuttled on 5.5.45 in Geltinger Bucht, in accordance
with* Operation Regenbogen *but contrary to the surrender terms.*

U 4711 Type XXIII

Built by Germania Werft, Kiel
Keel laid --.12.44 Launched 21.2.45
Commissioned 21.3.45 Feldpost Nr M 52 893

Scuttled 4.5.45 at Kiel

Served with
5 U-Flottille, Kiel March 1945 - 4.5.45 (ab)

Commanded by
OL Siegfried Endler March 1945 - 4.5.45

Patrols: None Ships sunk: None

*U 4711 was scuttled at Kiel on 4.5.45 to prevent her falling into
Allied hands.*

U 4712 Type XXIII

Built by Germania Werft, Kiel
Keel laid 3.1.45 Launched 1.3.45
Commissioned 3.4.45 Feldpost Nr M 52 911

Scuttled 4.5.45 at Kiel

Served with
5 U-Flottille, Kiel April 1945 - 4.5.45 (ab)

Commanded by
OL Karlheinz Rohlfing April 1945 4.5.45

Patrols: None Ships sunk: None

*U 4712 was scuttled at Kiel on 4.5.45 to prevent her falling into
Allied hands.*

*U 4713 and U 4714 were scuttled at Kiel on 3.5.45, shortly before
they were due for completion.*

UA Ex-Turkish *Batiray*

Built by Germania Werft, Kiel
Keel laid 10.2.37 Launched 28.9.38
Commissioned 20.9.39 Feldpost Nr M 00 073

Scuttled 3.5.45 at Kiel

*The boat was originally ordered by the Turkish Navy. She was taken
over by the Kriegsmarine at the outbreak of war, 3.9.39. She was
temporarily named* Optimist *but became UA on 21.9.39.*

Served with
U-Flottille Wegener, Kiel September - December 1939 (ab)
7 U-Flottille, Kiel January - May 1940 (ab/fb-t)
7 U-Flottille, Kiel/St Nazaire June 1940 - August 1942 (fb/fb-v)
U-Abwehrschule, Gotenhafen July 1942 - February 1943
4 U-Flottille, Stettin March 1943 - November 1944 (vb)
24 U-Flottille, Memel November 1944 - 3.5.45 (ab)

Commanded by
KL Hans Cohausz September 1939 - November 1940
KK Hans Eckermann November 1940 - January 1942
KK Hans Cohausz February - May 1942
OL Ebe Schnoor May - August 1942
KK Friedrich Schäfer October 1942 - March 1944
OL Ulrich-Philipp Graf von und zu Arco-Zinneberg
                              April 1944 - March 1945

Patrols: 7 Ships sunk: 7 (40,706 grt) + 1 damaged

1. 27.4.40 Left Kiel on transport duties, carrying aircraft bombs
and aviation fuel to Norway. Unloaded at Trondheim 2-5.5.40.
    The boat returned to Kiel **10.5.40**

2. 6.6.40 Left for the North Atlantic.
    UA patrolled initially S of Iceland and on the 16th she torpedoed
and sank the armed merchant cruiser *Andania* (br 13950t) ESE of
Vik, Iceland.
    The boat was ordered southwards and on the 26th she sank the
MV *Crux* (nw 3828t) W of Cape St Vincent. She became the first
boat to operate in the Central Atlantic. On 14.7.40 UA sank the
tanker SS *Sarita* (nw 5824t) just W of the Cape Verde Islands.
    On the 19th UA was refuelled and replenished by the German
auxiliary cruiser *Schiff 33/Pinguin* 650 miles NNW of St Paul Rocks.
The boat was taken in tow by *Pinguin* on the 25th and taken
towards Freetown. During the first night, UA cast off the line to
attack a tanker. The torpedo fired circled and almost hit the boat as
the tanker continued on her way.
    UA was taken in tow again but when the line parted on the 28th,
UA and *Pinguin* went their separate ways. The boat operated
only briefly off Freetown but engine trouble necessitated an earlier
return to base than planned.
    On 3.8.40 UA sank the SS *Rad* (yg 4201t) SW of Dakar, on the
15th the SS *Aspasia* (gr 4211t) NW of Madeira, on the 19th the
SS *Kelet* (hu 4295t) N of the Azores and on the 20th the SS *Tuira*
(pa 4397t) SW of Rockall.
    UA returned to Kiel **30.8.40**

3. 25.2.41 Left Kiel for the North Atlantic.
    UA was one of seven boats which formed a patrol line on 4.3.41
to intercept convoy OB 292 on the 5th W of the British Isles. The
convoy avoided the waiting boats. On the 8th UA attacked convoy
OB 293 S of Iceland and she torpedoed and damaged the
SS *Dunaff Head* (br 5258t).
    The boat put in to Lorient **18.3.41**

4. 14.4.41 Left Lorient for operations.

UA (continued)

The boat suffered damage to her rudder on the 20th and returned to Lorient **26.4.41**

5. 3.5.41   Left for the Central Atlantic.

UA was refuelled by the German supply ship *Egerland* on the 28th. The boat went on to operate off Freetown but she had no success. On 18.6.41 UA was scheduled for refuelling by the supply ship *Lothringen* but she had been sunk in early June.

UA returned to Lorient **30.7.41**

6. 7.10.41   Left Lorient and returned **9.10.41**

7. 21.10.41   Left for the Central Atlantic.

On 22.11 41 the supply ship *Schiff 16/Atlantis* was sunk NW of Ascension and survivors were picked up by U 126 and transferred to the German supply ship *Python* during the night of the 23/24th.

UA and U 68 rendezvoused with the *Python* during the night of November 30th/December 1st 780 miles S of St Helena. Whilst the two boats were being refuelled during daylight on the 1st, the *Python* was surprised by the cruiser HMS *Dorsetshire*. The boats dived and UA is believed to have fired five torpedoes at the cruiser, which all missed. *Python* stopped, those aboard abandoned ship and *Python* was sunk by gunfire from the *Dorsetshire*, which then promptly left the scene.

There were 414 survivors to be dealt with and UA and U 68 took aboard 100 men each and the other 214 were distributed in lifeboats or on rafts, which were then taken in tow by the two boats. The procession moved northwards and on 5.12.41 it rendezvoused with U 124 and U 129, which between them took aboard the 214 men being towed. All four boats continued northwards until the 16th, when they rendezvoused with four Italian submarines N of the Cape Verde Islands.

Between them, the *Torrelli*, *Tazzoli*, *Finzi* and *Calvi* took aboard half the survivors and the eight boats all headed for French ports. All the men were landed in the last week in December.

UA, with 54 survivors aboard, returned to Lorient **25.12.41**

8. 21.2.42   Left Lorient and returned **22.2.42**

9. 14.3.42   Left for Germany, via the North Atlantic.

En route, UA acted as an auxiliary tanker and supplied three boats, U 203 in late March and U 84 on 2.4.42, both outward-bound for the US east coast, and the returning U 202 on the 3rd. It was the first operation of this type, pioneering the supplying of one boat by another.

UA reached Bergen on 19.4.42 and then went on to Kiel, reaching there **24.4.42**

UA carried out no more operational patrols. She went on to training duties in July 1942 and may also have been used for experimental puposes at 4 U-Flottille.

UA was scuttled on 3.5.45 at Kiel to prevent her falling into Allied hands. The wreck was later broken up.

UB   Ex-British HMS *Seal*

Built in the Admiralty Dockyard, Chatham
Launched 27.9.38   Went into service May 1939

Commissioned into the Kriegsmarine at Kiel 30.11.40   No Feldpost Nr

Scuttled 3.5.45 at Kiel

Served with
1 U-Flottille, Kiel   November 1940 - May 1941 (vb)
3 U-Flottille, Kiel   May 1941 - 31.7.41 (vb)

Commanded by
FK Bruno Mahn   November 1940 - 31.7.41

Patrols: None   Ships sunk: None

In early January 1940 HMS *Seal*, a Porpoise class submarine, joined the 6th Submarine Flotilla at Rosyth, Firth of Forth. From that time she began to carry out convoy-escorts to Norway and patrols along the Norwegian coast.

On 29.4.40 *Seal* was on a minelaying operation, to lay 50 mines off Gothenburg, Sweden. *Seal's* presence in the area was known to the Germans. She had been sighted and attacked by aircraft on 3.5.40, sustaining some damage to her pressure hull.

After laying her mines on the 4th, *Seal* turned for home but was almost immediately located by a group of vessels of the German 12th Anti-Submarine Flotilla. The hunt for *Seal* went on for eight hours, into the evening.

At 19.00 hrs a tremendous explosion sent *Seal* to the bottom, with her bows inclined upward at an angle of some 10°. Six hours later, after several failed attempts, *Seal's* commander, Lt-Cdr Lonsdale, managed to resurface.

He radioed the Admiralty, advising of his serious situation. *Seal* was partly flooded, her rudder was jammed, the electric motors were out of action and only one diesel engine was partly working. Lonsdale stated his intent to head for neutral Sweden. The crew worked hard to made some sort of way but without success.

At first light the inevitable aircraft appeared, an Arado floatplane, and attacks began with machine guns and bombs. A second Arado arrived and joined the attack. *Seal* replied with her Lewis guns but when a He 115 appeared, *Seal's* situation was hopeless.

Lonsdale very reluctantly decided to surrender, rather than sacrifice his crew needlessly. On seeing the white table-cloth flying from the conning tower, one of the Arados landed near *Seal* and Lonsdale swam to it and was hauled aboard. The aircraft then took off to return to its base at Aalborg. The second Arado touched down and shouted for someone to swim over, as a hostage. Petty Officer Cousins obliged and the aircraft took off.

Almost immediately sub-chaser UJ-128 appeared. She hove to, lowered a motor-boat and made for *Seal*. The crew were eventually taken off and the submarine was taken in tow. She went into Frederikshavn, where she was made seaworthy for transfer to Kiel.

Early on 10.5.40 *Seal* was towed out with an escort of sub-chasers and He 115s and she arrived at Kiel in the afternoon of the 11th. Priority was arranged and she went to the Germania Werft yard for restoration and refit.

For a month Lonsdale and his crew remained at Kiel and were interrogated before being sent to PoW camps. After the war Lonsdale was court-martialled on charges of 'failure to engage the enemy' and 'allowing the submarine to fall into enemy hands'. He was honourably acquitted on both charges.

Seal was commissioned into the Kriegsmarine at Kiel on 30.11.40 as UB. She served with 1 and 3 U-Flottillen as an experimental boat until she was decommissioned on 31.7.41.

The boat was scuttled at Kiel on 3.5.45.

UC 1   Ex-Norwegian *B 5*

Built by Martinens Hivedwerft, Horten
Launched 17.6.29   Commissioned 1.10.29

Commissioned into the Kriegsmarine 20.11.40   Feldpost Nr M 10 850

Decommissioned 28.3.42, possibly at Bergen

Served with
U-Abwehrschule, Gotenhafen June 1941 - 28.3.42 (sb)

Commanded by
KL Wilhelm Kiesewetter   November 1940 - May 1941
KL Georg Lange   June - December 1941
Lt Karl Brockmann   December 1941 - 28.3.42

Patrols: None   Ships sunk: None

*UC 1 was originally submarine B 5 in the Royal Norwegian Navy.
She was taken as a prize to Kristiansand and commissioned into
the Kriegsmarine at Kiel on 20.11.40.*
   *The boat was at the U-Abwehrschule from June 1941 but was
taken out of service on 4.1.42 because of fire damage.*
   UC 1 was decommissioned on 28.3.42 and later broken up.

UC 2   Ex-Norwegian *B 6*

Built by Martinens Hivedwerft, Horten
Launched 4.8.29   Commissioned 1.5.30

Commissioned into the Kriegsmarine 17.11.41   Feldpost Nr M 43 628

Scuttled 3.5.45 at Kiel

Served with
U-Abwehrschule, Gotenhafen/Bergen
                           November 1941 - November 1943 (sb)

Commanded by
OL Otto Wollschläger November 1941 - November 1943

Patrols: None   Ships sunk: None

*UC 2 was originally submarine B 6 in the Royal Norwegian Navy.
She was taken as a prize to Florö and commissioned into the
Kriegsmarine on 17.11.41. Details of her units served with and
commanders up to her commissioning date are unknown.*
   *The boat was on training duties until she was decommissioned
in November 1943 at Kiel.*
   *She was scuttled on 3.5.45 at Kiel to prevent her falling into
Allied hands.*
   The wreck was later broken up.

UD 1   Ex-Norwegian *O 8*

Built by Canadian Vickers, Montreal   Launched August 1915

Commissioned into the Kriegsmarine 21.11.40   Feldpost Nr M 28 540

Scuttled 3.5.45 at Kiel

Served with
U-Abwehrschule, Gotenhafen November 1940 - May 1941 (sb/eb)
3 U-Flottille, Kiel May - August 1941 (vb)
5 U-Flottille, Kiel August - December 1941 (vb)
U-Abwehrschule, Gotenhafen/Bergen December 1941 - 23.11.43

Commanded by
KK Hermann Rigele   November 1940 - May 1941
KL Friedrich Schäfer   May - November 1941
KL Franz Venier November 1941 - December 1942
KL Wolfgang Ketelsen December 1942 - May 1943
OL Friedrich Weidner May 1943 - 23.11.43

Patrols: None   Ships sunk: None

*UD 1 was originally British submarine S 6 in the First World War.
She was interned after running aground at Schiermonnikoog on
18.1.16. The boat was later purchased by the Netherlands and
became submarine O 8.*
   *She was taken by the Germans as a prize on 14.5.40 at Den
Helder and was commissioned into the Kriegsmarine on 21.11.40
as UD 1.*
   *The boat was on training and experimental duties until she was
decommissioned on 23.11.43 at Kiel.*
   *UD 1 was scuttled on 3.5.45 at Kiel to prevent her falling into
Allied hands.*
   The wreck was later broken up.

UD 2   Ex-Netherlands *O 12*

Built by De Schelde, Flushing   Launched 8.11.30

Commissioned into the Kriegsmarine 28.1.41   Feldpost Nr M 35 992

Scuttled 3.5.45 at Kiel

Served with
U-Abwehrschule, Gotenhafen/Bergen January 1943 - 6.7.44 (sb)

Commanded by
KK Franz Venier January 1943 - April 1944
OL Günther Scholz April 1944 - 6.7.44

Patrols: None   Ships sunk: None

*UD 2 was originally submarine O 12 in the Royal Netherlands
Navy. She was scuttled on 14.5.40 at Willemsoord but was later
salved and taken as a prize by the Germans.*
   *The boat was commissioned into the Kriegsmarine on 28.1.41
and went on to training duties. She was decommissioned at Bergen
on 6.7.44.*
   *UD 2 was scuttled on 3.5.45 at Kiel to prevent her falling into
Allied hands.*
   The wreck was later broken up.

UD 3   Ex-Netherlands *O 25*

Built by Wilton-Fijenoord, Schiedam   Launched 1.5.40

Commissioned into the Kriegsmarine 8.6.41   Feldpost Nr M 38 047

Scuttled 3.5.45 at Kiel

Served with
3 U-Flottille, Kiel   June - July 1941 (vb)
5 U-Flottille, Kiel   July - August 1941 (ab)
2 U-Flottille, Kiel   August 1941 - September 1942 (ab)
10 U-Flottille, Lorient   September 1942 - February 1943 (fb)
U-Abwehrschule, Gotenhafen/Bergen   March 1943 - 13.10.44 (sb)

Commanded by
KK Hermann Rigele   June 1941 - October 1943
OL Joachim Seeger   October 1943 - 13.10.44

Patrols: 1   Ships sunk: 1 (5041 grt)

UD 3 was originally submarine O 25 in the Royal Netherlands Navy.   Uncompleted, she was scuttled in the dockyard in May 1940. The boat was raised in June, completed by the Germans and commissioned into the Kriegsmarine on 8.6.41. After experimental use and training duties, UD 3 became operational in October 1942.

1. 3.10.42   Left Kiel and arrived Lorient **22.10.42**

2. 3.11.42   Left for operations in the Central Atlantic.
   In mid-November UD 2 was refuelled by U 462 near the Cape Verde Islands. On the 26th she torpedoed and sank the MV *Indra* (nw 5041t) near St Paul Rocks. She returned to Lorient **7.1.43**

3. 10.2.43   Left Lorient and arrived Bergen **26.2.43**

4. 27.2.43   Left Bergen and arrived Gotenhafen **3.3.43**

U D 3 returned to Kiel and was taken out of service. She resumed training duties at the U-Abwehrschule. UD 3 was decommissioned on 13.10.43 after being damaged in a bombing raid on Kiel.
   She was scuttled there on 3.5.45.

UD 4   Ex-Netherlands submarine *O 26*

Built by Rotterdam Dry Dock Co.   Launched 23.11.40

Commissioned into the Kriegsmarine 28.1.41   Feldpost Nr M 30 414

Scuttled 3.5.45 at Kiel

Served with
3 U-Flottille, Kiel   May - August 1941 (vb)
5 U-Flottille, Kiel   August 1941 - December 1942 (ab)
27 U-Flottille, Gotenhafen   January 1943 - November 1944 (sb)
24 U-Flottille, Memel   November 1944 - January 1945 (sb)
18 U-Flottille, Gotenhafen   January - March 1945 (ab)

Commanded by
KK Helmut Brümmer-Patzig   January - October 1941
KK Rudolf Singule   November 1941 - April 1942
KL Hinrich-Oscar Bernbeck   April - October 1942
KK Friedrich Schäfer   April - November 1944
KL Fritz Bart   November 1944 - March 1945

Patrols: None   Ships sunk: None

UD 4 was originally submarine O 26 of the Royal Netherlands Navy. She was still under construction when taken by the Germans as a prize on 14.5.40. Work was completed and she was launched on 23.11.40 and commissioned into the Kriegsmarine on 28.1.41.
   UD 4 was on training duties. The early experiments with Alberich, the rubber anti-sonar coating, were carried out using this boat.
   She was scuttled on 3.5.45 at Kiel to prevent her falling into Allied hands.
   The wreck was later broken up.

UD 5   Ex-Netherlands *O 27*

Built by Rotterdam Dry Dock Co.   Launched 26.9.41

Commissioned into the Kriegsmarine 1.11.41   Feldpost Nr M 38 894

Surrendered at Bergen 9.5.45

Served with
5 U-Flottille, Kiel   November 1941 - August 1942 (ab)
10 U-Flottille, Lorient   August 1942 - January 1943 (fb)
U-Abwehrschule, Bergen   January 1943 - 9.5.45 (sb)

Commanded by
KzS Bruno Mahn   November 1941 - December 1942
OL Klaus-Dietrich König (temp)   December 1942
KL Horst-Tessen von Kameke   January - April 1943
KL Hans-Urich Scheltz   April 1943 - 9.5.45

Patrols: 1   Ships sunk: 1 (7628 grt)

UD 5 was originally submarine O 27 of the Royal Netherlands Navy. She was still under construction when taken by the Germans as a prize on 14.5.40. Work was completed and she was launched on 26.9.41 and commissioned into the Kriegsmarine on 1.11.41. The boat became operational in August 1942.

1. 27.8.42   Left Kiel and arrived Marviken **28.8.42**

2. 30.8.42   Left for the Central Atlantic.
   In October UD 5 was operating in an area W of Freetown. In late October the returning boat was refuelled W of the Cape Verde Islands by U 462.
   On the 29th UD 5 torpedoed and sank the SS *Primrose Hill* (br 7628t) NW of the Islands.
   The boat put in to Lorient **12.11.42**

3. 21.12.42   Left Lorient and arrived Bergen **3.1.43**

4. 4.1.43   Left Bergen and arrived Kiel **9.1.43**

UD 5 went on to training duties, as a school boat.
   She was surrendered at Bergen on 9.5.45 and left there on the 30th for an assembly area in Britain. On 13.7.45 the boat left Dundee to return to the Netherlands, where she was recommissioned into the Royal Netherlands Navy as O 27.
   The submarine was decommissioned on 14.11.59 and broken up in 1961.

UF 2 Ex-French *La Favorite*

Built by Chanier, Le Trait   Launched September 1938

Commissioned into the Kriegsmarine 24.11.42   Feldpost Nr M 50 058

Scuttled in early May 1945 at Gotenhafen

Served with
5 U-Flottille, Kiel   November - December 1942 (ab)
U-Abwehrschule, Gotenhafen/Bergen   January 1943 - 5.7.44 (sb)

Commanded by
KL Georg Lange   November 1942 - October 1943
OL Heinrich Gehrken   October 1943 - 5.7.44

Patrols: None   Ships sunk: None

UF 2 was originally submarine La Favorite *in the French Navy. She was taken as a German prize in June 1940. Work on her was completed at Le Trait, France on 5.11.42 and she was commissioned into the Kriegsmarine on 24.11.42.*

The boat was on training duties until decommissioned at Gotenhafen on 5.7.44. UF 2 was scuttled at Gotenhafen in early May 1945.

The wreck was later broken up.

UIT 21 Ex-Italian *Giuseppe Finzi*

Built by Odero-Terni-Orlando, Muggiano   Launched 29.6.35

Commissioned into the Kriegsmarine 14.10.43   Feldpost Nr M 55 490

Scuttled 25.8.44 at Bordeaux

Served with
12 U-Flottille, Bordeaux   October 1943 - 15.4.44 (fb-t-oE)

Commanded by
OL Friedrich Steinfeld   October 1943 - 15.4.44

Patrols: None   Ships sunk: None

UIT 21 was originally submarine Giuseppe Finzi *in the Italian Navy. She was taken over by the Germans in Bordeaux on 8.9.43, after the Italians surrendered.*

The boat was commissioned into the Kriegsmarine on 14.10.43 as a transport boat but was declared to be non-operational.

She was decommissioned at Bordeaux on 15.4.44 and scuttled there on 25.8.44 to prevent her falling into Allied hands.

UIT 22 Ex-Italian *Alpino Bagnolini*

Built by Franco Tosi, Taranto   Launched 28.10.39

Commissioned into the Kriegsmarine 11.10.43   Feldpost Nr M 55 509

Sunk 11.3.44 S of Cape Town (41°28′S 17°40′E)

Served with
12 U-Flottille, Bordeaux   October 1943 - 11.3.44 (fb-t)

Commanded by
OL Karl Wunderlich   October 1943 - 11.3.44

Patrols: Ships sunk: None

UIT 22 was originally submarine Alpino Bagnolini *in the Italian Navy. She was taken over by the Germans in Bordeaux on 8.9.43, after the Italians surrendered.*

The boat was commissioned into the Kriegsmarine on 11.10.43 as a transport boat and she became operational in January 1944.

1. 19.1.44   Left Bordeaux and returned **21.1.44**

2. 26.1.44   Left for the Far East.
En route through the south Atlantic, UIT 22 was attacked by a US aircraft SW of Ascension. She was badly damaged and lost fuel. The boat was ordered to rendezvous with U 178 600 miles S of Capetown.

UIT 22 reached the position but during the morning of 11.3.44 she was sighted on the surface by a Catalina of 262 Squadron (F/Lt F T Roddick). The aircraft attacked, dropping five depth-charges and strafing the boat. The badly-listing UIT 22 submerged, leaving a large oil slick. When she resurfaced, Roddick made another strafing atttack.

Other Catalinas arrived to relieve Roddick, whose aircraft had been damaged by return fire. UIT 22, which had again submerged, resurfaced and was straddled with six depth-charges by one of the Catalinas (F/Lt E S S Nash) and strafed by another (F/Lt A H Surridge). The boat was destroyed. U 178 arrived at the rendezvous 15 hours later. 43 men were lost from UIT 22.

UIT 23 Ex-Italian *Reginaldo Giuliani*

Built by Franco Tosi, Taranto   Launched 3.12.39

Commissioned into the Kriegsmarine 6.12.43   Feldpost Nr M 31 170

Sunk 15.2.44 in the Straits of Malacca (04°27′N 100°11′E)

Served with
12 U-Flottille, Bordeaux   October 1943 - 15.2.44 (fb-t)

Commanded by
KK Heinrich Schäfer   December 1943 - 15.2.44
OL Werner Striegler (temp)   February 1944

Patrols: 1   Ships sunk: None

UIT 23 was originally submarine Reginaldo Giuliani *in the Italian Navy. When Italy surrendered on 8.9.43, the boat was in Penang to pick up a cargo of strategic materials for passage to Europe. She was seized by the Japanese and subsequently handed over to the Germans and commissioned into the Kriegsmarine on 6.12.43.*

UIT 23 (continued)

UIT 23 left Shonan for Penang on 14.2.44, under the command of the 1 WO. On the 15th the boat was torpedoed and sunk by the submarine HMS Tally Ho *(Lt L W A Bennington) in the Straits of Malacca.*

31 men were lost and 14, including the commander, were picked up by Japanese forces.

UIT 24   Ex-Italian *Commandante Cappellini*

Built by Odero-Terni-Orlando, Muggiano   Launched 14.5.39

Commissioned into the Kriegsmarine 6.12.43   Feldpost Nr M 31 365

Handed over 10.5.45 at Kobe

Served with
12 U-Flottille, Bordeaux December 1943 - September 1944 (fb-t)
33 U-Flottille, Penang September 1944 - 10.5.45 (fb-t)

Commanded by
OL Heinrich Pahls December 1943 - 10.5.45

Patrols: 1   Ships sunk: None

UIT 24 was originally submarine Commandante Cappellini *in the Italian Navy.*

When Italy surrendered on 8.9.43, the boat was at Singapore to pick up a cargo of strategic materials for passage to Europe. She was seized by the Japanese, subsequently handed over to the Germans and commissioned into the Kriegsmarine on 6.12.43.

1. **2.2.44** Left Shonan and arrived Penang **3.2.44**

2. **8.2.44** Left Penang for Bordeaux.
UIT 24 had a cargo of 115 tons of rubber, 55 tons of tin and 10 tons of other materials. On 19.3.44 she was refuelled by U 532 after the supply tanker *Brake* was sunk on the 12th.
UIT 24 developed engine trouble and returned to Penang, reaching there on **3.4.44**

3. **5.4.44** Left Penang and arrived Shonan **6.4.44**

4. **25.5.44** Left Shonan and arrived Kobe **6.6.44**

5. **5.9.44** Left Kobe after an overhaul.
UIT 24 returned to Shonan **20.9.44**

6. **28.9.44** Left Shonan and arrived Penang **28.9.44**

7. **10.10.44** Left Penang and arrived Shonan **12.10.44**

8. **15.1.45** Left Shonan and arrived Kobe **18.2.45**

UIT 24 was to return to Europe in September 1944 after having an overhaul at Kobe but this was cancelled when there were no longer any refuelling facilities available en route.

The boat was at Kobe when Germany surrendered on 9.5.45. She was handed over to the Japanese on the 10th and became submarine I 503 in the Imperial Japanese Navy.

The submarine was surrendered to the Americans in August 1945. She was scuttled in April 1946.

UIT 25   Ex-Italian *Luigi Torelli*

Built by Odero-Terni-Orlando, Muggiano   Launched 6.1.40

Commissioned into the Kriegsmarine 6.12.43   Feldpost Nr M 32 441

Handed over 8.5.45 at Kobe

Served with
12 U-Flottille, Bordeaux December 1943 - September 1944 (fb-t)
33 U-Flottille, Penang September 1944 - 10.5.45 (fb-t)

Commanded by
OL Werner Striegler December 1943 - September 1944
KL Herbert Schrein September - November 1944
OL Alfred Meier November 1944 - 10.5.45

Patrols: None   Ships sunk: None

UIT 25 was originally submarine Luigi Torelli *in the Italian Navy.*

When Italy surrendered on 8.9.43, the boat was at Singapore to pick up a cargo of strategic materials for passage to Europe. She was seized by the Japanese, subsequently handed over to the Germans and commissioned into the Kriegsmarine on 6.12.43.

1. **8.2.44** Left Shonan and arrived Penang **10.2.44**

2. **7.3.44** Left Penang and arrived Surabaya **11.3.44**

3. **10.6.44** Left Surabaya and arrived Tama **25.6.44**

4. **--.7.44** Left Tama and arrived Kobe **--.7.44**

UIT 25 was to return to Europe in September 1944 but this was cancelled when there were no longer any refuelling facilities available en route.

When Germany surrendered on 9.5.45 the boat was at Kobe. She had been handed over to the Japanese on the 8th and became submarine I 504 in the Imperial Japanese Navy.

The submarine was surrendered to the Americans in August 1945.

APPENDICES

SKETCH MAPS

1. U-BOAT COMMANDERS   U 511 to UIT 25

Ackermann, Paul 235
Ackermann, Wolf 209
Ady, Gerhard 123, 127
Ahlers, Kurt 233
Albrecht, Karl 223
Altmeier, Friedrich 236
Andersen, Klaus 131
Angermann, Walter 245, 247,
von Arco-Zinneberg, Graf 185, 277
Auffermann, Hans-Jürgen 5
Aust, Eduard 124, 185

Baberg, Kurt 86, 168
Bach, Helmut 125
Bach, Joachim-Werner 226
Bade, Hans-Botho 92
Baden, Hans-Heinrich 190
Bahn, Rolf 181
Balduhn, Ernst-Ludwig 227
Baldus, Hugo 161
Balke, Diethelm 207
Ballert, René 231
Ballert, Sarto 228, 273
Baltz, Rudolf 72
Bargsten, Klaus 11, 37
Barch, Franz 239
Barschkis, Hans-Heinrich 244
Bart, Fritz 280
Bartels, Robert 35
Bartke, Erwin 225
Baum, Heinz 232, 242
Baumann, Heinz 247
Baur, Götz 114
Becker, Philipp 163
Becker, Richard 255
Beckmann, Hans 246
Behnisch, Günter 248
Behrens, Udo 170
Bender, Werner 168
Benker, Hans 91
Benthin, Karl-Dietrich 247
Berkemann, Paul 276
Bernardelli, Richard 166
Bernbeck, Hinrich-Oscar 100, 280
Bertelsmann, Hans-Joachim 72
Besold, Heinrich 243
Bielfeld, Heinz 126, 235
Bigalk, Gerhard 148
Bischoff, Gustav 252
Bitter, Otto 216, 260
von Bitter, Georg 147
Blaich, Ferdinand 267
Blaudow, Ernst-Ulrich 212
Blauert, Hans-Jörg 141
Blischke, Heinz 145
Block, Helmut 160
Blum, Otto-Ulrich 155
Boddenburg, Karl 194
Bode, Thilo 175
Böhm, Hermann 249
Boehmer, Wolfgang 50
Börner, Hans-Joachim 141
Bokelberg, Max 260
Boldt, Walter 138
Boos, Hans-Heinz 213, 217

Bopst, Eberhard 67
Borchardt, Gustav 37
Borchert, Ulrich 41, 58
Borm, Karl 62
Bornkessel, Dieter 247, 254
Bortfeld, Karl-Hermann 229
Bosüner, Harald 235
Brachmann, Hans-Günther 9
Braeucker, Friedrich 183
Brammer, Herbert 222
Brand, Wilhelm 231
Brandi, Albrecht 85, 197
Brans, Hans-Joachim 164
Brasack, Paul 142
Brauel, Wilhelm 201, 206, 275
Braun, Kurt 157
Breckwoldt, Friedrich 124
Breinlinger, Siegfried 266
Breithaupt, Wolfgang 69
von Bremen, Hanskurt 158
Breun, Gerhard 252
Brockmann, Karl 279
Brosin, Hans-Günther 97
Bruder, Hermann 221
Brückner, Werner 250
Brüllau, Heinz 184
Brümmer-Patzig, Helmut 280
Brünig, Matthias 269
Brüninghaus, Herbert 221
Brünner, Joachim 126
Brünning, Herbert 102, 273
Budzyn, Sigmund 251
Büchel, Paul 175
Bugs, Hans-Helmuth 94
Bungards, Hans 224, 257, 265
Burmeister, Walter 217
Buscher, Hans 243
Buttjer, Johann, 160, 161

Cabolet, Servais 184
Callsen, Peter 268
von Carlowitz, Dietrich 132
Carlsen, Klaus-Peter 140
Christiansen, Helmut 243
Christiansen, Uwe 253, 256
Christophersen, Erwin 268
Claussen, August-Wilhelm 236
Coester, Christian-Brandt 23
Cohausz, Hans 277
Collman, Herwig 36
Cordes, Ernst 35, 157, 231
Cremer, Peter Erich 258
Curio, Oskar 187, 259
Czekowski, Martin 253

Dahlhaus, Eberhard 97
Dahms, Hermann 202
Dankleff, Walter 160
Deecke, Joachim 55
Deetz, Friedrich 153
Degen, Horst 125
Deiring, Hugo 270
Dick, Hans-Peter 81
Dieterich, Max 99
Dingler, Gottfried 147

Dobberstein, Erich 206
Dobbert, Max 199, 261, 262
Dobratz, Kurt 238
Döhler, Hans 75
Drescher, Günther 267
Drewitz, Hans-Joachim 14
Drews, Ulrich 260
Dübler, Rudolf 224
Düppe, Joachim 255
Duis, Hans-Diederich 163
Dumrese, Adolf 111
Dunkelberg, Hans 136
Duppel, Martin 193

Eberbach, Heinz-Eugen 197
Eberlein, Otto 218
Ebersbach, Hans-Joachim 201
Ebert, Eberhard 233, 265
Ebert, Jürgen 186
Eck, Heinz-Wilhelm 172
Eckel, Kurt 245
Eckelmann, Heinz 98
Eckermann, Hans, 277
Ehrhardt, Walther 217
von Eickstedt, Wolfgang 120
Eisele, Wilhelm 224
Ellerlage, Hermann 249
Ellmenreich, Helmut 19
Elsinghorst, Josef 167
Emmermann, Carl 269
Endler, Siegfried 277
Endrass, Engelbert 43
Engel, Herbert 118
Eppen, Günter 10
Erdmann, Dieter 31, 183
Ernst, Hans-Joachim 218
von der Esch, Dietrich 57, 75, 177
Euler, Klaus 227
Ewerth, Klaus 172

Faber, Ulrich 217
Fabricius, Fritz 99
Fabricius, Ludwig 166
Fahr, Theodor 43
Falke, Hans (U 992) 207
Falke, Hans (U 1279) 241
Faust, Erich 86
Feiler, Gerhard 109
Feindt, Hans-Arend 153
Ferro, Otto 104
Feufel, Karl 242, 260
Fiebig, Günter 226
Fiedler, Hans 38, 211
Findeisen, Eberhard 181
Fischer, Ernst 147, 166, 264
Fischer, Klaus 194
Fitting, Hans-Hermann 240
Forster, Ludwig 111
Fraatz, Georg-Werner 16, 108
Fränzel, Otto 183, 265
Frahm, Karl 253
Franceschi, Gerhard 276
Franke, Hans-Heino 251
Franke, Heinz 255, 271
Franken, Wilhelm 40

Frerks, Paul 201
von Freyberg-Eisenberg-
  Allmendingen, Walter 79
von Friedeburg, Ludwig 277
Friedrich, Rudolf 155
Frischke, Karl-Heinz 182
Fritz, Detlef 31, 183
Fritze, Günther 234, 272
Frömmer, Heinz 185
Frömsdorf, Helmut 173
Frohberg, Günther 241
Fuchs, Karl-Heinz 16
Fuhlendorf, Harald 249

Gabert, Paul 235
Ganzer, Erwin 180
Gaude, Hans-Ludwig 249, 274
Gebauer, Werner 125
Gehrken, Heinrich 281
Geider, Horst 156
Geisler, Hans-Ferdinand 264
Gengelbach, Dietrich 50
Gerke, Ernst-August 122, 269
Gessner, Hans 215
Glaser, Wolfgang 216
Göing, Walter 152
Göllnitz, Heinrich 112
Götze, Hans 57, 259
Goldbeck, Heinz 229
Goschzik, Georg 250
Gosejakob, Henri 134
Gossler, Johann, Egbert 21
Graef, Adolf 116
Grasse, Martin 229, 271,
Grau, Peter 230
Grau, Peter-Ottmar 70, 180, 265
Grawert, Justus 147
Gretschel, Günter 130
Gréus, Friedrich-August 142
Grochowiak, Edmund 203
Grote, Heinrich 273
Groth, Gerhard 192
Günther, Horst 255, 260
Guggenberger, Friedrich 4, 171
Guse, Joachim 230
Gutteck, Hans-Joachim 219

Haelbich, Gerhard 122
Hänert, Klaus 27
Hagenau, Karl-Heinz 127
Hagene, Georg 234
Hamm, Horst 36
Hammer, Ulrich 140
Hansen, Hermann 212, 258
Hansen, Otto 70
Harms, Erich 267
Harney, Klaus 152
von Harpe, Richard 273
Hartel, Friedrich 251
Hartmann, Curt 31
von Hartmann, Götz 31, 37
Hartwig, Paul 9
Hasenschar, Heinrich 93
Hashagen, Berthold 171
Hass, Hans-Heinrich 245

2. U-BOAT GROUPS JUNE 1940 - APRIL 1945

The first attempts at controlled pack-operations were made in June 1940. The first was under the tactical command of Korvettekapitän Günther Prien and the second under Korvettekapitän Hans Rösing.

Neither was a success and a year passed before West group operated in the North Atlantic. There were further pack-operations during the second half of 1941 but it was not until 1942 that the 'wolf pack' came into its own, each group being controlled from U-Boat Headquarters.

U-Boat groups operated throughout the remaining years of the war, not only in all parts of the Atlantic Ocean but also in Northern Waters, against the Arctic convoys. Although there were some patrol lines formed in the Mediterranean, there were never pack-operations as such.

In operations in the Caribbean, Gulf of Mexico, Indian Ocean and the Baltic and Black Seas U-boats generally acted individually.

In this appendix there are several instances of the same group name being used more than once. When this occurs, the correct group can be identified by either its area of operation or its time of existence, both of which appear in brackets after the group name.

Adler (April 1943) U 84, U 188, U 257, U 267, U 404, U 571, U 613, U 615 and U 662

Amrum (December 1943) U 311, U 392, U 629, U 960 and U 976

Amsel (April 1943) U 186, U 223, U 266, U 359, U 377, U 383, U 403, U 448, U 454, U 466, U 525, U 634 and U 709

Amsel 1 (May 1943) U 107, U 402, U 504, U 575, U 621 and U 638

Amsel 2 (May 1943) U 223, U 266, U 377, U 383 and U 634

Amsel 3 (May 1943) U 448, U 468, U 525, U 569, U 709 and U 752

Amsel 4 (May 1943) U 186, U 359, U 403, U 454 and U 466

Arnauld (November 1941) U 81, U 205, U 433 and U 565

Benecke (November 1941) U 96, U 332, U 402 and U 552

Blitz (April 1944) U 277, U 355, U 711 and U 956

Blücher (August 1942) U 214, U 333, U 406, U 566, U 590, U 594 and U 653

Boreas (March 1944) U 278, U 288, U 307, U 315, U 361, U 366, U 472, U 739, U 959 and U 973

Borkum (December 1943) U 107, U 231, U 270, U 275, U 305, U 377, U 415, U 541, U 618, U 641, U 645, U 667, U 758, U 801, U 953 and U 962

Borkum 1 (January 1944) U 270, U 305 and U 382

Borkum 2 (January 1944) U 641 and U 758

Borkum 3 (January 1944) U 231, U 377 and U 953

Bosemüller (September 1941) U 71, U 83, U 95, U 98, U 557, U 558, U 561, U 562 and U 751

Brandenburg (September 1941) U 69, U 74, U 94, U 372, U 373, U 431, U 552, U 562, U 564, U 572 and U 575

Breslau (October 1941) U 71, U 83, U 204, U 206, U 563 and U 564

Büffel (December 1942) U 373, U 445 and U 663

Burggraf (March 1943) U 84, U 89, U 91, U 228, U 230, U 435, U 468, U 523, U 526, U 527, U 600, U 603, U 615, U 616, U 621, U 638, U 653, U 664 and U 758

Coronel (December 1943) U 92, U 107, U 269, U 311, U 415, U 421, U 541, U 543, U 544, U 618, U 625, U 629, U 653, U 667, U 672, U 734, U 761, U 801 and U 962

Coronel 1 (December 1943) U 92, U 311, U 421, U 544, U 625, U 629, U 653, U 672 and U 761

Coronel 2 (December 1943) U 284, U 364, U 471, U 741, U 976 and U 981

Coronel 3 (December 1943) U 107, U 269, U 415, U 541, U 543, U 618, U 667, U 801 and U 962

Dachs (September 1944) U 425, U 636, U 956, U 968, U 992 and U 995

Delphin (November 1942) U 259, U 380, U 407, U 595, U 596, U 617 and U 755

Delphin (December 1942 - February 1943) U 87, U 108, U 125, U 202, U 258, U 264, U 381, U 436, U 442, U 511, U 514, U 522, U 558, U 571, U 575 and U 620

Donau 1 (May 1943) U 258, U 304, U 340, U 381, U 418, U 636, U 645, U 731, U 760 and U 952

Donau 2 (May 1943) U 91, U 92, U 202, U 218, U 264, U 378, U 413, U 640, U 664, U 707, U 952 and U 954

Donner & Keil (April/May 1944) U 277, U 278, U 307, U 313, U 315, U 354, U 361, U 362, U 636, U 674, U 703, U 711, U 716, U 739, U 959 and U 990

Drachen (November 1942) U 262, U 445, U 454, U 522, U 611, U 623 and U 663

Dränger (March 1943) U 86, U 221, U 333, U 336, U 373, U 406, U 440, U 441, U 590 and U 608

Dragoner (May 1944) U 269, U 441, U 764, U 953 and U 984

Draufgänger (December 1942) U 221, U 455, U 553, U 569, U 600, U 604, U 609, U 610, U 611, U 615 and U 623

Drossel (May 1943) U 89, U 230, U 332, U 406, U 436, U 439, U 447, U 456, U 600, U 607 and U 659

Eisbär (August 1942) U 68, U 156, U 159, U 172 and U 504

Eisenbart (November/December 1943) U 277, U 307, U 314, U 354, U 360, U 387, U 601, U 636, U 713, U 716 and U 957

Eisenhart (November 1943) U 212, U 267, U 280, U 281, U 373, U 391, U 413, U 424, U 426, U 538, U 542, U 552, U 575, U 608, U 648, U 709, U 714, U 764, U 843, U 963, U 967 and U 969

Eisteufel (July 1942) U 88, U 251, U 355, U 376, U 457 and U 657

Elbe (May 1943) U 107, U 223, U 231, U 266, U 267, U 377, U 383, U 402, U 504, U 514, U 575, U 584, U 614, U 621, U 634 and U 650

Elbe 1 (May 1943) U 231, U 267, U 468, U 514, U 525, U 569, U 575, U 584, U 614, U 634, U 650, U 709 and U 752

Elbe 2 (May 1943) U 103, U 107, U 186, U 223, U 359, U 377, U 383, U 402, U 448, U 454, U 466, U 504 and U 621

288

Endrass (June 1942) U 84, U 89, U 132, U 134, U 437, U 552, U 571 and U 575

Falke (January 1943) U 69, U 71, U 167, U 201, U 226, U 257, U 333, U 384, U 404, U 414, U 441, U 444, U 525, U 563, U 572, U 584, U 606, U 607, U 631, U 632 and U 706

Faust (April 1945) U 286, U 295, U 307, U 313, U 363 and U 481

Fink (May 1943) U 92, U 125, U 134, U 168, U 188, U 192, U 209, U 226, U 231, U 258, U 260, U 264, U 270, U 358, U 378, U 381, U 413, U 438, U 533, U 552, U 584, U 614, U 628, U 630, U 648, U 650, U 662, U 707, U 732 and U 954

Föhr (December 1943) U 92, U 421, U 544, U 625, U 653 and U 672

Geier 1 (July 1943) U 228, U 603, U 608, U 641 and U 642

Geier 2 (July 1943) U 211, U 435, U 951 and U 953

Goeben (September/October 1941) U 75, U 79, U 97, U 331, U 371 and U 559

Gödecke (November 1941) U 69, U 98, U 201 and U 572

Greif (August 1943) U 278, U 362, U 365, U 711, U 739 and U 957

Grimm (September 1944) U 278, U 312, U 425, U 737, U 921, U 956 and U 997

Grube (November 1944) U 295, U 310, U 387, U 668, U 965, U 997 and U 1163

Habicht (January 1943) U 186, U 303, U 383, U 438, U 613, U 624, U 704 and U 752

Hagen (March 1945) U 307, U 312, U 363, U 711, U 716, U 968, U 997

Hai (July 1942) U 116, U 136, U 201, U 572, U 582 and U 752

Hai 1 & 2 (February 1944) U 91, U 212, U 256, U 264, U 281, U 386, U 406, U 437, U 441, U 546, U 549, U 603, U 608, U 650, U 709, U 764, U 963, U 985 and U 989

Hammer (April 1944) U 288, U 315, U 354 and U 968

Hartherz (February 1943) U 71, U 107, U 183, U 332, U 519, U 572, U 584, U 621, U 628, U 653 and U 753

Hartmut (February 1944) U 315, U 366, U 472 and U 673

Haudegen (January 1943) U 69, U 186, U 201, U 223, U 226, U 268, U 303, U 358, U 383, U 403, U 414, U 438, U 466, U 525, U 606, U 607, U 613, U 624, U 704, U 707 and U 752

Hecht (May 1942) U 94, U 96, U 124, U 406, U 569 and U 590

Hinein (January 1944) U 212, U 271, U 281, U 571, U 592 and U 650

Igel 1 (February 1944) U 212, U 283, U 386, U 406, U 441, U 545, U 546, U 547, U 549, U 666, U 714, U 764, U 984, U 985 and U 989

Igel 2 (February 1944) U 91, U 238, U 256, U 281, U 424, U 445, U 608, U 650, U 709, U 731, U 734, U 762 and U 963

Iller (May 1943) U 340, U 636, U 657, U 731 and U 760

Iltis (August/September 1942) U 87, U 107, U 214, U 333, U 406, U 566 and U 590

Inn (May 1943) U 258, U 381 and U 954

Isegrim (January 1944) U 278, U 314, U 360, U 425, U 601, U 716, U 737, U 739, U 957 and U 965

Jaguar (January 1943) U 96, U 123, U 266, U 337, U 413, U 594, U 598, U 662 and U 706

Jahn (November 1943) U 226, U 426, U 437, U 552, U 575, U 586, U 592, U 648, U 709 and U 842

Keil (See **Donner**)

Körner (November 1943) U 212, U 231, U 267, U 281, U 413, U 608, U 714, U 843, U 963, U 967 and U 969

Kreuzotter (November 1942) U 84, U 224, U 383, U 454, U 521, U 522, U 606, U 624 and U 753

Kurfürst (June 1941) U 73, U 201 and U 204

Kurfürst (September 1941) U 77, U 96, U 206, U 553, U 563, U 567, and U 568

Landsknecht (January 1943) U 71, U 187, U 257, U 262, U 265, U 267, U 333, U 384, U 402, U 404, U 444, U 454, U 456, U 465, U 553, U 572, U 584, U 609, U 614, U 631 and U 632

Landwirt (June 1944) U 212, U 228, U 255, U 256, U 260, U 262, U 269, U 270, U 275, U 281, U 333, U 373, U 382, U 413, U 415, U 437, U 441, U 445, U 608, U 621, U 629, U 650, U 714, U 740, U 758, U 764, U 766, U 821, U 953, U 963, U 970, U 981, U 984, U 985, U 989 and U 993

Lech (May 1943) U 91, U 202 and U 664

Leopard (October 1942) U 254, U 353, U 382, U 437, U 442, U 597, U 620 and U 662

Lerche (April 1943) U 168, U 191, U 203, U 260, U 270, U 532, U 563, U 584, U 630 and U 706

Letzte Ritter (November 1941) U 69, U 201 and U 402

Letzte Ritter (September 1942) U 216, U 404, U 410 and U 584

Leuthen (September 1943) U 229, U 238, U 260, U 270, U 275, U 305, U 338, U 377, U 378, U 386, U 402, U 422, U 584, U 641, U 645, U 666, U 731, U 758 and U 952

Löwenherz (April 1943) U 168, U 191, U 260, U 270, U 563, U 564, U 572, U 584, U 592, U 594, U 630, U 632, U 635 and U 706

Lohs (August/September 1942) U 135, U 174, U 176, U 256, U 259, U 373, U 410, U 432, U 438, U 569, U 596, U 599, U 605, U 660, U 705 and U 755

Luchs (October 1942) U 183, U 254, U 257, U 260, U 382, U 437, U 442, U 575, U 582, U 597, U 610, U 619, U 620, U 706, U 753 and U 755

Markgraf (August 1941) U 38, U 43, U 81, U 82, U 84, U 85, U 105, U 202, U 207, U 432, U 433, U 501, U 569 and U 652

Meise (April 1943) U 71, U 84, U 108, U 134, U 188, U 189, U 191, U 203, U 257, U 258, U 267, U 306, U 381, U 404, U 413, U 415, U 438, U 532, U 552, U 571, U 598, U 610, U 613, U 618, U 631, U 662, U 706 and U 732

Mitte (February - July 1944) U 242, U 276, U 286, U 294, U 295, U 299, U 317, U 319, U 397, U 677, U 745, U 771, U 975, U 982, U 987, U 994, U 999, U 1001, U 1007, U 1163, U 1165 and U 1192

Monsun (South Atlantic)(July 1943) U 168, U 183, U 188, U 506, U 509, U 514, U 516, U 532 and U 533

Monsun (Northern Waters)(October 1943) U 277, U 307, U 387, U 713 and U 956

Mordbrenner (October 1941) U 109, U 208, U 374 and U 573

Mosel (May 1943) U 218, U 221, U 228, U 231, U 305, U 336, U 378, U 468, U 552, U 558, U 569, U 575, U 603, U 607, U 621, U 641, U 642, U 650, U 666 and U 752

Nahe (May 1943) U 92, U 264 and U 707

Natter (November 1942) U 92, U 98, U 218, U 224, U 383, U 436, U 564, U 566, U 606, U 613, U 624 and U 653

Neptun (February 1943) U 135, U 359, U 376, U 405, U 413, U 448, U 566, U 608, U 659 and U 759

Neuland (March 1942) U 67, U 129, U 156, U 161 and U 502

Neuland (Northern Section)(March 1943) U 190, U 338, U 439, U 447, U 530, U 618, U 641, U 642, U 665 and U 666

Neuland (Southern Section)(March 1943) U 86, U 221, U 336, U 373, U 406, U 440, U 441, U 444, U 590, U 608 and U 757

Nordsturm (February 1942) U 186, U 223, U 268, U 358 and U 707

Oder (May 1943) U 221, U 228, U 336, U 558, U 603, U 607, U 642, U 666 and U 752

Ostmark (March 1943) U 190, U 338, U 439, U 447, U 530, U 618, U 633, U 641, U 642, U 665 and U 666

Panther (North Atlantic)(October 1942) U 71, U 84, U 89, U 132, U 254, U 260, U 301, U 353, U 381, U 382, U 402, U 437, U 438, U 441, U 442, U 443, U 563, U 571, U 575, U 597, U 602, U 609, U 610, U 620, U 621, U 658, U 662, U 704, U 706, U 753 and U 757

Panther (Northern Waters)(October 1944) U 293, U 295, U 310, U 315, U 363, U 365, U 387, U 425, U 636, U 668, U 737, U 771, U 956, U 965, U 968, U 992, U 995, U 997 and U 1163

Panzer (December 1942) U 135, U 211, U 254, U 439, U 465, U 524 and U 758

Pfadfinder (May 1942) U 135, U 213, U 404, U 432, U 455, U 566, U 578 and U 653

Pfeil (North Atlantic)(September 1942) U 216, U 221, U 258, U 356, U 615, U 617 and U 618

Pfeil (North Atlantic)(February 1943) U 89, U 187, U 262, U 267, U 402, U 413, U 454, U 465, U 594 and U 609

Pirat (August 1942) U 43, U 71, U 164, U 210, U 217, U 454, U 511, U 552, U 553, U 597, U 607 and U 704

Preussen (February/March 1944) U 91, U 92, U 212, U 255, U 256, U 262, U 267, U 281, U 302, U 311, U 333, U 358, U 437, U 441, U 448, U 549, U 603, U 608, U 625, U 653, U 667, U 672, U 709 U 741, U 744, U 764, U 962, U 963, U 985 and U 986

Prien (June 1940) U 25, U 28, U 30, U 32, U 47 and U 51

Puma (October 1942) U 301, U 436, U 441, U 443, U 563, U 575, U 602, U 621, U 624 and U 753

Rasmus (February 1945) U 286, U 307, U 425, U 711, U 716, U 739 and U 968

Raubgraf (March 1943) U 84, U 89, U 91, U 435, U 468, U 600, U 603, U 615, U 621, U 638, U 653, U 664 and U 758

Raubritter (November 1941) U 38, U 82, U 85, U 106, U 123, U 133, U 571 and U 577

Raufbold (December 1942) U 135, U 203, U 211, U 356, U 409, U 410, U 439, U 600, U 609, U 610, U 621 and U 664

Reissewolf (October 1941) U 73, U 77, U 101, U 432, U 502, U 568 and U 751

Rhein (May 1943) U 103, U 186, U 359, U 403, U 448, U 454, U 466, U 468, U 525, U 569, U 709 and U 752

Ritter (February 1943) U 225, U 332, U 377, U 454, U 468, U 529, U 603, U 621, U 623, U 628, U 653 and U 753

Robbe (February 1943) U 103, U 107, U 382, U 410, U 437, U 445, U 511 and U 569

Rochen (January/February 1943) U 43, U 66, U 87, U 202, U 218, U 258, U 264, U 504, U 521 and U 558

Rösing (June 1940) U 29, U 43, U 46, U 48 and U 101

Rossbach (September/October 1943) U 260, U 275, U 305, U 336, U 378, U 402, U 419, U 448, U 539, U 584, U 603, U 610, U 631, U 641, U 643, U 645, U 666, U 731, U 758 and U 952

Rügen (January 1944) U 92, U 212, U 260, U 271, U 281, U 302, U 309, U 311, U 364, U 390, U 392, U 471, U 545, U 547, U 571, U 592, U 650, U 666, U 731, U 741, U 762, U 846, U 972, U 976 and U 981

Rügen 1 (December 1943) U 364, U 972 and U 981

Rügen 2 (December 1943) U 545, U 744 and U 781

Rügen 3 (December 1943) U 390, U 471 and U 546

Rügen 4 (December 1943) U 302, U 392, U 960 and U 976

Rügen 5 (December 1943) U 92, U 311 and U 672

Rügen 6 (December 1943) U 421, U 625 and U 653

Schill (October 1943) U 211, U 228, U 262, U 306, U 333, U 358, U 441, U 466, U 707 and U 953

Schill 1 (November 1943) U 211, U 228, U 262, U 333, U 358, U 515 and U 600

Schill 2 (November 1943) U 238, U 343, U 426, U 536, U 586, U 608, U 648, U 709 and U 969

Schill 3 (November 1943) U 212, U 391, U 424, U 542, U 618, U 714, U 764, U 843 and U 967

Schlagetot (North Atlantic)(October 1941) U 38, U 82, U 84, U 85, U 93, U 123, U 202, U 203, U 569 and U 571

Schlagetot (Central Atlantic)(November 1942) U 103, U 108, U 130, U 173, U 509, U 510, U 511, U 572 and U 752

Schlei (January 1942) U 94, U 352, U 404, U 435, U 455, U 578, U 586, U 587, U 588, U 591, U 656 and U 753

Schlieffen (October 1943) U 91, U 231, U 267, U 281, U 309, U 413, U 426, U 437, U 448, U 540, U 608, U 631, U 762, U 841 and U 842

Seehund (January 1943) U 160, U 182, U 506, U 509 and U 516

Seeräuber (Central Atlantic)(December 1941) U 67, U 107, U 108, U 131 and U 434

Seeräuber (Central Atlantic)(March 1943) U 67, U 123, U 159, U 167, U 172, U 513 and U 515

Seeteufel (March 1943) U 134, U 168, U 188, U 191, U 260, U 306, U 415, U 523, U 526, U 564, U 572, U 592, U 598, U 610, U 632, U 663 and U 706

Seewolf (North Atlantic)(March 1943) U 84, U 86, U 257, U 305, U 333, U 336, U 373, U 440, U 441, U 527, U 530, U 590, U 591, U 615, U 618, U 631, U 641, U 642 and U 666

Seewolf (North Atlantic)(April 1945) U 518, U 546, U 805, U 858, U 880 and U 1235

Seydlitz (January 1942) U 71, U 84, U 93, U 203, U 552 and U 571

Siegfried (October 1943) U 91, U 226, U 231, U 267, U 309, U 373, U 413, U 426, U 437, U 552, U 575, U 608, U 709, U 762, U 842, U 963 and U 969

Siegfried 1 (October 1943) U 212, U 231, U 608, U 967 and U 969

Siegfried 2 (October 1943) U 267, U 281, U 413, U 426, U 437, U 552, U 592 and U 963

Siegfried 3 (October 1943) U 226, U 575, U 648, U 709 and U 842

Specht (April 1943) U 92, U 125, U 168, U 188, U 226, U 260, U 264, U 270, U 358, U 438, U 514, U 584, U 614, U 628, U 630, U 662, U 707 and U 732

Spitz (December 1942) U 123, U 203, U 225, U 260, U 356, U 406, U 440, U 659, U 662 and U 664

Star (April 1943) U 192, U 209, U 231, U 258, U 378, U 381, U 386, U 413, U 528, U 531, U 532, U 533, U 552, U 648, U 650 and U 954

Steinbrinck (August 1942) U 71, U 552, U 597, U 607 and U 704

Steuben (November 1941) U 43, U 105, U 372, U 434, U 574 and U 575

Stier (North Atlantic)(September 1942) U 96, U 380, U 404, U 584, U 594 and U 608

Stier (Northern Waters)(January 1945) U 956 and U 995

Stock (November 1944) U 286, U 293, U 299, U 313, U 315, U 318, U 363, U 365, U 992 and U 995

Störtebecker (Early November 1941) U 69, U 77, U 96, U 98, U 103, U 107, U 201, U 332, U 373, U 402, U 552, U 567 and U 572

Störtebecker (Late November 1941) U 85, U 133, U 571 and U 577

Stosstrupp (October/November 1941) U 96, U 133, U 552, U 567, U 571 and U 577

Strauchritter (April 1942) U 88, U 251, U 405, U 436, U 456, U 589 and U 703

Streitaxt (October 1942) U 134, U 203, U 409, U 509, U 510, U 572, U 604 and U 659

Stürmer (North Atlantic)(March 1943) U 134, U 190, U 305, U 338, U 384, U 439, U 523, U 526, U 530, U 598, U 610, U 618, U 631, U 641, U 642, U 665 and U 666

Stürmer (North Atlantic)(January 1944) U 309, U 386, U 390, U 406, U 441, U 545, U 547, U 666, U 731, U 762, U 764, U 984 and U 989

Sturmbock (February 1943) U 84, U 409, U 432, U 591, U 664 and U 758

Sylt (December 1943) U 302, U 364, U 471, U 741, U 972 and U 981

Taifun (February 1943) U 186, U 223, U 358 and U 707

Thor (April 1944) U 278, U 312, U 313 and U 674

Tiger (September 1942) U 216, U 221, U 258, U 356, U 410, U 595, U 599, U 607, U 615, U 617, U 618, and U 755

Tirpitz 1 to 5 (November 1943) U 212, U 226, U 231, U 267, U 280, U 281, U 373, U 413, U 426, U 437, U 552, U 575, U 586, U 592, U 608, U 648, U 709, U 714, U 842, U 843, U 963 and U 967

Trutz (Central Atlantic) (June 1943) U 92, U 211, U 217, U 221, U 228, U 232, U 336, U 435, U 558, U 603, U 608, U 641, U 642, U 666, U 951 and U 953

Trutz (Northern Waters)(August 1944) U 344, U 363, U 394, U 668, U 997

Trutz 1 (June 1943) U 228, U 558, U 608 and U 642

Trutz 2 (June 1943) U 232, U 336, U 603, U 641, U 666, U 951 and U 953

Trutz 3 (June 1943) U 193, U 211, U 217, U 221 and U 435

Tümmler (October 1942) U 458, U 593, U 605 and U 660

Tümmler (Central Atlantic)(March 1943) U 43, U 66, U 202, U 504, U 521 and U 558

Ulan (December 1941) U 134, U 454 and U 584

Ungestüm (December 1942) U 336, U 373, U 435, U 445, U 455, U 524, U 569, U 591, U 604, U 615 and U 628

Unverzagt (March 1943) U 106, U 130, U 167, U 172, U 513 and U 515

Veilchen (October 1942) U 71, U 84, U 89, U 132, U 381, U 402, U 437, U 438, U 442, U 454, U 571, U 658 and U 704

Vorwärts (August 1942) U 91, U 92, U 96, U 211, U 218, U 380, U 404, U 407, U 409, U 411, U 584, U 594, U 608, U 609, U 659 and U 756

Weddigen (November 1943) U 86, U 228, U 238, U 262, U 358, U 391, U 424, U 542, U 586, U 618, U 714, U 764, U 843 and U 969

Werwolf (January/February 1944) U 278, U 312, U 313, U 314, U 362, U 425, U 472, U 601, U 674, U 713, U 716, U 737, U 739, U 956, U 957, U 965, U 973 and U 990

West (June 1941) U 43, U 46, U 48, U 66, U 73, U 75, U 77, U 101, U 108, U 111, U 204, U 553, U 557, U 558 and U 751

Westmark (March 1943) U 228, U 230, U 332, U 359, U 405, U 409, U 432, U 448, U 523, U 526, U 527, U 566, U 591, U 616, U 634, U 659 and U 709

Westwall (November 1942) U 86, U 91, U 92, U 98, U 103, U 130, U 155, U 185, U 218, U 263, U 411, U 413, U 515, U 519, U 564, U 566 and U 653

Wiking (August/September 1943) U 302, U 354 and U 711

Wildfang (February 1943) U 84, U 89, U 409, U 432, U 591, U 638, U 664 and U 758

Wohlgemut (March 1943) U 67, U 103, U 109, U 159 and U 524

Wolf (July 1942) U 43, U 71, U 86, U 90, U 379, U 454, U 552, U 597, U 607 and U 704

Wotan (October 1942) U 216, U 221, U 258, U 356, U 410, U 599, U 607, U 615, U 618 and U 661

York (March 1942) U 135, U 553, U 569 and U 701

Ziethen (January 1942) U 84, U 86, U 87, U 135, U 203, U 333, U 552, U 553, U 582, U 654, U 701 and U 754

Zorn (September 1944) U 293, U 310, U 363, U 365, U 387, U 636, U 668, U 965, U 968, U 992 and U 995

3. *DEUTSCHE FELDPOST* NUMBERS U 511 - UIT 25

Every German military and naval unit had its own *Deutsche Feldpost* number. U-boats were each allocated a number, which in use was always preceded by the letter M, for Kriegsmarine.

The *Feldpost* number had other uses apart from being used as a postal address. In the case of a particular crew being called out in a public place to report back to base, the *Feldpost* number would be used and not the U-boat number, in the interests of security.

Feldpost	U-boat	Feldpost	U-boat	Feldpost	U-boat	Feldpost	U-boat	Feldpost	U-boat
00 073	UA	19 192	U 825	31 170	U 660	40 727	U 561	43 319	U1231
00 375	U 619	19 451	U 587	31 170	UIT 23	40 885	U 1167	43 347	U 706
00 375	U 683	19 451	U 871	31 365	U 661			43 381	U 973
00 412	U 775	19 456	U 875	31 365	UIT 24	41 096	U 1064	43 387	U 974
00 459	U 620	19 687	U 588	31 379	U 554	41 181	U 1109	43 405	U 658
00 459	U 874	19 687	U 880	31 936	U 1103	41 224	U 2321	43 405	U 3504
00 518	U 878	19 715	U 524			41 243	U 2322	43 508	U 1200
00 832	U 879	19 715	U 881	32 441	UIT 25	41 284	U 2323	43 526	U 2501
				32 765	U 883	41 306	U 741	43 628	UC 2
01 308	U 907	20 052	U 552	32 853	U 1166	41 384	U 2324	43 633	U 975
01 524	U 1014	20 725	U 525			41 387	U 2325	43 644	U 1230
				33 584	U 778	41 468	U 2326	43 666	U 929
02 062	U 621	21 203	U 630			41 495	U 2327	43 832	U 1065
		21 755	U 927	34 077	U 1003	41 556	U 2328	43 854	U 925
03 110	U 1016	21 775	U 589	34 971	U555	41 587	U 742	43 929	U 704
03 373	U 1017	21 922	U 1019			41 607	U 2329	43 973	U 574
				35 195	U 560	41 658	U 2502	43 973	U 1059
04 059	U 1055	22 458	U 631	35 647	U 651	41 704	U 2503		
04 155	U 622	22 623	U 632	35 882	U 826	41 779	U 845	44 068	U 575
04 237	U 623	22 623	U 1018	35 992	UD 2	41 815	U 2504	44 117	U 576
04 237	U 1106	22 922	U 633			41 858	U 850	44 117	U 1305
04 328	U 624	22 946	U 1020	36 167	U 558	41 903	U 2505	44 194	U 2330
04 328	U 1131			36 350	U 827	41 942	U 971	44 228	U 577
04 401	U 625	23 270	U 634	36 700	U 876	41 960	U 516	44 257	U 653
04 507	U 583	23 773	U 590	36 839	U 556	41 992	U 565	44 322	U 701
		23 789	U 553			41 996	U 517	44 322	U 2331
05 024	U 664	23 789	U 1021	37 084	U 543	41 996	U2506	44 381	U 2332
05 347	U 584	23 837	U 1056	37 230	U 591			44 442	U 752
05 459	U 1171			37 556	U 592	42 015	U 566	44 442	U 2333
05 506	U 585	24 797	U 656	37 886	U 544	42 090	U 2507	44 455	U 2334
05 593	U 1172	24 797	U 901	37 894	U 889	42 135	U 567	44 578	U 753
05 723	U 586			37 961	U 557	42 154	U 609	44 578	U 2335
05 834	U 1207	25 172	U 1057	37 961	U 673	42 154	U 2508	44 599	U 2336
05 973	U 1208	25 447	U 779			42 161	U 568	44 676	U 2337
		25 463	U 665	38 047	UD 3	42 293	U 569	44 690	U 518
06 051	U 655	25 463	U 828	38 314	U 593	42 293	U 3002	44 754	U 519
06 266	U 702	25 617	U 703	38 350	U 1022	42 302	U 3003	44 754	U 2338
06 857	U 522			38 516	U 594	42 381	U 570	44 892	U 613
06 935	U 523	26 026	U 551	38 782	U 559	42 483	U 571	44 892	U 2339
				38 782	U 1302	42 489	U 610	44 965	U 614
07 089	U 626	27 254	U 514	38 801	U 595	42 493	U 572	44 965	U 2340
07 089	U 1276	27 527	U 1108	38 801	U 1405	42 501	U 611		
07 218	U 627	27 582	U 604	38 859	U 928	42 501	U 3004	45 089	U 615
07 218	U 1277	27 945	U 1132	38 894	UD 5	42 508	U 573	45 089	U 2341
07 314	U 628	27 988	U 515	38 963	U 657	42 644	U 652	45 101	U 616
07 337	U 629			38 963	U 1023	42 792	U 511	45 175	U 663
07 970	U 1303	28 117	U 605			42 792	U 3005	45 175	U 2342
		28 390	U 606	39 246	U 756	42 884	U 596	45 207	U 2343
10 850	UC 1	28 509	U 607	39 246	U 1024	42 940	U 612	45 325	U 707
		28 540	UD 1	39 567	U 757	42 993	U 597	45 325	U 2344
14 151	U 772	28 568	U 708			42 993	U 3006	45 477	U 2371
		28 716	U 1209	40 175	U 564			45 671	U 2509
15 421	U 776	28 986	U 1210	40 175	U 1025	43 109	U 662	45 783	U 2510
				40 307	U 1058	43 135	U 972	45 912	U 2511
16 800	U 868	30 340	U 608	40 428	U 716	43 161	U 1199	45 926	U 2512
		30 414	UD 4	40 438	U 1063	43 201	U 598		
17 108	U 777	30 549	U 1278	40 564	U 563	43 202	U 599	46 136	U 578
17 549	U 806	30 807	U 751	40 608	U 562	43 288	U 3502	46 136	U 2513
17 865	U 822	30 807	U 1279	40 608	U 3501	43 302	U 3503	46 179	U 2514

46 268	U 579	49 383	U 535	49 972	U 841	50 627	U 921	51 907	U 846
46 289	U 3007	49 383	U 2530	49 972	U 3021	50 642	U 1204	51 963	U 527
46 323	U 580	49 394	U 2531	49 979	U 3022	50 646	U 4705	51 969	U 851
46 364	U 520	49 397	U 536	49 998	U 847	50 650	U 535	51 982	U 976
46 364	U 3008	49 401	U 2533	49 998	U 3023	50 650	U 4706	51 994	U 977
46 386	U 581	49 427	U 2534			50 655	U 961	51 997	U 978
46 411	U 521	49 432	U 870	50 010	U 3024	50 659	U 711		
46 411	U 3009	49 435	U 2535	50 029	U 957	50 679	U 962	52 015	U 2537
46 477	U 582	49 449	U 713	50 034	U 3025	50 693	U 648	52 021	U 2538
46 477	U 3010	49 449	U 2536	50 037	U 682	50 693	U 1205	52 044	U 2539
46 554	U 617	49 477	U 1052	50 044	U 958	50 698	U 4707	52 062	U 545
46 554	U 3011	49 500	U 1053	50 058	UF 2	50 702	U 963	52 062	U 2540
46 564	U 654	49 502	U 735	50 064	U 774	50 706	U 1234	52 068	U 3030
46 564	U 3012	49 527	U 669	50 076	U 959	50 718	U 964	52 101	U 3031
46 602	U 618	49 527	U 952	50 081	U 528	50 727	U 649	52 107	U 979
46 656	U 754	49 533	U 3511	50 081	U 3026	50 791	U 731	52 110	U 3032
46 656	U 3505	49 558	U 953	50 098	U 960	50 796	U 1235	52 146	U 2541
46 726	U 3506	49 566	U 3512	50 115	U 3027	50 801	U 650	52 184	U 1060
46 894	U 3507	49 566	U 531	50 141	U 3028	50 803	U 1273	52 191	U 3033
46 926	U 759	49 568	U 954	50 148	U 529	50 816	U 1274	52 197	U 3034
46 926	U 3508	49 568	U 3513	50 148	U 3029	50 824	U 906	52 251	U 3035
46 975	U 705	49 572	U 526	50 158	U 872	50 836	U 712	52 272	U 3524
		49 572	U 3514	50 159	U 2345	50 862	U 1275	52 280	U 3525
47 033	U 758	49 601	U 955	50 188	U 2346	50 883	U 733	52 300	U 3256
47 074	U 659	49 604	U 1233	50 196	U 639	50 897	U 1206	52 331	U 3527
47 074	U 930	49 612	U 643	50 196	U 2347	50 897	U 1301	52 347	U 3528
47 142	U 603	49 612	U 3515	50 203	U 2348	50 912	U 734	52 352	U 677
47 187	U 602	49 622	U 956	50 232	U 2349	50 939	U 926	52 359	U 3529
47 254	U 601	49 638	U 3516	50 247	U 2350	50 964	U 951	52 375	U 3530
47 389	U 600	49 683	U 644	50 271	U 873			52 381	U 678
47 389	U 1110	49 683	U 3517	50 291	U 640	51 083	U 541	52 386	U 2542
47 644	U 1304	49 689	U 1168	50 291	U 2351	51 100	U 761	52 395	U 2543
47 655	U 1406	49 693	U 1201	50 294	U 877	51 111	U 542	52 399	U 771
47 665	U 1407	49 695	U 3518	50 300	U 2352	51 111	U 2361	52 404	U 547
47 679	U 1307	49 699	U 3519	50 310	U 2353	51 115	U 2362	52 436	U 2544
47 884	U 2515	49 700	U 645	50 312	U 2354	51 135	U 672	52 467	U 2545
47 956	U 2516	49 700	U 3520	50 330	U 2355	51 222	U 715	52 470	U 548
47 966	U 2517	49 708	U 3521	50 346	U 1013	51 233	U 740	52 496	U 794
47 968	U 3509	49 751	U 646	50 346	U 2356	51 249	U 638	52 506	U 674
47 974	U 3510	49 751	U 3522	50 387	U 641	51 249	U 2363	52 544	U 803
47 986	U 512	49 757	U 1202	50 387	U 2357	51 254	U 763	52 546	U 792
47 994	U 513	49 759	U 1232	50 390	U 2358	51 307	U 801	52 552	U 3037
		49 765	U 709	50 396	U 1051	51 307	U 2364	52 559	U 717
48 818	U 3014	49 765	U 3523	50 416	U 539	51 370	U 843	52 580	U 3038
		49 790	U 1271	50 425	U 1054	51 377	U 666	52 607	U 857
49 036	U 681	49 799	U 647	50 444	U 1105	51 377	U 2365	52 636	U 745
49 039	U 1306	49 799	U 3013	50 445	U 540	51 391	U 844	52 646	U 858
49 058	U 773	49 804	U 537	50 445	U 2359	51 391	U 2366	52 652	U 3039
49 091	U 805	49 827	U 538	50 467	U 671	51 402	U 849	52 665	U 765
49 103	U 1308	49 827	U 3015	50 471	U 642	51 402	U 2367	52 673	U 3040
49 105	U 2518	49 834	U 668	50 495	U 714	51 414	U 965	52 685	U 862
49 106	U 2519	49 841	U 1272	50 520	U 1169	51 418	U 966	52 697	U 802
49 163	U 869	49 847	U 670	50 527	U 738	51 480	U 967	52 703	U 904
49 177	U 2520	49 847	U 3016	50 527	U 2360	51 536	U 968	52 715	U 821
49 231	U 2521	49 866	U 736	50 530	U 1170	51 543	U 969	52 749	U 998
49 263	U 905	49 880	U 732	50 536	U 4701	51 550	U 637	52 771	U 852
49 267	U 2522	49 880	U 3017	50 545	U 739	51 558	U 970	52 784	U 999
49 281	U 2523	49 907	U 737	50 558	U 4702	51 601	U 636	52 793	U 853
49 299	U 2524	49 924	U 710	50 566	U 842	51 783	U 635	52 805	U 1000
49 312	U 2526	49 924	U 3018	50 566	U 4703	51 783	U 2369	52 816	U 980
49 344	U 2527	49 943	U 762	50 568	U 667	51 791	U 546	52 852	U 1001
49 352	U 2528	49 943	U 3019	50 593	U 848	51 797	U 743	52 873	U 981
49 357	U 534	49 952	U 760	50 593	U 4704	51 807	U 744	52 880	U 1002
49 365	U 2525	49 952	U 3020	50 595	U 1203	51 813	U 2370	52 881	U 4710
49 368	U 2529			50 614	U 532	51 834	U 764	52 885	U 982

52 893 U 4711	53 569 U 719	54 065 U 989	54 806 U 771	55 209 U 1101
52 909 U 1162	53 610 U 766	54 093 U 990	54 813 U 860	55 214 U 1222
52 911 U 983	53 631 U 854	54 101 U 1004	54 842 U 864	55 256 U 1165
52 911 U 4712	53 631 U 2551	54 105 U 1005	54 873 U 861	55 261 U 1196
52 936 U 1163	53 677 U 679	54 124 U 1005	54 899 U 866	55 272 U 1197
52 982 U 1061	53 689 U 855	54 132 U 992	54 904 U 903	55 286 U 1228
52 991 U 1191	53 697 U 721	54 173 U 1006	54 950 U 867	55 295 U 1229
	53 706 U 859	54 196 U 1007	54 991 U 922	55 307 U 804
53 002 U 1062	53 733 U 2552	54 201 U 1164	54 999 U 924	55 331 U 1102
53 015 U 923	53 733 U 768	54 219 U 1194		55 392 U 746
53 051 U 1192	53 784 U 984	54 254 U 1195	55 038 U 993	55 404 U 750
53 099 U 1223	53 805 U 793	54 305 U 1226	55 064 U 1008	55 412 U 1161
53 122 U 1224	53 813 U 985	54 328 U 1227	55 083 U 994	55 433 U 747
53 122 U 2548	53 834 U 795	54 524 U 3001	55 087 U 1009	55 456 U 748
53 196 U 1225	53 856 U 986	54 607 U 676	55 095 U 995	55 485 U 749
53 434 U 549	53 881 U 863	54 671 U 720	55 109 U 1010	55 490 UIT 21
53 473 U 550	53 910 U 987	54 720 U 680	55 164 U 977	55 509 UIT 22
53 511 U 675	53 961 U 865	54 762 U 722	55 177 U 3041	55 611 U 3044
53 527 U 718	53 999 U 988	54 791 U 856	55 188 U 1221	

4. ALLIED WARSHIPS & AUXILIARIES SUNK, DAMAGED OR ATTACKED

British
Alisma 97
Alouette 29
Alnwick Castle 198
Ashanti 61
Asphodel 52
Audacity 148

Bedfordshire 33
Birdlip 26
Blackwood 159
Bluebell 133
Bredon 11
Bullen 162

Chanticleer 7
Commander Horton 28
Cossack 38
Convolvulous 50

Denbigh Castle 208

Ellesmere 233

Fame 13
Fidelity 83

Galatea 32
Gladiolus 33
Goodall 198
Goodson 204

Hardy 192
Hecla 6
Heythrop 109
Highlander 77
Holcombe 64
Hurricane 22

Itchen 118

Jaguar 109

Keppel 133
Kingston Ceylonite 126

LCI 162 67

British (continued)
LCT 1074 159
LCT 2335 77
LCT 2480 15
LST 362 146
Lapwing 198
Lark 198

Mahratta 207
Manners 220
Marne 6
Milne 127, 42
Mourne 160

Naiad 40
Notts Country 126

Partridge 41
Picotee 43
Pink 206
Polyanthus 188
Porcupine 72
Prince Leopold 90
Puckeridge 86

Redmill 225
Rose 151

St Issey 85
Salvia 44
Simoon 41
Snowflake 18
Somali 127
Stanley 50
Stella Capella 126
Swift 143

Trident 41
Tynedale 64

Vervain 241

Welshman 85

Zephyr 218
Zinnia 39

American
Barr 27
Block Island 27
Buck 84

Eagle 56 173
Ellyson 194

Fechteler 197
Fiske 165
Fogg 179
Frederick C Davis 25
Flaherty 25

Gannet 109

Jacob Jones 53

Kearny 43

LCI 99 120
LST 280 90
LST 333 64
LST 359 179
LST 387 64
LST 921 120

Muskeget 152

Plymouth 42

Reuben James 28

Skill 64

YP 389 126

Australian
Parramatta 35

Canadian
Chambly 56
Charlottetown 9
Chebogue 237
Clayoquot 166

Canadian (continued)
Columbia 12

Guysborough 179

HDML-163 238

Lunenburg 189

Magog 236
Matapedia 238
Moosejaw 11
Morden 118

Qu' Appelle 189

Regina 120
Restigouche 189

Saskatchewan 204
Shawinigan 237
Skeena 189
Spikenard 61

Toronto 235
Transcona 166
Trentonian 214

Vallyfield 26

French
Alysse 111

L'Enjoue 180

Netherlands
Colombia 8

Norwegian
Montbretia 91

Nordhav II 135
NYMS 382 219

Polish
Orkan 154

Russian
Archangel'sk 133

BMB-512 228
BMO-594 99
BO-224 210
BO-225 211
BO-229 211
BO-230 211
BPS-5 133

Karl Libknecht 211

M-108 133
M-175 55
MO-104 124

Nord 192

PS-70 108

Resitel'nyj 211

SKR-14 98
SKR-23 60
SKR-29 192

T-76 146
T-883 210
TSC-42 193
TSC-48 146
TSC-58 92
TSC-65 127
TSC-107 210
TSC-116 208
TSC-120 143
TSC-889 149
TSC-898 149

Zarkij 133
Zhivuchij 211

5. MERCHANT SHIPS SUNK, DAMAGED OR ATTACKED BY U 511 - UIT 25

British

Abosso 51
Aelybryn 31
Ainderby 28
Alexander Kennedy 214
Alhama 39
Alipore 8
Alliance 37
Alva 35
Amakura 33
Andania 277
Anglo Maersk 73
Ariosto 39
Ascanius 90
Ashmun J Clough 206
Athelduke 240
Athelprincess 12
Athelsultan 85
Athelviking 238
Avondale Park 248
Aymeric 112

Bandar Sharpur 6
Barberrys 116
Baron Erskine 125
Baron Jedburgh 18
Baron Kinnaird 89
Baron Pentland 108
Baron Semple 171
Baron Vernon 73
Beacon Grange 28
Berwickshire 176
Blackheath 180
Bombay 74
Brambleleaf 35
Bretwalda 38
British Ardour 129
British Consul 39
British Dominion 12, 88
British Freedom 126, 238
British Merit 29
British Promise 9
British Prudence 151
British Purpose 18
British Renown 9
British Security 31
British Splendour 28
British Vigilance 5
Brockley Hill 108
Broompark 29
Browning 66
Bulkoil 235
Bullmouth 113

Cadillac 27
California Star 6
Cameronia 41
Cap Padaran 67
Cape Race 114
Carperby 59
Carsbreck 39
Ceramic 6
Charles LD 31
Chaucer 31
Chinese Prince 28
Chumleigh 92
City of Cardiff 42
City of Guilford 64
City of Oxford 28
City of Singapore 7

British (continued)

Clan MacPherson 7
Clarissa Radcliffe 116
Clonlara 39
Comrade 51
Condylis 114
Consuelo 59
Corabella 6
Coral 159
Cordelia 96
Corinaldo 113
Cornwallis 5, 238
Cuba 231

Dafila 64
Dahomian 172
Darlington Court 31
Daronia 176
Dayrose 28
Devis 64
Diala 30
Dolius 100
Donald Stewart 9
Duchess of Bedford 128
Dumana 7
Dumfries 161
Dunaff Head 277

E P Theriault 150
Ebor Wyke 202
Eclipse 39
Egholm 244
Embassage 32
Empire Attendant 55
Empire Bede 31
Empire Byron 127
Empire Caribou 31
Empire Celt 59
Empire Cloud 39
Empire Corporal 68
Empire Dryden 48
Empire Explorer 51
Empire Geraint 162
Empire Gilbert 58
Empire Gold 225
Empire Hartebeeste 66
Empire Hawksbill 39
Empire Heron 43
Empire Housman 24, 145
Empire Impala 62
Empire Javelin 161
Empire Kohinoor 87
Empire Lancer 176
Empire Light 100
Empire Lugard 33
Empire Marvel 45
Empire Mersey 86
Empire Moonbeam 77
Empire Norseman 34
Empire Oak 39
Empire Oil 56, 113
Empire Portia 206
Empire Prairie 111
Empire Rainbow 76, 128
Empire Redshank 75
Empire Reindeer 114
Empire Sailor 9
Empire Sky 92
Empire Spenser 13
Empire Spring 52

British (continued)

Empire Standard 67
Empire Star 83
Empire Storm 32
Empire Sun 148
Empire Tourist 127
Empire Trader 74
Empire Turnstone 88
Empire Unity 202
Empire Wave 37
Empire Whale 115
Ensis 48
Erna III 37
Etrib 28
Everleigh 217

Fort à la Corne 67
Fort Bellingham 192
Fort Binger 59
Fort Cedar Lake 117
Fort Fidler 84
Fort la Reine 112
Fort Lamy 15
Fort Longueuil 18
Fort Norman 67
Fort Rampart 93
Fort Richepanse 43
Fort Thompson 236
Fresno City 38, 129

G S Walden 29, 84
Garmula 149
Gasray 244
Gilbert B Walters 49
Glacier 51
Glendinning 189
Glenlea 42
Goolistan 92
Grayburn 108
Grelhead 37
Guido 15

Harborough 6
Harbury 94
Harmala 82
Hartington 11, 12
Harvard 49
Hektoria 77
Helen Forsey 5
Helmspey 8
Hengist 44
Hertford 46
Holmpark 8

Inger Toft 139
Inverarder 33

Katvaldis 74
Kaying 64
Kelmscott 170
King Edgar 242
Kingswood 7
Kioto 5
Kirkland 40
Kitty's Brook 59

Lackenby 91
Laguna 112
Lavington Court 39
Leadgate 103

British (continued)

Lifland 79
Lindsay 148
Livingston 23
Llangibby Castle 48, 54
Lochkatrine 31
Lord Strathcona 4
Lorient 187
Lynton Grange 93

Maid of Orleans 206
Maja 220
Malaya II 38
Manchester Merchant 93
Margit 205
Margot 59
Maritima 12
Mattawin 30
Michael Jebsen 68
Monmouth Coast 243
Montreal City 62

Nagina 7
Nairung 176
Namaz 67
Nariva 70, 84
Nebraska 169
Nerissa 28
Nicoya 30
Nipiwan Park 238
Norfolk 28
Norfolk Coast 242
Normandy Coast 220
North Britain 130

Oakton 9
Ocean Vagabond 4
Ocean Vagabond 6
Ocean Venus 39
Ocean Viceroy 115
Opalia 39
Oregon 114
Otaio 33
Otina 89

PLM 27 9
Pacific Grove 38
Peisander 109
Pelayo 28
Perth 151
Phemius 7
Pontypridd 44
Port Hunter 55
Port Jackson 7
President Doumer 73
President Sergent 91
Primrose Hill 280

Queen Elizabeth 128

Radbury 176
Radhurst 14
Reedpol 6
Refast 54
Regent Lion 80
River Afton 127
Rose Castle 9
Roxby 81
Runo 64

British (continued)

Saganaga 4
St Lindsay 148
Samtucky 166
San Fabian 3
San Felix 31
San Gaspar 51
Saugor 32
Seminole 41
Sheaf Mount 74
Shillong 95
Shuntien 35
Silveray 148
Silvercedar 30
Silvermaple 190
Slemish 161
Southern Flower 218
Southern Prince 108
Southern Princess 70
Standella 68
Stockport 74
Stornest 129
Strathallan 37
Susan Maersk 30

Tahchee 108
Tahsinia 18
Tasmania 113
Tennessee 85
Terpsithea 37
Thurso 28
Tremoda 32
Triona 18
Troilus 175
Troisdoc 33
Tulagi 18

Umaria 115
Umtata 47

Vancouver Island 33
Victolite 39
Ville de Rouen 115
Vivian P Smith 69

Waiwera 151
Wallsend 29
Waroonga 98
Watuka 164
Wayfarer 176
Wentworth 94
Westmoreland 42
White Crest 33
William Wilberforce 3
Wrotham 36

Yorktown 87

Zarian 62

American

Alleghany 151
Andrew G Curtin 136
Angelina 86
Antinous 4, 6
Arlyn 9
Arthur Sewall 161
Atlantic States 174
Atlantic Sun 76
Atlas 28

MERCHANT SHIPS SUNK, DAMAGED OR ATTACKED BY U 511 - UIT 25 (continued)

American (continued)
Balladier 129
Barnegat 151
Beatrice 33
Black Hawk 161
Black Point 173
Byron T Benson 28

Caddo 9
Chapultepec 17
Charles C Pinckney 5
Chatham 9
Chattanooga City 75
Chilore 53
City of Flint 51
Coamo 74
Commercial Trader 33
Corneville 7
Cripple Creek 149
Cyrus H McCormick 225

Dan Beard 233
David H Atwater 28
Deer Lodge 8
Delisle 39
Delmundo 69

Eagle 5
Ebb 151
Edward B Dudley 83
Edward M House 204
Elihu B Washburne 5
Elizabeth Kellogg 8
Esso Aruba 3
Esso Augusta 126
Esso Harrisburg 8
Expositor 75
Ezra Weston 120

Fitzjohn Porter 9
Frances Salman 28
Frederick Douglass 105

George Ade 10
George Calvert 150
George Cleeve 199
George Hawley 232
Greylock 59
Gulftrade 59
Gurney E Newlin 75

Hahira 11
Henry G Blasdel 204
Henry Miller 179
Hollywood 22
Honolulan 55
Horace Bushnell 210
Horace Gray 133

Irenée du Pont 70
Isabela 148

J A Moffett Jr 47
Jack 33
Jack Carnes 7, 129
James A Farrell 204
James Gordon Bennett 188
James McKay 69
James Oglethorpe 154
James W Nesmith 219

American (continued)
John A Treutlen 204
John Barry 175
John Hancock 31
John R Park 231
John Winthrop 87
Jonas Lie 220
Jonathan Sturges 130

Kittaning 22

Louis Kossuth 206

McDowell 8
Mae 6
Maltran 155
Margaret 46
Martin van Buren 239
Mathew Luckenbach 13, 15
Melville E Stone 8
Menominee 151
Meriweather Lewis 97, 155
Michigan 41
Molly Pitcher 11

Nathaneal Green 41
Nicarao 148
Norlandia 51

Ohioan 39
Oklahoma 18
Oliver Ellsworth 60
Ontario 151
Otho 151

Pan New York 91
Pan Pennsylvania 27
Parismina 91
Patrick J Hurley 4
Pennsylvania Sun 47
Peter Silvester 177
Peter Skene Ogden 199
Pipestone County 52
Plow City 59
Point Breeze 8
Puerto Rican 58

R P Resor 53
Richard Caswell 5
Roanoke 220
Robert C Tuttle 126
Robert J Walker 177
Robin Goodfellow 176
Robin Hood 51
Rosario 116
Ruben Dario 167

Samuel Heintzelman 4
Santore 126
Sebastiano Cermeno 4
Sibert 217
Steel Navigator 80
Steel Scientist 5
Steel Voyager 188
Steelmaker 111
Stella Lykes 55
Sumner I Kimball 193
Sunoil 16, 38
Swiftscout 182
Syros 127

American (continued)
Tamaulipas 28
Thomas Donaldson 198
Thomas Hooker 110
Thomas Scott 198
Tiger 151

Walter Camp 18
West Imboden 149
West Madaket 56
Wichita 8
Will Rogers 219
William B Woods 188
William Boyce Thompson 33
William C Gorgas 153
William D Burnham 202
William Gaston 176
William Pierce Frye 80
William Rockefeller 126
William S Thayer 133
William W Gerhard 64

Yaka 12, 91
Yorkmar 105
Yukon 202

Greek
Annitsa 85
Aspasia 277

Carras 118

Fred 36

Icarion 151
Ilissos 176, 177
Ioannis Fafalios 176

Lily 59

Meropi 41
Mount Kitheron 151
Mount Olympos 36
Mount Pelion 12
Mount Pindus 9
Mount Taygetus 9

Nellie 76

Oropos 89

Parthenon 12
Peleus 172, 173

Stavros 64

Thetis 22

Netherlands
Adinda 37

Blitar 97
Bodegraven 26

Casandra 21
Corilla 148

Delfshaven 48

Netherlands (continued)
Fauna 33

Kota Tjandi 6

Leto 30

Maasdam 38
Madoera 62, 110, 151
Magdala 154
Mariso 9
Medea 112
Mendenau 149

Nieuw Amsterdam 238

Ocana 28

Poelau Roebiah 155
Polyphemus 53

Rosalia 83
Rotterdam 3

Saturnus 9
Spar 64
Suriname 33

Terkoelei 95
Triton 33
Tuva 50

Ulysses 38

Woensdrecht 6

Zaanland 154
Zuiderkerk 42

Norwegian
Abbekerk 73
Anna Knudsen 57
Annavore 43
Athene 35

Banffshire 18
Barbro 28
Belize 151
Bello 80
Berganger 53
Bidewind 149
Brand 72
Brant County 153
Bronxville 79

Cliona 47
Corona 85
Corvus 217
Crux 277

Daghild 77

Eidanger 33
Elin K 72
Erviken 33

Fernhill 153
Finnanger 33
Fjord 32

Norwegian (contiued)
Galatea 220
Glittre 72, 93

Haakon Hauan 150
Hallanger 67
Hamlet 150
Harboe Jensen 85
Hav 36
Heina 61
Hellen 49
Henrik 85
Hindanger 56

Idefjord 210, 211
Ila 30
Indra 280
Inger Elisabeth 9
Ingerfem 95
Ingerfire 81
Ingerto 53
Ingria 69, 93
Inneröy 30

Katy 182
Koll 46
Kollbjörg 65, 76
Kollskegg 151
Kongsgaard 38
Kosmos II 75, 91

Lancing 28
Leif 109
Leikanger 149
Lindvangen 6

Marit 67
Marit II 77
Minister Wedel 12, 51

N T Neilsen Alonso 151
Norfjell 198, 208
Norse King 62
Novasli 242

Polarland 238

Ranella 30
Reinholt 149
Ringen 157
Rynn 33

Sarita 277
Segundo 32
Skottland 59
Slemdal 28
Sneland I 248
Solör 167
Sörholt 6
Spind 28, 39
Stigstad 72
Sverre Helmersen 246

Taborfjell 52
Tamesis 126
Triton 42
Tropic Star 52

Vanja 47
Vardaas 39

Norwegian (continued)
Vibran 55
Vigsnes 230
Vilja 33

William Hansen 151

Swedish
Agra 111

Blankaholm 31

Industria 9

Magne 135
Milos 16

Suecia 66

Venezia 5

Other Countries

Belgium
Belgian Airman 182
Belgian Soldier 29, 76

Emile Francqui 116

Gand 31

Mokambo 7

Persier 217

Roumanie 85

Brazil
Antonico 8

Brasiloide 9

Lages 5

Brazil (continued)
Ozório 5

Pelotasloide 61

Tutóia 5

Vital d' Oliveira 176

Colombian
Ruby 8

Egyptian
Hamdiah 67

Nagwa 67

Samir 112
Sphinx 36

Faroese
Emanuel 31

Nyggjaberg 126

Tor II 85

Finnish
Linnea 193

Piikiö 193

French
Bamako 6

Lot 49

Mont Viso 64

Saint Basile 26
St Denis 108

Sergeant Gouarne 152
Sidi-Bel-Abbès 41
Simon Duhamel II 152

France (continued)
Wyoming 13

Greenland
Hans Egede 59

Honduran
Nicholas Cuneo 47

Hungary
Kelet 277

Icelandic
Dettifoss 223

Hekla 39

Reykjaborg 27

Indian
Jalabala 18

Irish
Irish Oak 77
Irish Pine 77

Latvian
Everelza 69

Mexican
Potrero del Llano 39

Nicaraguan
Bluefields 53

Panamanian
Alcedo 218

Bold Venture 30

C J Barkdull 96
Capira 79
Colin 175
Colombia 8
Crusader 36

Panamanian (continued)
Desert Light 48

El Lago 83

H H Rogers 116

J A Mowinckel 53

Lubrafol 39

Meridian 36

Nimba 6
Nortun 8
Norvik 12, 51

Persephone 64
Pillory 21
Pink Star 28
Pompoon 8

Soreldoc 162
Stanvac Melbourne 6
Stone Street 65

T J Williams 28
Tuira 277

Valera 10

W C Teagle 33
Winkler 93

Polish
Warszawa 35

Portuguese
Serpa Pinto 22

Russian
A Andreev 193
Archangel'sk 193

Ciolkovskij 60

Russian (continued)
Krest'janin 70
Kujbysev 70
Kuznec Lesov 71

Marija Uljanova 46
Mossovet 127
Murman 71

Onega 211

Proletarij 210

RT-52 210
Revoljucioner 227

Shchors 62
Sergej Kirov 127
Skval 92
Spokojnyj 211
Stalingrad 60

Tbilisi (7169t) 98
Tbilisi (7176t) 191

Varlaam Avaneson 109

ZM-93 149

Spanish
Monte Gorbea 4

Yugoslavian
Nikolina Matkovic 114

Rad 277

Senga 220

Vojvoda Putnik 62

6. OTHER MERCHANT SHIPS MENTIONED IN THE TEXT

American
Escape 10
Esso Buffalo 17

Shoemaker 244

William A Mann 176

British
Delilian 110

French
Île de France 159

Jazz Band 40

Portuguese
Alexandre Silva 173

Spanish
Fina 42

German
Angelburg 54
Anton 239

Belchen 32
Bessel 50
Brake 18, 19, 282

Charlotte Schliemann 18

German (continued)
Egerland 278

Osorno 22, 87, 111, 119, 154, 164, 194

Peter Wessel 220
Python 278

Rhakotis 113

German (continued)
Rio Grande 55

Spreewald 54

Thalia 39, 108

7. WARSHIPS AND AUXILIARIES MENTIONED IN THE TEXT

8. ALLIED AIR FORCE UNITS MENTIONED IN THE TEXT

British RAF Squadrons
8 172

9 178

36 85,194

38 37

47 35

48 65, 119

53 3, 19, 20, 79, 87, 95, 106, 195, 208

58 16, 34, 38, 77, 81, 118, 150, 171

59 22, 29, 89, 104, 136, 170, 207

61 148

77 129

86 19, 72, 77, 97, 99, 104, 107, 118, 145, 154, 170, 178, 184, 195, 198

120 13, 21, 22, 31, 38, 42, 47, 51, 65, 68, 75, 80, 91,96, 98, 104, 109, 122, 128, 139, 142, 144, 153, 157, 187, 214, 217

143 165, 224, 247, 252

144 223

172 14, 19, 42, 52, 82

179 23, 34, 42, 86, 87, 119, 156, 186

184 258

201 9, 15, 68, 190, 235

202 73, 88, 109, 156

203 40

206 52, 82, 93,132, 167, 246

209 45

210 71, 95, 145

220 52, 70, 83, 91, 101, 118, 130, 158, 180

224 6, 34, 69, 89, 92, 94, 141, 157 179, 206, 215, 222, 225, 237

228 38, 40, 77, 78, 81, 199

230 44

233 42, 49, 75, 119

235 165, 170, 224, 247, 252

British RAF Squadrons (continued)
236 104, 248, 255

244 19

248 104, 167, 179, 247

254 248, 255

262 175, 281

265 176

269 19, 21, 45, 87, 102, 105, 139

270 6

500 66, 194

502 38, 60, 148, 157, 203, 222

547 54, 70, 83

608 66, 81, 152

612 24, 94, 141,197

617 123, 178

618 193, 201

621 172

4(C)OTU 123, 209

10 OTU 13, 40, 62, 70, 83, 117

British FAA Squadrons
812 33, 44

813 185

815 53, 109

816 200, 220, 243

817 9

819 150

825 110, 159

842 119, 123, 193

846 134

853 134

882 134

892 150

1771 222

American USAF Squadrons
1st 13, 187

1st Composite 171

2nd 149

4th 130

10th 83, 84

19th 34

45th 111

99th 4, 5

396th 126

American USN Squadrons
VB-107 68, 74, 172, 177

VB-126 62

VB-128 42

VB-129 74

VB-130 84

VB-133 8

VC-1 14, 117, 171

VC-6 221

VC-9 15, 45, 57, 106, 176

VC-13 24

VC-19 25, 172, 182

VC-42 237

VC-58 24

VC-69 17

VP-32 155

VP-63 140, 156, 225

VP-73 55, 73

VP-74 5

VP-82 111

VP-84 16, 68, 80, 96, 101, 107, 112, 116, 140

VP-92 69

VP-94 61, 115

VP-103 197

VP-105 197

American USN Squadrons (continued)
VP-107 171

VP-110 63

VP-204 21, 83, 84

VP-205 49, 83, 84

VPB-14 166

VPB-103 125

VPB-127 156

VS-9 53

Australian RAAF Squadrons
10 10, 38, 106, 116

461 48, 70, 83, 190

Canadian RCAF Squadrons
10 11, 168, 170

113 9, 151

145 11, 113

162 135, 202, 236

404 223

407 121, 144, 161, 171, 197, 200, 206, 222

415 130

422 87, 92

423 80, 122, 151, 185

Czech Air Force Squadrons
311 53, 197, 200, 222

Norwegian Air Force Squadrons
330 75, 208

333 120, 160, 165, 177, 192, 211, 236, 247

Polish Air Force Squadrons
304 94, 230

South African SAAF Squadrons
26 47

9. SOURCES AND SELECTED BIBLIOGRAPHY

PRIMARY SOURCES

The Public Record Office, Kew
Imperial War Museum, London
Air Historical Branch, Ministry of Defence
Admiralty Historical Branch, Ministry of Defence
RAF Museum Library, Hendon
Royal Navy Submarine Museum, Gosport
National Maritime Museum, Greenwich
Bundesarchiv-Militärarchiv, Freiburg
U-Boat Archive, Altenbruch
Naval Historical Center, Washington DC
National Archives of Canada, Ottawa
Lloyd's Register of Shipping
Guildhall Library, London
Professor Dr Jürgen Rohwer of the Bibliothek für Zeitgeschichte, Stuttgart
Dr Axel Niestlé of Berlin
Flight Lieutenant E S Cheek AFC DFM
The late Dr Robert Holden
Herr Siewert Bahnsen and the U-Boot-Kameradschaft, Kiel

SELECTED BIBLIOGRAPHY

Beaver, Paul *U-boats in the Atlantic* Stephens 1979
Bekker, Cajus *Hitler's Naval War* Macdonald & Jane's 1974
Botting, Douglas and others *The U-boats* Time-Life Books 1979
Brennecke, Jochen *The Hunters and the Hunted* Burke 1958
Cameron, J (Editor) *The Peleus Trial* Hodge 1948
Campbell, Vice-Admiral Sir Ian and Capt Donald Macintyre *The Kola Run* Muller 1958
Chalmers, Rear-Admiral W S *Max Horton and the Western Approaches* Hodder & Stoughton 1954
Costello, John and Terry Hughes *The Battle of the Atlantic* Collins 1977
Cowling, Bill *1413 Days: in the Wake of a Canadian DEMS Gunner* Cowling 1994
Cremer, Peter *U 333 The story of a U-boat Ace* Bodley Head 1984
Divine, A D *The Merchant Navy Fights Tramps against U-boats* Murray 1940
Dönitz, Admiral Karl *Memoirs Ten Years and Twenty Days* Weidenfeld & Nicolson 1959
Dörr, Manfred *Die Ritterkreuzträger der U-Boot-Waffe* 2 Vols Biblio Verlag 1988-1989
Dorling, Capt Taprell *Western Mediterranean 1942-1945* Hodder & Stoughton 1947
Drummond, John *HM U-boat The story of U 570* Allen 1958
Edwards, B *The Merchant Navy goes to War* Hale 1990
Elliott, Peter *Allied Escort Ships of World War II* Macdonald & Jane's 1977
Frank, Wolfgang *Enemy Submarine The story of Günther Prien* Kimber 1954
------- *The Sea Wolves The story of German U-boats at war* Weidenfeld & Nicolson 1955
Franks, Norman *Conflict over the Bay* Kimber 1986
------- *Search, Find and Kill* Grub Street 1995
Gallery, Rear-Admiral Daniel V *We captured a U-boat The story of U 505* Sidgwick & Jackson 1957
Gannon, Michael *Operation Drumbeat* Harper & Row 1990
Gasaway, E B *Grey Wolf, Grey Sea The story of U 124* Barker 1972
Giese, Otto and Capt E J Wise *Shooting the War Memoirs of a U-boat officer* Cooper 1994
Gray, Edwyn *Captains of War They fought beneath the Sea* Cooper 1988
Gretton, Vice-Admiral Sir Peter *Convoy Escort Commander* Cassell 1964
Groner, Eric and Peter Mickel *U-boats and Mine Warfare Vessels* Conway Maritime 1991
Guske, Heinz F K *The War Diaries of U 764 Fact or Fiction?* Thomas 1992
Hadley, Michael *U-boats against Canada* McGill-Queen's University Press 1985
Hawkins, Doris M *Atlantic Torpedo Survivor's story of the* Laconia *sinking* Gollancz 1943
Hess, Hans Georg *Die Männer von U 995* Hess-Press 1987
Hessler, Günter *The U-boat War in the Atlantic* HMSO 1989
Hickam, Homer H *Torpedo Junction U-boat war off the US east coast 1942* Naval Institute Press 1989
HMSO *British Vessels Lost at Sea 1914-18 and 1939-45* Stephens 1988
Högel, Georg *Embleme Wappen Mallings U-boat emblems 1939-1945* Koehler 1987
Howarth, S and D Law *The Battle of the Atlantic 50th Anniversary Conference* Greenhill 1994
Irving, David *The Destruction of Convoy PQ 17* Corgi 1970
Jones, Geoffrey *Defeat of the Wolf Packs* Kimber 1986
------- *Submarines versus U-boats* Kimber 1986
------- *U-boat Aces and their Fates* Kimber 1988
------- *The Month of the Lost U-boats* Kimber 1977
------ *Autumn of the U-boats* Kimber 1984

SELECTED BIBLIOGRAPHY (continued)

Kelshall, Gaylord T M *U-boat War in the Caribbean* Naval Institute Press 1994
Köhl, Fritz and Eberhard Rössler *The Type XXI U-boat* Conway Maritime 1991
------- and Axel Niestlé *Vom Original zum Modell: Uboottyp VII C* Bernard & Graefe Verlag 1989
Korganoff, Alexandre *The Phantom of Scapa Flow The daring exploit of U 47* Allan 1974
Lenton, H T *German submarines* 2 vols Macdonald 1965
Lohmann, W & H H Hildebrand *Kriegsmarine 1939-45* Podzun Verlag 1956-1964
Lund, Paul and H Ludlam *Night of the U-boats* Foulsham 1973
Macintyre, Capt Donald *U-boat Killer* Weidenfeld & Nicolson 1956
Mars, Alastair *British Submarines at War 1939-1945* Kimber 1971
Metzler, Jost *The Laughing Cow An account of U 69* Kimber 1955
Middlebrook, Martin *Convoy The battle for convoys SC 122 and HX 229* Lane 1976
Mohr, Ulrich and A V Sellwood *Atlantis The story of a German surface raider* Laurie 1955
Morison, Samuel Eliot *History of United States Naval Operations in World War II* Little Brown 1990
Museum of Science and Industry *The story of U 505* Chicago 1978
Nowarra, Heinz J *German U-boat Type VII* Schiffer 1992
Padfield, Peter *Dönitz The Last Führer* Gollancz 1984
Pallud, Jean-Paul *Les Bases Brest-Lorient-St Nazaire-La Pallice-Bordeaux* Bayeux Cedex 1989
------- *U-Boote! Les sous-marins allemands* Bayeux Cedex 1989
Peillard, Léonce *U-boats to the Rescue The* Laconia *incident* Cape 1963
Piekalkiewicz, Janusz *Sea War 1939-1945* Blandford 1987
Porten, E von der *Pictorial History of the German Navy in World War II* Crowell 1976
Preston, A *U-boats* Bison 1978
Rachlis, Eugene *They Came to Kill* Random House 1961
Robertson,Terence *Walker RN The story of Captain F J Walker CB DSO* Evans 1956
-------- *The Golden Horseshoe The story of Otto Kretschmer* Evans 1955
Rodrigues, Georges *La Pallice Base sous-marine allemande* Jonzac 1992
Rohwer, Jürgen *U-Boote Eine Chronik in Bildern* Stalling Verlag 1962
------- *Axis Submarine Successes* Stephens 1983
------- *The Critical Convoy Battles of March 1943* Allan 1977
------- and Gerhard Hummelchen *Chronology of the War at Sea 1939-1945* Greenhill 1992
Roskill, Captain S W *The War at Sea 1939-1945* 4 Vols HMSO 1954-1961
------- *The Secret Capture The story of U 110* Collins 1959
Rössler, Eberhard *The U-boat The Evolution and Technical History* Arms and Armour Press 1989
Ruge, Vice-Admiral Friedrich *Der Seekrieg The German Navy's story 1939-1945* Naval Institute Press 1957
Runyan, T J and J M Copes *To Die Gallantly The Battle of the Atlantic* Westview Press 1994
Schaeffer, Heinz *U-boat 977* Kimber 1952
Sellwood, A V *The Warring Seas Concerning U 234* Werner Laurie 1956
Showell, J P Mallmann *U-boat Command and the Battle of the Atlantic* Conway Maritime 1989
------ *U-boats under the Swastika* Allan 1987
------- *The German Navy in World War Two* Naval Institute Press 1979
Smith, H A *The Law and Custom of the Sea* Stevens 1950
Southall, Ivan *They Shall Not Pass Unseen Flying boats against U-boats* Angus & Robertson 1956
Spooner, Tony *Coastal Ace The biography of Squadron Leader Terence Bulloch* Kimber 1986
Stern, Robert C *U-boats in Action* Squadron/Signal Publications 1977
Tarrant, E V *The U-boat Offensive 1914-1945* Arms and Armour Press 1989
------- *The Last Year of the Kriegsmarine May 1944-May 1945* Arms and Armour Press 1994
Terraine, John *Business in Great Waters The U-boat Wars 1916-1945* Cooper 1989
Time-Life Editors *Wolf Packs* Time-Life Books 1989
Turner, L and others *War in the Southern Oceans 1939-1945* Oxford University Press 1961
U-boat Commander's Handbook Thomas Publications 1989
Vat, Dan van der *The Atlantic Campaign* Grafton 1990
Vause, Jordan *U-boat Ace The story of Wolfgang Lüth* Airlife 1992
Watts, Anthony *The U-boat Hunters* Macdonald & Jane's 1976
------- *Axis Submarines* Macdonald & Jane's 1977
Wemyss, Cdr D E G *Relentless Pursuit The story of Captain F J Walker CB DSO* Kimber 1955
Wentzel, Fritz *Single or Return? German Pows in British camps* Kimber 1954
Werner, Herbert *Iron Coffins A personal account of the U-boat war* Mandarin 1972
Westwood, David *The Type VII U-boat* Conway Maritime 1984
Wetzel, Eckard *U 995 Das U-Boot vor dem Marine-Ehrenmal in Laboe* Kiel 1990
Whinney, Captain Reginald *The U-boat Peril* Arrow 1989
Woodman, Richard *Arctic Convoys 1941-1945* Murray 1994
Woodward, David *The Secret Raiders German merchant raiders* Kimber 1955
Young, John M *Britain's Sea War A diary of ship losses 1939-1945* Stephens 1989

1. THE ATLANTIC OCEAN

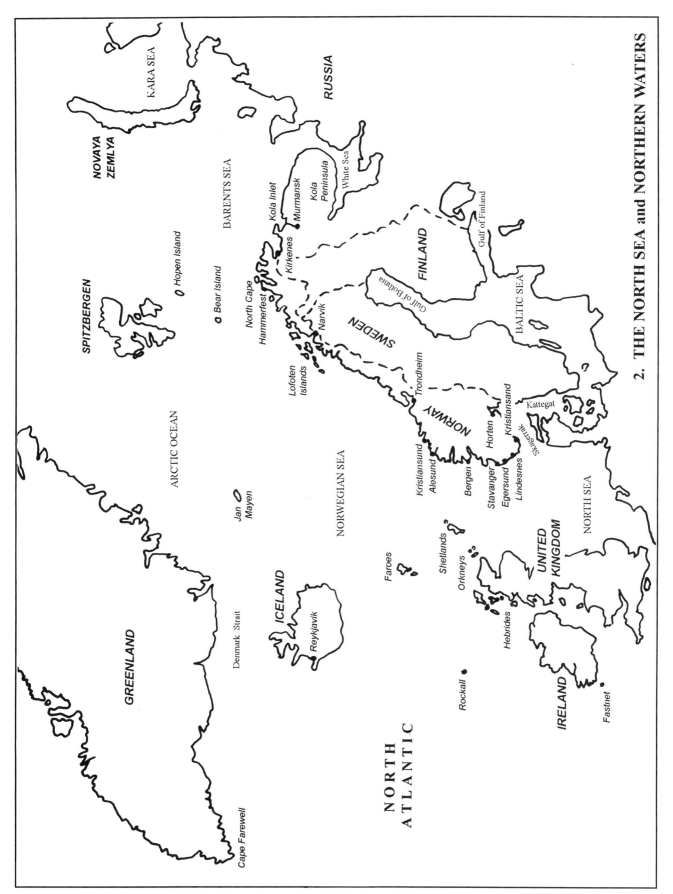

KARA SEA

RUSSIA

NOVAYA
ZEMLYA

BARENTS SEA

White Sea

Kola Inlet

Kola
Peninsula

Murmansk

Kirkenes

Gulf of Finland

Hopen Island

FINLAND

North Cape

Bear Island

Hammerfest

SPITZBERGEN

Gulf of Bothnia

Narvik

BALTIC SEA

Lofoten
Islands

SWEDEN

ARCTIC OCEAN

Trondheim

Kristiansand

Kattegat

NORWAY

Horten

Skagerrak

Jan
Mayen

Kristiansund
Alesund

Bergen

Stavanger
Egersund
Lindesnes

NORWEGIAN SEA

NORTH SEA

Shetlands

Faroes

Denmark Strait

Orkneys

UNITED
KINGDOM

GREENLAND

ICELAND

Reykjavik

Hebrides

Rockall

NORTH
ATLANTIC

IRELAND

Cape Farewell

Fastnet

2. THE NORTH SEA and NORTHERN WATERS

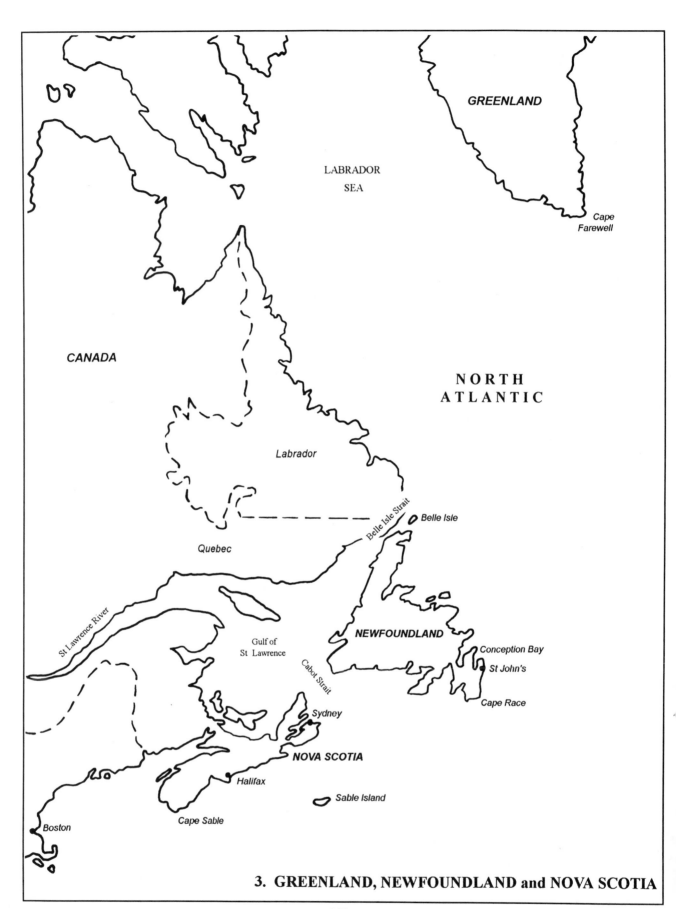

GREENLAND

LABRADOR
SEA

Cape
Farewell

CANADA

NORTH
ATLANTIC

Labrador

Belle Isle Strait
Belle Isle

Quebec

St Lawrence River

Gulf of
St Lawrence

NEWFOUNDLAND

Conception Bay
St John's

Cabot Strait

Cape Race

Sydney

NOVA SCOTIA

Halifax

Sable Island

Cape Sable

Boston

3. GREENLAND, NEWFOUNDLAND and NOVA SCOTIA

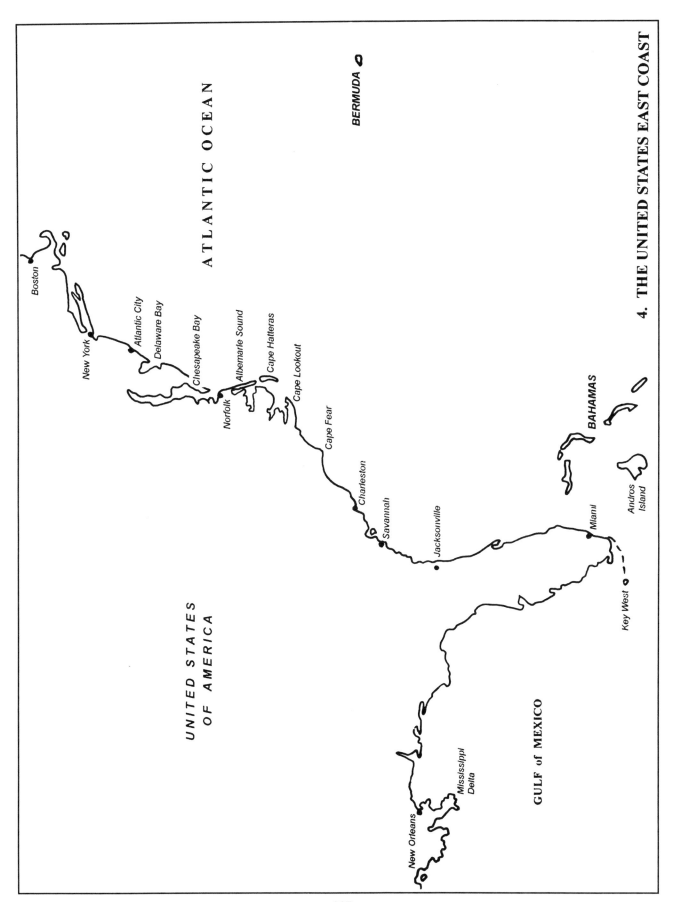

ATLANTIC OCEAN

BERMUDA

4. THE UNITED STATES EAST COAST

Boston

New York

Atlantic City

Delaware Bay

Chesapeake Bay

Norfolk

Albemarle Sound

Cape Hatteras

Cape Lookout

Cape Fear

Charleston

Savannah

Jacksonville

Miami

BAHAMAS

Andros Island

Key West

UNITED STATES
OF AMERICA

GULF of MEXICO

Mississippi
Delta

New Orleans

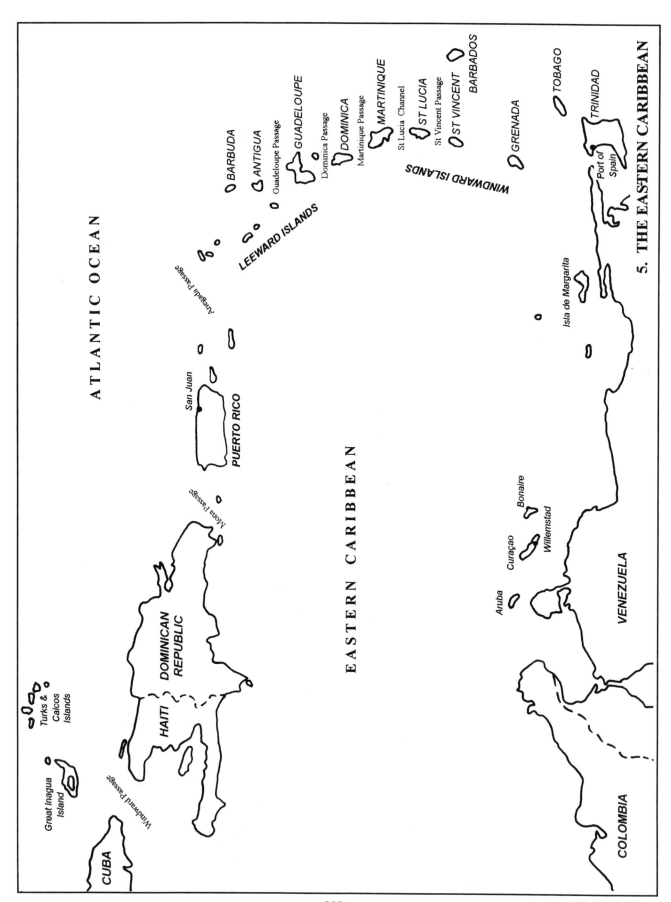

5. THE EASTERN CARIBBEAN

ATLANTIC OCEAN

EASTERN CARIBBEAN

CUBA

Great Inagua
Island

Turks &
Calcos
Islands

Windward Passage

HAITI

DOMINICAN
REPUBLIC

Mona Passage

San Juan

PUERTO RICO

Anegada Passage

LEEWARD ISLANDS

BARBUDA

ANTIGUA

Guadeloupe Passage

GUADELOUPE

Dominica Passage

DOMINICA

Martinique Passage

MARTINIQUE

St Lucia Channel

ST LUCIA

St Vincent Passage

ST VINCENT

BARBADOS

WINDWARD ISLANDS

GRENADA

TOBAGO

TRINIDAD

Port of
Spain

Isla de Margarita

Aruba

Curaçao

Bonaire

Willemstad

VENEZUELA

COLOMBIA

308

GULF OF MEXICO

FLORIDA

Key West
Florida Keys
Straits of Florida

BAHAMAS

Nicholas Channel

Santaren Channel

Andros
Island

Havana

CUBA

Old Bahama Channel

Cabo Catoche

Yucatan Channel

MEXICO

Yucatan Peninsula

Isla de la
Juventud

Manzanillo

Guantanamo

Cayman Islands

JAMAICA

Kingston

HONDURAS

WESTERN CARIBBEAN

NICARAGUA

Roncador Cay

Isla de San Andres

Cartagena

COSTA RICA

COLOMBIA

PACIFIC OCEAN

Colón

PANAMA

6. THE WESTERN CARIBBEAN

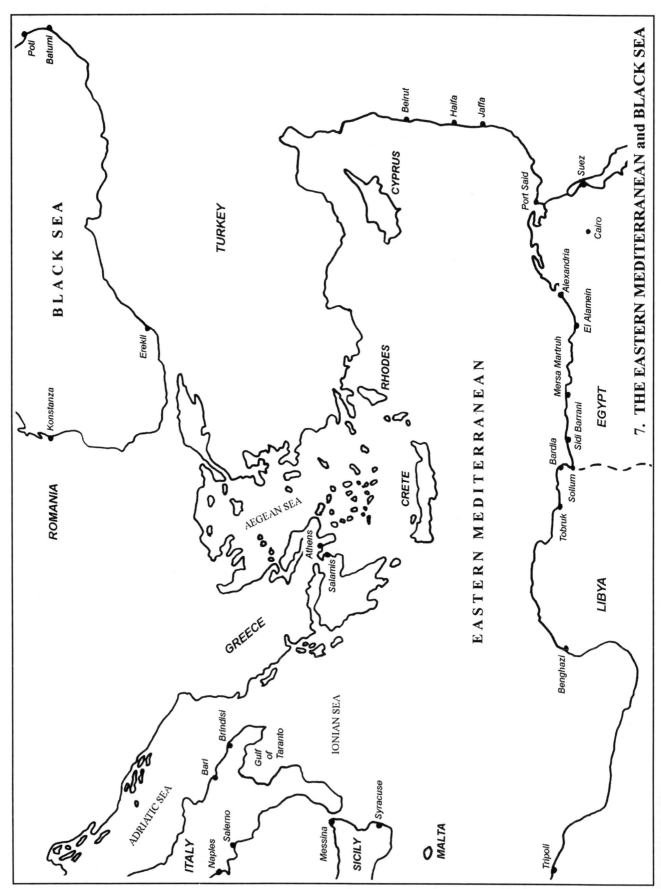

7. THE EASTERN MEDITERRANEAN and BLACK SEA

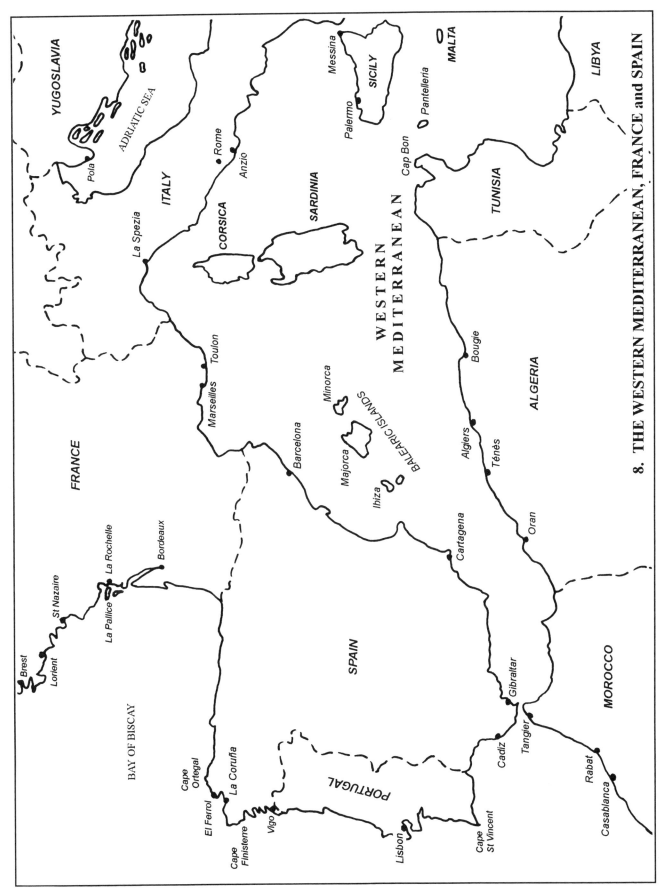

8. THE WESTERN MEDITERRANEAN, FRANCE and SPAIN

YUGOSLAVIA

ADRIATIC SEA

Pola

ITALY

La Spezia

Rome

Anzio

CORSICA

SARDINIA

MALTA

Messina

SICILY

Palermo

Pantelleria

Cap Bon

TUNISIA

LIBYA

WESTERN MEDITERRANEAN

FRANCE

Toulon

Marseilles

Minorca

BALEARIC ISLANDS

Barcelona

Majorca

Ibiza

Bougie

Algiers

Ténès

ALGERIA

Oran

Cartagena

SPAIN

Brest

Lorient

St Nazaire

La Pallice

La Rochelle

Bordeaux

BAY OF BISCAY

Cape Ortegal

El Ferrol

Cape Finisterre

La Coruña

Vigo

PORTUGAL

Lisbon

Cape St Vincent

Cadiz

Gibraltar

Tangier

Rabat

MOROCCO

Casablanca

311

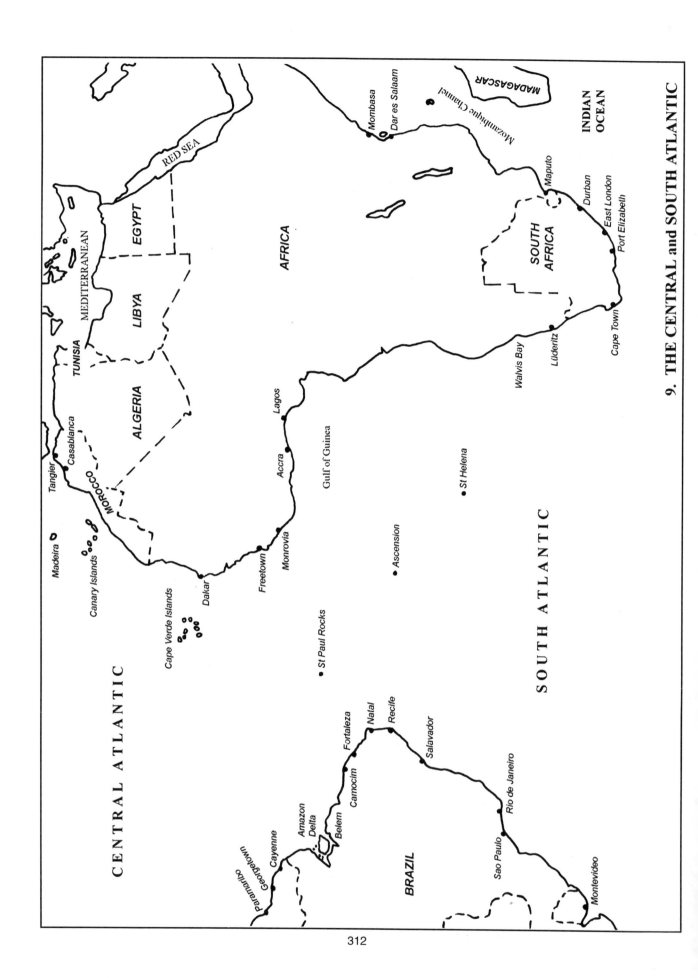

CENTRAL ATLANTIC

MEDITERRANEAN

RED SEA

EGYPT

AFRICA

LIBYA

TUNISIA

ALGERIA

MOROCCO

Tangier

Casablanca

Madeira

Canary Islands

Cape Verde Islands

Dakar

Freetown

Monrovia

Lagos

Accra

Gulf of Guinea

St Paul Rocks

Ascension

St Helena

Walvis Bay

Lüderitz

Cape Town

Port Elizabeth

East London

Durban

Maputo

SOUTH AFRICA

Mombasa

Dar es Salaam

Mozambique Channel

MADAGASCAR

INDIAN OCEAN

SOUTH ATLANTIC

Georgetown

Paramaribo

Cayenne

Amazon Delta

Belem

Camocim

Fortaleza

Natal

Recife

Salavador

BRAZIL

Rio de Janeiro

Sao Paulo

Montevideo

9. THE CENTRAL and SOUTH ATLANTIC